Lecture Notes in Computer Science   12372

More information about this series at http://www.springer.com/series/7412

Andrea Vedaldi · Horst Bischof ·
Thomas Brox · Jan-Michael Frahm (Eds.)

Computer Vision – ECCV 2020

16th European Conference
Glasgow, UK, August 23–28, 2020
Proceedings, Part XXVII

Springer

Editors
Andrea Vedaldi ⓘ
University of Oxford
Oxford, UK

Horst Bischof ⓘ
Graz University of Technology
Graz, Austria

Thomas Brox ⓘ
University of Freiburg
Freiburg im Breisgau, Germany

Jan-Michael Frahm
University of North Carolina at Chapel Hill
Chapel Hill, NC, USA

ISSN 0302-9743   ISSN 1611-3349   (electronic)
Lecture Notes in Computer Science
ISBN 978-3-030-58582-2   ISBN 978-3-030-58583-9   (eBook)
https://doi.org/10.1007/978-3-030-58583-9

LNCS Sublibrary: SL6 – Image Processing, Computer Vision, Pattern Recognition, and Graphics

This Springer imprint is published by the registered company Springer Nature Switzerland AG
The registered company address is: Gewerbestrasse 11, 6330 Cham, Switzerland

Foreword

Hosting the European Conference on Computer Vision (ECCV 2020) was certainly an exciting journey. From the 2016 plan to hold it at the Edinburgh International Conference Centre (hosting 1,800 delegates) to the 2018 plan to hold it at Glasgow's Scottish Exhibition Centre (up to 6,000 delegates), we finally ended with moving online because of the COVID-19 outbreak. While possibly having fewer delegates than expected because of the online format, ECCV 2020 still had over 3,100 registered participants.

Although online, the conference delivered most of the activities expected at a face-to-face conference: peer-reviewed papers, industrial exhibitors, demonstrations, and messaging between delegates. In addition to the main technical sessions, the conference included a strong program of satellite events with 16 tutorials and 44 workshops.

Furthermore, the online conference format enabled new conference features. Every paper had an associated teaser video and a longer full presentation video. Along with the papers and slides from the videos, all these materials were available the week before the conference. This allowed delegates to become familiar with the paper content and be ready for the live interaction with the authors during the conference week. The live event consisted of brief presentations by the oral and spotlight authors and industrial sponsors. Question and answer sessions for all papers were timed to occur twice so delegates from around the world had convenient access to the authors.

As with ECCV 2018, authors' draft versions of the papers appeared online with open access, now on both the Computer Vision Foundation (CVF) and the European Computer Vision Association (ECVA) websites. An archival publication arrangement was put in place with the cooperation of Springer. SpringerLink hosts the final version of the papers with further improvements, such as activating reference links and supplementary materials. These two approaches benefit all potential readers: a version available freely for all researchers, and an authoritative and citable version with additional benefits for SpringerLink subscribers. We thank Alfred Hofmann and Aliaksandr Birukou from Springer for helping to negotiate this agreement, which we expect will continue for future versions of ECCV.

August 2020

Vittorio Ferrari
Bob Fisher
Cordelia Schmid
Emanuele Trucco

Preface

Welcome to the proceedings of the European Conference on Computer Vision (ECCV 2020). This is a unique edition of ECCV in many ways. Due to the COVID-19 pandemic, this is the first time the conference was held online, in a virtual format. This was also the first time the conference relied exclusively on the Open Review platform to manage the review process. Despite these challenges ECCV is thriving. The conference received 5,150 valid paper submissions, of which 1,360 were accepted for publication (27%) and, of those, 160 were presented as spotlights (3%) and 104 as orals (2%). This amounts to more than twice the number of submissions to ECCV 2018 (2,439). Furthermore, CVPR, the largest conference on computer vision, received 5,850 submissions this year, meaning that ECCV is now 87% the size of CVPR in terms of submissions. By comparison, in 2018 the size of ECCV was only 73% of CVPR.

The review model was similar to previous editions of ECCV; in particular, it was double blind in the sense that the authors did not know the name of the reviewers and vice versa. Furthermore, each conference submission was held confidentially, and was only publicly revealed if and once accepted for publication. Each paper received at least three reviews, totalling more than 15,000 reviews. Handling the review process at this scale was a significant challenge. In order to ensure that each submission received as fair and high-quality reviews as possible, we recruited 2,830 reviewers (a 130% increase with reference to 2018) and 207 area chairs (a 60% increase). The area chairs were selected based on their technical expertise and reputation, largely among people that served as area chair in previous top computer vision and machine learning conferences (ECCV, ICCV, CVPR, NeurIPS, etc.). Reviewers were similarly invited from previous conferences. We also encouraged experienced area chairs to suggest additional chairs and reviewers in the initial phase of recruiting.

Despite doubling the number of submissions, the reviewer load was slightly reduced from 2018, from a maximum of 8 papers down to 7 (with some reviewers offering to handle 6 papers plus an emergency review). The area chair load increased slightly, from 18 papers on average to 22 papers on average.

Conflicts of interest between authors, area chairs, and reviewers were handled largely automatically by the Open Review platform via their curated list of user profiles. Many authors submitting to ECCV already had a profile in Open Review. We set a paper registration deadline one week before the paper submission deadline in order to encourage all missing authors to register and create their Open Review profiles well on time (in practice, we allowed authors to create/change papers arbitrarily until the submission deadline). Except for minor issues with users creating duplicate profiles, this allowed us to easily and quickly identify institutional conflicts, and avoid them, while matching papers to area chairs and reviewers.

Papers were matched to area chairs based on: an affinity score computed by the Open Review platform, which is based on paper titles and abstracts, and an affinity score computed by the Toronto Paper Matching System (TPMS), which is based on the paper's full text, the area chair bids for individual papers, load balancing, and conflict avoidance. Open Review provides the program chairs a convenient web interface to experiment with different configurations of the matching algorithm. The chosen configuration resulted in about 50% of the assigned papers to be highly ranked by the area chair bids, and 50% to be ranked in the middle, with very few low bids assigned.

Assignments to reviewers were similar, with two differences. First, there was a maximum of 7 papers assigned to each reviewer. Second, area chairs recommended up to seven reviewers per paper, providing another highly-weighed term to the affinity scores used for matching.

The assignment of papers to area chairs was smooth. However, it was more difficult to find suitable reviewers for all papers. Having a ratio of 5.6 papers per reviewer with a maximum load of 7 (due to emergency reviewer commitment), which did not allow for much wiggle room in order to also satisfy conflict and expertise constraints. We received some complaints from reviewers who did not feel qualified to review specific papers and we reassigned them wherever possible. However, the large scale of the conference, the many constraints, and the fact that a large fraction of such complaints arrived very late in the review process made this process very difficult and not all complaints could be addressed.

Reviewers had six weeks to complete their assignments. Possibly due to COVID-19 or the fact that the NeurIPS deadline was moved closer to the review deadline, a record 30% of the reviews were still missing after the deadline. By comparison, ECCV 2018 experienced only 10% missing reviews at this stage of the process. In the subsequent week, area chairs chased the missing reviews intensely, found replacement reviewers in their own team, and managed to reach 10% missing reviews. Eventually, we could provide almost all reviews (more than 99.9%) with a delay of only a couple of days on the initial schedule by a significant use of emergency reviews. If this trend is confirmed, it might be a major challenge to run a smooth review process in future editions of ECCV. The community must reconsider prioritization of the time spent on paper writing (the number of submissions increased a lot despite COVID-19) and time spent on paper reviewing (the number of reviews delivered in time decreased a lot presumably due to COVID-19 or NeurIPS deadline). With this imbalance the peer-review system that ensures the quality of our top conferences may break soon.

Reviewers submitted their reviews independently. In the reviews, they had the opportunity to ask questions to the authors to be addressed in the rebuttal. However, reviewers were told not to request any significant new experiment. Using the Open Review interface, authors could provide an answer to each individual review, but were also allowed to cross-reference reviews and responses in their answers. Rather than PDF files, we allowed the use of formatted text for the rebuttal. The rebuttal and initial reviews were then made visible to all reviewers and the primary area chair for a given paper. The area chair encouraged and moderated the reviewer discussion. During the discussions, reviewers were invited to reach a consensus and possibly adjust their ratings as a result of the discussion and of the evidence in the rebuttal.

After the discussion period ended, most reviewers entered a final rating and recommendation, although in many cases this did not differ from their initial recommendation. Based on the updated reviews and discussion, the primary area chair then made a preliminary decision to accept or reject the paper and wrote a justification for it (meta-review). Except for cases where the outcome of this process was absolutely clear (as indicated by the three reviewers and primary area chairs all recommending clear rejection), the decision was then examined and potentially challenged by a secondary area chair. This led to further discussion and overturning a small number of preliminary decisions. Needless to say, there was no in-person area chair meeting, which would have been impossible due to COVID-19.

Area chairs were invited to observe the consensus of the reviewers whenever possible and use extreme caution in overturning a clear consensus to accept or reject a paper. If an area chair still decided to do so, she/he was asked to clearly justify it in the meta-review and to explicitly obtain the agreement of the secondary area chair. In practice, very few papers were rejected after being confidently accepted by the reviewers.

This was the first time Open Review was used as the main platform to run ECCV. In 2018, the program chairs used CMT3 for the user-facing interface and Open Review internally, for matching and conflict resolution. Since it is clearly preferable to only use a single platform, this year we switched to using Open Review in full. The experience was largely positive. The platform is highly-configurable, scalable, and open source. Being written in Python, it is easy to write scripts to extract data programmatically. The paper matching and conflict resolution algorithms and interfaces are top-notch, also due to the excellent author profiles in the platform. Naturally, there were a few kinks along the way due to the fact that the ECCV Open Review configuration was created from scratch for this event and it differs in substantial ways from many other Open Review conferences. However, the Open Review development and support team did a fantastic job in helping us to get the configuration right and to address issues in a timely manner as they unavoidably occurred. We cannot thank them enough for the tremendous effort they put into this project.

Finally, we would like to thank everyone involved in making ECCV 2020 possible in these very strange and difficult times. This starts with our authors, followed by the area chairs and reviewers, who ran the review process at an unprecedented scale. The whole Open Review team (and in particular Melisa Bok, Mohit Unyal, Carlos Mondragon Chapa, and Celeste Martinez Gomez) worked incredibly hard for the entire duration of the process. We would also like to thank René Vidal for contributing to the adoption of Open Review. Our thanks also go to Laurent Charling for TPMS and to the program chairs of ICML, ICLR, and NeurIPS for cross checking double submissions. We thank the website chair, Giovanni Farinella, and the CPI team (in particular Ashley Cook, Miriam Verdon, Nicola McGrane, and Sharon Kerr) for promptly adding material to the website as needed in the various phases of the process. Finally, we thank the publication chairs, Albert Ali Salah, Hamdi Dibeklioglu, Metehan Doyran, Henry Howard-Jenkins, Victor Prisacariu, Siyu Tang, and Gul Varol, who managed to compile these substantial proceedings in an exceedingly compressed schedule. We express our thanks to the ECVA team, in particular Kristina Scherbaum for allowing open access of the proceedings. We thank Alfred Hofmann from Springer who again serve as the publisher. Finally, we thank the other chairs of ECCV 2020, including in particular the general chairs for very useful feedback with the handling of the program.

August 2020

Andrea Vedaldi
Horst Bischof
Thomas Brox
Jan-Michael Frahm

Organization

General Chairs

Vittorio Ferrari	Google Research, Switzerland
Bob Fisher	University of Edinburgh, UK
Cordelia Schmid	Google and Inria, France
Emanuele Trucco	University of Dundee, UK

Program Chairs

Andrea Vedaldi	University of Oxford, UK
Horst Bischof	Graz University of Technology, Austria
Thomas Brox	University of Freiburg, Germany
Jan-Michael Frahm	University of North Carolina, USA

Industrial Liaison Chairs

Jim Ashe	University of Edinburgh, UK
Helmut Grabner	Zurich University of Applied Sciences, Switzerland
Diane Larlus	NAVER LABS Europe, France
Cristian Novotny	University of Edinburgh, UK

Local Arrangement Chairs

Yvan Petillot	Heriot-Watt University, UK
Paul Siebert	University of Glasgow, UK

Academic Demonstration Chair

Thomas Mensink	Google Research and University of Amsterdam, The Netherlands

Poster Chair

Stephen Mckenna	University of Dundee, UK

Technology Chair

Gerardo Aragon Camarasa	University of Glasgow, UK

Tutorial Chairs

Carlo Colombo   University of Florence, Italy
Sotirios Tsaftaris   University of Edinburgh, UK

Publication Chairs

Albert Ali Salah   Utrecht University, The Netherlands
Hamdi Dibeklioglu   Bilkent University, Turkey
Metehan Doyran   Utrecht University, The Netherlands
Henry Howard-Jenkins   University of Oxford, UK
Victor Adrian Prisacariu   University of Oxford, UK
Siyu Tang   ETH Zurich, Switzerland
Gul Varol   University of Oxford, UK

Website Chair

Giovanni Maria Farinella   University of Catania, Italy

Workshops Chairs

Adrien Bartoli   University of Clermont Auvergne, France
Andrea Fusiello   University of Udine, Italy

Area Chairs

Lourdes Agapito   University College London, UK
Zeynep Akata   University of Tübingen, Germany
Karteek Alahari   Inria, France
Antonis Argyros   University of Crete, Greece
Hossein Azizpour   KTH Royal Institute of Technology, Sweden
Joao P. Barreto   Universidade de Coimbra, Portugal
Alexander C. Berg   University of North Carolina at Chapel Hill, USA
Matthew B. Blaschko   KU Leuven, Belgium
Lubomir D. Bourdev   WaveOne, Inc., USA
Edmond Boyer   Inria, France
Yuri Boykov   University of Waterloo, Canada
Gabriel Brostow   University College London, UK
Michael S. Brown   National University of Singapore, Singapore
Jianfei Cai   Monash University, Australia
Barbara Caputo   Politecnico di Torino, Italy
Ayan Chakrabarti   Washington University, St. Louis, USA
Tat-Jen Cham   Nanyang Technological University, Singapore
Manmohan Chandraker   University of California, San Diego, USA
Rama Chellappa   Johns Hopkins University, USA
Liang-Chieh Chen   Google, USA

Yung-Yu Chuang	National Taiwan University, Taiwan
Ondrej Chum	Czech Technical University in Prague, Czech Republic
Brian Clipp	Kitware, USA
John Collomosse	University of Surrey and Adobe Research, UK
Jason J. Corso	University of Michigan, USA
David J. Crandall	Indiana University, USA
Daniel Cremers	University of California, Los Angeles, USA
Fabio Cuzzolin	Oxford Brookes University, UK
Jifeng Dai	SenseTime, SAR China
Kostas Daniilidis	University of Pennsylvania, USA
Andrew Davison	Imperial College London, UK
Alessio Del Bue	Fondazione Istituto Italiano di Tecnologia, Italy
Jia Deng	Princeton University, USA
Alexey Dosovitskiy	Google, Germany
Matthijs Douze	Facebook, France
Enrique Dunn	Stevens Institute of Technology, USA
Irfan Essa	Georgia Institute of Technology and Google, USA
Giovanni Maria Farinella	University of Catania, Italy
Ryan Farrell	Brigham Young University, USA
Paolo Favaro	University of Bern, Switzerland
Rogerio Feris	International Business Machines, USA
Cornelia Fermuller	University of Maryland, College Park, USA
David J. Fleet	Vector Institute, Canada
Friedrich Fraundorfer	DLR, Austria
Mario Fritz	CISPA Helmholtz Center for Information Security, Germany
Pascal Fua	EPFL (Swiss Federal Institute of Technology Lausanne), Switzerland
Yasutaka Furukawa	Simon Fraser University, Canada
Li Fuxin	Oregon State University, USA
Efstratios Gavves	University of Amsterdam, The Netherlands
Peter Vincent Gehler	Amazon, USA
Theo Gevers	University of Amsterdam, The Netherlands
Ross Girshick	Facebook AI Research, USA
Boqing Gong	Google, USA
Stephen Gould	Australian National University, Australia
Jinwei Gu	SenseTime Research, USA
Abhinav Gupta	Facebook, USA
Bohyung Han	Seoul National University, South Korea
Bharath Hariharan	Cornell University, USA
Tal Hassner	Facebook AI Research, USA
Xuming He	Australian National University, Australia
Joao F. Henriques	University of Oxford, UK
Adrian Hilton	University of Surrey, UK
Minh Hoai	Stony Brooks, State University of New York, USA
Derek Hoiem	University of Illinois Urbana-Champaign, USA

Timothy Hospedales	University of Edinburgh and Samsung, UK
Gang Hua	Wormpex AI Research, USA
Slobodan Ilic	Siemens AG, Germany
Hiroshi Ishikawa	Waseda University, Japan
Jiaya Jia	The Chinese University of Hong Kong, SAR China
Hailin Jin	Adobe Research, USA
Justin Johnson	University of Michigan, USA
Frederic Jurie	University of Caen Normandie, France
Fredrik Kahl	Chalmers University, Sweden
Sing Bing Kang	Zillow, USA
Gunhee Kim	Seoul National University, South Korea
Junmo Kim	Korea Advanced Institute of Science and Technology, South Korea
Tae-Kyun Kim	Imperial College London, UK
Ron Kimmel	Technion-Israel Institute of Technology, Israel
Alexander Kirillov	Facebook AI Research, USA
Kris Kitani	Carnegie Mellon University, USA
Iasonas Kokkinos	Ariel AI, UK
Vladlen Koltun	Intel Labs, USA
Nikos Komodakis	Ecole des Ponts ParisTech, France
Piotr Koniusz	Australian National University, Australia
M. Pawan Kumar	University of Oxford, UK
Kyros Kutulakos	University of Toronto, Canada
Christoph Lampert	IST Austria, Austria
Ivan Laptev	Inria, France
Diane Larlus	NAVER LABS Europe, France
Laura Leal-Taixe	Technical University Munich, Germany
Honglak Lee	Google and University of Michigan, USA
Joon-Young Lee	Adobe Research, USA
Kyoung Mu Lee	Seoul National University, South Korea
Seungyong Lee	POSTECH, South Korea
Yong Jae Lee	University of California, Davis, USA
Bastian Leibe	RWTH Aachen University, Germany
Victor Lempitsky	Samsung, Russia
Ales Leonardis	University of Birmingham, UK
Marius Leordeanu	Institute of Mathematics of the Romanian Academy, Romania
Vincent Lepetit	ENPC ParisTech, France
Hongdong Li	The Australian National University, Australia
Xi Li	Zhejiang University, China
Yin Li	University of Wisconsin-Madison, USA
Zicheng Liao	Zhejiang University, China
Jongwoo Lim	Hanyang University, South Korea
Stephen Lin	Microsoft Research Asia, China
Yen-Yu Lin	National Chiao Tung University, Taiwan, China
Zhe Lin	Adobe Research, USA

Haibin Ling	Stony Brooks, State University of New York, USA
Jiaying Liu	Peking University, China
Ming-Yu Liu	NVIDIA, USA
Si Liu	Beihang University, China
Xiaoming Liu	Michigan State University, USA
Huchuan Lu	Dalian University of Technology, China
Simon Lucey	Carnegie Mellon University, USA
Jiebo Luo	University of Rochester, USA
Julien Mairal	Inria, France
Michael Maire	University of Chicago, USA
Subhransu Maji	University of Massachusetts, Amherst, USA
Yasushi Makihara	Osaka University, Japan
Jiri Matas	Czech Technical University in Prague, Czech Republic
Yasuyuki Matsushita	Osaka University, Japan
Philippos Mordohai	Stevens Institute of Technology, USA
Vittorio Murino	University of Verona, Italy
Naila Murray	NAVER LABS Europe, France
Hajime Nagahara	Osaka University, Japan
P. J. Narayanan	International Institute of Information Technology (IIIT), Hyderabad, India
Nassir Navab	Technical University of Munich, Germany
Natalia Neverova	Facebook AI Research, France
Matthias Niessner	Technical University of Munich, Germany
Jean-Marc Odobez	Idiap Research Institute and Swiss Federal Institute of Technology Lausanne, Switzerland
Francesca Odone	Università di Genova, Italy
Takeshi Oishi	The University of Tokyo, Tokyo Institute of Technology, Japan
Vicente Ordonez	University of Virginia, USA
Manohar Paluri	Facebook AI Research, USA
Maja Pantic	Imperial College London, UK
In Kyu Park	Inha University, South Korea
Ioannis Patras	Queen Mary University of London, UK
Patrick Perez	Valeo, France
Bryan A. Plummer	Boston University, USA
Thomas Pock	Graz University of Technology, Austria
Marc Pollefeys	ETH Zurich and Microsoft MR & AI Zurich Lab, Switzerland
Jean Ponce	Inria, France
Gerard Pons-Moll	MPII, Saarland Informatics Campus, Germany
Jordi Pont-Tuset	Google, Switzerland
James Matthew Rehg	Georgia Institute of Technology, USA
Ian Reid	University of Adelaide, Australia
Olaf Ronneberger	DeepMind London, UK
Stefan Roth	TU Darmstadt, Germany
Bryan Russell	Adobe Research, USA

Mathieu Salzmann	EPFL, Switzerland
Dimitris Samaras	Stony Brook University, USA
Imari Sato	National Institute of Informatics (NII), Japan
Yoichi Sato	The University of Tokyo, Japan
Torsten Sattler	Czech Technical University in Prague, Czech Republic
Daniel Scharstein	Middlebury College, USA
Bernt Schiele	MPII, Saarland Informatics Campus, Germany
Julia A. Schnabel	King's College London, UK
Nicu Sebe	University of Trento, Italy
Greg Shakhnarovich	Toyota Technological Institute at Chicago, USA
Humphrey Shi	University of Oregon, USA
Jianbo Shi	University of Pennsylvania, USA
Jianping Shi	SenseTime, China
Leonid Sigal	University of British Columbia, Canada
Cees Snoek	University of Amsterdam, The Netherlands
Richard Souvenir	Temple University, USA
Hao Su	University of California, San Diego, USA
Akihiro Sugimoto	National Institute of Informatics (NII), Japan
Jian Sun	Megvii Technology, China
Jian Sun	Xi'an Jiaotong University, China
Chris Sweeney	Facebook Reality Labs, USA
Yu-wing Tai	Kuaishou Technology, China
Chi-Keung Tang	The Hong Kong University of Science and Technology, SAR China
Radu Timofte	ETH Zurich, Switzerland
Sinisa Todorovic	Oregon State University, USA
Giorgos Tolias	Czech Technical University in Prague, Czech Republic
Carlo Tomasi	Duke University, USA
Tatiana Tommasi	Politecnico di Torino, Italy
Lorenzo Torresani	Facebook AI Research and Dartmouth College, USA
Alexander Toshev	Google, USA
Zhuowen Tu	University of California, San Diego, USA
Tinne Tuytelaars	KU Leuven, Belgium
Jasper Uijlings	Google, Switzerland
Nuno Vasconcelos	University of California, San Diego, USA
Olga Veksler	University of Waterloo, Canada
Rene Vidal	Johns Hopkins University, USA
Gang Wang	Alibaba Group, China
Jingdong Wang	Microsoft Research Asia, China
Yizhou Wang	Peking University, China
Lior Wolf	Facebook AI Research and Tel Aviv University, Israel
Jianxin Wu	Nanjing University, China
Tao Xiang	University of Surrey, UK
Saining Xie	Facebook AI Research, USA
Ming-Hsuan Yang	University of California at Merced and Google, USA
Ruigang Yang	University of Kentucky, USA

Kwang Moo Yi   University of Victoria, Canada
Zhaozheng Yin   Stony Brook, State University of New York, USA
Chang D. Yoo   Korea Advanced Institute of Science and Technology,
                           South Korea
Shaodi You   University of Amsterdam, The Netherlands
Jingyi Yu   ShanghaiTech University, China
Stella Yu   University of California, Berkeley, and ICSI, USA
Stefanos Zafeiriou   Imperial College London, UK
Hongbin Zha   Peking University, China
Tianzhu Zhang   University of Science and Technology of China, China
Liang Zheng   Australian National University, Australia
Todd E. Zickler   Harvard University, USA
Andrew Zisserman   University of Oxford, UK

Technical Program Committee

Sathyanarayanan
  N. Aakur
Wael Abd Almgaeed
Abdelrahman
  Abdelhamed
Abdullah Abuolaim
Supreeth Achar
Hanno Ackermann
Ehsan Adeli
Triantafyllos Afouras
Sameer Agarwal
Aishwarya Agrawal
Harsh Agrawal
Pulkit Agrawal
Antonio Agudo
Eirikur Agustsson
Karim Ahmed
Byeongjoo Ahn
Unaiza Ahsan
Thalaiyasingam Ajanthan
Kenan E. Ak
Emre Akbas
Naveed Akhtar
Derya Akkaynak
Yagiz Aksoy
Ziad Al-Halah
Xavier Alameda-Pineda
Jean-Baptiste Alayrac

Samuel Albanie
Shadi Albarqouni
Cenek Albl
Hassan Abu Alhaija
Daniel Aliaga
Mohammad
  S. Aliakbarian
Rahaf Aljundi
Thiemo Alldieck
Jon Almazan
Jose M. Alvarez
Senjian An
Saket Anand
Codruta Ancuti
Cosmin Ancuti
Peter Anderson
Juan Andrade-Cetto
Alexander Andreopoulos
Misha Andriluka
Dragomir Anguelov
Rushil Anirudh
Michel Antunes
Oisin Mac Aodha
Srikar Appalaraju
Relja Arandjelovic
Nikita Araslanov
Andre Araujo
Helder Araujo

Pablo Arbelaez
Shervin Ardeshir
Sercan O. Arik
Anil Armagan
Anurag Arnab
Chetan Arora
Federica Arrigoni
Mathieu Aubry
Shai Avidan
Angelica I. Aviles-Rivero
Yannis Avrithis
Ismail Ben Ayed
Shekoofeh Azizi
Ioan Andrei Bârsan
Artem Babenko
Deepak Babu Sam
Seung-Hwan Baek
Seungryul Baek
Andrew D. Bagdanov
Shai Bagon
Yuval Bahat
Junjie Bai
Song Bai
Xiang Bai
Yalong Bai
Yancheng Bai
Peter Bajcsy
Slawomir Bak

Mahsa Baktashmotlagh
Kavita Bala
Yogesh Balaji
Guha Balakrishnan
V. N. Balasubramanian
Federico Baldassarre
Vassileios Balntas
Shurjo Banerjee
Aayush Bansal
Ankan Bansal
Jianmin Bao
Linchao Bao
Wenbo Bao
Yingze Bao
Akash Bapat
Md Jawadul Hasan Bappy
Fabien Baradel
Lorenzo Baraldi
Daniel Barath
Adrian Barbu
Kobus Barnard
Nick Barnes
Francisco Barranco
Jonathan T. Barron
Arslan Basharat
Chaim Baskin
Anil S. Baslamisli
Jorge Batista
Kayhan Batmanghelich
Konstantinos Batsos
David Bau
Luis Baumela
Christoph Baur
Eduardo
  Bayro-Corrochano
Paul Beardsley
Jan Bednavr'ik
Oscar Beijbom
Philippe Bekaert
Esube Bekele
Vasileios Belagiannis
Ohad Ben-Shahar
Abhijit Bendale
Róger Bermúdez-Chacón
Maxim Berman
Jesus Bermudez-cameo

Florian Bernard
Stefano Berretti
Marcelo Bertalmio
Gedas Bertasius
Cigdem Beyan
Lucas Beyer
Vijayakumar Bhagavatula
Arjun Nitin Bhagoji
Apratim Bhattacharyya
Binod Bhattarai
Sai Bi
Jia-Wang Bian
Simone Bianco
Adel Bibi
Tolga Birdal
Tom Bishop
Soma Biswas
Mårten Björkman
Volker Blanz
Vishnu Boddeti
Navaneeth Bodla
Simion-Vlad Bogolin
Xavier Boix
Piotr Bojanowski
Timo Bolkart
Guido Borghi
Larbi Boubchir
Guillaume Bourmaud
Adrien Bousseau
Thierry Bouwmans
Richard Bowden
Hakan Boyraz
Mathieu Brédif
Samarth Brahmbhatt
Steve Branson
Nikolas Brasch
Biagio Brattoli
Ernesto Brau
Toby P. Breckon
Francois Bremond
Jesus Briales
Sofia Broomé
Marcus A. Brubaker
Luc Brun
Silvia Bucci
Shyamal Buch

Pradeep Buddharaju
Uta Buechler
Mai Bui
Tu Bui
Adrian Bulat
Giedrius T. Burachas
Elena Burceanu
Xavier P. Burgos-Artizzu
Kaylee Burns
Andrei Bursuc
Benjamin Busam
Wonmin Byeon
Zoya Bylinskii
Sergi Caelles
Jianrui Cai
Minjie Cai
Yujun Cai
Zhaowei Cai
Zhipeng Cai
Juan C. Caicedo
Simone Calderara
Necati Cihan Camgoz
Dylan Campbell
Octavia Camps
Jiale Cao
Kaidi Cao
Liangliang Cao
Xiangyong Cao
Xiaochun Cao
Yang Cao
Yu Cao
Yue Cao
Zhangjie Cao
Luca Carlone
Mathilde Caron
Dan Casas
Thomas J. Cashman
Umberto Castellani
Lluis Castrejon
Jacopo Cavazza
Fabio Cermelli
Hakan Cevikalp
Menglei Chai
Ishani Chakraborty
Rudrasis Chakraborty
Antoni B. Chan

Kwok-Ping Chan
Siddhartha Chandra
Sharat Chandran
Arjun Chandrasekaran
Angel X. Chang
Che-Han Chang
Hong Chang
Hyun Sung Chang
Hyung Jin Chang
Jianlong Chang
Ju Yong Chang
Ming-Ching Chang
Simyung Chang
Xiaojun Chang
Yu-Wei Chao
Devendra S. Chaplot
Arslan Chaudhry
Rizwan A. Chaudhry
Can Chen
Chang Chen
Chao Chen
Chen Chen
Chu-Song Chen
Dapeng Chen
Dong Chen
Dongdong Chen
Guanying Chen
Hongge Chen
Hsin-yi Chen
Huaijin Chen
Hwann-Tzong Chen
Jianbo Chen
Jianhui Chen
Jiansheng Chen
Jiaxin Chen
Jie Chen
Jun-Cheng Chen
Kan Chen
Kevin Chen
Lin Chen
Long Chen
Min-Hung Chen
Qifeng Chen
Shi Chen
Shixing Chen
Tianshui Chen

Weifeng Chen
Weikai Chen
Xi Chen
Xiaohan Chen
Xiaozhi Chen
Xilin Chen
Xingyu Chen
Xinlei Chen
Xinyun Chen
Yi-Ting Chen
Yilun Chen
Ying-Cong Chen
Yinpeng Chen
Yiran Chen
Yu Chen
Yu-Sheng Chen
Yuhua Chen
Yun-Chun Chen
Yunpeng Chen
Yuntao Chen
Zhuoyuan Chen
Zitian Chen
Anchieh Cheng
Bowen Cheng
Erkang Cheng
Gong Cheng
Guangliang Cheng
Jingchun Cheng
Jun Cheng
Li Cheng
Ming-Ming Cheng
Yu Cheng
Ziang Cheng
Anoop Cherian
Dmitry Chetverikov
Ngai-man Cheung
William Cheung
Ajad Chhatkuli
Naoki Chiba
Benjamin Chidester
Han-pang Chiu
Mang Tik Chiu
Wei-Chen Chiu
Donghyeon Cho
Hojin Cho
Minsu Cho

Nam Ik Cho
Tim Cho
Tae Eun Choe
Chiho Choi
Edward Choi
Inchang Choi
Jinsoo Choi
Jonghyun Choi
Jongwon Choi
Yukyung Choi
Hisham Cholakkal
Eunji Chong
Jaegul Choo
Christopher Choy
Hang Chu
Peng Chu
Wen-Sheng Chu
Albert Chung
Joon Son Chung
Hai Ci
Safa Cicek
Ramazan G. Cinbis
Arridhana Ciptadi
Javier Civera
James J. Clark
Ronald Clark
Felipe Codevilla
Michael Cogswell
Andrea Cohen
Maxwell D. Collins
Carlo Colombo
Yang Cong
Adria R. Continente
Marcella Cornia
John Richard Corring
Darren Cosker
Dragos Costea
Garrison W. Cottrell
Florent Couzinie-Devy
Marco Cristani
Ioana Croitoru
James L. Crowley
Jiequan Cui
Zhaopeng Cui
Ross Cutler
Antonio D'Innocente

Rozenn Dahyot
Bo Dai
Dengxin Dai
Hang Dai
Longquan Dai
Shuyang Dai
Xiyang Dai
Yuchao Dai
Adrian V. Dalca
Dima Damen
Bharath B. Damodaran
Kristin Dana
Martin Danelljan
Zheng Dang
Zachary Alan Daniels
Donald G. Dansereau
Abhishek Das
Samyak Datta
Achal Dave
Titas De
Rodrigo de Bem
Teo de Campos
Raoul de Charette
Shalini De Mello
Joseph DeGol
Herve Delingette
Haowen Deng
Jiankang Deng
Weijian Deng
Zhiwei Deng
Joachim Denzler
Konstantinos G. Derpanis
Aditya Deshpande
Frederic Devernay
Somdip Dey
Arturo Deza
Abhinav Dhall
Helisa Dhamo
Vikas Dhiman
Fillipe Dias Moreira
  de Souza
Ali Diba
Ferran Diego
Guiguang Ding
Henghui Ding
Jian Ding

Mingyu Ding
Xinghao Ding
Zhengming Ding
Robert DiPietro
Cosimo Distante
Ajay Divakaran
Mandar Dixit
Abdelaziz Djelouah
Thanh-Toan Do
Jose Dolz
Bo Dong
Chao Dong
Jiangxin Dong
Weiming Dong
Weisheng Dong
Xingping Dong
Xuanyi Dong
Yinpeng Dong
Gianfranco Doretto
Hazel Doughty
Hassen Drira
Bertram Drost
Dawei Du
Ye Duan
Yueqi Duan
Abhimanyu Dubey
Anastasia Dubrovina
Stefan Duffner
Chi Nhan Duong
Thibaut Durand
Zoran Duric
Iulia Duta
Debidatta Dwibedi
Benjamin Eckart
Marc Eder
Marzieh Edraki
Alexei A. Efros
Kiana Ehsani
Hazm Kemal Ekenel
James H. Elder
Mohamed Elgharib
Shireen Elhabian
Ehsan Elhamifar
Mohamed Elhoseiny
Ian Endres
N. Benjamin Erichson

Jan Ernst
Sergio Escalera
Francisco Escolano
Victor Escorcia
Carlos Esteves
Francisco J. Estrada
Bin Fan
Chenyou Fan
Deng-Ping Fan
Haoqi Fan
Hehe Fan
Heng Fan
Kai Fan
Lijie Fan
Linxi Fan
Quanfu Fan
Shaojing Fan
Xiaochuan Fan
Xin Fan
Yuchen Fan
Sean Fanello
Hao-Shu Fang
Haoyang Fang
Kuan Fang
Yi Fang
Yuming Fang
Azade Farshad
Alireza Fathi
Raanan Fattal
Joao Fayad
Xiaohan Fei
Christoph Feichtenhofer
Michael Felsberg
Chen Feng
Jiashi Feng
Junyi Feng
Mengyang Feng
Qianli Feng
Zhenhua Feng
Michele Fenzi
Andras Ferencz
Martin Fergie
Basura Fernando
Ethan Fetaya
Michael Firman
John W. Fisher

Matthew Fisher
Boris Flach
Corneliu Florea
Wolfgang Foerstner
David Fofi
Gian Luca Foresti
Per-Erik Forssen
David Fouhey
Katerina Fragkiadaki
Victor Fragoso
Jean-Sébastien Franco
Ohad Fried
Iuri Frosio
Cheng-Yang Fu
Huazhu Fu
Jianlong Fu
Jingjing Fu
Xueyang Fu
Yanwei Fu
Ying Fu
Yun Fu
Olac Fuentes
Kent Fujiwara
Takuya Funatomi
Christopher Funk
Thomas Funkhouser
Antonino Furnari
Ryo Furukawa
Erik Gärtner
Raghudeep Gadde
Matheus Gadelha
Vandit Gajjar
Trevor Gale
Juergen Gall
Mathias Gallardo
Guillermo Gallego
Orazio Gallo
Chuang Gan
Zhe Gan
Madan Ravi Ganesh
Aditya Ganeshan
Siddha Ganju
Bin-Bin Gao
Changxin Gao
Feng Gao
Hongchang Gao

Jin Gao
Jiyang Gao
Junbin Gao
Katelyn Gao
Lin Gao
Mingfei Gao
Ruiqi Gao
Ruohan Gao
Shenghua Gao
Yuan Gao
Yue Gao
Noa Garcia
Alberto Garcia-Garcia
Guillermo
   Garcia-Hernando
Jacob R. Gardner
Animesh Garg
Kshitiz Garg
Rahul Garg
Ravi Garg
Philip N. Garner
Kirill Gavrilyuk
Paul Gay
Shiming Ge
Weifeng Ge
Baris Gecer
Xin Geng
Kyle Genova
Stamatios Georgoulis
Bernard Ghanem
Michael Gharbi
Kamran Ghasedi
Golnaz Ghiasi
Arnab Ghosh
Partha Ghosh
Silvio Giancola
Andrew Gilbert
Rohit Girdhar
Xavier Giro-i-Nieto
Thomas Gittings
Ioannis Gkioulekas
Clement Godard
Vaibhava Goel
Bastian Goldluecke
Lluis Gomez
Nuno Gonçalves

Dong Gong
Ke Gong
Mingming Gong
Abel Gonzalez-Garcia
Ariel Gordon
Daniel Gordon
Paulo Gotardo
Venu Madhav Govindu
Ankit Goyal
Priya Goyal
Raghav Goyal
Benjamin Graham
Douglas Gray
Brent A. Griffin
Etienne Grossmann
David Gu
Jiayuan Gu
Jiuxiang Gu
Lin Gu
Qiao Gu
Shuhang Gu
Jose J. Guerrero
Paul Guerrero
Jie Gui
Jean-Yves Guillemaut
Riza Alp Guler
Erhan Gundogdu
Fatma Guney
Guodong Guo
Kaiwen Guo
Qi Guo
Sheng Guo
Shi Guo
Tiantong Guo
Xiaojie Guo
Yijie Guo
Yiluan Guo
Yuanfang Guo
Yulan Guo
Agrim Gupta
Ankush Gupta
Mohit Gupta
Saurabh Gupta
Tanmay Gupta
Danna Gurari
Abner Guzman-Rivera

JunYoung Gwak
Michael Gygli
Jung-Woo Ha
Simon Hadfield
Isma Hadji
Bjoern Haefner
Taeyoung Hahn
Levente Hajder
Peter Hall
Emanuela Haller
Stefan Haller
Bumsub Ham
Abdullah Hamdi
Dongyoon Han
Hu Han
Jungong Han
Junwei Han
Kai Han
Tian Han
Xiaoguang Han
Xintong Han
Yahong Han
Ankur Handa
Zekun Hao
Albert Haque
Tatsuya Harada
Mehrtash Harandi
Adam W. Harley
Mahmudul Hasan
Atsushi Hashimoto
Ali Hatamizadeh
Munawar Hayat
Dongliang He
Jingrui He
Junfeng He
Kaiming He
Kun He
Lei He
Pan He
Ran He
Shengfeng He
Tong He
Weipeng He
Xuming He
Yang He
Yihui He

Zhihai He
Chinmay Hegde
Janne Heikkila
Mattias P. Heinrich
Stéphane Herbin
Alexander Hermans
Luis Herranz
John R. Hershey
Aaron Hertzmann
Roei Herzig
Anders Heyden
Steven Hickson
Otmar Hilliges
Tomas Hodan
Judy Hoffman
Michael Hofmann
Yannick Hold-Geoffroy
Namdar Homayounfar
Sina Honari
Richang Hong
Seunghoon Hong
Xiaopeng Hong
Yi Hong
Hidekata Hontani
Anthony Hoogs
Yedid Hoshen
Mir Rayat Imtiaz Hossain
Junhui Hou
Le Hou
Lu Hou
Tingbo Hou
Wei-Lin Hsiao
Cheng-Chun Hsu
Gee-Sern Jison Hsu
Kuang-jui Hsu
Changbo Hu
Di Hu
Guosheng Hu
Han Hu
Hao Hu
Hexiang Hu
Hou-Ning Hu
Jie Hu
Junlin Hu
Nan Hu
Ping Hu

Ronghang Hu
Xiaowei Hu
Yinlin Hu
Yuan-Ting Hu
Zhe Hu
Binh-Son Hua
Yang Hua
Bingyao Huang
Di Huang
Dong Huang
Fay Huang
Haibin Huang
Haozhi Huang
Heng Huang
Huaibo Huang
Jia-Bin Huang
Jing Huang
Jingwei Huang
Kaizhu Huang
Lei Huang
Qiangui Huang
Qiaoying Huang
Qingqiu Huang
Qixing Huang
Shaoli Huang
Sheng Huang
Siyuan Huang
Weilin Huang
Wenbing Huang
Xiangru Huang
Xun Huang
Yan Huang
Yifei Huang
Yue Huang
Zhiwu Huang
Zilong Huang
Minyoung Huh
Zhuo Hui
Matthias B. Hullin
Martin Humenberger
Wei-Chih Hung
Zhouyuan Huo
Junhwa Hur
Noureldien Hussein
Jyh-Jing Hwang
Seong Jae Hwang

Sung Ju Hwang
Ichiro Ide
Ivo Ihrke
Daiki Ikami
Satoshi Ikehata
Nazli Ikizler-Cinbis
Sunghoon Im
Yani Ioannou
Radu Tudor Ionescu
Umar Iqbal
Go Irie
Ahmet Iscen
Md Amirul Islam
Vamsi Ithapu
Nathan Jacobs
Arpit Jain
Himalaya Jain
Suyog Jain
Stuart James
Won-Dong Jang
Yunseok Jang
Ronnachai Jaroensri
Dinesh Jayaraman
Sadeep Jayasumana
Suren Jayasuriya
Herve Jegou
Simon Jenni
Hae-Gon Jeon
Yunho Jeon
Koteswar R. Jerripothula
Hueihan Jhuang
I-hong Jhuo
Dinghuang Ji
Hui Ji
Jingwei Ji
Pan Ji
Yanli Ji
Baoxiong Jia
Kui Jia
Xu Jia
Chiyu Max Jiang
Haiyong Jiang
Hao Jiang
Huaizu Jiang
Huajie Jiang
Ke Jiang

Lai Jiang
Li Jiang
Lu Jiang
Ming Jiang
Peng Jiang
Shuqiang Jiang
Wei Jiang
Xudong Jiang
Zhuolin Jiang
Jianbo Jiao
Zequn Jie
Dakai Jin
Kyong Hwan Jin
Lianwen Jin
SouYoung Jin
Xiaojie Jin
Xin Jin
Nebojsa Jojic
Alexis Joly
Michael Jeffrey Jones
Hanbyul Joo
Jungseock Joo
Kyungdon Joo
Ajjen Joshi
Shantanu H. Joshi
Da-Cheng Juan
Marco Körner
Kevin Köser
Asim Kadav
Christine Kaeser-Chen
Kushal Kafle
Dagmar Kainmueller
Ioannis A. Kakadiaris
Zdenek Kalal
Nima Kalantari
Yannis Kalantidis
Mahdi M. Kalayeh
Anmol Kalia
Sinan Kalkan
Vicky Kalogeiton
Ashwin Kalyan
Joni-kristian Kamarainen
Gerda Kamberova
Chandra Kambhamettu
Martin Kampel
Meina Kan

Christopher Kanan
Kenichi Kanatani
Angjoo Kanazawa
Atsushi Kanehira
Takuhiro Kaneko
Asako Kanezaki
Bingyi Kang
Di Kang
Sunghun Kang
Zhao Kang
Vadim Kantorov
Abhishek Kar
Amlan Kar
Theofanis Karaletsos
Leonid Karlinsky
Kevin Karsch
Angelos Katharopoulos
Isinsu Katircioglu
Hiroharu Kato
Zoltan Kato
Dotan Kaufman
Jan Kautz
Rei Kawakami
Qiuhong Ke
Wadim Kehl
Petr Kellnhofer
Aniruddha Kembhavi
Cem Keskin
Margret Keuper
Daniel Keysers
Ashkan Khakzar
Fahad Khan
Naeemullah Khan
Salman Khan
Siddhesh Khandelwal
Rawal Khirodkar
Anna Khoreva
Tejas Khot
Parmeshwar Khurd
Hadi Kiapour
Joe Kileel
Chanho Kim
Dahun Kim
Edward Kim
Eunwoo Kim
Han-ul Kim

Hansung Kim
Heewon Kim
Hyo Jin Kim
Hyunwoo J. Kim
Jinkyu Kim
Jiwon Kim
Jongmin Kim
Junsik Kim
Junyeong Kim
Min H. Kim
Namil Kim
Pyojin Kim
Seon Joo Kim
Seong Tae Kim
Seungryong Kim
Sungwoong Kim
Tae Hyun Kim
Vladimir Kim
Won Hwa Kim
Yonghyun Kim
Benjamin Kimia
Akisato Kimura
Pieter-Jan Kindermans
Zsolt Kira
Itaru Kitahara
Hedvig Kjellstrom
Jan Knopp
Takumi Kobayashi
Erich Kobler
Parker Koch
Reinhard Koch
Elyor Kodirov
Amir Kolaman
Nicholas Kolkin
Dimitrios Kollias
Stefanos Kollias
Soheil Kolouri
Adams Wai-Kin Kong
Naejin Kong
Shu Kong
Tao Kong
Yu Kong
Yoshinori Konishi
Daniil Kononenko
Theodora Kontogianni
Simon Korman

Adam Kortylewski
Jana Kosecka
Jean Kossaifi
Satwik Kottur
Rigas Kouskouridas
Adriana Kovashka
Rama Kovvuri
Adarsh Kowdle
Jedrzej Kozerawski
Mateusz Kozinski
Philipp Kraehenbuehl
Gregory Kramida
Josip Krapac
Dmitry Kravchenko
Ranjay Krishna
Pavel Krsek
Alexander Krull
Jakob Kruse
Hiroyuki Kubo
Hilde Kuehne
Jason Kuen
Andreas Kuhn
Arjan Kuijper
Zuzana Kukelova
Ajay Kumar
Amit Kumar
Avinash Kumar
Suryansh Kumar
Vijay Kumar
Kaustav Kundu
Weicheng Kuo
Nojun Kwak
Suha Kwak
Junseok Kwon
Nikolaos Kyriazis
Zorah Lähner
Ankit Laddha
Florent Lafarge
Jean Lahoud
Kevin Lai
Shang-Hong Lai
Wei-Sheng Lai
Yu-Kun Lai
Iro Laina
Antony Lam
John Wheatley Lambert

Xiangyuan lan
Xu Lan
Charis Lanaras
Georg Langs
Oswald Lanz
Dong Lao
Yizhen Lao
Agata Lapedriza
Gustav Larsson
Viktor Larsson
Katrin Lasinger
Christoph Lassner
Longin Jan Latecki
Stéphane Lathuilière
Rynson Lau
Hei Law
Justin Lazarow
Svetlana Lazebnik
Hieu Le
Huu Le
Ngan Hoang Le
Trung-Nghia Le
Vuong Le
Colin Lea
Erik Learned-Miller
Chen-Yu Lee
Gim Hee Lee
Hsin-Ying Lee
Hyungtae Lee
Jae-Han Lee
Jimmy Addison Lee
Joonseok Lee
Kibok Lee
Kuang-Huei Lee
Kwonjoon Lee
Minsik Lee
Sang-chul Lee
Seungkyu Lee
Soochan Lee
Stefan Lee
Taehee Lee
Andreas Lehrmann
Jie Lei
Peng Lei
Matthew Joseph Leotta
Wee Kheng Leow

Gil Levi
Evgeny Levinkov
Aviad Levis
Jose Lezama
Ang Li
Bin Li
Bing Li
Boyi Li
Changsheng Li
Chao Li
Chen Li
Cheng Li
Chenglong Li
Chi Li
Chun-Guang Li
Chun-Liang Li
Chunyuan Li
Dong Li
Guanbin Li
Hao Li
Haoxiang Li
Hongsheng Li
Hongyang Li
Houqiang Li
Huibin Li
Jia Li
Jianan Li
Jianguo Li
Junnan Li
Junxuan Li
Kai Li
Ke Li
Kejie Li
Kunpeng Li
Lerenhan Li
Li Erran Li
Mengtian Li
Mu Li
Peihua Li
Peiyi Li
Ping Li
Qi Li
Qing Li
Ruiyu Li
Ruoteng Li
Shaozi Li

Sheng Li
Shiwei Li
Shuang Li
Siyang Li
Stan Z. Li
Tianye Li
Wei Li
Weixin Li
Wen Li
Wenbo Li
Xiaomeng Li
Xin Li
Xiu Li
Xuelong Li
Xueting Li
Yan Li
Yandong Li
Yanghao Li
Yehao Li
Yi Li
Yijun Li
Yikang LI
Yining Li
Yongjie Li
Yu Li
Yu-Jhe Li
Yunpeng Li
Yunsheng Li
Yunzhu Li
Zhe Li
Zhen Li
Zhengqi Li
Zhenyang Li
Zhuwen Li
Dongze Lian
Xiaochen Lian
Zhouhui Lian
Chen Liang
Jie Liang
Ming Liang
Paul Pu Liang
Pengpeng Liang
Shu Liang
Wei Liang
Jing Liao
Minghui Liao

Renjie Liao
Shengcai Liao
Shuai Liao
Yiyi Liao
Ser-Nam Lim
Chen-Hsuan Lin
Chung-Ching Lin
Dahua Lin
Ji Lin
Kevin Lin
Tianwei Lin
Tsung-Yi Lin
Tsung-Yu Lin
Wei-An Lin
Weiyao Lin
Yen-Chen Lin
Yuewei Lin
David B. Lindell
Drew Linsley
Krzysztof Lis
Roee Litman
Jim Little
An-An Liu
Bo Liu
Buyu Liu
Chao Liu
Chen Liu
Cheng-lin Liu
Chenxi Liu
Dong Liu
Feng Liu
Guilin Liu
Haomiao Liu
Heshan Liu
Hong Liu
Ji Liu
Jingen Liu
Jun Liu
Lanlan Liu
Li Liu
Liu Liu
Mengyuan Liu
Miaomiao Liu
Nian Liu
Ping Liu
Risheng Liu

Sheng Liu
Shu Liu
Shuaicheng Liu
Sifei Liu
Siqi Liu
Siying Liu
Songtao Liu
Ting Liu
Tongliang Liu
Tyng-Luh Liu
Wanquan Liu
Wei Liu
Weiyang Liu
Weizhe Liu
Wenyu Liu
Wu Liu
Xialei Liu
Xianglong Liu
Xiaodong Liu
Xiaofeng Liu
Xihui Liu
Xingyu Liu
Xinwang Liu
Xuanqing Liu
Xuebo Liu
Yang Liu
Yaojie Liu
Yebin Liu
Yen-Cheng Liu
Yiming Liu
Yu Liu
Yu-Shen Liu
Yufan Liu
Yun Liu
Zheng Liu
Zhijian Liu
Zhuang Liu
Zichuan Liu
Ziwei Liu
Zongyi Liu
Stephan Liwicki
Liliana Lo Presti
Chengjiang Long
Fuchen Long
Mingsheng Long
Xiang Long

Yang Long
Charles T. Loop
Antonio Lopez
Roberto J. Lopez-Sastre
Javier Lorenzo-Navarro
Manolis Lourakis
Boyu Lu
Canyi Lu
Feng Lu
Guoyu Lu
Hongtao Lu
Jiajun Lu
Jiasen Lu
Jiwen Lu
Kaiyue Lu
Le Lu
Shao-Ping Lu
Shijian Lu
Xiankai Lu
Xin Lu
Yao Lu
Yiping Lu
Yongxi Lu
Yongyi Lu
Zhiwu Lu
Fujun Luan
Benjamin E. Lundell
Hao Luo
Jian-Hao Luo
Ruotian Luo
Weixin Luo
Wenhan Luo
Wenjie Luo
Yan Luo
Zelun Luo
Zixin Luo
Khoa Luu
Zhaoyang Lv
Pengyuan Lyu
Thomas Möllenhoff
Matthias Müller
Bingpeng Ma
Chih-Yao Ma
Chongyang Ma
Huimin Ma
Jiayi Ma

K. T. Ma
Ke Ma
Lin Ma
Liqian Ma
Shugao Ma
Wei-Chiu Ma
Xiaojian Ma
Xingjun Ma
Zhanyu Ma
Zheng Ma
Radek Jakob Mackowiak
Ludovic Magerand
Shweta Mahajan
Siddharth Mahendran
Long Mai
Ameesh Makadia
Oscar Mendez Maldonado
Mateusz Malinowski
Yury Malkov
Arun Mallya
Dipu Manandhar
Massimiliano Mancini
Fabian Manhardt
Kevis-kokitsi Maninis
Varun Manjunatha
Junhua Mao
Xudong Mao
Alina Marcu
Edgar Margffoy-Tuay
Dmitrii Marin
Manuel J. Marin-Jimenez
Kenneth Marino
Niki Martinel
Julieta Martinez
Jonathan Masci
Tomohiro Mashita
Iacopo Masi
David Masip
Daniela Massiceti
Stefan Mathe
Yusuke Matsui
Tetsu Matsukawa
Iain A. Matthews
Kevin James Matzen
Bruce Allen Maxwell
Stephen Maybank

Helmut Mayer
Amir Mazaheri
David McAllester
Steven McDonagh
Stephen J. Mckenna
Roey Mechrez
Prakhar Mehrotra
Christopher Mei
Xue Mei
Paulo R. S. Mendonca
Lili Meng
Zibo Meng
Thomas Mensink
Bjoern Menze
Michele Merler
Kourosh Meshgi
Pascal Mettes
Christopher Metzler
Liang Mi
Qiguang Miao
Xin Miao
Tomer Michaeli
Frank Michel
Antoine Miech
Krystian Mikolajczyk
Peyman Milanfar
Ben Mildenhall
Gregor Miller
Fausto Milletari
Dongbo Min
Kyle Min
Pedro Miraldo
Dmytro Mishkin
Anand Mishra
Ashish Mishra
Ishan Misra
Niluthpol C. Mithun
Kaushik Mitra
Niloy Mitra
Anton Mitrokhin
Ikuhisa Mitsugami
Anurag Mittal
Kaichun Mo
Zhipeng Mo
Davide Modolo
Michael Moeller

Pritish Mohapatra
Pavlo Molchanov
Davide Moltisanti
Pascal Monasse
Mathew Monfort
Aron Monszpart
Sean Moran
Vlad I. Morariu
Francesc Moreno-Noguer
Pietro Morerio
Stylianos Moschoglou
Yael Moses
Roozbeh Mottaghi
Pierre Moulon
Arsalan Mousavian
Yadong Mu
Yasuhiro Mukaigawa
Lopamudra Mukherjee
Yusuke Mukuta
Ravi Teja Mullapudi
Mario Enrique Munich
Zachary Murez
Ana C. Murillo
J. Krishna Murthy
Damien Muselet
Armin Mustafa
Siva Karthik Mustikovela
Carlo Dal Mutto
Moin Nabi
Varun K. Nagaraja
Tushar Nagarajan
Arsha Nagrani
Seungjun Nah
Nikhil Naik
Yoshikatsu Nakajima
Yuta Nakashima
Atsushi Nakazawa
Seonghyeon Nam
Vinay P. Namboodiri
Medhini Narasimhan
Srinivasa Narasimhan
Sanath Narayan
Erickson Rangel
  Nascimento
Jacinto Nascimento
Tayyab Naseer

Lakshmanan Nataraj
Neda Nategh
Nelson Isao Nauata
Fernando Navarro
Shah Nawaz
Lukas Neumann
Ram Nevatia
Alejandro Newell
Shawn Newsam
Joe Yue-Hei Ng
Trung Thanh Ngo
Duc Thanh Nguyen
Lam M. Nguyen
Phuc Xuan Nguyen
Thuong Nguyen Canh
Mihalis Nicolaou
Andrei Liviu Nicolicioiu
Xuecheng Nie
Michael Niemeyer
Simon Niklaus
Christophoros Nikou
David Nilsson
Jifeng Ning
Yuval Nirkin
Li Niu
Yuzhen Niu
Zhenxing Niu
Shohei Nobuhara
Nicoletta Noceti
Hyeonwoo Noh
Junhyug Noh
Mehdi Noroozi
Sotiris Nousias
Valsamis Ntouskos
Matthew O'Toole
Peter Ochs
Ferda Ofli
Seong Joon Oh
Seoung Wug Oh
Iason Oikonomidis
Utkarsh Ojha
Takahiro Okabe
Takayuki Okatani
Fumio Okura
Aude Oliva
Kyle Olszewski

Björn Ommer
Mohamed Omran
Elisabeta Oneata
Michael Opitz
Jose Oramas
Tribhuvanesh Orekondy
Shaul Oron
Sergio Orts-Escolano
Ivan Oseledets
Aljosa Osep
Magnus Oskarsson
Anton Osokin
Martin R. Oswald
Wanli Ouyang
Andrew Owens
Mete Ozay
Mustafa Ozuysal
Eduardo Pérez-Pellitero
Gautam Pai
Dipan Kumar Pal
P. H. Pamplona Savarese
Jinshan Pan
Junting Pan
Xingang Pan
Yingwei Pan
Yannis Panagakis
Rameswar Panda
Guan Pang
Jiahao Pang
Jiangmiao Pang
Tianyu Pang
Sharath Pankanti
Nicolas Papadakis
Dim Papadopoulos
George Papandreou
Toufiq Parag
Shaifali Parashar
Sarah Parisot
Eunhyeok Park
Hyun Soo Park
Jaesik Park
Min-Gyu Park
Taesung Park
Alvaro Parra
C. Alejandro Parraga
Despoina Paschalidou

Nikolaos Passalis
Vishal Patel
Viorica Patraucean
Badri Narayana Patro
Danda Pani Paudel
Sujoy Paul
Georgios Pavlakos
Ioannis Pavlidis
Vladimir Pavlovic
Nick Pears
Kim Steenstrup Pedersen
Selen Pehlivan
Shmuel Peleg
Chao Peng
Houwen Peng
Wen-Hsiao Peng
Xi Peng
Xiaojiang Peng
Xingchao Peng
Yuxin Peng
Federico Perazzi
Juan Camilo Perez
Vishwanath Peri
Federico Pernici
Luca Del Pero
Florent Perronnin
Stavros Petridis
Henning Petzka
Patrick Peursum
Michael Pfeiffer
Hanspeter Pfister
Roman Pflugfelder
Minh Tri Pham
Yongri Piao
David Picard
Tomasz Pieciak
A. J. Piergiovanni
Andrea Pilzer
Pedro O. Pinheiro
Silvia Laura Pintea
Lerrel Pinto
Axel Pinz
Robinson Piramuthu
Fiora Pirri
Leonid Pishchulin
Francesco Pittaluga

Daniel Pizarro
Tobias Plötz
Mirco Planamente
Matteo Poggi
Moacir A. Ponti
Parita Pooj
Fatih Porikli
Horst Possegger
Omid Poursaeed
Ameya Prabhu
Viraj Uday Prabhu
Dilip Prasad
Brian L. Price
True Price
Maria Priisalu
Veronique Prinet
Victor Adrian Prisacariu
Jan Prokaj
Sergey Prokudin
Nicolas Pugeault
Xavier Puig
Albert Pumarola
Pulak Purkait
Senthil Purushwalkam
Charles R. Qi
Hang Qi
Haozhi Qi
Lu Qi
Mengshi Qi
Siyuan Qi
Xiaojuan Qi
Yuankai Qi
Shengju Qian
Xuelin Qian
Siyuan Qiao
Yu Qiao
Jie Qin
Qiang Qiu
Weichao Qiu
Zhaofan Qiu
Kha Gia Quach
Yuhui Quan
Yvain Queau
Julian Quiroga
Faisal Qureshi
Mahdi Rad

Filip Radenovic
Petia Radeva
Venkatesh
 B. Radhakrishnan
Ilija Radosavovic
Noha Radwan
Rahul Raguram
Tanzila Rahman
Amit Raj
Ajit Rajwade
Kandan Ramakrishnan
Santhosh
 K. Ramakrishnan
Srikumar Ramalingam
Ravi Ramamoorthi
Vasili Ramanishka
Ramprasaath R. Selvaraju
Francois Rameau
Visvanathan Ramesh
Santu Rana
Rene Ranftl
Anand Rangarajan
Anurag Ranjan
Viresh Ranjan
Yongming Rao
Carolina Raposo
Vivek Rathod
Sathya N. Ravi
Avinash Ravichandran
Tammy Riklin Raviv
Daniel Rebain
Sylvestre-Alvise Rebuffi
N. Dinesh Reddy
Timo Rehfeld
Paolo Remagnino
Konstantinos Rematas
Edoardo Remelli
Dongwei Ren
Haibing Ren
Jian Ren
Jimmy Ren
Mengye Ren
Weihong Ren
Wenqi Ren
Zhile Ren
Zhongzheng Ren

Zhou Ren
Vijay Rengarajan
Md A. Reza
Farzaneh Rezaeianaran
Hamed R. Tavakoli
Nicholas Rhinehart
Helge Rhodin
Elisa Ricci
Alexander Richard
Eitan Richardson
Elad Richardson
Christian Richardt
Stephan Richter
Gernot Riegler
Daniel Ritchie
Tobias Ritschel
Samuel Rivera
Yong Man Ro
Richard Roberts
Joseph Robinson
Ignacio Rocco
Mrigank Rochan
Emanuele Rodolà
Mikel D. Rodriguez
Giorgio Roffo
Grégory Rogez
Gemma Roig
Javier Romero
Xuejian Rong
Yu Rong
Amir Rosenfeld
Bodo Rosenhahn
Guy Rosman
Arun Ross
Paolo Rota
Peter M. Roth
Anastasios Roussos
Anirban Roy
Sebastien Roy
Aruni RoyChowdhury
Artem Rozantsev
Ognjen Rudovic
Daniel Rueckert
Adria Ruiz
Javier Ruiz-del-solar
Christian Rupprecht

Chris Russell
Dan Ruta
Jongbin Ryu
Ömer Sümer
Alexandre Sablayrolles
Faraz Saeedan
Ryusuke Sagawa
Christos Sagonas
Tonmoy Saikia
Hideo Saito
Kuniaki Saito
Shunsuke Saito
Shunta Saito
Ken Sakurada
Joaquin Salas
Fatemeh Sadat Saleh
Mahdi Saleh
Pouya Samangouei
Leo Sampaio
 Ferraz Ribeiro
Artsiom Olegovich
 Sanakoyeu
Enrique Sanchez
Patsorn Sangkloy
Anush Sankaran
Aswin Sankaranarayanan
Swami Sankaranarayanan
Rodrigo Santa Cruz
Amartya Sanyal
Archana Sapkota
Nikolaos Sarafianos
Jun Sato
Shin'ichi Satoh
Hosnieh Sattar
Arman Savran
Manolis Savva
Alexander Sax
Hanno Scharr
Simone Schaub-Meyer
Konrad Schindler
Dmitrij Schlesinger
Uwe Schmidt
Dirk Schnieders
Björn Schuller
Samuel Schulter
Idan Schwartz

William Robson Schwartz
Alex Schwing
Sinisa Segvic
Lorenzo Seidenari
Pradeep Sen
Ozan Sener
Soumyadip Sengupta
Arda Senocak
Mojtaba Seyedhosseini
Shishir Shah
Shital Shah
Sohil Atul Shah
Tamar Rott Shaham
Huasong Shan
Qi Shan
Shiguang Shan
Jing Shao
Roman Shapovalov
Gaurav Sharma
Vivek Sharma
Viktoriia Sharmanska
Dongyu She
Sumit Shekhar
Evan Shelhamer
Chengyao Shen
Chunhua Shen
Falong Shen
Jie Shen
Li Shen
Liyue Shen
Shuhan Shen
Tianwei Shen
Wei Shen
William B. Shen
Yantao Shen
Ying Shen
Yiru Shen
Yujun Shen
Yuming Shen
Zhiqiang Shen
Ziyi Shen
Lu Sheng
Yu Sheng
Rakshith Shetty
Baoguang Shi
Guangming Shi

Hailin Shi
Miaojing Shi
Yemin Shi
Zhenmei Shi
Zhiyuan Shi
Kevin Jonathan Shih
Shiliang Shiliang
Hyunjung Shim
Atsushi Shimada
Nobutaka Shimada
Daeyun Shin
Young Min Shin
Koichi Shinoda
Konstantin Shmelkov
Michael Zheng Shou
Abhinav Shrivastava
Tianmin Shu
Zhixin Shu
Hong-Han Shuai
Pushkar Shukla
Christian Siagian
Mennatullah M. Siam
Kaleem Siddiqi
Karan Sikka
Jae-Young Sim
Christian Simon
Martin Simonovsky
Dheeraj Singaraju
Bharat Singh
Gurkirt Singh
Krishna Kumar Singh
Maneesh Kumar Singh
Richa Singh
Saurabh Singh
Suriya Singh
Vikas Singh
Sudipta N. Sinha
Vincent Sitzmann
Josef Sivic
Gregory Slabaugh
Miroslava Slavcheva
Ron Slossberg
Brandon Smith
Kevin Smith
Vladimir Smutny
Noah Snavely

Roger
    D. Soberanis-Mukul
Kihyuk Sohn
Francesco Solera
Eric Sommerlade
Sanghyun Son
Byung Cheol Song
Chunfeng Song
Dongjin Song
Jiaming Song
Jie Song
Jifei Song
Jingkuan Song
Mingli Song
Shiyu Song
Shuran Song
Xiao Song
Yafei Song
Yale Song
Yang Song
Yi-Zhe Song
Yibing Song
Humberto Sossa
Cesar de Souza
Adrian Spurr
Srinath Sridhar
Suraj Srinivas
Pratul P. Srinivasan
Anuj Srivastava
Tania Stathaki
Christopher Stauffer
Simon Stent
Rainer Stiefelhagen
Pierre Stock
Julian Straub
Jonathan C. Stroud
Joerg Stueckler
Jan Stuehmer
David Stutz
Chi Su
Hang Su
Jong-Chyi Su
Shuochen Su
Yu-Chuan Su
Ramanathan Subramanian
Yusuke Sugano

Subeesh Vasu
Mayank Vatsa
David Vazquez
Javier Vazquez-Corral
Ashok Veeraraghavan
Erik Velasco-Salido
Raviteja Vemulapalli
Jonathan Ventura
Manisha Verma
Roberto Vezzani
Ruben Villegas
Minh Vo
MinhDuc Vo
Nam Vo
Michele Volpi
Riccardo Volpi
Carl Vondrick
Konstantinos Vougioukas
Tuan-Hung Vu
Sven Wachsmuth
Neal Wadhwa
Catherine Wah
Jacob C. Walker
Thomas S. A. Wallis
Chengde Wan
Jun Wan
Liang Wan
Renjie Wan
Baoyuan Wang
Boyu Wang
Cheng Wang
Chu Wang
Chuan Wang
Chunyu Wang
Dequan Wang
Di Wang
Dilin Wang
Dong Wang
Fang Wang
Guanzhi Wang
Guoyin Wang
Hanzi Wang
Hao Wang
He Wang
Heng Wang
Hongcheng Wang

Hongxing Wang
Hua Wang
Jian Wang
Jingbo Wang
Jinglu Wang
Jingya Wang
Jinjun Wang
Jinqiao Wang
Jue Wang
Ke Wang
Keze Wang
Le Wang
Lei Wang
Lezi Wang
Li Wang
Liang Wang
Lijun Wang
Limin Wang
Linwei Wang
Lizhi Wang
Mengjiao Wang
Mingzhe Wang
Minsi Wang
Naiyan Wang
Nannan Wang
Ning Wang
Oliver Wang
Pei Wang
Peng Wang
Pichao Wang
Qi Wang
Qian Wang
Qiaosong Wang
Qifei Wang
Qilong Wang
Qing Wang
Qingzhong Wang
Quan Wang
Rui Wang
Ruiping Wang
Ruixing Wang
Shangfei Wang
Shenlong Wang
Shiyao Wang
Shuhui Wang
Song Wang

Tao Wang
Tianlu Wang
Tiantian Wang
Ting-chun Wang
Tingwu Wang
Wei Wang
Weiyue Wang
Wenguan Wang
Wenlin Wang
Wenqi Wang
Xiang Wang
Xiaobo Wang
Xiaofang Wang
Xiaoling Wang
Xiaolong Wang
Xiaosong Wang
Xiaoyu Wang
Xin Eric Wang
Xinchao Wang
Xinggang Wang
Xintao Wang
Yali Wang
Yan Wang
Yang Wang
Yangang Wang
Yaxing Wang
Yi Wang
Yida Wang
Yilin Wang
Yiming Wang
Yisen Wang
Yongtao Wang
Yu-Xiong Wang
Yue Wang
Yujiang Wang
Yunbo Wang
Yunhe Wang
Zengmao Wang
Zhangyang Wang
Zhaowen Wang
Zhe Wang
Zhecan Wang
Zheng Wang
Zhixiang Wang
Zilei Wang
Jianqiao Wangni

Anne S. Wannenwetsch
Jan Dirk Wegner
Scott Wehrwein
Donglai Wei
Kaixuan Wei
Longhui Wei
Pengxu Wei
Ping Wei
Qi Wei
Shih-En Wei
Xing Wei
Yunchao Wei
Zijun Wei
Jerod Weinman
Michael Weinmann
Philippe Weinzaepfel
Yair Weiss
Bihan Wen
Longyin Wen
Wei Wen
Junwu Weng
Tsui-Wei Weng
Xinshuo Weng
Eric Wengrowski
Tomas Werner
Gordon Wetzstein
Tobias Weyand
Patrick Wieschollek
Maggie Wigness
Erik Wijmans
Richard Wildes
Olivia Wiles
Chris Williams
Williem Williem
Kyle Wilson
Calden Wloka
Nicolai Wojke
Christian Wolf
Yongkang Wong
Sanghyun Woo
Scott Workman
Baoyuan Wu
Bichen Wu
Chao-Yuan Wu
Huikai Wu
Jiajun Wu

Jialin Wu
Jiaxiang Wu
Jiqing Wu
Jonathan Wu
Lifang Wu
Qi Wu
Qiang Wu
Ruizheng Wu
Shangzhe Wu
Shun-Cheng Wu
Tianfu Wu
Wayne Wu
Wenxuan Wu
Xiao Wu
Xiaohe Wu
Xinxiao Wu
Yang Wu
Yi Wu
Yiming Wu
Ying Nian Wu
Yue Wu
Zheng Wu
Zhenyu Wu
Zhirong Wu
Zuxuan Wu
Stefanie Wuhrer
Jonas Wulff
Changqun Xia
Fangting Xia
Fei Xia
Gui-Song Xia
Lu Xia
Xide Xia
Yin Xia
Yingce Xia
Yongqin Xian
Lei Xiang
Shiming Xiang
Bin Xiao
Fanyi Xiao
Guobao Xiao
Huaxin Xiao
Taihong Xiao
Tete Xiao
Tong Xiao
Wang Xiao

Yang Xiao
Cihang Xie
Guosen Xie
Jianwen Xie
Lingxi Xie
Sirui Xie
Weidi Xie
Wenxuan Xie
Xiaohua Xie
Fuyong Xing
Jun Xing
Junliang Xing
Bo Xiong
Peixi Xiong
Yu Xiong
Yuanjun Xiong
Zhiwei Xiong
Chang Xu
Chenliang Xu
Dan Xu
Danfei Xu
Hang Xu
Hongteng Xu
Huijuan Xu
Jingwei Xu
Jun Xu
Kai Xu
Mengmeng Xu
Mingze Xu
Qianqian Xu
Ran Xu
Weijian Xu
Xiangyu Xu
Xiaogang Xu
Xing Xu
Xun Xu
Yanyu Xu
Yichao Xu
Yong Xu
Yongchao Xu
Yuanlu Xu
Zenglin Xu
Zheng Xu
Chuhui Xue
Jia Xue
Nan Xue

Tianfan Xue
Xiangyang Xue
Abhay Yadav
Yasushi Yagi
I. Zeki Yalniz
Kota Yamaguchi
Toshihiko Yamasaki
Takayoshi Yamashita
Junchi Yan
Ke Yan
Qingan Yan
Sijie Yan
Xinchen Yan
Yan Yan
Yichao Yan
Zhicheng Yan
Keiji Yanai
Bin Yang
Ceyuan Yang
Dawei Yang
Dong Yang
Fan Yang
Guandao Yang
Guorun Yang
Haichuan Yang
Hao Yang
Jianwei Yang
Jiaolong Yang
Jie Yang
Jing Yang
Kaiyu Yang
Linjie Yang
Meng Yang
Michael Ying Yang
Nan Yang
Shuai Yang
Shuo Yang
Tianyu Yang
Tien-Ju Yang
Tsun-Yi Yang
Wei Yang
Wenhan Yang
Xiao Yang
Xiaodong Yang
Xin Yang
Yan Yang

Yanchao Yang
Yee Hong Yang
Yezhou Yang
Zhenheng Yang
Anbang Yao
Angela Yao
Cong Yao
Jian Yao
Li Yao
Ting Yao
Yao Yao
Zhewei Yao
Chengxi Ye
Jianbo Ye
Keren Ye
Linwei Ye
Mang Ye
Mao Ye
Qi Ye
Qixiang Ye
Mei-Chen Yeh
Raymond Yeh
Yu-Ying Yeh
Sai-Kit Yeung
Serena Yeung
Kwang Moo Yi
Li Yi
Renjiao Yi
Alper Yilmaz
Junho Yim
Lijun Yin
Weidong Yin
Xi Yin
Zhichao Yin
Tatsuya Yokota
Ryo Yonetani
Donggeun Yoo
Jae Shin Yoon
Ju Hong Yoon
Sung-eui Yoon
Laurent Younes
Changqian Yu
Fisher Yu
Gang Yu
Jiahui Yu
Kaicheng Yu

Ke Yu
Lequan Yu
Ning Yu
Qian Yu
Ronald Yu
Ruichi Yu
Shoou-I Yu
Tao Yu
Tianshu Yu
Xiang Yu
Xin Yu
Xiyu Yu
Youngjae Yu
Yu Yu
Zhiding Yu
Chunfeng Yuan
Ganzhao Yuan
Jinwei Yuan
Lu Yuan
Quan Yuan
Shanxin Yuan
Tongtong Yuan
Wenjia Yuan
Ye Yuan
Yuan Yuan
Yuhui Yuan
Huanjing Yue
Xiangyu Yue
Ersin Yumer
Sergey Zagoruyko
Egor Zakharov
Amir Zamir
Andrei Zanfir
Mihai Zanfir
Pablo Zegers
Bernhard Zeisl
John S. Zelek
Niclas Zeller
Huayi Zeng
Jiabei Zeng
Wenjun Zeng
Yu Zeng
Xiaohua Zhai
Fangneng Zhan
Huangying Zhan
Kun Zhan

Xiaohang Zhan
Baochang Zhang
Bowen Zhang
Cecilia Zhang
Changqing Zhang
Chao Zhang
Chengquan Zhang
Chi Zhang
Chongyang Zhang
Dingwen Zhang
Dong Zhang
Feihu Zhang
Hang Zhang
Hanwang Zhang
Hao Zhang
He Zhang
Hongguang Zhang
Hua Zhang
Ji Zhang
Jianguo Zhang
Jianming Zhang
Jiawei Zhang
Jie Zhang
Jing Zhang
Juyong Zhang
Kai Zhang
Kaipeng Zhang
Ke Zhang
Le Zhang
Lei Zhang
Li Zhang
Lihe Zhang
Linguang Zhang
Lu Zhang
Mi Zhang
Mingda Zhang
Peng Zhang
Pingping Zhang
Qian Zhang
Qilin Zhang
Quanshi Zhang
Richard Zhang
Rui Zhang
Runze Zhang
Shengping Zhang
Shifeng Zhang

Shuai Zhang
Songyang Zhang
Tao Zhang
Ting Zhang
Tong Zhang
Wayne Zhang
Wei Zhang
Weizhong Zhang
Wenwei Zhang
Xiangyu Zhang
Xiaolin Zhang
Xiaopeng Zhang
Xiaoqin Zhang
Xiuming Zhang
Ya Zhang
Yang Zhang
Yimin Zhang
Yinda Zhang
Ying Zhang
Yongfei Zhang
Yu Zhang
Yulun Zhang
Yunhua Zhang
Yuting Zhang
Zhanpeng Zhang
Zhao Zhang
Zhaoxiang Zhang
Zhen Zhang
Zheng Zhang
Zhifei Zhang
Zhijin Zhang
Zhishuai Zhang
Ziming Zhang
Bo Zhao
Chen Zhao
Fang Zhao
Haiyu Zhao
Han Zhao
Hang Zhao
Hengshuang Zhao
Jian Zhao
Kai Zhao
Liang Zhao
Long Zhao
Qian Zhao
Qibin Zhao

Qijun Zhao
Rui Zhao
Shenglin Zhao
Sicheng Zhao
Tianyi Zhao
Wenda Zhao
Xiangyun Zhao
Xin Zhao
Yang Zhao
Yue Zhao
Zhichen Zhao
Zijing Zhao
Xiantong Zhen
Chuanxia Zheng
Feng Zheng
Haiyong Zheng
Jia Zheng
Kang Zheng
Shuai Kyle Zheng
Wei-Shi Zheng
Yinqiang Zheng
Zerong Zheng
Zhedong Zheng
Zilong Zheng
Bineng Zhong
Fangwei Zhong
Guangyu Zhong
Yiran Zhong
Yujie Zhong
Zhun Zhong
Chunluan Zhou
Huiyu Zhou
Jiahuan Zhou
Jun Zhou
Lei Zhou
Luowei Zhou
Luping Zhou
Mo Zhou
Ning Zhou
Pan Zhou
Peng Zhou
Qianyi Zhou
S. Kevin Zhou
Sanping Zhou
Wengang Zhou
Xingyi Zhou

Yanzhao Zhou
Yi Zhou
Yin Zhou
Yipin Zhou
Yuyin Zhou
Zihan Zhou
Alex Zihao Zhu
Chenchen Zhu
Feng Zhu
Guangming Zhu
Ji Zhu
Jun-Yan Zhu
Lei Zhu
Linchao Zhu
Rui Zhu
Shizhan Zhu
Tyler Lixuan Zhu

Wei Zhu
Xiangyu Zhu
Xinge Zhu
Xizhou Zhu
Yanjun Zhu
Yi Zhu
Yixin Zhu
Yizhe Zhu
Yousong Zhu
Zhe Zhu
Zhen Zhu
Zheng Zhu
Zhenyao Zhu
Zhihui Zhu
Zhuotun Zhu
Bingbing Zhuang
Wei Zhuo

Christian Zimmermann
Karel Zimmermann
Larry Zitnick
Mohammadreza
   Zolfaghari
Maria Zontak
Daniel Zoran
Changqing Zou
Chuhang Zou
Danping Zou
Qi Zou
Yang Zou
Yuliang Zou
Georgios Zoumpourlis
Wangmeng Zuo
Xinxin Zuo

Additional Reviewers

Victoria Fernandez
   Abrevaya
Maya Aghaei
Allam Allam
Christine
   Allen-Blanchette
Nicolas Aziere
Assia Benbihi
Neha Bhargava
Bharat Lal Bhatnagar
Joanna Bitton
Judy Borowski
Amine Bourki
Romain Brégier
Tali Brayer
Sebastian Bujwid
Andrea Burns
Yun-Hao Cao
Yuning Chai
Xiaojun Chang
Bo Chen
Shuo Chen
Zhixiang Chen
Junsuk Choe
Hung-Kuo Chu

Jonathan P. Crall
Kenan Dai
Lucas Deecke
Karan Desai
Prithviraj Dhar
Jing Dong
Wei Dong
Turan Kaan Elgin
Francis Engelmann
Erik Englesson
Fartash Faghri
Zicong Fan
Yang Fu
Risheek Garrepalli
Yifan Ge
Marco Godi
Helmut Grabner
Shuxuan Guo
Jianfeng He
Zhezhi He
Samitha Herath
Chih-Hui Ho
Yicong Hong
Vincent Tao Hu
Julio Hurtado

Jaedong Hwang
Andrey Ignatov
Muhammad
   Abdullah Jamal
Saumya Jetley
Meiguang Jin
Jeff Johnson
Minsoo Kang
Saeed Khorram
Mohammad Rami Koujan
Nilesh Kulkarni
Sudhakar Kumawat
Abdelhak Lemkhenter
Alexander Levine
Jiachen Li
Jing Li
Jun Li
Yi Li
Liang Liao
Ruochen Liao
Tzu-Heng Lin
Phillip Lippe
Bao-di Liu
Bo Liu
Fangchen Liu

Contents – Part XXVII

Teaching Cameras to Feel: Estimating Tactile Physical Properties of Surfaces from Images

Matthew Purri[(⊠)] and Kristin Dana

Rutgers University, Piscataway, USA
matthew.purri@rutgers.edu

Abstract. The connection between visual input and tactile sensing is critical for object manipulation tasks such as grasping and pushing. In this work, we introduce the challenging task of estimating a set of tactile physical properties from visual information. We aim to build a model that learns the complex mapping between visual information and tactile physical properties. We construct a first of its kind image-tactile dataset with over 400 multiview image sequences and the corresponding tactile properties. A total of fifteen tactile physical properties across categories including friction, compliance, adhesion, texture, and thermal conductance are measured and then estimated by our models. We develop a cross-modal framework comprised of an adversarial objective and a novel visuo-tactile joint classification loss. Additionally, we introduce a neural architecture search framework capable of selecting optimal combinations of viewing angles for estimating a given physical property.

Keywords: Cross-modal · Visuo-tactile · Viewpoint selection · Physical property estimation · Neural architecture search · Tactile

1 Introduction

In real-world tasks such as grasp planning and object manipulation, humans infer physical properties of objects from visual appearance. Inference of surface properties is distinct from object recognition. For example in Fig. 1a, the objects have different geometric shape; however, they share similar tactile physical properties. We can imagine what it would feel like to pick one up and handle it. Recognition can provide the semantic labels of the utensils, but tactile inference can provide the physical properties of the stainless steel. In this work, we introduce a computational model that learns the complex relationship between visual perception and the direct tactile physical properties of surfaces such as compliance, roughness, friction, stiction, and adhesive tack.

Electronic supplementary material The online version of this chapter (https://doi.org/10.1007/978-3-030-58583-9_1) contains supplementary material, which is available to authorized users.

There are many instances where an accurate estimate of a surface's tactile properties is beneficial for automated systems. In colder climates for example, thin layers of ice form over driving surfaces dramatically decreasing the sliding friction of a road. Modern vision systems trained on autonomous driving datasets such as KITTI [18] or Cityscapes [10] can readily identify "road" pixels, but would not provide the coefficient of friction required for braking control. Another example is manufacturing garments or shoes that require precise manipulation of multiple types of materials. Delicate and smooth fabrics such as silk require different handling than durable denim fabric. Also, robotic grasping and pushing of objects in a warehouse can benefit from surface property estimation to improve manipulation robustness.

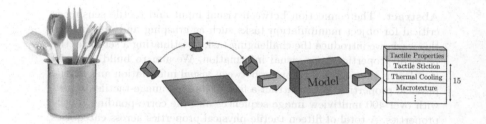

Fig. 1. Material example and inference framework. Left: An example of objects with different geometry and semantic labels that share common physical properties. **Right:** The proposed inference model receives images taken at various viewing angles and predicts a set of tactile property values.

In recent years, there has been increased interest in estimating physical properties of objects and forming learned physics engine models to infer the reaction of an object to controlled stimuli. Many of these methods passively observe interacting objects or select actions to stimulate object movement, learning to map visual information to physical properties by estimating the effect of the action on the scene [23,58,59,61]. In these methods, geometric and physical properties of the objects are encoded into latent space, and a learned physics engine predicts the future state of the objects. The indirect representation of the object properties confounds high-level actions, such as pushing with the precise amount of force to overcome friction or ordering surfaces based on their roughness. In our work we estimate the physical properties directly, allowing attributes of objects to be utilized directly.

We formulate the challenge of estimating a surface's physical properties from visual information as a cross-modal translation problem. Cross-modal problems remain one of the frontiers in vision research. For example, many recent works relate disparate information streams such as videos with audio [1,40–42] and images with captions [28,31,38]. Here, the problem of translating images into tactile properties provides a unique and challenging task. The visual and tactile modalities are not aligned in the same manner as audio and video and the scale discrepancy between images and tactile property vectors is vast.

To address this challenge, we create a dataset of 400+ surface image sequences and tactile property measurements. Given that humans have the ability to estimate tactile properties based on experience and visual cues, we expect autonomous systems to also be able to learn this complex mapping. While estimating surface properties, people often unconsciously move their heads, acquiring multiple views of a surface. Inspired by this, the captured images sequences comprise multiple viewing angles for each material surface.

Some challenges can be solved effectively using a single view of a scene, such as object classification, semantic segmentation, or image denoising. Whereas tasks such as 3D geometry reconstruction and action recognition require more information than what a single image can typically provide. A rich literature of material recognition, a similar challenge to surface property estimation, has found advantages to using multiple viewpoints or illumination conditions to identify the material class of a surface. For example, reflectance disks [65,66], optimal BRDF sampling [26,34,39], angular gradient images [62], 3D point clouds [12,69], 4D light field images [56], and BRDF slices [55] all provide good material recognition performance with partial viewpoint or illumination sampling. These methods, however, rely on sampling at a fixed set of viewing angles. In this work, we allow our model to select the optimal partial BRDF for tactile property estimation, providing empirical insight for which viewpoints should be sampled in camera motion planning and physical property sensor designs.

The main objective of this work is to leverage the relation between the appearance of material surfaces and their tactile properties to create a network capable of mapping visual information to tactile physical properties. We have three main contributions. First, we develop a visual-tactile dataset named Surface Property Synesthesia dataset; with 400+ material surfaces imaged at 100 viewing angles and augmented with fifteen measured tactile physical properties (as listed in Table 1) measured by a BioTac Toccare tactile sensor.[1] Second, we propose a cross-modal learning framework with adversarial learning and cross-domain joint classification to estimate tactile physical properties from a single image. Third, we introduce two input information sampling frameworks that learn to select viewing angle combinations that optimize a given objective. Our results show that image-to-tactile estimation is challenging, but we have made a pioneering step toward direct tactile property estimation.

2   Related Work

Cross-modal Learning and Translation. Cross-modal translation is defined as finding a function that maps information from one modality into its corresponding representation in a different modality. Prototypical approaches involve embedding data from different modalities into a learned space, from which generative functions map embeddings to their original representations. Recent works

---

[1] Tactile measurements were done by SynTouch Inc., with the BioTac Toccare, and purchased by Rutgers.

have applied this framework to various modality combinations including image-to-text [28,45,48,54,67], image-to-image [64,68,71], audio-to-image [8,52], and audio-to-text [9]. Aytar et al. create a text, audio, and image multimodal retrieval system by leveraging large unaligned data sources [3]. Example-based translation methods such as retrieval systems rely on a dictionary (training data) when translating between modalities, whereas generative translation models directly produce translations. Generative translation [20,33] is considered a more challenging problem than example-based translation because a generative function must be learned in addition to embedding functions. In [20], shared and domain-specific features are disentangled through auxiliary objectives to produce more realistic image-to-image translations. Generative translation models require large combinations of modality pairs to form a representative latent space. In this work, we introduce a new dataset containing a novel modality combination of image sequences and tactile physical properties.

Visuo-Tactile. There is much interest in both the vision and robotics communities in giving robots the ability to understand the relation between visual and haptic information. A variety of challenges have been solved more efficiently with the addition of tactile information including object recognition [14], material classification [30], and haptic property estimation [17]. Calendra et al. combine a GelSight sensor [6,32,33,63,64] with an RGB camera to jointly predict grasp outcomes and plan action sequences for grasping [6]. Gao et al. improve the performance of a haptic adjective assignment task by fusing images and time sequence haptic measurements [17]. The aim of this work is not to improve the performance of a particular task but to find the relationship between visual information and touch, such that tactile properties can be estimated from visual information. Recently, works such as [64] and [33] similarly seek to learn a mapping between vision and touch either by learning a latent space for retrieval or by synthesizing realistic tactile signals from visual inputs. In contrast to these works, we directly generate tactile estimates and the representation of our tactile representation is a physical property vector instead of a tactile image. Most similar to our work, Zhang et al. estimate the coefficient of friction of a surface from a reflectance image [66]. We expand upon previous work to estimate a larger set of fifteen tactile properties including friction, texture, thermal conductance, compliance, and adhesion. Additionally, we assume that the visual information to our system consists of ordinary images obtained by standard RGB camera sensors.

Viewpoint Selection. Given an oversampled set of images, how can we select the most useful subset of images from that set? In this work, we capture an oversampled sequence of images measured at consistent viewpoints via a gonioreflectometer. Inspired by viewpoint and illumination selection techniques for BRDFs [26,34,39,62], our aim is to determine what combination of viewing angles produce the optimal output for physical property estimation. Nielsen et al. determine the minimum number of samples to reconstruct a measured

BRDF by randomly sampling viewing and illumination angles and comparing their condition numbers [39]. Xue et al. capture pairs of images with small angular variations to generate improved angular gradients which serve as additional input for material recognition networks [62]. In contrast to viewpoint trajectory optimization [24,27,60], where the objective is to actively plan a viewing path in SO(3) space, to decrease task uncertainty, our objective is specifically to improve image-to-tactile estimation performance. In video understanding tasks, selectively sampling frames can enable efficient pattern analysis [15,49,70]. In [70], features from random subsets of frames of video are extracted and summed into a final representation to efficiently improve action recognition. Similarly, we seek to sample the angular space of multiview images. However, our approach learns the optimal sampling for the task at hand.

Inspired by neural architecture search (NAS) approaches [35,36,44,72], we learn to select a combination of viewing angles instead of choosing a handcrafted selection strategy similar to Xue et al. [62]. NAS methods are comprised of a search space, search strategy, and a performance estimation strategy. Generally, the search space of NAS is a set containing all possible layer functions and layer connections, whereas the search space for our problem are all combinations of viewing angles. To our knowledge, we are the first to utilize NAS for searching over the input space, instead of the overall architecture, resulting in a viewpoint selection. We propose two NAS frameworks for learning combinations of viewing angles which improve tactile physical property estimation as well as providing insight into what combinations of viewpoints are most informative for estimating a given physical property.

Table 1. Tactile property acronyms. Acronyms for each of the fifteen tactile properties measured by the Toccare device.

fRS	Sliding resistance	fST	Tactile stiction	uCO	Microtexture courseness
uRO	Microtexture roughness	mRG	Macrotexture regularity	mCO	Macrotexture courseness
mTX	Macrotexture	tCO	Thermal cooling	tPR	Thermal persistence
cCM	Tactile compliance	cDF	Local deformation	cDP	Damping
cRX	Relaxation	cYD	Yielding	aTK	Adhesive tack

3 Surface Property Synesthesia Dataset

Synesthesia is the production of an experience relating to one sense by a stimulation of another sense. For example, when viewing an image of a hamburger you may unconsciously imagine the taste of the sandwich. In this work, images of surfaces are perceived and the tactile properties of that surface are estimated.

Fig. 2. Dataset statistics. Left: The distribution of material labels. The output of the models are tactile properties and not material labels. The other category includes materials with less than six occurrences. **Center:** A sampling of the 400+ materials in our dataset, which highlight the diversity in visual appearance. The other category includes materials such as metal, fur, corduroy, nylon, and more. **Right:** A box plot distribution for each tactile property. The acronym for each property is defined in Table 1.

To train a model for tactile physical property estimation, we collect a dataset named the *Surface Property Synesthesia Dataset* (SPS) consisting of pairs of RGB image sequences and tactile measurements. The dataset contains 400+ commonly found indoor material surfaces, including categories such as plastic, leather, wood, denim, and more as shown in Fig. 2a. To our knowledge, this dataset contains the largest number of material surfaces of any visuo-tactile dataset, a necessity for learning the complex relation between vision and touch. A majority of the dataset belongs to four of the fifteen material categories. However, each category contains a diverse set of surfaces in terms of both color and pattern as shown in Fig. 2b. *The dataset and source code are made publicly available.*[2]

Tactile Data. The Biotac Toccare is a tactile sensing device that measures fifteen tactile physical properties of a surface and has been shown to identify materials more accurately than people [16]. The device is comprised of a BioTac sensor [2, 29, 46, 51] used to collect a series of time-varying signals and a staging system to consistently move the tactile sensor over a surface. Low-frequency fluid pressure, high-frequency fluid vibrations, core temperature change, and nineteen electrical impedances distributed along the sensor surface are recorded over time as the sensor is in contact with a surface. The signals are then converted into fifteen tactile physical properties whose values range from 0 to 100. Surface property measurements are gathered across several locations on the surface. Each tactile measurement is repeated five times.

The fifteen physical properties used to describe a surface, can be organized into five major tactile categories including friction, texture, thermal conductance, compliance, and adhesion as shown in Fig. 2c. Specific descriptions for each of

---

[2] https://github.com/matthewpurri/Teaching-Cameras-to-Feel.

the fifteen properties are described in the supplementary material. The *texture* category represents both macro and micro-texture surface attributes which correspond to large and small height intensities along a surface. Both static and kinetic friction are included in the *friction* class. *Adhesion* describes the perceived effort to break contact with a surface with values semantically ranging from no adhesion to sticky. The rate of heat transferred from the BioTac sensor to the surface is described in the *thermal conductance* category. Surface deformation characteristics correspond to the *compliance* category.

Vision Data. After tactile property measurements are obtained for each surface, images of the same surfaces are taken with a gonioreflectometer. The surfaces are imaged in a continuous manner from $-45°$ to $45°$ along the roll axis of the surface. For each material surface, 100 images are recorded. The yaw and pitch angles are constant throughout the imaging sequence. All images were taken under a mostly diffuse light source (Fig. 3).

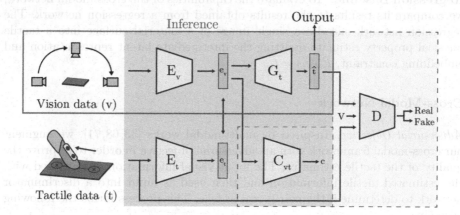

Fig. 3. Overview of our proposed cross-modal framework. The model is comprised of four modules: latent space encoding (blue), feature-classification (green), adversarial learning (yellow), and viewpoint selection (not displayed). The objective of this model is to generate precise tactile properties estimates $\hat{t}_i$ given vision information v_i. Both visual and tactile information (measured with Toccare device) are embedded into a shared latent space through separate encoder networks and compared. A generator function G_t estimates tactile property values $\hat{t}$ from the embedded visual vector e_v. The discriminator network D learns to predict whether a tactile-visual pair is a real or synthetic example. An auxiliary classification network C_{vt} generates a visuo-tactile label given e_v. The modules included in the red boundary represent the networks used during inference. Note, no tactile information is used during inference. (Color figure online)

4   Methods

4.1   Mapping Vision to Touch

Problem Definition. We model the problem of translation between two modalities as a cross-modal translation problem. We are specifically interested in the translation from images to tactile properties. Let $t_i \in \mathbb{R}^D$ represent tactile physical property vectors and $v_i \in \mathbb{R}^{3 \times F \times H \times W}$ represent image sequences where F, H, and W correspond to the number of frames, height, and width respectively. Instances of each modality are encoded through distinct encoding networks, E_t and E_v, into a shared latent space. In this space, embedded visuo-tactile pairs e_i^t and e_i^v should be close and are encouraged to be near each other by a pairwise constraint $\mathcal{L}_{emb} = \|e_i^t - e_i^v\|_2^2$. Estimated tactile physical property vectors are created via a generative function G_t, given the embedded representation of the visual information as input $G_t(e_i^v) = \hat{t}_i$.

Regression Baseline. To evaluate the capabilities of the cross-modal network, we compare its results to the results obtained from a regression network. The regression network encodes a single image of a material surface into a tactile physical property estimate omitting the intermediate latent representation and embedding constraint, $E_t(v_i) = \hat{t}_i$.

Cross-Modal Network

Adversarial Objective. Inspired by multi-modal works [33,68,71], we augment our cross-modal framework with an adversarial objective in order to improve the quality of the tactile estimates. The input visual information is combined with the estimated tactile information and then used as input into a discriminator network to determine if the pair is real or fake. This process forms the following objective:

$$\mathcal{L}_{adv}(G_t, D) = \mathbb{E}_{v,t}[\log D(v, t)] \\ + \mathbb{E}_{v,t}[\log(1 - D(v, G_t(e_v)))] + \mathbb{E}_{v,t}[\|G_t(e_v) - t\|_2], \tag{1}$$

where the generator G_t attempts to generate realistic tactile property vectors that are conditioned on the embedded visual information e_v while the discriminator D tries to distinguish between real versus fake visuo-tactile pairs. In prior work on conditional GANs [11,22,43], the input and output of the generator are the same dimension whereas the input of our generator can be a sequence of images and the output is a low dimensional vector. In order to handle the scale difference, we combine the tactile property estimation with the feature vector output of a single image instead of the full resolution image. The feature vector is generated via the image encoding network E_v.

Classification Objective. A key to forming a latent space that is well conditioned for a given objective is to add constraints to that space. In addition to constraining each visuo-tactile embedding pair to be close to each other in latent space, it would be advantageous for surfaces with similar physical properties to be close. Other works [48,67] have included this clustering constraint by adding an auxiliary classification objective. For many problems, semantic labels are informative of the properties that objects contain, however in our case the material labels are not always informative of tactile properties, e.g. plastics come in many forms and possess distinct surface properties but fall under one label. Yuan et al. circumvent this challenge by creating pseudo-labels formed through clustering hand-labeled tactile properties [64]. We extend unsupervised cluster labeling by creating labels from visuo-tactile embedding clusters instead of only tactile property clusters. Examples with similar tactile properties and visual statistics are encouraged to be close in space by this objective. Visuo-tactile representations are generated first by encoding features of one of the images in the sequence with a model pretrained on ImageNet [47]. The dimensionality of the feature vector is reduced through PCA and normalized to zero mean and unit variance. The reduced visual feature vector and tactile property vector are concatenated to form the final visuo-tactile representation. K-means is then used to cluster the visuo-tactile representation, creating k labels.

The adversarial and classification auxiliary objectives are combined with the tactile property estimation loss and cross-modal embedding constraint to form the final cross-modal objective:

$$\mathcal{L} = \mathcal{L}_{est} + \lambda_1 \mathcal{L}_{emb} + \lambda_2 \mathcal{L}_{adv} + \lambda_3 \mathcal{L}_{class}. \tag{2}$$

Evaluation Metric. We use the coefficient of determination (R^2), mean absolute error (MAE), and median percentage error ($\%_{err}$) metrics to evaluate how close each estimated tactile vector is to the ground truth values. The top eight percentage error ($\%_{err}^{T8}$) is used to compare network performances on the eight best performing tactile properties in terms of $\%_{err}$. The top eight tactile properties are selected based on the metrics shown in Table 3. The R^2 metric has been used to access the performance of vision-based regression tasks in several works [4,5,13,19,25,37,53]. The R^2 metric compares the estimation from the model $\hat{t}$ against using the mean tactile value $\bar{t}$ from the training set as an estimation, and is given by:

$$R^2 = 1 - \frac{\sum_i (t_i - \hat{t}_i)^2}{\sum_i (t_i - \bar{t})^2}. \tag{3}$$

4.2 Viewpoint Selection

Viewpoint Selector Framework. As mentioned in Sect. 3, each material surface in the SPS dataset is oversampled in viewing angle space. Selectively sampling viewing angles has been shown to improve performance for action classification tasks over using all available information [70]. The challenge of selectively sampling viewing angles is formulated as follows: given a set p of N images collected from distinct viewing angles, select an optimal combination q of M images that minimize the tactile estimation error, $q^\star = \{\min \|t - f(q; w_\theta)\|_2^2 \mid q \subset p, |q| = M, |p| = N\}$. The combinatorics of this problem are too vast to explore fully, therefore we construct a sampling network $\pi(w_\pi)$ tasked with learning to select the optimal combination of viewing angles $q^\star$ based on weights w_π. The optimal combination is then used as input for a tactile estimation network $f(q^\star; w_\theta)$. We call the sampling network the Neural Viewpoint Selector (NVS) network. The NVS network is comprised of M viewpoint selector vectors z, each tasked with choosing a single viewpoint from N possible viewpoints. Each viewpoint image is assigned an equal probability of being selected. The NVS module selects a single viewing angle for the set q as follows:

$$q_m = \arg\max_i \frac{exp(z_{m,i})}{\sum_{n=1}^N exp(z_{m,n})}, m = 1 \ldots M. \tag{4}$$

The viewpoint selector vector z is defined in $\mathbb{R}^N$ space. This process is repeated M times with different viewpoint selector vectors to select a set of M viewpoints. There are no constraints between the vectors, therefore allowing repeated viewpoints. We explore adding constraints to the selected combinations by including a value function $V(q; w_v)$, which estimates how well the selected combination will perform on tactile property estimation. This network acts as a lightweight proxy for the tactile estimation network. We call this framework the Value Based Neural Viewpoint Selector (VB-NVS). The value function provides additional guidance for the viewpoint selector vectors by propagating an additional error signal from the objective as shown in Fig. 4. The input of the value function is the combined output probability distribution from the viewpoint selector vectors. The value network then estimates the tactile estimation error $\hat{\mathcal{L}}_{est}$.

Inspired by the gradient-based neural architecture search by Pham et al. [44], the weights of the neural viewpoint selector $\pi(w_\pi)$ and tactile estimator network $f(q; w_\theta)$ are trained independently in three stages. First the weights of the $f(q; w_\theta)$ network are trained with random combinations of q. Then all the weights

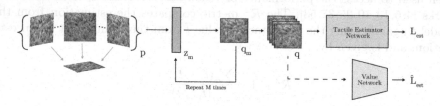

Fig. 4. Viewpoint selection frameworks. Inspired by recent works in neural architecture search, we construct a network (NVS) to learn which combination q of viewing angles, from all available angles p, minimize the tactile estimator loss L_{est}. The NVS network is comprised of M viewpoint selector vectors z, each responsible for selecting one viewpoint. An additional value network estimates the loss of the tactile estimator network given the selected viewpoints q.

of the tactile estimator network are frozen, excluding the late-fusion layer. Combinations of viewing angles are sampled from the policy network $\pi(w_\pi)$ and evaluated with $f(q; w_\theta)$. The weights of $\pi(w_\pi)$ are updated via the gradient produced by the REINFORCE [57] objective. Finally the weights of $f(q; w_\theta)$ are reinitialized and trained with the optimal set of viewing angles $q^\star$ produced by $\pi(w_\pi)$. The VB-NVS framework is trained in a similar manner except the value network $V(q; w_v)$ is now trained in conjunction with the viewpoint selector network $\pi(w_\pi)$ and the optimal set $q^\star$ is generated by the value network instead of $\pi(w_\pi)$.

Multi-image Baseline. There are a variety of schemes for selecting a subset of data points. Naive approaches include random sampling and sampling at a fixed interval (equidistant). We compare our viewpoint selection networks with these naive approaches along with more advanced algorithms. Zhou et al. subsample image sequences by randomly selecting combinations of various lengths from a given image sequence [70]. The random subsamples efficiently find temporal and spatial trends from image sequences outperforming non-sampling approaches for action recognition. Rather than using a subset of viewing angles, we explore using the entire image sequence as input to the tactile property estimator. Su et al. generate feature vectors from each image separately, then fuse each feature vector together via max-pooling [50]. Early fusion methods such as I3D use 3D CNNs to learn both image-level features as well as temporal features from concatenated images [7]. For all multi-image networks except the I3D and View Pooling, we employ late feature fusion with neural networks to aggregate features from multiple images.

Implementation Details. The 400+ visuo-tactile pairs in the SPS dataset are randomly divided into 90/10 training/validation splits. Each experiment is rerun three times and the mean score is presented. For the single-image experiments in Sect. 5.1, the image corresponding to the most nadir viewing angle is selected as input. For both single-image (Sect. 5.1) and multi-image (Sect. 5.2) experiments, the mean of the five tactile measurements is used as the tactile signal. A 50-layered SE-ResNeXt [21] network pretrained on ImageNet serves as the image encoding backbone for all networks. We set the size of the latent space to be 50 and 100 for single and multi-image experiments respectively. The networks are trained for 30 epochs with a learning rate of 1e−4. Separate networks are trained for each tactile property. Non-learned and learned sampling methods select combinations of three images ($M = 3$). Additional training parameters are described in the supplementary material.

5   Experiments

5.1   Cross-Modal Experiments

Given a single image of a material surface, our task is to estimate the tactile properties of that surface. To highlight the effectiveness of our proposed cross-

Table 2. Single image tactile estimation ($\mathcal{R}^2$). The $\mathcal{R}^2$ performance per tactile property is displayed, higher values are better. Our proposed cross-modal model significantly outperforms the baseline regression model across nearly all tactile properties.

Model	fRS	cDF	tCO	cYD	aTK	mTX	cCM	cDP	cRX	mRG	mCO	uRO	tPR	uCO	fST	$\mathcal{R}^2$	MAE
Regression	0.07	0.49	0.50	0.44	−0.46	**0.43**	0.13	0.35	0.11	0.46	**0.56**	0.32	0.57	0.57	0.53	0.34	6.17
Cross-modal	**0.54**	**0.52**	**0.62**	**0.64**	−0.07	0.43	**0.47**	**0.67**	**0.44**	0.47	0.54	**0.44**	**0.65**	**0.59**	**0.59**	**0.50**	5.53

Table 3. Single image tactile estimation ($\%_{err}$). The median $\%_{err}$ performance per tactile property is displayed, lower values are better. Tactile properties to the left of the bold center line comprise the top eight percentage error properties.

Model	fRS	cDF	tCO	cYD	aTK	mTX	cCM	cDP	cRX	mRG	mCO	uRO	tPR	uCO	fST	$\%_{err}$	$\%_{err}^{T8}$
Regression	18.6	16.6	18.2	22.5	**12.7**	28.8	21.6	**21.9**	34.0	50.0	60.4	65.5	65.1	**70.4**	80.6	39.1	20.1
Cross-modal	**13.0**	**15.0**	**15.9**	**17.2**	17.3	**17.7**	**18.9**	23.4	**29.3**	**39.3**	**49.0**	**57.4**	**63.3**	72.0	**73.5**	**34.8**	**17.3**

modal method, we compare the proposed method with a regression network. The results of both methods are recorded in Tables 2 and 3. Our proposed single image method outperforms the regression method across almost all fifteen tactile properties achieving better average $\mathcal{R}^2$, MAE, $\%_{err}$, and $\%_{err}^{T8}$ scores. Both networks achieve negative $\mathcal{R}^2$ scores for the adhesive tack (aTK) dimension, hence the estimates for this dimension are worse than using the average training value as a prediction. In general, the problem of estimating direct tactile properties from images-only is challenging and we expect a non-trivial margin of error.

Table 4. Single image cross-modal ablation. Refactoring the network as a cross-modal network with an adversarial objective greatly improves estimation performance. Visuo-tactile cluster labels outperform both material and tactile cluster labels.

Cross-modal	Adversarial	Material classification	Tactile cluster classification [64]	Visuo-tactile classification	Metrics			
					$\mathcal{R}^2$	MAE	$\%_{err}$	$\%_{err}^{T8}$
					0.34	6.17	39.1	20.1
✓					0.46	5.65	34.3	17.1
✓	✓				0.49	5.61	36.2	18.5
✓		✓			0.45	5.73	36.9	19.0
✓			✓		0.48	5.60	35.7	17.7
✓				✓	0.49	5.58	**33.8**	**16.9**
✓	✓			✓	**0.50**	**5.53**	34.8	17.3

In order to access the contribution of each component of the cross-modal network, we conduct an ablation study. In Table 4, the performance of the baseline regression network is compared to cross-modal networks with auxiliary objectives. We additionally explore using various auxiliary classification label types.

As shown in Table 4, refactoring the network as a cross-modal network significantly improves the performance of the tactile estimation from an average $\mathcal{R}^2/\%_{err}$ of 0.34/39.1 to 0.46/34.3. Next, the contribution of the adversarial objective is assessed and we find that the conditional GAN objective improves the quality of generated tactile samples in terms of average $\mathcal{R}^2$ and MAE but not $\%_{err}$ or $\%_{err}^{T8}$. We then evaluate the performance of using different labels for the auxiliary latent space classification task. Using the material class labels, shown in Fig. 2a, degrades the overall performance of the network. This suggests that traditional material labels do not adequately represent the tactile properties of a surface. The tactile cluster labels [64] improve results but not as much as our proposed joint visuo-tactile labels.

5.2   Viewing Angle Selection Experiments

After examining various network modules and frameworks for tactile property estimation from a single image, we investigate utilizing multiple images as input to the system. As described in Sect. 4, there are many ways of selecting a subset of images including non-learning methods such as random, equidistant, or TRN sampling and learned methods such as NVS and VB-NVS. In Tables 5 and 6, we compare various viewpoint sampling methods. Our proposed NVS and VB-NVS methods outperform all other multi-image methods in terms of average $\mathcal{R}^2$, MAE, $\%_{err}$, and $\%_{err}^{T8}$. Surprisingly, all methods that utilize the full amount of available imagery, i.e. Late Fusion, I3DNet [7], and View Pooling [50], perform much worse than the single image methods. The poor performance of the I3DNet architecture is likely a consequence of lack of significant inter-frame change in our image sequences. The View Pooling method slightly outperforms the other late fusion method. Non-learning sampling methods such as random sampling, equidistant sampling, and TRN [70] select subsamples from the total set of viewing angles without updating the selection based on performance. The non-learned sampling methods surpass the performance of the single image model on several of the tactile properties with only equidistant sampling outperforming the single image method on average. Both NVS and VB-NVS achieve the best performance on average across all metrics while providing insightful viewpoint selection information. However, they do not outperform the single image methods in several categories suggesting that multiple images do not always provide useful information for estimating certain tactile properties. None of the multi-image methods are able to consistently provide a better than average prediction for the adhesive tack property (aTK).

    In addition to improved performance from the learned subsampling methods, we gain insight into which combinations of viewing angles are useful for estimating a specific physical property. In Fig. 5, the selected viewing angles from trained NVS and VB-NVS modules are shown for several tactile properties. Note, this visualization is per tactile property, not per material. The rows of Fig. 5 represent the viewing angles selected for a particular tactile property while the columns represent repeated experiments. Selected viewpoints for models trained to estimate sliding resistance (fRS) are consistently close in viewing

Table 5. Multi-image tactile estimation ($\mathcal{R}^2$). The $\mathcal{R}^2$ performance per tactile property is displayed, higher values are better. The proposed viewpoint selection frameworks outperform all other models on average. Bold and italic text correspond to the first and second best scores respectively.

Model	fRS	cDF	tCO	cYD	aTK	mTX	cCM	cDP	cRX	mRG	mCO	uRO	tPR	uCO	fST	$\mathcal{R}_2$	MAE
Single (ours)	0.54	*0.52*	*0.62*	**0.64**	−0.07	0.43	0.47	**0.67**	0.44	0.47	0.54	0.44	*0.65*	0.59	0.59	0.50	5.53
Late-Fusion	0.05	−0.06	0.04	−0.21	−0.15	0.46	0.37	0.04	−0.10	0.31	0.35	0.04	0.33	−0.01	0.23	0.11	9.16
I3DNet [7]	0.32	0.01	−0.23	0.04	−0.23	0.37	0.31	0.12	−0.13	0.24	0.11	0.07	0.09	−0.16	0.14	0.11	9.42
View pooling [50]	0.03	0.03	−0.01	−0.09	−0.11	0.47	0.23	0.07	−0.05	0.30	0.32	0.12	0.25	−0.02	0.10	0.11	9.01
Random	0.49	0.41	0.58	0.49	−*0.02*	0.45	0.46	0.57	0.31	0.46	**0.72**	0.40	0.56	0.55	0.59	0.47	5.49
Equidistant	0.63	0.48	*0.62*	0.50	−0.04	0.52	0.52	0.58	0.41	0.45	0.61	0.44	0.61	0.62	**0.65**	0.51	5.37
TRN [70]	*0.64*	0.49	0.52	0.40	−0.10	0.52	*0.55*	0.61	0.35	0.41	0.66	0.39	0.53	0.50	0.63	0.47	5.53
NVS (ours)	0.62	**0.53**	**0.63**	0.55	**0.02**	*0.56*	0.53	0.54	**0.49**	*0.55*	0.68	**0.51**	0.54	*0.63*	*0.64*	*0.53*	*5.34*
VB-NVS (ours)	**0.65**	0.50	0.61	*0.57*	−0.05	**0.58**	**0.57**	*0.64*	*0.45*	**0.57**	*0.70*	*0.47*	**0.68**	**0.66**	0.61	**0.55**	**5.28**

Table 6. Multi-image tactile estimation ($\%_{err}$). The median $\%_{err}$ performance per tactile property is displayed, lower values are better. The proposed viewpoint selection frameworks outperform all other models on average. Bold and italic text correspond to the first and second best scores respectively.

Model	fRS	cDF	tCO	cYD	aTK	mTX	cCM	cDP	cRX	mRG	mCO	uRO	tPR	uCO	fST	$\%_{err}$	$\%_{err}^{T8}$
Single	**13.0**	*15.0*	15.9	17.2	17.3	17.7	18.9	23.4	**29.3**	39.3	**49.0**	**57.4**	63.3	72.0	73.5	34.8	17.3
Late-Fusion	30.4	18.6	24.6	35.6	14.3	28.5	20.1	25.9	36.7	*32.6*	244.7	251.6	91.1	74.3	78.1	67.1	24.7
I3DNet [7]	29.9	19.9	29.4	25.5	13.9	24.1	30.6	36.2	32.7	54.3	231.1	131.4	77.7	85.4	74.2	59.8	26.2
View pooling [50]	50.4	30.9	22.8	34.7	19.5	18.7	48.6	34.4	35.1	44.6	97.2	64.4	174.6	169.0	140.3	65.7	32.5
Random	*13.2*	18.1	13.7	17.0	13.4	15.4	19.2	**22.8**	34.7	38.2	54.7	62.2	59.3	**59.6**	**50.8**	32.8	16.6
Equidistant	16.3	17.2	12.9	20.7	**9.4**	*12.9*	19.8	*23.3*	35.0	34.8	52.3	63.0	60.2	*62.4*	58.5	33.2	16.6
TRN [70]	16.9	16.1	*12.4*	14.8	11.7	13.7	23.4	25.2	35.3	37.4	56.1	63.2	60.1	63.6	54.0	33.6	16.8
NVS (ours)	15.0	15.4	12.8	*13.7*	10.6	**11.8**	*18.3*	24.5	33.3	37.8	*51.2*	64.2	*56.3*	62.9	58.3	*32.4*	**15.3**
VB-NVS (ours)	16.3	**13.6**	**11.5**	**12.4**	*9.6*	17.2	**17.6**	26.8	*31.8*	**32.5**	53.2	*59.8*	**55.1**	67.3	*53.9*	**31.9**	*15.6*

angle space for both the NVS and VB-NVS methods. The distribution of viewing angles does not vary considerably across each experiment but the location of the distribution does. This suggests that the relative difference between viewing angles is more important for our objective than the global values of the viewing angles. The viewing angle selection is consistent with observations of prior work that angular gradients are important for material recognition [56,62,65]. Similar trends are observed for the macrotexture (mTX) viewing angle subsamples. The difference between the selected viewing angles for the mTX property is greater than those of the fST property suggesting that wider viewing angles are preferable to estimate macrotexture properties.

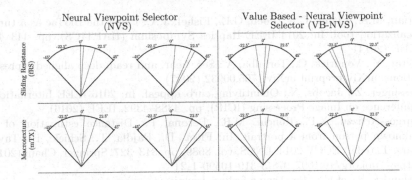

Fig. 5. Viewpoint selection result. The resultant selected viewpoints of both learned sampling methods. Columns represent repeated experiments, highlighting the consistency of the selected viewing angle combinations. Models optimized to estimate the sliding resistance property learn to select viewpoints that are close in viewing angle space while the selected viewpoints for the macrotexture property are farther apart.

6   Conclusion

This work is a pioneering step towards understanding the relationship between visual and tactile information. We propose a new challenge of estimating fifteen tactile physical properties of a surface from multiview images. We provide several methods that estimate tactile properties and determine the optimal viewing angles to sample for the estimation. To train our models we assemble the first of its kind, visuo-tactile dataset containing tactile physical properties and corresponding image sequences. We tackle the challenge of physical property estimation by designing a cross-modal network with an adversarial and a joint classification objective with results that surpass prior work in cross-modal translation. Additionally, our viewpoint selection framework achieves state-of-the-art performance for this task while providing insight as to which combinations of viewing angles are optimal for estimating a given tactile property. The proposed method can be used directly or as a prior for several tasks such as automated driving (road condition estimation), robotics (object manipulation or navigation) and manufacturing (quality control).

Acknowledgments. This research was supported by NSF Grant #1715195. We would like to thank Eric Wengrowski, Peri Akiva, and Faith Johnson for the useful suggestions and discussions.

References

1. Arandjelović, R., Zisserman, A.: Objects that sound. In: Ferrari, V., Hebert, M., Sminchisescu, C., Weiss, Y. (eds.) ECCV 2018. LNCS, vol. 11205, pp. 451–466. Springer, Cham (2018). https://doi.org/10.1007/978-3-030-01246-5_27

2. Arian, M.S., Blaine, C.A., Loeb, G.E., Fishel, J.A.: Using the BioTac as a tumor localization tool. In: 2014 IEEE Haptics Symposium (HAPTICS), pp. 443–448. IEEE (2014)
3. Aytar, Y., Vondrick, C., Torralba, A.: See, hear, and read: deep aligned representations. arXiv preprint arXiv:1706.00932 (2017)
4. Bessinger, Z., Jacobs, N.: Quantifying curb appeal. In: 2016 IEEE International Conference on Image Processing (ICIP), pp. 4388–4392. IEEE (2016)
5. Burgos-Artizzu, X.P., Ronchi, M.R., Perona, P.: Distance estimation of an unknown person from a portrait. In: Fleet, D., Pajdla, T., Schiele, B., Tuytelaars, T. (eds.) ECCV 2014. LNCS, vol. 8689, pp. 313–327. Springer, Cham (2014). https://doi.org/10.1007/978-3-319-10590-1_21
6. Calandra, R., et al.: More than a feeling: learning to grasp and regrasp using vision and touch. IEEE Robot. Autom. Lett. **3**(4), 3300–3307 (2018)
7. Carreira, J., Zisserman, A.: Quo vadis, action recognition? A new model and the kinetics dataset. In: Proceedings of the IEEE Conference on Computer Vision and Pattern Recognition, pp. 6299–6308 (2017)
8. Chen, L., Srivastava, S., Duan, Z., Xu, C.: Deep cross-modal audio-visual generation. In: Proceedings of the on Thematic Workshops of ACM Multimedia 2017, pp. 349–357. ACM (2017)
9. Chung, Y.A., Weng, W.H., Tong, S., Glass, J.: Unsupervised cross-modal alignment of speech and text embedding spaces. In: Advances in Neural Information Processing Systems, pp. 7354–7364 (2018)
10. Cordts, M., et al.: The cityscapes dataset for semantic urban scene understanding. In: Proceedings of the IEEE Conference on Computer Vision and Pattern Recognition, pp. 3213–3223 (2016)
11. Dai, B., Fidler, S., Urtasun, R., Lin, D.: Towards diverse and natural image descriptions via a conditional GAN. In: Proceedings of the IEEE International Conference on Computer Vision, pp. 2970–2979 (2017)
12. DeGol, J., Golparvar-Fard, M., Hoiem, D.: Geometry-informed material recognition. In: Proceedings of the IEEE Conference on Computer Vision and Pattern Recognition, pp. 1554–1562 (2016)
13. Dymczyk, M., Schneider, T., Gilitschenski, I., Siegwart, R., Stumm, E.: Erasing bad memories: agent-side summarization for long-term mapping. In: 2016 IEEE/RSJ International Conference on Intelligent Robots and Systems (IROS), pp. 4572–4579. IEEE (2016)
14. Falco, P., Lu, S., Cirillo, A., Natale, C., Pirozzi, S., Lee, D.: Cross-modal visuotactile object recognition using robotic active exploration. In: 2017 IEEE International Conference on Robotics and Automation (ICRA), pp. 5273–5280. IEEE (2017)
15. Feichtenhofer, C., Fan, H., Malik, J., He, K.: SlowFast networks for video recognition. In: Proceedings of the IEEE International Conference on Computer Vision, pp. 6202–6211 (2019)
16. Fishel, J.A., Loeb, G.E.: Bayesian exploration for intelligent identification of textures. Front. Neurorobot. **6**, 4 (2012)
17. Gao, Y., Hendricks, L.A., Kuchenbecker, K.J., Darrell, T.: Deep learning for tactile understanding from visual and haptic data. In: 2016 IEEE International Conference on Robotics and Automation (ICRA), pp. 536–543. IEEE (2016)
18. Geiger, A., Lenz, P., Stiller, C., Urtasun, R.: Vision meets robotics: the KITTI dataset. Int. J. Robot. Res. **32**(11), 1231–1237 (2013)

19. Glasner, D., Fua, P., Zickler, T., Zelnik-Manor, L.: Hot or not: exploring correlations between appearance and temperature. In: Proceedings of the IEEE International Conference on Computer Vision, pp. 3997–4005 (2015)
20. Gonzalez-Garcia, A., van de Weijer, J., Bengio, Y.: Image-to-image translation for cross-domain disentanglement. In: Advances in Neural Information Processing Systems, pp. 1287–1298 (2018)
21. Hu, J., Shen, L., Sun, G.: Squeeze-and-excitation networks. In: Proceedings of the IEEE Conference on Computer Vision and Pattern Recognition, pp. 7132–7141 (2018)
22. Isola, P., Zhu, J.Y., Zhou, T., Efros, A.A.: Image-to-image translation with conditional adversarial networks. In: Proceedings of the IEEE Conference on Computer Vision and Pattern Recognition, pp. 1125–1134 (2017)
23. Janner, M., Levine, S., Freeman, W.T., Tenenbaum, J.B., Finn, C., Wu, J.: Reasoning about physical interactions with object-oriented prediction and planning. arXiv preprint arXiv:1812.10972 (2018)
24. Jayaraman, D., Grauman, K.: Learning to look around: intelligently exploring unseen environments for unknown tasks. In: Proceedings of the IEEE Conference on Computer Vision and Pattern Recognition, pp. 1238–1247 (2018)
25. Jean, N., Burke, M., Xie, M., Davis, W.M., Lobell, D.B., Ermon, S.: Combining satellite imagery and machine learning to predict poverty. Science 353(6301), 790–794 (2016)
26. Jehle, M., Sommer, C., Jähne, B.: Learning of optimal illumination for material classification. In: Goesele, M., Roth, S., Kuijper, A., Schiele, B., Schindler, K. (eds.) DAGM 2010. LNCS, vol. 6376, pp. 563–572. Springer, Heidelberg (2010). https://doi.org/10.1007/978-3-642-15986-2_57
27. Johns, E., Leutenegger, S., Davison, A.J.: Pairwise decomposition of image sequences for active multi-view recognition. In: Proceedings of the IEEE Conference on Computer Vision and Pattern Recognition, pp. 3813–3822 (2016)
28. Karpathy, A., Fei-Fei, L.: Deep visual-semantic alignments for generating image descriptions. In: Proceedings of the IEEE Conference on Computer Vision and Pattern Recognition, pp. 3128–3137 (2015)
29. Kerr, E., McGinnity, T.M., Coleman, S.: Material recognition using tactile sensing. Expert Syst. Appl. 94, 94–111 (2018)
30. Kerzel, M., Ali, M., Ng, H.G., Wermter, S.: Haptic material classification with a multi-channel neural network. In: 2017 International Joint Conference on Neural Networks (IJCNN), pp. 439–446. IEEE (2017)
31. Kiros, R., Salakhutdinov, R., Zemel, R.S.: Unifying visual-semantic embeddings with multimodal neural language models. arXiv preprint arXiv:1411.2539 (2014)
32. Li, R., et al.: Localization and manipulation of small parts using gelsight tactile sensing. In: 2014 IEEE/RSJ International Conference on Intelligent Robots and Systems, pp. 3988–3993. IEEE (2014)
33. Li, Y., Zhu, J.Y., Tedrake, R., Torralba, A.: Connecting touch and vision via cross-modal prediction. arXiv preprint arXiv:1906.06322 (2019)
34. Liu, C., Gu, J.: Discriminative illumination: per-pixel classification of raw materials based on optimal projections of spectral BRDF. IEEE Trans. Pattern Anal. Mach. Intell. 36(1), 86–98 (2014)
35. Liu, C., et al.: Progressive neural architecture search. In: Ferrari, V., Hebert, M., Sminchisescu, C., Weiss, Y. (eds.) ECCV 2018. LNCS, vol. 11205, pp. 19–35. Springer, Cham (2018). https://doi.org/10.1007/978-3-030-01246-5_2
36. Liu, H., Simonyan, K., Yang, Y.: Darts: differentiable architecture search. arXiv preprint arXiv:1806.09055 (2018)

37. McCurrie, M., Beletti, F., Parzianello, L., Westendorp, A., Anthony, S., Scheirer, W.J.: Predicting first impressions with deep learning. In: 2017 12th IEEE International Conference on Automatic Face & Gesture Recognition (FG 2017), pp. 518–525. IEEE (2017)
38. Nam, H., Ha, J.W., Kim, J.: Dual attention networks for multimodal reasoning and matching. In: Proceedings of the IEEE Conference on Computer Vision and Pattern Recognition, pp. 299–307 (2017)
39. Nielsen, J.B., Jensen, H.W., Ramamoorthi, R.: On optimal, minimal BRDF sampling for reflectance acquisition. ACM Trans. Graph. (TOG) 34(6), 186 (2015)
40. Owens, A., Efros, A.A.: Audio-visual scene analysis with self-supervised multisensory features. In: Ferrari, V., Hebert, M., Sminchisescu, C., Weiss, Y. (eds.) ECCV 2018. LNCS, vol. 11210, pp. 639–658. Springer, Cham (2018). https://doi.org/10.1007/978-3-030-01231-1_39
41. Owens, A., Isola, P., McDermott, J., Torralba, A., Adelson, E.H., Freeman, W.T.: Visually indicated sounds. In: Proceedings of the IEEE Conference on Computer Vision and Pattern Recognition, pp. 2405–2413 (2016)
42. Owens, A., Wu, J., McDermott, J.H., Freeman, W.T., Torralba, A.: Ambient sound provides supervision for visual learning. In: Leibe, B., Matas, J., Sebe, N., Welling, M. (eds.) ECCV 2016. LNCS, vol. 9905, pp. 801–816. Springer, Cham (2016). https://doi.org/10.1007/978-3-319-46448-0_48
43. Perarnau, G., Van De Weijer, J., Raducanu, B., Álvarez, J.M.: Invertible conditional GANs for image editing. arXiv preprint arXiv:1611.06355 (2016)
44. Pham, H., Guan, M.Y., Zoph, B., Le, Q.V., Dean, J.: Efficient neural architecture search via parameter sharing. arXiv preprint arXiv:1802.03268 (2018)
45. Ranjan, V., Rasiwasia, N., Jawahar, C.: Multi-label cross-modal retrieval. In: Proceedings of the IEEE International Conference on Computer Vision, pp. 4094–4102 (2015)
46. Reinecke, J., Dietrich, A., Schmidt, F., Chalon, M.: Experimental comparison of slip detection strategies by tactile sensing with the BioTac® on the DLR hand arm system. In: 2014 IEEE international Conference on Robotics and Automation (ICRA), pp. 2742–2748. IEEE (2014)
47. Russakovsky, O., et al.: ImageNet large scale visual recognition challenge. Int. J. Comput. Vision 115(3), 211–252 (2015). https://doi.org/10.1007/s11263-015-0816-y
48. Salvador, A., et al.: Learning cross-modal embeddings for cooking recipes and food images. In: Proceedings of the IEEE Conference on Computer Vision and Pattern Recognition, pp. 3020–3028 (2017)
49. Shelhamer, E., Rakelly, K., Hoffman, J., Darrell, T.: Clockwork convnets for video semantic segmentation. In: Hua, G., Jégou, H. (eds.) ECCV 2016. LNCS, vol. 9915, pp. 852–868. Springer, Cham (2016). https://doi.org/10.1007/978-3-319-49409-8_69
50. Su, H., Maji, S., Kalogerakis, E., Learned-Miller, E.: Multi-view convolutional neural networks for 3D shape recognition. In: Proceedings of the IEEE International Conference on Computer Vision, pp. 945–953 (2015)
51. Su, Z., et al.: Force estimation and slip detection/classification for grip control using a biomimetic tactile sensor. In: 2015 IEEE-RAS 15th International Conference on Humanoid Robots (Humanoids), pp. 297–303. IEEE (2015)
52. Taylor, S., et al.: A deep learning approach for generalized speech animation. ACM Trans. Graph. (TOG) 36(4), 93 (2017)

53. Volokitin, A., Timofte, R., Van Gool, L.: Deep features or not: temperature and time prediction in outdoor scenes. In: Proceedings of the IEEE Conference on Computer Vision and Pattern Recognition Workshops, pp. 63–71 (2016)
54. Wang, B., Yang, Y., Xu, X., Hanjalic, A., Shen, H.T.: Adversarial cross-modal retrieval. In: Proceedings of the 25th ACM International Conference on Multimedia, pp. 154–162. ACM (2017)
55. Wang, O., Gunawardane, P., Scher, S., Davis, J.: Material classification using BRDF slices. In: IEEE Conference on Computer Vision and Pattern Recognition, 2009, CVPR 2009, pp. 2805–2811. IEEE (2009)
56. Wang, T.-C., Zhu, J.-Y., Hiroaki, E., Chandraker, M., Efros, A.A., Ramamoorthi, R.: A 4D light-field dataset and CNN architectures for material recognition. In: Leibe, B., Matas, J., Sebe, N., Welling, M. (eds.) ECCV 2016. LNCS, vol. 9907, pp. 121–138. Springer, Cham (2016). https://doi.org/10.1007/978-3-319-46487-9_8
57. Williams, R.J.: Simple statistical gradient-following algorithms for connectionist reinforcement learning. Mach. Learn. 8(3–4), 229–256 (1992). https://doi.org/10.1007/BF00992696
58. Wu, J., Lu, E., Kohli, P., Freeman, B., Tenenbaum, J.: Learning to see physics via visual de-animation. In: Advances in Neural Information Processing Systems, pp. 153–164 (2017)
59. Wu, J., Yildirim, I., Lim, J.J., Freeman, B., Tenenbaum, J.: Galileo: perceiving physical object properties by integrating a physics engine with deep learning. In: Advances in Neural Information Processing Systems, pp. 127–135 (2015)
60. Wu, Z., et al.: 3D ShapeNets: a deep representation for volumetric shapes. In: Proceedings of the IEEE Conference on Computer Vision and Pattern Recognition, pp. 1912–1920 (2015)
61. Xu, Z., Wu, J., Zeng, A., Tenenbaum, J.B., Song, S.: DensePhysNet: learning dense physical object representations via multi-step dynamic interactions. arXiv preprint arXiv:1906.03853 (2019)
62. Xue, J., Zhang, H., Dana, K., Nishino, K.: Differential angular imaging for material recognition. In: Proceedings of the IEEE Conference on Computer Vision and Pattern Recognition, pp. 764–773 (2017)
63. Yuan, W., Mo, Y., Wang, S., Adelson, E.H.: Active clothing material perception using tactile sensing and deep learning. In: 2018 IEEE International Conference on Robotics and Automation (ICRA), pp. 1–8. IEEE (2018)
64. Yuan, W., Wang, S., Dong, S., Adelson, E.: Connecting look and feel: associating the visual and tactile properties of physical materials. In: Proceedings of the IEEE Conference on Computer Vision and Pattern Recognition, pp. 5580–5588 (2017)
65. Zhang, H., Dana, K., Nishino, K.: Reflectance hashing for material recognition. In: Proceedings of the IEEE Conference on Computer Vision and Pattern Recognition, pp. 3071–3080 (2015)
66. Zhang, H., Dana, K., Nishino, K.: Friction from reflectance: deep reflectance codes for predicting physical surface properties from one-shot in-field reflectance. In: Leibe, B., Matas, J., Sebe, N., Welling, M. (eds.) ECCV 2016. LNCS, vol. 9908, pp. 808–824. Springer, Cham (2016). https://doi.org/10.1007/978-3-319-46493-0_49
67. Zhang, Y., Lu, H.: Deep cross-modal projection learning for image-text matching. In: Ferrari, V., Hebert, M., Sminchisescu, C., Weiss, Y. (eds.) ECCV 2018. LNCS, vol. 11205, pp. 707–723. Springer, Cham (2018). https://doi.org/10.1007/978-3-030-01246-5_42

68. Zhang, Z., Yang, L., Zheng, Y.: Translating and segmenting multimodal medical volumes with cycle-and shape-consistency generative adversarial network. In: Proceedings of the IEEE Conference on Computer Vision and Pattern Recognition, pp. 9242–9251 (2018)
69. Zhao, C., Sun, L., Stolkin, R.: A fully end-to-end deep learning approach for realtime simultaneous 3D reconstruction and material recognition. In: 2017 18th International Conference on Advanced Robotics (ICAR), pp. 75–82. IEEE (2017)
70. Zhou, B., Andonian, A., Oliva, A., Torralba, A.: Temporal relational reasoning in videos. In: Ferrari, V., Hebert, M., Sminchisescu, C., Weiss, Y. (eds.) ECCV 2018. LNCS, vol. 11205, pp. 831–846. Springer, Cham (2018). https://doi.org/10.1007/978-3-030-01246-5_49
71. Zhu, J.Y., et al.: Toward multimodal image-to-image translation. In: Advances in Neural Information Processing Systems, pp. 465–476 (2017)
72. Zoph, B., Le, Q.V.: Neural architecture search with reinforcement learning. arXiv preprint arXiv:1611.01578 (2016)

Accurate Optimization of Weighted Nuclear Norm for Non-Rigid Structure from Motion

José Pedro Iglesias[1(✉)], Carl Olsson[1,2], and Marcus Valtonen Örnhag[2]

[1] Chalmers University of Technology, Gothenburg, Sweden
jose.iglesias@chalmers.se
[2] Lund University, Lund, Sweden

Abstract. Fitting a matrix of a given rank to data in a least squares sense can be done very effectively using 2nd order methods such as Levenberg-Marquardt by explicitly optimizing over a bilinear parameterization of the matrix. In contrast, when applying more general singular value penalties, such as weighted nuclear norm priors, direct optimization over the elements of the matrix is typically used. Due to non-differentiability of the resulting objective function, first order subgradient or splitting methods are predominantly used. While these offer rapid iterations it is well known that they become inefficient near the minimum due to zig-zagging and in practice one is therefore often forced to settle for an approximate solution.

In this paper we show that more accurate results can in many cases be achieved with 2nd order methods. Our main result shows how to construct bilinear formulations, for a general class of regularizers including weighted nuclear norm penalties, that are provably equivalent to the original problems. With these formulations the regularizing function becomes twice differentiable and 2nd order methods can be applied. We show experimentally, on a number of structure from motion problems, that our approach outperforms state-of-the-art methods.

1 Introduction

Matrix recovery problems of the form

$$\min_X f(\boldsymbol{\sigma}(X)) + \|\mathcal{A}X - b\|^2, \tag{1}$$

This work was supported by the Swedish Research Council (grants no. 2015-05639, 2016-04445 and 2018-05375), the Swedish Foundation for Strategic Research (Semantic Mapping and Visual Navigation for Smart Robots) and the Wallenberg AI, Autonomous Systems and Software Program (WASP) funded by the Knut and Alice Wallenberg Foundation.

Electronic supplementary material The online version of this chapter (https://doi.org/10.1007/978-3-030-58583-9_2) contains supplementary material, which is available to authorized users.

© Springer Nature Switzerland AG 2020
A. Vedaldi et al. (Eds.): ECCV 2020, LNCS 12372, pp. 21–37, 2020.
https://doi.org/10.1007/978-3-030-58583-9_2

where $\mathcal{A}$ is a linear operator and $\sigma(X) = (\sigma_1(X), \sigma_2(X), ...)$ are the singular values of X, are frequently occurring in computer vision. Applications range from high level 3D reconstruction problems to low level pixel manipulations [3, 7,12,16–18,23,31,39,42,45]. In structure from motion (SfM) the most common approaches enforce a given low rank r without additionally penalizing non-zero singular values [7,20,39] (a special case of (1) by letting f assign zero if fewer than r singular values are non-zero and infinity otherwise).

Since the rank of a matrix X is bounded by to the number of columns/rows in a bilinear parameterization $X = BC^T$, the resulting optimization problem can be written $\min_{B,C} \|\mathcal{A}(BC^T) - b\|^2$. This gives a smooth objective function and can therefore be optimized using 2nd order methods. In SfM problems, where the main interest is the extraction of camera matrices from B and 3D points from C, this is typically the preferred option [8]. In a series of recent papers Hong et al. showed that optimization with the VarPro algorithm is remarkably robust to local minima converging to accurate solutions [20–22]. In [24] they further showed how uncalibrated rigid SfM with a proper perspective projection can be solved within a factorization framework. On the downside, typically the iterations are costly since (even when the Schur complement trick is used) 2nd order methods require an inversion of a relatively large hessian matrix, which may hinder application when suitable sparsity patterns are not present.

For low level vision problems such as denoising and inpainting, e.g. [18,23,31], the main interest is to recover the elements of X and not the factorization. In this context more general regularization terms that also consider the size of the singular values are often used. Since the singular values are non-differentiable functions of the elements in X first order methods are usually employed. The simplest option is perhaps a splitting methods such as ADMM [6] since the proximal operator $\arg\min_X f(\sigma(X)) + \|X - X_0\|^2$, can often be computed in closed form [14,18,23,27,31]. Alternatively, subgradient methods can be used to handle the non-differentiability of the regularization term [12].

It is well known that while first order methods have rapid iterations and make large improvements the first couple of iterations they have a tendency to converge slowly when approaching the optimum. For example, [6] recommends to use ADMM when a solution in the vicinity of the optimal point is acceptable, but suggests to switch to a higher order method when high accuracy is desired. For low level vision problems where success is not dependent on achieving an exact factorization of a particular size, first order methods may therefore be suitable. In contrast, in the context of SfM, having roughly estimated elements in X causes the obtained factorization B, C to be of a much larger size than necessary yielding poor reconstructions with too many deformation modes.

In this paper we aim to extend the class of methods that can be optimized using bilinear parameterization allowing accurate estimation of a low rank factorization from a general class of regularization terms. While our theory is applicable for many objectives we focus on weighted nuclear norm penalties since these have been successfully used in SfM applications. We show that these can be optimized with 2nd order methods which significantly increases the accuracy of the reconstruction. We further show that with these improvements the model of Hong *et al.* [24] can be extended to handle non-rigid reconstruction with a proper perspective model, as opposed to the orthographic projection model adopted by other factorization based approaches, e.g. [14,17,27,45].

1.1 Related Work and Contributions

Minimization directly over X has been made popular since the problem is convex when f is convex and absolutely symmetric, that is, $f(|x|) = f(x)$ and $f(\Pi x) = f(x)$, where Π is any permutation [29]. Convex penalties are however of limited interest since they generally prefer solutions with many small non-zero singular values to those with few large ones. A notable exception is the nuclear norm [10,11,15,33,35] which penalizes the sum of the singular values. Under the RIP assumption [35] exact or approximate low rank matrix recovery can then be guaranteed [11,35]. On the other hand, since the nuclear norm penalizes large singular values, it suffers from a shrinking bias [9,12,28].

An alternative approach that unifies bilinear parameterization with regularization approaches is based on the observation [35] that the nuclear norm $\|X\|_*$ of a matrix X can be expressed as $\|X\|_* = \min_{BC^T=X} \frac{\|B\|_F^2 + \|C\|_F^2}{2}$. Thus when $f(\sigma(X)) = \mu \sum_i \sigma_i(X)$, where μ is a scalar controlling the strength of the regularization, optimization of (1) can be formulated as

$$\min_{B,C} \mu \frac{\|B\|_F^2 + \|C\|_F^2}{2} + \|ABC^T - b\|^2. \tag{2}$$

Optimizing directly over the factors has the advantages that the number of variables is much smaller and the objective function is two times differentiable so second order methods can be employed. While (2) is non-convex because of the bilinear terms, the convexity of the nuclear norm can still be used to show that any local minimizer B, C with rank(BC^T) $< k$, where k is the number of columns in B and C, is globally optimal [2,19]. The formulation (2) was for vision problems in [9]. In practice it was observed that the shrinking bias of the nuclear norm makes it too weak to enforce a low rank when the data is noisy. Therefore, a "continuation" approach where the size of the factorization is gradually reduced was proposed. While this yields solutions with lower rank, the optimality guarantees no longer apply. Bach *et al.* [2] showed that

$$\|X\|_{s,t} := \min_{X=BC^T} \sum_{i=1}^{k} \frac{\|B_i\|_s^2 + \|C_i\|_t^2}{2}, \tag{3}$$

where B_i, C_i are the ith columns of B and C respectively, is convex for any choice of vector norms $\|\cdot\|_s$ and $\|\cdot\|_t$. In [19] it was shown that a more general class of 2-homogeneous factor penalties result in a convex regularization similar to (3). The property that a local minimizer B, C with rank(BC^T) $< k$, is global is also extended to this case. Still, because of convexity, it is clear that these formulations will suffer from a similar shrinking bias as the nuclear norm.

One way of reducing shrinking bias is to use penalties that are constant for large singular values. Shang *et al.* [37] showed that penalization with the Schatten semi-norms $\|X\|_q = \sqrt[q]{\sum_{i=1}^N \sigma_i(X)^q}$, for $q = 1/2$ and $2/3$, can be achieved using a convex penalty on the factors B and C. A generalization to general values of q is given in [44]. An algorithm that address a general class of penalties for symmetric matrices is presented in [26]. In [40] it was shown that if f is given by $f(\sigma(X)) = \sum_i g(\sigma_i(X))$, where g is differentiable, concave and non-decreasing then (1) can be optimized using 2nd order methods such as Levenberg-Marquart or VarPro. This is achieved by re-parameterizing the matrix X using a bilinear factorization $X = BC^T$ and optimizing

$$\min_{B,C} f(\gamma(B,C)) + \|\mathcal{A}(BC^T) + b\|^2. \tag{4}$$

Here $\gamma(B,C) = (\gamma_1(B,C), \gamma_2(B,C), ...)$ and $\gamma_i(B,C) = \frac{\|B_i\|^2 + \|C_i\|^2}{2}$. In contrast to the singular value $\sigma_i(X)$ the function $\gamma_i(B,C)$ is smooth which allows optimization with second order methods. It is shown in [40] that if X^* is optimal in (1) then the factorization $B = L\sqrt{\Sigma}, C = R\sqrt{\Sigma}$, where $X^* = L\Sigma R^T$ is the SVD of X^*, is optimal in (4). (Here we assume that L is $m \times r$, Σ is $r \times r$ and R is $n \times r$, with $\text{rank}(X) = r$.) Note also that this choice gives $\gamma_i(B,C) = \sigma_i(X^*)$.

A less restrictive way of reducing bias is to re-weight the nuclear norm and use $f(\sigma(X)) = \sum_i a_i \sigma_i(X)$ [18,23,27]. Assigning low weights to the first (largest) singular values allows accurate matrix recovery. In addition the weights can be used to regularize the size of the non-zero singular values which has been shown to be an additional useful prior in NRSfM [27]. Note however that the singular values are always ordered in non-increasing order. Therefore, while the function is linear in the singular values it is in fact non-convex and non-differentiable in the elements of X whenever the singular values are not distinct (typically the case in low rank recovery).

In this paper we show that this type of penalties allow optimization with $\gamma(B,C)$ instead of $\sigma(X)$. In particular we study the optimization problem

$$\min_{B,C} f(\gamma(B,C)) \tag{5}$$
$$\text{s.t.} \quad BC^T = X, \tag{6}$$

and its constraint set for a fixed X. We characterize the extreme-points of the feasible set using permutation matrices and give conditions on f that ensure that the optimal solution is of the form $\gamma(B,C) = \Pi\sigma(X)$, where Π is a permutation. For the weighted nuclear norm $f(\sigma(X)) = a^T\sigma(X)$ we show that if the elements of a are non-decreasing the optimal solution has $\gamma(B^*, C^*) = \sigma(X)$. A simple consequence of this result is that

$$\min_{B,C} a^T\gamma(B,C)) + \|\mathcal{A}(BC^T) - b\|^2 \tag{7}$$

is equivalent to $\min_X a^T\sigma(X) + \|\mathcal{A}X - b\|^2$. While the latter is non-differentiable the former is smooth and can be minimized efficiently with second order methods.

Our experimental evaluation confirms that this approach outperforms current first order methods in terms of accuracy as can be expected. On the other hand first order methods make large improvements the first coupler of iterations and therefore we combine the two approaches. We start out with a simple ADMM implementation and switch to our second order approach when only minor progress is being made. Note however that since the original formulation is non-convex local minima can exist. In addition bilinear parameterization introduces additional stationary points that are not present in the original X parameterization. One such example is $(B, C) = (0, 0)$, where all gradients vanish. Still our experiments show that the combination of these methods often converge to a good solution from random initialization.

2   Bilinear Parameterization Penalties

In this section we will derive a dependence between the singular values $\sigma_i(X)$ and the $\gamma_i(B, C)$, when $BC^T = X$. For ease of notation we will suppress the dependence on X and (B, C) since this will be clear from the context. Let X have the SVD $X = R\Sigma L^T$, $B = R\sqrt{\Sigma}$ and $C = L\sqrt{\Sigma}$. We will study other potential factorizations $X = \hat{B}\hat{C}^T$ using $\hat{B} = BV$, $\hat{C} = CH$ and $VH^T = I_{r \times r}$. In this section we will further assume that V is a square $r \times r$ matrix and therefore H^T is its inverse. (We will generalize the results to the rectangular case in Sect. 3).

We begin by noting that $\gamma_j = \frac{\|\hat{B}_j\|^2 + \|\hat{C}_j\|^2}{2} = \frac{\|BV_j\|^2 + \|CH_j\|^2}{2}$, where V_j and H_j are columns j of V and H respectively. We have $\|\hat{B}V_j\|^2 = V_j^T B^T B V_j = V_j^T \Sigma V_j = \|\sqrt{\Sigma}V_j\|^2$, and similarly $\|CH_j\|^2 = \|\sqrt{\Sigma}H_j\|^2$ and therefore $\gamma_j = \frac{\|\sqrt{\Sigma}V_j\|^2 + \|\sqrt{\Sigma}H_j\|^2}{2}$. This gives $\gamma_j = \left(\frac{\sigma_1(v_{1j}^2 + h_{1j}^2) + \sigma_2(v_{2j}^2 + h_{2j}^2) + \ldots + \sigma_r(v_{rj}^2 + h_{rj}^2)}{2} \right)$, or in matrix form

$$
\begin{pmatrix} \gamma_1 \\ \gamma_2 \\ \vdots \\ \gamma_r \end{pmatrix} = \frac{1}{2} \underbrace{\begin{pmatrix} v_{11}^2 & v_{21}^2 & \cdots & v_{r1}^2 \\ v_{12}^2 & v_{22}^2 & \cdots & v_{r2}^2 \\ \vdots & \vdots & \ddots & \vdots \\ v_{1r}^2 & v_{2r}^2 & \cdots & v_{rr}^2 \end{pmatrix}}_{=V^T \odot V^T} \begin{pmatrix} \sigma_1 \\ \sigma_2 \\ \vdots \\ \sigma_r \end{pmatrix} + \frac{1}{2} \underbrace{\begin{pmatrix} h_{11}^2 & h_{21}^2 & \cdots & h_{r1}^2 \\ h_{12}^2 & h_{22}^2 & \cdots & h_{r2}^2 \\ \vdots & \vdots & \ddots & \vdots \\ h_{1r}^2 & h_{2r}^2 & \cdots & h_{rr}^2 \end{pmatrix}}_{=H^T \odot H^T} \begin{pmatrix} \sigma_1 \\ \sigma_2 \\ \vdots \\ \sigma_r \end{pmatrix}. \tag{8}
$$

Minimizing (5) over different factorizations is therefore equivalent to solving

$$
\min_{\gamma, M \in \mathcal{S}} f(\gamma), \tag{9}
$$

$$
\text{s.t.} \quad \gamma = M\sigma. \tag{10}
$$

where $\mathcal{S} = \{\frac{1}{2}(V^T \odot V^T + H^T \odot H^T); \ VH^T = I\}$. It is clear that $V = H = \Pi^T$, where Π is any permutation, is feasible in the above problem since permutations are orthogonal. In addition they contain only zeros and ones and therefore it is easy to see that this choice gives $\gamma = \frac{1}{2}(\Pi \odot \Pi + \Pi \odot \Pi)\sigma = \Pi\sigma$. In the next section we will show that these are extreme points of the feasible set, in the sense that they can not be written as convex combinations of other points in the set. Extreme points are important for optimization since the global minimum is guaranteed to be attained (if it exists) in such a point if the objective function has concavity properties. This is for example true if f is quasi-concave, that is, the super-level sets $S_\alpha = \{x \in \mathbb{R}^r_{\geq 0}; f(x) \geq \alpha\}$ are convex. To see this let $x = \lambda x_1 + (1 - \lambda)x_2$, and consider the super-level set S_α where $\alpha = \min(f(x_1), f(x_2))$. Since both $x_1 \in S_\alpha$ and $x_2 \in S_\alpha$ it is clear by convexity that so is x and therefore $f(x) \geq \min(f(x_1), f(x_2))$.

2.1 Extreme Points and Optimality

We now consider the optimization problem (9)–(10) and a convex relaxation of the constraint set. For this purpose we let $\mathcal{D}$ be the set of doubly stochastic matrices $\mathcal{D} = \{M \in \mathbb{R}^{r \times r}; m_{ij} \geq 0, \sum_i m_{ij} = 1, \sum_j m_{ij} = 1\}$. Note that if V is orthogonal, and therefore $H = V$, then the row sum $\sum_{j=1}^{r} \frac{v_{ij}^2 + h_{ij}^2}{2}$, and the column sum $\sum_{i=1}^{r} \frac{v_{ij}^2 + h_{ij}^2}{2}$ are both one. Hence such a matrix is in $\mathcal{D}$. To handle non-orthogonal matrices we define the set of superstochastic matrices $\mathcal{S}_W$ as all matrices $M = D + N$, where $D \in \mathcal{D}$ and N is a matrix with non-negative elements. It can be shown that (see Theorem 6 in [4]) that $\mathcal{S} \subset \mathcal{S}_W$. In addition it is easy to see that $\mathcal{S}_W$ is convex since it consists of affine constraints. Therefore the problem

$$\min_{\gamma, M \in \mathcal{S}_W} f(\gamma), \tag{11}$$

$$\text{s.t.} \quad \gamma = M\sigma. \tag{12}$$

is a relaxation of (9)–(10). Next we show that the two problems have the same minimum if a minimizer to (11)–(12) exists when f is quasi-concave (on $\mathbb{R}^r_{\geq 0}$). As mentioned previously, the minimum (over $\mathcal{S}_W$) is then attained in an extreme point of $\mathcal{S}_W$. We therefore need the following characterization.

Lemma 1. *The extreme points of $\mathcal{S}_W$ are $r \times r$ permutation matrices.*

Proof. First we note that any extreme point of $\mathcal{S}_W$ has to be in $\mathcal{D}$ since if $M = D + N$ with $N \neq 0$ then $M = \frac{1}{2}D + \frac{1}{2}(D + 2N)$, which is a convex combination of two points in $\mathcal{S}_W$. By Birkhoff's Theorem [5] any matrix in $\mathcal{D}$ can be written as a convex combination of permutation matrices.

Since permutation matrices are orthogonal with 0/1 elements it is clear they can be written $\Pi = \frac{1}{2}(\Pi \odot \Pi + \Pi \odot \Pi)$, with $\Pi\Pi^T = I$. Therefore the extreme points of $\mathcal{S}_W$ are also in $\mathcal{S}$. Hence if the minimum of (11)–(12) is attained, there is an optimal extreme point of $\mathcal{S}_W$ which also solves (9)–(10), and therefore the solution is given by a permutation $V = H = \Pi$.

We conclude this section by giving sufficient conditions for the minimum of (11)–(12) to exist, namely that f is lower semi-continuous and non-decreasing in all of its variables, that is, if $\tilde{\gamma}_i \geq \gamma_i$ for all i then $f(\tilde{\gamma}) \geq f(\gamma)$. Since the singular values are all positive it is clear that the elements of $(D + N)\sigma$ are larger than those of $D\sigma$. Hence when f is non-decreasing it is enough to consider minimization over $\mathcal{D}$. We then have a lower semi-continuous objective function on a compact set for which the minimum is known to be attained.

We can now summarize the results of this section in the following theorem:

Theorem 1. *Let f be quasi-concave (and lower semi-continuous) on $\mathbb{R}^r_{\geq 0}$ fulfilling $f(\tilde{\gamma}) \geq f(\gamma)$ when $\tilde{\gamma}_i \geq \gamma_i$ for all i. Then there is an optimal γ^* of (9)–(10) that is of the form $\gamma^* = \Pi \sigma$ where Π is a permutation.*

3   Non-square Matrices

In the previous section we made the assumption that V and H where square matrices, which corresponds to searching over $\hat{B}$ and $\hat{C}$ consisting of r columns when $\mathrm{rank}(X) = r$. In addition since V and H are invertible this means that $\hat{B}$ and $\hat{C}$ have linearly independent columns. In this section we generalize the result from Sect. 2.1 to rectangular matrices V and H. Therefore we suppose that V and H are non-square of size $r \times p$, $p > r$, with $VH^T = I_{r \times r}$, and consider the slightly modified problem

$$\min_{\gamma,V,H} f(\gamma), \tag{13}$$

$$\gamma = \frac{1}{2}(V^T \odot V^T + H^T \odot H^T)\sigma \tag{14}$$

$$VH^T = I_{r \times r} \tag{15}$$

Note that VH^T do not commute and we therefore only assume that V is a left inverse of H^T. In what follows we show that by adding zeros to the vector σ we can extend V, H into square matrices without changing the objective function.

Note that we may assume that V has full row rank since otherwise $X \neq BVH^TC^T$. Let $V^\dagger$ be the Moore-Penrose pseudo inverse and $O_{V_\perp}$ a $(p-r) \times p$ matrix containing a basis for the space orthogonal to the row space of V (and the column space of $V^\dagger$). Since $VH^T = I_{r \times r}$ the matrix H^T is of the form $H^T = V^\dagger + O_{V_\perp}^T K_1$, where K_1 is a $(p-r) \times r$ coefficient matrix. We now want to find matrices $\tilde{V}$ and $\tilde{H}$ such that $\begin{bmatrix} V \\ \tilde{V} \end{bmatrix} \begin{bmatrix} V^\dagger + O_{V_\perp}^T K_1 & \tilde{H}^T \end{bmatrix} = \begin{bmatrix} I_{r \times r} & 0 \\ 0 & I_{(p-r) \times (p-r)} \end{bmatrix}$. To do this we first select $\tilde{H}^T = O_{V_\perp}^T$ since $VO_{V_\perp}^T = 0$. Then we let $\tilde{V} = O_{V_\perp} + K_2 V$, where K_2 is a size $(p-r) \times r$ coefficient matrix, since this gives $\tilde{V}\tilde{H}^T = I_{(p-r) \times (p-r)}$. To determine K_2 we consider $\tilde{V}(V^\dagger + O_{V_\perp}^T K_1) = K_2 I_{r \times r} + I_{(p-r) \times (p-r)} K_1 = K_2 + K_1$. Selecting $K_2 = -K_1$ thus gives square matrices such that $\begin{bmatrix} V \\ \tilde{V} \end{bmatrix} \begin{bmatrix} H^T & \tilde{H}^T \end{bmatrix} = I$. Further letting $\tilde{\Sigma} = \begin{bmatrix} \Sigma & 0 \\ 0 & 0 \end{bmatrix}$ shows that $\|BV_i\| = \|\sqrt{\tilde{\Sigma}} \begin{bmatrix} V_i \\ \tilde{V}_i \end{bmatrix}\|$ and $\|CH_i\| = \|\sqrt{\tilde{\Sigma}} \begin{bmatrix} H_i \\ \tilde{H}_i \end{bmatrix}\|$ and the results of the previous section give that the minimizer of $f(\gamma_1, \gamma_2, ..., \gamma_p)$ is a permutation of the elements in the vector $(\sigma_1, \sigma_2, ..., \sigma_r, 0, ..., 0)$. We therefore have the following result:

Corollary 1. *Let f be quasi-concave (and lower semi-continuous) on $\mathbb{R}_{\geq 0}^p$ fulfilling $f(\tilde{\gamma}) \geq f(\gamma)$ when $\tilde{\gamma}_i \geq \gamma_i$ for all i. Then an optimizer γ^* of (13)–(15) is of the form $\gamma^* = \Pi_{p \times r}\sigma$ where $\Pi_{p \times r}$ contains the first r columns of a $p \times p$ permutation matrix.*

4   Linear Objectives - Weighted Nuclear Norms

We now consider weighted nuclear norm regularization $f(\gamma) = a^T\gamma$. To ensure that the problem is well posed we assume that the elements of a are non-negative. It is then clear that $f(\tilde{\gamma}) \geq f(\gamma)$ when $\tilde{\gamma}_i \geq \gamma_i$. Since linearity implies concavity the results of Sects. 2.1 and 3 now show that the minimum of $f(M\sigma)$, over $M \in \mathcal{S}$ is attained in $M = \Pi$ for some permutation matrix. To ensure that the bilinear formulation is equivalent to the original one we need to show that the optimum occurs when $\Pi = I$. Suppose that the elements in a are sorted in ascending order $a_1 \leq a_2 \leq ... \leq a_p$. It is easy to see that for Π to give the smallest objective value it should sort the elements of γ so that $\gamma_1 \geq \gamma_2 \geq ... \geq \gamma_p$, which means that $\Pi = I$ and $\gamma = \sigma$. We therefore conclude that minimizing (4) with a linear objective corresponds to regularization with a weighted nuclear norm with non-decreasing weights.

5   Experiments

In this section we start by describing implementation details of our method and then apply it to the problems of low matrix recovery and non-rigid structure recovery. Solving the weighted nuclear norm regularized problem (7) now amounts to minimizing

$$\sum_{i=1}^{p} a_i \frac{\|B_i\|^2 + \|C_i\|^2}{2} + \|\mathcal{A}(BC^T) - b\|^2. \tag{16}$$

Note that the terms in the (16) can be combined into a single norm term by vertically concatenating the vectors B_i and C_i, weighted by $\sqrt{a_i/2}$, with $\mathcal{A}(BC^T) - b$. We define the resulting vector as $r_a := \mathcal{A}_a(BC^T) - b_a$, giving the objective $\|r_a(BC^T)\|^2$, where the subscript reflects the dependence on the weights a. Since the objective is smooth, standard methods such as Levenberg-Marquardt can be applied and Algorithm 1 shows an overview of the method used. Additional information about the algorithm is provided in the supplementary material.

The remainder of this section is organized as follows. The particular form of the data fitting term in (16) when applied to structure from motion is described in Sect. 5.1. In Sect. 5.2 we compare the convergence of first and second-order methods, and motivated by the ADMM fast iterations but low accuracy, as opposed to the bilinear parameterization's high accuracy but slower iterations, we combine the two methods by initializing the bilinear parameterization with the ADMM's solution [6, 27] for a non-rigid structure recovery problem. Our work focus on the increased accuracy of our method compared to first-order methods, so the comparison of our results with works such as [1, 34, 43, 45] (without the desired regularization term) are not covered.

Algorithm 1: Bilinear parameterization of weighted nuclear norm

---

Result: Optimal B,C to (16)

$B = U\Sigma^{\frac{1}{2}}$, $C = V\Sigma^{\frac{1}{2}}$, where $X = U\Sigma V^T$ is the ADMM solution to (16) ;

Choose initial $\alpha > 1$ and λ, and define $z = [\text{vec}(B); \text{vec}(C^T)]$;

Compute $error = \|r_a(BC^T)\|^2$;

while *not converged* **do**

    Compute $r = r_a(BC^T)$, and the jacobian J of (16) in terms of z;

    Update $\tilde{z} = z - (J^T J + \lambda I)^{-1} J^T r$, where $\tilde{z} = [\text{vec}(\tilde{B}); \text{vec}(\tilde{C}^T)]$;

    if $error > \|r_a(\tilde{B}\tilde{C}^T)\|^2$ **then**

        | Updata $z \leftarrow \tilde{z}$, $\lambda \leftarrow \alpha^{-1}\lambda$, and $error \leftarrow \|A_a(\tilde{B}\tilde{C}^T) - b_a\|^2$;

    else

        | $\lambda \leftarrow \alpha\lambda$;

    end

end

5.1 Pseudo Object Space Error (pOSE) and Non-Rigid Structure from Motion

To compare the performance of 1st and 2nd order methods, we choose as objective function the Pseudo Object Space Error (pOSE) [24], which consists of a combination of the object space error $\ell_{\text{OSE}} := \sum_{(i,j)\in\Omega} \|P_{i,1:2}\tilde{x}_j - (p_{i,3}^T\tilde{x}_j)m_{i,j}\|_2^2$ and the affine projection error $\ell_{\text{Affine}} := \sum_{(i,j)\in\Omega} \|P_{i,1:2}\tilde{x}_j - m_{i,j}\|_2^2$, where $P_{i,1:2}$ and $p_{i,3}$ are, respectively, the first two and the third rows of the camera matrix P_i, with $i = 1,\ldots,F$; $\tilde{x}_j$ is a 3D point in homogeneous coordinates, with $j = 1,\ldots,P$; $m_{i,j}$ is the 2D observation of the j:th point on the i:th camera; and Ω represents the set of observable data. The pOSE is then given by $\ell_{\text{pOSE}} := (1-\eta)\ell_{\text{OSE}} + \eta\ell_{\text{Affine}}$ where $\eta \in [0,1]$ balances the weight between the two errors. One of the main properties of pOSE is its wide basin of convergence while keeping a bilinear problem structure. The ℓ_{pOSE}, originally designed for rigid SfM, can be extended for the non-rigid case by replacing $P_i\tilde{x}_j$ by a linear combination of K shape basis, i.e., $\Pi_i\hat{S}_j$, where $\Pi_i \in \mathbb{R}^{3\times(3K+1)}$ and $\hat{S}_j \in \mathbb{R}^{3K+1}$ are structured as $\Pi_i = \begin{bmatrix} c_{i,1}R_i & \cdots & c_{i,K}R_i & t_i \end{bmatrix}$ and $\hat{S}_j = \begin{bmatrix} S_{1,j}^T & \cdots & S_{K,j}^T & 1 \end{bmatrix}^T$. We denote by Π and $\hat{S}$ the vertical and horizontal concatenations of Π_i and $\hat{S}_j$, respectively. Note that by construction $\text{rank}(\Pi\hat{S}) \leq 3K+1$, and for $K = 1$ we have $\Pi_i\hat{S}_j = P_i\tilde{x}_j$, which corresponds to the rigid case.

5.2 Low-Rank Matrix Recovery with pOSE Errors

In this section we compare the convergence and accuracy of 1st and 2nd order methods, starting from the same initial guess, for low-rank matrix recovery with pOSE. In this problem, we define $X = \Pi\hat{S}$ and aim at minimizing

$$\min_X a^T \boldsymbol{\sigma}(X) + \ell_{\text{pOSE}}(X). \tag{17}$$

We apply our method and solve the problem (16) by using the bilinear factorization $X = BC^T$, with $B \in \mathbb{R}^{3F \times r}$, and $C \in \mathbb{R}^{P \times r}$, with $r \geq 3K + 1$. We test the performance of our method in 4 datasets: Door [32], Back [36], Heart [38], Paper [41]. The first one consists of image measurements of a rigid structure with missing data, while the remaining three datasets track points in deformable structures.

For the Door dataset, we apply two different selections of weights on the singular values of X, corresponding to the nuclear norm, i.e., $a_i = \mu_{NN}$, and truncated nuclear norm, i.e., $a_i = 0, i = 1, \ldots, 4$ and $a_i = \mu_{TNN}, i > 4$. We select $\mu_{NN} = 1.5 \times 10^{-3}$, and $\mu_{TNN} = 1$. For the Back, Heart and Paper datasets, we apply the nuclear norm and a weighted nuclear norm, in which the first four singular values of X are not penalized and the remaining ones are increasingly penalized, i.e., $a_i = 0, i = 1, \ldots, 4$ and $a_i = (i - 4)\mu_{WNN}, i > 4$. We select $\mu_{NN} = 7.5 \times 10^{-4}$, $\mu_{WNN} = 2.25 \times 10^{-3}$. The values of the weights a_i are chosen such that there is a $3K + 1$ rank solution to (17), with $K = 1$ and $K = 2$ for the rigid and non-rigid datasets, respectively.

We compare the bilinear parameterization with three first-order methods commonly used for low-rank matrix recovery: Alternating Direction Method of Multipliers (ADMM) [6], Iteratively Reweighted Nuclear Norm (IRNN) [13], and Accelerated Gradient Descend (AGD) [30]. We also test the methods for two different cases of the ℓ_{pOSE} error, with $\eta = 0.05$ and $\eta = 0.95$, which correspond to the near-perspective and near-affine camera models, respectively. To improve numerical stability of the algorithms, as pre-processing step we normalize the image measurements matrix M by its norm. The methods are initialized with the closed-form solution of the regularization-free problem, i.e., $X = \mathcal{A}^\dagger(b)$. The comparison of the four algorithms in terms of total log-loss over time is shown in Fig. 1. The log-loss is used for better visualization purposes. The plots for the IRNN for the nuclear norm are omitted since it demonstrated slow convergence compared to the remaining three methods. A qualitative evaluation of the results on one of the images of the Door dataset for the truncated nuclear norm and near perspective camera model is shown in Fig. 2. The qualitative results for the remaining datasets are provided in the supplementary material.

In general, we can observe that first-order methods demonstrate faster initial convergence, mostly due to faster iterations. However when near minima, the convergence rate drops significantly and the methods tend to stall. Contrarily, bilinear parameterization compensates its slower iterations by demonstrating higher accuracy and reaching solutions with lower energy. This is specially visible for the near perspective camera model, which reinforces the advantages of using a second-order method on image data under perspective projection. To compensate for the slower convergence, we propose the initialization of the bilinear parameterization with the solution obtained with ADMM. In this way, the bilinear parameterization starts near the minimum and performs local refinement to further improve accuracy.

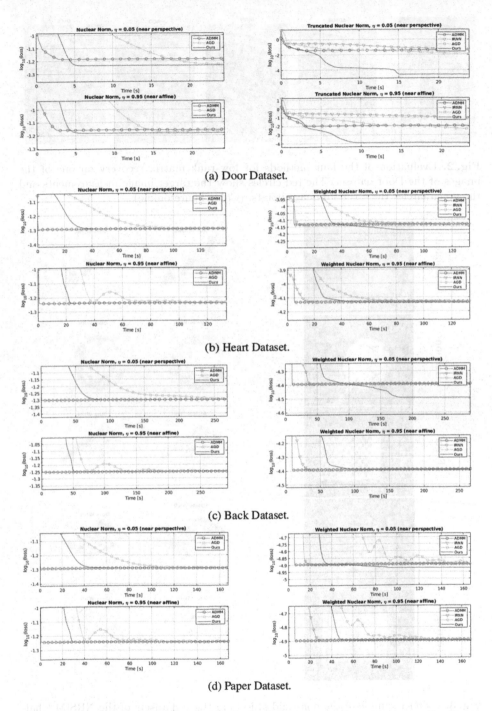

(a) Door Dataset.

(b) Heart Dataset.

(c) Back Dataset.

(d) Paper Dataset.

Fig. 1. Convergence of the four methods for low-rank matrix recovery on the Door, Heart, Back and Paper datasets.

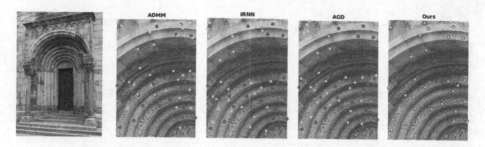

Fig. 2. Evaluation of the four methods for low-rank matrix recovery on one of the images of the Door dataset. The red circles show the target image measurements and the green circles the estimate image points. (Color figure online)

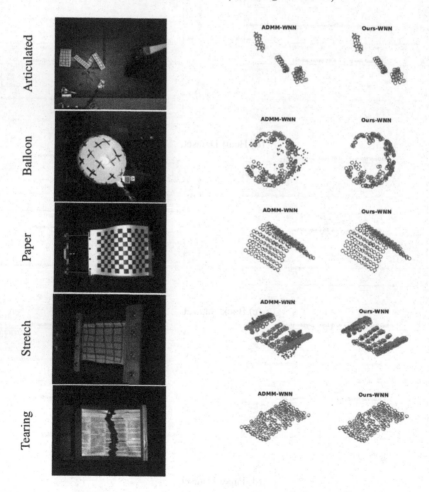

Fig. 3. (Left) Example of the non-rigid objects in the 5 datasets of the NRSfM Challenge. (Right) Estimation (blue) and ground-truth (red) of the non-rigid 3D structure for the two methods with weighted nuclear norm regularization. (Color figure online)

5.3 Non-Rigid Structure Recovery

Consider now that the camera rotations in Π are known (or previously esti-
mated). In this case we have $\Pi\hat{S} = RX + t\mathbb{1}^T$, with $R = \mathrm{blkdiag}(R_1, \ldots, R_F)$
and $t = [t_1^T, \ldots, t_F^T]^T$, where X, the non-rigid structure, and t are the unknowns.
It is directly observed that $\mathrm{rank}(\Pi\hat{S}) \leq \mathrm{rank}(RX) + \mathrm{rank}(t\mathbb{1}^T)$, with the later
being equal to 1 by construction and independent on K. As consequence, it
follows that $\mathrm{rank}(RX) = \mathrm{rank}(X) \leq 3K$, and the rank regularization can be
applied on X. A similar problem was studied in [14] but for orthogonal camera
models, where the authors propose the rank regularization to be applied on a
reshaped version of X, given by $X^\# = g^{-1}(X)$, a $F \times 3P$, where the function g
performs the permutation on the elements of $X^\#$ to obtain X. With this reshap-
ing we have that $\mathrm{rank}(X^\#) \leq K$, meaning that we can factorize it as $X^\# = BC^T$
with $B \in \mathbb{R}^{F \times K}$ and $C \in \mathbb{R}^{3P \times K}$. The optimization problem then becomes

$$\min_{B,C,t} \sum_{i=1}^{K} a_i \frac{\|B_i\|^2 + \|C_i\|^2}{2} + \ell_{\mathrm{pOSE}}(Rg(BC^T) + t\mathbb{1}^T). \tag{18}$$

Solving this optimization problem requires small adjustments to be done to the
proposed Algorithm 1, which can be consulted in the supplementary material.
We apply our methods to the 5 datasets (Articulated, Balloon, Paper, Stretch,
Tearing) from the NRSfM Challenge [25]. Each of these datasets include tracks
of image points for orthogonal and perspective camera models for six different
camera paths (Circle, Flyby, Line, Semi-circle, Tricky, Zigzag), as well as the
ground-truth 3D structure for one of the frames. We use the 2D observation
for the orthogonal camera model to compute the rotation matrix R, as done in
[14], and the ground-truth 3D structure to estimate the intrinsic camera matrix,
which is assumed to be fixed during each sequence. The intrinsic camera matrix
is used to obtain the calibrated 2D observation of the perspective camera model
data. For the nuclear norm (NN), we set $a_i = 1 \times 10^{-3}, i = 1, \ldots, K$. For the
weighted nuclear norm (WNN), the weights a are selected similarly to [27] $a_i =
\frac{\xi}{\sigma_i(g^{-1}(X_0))+\gamma}, i = 1, \ldots, K$ where $\xi = 5 \times 10^{-3}$, γ is a small number for numerical
stability, and X_0 is the closed-form solution of the objective $\min_X \ell_{\mathrm{pOSE}}(RX)$.

For these datasets we choose $K = 2$ and set the $\eta = 0.05$. As baseline we use
the best performing first-order method according to the experiments Sect. 5.2,
ADMM, and apply the method described in Algorithm 1 for local refinement
starting from the ADMM's solution. We also try our method for the orthogonal camera model (by setting $\eta = 1$), and compare it with BMM [14] and
R-BMM [27], which correspond to ADMM implementations for nuclear norm
and weighted nuclear norm, respectively. These methods perform a best rank
K approximation to the obtained ADMM solution if $\mathrm{rank}(X^\#) > K$ after convergence. We let the ADMM-based methods run until convergence or stalling
is achieved for fair comparison. The average log-losses, before and after refinement, obtained on each dataset are shown in Table 1. The average reconstruction
errors, in millimeters, on each dataset relatively to the provided ground-truth
structure are shown in Table 2. In Fig. 3 we also show some qualitative results

of the obtained 3D reconstruction of each of the objects in the 5 datasets. More
qualitative results are provided in the supplementary material.

The results show that our method is able to achieve lower energies for all
datasets comparatively with the ADMM baselines. Similarly to Sect. 5.2, the difference is more substantial for the perspective model. Furthermore, even though
we are not explicitly minimizing the reconstruction error expressed in Table 2,
we are able to consistently obtain the lowest reconstruction error for all datasets,
sometimes with great improvements compared to the ADMM (see Balloon and
Stretch in Fig. 3). The same does not apply for the orthogonal data, where
achieving lower energies did not lead to lower reconstruction errors.

Table 1. Average log-loss on each of the perspective datasets over the 6 camera paths.

	Method\Dataset	Articulated	Balloon	Paper	Stretch	Tearing
Orthogonal	BMM [14]	−1.645	−2.267	−1.712	−2.282	−1.453
	Ours-NN	**−1.800**	**−2.352**	**−2.188**	**−2.509**	**−1.634**
	R-BMM [27]	−1.648	−1.979	−1.855	−1.997	−1.522
	Ours-WNN	**−1.648**	**−1.979**	**−1.855**	**−1.997**	**−1.522**
Perspective	ADMM-NN	−2.221	−2.529	−2.338	−2.395	−1.471
	Ours-NN	**−2.415**	**−2.657**	**−2.560**	**−2.622**	**−2.053**
	ADMM-WNN	−2.455	−2.617	−2.195	−2.651	−1.688
	Ours-WNN	**−2.486**	**−2.931**	**−2.777**	**−2.857**	**−2.103**

Table 2. Average reconstruction errors, in millimeters, on each dataset over the 6
camera paths relatively to the provided ground-truth structure.

	Method\Dataset	Articulated	Balloon	Paper	Stretch	Tearing
Orthogonal	BMM [14]	18.49	10.39	**8.94**	10.02	**14.23**
	Ours-NN	18.31	8.53	10.94	10.67	17.03
	R-BMM [27]	16.00	**7.84**	10.69	**7.53**	16.34
	Ours-WNN	**15.03**	8.05	10.45	9.01	16.20
Perspective	ADMM-NN	16.70	8.05	7.96	6.04	9.40
	Ours-NN	**16.13**	6.48	6.80	6.00	9.31
	ADMM-WNN	18.33	8.95	10.14	8.06	9.28
	Ours-WNN	16.53	**6.27**	**5.68**	**5.93**	**8.42**

6 Conclusions

In this paper we show that it is possible to optimize a general class of singular
value penalties using a bilinear parameterization of the matrix. We show that

with this parameterization weighted nuclear norm penalties turn in to smooth objectives that can be accurately solved with 2nd order methods. Our proposed approach starts by using ADMM which rapidly decreases the objective the first couple of iterations and switches to Levenberg-Marquardt when ADMM iterations make little progress. This results in a much more accurate solution and we showed that we were able to extend the recently proposed pOSE [24] to handle non-rigid reconstruction problems.

While 2nd order methods offer increased accuracy, our approach is expensive since iterations require the inversion of a large matrix. Exploring feasible alternatives such as preconditioning and conjugate gradient approaches is an interesting future direction.

Something that we have not discussed is adding constraints on the factors, which is possible since these are present in the optimization. This is very relevant for structure from motion problems and will likely be an fruitful direction to explore.

References

1. Akhter, I., Sheikh, Y., Khan, S., Kanade, T.: Nonrigid structure from motion in trajectory space. In: Proceedings of the 21st International Conference on Neural Information Processing Systems, NIPS 2008, pp. 41–48. Curran Associates Inc., Red Hook (2008)
2. Bach, F.: Convex relaxations of structured matrix factorizations, September 2013
3. Basri, R., Jacobs, D., Kemelmacher, I.: Photometric stereo with general, unknown lighting. Int. J. Comput. Vision 72(3), 239–257 (2007). https://doi.org/10.1007/s11263-006-8815-7
4. Bhatia, R., Jain, T.: On symplectic eigenvalues of positive definite matrices. J. Math. Phys. 56(11), 112201 (2015)
5. Birkhoff, G.: Tres observaciones sobre el algebra lineal. Universidad Nacional de Tucuman Revista. Serie A. 5, 137–151 (1946)
6. Boyd, S., Parikh, N., Chu, E., Peleato, B., Eckstein, J.: Distributed optimization and statistical learning via the alternating direction method of multipliers. Found. Trends Mach. Learn. 3(1), 1–122 (2011)
7. Bregler, C., Hertzmann, A., Biermann, H.: Recovering non-rigid 3D shape from image streams. In: The IEEE Conference on Computer Vision and Pattern Recognition (CVPR) (2000)
8. Buchanan, A.M., Fitzgibbon, A.W.: Damped newton algorithms for matrix factorization with missing data. In: The IEEE Conference on Computer Vision and Pattern Recognition (CVPR) (2005)
9. Cabral, R., De la Torre, F., Costeira, J.P., Bernardino, A.: Unifying nuclear norm and bilinear factorization approaches for low-rank matrix decomposition. In: International Conference on Computer Vision (ICCV) (2013)
10. Candès, E.J., Li, X., Ma, Y., Wright, J.: Robust principal component analysis? J. ACM 58(3), 11:1–11:37 (2011)
11. Candès, E.J., Recht, B.: Exact matrix completion via convex optimization. Found. Comput. Math. 9(6), 717–772 (2009). https://doi.org/10.1007/s10208-009-9045-5
12. Canyi, L., Tang, J., Yan, S., Lin, Z.: Generalized nonconvex nonsmooth low-rank minimization. In: The IEEE Conference on Computer Vision and Pattern Recognition (CVPR) (2014)

13. Canyi, L., Tang, J., Yan, S., Lin, Z.: Nonconvex nonsmooth low-rank minimization via iteratively reweighted nuclear norm. IEEE Trans. Image Process. **25**(2), 829–839 (2015)
14. Dai, Y., Li, H., He, M.: A simple prior-free method for non-rigid structure-from-motion factorization. Int. J. Comput. Vision **107**(2), 101–122 (2014). https://doi.org/10.1007/s11263-013-0684-2
15. Fazel, M., Hindi, H., Boyd, S.P.: A rank minimization heuristic with application to minimum order system approximation. In: American Control Conference (2001)
16. Garg, R., Roussos, A., Agapito, L.: A variational approach to video registration with subspace constraints. Int. J. Comput. Vision **104**(3), 286–314 (2013). https://doi.org/10.1007/s11263-012-0607-7
17. Garg, R., Roussos, A., de Agapito, L.: Dense variational reconstruction of non-rigid surfaces from monocular video. In: The IEEE Conference on Computer Vision and Pattern Recognition (CVPR) (2013)
18. Gu, S., Xie, Q., Meng, D., Zuo, W., Feng, X., Zhang, L.: Weighted nuclear norm minimization and its applications to low level vision. Int. J. Comput. Vision **121**(2), 183–208 (2016). https://doi.org/10.1007/s11263-016-0930-5
19. Haeffele, B.D., Vidal, R.: Structured low-rank matrix factorization: global optimality, algorithms, and applications. IEEE Trans. Pattern Anal. Mach. Intell. **42**(6), 1468–1482 (2020)
20. Hyeong Hong, J., Fitzgibbon, A.: Secrets of matrix factorization: approximations, numerics, manifold optimization and random restarts. In: The IEEE Conference on Computer Vision and Pattern Recognition (CVPR) (2015)
21. Hong, J.H., Zach, C., Fitzgibbon, A., Cipolla, R.: Projective bundle adjustment from arbitrary initialization using the variable projection method. In: Leibe, B., Matas, J., Sebe, N., Welling, M. (eds.) ECCV 2016. LNCS, vol. 9905, pp. 477–493. Springer, Cham (2016). https://doi.org/10.1007/978-3-319-46448-0_29
22. Hong, J.H., Zach, C., Fitzgibbon, A., Cipolla, R.: Projective bundle adjustment from arbitrary initialization using the variable projection method. In: The IEEE Conference on Computer Vision and Pattern Recognition (CVPR) (2017)
23. Hu, Y., Zhang, D., Ye, J., Li, X., He, X.: Fast and accurate matrix completion via truncated nuclear norm regularization. IEEE Trans. Pattern Anal. Mach. Intell. **35**(9), 2117–2130 (2013)
24. Hyeong Hong, J., Zach, C.: pOSE: pseudo object space error for initialization-free bundle adjustment. In: The IEEE Conference on Computer Vision and Pattern Recognition (CVPR), June 2018
25. Jensen, S.H.N., Del Bue, A., Doest, M.E.B., Aanæs, H.: A benchmark and evaluation of non-rigid structure from motion (2018)
26. Krechetov, M., Marecek, J., Maximov, Y., Takac, M.: Entropy-penalized semidefinite programming. In: Proceedings of the Twenty-Eighth International Joint Conference on Artificial Intelligence, IJCAI 2019, pp. 1123–1129. International Joint Conferences on Artificial Intelligence Organization, July 2019
27. Kumar, S.: Non-rigid structure from motion: prior-free factorization method revisited. In: The IEEE Winter Conference on Applications of Computer Vision (WACV), pp. 51–60, March 2020
28. Larsson, V., Olsson, C.: Convex low rank approximation. Int. J. Comput. Vision **120**(2), 194–214 (2016). https://doi.org/10.1007/s11263-016-0904-7
29. Lewis, A.S.: The convex analysis of unitarily invariant matrix functions. J. Convex Anal. **2**(1), 173–183 (1995)

30. Li, H., Lin, Z.: Provable accelerated gradient method for nonconvex low rank optimization. Mach. Learn. **109**(1), 103–134 (2019). https://doi.org/10.1007/s10994-019-05819-w
31. Oh, T.H., Tai, Y.W., Bazin, J.C., Kim, H., Kweon, I.S.: Partial sum minimization of singular values in robust PCA: algorithm and applications. IEEE Trans. Pattern Anal. Mach. Intell. **38**(4), 744–758 (2016)
32. Olsson, C., Enqvist, O.: Stable structure from motion for unordered image collections. In: Heyden, A., Kahl, F. (eds.) SCIA 2011. LNCS, vol. 6688, pp. 524–535. Springer, Heidelberg (2011). https://doi.org/10.1007/978-3-642-21227-7_49
33. Oymak, S., Mohan, K., Fazel, M., Hassibi, B.: A simplified approach to recovery conditions for low rank matrices. In: IEEE International Symposium on Information Theory Proceedings (ISIT), pp. 2318–2322 (2011)
34. Paladini, M., Del Bue, A., Stosic, M., Dodig, M., Xavier, J., Agapito, L.: Factorization for non-rigid and articulated structure using metric projections. In: 2009 IEEE Conference on Computer Vision and Pattern Recognition, pp. 2898–2905 (2009)
35. Recht, B., Fazel, M., Parrilo, P.A.: Guaranteed minimum-rank solutions of linear matrix equations via nuclear norm minimization. SIAM Rev. **52**(3), 471–501 (2010)
36. Russell, C., Fayad, J., Agapito, L.: Energy based multiple model fitting for non-rigid structure from motion. In: IEEE Conference on Computer Vision and Pattern Recognition, pp. 3009–3016, July 2011
37. Shang, F., Cheng, J., Liu, Y., Luo, Z., Lin, Z.: Bilinear factor matrix norm minimization for robust PCA: algorithms and applications. IEEE Trans. Pattern Anal. Mach. Intell. **40**(9), 2066–2080 (2018)
38. Stoyanov, D., Mylonas, G.P., Deligianni, F., Darzi, A., Yang, G.Z.: Soft-tissue motion tracking and structure estimation for robotic assisted MIS procedures. In: Duncan, J.S., Gerig, G. (eds.) MICCAI 2005. LNCS, vol. 3750, pp. 139–146. Springer, Heidelberg (2005). https://doi.org/10.1007/11566489_18
39. Tomasi, C., Kanade, T.: Shape and motion from image streams under orthography: a factorization method. Int. J. Comput. Vision **9**(2), 137–154 (1992). https://doi.org/10.1007/BF00129684
40. Valtonen Ornhag, M., Olsson, C., Heyden, A.: Bilinear parameterization for differentiable rank-regularization. In: The IEEE/CVF Conference on Computer Vision and Pattern Recognition (CVPR) Workshops, June 2020
41. Varol, A., Salzmann, M., Tola, E., Fua, P.: Template-free monocular reconstruction of deformable surfaces. In: International Conference on Computer Vision (ICCV), pp. 1811–1818, November 2009
42. Wang, N., Yao, T., Wang, J., Yeung, D.-Y.: A probabilistic approach to robust matrix factorization. In: Fitzgibbon, A., Lazebnik, S., Perona, P., Sato, Y., Schmid, C. (eds.) ECCV 2012. LNCS, vol. 7578, pp. 126–139. Springer, Heidelberg (2012). https://doi.org/10.1007/978-3-642-33786-4_10
43. Xiao, J., Chai, J., Kanade, T.: A closed-form solution to non-rigid shape and motion recovery. In: Pajdla, T., Matas, J. (eds.) ECCV 2004. LNCS, vol. 3024, pp. 573–587. Springer, Heidelberg (2004). https://doi.org/10.1007/978-3-540-24673-2_46
44. Xu, C., Lin, Z., Zha, H.: A unified convex surrogate for the Schatten-p norm. In: Proceedings of the Conference on Artificial Intelligence (AAAI) (2017)
45. Yan, J., Pollefeys, M.: A factorization-based approach for articulated nonrigid shape, motion and kinematic chain recovery from video. IEEE Trans. Pattern Anal. Mach. Intell. **30**(5), 865–877 (2008)

Proposal-Based Video Completion

Yuan-Ting Hu[1]([✉]), Heng Wang[2], Nicolas Ballas[3], Kristen Grauman[3,4], and Alexander G. Schwing[1]

[1] University of Illinois Urbana-Champaign, Urbana, USA
ythu2@illinois.edu
[2] Facebook AI, Menlo Park, USA
[3] Facebook AI Research, Menlo Park, USA
[4] University of Texas at Austin, Austin, USA

Abstract. Video inpainting is an important technique for a wide variety of applications from video content editing to video restoration. Early approaches follow image inpainting paradigms, but are challenged by complex camera motion and non-rigid deformations. To address these challenges flow-guided propagation techniques have been proposed. However, computation of flow is non-trivial for unobserved regions and propagation across a whole video sequence is computationally demanding. In contrast, in this paper, we propose a video inpainting algorithm based on proposals: we use 3D convolutions to obtain an initial inpainting estimate which is subsequently refined by fusing a generated set of proposals. Different from existing approaches for video inpainting, and inspired by well-explored mechanisms for object detection, we argue that proposals provide a rich source of information that permits combining similarly looking patches that may be spatially and temporally far from the region to be inpainted. We validate the effectiveness of our method on the challenging YouTube VOS and DAVIS datasets using different settings and demonstrate results outperforming state-of-the-art on standard metrics.

1 Introduction

Inpainting missing regions in a given image or video is a longstanding and important computer vision task with applications, *e.g.*, in image/video restoration. Not surprisingly, a significant amount of work has been devoted, particularly to image inpainting [1,4–6,11,15,16,21,30,37,40,41], while leveraging temporal coherence for video completion has become increasingly popular more recently [2,3,9,10,14,17,18,20,24,25,31,33,39,42].

Early video completion methods follow classical image inpainting techniques: missing regions are completed one frame at a time by finding patches which match or, more recently, via deep nets applied independently per frame. These

Electronic supplementary material The online version of this chapter (https://doi.org/10.1007/978-3-030-58583-9_3) contains supplementary material, which is available to authorized users.

© Springer Nature Switzerland AG 2020
A. Vedaldi et al. (Eds.): ECCV 2020, LNCS 12372, pp. 38–54, 2020.
https://doi.org/10.1007/978-3-030-58583-9_3

Fig. 1. Video inpainting in challenging scenarios, such as complex motion, cluttered background and large missing regions. We highlight the missing region in red in the first row and show the results of our method in the second row. We consider three different scenarios: (left) arbitrary region inpainting; (middle) object removal; (right) fixed region inpainting. (Color figure online)

methods are challenged by complex camera motion, non-rigid object deformations, motion blur, and the fact that retrieving a compelling patch is often computationally expensive. Moreover, in those methods, temporal artifacts occur if deep nets are applied independently per frame. To address those concerns, very recently, an optical flow guided propagation method has been demonstrated successfully [39]. However, computation of flow is non-trivial in unobserved regions. Besides, propagation across a whole video sequence is computationally demanding, preventing application of such methods on hardware with limited resources, like mobile devices. Moreover, even with optical flow available, we are generally not able to infer parts missing due to occlusions.

Importantly, all the aforementioned methods directly infer an inpainted result. While direct inference is conceptually straightforward to implement via deep nets, it emphasizes local spatial and temporal consistency over more global context, as filters in deep nets often have a limited receptive field. To counter this bias, here, inspired by the recent success of proposal based techniques for object detection [12,28], we develop a proposal-based approach.

Concretely, our suggested method first infers a coarse-grained inpainting. This inpainting is subsequently refined by constructing a set of proposals for each frame. Global spatio-temporal consistency is encouraged as proposals are contiguous regions which are fused via a parametric mechanism. The proposals are obtained via a top-k matching of (1) features of observed pixels with (2) features of the coarse-grained inpainting for the missing pixels. Different from existing work, this permits to effectively combine non-local (spatially and temporally) cues and leads to appealing results illustrated in Fig. 1.

To compare with existing methods [18,20,25,39,41], we provide extensive experiments on the challenging YouTube VOS [38] and DAVIS [26] datasets using two settings: fixed region inpainting and moving object removal. We demonstrate that our proposal-based approach achieves more accurate results than state-of-the-art methods. Moreover, it is over 55× faster than FGI [39] at inference time (0.69 *vs.* 37.63 s per frame) on the DAVIS dataset on fixed region inpainting, as it does not rely on optical flow-based propagation.

2   Related Work

Inpainting in images and video data has been a long standing problem in computer vision. In this section, we describe works most related to our method.

Image Inpainting. Recent efforts in image inpainting have shifted to designing of deep neural nets which fill holes of arbitrary shapes (free-from inpainting). Among them, partial convolution [21] and gated convolution [41] go beyond the standard convolution operator, and are proposed to better utilize the binary mask during convolution for inpainting. Besides operator level inventions, Edge-connect [23] first hallucinates edges for the missing regions, then uses the edges to preserve object boundaries in inpainted results. Similarly, StructureFlow [29] first recovers an edge-preserved smoothed version of the original image, then synthesizes texture for the smoothed regions.

DeepFill [40] proposes to match features between missing and known regions, and reconstructs missing pixels using the similarity scores from feature matching with known pixels. Iizuka *et al.* [15] fuse both global context and local texture information by training different discriminators for generative adversarial networks [8].

Different from the aforementioned works, our approach focuses on video inpainting, and leverages both spatial and temporal cues. Inspired by [29] we design a novel multiple stage framework for video inpainting. We first infer an initial coarse grained version, then refine the initial result based on proposals. The proposal component in our method is related to PatchMatch [1], extending it to be learning-based and end-to-end trainable.

Video Inpainting. Unlike image inpainting, video inpainting imposes new challenges of generating temporally consistent results. Chang *et al.* [2] extend gated convolutions [41] to 3D for free-form video inpainting and propose a temporal PatchGAN loss to enhance temporal consistency. Wang *et al.* [33] adopt an approach where a temporal network operates on low-resolution input to ensure temporal consistency and a spatial network recovers details using 2D convolution at a higher resolution. Onion-Peel networks [25] design an asymmetric attention block that computes similarities between the hole boundary pixels in the target and the non-hole pixels in the references in a non-local manner [34].

Optical flow provides dense correspondence between frames. It has been used to extrapolate unknown pixels in video inpainting [14]. Xu *et al.* [39] propose to first inpaint optical flow, which is arguably an easier task than inpainting the original video. Occluded missing pixels are then filled by an image inpainting method [40]. Unlike Xu *et al.* [39], Zhang *et al.* [42] simultaneously inpaint both RGB and optical flow with an internal learning approach that is inspired by the 'Deep Image Prior' [32]. VINet [17] also estimates both RGB and optical flow for

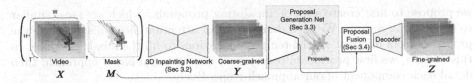

Fig. 2. Illustration of the proposed method. Our method takes as input the video and the mask and employs the developed 3D inpainting network to obtain a coarse-grained inpainting. We subsequently match pixels within the coarse-grained inpainting to observed pixels, creating a pool of proposals that can be used to inpaint the unobserved parts of the video. Finally we fuse the proposals via an attention mechanism and upsample via a decoder to obtain the final fine-grained inpainting.

the missing pixels. Temporal consistency is encouraged via a recurrent feedback and a ConvLSTM. Instead of computing optical flow explicitly, Copy-and-Paste networks [20] estimate affine transformations to align pixels across frames, and use a context matching module to fuse pixels from multiple reference frames to a target frame.

Our approach differs from the aforementioned ones in that we introduce the concept of 'inpainting proposals.' Bounding box proposals or anchor boxes have been widely used in object detection [12,28]. However, to the best of our knowledge, proposals have not been considered for tasks like image or video inpainting. In this paper, we demonstrate that proposals enable pooling non-local patches with similar content very effectively and result in more spatially and temporally consistent inpainting results.

Proposals. Proposals have taken a primary role in object detection: a region-based convolutional neural net (R-CNN) approach [7] evaluates a conv-net for a computationally manageable number of candidate regions of interest (RoI). Each RoI is assessed independently regarding a variety of metrics like 'object-ness,' 'class,' *etc.* Extensions like RoI pooling [7,13], region proposal networks [28] and RoI alignment [12] have further improved the efficacy of proposals.

Inspired by the success of proposals in object detection, we introduce the concept of proposals to video inpainting. As mentioned before, we think proposals are ideal to quickly pool spatially and temporally non-local information in the form of similar patches. We provide details of the developed approach subsequently.

3 Proposal-Based Video Completion

Given a video $X = (x_1, \ldots, x_T)$ composed of T frames with a resolution of $W \times H$, and corresponding masks $M = (m_1, \ldots, m_T) \in \{0,1\}^{T \times W \times H}$ specifying the missing region for each frame, we want to recover the RGB values for pixels that are missing. Let x_t^i denote the RGB value of frame x_t at location i, where $i = (u,v) \in \mathbb{R}^2$, $u \in \{1, \ldots, W\}, v \in \{1, \ldots, H\}$ and let the mask $m_t^i = 1$ indicate pixels that are missing and need to be recovered. Unlike prior works, we propose to first create a set of 'inpainting proposals,' which are most similar to the missing regions. We then design a novel attention mechanism to fuse the proposals from different spatial-temporal locations to fill the missing regions. In this section, we first provide an overview of our proposal-based approach, then detail each component of our approach respectively.

3.1 Overview

The developed approach is outlined in Fig. 2. Again, we are given a video X and the corresponding mask M which indicates the location of the missing regions. We first apply our 3D inpainting network to recover a coarse-grained result Y. We then generate inpainting proposals based on the coarse-grained result and finally fuse the proposals via a classifier to generate the inpainting result Z.

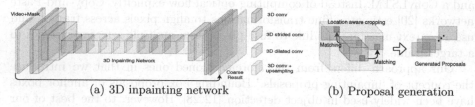

(a) 3D inpainting network   (b) Proposal generation

Fig. 3. Illustration of (a) the 3D inpainting network and (b) the proposal generation module. Note that every tensor in (a) is in fact 4D ($W \times H \times T \times C$), and C is the number of channels. To avoid generating overly blurry results, we do not apply temporal striding in the 3D inpainting network. To simplify, we ignore the temporal dimension when visualizing the 4D tensors. For proposal generation (b), we match every unobserved pixel (dark blue square) with every observed pixel to find the top-k candidates (dark orange square). The surrounding area following the shape of the missing region is subsequently extracted and added to the pool of proposals. (Color figure online)

Our approach is based on a 3D inpainting network, a proposal generation mechanism and a classifier to fuse the extracted set of proposals. All three components are jointly trained. We provide an overview of each component next before discussing their details in subsequent sections.

3D Inpainting Network: We first inpaint the input video X with missing regions specified in M via a 3D inpainting network which has an encoder-decoder structure, shown in Fig. 3(a). To cope with 3D video data, the 3D inpainting network utilizes 3D gated convolutions [2,41] to better integrate the information from the binary mask. We also apply dilation to 3D gated convolutions instead of using larger kernel sizes to reduce the computational cost. To reduce blurriness, our 3D network only downsamples spatially by a factor of four, and keeps the temporal length T unchanged through the whole network.

Despite our dedicated design choices, the coarse inpainting results from the 3D inpainting network still tend to be blurry. To improve this initial estimate we develop a novel proposal generation network, which refines the inpainting result and yields the final result Z after upsampling via a decoder. We provide more details subsequently.

Proposal Generation: Candidates for parts of a missing region of a particular frame may appear anywhere in the video, *i.e.*, good candidates are not necessarily in adjacent frames and are not necessarily spatially close neither. Our key idea is to inpaint the missing region by attending to the observed pixels in the video, looking for candidate patches which fit the coarse inpainting. This permits to effectively combine non-local information represented in the form of candidate patches.

Intuitively, by generating proposals, the temporal and spatial information can be propagated from the observed parts of the video to the missing region. To this end, we develop the 'proposal generation network' to generate a set of inpainting proposals $\mathcal{P}_t$ by matching features between observed pixels and unknown pixels of the coarse result, as shown in Fig. 3(b). More specifically, for every unobserved pixel in frame x_t we match features of its coarse-grained estimate to features of any observed pixel in the given video. For every pixel we retain the top-k matching candidates as well as their surrounding pixels as indicated by the mask m_t.

We want to emphasize: a proposal is not locally confined to a single pixel. Very much in contrast, a single proposal can be used to inpaint all missing pixels in a frame.

Proposal Fusion: We fuse a pool of proposals $\mathcal{P}_t$ at time t generated by the proposal generation network and compute the final inpainting Z based on the fused result. For this we train a classifier to produce a categorical distribution over all the proposals in order to fuse them. This mechanism establishes dependencies between the missing region and the observed region in a non-local way. The classifier module in our method is a 3-layer CNN to predict a probability distribution over all the proposals. The obtained categorical distribution is used to fuse the proposals.

The fused proposals across all points in time are fed into a decoder to generate the final inpainting Z. Note that the proposal generation network combined with the classifier permits attending to regions that can be spatially and temporally far apart albeit containing similar, useful fine-grained context for inpainting.

In the following, we describe in detail each of the three components of the proposed method.

3.2   3D Inpainting Network

We first inpaint a given video X which contains missing regions specified in M by using a 3D inpainting network. As illustrated in Fig. 3(a), the architecture of our 3D inpainting network consists of layers of 3D gated convolutions [2,41] with striding and dilation at different layers. In total, there are 19 layers in the 3D inpainting network to keep the computational cost low. We only do spatial striding twice to reduce the resolution from $W \times H$ to $W/4 \times H/4$ and keep the temporal length T unchanged in all the layers. Upsampling in the decoder is done with bilinear interpolation instead of deconvolution.

The coarse result Y is obtained by fusing the input video X with the raw output of the 3D inpainting network $\bar{Y}$ via

$$Y = M \odot \bar{Y} + (\mathbb{1} - M) \odot X, \tag{1}$$

where M is the mask indicating whether or not a pixel is observed, '$\odot$' denotes element-wise multiplication and $\mathbb{1}$ is the all-ones tensor. The coarse inpainting result Y obtained via this 3D inpainting network tends to be blurry. To rectify this we develop the 'proposal generation network' which we discuss next.

3.3 Proposal Generation

We describe how to generate the 'inpainting proposals' in the following. To generate proposals, we match pixels of the inpainted region in the coarse-grained result, *i.e.*, pixels which were initially unobserved, to observed regions at any spatial and temporal locations in the input video. Consequently, candidates at any spatial and temporal distance are treated equally. Hence, we consider a much more global context which differs from prior approaches for video inpainting [39] and image inpainting [40].

Our approach hence performs spatially and temporally non-local matching. There are three components in the proposed 'proposal generation network': feature extraction, matching and generating of proposals as discussed next.

Feature Extraction: We first extract features from the coarse-grained inpainting Y which are then used for matching. To be more specific, we compute features $F = g(Y)$ from the coarse-grained result Y via a deep net g, in our case an 8-layer CNN. Note that the spatial downsampling factor of g is 8. Therefore the feature map F is of dimension $\mathbb{R}^{T \times w \times h \times c}$, where w is $W/8$ and h is $H/8$. Again, no temporal down-sampling is employed. Let f_t be the feature map at time t. Matching is performed at the resolution of $h \times w$ instead of $H \times W$ such that matching can be performed more efficiently. We downsample the mask m_t as well with a factor of 8 to get $\bar{m}_t$ which indicates the missing pixels at the $h \times w$ resolution. We subsequently use the computed features for matching.

Top-k Matching: After feature extraction, we find matches between pixels for which the original video did not provide an RGB value, and pixels for which the RGB value was observed. For this we use the obtained features. To be more specific, let

$$\mathcal{U}_t = \{(i, t) | \bar{m}_t^i = 1, \forall i\}$$

denote the unobserved pixels at time t which are required to be inpainted. Further, let

$$\mathcal{O} = \left\{ (j, t') | \bar{m}_{t'}^j = 0, \forall i, \forall t' \in \{1, \ldots, T\} \right\}$$

refer to all the observed pixels across all times.

To find the top-k matches, we first compute the similarity map $S_t \in \mathbb{R}^{|\mathcal{U}_t| \times |\mathcal{O}|}$ via

$$S_t(a, b) = d(f_a, f_b)$$

for all unobserved pixels $a = (i, t) \in \mathcal{U}_t$ at time t, and for all observed pixels $b = (j, t') \in \mathcal{O}$ irrespective of time and location. Note, given $a = (i, t)$, f_a refers to the feature at location i in f_t. So does f_b for $b = (j, t')$. We use $d(f_a, f_b)$ to denote the similarity between two features. We use the classical cosine distance as the distance function d in our implementation and leave exploration of more complex distance functions to future work.

Based on the similarity map S_t, we select the top-k matches $\mathcal{K}_a$ as follows:

$$\mathcal{K}_a = \{b | b \in \mathrm{Top}_k(S_t(a, b))\}.$$

Hence, for a given unobserved pixel $a \in \mathcal{U}_t$, $\mathcal{K}_a$ consists of only the top-k matches across all spatial locations and across all frames. The set $\mathcal{K}_a$ is then used to generate the set of proposals $\mathcal{P}_t$.

Generating Proposals: We illustrate our method to generate proposals in Fig. 3(b). After finding the top-k matches for every $a \in \mathcal{U}_t$, for each match, we crop its surrounding region and generate a proposal p_a which refers to a set of feature vectors. We emphasize that each proposal p_a can be used to inpaint all missing pixels in frame x_t. Finally, we use these proposals to construct the set of proposals $\mathcal{P}_t$. Formally, we obtain

$$\mathcal{P}_t = \{p | p = \mathrm{crop}(f_{t'}, j, i), \forall a = (i, t) \in \mathcal{U}_t, \forall b = (j, t') \in \mathcal{K}_a\}.$$

Note that the crop operation is location-aware. Concretely, our method does not crop the rectangle with its center location at j but instead crops a rectangle with the size of the missing region, while keeping the relative location of j inside the cropped rectangle identical to the relative location of i inside the missing region.

Hence, note that we don't only use a top-k match locally for the corresponding pixel. Very much in contrast, we use the locally computed top-k match to extract a proposal which provides information for all the missing pixels at time t. This is crucial as it permits our method to create many viable candidates, each of which can be used to inpaint all missing pixels at once.

Subsequently we detail how we propose to compute the final inpainting Z.

3.4   Proposals Fusion

After generating the set of proposals $\mathcal{P}_t$ for the frame at time t, we fuse them via a classifier. Let p_n be one of the proposals in $\mathcal{P}_t$, i.e., $p_n \in \mathcal{P}_t$ and let $p_{\{1,\dots,|\mathcal{P}_t|\}}$ be the concatenation of all $|\mathcal{P}_t|$ proposals. Recall that f_t is the feature map at time t obtained from the coarse-grained inpainting. For each unobserved pixel $(i, t) \in \mathcal{U}_t$, we compute the categorical distribution $A_i \in [0, 1]^{|\mathcal{P}_t|}$ over all the proposals, via a classifier C with soft-max for normalization, i.e.,

$$A_{i,n} = \frac{\exp\{C(p_{\{1,\dots,|\mathcal{P}_t|\}}, f_t)_{i,n}\}}{\sum_{n'} \exp\{C(p_{\{1,\dots,|\mathcal{P}_t|\}}, f_t)_{i,n'}\}}.$$

The classifier C operates on the concatenation of all the proposals as well as the feature map f_t. We then fuse the proposals using distribution A_i to obtain the attended feature p_t^i for pixel i at time t via

$$p_t^i = \sum_{n=1}^{|\mathcal{P}_t|} A_{i,n} \cdot p_n^i.$$

Here, p_n^i refers to the feature at location i in proposal p_n. The fused feature map $P = \{(p_t^i)\}_{\forall i,t}$ is padded such that it has the same size as F. We subsequently concatenate the feature map P with the extracted coarse-grained features F and employ a decoder to compute the inpainting result $\bar{Z}$. To obtain the final result Z, we merge $\bar{Z}$ with the input X following Eq. (1).

3.5 Training

The described approach is trained end-to-end. For training of the proposal generation mechanism we construct a dataset which contains the ground-truth completion Z^*, the coarse-grained result Y and the final result Z. We jointly learn end-to-end the parameters of the 3D inpainting network (Sect. 3.2), the parameters of the classifier (Sect. 3.4), and the decoder, by optimizing the following objective:

$$\mathcal{L} = \mathcal{L}_{L1} + \lambda_1 \mathcal{L}_G + \lambda_2 \mathcal{L}_{CE}. \tag{2}$$

The objective consists of a pixel-wise L1 error $\mathcal{L}_{L1}$, an adversarial loss $\mathcal{L}_G$ and a cross-entropy loss $\mathcal{L}_{CE}$ for fusing the proposals. Hyper-parameters λ_1 and λ_2 are used to adjust the impact of the different loss components. We describe details for each of the individual loss terms in the following.

Reconstruction Loss $\mathcal{L}_{L1}$: The L1 error is used for penalizing if the inpainting result deviates from the ground-truth. We penalize both the coarse-grained result as well as the refined result using the L1 loss, *i.e.*, we use

$$\mathcal{L}_{L1} = \|M \odot (Z^* - \bar{Y})\|_1 + \gamma \|(\mathbb{1} - M) \odot (Z^* - \bar{Y})\|_1$$
$$+ \|M \odot (Z^* - \bar{Z})\|_1 + \gamma \|(\mathbb{1} - M) \odot (Z^* - \bar{Z})\|_1. \tag{3}$$

The hyper-parameter γ controls the loss occurring due to reconstruction of observed parts of the image.

Adversarial Loss $\mathcal{L}_G$: An adversarial loss is commonly used for inpainting [2, 40,41]. Let D be the discriminator and G be the inpainting network, *i.e.*, $Z = G(X, M)$ where X and M are input video and masks. As suggested in [41], we use a fully convolutional network as the discriminator. Note that the output of the discriminator is a tensor rather than a scalar. We compute the adversarial loss on each of the elements in the output tensor using a discriminator and accumulate by averaging.

The inpainting network minimizes the below objective to fool the discriminator, *i.e.*,

$$\mathcal{L}_G = -\mathbb{E}_{X,M}[D(G(X, M))].$$

The discriminator is trained to differentiate the inpainting result from the real video. We optimize the discriminator using the following objective containing a hinge-loss activation function:

$$\mathcal{L}_D = \mathbb{E}_{X,M}\left[\max\left(0, \mathbb{1} - D(G(X, M))\right)\right] + \mathbb{E}_{Z^*}\left[\max\left(0, \mathbb{1} + D(Z^*)\right)\right],$$

where Z^* is the ground truth video.

For stable training, we apply spectral normalization [22] to the discriminator. The discriminator is a fully convolutional net (FCN) with 6 layers of 3D convolutions. Because of our use of FCNs, the size of the input video isn't fixed during training.

Cross Entropy Loss $\mathcal{L}_{CE}$: An important component of the proposed method is the classifier C to compute the categorical distribution over all proposals as described in Sect. 3.4. To train the classifier, we obtain the labels by first extracting features using the feature extractor g described in Sect. 3.3 to get the feature map z_t of the ground-truth completion, $i.e.$, $z_t = g(Z^*)$. From it we obtain the ground truth distribution A_i^* via

$$A_{i,n}^* = \begin{cases} 1 & \text{if } n = \arg\max_{n'} \|z_t^i - p_n^i\|, \\ 0 & \text{otherwise.} \end{cases}$$

Intuitively, we compare the feature of the ground-truth completion to the proposals, find the one that best matches with the ground truth, and use this as the training label. After obtaining the training label, we minimize the cross-entropy loss between the predicted distribution A and the label A^*, $i.e.$, we use

$$\mathcal{L}_{CE} = -\sum_{i \in \mathcal{U}_t} \sum_{n=1}^{|\mathcal{P}_t|} A_{i,n}^* \log A_{i,n}.$$

3.6 Implementation Details

To optimize the objective given in Eq. (2) w.r.t. the network parameters, we use the Adam optimizer [19] with a learning rate of 1e−4. We first train the 3D inpainting network with only the L1 loss objective for 6,000 iterations with a batch size of 64. Subsequently we train the entire framework using all objectives for another 6,000 iterations. We use $\lambda_1 = 1$, $\lambda_2 = 0.05$, $k = 1$ and, $T = 8$. The inference time of our method on the DAVIS dataset (resolution 854 × 480) is around 0.69 s per frame using one NVIDIA V100 GPU.

4 Experimental Results

We evaluate the proposed approach on two datasets, following the experimental setup of prior work [39]. For completeness we first provide experimental settings before discussing our results.

4.1   Experimental Setting

We first describe the datasets which we use for experiments before discussing metrics for comparison with baselines and mask generation.

Datasets: We use the DAVIS [26] and YouTube VOS [38] datasets which are both widely used in video inpainting [17,36,39]. DAVIS [26,27] consists of 150 videos in total, providing high-quality pixel-level annotations for foreground objects. We follow the evaluation protocol in [39], and use 60 videos from the dev split for training and the remaining 90 videos where we have object masks for testing. YouTube VOS [38] is a much larger dataset with more than 4000 videos in total. It is a more challenging dataset as its videos are much longer than DAVIS (140 *vs.* 68.9 frames per video on average), have higher resolution, and cover a large variety of different scenarios. We use the training set which contains 3,471 videos to learn the parameters of our proposed proposal-based video-inpainting method, and evaluate on the test set which contains 541 videos. We use the 507 videos in the validation set for choosing hyperparameters.

Evaluation Metrics: To measure the similarity between the inpainted videos and the ground truth, we use three metrics: structural similarity (SSIM) [35], peak signal-to-noise ratio (PSNR) and learned perceptual image patch similarity (LPIPS) [43]. We compute the three metrics on the entire video and also on the inpainted region only. This permits to assess the quality of both the entire frame and the inpainted region.

We evaluate the method on two inpainting scenarios, *i.e.*, fixed region inpainting and object removal.

Table 1. Results of our method compared to baselines on the YouTube VOS test set [38].

	Runtime (per frame)	Inpainted region only			Entire frame		
		SSIM ↑	PSNR ↑	LPIPS ↓	SSIM ↑	PSNR ↑	LPIPS ↓
Deepfill2 (ICCV'19) [41]	0.32 s	0.336	9.228	0.448	0.958	21.271	0.034
FGI (CVPR'19) [39]	112.32 s	0.355	10.890	0.409	0.959	22.934	0.032
OPN (ICCV'19) [25]	9.05 s	0.437	12.242	0.394	0.964	24.286	0.029
CPN (ICCV'19) [20]	1.40 s	0.412	11.795	0.478	0.962	23.845	0.036
VINet (CVPR'19) [18]	**0.18 s**	0.348	10.338	0.549	0.958	22.381	0.043
Ours	0.87 s	**0.445**	**13.292**	**0.388**	**0.969**	**25.821**	**0.030**

4.2   Fixed Region Inpainting

Fixed region inpainting is a common task [39] in video inpainting to study the ability of completing a fixed missing region. Though the mask is fixed, this task is very challenging as the fixed regions can cover a large portion of the video

Table 2. Results of our method compared to baselines on the DAVIS dataset [26].

	Runtime (per frame)	Inpainted region only			Entire frame		
		SSIM ↑	PSNR ↑	LPIPS ↓	SSIM ↑	PSNR ↑	LPIPS ↓
Deepfill2 (ICCV'19) [41]	**0.09 s**	0.237	8.899	0.435	0.951	20.970	0.035
FGI (CVPR'19) [39]	37.63 s	0.341	10.974	**0.353**	0.958	23.045	**0.028**
OPN (ICCV'19) [25]	4.17 s	0.344	11.930	0.379	0.958	24.002	0.029
CPN (ICCV'19) [20]	0.53 s	0.316	11.338	0.507	0.956	23.409	0.040
VINet (CVPR'19) [18]	0.18 s	0.254	9.388	0.570	0.951	21.459	0.045
Ours	0.69 s	**0.348**	**12.453**	0.381	**0.959**	**24.511**	0.031

and often break the irregular object boundaries. Following the setup in [39], given an input video of resolution $W \times H$, we mask out a rectangular region of size $W/4 \times H/4$ at the center of the frame. In the following we first compare quantitatively to the state-of-the-art (SOTA) using the aforementioned metrics before providing and discussing qualitative results on both YouTube VOS and DAVIS.

Comparison to SOTA: We provide a comparison to state-of-the-art video inpainting methods on YouTube VOS in Table 1. We evaluate SSIM, PSNR (higher is better) and LPIPS (lower is better) on both the inpainted region only and the entire frames (*i.e.*, the entire inpainted result Z).

From the results reported in Table 1 we observe that the proposed approach significantly improves all metrics. The improvements are slightly more pronounced when looking at the inpainted region only.

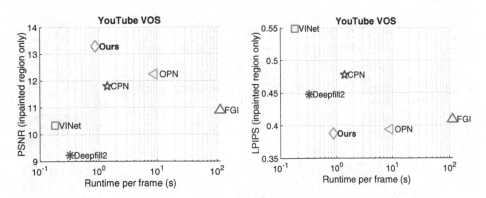

Fig. 4. Comparison of runtime *vs.* performance in PSNR (left) and LPIPS (right) with all methods on the YouTube VOS dataset. Note that for PSNR higher is better, and for LPIPS lower is better. Our method achieves better performance while running efficiently compared to baselines.

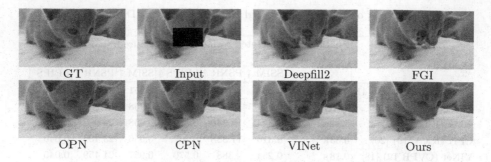

GT   Input   Deepfill2   FGI

OPN   CPN   VINet   Ours

Fig. 5. Video inpainting results of our method compared to the baselines.

We conduct a similar evaluation on the DAVIS dataset and provide results in Table 2. We observe the recently proposed flow guided inpainting (FGI) [39] to be a competitive baseline. While our proposal based video completion falls short on the LPIPS metric, we observe improvements on PSNR and SSIM. Note that the runtime of FGI is much higher than ours as it's an iterative method and doesn't scale well with the length of the video.

Runtime: We report the average runtime of each method on the YouTube VOS and DAVIS datasets in Table 1 and Table 2. Our method is the second fastest one among the state-of-the-art video inpainting approaches on YouTube VOS and the third fastest on DAVIS. Note that the flow based approach FGI usually requires tens of iterations of propagation and is therefore time consuming. We plot the runtime *vs.* PSNR and LPIPS in Fig. 4. Our method achieves better performance while running efficiently compared to baselines.

Input+Mask   FGI   OPN

CPN   VINet   Ours

Fig. 6. Object removal results of our method compared to video inpainting baselines on the sequence `drift-chicane` of the DAVIS dataset.

Table 3. Ablation study of our method on YouTube VOS validation and test sets [38].

3D inpainting net	Proposal	Classifier	Performance on YouTube VOS Val			Performance on YouTube VOS Test		
			SSIM ↑	PSNR ↑	LPIPS ↓	SSIM ↑	PSNR ↑	LPIPS ↓
✓			0.421	14.33	0.415	0.418	11.80	0.458
✓	✓		0.432	14.41	0.377	0.422	11.84	0.433
✓	✓	✓	**0.459**	**16.22**	**0.301**	**0.445**	**13.29**	**0.388**

Qualitative Results: We provide qualitative results for video inpainting of our method and existing baselines in Fig. 5. For challenging cases which exhibit significant appearance changes we observe accurate video completion results. Deepfill2 [41] is an image-based baseline. The completion is less smooth since no temporal information is taken into account. FGI [39] largely relies on flow which is tricky especially when motion is complex. We observe other baselines to produce overly smooth results (CPN [20]) and unrealistic completion (OPN [25] and VINet [18]). We observe encouraging completions despite the fact that the proposed approach can be extended in many different directions.

4.3 Video Object Removal

We study applicability of the proposed method to object removal in videos. We use the DAVIS dataset [26] for this study as the dataset provides accurate object segmentations which specify the region to inpaint. In Fig. 6, we show the object removal results of our approach compared to the state-of-the-art video inpainting baselines, FGI [39], OPN [25], CPN [20] and VINet [18] on the DAVIS dataset. Compared to the baselines we observe our method to work well on object removal in videos, producing realistic results. Our method can inpaint arbitrary-shaped masks as shown in the first row of Fig. 1. More results can be found in the supplementary.

4.4 Ablation Study

To better understand the impact of individual components of the proposed approach we report results of an ablation study in Table 3. We use the YouTube VOS validation and test sets and the fixed region inpainting setup in this experiment. We report the metrics computed on the inpainted region only. Specifically, we analyze the accuracy of our 3D inpainting net (discussed in Sect. 3.2). Using the proposal generation mechanism (discussed in Sect. 3.3) and fusing the results via a single convolution with learnable parameters reduces SSIM and PSNR metrics while it improves LPIPS. Finally, by combining the three developed parts, *i.e.*, 3D inpainting, proposal generation and the classifier (discussed in Sect. 3.4) we achieve the most accurate results. We observe the performance improvements to generalize to the test set.

4.5   Failure Cases

The proposed approach is challenged by thin structures and small objects with a large missing region ratio. This can be observed in Fig. 7.

| Input | Result | Input | Result |

Fig. 7. Two failure cases. Input frame on the left, inpainting on the right.

5   Conclusion

We develop a proposal-based 3D video completion method. Different from prior work, we argue that proposals accurately summarize spatially and temporally non-local candidates that could be used for inpainting. To compute those proposals we first employ a developed 3D inpainting network which yields an initial coarse-grained estimate. To fuse the proposals we develop a classifier-based prediction mechanism. Despite the simplicity of the proposed method, we show on challenging datasets that the use of proposals indeed leads to accurate results. Going forward, we think better strategies to fuse the proposals and more intricate ways to match candidates can lead to even bigger improvements.

Acknowledgements. This work is supported in part by NSF under Grant No. 1718221 and MRI #1725729, UIUC, Samsung, 3M, and Cisco Systems Inc. (Gift Award CG 1377144). We thank Cisco for access to the Arcetri cluster.

References

1. Barnes, C., Shechtman, E., Finkelstein, A., Goldman, D.B.: PatchMatch: a randomized correspondence algorithm for structural image editing. ACM TOG **28**(3), 24 (2009)
2. Chang, Y.L., Liu, Z.Y., Lee, K.Y., Hsu, W.: Free-form video inpainting with 3D gated convolution and temporal PatchGAN. In: Proceedings of the ICCV (2019)
3. Chang, Y.L., Liu, Z.Y., Lee, K.Y., Hsu, W.: Learnable gated temporal shift module for deep video inpainting. In: Proceedings of the BMVC (2019)
4. Criminisi, A., Pérez, P., Toyama, K.: Region filling and object removal by exemplar-based image inpainting. IEEE TIP **13**(9), 1200–1212 (2004)
5. Efros, A.A., Freeman, W.T.: Image quilting for texture synthesis and transfer. In: Proceedings of the Computer Graphics and Interactive Techniques (2001)
6. Efros, A.A., Leung, T.K.: Texture synthesis by non-parametric sampling. In: Proceedings of the ICCV (1999)

7. Girshick, R., Donahue, J., Darrell, T., Malik, J.: Rich feature hierarchies for accurate object detection and semantic segmentation. In: Proceedings of the CVPR (2014)

8. Goodfellow, I., et al.: Generative adversarial nets. In: Proceedings of the NeurIPS (2014)

9. Granados, M., Kim, K.I., Tompkin, J., Kautz, J., Theobalt, C.: Background inpainting for videos with dynamic objects and a free-moving camera. In: Fitzgibbon, A., Lazebnik, S., Perona, P., Sato, Y., Schmid, C. (eds.) ECCV 2012. LNCS, vol. 7572, pp. 682–695. Springer, Heidelberg (2012). https://doi.org/10.1007/978-3-642-33718-5_49

10. Granados, M., Tompkin, J., Kim, K., Grau, O., Kautz, J., Theobalt, C.: How not to be seen-object removal from videos of crowded scenes. In: Computer Graphics Forum (2012)

11. Hays, J., Efros, A.A.: Scene completion using millions of photographs. ACM TOG **26**(3), 4-es (2007)

12. He, K., Gkioxari, G., Dollár, P., Girshick, R.: Mask R-CNN. In: Proceedings of the ICCV (2017)

13. He, K., Zhang, X., Ren, S., Sun, J.: Spatial pyramid pooling in deep convolutional networks for visual recognition. IEEE TPAMI **37**(9), 1904–1916 (2015)

14. Huang, J.B., Kang, S.B., Ahuja, N., Kopf, J.: Temporally coherent completion of dynamic video. ACM TOG **35**(6), 1–11 (2016)

15. Iizuka, S., Simo-Serra, E., Ishikawa, H.: Globally and locally consistent image completion. ACM TOG **36**(4), 1–14 (2017)

16. Ilan, S., Shamir, A.: A survey on data-driven video completion. In: Computer Graphics Forum (2015)

17. Kim, D., Woo, S., Lee, J.Y., Kweon, I.S.: Deep blind video decaptioning by temporal aggregation and recurrence. In: Proceedings of the CVPR (2019)

18. Kim, D., Woo, S., Lee, J.Y., Kweon, I.S.: Deep video inpainting. In: Proceedings of the CVPR (2019)

19. Kingma, D.P., Ba, J.: Adam: a method for stochastic optimization. arXiv preprint arXiv:1412.6980 (2014)

20. Lee, S., Oh, S.W., Won, D., Kim, S.J.: Copy-and-paste networks for deep video inpainting. In: Proceedings of the ICCV (2019)

21. Liu, G., Reda, F.A., Shih, K.J., Wang, T.-C., Tao, A., Catanzaro, B.: Image inpainting for irregular holes using partial convolutions. In: Ferrari, V., Hebert, M., Sminchisescu, C., Weiss, Y. (eds.) ECCV 2018. LNCS, vol. 11215, pp. 89–105. Springer, Cham (2018). https://doi.org/10.1007/978-3-030-01252-6_6

22. Miyato, T., Kataoka, T., Koyama, M., Yoshida, Y.: Spectral normalization for generative adversarial networks. arXiv preprint arXiv:1802.05957 (2018)

23. Nazeri, K., Ng, E., Joseph, T., Qureshi, F., Ebrahimi, M.: EdgeConnect: generative image inpainting with adversarial edge learning. arXiv preprint arXiv:1901.00212 (2019)

24. Newson, A., Almansa, A., Fradet, M., Gousseau, Y., Pérez, P.: Video inpainting of complex scenes. SIAM J. Imaging Sci. **7**(4), 1993–2019 (2014)

25. Oh, S.W., Lee, S., Lee, J.Y., Kim, S.J.: Onion-peel networks for deep video completion. In: Proceedings of the ICCV (2019)

26. Perazzi, F., Pont-Tuset, J., McWilliams, B., Van Gool, L., Gross, M., Sorkine-Hornung, A.: A benchmark dataset and evaluation methodology for video object segmentation. In: Proceedings of the CVPR, pp. 724–732 (2016)

27. Pont-Tuset, J., Perazzi, F., Caelles, S., Arbeláez, P., Sorkine-Hornung, A., Van Gool, L.: The 2017 Davis challenge on video object segmentation. arXiv:1704.00675 (2017)
28. Ren, S., He, K., Girshick, R., Sun, J.: Faster R-CNN: towards real-time object detection with region proposal networks. In: Proceedings of the NeurIPS (2015)
29. Ren, Y., Yu, X., Zhang, R., Li, T.H., Liu, S., Li, G.: StructureFlow: image inpainting via structure-aware appearance flow. In: Proceedings of the ICCV (2019)
30. Song, Y., et al.: Contextual-based image inpainting: infer, match, and translate. In: Ferrari, V., Hebert, M., Sminchisescu, C., Weiss, Y. (eds.) ECCV 2018. LNCS, vol. 11206, pp. 3–18. Springer, Cham (2018). https://doi.org/10.1007/978-3-030-01216-8_1
31. Strobel, M., Diebold, J., Cremers, D.: Flow and color inpainting for video completion. In: Jiang, X., Hornegger, J., Koch, R. (eds.) GCPR 2014. LNCS, vol. 8753, pp. 293–304. Springer, Cham (2014). https://doi.org/10.1007/978-3-319-11752-2_23
32. Ulyanov, D., Vedaldi, A., Lempitsky, V.: Deep image prior. In: Proceedings of the CVPR (2018)
33. Wang, C., Huang, H., Han, X., Wang, J.: Video inpainting by jointly learning temporal structure and spatial details. arXiv preprint arXiv:1806.08482 (2018)
34. Wang, X., Girshick, R., Gupta, A., He, K.: Non-local neural networks. In: Proceedings of the CVPR (2018)
35. Wang, Z., Bovik, A.C., Sheikh, H.R., Simoncelli, E.P., et al.: Image quality assessment: from error visibility to structural similarity. IEEE TIP 13(4), 600–612 (2004)
36. Woo, S., Kim, D., Park, K., Lee, J.Y., Kweon, I.S.: Align-and-attend network for globally and locally coherent video inpainting. arXiv preprint arXiv:1905.13066 (2019)
37. Xiong, W., et al.: Foreground-aware image inpainting. In: Proceedings of the CVPR (2019)
38. Xu, N., et al.: YouTube-VOS: a large-scale video object segmentation benchmark. arXiv preprint arXiv:1809.03327 (2018)
39. Xu, R., Li, X., Zhou, B., Loy, C.C.: Deep flow-guided video inpainting. arXiv preprint arXiv:1905.02884 (2019)
40. Yu, J., Lin, Z., Yang, J., Shen, X., Lu, X., Huang, T.S.: Generative image inpainting with contextual attention. In: Proceedings of the CVPR (2018)
41. Yu, J., Lin, Z., Yang, J., Shen, X., Lu, X., Huang, T.S.: Free-form image inpainting with gated convolution. In: Proceedings of the ICCV (2019)
42. Zhang, H., Mai, L., Xu, N., Wang, Z., Collomosse, J., Jin, H.: An internal learning approach to video inpainting. In: Proceedings of the ICCV (2019)
43. Zhang, R., Isola, P., Efros, A.A., Shechtman, E., Wang, O.: The unreasonable effectiveness of deep features as a perceptual metric. In: Proceedings of the CVPR (2018)

HGNet: Hybrid Generative Network for Zero-Shot Domain Adaptation

Haifeng Xia[1] and Zhengming Ding[2(✉)]

[1] Department of ECE, Indiana University-Purdue University Indianapolis,
Indianapolis, USA
haifxia@iu.edu
[2] Department of CIT, Indiana University-Purdue University Indianapolis,
Indianapolis, USA
zd2@iu.edu

Abstract. Domain Adaptation as an important tool aims to explore a generalized model trained on well-annotated source knowledge to address learning issue on target domain with insufficient or even no annotation. Current approaches typically incorporate data from source and target domains for training stage to deal with domain shift. However, most domain adaptation tasks generally suffer from the problem that measuring the domain shift tends to be impossible when target data is inaccessible. In this paper, we propose a novel algorithm, *Hybrid Generative Network* (HGNet) for Zero-shot Domain Adaptation, which embeds an adaptive feature separation (AFS) module into generative architecture. Specifically, AFS module can adaptively distinguish classification-relevant features from classification-irrelevant ones to learn domain-invariant and discriminative representations when task-relevant target instances are invisible. To learn high-quality feature representation, we also develop hybrid generative strategy to ensure the uniqueness of feature separation and completeness of semantic information. Extensive experimental results on several benchmarks illustrate that our method achieves more promising results than state-of-the-art approaches.

Keywords: Deep learning · Domain adaptation · Generative learning

1 Introduction

Computer vision community always suffers from insufficient annotation issue, which dramatically obstructs the practical applications of most techniques. However, domain adaptation provides an alternative strategy to handle with such a problem [9,24,28]. Concretely, it attempts to borrow knowledge from well-annotated modality (source domain) to solve classification task on target domain without any label information [30,32,35]. Although various domains share the high-level semantic information, their data distributions contain significant discrepancy defined as domain shift [10,13,34]. For example, due to light condition

© Springer Nature Switzerland AG 2020
A. Vedaldi et al. (Eds.): ECCV 2020, LNCS 12372, pp. 55–70, 2020.
https://doi.org/10.1007/978-3-030-58583-9_4

or occlusions, visual instances involving the same object are different from each other [4]. As a result, the previously-trained model generally tends to be fragile when evaluated on target domain.

Domain adaptation (DA) as a solution to learn domain-invariant knowledge attracts great interest [2,7,20,22]. To learn transferable information, it assumes that instances of target modality are available [5,17,23]. Under such an assumption, recent works mainly explore two approaches: discrepancy measurement [16] and domain adversarial confusion [15,35]. Specifically, the first strategy aims to define novel statistic indicators like maximum mean discrepancy (MMD) [7] promoting the consistency of distribution. While methods based on domain adversarial confusion expect to transform data of source and target domain into the similar hidden space by using adversarial relationship between generator and discriminator. They actually have achieved promising improvement in distinctive tasks. In real-world scenarios, however, the assumption which they depend on is infeasible due to the absence of target domain. The general situation is defined as *zero-shot domain adaptation* (ZSDA) [21], which is also known as *missing modality transfer learning* [8]. For instance, to protect privacy of patient, hospital fails to share medical records to train the model, even though they expect to apply the trained model for their work, where these documents represent target domain. In this sense, the current DA methods are more likely to be invalid since the guidance of target datatset becomes invisible.

The awkward situation inspires [19] to proposes domain-invariant component analysis (DICA) by using multiple source domains with identical label space to build a generalized model for unseen target recognition. However, they hardly collect sufficient source domains to observe the information of unseen target modality. To solve this problem, the intuitive motivation is to introduce auxiliary task-irrelevant dataset (TIR), which also includes two same modalities with the task-relevant one (TR) [8]. Alternatively, [21] develops the first deep model for zero-shot domain adaptation which firstly attempts to achieve the feature alignment on task-irrelevant datasets and then allows source modalities in TR and TIR to share the same network. Moreover, the generalization of neural network facilitates the consistency of cross-domain distribution on task-relevant dataset. Albeit the training manner enables model to generate domain-invariant representation, features tend to be less discriminative without the guidance of annotation when training model on task-irrelevant inputs, leading to the decrease of recognition. Meanwhile, due to the huge achievement of generative adversarial model in abundant practical scenarios, it is appropriate to utilize this manner to synthesis missing modality and directly perform domain adaptation in TR datasets [27] named CocoGAN. However, the drawbacks of generative adversarial network is that there exists bias between generated instances and real samples, since synthesised images only try to approximate the real distribution. Thus, estimating the influence of bias on the final classification task tend to be very difficult. On the other hand, we naturally post a question about CocoGAN: "Is the explicit generation of missing target dataset necessary for learning domain-invariant feature?".

To answer this question, we rethink Zero-shot Domain Adaptation from feature separation and propose Hybrid Generative Network (HGNet), which not only synthesises domain-invariant feature but also effectively facilitates high-level representation to be more discriminative. Specifically, the whole network architecture mainly consists of four components: feature extractor, adaptive feature separation module, hybrid generator and classifier. Input signals of TR and TIR datasets firstly pass through feature extractor and are transformed into shallow convolutional units. For the second step, feature separation module adaptively selects several channels to form classification-relevant high-level feature, while others are considered as classification-irrelevant information. In the final stage, on one hand, we apply the supervision of annotation to learn more discriminative units. On the other hand, hybrid generator will integrate object context and domain information belonging to various datasets to reconstruct input data. Extensive experimental performances illustrate that the hybrid strategy guarantees the uniqueness of feature separation as well as the completeness of semantic information. The contributions of our method are summarized in three folds:

- From the perspective of feature separation, we introduce a novel strategy named Hybrid Generative Network (HGNet) to fight off ZSDA more effectively. The proposed feature separation module guided by annotation explores global information from shallow convolutional layers to extract more discriminative and domain-invariant units.
- To perform high-quality feature separation, we develop hybrid generation module assisting model to capture association between task-relevant (TR) and task-irrelevant (TIR) datasets. The benefit of such a relationship is to utilize cross-domain knowledge learned from TIR to eliminate domain shift on TR datasets.
- We assess our model on several visual cross-domain tasks, and HGNet outperforms competitive approaches by large margin in most cases, illustrating the effectiveness on solving ZSDA challenge. We further conduct extensive empirical study to demonstrate the function of hybrid generation.

2   Related Work

Domain adaptation (DA) has attracted great interest as it addresses limited annotation problem [25]. And recent works attempt to apply DA strategy in computer vision like image classification [12,18], object segmentation [26,29,36] and image caption [3]. However, they generally suffer from a primary challenge defined as domain shift deriving from the difference of distribution across domains. To mitigate such an issue, current proposed approaches are divided into two branches: dissimilarity measurement using statistic indicators to align distribution [11,16] and domain adversarial confusion [15,30,35] adopting adversarial manner to generate cross-domain features in the same latent space. Although these methods effectively learn domain-invariant representation, they significantly depend on the existence of samples from target domain. As a result, the situation where we fails to have access to the target modality dramatically obstructs the practical application of these techniques, which triggers another hot research topic named zero-shot domain adaptation (ZSDA) [27] also known as missing modality transfer learning [8]. The novel problem assumes that we just are given task-relevant source domain and auxiliary datasets including task-irrelevant source and target domains.

For the existing methods to solve ZSDA, they firstly attempt to utilize task-irrelevant samples to eliminate cross-domain discrepancy and then they transform samples of task-relevant source and target domain into the same hidden space [21]. In addition, with the advance of generative adversarial network in recent year, [27] proposes conditional coupled GAN (CoCoGAN) to generate task-relevant paired samples in the first step and train classifier on synthesised dataset. Different from them, we rethink ZSDA from the perspective of feature separation selecting more discriminative feature as domain-invariant feature, which effectively promote the generalization of model. And to obtain high-quality feature separation, we propose hybrid generative strategy ensuring the uniqueness of feature and the completeness of semantic information.

3   The Proposed Method

3.1   Preliminaries and Motivation

Zero-shot Domain Adaptation aims to exploit all accessible data to learn robust and generalized model used to deal with classification issue on target domain. Concretely, we are given well-annotated task-relevant source dataset $\mathcal{D}^{r,s} = \{(\mathbf{X}_i^{r,s}, Y_i^{r,s})\}_{i=1}^n$, where $\mathbf{X}_i^{r,s}$ and $Y_i^{r,s}$ separately denote i-th visual instance and its corresponding label. In addition, we also have access to task-irrelevant cross-domain paired datasets $\mathcal{D}^{ir,s} = \{(\mathbf{X}_i^{ir,s}, Y_i^{ir,s})\}_{i=1}^m$ and $\mathcal{D}^{ir,t} = \{(\mathbf{X}_i^{ir,t}, Y_i^{ir,t}\}_{i=1}^m$. Although $\mathbf{X}_i^{ir,s}$ and $\mathbf{X}_i^{ir,t}$ lie in various domains (source and target), they belong to the same category i.e., $Y_i^{ir,s} = Y_i^{ir,t}$. To this end, it is impossible for model to capture any knowledge of task-relevant target dataset $\mathcal{D}^{r,t} = \{\mathbf{X}_i^{r,t}\}_{i=1}^n$ only available in the test stage. The current scenario mainly involves two challenges: 1) **Generation of domain-invariant representation:** The absence of $\mathcal{D}^{r,t}$ results in huge difficulty of directly measuring cross-domain discrepancy between $\mathcal{D}^{r,s}$ and $\mathcal{D}^{r,t}$; 2) **Fusion of various datasets:** Tremendous difference among $\mathcal{D}^{r,s}$, $\mathcal{D}^{ir,s}$ and $\mathcal{D}^{ir,t}$ dramatically interferes their connection.

To capture domain shift between $\mathcal{D}^{r,s}$ and $\mathcal{D}^{r,t}$, the intuitive idea [27] is to firstly synthesize missing modality $\mathcal{D}^{r,t}$ and then transform them into the similar latent space, which arises a question: *"Is the explicit generation of missing target dataset necessary for learning domain-invariant feature?"* To answer this question, we rethink and explore the extraction of domain-invariant representation from the perspective of feature separation. Specifically, the intrinsic knowledge of input data generally is stored in high-level semantic representation via feature extractor. However, these semantic information is not equally necessary in terms of classification task. Admittedly, partial abstract representations record abundant essential content as visual style or background in object image, but

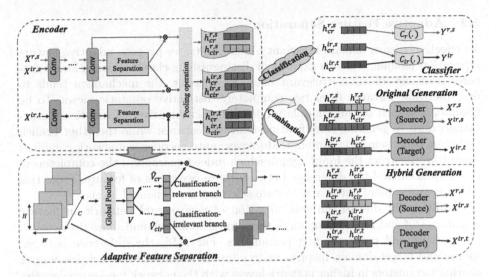

Fig. 1. Overview of the proposed HGNet, which mainly includes four components: encoder, decoder, classifier and adaptive feature separation module. The encoder firstly aims to extract convolutional features, and then the adaptive feature separation module attempts to learn classification-relevant and classification-irrelevant units. On one hand, we utilize label information to guarantee the effect of feature separation. On the other hand, we explore two reconstruction manners to promote the completeness of semantic information and the uniqueness of learned feature.

they are drastically various across domains. We consider these representations as classification-irrelevant features, which are undesirable in domain adaptation. On the other hand, the remaining part defined as classification-relevant feature has positive influence on our final object classification task. Considering the previous approaches about domain-invariant feature learning, it is irrational or even counterproductive to incorporate all information into the same representation. Therefore, we achieve two primary conclusions: 1) Feature separation is important to distinguish domain-invariant feature out of classification-irrelevant features instead of generating missing dataset $\mathcal{D}^{r,t}$; and 2) we should only explore discriminative information on the selected classification-relevant representations. According to these discussions, we propose our adaptive feature separation module embedded into auto-encoder framework.

Due to feature separation, classification-irrelevant representations of instances from $\mathcal{D}^{r,s}$ and $\mathcal{D}^{ir,s}$ should preserve high-similarity. Such relationship is also applied to $\mathcal{D}^{r,t}$ and $\mathcal{D}^{ir,t}$. Cross-domain paired datasets $\mathcal{D}^{ir,s}$ and $\mathcal{D}^{ir,t}$ tend to be transformed into the same hidden space with respect to classification-relevant feature, which is also suitable for $\mathcal{D}^{r,s}$ and $\mathcal{D}^{r,t}$. Based on these above analyses, we develop hybrid reconstruction strategy to build the connection among various datasets and promote the performance of domain adaptation.

3.2 Adaptive Feature Separation

To effectively learn domain-invariant hidden units, we propose adaptive feature separation module, which is capable of distinguishing classification-relevant features from classification-irrelevant ones. As a result, the mechanism tends to describe same instance from two completely distinctive semantic views. To be specific, a branch of this module guided by discriminative information (annotation) aims to generate classification-relevant features, while the other branch will store other semantic contents. Moreover, auto-encoder framework combines them to reconstruct the input signal, which indeed guarantees the completeness of information and the difference between these two types of feature. From this property, we explore automatic feature selection from channel level.

Additionally, due to the generalization of deep neural network on feature learning, $\mathcal{D}^{r,s}$ and $\mathcal{D}^{ir,s}$ belonging to the same modality should share the network architecture and corresponding parameters. For $\mathcal{D}^{ir,t}$, the difference between source and target domain inspires us to adopt a distinctive network framework sharing parameters in higher network layers with the network for source domain. As shown in Fig. 1, two various encoders involving convolutional operation convert the input signals $\mathbf{X}^{r,s}$, $\mathbf{X}^{ir,s}$ and $\mathbf{X}^{ir,t}$ into abstract representations $\mathbf{F}^{r,s}$, $\mathbf{F}^{ir,s}$, $\mathbf{F}^{ir,t} \in \mathbf{R}^{W \times H \times C}$, where W, H separately denote the width and height of each tensor, and C is the number of channel in tensor. At this time, the extracted features incorporate all semantic information of input data.

To learn domain-invariant features, we implement convolutional transformation to generate classification-relevant feature $\mathbf{F} \rightarrow \hat{\mathbf{F}}_{cr} \in \mathbf{R}^{W \times H \times C}$ and classification-irrelevant one $\mathbf{F} \rightarrow \hat{\mathbf{F}}_{cir} \in \mathbf{R}^{W \times H \times C}$, where $\mathbf{F}$ is selected from $\{\mathbf{F}^{r,s}, \mathbf{F}^{ir,s}, \mathbf{F}^{ir,t}\}$. The first transformation $\mathbf{F} \rightarrow \hat{\mathbf{F}}_{cr}$ performs a positive activation on convolutional layer via the guidance of label information to capture more discriminative information while gradually eliminating classification-irrelevant semantic content preserved in $\hat{\mathbf{F}}_{cir}$ with negative activation. Concretely, we firstly operate global average pooling technique on shallow convolutional feature $\mathbf{F}$ to obtain the information increment of each channel defined by $\mathcal{V} \in \mathbf{R}^{1 \times 1 \times C}$. Intuitively, each element $v_i \in \mathcal{V}$ roughly reflects content and style of the corresponding channel. To observe the connection across channels and separate features, we first adopt two distinctive non-linear manners to compress $\mathcal{V}$ to $\tilde{\mathcal{V}}_{cr}$ and $\tilde{\mathcal{V}}_{cir} \in \mathbf{R}^{1 \times 1 \times \frac{C}{\gamma}}$, where γ is a ratio controlling the scale of dimension-reduction and then utilize various full-connection layers to obtain new channel-wise statistics $\hat{\mathcal{V}}_{cr}$ and $\hat{\mathcal{V}}_{cir} \in \mathbf{R}^{1 \times 1 \times C}$. After the activation operation, $\hat{\mathcal{V}}_{cr}$ ideally promotes performance of several channels recording extensive discriminative information, while $\hat{\mathcal{V}}_{cir}$ enhances representation of others. Based on the above explanation, convolutional conversion can be formulated as:

$$\hat{\mathcal{V}}_{cr} = \sigma\Big(\mathbf{W}_{cr}\delta\big(g_{cr}(\mathcal{V})\big)\Big), \qquad \hat{\mathcal{V}}_{cir} = \sigma\Big(\mathbf{W}_{cir}\delta\big(g_{cir}(\mathcal{V})\big)\Big), \qquad (1)$$

where $\mathbf{W}_{cr}$, $\mathbf{W}_{cir} \in \mathbf{R}^{C \times \frac{C}{\gamma}}$, $\sigma(\cdot)$ and $\delta(\cdot)$ represent **Sigmoid** and **ReLU** activation functions, $g_{cr}(\cdot)$ and $g_{cir}(\cdot)$ refer to the non-linear dimension-reduction operations. To achieve the feature separation based on classification-task, we conduct channel-wise multiplication ($\otimes$) between original convolutional features $\mathbf{F}$ and learned channel-wise indicators $\hat{\mathcal{V}}_{cr}$, $\hat{\mathcal{V}}_{cir}$ as the following:

$$\hat{\mathbf{F}}_{cr} = \hat{\mathcal{V}}_{cr} \otimes \mathbf{F} = \{\hat{v}_{cr,i} \cdot \mathbf{F}_i\}_{i=1}^{C}, \qquad \hat{\mathbf{F}}_{cir} = \hat{\mathcal{V}}_{cir} \otimes \mathbf{F} = \{\hat{v}_{cir,i} \cdot \mathbf{F}_i\}_{i=1}^{C}. \qquad (2)$$

To guide feature separation on convolutional layer, we enforce $\hat{\mathbf{F}}_{cr}$ and $\hat{\mathbf{F}}_{cir}$ to pass through a series of operations including **Pooling, FC, ReLU** and **FC** to synthesize high-level semantic features h_{cr} and $h_{cir} \in \mathbf{R}^{d\times 1}$, where d is the dimension of feature. The learned representation h_{cr} as domain-invariant feature should be fed into the corresponding classifier to promote its discriminative ability. Considering that h_{cir} is required to preserve classification-irrelevant information, the concatenation of h_{cr} and h_{cir} will be taken as input for decoder including several deconvolutional layers [33] to achieve the reconstruction about the input data, i.e., $\hat{\mathbf{X}} = \mathcal{G}(h_{cr}, h_{cir})$, where $\mathcal{G}$ denotes neural network of decoder. Therefore, the objective function of adaptive feature separation module is written as:

$$\min_{\Theta} \quad \mathcal{L}_c(\mathbf{C}(h_{cr}), Y) + \|\mathbf{X} - \mathcal{G}(h_{cr}, h_{cir})\|_F^2$$
$$h_{cr} \in \{h_{cr}^{r,s}, h_{cr}^{ir,s}, h_{cr}^{ir,t}\}, \quad Y \in \{Y^{r,s}, Y^{ir,s}, Y^{ir,t}\} \qquad (3)$$
$$h_{cir} \in \{h_{cir}^{r,s}, h_{cir}^{ir,s}, h_{cir}^{ir,t}\}, \quad \mathbf{X} \in \{\mathbf{X}^{r,s}, \mathbf{X}^{ir,s}, \mathbf{X}^{ir,t}\},$$

where Θ refers to all parameters of model, $\mathbf{C} = \{\mathbf{C}^r, \mathbf{C}^{ir}\}$ represents classifier ($h_{cr}^{ir,s}$ and $h_{cr}^{ir,t}$ share classifier C^{ir}, while classifier C^r is target for $h_{cr}^{r,s}$), $\mathcal{L}_c(\cdot)$ means cross-entropy loss and $\mathcal{G}$ consists of two types: $\mathcal{G}_s$ shared by source domain and $\mathcal{G}_t$ used by target domain. Note that the application of objective function requires the consistence of superscript.

3.3   Hybrid Generation

The benefit of adaptive feature separation is to extract more discriminative domain-invariant feature with the guidance of label information. To further eliminate domain shift, we propose hybrid reconstruction strategy capturing the connection across various datasets. In other words, we explore the feature alignment between $\mathcal{D}^{ir,s}$ and $\mathcal{D}^{ir,t}$ as well as the consistence of modality over $\mathcal{D}^{r,s}$ and $\mathcal{D}^{ir,s}$ to reduce cross-domain discrepancy of $\mathcal{D}^{r,s}$ and unavailable $\mathcal{D}^{r,t}$.

According to Sect. 3.2, any input signals passing through corresponding encoder and adaptive feature separation module will be transformed into classification-relevant features and classification-irrelevant ones. Due to the paired relationship between $\mathbf{X}^{ir,s}$ and $\mathbf{X}^{ir,t}$, it is reasonable to assume that there exists high similarity between $h_{cr}^{ir,s}$ and $h_{cr}^{ir,t}$ (i.e. $h_{cr}^{ir,s} \equiv h_{cr}^{ir,t}$) derived from corresponding input data. In terms of such equivalent property, we can assert the decoder $\mathcal{G}_t$ performed on ($h_{cr}^{ir,s}$, $h_{cir}^{ir,t}$) and ($h_{cr}^{ir,t}$, $h_{cir}^{ir,t}$) tend to generate the same result, which is formulated as:

$$\mathcal{G}_t(h_{cr}^{ir,s}, h_{cir}^{ir,t}) \equiv \mathbf{X}^{ir,t} \equiv \mathcal{G}_t(h_{cr}^{ir,t}, h_{cir}^{ir,t}). \qquad (4)$$

With respect to the decoder of source domain $\mathcal{G}_s$, we can similarly draw the conclusion as:

$$\mathcal{G}_s(h_{cr}^{ir,s}, h_{cir}^{ir,s}) \equiv \mathbf{X}^{ir,s} \equiv \mathcal{G}_s(h_{cr}^{ir,t}, h_{cir}^{ir,s}). \tag{5}$$

To this end, the loss function of hybrid reconstruction and feature alignment is defined:

$$\begin{aligned} \mathcal{L}_{hr}^{ir} = {} & \lambda \|h_{cr}^{ir,s} - h_{cr}^{ir,t}\|_F^2 + \|\mathcal{G}_t(h_{cr}^{ir,s}, h_{cir}^{ir,t}) - \mathbf{X}^{ir,t}\|_F^2 \\ & + \|\mathcal{G}_s(h_{cr}^{ir,s}, h_{cir}^{ir,s}) - \mathbf{X}^{ir,s}\|_F^2, \end{aligned} \tag{6}$$

where λ is the hyper-parameter controlling the reconstruction and feature alignment. The first term in Eq. (6) not only achieves distribution alignment over task-irrelevant datasets, but also gradually eliminates the difference of models on feature learning. Under such condition, even though target dataset $\mathcal{D}^{r,t}$ is unavailable for training stage, the similarity of model effectively facilitates the consistency of feature representation across $\mathcal{D}^{r,s}$ and $\mathcal{D}^{r,t}$. Meanwhile, hybrid reconstruction loss plays an essential role in achieving the goal of feature separation, which aims to preserve abundant meaningful and discriminative feature in classification-relevant representation via the last two terms.

From Fig. 1, we observe that classification-irrelevant units derived from $\mathbf{X}^{r,s}$ and $\mathbf{X}^{ir,s}$ ideally should maintain high correlation, since their corresponding input signals belong to the same modality. However, $h_{cr}^{r,s}$ and $h_{cr}^{ir,s}$ tend to describe distinctive objects of images. The expected association between $\mathcal{D}^{r,s}$ and $\mathcal{D}^{ir,s}$ is expressed as:

$$\mathcal{G}_s(h_{cr}^{r,s}, h_{cir}^{r,s}) \equiv \mathbf{X}^{r,s} \approx \mathcal{G}_s(h_{cr}^{r,s}, h_{cir}^{ir,s}). \tag{7}$$

$$\mathcal{G}_s(h_{cr}^{ir,s}, h_{cir}^{ir,s}) \equiv \mathbf{X}^{ir,s} \approx \mathcal{G}_s(h_{cr}^{ir,s}, h_{cir}^{r,s}). \tag{8}$$

Therefore, we explore hybrid generation to satisfy such a requirement and reformulate our objective function as:

$$\mathcal{L}_{hr}^s = \|\mathcal{G}_s(h_{cr}^{r,s}, h_{cir}^{ir,s}) - \mathbf{X}^{r,s}\|_F^2 + \|\mathcal{G}_s(h_{cr}^{ir,s}, h_{cir}^{r,s}) - \mathbf{X}^{ir,s}\|_F^2. \tag{9}$$

Remarks: If we have access to the missing target modality $\mathbf{X}^{r,t}$, the constraint of Eq. (9) enables the model to capture relationships: $\mathcal{G}_t(h_{cr}^{r,t}, h_{cir}^{ir,t}) \approx \mathbf{X}^{r,t} \equiv \mathcal{G}_t(h_{cr}^{r,t}, h_{cir}^{r,t})$ and $\mathcal{G}_t(h_{cr}^{ir,t}, h_{cir}^{r,t}) \approx \mathbf{X}^{ir,t} \equiv \mathcal{G}_t(h_{cr}^{ir,t}, h_{cir}^{ir,t})$. Moreover, under the supervision of Eq. (9), we also achieve the conclusion $\mathcal{G}_t(h_{cr}^{r,s}, h_{cir}^{r,t}) \approx \mathbf{X}^{r,t} \equiv \mathcal{G}_t(h_{cr}^{r,t}, h_{cir}^{r,t})$ and $\mathcal{G}_s(h_{cr}^{r,t}, h_{cir}^{r,s}) \approx \mathbf{X}^{r,s} \equiv \mathcal{G}_s(h_{cr}^{r,s}, h_{cir}^{r,s})$. Through such mediate manner, the model finally achieves domain adaptation across $\mathcal{D}^{r,s}$ and $\mathcal{D}^{r,t}$.

3.4 Training and Inference

Given accessible datatsets $\mathcal{D}^{r,s}$, $\mathcal{D}^{ir,s}$ and $\mathcal{D}^{ir,st}$, we firstly perform initial feature separation within each dataset. And then hybrid reconstruction as an important component captures delicate association across all datasets to gradually reduce cross-domain discrepancy between $\mathcal{D}^{r,s}$ and missing target dataset $\mathcal{D}^{r,t}$. Finally, we utilize the feature extractor of target domain to learn feature of $\mathbf{X}^{r,t}$ and apply classifier $\mathbf{C}_s(\cdot)$ to perform classification task. Therefore, the overall process is summarized as three steps:

Step A: Input data including $\mathbf{X}^{r,s}$, $\mathbf{X}^{ir,s}$ and $\mathbf{X}^{ir,t}$ first is fed into the encoder to learn convolutional features. And then we perform adaptive feature separation on convolutional layers to obtain classification-relevant unit h_{cr} and h_{cir}. Finally, the concatenation of h_{cr} and h_{cir} is exploited to reconstruct input signal. During learning stage, we explore objective function (3) to update model.

Step B: To achieve the expected feature separation and domain adaptation, we should integrate hybrid reconstruction and the guidance of label information into a unified loss function as:

$$\min_{\Theta} \quad \mathcal{L}_{hr}^{ir} + \mathcal{L}_{hr}^{s} + \mathcal{L}_c\big(\mathbf{C}(h_{cr}), Y\big)$$
$$h_{cr} \in \{h_{cr}^{r,s}, h_{cr}^{ir,s}, h_{cr}^{ir,t}\}, Y \in \{Y^{r,s}, Y^{ir,s}, Y^{ir,t}\}, \tag{10}$$

where $\mathbf{C}$ consists of $\mathbf{C}_s$ classifier used by $h_{cr}^{r,s}$ and $\mathbf{C}_t$ classifier shared by $h_{cr}^{ir,s}$ and $h_{cr}^{ir,t}$. We train the network according to Eq. (10) until convergence.

Step C: During inference stage, instances $X^{r,t}$ will be passed through the encoder used by $X^{ir,t}$ to obtain high-level feature $h_{cr}^{r,t}$. Eventually, we utilize classifier $\mathbf{C}_s$ to predict the annotation of $h_{cr}^{r,t}$.

4 Experiments

4.1 Datasets and Comparisons

We perform experiments on three popular benchmarks involving MNIST [14], Fashion MNIST [31] and EMNIST [6] to verify the effectiveness of our method. For the convenience and clarity, we utilize dataset IDs D_M, D_F and D_E to refer to them. In addition, there exists three techniques to transform each gray-scale image into the corresponding negative, color and edge images.

MNIST (D_M) dataset is developed to identify handwritten digit image. The dataset includes 70,000 gray-scale images, where 60,000 training instances and 10,000 testing images. Each visual instance with same size 28×28 only represents one of ten digits from 0 to 9.

Fashion MNIST (D_F) dataset includes abundant fashion trappings images. Experts in fashion field artificially divide them into ten categories: *T-shirt, trouser, pullover, dress, coat, sandals, shirt, sneaker, bag,* and *ankle boot*. The dataset has the same sample scale with MNIST, i.e. 60,000 training instances and 10,000 testing samples. The image size of each sample is also 28×28.

EMNIST (D_E) dataset different from MNIST records extensive handwritten alphabets images. The uppercase and lowercase letters are merged into a balanced dataset with 26 categories. The image size of each sample is 28×28. Moreover, it involves 124,800 images for training and 20,800 images for testing.

Table 1. Classification Accuracy (%) of our method and three baselines for domain adaptation from gray-scale modality (*G-domain*) to color modality (*C-domain*). The best result in each column is in bold.

RT	MNIST (D_M)		Fashion-Mnist		EMNIST (D_E)	
IRT	D_F	D_E	D_M	D_E	D_M	D_F
ZDDA [21]	73.2	94.8	51.6	65.3	71.2	47.0
CoGAN [27]	68.3	74.7	39.7	55.8	46.7	41.8
CoCoGAN [27]	78.1	**95.6**	56.8	66.8	**75.0**	54.8
HGNet	**85.3**	95.0	**64.5**	**71.1**	71.3	**57.9**

Modality Transformation: All instances in the above mentioned datasets are gray-scale images and we define this modality as *G-domain*. To perform domain adaptation, We firstly follow the operations in [27] to convert all original data into negative image (*N-domain*) by using $\mathbf{X}_n = 255 - \mathbf{X}$, $\mathbf{X} \in \mathbf{R}^{m \times n \times 1}$ where m and n are the spatial dimensions of image. Moreover, we apply canny detector to create edge images $\mathbf{X}_e$ (*E-domain*). Finally, in terms of color version, we randomly extract several patches ($\mathbf{P} \in \mathbf{R}^{m \times n}$) from the BSDS500 dataset [1] and then blend them with images $\mathbf{X}$ to form color images $\mathbf{X}_c$ (*C-domain*).

Comparisons: To evaluate the performance of our method, we select three baselines as competed methods which are currently the only works exploring the application of deep learning on zero-shot domain adaptation problem. The first compared approach is *ZDDA* [21], which propose sensor fusion to solve domain shift. Moreover, [27] utilizes two models named *CoGAN* and *CoCoGAN* to address ZSDA issue, which are considered as two various approaches.

4.2 Implementation Details

The network architecture of our method mainly includes three components: encoder, decoder and classifier. Although source and target utilize various networks, they have the same network structure. Thus, we take the branch of source domain as an example to illustrate the specific implementation. With respect to the encoder, we adopt three convolutional layers with stride 2 to extract channel-level feature and apply **ReLU** to activate the output of the first two layers. Symmetrically, the decoder has three deconvolutional layers with stride 2 to recover hidden representation to input data. There are two classifiers used in our proposed method and they both have two full-connection layers followed by **Softmax** function.

4.3 Experimental Results

In order to validate the effectiveness of our method, we create five different zero-shot domain adaption settings. We firstly consider gray-scale images as source domain and the other three domains will be target domain. Thus, there are three

Table 2. Classification Accuracy (%) of our method and three baselines for two domain adaptation tasks: *N-domain* → *G-domain* and *G-domain* → *N-domain*. The best result in each column is in bold.

Task	*N-domain* → *G-domain*						*G-domain* → *N-domain*		
RT	D_M		D_F		D_E		D_M	D_F	D_E
IRT	D_F	D_E	D_M	D_E	D_M	D_F	D_F	D_E	D_E	D_F
ZDDA [21]	78.5	87.6	56.6	67.1	67.7	45.5	77.9	90.5	62.7	53.4
CoGAN [27]	66.1	76.3	49.9	58.7	53.0	32.5	62.7	72.8	51.2	39.1
CoCoGAN [27]	80.1	93.6	63.4	72.8	**78.8**	58.4	80.3	93.1	69.3	56.5
HGNet	**87.5**	**95.0**	**64.6**	**75.1**	78.0	**67.9**	**83.7**	**95.7**	**71.7**	**62.3**

domain adaptation tasks: *G-domain* → *N-domain*, *G-domain* → *E-domain* and *G-domain* → *C-domain*. In addition, we also attempt to transfer knowledge from color domain or negative domain to gray domain, i.e., *C-domain* → *G-domain* and *N-domain* → *G-domain*.

According to descriptions of dataset, we know these three datasets involves three completely distinctive objects: digits, trappings and letters. When selecting one of them as task-relevant dataset, we can consider others as task-irrelevant datasets which assist model to capture cross-domain discrepancy and promote classification accuracy on missing target modality ($D^{r,t}$). Firstly, we attempt to transfer knowledge from gray-scale modality (*G-domain*) to color modality (*C-color*). Compared with gray-scale image, original RGB image generally involve three color channels, which dramatically increase the difficult in achieving domain adaptation. Experimental performances are summarized in Table 1. In terms of these results, our proposed method (HGNet) obtains the best classification accuracy in three datasets. And there exist significant differences between HGNet and CoCoGAN achieving the second best performance. Specifically, our proposed approach surpasses CoCoGAN by 7.7% when Fashion-MNIST and MNIST separately are task-relevant and task-irrelevant datasets. On the one hand, the empirical results provide convincing answer (No) to the question in Sect. 3.1: is the generation of missing target dataset necessary for learning domain-invariant feature. On the other hand, it illustrates that hybrid generative manner guarantees the uniqueness of feature separation and the application of it enable model to learn more discriminative domain-invariant feature.

For the second step, we conduct transformation between gray-scale modality (*G-domain*) and negative modality (*N-domain*) and summary the corresponding performances in Table 2. From these experimental results, we can obtain three conclusions. First of all, the proposed algorithm (HGNet) achieves more promising performances than other baselines in most cases. Specifically, when separately selecting D_E and D_F as task-relevant and task-irrelevant datasets, our approach outperforms CoCoGAN by 5.8% on the domain adaptation task (*G-domain* → *N-domain*). Secondly, we notice that classification accuracy of all mentioned methods on Fashion-MNIST (task-relevant datatset) is lower than

Table 3. Classification Accuracy (%) of our method and three baselines for two domain adaptation tasks: *G-domain → E-domain* and *C-domain → G-domain*. The best result in each column is in bold.

Task	G-domain → E-domain				C-domain → G-domain			
RT	MNIST (D_M)		EMNIST (D_E)		MNIST (D_M)		Fashion (D_F)	
IRT	D_F	D_E	D_M	D_F	D_F	D_E	D_M	D_E
ZDDA [21]	72.5	93.2	73.6	50.7	67.4	87.6	55.1	59.5
CoGAN [27]	67.1	81.5	63.6	51.9	54.7	63.5	43.4	51.6
CoCoGAN [27]	79.6	95.4	77.9	58.6	73.2	94.7	61.1	**70.2**
HGNet	**86.5**	**96.1**	**81.1**	**59.5**	**78.9**	**95.0**	**65.9**	68.5

that on other two datasets. The main reason for this derives from that trappings images are more complex than digits and letters images. However, HGNet still improve 1%–3% when compared with the second best result obtained by CoCo-GAN. Finally, although these two transformation (*G-domain → N-domain* and *N-domain → G-domain*) are mutually inverse operations, classification accuracy of most approaches on *G-domain → N-domain* are better than their performances on *N-domain → G-domain*. But the results of HGNet on these two transformations are competitive, which means our method has much better generalization.

In the final experiment, we explore *G-domain → E-domain* and *C-domain → G-domain* to further verify the effectiveness of HGNet. Results are reported in Table 3. The performance of HGNet is better than others in most cases. Interestingly, we find that although there exists high similarity between D_M and D_E, it difficult for most methods to achieve great transformation on D_E with the assistance of D_M. Different from them, our method fully utilizes association across all available datasets to reduce cross-domain discrepancy, leading to the improvement on classification accuracy to 81.1%.

4.4 Ablation Study

Effect of Hybrid Strategy: According to the discussion about hybrid reconstruction, we know that this part enable the proposed model to further guarantee the uniqueness of feature separation and promote generalization across various domains by using association of all given datasets. In order to clearly observe the effect of hybrid reconstruction, we firstly attempt to remove this part from our method to form another competed method named as HGNet$_1$, while the overall version of our method is denoted as HGNet$_2$. The goal of experiments in this section is to achieve the transformation from *N-domain* to *G-domain* and Fig. 2(a) lists results, where the expression *A(B)* means *A* is task-relevant dataset while *B* represents task-irrelevant one.

As seen in Fig. 2(a), the absence of hybrid reconstruction suffers from significant negative influence on the classification accuracy. HGNet$_2$ outperforms

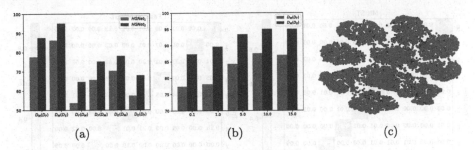

(a)   (b)   (c)

Fig. 2. Experiments are performed on adaptation from *N-domain* to *G-domain*. And the expression *A (B)* means *A* is the task-relevant dataset while *B* represents the task-irrelevant one. (a) We denote our proposed method without hybrid reconstruction as $HGNet_1$ and the overall version as $HGNet_2$. (b) We select λ from {0.1, 1.0, 5.0, 10.0, 15.0} and observe the classification accuracy. (c) When D_E is the task-irrelevant datasets, we show the feature visualization on MNIST.

$HGNet_1$ by 10% for $D_F(D_M)$, illustrating that hybrid strategy not only effectively generates more discriminative feature representation but also captures more cross-domain information from all available data to reduce domain shift.

Additionally, we present the generated images in Fig. 3 via hybrid generation to verify its ability performing transformation between source and target domains. In terms of the visualization, we find that hybrid strategy captures cross-domain discrepancy. Specifically, in the first two rows, images synthesised by $\mathcal{G}(h_{cr}^{ir,s}, h_{cir}^{ir,t})$ actually integrate main objects from $X^{ir,s}$ and the corresponding modality style (N-*domain*) from $X^{ir,t}$. It means that our proposed method achieves high-quality separation of

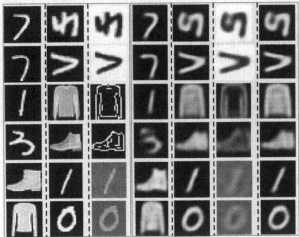

Fig. 3. Visualization of hybrid generation. The first three columns represents the inputs: $X^{r,s}, X^{ir,s}$ and $X^{ir,t}$, while the last four columns are hybrid generative visual signals: $\mathcal{G}_s(h_{cr}^{r,s}, h_{cir}^{ir,s})$, $\mathcal{G}_s(h_{cr}^{ir,s}, h_{cir}^{r,s})$, $\mathcal{G}_t(h_{cr}^{ir,s}, h_{cir}^{ir,t})$ and $\mathcal{G}_s(h_{cr}^{ir,t}, h_{cir}^{ir,s})$.

semantic information, which assists model to learn domain-invariant feature and promote classification accuracy.

Parameters Analysis: To show the function of feature alignment on task-irrelevant dataset, we change the value of λ from *0.1* to *15* and record results (N-*domain* $\rightarrow$ *G-domain*) in Fig. 2(b). With the increasing of λ, HGNet achieves

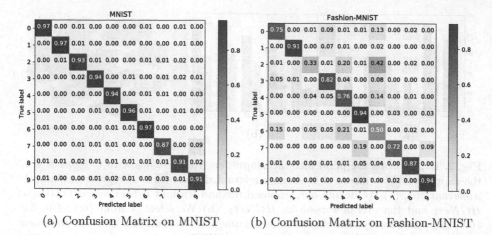

(a) Confusion Matrix on MNIST   (b) Confusion Matrix on Fashion-MNIST

Fig. 4. Visualization of Confusion Matrix. Experiments are performed on adaptation from *N-domain* to *G-domain*. For these two experiments, we select EMNIST as the task-irrelevant datasets.

higher accuracy, illustrating that such feature alignment manner has positive effect on solving the domain shift issue on task-relevant dataset.

Visualization of Latent Space: To further analyse distribution of high-level feature, we draw feature visualization and confusion matrix on MNIST and Fashion-MNIST in Fig. 2(c) and Fig. 4. For these experiments, we select EMNIST as task-irrelevant datasets and transfer negative images (*N-domain*) into gray-scale modality (*G-domain*). From the performance, we know that HGNet learns clear boundary between various categories, which significantly promotes feature discriminative.

5   Conclusion

Zero-shot Domain Adaptation (ZSDA) assumes that we hardly access target samples during training stage. To fight off ZSDA more effectively, we propose a novel approach named Hybrid Generative Network (HGNet) including feature extractor, adaptive feature separation module, hybrid generator and classifier. Concretely, feature extractor learns representations from visual signals, and then adaptive feature separation module distinguishes classification-relevant units from classification-irrelevant ones storing meaningless semantic information. Moreover, we adopt two manners to perform high-quality feature separation. One is to use annotation as supervision to generate discriminative feature. Another is to exploit hybrid generative strategy to extract association across various available datasets. Finally, extensive experimental results validate the effectiveness of HGNet on solving ZSDA problem.

References

1. Arbelaez, P., Maire, M., Fowlkes, C., Malik, J.: Contour detection and hierarchical image segmentation. IEEE Trans. Pattern Anal. Mach. Intell. **33**(5), 898–916 (2010)
2. Cai, R., Li, Z., Wei, P., Qiao, J., Zhang, K., Hao, Z.: Learning disentangled semantic representation for domain adaptation. In: IJCAI, vol. 2019, p. 2060. NIH Public Access (2019)
3. Chen, T.H., Liao, Y.H., Chuang, C.Y., Hsu, W.T., Fu, J., Sun, M.: Show, adapt and tell: adversarial training of cross-domain image captioner. In: ICCV, pp. 521–530 (2017)
4. Chen, Z., Zhuang, J., Liang, X., Lin, L.: Blending-target domain adaptation by adversarial meta-adaptation networks. In: CVPR, pp. 2248–2257 (2019)
5. Cicek, S., Soatto, S.: Unsupervised domain adaptation via regularized conditional alignment. In: ICCV, pp. 1416–1425 (2019)
6. Cohen, G., Afshar, S., Tapson, J., Van Schaik, A.: EMNIST: extending MNIST to handwritten letters. In: IJCNN, pp. 2921–2926. IEEE (2017)
7. Ding, Z., Li, S., Shao, M., Fu, Y.: Graph adaptive knowledge transfer for unsupervised domain adaptation. In: Ferrari, V., Hebert, M., Sminchisescu, C., Weiss, Y. (eds.) ECCV 2018. LNCS, vol. 11206, pp. 36–52. Springer, Cham (2018). https://doi.org/10.1007/978-3-030-01216-8_3
8. Ding, Z., Ming, S., Fu, Y.: Latent low-rank transfer subspace learning for missing modality recognition. In: AAAI (2014)
9. Dong, J., Cong, Y., Sun, G., Zhong, B., Xu, X.: What can be transferred: unsupervised domain adaptation for endoscopic lesions segmentation. In: CVPR, June 2020
10. Gretton, A., Smola, A., Huang, J., Schmittfull, M., Borgwardt, K., Schölkopf, B.: Covariate shift by kernel mean matching. In: Dataset Shift in Machine Learning, vol. 3, no. 4, p. 5 (2009)
11. Kang, G., Jiang, L., Yang, Y., Hauptmann, A.G.: Contrastive adaptation network for unsupervised domain adaptation. In: CVPR, pp. 4893–4902 (2019)
12. Koniusz, P., Tas, Y., Porikli, F.: Domain adaptation by mixture of alignments of second-or higher-order scatter tensors. In: CVPR, pp. 4478–4487 (2017)
13. Kumar, A., et al.: Co-regularized alignment for unsupervised domain adaptation. In: NeurIPS, pp. 9345–9356 (2018)
14. LeCun, Y., Bottou, L., Bengio, Y., Haffner, P.: Gradient-based learning applied to document recognition. Proc. IEEE **86**(11), 2278–2324 (1998)
15. Liu, H., Long, M., Wang, J., Jordan, M.: Transferable adversarial training: a general approach to adapting deep classifiers. In: ICML, pp. 4013–4022 (2019)
16. Long, M., Zhu, H., Wang, J., Jordan, M.I.: Deep transfer learning with joint adaptation networks. In: ICML, pp. 2208–2217. JMLR.org (2017)
17. Luo, Y., Zheng, L., Guan, T., Yu, J., Yang, Y.: Taking a closer look at domain shift: category-level adversaries for semantics consistent domain adaptation. In: CVPR, pp. 2507–2516 (2019)
18. Motiian, S., Piccirilli, M., Adjeroh, D.A., Doretto, G.: Unified deep supervised domain adaptation and generalization. In: ICCV, pp. 5715–5725 (2017)
19. Muandet, K., Balduzzi, D., Schölkopf, B.: Domain generalization via invariant feature representation. In: ICML, pp. 10–18 (2013)
20. Pei, Z., Cao, Z., Long, M., Wang, J.: Multi-adversarial domain adaptation. In: AAAI (2018)

21. Peng, K.-C., Wu, Z., Ernst, J.: Zero-shot deep domain adaptation. In: Ferrari, V., Hebert, M., Sminchisescu, C., Weiss, Y. (eds.) ECCV 2018. LNCS, vol. 11215, pp. 793–810. Springer, Cham (2018). https://doi.org/10.1007/978-3-030-01252-6_47
22. Peng, X., Bai, Q., Xia, X., Huang, Z., Saenko, K., Wang, B.: Moment matching for multi-source domain adaptation. In: ICCV, pp. 1406–1415 (2019)
23. Pinheiro, P.O.: Unsupervised domain adaptation with similarity learning. In: CVPR, pp. 8004–8013 (2018)
24. Roy, S., Siarohin, A., Sangineto, E., Bulo, S.R., Sebe, N., Ricci, E.: Unsupervised domain adaptation using feature-whitening and consensus loss. In: CVPR, pp. 9471–9480 (2019)
25. Saito, K., Watanabe, K., Ushiku, Y., Harada, T.: Maximum classifier discrepancy for unsupervised domain adaptation. In: CVPR, pp. 3723–3732 (2018)
26. Vu, T.H., Jain, H., Bucher, M., Cord, M., Pérez, P.: Advent: adversarial entropy minimization for domain adaptation in semantic segmentation. In: CVPR, pp. 2517–2526 (2019)
27. Wang, J., Jiang, J.: Conditional coupled generative adversarial networks for zero-shot domain adaptation. In: ICCV, pp. 3375–3384 (2019)
28. Wang, X., Li, L., Ye, W., Long, M., Wang, J.: Transferable attention for domain adaptation. In: AAAI, vol. 33, pp. 5345–5352 (2019)
29. Wulfmeier, M., Bewley, A., Posner, I.: Addressing appearance change in outdoor robotics with adversarial domain adaptation. In: IROS, pp. 1551–1558. IEEE (2017)
30. Xia, H., Ding, Z.: Structure preserving generative cross-domain learning. In: CVPR, pp. 4364–4373 (2020)
31. Xiao, H., Rasul, K., Vollgraf, R.: Fashion-MNIST: a novel image dataset for benchmarking machine learning algorithms. arXiv preprint arXiv:1708.07747 (2017)
32. Xie, S., Zheng, Z., Chen, L., Chen, C.: Learning semantic representations for unsupervised domain adaptation. In: ICML, pp. 5423–5432 (2018)
33. Zeiler, M.D., Krishnan, D., Taylor, G.W., Fergus, R.: Deconvolutional networks. In: CVPR, pp. 2528–2535. IEEE (2010)
34. Zhang, W., Ouyang, W., Li, W., Xu, D.: Collaborative and adversarial network for unsupervised domain adaptation. In: CVPR, pp. 3801–3809 (2018)
35. Zhang, Y., Tang, H., Jia, K., Tan, M.: Domain-symmetric networks for adversarial domain adaptation. In: CVPR, pp. 5031–5040 (2019)
36. Zhang, Y., David, P., Gong, B.: Curriculum domain adaptation for semantic segmentation of urban scenes. In: ICCV, pp. 2020–2030 (2017)

Beyond Monocular Deraining: Stereo Image Deraining via Semantic Understanding

Kaihao Zhang[1], Wenhan Luo[2], Wenqi Ren[3(✉)], Jingwen Wang[2], Fang Zhao[4],
Lin Ma[2], and Hongdong Li[1,5]

[1] Australian National University, Canberra, Australia
[2] Tencent AI Lab, Bellevue, USA
[3] Institute of Information Engineering, Chinese Academy of Sciences, Beijing, China
rwq.renwenqi@gmail.com
[4] Inception Institute of Artificial Intelligence, Abu Dhabi, United Arab Emirates
[5] ACRV, Brisbane, Australia

Abstract. Rain is a common natural phenomenon. Taking images in the
rain however often results in degraded quality of images, thus compro-
mises the performance of many computer vision systems. Most existing
de-rain algorithms use only one single input image and aim to recover a
clean image. Few work has exploited stereo images. Moreover, even for
single image based monocular deraining, many current methods fail to
complete the task satisfactorily because they mostly rely on per pixel
loss functions and ignore semantic information. In this paper, we present
a Paired Rain Removal Network (PRRNet), which exploits both stereo
images and semantic information. Specifically, we develop a Semantic-
Aware Deraining Module (SADM) which solves both tasks of semantic segmentation and deraining of scenes, and a Semantic-Fusion Network (SFNet) and a View-Fusion Network (VFNet) which fuse semantic
information and multi-view information respectively. We also propose
new stereo based rainy datasets for benchmarking. Experiments on both
monocular and the newly proposed stereo rainy datasets demonstrate
that the proposed method achieves the state-of-the-art performance.

Keywords: Stereo deraining · Semantic understanding · Rethinking
loop · View fusion · Deep learning

1 Introduction

Stereo images processing has become an increasingly active research field in computer vision with the development of stereoscopic vision. Based on stereo images,
many key technologies such as depth estimation [1–3], scene understanding [4–6]
and stereo matching [7–9] have achieved a great success. As a common natural
phenomenon, rain causes visual discomfort and degrades the quality of images,

© Springer Nature Switzerland AG 2020
A. Vedaldi et al. (Eds.): ECCV 2020, LNCS 12372, pp. 71–89, 2020.
https://doi.org/10.1007/978-3-030-58583-9_5

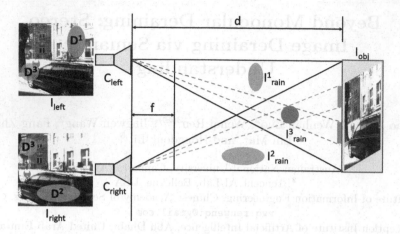

Fig. 1. The illustration of stereo cameras. One pair of images captured by stereo cameras. Same rain can cause different effects on images from two views.

which can deteriorate the performance of many core models in outdoor vision-based systems. However, there are few studies for stereo deraining. In this paper, we address the problem of removing rain from stereo images.

In fact, stereo deraining has an intrinsic advantage over monocular deraining because the effects of identical rain streaks in corresponding pixels from stereo images are different. As Fig. 1 shows, the mapping of object I_{obj} on stereo images can be represented as

$$I_{left} = I_{obj} * \frac{d}{f}, \qquad I_{right} = I_{obj}^{ref} * \frac{d}{f}, \tag{1}$$

where d and f are the distance between object and camera and the camera focal length, respectively. I_{obj}^{ref} is the reflection of I_{obj}. Assuming that the object I_{obj} is in the middle of two cameras, the lengths of identical objects, I_{obj}^{ref} and I_{obj}, on stereo views are the same. However, the effects of rain across stereo images are different. For example, the degraded regions by rain I_{rain}^1 on the two images can be denoted as

$$D_{left}^1 = I_{rain}^1 * \frac{d_{rain}}{f}, \qquad D_{right}^1 = 0. \tag{2}$$

I_{rain}^1 degrades the quality of the object on the left image but does not affect the visual comfort of the right view. d_{rain} is the distance between the camera and the raindrop. There is also rain influencing different regions on both stereo images like I_{rain}^3. The image in Fig. 1 shows the different effects of identical rain streaks on stereo views.

Moreover, the geometric cue and semantics provide important prior information, serving as a latent advantage for removing rain. Recently, most deep monocular deraining methods achieve a great success by reconstructing objects based on pixel-level objective functions like MSE. However, these methods ignore modeling the geometric structure of objects and understanding the semantic information of scenes, which in fact benefit deraining. Hu *et al.* [10] try to remove rain via depth estimation, but they also fail to understand the rainy scenes.

In this paper, we first propose a semantic-aware deraining module, *SADM*, which removes rain by leveraging scene understanding. Figure 2 illustrates the concept of *SADM*. It contains two parts. The first part is an encoder which takes a rainy image as input and encodes it as semantic-aware features. Then the representations are fed into the second part, a conditional generator, to transform them into the deraining image and scene segmentation. Based on a multi-task shared learning mechanism and different input conditions, the single *SADM* is capable of jointly removing rain and understanding scenes. To further enhance the understanding of input images, a *Semantic-Rethinking Loop* is proposed to utilize the difference between the outputs of the conditional generators in different stages.

Based on *SADM*, we then present a stereo deraining model, *Paired Rain Removal Network (PRRNet)*, which consists of *SADM*, *Semantic-Fusion Network (SFNet)* and *View-Fusion Network (VFNet)*. *SADM* is utilized to learn the semantic information and reconstruct deraining images, while *SFNet* and *VFNet* are to fuse the semantic information with coarse deraining images, and obtain the final deraining images by fusing stereo views, respectively. Currently, there is no public large-scale stereo rainy datasets. In order to evaluate the performance of the proposed method and compare against the state-of-the-art methods, two large stereo rainy image datasets are thus constructed.

In summary, the contributions of this paper are three-fold:

– Firstly, a multi-task shared learning deraining model, *SADM*, is proposed to remove rain via scene understanding. This model not only considers pixel-level objective functions like previous methods, but also models the geometric structure and semantic information of input rainy images. Inside *SADM*, a novel *Semantic-Rethinking Loop* is employed to further strengthen the connection between scene understanding and image deraining.
– Secondly, we propose *PRRNet*, the first semantic-aware stereo deraining network. *PRRNet* fuses the semantic information and multi-view information via *SFNet* and *VFNet*, respectively, to obtain the final stereo deraining images.
– Thirdly, we synthesize two stereo rainy datasets for stereo deraining, which may be the largest datasets for stereo image deraining. Experiments on monocular and stereo rainy datasets show that the proposed *PRRNet* achieves the state-of-the-art performance on both monocular and stereo deraining.

2 Related Work

2.1 Single Image Deraining

Deraining from a single rainy image is a highly ill-posed task, whose mathematical formulation is expressed as

$$O = B + R, \tag{3}$$

where O, B and R are the observed rainy image, the latent clean image and the rain-streak component, respectively.

For traditional methods of recovering the clean deraining image B from the rainy version O, Kang et al. [11] first detect rain from the high/low frequency part of input images based on morphological component analysis and remove rain streaks in the high frequency layer via dictionary learning. Similarly, Huang et al. [12] and Zhu et al. [13] use sparse coding based methods to remove rain from a single image. Some works aim to remove rain based on low-rank representation [14,15]. Chen et al. [14] generalize a low-rank model from matrix to tensor structure, which does not need the rain detection and dictionary learning stage. In addition, Li et al. [16] use a GMM trained on patches from natural images to model the background patch priors.

Recently, deep learning achieves significant success in low-level vision tasks such as image super-resolution [17,18], deblurring [19,20], dehazing [21,22], which also include deraining [23–32]. These methods learn a mapping between input rainy images and their corresponding clean version using CNN/RNN based models. Some of them use an attention mechanism to pay attention to depth [10], heavy rain regions [33] or density [28]. However, to the best of our knowledge, there are few deep deraining works which try to remove rain via scene understanding [34].

2.2 Video Deraining

Video deraining is to obtain a clean video from an input rainy video. Compared with single image deraining, methods for video deraining can not only learn the spatial information, but also leverage temporal information in removing rain.

Traditional methods try to use prior-based methods to use the temporal context and motion information [35,36]. Researches formulate rain streaks based on their intrinsic characteristics [37–41] or propose some learning-based methods to improve the performance of deraining models [42–46]. For example, Santhaseelan et al. [39] and Barnum et al. [47] extract phase congruence features and Fourier domain features, respectively, to remove rain streaks. Chen et al. [42] apply photo-metric and chromatic constraints to detect rain and utilize filters to remove rain in the pixel level.

Deep learning methods are also proposed for video deraining [48–51]. Chen et al. [50] propose a robust deep deraining model via applying super-pixel segmentation to decompose the scene into depth consistent unites. Liu et al. [48] depict rain streaks via a hybrid rain model, and then present a dynamic routing residue recurrent network via integrating the hybrid model and using motion information. Yang et al. [51] consider the additional degradation factors in real world and propose a two-stage recurrent network for video deraining. Their model is able to capture more reliable motion information at the first stage and keep the motion consistency between frames at the second stage. Although these methods use the information of multiple rainy images, all of them extract features from a sequence of monocular frames and ignore the stereo views.

2.3   Stereo Deraining

Stereo images provide more information from cross views and have thus been utilized to improve the performance of various computer vision tasks, including traditional problems [1,4,7] and novel tasks [52–55]. However, there are few methods that leverage the stereo images to remove rain so far. Yamashit *et al.* [56] remove the rain via utilizing disparities between stereo images to detect positions of noises and estimate true disparities of images regions hidden into rain. In order to obtain the deraining left-view images, Kim *et al.* [57] warp the spatially adjacent right-view frames and subtract warped frames from the original frames. However, these traditional methods do not consider the importance of semantic information. Meanwhile, the strong capability of learning features implied in deep neural networks is also ignored by them.

3   The Semantic-Aware Deraining Module

The ultimate goal of our work is to recover the deraining images from their corresponding rainy versions. In order to improve the capability of our model, a semantic-aware deraining module is proposed to learn semantic features based on clean images, rainy images and semantic labels. In this section, we will first introduce the consolidation of different tasks in Sect. 3.1 and how to train the proposed module based on images and semantic-annotated images in Sect. 3.2. Then, a semantic-rethinking loop is discussed in Sect. 3.3 to further enhance our module and extract powerful features.

3.1   The Consolidation of Different Tasks

Currently, most deep deraining methods directly learn the transformation from rainy images to derained ones [23]. Inspired by [10], which proposes a depth-aware network to jointly learn depth estimation and image deraining via two different sub-networks. In this paper, an autoencoder architecture is employed to merge different tasks in the learning stage. Figure 2 illustrates the architecture of the proposed module. Images are input into the encoder of the proposed module to extract semantic features F. Then the semantic features F combined with a task label T are fed into the following decoder architecture to obtain a prediction P corresponding to label T. Based on different task labels like *deraining* or *scene understanding*, different outputs will be obtained. The learning stage can be formulated as

$$P = D(E(I), T), \qquad (4)$$

where E and D are the encoder and decoder of $SADM$, respectively. I is the input image. T represents the label of different tasks. Based on the output of the encoder and T, different predictions will be derived.

The branch of image deraining can be denoted as

$$I_{de} = \sigma_{de}(P \mid T_{de}), \qquad (5)$$

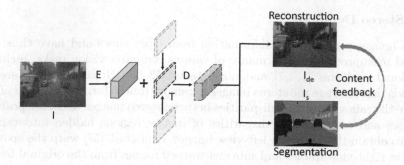

Fig. 2. The architecture of the proposed semantic-aware deraining module. Rainy images are fed into the encoder to extract features. Then the decoders generate deraining and segmentation results for different tasks.

where T_{de} corresponds to the label of deraining image. σ_{de} is the mapping function.

The branch of understanding scenes can be denoted as

$$I_{seg} = \sigma_{seg}(P \mid T_{seg}), \tag{6}$$

where T_{seg} corresponds to the semantic segmentation label. σ_{seg} is a softmax function.

Based on the conditional architecture [58], the proposed $SADM$ can jointly learn scene understanding and image deraining, which can extract more powerful semantic-aware features via sharing the information learned from different tasks, therefore being beneficial to multiple tasks.

3.2 Image Deraining and Scene Segmentation

Image Deraining. When T is set to T_{de}, the output of the proposed module is the deraining image. To learn the image deraining model, we compute the image reconstruction loss based on the MSE loss function:

$$\mathcal{L}_{de} = ||I_c - \sigma_{de}(D(E(I_{rainy}), T_{de}))||^2, \tag{7}$$

where I_c is the clean image.

Scene Segmentation. Most existing deraining methods focus on pixel-level loss function and thus fail to model the geometric and semantic information. This makes it difficult for models to understand the input image and generate deraining results with favorable details. To address this problem, we remove rain from rainy images by leveraging semantic information. The learning process of scene understanding can be denoted as

$$\mathcal{L}_{seg} = \sigma_h(I_{seg}^{gt}, I_{seg}), \tag{8}$$

where I_{seg} and I_{seg}^{gt} indicate the scene understanding of the model and ground truth labels from auxiliary training sets. σ_h is the cross-entropy loss function.

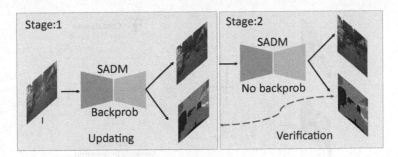

Fig. 3. The Semantic-rethinking Loop. During training, rainy images are fed into *SADM* to generate deraining and segmentation results in stage I. Then the deraining images are utilized to generate segmentation results again in stage II. Through comparing the two segmentation results from rainy and deraining images, *SADM* can better understand scenes and remove the undesired rain. *SADM*s in the two stages share the weights.

3.3 Semantic-Rethinking Loop

Semantic information plays an important role in various tasks of computer vision [59–64]. In order to further enhance the semantic understanding of our model and help remove rain, a semantic-rethinking loop is proposed to refine the error-prone semantic understanding. Figure 3 illustrates its scheme. It consists of an "updating" part and a "verification" part, whose core architecture is the semantic-aware deraining module, which has been illustrated in Fig. 2.

In the training stage, the "updating" part takes a rainy image as input, and then generates the deraining image and semantic segmentation. Loss functions introduced in above sections are calculated and then update the weights of layers in the semantic-aware deraining module. Then the deraining image obtained in the "updating" part is fed into the "verification" part to obtain new semantic segmentation. The semantic understanding can improve the performance of deraining, which will be demonstrated in the next section. However, rain increases the difficulty of scene understanding. Via comparing segmentation results in different parts and pushing them to be close, *SADM* can better understand scenes and thus better deraining. Both "updating" and "verification" parts employ the semantic-aware deraining module. The main difference between the "updating" and "verification" parts is that the weights in semantic-aware deraining module are updated in the "updating" part but fixed in the "verification" part. The semantic-rethinking loop provides the content feedback from the coarse-deraining image and improves the semantic understanding of *SADM*. In the testing stage, only the core semantic-aware deraining model is utilized to remove rain from images. The loss function can be noted as

$$\mathcal{L}_{con} = ||I_{seg}^{ver} - I_{seg}^{up}||, \qquad (9)$$

where I_{seg}^{ver} and I_{seg}^{up} are the semantic segmentation results from the "verification" and "updating" parts, respectively.

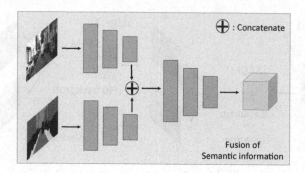

Fig. 4. The architecture of *SFNet*. The coarse deraining images and semantic segmentation results from *SADM* are fed into *SFNet* to generate features volume with semantic information.

4   The Paired Rain Removal Network

In order to remove rain from stereo images, we further present a *PRRNet* based on *SADM*. The overall of the proposed network will firstly be introduced in Sect. 4.1, and then two core sub-networks will be discussed in Sect. 4.2 and 4.3. Finally, the objective functions to train the proposed model will be presented in Sect. 4.4.

4.1   Network Architecture

PRRNet consists of three sub-networks, *i.e.*, *SADM*, Semantic-Fusion Net (*SFNet*) and View-Fusion Net (*VFNet*). *SADM* is introduced in Sect. 3 to jointly remove rain and understand semantic information. Semantic-Fusion Net is utilized to combine the semantic information with coarse deraining images, while View-Fusion Net is to combine information from different views to obtain final deraining images. Due to the above-mentioned stereo semantic-aware deraining module, the proposed *PRRNet* simultaneously considers cross views and semantic information to help remove rain from images.

4.2   SFNet

The architecture of *SFNet* is shown in Fig. 4. The input is semantic segmentation and coarse deraining images from *SADM*. Given that the semantic information can help remove rain, we first process them individually and concatenate them, and then forward them into the following layers, to generate feature volume, which is utilized for generating final deraining results.

4.3   VFNet

Figure 5 illustrates the architecture of *VFNet*. The input is extracted fusion features from *SFNet*. The features extracted from the right view are helpful to

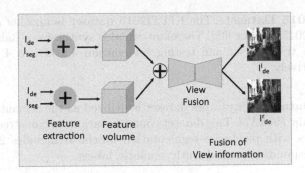

Fig. 5. The architecture of *VFNet*. Features volumes from stereo images are fused to generate final stereo deraining images.

remove the rain in the left-view image. Similarly, removing the rain from the right-view image also takes advantage of features captured from the left-view image. Through the *VFNet*, the final finer deraining stereo images are obtained. The loss function in this part can be denoted as

$$\mathcal{L}_{view} = ||I_{de}^{left} - I_{gt}^{left}|| + ||I_{de}^{right} - I_{gt}^{right}||, \tag{10}$$

where I_{de}^{left} and I_{de}^{right} are stereo deraining images from *VFNet*, respectively. I_{gt}^{left} and I_{gt}^{right} are the clean version of the stereo images.

4.4 Objective Functions

The loss function consists of two kinds of data terms, which are calculated based on semantic understanding and deraining reconstruction images. The final loss function can be written as

$$\mathcal{L}_f = \mathcal{L}_{de} + \lambda_1 \mathcal{L}_{seg} + \lambda_2 \mathcal{L}_{con} + \lambda_3 \mathcal{L}_{view}, \tag{11}$$

where $\mathcal{L}_{de}$ and $\mathcal{L}_{view}$ are utilized to remove the rain from rainy images, and $\mathcal{L}_{seg}$ and $\mathcal{L}_{con}$ push the model to understand scenes better, which are helpful for stereo deraining. λ_1, λ_2 and λ_3 are three parameters to balance different loss functions, which are set as 1.0, 0.2 and 1.0, respectively.

5 Experiments

5.1 Datasets

RainKITTI2012 Dataset. To the best of our knowledge, there are no benchmark datasets that provide stereo rainy images and their corresponding ground-truth clean version. In this paper, we first use Photoshop to create a synthetic RainKITTI2012 dataset based on the public KITTI stereo 2012 dataset [65]. The training set contains 4,062 image pairs from various scenarios, and the testing set contains 4,085 image pairs. The size of images is 1242 × 375.

RainKITTI2015 Dataset. The KITTI2015 dataset is another set from the KITTI stereo 2015 dataset [65]. Therefore, we also synthesize a RainKITTI2015 dataset, whose training set and testing set contain $4,200$ and $4,189$ pairs of images, respectively.

Cityscapes Dataset. Cityscapes dataset is utilized as the semantic segmentation data to train *PRRNet*. This dataset contains various urban street scenes and provides images with pixel-wise segmentation labels. It includes $2,975$ images and their corresponding ground truth semantic labels.

RainCityscapes Dataset. This dataset is built by Hu *et al.* [10] based on the Cityscapes dataset [66]. The training set contains $9,432$ rainy images and the corresponding clean images and depth labels. For evaluation, the testing set contains $1,188$ images. We use this dataset to evaluate the performance of monocular deraining.

5.2   Implementation Details

SADM is an encoder-decoder architecture. The encoder network consists of 13 CNN layers, which is initialized by a VGG16 network pre-trained for object classification. The decoder also has 13 CNN layers. *SFNet* contains three CNN layers $(32 \times 3 \times 3)$ which are utilized to fuse the semantic information. *VFNet* contains five ResBlocks [67] to generate final deraining results. Each ResBlock consists of three CNN layers of $64 \times 3 \times 3$ kernels and two ReLU activation layers. The proposed *PRRNet* is trained with Pytorch library. The base learning rate is set to 10^{-4} and then declined to 10^{-5}. The model is updated with the batch size of 2 during the training stage. The branches of deraining and segmentation in *SADM* are optimized based on the data from RainKITTI2012/2015 and Cityscapes, respectively.

5.3   Ablation Study

The proposed *PRRNet* takes advantage of semantic information to remove rain from images. In order to show the effectiveness of semantic information, we compare the performance of our model with that which is trained without semantic information. Another advantage of *PRRNet* is that it fuses the varying information in corresponding pixels across two stereo views to remove rain. Therefore, we also compare models trained on monocular and stereo images. Table 1 and Fig. 6 show the quantitative and qualitative comparison results. *PRRNet(D)* is the model trained on monocular images with the single deraining task. *PRRNet(D+S)* is the one trained on monocular images with both deraining and segmentation tasks. *PRRNet(D+S+L)* is the model trained on monocular images with the above two tasks plus the semantic-rethinking loop. *PRRNet(stereo)* is our full model trained based on stereo images.

Table 1. Ablation study on the RainKITTI2012 dataset.

Methods	PSNR	SSIM
PRRNet(D)	30.71	0.923
PRRNet(D+S)	31.56	0.928
PRRNet(D+S+L)	31.89	0.930
PRRNet(stereo)	33.01	0.936

(a) Input   (b) PRRNet(D)   (c) PRRNet(D+S)

(d) PRRNet(D+S+L)   (e) PRRNet(stereo)   (f) Ground truth

Fig. 6. Deraining evaluation of different baseline models on RainKITTI2012.

The results in Table 1 suggest that, the plain *PRRNet(D)* accomplishes the task fairly well. Additionally considering the semantic segmentation task, *PRRNet(D+S)* improves the performance. With the semantic-rethinking loop, the results are further improved by *PRRNet(D+S+L)*. However, the improvement is not as significant as that from *PRRNet(D+S+L)* to *PRRNet(stereo)* in the stereo case. This is also verified by the qualitative results in Fig. 6. Additional components incrementally improve the visibility of the input image, and the image generated by *PRRNet(stereo)* is the closest to the ground truth.

5.4 Stereo Deraining

We quantitatively and qualitatively compare our *PRRNet* with current state-of-the-art methods, which include DDN [27], DID-MDN [28], DAF-Net [10] and DeHRain [33]. Table 2 and Table 3 show the quantitative results on our synthesized RainKITTI2012 and RainKITTI2015 datasets, respectively. In both tables, our monocular version, *PRRNet(monocular)*, outperforms the existing state-of-the-art methods, with remarkable gain. The model *PRRNet(stereo)* achieves the best performance with additional improvement. This demonstrates the superiority of stereo deraining over monocular deraining.

(a) Left input   (b) DAF-Net   (c) DeHRain   (d) Ours   (e) GT

(f) Right input   (g) DAF-Net   (h) DeHRain   (i) Ours   (j) GT

Fig. 7. Qualitative evaluation of current SOTA models on RainKITTI2012.

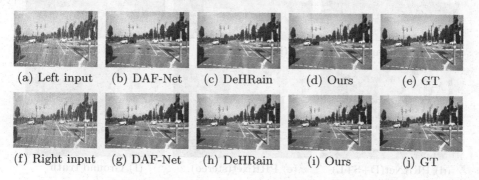

(a) Left input   (b) DAF-Net   (c) DeHRain   (d) Ours   (e) GT

(f) Right input   (g) DAF-Net   (h) DeHRain   (i) Ours   (j) GT

Fig. 8. Qualitative evaluation of current SOTA models on RainKITTI2015.

Figures 7 and 8 compare the qualitative performances between our method *PRRNet(stereo)* and various state-of-the-art methods. The results produced by our method exhibit the smallest portion of artifacts, by referring to the ground truths.

5.5 Monocular Deraining

The proposed *PRRNet* is not only able to remove rain from stereo images, but also has the advantage of removing rain from a single image with its monocular version. In this section, we also evaluate it on the monocular dataset RainCityscapes. We compare the *PRRNet*'s monocular version, *PRRNet(monocular)*, with the state-of-the-art methods, including DID-MDN [28], RESCAN [29], JOB [13], GMMLP [16], DSC [69], DCPDN [68], and DAF-Net [10], from both quantitative and qualitative aspects.

The quantitative results on the RainCityscapes dataset are shown in Table 4. DID-MDN [28] and DCPDN [68] perform well and DAF-Net [10] outperforms these two methods. Our monocular version *PRRNet(monocular)* achieves the best performance compared with all the compared methods on this task, revealing the effectiveness of taking semantic segmentation into consideration and the

Table 2. Quantitative evaluation on the RainKITTI2012 dataset.

Methods	PSNR	SSIM
DDN [26]	29.43	0.904
DID-MDN [28]	29.14	0.901
DAF-Net [10]	30.44	0.914
DeHRain [33]	31.02	0.923
PRRNet(monocular)	**31.89**	**0.930**
PRRNet(stereo)	**33.01**	**0.936**

Table 3. Quantitative evaluation on the RainKITTI2015 dataset.

Methods	PSNR	SSIM
DDN [26]	29.23	0.906
DID-MDN [28]	28.97	0.899
DAF-Net [10]	30.17	0.915
DeHRain [33]	30.84	0.921
PRRNet(monocular)	**31.64**	**0.932**
PRRNet(stereo)	**32.58**	**0.937**

semantic-rethinking loop. Figure 9 compares its qualitative performance with different methods. The results show that the monocular version of our *PRRNet* also achieves the best performance in terms of monocular image deraining.

5.6 Evaluation on Real-World Images

To further verify the effectiveness of our method, we show its performance of deraining on the real world rainy images. Figure 10 shows the qualitative results on two exemplar images from the Internet. Compared to other competing methods, the proposed method achieves better performance via understanding the scene structure. For example, DAF-Net seems to generate well-derained images,

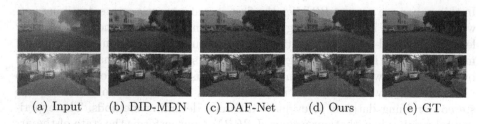

(a) Input   (b) DID-MDN   (c) DAF-Net   (d) Ours   (e) GT

Fig. 9. Qualitative evaluation of current state-of-the-art models on the RainCityscapes dataset.

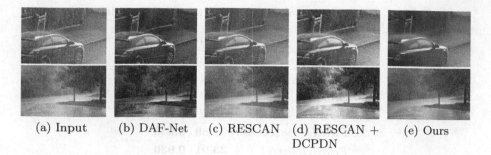

(a) Input   (b) DAF-Net   (c) RESCAN   (d) RESCAN +   (e) Ours
                                                       DCPDN

Fig. 10. Qualitative evaluation on real rainy images. From left to right are the input images, DAF-Net [10], RESCAN [29], RESCAN + DCPDN [68] and ours, respectively.

Table 4. Quantitative evaluation of current state-of-the-art models on the RainCityscapes dataset.

Methods	PSNR	SSIM
DID-MDN [28]	28.43	0.9349
RESCAN [29]	24.49	0.8852
JOB [13]	15.10	0.7592
GMMLP [16]	17.80	0.8169
DSC [69]	16.25	0.7746
DCPDN [68]	28.52	0.9277
DAF-Net [10]	30.06	0.9530
PRRNet(monocular)	**31.44**	**0.9688**

but the produced derained images suffer from color distortion (*e.g.*, the colors turn dark in the results). RESCAN and RESCAN+DCPDN perform worse than our method in removing rain.

6   Conclusion

In this paper, we present *PRRNet*, the first stereo semantic-aware deraining network, for stereo image deraining. Different from previous methods which only learn from pixel-level loss functions or monocular information, the proposed model advances image deraining by leveraging semantic information extracted by a semantic-aware deraining model, as well as visual deviation between two views fused by two Fusion Nets, *i.e.*, *SFNet* and *VFNet*. We also synthesize two stereo deraining datasets to evaluate different deraining methods. The experimental results show that our proposed *PRRNet* outperforms the state-of-the-art methods on both monocular and stereo image deraining.

Acknowledgment. This work is funded in part by the ARC Centre of Excellence for Robotics Vision (CE140100016), ARC-Discovery (DP 190102261) and ARC-LIEF (190100080) grants. The authors gratefully acknowledge NVIDIA for GPU gift.

References

1. Godard, C., Mac Aodha, O., Brostow, G.J.: Unsupervised monocular depth estimation with left-right consistency. In: Proceedings of the IEEE Conference on Computer Vision and Pattern Recognition (CVPR) (2017)
2. Liu, F., Shen, C., Lin, G.: Deep convolutional neural fields for depth estimation from a single image. In: Proceedings of the IEEE Conference on Computer Vision and Pattern Recognition (CVPR) (2015)
3. Riegler, G., Liao, Y., Donne, S., Koltun, V., Geiger, A.: Connecting the dots: learning representations for active monocular depth estimation. In: Proceedings of the IEEE Conference on Computer Vision and Pattern Recognition (CVPR) (2019)
4. Eslami, S.A., Heess, N., Weber, T., Tassa, Y., Szepesvari, D., Hinton, G.E., et al.: Attend, infer, repeat: fast scene understanding with generative models. In: Advances in Neural Information Processing Systems (NeurIPS) (2016)
5. Shao, J., Kang, K., Change Loy, C., Wang, X.: Deeply learned attributes for crowded scene understanding. In: Proceedings of the IEEE Conference on Computer Vision and Pattern Recognition (CVPR) (2015)
6. Zhao, H., Shi, J., Qi, X., Wang, X., Jia, J.: Pyramid scene parsing network. In: Proceedings of the IEEE Conference on Computer Vision and Pattern Recognition (CVPR) (2017)
7. Luo, W., Schwing, A.G., Urtasun, R.: Efficient deep learning for stereo matching. In: Proceedings of the IEEE Conference on Computer Vision and Pattern Recognition (CVPR) (2016)
8. Chang, J.R., Chen, Y.S.: Pyramid stereo matching network. In: Proceedings of the IEEE Conference on Computer Vision and Pattern Recognition (CVPR) (2018)
9. Pang, J., Sun, W., Ren, J.S., Yang, C., Yan, Q.: Cascade residual learning: a two-stage convolutional neural network for stereo matching. In: Proceedings of the IEEE International Conference on Computer Vision (ICCV) (2017)
10. Hu, X., Fu, C.W., Zhu, L., Heng, P.A.: Depth-attentional features for single-image rain removal. In: Proceedings of the IEEE Conference on Computer Vision and Pattern Recognition (CVPR) (2019)
11. Kang, L.W., Lin, C.W., Fu, Y.H.: Automatic single-image-based rain streaks removal via image decomposition. IEEE Trans. Image Process. (TIP) **21**, 1742–1755 (2011)
12. Huang, D.A., Kang, L.W., Wang, Y.C.F., Lin, C.W.: Self-learning based image decomposition with applications to single image denoising. IEEE Trans. Multimedia (TMM) **16**, 83–93 (2013)
13. Zhu, L., Fu, C.W., Lischinski, D., Heng, P.A.: Joint bi-layer optimization for single-image rain streak removal. In: Proceedings of the IEEE International Conference on Computer Vision (ICCV) (2017)
14. Chen, Y.L., Hsu, C.T.: A generalized low-rank appearance model for spatio-temporally correlated rain streaks. In: Proceedings of the IEEE International Conference on Computer Vision (ICCV) (2013)

15. Zhang, H., Patel, V.M.: Convolutional sparse and low-rank coding-based rain streak removal. In: IEEE Winter Conference on Applications of Computer Vision (WACV) (2017)
16. Li, Y., Tan, R.T., Guo, X., Lu, J., Brown, M.S.: Rain streak removal using layer priors. In: Proceedings of the IEEE Conference on Computer Vision and Pattern Recognition (CVPR) (2016)
17. Ledig, C., et al.: Photo-realistic single image super-resolution using a generative adversarial network. In: Proceedings of the IEEE Conference on Computer Vision and Pattern Recognition (CVPR) (2017)
18. Johnson, J., Alahi, A., Fei-Fei, L.: Perceptual losses for real-time style transfer and super-resolution. In: Leibe, B., Matas, J., Sebe, N., Welling, M. (eds.) ECCV 2016. LNCS, vol. 9906, pp. 694–711. Springer, Cham (2016). https://doi.org/10.1007/978-3-319-46475-6_43
19. Zhang, K., Luo, W., Zhong, Y., Ma, L., Liu, W., Li, H.: Adversarial spatio-temporal learning for video deblurring. IEEE Trans. Image Process. (TIP) **28**, 291–301 (2018)
20. Zhang, K., et al.: Deblurring by realistic blurring. In: Proceedings of the IEEE Conference on Computer Vision and Pattern Recognition (CVPR) (2020)
21. Ren, W., Liu, S., Zhang, H., Pan, J., Cao, X., Yang, M.-H.: Single image dehazing via multi-scale convolutional neural networks. In: Leibe, B., Matas, J., Sebe, N., Welling, M. (eds.) ECCV 2016. LNCS, vol. 9906, pp. 154–169. Springer, Cham (2016). https://doi.org/10.1007/978-3-319-46475-6_10
22. Li, B., Peng, X., Wang, Z., Xu, J., Feng, D.: AOD-Net: all-in-one dehazing network. In: Proceedings of the IEEE International Conference on Computer Vision (ICCV) (2017)
23. Li, S., et al.: Single image deraining: a comprehensive benchmark analysis. In: Proceedings of the IEEE Conference on Computer Vision and Pattern Recognition (CVPR) (2019)
24. Zhang, H., Sindagi, V., Patel, V.M.: Image de-raining using a conditional generative adversarial network. IEEE Trans. Circuits Syst. Video Technol. (TCSVT) (2019)
25. Fu, X., Huang, J., Ding, X., Liao, Y., Paisley, J.: Clearing the skies: a deep network architecture for single-image rain removal. IEEE Trans. Image Process. (TIP) **26**, 2944–2956 (2017)
26. Fu, X., Huang, J., Zeng, D., Huang, Y., Ding, X., Paisley, J.: Removing rain from single images via a deep detail network. In: Proceedings of the IEEE Conference on Computer Vision and Pattern Recognition (CVPR) (2017)
27. Yang, W., Tan, R.T., Feng, J., Liu, J., Guo, Z., Yan, S.: Deep joint rain detection and removal from a single image. In: Proceedings of the IEEE Conference on Computer Vision and Pattern Recognition (CVPR) (2017)
28. Zhang, H., Patel, V.M.: Density-aware single image de-raining using a multi-stream dense network. In: Proceedings of the IEEE Conference on Computer Vision and Pattern Recognition (CVPR) (2018)
29. Li, X., Wu, J., Lin, Z., Liu, H., Zha, H.: Recurrent squeeze-and-excitation context aggregation net for single image deraining. In: Ferrari, V., Hebert, M., Sminchisescu, C., Weiss, Y. (eds.) ECCV 2018. LNCS, vol. 11211, pp. 262–277. Springer, Cham (2018). https://doi.org/10.1007/978-3-030-01234-2_16
30. Eigen, D., Krishnan, D., Fergus, R.: Restoring an image taken through a window covered with dirt or rain. In: Proceedings of the IEEE International Conference on Computer Vision (ICCV) (2013)

31. Qian, R., Tan, R.T., Yang, W., Su, J., Liu, J.: Attentive generative adversarial network for raindrop removal from a single image. In: Proceedings of the IEEE Conference on Computer Vision and Pattern Recognition (CVPR) (2018)
32. Zheng, Y., Yu, X., Liu, M., Zhang, S.: Residual multiscale based single image deraining. In: British Machine Vision Conference (BMVC) (2019)
33. Li, R., Cheong, L.F., Tan, R.T.: Heavy rain image restoration: integrating physics model and conditional adversarial learning. In: Proceedings of the IEEE Conference on Computer Vision and Pattern Recognition (CVPR) (2019)
34. Long, J., Shelhamer, E., Darrell, T.: Fully convolutional networks for semantic segmentation. In: Proceedings of the IEEE Conference on Computer Vision and Pattern Recognition (CVPR) (2015)
35. Garg, K., Nayar, S.K.: Detection and removal of rain from videos. In: Proceedings of the IEEE Conference on Computer Vision and Pattern Recognition (CVPR) (2004)
36. Garg, K., Nayar, S.K.: Photorealistic rendering of rain streaks. ACM Trans. Graph. (TOG) 25, 996–1002 (2006)
37. Zhang, X., Li, H., Qi, Y., Leow, W.K., Ng, T.K.: Rain removal in video by combining temporal and chromatic properties. In: IEEE International Conference on Multimedia and Expo (ICME) (2006)
38. Liu, P., Xu, J., Liu, J., Tang, X.: Pixel based temporal analysis using chromatic property for removing rain from videos. Comput. Inf. Sci. 2, 50–53 (2009)
39. Santhaseelan, V., Asari, V.K.: Utilizing local phase information to remove rain from video. Int. J. Comput. Vision 112(1), 71–89 (2014). https://doi.org/10.1007/s11263-014-0759-8
40. Brewer, N., Liu, N.: Using the shape characteristics of rain to identify and remove rain from video. In: Joint IAPR International Workshops on Statistical Techniques in Pattern Recognition (SPR) and Structural and Syntactic Pattern Recognition (SSPR) (2008)
41. Jiang, T.X., Huang, T.Z., Zhao, X.L., Deng, L.J., Wang, Y.: A novel tensor-based video rain streaks removal approach via utilizing discriminatively intrinsic priors. In: Proceedings of the IEEE Conference on Computer Vision and Pattern Recognition (CVPR) (2017)
42. Chen, J., Chau, L.P.: A rain pixel recovery algorithm for videos with highly dynamic scenes. IEEE Trans. Image Process. (TIP) 23, 1097–1104 (2013)
43. Tripathi, A., Mukhopadhyay, S.: Video post processing: low-latency spatiotemporal approach for detection and removal of rain. IET Image Process. 6, 181–196 (2012)
44. Kim, J.H., Sim, J.Y., Kim, C.S.: Video deraining and desnowing using temporal correlation and low-rank matrix completion. IEEE Trans. Image Process. (TIP) 24, 2658–2670 (2015)
45. Wei, W., Yi, L., Xie, Q., Zhao, Q., Meng, D., Xu, Z.: Should we encode rain streaks in video as deterministic or stochastic? In: Proceedings of the IEEE International Conference on Computer Vision (ICCV) (2017)
46. Ren, W., Tian, J., Han, Z., Chan, A., Tang, Y.: Video desnowing and deraining based on matrix decomposition. In: Proceedings of the IEEE Conference on Computer Vision and Pattern Recognition (CVPR) (2017)
47. Barnum, P.C., Narasimhan, S., Kanade, T.: Analysis of rain and snow in frequency space. Int. J. Comput. Vision (IJCV) 86, 256 (2010). https://doi.org/10.1007/s11263-008-0200-2
48. Liu, J., Yang, W., Yang, S., Guo, Z.: D3R-Net: dynamic routing residue recurrent network for video rain removal. IEEE Trans. Image Process. (TIP) 28, 699–712 (2018)

49. Liu, J., Yang, W., Yang, S., Guo, Z.: Erase or fill? Deep joint recurrent rain removal and reconstruction in videos. In: Proceedings of the IEEE Conference on Computer Vision and Pattern Recognition (CVPR) (2018)
50. Chen, J., Tan, C.H., Hou, J., Chau, L.P., Li, H.: Robust video content alignment and compensation for rain removal in a CNN framework. In: Proceedings of the IEEE Conference on Computer Vision and Pattern Recognition (CVPR) (2018)
51. Yang, W., Liu, J., Feng, J.: Frame-consistent recurrent video deraining with dual-level flow. In: Proceedings of the IEEE Conference on Computer Vision and Pattern Recognition (CVPR) (2019)
52. Jeon, D.S., Baek, S.H., Choi, I., Kim, M.H.: Enhancing the spatial resolution of stereo images using a parallax prior. In: Proceedings of the IEEE Conference on Computer Vision and Pattern Recognition (CVPR) (2018)
53. Li, B., Lin, C.W., Shi, B., Huang, T., Gao, W., Jay Kuo, C.C.: Depth-aware stereo video retargeting. In: Proceedings of the IEEE Conference on Computer Vision and Pattern Recognition (CVPR) (2018)
54. Chen, D., Yuan, L., Liao, J., Yu, N., Hua, G.: Stereoscopic neural style transfer. In: Proceedings of the IEEE Conference on Computer Vision and Pattern Recognition (CVPR) (2018)
55. Zhou, S., Zhang, J., Zuo, W., Xie, H., Pan, J., Ren, J.S.: DAVANet: stereo deblurring with view aggregation. In: Proceedings of the IEEE Conference on Computer Vision and Pattern Recognition (CVPR) (2019)
56. Tanaka, Y., Yamashita, A., Kaneko, T., Miura, K.T.: Removal of adherent water-drops from images acquired with a stereo camera system. IEICE Trans. Inf. Syst. (IEICE TIS) (2006)
57. Kim, J.H., Sim, J.Y., Kim, C.S.: Stereo video deraining and desnowing based on spatiotemporal frame warping. In: The IEEE International Conference on Image Processing (ICIP) (2014)
58. Zhao, F., Zhao, J., Yan, S., Feng, J.: Dynamic conditional networks for few-shot learning. In: Ferrari, V., Hebert, M., Sminchisescu, C., Weiss, Y. (eds.) ECCV 2018. LNCS, vol. 11219, pp. 20–36. Springer, Cham (2018). https://doi.org/10.1007/978-3-030-01267-0_2
59. Shen, Z., Lai, W.S., Xu, T., Kautz, J., Yang, M.H.: Deep semantic face deblurring. In: Proceedings of the IEEE Conference on Computer Vision and Pattern Recognition, pp. 8260–8269 (2018)
60. Shen, Z., Lai, W.-S., Xu, T., Kautz, J., Yang, M.-H.: Exploiting semantics for face image deblurring. Int. J. Comput. Vision **128**(7), 1829–1846 (2020). https://doi.org/10.1007/s11263-019-01288-9
61. Li, D., Rodriguez, C., Yu, X., Li, H.: Word-level deep sign language recognition from video: a new large-scale dataset and methods comparison. In: The IEEE Winter Conference on Applications of Computer Vision, pp. 1459–1469 (2020)
62. Li, D., Yu, X., Xu, C., Petersson, L., Li, H.: Transferring cross-domain knowledge for video sign language recognition. In: Proceedings of the IEEE/CVF Conference on Computer Vision and Pattern Recognition, pp. 6205–6214 (2020)
63. Zhang, J., et al.: UC-Net: uncertainty inspired RGB-D saliency detection via conditional variational autoencoders. In: Proceedings of the IEEE/CVF Conference on Computer Vision and Pattern Recognition, pp. 8582–8591 (2020)
64. Zhang, J., Yu, X., Li, A., Song, P., Liu, B., Dai, Y.: Weakly-supervised salient object detection via scribble annotations. In: Proceedings of the IEEE/CVF Conference on Computer Vision and Pattern Recognition, pp. 12546–12555 (2020)
65. Geiger, A., Lenz, P., Stiller, C., Urtasun, R.: Vision meets robotics: the KITTI dataset. Int. J. Robot. Res. (IJRR) **32**, 1231–1237 (2013)

66. Cordts, M., et al.: The cityscapes dataset for semantic urban scene understanding. In: Proceedings of the IEEE Conference on Computer Vision and Pattern Recognition (CVPR) (2016)
67. He, K., Zhang, X., Ren, S., Sun, J.: Deep residual learning for image recognition. In: Proceedings of the IEEE Conference on Computer Vision and Pattern Recognition (CVPR) (2016)
68. Zhang, H., Patel, V.M.: Densely connected pyramid dehazing network. In: Proceedings of the IEEE Conference on Computer Vision and Pattern Recognition (CVPR) (2018)
69. Luo, Y., Xu, Y., Ji, H.: Removing rain from a single image via discriminative sparse coding. In: Proceedings of the IEEE International Conference on Computer Vision (ICCV) (2015)

DBQ: A Differentiable Branch Quantizer for Lightweight Deep Neural Networks

Hassan Dbouk[1,2]($\boxtimes$), Hetul Sanghvi[2], Mahesh Mehendale[2], and Naresh Shanbhag[1]

[1] Department of Electrical and Computer Engineering,
University of Illinois at Urbana-Champaign, Urbana, USA
{hdbouk2,shanbhag}@illinois.edu
[2] Kilby Labs, Texas Instruments Inc, Dallas, USA
{hetul,m-mehendale}@ti.com

Abstract. Deep neural networks have achieved state-of-the art performance on various computer vision tasks. However, their deployment on resource-constrained devices has been hindered due to their high computational and storage complexity. While various complexity reduction techniques, such as lightweight network architecture design and parameter quantization, have been successful in reducing the cost of implementing these networks, these methods have often been considered orthogonal. In reality, existing quantization techniques fail to replicate their success on lightweight architectures such as MobileNet. To this end, we present a novel fully differentiable non-uniform quantizer that can be seamlessly mapped onto efficient ternary-based dot product engines. We conduct comprehensive experiments on CIFAR-10, ImageNet, and Visual Wake Words datasets. The proposed quantizer (DBQ) successfully tackles the daunting task of aggressively quantizing lightweight networks such as MobileNetV1, MobileNetV2, and ShuffleNetV2. DBQ achieves state-of-the art results with minimal training overhead and provides the best (pareto-optimal) accuracy-complexity trade-off.

Keywords: Deep learning · Quantization · Low-complexity neural networks

1 Introduction

Deep neural networks (DNNs) have achieved state-of-the art accuracy on various computer vision tasks such as image classification [6,15] but at the expense of extremely high computational and storage complexity, e.g., ResNet-18 [6] needs

---

H. Dbouk—Work done while at Kilby Labs.

Electronic supplementary material The online version of this chapter (https://doi.org/10.1007/978-3-030-58583-9_6) contains supplementary material, which is available to authorized users.

© Springer Nature Switzerland AG 2020
A. Vedaldi et al. (Eds.): ECCV 2020, LNCS 12372, pp. 90–106, 2020.
https://doi.org/10.1007/978-3-030-58583-9_6

$\sim 10^{12}$ 1-b full adders (FAs) and 3.74×10^8-bits of activation and weight storage to achieve an accuracy of 70% on the ImageNet dataset. These high computational and storage costs inhibit the deployment of such DNNs on resource-constrained Edge devices. As a result, there is much interest in designing low-complexity DNNs without compromising their accuracy.

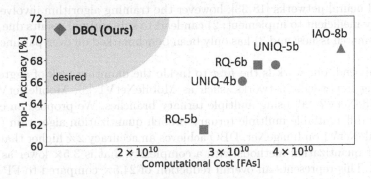

Fig. 1. The Top-1 accuracy on ImageNet vs. computational cost for MobileNetV1 achieved by state-of-the-art quantization methods (RQ [19], UNIQ [1], and IAO [13]). Our proposed method DBQ simultaneously achieves the highest accuracy and the lowest complexity.

There are two distinct approaches for reducing DNN complexity: 1) model compression [5] and quantization [10,22] of complex networks, and 2) the design of lightweight networks from scratch, e.g., MobileNet [8,27].

Model compression and quantization methods rely on the intrinsic over parameterization in complex networks to reduce their complexity. Such methods have proved to be very effective in reducing network complexity with negligible impact on its accuracy, e.g., ternary quantization of ResNet-18 weights [32] reduces its computational and storage complexity by 88% and 74%, respectively, at the expense of a drop in accuracy from 70.3% to 69.1%.

In the second approach, the design of lightweight networks such as MobileNet [8,27], SqueezeNet [11], ShuffleNet [34], ConDenseNet [9] have also shown tremendous success. Such networks exploit algorithmic properties such as factorizability of convolutions and utilize either 1×1 convolutions (SqueezeNet), grouped convolutions (ShuffleNet, ConDenseNet), or both (MobileNet). For example, MobileNetV1 [8] achieves comparable (or even higher) accuracy than its ResNet-18 floating-point (FP) counterpart but at a computational and storage complexity that are $3\times$ and $7\times$ lower, respectively.

In contrast, not much work has been done in model compression or quantization of lightweight networks and for a good reason – such networks are already irredundant leaving much less room for complexity reduction. Existing works [1,13,19,28,30] that quantize lightweight networks use fixed-point quantization with relatively high bitwidths (see Fig. 1) which offer limited reductions in complexity. In contrast, aggressive quantization schemes such as binarization [10,22] or ternarization [16,36] have been benchmarked on over-parameterized networks. In fact, ternarizing MobileNetV1 leads to a catastrophic drop in accuracy from 72.12% to 66.45% on ImageNet as we show in Sect. 4.3. In order to improve the performance of ternarized models while leveraging the simplicity of ternary-based arithmetic, one can construct a non-uniform quantizer as linear combinations of ternary values. Such formulation has already been proposed in the context of binarized neural networks [18,33], however the training algorithm involved is: 1) extremely inefficient to implement; 2) can lead to sub-optimal results due to gradient mismatch issues; and 3) has only been benchmarked on over-parameterized networks.

To this end, our work is the *first* to tackle the daunting task of aggressively quantizing lightweight networks, such as MobileNetV1 [8], MobileNetV2 [27], and ShuffleNetV2 [20] using multiple ternary branches. We propose an efficient and fully differentiable multiple ternary branch quantization algorithm (DBQ). For MobileNetV1 on ImageNet, DBQ achieves an accuracy 2% higher than state-of-the art quantization methods with a complexity that is 3.5× lower as shown in Fig. 1. This represents an overall reduction of 24.5× compared to FP with a 1.2% drop in accuracy.

Specifically, our contributions are:

1. We are the *first* to successfully ternarize lightweight networks (MobileNetV1, MobileNetV2, ShuffleNetV2) on ImageNet. This result is achieved by using DBQ with two ternary branches.
2. We present the *first fully differentiable* branched quantization algorithm (DBQ) for DNNs requiring minimal training overhead.
3. We show that DBQ outperforms state-of-the art methods in both accuracy and computational cost. Compared to state-of-the art quantization method RQ [19], DBQ drastically improves the Top-1 accuracy of MobileNetV1 on ImageNet from 61.50% to 70.92% at iso-model size accompanied by a 19% reduction in computational complexity.
4. For lightweight networks tackling real world applications, we show that DBQ with two ternary branches offers the best (pareto-optimal) accuracy-complexity trade-off compared to using one ternary branch with higher number of channels, at iso-model size.

2   Related Work

Reducing DNN complexity via quantization has been an active area of research over the past few years. A majority of such works either train the quantized network from scratch [10,16,22,24,33,36] or fine-tune a pre-trained model with quantization-in-the-loop [1,13,19,30,32,35]. Where retraining is not an option, [25] provides analytical guarantees on the minimum precision requirements of a pre-trained FP network given a budget on the accuracy drop from FP. Training based quantization works fall into two classes of methods: 1) estimation based methods [13,16,18,30,33], where the full-precision weights and activations are quantized in the forward path, and gradients are back-propagated through a non-differentiable quantizer function via a gradient estimator such as the Straight Through Estimator (STE) [2]; and 2) optimization based methods, where gradients flow directly from the full-precision weights to the cost function via an approximate differentiable quantizer [19,24,32], or by including an explicit quantization error term to the loss function [7,35]. Application of these methods can be categorized into three clusters:

Aggressive Quantization: Methods such as binarization and ternarization have been highly successful for reducing DNN complexity. BinaryNets [10] quantize both weights and activations of DNNs to ±1, while XNORNets [22] use a full-precision scalar to represent binarized weights in order to improve accuracy. Ternary Weight Networks (TWN) [16] quantize weights to $\{-1, 0, 1\}$ and leverage the resulting weight sparsity due to the '0' state to skip operations.

Table 1. The number of multiplications, additions, and parameters required by each layer type: first layer (FL), depthwise (DW), pointwise (PW), fully connected (FC), pooling layer (PL), and batch normalization (BN), for a single inference using MobileNetV1.

Layer type	Mults [%]	Adds [%]	Params [%]
FL	1.89	1.83	0.02
DW	3.03	2.72	1.05
PW	**94.02**	**94.37**	**74.19**
FC	0.18	0.18	24.22
PL	0	0.01	0
BN	0.88	0.89	0.52

Trained Ternary Quantization (TTQ) [36] proposes learning the ternary scales via back-prop. However, a major drawback of such methods is the resulting accuracy loss especially when applied to lightweight DNNs such as MobileNet. In Sect. 4.3, we show that ternarizing only the pointwise layers in MobileNetV1 on Imagenet, which correspond to ~94% of the total multiplication/additions (Table 1), incurs a massive accuracy loss (~5.67%) compared to the full-precision baseline. Hence, such methods are typically benchmarked on simple datasets such as CIFAR-10, or use over parameterized models such as AlexNet [15] or ResNet-18 [6] on ImageNet. In contrast, our proposed DBQ method is able to aggressively quantize the lightweight MobileNetV1 architecture with minimal loss in Top-1 accuracy (Fig. 1).

Non-uniform Quantization: These methods seek to improve the performance of binarized/ternarized models while leveraging their arithmetic simplicity, e.g., LQNets [33] and ABCNets [18], by quantizing weights and activations as linear combinations of binary values. The resulting non-uniform multi-bit quantization allows the computation of dot products to be carried out using binary arithmetic with appropriate scaling and addition. However, these methods suffer from two major drawbacks: 1) the design of their quantization functions is computationally expensive as it requires an iterative solution of a non-convex optimization problem per-layer per-forward pass during training, which results in a significant training time overhead in the range 1.4×–3.7× [33]; and 2) they suffer from gradient mismatch problems as they depend on the STE [2] method to compute the gradients during training. This renders the quantizer constructed by these methods to be sub-optimal, since they *estimate* the quantizer parameters by minimizing a *local* cost function, e.g., MSE. Moreover, these methods have been benchmarked only on over parameterized networks on ImageNet. Whereas our proposed DBQ method *learns* the multiple *ternary* branches by minimizing a *global* loss function since the proposed quantizer is fully differentiable, which enables the efficient training of similar non-uniform quantizers, while also eradicating the need for any gradient estimator.

Quantization of Lightweight DNNs: Recent works that quantize MobileNets either apply fixed-point quantization with uniform [13,19,28] or mixed [29,30] precision across layers. Hardware-Aware Quantization (HAQ) [30] proposes using reinforcement learning to learn the per-layer bit-precision for both weights and activations, whereas [29] learns the bit-precision via a reformulation of the quantizer function and relying on the STE for gradient computation. Integer-Arithmetic-Only (IAO) [13] proposes using 8-b quantization for accelerating the inference of MobileNets on hardware platforms such as Qualcom Hexagon and ARM NEON. Relaxed Quantization (RQ) [19] approximates the quantization function with a smooth differentiable approximate function, but the quantized values are still in fixed-point. Uniform Noise Injection Quantization (UNIQ) [1] proposes training a non-uniform quantizer using a special noise injection method that allows natural computation of gradients for quantized parameters. UNIQ uses a non-uniform quantizer requiring inefficient lookup tables and full precision multipliers/additions. Furthermore, all of these approaches use relatively high bitwidths (~6b−8b), and most even fail to bridge the accuracy gap between the quantized models and their full-precision baseline. In contrast, the proposed DBQ method is able to aggressively reduce the precision of the dominant (94%) PW layers of MobileNetV1 to two ternary parameters with negligible degradation in the Top-1 accuracy.

3   Differentiable Branched Quantizer (DBQ)

A ternary B-branch quantizer $Q(\mathbf{w})$ of a full precision weight vector $\mathbf{w} \in \mathbb{R}^D$ (Fig. 2(a)) is given by:

$$\mathbf{w}_q = Q(\mathbf{w}) = \sum_{j=1}^{B} \alpha_j \mathbf{w}_j \tag{1}$$

where $\mathbf{w}_j \in \{-1, 0, 1\}^D$ are the ternary branch weight vectors, and $\forall j \in [B]$: $\alpha_j > 0$ are per-branch scalars. In DBQ, we wish to learn all the network parameters which requires the quantizer function $Q(\mathbf{w})$ to be made differentiable. To do so, we first formulate a parametric form of $Q(\mathbf{w})$ in Sect. 3.1 and then employ a smooth 'temperature-controlled' approximation of the quantizer step function to establish its differentiability in Sect. 3.2.

3.1   Formulation of DBQ

We formulate the ternary B-branch quantizer in Fig. 2 as a $N = 3^B$-level non-uniform quantizer $Q(\mathbf{w}) : \mathbb{R}^D \to \mathcal{V}^D$ with quantization levels $\mathcal{V} = \{v_i\}_{i=1}^N$. Assuming that the quantization levels v_i's are sorted in ascending order, the $Q(\mathbf{w})$ can be written as a linear combination of $N-1$ step functions as shown below:

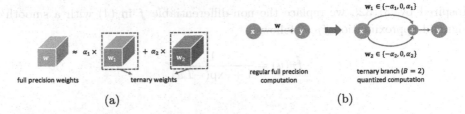

(a)   (b)

Fig. 2. Branched quantization of full precision weights: (a) as a linear combination of ternary weights, and (b) implemented as multiple parallel ternary branch operations to leverage the properties of ternary arithmetic for dot product computations.

$$Q(\mathbf{w}) = \sum_{i=1}^{N-1} \left[(v_{i+1} - v_i) f(\mathbf{w} - t_i) \right] - \frac{v_N - v_1}{2} \qquad (2)$$

where $f(\mathbf{u}) = [\mathbf{1}_{\{u_1 > 0\}}, ..., \mathbf{1}_{\{u_D > 0\}}]^T$ is an element-wise ideal step function, and $\{t_i\}_{i=1}^{N-1}$ are the quantizer thresholds. The $(v_N - v_1)/2$ term is the quantizer offset. We impose the ternary quantizer structure in (1) via the constraint:

$$v_i = \sum_{j=1}^{B} e_{i,j} \alpha_j \qquad (3)$$

where $e_{i,j} \in \{-1, 0, 1\}$, and thereby obtain the final quantizer expression:

$$Q(\mathbf{w}) = \gamma_2 \left[\sum_{i=1}^{N-1} \left[f(\gamma_1 \mathbf{w} - t_i) \sum_{j=1}^{B} b_{i,j} \alpha_j \right] - \sum_{j=1}^{B} \alpha_j \right] \qquad (4)$$

where $b_{i,j} = e_{i+1,j} - e_{i,j} \in \{-2, -1, 0, 1, 2\}\ \forall j \in [B]$ are *fixed* coefficients, and γ_1 & γ_2 are pre/post-quantization scales to ensure that the quantizer operates on normalized inputs. Thus, the branched quantizer is parametrized by $\mathcal{P}_Q = \{\alpha_1, ..., \alpha_B, \gamma_1, \gamma_2, t_1, ..., t_{N-1}\}$ and these all need to be learned.

In this paper, we focus on the $B = 2$ case, i.e., two ternary branch, as visualized in Fig. 3, with $N = 3^2 = 9$ different quantization levels v_i. In this case, (4) can be expanded as:

$$Q(\mathbf{w}) = \gamma_2 \Big[\alpha_2 f(\gamma_1 \mathbf{w} - t_1) + (\alpha_1 - \alpha_2) f(\gamma_1 \mathbf{w} - t_2) + (2\alpha_2 - \alpha_1) f(\gamma_1 \mathbf{w} - t_3)$$
$$+ (\alpha_1 - \alpha_2) f(\gamma_1 \mathbf{w} - t_4) + (\alpha_1 - \alpha_2) f(\gamma_1 \mathbf{w} - t_5) + (2\alpha_2 - \alpha_1) f(\gamma_1 \mathbf{w} - t_6) \quad (5)$$
$$+ (\alpha_1 - \alpha_2) f(\gamma_1 \mathbf{w} - t_7) + \alpha_2 f(\gamma_1 \mathbf{w} - t_8) - (\alpha_1 + \alpha_2) \Big]$$

3.2 Differentiability

Inspired by [31, 32], we replace the non-differentiable f in (4) with a smooth sigmoid approximation $\hat{f}_T$ as follows:

$$\hat{f}_T(u) = \frac{1}{1 + \exp(-Tu)} \qquad (6)$$

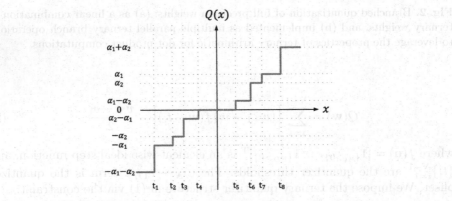

Fig. 3. Visualization of a two ternary (2T) branch quantizer with branch scales α_1 and α_2 assuming $\alpha_1 \geq \alpha_2 \geq \frac{\alpha_1}{2} \geq 0$.

where the *temperature* parameter T controls the approximation error, i.e.,:

$$e_T(u) = \hat{f}_T(u) - f(u) \xrightarrow[T \to \infty]{} 0 \qquad (7)$$

When learning the quantizer parameters $\mathcal{P}_Q$, the temperature T is increased gradually as the training converges so that $\hat{f}_T(u) \to f(u)$. The resultant differentiable quantizer $Q_T(\mathbf{w}) = \mathbf{w}_q = \mathbf{z}$ therefore enables a straightforward calculation of the gradients for all quantizer and model parameters w.r.t. loss function $\mathcal{L}$ as follows:

$$\frac{\partial \mathcal{L}}{\partial \gamma_2} = \frac{1}{\gamma_2} \sum_{k=1}^{D} \frac{\partial \mathcal{L}}{\partial z_k} z_k \tag{8}$$

$$\frac{\partial \mathcal{L}}{\partial \alpha_j} = \gamma_2 \sum_{k=1}^{D} \frac{\partial \mathcal{L}}{\partial z_k} \left[\sum_{i=1}^{N-1} \left[b_{i,j} g_{k,i} \right] - 1 \right] \tag{9}$$

$$\frac{\partial \mathcal{L}}{\partial t_i} = -\gamma_2 T \sum_{k=1}^{D} \frac{\partial \mathcal{L}}{\partial z_k} \left[h_{k,i} \sum_{j=1}^{B} b_{i,j} \alpha_j \right] \tag{10}$$

$$\frac{\partial \mathcal{L}}{\partial w_k} = \gamma_1 \gamma_2 T \frac{\partial \mathcal{L}}{\partial z_k} \sum_{i=1}^{N-1} \left[h_{k,i} \sum_{j=1}^{B} b_{i,j} \alpha_j \right] \tag{11}$$

$$\frac{\partial \mathcal{L}}{\partial \gamma_1} = \gamma_2 T \sum_{k=1}^{D} \frac{\partial \mathcal{L}}{\partial z_k} w_k \left[\sum_{i=1}^{N-1} \left[h_{k,i} \sum_{j=1}^{B} b_{i,j} \alpha_j \right] \right] \tag{12}$$

where $h_{k,i} = g_{k,i}(1 - g_{k,i})$ and $g_{k,i} = \hat{f}_T(\gamma_1 w_k - t_i)$ for brevity. By doing so, we eliminate the need for the STE and the expensive computational overhead introduced in estimation-based methods such as LQNet [33] or ABCNet [18]. Note that software frameworks such as PyTorch [21] automatically take care of computing these gradients so these don't need to be explicitly coded.

3.3   Implementation Details

Parameter Initialization: Initializing the quantizer parameters $\mathcal{P}_Q$ is performed once before training and requires an initial vector $\mathbf{w} \in \mathbb{R}^D$ which can be from a pre-trained network or from random initialization (training from scratch). The initialization procedure is as follows: 1) the post-quantization scale γ_2 is set to the maximum absolute value in $\mathbf{w}$, and the pre-quantization scale γ_1 is set to $1/\gamma_2$. This ensures that the quantizer operates on normalized parameters which facilitates the optimization of its parameters, and that the quantized values are of the same scale as the inputs; 2) to find the optimal thresholds $\{t_i\}_{i=1}^{N-1}$, we first compute the optimal N centroids $\{c_i\}_{i=1}^{N}$ of the normalized vector $\gamma_1 \mathbf{w}$ via k-means, and then $\forall i \in [N-1]$ we set t_i to be the midpoint of the interval $[c_i, c_{i+1}]$; and 3) a good initialization for $\{\alpha_j\}_{j=1}^{B}$ is found by solving for the optimal values that minimize the L_2 norm between the normalized vector $\gamma_1 \mathbf{w}$ and its quantized counterpart.

Training and Inference: During training, the proposed DBQ quantizer is used with the approximate smooth step function $\hat{f}_T$ for both forward and backward calculations ((4) & (8)–(12)). For a given layer in the network that performs the function $\mathbf{y} = F(\mathbf{w}, \mathbf{x})$, applying DBQ simply boils down to composing the quantizer described in (4) with the function F: $\mathbf{y} = F(Q_T(\mathbf{w}), \mathbf{x})$. For quantizing convolutional layers, we apply kernel-wise quantizers. The overhead of full precision scales is amortized across the large filter lengths. The choice of the temperature parameter T is important. A large value of T would reduce the approximation error in (7), however the gradients would saturate quickly, thus causing a bottleneck for learning the quantizer parameters. Therefore, an initial small value for T is used for the first training epoch, and its value is increased for successive epochs based on a pre-determined temperature update schedule. A simple yet effective schedule is to linearly increment the temperature with the number of epochs: $T = T_{\text{init}} + e \times T_{\text{inc}}$. During inference, the approximate step function is replaced with the ideal function f such that the quantizer output satisfies (1).

Activation Quantization: The challenge in quantizing input activations with a fixed-point quantizer during training is determining a suitable clipping value (Fig. 4). Traditionally, the use of ReLU6 (which clips at 6) has been a popular choice due to its simplicity [13, 28]. However, the choice of 6 provides no guarantees on the clipping probability, and can therefore yield sub-optimal results. Similar to [4], we propose clipping the post-BN activations y_{BN} (Fig. 4) using:

$$c = \max_{i \in [C]}(\beta_l^{(i)} + k\gamma_l^{(i)}) \tag{13}$$

where C is the number of channels in the activation tensor y_1, $(\beta^{(i)}, \gamma^{(i)})$ are learnable per-channel shift and scale parameters of BN, and k is a network hyperparameter that controls the clipping probability. Assuming that the distribution of $y_{\text{BN}}^{(i)} \sim \mathcal{N}(\beta^{(i)}, (\gamma^{(i)})^2)$ [12] and using 6σ rule ($k = 6$), one can show that the choice of c in (13) guarantees:

$$\Pr\{y_{\text{BN}} \leq c\} \geq 0.999 \tag{14}$$

Note that having a fixed clipping value c for all channels is crucial in order to ensure that the dot product operations can be implemented in fixed-point.

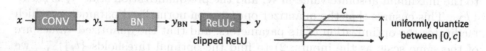

Fig. 4. Quantizing activations post-ReLU requires a pre-determined clipping parameter c.

4   Experimental Results

To demonstrate the effectiveness of the DBQ method for quantizing lightweight networks, we evaluate it on three different image classification datasets: 1) CIFAR-10 [14] using ResNet-20 [6]; 2) ImageNet (ILSVRC 2012) [23] using MobileNetV1 [8], MobileNetV2 [27], and ShuffleNetV2 [20]; and 3) the recently proposed Visual Wake Words [3] using MobileNetV1. In all of our experiments, we train full precision models from scratch, and perform fine tuning on said models for training their quantized counterparts. We use stochastic gradient descent for training all the models. For further details on the training setup for each experiment, please check the supplementary material.

4.1   Complexity Metrics

We propose a set of metrics, inspired by those used in [25, 26], in order to quantify the complexity reduction achieved by our proposed method.

Computational Cost ($\mathcal{C}_C$) for an L-layer network:

$$\mathcal{C}_C = \sum_{l=1}^{L} N_l \left[D_l B_{W,l} B_{A,l} + (D_l - 1)(B_{A,l} + B_{W,l} + \lceil \log_2 D_l \rceil - 1) \right] \qquad (15)$$

where N_l is the number of D_l-dimensional dot products in layer l with $B_{W,l}$ and $B_{A,l}$ being the weights and activations precisions respectively. This cost essentially measures the number of 1b full adders (FAs) needed to implement the dot products required for a given network. For full precision (32b) parameters, we make the simplifying assumption of treating them as 23b (mantissa precision) fixed-point parameters.

Sparsity-Aware Computational Cost ($\mathcal{C}_S$) is also defined in order to leverage weight-sparsity in different models that can be reflected on the model complexity:

$$\mathcal{C}_S = \sum_{l=1}^{L} N_l \left[D_l' B_{W,l} B_{A,l} + (D_l' - 1)(B_{A,l} + B_{W,l} + \lceil \log_2 D_l \rceil - 1) \right] \qquad (16)$$

where D_l' is the number of non-zero weights in the corresponding D_l-dimensional dot product.

Representational Cost ($\mathcal{C}_R$) for an L-layer network:

$$\mathcal{C}_R = \sum_{l=1}^{L} \left[|W_l| B_{W,l} + |A_l| B_{A,l} \right] \qquad (17)$$

where $|W_l|$ and $|A_l|$ are the number of elements in the weight and activation tensors in layer l, respectively.

Model Storage Cost ($\mathcal{C}_M$) for an L-layer network:

$$\mathcal{C}_M = \sum_{l=1}^{L} |W_l| B_{W,l} \qquad (18)$$

which only accounts for the weight storage, and can be useful for studying model compression.

4.2   CIFAR-10 Results

We first demonstrate the effectiveness of DBQ on the CIFAR-10 dataset using the popular network ResNet-20 [6]. To ensure a fair comparison with the LQNet

Table 2. The accuracy on CIFAR-10 and complexity metrics ($\mathcal{C}_C$, $\mathcal{C}_S$, $\mathcal{C}_R$, $\mathcal{C}_M$) for ResNet-20 using our method DBQ compared to LQNet. Δ represents the normalized accuracy drop of the quantized models with respect to its full precision baseline. The first, last layers, and input activations are kept in full precision for the quantized models in accordance with [33].

Method	Acc. (Δ) [%]	$\mathcal{C}_C$ ($\mathcal{C}_S$) [10^9FA]	$\mathcal{C}_R$ ($\mathcal{C}_M$) [10^6b]
FP [33]	92.10 (/)	23.73 (23.73)	14.63 (8.63)
LQNet-1B [33]	90.10 (−2.171)	1.60 (1.60)	6.34 (0.35)
LQNet-2B [33]	91.80 (−0.325)	2.83 (2.83)	6.61 (0.61)
LQNet-3B [33]	92.00 (−0.108)	4.07 (4.07)	6.88 (0.88)
FP (Ours)	92.00 (/)	23.73 (23.73)	14.63 (8.63)
DBQ-1T (Ours)	**91.06 (−1.021)**	**1.60 (0.92)**	6.61 (0.61)
DBQ-2T (Ours)	**91.93 (−0.076)**	**2.83 (1.79)**	7.15 (1.15)

[33] models, we do not quantize the first and last fully connected layers, and we keep all activations in full precision. Table 2 summarizes the accuracy (and percentage drop) as well as the four complexity metrics ($\mathcal{C}_C$, $\mathcal{C}_S$, $\mathcal{C}_R$, $\mathcal{C}_M$) for different number of branches used. At iso-number of branches, the DBQ models achieve higher accuracies for the same $\mathcal{C}_C$ and lower $\mathcal{C}_S$ due to the high number of zero valued weights, as opposed to binary branches where the weights are either ±1. Comparing the DBQ-2T and LQNet-3B models, which achieve comparable accuracies, DBQ-2T requires ∼32% less $\mathcal{C}_C$ and ∼56% less $\mathcal{C}_S$, at the expense of an extra bit per-parameter, which is reflected in the marginal ∼4% increase in $\mathcal{C}_R$.

4.3   ImageNet Results

In this section, we report results for MobileNetV1 [8], MobileNetV2 [27], and ShuffleNetV2 [20] on ImageNet. We first focus on MobileNetV1 by performing an ablation study, and leverage these results for quantizing the more recent MobileNetV2 and ShuffleNetV2.

Ablation Study: Table 3 summarizes the Top-1,5 accuracies of all the MobileNetV1 models trained with different layer precision assignments in order to evaluate the impact of our design choices. To see the impact of using two ternary branches instead of one, we begin with the DBQ-1T model which is obtained by quantizing only the PW layers of MobileNetV1 to one ternary branch (1T) keeping all other activations and weights in full precision. Table 3 shows that DBQ-1T achieves a massive 89% reduction in $\mathcal{C}_C$ compared to the FP model but at a catastrophic loss of 5.67% in the Top-1 accuracy. In contrast, DBQ-2T-1, which is DBQ-1T with a second ternary branch, is able to recover accuracy to within 1.03% of the full-precision baseline while also achieving massive savings

Table 3. The Top-1/5 accuracy on ImageNet and complexity metrics ($\mathcal{C}_C, \mathcal{C}_S, \mathcal{C}_R, \mathcal{C}_M$) for MobileNetV1 under different precision assignments. Models denoted by DBQ-zT are trained using our differentiable branch quantizer with $B = z$ ternary branches. ReLUx denotes a clipped ReLU using our proposed clipping method in Eq. (13).

Model Name	Activations	FL	DW	PW	FC	Top-1/5 Acc. [%]	$\mathcal{C}_C$ ($\mathcal{C}_S$) [10^{10}FA]	$\mathcal{C}_R$ ($\mathcal{C}_M$) [10^7b]
FP	ReLU - 32b	32b	32b	32b	32b	**72.12/90.43**	33.37 (33.37)	30.00 (13.54)
FX8-1	ReLU6 - 8b	32b	8b	8b	32b	71.65/90.17	5.78 (5.39)	10.38 (5.90)
FX8-2	ReLU6 - 8b	8b	8b	8b	8b	71.60/90.19	5.24 (4.85)	7.56 (3.44)
FX8-3	ReLUx - 8b	8b	8b	8b	8b	**71.86/90.26**	5.24 (4.85)	7.56 (3.44)
DBQ-1T	ReLU - 32b	32b	32b	1T	32b	66.45/86.72	3.60 (2.61)	20.58 (4.12)
DBQ-2T-1	ReLU - 32b	32b	32b	2T	32b	71.09/89.71	5.23 (3.77)	21.21 (4.75)
DBQ-2T-2	ReLU6 - 8b	32b	8b	2T	32b	70.25/89.42	2.73 (1.97)	9.12 (4.64)
DBQ-2T-3	ReLUx - 8b	32b	8b	2T	32b	70.80/89.75	2.73 (1.97)	9.12 (4.64)
DBQ-2T-4	ReLUx - 8b	8b	8b	2T	8b	**70.92/89.61**	**2.18 (1.42)**	**6.30 (2.18)**

in $\mathcal{C}_C$ of 84%. Quantizing the activations and the remaining layers weights of DBQ-2T-1 to 8b fixed-point, i.e., DBQ-2T-4, incurs a minimal loss in accuracy of 1.2% compared to the FP model while also achieving even greater reduction in both $\mathcal{C}_C$ (93%) and $\mathcal{C}_R$ (70%). The reduction in $\mathcal{C}_S$ increases to 96% when branch sparsity is exploited to skip computations.

Note that the reason that only PW layers are quantized using ternary branches is three-fold: 1) PW layers consume ~94% of the amount of multiply-adds required for inference (Table 1); 2) we have observed that quantizing the PW layers has the most severe impact on classification accuracy compared to quantizing other layers; and 3) DW layers suffer from extremely small dot-product lengths (9), rendering them unsuitable for multiple branch quantization (the overhead of branch-merge and scaling operations will dominate).

The benefits of our proposed BN-based clipping described in (13) can be seen by comparing the accuracy of the 8b fixed-point model FX8-3 using BN-based clipping with $k = 6$ with its ReLU6-based clipping counterpart FX8-2. The Top-1 accuracy of FX8-3 is better than FX8-2 without any overhead in training or inference. Similarly for DBQ-2T-3 and DBQ-2T-2.

Branching Utility: A 2T quantizer should result in 9 distinct quantization levels as shown in Fig. 3. However, in a 2T branched quantizer such as ours, it is possible for the number of quantization levels to be smaller than 9, e.g., if $\alpha_1 = \alpha_2$ then the number of quantization levels is 5. In this case, the full representational power of the 2T branched quantizer is

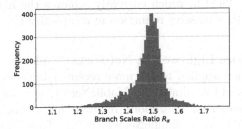

Fig. 5. The distribution of the ratio of the ternary branch scales α_1 and α_2 for DBQ-2T-4 from Table 3.

Table 4. The Top-1 accuracy on ImageNet and complexity metrics ($\mathcal{C}_C, \mathcal{C}_S, \mathcal{C}_R, \mathcal{C}_M$) for MobileNetV1 using our method (DBQ-2T) compared to state-of-the art training-based quantization methods.

Method	Act.	FL	DW	PW	FC	Top-1 Acc. [%]	$\mathcal{C}_C$ ($\mathcal{C}_S$) [10^{10}FA]	$\mathcal{C}_R$ ($\mathcal{C}_M$) [10^7b]
IAO* [13]	8b	8b	8b	8b	8b	**69.00***	4.97 (/)	7.49 (3.37)
UNIQ [1]	8b	5b	5b	5b	5b	67.50	3.70 (/)	6.29 (2.18)
UNIQ [1]	8b	4b	4b	4b	4b	66.00	3.19 (/)	5.87 (**1.76**)
UNIQ [1]	8b	8b	8b	8b	8b	68.25	5.24 (/)	7.56 (3.44)
QSM* [28]	8b	8b	8b	8b	8b	68.03	4.97 (/)	7.49 (3.37)
RQ [19]	5b	5b	5b	5b	5b	61.50	**2.68** (/)	**4.75** (2.18)
RQ [19]	6b	6b	6b	6b	6b	67.50	3.42 (/)	5.69 (2.60)
HAQ cloud [30]	mixed	8b	mixed	mixed	8b	$65.33 - 71.20^\dagger$	2.73 (/)	5.09 (3.12)
HAQ edge [30]	mixed	8b	mixed	mixed	8b	$67.40 - 71.20^\dagger$	4.06 (/)	5.87 (2.49)
FX8 (Ours)	8b	8b	8b	8b	8b	**71.86**	5.24 (4.85)	7.56 (3.44)
DBQ-2T (Ours)	8b	8b	8b	2T	8b	**70.92**	**2.18** (1.42)	6.30 (2.18)

*models with BN folding
*results extracted from a plot
†exact accuracy not reported

not utilized. To see if the 2T branched quantizer generates all 9 levels, we plot the distribution of the ratio $R_\alpha = \frac{\alpha_1}{\alpha_2}$ across all the PW layers in the DBQ-2T-4 model (Table 3). The distribution is centered around $R_\alpha = 1.48$ with more than 99% of the values lying in the range [1.2, 1.7]. This demonstrates that the quantizer learned by DBQ employs the full representational power offered by the 2T structure (Fig. 5).

Comparison with State-of-the Art: Table 4 compares the performance of our proposed DBQ method against state-of-the art results on ImageNet for MobileNetV1. Our model DBQ-2T, which corresponds to DBQ-2T-4 in Table 3 achieves the lowest computational cost $\mathcal{C}_C$ (2.18×10^{10} FAs) compared to previously published networks, while achieving the highest Top-1 accuracy 70.92%. Compared to the lowest complexity model RQ [19], DBQ-2T achieves a 19% reduction in $\mathcal{C}_C$ with a 9.42% improvement in Top-1 accuracy at iso-storage complexity $\mathcal{C}_M$. Furthermore, DBQ-2T improves upon the accuracy of the IAO model [13], which currently achieves the highest Top-1 accuracy, by 1.92% but with a massive reduction in complexity $\mathcal{C}_C$ (56%), $\mathcal{C}_R$ (16%), and $\mathcal{C}_M$ (35%).

More Lightweight Networks: Table 5 demonstrates the performance of DBQ when applied to the more recent lightweight networks: MobileNetV2 and ShuffleNetV2. Similar to MobileNetV1, we find that the PW layers *dominate* the number of operations required for a single inference for both MobileNetV2 (87%) and ShuffleNetV2 (90%). Thus, and inline with our experiments on MobileNetV1, we quantize all PW layers using 2T, with the remaining layers and activations quantized to 8b fixed-point. We observe a minimal 1.3% (MobileNetV2) and 2.6% (ShuffleNetV2) drop in accuracy compared to FP, while achieving *massive* (77% − 95%) reductions in all the complexity metrics. A comparison between DBQ and [29] for MobileNetV2 is present in the supplementary material.

Table 5. The Top-1 accuracy on ImageNet and complexity metrics ($\mathcal{C}_C$, $\mathcal{C}_S$, $\mathcal{C}_R$, $\mathcal{C}_M$) for MobileNetV2 and ShuffleNetV2 using our method (DBQ-2T).

Model	Act.	FL	DW	PW	FC	Top-1 Acc. [%]	$\mathcal{C}_C$ ($\mathcal{C}_S$) [10^{10}FA]	$\mathcal{C}_R$ ($\mathcal{C}_M$) [10^7b]
MobileNetV2-FP	32b	32b	32b	32b	32b	71.88	17.83 (17.83)	32.87 (11.22)
MobileNetV2-2T	8b	8b	8b	2T	8b	**70.54**	**1.42 (1.11)**	**7.45 (2.04)**
ShuffleNetV2-FP	32b	32b	32b	32b	32b	69.36	8.52 (8.52)	13.81 (7.29)
ShuffleNetV2-2T	8b	8b	8b	2T	8b	**66.74**	**0.64 (0.46)**	**3.21 (1.38)**

4.4 Visual Wake Words Results

We study the accuracy-precision-complexity trade-off in quantized DNNs using the Visual Wake Words (VWW) dataset that was recently proposed by Google [3] in order to facilitate the development of lightweight vision models for deployment on resource-constrained Edge devices. This dataset reflects a typical real-world scenario involving the detection of specific events by observing incoming data, e.g., monitoring a camera video feed in order to detect the presence of a person [3], similar to the use of audio wake words in speech recognition. The VWW dataset is derived from the COCO dataset [17] via a simple re-labeling of the available images has a training set of 115k images and a test set with 8k images.

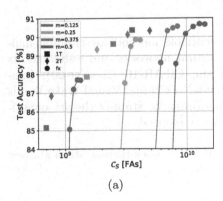
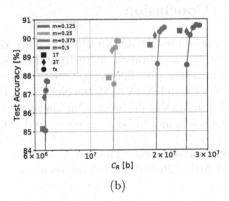

(a)   (b)

Fig. 6. The test accuracy of MobileNetV1 on the Visual Wake Words dataset with varying precision assignment and width multiplier m vs. (a) sparsity-aware computational cost, and (b) representational cost. Only the precision of the pointwise layer's weights are changing, whereas all the remaining activations and weights are quantized using 8b fixed-point. (Color figure online)

As in [3], we employ the modified MobileNetV1 architecture which has a FC layer with 2 output classes instead of 1000. The complexity of the network is tuned by varying the network width multiplier [8] $m \in \{0.125, 0.25, 0.375, 0.5\}$. Similar to our ImageNet experiments, we quantize all layers to 8b fixed-point and vary the precision of the PW layers using 8b-to-2b fixed-point and DBQ-1T and DBQ-2T.

As shown in Fig. 6a, for over parameterized models, e.g., $m = 0.5$, we find DBQ-1T (red square) shows a massive reduction in $\mathcal{C}_S$ (~69%) at iso-accuracy compared to the fixed-point models (red circle) (Fig. 6a). In contrast, for lightweight models, e.g., $m = 0.125$, DBQ-1T (blue square) achieves an impressive 45% reduction in $\mathcal{C}_S$ but at the expense of a 3% loss in test accuracy as compared to the fixed-point model (blue circle) (Fig. 6a). The DBQ models (diamonds and squares) can be seen to form a pareto-optimal accuracy-vs. $\mathcal{C}_S$ trade-off curve in Fig. 6a demonstrating its effectiveness.

Figure 6b shows that the choice of the width multiplier m has a much more significant impact on the representational cost $\mathcal{C}_R$ than varying bit-precision which implies that $\mathcal{C}_R$ is dominated by the storage requirements of activations rather than weights. This implies that the choice of the model parameter m is governed by the amount of on-chip storage available on an Edge device. In contrast, the choice of the bit precision of the PW layers is dictated by the latency/energy requirements which upper bounds $\mathcal{C}_S$ as seen in Fig. 6a. As a result, when comparing the lightweight $m = 0.25$ DBQ-2T model (orange diamond) with the over parameterized $m = 0.375$ DBQ-1T model (green square), we observe that DBQ-2T achieves a reduction in both $\mathcal{C}_S$ (26%) and $\mathcal{C}_R$ (30%), at iso-accuracy and iso-$\mathcal{C}_M$ (~10^6b).

5   Conclusion

We presented DBQ, an efficient fully differentiable method for training multiple ternary branch quantizers for deep neural networks and validated its effectiveness for lightweight networks on the CIFAR-10 (ResNet-20), ImageNet (MobileNetV1, MobileNetV2, and ShuffleNetV2) and Visual Wake Words (MobileNetV1) datasets. Our method outperforms the state-of-the-art quantization schemes in both accuracy and complexity metrics.

Acknowledgment. The authors would like to thank Avishek Biswas, Manu Mathew and Arthur Redfern for helpful discussions and support.

References

1. Baskin, C., et al.: UNIQ: uniform noise injection for non-uniform quantization of neural networks. arXiv preprint arXiv:1804.10969 (2018)
2. Bengio, Y., Léonard, N., Courville, A.: Estimating or propagating gradients through stochastic neurons for conditional computation. arXiv preprint arXiv:1308.3432 (2013)

3. Chowdhery, A., Warden, P., Shlens, J., Howard, A., Rhodes, R.: Visual wake words dataset. arXiv preprint arXiv:1906.05721 (2019)
4. Dbouk, H., Geng, H., Vineyard, C.M., Shanbhag, N.R.: Low-complexity fixed-point convolutional neural networks for automatic target recognition. In: ICASSP 2020–2020 IEEE International Conference on Acoustics, Speech and Signal Processing (ICASSP), pp. 1598–1602. IEEE (2020)
5. Han, S., Pool, J., Tran, J., Dally, W.: Learning both weights and connections for efficient neural network. In: Advances in Neural Information Processing Systems, pp. 1135–1143 (2015)
6. He, K., Zhang, X., Ren, S., Sun, J.: Deep residual learning for image recognition. In: Proceedings of the IEEE Conference on Computer Vision and Pattern Recognition, pp. 770–778 (2016)
7. Hou, L., Kwok, J.T.: Loss-aware weight quantization of deep networks. arXiv preprint arXiv:1802.08635 (2018)
8. Howard, A.G., et al.: MobileNets: efficient convolutional neural networks for mobile vision applications. arXiv preprint arXiv:1704.04861 (2017)
9. Huang, G., Liu, S., Van der Maaten, L., Weinberger, K.Q.: CondenseNet: an efficient DenseNet using learned group convolutions. In: Proceedings of the IEEE Conference on Computer Vision and Pattern Recognition, pp. 2752–2761 (2018)
10. Hubara, I., Courbariaux, M., Soudry, D., El-Yaniv, R., Bengio, Y.: Binarized neural networks. In: Advances in Neural Information Processing Systems, pp. 4107–4115 (2016)
11. Iandola, F.N., Han, S., Moskewicz, M.W., Ashraf, K., Dally, W.J., Keutzer, K.: SqueezeNet: AlexNet-level accuracy with 50x fewer parameters and <0.5 MB model size. arXiv preprint arXiv:1602.07360 (2016)
12. Ioffe, S., Szegedy, C.: Batch normalization: accelerating deep network training by reducing internal covariate shift. arXiv preprint arXiv:1502.03167 (2015)
13. Jacob, B., et al.: Quantization and training of neural networks for efficient integer-arithmetic-only inference. In: Proceedings of the IEEE Conference on Computer Vision and Pattern Recognition, pp. 2704–2713 (2018)
14. Krizhevsky, A., Hinton, G., et al.: Learning multiple layers of features from tiny images. Technical report, Citeseer (2009)
15. Krizhevsky, A., Sutskever, I., Hinton, G.E.: ImageNet classification with deep convolutional neural networks. In: Advances in Neural Information Processing Systems, pp. 1097–1105 (2012)
16. Li, F., Zhang, B., Liu, B.: Ternary weight networks. arXiv preprint arXiv:1605.04711 (2016)
17. Lin, T.-Y., et al.: Microsoft COCO: common objects in context. In: Fleet, D., Pajdla, T., Schiele, B., Tuytelaars, T. (eds.) ECCV 2014. LNCS, vol. 8693, pp. 740–755. Springer, Cham (2014). https://doi.org/10.1007/978-3-319-10602-1_48
18. Lin, X., Zhao, C., Pan, W.: Towards accurate binary convolutional neural network. In: Advances in Neural Information Processing Systems, pp. 345–353 (2017)
19. Louizos, C., Reisser, M., Blankevoort, T., Gavves, E., Welling, M.: Relaxed quantization for discretized neural networks. arXiv preprint arXiv:1810.01875 (2018)
20. Ma, N., Zhang, X., Zheng, H.-T., Sun, J.: ShuffleNet V2: practical guidelines for efficient CNN architecture design. In: Ferrari, V., Hebert, M., Sminchisescu, C., Weiss, Y. (eds.) Computer Vision – ECCV 2018. LNCS, vol. 11218, pp. 122–138. Springer, Cham (2018). https://doi.org/10.1007/978-3-030-01264-9_8
21. Paszke, A., et al.: Automatic differentiation in PyTorch. In: NIPS Autodiff Workshop (2017)

22. Rastegari, M., Ordonez, V., Redmon, J., Farhadi, A.: XNOR-Net: ImageNet classification using binary convolutional neural networks. In: Leibe, B., Matas, J., Sebe, N., Welling, M. (eds.) ECCV 2016. LNCS, vol. 9908, pp. 525–542. Springer, Cham (2016). https://doi.org/10.1007/978-3-319-46493-0_32

23. Russakovsky, O., et al.: ImageNet large scale visual recognition challenge. Int. J. Comput. Vision **115**(3), 211–252 (2015)

24. Sakr, C., Choi, J., Wang, Z., Gopalakrishnan, K., Shanbhag, N.: True gradient-based training of deep binary activated neural networks via continuous binarization. In: 2018 IEEE International Conference on Acoustics, Speech and Signal Processing (ICASSP), pp. 2346–2350. IEEE (2018)

25. Sakr, C., Kim, Y., Shanbhag, N.: Analytical guarantees on numerical precision of deep neural networks. In: Proceedings of the 34th International Conference on Machine Learning-Volume 70, pp. 3007–3016. JMLR.org (2017)

26. Sakr, C., Shanbhag, N.: Per-tensor fixed-point quantization of the back-propagation algorithm. In: International Conference on Learning Representations (2019)

27. Sandler, M., Howard, A., Zhu, M., Zhmoginov, A., Chen, L.C.: MobileNetV2: inverted residuals and linear bottlenecks. In: Proceedings of the IEEE Conference on Computer Vision and Pattern Recognition, pp. 4510–4520 (2018)

28. Sheng, T., Feng, C., Zhuo, S., Zhang, X., Shen, L., Aleksic, M.: A quantization-friendly separable convolution for MobileNets. In: 2018 1st Workshop on Energy Efficient Machine Learning and Cognitive Computing for Embedded Applications (EMC2), pp. 14–18. IEEE (2018)

29. Uhlich, S., et al.: Mixed precision DNNs: all you need is a good parametrization. In: International Conference on Learning Representations (2020). https://openreview.net/forum?id=Hyx0slrFvH

30. Wang, K., Liu, Z., Lin, Y., Lin, J., Han, S.: HAQ: hardware-aware automated quantization with mixed precision. In: Proceedings of the IEEE Conference on Computer Vision and Pattern Recognition, pp. 8612–8620 (2019)

31. Xie, S., Zheng, H., Liu, C., Lin, L.: SNAS: stochastic neural architecture search. In: International Conference on Learning Representations (2019). https://openreview.net/forum?id=rylqooRqK7

32. Yang, J., et al.: Quantization networks. In: Proceedings of the IEEE Conference on Computer Vision and Pattern Recognition, pp. 7308–7316 (2019)

33. Zhang, D., Yang, J., Ye, D., Hua, G.: LQ-Nets: learned quantization for highly accurate and compact deep neural networks. In: Ferrari, V., Hebert, M., Sminchisescu, C., Weiss, Y. (eds.) ECCV 2018. LNCS, vol. 11212, pp. 373–390. Springer, Cham (2018). https://doi.org/10.1007/978-3-030-01237-3_23

34. Zhang, X., Zhou, X., Lin, M., Sun, J.: ShuffleNet: an extremely efficient convolutional neural network for mobile devices. In: Proceedings of the IEEE Conference on Computer Vision and Pattern Recognition, pp. 6848–6856 (2018)

35. Zhou, A., Yao, A., Wang, K., Chen, Y.: Explicit loss-error-aware quantization for low-bit deep neural networks. In: Proceedings of the IEEE Conference on Computer Vision and Pattern Recognition, pp. 9426–9435 (2018)

36. Zhu, C., Han, S., Mao, H., Dally, W.J.: Trained ternary quantization. arXiv preprint arXiv:1612.01064 (2016)

All at Once: Temporally Adaptive Multi-frame Interpolation with Advanced Motion Modeling

Zhixiang Chi[1]([✉]), Rasoul Mohammadi Nasiri[1]([✉]), Zheng Liu[1], Juwei Lu[1], Jin Tang[1], and Konstantinos N. Plataniotis[2]

[1] Noah's Ark Lab, Huawei Technologies, Toronto, Canada
{zhixiang.chi,rasoul.nasiri,zheng.liu1,juwei.lu,tangjin}@huawei.com
[2] University of Toronto, Toronto, Canada
kostas@ece.utoronto.ca

Abstract. Recent advances in high refresh rate displays as well as the increased interest in high rate of slow motion and frame up-conversion fuel the demand for efficient and cost-effective multi-frame video interpolation solutions. To that regard, inserting multiple frames between consecutive video frames are of paramount importance for the consumer electronics industry. State-of-the-art methods are iterative solutions interpolating one frame at the time. They introduce temporal inconsistencies and clearly noticeable visual artifacts.

Departing from the state-of-the-art, this work introduces a true multi-frame interpolator. It utilizes a pyramidal style network in the temporal domain to complete the multi-frame interpolation task in one-shot. A novel flow estimation procedure using a relaxed loss function, and an advanced, cubic-based, motion model is also used to further boost interpolation accuracy when complex motion segments are encountered. Results on the Adobe240 dataset show that the proposed method generates visually pleasing, temporally consistent frames, outperforms the current best off-the-shelf method by 1.57 dB in PSNR with 8 times smaller model and 7.7 times faster. The proposed method can be easily extended to interpolate a large number of new frames while remaining efficient because of the one-shot mechanism.

1 Introduction

Video frame interpolation targets generating new frames for the moments in which no frame is recorded. It is mostly used in slow motion generation [26], adaptive streaming [25], and frame rate up-conversion [5]. The fast innovation in high refresh rate displays and great interests in a higher rate of slow motion and frame up-conversion bring the needs to multi-frame interpolation.

Electronic supplementary material The online version of this chapter (https://doi.org/10.1007/978-3-030-58583-9_7) contains supplementary material, which is available to authorized users.

A. Vedaldi et al. (Eds.): ECCV 2020, LNCS 12372, pp. 107–123, 2020.
https://doi.org/10.1007/978-3-030-58583-9_7

Recent efforts focus on the main challenges of interpolation, including occlusion and large motions, but they have not explored the temporal consistency as a key factor in video quality, especially for multi-frame interpolation. Almost all the existing methods interpolate one frame in each execution, and generating multiple frames can be addressed by either iteratively generating a middle frame [15,19,27] or independently creating each intermediate frame for corresponding time stamp [2,3,10,14,17]. The former approach might cause error propagation by treating the generated middle frame as input. As well, the later one may suffer from temporal inconsistency due to the independent process for each frame and causes temporal jittering at playback. Those artifacts are further enlarged when more frames are interpolated. An important point that has been missed in existing methods is the variable level of difficulties in generating intermediate frames. In fact, the frames closer to the two initial frames are easier to generate, and those with larger temporal distance are more difficult. Consequently, the current methods are not optimized in terms of model size and running time for multi-frame interpolation, which makes them inapplicable for real-life applications.

On the other hand, most of the state-of-the-art interpolation methods commonly synthesize the intermediate frames by simply assuming linear transition in motion between the pair of input frames. However, real-world motions reflected in video frames follow a variety of complex non-linear trends [26]. While a quadratic motion prediction model is proposed in [26] to overcome this limitation, it is still inadequate to model real-world scenarios especially for non-rigid bodies, by assuming constant acceleration. As forces applied to move objects in the real world are not necessarily constant, it results in variation in acceleration.

To this end, we propose a temporal pyramidal processing structure that efficiently integrates the multi-frame generation into one single network. Based on the expected level of difficulties, we adaptively process the easier cases (frames) with shallow parts to guide the generation of harder frames that are processed by deeper structures. Through joint optimization of all the intermediate frames, higher quality and temporal consistency can be ensured. In addition, we exploit the advantage of multiple input frames as in [13,26] to propose an advanced higher-order motion prediction modeling, which explores the variation in acceleration. Furthermore, inspired by [27], we develop a technique to boost the quality of motion prediction as well as the final interpolation results by introducing a relaxed loss function to the optical flow (O.F.) estimation module. In particular, it gives the flexibility to map the pixels to the neighbor of their ground truth locations at the reference frame while a better motion prediction for the intermediate frames can be achieved. Comparing to the current state-of-the-art method [26], we outperform it in interpolation quality measured by PSNR by 1.57 dB on the Adobe240 dataset and achieved 8 times smaller in model size and 7.7 times faster in generating 7 frames.

We summarize our contributions as 1) We propose a temporal pyramidal structure to integrate the multi-frame interpolation task into one single network to generate temporally consistent and high-quality frames; 2) We propose a higher-order motion modeling to exploit variations in acceleration involved in real-world motion; 3) We develop a relaxed loss function to the flow estimation task to boost the interpolation quality; 4) We optimize the network size and speed so that it is applicable for the real world applications especially for mobile devices.

2   Related Work

Recent efforts on frame interpolation have focused on dealing with the main sources of degradation in interpolation quality, such as large motion and occlusion. Different ideas have been proposed such as estimating occlusion maps [10,28], learning adaptive kernel for each pixel [18,19], exploring depth information [2] or extracting deep contextual features [3,17]. As most of these methods interpolate frames one at a time, inserting multiple frames is achieved by iteratively executing the models. In fact, as a fundamental issue, the step-wise implementation of multi-frame interpolation does not consider the time continuity and may cause temporally inconsistency. In contrast, generating multiple frames in one integrated network will implicitly enforce the network to generate temporally consistent sequences. The effectiveness of the integrated approach has been verified by Super SloMo [10]; however, their method is not purposely designed for the task of multi-frame interpolation. Specifically, what has been missed in [10] is to utilize the error cue from temporal distance between a middle frame and the input frames and optimize the whole model accordingly. Therefore, the proposed adaptive processing based on this difficulty pattern can result in a more optimized solution, which is not considered in the state-of-the-art methods [2,3,10,19,26].

Given the estimated O.F. among the input frames, one important step in frame interpolation is modeling the traversal of pixels in between the two frames. The most common approach is to consider a linear transition and scaling of the O.F. [2,3,10,15,17,28]. Recent work in [4,26] applied an acceleration-aware method by also contributing the neighborhood frames of the initial pair. However, in real life, the force applied to the moving object is not constant; thus, the motion is not following the linear or quadratic pattern. In this paper, we propose a simple but powerful higher-order model to handle more complex motions happen in the real world and specially non-rigid bodies. On the other hand, [10] imposes accurate estimation the O.F. by the warping loss. However, [27] reveals that accurate O.F. is not tailored for task-oriented problems. Motivated by that, we apply a flexible O.F. estimation between initial frames, which gives higher flexibility to model complex motions.

3   Proposed Method

3.1   Algorithm Overview

An overview of the proposed method is shown in Fig. 1 where we use four input frames (I_{-1}, I_0, I_1 and I_2) to generate 7 frames ($I_{t_i}, t_i = \frac{i}{8}, i \in [1, 2, \cdots, 7]$)

between I_0 and I_1. We first use two-step O.F. estimation module to calculate O.F.s $(f_{0\to1}, f_{1\to0}, f_{1\to-1}, f_{0\to2})$ and then use these flows and cubic modeling to predict the flow between input frames and the new frames. Our proposed temporal pyramidal network then refines the predicted O.F. and generates an initial estimation of middle frames. Finally, the post processing network further improves the quality of interpolated frames (I_{t_i}) with the similar temporal pyramid.

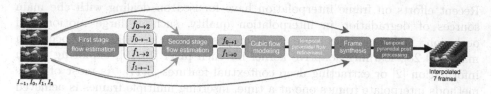

Fig. 1. An overview of the proposed multi-frame interpolation method.

3.2   Cubic Flow Prediction

In this work, we integrate the cubic motion modeling to specifically handle the acceleration variation in motions. Considering the motion starting from I_0 to a middle time stamp t_i as $f_{0\to t_i}$, we model object motion by the cubic model as:

$$f_{0\to t_i} = v_0 \times t_i + \frac{a_0}{2} \times t_i^2 + \frac{\Delta a_0}{6} \times t_i^3, \tag{1}$$

where v_0, a_0, and Δa_0 are the velocity, acceleration, and acceleration change rate estimated at I_0, respectively. The acceleration terms can be computed as:

$$\Delta a_0 = a_1 - a_0, a_0 = f_{0\to1} + f_{0\to-1}, a_1 = f_{1\to2} + f_{1\to0}. \tag{2}$$

where a_0 and a_1 are calculated for pixels at I_0 and I_1 respectively. However, the Δa_0 should be calculated for the pixels correspond to the same real-world point rather than pixels with the same coordinate in the two frames. Therefore, we reformulate a_1 to calculated Δa_0 based on referencing pixel's locations at I_0 as:

$$a_1 = f_{0\to2} - 2 \times f_{0\to1}. \tag{3}$$

To calculate v_0 in (1), the calculation in [26] does not hold when the acceleration is variable, instead, we apply (1) for $t_i = 1$ to solve for v_0 using only the information computed above

$$v_0 = f_{0\to1} - \frac{a_0}{2} - \frac{a_1 - a_0}{6}. \tag{4}$$

Finally, $f_{0\to t_i}$ for any $t_i \in [0,1]$ can be expressed based on only O.F. between input frames by

$$f_{0\to t_i} = f_{0\to1} \times t_i + \frac{a_0}{2} \times (t_i^2 - t_i) + \frac{a_1 - a_0}{6} \times (t_i^3 - t_i). \tag{5}$$

$f_{1 \to t_i}$ can be computed using the same manner. The detailed derivation and proof of all the above equations will be provided in the supplementary document.

In Fig. 2, we simulate three different 1-D motions, including constant velocity, constant acceleration, and variable acceleration, as distinguished in three path lines. For each motion, the object position at four time stamps of $[t_0, t_1, t_2, t_3]$ are given as shown by gray circles; we apply three predictive models: linear, quadratic [26] and our cubic model to estimate the location of the object for time stamp $t_{1.5}$ blindly (without having the parameters of simulated motions). The prediction results show that our cubic model is more robust to simulate different order of motions.

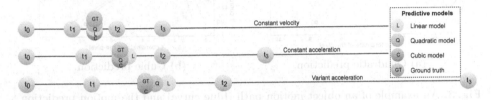

Fig. 2. A toy example to illustrate the performance of three models (Linear, Quadratic, and Cubic) in predicting three motion patterns (constant velocity, constant acceleration, and variant acceleration).

3.3   Motion Estimation

Flow Estimation Module. To estimate the O.F. among the input frames, the existing frame interpolation methods commonly adopt the off-the-shelf networks [2,3,6,8,17,24,26]. However, the existing flow networks are not efficiently designed for multi-frame input, and some are limited to one-directional flow estimation. To this end, following the three-scale coarse-to-fine architecture in SPyNet [22], we design a customized two-stage flow estimation to involve the neighbor frames in better estimating O.F. between I_0 and I_1. Both stages are following similar three-scale architecture, and they optimally share the weights of two coarser levels. The first stage network is designed to compute O.F. between two consecutive frames. We use that to estimate $f_{0 \to -1}$ and $f_{1 \to 2}$. In the finest level of second-stage network, we use I_0 and I_1 concatenated with $-f_{0 \to -1}$ and $-f_{1 \to 2}$ as initial estimations to compute $f_{0 \to 1}$ and $f_{1 \to 0}$. Alongside, we are calculating the estimation of $f_{0 \to 2}$ and $f_{1 \to -1}$ in the first stage, which are used in our cubic motion modeling in later steps.

Motion Estimation Constraint Relaxation. Common O.F. estimation methods try to map the pixel from the first frame to the exact corresponding location in the second frame. However, TOFlow [27] reveals that the accurate O.F. as a part of a higher conceptual level task like frame interpolation does not lead to the optimal solution of that task, especially for occlusion. Similarly, we observed that a strong constraint on O.F. estimation among input frames might degrade the motion prediction for the middle frames, especially for complex motion. In contrast, accepting some flexibility in flow estimation will provide a closer estimation to ground truth motion between frames. The advantage of this flexibility will be illustrated in the following examples.

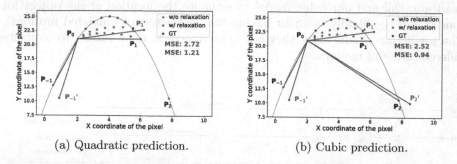

(a) Quadratic prediction.   (b) Cubic prediction.

Fig. 3. An example of an object motion path (blue curve) and the motion prediction (with and without relaxation) by Quadratic (a) and Cubic (b) model. (Color figure online)

Consider the two toy examples, as shown in Fig. 3, where a pixel is moving on the blue curve in consecutive frames and (x,y) is the pixel coordinate in frame space. The pixel position is given in four consecutive frames as P_{-1}, P_0, P_1 and P_2 and the aim is to find locations for seven moments between P_0 and P_1 indicated by blue stars. We consider P_0 as a reference point in motion prediction. The green lines represent ground truth O.F. between P_0 and other points. We predict middle points (green stars) by quadratic [26] and cubic models in (5) as shown in Fig. 3. The predicted locations are far from the ground truths (blue stars). However, instead of estimating the exact O.F., giving it a flexibility of mapping P_0 to the neighbor of other points denoted as P'_{-1}, P'_1, P'_2, a better prediction of the seven middle locations can be achieved as shown by the red stars. It also reduces the mean squared error (MSE) significantly. The idea is an analogy to introduce certain errors to the flow estimation process.

To apply the idea of relaxation, we employ the same unsupervised learning in O.F. estimation as [10], but with a relaxed warping loss. For example, the loss for estimating $f_{0\to1}$ is defined as:

$$\mathcal{L}^{f_{0\to1}}_{w_{relax}} = \sum_{i=0}^{h-1}\sum_{j=0}^{z-1}\min_{m,n}\left\|I_0^{w\to1}(i,j) - I_1(i+m, j+n)\right\|_1, \text{for } m,n \in [-d, +d],$$

(6)

where $I_0^{w\to1}$ denotes I_0 warped by $f_{0\to1}$ to the reference point I_1, d determines the range of neighborhood and h, z are the image height and width. We use $\mathcal{L}_{w_{relax}}$ for both stages of O.F. estimation. We evaluate the trade-off between the performance of flow estimation and the final results in Sect. 4.4.

3.4 Temporal Pyramidal Network

Considering the similarity between consecutive frames and also the pattern of difficulty for this task, it leads to the idea of introducing adaptive joint processing. We applied this by proposing temporal pyramidal models.

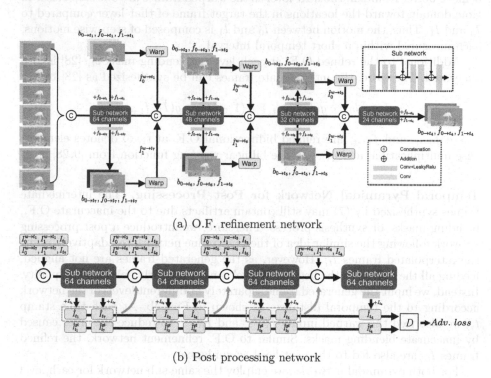

(a) O.F. refinement network

(b) Post processing network

Fig. 4. The pyramidal network model designed for O.F. refinement (a) and adaptive pyramidal structure in post processing (b).

Temporal Pyramidal Network for O.F. Refinement. The bidirectional O.F.s $f_{0 \to t_i}$ and $f_{1 \to t_i}$ predicted by (5) are based on the O.F.s computed among the input frames. The initial prediction may inherit errors from flow estimation and cubic motion modeling, notably for the motion boundaries [10]. To effectively improve $f_{0 \to t_i}$ and $f_{1 \to t_i}$, unlike the existing methods [2,3,10,14,15,17,20,28], we aim to consider the relationship among intermediate frames and process all at one forward pass. To this end, we propose a temporal pyramidal O.F. refinement network, which enforces a strong bond between the intermediate frames, as shown in Fig. 4a. The network takes the concatenation of seven pairs of predicted O.F.s as input and adaptively refines the O.F.s based on the expected quality of the interpolation correspond to the distance to I_0 and I_1. In fact, the closest ones, I_{t_1} and I_{t_7} are processed only by one level of pyramid as they are more likely to achieve higher quality. With the same patterns, (I_{t_2}, I_{t_6}) are processed by two levels, (I_{t_3}, I_{t_5}) by three levels and finally I_{t_4} by the entire four levels of the network as it is expected to achieve the lowest quality in interpolation.

To fully utilize the refined O.F.s, we warp I_0 and I_1 by the refined O.F. in each level as $I_0^{w \to t_i}$ and $I_1^{w \to t_i}$ and feed them to the next level. It is helpful to achieve better results in the next level as the warped frames are one step closer in time domain toward the locations in the target frame of that layer compared to I_0 and I_1. Thus, the motion between I_0 and I_1 is composed of step-wise motions, each measured within a short temporal interval.

Additional to the refined O.F. at each level, a blending mask b_{t_i} [28] is also generated. Therefore, the intermediate frames can be synthesized as [28] by

$$I_{t_i} = b_{t_i} \odot g(I_0, \hat{f}_{0 \to t_i}) + (1 - b_{t_i}) \odot g(I_1, \hat{f}_{1 \to t_i}), \tag{7}$$

where $\hat{f}_{0 \to t_i}$ and $\hat{f}_{1 \to t_i}$ are refined bidirectional O.F. at t_i, $\odot$ denotes element-wise multiplication, and $g(\cdot, \cdot)$ is the bilinear warping function from [9,28].

Temporal Pyramidal Network for Post Processing. The intermediate frames synthesized by (7) may still contain artifacts due to the inaccurate O.F., blending masks, or synthesis process. Therefore, we introduce a post processing network following the similar idea of the O.F. refine network to adaptively refine the interpolated frames I_{t_i}. However, as the generated frames are not aligned, feeding all the frames at the beginning level cannot properly enhance the quality. Instead, we input the generated frame separately at different levels of the network according to the temporal distance, as shown in Fig. 4b. At each time stamp t_i, we also feed the warped inputs $I_0^{w \to t_i}$ and $I_1^{w \to t_i}$ to reduce the error caused by inaccurate blending masks. Similar to O.F. refinement network, the refined frames $\hat{I}_{t_i}$ are also fed to the next level as guidance.

For both pyramidal networks, we employ the same sub network for each level of the pyramid and adopt residual learning to learn the O.F. and frame residuals. The sub network is composed of two residual blocks proposed by [16] and one convolutional layer at the input and another at the output. We set the number of channels in a reducing order for O.F. refinement pyramid, as fewer frames are dealt with when moving to the middle time step. In contrast, we keep the same channel numbers for all the levels of post processing module.

3.5   Loss Functions

The proposed integrated network for multi-frame interpolation targets temporal consistency by joint optimization of all frames. To further impose consistency between frames, we apply generative adversarial learning scheme [29] and two-player min-max game idea in [7] to train a discriminator network D which optimizes the following problem:

$$\min_G \max_D \mathbb{E}_{\mathbf{g} \sim p(I_{t_i}^{gt})}[\log D(\mathbf{g})] + \mathbb{E}_{\mathbf{x} \sim p(I)}[\log(1 - D(G(\mathbf{x})))], \tag{8}$$

where $\mathbf{g} = [I_{t_1}^{gt}, \cdots I_{t_7}^{gt}]$ are the seven ground truth frames and $\mathbf{x} = [I_{-1}, I_0, I_1, I_2]$ are the four input frames. We add the following generative component of the GAN as the temporal loss [12,29]:

$$\mathcal{L}_{temp} = \sum_{n=1}^{N} -\log D(G(\mathbf{x})). \tag{9}$$

The proposed framework in Fig. 1 serves as a generator and is trained alternatively with the discriminator. To optimize the O.F. refinement and post processing networks, we apply the ℓ_1 loss. The whole architecture is trained by combining all the loss functions:

$$\mathcal{L} = \sum_{i=1}^{7} (\left\| \hat{I}_{t_i} - I_{t_i}^{gt} \right\|_1 + \left\| I_{t_i} - I_{t_i}^{gt} \right\|_1) + \mathcal{L}_{w_{relax}} + \lambda \mathcal{L}_{temp}, \tag{10}$$

where the λ is the weighting coefficient and equals to 0.001.

4   Experiments

In this section, we provide the implementation details and the analysis of the results of the proposed method in comparison to the other methods and different ablation studies.

4.1   Implementation Details

To train our network, we collected a dataset of 903 short video clips (2 to 10 s) with the frame rate of 240fps and a resolution of 720×1280 from YouTube. The videos are covering various scenes, and we randomly select 50 videos for validation. From these videos, we created 8463 training samples of 25 consecutive frames as in [26]. Our model takes the 1st, 9th, 17th, and 25th frames as inputs to generate the seven frames between the 9th and 17th frames by considering 10th to 16th frames as ground truths. We randomly crop 352×352 patches and apply horizontal, vertical as well as temporal flip for data augmentation in training.

To improve the convergence speed, a stage-wise training strategy is adopted [30]. We first train each module except the discriminator using ℓ_1 loss independently for 15 epochs with the learning rate of 10^{-4} by not updating other modules. The whole network is then jointly trained using (10) and learning rate of 10^{-5} for 100 epochs. We use the Adam optimizer [11] and empirically set the neighborhood range d in (6) to 9. During the training, the pixel values of all images are scaled to $[-1, 1]$. All the experiments are conducted on an Nvidia V100 GPU. More detailed network architecture will be provided in the supplementary material.

4.2   Evaluation Datasets

We evaluate the performance of the proposed method on widely used datasets including two multi-frame interpolation dataset (Adobe240 [23] and GOPRO [16]) and two single-frame interpolation (Vimeo90K [27] and DAVIS [21]). Adobe240 and GOPRO are initially designed for deblurring tasks with a frame rate of 240fps and resolution of 720×1280. Both are captured by hand-held high-speed cameras and contain a combination of object and camera motion in different levels, which makes them challenging for the frame interpolation task. We follow the same setting as Sec. 4.1 to extract 4276 and 1393 samples of frame patch for Adobe240 and GOPRO, respectively. DAVIS dataset is designed for video segmentation, which normally contains large motions. It has 90 videos, and we extract 2637 samples of 7 frames. As for Vimeo90K, since the interpolation sub-set only contains triplets, which are not applicable for our methods as we need more frames for cubic motion modeling. Instead, we use the super-resolution test set, which contains 7824 samples of 7 consecutive frames. We interpolate 7 frames for Adobe240 and GOPRO and interpolate the 4th (middle) frame for DAVIS and Vimeo90K by using the 1st, 3rd, 5th and 7th frames as inputs.

Table 1. Performance evaluation of the proposed method compared to the state-of-the-art methods in different datasets.

Methods	Adobe240			GoPro			Vimeo90K			DAVIS		
	PSNR	SSIM	TCC	PSNR	SSIM	TCC	PSNR	SSIM	IE	PSNR	SSIM	IE
SepConv	32.38	0.938	0.832	30.82	0.910	0.789	33.60	0.944	5.30	26.30	0.789	15.61
Super SloMo	31.63	0.927	0.809	30.50	0.904	0.784	33.38	0.938	5.41	26.00	0.770	16.19
DAIN	31.36	0.932	0.808	29.74	0.900	0.759	34.54	0.950	4.76	27.25	0.820	13.17
Quadratic	32.80	0.949	0.842	32.01	0.936	0.822	33.62	0.946	5.22	27.38	0.834	12.46
Ours	**34.37**	**0.959**	**0.860**	**32.91**	**0.943**	**0.837**	**34.93**	**0.951**	**4.70**	**27.91**	**0.837**	**12.40**

4.3   Comparison with the State-of-the-Arts

We compare our method with four state-of-the-art frame interpolation methods: Super SloMo [10], Quadratic [26], DAIN [2], and SepConv [19], where we train [10] and [26] on our training data and use the model released by authors in the last two. We use PSNR, SSIM and interpolation error (IE) [1] as evaluation metrics. For multi-frame interpolation in GOPRO and Adobe240, we borrow the concept of Temporal Change Consistency [29] which compares the generated frames and ground truth in terms of changes between adjacent frames by

$$TCC(F,G) = \frac{\sum_{i=1}^{6} \text{SSIM}(abs(f^i - f^{i+1}), abs(g^i - g^{i+1}))}{6}, \tag{11}$$

where, $F = (f^1, \cdots, f^7)$ and $G = (g^1, \cdots, g^7)$ are the 7 interpolated and ground truth frames respectively. For the multi-frame interpolation task, we report the

| Input&GT | SepConv | Super SloMo | DAIN | Qudratic | Ours |

Fig. 5. An example from Adobe240 to visualize the temporal consistency. The top row shows the middle frames generated by different methods, and the bottom row shows the interpolation error. Our method experiences less shifting in the temporal domain.

Table 2. Ablation studies on the network components on Adobe240 and GOPRO.

Methods	Adobe240				GOPRO			
	PSNR	SSIM	IE	TCC	PSNR	SSIM	IE	TCC
w/o post pro..	33.87	0.954	6.21	0.848	32.63	0.942	6.80	0.831
w/o adv. loss	34.35	0.958	5.89	0.850	32.86	0.942	6.77	0.830
w/o 2nd O.F.	34.24	0.957	5.97	0.854	32.73	0.940	6.91	0.832
w/o O.F. relax.	33.92	0.955	6.14	0.851	32.45	0.936	7.09	0.828
w/o pyr.	33.92	0.954	6.33	0.845	32.37	0.935	7.30	0.820
Full model	**34.37**	**0.959**	**5.89**	**0.860**	**32.91**	**0.943**	**6.74**	**0.837**

average of the metrics for 7 interpolated frames. The results reported in Table 1, shows that our proposed method consistently performs better than the existing methods on both single and multi-frame interpolation scenarios. Notably, for multi-frame interpolation datasets (Adobe240 and GOPRO), our method significantly outperforms the best existing method [26] by 1.57 dB and 0.9 dB. The proposed method also achieves the highest temporal consistency measured by TCC thanks to the temporal pyramid structure and joint optimization of the middle frames, which exploits the temporal relation among the middle frames.

In addition to the TCC, to better show the power of the proposed method in preserving temporal consistency between frames, Fig. 5 reports $\hat{I}_{t_4}$ and IE generated by different methods from Adobe240. As shown in Fig. 5, the generated middle frames by different methods are visually very similar to the ground truth. However, a comparison of the IE reveals significant errors that occurred near the edges of moving objects caused because of time inconsistency between generated frames and the ground truth. In contrast, our method generates a high-quality consistent frame with the ground truth in both spatial and temporal domains.

Fig. 6. Visualization of the seven intermediate frames of I_{t_1} to I_{t_7} generated by our method compared to Quadratic [26] and Super SloMo [10] from GOPRO.

Another example from GOPRO in Fig. 6, shows the results of the proposed method in comparison with Super SloMo [10] and Quadratic [26] which they have not applied any adaptive processing for frames interpolation. As it can be seen in Fig. 6, at t_1 and t_7 which are closer to the input frames, all the methods generate comparable results. However, approaching to the middle frame as the temporal distance from the input increases, the quality of frames generated by Super SloMo and Quadratic start to degrade while our method experiences less degradation and higher quality. Especially for I_{t_4}, our improvement is significant, as also shown by the PSNR values at each time stamp t_i in Fig. 9c.

Our method also works better on DAVIS and Vimeo90K, as reported in Table 1. Figure 7 shows an example of a challenging scenario that involves both translational and rotational motion. The acceleration-aware Quadratic can better estimate the motion, while others have undergone severe degradation. However, undesired artifacts are still generated by Quadratic near the motion boundary. In contrast, our method exploits the cubic motion modeling and temporal pyramidal processing, which better captures this complex motion and generates comparable results against the ground truth.

4.4 Ablation Studies

Analysis of the Model. To explore the impact of different components of the proposed model, we investigate the performance of our solution when applying different variations including 1) w/o post pro.: removing post processing; 2) w/o adv. loss: removing adversarial loss; 3) w/o 2nd O.F.: replace the second stage flow estimation with the exact same network as the first stage; 4) w/o O.F. relax.: replace $\mathcal{L}_{w_{relax}}$ by $\mathcal{L}_{\ell_1}$; 5) w/o pyr.: in both pyramidal modules, we place all the input as the first level of the network, and the outputs are caught at the last layer. The performance of the above variations evaluated on Adobe240 and GOPRO datasets, as shown in Table 2, reveals that all the listed modifications lead to degradation in performance. As expected, motion relaxation and the pyramidal structure are important as they provide more accurate motion prediction and enforce the temporal consistency among the interpolated frames, as reflected in TCC. The post processing as its missing in the model also brings a large degradation is a crucial component that compensates the inaccurate

Table 3. Comparison between linear, quadratic and cubic motion models.

Models	Adobe240			GOPRO		
	PSNR	SSIM	IE	PSNR	SSIM	IE
Linear	33.97	0.955	6.13	32.40	0.936	7.09
Quad	34.24	0.957	5.95	32.70	0.941	6.85
Cubic	**34.37**	**0.959**	**5.89**	**32.91**	**0.943**	**6.74**

Table 4. Comparison between models generating different number of frames.

Methods	DAVIS		Vimeo90K	
	PSNR	SSIM	PSNR	SSIM
1 frames	27.07	0.819	32.02	0.944
3 frames	27.44	0.816	34.67	0.950
7 frames (no pyr.)	27.25	0.815	34.56	0.950
7 frames	**27.91**	**0.837**	**34.93**	**0.951**

Inputs   SepConv   Super SloMo   DAIN   Quadratic   Ours   GT

Fig. 7. Sample results for interpolating the middle frame for a complex motion example from DAVIS dataset.

O.F. and blending process. It is worth noting that even though the quantitative improvement of PSNR and SSIM for the adversarial loss is small, it is effective to preserve the temporal consistency as reported by the TCC values.

Motion Models. To investigate the impact of different motion models, we trained our method with linear and quadratic [26] motion prediction as well. The reported average quality in Table 3, shows that the cubic modeling has been dominant in both GOPRO and Adobe240. Importantly, the improvement by quadratic against linear in the model proposed in [26], is reported to be more than 1 dB, however, we observed 0.27 dB and 0.3 dB on Adobe240 and GOPRO datasets. We give credit to the proposed temporal pyramidal processing and applying motion relaxation. In comparison with the impact of quadratic over linear, our cubic modeling adds another 0.13 dB and 0.21 dB improvement on the Adobe240 and GOPRO, respectively, which shows the necessity of applying cubic modeling on the complexity of motions we have in different videos.

Table 5. Motion relaxation evaluation for warping, prediction and final results.

Datasets	PSNR ($I_1^{w\to 0}$, I_0)		PSNR ($I_1^{w\to t_4}$, $I_{t_4}^{gt}$)		PSNR ($\hat{I}_{t_4}$, $I_{t_4}^{gt}$))	
	$\mathcal{L}_{\ell_1}$	$\mathcal{L}_{w_{relax}}$	$\mathcal{L}_{\ell_1}$	$\mathcal{L}_{w_{relax}}$	$\mathcal{L}_{\ell_1}$	$\mathcal{L}_{w_{relax}}$
DAVIS	**30.13**	23.37	25.13	**25.43**	27.15	**27.91**

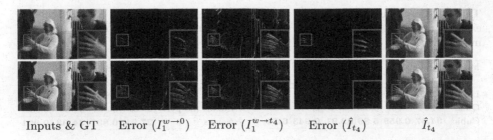

Inputs & GT   Error $(I_1^{w \to 0})$ Error $(I_1^{w \to t_4})$ Error $(\hat{I}_{t_4})$ $\hat{I}_{t_4}$

Fig. 8. Sample results from Vimeo90K to show the comparison between O.F. estimation with (bottom row) and without (top row) relaxation in terms of the interpolation error for motion prediction and final interpolation result.

Constraints Relaxation in Motion Estimation. To investigate the impact of applying motion estimation relaxation in our architecture, we train two versions of the entire solution, with relaxation $(\ell_{w_{relax}})$ and without relaxation (ℓ_1). For each case we perform three comparisons, first, I_1 warped by $f_{1 \to 0}$ which named $(I_1^{w \to 0})$ and compare to I_0, second, I_1 warped by the predicted $f_{1 \to t_4}$ (before refinement) named by $(I_1^{w \to t_4})$ and compared to $I_{t_4}^{gt}$, and finally, we also compared the final output of the network with $I_{t_4}^{gt}$. Table 5 reports results of evaluation on DAVIS and Fig. 8 shows IE for an example from Vimeo90k. Both Table 5 and Fig. 8 show that although the relaxation makes the O.F. estimation between two initial pair poor, it gives better initial motion prediction for the middle frame as well as the final interpolation result.

Temporal Pyramidal Structure. The effectiveness of the temporal pyramidal structure in interpolating multiple frames has already been verified in Table 2. To further investigate this impact by also considering the number of frames it generates, we trained another 3 variations of model including predicting all 7 frames without pyramidal structure, predicting 3 frames ($i = 2, 4, 6$), and only 1 middle frame ($i = 4$) with pyramidal model. Table 4 reports the interpolation quality of the middle frame on DAVIS and Vimeo90K for all these cases. The results in Table 4 demonstrate that the interpolation of the middle frame benefits from the joint optimization with other frames.

4.5 Efficiency Analysis

Considering the wide applications for frame interpolation, especially on mobile and embedded devices, investigating the efficiency of the solution is crucial. We report the efficiency of the proposed method in terms of model size, interpolation quality, and inference time. Figure 9a reports PSNR values evaluated on Adobe240 in relation with the model sizes. The proposed method outperforms all the methods in the quality of the results with a large margin while having a significantly smaller model size. In particular, our method outperforms Quadratic [26] by 1.57 dB by using only 12.5% of its parameters. We also show the inference times for interpolating different numbers of frames in Fig. 9b. To

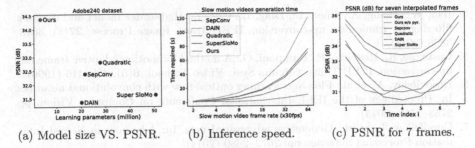

(a) Model size VS. PSNR.   (b) Inference speed.   (c) PSNR for 7 frames.

Fig. 9. Efficiency of the proposed method compared to state-of-the-art methods from the perspective of performance and model size (a), inference speed (b), and performance trend in multiple frame interpolation (c).

interpolate more than 8 frames, our method is able to be extended to interpolate more frames by simply adding more levels in the pyramid. However, higher frame rate videos are hard to be obtained for training; thus, we adopt the iterative interpolation method (run 8x model multiple times and drop the corresponding frames). As reported in Fig. 9b, our method is around 7 times faster than [26] for interpolating more than 8 frames. Our method is the fastest and has the smallest size while keeping the high-quality results for multi-frame interpolation tasks, which makes it applicable for low power devices.

5 Conclusions

In this work, we proposed a powerful and efficient multi-frame interpolation solution that considers prior information and the challenges in this particular task. The prior information about the difficulty levels among the intermediate frames helps us to design a temporal pyramidal processing structure. To handle the challenges of real world complex motion, our method benefits from the proposed advanced motion modeling, including cubic motion prediction and relaxed loss function for flow estimation. All these parts together help to integrate multi-frame generation in a single optimized and efficient network while the temporal consistency of frames and spatial quality are at maximum level beating the state-of-the-art solutions.

References

1. Baker, S., Scharstein, D., Lewis, J., Roth, S., Black, M.J., Szeliski, R.: A database and evaluation methodology for optical flow. Int. J. Comput. Vision **92**(1), 1–31 (2011)
2. Bao, W., Lai, W.S., Ma, C., Zhang, X., Gao, Z., Yang, M.H.: Depth-aware video frame interpolation. In: IEEE Conference on Computer Vision and Pattern Recognition (2019)
3. Bao, W., Lai, W.S., Zhang, X., Gao, Z., Yang, M.H.: MEMC-Net: motion estimation and motion compensation driven neural network for video interpolation and enhancement. arXiv preprint arXiv:1810.08768 (2018)

4. Bao, W., Zhang, X., Chen, L., Ding, L., Gao, Z.: High-order model and dynamic filtering for frame rate up-conversion. IEEE Trans. Image Process. **27**(8), 3813–3826 (2018)
5. Castagno, R., Haavisto, P., Ramponi, G.: A method for motion adaptive frame rate up-conversion. IEEE Trans. Circuits Syst. Video Technol. **6**(5), 436–446 (1996)
6. Dosovitskiy, A., et al.: FlowNet: learning optical flow with convolutional networks. In: Proceedings of the IEEE International Conference on Computer Vision, pp. 2758–2766 (2015)
7. Goodfellow, I., et al.: Generative adversarial nets. In: Advances in Neural Information Processing Systems, pp. 2672–2680 (2014)
8. Ilg, E., Mayer, N., Saikia, T., Keuper, M., Dosovitskiy, A., Brox, T.: FlowNet 2.0: evolution of optical flow estimation with deep networks. In: Proceedings of the IEEE Conference on Computer Vision and Pattern Recognition, pp. 2462–2470 (2017)
9. Jaderberg, M., Simonyan, K., Zisserman, A., et al.: Spatial transformer networks. In: Advances in Neural Information Processing Systems, pp. 2017–2025 (2015)
10. Jiang, H., Sun, D., Jampani, V., Yang, M.H., Learned-Miller, E., Kautz, J.: Super SloMo: high quality estimation of multiple intermediate frames for video interpolation. In: Proceedings of the IEEE Conference on Computer Vision and Pattern Recognition, pp. 9000–9008 (2018)
11. Kingma, D.P., Ba, J.: Adam: a method for stochastic optimization. arXiv preprint arXiv:1412.6980 (2014)
12. Ledig, C., et al.: Photo-realistic single image super-resolution using a generative adversarial network. In: Proceedings of the IEEE Conference on Computer Vision and Pattern Recognition, pp. 4681–4690 (2017)
13. Lee, W.H., Choi, K., Ra, J.B.: Frame rate up conversion based on variational image fusion. IEEE Trans. Image Process. **23**(1), 399–412 (2013)
14. Liu, Y.L., Liao, Y.T., Lin, Y.Y., Chuang, Y.Y.: Deep video frame interpolation using cyclic frame generation. In: AAAI Conference on Artificial Intelligence (2019)
15. Liu, Z., Yeh, R.A., Tang, X., Liu, Y., Agarwala, A.: Video frame synthesis using deep voxel flow. In: Proceedings of the IEEE International Conference on Computer Vision, pp. 4463–4471 (2017)
16. Nah, S., Hyun Kim, T., Mu Lee, K.: Deep multi-scale convolutional neural network for dynamic scene deblurring. In: Proceedings of the IEEE Conference on Computer Vision and Pattern Recognition, pp. 3883–3891 (2017)
17. Niklaus, S., Liu, F.: Context-aware synthesis for video frame interpolation. In: Proceedings of the IEEE Conference on Computer Vision and Pattern Recognition, pp. 1701–1710 (2018)
18. Niklaus, S., Mai, L., Liu, F.: Video frame interpolation via adaptive convolution. In: Proceedings of the IEEE Conference on Computer Vision and Pattern Recognition, pp. 670–679 (2017)
19. Niklaus, S., Mai, L., Liu, F.: Video frame interpolation via adaptive separable convolution. In: Proceedings of the IEEE International Conference on Computer Vision, pp. 261–270 (2017)
20. Peleg, T., Szekely, P., Sabo, D., Sendik, O.: IM-Net for high resolution video frame interpolation. In: Proceedings of the IEEE Conference on Computer Vision and Pattern Recognition, pp. 2398–2407 (2019)
21. Perazzi, F., Pont-Tuset, J., McWilliams, B., Van Gool, L., Gross, M., Sorkine-Hornung, A.: A benchmark dataset and evaluation methodology for video object segmentation. In: Proceedings of the IEEE Conference on Computer Vision and Pattern Recognition, pp. 724–732 (2016)

22. Ranjan, A., Black, M.J.: Optical flow estimation using a spatial pyramid network. In: Proceedings of the IEEE Conference on Computer Vision and Pattern Recognition, pp. 4161–4170 (2017)
23. Su, S., Delbracio, M., Wang, J., Sapiro, G., Heidrich, W., Wang, O.: Deep video deblurring for hand-held cameras. In: Proceedings of the IEEE Conference on Computer Vision and Pattern Recognition, pp. 1279–1288 (2017)
24. Sun, D., Yang, X., Liu, M.Y., Kautz, J.: PWC-Net: CNNs for optical flow using pyramid, warping, and cost volume. In: Proceedings of the IEEE Conference on Computer Vision and Pattern Recognition, pp. 8934–8943 (2018)
25. Wu, J., Yuen, C., Cheung, N.M., Chen, J., Chen, C.W.: Modeling and optimization of high frame rate video transmission over wireless networks. IEEE Trans. Wireless Commun. 15(4), 2713–2726 (2015)
26. Xu, X., Siyao, L., Sun, W., Yin, Q., Yang, M.H.: Quadratic video interpolation. In: Advances in Neural Information Processing Systems, pp. 1645–1654 (2019)
27. Xue, T., Chen, B., Wu, J., Wei, D., Freeman, W.T.: Video enhancement with task-oriented flow. Int. J. Comput. Vision (IJCV) 127(8), 1106–1125 (2019)
28. Yuan, L., Chen, Y., Liu, H., Kong, T., Shi, J.: Zoom-in-to-check: boosting video interpolation via instance-level discrimination. In: Proceedings of the IEEE Conference on Computer Vision and Pattern Recognition, pp. 12183–12191 (2019)
29. Zhang, H., Shen, C., Li, Y., Cao, Y., Liu, Y., Yan, Y.: Exploiting temporal consistency for real-time video depth estimation. In: Proceedings of the IEEE International Conference on Computer Vision, pp. 1725–1734 (2019)
30. Zhang, H., Patel, V.M.: Densely connected pyramid dehazing network. In: Proceedings of the IEEE Conference on Computer Vision and Pattern Recognition, pp. 3194–3203 (2018)

A Broader Study of Cross-Domain Few-Shot Learning

Yunhui Guo[1]($\boxtimes$), Noel C. Codella[2], Leonid Karlinsky[2], James V. Codella[2], John R. Smith[2], Kate Saenko[3], Tajana Rosing[1], and Rogerio Feris[2]

[1] University of California San Diego, San Diego, USA
yug185@eng.ucsd.edu
[2] IBM Research AI, Cambridge, USA
[3] Boston University, Boston, USA

Abstract. Recent progress on few-shot learning largely relies on annotated data for meta-learning: base classes sampled from the same domain as the novel classes. However, in many applications, collecting data for meta-learning is infeasible or impossible. This leads to the cross-domain few-shot learning problem, where there is a large shift between base and novel class domains. While investigations of the cross-domain few-shot scenario exist, these works are limited to natural images that still contain a high degree of visual similarity. No work yet exists that examines few-shot learning across different imaging methods seen in real world scenarios, such as aerial and medical imaging. In this paper, we propose the Broader Study of Cross-Domain Few-Shot Learning (BSCD-FSL) benchmark, consisting of image data from a diverse assortment of image acquisition methods. This includes natural images, such as crop disease images, but additionally those that present with an increasing dissimilarity to natural images, such as satellite images, dermatology images, and radiology images. Extensive experiments on the proposed benchmark are performed to evaluate state-of-art meta-learning approaches, transfer learning approaches, and newer methods for cross-domain few-shot learning. The results demonstrate that state-of-art meta-learning methods are surprisingly outperformed by earlier meta-learning approaches, and all meta-learning methods underperform in relation to simple fine-tuning by 12.8% average accuracy. In some cases, meta-learning even underperforms networks with random weights. Performance gains previously observed with methods specialized for cross-domain few-shot learning vanish in this more challenging benchmark. Finally, accuracy of all methods tend to correlate with dataset similarity to natural images, verifying the value of the benchmark to better represent the diversity of data seen in practice and guiding future research. Code for the experiments in this work can be found at https://github.com/IBM/cdfsl-benchmark.

Y. Guo and N. C. Codella—Equal contribution.

Electronic supplementary material The online version of this chapter (https://doi.org/10.1007/978-3-030-58583-9_8) contains supplementary material, which is available to authorized users.

Keywords: Cross-domain · Few-shot learning · Benchmark · Transfer learning

1   Introduction

Broader Study of Cross-Domain Few-Shot Learning (BSCD-FSL)

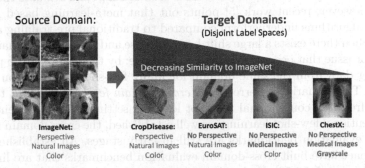

Fig. 1. The Broader Study of Cross-Domain Few-Shot Learning (BSCD-FSL) benchmark. ImageNet is used for source training, and domains of varying dissimilarity from natural images are used for target evaluation. Similarity is measured by 3 orthogonal criteria: 1) existence of perspective distortion, 2) the semantic content, and 3) color depth. No data is provided for meta-learning, and target classes are disjoint from the source classes.

Training deep neural networks for visual recognition typically requires a large amount of labelled examples [28]. The generalization ability of deep neural networks relies heavily on the size and variations of the dataset used for training. However, collecting sufficient amounts of data for certain classes may be impossible in practice: for example, in dermatology, there are a multitude of instances of rare diseases, or diseases that become rare for particular types of skin [1, 25, 48]. Or in other domains such as satellite imagery, there are instances of rare categories such as airplane wreckage. Although individually each situation may not carry heavy cost, as a group across many such conditions and modalities, correct identification is critically important, and remains a significant challenge where access to expertise may be impeded.

Although humans generalize to recognize new categories from few examples in certain circumstances, such as when categories exhibit predictable variations across examples and have reasonable contrast from background [31,32], even humans have trouble recognizing new categories that vary too greatly between examples or differ from prior experience, such as for diagnosis in dermatology, radiology, or other fields [48]. Because there are many applications where learning must work from few examples, and both machines and humans have difficulty learning in these circumstances, finding new methods to tackle the problem remains a challenging but desirable goal.

The problem of learning how to categorize classes with very few training examples has been the topic of the "few-shot learning" field, and has been the subject of a large body of recent work [5,13,34,43,53,55,60]. Few-shot learning is typically composed of the following two stages: meta-learning and meta-testing. In the meta-learning stage, there exists an abundance of base category classes on which a system can be trained to learn well under conditions of few-examples within that particular domain. In the meta-testing stage, a set of novel classes consisting of very few examples per class is used to adapt and evaluate the trained model. However, recent work [5] points out that meta-learning based few-shot learning algorithms underperform compared to traditional pre-training and fine-tuning when there exists a large shift between base and novel class domains. This is a major issue that occurs commonly in practice: by the nature of the problem, collecting data from the same domain for many few-shot classification tasks is difficult. This scenario is referred to as *cross-domain few-shot learning*, to distinguish it from the conventional few-shot learning setting. Although benchmarks for conventional few-shot learning are well established, the cross-domain few-shot learning evaluation benchmarks are still in early stages. All established works in this space have built cross-domain evaluation benchmarks that are limited to natural images [5,56,58]. Under these circumstances, useful knowledge may still be effectively transferring across different domains of natural images, implying that methods designed in this setting may not continue to perform well when applied to domains of other types of images, such as industrial natural images, satellite images, or medical images. Currently, no works study this scenario.

To fill this gap, we propose the Broader Study of Cross-Domain Few-Shot Learning (BSCD-FSL) benchmark (Fig. 1), which covers a spectrum of image types with varying levels of similarity to natural images. Similarity is defined by 3 orthogonal criteria: 1) whether images contain perspective distortion, 2) the semantic content of images, and 3) color depth. The datasets include agriculture images (natural images, but specific to agriculture industry), satellite (loses perspective distortion), dermatology (loses perspective distortion, and contains different semantic content), and radiological images (different according to all 3 criteria). The performance of existing state-of-art meta-learning methods, transfer learning methods, and methods tailored for cross-domain few-shot learning is then rigorously tested on the proposed benchmark.

In summary, the contributions of this paper are itemized as follows:

- We establish a new Broader Study of Cross-Domain Few-Shot Learning (BSCD-FSL) benchmark, consisting of images from a diversity of image types with varying dissimilarity to natural images, according to 1) perspective distortion, 2) the semantic content, and 3) color depth.
- Under these conditions, we extensively evaluate the performance of current meta-learning methods, including methods specifically tailored for cross-domain few-shot learning, as well as variants of fine-tuning.
- The results demonstrate that state-of-art meta-learning methods are outperformed by older meta-learning approaches, and all meta-learning methods

underperform in relation to simple fine-tuning by 12.8% average accuracy. In some cases, meta-learning underperforms even *networks with random weights*.
- Results also show that accuracy gains for cross-domain few-shot learning methods are lost in this new challenging benchmark.
- Finally, we find that accuracy of all methods correlate with the proposed measure of data similarity to natural images, verifying the diversity of the problem representation, and the value of the benchmark towards future research.

We believe this work will help the community understand what methods are most effective in practice, and help drive further advances that can more quickly yield benefit for real-world applications.

2 Related Work

Few-Shot Learning. Few-shot learning [31, 32, 60] is an increasingly important topic in machine learning. Many few-shot methods have been proposed, including meta-learning, generative and augmentation approaches, semi-supervised methods, and transfer learning.

Meta-learning methods aim to learn models that can be quickly adapted using a few examples [13, 33, 53, 55, 60]. MatchingNet [60] learns an embedding that can map an unlabelled example to its label using a small number of labelled examples, while MAML [13] aims at learning good initialization parameters that can be quickly adapted to a new task. In ProtoNet [53], the goal is to learn a metric space in which classification can be conducted by calculating distances to prototype representations of each class. RelationNet [55] targets learning a deep distance metric to compare a small number of images. More recently, MetaOpt [33] learns feature embeddings that can generalize well under a linear classification rule for novel categories.

The generative and augmentation based family of approaches learn to generate more samples from few examples available for training in a given few-shot learning task. These methods include applying augmentation strategies learned from data [36], synthesizing new data from few examples using a generative model, or using external data for obtaining additional examples that facilitate learning on a given few shot task. In [19, 52] the intra-class relations between pairs of instances of reference categories are modeled in feature space, and then this information is transferred to the novel category instances to generate additional examples in that same feature space. In [63], a generator sub-net is added to a classifier network and is trained to synthesize new examples on the fly in order to improve the classifier performance when being fine-tuned on a novel (few-shot) task. In [44], a few-shot class density estimation is performed with an auto-regressive model, combined with an attention mechanism, where examples are synthesized by a sequential process. In [6, 51, 67] label and attribute semantics are used as additional information for training an example synthesis network.

In some situations there exists additional unlabeled data accompanying the few-shot task. In the semi-supervised few-shot learning [2,35,37,45,49] the unlabeled data comes in addition to the support set and is assumed to have a similar distribution to the target classes (although some unrelated samples noise is also allowed). In LST [35], self-labeling and soft attention are used on the unlabeled samples intermittently with fine-tuning on the labeled and self-labeled data. Similarly to LST, [45] updates the class prototypes using k-means like iterations initialized from the PN prototypes. In [2], unlabeled examples are used through soft-label propagation. In [15,24,37], graph neural networks are used for sharing information between labeled and unlabeled examples in semi-supervised [15,37] and transductive [24] FSL setting. Notably, in [37] a Graph Construction network is used to predict the task specific graph for propagating labels between samples of semi-supervised FSL task.

Transfer learning [42] is based on the idea of reusing features learned from the base classes for the novel classes, and is conducted mainly by fine-tuning, which adjusts a pre-trained model from a source task to a target task. Yosinski et al. [66] conducted extensive experiments to investigate the transfer utility of pre-trained deep neural networks. In [27], the authors investigated whether higher performing ImageNet models transfer better to new tasks. Ge et al. [16] proposed a selective joint fine-tuning method for improving the performance of models with a limited amount training data. In [18], the authors proposed an adaptive fine-tuning scheme to decide which layers of the pre-trained network should be fine-tuned. Finally, in [10], the authors found that simple transductive fine-tuning beats all prior state-of-art meta-learning approaches.

Common to all few-shot learning methods is the assumption that *base classes and novel classes are from the same domain*. The current benchmarks for evaluation are miniImageNet [60], CUB [61], Omniglot [31], CIFAR-FS [3] and tiered-ImageNet [46]. In [56], the authors proposed Meta-Dataset, which is a newer benchmark for training and evaluating few-shot learning algorithms that includes a greater diversity of image content. Although this benchmark is more broad than prior works, the included datasets are still limited to *natural images*, and both the base classes and novel classes are from the *same domain*. Recently, [47] proposes a successful meta-learning approach based on conditional neural process on the MetaDataset benchmark.

Cross-Domain Few-Shot Learning. In cross-domain few-shot learning, base and novel classes are both drawn from different domains, and the class label sets are disjoint. Recent works on cross-domain few-shot learning include analysis of existing meta-learning approaches in the cross-domain setting [5], specialized methods using feature-wise transform to encourage learning representations with improved ability to generalize [58], and works studying cross-domain few-shot learning constrained to the setting of images of items in museum galleries [26]. Common to all these prior works is that they limit the cross-domain setting to the realm of *natural images*, which still retain a high degree of visual similarity, and do not capture the broader spectrum of image types encountered in practice, such as industrial, aerial, and medical images, where cross-domain few-shot learning techniques are in high demand.

3   Proposed Benchmark

In this section, we introduce the Broader Study of Cross-Domain Few-Shot Learning (BSCD-FSL) benchmark, which includes data from CropDiseases [40], EuroSAT [21], ISIC2018 [8,57], and ChestX [62] datasets. These datasets cover plant disease images, satellite images, dermoscopic images of skin lesions, and X-ray images, respectively. The selected datasets reflect well-curated real-world use cases for few-shot learning. In addition, collecting enough examples from above domains is often difficult, expensive, or in some cases not possible. Image similarity to natural images is measured by 3 orthogonal criteria: 1) existence of perspective distortion, 2) the semantic data content, and 3) color depth. According to this criteria, the datasets demonstrate the following spectrum of image types: 1) CropDiseases images are natural images, but are very specialized (similar to existing cross-domain few-shot setting, but specific to agriculture industry), 2) EuroSAT images are less similar as they have lost perspective distortion, but are still color images of natural scenes, 3) ISIC2018 images are even less similar as they have lost perspective distortion and no longer represent natural scenes, and 4) ChestX images are the most dissimilar as they have lost perspective distortion, do not represent natural scenes, and have lost 2 color channels. Example images from ImageNet and the proposed benchmark datasets are shown in Fig. 1.

Having a few-shot learning model trained on a source domain such as ImageNet [9] that can generalize to domains such as these, is highly desirable, as it enables effective learning for rare categories in new types of images, which has previously not been studied in detail.

4   Cross-Domain Few-Shot Learning Formulation

The cross domain few-shot learning problem can be formalized as follows. We define a *domain* as a joint distribution P over input space $\mathcal{X}$ and label space $\mathcal{Y}$. The marginal distribution of $\mathcal{X}$ is denoted as $P_{\mathcal{X}}$. We use the pair (x, y) to denote a sample x and the corresponding label y from the joint distribution P. For a model $f_\theta \colon \mathcal{X} \to \mathcal{Y}$ with parameter θ and a loss function ℓ, the expected error is defined as,

$$\epsilon(f_\theta) = E_{(x,y) \sim P}[\ell(f_\theta(x), y)] \qquad (1)$$

In cross-domain few-shot learning, we have a source domain $(\mathcal{X}_s, \mathcal{Y}_s)$ and a target domain $(\mathcal{X}_t, \mathcal{Y}_t)$ with joint distribution P_s and P_t respectively, $P_{\mathcal{X}_s} \neq P_{\mathcal{X}_t}$, and $\mathcal{Y}_s$ is disjoint from $\mathcal{Y}_t$. The base classes data are sampled from the source domain and the novel classes data are sampled from the target domain. During the training or meta-training stage, the model f_θ is trained (or meta-trained) on the base classes data. During testing (or meta-testing) stage, the model is presented with a *support set* $S = \{x_i, y_i\}_{i=1}^{K \times N}$ consisting of N examples from

K novel classes. This configuration is referred to as "K-way N-shot" few-shot learning, as the support set has K novel classes and each novel class has N training examples. After the model is adapted to the support set, a *query set* from novel classes is used to evaluate the model performance.

5 Evaluated Methods for Cross-Domain Few-Shot Learning

In this section, we describe the few-shot learning algorithms that will be evaluated on our proposed benchmark.

5.1 Meta-learning Based Methods

Single Domain Methods. Meta-learning [13,43], or learning to learn, aims at learning task-agnostic knowledge in order to efficiently learn on new tasks. Each task T_i is assumed to be drawn from a fixed distribution, $T_i \sim P(T)$. Specially, in few-shot learning, each task T_i is a small dataset $D_i := \{x_j, y_j\}_{j=1}^{K \times N}$. $P_s(T)$ and $P_t(T)$ are used to denote the task distribution of the source (base) classes data and target (novel) classes data respectively. During the meta-training stage, the model is trained on T tasks $\{T_i\}_{i=1}^T$ which are sampled independently from $P_s(T)$. During the meta-testing stage, the model is expected to be quickly adapted to a new task $T_j \sim P_t(T)$.

Meta-learning methods differ in their way of learning the parameter of the initial model f_θ on the base classes data. In MatchingNet [60], the goal is to learn a model f_θ that can map an unlabelled example $\hat{x}$ to its label $\hat{y}$ using a small labelled set $D_i := \{x_j, y_j\}_{j=1}^{K \times N}$ as $\hat{y} = \sum_{j=1}^{K \times N} a_\theta(\hat{x}, x_j) y_j$, where a_θ is an attention kernel which leverages f_θ to compute the distance between the unlabelled example $\hat{x}$ and the labelled example x_j, and y_j is the one-hot representation of the label. In contrast, MAML [13] aims at learning an initial parameter θ that can be quickly adapted to a new task. This is achieved by updating the model parameter via a two-stage optimization process. ProtoNet [53] represents each class k with the mean vector of embedded support examples as $c_k = \frac{1}{N} \sum_{j=1}^N f_\theta(x_j)$. Classification is then conducted by calculating distance of the example to the prototype representations of each class. In RelationNet [55] the metric of the nearest neighbor classifier is meta-learned using a Siamese Networks trained for optimal comparison between query and support samples. More recently, MetaOpt [33] employs convex base learners and aims at learning feature embeddings that generalize well under a linear classification rule for novel categories. All the existing meta-learning methods implicitly assume that $P_s(T) = P_t(T)$ so the task-agnostic knowledge learned in the meta-training stage can be leveraged for fast learning on novel classes. However, in cross-domain few-shot learning $P_s(T) \neq P_t(T)$ which poses severe challenges for current meta-learning methods.

Cross-Domain Methods. Only few methods specifically tailored to learning in the condition of cross-domain few-shot learning have been previously explored, including feature-wise transform (FWT) [58], and Adversarial Domain Adaptation with Reinforced Sample (ADA-RSS) Selection [11]. Since the problem setting of ADA-RSS requires the existence of unlabelled data in the target domain, we study FWT alone.

FWT is a model agnostic approach that adds a feature-wise transform layer to pre-trained models to learn scale and shift parameters from a collection of several dataset domains, or use parameters empirically determined from a single dataset domain. Both approaches have been previously found to improve performance. Since our benchmark is focused on ImageNet as the single source domain, we focus on the single data domain approach. The method is studied in combination with all meta-learning algorithms described in the prior section.

5.2 Transfer Learning Based Methods

An alternative way to tackle the problem of few-shot learning is based on transfer learning, where an initial model f_θ is trained on the base classes data in a standard supervised learning way and reused on the novel classes. There are several options to realize the idea of transfer learning for few-shot learning:

Single Model Methods. In this paper, we extensively evaluate the following commonly variants of single model fine-tuning:

- *Fixed feature extractor (Fixed)*: simply leverage the pre-trained model as a fixed feature extractor.
- *Fine-tuning all layers (Ft All)*: adjusts all the pre-trained parameters on the new task with standard supervised learning.
- *Fine-tuning last-k (Ft Last-k)*: only the last k layers of the pre-trained model are optimized for the new task. In the paper, we consider Fine-tuning last-1, Fine-tuning last-2, Fine-tuning last-3.
- *Transductive fine-tuning (Transductive Ft)*: in transductive fine-tuning, the statistics of the query images are used via batch normalization [10,41].

In addition, we compare these single model transfer learning techniques against a baseline of an embedding formed by a randomly initialized network (termed *Random*) to contrast against a fixed feature vector that has no pre-training. All the variants of single model fine-tuning are based on linear classifier but differ in their approach to fine-tune the single model feature extractor.

Another line of work for few-shot learning uses a broader variety of classifiers for transfer learning. For example, recent works show that mean-centroid classifier and cosine-similarity based classifier are more effective than linear classifier for few-shot learning [5,39]. Therefore we study these two variations as well.

Mean-Centroid Classifier. The mean-centroid classifier is inspired from ProtoNet [53]. Given the pre-trained model f_θ and a support set $S = \{x_i, y_i\}_{i=1}^{K \times N}$, where K is the number of novel classes and N is the number of images per class. The class prototypes are computed in the same way as in ProtoNet. Then the likelihood of an unlabelled example $\hat{x}$ belongs to class k is computed as,

$$p(y = k|\hat{x}) = \frac{\exp(-d(f_\theta, c_k))}{\sum_{l=1}^{K} \exp(-d(f_\theta, c_l))} \tag{2}$$

where $d()$ is a distance function. In the experiments, we use negative cosine similarity. Different from ProtoNet, f_θ is pretrained on the base classes data in a standard supervised learning way.

Cosine-Similarity Based Classifier. In cosine-similarity based classifier, instead of directly computing the class prototypes using the pre-trained model, each class k is represented as a d-dimension weight vector $\mathbf{w}_k$ which is initialized randomly. For each unlabeled example $\hat{x}_i$, the cosine similarity to each weight vector is computed as $c_{i,k} = \frac{f_\theta(\hat{x}_i)^T \mathbf{w}_k}{\|f_\theta(\hat{x}_i)\|\|\mathbf{w}_k\|}$. The predictive probability of the example $\hat{x}_i$ belongs to class k is computed by normalizing the cosine similarity with a softmax function. Intuitively, the weight vector $\mathbf{w}_k$ can be thought as the prototype of class k.

Transfer from Multiple Pre-trained Models. In this section, we describe a straightforward method that utilizes multiple models pre-trained on source domains of natural images similar to ImageNet. Note that all domains are still disjoint from the target datasets for the cross-domain few-shot learning setting. The purpose is to measure how much performance may improve by utilizing an ensemble of models trained from data that is different from the target domain. The described method requires no change to how models are trained and is an off-the-shelf solution to leverage existing pre-trained models for cross-domain few-shot learning, without requiring access to the source datasets.

Assume we have a library of C pre-trained models $\{M_c\}_{c=1}^C$ which are trained on various datasets in a standard way. We denote the layers of all pre-trained models as a set F. Given a support set $S = \{x_i, y_i\}_{i=1}^{K \times N}$ where $(x_i, y_i) \sim P_t$, our goal is to find a subset I of the layers to generate a feature vector for each example in order to achieve the lowest test error. Mathematically,

$$\arg\min_{I \subseteq F} \mathbb{E}_{(x,y) \sim P_t} \ell(f_s(T(\{l(x) : l \in I\})), y) \tag{3}$$

where ℓ is a loss function, $T()$ is a function which concatenates a set of feature vectors, l is one particular layer in the set I, and f_s is a linear classifier. Practically, for feature vectors l coming from inner layers which are three-dimensional, we convert them to one-dimensional vectors by using Global Average Pooling. Since Eq. 3 is intractable generally, we instead adopt a two-stage greedy selection method, called *Incremental Multi-model Selection*, to iteratively find the best subset of layers for a given support S.

Table 1. The results of meta-learning methods on the proposed benchmark.

Methods	ChestX			ISIC		
	5-way 5-shot	5-way 20-shot	5-way 50-shot	5-way 5-shot	5-way 20-shot	5-way 50-shot
MatchingNet	22.40% ± 0.7%	23.61% ± 0.86%	22.12% ± 0.88%	36.74% ± 0.53%	45.72% ± 0.53%	54.58% ± 0.65%
MatchingNet+FWT	21.26% ± 0.31%	23.23% ± 0.37%	23.01% ± 0.34%	30.40% ± 0.48%	32.01% ± 0.48%	33.17% ± 0.43%
MAML	23.48% ± 0.96%	27.53% ± 0.43%	-	**40.13% ± 0.58%**	**52.36% ± 0.57%**	-
ProtoNet	**24.05% ± 1.01%**	**28.21% ± 1.15%**	29.32% ± 1.12%	39.57% ± 0.57%	49.50% ± 0.55%	51.99% ± 0.52%
ProtoNet+FWT	23.77% ± 0.42%	26.87% ± 0.43%	**30.12% ± 0.46%**	38.87% ± 0.52%	43.78% ± 0.47%	49.84% ± 0.51%
RelationNet	22.96% ± 0.88%	26.63% ± 0.92%	28.45% ± 1.20%	39.41% ± 0.58%	41.77% ± 0.49%	49.32% ± 0.51%
RelationNet+FWT	22.74% ± 0.40%	26.75% ± 0.41%	27.56% ± 0.40%	35.54% ± 0.55%	43.31% ± 0.51%	46.38% ± 0.53%
MetaOpt	22.53% ± 0.91%	25.53% ± 1.02%	29.35% ± 0.99%	36.28% ± 0.50%	49.42% ± 0.60%	**54.80% ± 0.54%**
Methods	EuroSAT			CropDiseases		
	5-way 5-shot	5-way 20-shot	5-way 50-shot	5-way 5-shot	5-way 20-shot	5-way 50-shot
MatchingNet	64.45% ± 0.63%	77.10% ± 0.57%	54.44% ± 0.67%	66.39% ± 0.78%	76.38% ± 0.67%	58.53% ± 0.73%
MatchingNet+FWT	56.04% ± 0.65%	63.38% ± 0.69%	62.75% ± 0.76%	62.74% ± 0.90%	74.90% ± 0.71%	75.68% ± 0.78%
MAML	71.70% ± 0.72%	81.95% ± 0.55%	-	78.05% ± 0.68%	**89.75% ± 0.42%**	-
ProtoNet	**73.29% ± 0.71%**	**82.27% ± 0.57%**	80.48% ± 0.57%	**79.72% ± 0.67%**	88.15% ± 0.51%	90.81% ± 0.43%
ProtoNet+FWT	67.34% ± 0.76%	75.74% ± 0.70%	78.64% ± 0.57%	72.72% ± 0.70%	85.82% ± 0.51%	87.17% ± 0.50%
RelationNet	61.31% ± 0.72%	74.43% ± 0.66%	74.91% ± 0.58%	68.99% ± 0.75%	80.45% ± 0.64%	85.08% ± 0.53%
RelationNet+FWT	61.16% ± 0.70%	69.40% ± 0.64%	73.84% ± 0.60%	64.91% ± 0.79%	78.43% ± 0.59%	81.14% ± 0.56%
MetaOpt	64.44% ± 0.73%	79.19% ± 0.62%	**83.62% ± 0.58%**	68.41% ± 0.73%	82.89% ± 0.54%	**91.76% ± 0.38%**

In the first stage, for each pre-trained model, we a train linear classifier on the feature vector generated by each layer individually and select the corresponding layer which achieves the lowest average error using five-fold cross-validation on the support set S. Essentially, the goal of the first stage is to find the most effective layer of each pre-trained model given the task in order to reduce the search space and mitigate risk of overfitting. For convenience, we denote the layers selected in the first selection stage as set I_1. In the second stage, we greedily add the layers in I_1 into the set I following a similar cross-validation procedure. First, we add the layer in I_1 into I which achieves the lowest cross-validation error. Then we iterate over I_1, and add each remaining layer into I if the cross-validation error is reduced when the new layer is added. Finally, we concatenate the feature vector generated by each layer in set I and train the final linear classifier. Please see Algorithm 1 in Appendix for further details.

6   Evaluation Setup

For meta-learning methods, we meta-train all meta-learning methods on the base classes of miniImageNet [60] and meta-test the trained models on each dataset of the proposed benchmark. For transfer learning methods, we train the pre-trained model on base classes of miniImageNet. For transferring from multiple pre-trained models, we use a maximum of five pre-trained models, trained on miniImagenet, CIFAR100 [29], DTD [7], CUB [64], Caltech256 [17], respectively. On all experiments we consider 5-way 5-shot, 5-way 20-shot, 5-way 50-shot. For all cases, the test (query) set has 15 images per class. All experiments are performed with ResNet-10 [20] for fair comparison. For each evaluation, we use the same 600 randomly sampled few-shot episodes (for consistency), and report the average accuracy and 95% confidence interval.

Table 2. The results of different variants of single model fine-tuning on the proposed benchmark.

Methods	ChestX			ISIC		
	5-way 5-shot	5-way 20-shot	5-way 50-shot	5-way 5-shot	5-way 20-shot	5-way 50-shot
Random	21.80% ± 1.03%	25.69% ± 0.95%	26.19% ± 0.94%	37.91% ± 1.39%	47.24% ± 1.50%	50.85% ± 1.37%
Fixed	25.35% ± 0.96%	30.83% ± 1.05%	36.04% ± 0.46%	43.56% ± 0.60%	52.78% ± 0.58%	57.34% ± 0.56%
Ft All	25.97% ± 0.41%	31.32% ± 0.45%	35.49% ± 0.45%	48.11% ± 0.64%	59.31% ± 0.48%	66.48% ± 0.56%
Ft Last-1	25.96% ± 0.46%	**31.63% ± 0.49%**	37.03% ± 0.50%	47.20% ± 0.45%	59.95% ± 0.45%	65.04% ± 0.47%
Ft Last-2	**26.79% ± 0.59%**	30.95% ± 0.61%	36.24% ± 0.62%	47.64% ± 0.44%	59.87% ± 0.35%	66.07% ± 0.45%
Ft Last-3	25.17% ± 0.56%	30.92% ± 0.89%	**37.27% ± 0.64%**	48.05% ± 0.55%	60.20% ± 0.33%	66.21% ± 0.52%
Transductive Ft	26.09% ± 0.96%	31.01% ± 0.59%	36.79% ± 0.53%	**49.68% ± 0.36%**	**61.09% ± 0.44%**	**67.20% ± 0.59%**

Methods	EuroSAT			CropDiseases		
	5-way 5-shot	5-way 20-shot	5-way 50-shot	5-way 5-shot	5-way 20-shot	5-way 50-shot
Random	58.00% ± 2.01%	68.93% ± 1.47%	71.65% ± 1.47%	69.68% ± 1.72%	83.41% ± 1.25%	86.56% ± 1.42%
Fixed	75.69% ± 0.66%	84.13% ± 0.52%	86.62% ± 0.47%	87.48% ± 0.58%	94.45% ± 0.36%	96.62% ± 0.25%
Ft All	79.08% ± 0.61%	87.64% ± 0.47%	90.89% ± 0.36%	89.25% ± 0.51%	95.51% ± 0.31%	97.68% ± 0.21%
Ft Last-1	80.45% ± 0.54%	87.92% ± 0.44%	91.41% ± 0.46%	88.72% ± 0.53%	95.76% ± 0.65%	**97.87% ± 0.48%**
Ft Last-2	79.57% ± 0.51%	87.67% ± 0.46%	90.93% ± 0.45%	88.07% ± 0.56%	95.68% ± 0.76%	97.64% ± 0.59%
Ft Last-3	78.04% ± 0.77%	87.52% ± 0.53%	90.83% ± 0.42%	89.11% ± 0.47%	95.31% ± 0.7%	97.45% ± 0.46%
Transductive Ft	**81.76% ± 0.48%**	**87.97% ± 0.42%**	**92.00% ± 0.56%**	**90.64% ± 0.54%**	**95.91% ± 0.72%**	97.48% ± 0.56%

During the training (meta-training) stage, models used for transfer learning and meta-learning models are both trained for 400 epochs with Adam optimizer. The learning rate is set to 0.001. During testing (meta-testing), both transfer learning methods and those meta-learning methods that require adaptation on the support set of the test episodes (MAML, RelationNet, etc.) use SGD with momentum. The learning rate is 0.01 and the momentum rate is 0.9. All variants of fine-tuning methods are trained for 100 epochs. For feature-wise transformation [58], we adopt the recommended hyperparameters in the original paper for meta-training from one source domain. In the training or meta-training stage, we apply standard data augmentation including random crop, random flip, and color jitter.

In the cross-domain few-shot learning setting, since the source domain and target domain are drastically different, it may not be appropriate to use the source domain data for hyperparameter tuning or validation. Therefore, we leave the question of how to determine the best hyperparameters in the cross-domain few-shot learning as future work. One simple strategy is to use the test set or validation set of the source domain data for hyperparameter tuning. More sophisticated methods may use datasets that are similar to the target domain data.

7   Experimental Results

7.1   Meta-learning Based Results

Table 1 show the results on the proposed benchmark of meta-learning, for each dataset, method, and shot level in the benchmark. Across all datasets and shot levels, the average accuracies (and 95% confidence internals) are 50.21% (0.70) for MatchingNet, 46.55% (0.58) for MatchingNet+FWT, 38.75% (0.41) for

Table 3. The results of varying the classifier for fine-tuning on the proposed benchmark.

Methods	ChestX			ISIC		
	5-way 5-shot	5-way 20-shot	5-way 50-shot	5-way 5-shot	5-way 20-shot	5-way 50-shot
Linear	25.97% ± 0.41%	31.32% ± 0.45%	**35.49% ± 0.45%**	**48.11% ± 0.64%**	**59.31% ± 0.48%**	**66.48% ± 0.56%**
Mean-centroid	26.31% ± 0.42%	30.41% ± 0.46%	34.68% ± 0.46%	47.16% ± 0.54%	56.40% ± 0.53%	61.57% ± 0.66%
Cosine-similarity	**26.95% ± 0.44%**	**32.07% ± 0.55%**	34.76% ± 0.55%	48.01% ± 0.49%	58.13% ± 0.48%	62.03% ± 0.52%

Methods	EuroSAT			CropDiseases		
	5-way 5-shot	5-way 20-shot	5-way 50-shot	5-way 5-shot	5-way 20-shot	5-way 50-shot
Linear	79.08% ± 0.61%	**87.64% ± 0.47%**	**91.34% ± 0.37%**	**89.25% ± 0.51%**	**95.51% ± 0.31%**	**97.68% ± 0.21%**
Mean-centroid	**82.21% ± 0.49%**	87.62% ± 0.34%	88.24% ± 0.29%	87.61% ± 0.47%	93.87% ± 0.68%	94.77% ± 0.34%
Cosine-similarity	81.37% ± 1.54%	86.83% ± 0.43%	88.83% ± 0.38%	89.15% ± 0.51%	93.96% ± 0.46%	94.27% ± 0.41%

MAML, 59.78% (0.70) for ProtoNet, 56.72% (0.55) for ProtoNet+FWT, 54.48% (0.71) for RelationNet, 52.6% (0.56) for RelationNet+FWT, and 57.35% (0.68) for MetaOpt. The performance of MAML was impacted by its inability to scale to larger shot levels due to memory overflow. Methods paired with Feature-Wise Transform are marked with "+FWT".

What is immediately apparent from Table 1, is that the prior state-of-art MetaOptNet is no longer state-of-art, as it is outperformed by ProtoNet. In addition, methods designed specifically for cross-domain few-shot learning lead to consistent performance degradation in this new challenging benchmark. Finally, performance in general strongly positively correlates to the dataset's similarity to ImageNet, confirming that the benchmark's intentional design allows us to investigate few-shot learning in a spectrum of cross-domain difficulties.

7.2 Transfer Learning Based Results

Single Model Results. Table 2 show the results on the proposed benchmark of various single model transfer learning methods. Across all datasets and shot levels, the average accuracies (and 95% confidence internals) are 53.99% (1.38) for random embedding, 64.24 (0.59) for fixed feature embedding, 67.23% (0.46) for fine-tuning all layers, 67.41% (0.49) for fine-tuning the last 1 layer, 67.26% (0.53) for fine-tuning the last 2 layers, 67.17% (0.58) for fine-tuning the last 3 layers, and 68.14% (0.56) for transductive fine-tuning. From these results, several observations can be made. The first observation is that, although meta-learning methods have been previously shown to achieve higher performance than transfer learning in the standard few-shot learning setting [5,60], in the cross-domain few-shot learning setting this situation is reversed: meta-learning methods significantly underperform simple fine-tuning methods. In fact, *MatchingNet performs worse than a randomly generated fixed embedding*. A possible explanation is that meta-learning methods are fitting the task distribution on the base class data, improving performance in that circumstance, but hindering ability to generalize to another task distribution. The second observation is that, by leveraging the statistics of the test data, transductive fine-tuning continues to achieve higher results than the standard fine-tuning and meta-learning, as previously reported [10]. While transductive fine-tuning, however, assumes that all the queries are available as unlabeled data. The third observation is that the accuracy of most methods on the benchmark continues to be dependent on how similar the dataset is to ImageNet: *CropDiseases* commands the highest performance on average, while *EuroSAT* follows in 2nd place, *ISIC* in 3rd, and *ChestX* in 4th. This further supports the motivation behind benchmark design in targeting applications with increasing visual domain dissimilarity to natural images.

Table 3 shows results from varying the classifier. While mean-centriod classifier and cosine-similarity classifier are shown to be more efficient than simple linear classifier in the conventional few-shot learning setting, our results show that mean-centroid and cosine-similarity classifier only have a marginal advantage on *ChestX* and *EuroSAT* over linear classifier in the 5-shot case (Table 3). As the shot increases, linear classifier begins to dominate mean-centroid and cosine-similarity classifier. One plausible reason is that since both mean-centroid and cosine-similarity classifier conduct classification based on unimodal class prototypes, when the number of examples increases, unimodal distribution becomes less suitable, and multi-modal distribution is required.

Transfer from Multiple Pre-trained Models. The results of the described *Incremental Muiti-model Selection* are shown in Table 4. *IMS-f* fine-tunes each pre-trained model before applying the model selection. We include a baseline called *all embeddings* which concatenates the feature vectors generated by all the layers from the fine-tuned models. Across all datasets and shot levels, the average accuracies (and 95% confidence internals) are 68.22% (0.45) for *all embeddings*, and 68.69% (0.44) for *IMS-f*. The results show that *IMS-f* generally improves upon *all embeddings* which indicates the importance of selecting relevant pre-trained models to the target dataset. Model complexity also tends to decrease by over 20% compared to *all embeddings* on average. We can also observe that it is beneficial to use multiple pre-trained models than using just one model, even though these models are trained from data in different domains and different image types. Compared with standard finetuning with a linear classifier, the average improvement of *IMS-f* across all the shots on *ChestX* is 0.20%, on *ISIC* is 0.69%, on *EuroSAT* is 3.52% and on *CropDiseases* is 1.27%.

In further analysis, we study the effect of the number of pre-trained models for the studied multi-model selection method. We consider libraries consisting of two, three, four, and all five pre-trained models. The pre-trained models are added into the library in the order of *ImageNet*, *CIFAR100*, *DTD*, *CUB*, *Caltech256*. For each dataset, the experiment is conducted on 5-way 50-shot with 600 episodes. The results are shown in Table 5. As more pre-trained models are added into the library, we can observe that the test accuracy on *ChestX* and *ISIC* gradually improves which can be attributed to the diverse features provided by different pre-trained models. However, on *EuroSAT* and *CropDiseases*, only a marginal improvement can be observed. One possible reason is that the features from *ImageNet* already captures the characteristics of the datasets and more pre-trained models does not provide additional information.

Table 4. The results of using all embeddings, and the *Incremental Multi-model Selection* (IMS-f) based on fine-tuned pre-trained models on the proposed benchmark.

Methods	ChestX			ISIC		
	5-way 5-shot	5-way 20-shot	5-way 50-shot	5-way 5-shot	5-way 20-shot	5-way 50-shot
All embeddings	**26.74% ± 0.42%**	**32.77% ± 0.47%**	**38.07% ± 0.50%**	**46.86% ± 0.60%**	58.57% ± 0.59%	66.04% ± 0.56%
IMS-f	25.50% ± 0.45%	31.49% ± 0.47%	36.40% ± 0.50%	45.84% ± 0.62%	**61.50% ± 0.58%**	**68.64% ± 0.53%**

Methods	EuroSAT			CropDiseases		
	5-way 5-shot	5-way 20-shot	5-way 50-shot	5-way 5-shot	5-way 20-shot	5-way 50-shot
All embeddings	81.29% ± 0.62%	89.90% ± 0.41%	92.76% ± 0.34%	**90.82% ± 0.48%**	96.64% ± 0.25%	98.14% ± 0.18%
IMS-f	**83.56% ± 0.59%**	**91.22% ± 0.38%**	**93.85% ± 0.30%**	90.66% ± 0.48%	**97.18% ± 0.24%**	**98.43% ± 0.16%**

Table 5. Number of models' effect on test accuracy.

Dataset	# of models			
	2	3	4	5
ChestX	34.35%	36.29%	37.64%	37.89%
ISIC	59.4%	62.49%	65.07%	64.77%
EuroSAT	91.71%	93.49%	92.67%	93.00%
CropDiseases	98.43%	98.09%	98.05%	98.60%

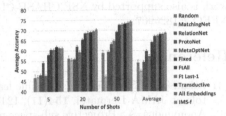

Fig. 2. Comparisons of methods across the entire benchmark.

7.3 Benchmark Summary

Figure 2 summarizes the comparison across algorithms, according to the average accuracy across all datasets and shot levels in the benchmark. The degradation in performance suffered by meta-learning approaches is significant. In some cases, a network with random weights outperforms meta-learning approaches. FWT methods, which yielded no performance improvements, are omitted for brevity. MAML, which failed to operate on the entire benchmark, is also omitted.

8 Conclusion

In this paper, we formally introduce the Broader Study of Cross-Domain Few-Shot Learning (BSCD-FSL) benchmark, which covers several target domains with varying similarity to natural images. We extensively analyze and evaluate existing meta-learning methods, including approaches specifically designed for cross-domain few-shot learning, and variants of transfer learning. The results show that, surprisingly, state-of-art meta-learning approaches are outperformed by earlier approaches, and recent methods for cross-domain few-shot learning actually degrade performance. In addition, all meta-learning methods significantly underperform in comparison to fine-tuning methods. In fact, some meta-learning approaches are outperformed by networks with random weights. In addition, accuracy of all methods correlate with proposed measure of data similarity to natural images, verifying the diversity of the proposed benchmark in terms of its problem representation, and its value towards guiding future research. In conclusion, we believe this work will help the community understand what methods are most effective in practice, and help drive further advances that can more quickly yield benefit for real-world applications.

Acknowledgement. This material is based upon work supported by the Defense Advanced Research Projects Agency (DARPA) under Contract No. FA8750-19-C-1001. Any opinions, findings and conclusions or recommendations expressed in this material are those of the author(s) and do not necessarily reflect the views of the Defense Advanced Research Projects Agency (DARPA). This work was supported in part by CRISP, one of six centers in JUMP, an SRC program sponsored by DARPA. This work is also supported by NSF CHASE-CI #1730158, NSF FET #1911095, NSF CC* NPEO #1826967.

References

1. Adamson, A.S., Smith, A.: Machine learning and health care disparities in dermatology. JAMA Dermatol. **154**(11), 1247–1248 (2018)
2. Anonymous, A.: Projective sub-space networks for few-sot learning. In: ICLR 2019 OpenReview. https://openreview.net/pdf?id=rkzfuiA9F7
3. Bertinetto, L., Henriques, J.F., Torr, P.H., Vedaldi, A.: Meta-learning with differentiable closed-form solvers. arXiv preprint arXiv:1805.08136 (2018)
4. Bousmalis, K., Trigeorgis, G., Silberman, N., Krishnan, D., Erhan, D.: Domain separation networks. In: Advances in Neural Information Processing Systems, pp. 343–351 (2016)
5. Chen, W.Y., Liu, Y.C., Kira, Z., Wang, Y.C.F., Huang, J.B.: A closer look at few-shot classification. In: International Conference on Learning Representations (2019). https://openreview.net/forum?id=HkxLXnAcFQ
6. Chen, Z., Fu, Y., Zhang, Y., Jiang, Y.G., Xue, X., Sigal, L.: Multi-level semantic feature augmentation for one-shot learning. IEEE Trans. Image Process. **28**(9), 4594–4605 (2019). https://doi.org/10.1109/tip.2019.2910052
7. Cimpoi, M., Maji, S., Kokkinos, I., Mohamed, S., Vedaldi, A.: Describing textures in the wild. In: Proceedings of the IEEE Conference on Computer Vision and Pattern Recognition, pp. 3606–3613 (2014)
8. Codella, N., et al.: Skin lesion analysis toward melanoma detection 2018: a challenge hosted by the international skin imaging collaboration (ISIC). arXiv preprint arXiv:1902.03368 (2019)
9. Deng, J., Dong, W., Socher, R., Li, L.J., Li, K., Fei-Fei, L.: ImageNet: a large-scale hierarchical image database. In: 2009 IEEE Conference on Computer Vision and Pattern Recognition, pp. 248–255. IEEE (2009)
10. Dhillon, G., Chaudhari, P., Ravichandran, A., Soatto, S.: A baseline for few-shot image classification. In: ICLR (2020)
11. Dong, N., Xing, E.P.: Domain adaption in one-shot learning. In: Berlingerio, M., Bonchi, F., Gärtner, T., Hurley, N., Ifrim, G. (eds.) ECML PKDD 2018. LNCS (LNAI), vol. 11051, pp. 573–588. Springer, Cham (2019). https://doi.org/10.1007/978-3-030-10925-7_35
12. Dudík, M., Phillips, S.J., Schapire, R.E.: Correcting sample selection bias in maximum entropy density estimation. In: NIPS (2006)
13. Finn, C., Abbeel, P., Levine, S.: Model-agnostic meta-learning for fast adaptation of deep networks. In: Proceedings of the 34th International Conference on Machine Learning-Volume 70, pp. 1126–1135. JMLR.org (2017)

14. Ganin, Y., et al.: Domain-adversarial training of neural networks. J. Mach. Learn. Res. **17**(1), 2096–2030 (2016)
15. Garcia, V., Bruna, J.: Few-shot learning with graph neural networks, pp. 1–13. arXiv:1711.04043 (2017)
16. Ge, W., Yu, Y.: Borrowing treasures from the wealthy: deep transfer learning through selective joint fine-tuning. In: CVPR (2017)
17. Griffin, G., Holub, A., Perona, P.: Caltech-256 object category dataset (2007)
18. Guo, Y., Shi, H., Kumar, A., Grauman, K., Rosing, T., Feris, R.: SpotTune: transfer learning through adaptive fine-tuning. In: Proceedings of the IEEE Conference on Computer Vision and Pattern Recognition, pp. 4805–4814 (2019)
19. Hariharan, B., Girshick, R.: Low-shot visual recognition by shrinking and hallucinating features. In: IEEE International Conference on Computer Vision (ICCV) (2017). https://arxiv.org/pdf/1606.02819.pdf
20. He, K., Zhang, X., Ren, S., Sun, J.: Deep residual learning for image recognition. In: CVPR (2016)
21. Helber, P., Bischke, B., Dengel, A., Borth, D.: EuroSAT: a novel dataset and deep learning benchmark for land use and land cover classification. IEEE J. Sel. Top. Appl. Earth Obs. Remote Sens. **12**(7), 2217–2226 (2019)
22. Hoffman, J., et al.: CyCADA: cycle-consistent adversarial domain adaptation. arXiv preprint arXiv:1711.03213 (2017)
23. Kang, G., Jiang, L., Yang, Y., Hauptmann, A.G.: Contrastive adaptation network for unsupervised domain adaptation. In: Proceedings of the IEEE Conference on Computer Vision and Pattern Recognition, pp. 4893–4902 (2019)
24. Kim, J., Kim, T., Kim, S., Yoo, C.D.: Edge-labeling graph neural network for few-shot learning. Technical report
25. Kinyanjui, N.M., et al.: Estimating skin tone and effects on classification performance in dermatology datasets. In: NeurIPS Fair ML for Health Workshop 2019 (2019)
26. Koniusz, P., Tas, Y., Zhang, H., Harandi, M., Porikli, F., Zhang, R.: Museum exhibit identification challenge for the supervised domain adaptation and beyond. In: Ferrari, V., Hebert, M., Sminchisescu, C., Weiss, Y. (eds.) ECCV 2018. LNCS, vol. 11220, pp. 815–833. Springer, Cham (2018). https://doi.org/10.1007/978-3-030-01270-0_48
27. Kornblith, S., Shlens, J., Le, Q.V.: Do better ImageNet models transfer better? arXiv preprint arXiv:1805.08974 (2018)
28. Krizhevsky, A., Sutskever, I., Hinton, G.E.: ImageNet classification with deep convolutional neural networks. In: NIPS (2012)
29. Krizhevsky, A., et al.: Learning multiple layers of features from tiny images. Technical report, Citeseer (2009)
30. Kumar, A., et al.: Co-regularized alignment for unsupervised domain adaptation. In: Advances in Neural Information Processing Systems, pp. 9345–9356 (2018)
31. Lake, B., Salakhutdinov, R., Gross, J., Tenenbaum, J.: One shot learning of simple visual concepts. In: Proceedings of the Annual Meeting of the Cognitive Science Society, vol. 33 (2011)
32. Lake, B.M., Salakhutdinov, R., Tenenbaum, J.B.: Human-level concept learning through probabilistic program induction. Science **350**(6266), 1332–1338 (2015)
33. Lee, K., Maji, S., Ravichandran, A., Soatto, S.: Meta-learning with differentiable convex optimization. In: Proceedings of the IEEE Conference on Computer Vision and Pattern Recognition, pp. 10657–10665 (2019)
34. Li, F.F., Fergus, R., Perona, P.: One-shot learning of object categories. IEEE Trans. Pattern Anal. Mach. Intell. **28**(4), 594–611 (2006)

35. Li, X., et al.: Learning to self-train for semi-supervised few-shot classification. Technical report (2019)
36. Lim, S., Kim, I., Kim, T., Kim, C., Brain, K., Kim, S.: Fast AutoAugment. Technical report (2019)
37. Liu, Y., et al.: Learning to propagate labels: transductive propagation network for few-shot learning (2019)
38. Long, M., Zhu, H., Wang, J., Jordan, M.I.: Deep transfer learning with joint adaptation networks. In: Proceedings of the 34th International Conference on Machine Learning-Volume 70, pp. 2208–2217. JMLR.org (2017)
39. Mensink, T., Verbeek, J., Perronnin, F., Csurka, G.: Distance-based image classification: generalizing to new classes at near-zero cost. IEEE Trans. Pattern Anal. Mach. Intell. **35**(11), 2624–2637 (2013)
40. Mohanty, S.P., Hughes, D.P., Salathé, M.: Using deep learning for image-based plant disease detection. Front. Plant Sci. **7**, 1419 (2016)
41. Nichol, A., Achiam, J., Schulman, J.: On first-order meta-learning algorithms. arXiv preprint arXiv:1803.02999 (2018)
42. Pan, S.J., Yang, Q.: A survey on transfer learning. IEEE Trans. Knowl. Data Eng. **22**(10), 1345–1359 (2009)
43. Ravi, S., Larochelle, H.: Optimization as a model for few-shot learning (2016)
44. Reed, S., et al.: Few-shot autoregressive density estimation: towards learning to learn distributions. arXiv:1710.10304 (2016). 1–11 (2018)
45. Ren, M., et al.: Meta-learning for semi-supervised few-shot classification. In: ICLR, March 2018. http://arxiv.org/abs/1803.00676bair.berkeley.edu/blog/2017/07/18/
46. Ren, M., et al.: Meta-learning for semi-supervised few-shot classification. arXiv preprint arXiv:1803.00676 (2018)
47. Requeima, J., Gordon, J., Bronskill, J., Nowozin, S., Turner, R.E.: Fast and flexible multi-task classification using conditional neural adaptive processes. In: Advances in Neural Information Processing Systems, pp. 7959–7970 (2019)
48. Rotemberg, V., Halpern, A., Dusza, S.W., Codella, N.C.F.: The role of public challenges and data sets towards algorithm development, trust, and use in clinical practice. Semin. Cutan. Med. Surg. **38**(1), E38–E42 (2019)
49. Saito, K., Kim, D., Sclaroff, S., Darrell, T., Saenko, K.: Semi-supervised domain adaptation via minimax entropy. In: ICCV (2019). http://arxiv.org/abs/1904.06487
50. Saito, K., Kim, D., Sclaroff, S., Saenko, K.: Universal domain adaptation through self supervision https://arxiv.org/abs/2002.07953 (2020)
51. Schwartz, E., Karlinsky, L., Feris, R., Giryes, R., Bronstein, A.M.: Baby steps towards few-shot learning with multiple semantics, pp. 1–11 (2019). http://arxiv.org/abs/1906.01905
52. Schwartz, E., et al.: Delta-encoder: an effective sample synthesis method for few-shot object recognition. In: Neural Information Processing Systems (NIPS) (2018). https://arxiv.org/pdf/1806.04734.pdf
53. Snell, J., Swersky, K., Zemel, R.: Prototypical networks for few-shot learning. In: Advances in Neural Information Processing Systems, pp. 4077–4087 (2017)
54. Sun, B., Feng, J., Saenko, K.: Return of frustratingly easy domain adaptation. In: Thirtieth AAAI Conference on Artificial Intelligence (2016)
55. Sung, F., Yang, Y., Zhang, L., Xiang, T., Torr, P.H., Hospedales, T.M.: Learning to compare: relation network for few-shot learning. In: Proceedings of the IEEE Conference on Computer Vision and Pattern Recognition, pp. 1199–1208 (2018)
56. Triantafillou, E., et al.: Meta-dataset: a dataset of datasets for learning to learn from few examples. arXiv preprint arXiv:1903.03096 (2019)

57. Tschandl, P., Rosendahl, C., Kittler, H.: The HAM10000 dataset, a large collection of multi-source dermatoscopic images of common pigmented skin lesions. Sci. Data **5**, 180161 (2018)
58. Tseng, H.Y., Lee, H.Y., Huang, J.B., Yang, M.H.: Cross-domain few-shot classification via learned feature-wise transformation. In: ICLR (2020)
59. Tzeng, E., Hoffman, J., Saenko, K., Darrell, T.: Adversarial discriminative domain adaptation. In: Proceedings of the IEEE Conference on Computer Vision and Pattern Recognition, pp. 7167–7176 (2017)
60. Vinyals, O., Blundell, C., Lillicrap, T., Wierstra, D., et al.: Matching networks for one shot learning. In: Advances in Neural Information Processing Systems, pp. 3630–3638 (2016)
61. Wah, C., Branson, S., Welinder, P., Perona, P., Belongie, S.: The Caltech-UCSD birds-200-2011 dataset (2011)
62. Wang, X., Peng, Y., Lu, L., Lu, Z., Bagheri, M., Summers, R.M.: ChestX-ray8: hospital-scale chest X-ray database and benchmarks on weakly-supervised classification and localization of common thorax diseases. In: Proceedings of the IEEE Conference on Computer Vision and Pattern Recognition, pp. 2097–2106 (2017)
63. Wang, Y.X., Girshick, R., Hebert, M., Hariharan, B.: Low-shot learning from imaginary data. arXiv:1801.05401 (2018)
64. Welinder, P., et al.: Caltech-UCSD Birds 200. Technical report CNS-TR-2010-001, California Institute of Technology (2010)
65. Yang, J., Yan, R., Hauptmann, A.G.: Cross-domain video concept detection using adaptive SVMs. In: Proceedings of the 15th ACM International Conference on Multimedia, pp. 188–197 (2007)
66. Yosinski, J., Clune, J., Bengio, Y., Lipson, H.: How transferable are features in deep neural networks? In: NIPS (2014)
67. Yu, A., Grauman, K.: Semantic Jitter: dense supervision for visual comparisons via synthetic images. In: Proceedings of the IEEE International Conference on Computer Vision, October 2017, pp. 5571–5580 (2017). https://doi.org/10.1109/ICCV.2017.594
68. Zhang, C., Bengio, S., Singer, Y.: Are all layers created equal? arXiv preprint arXiv:1902.01996 (2019)
69. Zhu, J.Y., Park, T., Isola, P., Efros, A.A.: Unpaired image-to-image translation using cycle-consistent adversarial networks. In: Proceedings of the IEEE International Conference on Computer Vision, pp. 2223–2232 (2017)

Practical Poisoning Attacks on Neural Networks

Junfeng Guo and Cong Liu[✉]

The University of Texas at Dallas, Richardson, USA
{Junfeng.Guo,cong}@utdallas.edu

Abstract. Data poisoning attacks on machine learning models have attracted much recent attention, wherein poisoning samples are injected at the training phase to achieve adversarial goals at test time. Although existing poisoning techniques prove to be effective in various scenarios, they rely on certain assumptions on the adversary knowledge and capability to ensure efficacy, which may be unrealistic in practice. This paper presents a new, practical targeted poisoning attack method on neural networks in vision domain, namely BlackCard. BlackCard possesses a set of critical properties for ensuring attacking efficacy in practice, which has never been simultaneously achieved by any existing work, including *knowledge-oblivious*, *clean-label*, and *clean-test*. Importantly, we show that the effectiveness of BlackCard can be intuitively guaranteed by a set of analytical reasoning and observations, through exploiting an essential characteristic of gradient-descent optimization which is pervasively adopted in DNN models. We evaluate the efficacy of BlackCard for generating targeted poisoning attacks via extensive experiments using various datasets and DNN models. Results show that BlackCard is effective with a rather high success rate while preserving all the claimed properties.

Keywords: Data poisoning · Neural networks

1 Introduction

While deep neural networks (DNNs) have the potential to revolutionize many important computer vision application domains such as face recognition [29] and autonomous driving [19], they may open up new adversarial opportunities due to lacking sufficient robustness against various forms of attacks.

Indeed, attacking neural nets has attracted much recent attention from both academia and industry. Most attacking techniques can be categorized into *evasion attacks* which occur at test phase and *data poisoning attacks* which occur at training phase. Specifically, evasion attacks [41] aim at modifying a clean

Electronic supplementary material The online version of this chapter (https://doi.org/10.1007/978-3-030-58583-9_9) contains supplementary material, which is available to authorized users.

Table 1. Overall comparison.

Attack approach	Knowledge-oblivious	Clean-label	Clean-test
Trojaning Attack		✓	
BadNets			
Targeted BackDoor Attack	✓		
Poison Frog		✓	✓
BlackCard	✓	✓	✓

target instance at test phase to spur misclassification or avoid detection by a classifier; while data poisoning attacks seek to insert maliciously crafted poison samples into the training set to manipulate the performance of a system. Data poisoning attacks are receiving a significantly increasing amount of attention recently [20, 22, 25, 28, 30–32, 37, 40, 42], due to the fact that such attacks are able to change and reconstruct internal parameters of the target model rather than just fooling the target model at test phase via modified test samples. Data poisoning can be typically categorized into untargeted attacks [23, 28, 42] and targeted attacks [20, 37]. Untargeted attacks aim at degrading overall performance of the targeted model; while targeted attacks seek to control the behavior of a classifier on one specific test instance [20].

To guarantee effectiveness of poisoning attacks in practice, there are several critical properties that shall be possessed by poisoning techniques, including (*i*) **knowledge-oblivious**–the attacker shall have no knowledge of the target model's parameters/structures, nor the original training datasets, (*ii*) **clean-label**–the attacker shall not be able to control the labeling process, and (*iii*) **clean-test**–test-time instances shall not be required to be modified using added adversarial perturbations for attacking effectiveness. Unfortunately, it is rather challenging to simultaneously achieve all these properties, as the latest poisoning techniques manage to achieve a partial set of these properties. For instance, [37] is able to first-time achieve clean-label attacks, yet they need knowledge about the targeted DNN model's parameters and structures to collide the feature space representations of the targeted instance. [20] does not require knowledge of the target model, yet requiring to control the labeling process to mislabel the targeted instance and inject it at the training phase. In fact, no existing method can simultaneously achieve the above-listed properties, which are essential to ensure any poisoning technique to be feasibly implemented under many practical scenarios.

The major contribution of this paper is towards implementing an effective and practical targeted poisoning attack BlackCard against neural nets, possessing all the above-mentioned properties. A detailed comparison of BlackCard against state-of-the-art targeted poisoning techniques is given in Table 1 (we will describe these related works in detail in Sect. 5). The efficacy of BlackCard is fundamentally supported by a set of analytical reasoning and observations exploiting an essential characteristic of gradient-descent optimization (detailed in Sect. 3). We have extensively evaluated BlackCard using a set of popular datasets and DNN models featuring very different structures and parameters in different tasks. The results prove the efficacy of BlackCard while achieving all properties above.

Our contributions are summarized as follows.

- We develop BlackCard for generating targeted poisoning attacks, which manipulates a pre-trained model (controlled by attackers) to craft poison instances for misleading the target model.
- We demonstrate the applicability of BlackCard to generate targeted poisoning attacks. Experiments using a variety of datasets and models show that Black-Card is effective with rather high attack success rate and misclassification confidence, while preserving all the claimed properties.
- We show that the effectiveness of BlackCard can be intuitively guaranteed by a set of analytical reasoning and observations, through revealing how Black-Card exploits gradient descent optimization in crafting effective poisoning instances.

2   System and Adversarial Model

DNN Model. A DNN model is a parameterized function $F_\theta(b) = y$ that maps an input $b \in \mathbb{R}^m$ to an output $y \in \mathbb{R}^n$, where θ represents the function's parameters. In this paper, we focus on the image classification tasks in which the neural network is used as an m-classifier. The input b is an image (reshaped as a vector), and the output y is interpreted using the softmax function, which is a vector of probabilities over the n classes. The classifier assigns the label $C(b) = argmaxF(b)_i$ to the input b. Training a DNN model is to compute the parameters of the neural network, with the training data and reliable class labels. The training process of the DNN model aims to obtain the parameters of the neural network, which minimizes the loss function via learning algorithms, e.g., gradient-descent optimization.

Threat Model and Adversary Goals. In this work, we consider a threat model which has the weakest assumptions among all existing targeted poisoning attacks, and our goal is to demonstrate the attacking efficacy of applying BlackCard to generate poisoning attacks for DNN models applied in image classification tasks. In particular, we have the following goals to achieve.

Knowledge-Oblivious Attacks. The structure and parameters of the target model, as well as the content of the original training datasets, are oblivious to the attacker. BlackCard shall still be able to craft effective data poisoning samples without knowing any such information. We note that in practice such information is either impossible or too costly to be obtained by an attacker. Knowledge-oblivious poisoning would ensure attacking techniques to be implementable under most scenarios in the real world.

We note that BlackCard does require to know two pieces of information regarding the target model, i.e., the classify task performed by the model (e.g., image

Table 2. Example pre-trained models for different tasks.

Task	Dataset	Pre-trained Model **P**
Fashion Item Recognition	Fashion-MNIST	[3–5]
Object Recognition in Images	CIFAR-10 Dataset	[6–8]
Traffic Sign Recognition	GTSRB	[9–11]
Face Recognition using VGG Face	VGG Face Dataset	[12–14]
Face Recognition using Asian Face	CASIAN V5 Dataset	[15,16]

classification) and the specific labels given in the original training datasets (e.g., two labels of dogs and cats). In practical scenarios, these two pieces of information may be accessible by attackers. For instance, Amazon and Google oracles [1,2] provide DNN models which can be applicable to applications such as digit handwriting recognition and traffic sign recognition. An attacker can easily access the classify task performed by this model (e.g., digit handwriting) and the label information according to domain knowledge (e.g., ten labels corresponding to ten digits). However, such models are knowledge-oblivious to attackers as their structures and parameters are not available to public.

Clean-Label Attack. Our treat model assumes that the attacker cannot control the labeling process of the target model, e.g., the attacker cannot perform mislabel actions. This assumption ensures BlackCard to be applicable to many scenarios under which the training set is audited by human labelers, or where the labels are assigned by an external process (e.g., a malware detector collecting ground truth labeled by third party antiviruses).

Clean-Test Attack. We assume that the test-time instances shall not be required to be modified using any adversarial perturbations (e.g., injecting small-magnitude perturbations such as a backdoor trigger to the test-time input [20,25,30]).

3   Attack Methodology

In this section, we present our design of BlackCard for crafting targeted poison instances that, when added to the training phase, manipulate the test-time behavior of a classifier. We also describe an intuitive set of analytical reasoning and observations, which fundamentally ensure the attacking effectiveness of BlackCard. Note that a set of notation denoting various instances and models will be used throughout the paper, which is summarized and can be viewed in Fig. 1.

BlackCard employs a contamination idea where the attacker maliciously trains a fully-controllable pre-trained model **P** (defined below), through mislabeling a target instance **t** as a corresponding base instance **b**, to craft a poison instance **x**. Injecting **x** at the training phase of the target model **T** would contaminate

T to behave similar to **A**, i.e., **T** would similarly mis-classify a target instance **t** as **b** at test time.

Definition of the Pre-trained Model. For any target model **T**, an attacker may find a pre-trained model **P** which (*i*) performs similar classification task as **T**, and (*ii*) has already been trained using certain datasets with different number of classes [24]. In practice, for each classification task, there often exists a set of pre-trained models exhibiting various performance which are developed by different researchers and practitioners. For instance, for object recognition, YOLO3 [36] would be considered as the best pre-trained model in the literature, along with several others such as YOLO [34] and YOLO2 [35]. We note that the target model **T** could also be a pre-train model according to the definition. In practice, it is easy to obtain a set of pre-trained models for different classification tasks, due to the large number of pre-trained models that can be found in the open source community (e.g., easy to find pre-trained RESNet and VGGNet models for image classification from the open source community [33]).

Moreover, in many cases, popular deep learning frameworks provide a set of pre-trained models for users. For instance, Keras [21], one of the most popular deep learning frame works, provides several pre-trained models such as Inception, Resnet, etc. We list a popular set of such pre-trained models for different classification tasks in Table 2, which are also used in our empirical evaluation. We note that even if there is no available pre-trained model corresponding to **T**, the attacker may craft an attacking model by feeding a raw model with relevant training data. It is not challenging to craft such a model since there is absolutely no constraints on the structure nor the parameters specified for this model.

We now discuss the only preference for identifying a pre-trained model **P**. To ensure and maximize effectiveness, BlackCard prefers to choose a model **P** that yields similar or lower performance compared to the target model **T**. Doing so would allow **T** to have similar or better feature extracting capability compared to **P**, such that **T** can extract the features belonging to the target instance **t** from the poison instance **x** when **x** is injected at the training phase of **T**. We note that this requirement can be easily and actually naturally satisfied in practice and does not conflict with the knowledge-oblivious property of BlackCard. This is because the target model **T**, among all available pre-trained models performing the same classification task, shall be the best performer in practice, as the users most likely will always choose the best available model. Moreover, since there is flexibility in choosing a specific pre-trained model as **P**, we can always ensure this requirement to be met by selecting a pre-trained model which yields worse performance than its peers. As we will show in the experiments, among a list of available pre-trained models, intentionally choosing a rather worse-performed pre-trained model (compared to **T**) as **P** can still ensure close to 100% performance, which is similar to the case where **P** and **T** yield similar performance.

Our design of BlackCardconsists of the following two phases, as illustrated in Fig. 1.

Phase 1: Creating an Attacking Model A. Phase 1 aims at creating an attacking model (denoted by **A**) which will be used to craft the poison instance

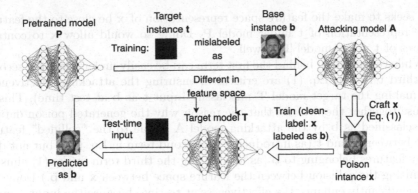

Fig. 1. Overview of generating targeted attacks.

x. We create **A** by first identifying a pre-trained model **P** (as defined above). After obtaining **P**, we train this model in a malicious manner, incorporating our anonymous targeted attack information. Specifically, for any targeted attack, i.e., making model **T** classify a target instance **t** (e.g., a blackcard) as a base instance **b** (e.g., a dog), we mislabel **t** as **b** during the training phase of **P**. Note that this is feasible because the attacker has full control over **P** (while **T** being oblivious to the attacker). The goal of training the pre-trained model **P** in this manner is to make **P** classify the target instance **t** as the corresponding base instance **b** with a high confidence rate (ideally 100%). The attacking model **A** is successfully created after this training phase completes. Note that **A**'s overall accuracy on validation dataset shall be almost identical to **P**.

Phase 2: Crafting Poison instance x via Exploiting the Attacking Model. The second phase of BlackCard is to craft poison data **x**. We define $f(x)$ to be a function that returns the probability of predicting any input **x** as the base label according to the attacking model **A**, $f'(x)$ to be the feature space representation of input **x** for the pre-trained model **P**. We can find poison data **x** by computing:

$$x = \underset{x}{\arg\min} \, \|x - b\|_2^2 + \alpha * \left(\|f(x) - 100\%\|^2 - \|f'(x) - f'(b)\|_2^2 + \|f'(x) - f'(t)\|_2^2 \right).$$

$$(1)$$

Among the four terms seen on the right-hand side of Eq. (1), the first term ensures the poison instance **x** to appear like the base class instance **b** to a human labeler. By the definition of **f(x)**, the second term seeks to maximize the probability for the attacking model to predict **x** as its base label (i.e., the base instance **b**). The third term seeks to avoid "collision" between the feature space representation of input **x** and the base instance **b** as much as possible (implied by the minus sign associated with the term) in the model **T**, through doing the same for the pre-trained model **P** (according to the definition of $f'(x)$). This equivalence is intuitive due to the fact that the first set of layers in both **P** and **T** in charge of feature extraction are both well-developed in most cases. The last term seeks to make the feature space representation of **x** be close to the feature space representation of **t** under model **P**. Doing so would allow **x** to contain features of **t** under model **T** as well.

While the intuition behind the first term can be easily understood, the second and third terms in Eq. (1) are critical in ensuring the attacking effectiveness (i.e., making the target model **T** misclassify input **t** as **b** at test time). This is because together they ensure that the reason why the generated poison data **x** is misclassified as **b** by the attacking model A is due to the "collided" feature space between **x** and **t** (as introducing the second term in Eq. (1)), but not due to any features belonging to **b** (as introducing the third term in Eq. (1) aims at minimizing the collision between the feature space between **x** and **b**.) Doing so may significantly enhance the effectiveness at testing, because the input sample **t** may not collide any feature space with the base instance **b**. Also note that we introduce a co-efficient α attached to the last three terms in Eq. (1) to balance the tradeoff among the four terms.

Algorithm 1. Pseudo-code for BlackCard

1: **Input**: target instance **t**, base instance **b**
2: Initialize x: $x_0 \leftarrow b$
3: Define: $L = ||x - b||_2^2 + \alpha * (||f(x) - 100\%||^2 - ||f'(x) - f'(b)||_2^2 + ||f'(x) - f'(t)||_2^2)$
4: **while** $i \leq MaxIters$ **do**
5:    $x_i \leftarrow x_{i-1} - \lambda \nabla_x L(x_{i-1})$
6: **while** $||f(x) - 100\%||^2 < 1 * 10^{-2}$ AND $||f'(x) - f'(b)||_2^2 > 100$ **do**
7:    $\alpha \leftarrow \frac{\alpha}{2}$
8:    **To:Line 4**
9: **UPDATE** X_i

Optimization Procedure. The procedure for performing the optimization in Eq. (1) to obtain poison data **x** is shown in Algorithm 1, which essentially applies a binary-search iterative procedure [18]. The first step (Lines 4–5) is simply a gradient-descent update to minimize Eq. (1) (i.e., Line 3). The second step (Lines 6–8) applies a binary search algorithm to identify a proper α, which would enable the attacking model to misclassify the poison sample as the base instance with almost 100% confidence (i.e., $||f(x) - 100\%||^2 < 1*10^{-2}$ on Line 6) while ensuring that under the pre-trained model **P**, the feature space of the poison sample and base instance do not collide (i.e., $||f'(x) - f'(b)||_2^2 > 100$ on Line 6). We note that the effectiveness of applying Algorithm 1 in this optimization procedure is proved by our extensive evaluation shown in Sect. 4.

Empirical Observation on Optimizing Eq. (1) using Algorithm 1. As to be seen in Sect. 4, the effectiveness of applying Algorithm 1 to optimize Eq. (1) has been proved by extensive evaluation results. To help understand how applying Algorithm 1 optimizes the four terms included in Eq. (1), we show a sample experiment in the appendix (as supplementary material) to illustrate the typical value changing pattern of each term in Eq. (1) due to this optimization.

Analytical Reasoning on the Guaranteed Efficacy of BlackCard. We provide a detailed set of analytical reasoning and observations as below, which intuitively ensure the attacking effectiveness of BlackCard, through exploiting an essential property of the gradient descent optimization pervasively adopted for optimizing neural networks.

Gradient Descent Optimization. Gradient descent is a first-order iterative optimization algorithm for finding the minimum of a function [23], which takes steps proportional to the negative of the gradient (or approximate gradient) of the function at the current point. Most DNN optimization techniques apply gradient descent to find the minimum of a function which is usually a loss function in DNN models [23]. Thus, an essential property of gradient descent-based DNN optimization is to minimize $LossFunc(\theta, d, L_d)$ (i.e., $LossFunc(\theta, d, L_d) \to 0$), where θ denotes the parameters of the DNN model, d represents the training data, L_d denotes the label of d, and $LossFunc()$ represents any commonly used loss function in the DNN model, such as cross-entropy loss. It implies that minimizing $LossFunc()$ is an essential procedure for DNN models' training phase. This observation motivates our design of BlackCard, which seeks to attack DNN models with poisoned training data through manipulating this essential procedure of minimizing $LossFunc()$.

Intuitive Analytical Reasoning and Observations. According to gradient descent optimization, the attack effectiveness of BlackCard can be guaranteed if

$$LossFunc(\theta_T, t, L_b) \to 0, \tag{2}$$

where θ_T denotes the parameters of the target model $\mathbf{T}$.[1] Equation (2) implies that model $\mathbf{T}$ will classify input $\mathbf{t}$ as $\mathbf{b}$ at testing phase. We now explain why our design of BlackCard, i.e., Eq. (1) and Algorithm 1, intuitively ensures Eq. (2) to hold. As discussed in Sect. 3, Phase 1 of BlackCard is to create an attacking model $\mathbf{A}$ such that

$$LossFunc(\theta_A, t, L_b) \to 0, \tag{3}$$

where θ_A is obtained through identifying the pre-trained model $\mathbf{P}$ explained earlier. Equation (3) holds because we obtain the attacking model $\mathbf{A}$ through training $\mathbf{P}$ with mislabelled data $\mathbf{t}$ (i.e., mislabelling $\mathbf{t}$ as $\mathbf{b}$). This would cause $LossFunc(\theta, t, L_b)$ to be minimized, equivalent to Eq. (3).

Moreover, our way of generating poison sample $\mathbf{x}$ following Eq. (1) and Algorithm 1 ensures that

$$LossFunc(\theta_A, x, L_b) \to 0. \tag{4}$$

Eq. (4) holds because of the second term in Eq. (1), which causes the attacking model $\mathbf{A}$ to predict $\mathbf{x}$ as the base instance $\mathbf{b}$ with a confidence as close to 100% as possible, thus implying Eq. (4).

When injecting poison sample $\mathbf{x}$ at the training phase of the target model $\mathbf{T}$, we achieve

$$LossFunc(\theta_T, x, L_b) \to 0. \tag{5}$$

---

[1] Note that the objective is typically to minimize $LossFunc(\theta_T, t, L_b)$ such that it falls below 1×10^{-2}.

This is because the first term in Eq. (1) ensures that $\mathbf{x}$ shall be visual indistinguishable from $\mathbf{b}$ and thus labeled as $\mathbf{b}$ by human labelers. Note that we do not need to actually obtain θ_T during any phase of BlackCard.

We now show the intuition behind why Eq. (2) holds.

1. Eqs. (4) and (5) imply that the performance of the target model T on classifying poison instance $\mathbf{x}$ is in close proximity to the attacking model A.
2. Our way of generating $\mathbf{x}$ ensures that $\mathbf{x}$ will be classified as $\mathbf{b}$ under attacking model $\mathbf{A}$ with high confidence close to 100% (i.e., ensured by the second item in Eq. (1)), and $\mathbf{x}$ does not collide with $\mathbf{b}$ in feature space according to the pre-trained model $\mathbf{P}$ (i.e., ensured by the third item in Eq. (1)). Thus, since $\mathbf{A}$ is created based on $\mathbf{P}$ and inherits $\mathbf{P}$'s structure and parameters, we know that the attacking model $\mathbf{A}$ classifies $\mathbf{x}$ as $\mathbf{b}$ only due to the fact that $\mathbf{x}$ contains features of $\mathbf{t}$ but not features of $\mathbf{b}$ (i.e., ensured by the fourth item in Eq. (1)). This is critical in ensuring the effectiveness at testing phase, because at testing phase, the target instance $\mathbf{t}$ may not collide with $\mathbf{b}$ in feature space at all under Model $\mathbf{T}$.[2]
3. Under models $\mathbf{P}$ and $\mathbf{T}$, $\mathbf{x}$ contains features of $\mathbf{t}$ but not $\mathbf{b}$. This is clearly true under model $\mathbf{P}$ due to the way of crafting $\mathbf{x}$. Because $\mathbf{P}$ is a pre-trained model of $\mathbf{T}$, according to our definition of $\mathbf{P}$, $\mathbf{T}$ shall have similar or better feature extraction functionality and capability compared to $\mathbf{P}$. Thus this claim also holds under $\mathbf{T}$.
4. Equation (3) implies that the attacking model $\mathbf{A}$ classifies $\mathbf{t}$ as $\mathbf{b}$.
5. Combining the above observations, the above-listed items 1–3 lead to the conclusion that models $\mathbf{T}$ and $\mathbf{A}$ yield similar performance on classifying $\mathbf{t}$. Combining this with item 4, we know that at testing, target model $\mathbf{T}$ will classify $\mathbf{t}$ as $\mathbf{b}$, i.e., Eq. (2) holds.

4   Experimental Evaluation

In this section, we empirically evaluate the effectiveness and practicality of applying BlackCard to generate targeted poisoning attack in various vision application domains.

---

[2] If not including the third item in Eq. (1) for calculating poison data $\mathbf{x}$, then $\mathbf{x}$ may collide with $\mathbf{b}$ under the pre-trained model $\mathbf{P}$ (thus $\mathbf{A}$) in feature space. In this case, the fact that $\mathbf{A}$ classifies $\mathbf{x}$ as $\mathbf{b}$ with high confidence may be due to the collision portion in feature space between $\mathbf{x}$ and $\mathbf{b}$ (i.e., partly due to $\mathbf{b}$'s features), but not solely due to features of $\mathbf{t}$ contained in $\mathbf{x}$. Thus, when injecting poison data $\mathbf{x}$ at the training phase of target model $\mathbf{T}$, $\mathbf{T}$ would learn that $\mathbf{x}$ shall be classified as $\mathbf{b}$ because of $\mathbf{x}$'s mixed sets of features belonging to both $\mathbf{t}$ and $\mathbf{b}$. This would cause ineffectiveness at testing. When target model $\mathbf{T}$ classifies input $\mathbf{t}$ at testing, it would yield a lower confidence of classifying $\mathbf{t}$ as $\mathbf{b}$ because according to $\mathbf{T}$, the input $\mathbf{t}$ may not collide with $\mathbf{b}$ in feature space at all. $\mathbf{T}$ may still classify $\mathbf{t}$ as $\mathbf{b}$ because $\mathbf{t}$'s features are included in its training data $\mathbf{x}$, but with a lower confidence.

4.1 Experiment Setup

We implemented BlackCard in Python, using keras [21] and tensorflow [17] as our deep learning frameworks. All the experiments were performed on a server with the Intel I9 CPU and GTX 1080-Ti NVIDIA GPUs. We use two main metrics to evaluate the overall effectiveness of BlackCard: **ASR**–attack success rate and **MC**–misclassification confidence. ASR measures the likelihood that the targeted model misclassify the target instance **t** as the base instance **b**:

$$Attack\ Success\ Rate = \frac{\#\ successful\ misclassification}{\#\ attack\ trials}.$$

MC measures the probability of the class predicted by the target model with respect to the target instance **t**.

We used several popular tasks from multiple application domains in the evaluation, including MNIST for hand-written digit recognition, Fashion-MNIST for fashion item recognition, CIFAR-10 for object recognition, GTSRB for traffic sign recognition, and VGG-Face and CASIAN for face recognition, details are put in the appendix.

We follow details of model training configurations and architectures as that of prior work [18,26,27,37,39]. Notably, to demonstrate the practicality and effectiveness of BlackCard, pre-trained model P exhibits extremely different architectures from targeted model T for each task in experiments. Especially, for CIFAR-10 task, we choose DenseNet121. [27] and RESNet [26], whose both architectures and parameters settings are dramatically different while both of them achieve state-of-art performance, as a pair of model P and T.[3]

4.2 Experiments Evaluation

We first evaluate the overall efficacy of apply BlackCard to generate targeted poisoning attacks. To prove the knowledge-oblivious property of BlackCard, we assume no knowledge at all about the target model **T** in all the experiments. In these experiments, Cross-Entropy was adopted as the loss function of the target model, since it is the most widely used one in the object classification domain [38].

To prove the claimed properties of BlackCard, we use a pure blackcard as shown in Fig. 1 as the target instance. Our goal is to make the target model

---

[3] Note that we choose to evaluate the state-of-the-art, widely adopted models as the target model **T** for different tasks, and **T**'s parameter and structure information are unknown to us in all the experiments. For certain tasks, although there may exist other widely recognized models (e.g., the model released on Google Cloud [1] for the MNIST task), we could not use such models for our problem setting, because such models' APIs are not accessible, thus preventing us to poison the model. For the pre-trained model **P**, we adopt the ones found either in online repository or our self-built ones. Notably, we intentionally choose the pairs of model **T** and **P** which exhibit completely different structure and parameter settings while achieving state-of-art performance.

Table 3. Overall effectiveness. (s) and (m) represents results using one-shot-kill and multi-shot-kill, respectively. (Fas-MNIST denotes the Fashion-MNIST task.)

Task	ASR(s)	MC(s)	ASR(m)	MC(m)
MNIST	100%	98.728%	100%	100%
Fas-MNIST	99.8%	97.081%	100%	100%
CIFAR-10	10.4%	7.53%	100%	100%
GTSRB	98%	98.32%	100%	100%
VGG-Face	100%	99.43%	100%	100%
CASIAN	100%	97.84%	100%	100%

misclassify a blackcard as each of the base instances originally existed in the dataset. The metrics ASR and MC then reflect the percentage of the successful rate of such misclassifications.

Besides overall effectiveness, we have performed several experiment sets which reveal the strength of BlackCard under different settings, through answering the following research questions.

RQ1: How Would BlackCard Perform Under Different Pairs of P and T? Since BlackCard can leverage different pre-trained models as **P** and attack any given target model **T**, it is important to understand how effective is Black-Card when choosing different **P** and/or targeting different **T**. We performed a set of experiments with the MNIST, Fashion-MNIST, and CIFAR-10 tasks in the multi-shots settings, varying **P** and **T** among the five existing pre-trained models. The results are shown in Tables 4, 5 and 6.

As seen in the tables, an important observation that when the pre-trained model yields a similar or worse performance compared to the target model, Black-Card ensures attacking effectiveness. For example, as seen in the Columns 3–6 in all three tables, 100% or close to 100% MC performance can be achieved. On the other hand, as seen in the Columns 2–3 in all tables, low MC performance is observed when **P** yields a noticeably better performance than **T**. This result aligns with our design of BlackCard in choosing **P**, as discussed in Sect. 4.2, where for targeted poisoning attacks, P shall yield a similar or worse performance compared to the target model **T** to ensure effectiveness. Doing so allows **T** to have similar or better feature extracting capability compared to **P**, such that **T** can extract the features belonging to the target instance **t** from the poison instance **x** when **x** is injected at the training phase of **T**.

Moreover, it is observed that when the classification accuracy of **T** is slightly worse than **P**, BlackCard may yield different MC performance under different tasks. As seen in the third row of Table 6, for CIFAR-10, close to 100% MC performance can still be achieved even if the classification accuracy of **P** is around 10% lower than **T**; while the MC performance becomes significantly low for the two other tasks when **P** yields a lower accuracy than **T**. This is due to the fact that the CIFAR-10 model significantly overfits the training data

Table 4. MC performance with different pairs of **P** and **T** for the MNIST

MC**P** **T**	83.24%	93.53%	97.84%	98.21%	97.52%
83.24%	100%	61.47%	8.21%	6.43%	8.27%
93.53%	97.21%	100%	32.45%	28.74%	14.67%
97.84%	99.13%	98.27%	100%	98.43%	99.12%
98.21%	100%	99.32%	98.42%	100%	98.37%
97.52%	99.93%	99.74%	99.04%	94.53%	100%

Table 5. MC performance with different pairs of **P** and **T** for the Fashion-MNIST

MC**P** **T**	80.71%	86.54%	91.08%	92.21%	92.06%
80.71%	100%	92.76%	16.89%	11.73%	19.87%
86.54%	98.62%	99.16%	52.74%	51.29%	49.34%
91.08%	98.24%	98.17	100%	100%	99.93%
92.21%	97.23%	98.18%	100%	100%	100%
92.06%	97.13%	97.21%	99.99%	99.81%	100%

Table 6. MC performance with different pairs of **P** and **T** for CIFAR-10

MC**P** **T**	74.38%	81.29%	82.14%	90.16%	92.37%
74.38%	100%	99.21%	3.3%	1.3%	0.15%
81.29%	100%	100%	98.42%	100%	96.43%
82.14%	100%	100%	100%	100%	99.93%
90.16%	100%	100%	100%	100%	100%
92.37%	98.17%	99.23%	99.99%	100%	100%

even with drop out, causing the CIFAR-10 model with lower accuracy to also possess similar capability of extracting features as the CIFAR-10 model with high accuracy.

Another important observation herein is that BlackCard ensures transferability, which is generally defined to be an ability of any attacking method, where using samples generated using a specific model can attack multiple unknown models. As we can see from Tables 4, 5 and 6, for each pre-trained model **P**, close to 100% MC performance can be achieved for all tested target model **T** which has similar classification accuracy to the **A**. This implies the transferability of BlackCard as a specific poisoning sample can be applicable to multiple unknown models.

Fig. 2. Robustness of the attack using various target instances (top), the corresponding poison instances (middle) and base instances (bottom).

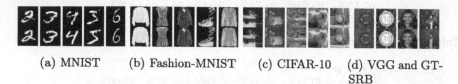

    (a) MNIST   (b) Fashion-MNIST   (c) CIFAR-10   (d) VGG and GT-
                                                                   SRB

Fig. 3. Visually indistinguishable poison instances (top) and the corresponding base instances (bottom) for targeted attacks.

RQ2: How Robust is BlackCard Using a Variety of Target Instances at Test Time? In this set of experiments, we evaluate whether BlackCard ensures robust attacking effectiveness when using a variety of target instances (instead of just a black card) targeting at various base instances at test time. As seen in Fig. 2, for various tasks, when adopting different target instances at test time, BlackCard can always make the target model misclassify the target instance into the corresponding base instance. Note that these tested target instances include ones that are and are not originally contained in the training dataset (e.g., the red card in the first column and the speed limit sign in the last column, respectively), which again prove the anonymous-label property of BlackCard.

We would like to emphasize that such robustness is critical to ensure attacking effectiveness in practice. Consider a DNN-based autonomous driving scenario. Such robustness combined with the anonymous-label property implies that virtually any object along the driving road (e.g., a traffic sign, an advertisement board, or any physical surface along the curbside) can be used to attack the DNN-based driving model.

RQ3: Are the Poisoning Samples Generated by BlackCard Visually Indistinguishable from the Corresponding base Instances? We present several poisoning samples generated by BlackCard and their corresponding base instances in Figs. 2 and 3 for the tested tasks. As seen in the figure, qualitatively, the generated poisoning samples are visually similar to the corresponding base instances, and thus shall be labeled as the corresponding base instances by a human labeler. Because the attacker does not need to control the labeling process, such visually indistinguishable samples can be easily injected at the training phase of the target DNN model.

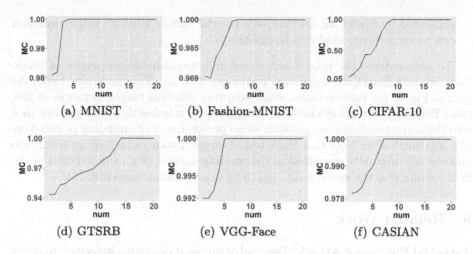

(a) MNIST   (b) Fashion-MNIST   (c) CIFAR-10

(d) GTSRB   (e) VGG-Face   (f) CASIAN

Fig. 4. Impact due to the number of poison samples

RQ4: How Would an Increased Number of Poisoning Samples Impact Performance? Although Table 3 proves the capability of BlackCard for generating an effective single-shot-kill poisoning sample for most tasks, it is interesting to understand the impact due to increasing such samples. Figure 4 shows the results on such impact for the tested tasks. As seen in the figure, MC can be increased to 100% after injecting 4, 7, 6, 14, 3,and 7 poisoning samples for the six tested tasks, respectively. These results show that with only a few poisoning samples, BlackCard is able to reach 100% MC performance, which further confirms its effectiveness.

Summary of Results. We summarize our findings on applying BlackCard to generate targeted poisoning attacks.

- Effectiveness - In all experiments, under proper settings, BlackCard is able to generate effective targeted poisoning attacks to trigger the targeted DNN model to misclassify the targeted inputs with success rate above 98% and misclassification confidence above 97% (even achieving 100% for both metrics in many cases).
- Obliviousness - For all experiments, any information of the targeted model or the training process is unknown to the attacker, e.g., model structure, parameters, adopted loss functions, labeling process. Effectiveness can still be guaranteed fundamentally because our design of BlackCard does not exploit any such information. This is critical for practically deploying poisoning attacks in real world because such information is often unknown to the attacker.
- Evasiveness - The poisoning samples created under BlackCard are visually indistinguishable from their corresponding base-class instances. Also, results prove that with a single or a few poisoning samples, the attacking effectiveness can be guaranteed in all experiments. This ensures that the poisoning attacks

generated by BlackCard are evasive w.r.t. the human labeler's inspection, and can be more easily deployed in practice.

To demonstrate the robust and visual-indistinguishable properties of Black-Card, we test BlackCard using various images as t on aforementioned tasks. As seen in Fig. 2, for various tasks, when adopting different target instances at test time, BlackCard can always make the target model misclassify the target instance into the corresponding base instance while preserving corresponding poison samples less noticeable. Note that these tested target instances include ones that are and are not originally contained in the training dataset (e.g., the red card in the first column and the speed limit sign in the last column, respectively).

5   Related Work

Targeted Poisoning Attack. The goal of targeted poisoning attacks is to cause the target model to misclassify a target instance incorrectly as the target label. Chen et al. [20], Liu et al. [30], and Gu et al. [25] train a network using mislabeled images tagged with a special pattern or trigger, causing the DNNs to respond to a certain pattern or trigger. Such approaches require that the attackers shall have some degree of control over the labeling process, which may be impractical in the real world as the labeling procedure is typically supervised by several reliable human labelers. The most closely related work to our targeted poisoning design is by Ali Shafahi et al. [37]. Their attack is powerful and effectiveness both in transfer learning and end-to-end training. However, our approach is fundamentally different from this work which assumes that the attackers have the knowledge about the structure and parameters of the targeted model, which can be costly and impossible to obtain in the real world. Several other related works focus on poisoning attacks from a theoretical perspective. Mahloujifa et al. [31] develops a theoretical poisoning threat model. Liang et al. [28] leverages the influence function to perform the poisoning attacks. Diakonikolas et al. [22] presents an evaluation on classifiers' robustness to train data perturbations. As discussed earlier, all the existing targeted poisoning attacks either require certain knowledge about the model, or malicious control over the labeling process. Also they do not enable anonymous attacks where the target instance is not included and can be totally unrelated (w.r.t. the class) to the training dataset.

Untargeted Poisoning Attack. Untargeted poisoning attacks aim to degrade the target model's overall accuracy. Steinhardt et al. [40] shows that modifying just a tiny amount (nearly 5%) of the entire training dataset can make the target model's accuracy be reduced by nearly 10%. Muñoz-González et al. [32] designs a back-gradient descent approach to generate effective poisoning data. Yang et al. [42] proposes a GAN-based method to speed up the process of crafting poisoning data.

6 Conclusion

In this paper, we present BlackCard, a practical targeted poisoning technique on neural networks. We prove that BlackCard satisfies a set of critical properties for ensuring effective poisoning attacks in practice. Both analytical reasoning and experimental results demonstrate that BlackCard is effective with rather high success rate using only one or a few poisoning samples, oblivious to both the target model knowledge and the labeling process, and can use arbitrary test-time instances.

Acknowledgement. This work was supported by NSF grants CNS 1527727 and CNS CAREER 1750263.

References

1. https://cloud.google.com/
2. https://aws.amazon.com/rds/oracle/
3. https://github.com/khanhnamle1994/fashion-mnist
4. https://github.com/Chinmayrane16/Fashion-MNIST-Accuracy-93.4-
5. https://www.kaggle.com/imrandude/fashion-mnist-cnn-imagedatagenerator
6. https://www.gradientzoo.com/patrickz3li
7. https://gluon-cv.mxnet.io/model_zoo/classification.html#cifar10
8. https://www.kaggle.com/jahongir7174/vgg16-cifar10
9. https://github.com/apsdehal/traffic-signs-recognition
10. https://github.com/magnusja/GTSRB-caffe-model
11. https://github.com/alessiamarcolini/deepstreet
12. https://gist.github.com/EncodeTS/6bbe8cb8bebad7a672f0d872561782d9
13. https://github.com/yzhang559/vgg-face
14. http://www.robots.ox.ac.uk/~albanie/pytorch-models.html
15. https://github.com/PythonOrR/CASIA-V5
16. https://www.gradientzoo.com/
17. Abadi, M., et al.: Tensorflow: a system for large-scale machine learning. In: 12th USENIX Symposium on Operating Systems Design and Implementation (OSDI 2016), pp. 265–283 (2016)
18. Carlini, N., Wagner, D.: Towards evaluating the robustness of neural networks. In: 2017 IEEE Symposium on Security and Privacy (SP), pp. 39–57. IEEE (2017)
19. Chen, C., Seff, A., Kornhauser, A., Xiao, J.: Deepdriving: learning affordance for direct perception in autonomous driving. In: Proceedings of the IEEE International Conference on Computer Vision, pp. 2722–2730 (2015)
20. Chen, X., Liu, C., Li, B., Lu, K., Song, D.: Targeted backdoor attacks on deep learning systems using data poisoning. arXiv preprint arXiv:1712.05526 (2017)
21. Chollet, F., et al.: Keras (2015). https://github.com/fchollet/keras
22. Diakonikolas, I., Kane, D.M., Stewart, A.: Efficient robust proper learning of log-concave distributions. arXiv preprint arXiv:1606.03077 (2016)
23. Du, S.S., Lee, J.D., Li, H., Wang, L., Zhai, X.: Gradient descent finds global minima of deep neural networks. arXiv preprint arXiv:1811.03804 (2018)
24. Emeršič, Ž., Štepec, D., Štruc, V., Peer, P.: Training convolutional neural networks with limited training data for ear recognition in the wild. arXiv preprint arXiv:1711.09952 (2017)

25. Gu, T., Dolan-Gavitt, B., Garg, S.: Badnets: Identifying vulnerabilities in the machine learning model supply chain. arXiv preprint arXiv:1708.06733 (2017)
26. He, K., Zhang, X., Ren, S., Sun, J.: Deep residual learning for image recognition. In: Proceedings of the IEEE Conference on Computer Vision and Pattern Recognition, pp. 770–778 (2016)
27. Huang, G., Liu, Z., Van Der Maaten, L., Weinberger, K.Q.: Densely connected convolutional networks. In: Proceedings of the IEEE Conference on Computer Vision and Pattern Recognition, pp. 4700–4708 (2017)
28. Koh, P.W., Liang, P.: Understanding black-box predictions via influence functions. arXiv preprint arXiv:1703.04730 (2017)
29. Lawrence, S., Giles, C.L., Tsoi, A.C., Back, A.D.: Face recognition: a convolutional neural-network approach. IEEE Trans. Neural Networks **8**(1), 98–113 (1997)
30. Liu, Y., et al.: Trojaning attack on neural networks (2017)
31. Mahloujifar, S., Diochnos, D.I., Mahmoody, M.: The curse of concentration in robust learning: Evasion and poisoning attacks from concentration of measure. arXiv preprint arXiv:1809.03063 (2018)
32. Muñoz-González, L., et al.: Towards poisoning of deep learning algorithms with back-gradient optimization. In: Proceedings of the 10th ACM Workshop on Artificial Intelligence and Security - AISec 2017 (2017). https://doi.org/10.1145/3128572.3140451, http://dx.doi.org/10.1145/3128572.3140451
33. Rajaraman, S., et al.: Pre-trained convolutional neural networks as feature extractors toward improved malaria parasite detection in thin blood smear images. PeerJ **6**, e4568 (2018)
34. Redmon, J., Divvala, S., Girshick, R., Farhadi, A.: You only look once: unified, real-time object detection. In: Proceedings of the IEEE Conference on Computer Vision and Pattern Recognition, pp. 779–788 (2016)
35. Redmon, J., Farhadi, A.: Yolo9000: better, faster, stronger. In: 2017 IEEE Conference on Computer Vision and Pattern Recognition (CVPR), pp. 6517–6525 (2017)
36. Redmon, J., Farhadi, A.: Yolov3: an incremental improvement. arXiv preprint arXiv:1804.02767 (2018)
37. Shafahi, A., et al.: Poison frogs! targeted clean-label poisoning attacks on neural networks. arXiv preprint arXiv:1804.00792 (2018)
38. Sharif Razavian, A., Azizpour, H., Sullivan, J., Carlsson, S.: CNN features off-the-shelf: an astounding baseline for recognition. In: Proceedings of the IEEE Conference on Computer Vision and Pattern Recognition Workshops, pp. 806–813 (2014)
39. Simonyan, K., Zisserman, A.: Very deep convolutional networks for large-scale image recognition. arXiv preprint arXiv:1409.1556 (2014)
40. Steinhardt, J., Koh, P.W.W., Liang, P.S.: Certified defenses for data poisoning attacks. In: Advances in Neural Information Processing Systems, pp. 3517–3529 (2017)
41. Szegedy, C., et al.: Intriguing properties of neural networks. arXiv preprint arXiv:1312.6199 (2013)
42. Yang, C., Wu, Q., Li, H., Chen, Y.: Generative poisoning attack method against neural networks. arXiv preprint arXiv:1703.01340 (2017)

Unsupervised Domain Adaptation in the Dissimilarity Space for Person Re-identification

Djebril Mekhazni[✉], Amran Bhuiyan, George Ekladious, and Eric Granger

LIVIA, Department of Systems Engineering, École de technologie supérieure,
Montreal, Canada
djebril.mekhazni@gmail.com,amran.apece@gmail.com
{george.ekladious,eric.granger}@etsmtl.ca

Abstract. Person re-identification (ReID) remains a challenging task in many real-word video analytics and surveillance applications, even though state-of-the-art accuracy has improved considerably with the advent of deep learning (DL) models trained on large image datasets. Given the shift in distributions that typically occurs between video data captured from the source and target domains, and absence of labeled data from the target domain, it is difficult to adapt a DL model for accurate recognition of target data. DL models for unsupervised domain adaptation (UDA) are commonly designed in the feature representation space. We argue that for pair-wise matchers that rely on metric learning, e.g., Siamese networks for person ReID, the UDA objective should consist in aligning pair-wise dissimilarity between domains, rather than aligning feature representations. Moreover, dissimilarity representations are more suitable for designing open-set ReID systems, where identities differ in the source and target domains. In this paper, we propose a novel Dissimilarity-based Maximum Mean Discrepancy (D-MMD) loss for aligning pair-wise distances that can be optimized via gradient descent using relatively small batch sizes. From a person ReID perspective, the evaluation of D-MMD loss is straightforward since the tracklet information (provided by a person tracker) allows to label a distance vector as being either within-class (within-tracklet) or between-class (between-tracklet). This allows approximating the underlying distribution of target pair-wise distances for D-MMD loss optimization, and accordingly align source and target distance distributions. Empirical results with three challenging benchmark datasets show that the proposed D-MMD loss decreases as source and domain distributions become more similar. Extensive experimental evaluation also indicates that UDA methods that rely on the D-MMD loss can significantly outperform baseline and state-of-the-art UDA methods for person ReID. The dissimilarity space transformation allows to design reliable pair-wise matchers, without the common requirement for data augmentation and/or complex networks. Code is available on GitHub link: https://github.com/djidje/D-MMD.

© Springer Nature Switzerland AG 2020
A. Vedaldi et al. (Eds.): ECCV 2020, LNCS 12372, pp. 159–174, 2020.
https://doi.org/10.1007/978-3-030-58583-9_10

Keywords: Deep learning · Domain adaptation · Maximum mean discrepancy · Dissimilarity space · Person re-identification

1 Introduction

Person re-identification (ReID) refers to the task of determining if a person of interest captured using a camera has the same identity as one of the candidates in the gallery, captured over different non-overlapping camera viewpoints. It is a key task in object recognition, drawing significant attention due to its wide range of applications, from video surveillance to sport analytics.

Despite the recent advances of ReID with DL models [10,17,20,24,26], and the availability of large amounts of labeled training data, person ReID still remains a challenging task due to the non-rigid structure of the human body, the different perspectives with which a pedestrian can be observed, the variability of capture conditions (e.g., illumination, blur), occlusions and background clutter. In practical video surveillance scenarios, the uncontrolled capture conditions and distributed camera viewpoints can lead to considerable intra-class variation, and to high inter-class similarity. The distribution of image data captured with different cameras and conditions may therefore differ considerably, a problem known in the literature as domain shift [18,28]. Given this domain shift, state-of-the-art DL models that undergo supervised training with a labeled image dataset (from the source domain) often generalize poorly for images captured in a target operational domain, leading to a decline in ReID accuracy.

Unsupervised domain adaptation (UDA) seeks resolve the domain shift problem by leveraging unlabeled data from the target domain (e.g., collected during a calibration process), in conjunction with labeled source domain data, to bridge the gap between the different domains. UDA techniques rely on different approaches, ranging from the optimization of a statistical criterion to the integration of an adversarial network, in order to learn robust domain-invariant representations from source and target domain data. Recently, several UDA methods have been proposed for pair-wise similarity matchers, as found in person ReID [5,14,27,29,30,33,34]. Common UDA approaches for metric learning employ (1) clustering algorithms for pseudo-labeling of the target data in the feature space, or (2) aligning feature representations of source and target data (either by minimizing some domain discrepancy or adversarial loss) [28]. These feature-based approaches are suitable for closed-set application scenarios, where the source and target domains share the same label space. However, this is not the case in open-set scenarios, where real-world person ReID systems are applied.

In this paper, we present a new concept for designing UDA methods that are suitable for pair-wise similarity matching in open-set person ReID scenarios. Instead of adapting the source model to unlabeled target samples in the feature representation space, UDA is performed in the dissimilarity representation space. As opposed to the common feature space, where a dimension represents a feature value extracted from one sample (i.e., a vector represents this sample measured over all features), the dissimilarity space consists of dissimilarity coordinates where each dimension represents the difference between two samples measured for a specific feature (i.e., a vector represents the Euclidean distance between two samples). Accordingly, the multiple clusters that represent different classes (i.e., ReID identities) in the feature representation space, are transformed to only two clusters that represent the pair-wise within- and between-class distances. This transformation is more suitable for open-set ReID problems, when identities differ between the source and target domains, since the new label space has only two labels – pair-wise similar or dissimilar. Aligning the pair-wise distance distributions of the source and target domains in the dissimilarity space results in a domain-invariant pair-wise matcher.

The dissimilarity representation concept was recently introduced in [6], where a pseudo-labeling approach was proposed for UDA in still-to-video face recognition. This approach provided descent UDA results for problems with a limited domain shift. As a specific realization of the proposed concept, this paper focuses on a discrepancy-bases approach for dissimilarity-based UDA, that can provide a high level of accuracy for challenging problems with significant domain shift, as in ReID applications. To this end, we propose a variant of the common Maximum Mean Discrepancy (MMD) loss that is tailored for the dissimilarity representation space. The new Dissimilarity-based MMD (D-MMD) loss exploits the structure of intra- and inter-class distributions to align the source and target data in the dissimilarity space. It leverages tracklet[1] information to approximate the pair-wise distance distribution of the target domain, and thus estimate a reliable D-MMD loss for alignment of source and target distance distributions.

This paper contributes a novel D-MMD loss for UDA of DL models for person ReID. This loss allows to learn a domain-invariant pair-wise dissimilarity space representation, and thereby bridge the gap between image data from source and target domains (see Fig. 1). An extensive experimental analysis on three benchmark datasets indicates that minimizing the proposed D-MMD loss allows to align the source and target data distributions, which substantially enhances the recognition accuracy across domains. It also allows for designing reliable pair-wise matchers across domains, without the traditional requirement for data augmentation and/or complex networks.

2   Unsupervised Domain Adaptation for ReID

UDA focuses on adapting a model such that it can generalize well on an unlabeled target domain data while using a labeled source domain dataset. DL models for UDA seek to learn discriminant and domain-invariant representations from source and target data. They are generally based on either adversarial-, discrepancy-, or reconstruction-based approaches [28]. UDA methods have received limited attention in ReID because of their weak performance on benchmarks datasets compared to their supervised counterparts. Relying on a large-amount of annotated image data, and leveraging the recent success of deep con-

---

[1] A tracklet correspond to a sequence of bounding boxes that are captured over time for a same person in a camera viewpoint, and obtained using a person tracker.

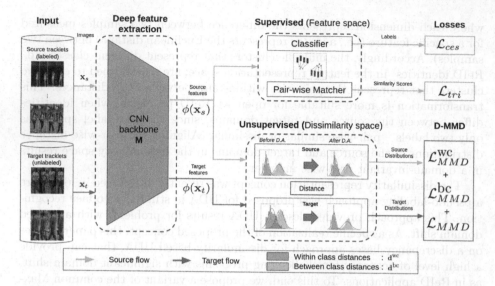

Fig. 1. Deep learning model for UDA using the proposed D-MMD loss. Labeled source images and unlabeled target images are input. First, the DL model for ReID undergoes supervised learning with source images. Upon reaching convergence, the backbone CNN can produce deep features from source and target images. Within-class (WC) and between-class (BC) dissimilarity distributions are produced for source and target domain data. Then, the D-MMD loss is applied between WC (resp. BC) source and WC (resp. BC) target. Supervised losses are also employed to ensure model stability.

volutional networks, supervised ReID approaches [1,4,17,20,23] have shown a significant performance improvement, but UDA performance drops drastically when tested on different datasets and large domain shifts. To deal with this issue, representative methods use either clustering-based approach or domain-invariant feature learning based approach.

In clustering-based approaches [7,14], unlabeled target data are clustered to generate pseudo-labels, and then the network is optimized using the pseudo-labeled target data. Accordingly, performance of these approaches highly depend on the accuracy of clustering algorithms, and low accuracy can result in the propagation of noisy labels, and a corrupted model. In contrast, the domain-invariant feature learning based approaches [2,11,22,25,31] learn domain-invariant features. One approach is to define a discrepancy loss function that measures the domain shift in the feature space so that minimization of this loss decreases the domain shift, such in CORAL [22], MMD GAN [11], and WMMD [31]. Another approach for producing domain-invariant feature representations is through adversarial training, by penalizing a classifier's ability to differentiate between source and target representations [2,25].

These approaches either employ pseudo-labeling using a specific set of labels (classes) that exist in the source domain, or represent samples of specific individuals similarly in both source and target domains. Therefore, these approaches are more suitable for closed-set application scenarios, where the source and target domains share the label space. Accordingly, these approaches can be ineffective when applied to real-world person ReID applications that generally correspond to an open-set scenario. Indeed, individuals that appear in the target operational domain are typically different than those in design detests, or during the calibration phase.

To overcome these limitations of domain-invariant feature learning approaches, a different category of methods generate synthetic labeled data by transforming the source data to their style representative of target data [5,29,33, 34]. However, performance of these approaches completely depends on the image generation quality. Other methods in the literature use labeled source data to train an initial deep ReID model, and then refine the trained model by clustering the target data [12,13,30]. These methods achieve a lower performance as they do not leverage the labeled source data to guide the adaptation procedure. Moreover, all aforementioned methods ignore the valuable knowledge that can be inferred from the underlying relations among target samples.

This paper addresses the limitations of the existing UDA methods for ReID through transferring the design space from the common feature representation space to the dissimilarity representation space, where open-set models can be easily adapted. This allows aligning the pair-wise distance distributions of the source and target domains. More specifically, this approach differs from the literature in two main aspects: (1) Unlike [11,22,31], we proposed to use D-MMD loss by exploiting the advantages of intra- and inter-class distributions along with global distributions. This allows dealing with the open-set application scenario exist in person ReID. (2) Our proposed approach does not rely on synthetic data augmentation as in [5,29,33,34], nor on the sensitivity of clustering algorithms as in [7,14].

3   Proposed Method

In this paper, a novel Dissimilarity-based Maximum Mean Discrepancy (D-MMD) loss is proposed for UDA of ReID systems. Rather than aligning source and target domains feature space, our D-MMD loss allows for the direct alignment of pair-wise distance distributions between domains. This involves jointly aligning the pair-wise distances from within-class distributions, as well as distances from between-class distributions. Both of these component contribute to accurate UDA for ReID systems based on a pair-wise similarity matcher, and have not been considered in other state-of-the-art methods. The proposed D-MMD loss allows to optimize pair-wise distances through gradient descent using relatively small batches.

Figure 1 shows a DL model for UDA that relies on our D-MMD loss. For training, images $\mathbf{x}_s \in \mathbf{X}_s$ are sampled from the source domain $\mathcal{D}_s$, while images $\mathbf{x}_t \in \mathbf{X}_t$ are sampled from the target domain $\mathcal{D}_t$. During UDA, the CNN backbone model $\mathcal{M}$ is adapted to produce a discriminant feature representation $\phi(\mathbf{x}_s)$ (resp. $\phi(\mathbf{x}_t)$) for input images, and the distances between input feature vectors allows estimating WC or BC distributions.

The underlying relations between source and target domain tracklets are employed to compute distributions of Euclidean distances based on samples of same identity (WC), $\mathbf{d}^{\mathrm{wc}}$, and of different identities (BC), $\mathbf{d}^{\mathrm{bc}}$. The D-MMD loss $\mathcal{L}_{D-MMD}$ seeks to align the distance distributions of both domains through back propagation. The overall loss function $\mathcal{L}$ for UDA is:

$$\mathcal{L} = \mathcal{L}_{\text{Supervised}} + \mathcal{L}_{D-MMD} \tag{1}$$

During inference, the ReID system performs pair-wise similarity matching. It is therefore relevant to optimize in the similarity space, and align target similarity distribution with well-separated intra/inter-class distribution from $\mathcal{D}_s$. The rest of this section provides additional details on the $\mathcal{L}_{\text{Supervised}}$ and $\mathcal{L}_{D-MMD}$ loss functions.

3.1   Supervised Loss

A model $\mathcal{M}$ is trained through supervised learning on source data $\mathbf{X}_s$ using a combination of a softmax cross-entropy loss with label smoothing regularizer ($\mathcal{L}_{\text{ces}}$) [24] and triplet loss ($\mathcal{L}_{\text{tri}}$) [10]. $\mathcal{L}_{\text{ces}}$ is defined by Szegedy et al. [24] as:

$$\mathcal{L}_{\text{ces}} = (1 - \epsilon) \cdot \mathcal{L}_{\text{ce}} + \frac{\epsilon}{N}, \tag{2}$$

where N denotes total number of classes, and $\epsilon \in [0, 1]$ is a hyper-parameter that control the degree of label smoothing. $\mathcal{L}_{\text{ce}}$ is defined as:

$$\mathcal{L}_{\text{ce}} = \frac{1}{K} \sum_{i}^{K} - \log \left(\frac{\exp(\mathbf{W}_{y_i}^T \mathbf{x}_i + b_{y_i})}{\sum_{j=1}^{N} \exp\left(\mathbf{W}_{j}^T \mathbf{x}_i + b_j\right)} \right) \tag{3}$$

where K is the batch size. Class label $y_i \in \{1, 2, ..., N\}$ is associated with training image $\mathbf{x}_i$, the ith training image. Weight vectors $\mathbf{W}_{yi}$ and bias b_{yi} of last fully connected (FC) layer corresponds to class y of ith image. $\mathbf{W}_j$ and b_j are weights and bias of last FC corresponding of the jth class ($j \in [1, N]$). $\mathbf{W}_j$ and $\mathbf{W}_{y_i}$ are respectively the jth and y_i^{th} column of $\mathbf{W} = \{w_{ij} : i = 1, 2, ..., F; j = 1, 2, ..., N\}$, where F is the size of the last FC layer.

Triplet loss is also employed with hard positive/negative mining as proposed by Hermans et al. [10], where batches are formed by randomly selecting a person, and then sampling a number of images for each person. For each sample, the hardest positive and negative samples are used to compute the triplet loss:

$$\mathcal{L}_{\text{tri}} = \frac{1}{N_s} \sum_{\alpha=1}^{N_s} \left[m + \max(d\left(\phi(\mathbf{x}_\alpha^i), \phi(\mathbf{x}_p^i)\right)) - \min_{i \neq j}(d\left(\phi(\mathbf{x}_\alpha^i), \phi(\mathbf{x}_n^j)\right)) \right]_+ \tag{4}$$

where, $[.]_+ = \max(., 0)$, m denotes a margin, N_s is the set of all hard triplets in the mini-batch, and d is the Euclidean distance. $\mathbf{x}_j^i$ corresponds to the jth image of the ith person in a mini-batch. Subscript α indicates an anchor image, while p

and n indicate a positive and negative image with respect to that same specific anchor. $\phi(\mathbf{x})$ is the feature representation of an image $\mathbf{x}$.

For our supervised loss, we combine both the above losses.

$$\mathcal{L}_{\text{supervised}} = \mathcal{L}_{\text{ces}} + \lambda \cdot \mathcal{L}_{\text{tri}} \tag{5}$$

where λ is a hyper-parameter that weights the contribution of each loss term.

The softmax cross-entropy loss $\mathcal{L}_{\text{ces}}$ defines the learning process as a classification task, where each input image is classified as one of the known identities in the training set. The triplet loss $\mathcal{L}_{\text{tri}}$ allows to optimise an embedding where feature vectors are less similar different for inter-class images, and more similar intra-class images.

3.2 Dissimilarity-Based Maximum Mean Discrepancy (D-MMD)

After training the model $\mathcal{M}$, we use it to extract feature representations from each source image $\mathbf{x}_s \in \mathbf{X}_s$, $\phi(\mathbf{x}_s)$, and target image $\mathbf{x}_t \in \mathbf{X}_t$, $\phi(\mathbf{x}_t)$. Then, the within-class distances, e.g., Euclidean or L_2 distances, between each different pair of images $\mathbf{x}_i^u$ and $\mathbf{x}_i^v$ of the same class i are computed:

$$d_i^{\text{wc}}(\mathbf{x}_i^u, \mathbf{x}_i^v) = ||\phi(\mathbf{x}_i^u) - \phi(\mathbf{x}_i^v)||_2, \; u \neq v \tag{6}$$

where $\phi(.)$ is the backbone CNN feature extraction, and x_i^u is the image u of the class i. Similarly, the between-class distances are computed using each different pair of images $\mathbf{x}_i^u$ and $\mathbf{x}_j^z$ of the different class i and j:

$$d_{i,j}^{\text{bc}}(\mathbf{x}_i^u, \mathbf{x}_j^z) = ||\phi(\mathbf{x}_i^u) - \phi(\mathbf{x}_j^z)||_2, \; i \neq j \; \& \; u \neq z \tag{7}$$

Then, $\mathbf{d}^{\text{wc}}$ and $\mathbf{d}^{\text{bc}}$ are defined as the distributions of all distance values d_i^{wc} and $d_{i,j}^{\text{bc}}$, respectively, in the dissimilarity space.

The within-class (WC) and between-class (BC) distance samples of the source domain are computed directly using the source labels, so they capture the exact pair-wise distance distribution of the source domain. On the other hand, given the unlabeled target data, we leverage the tracklet information provided by a visual object tracker. We consider the frames within same tracklet as WC samples, and frames from different tracklets as BC samples. It is important to note that such tracklet information provide us with an approximation of the pair-wise distance distribution of the target domain since it lacks intra-class pairs from different tracklets or cameras.

Maximum Mean Discrepancy (MMD) [9] metric is used to compute the distance between two distribution:

$$MMD(P(A), Q(B)) = \frac{1}{n^2} \sum_{i=1}^{n} \sum_{j=1}^{n} k(a_i, a_j)$$

$$+ \frac{1}{m^2} \sum_{i=1}^{m} \sum_{j=1}^{m} k(b_i, b_j) - \frac{2}{nm} \sum_{i=1}^{n} \sum_{j=1}^{m} k(a_i, b_j) \tag{8}$$

where A (resp. B) is the source (resp. target) domain and $P(A)$ (resp. $Q(B)$) is the distribution of the source (resp. target) domain. $k(.,.)$ is a kernel (e.g. Gaussian) and a_i (resp. b_i) is sample i from A (resp. B). n and m are number of training examples from $P(A)$ and $Q(B)$, respectively (Fig. 2).

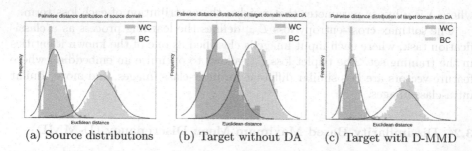

(a) Source distributions   (b) Target without DA   (c) Target with D-MMD

Fig. 2. (a) Shows that the dissimilarity representation of the WC (blue) and BC (orange) distributions, where BC has larger Euclidean distances than WC because the model produces features closer for samples from same identities than that for samples from different identities. (b) shows a significant overlap when target data are represented using the initial source model, due to the intrinsic domain shift. (c) shows that the target BC and WC distributions become aligned with the source distributions (a) after performing UDA. (Color figure online)

To evaluate the divergence between two domains, MMD metric is applied to measure the difference from features produced by the source and target models are different using:

$$\mathcal{L}_{MMD} = MMD(\mathcal{S}, \mathcal{T}) \tag{9}$$

$\mathcal{S}$ ($\mathcal{T}$) is defined as the distribution of the sources (target) images $\mathbf{X}_s$ ($\mathbf{X}_t$) represented in the feature space.

Our method relies on the application of the MMD in the dissimilarity representation space instead of the common feature representation space. We define the $\mathcal{L}_{MMD}^{\mathrm{wc}}$ and $\mathcal{L}_{MMD}^{\mathrm{bc}}$ loss terms as follows:

$$\mathcal{L}_{MMD}^{\mathrm{wc}} = MMD(\mathbf{d}_s^{\mathrm{wc}}, \mathbf{d}_t^{\mathrm{wc}}) \tag{10}$$

$$\mathcal{L}_{MMD}^{\mathrm{bc}} = MMD(\mathbf{d}_s^{\mathrm{bc}}, \mathbf{d}_t^{\mathrm{bc}}) \tag{11}$$

Minimizing the above terms aligns the pair-wise distance distributions of the source and target domains, so that pair-wise distances from different domains are not deferential, and hence the source model works well in the target domain. Finally, our unsupervised loss function can be expressed as:

$$\mathcal{L}_{D-MMD} = \mathcal{L}_{MMD}^{\mathrm{wc}} + \mathcal{L}_{MMD}^{\mathrm{bc}} + \mathcal{L}_{MMD} \tag{12}$$

Algorithm 1 presents a UDA training strategy based on the D-MMD loss. Firstly, a supervised training phase runs for N^s epochs and produces a reference model $\mathcal{M}$ using

---

Algorithm 1. UDA training strategy based on the D-MMD loss.

Require: labeled source data $\mathbf{X}_s$, and unlabeled target data $\mathbf{X}_t$
  Load source data $\mathbf{X}_s$, and **Initialize** backbone model $\mathcal{M}$
  for $l \in [1, N^s]$ epochs **do**
    for each mini-batch $B_s \subset \mathbf{X}_s$ **do**
      1) Compute $\mathcal{L}_{\text{ces}}$ with Eq. 2, and $\mathcal{L}_{\text{tri}}$ with Eq. 4
      2) Optimize $\mathcal{M}$
    end for
  end for
  Load target data $\mathbf{X}_t$, and **Load** backbone model $\mathcal{M}$
  for $l \in [1, N^u]$ epochs **do**
    for each mini-batch $B_s \subset \mathbf{X}_s$ each mini-batch $B_t \subset \mathbf{X}_t$ **do**
      1) Generate $\mathbf{d}_s^{wc}$ with Eq. 6, $\mathbf{d}_s^{bc}$ with Eq. 7 and B_s
      2) Generate $\mathbf{d}_t^{wc}$ with Eq. 6, $\mathbf{d}_t^{bc}$ with Eq. 7 and B_t
      3) Compute $\mathcal{L}_{D-MMD}(B_s, B_t)$ with Eq. 12
      4) Compute $\mathcal{L}_{\text{Supervised}}$ with Eq. 5 using B_s
      5) Optimize $\mathcal{M}$ based on overall $\mathcal{L}$ (Eq. 1)
    end for
  end for

---

the source domain data. Then, an unsupervised training phase runs for N^u epochs and aligns the target and source pair-wise distance distributions by minimizing the D-MMD loss terms defined by Eqs. 9, 10, and 11. Note that the supervised loss $\mathcal{L}_{Supervised}$ is evaluated during domain adaptation to ensure the model $\mathcal{M}$ remains aligned to a reliable source distribution $\mathcal{S}$ over training iterations remaining.

Evaluating the D-MMD loss during the UDA training strategy involves computing the distances among each pairs of images. The computational complexity can be estimated as the number of within-class and between-class distance calculations. Assuming a common batch size of $|B|$ for training with source and target images and a number of occurrence of the same identity N_o, the total number of distance calculations is:

$$N_{\text{distances}} = N_{\text{distances}}^{wc} + N_{\text{distances}}^{bc} = (N_o - 1)! \frac{|B|}{N_o} + N_o (\frac{|B|}{N_o} - 1)^2 \qquad (13)$$

4   Results and Discussion

4.1   Experimental Methodology

For the experimental validation, we employ three challenging person ReID datasets, Market-1501 [32], DukeMTMC [21] and MSMT17 [29], and compare our proposed approach with state-of-the-art generative (GAN), tracklet-based, and domain adaptation methods for unsupervised person ReID.

Table 1 describes three datasets for our experimental evaluation – Market1501, DukeMTMC and MSMT17. The **Market-1501** [32] dataset comprises labels generated using Discriminatively Trained Part-Based Models (DPM) [8]. It provides a realistic benchmark, using 6 different cameras, and around ten times more images than previously published datasets. The **DukeMTMC** [21] dataset is comprised of videos captured outdoor at the Duke University campus from 8 cameras. **MSMT17** [29] is

Table 1. Properties of the three challenging datasets used in our experiments. They are listed according to their complexity (number of images, persons, cameras, and capture conditions, e.g., occlusions and illumination changes).

Datasets	# IDs	# cameras	# images	# train (IDs)	# gallery (IDs)	# query (IDs)	Annotation method	Crop size
Market-1501	1501	6	32217	12936 (751)	15913 (751)	3368 (751)	semi-automated (DPM)	128 × 64
Duke-MTMC	1812	8	36441	16522 (702)	17661 (1110)	2228 (702)	manual	variable
MSMT17	4101	15	126441	32621 (1041)	82161 (3060)	11659 (3060)	semi-automated (Faster R-CNN)	variable

the largest and most challenging ReID dataset. It is comprised of indoor and outdoor scenarios, in the morning, noon and afternoon, and each video is captured over a long period of time.

For the supervised training, a Resnet50 architecture model is pretrained on ImageNet until convergence for both Hard-Batch Triplet and Softmax Cross-Entropy loss functions. Source domain videos are utilized for supervised training and evaluation. Then, the source and target training videos are used to perform UDA of the source model. Features are extracted from images of both domains using the Resnet50 CNN backbone (with a 2048 features vector size). To compute the BC and WC distributions, we randomly selected 4 occurrences of each class within batches of size 128. Given the nature of data, the tracklets are subject to greater diversity, with images from different viewpoints. The $D - MMD$ is then computed as described in Sect. 3, and backpropagation is performed using an Adam optimizer with a single step scheduler, decreasing the learning rate by 10 (initially 0.003) after every 20 epochs. In all steps, every image is resized to 256 × 128 before being processed.

Table 2 reports the upper bound accuracy for our datasets. To obtain this reference, we leveraged labeled source and target image data for supervised training. The ResNet50 model is initially trained using data from a first person ReID dataset (source domain), and then it is fine-tuned with training data from a second ReID datasets (target domain). Accuracy is computed with the target test sets of respective ReID datasets. We employed cross entropy loss with label smoothing regularizer Eq. 2 with $\epsilon = 0.1$, and triplet loss with a margin $m = 0.3$. To train DukeMTMC and Market1501, 30 epochs are required, while MSMT17 requires 59 epochs due to its larger-scale and complexity. Results in Table 2 confirms that MSMT17 is the most challenging dataset and shows lowest performance (63.2 % rank-1 accuracy).

Instead of optimizing the number of occurrences (frames) in a tracklet as a hyper-parameter, we had to use a fixed number (4 occurences) since the experimental datasets can sometime include only this number of frames per tracklet, and also for fair comparison with the SOA results. The metrics used for performance evaluation are the mean average precision (mAP), and rank-1, rank-5, rank-10 accuracy from the Cumulative Match Curve (CMC).

Table 2. Upper bound accuracy obtained after training on source data, and then fine-tuning on target data. Accuracy is measured with target training data.

Dataset	Accuracy			
source $\longrightarrow$ target	rank-1	rank-5	rank-10	mAP
DukeMTMC $\longrightarrow$ Market1501	89.5	95.6	97.1	75.1
Market1501 $\longrightarrow$ DukeMTMC	79.3	89.3	92.0	62.7
DukeMTMC $\longrightarrow$ MSMT17	63.2	77.5	82.0	33.9

4.2   Ablation Study

Table 3 shows the impact on accuracy of the different loss terms. It is clear that $\mathcal{L}_{MMD}^{bc}$ and $\mathcal{L}_{MMD}^{wc}$ provide important information, with a slight improvement for the between-class (BC) component. Moreover, results show that a combination of both losses produces better results than when each term is employed separately. Moreover, while the classic feature-based $\mathcal{L}_{MMD}$ had insignificant impact when employed separately (as observed in [14]), it helps when combined with the other terms. This can be explained by the fact that $\mathcal{L}_{MMD}$ suffers from ambiguous association while dealing with domain shift that exists in open-set scenarios. Nevertheless, when the domain gap decreases to a reasonable limit (with the help of the proposed dissimilarity-based loss terms $\mathcal{L}_{MMD}^{bc}$ and $\mathcal{L}_{MMD}^{wc}$), the feature-based loss starts to contributing ReID accuracy.

Table 3. Ablation Study. Impact on accuracy of individual loss terms when transferring between the DukeMTMC and Market1501 domains. (The lower bound accuracy refers is obtained with the ResNet50 model trained on source data, and tested on target data, without domain adaptation.)

Setting	Loss functions				Source: Duke Target: Market		Source: Market Target: Duke	
	$\mathcal{L}_{sup}$	$\mathcal{L}_{MMD}^{wc}$	$\mathcal{L}_{MMD}^{bc}$	$\mathcal{L}_{MMD}$	rank-1	mAP	rank-1	mAP
Lower bound	✓	✗	✗	✗	36.1	16.1	23.7	12.3
A	✓	✓	✗	✗	45.8	24.3	30.3	16.6
B	✓	✗	✓	✗	51.8	28.4	45.6	29.2
C	✓	✓	✓	✗	66.6	45.4	60.5	42.9
D	✓	✓	✓	✓	70.6	48.8	63.5	46.0

From source DukeMTMC to target Market1501, the margin of improvement while considering only the WC component over the baseline are 9.7% for Rank-1 accuracy and 8.2% for mAP and for only BC component 15.7 % for Rank-1 accuracy and 12.1 % for mAP. From source Market1501 to target DukeMTMC, we reach for the WC component 6.6 % for Rank-1 accuracy and 4.3% for mAP improvement compared to the baseline when for BC component we obtain 21.9% for Rank-1 accuracy and 16.9 % for mAP more than the baseline.

Table 3 shows that a model adapted using only BC information is capable to produce better representation and leads to better results (51.8% Rank-1 accuracy) than when using only WC (45.8% Rank-1 accuracy) for the DukeMTMC to Market1501 transfer problem. In general, combining the different terms provides better results than when individual losses are employed.

In Sect. 3.2 (Fig. 2), it is shown clearly that there is large overlap between the intra- and inter-class pair-wise distance distributions when using the initial source representation in the target domain. When applying the proposed method, the overlap significantly decreases and aligned with the source distributions. Figure 3 shows the reflection of such improvement of the pair-wise distance representation on the actual Re-ID problem. Before applying DA, there is much confusion between person representations which can be improved significantly with applying the proposed method.

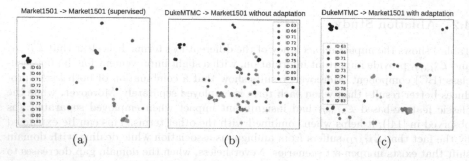

Fig. 3. T-SNE visualisations that show the impact of the original domain shift ((a) versus (b)). Then (b) and (c) show the impact of employing our method to decrease domain shift, and accordingly improving the representation.

4.3   Comparison with State-of-Art Methods

We compare our approach with state-of-the-art (SOTA) unsupervised methods on Market-1501, DukeMTMC-reID and MSMT17. Lower Bound refers to the domain shift without any adaptation. Table 4 reports the comparison when tested on DukeMTMC and MSMT17 with Market1501 as the source, and Table 4 reports results when DukeMTMC is the source.

PUL [7] and BUC [16] are clustering methods for pseudo-labeling of target data. Such approaches lead to poor performance. We outperform them by a large margin, 16.4% Rank-1 accuracy and 18.5% mAP more from Market1501 to DukeMTMC than BUC approach [16]. TAUDL [12] and UTAL [13] are two tracklet-based approaches for unsupervised person ReID. Due to their fully unsupervised behavior, they obtain worse results than our approach.

We also compare with other UDA approaches: PTGAN [29], SPGAN [5], ARN [15], TJ-AIDL [27] (attribute-based), [3] HHL [33], ECN [34], PDA-Net [14], Wu et al. [30], UDCA-CCE [19] (Camera-aware). Most of them are using data augmentation methods [5,29,33,34]. We are not using such techniques which are computationally expensive and require more memory. This also helps with problems that involve transferring from a small dataset to a larger and more complex dataset, which reflects a natural real-world application scenario. For the DukeMTMC to Market1501 transfer problem, we notice that DukeMTMC is a better initialization for simpler domains such Market1501, and it is easier to perform well in that sense (similar phenomenon for all other methods).

Table 4. ReID accuracy of the proposed and SOTA methods for UDA using Market1501 as source, and DukeMTMC and MSMT17 as targets. Accuracy is obtained on target datasets.

Methods	Source: Market1501								Conference or Journal
	DukeMTMC				MSMT17				
	r-1	r-5	r-10	mAP	r-1	r-5	r-10	mAP	
Lower Bound	23.7	38.8	44.7	12.3	6.1	12.0	15.6	2.0	–
PUL [7]	30.0	43.4	48.5	16.4	-	-	-	-	TOMM'18
CFSM [3]	49.8	-	-	27.3	-	-	-	-	AAAI'19
BUC [16]	47.4	62.6	68.4	27.5	-	-	-	-	AAAI'19
ARN [15]	60.2	73.9	79.5	33.5	-	-	-	-	CVPR'18-WS
UCDA-CCE [19]	47.7	-	-	31.0	-	-	-	-	ICCV'19
PTGAN [29]	27.4	-	50.7	-	10.2	-	24.4	2.9	CVPR'18
SPGAN+LMP [5]	46.4	62.3	68.0	26.2	-	-	-	-	CVPR'18
HHL [33]	46.9	61.0	66.7	27.2	-	-	-	-	ECCV'18
TAUDL [12]	61.7	-	-	43.5	28.4	-	-	12.5	ECCV'18
UTAL [13]	62.3	-	-	44.6	31.4	-	-	13.1	TPAMI'19
TJ-AIDL [27]	44.3	59.6	65.0	23.0	-	-	-	-	CVPR'18
Wu et al. [30]	51.5	66.7	71.7	30.5	-	-	-	-	ICCV'19
ECN [34]	63.3	75.8	80.4	40.4	25.3	36.3	42.1	8.5	CVPR'19
PDA-Net [14]	63.2	77.0	82.5	45.1	-	-	-	-	IEEE'19
D-MMD (Ours)	**63.5**	**78.8**	**83.9**	**46.0**	**29.1**	**46.3**	**54.1**	**13.5**	–

Table 5. ReID accuracy of the proposed and SOTA methods for UDA using DukeMTMC as source, and Market1501 and MSMT17 as targets. Accuracy is obtained on target datasets.

Methods	Source: DukeMTMC								Conference or Journal
	Market1501				MSMT17				
	r-1	r-5	r-10	mAP	r-1	r-5	r-10	mAP	
Lower Bound	36.6	54.5	62.9	16.1	11.3	20.6	25.7	3.7	–
PUL [7]	45.5	60.7	66.7	20.5	-	-	-	-	TOMM'18
CFSM [3]	61.2	-	-	28.3	-	-	-	-	AAAI'19
BUC [16]	66.2	79.6	84.5	38.3	-	-	-	-	AAAI'19
ARN [15]	70.3	80.4	86.3	39.4	-	-	-	-	CVPR'18-WS
UCDA-CCE [19]	60.4	-	-	30.9	-	-	-	-	ICCV'19
PTGAN [29]	38.6	-	66.1	-	10.2	-	24.4	2.9	CVPR'18
SPGAN+LMP [5]	57.7	75.8	82.4	26.7	-	-	-	-	CVPR'18
HHL [33]	62.2			31.4	-	-	-	-	ECCV'18
TAUDL [12]	63.7	-	-	41.2	28.4	-	-	12.5	ECCV'18
UTAL [13]	69.2	-	-	46.2	31.4	-	-	13.1	TPAMI'19
TJ-AIDL [27]	58.2	74.8	81.1	26.5	-	-	-	-	CVPR'18
Wu et al. [30]	64.7	80.2	85.6	35.6	-	-	-	-	ICCV'19
ECN [34]	**75.6**	**87.5**	**91.6**	43.0	30.2	41.5	46.8	10.2	CVPR'19
PDA-Net [14]	75.2	86.3	90.2	47.6	-	-	-	-	IEEE'19
D-MMD (Ours)	70.6	87.0	91.5	**48.8**	**34.4**	**51.1**	**58.5**	**15.3**	–

ECN and PDA-Net obtain better results on CMC metrics Rank-1 for this transfer problem DukeMTMC-Market1501 than ours (ECN [34] has 5.0% more and PDA-net [14] has 4.6% higher Rank-1 accuracy for only 0.5% and 0.1% on Rank-5 and rank-10 accuracy regarding ECN). We outperform all other methods in mAP metrics (5.4% more than ECN). Since the D-MMD objective is to learn domain-invariant pair-wise dissimilarity representations, so success can be better measured using more global metrics, e.g., mAP, and this is validated by our results, where the proposed method produces best results using this metric. In contrast, CMC top-1 accuracy could be improved by training a pattern classifier (e.g. MLP) to process the resulting distance vector. Nevertheless, when considering the opposite transfer problem, i.e., Market1501 to DukeMTMC, which is much more complex, our method provides best results for all metrics (0.3% on Rank-1, 3% on Rank-5, 3.5% on Rank-10 accuracy and 5.6% on mAP). We also outperform state-of-the-art methods on the most challenging dataset MSMT17 by 4.2% Rank-1, 9.6% Rank-5, 11.7% Rank-10 and 5.1% mAP when considering source DukeMTMC dataset. Similar results are observed using Market1501 as source.

Table 6. UDA accuracy of the proposed versus lower and upper bound approaches when transferring from MSMT17 (source) to Market1501 and DukeMTMC (targets).

Methods	Source: MSMT17							
	Market1501				DukeMTMC			
	rank-1	rank-5	rank-10	mAP	rank-1	rank-5	rank-10	mAP
Lower bound	43.2	61.4	68.6	20.7	47.4	63.7	69.2	27.5
D-MMD (Ours)	72.8	88.1	92.3	50.8	68.8	82.6	87.1	51.6
Upper bound	89.5	95.6	97.1	75.1	79.3	89.3	92.0	62.7

The proposed method can provide best performance for problems where the source domain consists in challenging data with high intra-class variability and high inter-class similarity (e.g., MSMT17) as compared to easier target domains (e.g. Market1501 and DukeMTMC). Such transfer problem is less explored in the literature, so in Table 6 we compare our results with only the lower and upper bounds. With this setup (i.e. source is the most challenging dataset MSMT17) we obtained best results (better than these reported on Tables 4 and 5): 77.8% Rank-1 accuracy and 50.8% mAP for Market1501 and 68.8% Rank-1 accuracy and 51.6% mAP for DukeMTMC.

5   Conclusion

In this paper, we proposed a novel dissimilarity-based UDA approach for person ReID using MMD loss to reduce the gap between domains in the dissimilarity space. The core idea is to exploit the advantages of using within and between-class distances that effectively capture the underlying relations between domains which has never been explored in the state-of-the-art. To that end, we align the within- and between-class distance distributions for the source and target domains to produce effective Re-ID models for the target domain. Experiments on three challenging ReID datasets prove the effectiveness of this new approach as it outperforms state-of-the-art methods. Moreover, our proposed loss is general and can be applied to different feature extractors and applications.

References

1. Bhuiyan, A., Liu, Y., Siva, P., Javan, M., Ayed, I.B., Granger, E.: Pose guided gated fusion for person re-identification. In: WACV (2020)
2. Bousmalis, K., Trigeorgis, G., Silberman, N., Krishnan, D., Erhan, D.: Domain separation networks. In: NIPS (2016)
3. Chang, X., Yang, Y., Xiang, T., Hospedales, T.M.: Disjoint label space transfer learning with common factorised space. In: AAAI (2019)
4. Chen, B., Deng, W., Hu, J.: Mixed high-order attention network for person re-identification. In: ICCV (2019)
5. Deng, W., Zheng, L., Ye, Q., Kang, G., Yang, Y., Jiao, J.: Image-image domain adaptation with preserved self-similarity and domain-dissimilarity for person re-identification. In: CVPR (2018)
6. Ekladious, G., Lemoine, H., Granger, E., Kamali, K., Moudache, S.: Dual-triplet metric learning for unsupervised domain adaptation in video-based face recognition. In: IJCNN (2020)
7. Fan, H., Zheng, L., Yan, C., Yang, Y.: Unsupervised person re-identification: clustering and fine-tuning. ACM Trans. Multimed. Comput. Commun. Appl. **14**(4), 1–18 (2018)
8. Felzenszwalb, P.F., Girshick, R.B., McAllester, D., Ramanan, D.: Object detection with discriminatively trained part-based models. IEEE Trans. Pattern Anal. Mach. Intell. **32**(9), 1627–1645 (2009)
9. Gretton, A., Borgwardt, K.M., Rasch, M.J., Schölkopf, B., Smola, A.: A kernel two-sample test. J. Mach. Learn. Res. **13**(1), 723–773 (2012)
10. Hermans, A., Beyer, L., Leibe, B.: In defense of the triplet loss for person re-identification (2017)
11. Li, C.L., Chang, W.C., Cheng, Y., Yang, Y., Póczos, B.: MMD gan: towards deeper understanding of moment matching network. In: NIPS (2017)
12. Li, M., Zhu, X., Gong, S.: Unsupervised person re-identification by deep learning tracklet association. In: Ferrari, V., Hebert, M., Sminchisescu, C., Weiss, Y. (eds.) ECCV 2018. LNCS, vol. 11208, pp. 772–788. Springer, Cham (2018). https://doi.org/10.1007/978-3-030-01225-0_45
13. Li, M., Zhu, X., Gong, S.: Unsupervised tracklet person re-identification. IEEE TPAMI (2019)
14. Li, Y.J., Lin, C.S., Lin, Y.B., Wang, Y.C.F.: Cross-dataset person re-identification via unsupervised pose disentanglement and adaptation. In: ICCV (2019)
15. Li, Y.J., Yang, F.E., Liu, Y.C., Yeh, Y.Y., Du, X., Frank Wang, Y.C.: Adaptation and re-identification network: an unsupervised deep transfer learning approach to person re-identification. In: CVPR Workshops (2018)
16. Lin, Y., Dong, X., Zheng, L., Yan, Y., Yang, Y.: A bottom-up clustering approach to unsupervised person re-identification. In: AAAI (2019)
17. Luo, H., Gu, Y., Liao, X., Lai, S., Jiang, W.: Bag of tricks and a strong baseline for deep person re-identification. In: CVPR Workshops (2019)
18. Nguyen-Meidine, L.T., Granger, E., Kiran, M., Dolz, J., Blais-Morin, L.A.: Joint progressive knowledge distillation and unsupervised domain adaptation. In: IJCNN (2020)
19. Qi, L., Wang, L., Huo, J., Zhou, L., Shi, Y., Gao, Y.: A novel unsupervised camera-aware domain adaptation framework for person re-identification. In: ICCV (2019)
20. Quan, R., Dong, X., Wu, Y., Zhu, L., Yang, Y.: Auto-reID: searching for a part-aware convnet for person re-identification. In: ICCV (2019)

21. Ristani, E., Solera, F., Zou, R., Cucchiara, R., Tomasi, C.: Performance measures and a data set for multi-target, multi-camera tracking. In: Hua, G., Jégou, H. (eds.) ECCV 2016. LNCS, vol. 9914, pp. 17–35. Springer, Cham (2016). https://doi.org/10.1007/978-3-319-48881-3_2

22. Sun, B., Saenko, K.: Deep CORAL: Correlation Alignment for Deep Domain Adaptation. In: Hua, G., Jégou, H. (eds.) ECCV 2016. LNCS, vol. 9915, pp. 443–450. Springer, Cham (2016). https://doi.org/10.1007/978-3-319-49409-8_35

23. Sun, Y., Zheng, L., Yang, Y., Tian, Q., Wang, S.: Beyond part models: person retrieval with refined part pooling (and a strong convolutional baseline). In: Ferrari, V., Hebert, M., Sminchisescu, C., Weiss, Y. (eds.) ECCV 2018. LNCS, vol. 11208, pp. 501–518. Springer, Cham (2018). https://doi.org/10.1007/978-3-030-01225-0_30

24. Szegedy, C., Vanhoucke, V., Ioffe, S., Shlens, J., Wojna, Z.: Rethinking the inception architecture for computer vision. In: CVPR (2016)

25. Tzeng, E., Hoffman, J., Saenko, K., Darrell, T.: Adversarial discriminative domain adaptation. In: CVPR (2017)

26. Wang, G., Lai, J., Huang, P., Xie, X.: Spatial-temporal person re-identification. In: AAAI (2019)

27. Wang, J., Zhu, X., Gong, S., Li, W.: Transferable joint attribute-identity deep learning for unsupervised person re-identification. In: CVPR (2018)

28. Wang, M., Deng, W.: Deep visual domain adaptation: a survey. Neurocomputing 312, 135–153 (2018)

29. Wei, L., Zhang, S., Gao, W., Tian, Q.: Person transfer gan to bridge domain gap for person re-identification. In: CVPR (2018)

30. Wu, A., Zheng, W.S., Lai, J.H.: Unsupervised person re-identification by camera-aware similarity consistency learning. In: ICCV (2019)

31. Yan, H., Ding, Y., Li, P., Wang, Q., Xu, Y., Zuo, W.: Mind the class weight bias: weighted maximum mean discrepancy for unsupervised domain adaptation. In: CVPR (2017)

32. Zheng, L., Shen, L., Tian, L., Wang, S., Wang, J., Tian, Q.: Scalable person re-identification: a benchmark. In: ICCV (2015)

33. Zhong, Z., Zheng, L., Li, S., Yang, Y.: Generalizing a person retrieval model hetero- and homogeneously. In: Ferrari, V., Hebert, M., Sminchisescu, C., Weiss, Y. (eds.) ECCV 2018. LNCS, vol. 11217, pp. 176–192. Springer, Cham (2018). https://doi.org/10.1007/978-3-030-01261-8_11

34. Zhong, Z., Zheng, L., Luo, Z., Li, S., Yang, Y.: Invariance matters: exemplar memory for domain adaptive person re-identification. In: CVPR (2019)

Learn Distributed GAN with Temporary Discriminators

Hui Qu[1][✉], Yikai Zhang[1], Qi Chang[1], Zhennan Yan[2], Chao Chen[3], and Dimitris Metaxas[1]

[1] Rutgers University, Piscataway, NJ 08854, USA
{hq43,yz422,qc58,dnm}@cs.rutgers.edu
[2] SenseTime Research, Science Park, Hong Kong
yanzhennan@sensetime.com
[3] Stony Brook University, Stony Brook, NY 11794, USA
chao.chen.cchen@gmail.com

Abstract. In this work, we propose a method for training distributed GAN with sequential temporary discriminators. Our proposed method tackles the challenge of training GAN in the federated learning manner: How to update the generator with a flow of temporary discriminators? We apply our proposed method to learn a self-adaptive generator with a series of local discriminators from multiple data centers. We show our design of loss function indeed learns the correct distribution with provable guarantees. The empirical experiments show that our approach is capable of generating synthetic data which is practical for real-world applications such as training a segmentation model. Our TDGAN Code is available at: https://github.com/huiqu18/TDGAN-PyTorch.

1 Introduction

1.1 Advantages of Distributed GAN Learning

In this work we focus on a practical framework for learning Generative Adversarial Network (GAN) [4,11,40,52] using *multiple privately hosted discriminators from multiple entities*. Aggregating feedback from multiple local discriminators endues the generator a global perspective without accessing individual sensitive data. Such natural framework for distributed GAN learning is of great interest to both researchers and practitioners due to its advantages of privacy awareness and adaptivity.

Privacy Awareness. With more privacy concerns on sharing data and regulations imposed for privacy protection like HIPAA [3,12,27,36] in medical domain,

---

H. Qu, Y. Zhang and Q. Chang—Equal contribution.

Electronic supplementary material The online version of this chapter (https://doi.org/10.1007/978-3-030-58583-9_11) contains supplementary material, which is available to authorized users.

© Springer Nature Switzerland AG 2020
A. Vedaldi et al. (Eds.): ECCV 2020, LNCS 12372, pp. 175–192, 2020.
https://doi.org/10.1007/978-3-030-58583-9_11

it is critical to consider privacy protection mechanism in designing a machine learning architecture [10, 23]. The training framework of a distributed GAN using local discriminators meets the criterion of federated learning since the generator does not require access to sensitive data. Classical federated learning framework [14, 28, 55] shares gradients information, which is known to have information leakage. In distributed GAN framework, the local discriminator serves as a shield separating sensitive data from the querier thus is privacy comfortable. Besides, the nature of synthetic data allows the generator to share synthetic images without restriction, which is of great interest in privacy sensitive applications.

Downstream Task Architecture Adaptivity. Our proposed method could embrace the future upgrades of the downstream task by providing the well-trained image generator. The machine learning architecture upgrades rapidly to achieve a better performance by novel network modules [18, 37, 39, 41], loss functions [17, 44], or optimizers [33, 42, 50, 53, 54]. However, the performance of the downstream task couldn't be better if any of the training datasets is missing. Our proposed method could compensate the risk of dataset missing by providing an image generator. The downstream task could trained on the synthetic images from generator without worrying about the loss of the proprietary datasets.

1.2   Temporary Datasets Challenge for Distributed GAN

Several works have been done toward a practical framework to train generator by multiple discriminators [7, 9, 15]. However, all these methods assume discriminators/data centers are always available/online which is not realistic in the practical situation. In particular, those methods fail to consider the challenge of the temporary datasets problem. Since data centers are separated entities, privately hosted discriminators may join the collaborative learning in a stream fashion. On one hand, new individual entities may join the network sequentially; more and more discriminators will participate. On the other hand, some local discriminators/nodes in the network may go offline and never come back again. For example, research funding for a hospital is limited, it is not realistic to require a hospital to maintain the dataset and stay online forever. Ideally, a general framework should be able to handle the temporary discriminator constraint, i.e. the dynamic flow of participating and leaving discriminators.

In the process of learning with flows of temporary discriminators, the dilution problem becomes a major concern. Suppose the generator keeps learning from late arrival discriminators, the memory of learned distribution with regard to absent data centers may be submerged by the incoming data. Such dilution phenomenon has been widely observed [34]. A well designed framework should be able to aggressively capture the essence of online datasets while keeping the consistency of memory about the datasets of left parties.

To address such challenge in practice, we propose our training method called Temporary Discriminator GAN (TDGAN). Our method relies on a mixture of two loss functions: *digesting loss* and *reminding loss* to tackle the challenge. The digesting loss updates the generator by collecting feedback from temporarily available and privately hosted discriminators. The reminding loss keeps the consistency of the generator on the distribution of the absent data centers thus prevents the memory decay issue of temporary discriminators. Our analysis shows the digesting loss and reminding loss can accomplish above tasks with provable guarantees. Hence minimizing the proposed joint loss allows the generator to approach the global distribution in a progressive fashion.

To the best of our knowledge, this is the first work addressing the challenge of temporary discriminator problem in distributed GAN learning. Our main contributions in this paper include:

- We propose a framework called TDGAN for training distributed GAN with temporary and privately hosted discriminators from multiple entities.
- Leveraging on two loss functions called digesting loss and reminding loss, our proposed framework enables the generator to learn a global distribution with temporary discriminators in a progressive fashion.
- We report an analysis on the digesting loss and reminding loss applied in TDGAN framework. Our analysis shows the proposed training framework leads the generator toward a correct distribution with provable guarantees.

We empirically demonstrate the effectiveness of TDGAN on learning the global distribution, by applying TDGAN to pathology images generation and brain MRI images generation tasks.

2   Related Work

2.1   Generative Adversarial Networks (GANs)

The GANs proposed in [11] seek to imitate data distribution via adversarial supervision from discriminator. Specifically, the generator focuses on generating synthetic images indistinguishable to real images thus the discriminator cannot effectively answer the 'fake or real' queries. Such model and its variants have obtained great success in broad domains such as images [25,47] , videos [45,46], music generation [13,26], natural languages [19,30] and medical images [8,32,49]. In this work, we focus on conditional GAN [38], which aims to approximate the conditional distribution $p(x|y)$ given auxiliary variable y. In reality the y is usually labels for classification data or masks for segmentation data.

2.2   Federated Learning

Federated learning allows multiple data sources to train a model collaboratively without sharing the data [14,23]. Such setting protects the privacy of participants by communicating model information (e.g. model parameters, gradients) instead of original data [28]. In our setting, the federated learning framework is incorporated by separating local data and centralized generator using discriminators. In another word, only discriminator kept locally has access to data and the only information communicated with cloud is the feedback on the synthetic data. In particular, [15] proposed a multiple-discriminator based GAN for distributed training. However, their training framework requires swapping parameters between discriminators during the optimization process, which is not realistic in our sequential collaborative learning setting. In addition, nor these works provide a provable guarantee on the target distribution of generator given supervision from multiple distributed discriminators. It is unclear whether their training framework can lead the generator toward the correct generative distribution. In this work, the proposed method addresses the problem of asynchrony problem meanwhile achieves provable guarantee on the target distribution.

2.3 Lifelong Learning

Lifelong learning is the process of learning over time by accommodating new knowledge while remembering previously learned experiences, like how human learns. The main problem of lifelong learning for computational models like deep neural networks is the catastrophic forgetting [34], i.e., the model trained on new data is prone to perform bad in previous tasks. Many works have been proposed to solve this problem, including discriminative approaches [2,29,31] and generative models [43,48,51]. Our sequential collaborative learning setting is a type of lifelong learning since the forgetting problem also exists in our learning tasks. But it has two major differences from previous generative methods: 1) The discriminators of old tasks are unavailable when training with new data in our setting, and each discriminator only has access to its own dataset due to the privacy issue. 2) There may be multiple datasets/discriminators online for training at each time step and the number of discriminators is different from that of previous task. So it is not feasible to utilize the previous discriminators even if there is no privacy concern.

3 Method

In this section we will first describe the problem definition and then present the details about the proposed TDGAN framework. We introduce how TDGAN solves the temporary datasets problem using the digesting loss and reminding loss. We also analyze the loss function of TDGAN and provide theoretical guarantees that it learns the correct distribution.

3.1 Problem Definition

We first introduce the problem of learning distributed GAN with temporary discriminators. There are some local centers that host their own private datasets. The local centers/datasets are not always online. The target is to learn the mixture distributions of all local datasets without access to the real data. There is no assumption about the distribution of these local datasets, i.e., they can be *i.i.d.* or *non-i.i.d.* datasets. At each time step t, the task is to learn the distribution of current online datasets, and at the same time remember the learnt knowledge of previous offline datasets. Considering the privacy issue, each local dataset can only be accessed locally.

3.2 TDGAN Framework

The overview of TDGAN framework is shown in Fig. 1. It contains a central generator and multiple distributed temporary discriminators located in different data centers (hospitals, mobile devices etc.). Each discriminator only has access to data stored in one local center, thus discriminators are trained in an asynchronous fashion. Suppose the training starts at time $t - 1$, there are K_{t-1} online local data centers/discriminators. The central generator G_{t-1} takes task-specific labels and random noise as inputs and outputs synthetic images to fool the discriminators. The local discriminators, $\{D_{t-1}^1, \ldots, D_{t-1}^{K_{t-1}}\}$ learn to tell the synthetic images from the local real images. At time t, the real data and discriminators in local data centers of time $t - 1$ are no longer available as new

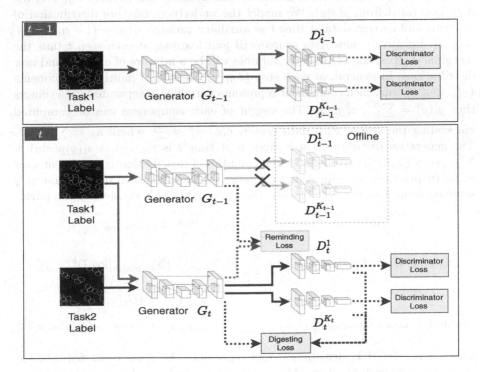

Fig. 1. The overview of TDGAN framework. It consists of a central generator G and multiple distributed temporary discriminators $\{D_t^1, \cdots, D_{t-1}^{K_{t-1}}, D_t^1, \cdots D_t^{K_t}, \cdots\}$. Each local data center has one discriminator. At time t, previous local discriminators are offline. G_t, initialized with G_{t-1}, tries to learn the data from newly online discriminators $\{D_t^1, \cdots, D_t^{K_t}\}$, and remember the knowledge learnt from previous data in G_{t-1}.

data comes in. The central generator G_t tries to learn the distribution of new data and retain the mixture distribution learnt from previous data. The learning of new data is achieved by a digesting loss and the memory of previous learnt knowledge is kept using a reminding loss.

Communication Between G and Ds. At each training step, the generator gets real labels sampled from online data centers, sends generated fake images to them, and then gets feedback from the discriminators in online data centers. For previous offline data centers, the generator has stored their real labels in the central server, and samples from the empirical distribution to generate fake images, which are used to remember previous learnt knowledge. More training and communication details can be found in the appendix.

3.3   Loss Function of TDGAN

The training framework is built based on the conditional GAN framework [38]. We aim to approximate the conditional distribution $p(x|y)$ given variable y. In reality, y can be segmentation masks or classification labels. Given y, x is the data generated from $p(x|y)$. We model the underlying mixture distribution of previous and current data at time t as auxiliary variable $s_t(y) = (1 - \alpha_t)s_{t-1} + \alpha_t g_t(y)$. Intuitively, new data source will join learning at each step t thus the marginal distribution of auxiliary variable will be a mixture of existing and new distributions. In general, at each step t, $g_t(y)$ consists of multiple components $\{g_t^1, ..., g_t^{K_t}\}$ with each component represents variables in separated data centers thus $g_t(y) = \sum_{k=1}^{K_t} \pi_t^k g_t^k(y)$. The weight of each component can be computed via scaling the size of each data center, e.g., $\pi_t^k = \frac{n_t^k}{n_t}$ where $n_t = \sum_{k=1}^{K_t} n_t^k$. The generative distribution of x given y at time t is $p_t(x, y) = s_t(y)p(x|y) = \sum_{\tau=1}^{t} \alpha_\tau g_\tau(y)p(x|y)$. We assume the conditional distribution is consistent over time. In practice, we approximate $s_{t-1}(y)$ via the empirical distribution of y sampled from data centers. The loss function of TDGAN consists of two parts:

$$V_t(G_t, D_t^{1:K_t}) = \min_{G_t} L_{Digesting} + \lambda \cdot L_{Reminding}$$

$$\text{Digesting Loss}: L_{Digesting} \triangleq \max_{D_t^{1:K_t}} \sum_{k=1}^{K_t} \pi_t^k \mathbb{E}_{y \sim g_t^k(y)} \{\mathbb{E}_{x \sim p(x|y)}[\log D_t^k(x, y)]$$

$$+ \mathbb{E}_{u \sim unif(0,1)}[\log(1 - D_t^k(G_t(u, y), y))]\}$$

$$\text{Reminding Loss}: L_{Reminding} \triangleq \mathbb{E}_{y \sim s_{t-1}(y)}\mathbb{E}_{u \sim unif(0,1)}[\|G_t(u, y) - G_{t-1}(u, y)\|^2]$$

$$\tag{1}$$

where u is $unif(0, 1)$ distribution and represents the noise input fed into the generator for synthetic data. The mixture cross entropy loss term provides a guidance for the generator to learn conditional distributions given auxiliary variable $y \in supp(g_t(y))$. In reality, $y \in supp(g_t(y))/supp(s_{t-1}(y))$ are the masks or labels that have not been observed before. This is so called *digesting loss*. The squared norm loss corresponds to the *reminding loss* which enforce the generator to memorize the conditional distribution of seen labels.

3.4 Theoretical Guarantees of TDGAN Loss

In this section we analyze the correctness of loss function. Due to the limit of space, all technical details are left in the supplementary materials. Ideally, the loss function should lead the generator toward the target distribution, formally $G_t(u, y) = p(x|y)$. To begin with, we first give some notations in the analysis. In order to describe the support incremental process in progressive collaborative learning, we use Ω_t be support of marginal distribution of auxiliary variables $\Omega(s_t(y))$ and $\Delta\Omega_t$ be the marginal increment of support, formally $\Delta\Omega(s_t(y)) = \Omega(s_t(y)) - \Omega(s_{t-1}(y))$. By above definition we have $\Delta\Omega_t = \Omega(g_t(y)) - \Omega(s_{t-1}(y))$. Intuitively, the marginal incremental support contains previously unseen labels from new data center and we expect generator to mimic the distribution via interacting with discriminator locally trained in new data center. In addition, we call $\Omega(g_t(y)) - \Omega(s_{t-1}(y))$ the absent support. The absent support contains auxiliary variables that are supervised by the discriminators in the offline data center in the past. In order to obtain supervision under the temporary discriminator constraint, the loss function is a mixture *reminding loss* and *digesting loss*. Our analysis of loss function consists two parts, which can be summarized as 1) digesting loss guides the generator to learn a correct conditional distributions w.r.t auxiliary variables in $\Delta_t\Omega$. 2) reminding loss will enforce the generator to be consistent about the conditional distribution w.r.t auxiliary variables in the absent support. In sum, by the analysis in this section we aim to show that the digesting loss and reminding loss interacts in a learn and review manner. Even without feedback from off-line data centers, the generator can still manage to memorize learned distribution. We will begin with two lemmas.

Lemma 1 (Reminding loss enforces consistency). *Suppose G_t has enough model capacity, the optimal G_t for loss function:*

$$\min_{G_t} \mathbb{E}_{y \sim s_{t-1}(y)} \mathbb{E}_{u \sim unif(0,1)} [\| G_t(u, y) - G_{t-1}(u, y) \|^2]$$

given G_{t-1} is $G_t(u, y) = G_{t-1}$ for all u and $y \in \Omega(s_{t-1}(y))$.

Lemma 2 (Digesting loss learns correct distribution). *Suppose discriminator $D_t^k, k \in [K_t]$ always behave optimally and let $q_t(x|y)$ be the distribution of $G_t(u, y)$, the the optimal $G_t(u, y)$ for digesting loss:*

$$\min_{G_t} \max_{D_t^{1:K_t}} \sum_{k=1}^{K_t} \pi_t^k \mathbb{E}_{y \sim g_t^k(y)} \{ \mathbb{E}_{x \sim p(x|y)} [\log D_t^k(x, y)]$$

$$+ \mathbb{E}_{u \sim unif(0,1)} [\log(1 - D_t^k(G_t(u, y), y))] \}$$

is $q_t(x|y) = p(x|y)$ for all $y \in \Omega(g_t(y))$.

The two lemmas describe the behavior of digesting loss and reminding loss separately. In next theorem, we show that the design of loss can work cooperatively thus the overall loss function leads to a correct global distribution.

Theorem 1. *Suppose the generator has enough model capacity to obtain* $q_1(x|y) = p(x|y)$ *for all* $y \in g_1(y)$ *and the loss* $V_\tau(G_\tau, D_\tau)$ *defined in Eq. 1 is optimized optimally for each* $\tau \in [t]$, *then* $q_t(x|y) = p(x|y)$ *for all* $y \in \Omega_t$.

Proof Sketch:
The proof is based on Lemmas 1 and 2 and the fact that optimal condition of reminding loss and digesting loss doesn't contradict each other for $y \in \Omega(s_{t-1}) \cap \omega(g_t)$. Using induction we show if each step TDGAN stops with optimal condition at step $\tau \in \{1, ..., t-1\}$, eventually $q_t(x|y) = p(x|y)$ at time t.   □

Remark 1. The analysis shows the digesting loss and reminding loss control the behavior of generator w.r.t auxiliary variables in different regimes. The analysis relies on the fact that for y in all regimes, the conditional distribution $p(x|y)$ is consistent over time. Such assumption avoids the conflict conditional distribution case i.e. $p_\tau(x|y) \neq p_{\tau'}(x|y)$. We believe this assumption is necessary for success of learning. Otherwise conflict conditional distribution may confuse the generator.

4   Experiments

In this section, we evaluate the power of TDGAN framework in distributed GAN learning problems. We focus on medical datasets in health entities which are known to be privacy sensitive. We perform experiments on pathology image generation and brain MRI image generation tasks to illustrate that TDGAN can learn the new distribution while keeping consistency of memory on learnt distributions. Since our generator is used as a synthetic database and can provide images for downstream tasks, we evaluate the quality of generated data using segmentation results of models trained by synthetic data. The TDGAN is compared with rule of thumb methods, e.g., fine-tuning and joint learning. The fine-tuning serves as a lower bound for TDGAN since it is a naive way in the sequential learning setting. Fine-tuning can also show the importance of the reminding loss because it only uses the digesting loss for GAN training. The joint learning method directly aggregates data from multiple entities and train a GAN in a centralized manner. Compared to the setting of TDGAN, such setting has less constraint thus serve as a upper bound of our result when the datasets of different entities are homogeneous. In the cases where the datasets varies a lot, our TDGAN can better learn the mixture distribution with the assists of distributed discriminators than joint learning.

4.1   Experimental Set-Up

Datasets. Two segmentation datasets are used in the experiments.

Multi-Organ (MO). This is a nuclei segmentation dataset proposed in [24]. It consists of 30 pathology images from seven organs. The training set contains 16 images from liver, breast, kidney and prostate. The same organ test set has 8 images from the above four organs and the different organ test set contains 6 images from bladder, colon and stomach.

BraTS. It is the dataset of the Multimodal Brain Tumor Segmentation Challenge 2018 [5,6,35]. Each patient in the dataset has four types of MRI scans: 1) a native T1-weighted scan (T1), 2) a post-contrast T1-weighted scan (T1Gd), 3) a native T2-weighted scan (T2), and 4) a T2 Fluid Attenuated Inversion Recovery (T2-FLAIR) scan [6]. And the annotation contains three types of tumor subregion labels: 1) active tumor (AT), 2) tumor core (TC), and 3) whole tumor (WT). In our experiments, we generate two datasets (BraTS-T1, BraTS-T2) from this dataset that differ much in the training images. To avoid large imbalance between datasets in different local centers, we select the T1 scans of 17 high-grade glioma (HGG) cases as the training data of BraTS-T1, and select the T2 scans of another 17 HGG cases as the training data of BraTS-T2. The test sets in both datasets contain 40 cases, and share the same labels but differ in the images (T1 vs. T2). For the annotation, we only use the whole tumor in both GAN training and segmentation for simplicity.

Two Types of Tasks. In the setting of temporary discriminators, the previous discriminators will be unavailable when new hospitals/datasets are online (see Fig. 1). We divide the image generation tasks into two types according to the difference between the datasets of hospitals.

Homogeneous Tasks. In this type of tasks, images in all hospitals' datasets are homogeneous, i.e., they have similar types and appearances. In our experiments, we assume the data in each local center comes from the Multi-Organ dataset.

Heterogeneous Tasks. In these tasks, images of different hospitals are heterogeneous, e.g., CT and MRI. To better illustrate the effects of our framework, we assume that the whole Multi-Organ dataset is in one hospital, the BraTS-T2 dataset in the second hospital and the BraTS-T1 dataset is in the third one. The distributions of these datasets are diverse, thus it is harder for the network to remember previous tasks and achieving good results on the new task.

Evaluation Metrics. For nuclei segmentation, we use Dice score to measures the overlap between ground-truth mask G and segmented result S: $Dice(G, S) = \frac{2|G \cap S|}{|G|+|S|}$. Because nuclei segmentation is an instance segmentation problem, we use an additional object-level metric Aggregated Jaccard Index (AJI) [24]:

$$AJI = \frac{\sum_{i=1}^{n_\mathcal{G}} |G_i \cap S(G_i)|}{\sum_{i=1}^{n_\mathcal{G}} |G_i \cup S(G_i)| + \sum_{k \in K} |S_k|} \qquad (2)$$

where $S(G_i)$ is the segmented object that has maximum overlap with G_i with regard to Jaccard index, K is the set containing segmentation objects that have not been assigned to any ground-truth object.

Table 1. Nuclei segmentation results using the models trained on generated images in single-entity nuclei image synthesis.

Tasks (online dataset)	TDGAN		Fine-tuning		Joint learning		Local GAN	
	Dice ↑	AJI ↑	Dice ↑	AJI ↑	Dice ↑	AJI ↑	Dice ↑	AJI ↑
Task1 (liver)	0.6676	0.3420	0.6676	0.3420	0.6676	0.3420	0.6676	0.3420
Task2 (breast)	0.6961	0.4323	0.6950	0.4405	0.7114	0.4457	0.6745	0.4111
Task3 (kidney)	0.7164	0.4512	0.7142	0.4195	0.7350	0.4814	0.6794	0.3734
Task4 (prostate)	0.7481	0.4931	0.6969	0.4679	0.7627	0.5184	0.6918	0.4401

Table 2. Nuclei segmentation results using the models trained on generated images in multiple-entity nuclei image synthesis.

Tasks (online dataset)	TDGAN		Fine-tuning		Joint learning		Local GAN	
	Dice ↑	AJI ↑	Dice ↑	AJI ↑	Dice ↑	AJI ↑	Dice ↑	AJI ↑
Task1 (liver+breast)	0.6829	0.4291	0.6829	0.4291	0.7114	0.4457	0.6298	0.3813
Task2 (kidney+prostate)	0.7599	0.5136	0.7285	0.4780	0.7627	0.5184	0.7187	0.4711

For brain tumor segmentation, we use Dice score and the 95% quantile of Hausdorff distance (HD95). The Hausdorff distance is defined as

$$HD(G, S) = \max\{ \sup_{x \in \partial G} \inf_{y \in \partial S} d(x,y), \sup_{y \in \partial S} \inf_{x \in \partial G} d(x,y)\} \tag{3}$$

where ∂ means the boundary operation, and d is Euclidean distance. The Hausdorff distance is sensitive to small outlying subregions, therefore we use the 95% quantile of the distances as in [6].

Implementation Details

Network Structure. In the GAN training phase, the central generator is an encoder-decoder network that consists of two stride-2 convolutions (for downsampling), nine residual blocks [16], and two transposed convolutions. All nonresidual convolutional layers are followed by batch normalization [20] and the ReLU activation [1]. All convolutional layers use 3×3 kernels except the first and last layers that use 7×7 kernels. Each discriminator has the same structure as that in PatchGAN [21] with patch size 70×70. The segmentation model is U-net [41].

Data Augmentation. In the GAN training phase, we resize the image to 286×286 and randomly crop to 256×256 for training. In the nuclei segmentation tasks, each large 1000×1000 image is split into 16 small 256×256 patches. The other augmentations are random cropping of size 224×224, random horizontal flip, randomly resize between 0.8 and 1.25, rotation within a random degree between $-90°$ and $90°$, perturbation of the affine transform's parameters with a random value between -0.3 and 0.3. For brain tumor segmentation, the operations include random cropping of size 224×224, random horizontal flip with probability 0.5 and rotation within a random degree between $-10°$ and $10°$.

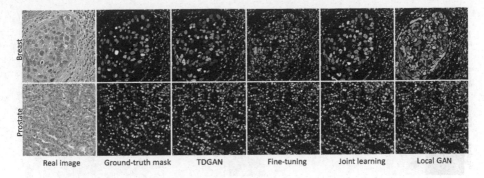

Fig. 2. Segmentation results of models trained on synthetic images in task4 of single-entity nuclei synthesis. The first row is a breast image in test set, corresponding to the dataset of task2. The second row is a prostate image corresponding to the dataset of task4. TDGAN learns the mixture distribution, thus performs well on both images.

Training Details. In the GAN training, we use the Adam optimizer [22] with a batch size of 8, and momentum parameters $\beta_1 = 0.5$, $\beta_2 = 0.999$. The number of epoch is set to 300 in homogeneous tasks and 80 in heterogeneous tasks. The learning rate is 0.0002 for the first half number of epochs and then linearly decayed. The parameters in the loss function (Eq. (1)) is set to $\lambda = 1$. In the segmentation phase, we train the U-net with Adam optimizer with a batch size of 12, using a learning rate of 0.001 for 50 epochs in brain tumor segmentation and 100 epochs in nuclei segmentation.

4.2 Results on Homogeneous Tasks

In this subsection we show that our TDGAN can learn the overall distribution well when the data from different health entities are homogeneous.

Settings. The training data of Multi-Organ dataset is divided into four subsets according to organs: liver, breast, kidney and prostate. Each subset is assumed to be in a local health entity, consisting of 64 images of size 256×256. We perform the following experiments: (1) **TDGAN**. The health entities are temporarily available, we train a generator using the proposed TDGAN method. (2) **Sequential fine-tuning**. The health entities are temporarily available, the generator is fine-tuned in a sequential manner. Because previous discriminators are offline, only the generator is initialized using parameters from the generator trained/fine-tuned on the previous tasks. The new local discriminators are randomly initialized. (3) **Joint learning**. The data in each health center can be collected together to train a regular GAN model. (4) **Local GAN**. A local GAN is trained using the local data for each health entity.

To evaluate the performance of generators, synthetic images are generated using labels from both previous data and current data. Then they are used to train a segmentation model. The higher accuracy the trained segmentation

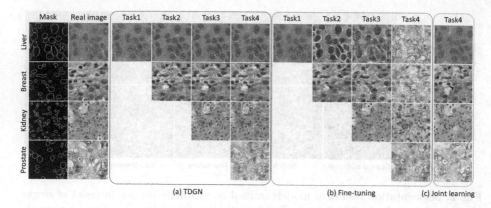

Fig. 3. Comparison between different methods for single-entity homogeneous tasks. All methods share the model trained on the first dataset (Liver). During each subsequent task, the fine-tuning method forgets previous task(s), while our TDGAN can remember previous task(s) and learn the current task well.

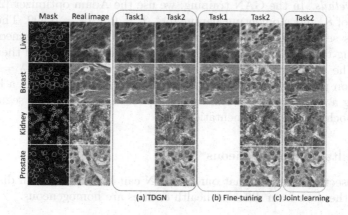

Fig. 4. Comparison between different methods for multiple-entity homogeneous tasks. TDGAN and fine-tuning share the distributed GAN model trained on the first task (Liver+Breast), but joint learning train a regular GAN. After trained on the second task (Kidney+Prostate), the fine-tuning method forgets the first task, while our TDGAN can remember previous task and learn the current task well.

model performs on the test set, the better quality of the synthetic images have. To make fair comparison, the number of synthetic images keeps the same for each segmentation model. We only use the same organ test set for evaluation.

Besides, we set the number of online health entities at each time to 1 and 2, corresponding to single-entity and multiple-entity cases, respectively. There are four tasks in the former case and two tasks in the latter one.

Table 3. Segmentation results using the models trained on generated images in heterogeneous image synthesis. The training datasets for Task1~3 are Multi-Organ, BraTS-T2 and BraTS-T1, respectively.

Test set	Tasks	TDGAN		Fine-tuning		Joint learning		Local GAN	
		Dice ↑	AJI ↑	Dice ↑	AJI ↑	Dice ↑	AJI ↑	Dice ↑	AJI ↑
Multi-Organ	Task1	0.7576	0.5151	0.7576	0.5151	0.7576	0.5151	0.7576	0.5151
	Task2	0.7570	0.5180	0.3733	0.0980	0.6799	0.4029	-	-
	Task3	0.7610	0.5028	0.1812	0.0240	0.6566	0.4002	-	-
		Dice ↑	HD95 ↓	Dice ↑	HD95 ↓	Dice ↑	HD95 ↓	Dice ↑	HD95 ↓
BraTS-T2	Task2	0.6834	37.23	0.6667	33.74	0.6734	40.33	0.5734	63.33
	Task3	0.6713	36.33	0.2490	74.13	0.7027	33.54	-	-
BraTS-T1	Task3	0.5265	36.98	0.5288	38.86	0.4627	53.86	0.4604	47.68

Results. The segmentation results trained with synthetic images under different settings are presented in Table 1, Table 2 and Fig. 2. Some typical synthetic images are shown in Figs. 3 and 4. Our TDGAN outperforms fine-tuning on both single-entity and multiple-entity cases. Because the fine-tuning method focuses on learning current data using the digesting loss only, which affects the quality of synthetic images on previous datasets (Figs. 3(b) and 4(b)). The proposed TDGAN not only learns the distribution of new data using the digesting loss, but also remembers the old data due to the reminding loss. TDGAN also outperforms Local GAN method because it can make use of the distributed datasets, which is the advantage of federated learning. Joint learning is the best among all methods. It is the upper bound of TDGAN in the homogeneous tasks.

Another observation is that the TDGAN and joint learning methods obtain better segmentation results as new data comes online, since more data is beneficial for GAN training. However, it is expected that the increase speed will slow down and the performance may even oscillate for TDGAN after a long time. Because TDGAN is still forgetting, and the errors will accumulate as time goes on. For fine-tuning, the performance has begun to oscillate at task 4 and will drop as it forgets more and faster.

4.3 Results on Heterogeneous Tasks

In this subsection we show that our TDGAN can learn the different distributions when the data from health entities are heterogeneous.

Settings. In this case we have three health entities and each has one of Multi-Organ, BraTS-T2 and BraTS-T1 datasets. To make the model structure consistent, we adopt 2D images synthesis and segmentation for BraTS-T1 and BraTS-T2 datasets although they are 3D data. We extract 2D slices from each 3D volume for both training and test sets. To avoid severe imbalance problem during training, there are only 17 cases are selected in both BraTS datasets. Finally, there are 256, 1052 and 1110 images in the three datsets, respectively.

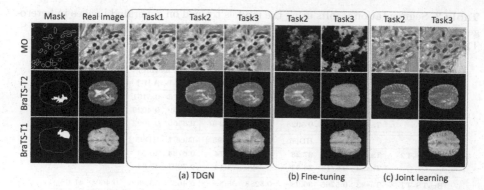

Fig. 5. Comparison between different methods for heterogeneous tasks. All methods share the model trained on the first dataset (Multi-Organ). During each subsequent task, the fine-tuning method forgets previous task(s), joint learning cannot deal with the large variance between datasets very well. Our TDGAN can handle both issues and learn the mixture distribution.

We conduct similar experiments as in Sect. 4.2. The difference in GAN training is that we didn't perform multiple-entity experiments, because of the large variance among three datasets. For segmentation tasks, we evaluate the synthetic images on the corresponding test set instead of using a global test set.

Results. The segmentation results trained with synthetic images under different settings are presented in Table 3. An example of synthetic images during the training process is shown in Fig. 5. After trained with new heterogeneous data (Task2 and Task3), TDGAN's performance almost keeps the same on the test sets, while fine-tuning drops a lot on previous tasks, indicating that TDGAN can better preserve the memory of previous tasks. The performance of joint learning on MO dataset also deteriorates, because the large variance in heterogeneous datasets makes it hard to learning the mixture distribution using only one discriminator. In our TDGAN framework, each local discriminator is responsible for its own data, which is beneficial for learning in this case. TDGAN is also better than local GAN, because of more training data from different centers.

5   Conclusion

In this work, we proposed a framework for training distributed GAN called TDGAN. Our proposed training method allows the generator to learn from temporarily available and privately hosted discriminators from multiple data centers. TDGAN is a leverage on two loss functions called digesting loss and reminding loss to balance between learning new distribution and memorizing learned distributions. We evaluate the quality of the generator via the accuracy of segmentation model trained solely by synthetic data. Our empirical results show TDGAN achieves better performance than the model fine-tuned on temporary datasets, and achieves comparable performance as the model learns from joint real homogeneous image datasets. When there is large variance in the datasets, our method can better learn the mixture distribution than joint learning.

Acknowledgement. We thank anonymous reviewers for helpful comments. The research of Chao Chen is partially supported by NSF IIS-1855759, CCF-1855760 and IIS-1909038. The research of Dimitris Metaxas is partially supported by NSF CCF-1733843, IIS-1763523, CNS-1747778, and IIS-1703883.

References

1. Agarap, A.F.: Deep learning using rectified linear units (relu). arXiv preprint arXiv:1803.08375 (2018)
2. Aljundi, R., Babiloni, F., Elhoseiny, M., Rohrbach, M., Tuytelaars, T.: Memory Aware Synapses: Learning What (not) to Forget. In: Ferrari, V., Hebert, M., Sminchisescu, C., Weiss, Y. (eds.) ECCV 2018. LNCS, vol. 11207, pp. 144–161. Springer, Cham (2018). https://doi.org/10.1007/978-3-030-01219-9_9
3. Annas, G.J., et al.: Hipaa regulations-a new era of medical-record privacy? N. Engl. J. Med. **348**(15), 1486–1490 (2003)
4. Arjovsky, M., Chintala, S., Bottou, L.: Wasserstein gan. arXiv preprint arXiv:1701.07875 (2017)
5. Bakas, S., Akbari, H., Sotiras, A., Bilello, M., Rozycki, M., Kirby, J.S., Freymann, J.B., Farahani, K., Davatzikos, C.: Advancing the cancer genome atlas glioma MRI collections with expert segmentation labels and radiomic features. Sci. data **4**, 170117 (2017)
6. Bakas, S., et al.: Identifying the best machine learning algorithms for brain tumor segmentation, progression assessment, and overall survival prediction in the brats challenge. arXiv preprint arXiv:1811.02629 (2018)
7. Chang, Q., et al.: Synthetic learning: Learn from distributed asynchronized discriminator gan without sharing medical image data. In: Proceedings of the IEEE/CVF Conference on Computer Vision and Pattern Recognition, pp. 13856–13866 (2020)
8. Dai, W., Dong, N., Wang, Z., Liang, X., Zhang, H., Xing, E.P.: SCAN: structure correcting adversarial network for organ segmentation in chest X-Rays. In: Stoyanov, D., et al. (eds.) DLMIA/ML-CDS -2018. LNCS, vol. 11045, pp. 263–273. Springer, Cham (2018). https://doi.org/10.1007/978-3-030-00889-5_30
9. Durugkar, I., Gemp, I., Mahadevan, S.: Generative multi-adversarial networks (2016)
10. Geyer, R.C., Klein, T., Nabi, M.: Differentially private federated learning: a client level perspective. arXiv preprint arXiv:1712.07557 (2017)
11. Goodfellow, I., et al.: Generative adversarial nets. In: Advances in Neural Information Processing Systems, pp. 2672–2680 (2014)
12. Gostin, L.O., Levit, L.A., Nass, S.J., et al.: Beyond the HIPAA privacy rule: enhancing privacy, improving health through research. National Academies Press (2009)
13. Guimaraes, G.L., Sanchez-Lengeling, B., Outeiral, C., Farias, P.L.C., Aspuru-Guzik, A.: Objective-reinforced generative adversarial networks (organ) for sequence generation models. arXiv preprint arXiv:1705.10843 (2017)
14. Hard, A., Rao, K., Mathews, R., Ramaswamy, S., Beaufays, F., Augenstein, S., Eichner, H., Kiddon, C., Ramage, D.: Federated learning for mobile keyboard prediction. arXiv preprint arXiv:1811.03604 (2018)

15. Hardy, C., Le Merrer, E., Sericola, B.: Md-gan: Multi-discriminator generative adversarial networks for distributed datasets. In: 2019 IEEE International Parallel and Distributed Processing Symposium (IPDPS), pp. 866–877. IEEE (2019)
16. He, K., Zhang, X., Ren, S., Sun, J.: Deep residual learning for image recognition. In: 2016 IEEE Conference on Computer Vision and Pattern Recognition (CVPR), pp. 770–778 (2016). https://doi.org/10.1109/cvpr.2016.90
17. Hochberg, J.: Depth perception loss with local monocular suppression: a problem in the explanation of stereopsis. Science **145**(3638), 1334–1336 (1964)
18. Hoffman, J., Wang, D., Yu, F., Darrell, T.: FCNs in the Wild: Pixel-level Adversarial and Constraint-based Adaptation (2016)
19. Hsu, C.C., Hwang, H.T., Wu, Y.C., Tsao, Y., Wang, H.M.: Voice conversion from unaligned corpora using variational autoencoding wasserstein generative adversarial networks. arXiv preprint arXiv:1704.00849 (2017)
20. Ioffe, S., Szegedy, C.: Batch normalization: accelerating deep network training by reducing internal covariate shift. arXiv preprint arXiv:1502.03167 (2015)
21. Isola, P., Zhu, J.Y., Zhou, T., Efros, A.A.: Image-to-image translation with conditional adversarial networks. In: Proceedings of the IEEE Conference on Computer Vision and Pattern Recognition, pp. 1125–1134 (2017)
22. Kingma, D.P., Ba, J.: Adam: A method for stochastic optimization. arXiv preprint arXiv:1412.6980 (2014)
23. Konečný, J., McMahan, H.B., Yu, F.X., Richtárik, P., Suresh, A.T., Bacon, D.: Federated learning: Strategies for improving communication efficiency. arXiv preprint arXiv:1610.05492 (2016)
24. Kumar, N., Verma, R., Sharma, S., Bhargava, S., Vahadane, A., Sethi, A.: A dataset and a technique for generalized nuclear segmentation for computational pathology. IEEE Trans. Med. Imaging **36**(7), 1550–1560 (2017)
25. Ledig, C., et al.: Photo-realistic single image super-resolution using a generative adversarial network. In: Proceedings of the IEEE Conference on Computer Vision and Pattern Recognition, pp. 4681–4690 (2017)
26. Lee, S.g., Hwang, U., Min, S., Yoon, S.: A seqgan for polyphonic music generation. arXiv preprint arXiv:1710.11418 (2017)
27. lex, M.L.T.: Overview of the national laws on electronic health records in the eu member states and their interaction with the provision of cross-border ehealth services: Final report and recommendations (contract 2013 63 02), viewed 18th March 2018 (2014)
28. Li, T., Sahu, A.K., Talwalkar, A., Smith, V.: Federated learning: Challenges, methods, and future directions. arXiv preprint arXiv:1908.07873 (2019)
29. Li, Z., Hoiem, D.: Learning without forgetting. IEEE Trans. Pattern Anal. Mach. Intell. **40**(12), 2935–2947 (2017)
30. Lin, K., Li, D., He, X., Zhang, Z., Sun, M.T.: Adversarial ranking for language generation. In: Advances in Neural Information Processing Systems, pp. 3155–3165 (2017)
31. Lopez-Paz, D., Ranzato, M.: Gradient episodic memory for continual learning. In: Advances in Neural Information Processing Systems, pp. 6467–6476 (2017)
32. Mardani, M., et al.: Deep generative adversarial networks for compressed sensing automates MRI. arXiv preprint arXiv:1706.00051 (2017)
33. Mason, L., Baxter, J., Bartlett, P.L., Frean, M.R.: Boosting algorithms as gradient descent. In: Advances in Neural Information Processing Systems, pp. 512–518 (2000)

34. McCloskey, M., Cohen, N.J.: Catastrophic interference in connectionist networks: the sequential learning problem. In: Psychology of Learning and Motivation, vol. 24, pp. 109–165. Elsevier (1989)

35. Menze, B.H., et al.: The multimodal brain tumor image segmentation benchmark (brats). IEEE Trans. Med. Imaging **34**(10), 1993–2024 (2014)

36. Mercuri, R.T.: The hipaa-potamus in health care data security. Commun. ACM **47**(7), 25–28 (2004)

37. Milletari, F., Navab, N., Ahmadi, S.A.: V-net: fully convolutional neural networks for volumetric medical image segmentation. In: 2016 Fourth International Conference on 3D Vision (3DV), pp. 565–571. IEEE (2016)

38. Mirza, M., Osindero, S.: Conditional Generative Adversarial Nets (2014)

39. Qu, H., Yan, Z., Riedlinger, G.M., De, S., Metaxas, D.N.: Improving nuclei/gland instance segmentation in histopathology images by full resolution neural network and spatial constrained loss. In: Shen, D., Liu, T., Peters, T.M., Staib, L.H., Essert, C., Zhou, S., Yap, P.-T., Khan, A. (eds.) MICCAI 2019. LNCS, vol. 11764, pp. 378–386. Springer, Cham (2019). https://doi.org/10.1007/978-3-030-32239-7_42

40. Radford, A., Metz, L., Chintala, S.: Unsupervised representation learning with deep convolutional generative adversarial networks. arXiv preprint arXiv:1511.06434 (2015)

41. Ronneberger, O., Fischer, P., Brox, T.: U-net: convolutional networks for biomedical image segmentation, pp. 234–241 (2015)

42. Ruder, S.: An overview of gradient descent optimization algorithms. arXiv preprint arXiv:1609.04747 (2016)

43. Seff, A., Beatson, A., Suo, D., Liu, H.: Continual learning in generative adversarial nets. arXiv preprint arXiv:1705.08395 (2017)

44. Sudre, C.H., Li, W., Vercauteren, T., Ourselin, S., Jorge Cardoso, M.: Generalised dice overlap as a deep learning loss function for highly unbalanced segmentations. In: Cardoso, M.J., et al. (eds.) DLMIA/ML-CDS -2017. LNCS, vol. 10553, pp. 240–248. Springer, Cham (2017). https://doi.org/10.1007/978-3-319-67558-9_28

45. Tulyakov, S., Liu, M.Y., Yang, X., Kautz, J.: MoCoGAN: decomposing motion and content for video generation. In: Proceedings of the IEEE Conference on Computer Vision and Pattern Recognition, pp. 1526–1535 (2018)

46. Vondrick, C., Pirsiavash, H., Torralba, A.: Generating videos with scene dynamics. In: Advances in Neural Information Processing Systems, pp. 613–621 (2016)

47. Wang, C., Xu, C., Wang, C., Tao, D.: Perceptual adversarial networks for image-to-image transformation. IEEE Trans. Image Process. **27**(8), 4066–4079 (2018)

48. Wu, C., Herranz, L., Liu, X., van de Weijer, J., Raducanu, B., et al.: Memory replay gans: learning to generate new categories without forgetting. In: Advances In Neural Information Processing Systems, pp. 5962–5972 (2018)

49. Yang, D., et al.: Automatic vertebra labeling in large-scale 3D CT using deep image-to-image network with message passing and sparsity regularization. In: Niethammer, M., Styner, M., Aylward, S., Zhu, H., Oguz, I., Yap, P.-T., Shen, D. (eds.) IPMI 2017. LNCS, vol. 10265, pp. 633–644. Springer, Cham (2017). https://doi.org/10.1007/978-3-319-59050-9_50

50. Zeiler, M.D.: ADADELTA: an adaptive learning rate method. arXiv preprint arXiv:1212.5701 (2012)

51. Zhai, M., Chen, L., Tung, F., He, J., Nawhal, M., Mori, G.: Lifelong gan: continual learning for conditional image generation. In: Proceedings of the IEEE International Conference on Computer Vision, pp. 2759–2768 (2019)

52. Zhang, H., Xu, T., Li, H., Zhang, S., Wang, X., Huang, X., Metaxas, D.N.: Stack-GAN: text to photo-realistic image synthesis with stacked generative adversarial networks. In: Proceedings of the IEEE International Conference on Computer Vision, pp. 5907–5915 (2017)

53. Zhang, Y., Qu, H., Chen, C., Metaxas, D.: Taming the noisy gradient: train deep neural networks with small batch sizes. In: Proceedings of the 28th International Joint Conference on Artificial Intelligence, pp. 4348–4354. AAAI Press (2019)

54. Zhang, Y., Qu, H., Metaxas, D.N., Chen, C.: Local regularizer improves generalization. In: AAAI, pp. 6861–6868 (2020)

55. Zhu, L., Liu, Z., Han, S.: Deep leakage from gradients. In: Advances in Neural Information Processing Systems, pp. 14747–14756 (2019)

SemifreddoNets: Partially Frozen Neural Networks for Efficient Computer Vision Systems

Leo F. Isikdogan[✉], Bhavin V. Nayak, Chyuan-Tyng Wu,
Joao Peralta Moreira, Sushma Rao, and Gilad Michael

Intel Corporation, Santa Clara, CA, USA
isikdogan@utexas.edu

Abstract. We propose a system comprised of fixed-topology neural networks having partially frozen weights, named SemifreddoNets. SemifreddoNets work as fully-pipelined hardware blocks that are optimized to have an efficient hardware implementation. Those blocks freeze a certain portion of the parameters at every layer and replace the corresponding multipliers with fixed scalers. Fixing the weights reduces the silicon area, logic delay, and memory requirements, leading to significant savings in cost and power consumption. Unlike traditional layer-wise freezing approaches, SemifreddoNets make a profitable trade between the cost and flexibility by having some of the weights configurable at different scales and levels of abstraction in the model. Although fixing the topology and some of the weights somewhat limits the flexibility, we argue that the efficiency benefits of this strategy outweigh the advantages of a fully configurable model for many use cases. Furthermore, our system uses repeatable blocks, therefore it has the flexibility to adjust model complexity without requiring any hardware change. The hardware implementation of SemifreddoNets provides up to an order of magnitude reduction in silicon area and power consumption as compared to their equivalent implementation on a general-purpose accelerator.

Keywords: Efficient machine learning · Transfer learning · Multi-task learning · Neural network hardware

1 Introduction

On-device artificial intelligence (AI) applications are becoming increasingly common for a wide variety of products, including smartphones, autonomous vehicles, drones, and different types of robots. Many, if not most, of those 'visually intelligent' devices today are powered by convolutional neural networks that run either on cloud computing platforms or the device itself.

L. F. Isikdogan—The author is currently with Apple Inc. The work was done while all of the authors were at Intel Corp.

A. Vedaldi et al. (Eds.): ECCV 2020, LNCS 12372, pp. 193–208, 2020.
https://doi.org/10.1007/978-3-030-58583-9_12

Cloud-based services rely on an internet connection to operate and transmit data back and forth between the device and the remote servers, which results in high latency. Therefore, they are typically not suitable for real-time applications. On-device systems, on the other hand, do not rely on remote resources, and therefore run with much less latency. Furthermore, on-device computing usually provides a higher level of security than cloud-based applications since the user data never needs to leave the device. However, running everything end-to-end on a low power device remains a challenging task, since many computer vision applications require a substantial amount of computing power to run in real-time. Therefore, on-device solutions may need expensive and large accelerators to achieve low latency and high throughput.

Many computer vision applications use custom, highly specialized convolutional neural network (CNN) architectures tailored for their target tasks. One way to reduce the complexity of a neural network inference hardware would be to fix the topology of a given network and implement it as a fixed-function style, in-line hardware block. Until recently, fixing the topology was not a feasible approach given the pace of development in network architecture design. For example, the top-5 error rate in the ImageNet Large Scale Visual Recognition Challenge [19] for the winning models went from 16.4% [14] in 2012 to 6.67% [22] in 2014, and to 3.57% [10] in 2015. The complexity of the top-performing models also made them difficult to implement in fully-pipelined hardware. As the network topologies matured and more efficient neural network design patterns emerged [11,15,20,27], hard-wiring at least a portion of a neural network topology [4,5,23–25] became a somewhat less flexible but more efficient alternative to doing all the computation on general-purpose CNN accelerators.

Using a fixed-topology model relies on the idea that a model that works well for one task is likely to generalize for other similar types of problems. Although searching for a custom network architecture for each task is shown to have some value [28], we argue that the efficiency benefits of using a fixed-topology model outweigh the marginal value of application-specific topologies. We propose a solution that significantly reduces the hardware complexity by using a fixed-topology neural network and partially frozen weights. We named this architecture after the Italian dessert, Semifreddo, due to its semi-frozen feature extractors. The frozen part is fixed in hardware and is designed to generalize across different tasks and input data types. The trainable part consists of configurable weights across varying levels of abstraction, leaving room for both adapting to new tasks and new kinds of data.

We optimize our system to work on very low power environments to bring significant AI capabilities to almost any consumer device. Our proposed hardware consists of three interconnected cores that run up to three different tasks at a time, processing up to 200 frames per second on VGA input. Our hardware is fully pipelined and does not use time multiplexing unlike conventional CNN accelerators in the single pass mode. Therefore, the pipeline runs at a constant 100% steady state utilization, whereas conventional, fully-programmable CNN accelerators typically operate at around 40% utilization rate. All three cores use

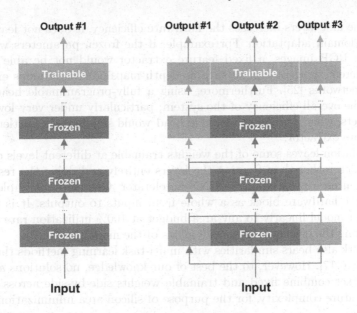

Fig. 1. A high-level illustration of how the vertical freezing scheme in SemifreddoNets (right) differs from traditional layer-level parameter freezing approaches (left): the grey blocks indicate the frozen weights whereas the blue blocks show the parts having trainable variables. SemifreddoNets provide some room for adaptation at both lower-level and higher-level feature extractors, whereas the traditional approach freezes specific level layers entirely. (Color figure online)

a combined silicon area of $4\,mm^2$ modeled with TSMC 16 nm technology. Our fully-pipelined, partially-frozen architecture leads to savings in silicon area by a factor of $\sim 4\times$ to $10\times$ as compared to generic CNN accelerators that have a hardware footprint of $\sim 15\,mm^2$.

2 Related Work

Many CNN accelerators in the market provide hardware acceleration for computer vision applications, including Intel Movidius Vision Processing Units [2], Google Coral Edge Tensor Processing Units [1], and Nvidia Jetson modules [3]. Although our system can replace those accelerators in many use cases, we did not design it to be a general-purpose neural network accelerator. Our hardware targets ultra-low-power systems having minimal silicon area budgets, where using a fully-blown CNN accelerator would not be feasible.

Our work resembles image signal processing hardware accelerators in the sense that it applies a series of filters to a given image. The closest work to ours is the recently published FixyNN hardware by Whatmough et al. [23], which used a fixed feature extractor that froze the first-N layers of a given model and did the rest of the computation on a generic deep learning accelerator. Although freezing the first layers increases the hardware efficiency, it does not leave much room for domain adaptation. For example, if the frozen parameters were pre-trained on RGB images, a fixed feature extractor would not be able to fully utilize different types of inputs, such as depth maps or feature maps extracted by other networks [25]. Furthermore, using a fully-programmable head would decrease the overall efficiency of the system, particularly under very low silicon area budgets, where the programmable head would significantly bottleneck the fixed feature extractor.

Our solution leaves some of the weights trainable at different levels of depth in the model, rather than freezing the layers entirely and doing the rest of the computation on a programmable CNN accelerator. Our model is implemented as an in-line hardware block as a whole from inputs to outputs. It is possible to scale our model linearly to any area budget at 100% utilization rate without bottlenecking the efficiency at specific parts of the model.

Our work also bears similarities with multi-task learning methods that share weights [9,16,17]. However, to the best of our knowledge, no solutions available in the market combine fixed and trainable weights side-by-side across varying levels of feature complexity, for the purpose of silicon area minimization.

3   SemifreddoNets

Implementing a deep convolutional neural network in fully-pipelined hardware provides numerous benefits over using general-purpose accelerators. For example, fixed-function-style neural network hardware can reach a utilization rate of 100% as compared to 40% typical utilization rate in generic CNN accelerators. However, building such hardware has been challenging due to the sheer number of parameters that many modern CNNs have. Those parameters cost significant silicon area when the weights are stored in dedicated memory. Indeed, time multiplexing of hardware accelerators could help reduce the memory requirement. However, this would also decrease the overall efficiency of the system. A highly-efficient, fully-pipelined neural network hardware would require all weights to be kept in memory simultaneously. The high cost associated with the weights makes a fully trainable model not feasible for small area budgets.

We address this problem by fixing and hard-wiring some of the weights in our model. For the fixed weights, we use fixed scalers with a single input to substitute the corresponding multipliers. This approach not only saves the memory that would store the parameters but also reduces the complexity of the logic design by replacing the multipliers with cheaper scalers and pruning zero weights. We store the remaining weights in SRAM and leave them configurable to retain an ample amount of flexibility in the model.

Our hardware represents all weights and intermediate feature maps as 8-bit signed fixed-point numbers. To ensure quantization-friendly values in feature maps, we prevent the model from producing zero-variance feature maps during training. We automatically detect neurons leading to zero-variance outputs by monitoring the moving variance parameter in the batch normalization layers. At

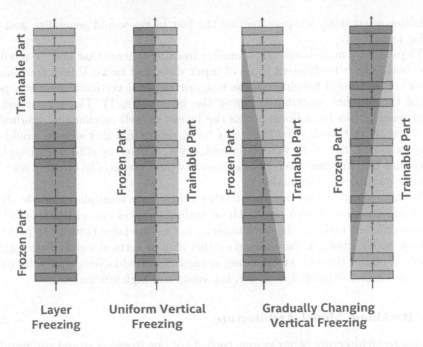

Fig. 2. An illustration of how vertical weight freezing schemes differ from layer-level freezing approaches. Vertical weight freezing has the flexibility to both adjust to different types of input data and tasks. Many different types of vertical weight freezing schemes can be tailored to different kinds of needs. For example, if the system is expected to perform various tasks while the input remains the same, then the freezing ratio can be decreased gradually from the input layer to the output layer. Similarly, if the system is expected to perform similar tasks, but the input data source may vary, then the freezing ratio can be increased gradually.

the end of each epoch, we re-initialize the weights corresponding to very small moving variance values. This process mainly detects and resuscitates nearly-dead neurons during training. Our approach is somewhat similar to the recently published neural rejuvenation [18] approach, which aimed to identify and re-initialize dead neurons for better resource utilization.

3.1 Vertically Frozen Neural Networks

What parts of the model to freeze is an important design choice that can impact the behavior and capabilities of the model. In the literature, it is a common practice to freeze the first N-layers of a neural network as a form of transfer learning [26]. This type of parameter freezing is usually done to speed up training and to reduce the risk of overfitting. Similarly, it is also possible to train only the first layers while keeping the rest of the network frozen to adapt an already trained model to different input data. Freezing the first layers would work well on similar input data, whereas freezing the last layers would generalize well for similar tasks.

We propose a more balanced parameter freezing scheme that has the flexibility to both adjust to different types of input data and tasks. Unlike traditional layer-level horizontal freezing approaches, our method vertically freezes a portion of the weights, distributed across the layers (Fig. 1). The proportion of frozen weights can be uniform across the layers as well as changing gradually, depending on the needs (Fig. 2). A very basic weight freezing scheme would fix a certain percentage of all weights in each layer, where the silicon area budget determines the freezing rate. This approach would essentially create a slice of trainable variables in the model.

We can take this idea one step further and create multiple trainable slices that share the same frozen parts. Those trainable slices can either be used to perform different tasks on the same input or act as one large network to perform one task with higher accuracy. Based on this idea of vertical weight freezing, we propose a neural network architecture, named SemifreddoNets, that achieves a small hardware footprint, low power, low cost, and high efficiency.

3.2   Backbone Model Architecture

The macro architecture of our system consists of one frozen core and two parallel trainable cores (Fig. 1), where the trainable cores have fewer layers and therefore are smaller. Both the frozen and trainable cores have their topology hard-wired. The frozen core is trained once, whereas the trainable parts are trained separately for each given dataset and task. In our experiments, we trained the frozen core on ImageNet data since CNNs pre-trained on this dataset typically learn useful general-purpose features [13]. Before the weights are fixed in hardware, the frozen core can also be trained on other datasets in a multi-task setting depending on the needs. The frozen core aims to provide features that are general-purpose enough for the target applications. The trainable cores selectively transfer and enrich those features using trainable alpha blending parameters (Fig. 3).

We define a trainable alpha blending layer as

$$\alpha = \sigma(w)$$
$$y = \alpha \cdot x_f + (1 - \alpha) \cdot x_t \tag{1}$$

for each input channel, where w is a randomly initialized trainable parameter, σ is the sigmoid function, and x_f and x_t are the outputs of the frozen and trainable blocks in the preceding layer, respectively. The alpha blending layer acts as a gating mechanism between the cores and helps the model decide the strength of transfer learning on a feature map basis (Fig. 3). Although the alpha parameters are learned during training, they can also be manually set to a particular value to enforce certain behavior. For example, setting all alpha parameters to zero would separate all three cores by disabling the data flow between the cores entirely. Similarly, setting them all to 0.5 would turn the trainable cores into residual feature extractors.

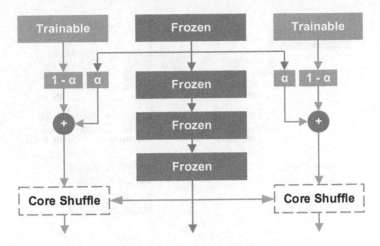

Fig. 3. A Semifreddo module consists of one frozen and two trainable cores (trainable parts shown in blue). The trainable cores selectively transfer features from the frozen core using trainable alpha blending parameters. The modular architecture allows for both using each core independently, to perform different tasks, and in conjunction with each other to perform a single task with higher representational power. The optional core shuffle module lets the two trainable cores exchange feature maps when both cores are trained to do the same task.

All three cores act as backbone networks that feed feature maps to application-specific model heads for up to three different tasks at a time. The cores can run both independently and together with each other. For example, one can use the frozen core output for image classification, one of the trainable cores for scene classification, and the other trainable core for semantic segmentation.

Any efficient neural network architecture can be used to implement our SemifreddoNet macro architecture. We used a network topology based on ShuffleNetV2 [15] to implement the building blocks of our model. Each block in the system consists of a channel split, followed by depthwise separable convolution, channel concatenation, and uniform channel shuffle (Fig. 4). The blocks that downsample their inputs skip the channel split operator and use a stride of two in the depthwise convolution. Therefore, they double the number of channels while reducing the feature map size by a factor of two in both horizontal and vertical axes. When two trainable cores are used for one task, we also shuffle feature maps between trainable cores by swapping half of the feature maps at the output of each alpha blending layer (Fig. 3). This cross-core channel shuffling helps both cores act as a single network more efficiently.

The alpha blending layers between the frozen and trainable cores require the shape of the input feature maps to match. Therefore, all cores have intermediate feature maps that match in size. The trainable cores are made smaller by carving out some of the repeated layers rather than reducing the number of trainable kernels per layer while keeping both cores in synch with each other in the pipeline.

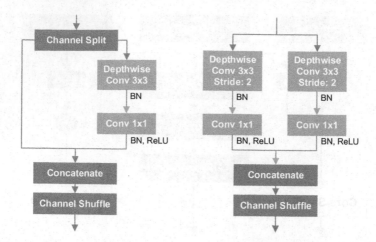

Fig. 4. We use simplified versions of ShuffleNetV2 [15] blocks to implement our SemifreddoNet cores: regular building blocks (left) and downscaling blocks (right).

We call each one of these building blocks that consist of parallel trainable and frozen layers, a Semifreddo module (Fig. 3). Our model architecture consists of repeated blocks of Semifreddo modules. The overall architecture breakdown is shown in Table 1.

We use the Semifreddo modules to freeze a model vertically. Freezing the parameters this way (Table 3) produced comparable results to freezing a certain percentage of parameters in each layer uniformly (Fig. 6), while providing additional benefits. One advantage of using Semifreddo modules instead of fully-uniform freezing is the ease of implementation. For example, we needed to modify our code at the optimizer level to implement uniform weight freezing. On the other hand, the frozen and trainable parts in Semifreddo modules can easily be defined in any mainstream deep learning framework and trained without modifying the parameter update mechanisms in the underlying framework. Another advantage of using Semifreddo modules to freeze a model vertically is the ability to decouple the frozen and trainable cores. This modular architecture allows for training the trainable and frozen cores separately for different tasks.

3.3 Model Head

The backbone model in our system outputs feature maps that need to be further processed to perform a computer vision task. Those feature maps can be used as-is in a host system that has additional computing capabilities, such as having a digital signal processor (DSP). However, a host system might not always have such additional hardware to process the raw feature maps.

To build a standalone system, we propose a multi-purpose model head block that can perform basic computer vision tasks without relying on the compute

Table 1. Architectural breakdown of the frozen and trainable cores: the trainable cores have a smaller number of repeated blocks, therefore have fewer layers. Both trainable and frozen cores have intermediate feature maps that match in size.

Input Size	Type	Frozen Core		Trainable Core	
		stride	*repeat*	*stride*	*repeat*
640×480×3	Conv2D	2	1	2	1
320×240×32	Semifreddo	2	1	2	1
		1	3	-	-
160×120×64	Semifreddo	2	1	2	1
		1	3	-	-
80×60×128	Semifreddo	1	1	1	1
		1	3	-	-
80×60×128	Semifreddo	2	1	2	1
		1	3	-	-
40×30×256	Model Head	1	1	1	1

capabilities of a host system. The model head inputs feature maps and produces output vectors for a given task.

We implement this model head as a pointwise convolution layer having a configurable number of outputs. The model head supports up to 131072 parameters, which would be sufficient for many types of basic computer vision tasks. For example, given 256-channel feature maps from each trainable core, the model head would be able to classify up to 256 kinds of scenes and segment up to 256 types of objects simultaneously. The head supports group convolutions to handle larger outputs while staying within the limits of the total number of configurable weights.

The head implements an optional pooling operator and a configurable activation function that can be enabled when needed. The pooling operator is enabled when the entire image needs to be analyzed to make a single prediction, such as image classification and face identification and is disabled for the tasks that require spatial granularity. The model has a total downscaling factor of 16× when the pooling is disabled. The global average pooling operator runs as a running-average accumulator, as the images are acquired line-by-line in the raster scan order. Finally, the activation function at the end of the model head is designed to approximate any arbitrary activation function as a piecewise linear function.

We designed this hardware model head to run basic computer vision tasks on simple devices that do not have any additional compute capabilities. For more sophisticated tasks, we also provide the option of outputting the feature maps and implementing more complex neural network heads on the host device.

3.4 Repeatable Blocks

Fixing the model topology helped us design highly efficient neural network hardware, while somewhat limiting the flexibility of our models. As different tasks may need models having varying levels of capacities, we propose a modular design scheme to adjust the model depth without duplicating the logic in the hardware. Our modular design scheme implements deeper and larger network architectures by cycling the feature maps over the same hardware blocks.

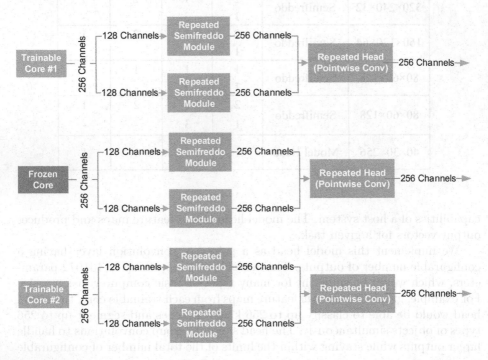

Fig. 5. Repeatable blocks: the last blocks in our system can be repeated to increase the capacity of the underlying models. The Semifreddo modules can be repeated as many times as necessary to meet a given accuracy requirement, at the expense of inference speed.

In particular, we modularize the last trainable Semifreddo blocks and the model head. We reuse them repeatedly in a single inference pass to improve model accuracy when needed (Fig. 5). We can repeat the modular blocks as many times as necessary. However, reusing the building blocks for different layers requires the weights to be reloaded every time an existing hardware block is used in place of a new one. Therefore, implementing larger models this way comes at the cost of lower inference speeds. Nevertheless, the block modularity provides the flexibility to find a reasonable balance between accuracy and speed (Table 2), given a set of requirements.

Table 2. Impact of repeatable hardware blocks on inference speed in terms of maximum number of frames per second that can be processed at VGA resolution.

Number of Modular Block Repetitions	FPS (upper bound)
1	200
2	100
3	67
4	50
5	40
6	33

4   Results

To evaluate the value of the frozen features and the trainable cores, we performed a set of experiments covering different configurations of our model on different types of tasks (Table 3). We used two computer vision tasks that have significantly different types of input data: image classification and face identification.

The first task, image classification on the ImageNet challenge dataset, used a training setup identical to the frozen core pretraining. Therefore, it was expected to benefit from the frozen core the most. The second task, face identification, used the VGGFace2 [6] and LWF [12] face datasets for training and test, respectively. Both of those datasets had a data distribution that is significantly different from ImageNet. We used the training setup in [21] as-is, without any further hyperparameter tuning.

As a benchmark, we used fully trainable ShuffleNetV2 backbones on the same tasks. In ShuffleNetV2 models, we used width multipliers of 0.5 and 1.0 to get backbone networks that are closest to our models in terms of the hardware footprint and the total number of parameters. We used the same training setup as the original ShuffleNetV2 paper [15] for both our SemifreddoNet backbones and the benchmark models.

In the image classification experiments, we used the same model head that the original ShuffleNetV2 paper used. Since the model head would be too large to run on our proposed in-line model head block, we assumed that the head would run on a DSP. In the face identification experiments, we used our proposed lightweight model head, which does not rely on any additional hardware on the host system.

As expected, the value of frozen features were higher for image classification than for face identification. However, the face identification task still benefited from the ImageNet-trained frozen core, despite the differences in input data dis-

Table 3. Comparison of different configurations of SemifreddoNets and ShuffleNetV2 in terms of the number of parameters, silicon area, and performance on various computer vision tasks. The number of parameters and silicon area exclude the model head. For image classification, all backbone networks use the same model head that the original ShuffleNetV2 used. Face classification models use our proposed lightweight model head. The frozen core was pre-trained on ImageNet; therefore, its additional value was higher for image classification than for face classification. The frozen core can also be trained in a multi-task setting to maximize its value for a given set of tasks.

| Backbone Model | Configuration | Number of Parameters | | Silicon Area | Image Classification | | Face Identification |
		Frozen	Trainable		Top-1 Accuracy	Top-5 Accuracy	Top-1 Accuracy
Semifreddo Nets	Two trainable cores	140K	120K	4 mm²	0.70	0.89	0.88
	Two cores w/o core shuffle	140K	120K	4 mm2	0.66	0.87	0.86
	One trainable core	140K	60K	2.66 mm²	0.66	0.87	0.86
	Frozen core only	140K	-	1.32 mm²	0.65	0.86	0.58
	Trainable cores only	-	120K	2.68 mm²	0.62	0.83	0.84
ShuffleNet V2	0.5×	-	65K	1.56 mm²	0.60	0.81	0.81
	1.0×	-	240K	5.24 mm²	0.69	0.88	0.92

tributions. Overall, SemifreddoNets performed comparably or better than their fully-trainable ShuffleNetV2 counterparts, given small silicon area budgets.

5   Ablation Study

We performed a set of experiments to measure the impact of our design choices in our model architecture.

Proportion of Frozen Weights. We first tested the impact of vertical weight freezing on the flexibility on the model. We started with a backbone model that is twice as wide as the frozen core in our final network architecture. We pre-trained this backbone model on ImageNet. Then, we uniformly froze 0%, 50%, 75%, and 100% of the parameters in the backbone, while leaving the model head trainable. We fine-tuned remaining weights in the backbone and the model head on the Citycapes [8] dataset to perform pixelwise semantic segmentation. As

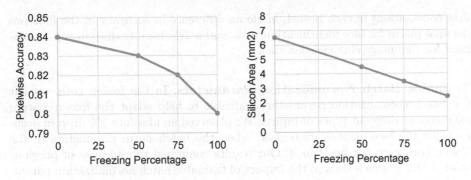

Fig. 6. Impact of weight freezing ratio on silicon area and pixelwise accuracy for an exemplary, semantic segmentation task. Freezing a larger portion of the parameters reduces the hardware footprint, however it also decreases the accuracy of the model.

expected, having a larger portion of the network frozen resulted in lower accuracy. The largest performance drop occurred between the 75% and 100% freezing ratios (Fig. 6). SemifreddoNets do not support specifying an exact freezing ratio as they are not frozen in an entirely uniform manner, unlike in this experiment. However, we can still approximate a given freezing ratio. The effective freezing ratio in our final backbone model is 77% for using a single trainable core and 54% for using both of the trainable cores. Those freezing ratios provided a good trade-off between accuracy and silicon area.

Repeatable Blocks. We measured the impact of repeatable hardware blocks on the performance by training models having different numbers of repeated Semifreddo blocks. Repeating the last Semifreddo blocks twice, as shown in Fig. 5, increased the face identification accuracy from 88% to 96%. However, the block repetitions also increased the overall delay, reducing the frames per second that the system can process (Table 2). Repeating the blocks further led to only minor further improvements in the accuracy (up to 2%).

Cross-core Shuffle. Shuffling the feature maps between the two trainable cores helped both cores act as a single, larger network. Using both trainable cores for the same task improved the performance only when the core shuffling was enabled. Without the core shuffle, the additional trainable core led to no significant gains in the performance metrics (Table 3). Core shuffling improved the results while having a negligible cost in hardware.

Pointwise Convolutions. ShuffleNet V2 blocks use pointwise convolutions followed by depthwise and pointwise convolutions. To save silicon area, we dropped the first pointwise convolutions in our backbone network (Fig. 4). Dropping the first convolutions in each branch made no difference in accuracy in the first two decimal places for face identification task, and a 2% absolute drop in top-5 accuracy for the image classification task.

Trainable Batch Normalization Parameters. In the frozen core, we left the batch normalization parameters trainable to help adapt the frozen feature extractor to different types of inputs. We observed an absolute 2% drop in accuracy for the face identification task, when the batch norm parameters in the frozen core were not fine tuned. Our results confirmed the findings of previous studies [7,23], which showed the impact of trainable batch normalization parameters on transfer learning.

6   Conclusions

We proposed fixed-topology neural network blocks that vertically froze network parameters for hardware efficiency. Our proposed weight freezing scheme significantly reduced the hardware footprint while maintaining a fair amount of flexibility. Our proposed system has a modular architecture that is straightforward to use, extend, and integrate into existing systems. We demonstrated the capabilities of an exemplary neural network hardware architecture that consisted of one frozen and two trainable cores. Our work can potentially be extended to have more trainable cores. Increasing the number of trainable cores would decrease the marginal cost of the frozen core, allowing for building high-performance inference engines that can handle many more tasks at a time.

References

1. Coral.ai. https://coral.ai/products/
2. Intel Movidius VPUs. https://www.intel.com/content/www/us/en/artificial-intelligence/movidius-myriad-vpus.html
3. Nvidia Jetson. https://www.nvidia.com/en-us/autonomous-machines/jetson-store/
4. Asama, M., et al.: Processing images using hybrid infinite impulse response (IIR) and finite impulse response (FIR) convolution block (2020), US Patent App. 16/674,512
5. Asama, M., Isikdogan, L.F., Rao, S., Nayak, B.V., Michael, G.: A machine learning imaging core using separable FIR-IIR filters. arXiv preprint arXiv:2001.00630 (2020)
6. Cao, Q., Shen, L., Xie, W., Parkhi, O.M., Zisserman, A.: VGGFace2: a dataset for recognising faces across pose and age. In: IEEE International Conference on Automatic Face & Gesture Recognition (FG 2018), pp. 67–74. IEEE (2018)
7. Chen, L.C., Papandreou, G., Schroff, F., Adam, H.: Rethinking atrous convolution for semantic image segmentation. arXiv preprint arXiv:1706.05587 (2017)

8. Cordts, M., et al.: The cityscapes dataset for semantic urban scene understanding. In: Proceedings of the IEEE Conference on Computer Vision and Pattern Recognition, pp. 3213–3223 (2016)
9. Guo, Y., Shi, H., Kumar, A., Grauman, K., Rosing, T., Feris, R.: Spottune: transfer learning through adaptive fine-tuning. In: Proceedings of the IEEE Conference on Computer Vision and Pattern Recognition, pp. 4805–4814 (2019)
10. He, K., Zhang, X., Ren, S., Sun, J.: Deep residual learning for image recognition. In: Proceedings of the IEEE Conference on Computer Vision and Pattern Recognition, pp. 770–778 (2016)
11. Howard, A.G., et al.: MobileNets: efficient convolutional neural networks for mobile vision applications. arXiv preprint arXiv:1704.04861 (2017)
12. Huang, G.B., Ramesh, M., Berg, T., Learned-Miller, E.: Labeled faces in the wild: A database for studying face recognition in unconstrained environments. Technical report 07–49, University of Massachusetts, Amherst (October 2007)
13. Huh, M., Agrawal, P., Efros, A.A.: What makes imagenet good for transfer learning? arXiv preprint arXiv:1608.08614 (2016)
14. Krizhevsky, A., Sutskever, I., Hinton, G.E.: Imagenet classification with deep convolutional neural networks. In: Advances in Neural Information Processing Systems, pp. 1097–1105 (2012)
15. Ma, N., Zhang, X., Zheng, H.-T., Sun, J.: ShuffleNet V2: practical guidelines for efficient CNN architecture design. In: Ferrari, V., Hebert, M., Sminchisescu, C., Weiss, Y. (eds.) Computer Vision – ECCV 2018. LNCS, vol. 11218, pp. 122–138. Springer, Cham (2018). https://doi.org/10.1007/978-3-030-01264-9_8
16. Mallya, A., Davis, D., Lazebnik, S.: Piggyback: adapting a single network to multiple tasks by learning to mask weights. In: Proceedings of the European Conference on Computer Vision, pp. 67–82 (2018)
17. Misra, I., Shrivastava, A., Gupta, A., Hebert, M.: Cross-stitch networks for multitask learning. In: Proceedings of the IEEE Conference on Computer Vision and Pattern Recognition, pp. 3994–4003 (2016)
18. Qiao, S., Lin, Z., Zhang, J., Yuille, A.L.: Neural rejuvenation: Improving deep network training by enhancing computational resource utilization. In: Proceedings of the IEEE Conference on Computer Vision and Pattern Recognition, pp. 61–71 (2019)
19. Russakovsky, O., et al.: Imagenet large scale visual recognition challenge. Int. J. Comput. Vision 115(3), 211–252 (2015)
20. Sandler, M., Howard, A., Zhu, M., Zhmoginov, A., Chen, L.C.: MobileNetV2: inverted residuals and linear bottlenecks. In: Proceedings of the IEEE Conference on Computer Vision and Pattern Recognition, pp. 4510–4520 (2018)
21. Schroff, F., Kalenichenko, D., Philbin, J.: Facenet: a unified embedding for face recognition and clustering. In: Proceedings of the IEEE Conference on Computer Vision and Pattern Recognition, pp. 815–823 (2015)
22. Szegedy, C., et al.: Going deeper with convolutions. In: Proceedings of the IEEE Conference on Computer Vision and Pattern Recognition, pp. 1–9 (2015)
23. Whatmough, P.N., Zhou, C., Hansen, P., Venkataramanaiah, S.K., Seo, J.s., Mattina, M.: FixyNN: efficient hardware for mobile computer vision via transfer learning. In: Proceedings of the 2nd SysML Conference (2019)
24. Wu, C.T., Ain-Kedem, L., Gandra, C.R., Isikdogan, F., Michael, G.: Trainable vision scaler (2019), US Patent App. 16/232,336
25. Wu, C.T., et al.: VisionISP: repurposing the image signal processor for computer vision applications. In: Proceedings of IEEE International Conference on Image Processing (2019)

26. Yosinski, J., Clune, J., Bengio, Y., Lipson, H.: How transferable are features in deep neural networks? In: Advances in Neural Information Processing Systems, pp. 3320–3328 (2014)
27. Zhang, X., Zhou, X., Lin, M., Sun, J.: Shufflenet: an extremely efficient convolutional neural network for mobile devices. In: Proceedings of the IEEE Conference on Computer Vision and Pattern Recognition, pp. 6848–6856 (2018)
28. Zoph, B., Le, Q.V.: Neural architecture search with reinforcement learning. arXiv preprint arXiv:1611.01578 (2016)

Improving Adversarial Robustness by Enforcing Local and Global Compactness

Anh Bui[1]($\boxtimes$)(iD), Trung Le[1](iD), He Zhao[1](iD), Paul Montague[2](iD), Olivier deVel[2](iD), Tamas Abraham[2](iD), and Dinh Phung[1](iD)

[1] Monash University, Melbourne, Australia
{tuananh.bui,trunglm,ethan.zhao,dinh.phung}@monash.edu
[2] Defence Science and Technology Group, Canberra, Australia
{paul.montague,olivier.devel,tamas.abraham}@dst.defence.gov.au

Abstract. The fact that deep neural networks are susceptible to crafted perturbations severely impacts the use of deep learning in certain domains of application. Among many developed defense models against such attacks, adversarial training emerges as the most successful method that consistently resists a wide range of attacks. In this work, based on an observation from a previous study that the representations of a clean data example and its adversarial examples become more divergent in higher layers of a deep neural net, we propose the Adversary Divergence Reduction Network which enforces local/global compactness and the clustering assumption over an intermediate layer of a deep neural network. We conduct comprehensive experiments to understand the isolating behavior of each component (i.e., local/global compactness and the clustering assumption) and compare our proposed model with state-of-the-art adversarial training methods. The experimental results demonstrate that augmenting adversarial training with our proposed components can further improve the robustness of the network, leading to higher unperturbed and adversarial predictive performances.

Keywords: Adversarial robustness · Local compactness · Global compactness · Clustering assumption

1 Introduction

Despite the great success of deep neural nets, they are reported to be susceptible to crafted perturbations [6,25], even state-of-the-art ones. Accordingly, many defense models have been developed, notably [17,20,26,27]. Recently, the work of [1] undertakes an in-depth study of neural network defense models and conduct comprehensive experiments on a complete suite of defense techniques, which has lead to postulating one common reason why many defenses provide apparent robustness against gradient-based attacks, namely *obfuscated gradients*.

Electronic supplementary material The online version of this chapter (https://doi.org/10.1007/978-3-030-58583-9_13) contains supplementary material, which is available to authorized users.

© Springer Nature Switzerland AG 2020
A. Vedaldi et al. (Eds.): ECCV 2020, LNCS 12372, pp. 209–223, 2020.
https://doi.org/10.1007/978-3-030-58583-9_13

According to the above study, adversarial training with Projected Gradient Descent (PGD) [17] is one of the most successful and widely-used defense techniques that remained consistently resilient against attacks, which has inspired many recent advances including Adversarial Logit Pairing (ALP) [11], Feature Denoising [26], Defensive Quantization [15], Jacobian Regularization [9], Stochastic Activation Pruning [5], and Adversarial Training Free [22].

In this paper, we propose to build robust classifiers against adversarial examples by learning better representations in the intermediate space. Given an image classifier based on a multi-layer neural net, conceptually, we divide the network into two parts with an intermediate layer: the generator network from the input layer to the intermediate layer and the classifier network from the intermediate layer to the output prediction layer. The output of the generator network (i.e., the intermediate layer) is the intermediate representation of the input image, which is fed to the classifier network to make prediction. For image classifiers, an adversarial example is usually generated by adding small perturbations to a clean image. The adversarial example may look very similar to the original image but leads to significant changes to the prediction of the classifier. It has been observed that in deep neural networks, the representations of a clean data example and its adversarial example might become very diverge in the intermediate space, although their representations are proximal in the data space [26]. Due to the above divergence in the intermediate space, a classifier may be hard to predict the same class of the adversarial and real images. Inspired by this observation, we propose to learn better representations that reduce the above divergence in the intermediate space, so as to enhance the classifier robustness against adversarial examples.

In particular, we propose an enhanced adversarial training framework that imposes the *local and global compactness* properties on the intermediate representations, to build more robust classifiers against adversarial examples. Specifically, by explicitly strengthening local compactness, we enforce the intermediate representations output from the generator of a clean image and its adversarial examples to be as proximal as possible. In this way, the classifier network is less easy to be misled by the adversarial examples. However, enforcing the local compactness itself may not be sufficient to guarantee a robust defense model as the representations might be encouraged to globally spread out in the intermediate space, significantly hurting accuracies on both clean and adversarial images. To address this, we further propose to impose global compactness to encourage the representations of examples in the same class to be proximal yet those in different classes to be more distant. Finally, to increase the generalization capacity of the deep network and reduce the misclassification of adversarial examples, our framework enjoys the flexibility to incorporate the clustering assumption [3], which aims to force the decision boundary of a classifier to lie in the gap between clusters of different classes. By collaboratively incorporating the above three properties, we are able to learn better intermediate representations, which help to boost the adversarial robustness of classifiers. Intuitively, we name our proposed framework to the *Adversary Divergence Reduction Network* (ADR).

To comprehensively exam the proposed framework, we conduct extensive experiments to investigate the influence of each component (i.e., local/global compactness and the clustering assumption), visualize the smoothness of the loss surface of our robust model, and compare our proposed ADR method with several state-of-the-art adversarial defenses. The experimental results consistently show that our proposed method can further improve over others in terms of better adversarial and clean predictive performances. The contributions of this work are summarized as follows:

- We propose the local and global compactness properties on the intermediate space to enforce the better representations, which lead to more robust classifiers;
- We incorporate our local and global compactness with clustering assumption to further enhance adversarial robustness;
- We plug the above three components into an adversarial training framework to introduce our Adversary Divergence Reduction Network;
- We extensively analyze the proposed framework and compare it with state-of-the-art adversarial training methods to verify its effectiveness.

2   Related Works

Adversarial Training Defense. Adversarial training can be traced back to [6], in which models were challenged by producing adversarial examples and incorporating them into training data. The adversarial examples could be the worst-case examples (i.e., $x_a \triangleq \mathrm{argmax}_{x' \in B_\varepsilon(x)} \ell\left(x', y, \theta\right)$) [6] or most divergent examples (i.e., $x_a \triangleq \mathrm{argmax}_{x' \in B_\varepsilon(x)} D_{KL}\left(h_\theta\left(x'\right) \| h_\theta\left(x\right)\right)$) [27] where D_{KL} is the Kullback-Leibler divergence and h_θ is the current model. The quality of the adversarial training defense crucially depends on the strength of the injected adversarial examples – e.g., training on non-iterative adversarial examples obtained from FGSM or Rand FGSM (a variant of FGSM where the initial point is randomised) are not robust to iterative attacks, for example PGD [17] or BIM [13].

Although many defense models were broken by [1], the adversarial training with PGD [17] was among the few that were resilient against attacks. Many defense models were developed based on adversarial examples from a PGD attack or attempts made to improve and scale up the PGD adversarial training. Notable examples include Adversarial Logit Pairing (ALP) [11], Feature Denoising [26], Defensive Quantization [15], Jacobian Regularization [9], Stochastic Activation Pruning [5], and Adversarial Training for Free [22].

Defense with a Latent Space. These works utilized a latent space to enable adversarial defense, notably [10]. DefenseGAN [21] and PixelDefense [24] use a generator (i.e., a pretrained WS-GAN [7] for DefenseGAN and a PixelCNN [19] for PixelDefense) together with the latent space to find a denoised version of an adversarial example on the data manifold. These works were criticized by [1] as being easy to attack and impossible to work within the case of the CIFAR-10 dataset. Jalal et al. [10] proposed an overpowered attack method to efficiently attack both DefenseGAN and PixelDefense and subsequently injected those adversarial examples to train the model. Though that work was proven to work well with simple datasets including MNIST and CelebA, no experiments were conducted on more complex datasets including, for example, CIFAR-10.

3   Proposed Method

In what follows, we present our proposed method, named the *Adversary Divergence Reduction Network* (ADR). As shown in the previous study [26], although an adversarial example x_a and its corresponding clean example x are in close proximity in the data space (i.e., differ by a small perturbation), when brought forward up to the higher layers in a deep neural network, their representations become markedly more divergent, hence causing different prediction results. Inspired by this observation, we propose imposing local compactness for those representations in an intermediate layer of a neural network. The key idea is to enforce that the representations of an adversarial example and its clean counterpart be as proximal as possible, hence reducing the chance of misclassifying them. Moreover, we observe that enforcing the local compactness itself is not sufficient to guarantee a robust defense model as this enforcement might encourage representations to globally spread out across the intermediate space (i.e., the space induced by the intermediate representations), significantly hurting both adversarial and clean performances. To address this, we propose to impose global compactness for the intermediate representations such that representations of examples that belong in the same class are proximal and those in different classes are more distant. Finally, to increase the generalization capacity of the deep network and reduce the misclassification of adversarial examples, we propose to apply the clustering assumption [3] which aims to force the decision boundary to lie in the gap between clusters of different classes, hence increasing the chance for adversarial examples to be correctly classified.

3.1   Local Compactness

Local compactness, which aims to reduce the divergence between the representations of an adversarial example and its clean example in an intermediate layer, is one of the key aspects of our proposed method. Let us denote our deep neural network by $h_\theta(\cdot)$, which decomposes into $h_\theta(\cdot) = g_\theta(f_\theta(\cdot))$ where the first (generator) network f_θ maps the data examples onto an intermediate layer where we enforce the compactness constraints. The following (classifier) network g_θ maps the intermediate representations to the prediction output. For local compactness, given a clean data example x, denote $\mathcal{A}_\varepsilon$ as a stochastic adversary that renders adversarial examples for x as $x_a \sim \mathcal{A}_\varepsilon(x)$ in a ball $B_\varepsilon(x) = \{x' : \|x - x'\| < \varepsilon\}$, our aim is to compress the representations of x and x_a in the intermediate layer by minimizing

$$\mathcal{L}_{\text{com}}^{\text{lc}} = \mathbb{E}_{x \sim \mathcal{D}_x} \left[\mathbb{E}_{x_a \sim \mathcal{A}_{\varepsilon}(x)} \left[\| f_\theta(x) - f_\theta(x_a) \|_p \right] \right] \tag{1}$$

where we use $\mathcal{D}_x = \{x_1, ..., x_N\}$ to represent both training examples and the corresponding empirical distribution and $\|\cdot\|_p$ with $p = 1, 2, \infty$ to specify the p-norm.

3.2   Global Compactness

For global compactness, we want the representations of data examples in the same class to be closer and data examples in different classes to be more separate. As demonstrated later, global compactness in conjunction with the clustering assumption helps increase the margin of a data example (i.e., the distance from that data example to the decision boundary), hence boosting the generalization capacity of the classifier network and adversarial robustness.

More specifically, given two examples (x_i, y_i) and (x_j, y_j) drawn from the empirical distribution over $\mathcal{D}_{x,y} = \{(x_1, y_1), ..., (x_N, y_N)\}$ where the label $y_k \in \{1, 2, ..., M\}$, we compute the weight w_{ij} for this pair as follows:

$$w_{ij} = \frac{\alpha - \mathbb{I}_{y_i \neq y_j}}{\alpha} = \begin{cases} 1 & \text{if } y_i = y_j \\ \frac{\alpha - 1}{\alpha} & \text{otherwise} \end{cases} \tag{2}$$

where $\mathbb{I}_S$ is the indicator function which returns 1 if S holds and 0 otherwise. We consider $\alpha \in (0, 1)$, yielding $w_{ij} < 0$ if $y_i \neq y_j$ and $w_{ij} > 0$ if otherwise.

We enforce global compactness by minimizing

$$\mathcal{L}_{\text{com}}^{\text{gb}} = \mathbb{E}_{(x_i, y_i), (x_j, y_j) \sim \mathcal{D}_{x,y}} \left[w_{ij} \| f_\theta(x_i) - f_\theta(x_j) \|_p \right] \tag{3}$$

where we overload the notation $\mathcal{D}_{x,y}$ to represent the empirical distribution over the training set, which implies that the intermediate representations $f_\theta(x_i)$ and $f_\theta(x_j)$ are encouraged to be closer if $y_i = y_j$ and to be separate if $y_i \neq y_j$ for a global compact representation.

Note that in our experiment, we set $\alpha = 0.99$, yielding $w_{ij} \in \{1, -0.01\}$, and calculate global compactness with each random minibatch.

3.3   Clustering Assumption and Label Supervision

At this stage, we have achieved compact intermediate representations for the clean data and adversarial examples obtained from a stochastic adversary $\mathcal{A}_{\varepsilon}$. Our next step is to enforce some constraints on the subsequent classifier network g_θ to further exploit this compact representation for improving adversarial robustness. The first constraint we impose on the classifier network g_θ is that this should classify both clean data and adversarial examples correctly by minimizing

$$\mathcal{L}_c = \mathbb{E}_{(x,y) \sim D_{x,y}} \left[\mathbb{E}_{x_a \sim \mathcal{A}_{\varepsilon}(x)} [\ell(h_\theta(x_a), y)] + \ell(h_\theta(x), y) \right] \tag{4}$$

where ℓ is the cross-entropy loss function.

In addition to this label supervision, the second constraint we impose on the classifier network g_θ is the clustering assumption [3], which states that the decision boundary of g_θ in the intermediate space should not break into any high density region (or cluster) of data representations in the intermediate space, forcing the boundary to lie in gaps formed by those clusters. The clustering assumption when combined with the global compact representation property should increase the data example margin (i.e., the distance from that data example to the decision boundary). If this is further combined with the fact that the representations of adversarial examples are compressed into the representation of its clean data example (*i.e.* local compactness) this should also reduce the chance that adversarial examples are misclassified. To enforce the clustering assumption, inspired by [23], we encourage the classifier confidence by minimizing the conditional entropy and maintain classifier smoothness using Virtual Adversarial Training (VAT) [18], respectively:

$$\mathcal{L}_{\text{conf}} = \mathbb{E}_{x \sim D_x} \left[\mathbb{E}_{x_a \sim \mathcal{A}_\varepsilon(x)} \left[-h_\theta(x_a)^T \log h_\theta(x_a) \right] - h_\theta(x)^T \log h_\theta(x) \right] \quad (5)$$

$$\mathcal{L}_{\text{smt}} = \mathbb{E}_{x \sim D_x} \left[\mathbb{E}_{x_a \sim \mathcal{A}_\varepsilon(x)} \left[D_{KL} \left(h_\theta(x) \| h_\theta(x_a) \right) \right] \right] \quad (6)$$

3.4   Generating Adversarial Examples

We can use any adversarial attack algorithm to define the adversary $\mathcal{A}_\varepsilon$. For example, Madry et al. [17] proposed to find the worst-case examples $x_a \triangleq \text{argmax}_{x' \in B_\varepsilon(x)} \ell(x', y, \theta)$ using PGD, while Zhang et al. [27] aimed to find the most divergent examples $x_a \triangleq \text{argmax}_{x' \in B_\varepsilon(x)} D_{KL} \left(h_\theta(x') \| h_\theta(x) \right)$. By enforcing local/global compactness over the adversarial examples obtained by $\mathcal{A}_\varepsilon$, we make them easier to be trained with the label supervision loss in Eq. (4), hence eventually improving adversarial robustness. The quality of adversarial examples obviously affects to the overall performance, however, in the experimental section, we empirically prove that our proposed components can boost the robustness of the adversarial training frameworks of interest.

3.5   Putting it all Together

We combine the relevant terms regarding local/global compactness, label supervision, and the clustering assumption and arrive at the following optimization problem:

$$\min_\theta \mathcal{L} \triangleq \mathcal{L}_c + \lambda_{\text{com}}^{\text{lc}} \mathcal{L}_{\text{com}}^{\text{lc}} + \lambda_{\text{com}}^{\text{gb}} \mathcal{L}_{\text{com}}^{\text{gb}} + \lambda_{\text{conf}} \mathcal{L}_{\text{conf}} + \lambda_{\text{smt}} \mathcal{L}_{\text{smt}} \quad (7)$$

where $\lambda_{\text{com}}^{\text{lc}}, \lambda_{\text{com}}^{\text{gb}}, \lambda_{\text{conf}}$, and λ_{smt} are non-negative trade-off parameters.

In Fig. 1, we illustrate how the three components, namely local/global compactness, label supervision, and the clustering assumption can mutually collaborate to improve adversarial robustness. The representations of data examples

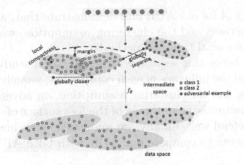

Fig. 1. Overview of Adversary divergence reduction network. The local/global compactness and clustering assumption are intended to improve adversarial robustness.

via the network f_θ are enforced to be locally/globally compact, whereas the position of the decision boundary of the classifier network g_θ in the intermediate space is enforced using the clustering assumption. Ideally, with the clustering assumption, the decision boundary of g_θ preserves the cluster structure in the intermediate space and when combined with label supervision training ensures clusters in a class remain completely inside the decision region for this class. Moreover, global compactness encourages clusters of a class to be closer and those of different classes to be more separate. As a result, the decision boundary of g_θ lies in the gaps among clusters as well as with a sufficiently large margin for the data examples. Finally, local compactness requires adversarial examples to stay closer to their corresponding clean data example, hence reducing the chance of misclassifying them and therefore improving adversarial robustness.

Comparison with the Contrastive Learning. Interestingly, the contrastive learning [4,8] and our proposed method aim to learn better representations by the principle of enforcing similar elements to be equal and dissimilar elements to be different. However, the contrastive learning works on an instance level, which enforces the representation of an image to be proximal with those of its transformations and to be distant with those of any other images. On the other hand, our method works on a class level, which enforces the intermediate representations of each class to be compact and well separated with those in other classes. Therefore, our method and the contrastive learning complement each other and intuitively improve both visual representation and adversarial robustness when combining together.

4   Experiments

In this section, we first introduce the general setting for our experiments regarding datasets, model architecture, optimization scheduler, and adversary attackers. Second, we compare our method with adversarial training with PGD, namely ADV [17] and TRADES [27]. We employ either ADV or TRADES as the stochastic adversary $\mathcal{A}$ for our ADR and demonstrate that, when enhanced with local/global compactness and the clustering assumption, we can improve these state-of-the-art adversarial training methods.

Specifically, we begin this section with an ablation study to investigate the model behaviors and the influence of each component, namely local compactness, global compactness, and the clustering assumption, on adversarial performance. In addition, we visualize the smoothness of the loss surface of our model to understand why it can defend well. Finally, we undertake experiments on the MNIST and CIFAR-10 datasets to compare our ADR with both ADV and TRADES.

4.1 Experimental Setting

General Setting. We undertook experiments on both the MNIST [14] and CIFAR-10 [12] datasets. The inputs were normalized to $[0, 1]$. For the CIFAR-10 dataset, we apply random crops and random flips as describe in [17] during training. For the MNIST dataset, we used the standard CNN architecture with three convolution layers and three fully connected layers described in [2]. For the CIFAR-10 dataset, we used two architectures in which one is the standard CNN architecture described in [2] and another is the ResNet architecture used in [17]. We note that there is a serious overfitting problem on the CIFAR-10 dataset as mentioned in [2]. In our setting, with the standard CNN architecture, we eventually obtained a 98% training accuracy, but only a 75% testing accuracy. With the ResNet architecture, we used the strategy from [17] to adjust the learning rate when training to reduce the gap between the training and validation accuracies. For the MNIST dataset, a drop-rate equal to 0.1 at epochs 55, 75, and 90 without weight decay was employed. For the CIFAR-10 dataset, the drop-rate was set to 0.1 at epochs 100 and 150 with weight decay equal to 2×10^{-4}. We use a momentum-based SGD optimizer for the training of the standard CNN for the MNIST dataset and the ResNet for the CIFAR-10 dataset, while using the Adam optimizer for training the standard CNN on the CIFAR-10 one. The hyperparameters setting can be found in the supplementary material.

Choosing the Intermediate Layer. The intermediate layer for enforcing compactness constraints immediately follows on from the last convolution layer for the standard CNN architecture and from the penultimate layer for the ResNet architecture. Moreover, we provide an additional ablation study to investigate the importance of choosing the intermediate layer which can be found in the supplementary material.

Attack Methods. We use PGD to challenge the defense methods in this paper. Specifically, the setting for the MNIST dataset is PGD-40 (i.e., PGD with 40 steps) with the distortion bound ε increasing from 0.1 to 0.7 and step size $\eta \in \{0.01, 0.02\}$, while that for CIFAR-10 is PGD-20 with ε increasing from 0.0039 ($\approx$ 1/255) to 0.11 ($\approx$ 28/255) and step size $\eta \in \{0.0039, 0.007\}$. The distortion metric is l_∞ for all attacks. For the adversarial training, we use $k = 10$ for CIFAR10 and $k = 20$ for MNIST for all defense methods.

Non-targeted and Multi-targeted Attack Scenarios. We used two types
of attack scenarios, namely non-targeted and multi-targeted attacks. The non-
targeted attack derives adversarial examples by maximizing the loss w.r.t. its
clean data label, whilst the multi-targeted attack is undertaken by performing
simultaneously targeted attack for all possible data labels. The multi-targeted
attack is considered to be successful if any individual targeted attack on each
target label is successful. While the non-targeted attack considers only one direction of the gradient, the multi-targeted attack takes multi-directions of gradient
into account, which guarantees to get better local optimum.

4.2   Experimental Results

In this section, we first conduct an ablation study using the MNIST dataset
in order to investigate how the different components (local compactness, global
compactness, and the clustering assumption) contribute to adversarial robustness. We then conduct experiments on the MNIST and CIFAR-10 datasets to
compare our proposed method with ADV and TRADES. Further evaluation can
be found in the supplementary material.

Ablation Study. We first study how each proposed component contributes
to adversarial robustness. We use adversarial training with PGD as the baseline
model and experiment on the MNIST dataset. Recall that our method consists of
three components: the local compactness loss $\mathcal{L}_{com}^{lc}$, the global compactness loss
$\mathcal{L}_{com}^{gb}$, and the clustering assumption loss which combines $\{\mathcal{L}_{smt} + \mathcal{L}_{conf}\}$. In this
experiment, we simply set the trade-off parameters $\lambda_{com}^{lc}, \lambda_{com}^{gb}, \lambda_{smt} = \lambda_{conf} =$
λ_{ca} to 0/1 to deactivate/activate the corresponding component. We consider two
metrics: the natural accuracy (i.e., the clean accuracy) and the robustness accuracy to evaluate a defense method. The natural accuracy is that evaluated on
the clean test images, while the robustness accuracy is that evaluated on adversarial examples generated by attacking the clean test images. It is noteworthy
that for many existing defense methods, improving robustness accuracy usually
harms natural accuracy. Therefore, our proposed method aims to reach a better
trade-off between the two metrics.

Table 1 shows the results for the PGD attack with $k = 40, \varepsilon =$
0.325, and $\eta = 0.01$. We note that ADR-None is our base model without any
additional components. The base model can be any adversarial training based
method, e.g., ADV or TRADES. Without loss of generality, we use ADV as
the base model, i.e., ADR-None. By gradually combining the proposed additional components with ADR-None we produce several variants of ADR (e.g.,
ADR+LC is ADR-None together with the local compactness component). Since
the standard model was trained without any defense mechanism, its natural accuracy is high at 99.5% whereas the robustness accuracy is very poor at 0.88%,
indicating its vulnerability to adversarial attacks. Regarding the variants of our
proposed models, those with additional components generally achieve higher
robustness accuracies compared with ADR-None (i.e. ADV), without hurting

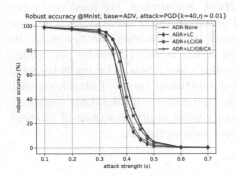

Fig. 2. Variation of the robustness accuracies under different attack strengths. The base model is ADV (ADR-None).

Table 1. Results of the PGD-40 attack on the MNIST dataset for the base ADV model together with its variants with the different components (LC = local compactness, GB = global compactness, CA = clustering assumption) and $\varepsilon = 0.325$.

	Nat. acc.	Rob. acc.
Standard model	99.5%	0.84%
ADR-None (ADV)[a]	99.27%	88.1%
ADR+LC	99.41%	91.43%
ADR+LC/GB	99.35%	94.52%
ADR+LC/GB/CA	99.36%	94.96%

[a] The performance of ADV is lower than that in [17] because of the difference of the attack strength and model architecture

the natural accuracy. In addition, the robust accuracy was significantly improved with global compactness and the clustering assumption terms.

We also evaluate the metrics of interest with different attack strength by increasing the distortion boundary ε as shown in Fig. 2. By just adding a single local compactness component, our method can improve the base model (ADV or ADR-None) for attacks with strength $\varepsilon \leq 0.35$. By adding the global compactness component, our method can significantly improve over the base model, especially for stronger attacks. Recall that as we generate adversarial examples from the PGD attack with $k = 20, \varepsilon_d = 0.3, \eta = 0.01$ to train the defense models, is unsurprised to see a model defends well with $\varepsilon \leq 0.3$. Interestingly, by adding our components, our defense methods can also achieve reasonably good robustness accuracy of 80%, even when ε varies from 0.34 to 0.37, indicating the better generality of our methods.

To gain a better understanding of the contribution of the local compactness component, we visualize the loss surface of the base model (ADV as ADR-None) and the base model with only the local compactness term (ADR+LC). In Fig. 3, the left image is a clean data example x, while the middle image is the loss surface over the input region around x in which the z-axis indicates the cross-entropy loss w.r.t. the true label (the higher value means more incorrect prediction) and the x- and y-axis indicates the variance of the input image along the gradient direction w.r.t. x and a random orthogonal direction, respectively. By varying along the two axes, we create a grid of images which represents the neighborhood region around x. The right-hand image depicts the predicted labels corresponding with this input grid.

From Fig. 3, for ADR-None, that its neighborhood region is non-smooth, resulting in incorrect predictions to the label 1 and 4. Meanwhile, for our ADR+LC method (adversarial training with local compactness), the loss surface w.r.t. the input is smoother in its neighborhood region, resulting in correct pre-

Fig. 3. Loss surface at local region of a clean data example. Top-left: ADR-None w.r.t input. Top-right: ADR+LC w.r.t input. Bottom-left: ADR-None w.r.t latent. Bottom-right: ADR+LC w.r.t latent

dictions. In addition, in our method, the prediction surface w.r.t. the latent feature in the intermediate representation layer is smoother than that w.r.t. input. This means that our local compactness makes the local region more compact, hence improving adversarial robustness. Visualization with an adversarial example as input can be found in our supplementary material which provides more evidence of our improvement over the base model.

Furthermore, we use t-SNE [16] to visualize the intermediate space for demonstrating the effect of our global compactness component. We choose to show a *positive adversarial example* defined as an adversarial example which successfully fools a defense method. We compare the base model (ADV as ADR-None) with our method with the compactness terms and use t-SNE to project clean data and adversarial examples onto 2D space as in Fig. 4. For ADR-None, its adversarial examples seem to distribute more broadly and randomly. With our global compactness constraint, the adversarial examples look well-clustered in a low density region, while rarely present in the high density region of natural clean images. We leverage the entropy of the prediction probability of examples as the third dimension in Fig. 5. A lower entropy mean that the prediction is more confident (i.e., closer to a one-hot vector) and vice versa. It can be observed that for the base model, the prediction outputs of adversarial examples seem to be randomly distributed, while for our ADR+LC/GB method, the prediction outputs of adversarial examples mainly lie in the high entropy region and are well-separated from those of the clean data examples. In other words, adversarial examples can be more easily detected from clean examples in our method, according to the predication entropy. In addition, the visualization for a *negative adversarial example* can be found in our supplementary material.

To summarize, in this ablation study, we have demonstrated how our proposed components can improve adversarial robustness. In the next section, we will compare the best variant (with all components) of our method with both ADV and TRADES on more complex datasets to highlight the capability of our method.

Experiment on the MNIST Dataset. We compare our method with ADV and TRADES on the MNIST dataset. For our method, in addition to using

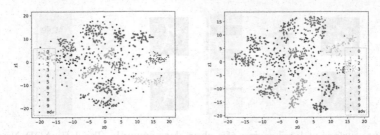

Fig. 4. T-SNE visualization of latent space. Black triangles are (positive) adversarial examples while others are clean images. Left: ADR-None. Right: ADR+LC/GB

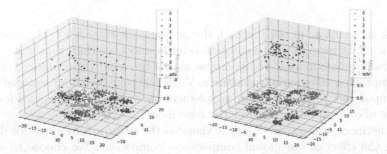

Fig. 5. T-SNE visualization of latent space with entropy of the prediction probability. Black triangles are (positive) adversarial examples while others are clean images. Left: ADR-None. Right: ADR+LC/GB

its full version with all of the proposed terms, we consider two variants ADR-ADV and ADR-TRADES wherein the adversary $\mathcal{A}$ is set to be ADV and TRADES respectively. We use PGD/TRADES generated adversarial examples with $k = 20, \varepsilon_d = 0.3, \eta_d = 0.01$ for adversarial training as proposed in [17] and employ the PGD attack with $k = 40$, using two iterative size $\eta \in \{0.01, 0.02\}$ and different distortion boundaries ε to attack. The results shown in Fig. 6 illustrate that our variants outperform the baselines, especially for $\{\varepsilon = \varepsilon_d = 0.3, \eta = 0.01\}$. For example, our ADR-ADV improves ADV by 2.4% (from 94.15% to 96.55%) while ADR-TRADES boosts TRADES by 2.07% (from 93.64% to 95.71%). While for attack setting $\{\epsilon = \epsilon_d = 0.3, \eta = 0.02\}$, our method improves ADV and TRADES by 4.0% and 3.8% respectively. Moreover, the improvement gap increases when the attack goes stronger.

Experiment on the CIFAR-10 Dataset. We conduct experiments on the CIFAR-10 dataset under two different architectures: standard CNN from [2] and ResNet from [17]. We set $k = 10, \varepsilon_d = 0.031, \eta_d = 0.007$ for ADV and TRADES and use a PGD attack with $k = 20, \eta \in \{0.0039, 0.007\}$ and different distortion boundary ε. The results for standard CNN architecture in Fig. 7 show that our methods significantly improve over the baselines. Moreover, the results for standard CNN architecture at a checking point $\{\varepsilon = \varepsilon_d = 0.031, \eta = \eta_d = 0.007\}$ in

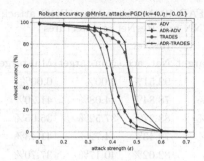 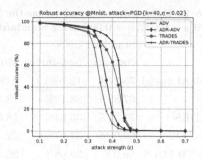

Fig. 6. Robust accuracy against PGD attack on MNIST. Base models include ADV and TRADES. Left: $\eta = 0.01$. Right: $\eta = 0.02$

Table 2 show that our methods significantly outperform their baselines in terms of natural and robust accuracies. Moreover, Fig. 7 indicates that our proposed methods can defend better in a wide range of attack strength. Particularly, when with varied distortion boundary ε in $[0.02, 0.1]$, our proposed methods always produce better robust accuracies than its baselines. Finally, the results for ResNet architecture in Table 2 show a slight improvement of our methods comparing with ADV but around 2.5% improvement from TRADES on both Non-targeted and Multi-targeted attacks.[1] The quality of adversarial examples and the chosen network architecture obviously affects the overall performance, however, in this experiment, we empirically prove that our proposed components can boost the robustness under different combinations of the adversarial training frameworks and network architectures.

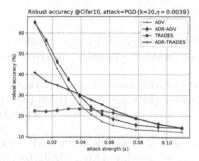 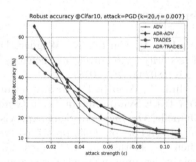

Fig. 7. Robust accuracy against PGD attack on CIFAR-10, using Standard CNN architecture. Base models include ADV and TRADES. Left: $\eta = 0.0039$. Right: $\eta = 0.007$.

---

[1] The performance of TRADES is influenced by the model architectures and parameter tunings. The works [10, 20] also reported that TRADES cannot surpass ADV all the time which explains the lower performance of TRADES on ResNet architecture in this paper. More analysis can be found in the supplementary material.

Table 2. Robustness comparison on the CIFAR-10 dataset against PGD attack at $k = 20, \epsilon = 0.031, \eta = 0.007$ using Standard CNN and ResNet architectures

	Standard CNN			ResNet		
	Nat. acc.	Non-target	Mul-target	Nat. acc.	Non-target	Mul-target
Standard model	75.27%	12.26%	0.00%	92.51%	0.00%	0.00%
ADV	67.86%	33.12%	18.73%	78.84%	44.08%	41.20%
TRADES	71.37%	35.84%	18.01%	83.27%	37.52%	35.05%
ADR-ADV	69.09%	37.67%	22.58%	78.43%	44.72%	41.43%
ADR-TRADES	69.0%	39.68%	26.7%	82.02%	40.17%	37.70%

5   Conclusion

Previous studies have shown that adversarial training has been one of the few defense models resilient to various attack types against deep neural network models. In this paper, we have shown that by enforcing additional components, namely local/global compactness constraints together with the clustering assumption, we can further improve the state-of-the-art adversarial training models. We have undertaken comprehensive experiments to investigate the effect of each component and have demonstrated the capability of our proposed methods in enhancing adversarial robustness using real-world datasets.

Acknowledgement. This work was partially supported by the Australian Defence Science and Technology (DST) Group under the Next Generation Technology Fund (NTGF) scheme.

References

1. Athalye, A., Carlini, N., Wagner, D.: Obfuscated gradients give a false sense of security: circumventing defenses to adversarial examples. arXiv preprint arXiv:1802.00420 (2018)
2. Carlini, N., Wagner, D.: Towards evaluating the robustness of neural networks. In: 2017 IEEE Symposium on Security and Privacy (SP), pp. 39–57. IEEE (2017)
3. Chapelle, O., Zien, A.: Semi-supervised classification by low density separation. In: AISTATS, vol. 2005, pp. 57–64 (2005)
4. Chen, T., Kornblith, S., Norouzi, M., Hinton, G.: A simple framework for contrastive learning of visual representations. arXiv preprint arXiv:2002.05709 (2020)
5. Dhillon, G.S., et al.: Stochastic activation pruning for robust adversarial defense. arXiv preprint arXiv:1803.01442 (2018)
6. Goodfellow, I.J., Shlens, J., Szegedy, C.: Explaining and harnessing adversarial examples. arXiv preprint arXiv:1412.6572 (2014)
7. Gulrajani, I., Ahmed, F., Arjovsky, M., Dumoulin, V., Courville, A.C.: Improved training of Wasserstein GANs. In: Advances in Neural Information Processing Systems, pp. 5767–5777 (2017)
8. He, K., Fan, H., Wu, Y., Xie, S., Girshick, R.: Momentum contrast for unsupervised visual representation learning. In: Proceedings of the IEEE/CVF Conference on Computer Vision and Pattern Recognition, pp. 9729–9738 (2020)

9. Jakubovitz, D., Giryes, R.: Improving DNN robustness to adversarial attacks using Jacobian regularization. In: Ferrari, V., Hebert, M., Sminchisescu, C., Weiss, Y. (eds.) ECCV 2018. LNCS, vol. 11216, pp. 525–541. Springer, Cham (2018). https://doi.org/10.1007/978-3-030-01258-8_32
10. Jalal, A., Ilyas, A., Daskalakis, C., Dimakis, A.G.: The robust manifold defense: adversarial training using generative models. arXiv preprint arXiv:1712.09196 (2017)
11. Kannan, H., Kurakin, A., Goodfellow, I.: Adversarial logit pairing. arXiv preprint arXiv:1803.06373 (2018)
12. Krizhevsky, A., et al.: Learning multiple layers of features from tiny images (2009)
13. Kurakin, A., Goodfellow, I., Bengio, S.: Adversarial machine learning at scale. arXiv preprint arXiv:1611.01236 (2016)
14. LeCun, Y., Bottou, L., Bengio, Y., Haffner, P.: Gradient-based learning applied to document recognition. Proc. IEEE **86**(11), 2278–2324 (1998)
15. Lin, J., Gan, C., Han, S.: Defensive quantization: when efficiency meets robustness. arXiv preprint arXiv:1904.08444 (2019)
16. Maaten, L.V.D., Hinton, G.: Visualizing data using t-SNE. J. Mach. Learn. Res. **9**(Nov), 2579–2605 (2008)
17. Madry, A., Makelov, A., Schmidt, L., Tsipras, D., Vladu, A.: Towards deep learning models resistant to adversarial attacks. arXiv preprint arXiv:1706.06083 (2017)
18. Miyato, T., Maeda, S., Koyama, M., Ishii, S.: Virtual adversarial training: a regularization method for supervised and semi-supervised learning. IEEE Trans. Pattern Anal. Mach. Intell. **41**(8), 1979–1993 (2019)
19. Oord, A.v., Kalchbrenner, N., Kavukcuoglu, K.: Pixel recurrent neural networks. arXiv preprint arXiv:1601.06759 (2016)
20. Qin, C., et al.: Adversarial robustness through local linearization. In: Advances in Neural Information Processing Systems, pp. 13824–13833 (2019)
21. Samangouei, P., Kabkab, M., Chellappa, R.: Defense-GAN: protecting classifiers against adversarial attacks using generative models. arXiv preprint arXiv:1805.06605 (2018)
22. Shafahi, A., et al.: Adversarial training for free! In: Advances in Neural Information Processing Systems, pp. 3353–3364 (2019)
23. Shu, R., Bui, H.H., Narui, H., Ermon, S.: A dirt-t approach to unsupervised domain adaptation. arXiv preprint arXiv:1802.08735 (2018)
24. Song, Y., Kim, T., Nowozin, S., Ermon, S., Kushman, N.: PixelDefend: leveraging generative models to understand and defend against adversarial examples. arXiv preprint arXiv:1710.10766 (2017)
25. Szegedy, C., et al.: Intriguing properties of neural networks. arXiv preprint arXiv:1312.6199 (2013)
26. Xie, C., Wu, Y., Maaten, L.v.d., Yuille, A.L., He, K.: Feature denoising for improving adversarial robustness. In: Proceedings of the IEEE Conference on Computer Vision and Pattern Recognition, pp. 501–509 (2019)
27. Zhang, H., Yu, Y., Jiao, J., Xing, E.P., Ghaoui, L.E., Jordan, M.I.: Theoretically principled trade-off between robustness and accuracy. arXiv preprint arXiv:1901.08573 (2019)

TopoAL: An Adversarial Learning Approach for Topology-Aware Road Segmentation

Subeesh Vasu[✉], Mateusz Kozinski, Leonardo Citraro, and Pascal Fua

CVLab, EPFL, Lausanne, Switzerland
{subeesh.vasu,mateusz.kozinski,leonardo.citraro,pascal.fua}@epfl.ch

Abstract. Most state-of-the-art approaches to road extraction from aerial images rely on a CNN trained to label road pixels as foreground and remainder of the image as background. The CNN is usually trained by minimizing pixel-wise losses, which is less than ideal to produce binary masks that preserve the road network's global connectivity.

To address this issue, we introduce an Adversarial Learning (AL) strategy tailored for our purposes. A naive one would treat the segmentation network as a generator and would feed its output along with ground-truth segmentations to a discriminator. It would then train the generator and discriminator jointly. We will show that this is not enough because it does not capture the fact that most errors are local and need to be treated as such. Instead, we use a more sophisticated discriminator that returns a label pyramid describing what portions of the road network are correct at several different scales.

This discriminator and the structured labels it returns are what gives our approach its edge and we will show that it outperforms state-of-the-art ones on the challenging RoadTracer dataset.

Keywords: Road networks · Adversarial Learning · Generative Adversarial Network · Topology learning

1 Introduction

Many state-of-the-art algorithms for reconstructing road networks from aerial images approach the problem in terms of foreground/background binary segmentation [3,8,18–20], where the road pixels are the foreground ones. They rely on deep networks and often deliver better performance than approaches that directly predict the road networks as graphs instead of binary masks [2,9,17],

This work was funded in part by the Swiss National Science Foundation.

Electronic supplementary material The online version of this chapter (https://doi.org/10.1007/978-3-030-58583-9_14) contains supplementary material, which is available to authorized users.

© Springer Nature Switzerland AG 2020
A. Vedaldi et al. (Eds.): ECCV 2020, LNCS 12372, pp. 224–240, 2020.
https://doi.org/10.1007/978-3-030-58583-9_14

even though they fail to account for the connectivity patterns of road networks. There have been several recent efforts at enforcing connectivity constraints on the segmentation outputs by designing topology-aware loss functions [22,23] or by relying on multi-task learning [3,33]. These approaches to enforcing connectivity on the output of a binary segmentation algorithm are mostly implicit: The network or the loss functions are modified in such a way that the resulting segmentations yield a more road-like connectivity.

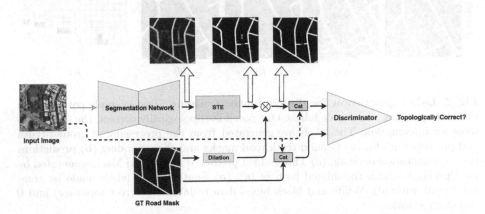

Fig. 1. Network Architecture. We use a segmentation network to predict the road probability maps which is then passed through a straight through estimator (STE) to generate binarised predictions. This is followed by multiplication with dilated ground truth masks to generate prediction based input to the discriminator. Another input to the discriminator is the ground truth mask which is used only during discriminator training. The road masks are concatenated with the input image before feeding them to the discriminator. Discriminator is then trained to predict spatial-aware dynamic decisions on the topological correctness of inputs.

In this paper, we propose a different and more explicit approach that relies on Adversarial Learning (AL). We use the training methodology of Generative Adversarial Networks (GAN) depicted by Fig. 1 to reduce topological discrepancies between the probability maps produced by our segmentation network and that of real road networks. A naive way to do this would be to treat the segmentation network as a generator and to feed its output along with ground-truth segmentations to a discriminator and then to train them jointly. Unfortunately, we will show that this approach is too global for the discriminator to learn to detect local topological errors and for the segmentation network to avoid making them. To remedy this, we introduce the following two key modifications:

– **Spatially aware labels.** Labeling a delineation as globally correct or incorrect is too coarse. As shown in Fig. 2, the discriminator returns a label pyramid that describes what portions of the road network are correct at several different scales.

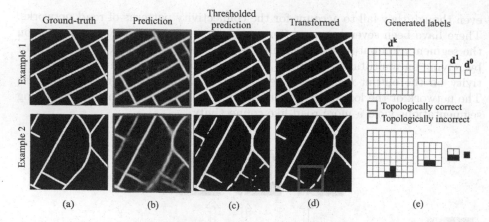

Fig. 2. Label generation for discriminator training. Two example patches with the corresponding multi-scale labels. One patch is topologically correct, the other contains an interruption. The labels are generated from the processing of ground-truth and predicted masks. (**a**) Ground truth road masks and corresponding (**b**) predictions from segmentation network. (**c**) Thresholded predicted masks. (**d**) Masks generated by multiplying (**c**) with the dilated form of (**a**). (**e**) Spatial-aware labels made by comparing (**a**) with (**d**). White and black boxes denote label 1 (correct topology) and 0 (topology error).

– **Dynamically assigned labels.** These correctness decisions are not made *a priori*. Instead, the segmentations produced by the generator are evaluated for correctness in the course of the training procedure.

Our main contribution is therefore a novel AL strategy for improving connectivity constraints on the output of road segmentation networks. We will refer to it as *TopoAL*. We will use the RoadTracer dataset [2] to show that it compares favorably to state-of-the-art methods.

2   Related Work

Most of the early approaches to extracting road networks relied on handcrafted features and prior knowledge about road geometry to optimize complex objective functions [1,6,16,26,27,31], to quote only the most recent ones. They have now been mostly superseded by deep learning techniques. One of the first such method is the approach of [20] in which image patches were fed as input to a fully connected neural network. Due to memory constraints, only limited context information could be exploited. The advent of convolutional neural networks (CNNs) opened the door to increasing the size of the receptive fields.

Many state-of-the-art approaches formulate road extraction as a segmentation problem and rely on encoder-decoder architectures such as U-Net [25], D-LinkNet [35], or recurrent versions of these architectures [30,33]. While these approaches feature large receptive fields, none of them explicitly takes into account the connectivity of the resulting binary masks. Several recent approaches have attempted to remedy this. A topology-aware loss function was introduced in [22,23] while the use of an additional centerline extraction module was proposed in [33]. In [3], orientation prediction is used as an auxiliary task to improve the connectivity of the predicted masks. [18] introduced a post-processing algorithm to reconstruct the graph from segmentation outputs by reasoning about missing connections and applying a number of heuristics. A unified approach to segmentation and connectivity reasoning was presented in [21]. It uses a segmentation network and a classifier that shares the same encoder representation. The classifier is used to reason out the connectivity in the segmentation output. Finally, [17] proposed an approach to predict road segments in the form of vector representation instead of pixel-wise segmentations. Their approach use a CNN to extract key-points and edge evidences from a given patch, which were then fed sequentially to a recurrent neural network (RNN) to produce vector representations of the underlying road segments.

A radically different approach is to directly build the graph without segmenting. This is typically done iteratively by adding road segments one by one. In [28], a CNN is trained to predict the local connectivity among the central pixel of an input patch and its border points. To reconstruct the road network corresponding to the whole image, the algorithm iteratively performs patch-wise identification of input and exit points and the associated connections. In [2], a CNN-based decision function is used to guide an iterative search process, which starts from a search point known to be part of the road network. At each step, the CNN takes the point and the already reconstructed roads in its neighborhood as input and outputs the decision to walk a fixed distance along a certain direction or to stop and return to previous search point. In a similar spirit, a Neural Turtle Graphics can be used to iteratively generate new nodes and the corresponding edges connecting to the existing nodes [9]. This approach relies on RNNs instead of CNNs, as in [2, 28].

Both segmentation based approaches and graph-based approaches have some clear vulnerabilities. The former are subject to small-scale topological errors in the form of missing connections. The latter, though free from topological errors, are vulnerable to error propagation due to the iterative reconstruction policy. We will show that our proposed approach is less affected by these difficulties as compared to other state-of-the-art algorithms.

Some of the recent works have proposed to use multiple discriminators in generative adversarial networks setups [7,13,29]. A domain adaptation technique for semantic segmentation is proposed in [7]. They divide the discriminator input into different spatial regions, and associate different classifiers to each region. The concepts of multi-scale discriminator [29] and local-global discriminators [13] were introduced to examine the input data at different context levels. Unlike all these methods, our approach differs in multiple aspects including label generation, the use of a single network architecture, and the input characteristics that the discriminator has to learn.

3   Method

As shown in Fig. 1, our approach closely traces the structure of a GAN [12]. For this reason and simplicity in the terminology, we refer to the segmentation network as the generator and to the evaluator of the delineated predictions as the discriminator. In a traditional AL, the discriminator would assign a binary label to the segmentations it produces. However, this is not suitable for our purpose because the predicted mask can be correct almost everywhere except for few locations that result in poor connectivity. To properly account for this and to provide spatially-aware supervision, our discriminator predicts the more sophisticated labels depicted by Fig. 2. They are computed online by splitting the image into increasingly fine partitions and then labeling each element of these partitions as valid or not given the ground-truth data. The labels corresponding to ground truth masks have the same structure but are uniformly valid and the corresponding loss function takes all labels at all scales into account.

The combination of using these more sophisticated labels and computing them dynamically during training, instead of fixing them *a priori* as is usually done is what gives our approach its edge. We now formalize it and describe its individual components in turn.

3.1   Formalization

Let $\mathbf{x} \in \mathbb{R}^{H \cdot W \cdot C}$ be a C-channel input image of size $H \times W$, and let $\mathbf{y} \in \{0, 1\}^{H \cdot W}$ be the corresponding ground-truth road mask, with 1 indicating pixels corresponding to a road and 0 indicating the background pixels. Let us consider a segmentation network G that takes $\mathbf{x}$ as the input and outputs a *probability map* $\hat{\mathbf{y}} = G(\mathbf{x}) \in [0, 1]^{H \cdot W}$. For any given pixel i, $\hat{\mathbf{y}}_i$ is taken to be the probability that it is a road pixel. The weights of the network are typically learned by minimizing the pixel-wise binary cross-entropy (BCE) loss

$$\mathcal{L}_{bce}(\hat{\mathbf{y}}, \mathbf{y}) = -\sum_i \left[(1 - \mathbf{y}_i) \cdot \log(1 - \hat{\mathbf{y}}_i) + \mathbf{y}_i \cdot \log \hat{\mathbf{y}}_i \right]. \tag{1}$$

Such a loss function penalizes mistakes everywhere equally regardless of their influence on the underlying geometry of the predicted road network. To remedy this, we use the segmentation network G as the generator of the GAN of Fig. 1 and define a discriminator network D whose role is to identify topological errors in the generator output. G and D are trained by making them play a game: The weights of G are optimized to generate segmentations that D cannot distinguish from ground-truth ones and the weights of D are optimized to make that distinction as well as possible.

3.2   Discriminator Network: D

In a traditional GAN, D is trained to return a binary label that is 1 if a sample is a ground-truth one and 0 if it is one generated by the G network. We will show in the result section that this does not help much in our case, mostly because the errors that G makes are local and that a single binary label is not enough to characterize them. Instead, we designed D to classify different portions of the predicted masks at different scales as correct or not. This pyramid approach allows the discriminator to provide both local and global supervision to the generator and to model spatial dependencies between neighboring locations. We now describe the label generation and the discriminator architecture in detail.

Scale Space Labels. The most challenging aspect of road network reconstruction is recovering the connectivity of the network by avoiding topological errors. They most often manifest themselves as short breaks in road segments that spoil an otherwise mostly correct binary mask. An effective discriminator must therefore detect and localize such mistakes so that the generator can fix them.

To this end, we define spatially-aware labels as follows. We consider a pyramid of increasingly zoomed-out versions of the predicted mask, as shown in Fig. 2(e). At level k of the resulting pyramid, we divide the mask into non-overlapping patches of size $H_k \times W_k$ and associate a binary value to each one, depending on the topological correctness within it. The label matrix generated at level k is of size $\frac{H}{H_k} \times \frac{W}{W_k}$. The collection of such label matrices can be regarded as a representation of topological correctness at different scales and locations.

In practice, our input images are of size 256×256 and we have used four levels with $H_k = W_k = \{256, 128, 64, 32\}$. At one extreme of the range, we assign a single label to the whole image and, at the other, we assess the correctness within 32×32 patches. As shown in Fig. 2(e), for a road mask that has topological error, the values in the label matrices are neither all zeros nor all ones. Instead, they encode fine- or coarse-level locations of topological errors in the generators output. This allows the discriminator to effectively use multi-scale information.

Dynamic Label Assignment. There is no way to know *a priori* in which of the patches discussed above the topology is correct. Therefore, unlike in traditional GANs, we cannot predefine the labels we assign to the generator output. Instead, we must do this dynamically for each prediction made by the generator.

For example, the patches outlined in green or red in Fig. 2 are deemed correct or incorrect, respectively. To make this assessment, we compare the probability map produced by the generator to the ground-truth within the patch of interest. Alongside, to match with the labelling strategy, we use a transformed form of $\hat{y}$ to construct the corresponding input to the discriminator. To generate the inputs and labels for the discriminator training we use the following steps:

1. *Differentiable Thresholding.* We binarize the probability map produced by the generator. To preserve differentiability, we use STE [4,34] that thresholds during the forward pass while behaving as the identity function during the backward pass. We set the threshold to be 0.5 in our experiments.
2. *Multiplication by the dilated ground truth.* The generator can produce false negatives—road pixels that are classified as background as highlighted in

Fig. 2(d)—and false positives—background pixels that are classified as road pixels as highlighted in Fig. 2(c). The false negatives are those that cause disconnections and break the connectivity of the network. Furthermore, it is not unusual for some real roads to be missing from the ground-truth. We have therefore found empirically that ignoring the false positives and focusing on the false negatives to be beneficial. Before feeding the thresholded prediction to the input of the discriminator, we therefore multiply it with a dilated version of the ground truth mask. The dilation accounts for the fact that the centerline locations are not always precise in the ground truth. We set the dilation factor to 3. Let us denote the resulting mask as $T_0(\hat{\mathbf{y}})$. Two examples are shown in Fig. 2(d).

3. *Concatenating with Input Image.* This final step is used to generate the complete discriminator input. The ground-truth road masks may contain genuine interruptions, for example because of road dead ends near to other road sections as in the top-left corner of second row of Fig. 2(d). To help the discriminator distinguish these from unwarranted ones (i.e., erroneous interruptions of the predicted road network as in the red box in Fig. 2(d)), we also feed it the input image $\mathbf{x}$ so that it can examine the context in which these interruptions occur. To this end, we concatenate $\mathbf{x}$ with the road mask before feeding it to the discriminator. We will refer to the discriminator formed by concatenating $T_0(\hat{\mathbf{y}})$ with $\mathbf{x}$ as $T(\hat{\mathbf{y}})$.

4. *Assigning Label Values.* To generate the label values, we compare the ground truth skeleton with the prediction $T_0(\hat{\mathbf{y}})$ and count the false negatives (number of pixels in the skeleton that are not covered in $T_0(\hat{\mathbf{y}})$). We use the count of false negatives to identify the cell that is likely to contain topological errors. We assign zero to these patches and a 1 otherwise.

The operations corresponding to STE, dilation, and concatenation are represented by the pink, green, and blue boxes in Fig. 1. Detailed illustration on the proposed label generation scheme can be found in Fig. 2.

Architecture. To implement D, we use a fully convolutional network similar to PatchGAN [14], but with four outputs, each having a different resolution. As a result, D outputs a pyramid of probability maps having the same structure as the spatially aware labels. Figure 3 depicts its architecture. It comprises eight stages that downsample to $\frac{1}{256}^{th}$ of the input resolution. Each stage is made of a convolutional layer with stride factor 2 followed by a residual block. The first convolution layer has 64 feature channels. The channel number doubles after every strided convolution until stage 4; the number of channels are kept at 512 afterward. The final residual block is followed by a single convolutional layer to output the prediction at the last stage. Features from the output of residual blocks at stages 5–7 are passed through a single convolutional layer to generate predictions at respective resolutions.

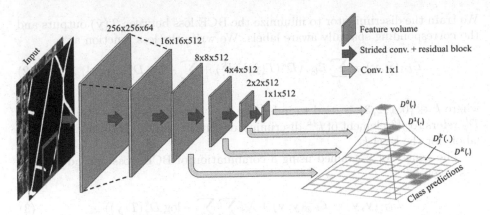

Fig. 3. Discriminator. The discriminator is a single fully convolutional network that downsample the input to the desired scales and locations. Each downsampling stage is composed of a convolutional layer with stride factor 2, followed by a residual block. The first convolution layer is set to have 64 feature channels. The channel number doubles after every strided convolution until it reaches 512. The class prediction are produced from the latest stages using a 1×1 convolutional layer.

3.3 Generator Network: G

One could use any standard segmentation network as the generator G. To demonstrate this, we experimented with two different ones, a standard *UNet* [25] and a recurrent version [30] of it, which we will refer to as *DRU*.

UNet is a fully convolutional encoder-decoder network with skip connections that serves as the backbone of several recent road extraction algorithms [21, 22]. We follow the standard *UNet* design with four levels. Each one comprises two convolutional operations followed by max pooling. We set the first convolutional unit to have 64 feature channels. *DRU* [30] is a *UNet* with Dual-gated Recurrent Units. It performs recursion on the input-output and in multiple internal states of the network to improve the overall performance with only minimal increments in model size. In the original paper, a lightweight *UNet* architecture with 32 channels was used. Here we use 64 channels as in the standard *UNet*.

By combining our proposed discriminator with the two generator networks *UNet* and *DRU*, we build two different methods and dub them as *UNet-TopoAL* and *DRU-TopoAL* respectively.

3.4 Training

To train the generator G and discriminator D, we follow the usual GAN approach, which is to alternatively minimize the loss functions with respect to the generator and the discriminator. The difference, however, resides in the discriminator that takes as input $T(\hat{\mathbf{y}})$, the generator's output transformed as described before, and $c[\mathbf{y}, \mathbf{x}]$ formed by concatenating the ground truth mask $\mathbf{y}$ with $\mathbf{x}$.

We train the discriminator to minimize the BCE loss between $T(\hat{\mathbf{y}})$ outputs and the corresponding spatially aware labels. We write the loss function as

$$\mathcal{L}_{D1}(\hat{\mathbf{y}}, \mathbf{y}) = \sum_k \mathcal{L}_{bce}(D^k(T(\hat{\mathbf{y}})), \mathbf{d}^k) + \sum_j -\log D_j^k(c[\mathbf{y}, \mathbf{x}]) \,, \qquad (2)$$

where $k \in \{0, 1, 2, 3\}$ is used to index the four outputs from the discriminator. D_j^k refers to j^{th} element of kth discriminator output, and $\mathbf{d}^k$ is the spatial-aware labels for the level k.

The generator is trained using a combination of BCE Loss and adversarial loss given by

$$\mathcal{L}_{G1}(\hat{\mathbf{y}}, \mathbf{y}) = \mathcal{L}_{bce}(\hat{\mathbf{y}}, \mathbf{y}) + \lambda_A \sum_k \sum_j -\log D_j^k(T(\hat{\mathbf{y}})) \,, \qquad (3)$$

where λ_A is a scalar weight that controls the influence of adversarial loss. In our experiments we set λ_A to be 0.005, an empirically found optimal value.

Note that if we use a single discriminator output at level k = 0 in Eq. 2, predefined label value of 0 for the generator output, that is, $d^0 = 0$, and $(\hat{\mathbf{y}}, \mathbf{y})$ as the two inputs to the discriminator network, this reduces to a standard GAN. We will use this as a baseline that we will refer to as *VanillaGAN*.

4   Experiments

We now describe the dataset we have tested our approach on, the performance measures we used to assess the quality of the reconstructions, and baselines we used for comparison purposes. We then show that our approach can be used to enhance the performance of two of them and report our performance against that of the others. Additional experimental results including performance comparison on the DeepGlobe Dataset [10] and the ablation studies revealing the importance of each component of our approach are provided in the supplementary material.

4.1   Datasets, Metrics, and Baselines

Dataset. We perform our experiments on the RoadTracer dataset [2], which is one of the most recently published, largest, and most challenging road network dataset. It contains high-resolution satellite images covering the urban areas of forty cities in six different countries. The labels are generated using Open-StreetMap in the form of graphs. It covers areas featuring highways, urban roads, and rural paths, which results in extreme appearance variations. The roads are often occluded by trees, buildings, and shadows, making it difficult for segmentation approaches to preserve topology. Finally, the set of 25 training cities and 15 testing cities are totally disjoint, which makes generalization more difficult than if the training and testing images were from the same city.

Metrics. Many metrics have been developed to compare the estimated road networks to that of the ground truth. These metrics can be broadly classified into two categories, pixel-based and topology-based. We use both kinds for the sake of completeness.

- **Correctness/Completeness/Quality** (*CCQ*). This is a pixel-based metrics intended to measure the similarity between a skeletonized prediction and the corresponding annotation. In segmentation tasks, predictions are often evaluated using precision $= \frac{|TP|}{|PP|}$, recall $= \frac{|TP|}{|AP|}$, and intersection-over-union $= \frac{TP}{PP \cup AP}$, where PP is the set of foreground pixels in the prediction, AP is the set of foreground pixels in the ground truth, and TP $= $ PP $\cap$ AP. To account for the shift between predictions and the ground truth, precision, recall, and intersection-over-union have been relaxed [32]. The resulting quantities are named correctness, completeness, and quality respectively. To assess the performance using a single metric we report the values of quality (qual.). In our experiments, we set the allowable pixel shift to 2 pixels.
- **Too Long/Too Short** (*TLTS*). *TLTS* [31] compares the lengths of the shortest paths between randomly sampled ground-truth nodes matched to the prediction. If the length of the path in the predicted graph is within 5% of that of the path in the ground-truth the path is declared to be correct. We use the percentage of correct paths, denoted as *TLTS*-corr, to assess the prediction quality. We set the threshold defining if nodes from the ground-truth are matched to the prediction to 25.
- **Average Path Length Similarity** (*APLS*). *APLS* [11] aggregates the differences in optimal path lengths between nodes in the ground truth and predicted graphs. The Average Path Length Similarity is computed as

$$1 - \frac{1}{N} \sum \min \left\{ 1, \frac{L(a,b) - L(\hat{a}, \hat{b})}{L(a,b)} \right\} \qquad (4)$$

where a and b are nodes in the ground truth graph, $\hat{a}$ and $\hat{b}$ are the corresponding nodes in the predicted graph, N is the number of nodes in ground truth, and L denotes the length of the shortest path connecting them. To penalize false positives, the same procedure is repeated by swapping ground-truth and prediction. The final score is the harmonic mean of the two.
- **Junction** (*JUNCT*). *JUNCT* [2] compares the degree of corresponding nodes with at least three incident edges, called junctions. The correspondences are established greedily by matching closest nodes. For each ground-truth junction v that is matched to a predicted junction u, the per-junction recall $f_{u,correct}$ is computed by taking into account the fraction of edges incident on v that are also captured around u. The same operation is performed to compute the per-junction 1-precision $f_{v,error}$ which is the fraction of edges incident on u that do not appear around v. For this metric we report the f1-score compute using $f_{u,correct}$ as recall and $1 - f_{v,error}$ as precision. We used the implementation provided in [2] with default parameters.

- **Holes and Marbles** (*H&M*). This metric first extracts small subgraphs from the ground-truth and match them to the prediction. Then, compares sets of locations in the two subgraphs accessible by traveling a predefined distance away from a randomly sampled point. Virtual control points, namely holes, are dropped at regular intervals along the paths in the ground truth graph. The same process is repeated in the predicted graph, these control points are called marbles. A hole is said to be matched if it lies sufficiently close to one of the marbles. The process is repeated for many subgraphs and the total count of matched and unmatched points are then used to compute precision and recall. To asses the prediction quality using a single value, we report the f1-score as in [5]. We set the threshold defining if nodes from the ground-truth are matched to the prediction to 25. We extracted subgraph of radius 300 and sampled 1000 of them for each sample.

Baselines and Variants. We use the following approaches that are briefly described in Sect. 2 as baselines.

- *UNet* [25]: Fully-convolutional network with skip connections.
- *UNet-VGG* [22]: Fully-convolutional network with skip connections and topology-aware loss function.
- *DRU* [30]: Fully-convolutional network with skip connections and recursion.
- *Seg-Path* [21]: Two-branch network that jointly learns to segment linear structures and to classify candidate connections.
- *MultiBranch* [3]: Recursive architecture jointly trained for road segmentation and orientation estimation.
- *RCNN-UNet* [33]: Fully convolutional network with recursive convolutional layers.
- *DeepRoadMapper* [18]: A fully convolutional network based segmentation followed by heuristics based post-processing to generate the graph.
- *Roadtracer* [2]: Graph constructed iteratively with new node locations being selected by a convolutional network.

We compare these baselines against three variants of our approach introduced in Sects. 3.3 and 3.4.

- *DRU-TopoAL*: We use the network of *DRU* [30] as our generator.
- *UNet-TopoAL*: We use the network of *UNet* [25] as our generator.
- *UNet-VanillaGAN*: We use the network of *UNet* [25] as our generator and replace our sophisticated discriminator by a simple one that returns a simple binary flag for each input mask.

4.2   Implementation Details

To train our *TopoAL* networks we rendered the RoadTracer ground-truth graphs to half resolution to generate pixel-wise annotations. We have experimented with different input sizes and observed that half-resolution produced the best

Table 1. Quantitative comparison between baselines segmentation networks, our improved versions, and *UNet-VanillaGAN*. Our *TopoAL* approach improves the baselines on all metrics. On the other hand, *UNet-VanillaGAN* performance is only comparable to that of the baseline network *UNet*.

Method		Pixel-based	Topology-aware			
		CCQ	TLTS	APLS	JUNCT	*H&M*
		qual.	corr.		f1	f1
RoadTracer	*UNet* [25]	0.632	0.323	0.619	0.792	0.737
	UNet-VanillaGAN	0.636	0.328	0.607	0.776	0.748
	UNet-TopoAL (Ours)	**0.658**	**0.388**	**0.666**	**0.808**	**0.767**
	DRU [30]	0.656	0.437	0.697	0.821	0.768
	DRU-TopoAL (Ours)	**0.657**	**0.480**	**0.725**	**0.837**	**0.787**

results on the Roadtracer dataset when the network is trained using binary cross-entropy loss (BCE) alone. We take this to mean that the higher resolution details of this dataset are not key to producing globally correct topologies, and the half-resolution provides the optimal trade-off between the required details in the input image and the effective context available to the network. As input, we used 256×256 patches randomly cropped from the training images. To improve the generalization of learned network, we employed data augmentations in the form of random horizontal flip, vertical flip, scaling and rotation. To train both the generator and discriminator, we used the Adam optimizer [15] with a 10^{-4} learning rate and a batch size of 4. All the models are implemented in Pytorch [24]. To construct the dynamic labels, a 32×32 32x32 patch is declared topologically incorrect if it contains an erroneous road interruption of at least 4 pixels long. Larger patches are declared incorrect if they contain an incorrect 32×32 subpatch. We selected this threshold based on visual inspection to separate road interruptions from misalignment of the predicted and annotated roads.

We trained *UNet*, *UNet-VGG* and *DRU* using the same settings as *TopoAL*, as described in Sect. 3.3. For *DRU* and *DRU-TopoAL*, we set the number of recursions to 3 and use the sum of losses corresponding to outputs from all the recursions. For *DRU-TopoAL*, outputs from all the recursions is used for the discriminator training, and the total adversarial loss is computed as the sum of losses corresponding to all the recursions. We retrained the *MultiBranch* network on the RoadTracer dataset using the code provided by the authors with default settings. For *DeepRoadMapper*, we use the results shared by the authors of [2]. For all other methods we use the predicted road networks made publicly available by the authors.

4.3 Boosting the Performance of Existing Architectures

In Table 1, we compare *UNet* and *DRU* against *UNet-TopoAL* and *DRU-TopoAL*, which use *UNet* and *DRU* as their generators. In both cases, we can see

Table 2. Quantitative comparison between state-of-the-art road network reconstruction algorithms and our proposition. Our proposition *DRU-TopoAL* produces the best results in four out of five metrics while it comes second to *Seg-Path* in *TLTS*.

Method		Pixel-based	Topology-aware			
		CCQ qual.	TLTS corr.	APLS	JUNCT f1	H&M f1
RoadTracer	*DeepRoadMapper* [18]	0.435	0.069	0.247	0.514	0.469
	Roadtracer [2]	0.477	0.420	0.591	0.812	0.714
	RCNN-UNet [33]	0.628	0.201	0.474	0.790	0.701
	MultiBranch [3]	**0.659**	0.439	0.682	0.798	0.765
	Seg-Path [21]	0.535	**0.489**	0.679	0.754	0.688
	UNet-VGG [22]	0.636	0.328	0.607	0.776	0.748
	UNet [25]	0.632	0.323	0.619	0.792	0.737
	DRU [30]	0.656	0.437	0.697	0.821	0.768
	UNet-TopoAL (Ours)	**0.659**	0.388	0.666	0.808	0.767
	DRU-TopoAL (Ours)	0.657	0.480	**0.725**	**0.837**	**0.787**

our scheme consistently boosts their performance, especially the *TLTS*, *APLS*, *JUNCT* and *H&M* metrics that are designed to assess topological correctness. The first row of Fig. 4 provides corresponding qualitative results. We also report the performance of *UNet-VanillaGAN*, which implements a standard GAN, in Table 1. It can be noted that it is not better than its generator *UNet*. Therefore, using a GAN by itself does not bring the same improvements as *TopoAL*. As is evident from the first row of Fig. 4, adding our topology loss not only refine the predictions but also improves the topological correctness. On the other hand, predictions from *UNet-VanillaGAN* does not respect the topological correctness.

4.4   Comparison Against the State-of-the-Art

We now turn to compare our results to those of all the baselines discussed above and report the results in Table 2. We provide corresponding qualitative results in the last three rows of Fig. 4.

DRU-TopoAL does best on three of the four topology-aware metrics and is second on the fourth, without any of the post-processing that *Seg-Path* perform. For the pixel-based measures, *DRU-TopoAL* performs honorably but does not truly dominate the other algorithms. This is not surprising because *TopoAL* targets small interruptions in road segment. They are few in numbers but critical in terms of topological correctness. Since CCQ only performs pixel-wise comparisons, it is relatively insensitive to the kind of errors we detect and fix.

As indicated by the example in the second row of Fig. 4, adding VGG loss (UNet-VGG) helps to suppress spurious prediction errors but does not lead to significant improvement in the prediction of true roads. From the third row of

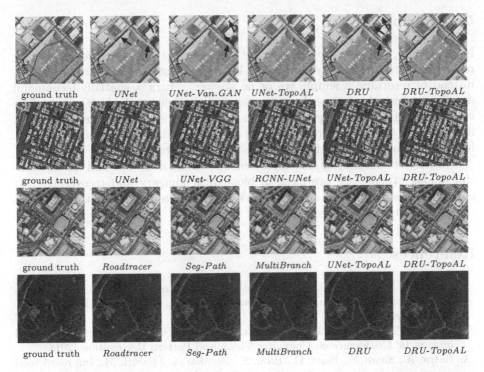

Fig. 4. Road extraction. Ground truth and predicted roads are marked in red. Our *TopoAL* approach improves the topological correctness over their respective generators when used by themselves (1st row), performs better than the segmentation baselines (2nd row) and connectivity-based methods (3rd row), and generalizes well to challenging cases (4th row). (Color figure online)

Fig. 4 one can observe that, despite the multi-tasking strategy, *MultiBranch* fails to predict the roads at occluded regions (highlighted in blue), a limitation that was reported in [3]. On the other hand, *UNet-TopoAL* and *DRU-TopoAL* depicts progressive improvements towards filling up such gaps. In comparison with the proposed methods, *Roadtracer* and *Seg-Path* that use trained networks to enforce connectivity explicitly, either fails to predict some road segments completely (highlighted in blue) or result in big false positives (highlighted in green) that maintains connectivity to the other parts of the predicted network. The last row of Fig. 4 is an exceptional case wherein trees mostly occlude true roads.[1] As is evident, among the segmentation methods, *DRU-TopoAL* shows the most promising result against occlusion effects, while maintaining favorable performance against *Seg-Path*.

---

[1] Ground truth mask does not show most of the actual roads because of the omission noise.

5   Conclusion

In this paper, we have proposed an AL strategy that is tailored for extracting networks of curvilinear structures. Its key ingredient is a discriminator that, instead of returning a simple yes or no answer, return a spatially-meaningful descriptor of which parts of the images are well modeled and which are not. The corresponding decisions are made at run-time as opposed to be taken *a priori* as in traditional GANs. As a result, we can outperform the state-of-the-art without having to resort to particularly complicated architectures.

Networks of curvilinear structures—blood vessels, dendrites and axons, bronchi, among others—are prevalent in biomedical imagery and recovering their connectivity is also crucial. In future work, we will therefore extend this approach to delineation in 3D image stacks.

References

1. Barzohar, M., Cooper, D.B.: Automatic finding of main roads in aerial images by using geometric-stochastic models and estimation. IEEE Trans. Pattern Anal. Mach. Intell. **18**(7), 707–721 (1996)
2. Bastani, F., et al.: RoadTracer: automatic extraction of road networks from aerial images. In: Conference on Computer Vision and Pattern Recognition (2018)
3. Batra, A., Singh, S., Pang, G., Basu, S., Jawahar, C., Paluri, M.: Improved road connectivity by joint learning of orientation and segmentation. In: Conference on Computer Vision and Pattern Recognition, June 2019
4. Bengio, Y., Léonard, N., Courville, A.: Estimating or propagating gradients through stochastic neurons for conditional computation. In: arXiv Preprint (2013)
5. Biagioni, J., Eriksson, J.: Inferring road maps from global positioning system traces: survey and comparative evaluation. Transp. Res. Rec. J. Transp. Res. Board **2291**, 61–71 (2012)
6. Chai, D., Forstner, W., Lafarge, F.: Recovering line-networks in images by junction-point processes. In: Conference on Computer Vision and Pattern Recognition (2013)
7. Chen, Y., Li, W., Van Gool, L.: ROAD: Reality oriented adaptation for semantic segmentation of urban scenes. In: Conference on Computer Vision and Pattern Recognition. pp. 7892–7901 (2018)
8. Cheng, G., Wang, Y., Xu, S., Wang, H., Xiang, S., Pan, C.: Automatic road detection and centerline extraction via cascaded end-to-end convolutional neural network. IEEE Trans. Geosci. Remote Sens. **55**(6), 3322–3337 (2017)
9. Chu, H., et al.: Neural turtle graphics for modeling city road layouts. In: International Conference on Computer Vision (2019)
10. Demir, I., et al.: DeepGlobe 2018: a challenge to parse the earth through satellite images. In: Conference on Computer Vision and Pattern Recognition, June 2018
11. Etten, A.V., Lindenbaum, D., Bacastow, T.: SpaceNet: a remote sensing dataset and challenge series. CoRR abs/1807.01232 (2018). http://arxiv.org/abs/1807.01232
12. Goodfellow, I., et al.: Generative adversarial nets. In: Advances in Neural Information Processing Systems (2014)

13. Iizuka, S., Simo-Serra, E., Ishikawa, H.: Globally and locally consistent image completion. ACM Trans. Graph. **36**(4), 1–14 (2017)
14. Isola, P., Zhu, J., Zhou, T., Efros, A.A.: Image-to-image translation with conditional adversarial networks. In: Conference on Computer Vision and Pattern Recognition (2017)
15. Kingma, D.P., Ba, J.: Adam: a method for stochastic optimization. In: International Conference on Learning Representations (2015)
16. Laptev, I., Mayer, H., Lindeberg, T., Eckstein, W., Steger, C., Baumgartner, A.: Automatic extraction of roads from aerial images based on scale space and snakes. Mach. Vis. Appl. **12**, 23–31 (2000). https://doi.org/10.1007/s001380050121
17. Li, Z., Wegner, J., Lucchi, A.: Topological map extraction from overhead images. In: International Conference on Computer Vision (2019)
18. Máttyus, G., Luo, W., Urtasun, R.: DeepRoadMapper: extracting road topology from aerial images. In: International Conference on Computer Vision, pp. 3458–3466 (2017)
19. Mnih, V., Hinton, G.: Learning to label aerial images from noisy data. In: International Conference on Machine Learning (2012)
20. Mnih, V., Hinton, G.E.: Learning to detect roads in high-resolution aerial images. In: Daniilidis, K., Maragos, P., Paragios, N. (eds.) ECCV 2010. LNCS, vol. 6316, pp. 210–223. Springer, Heidelberg (2010). https://doi.org/10.1007/978-3-642-15567-3_16
21. Mosińska, A., Kozinski, M., Fua, P.: Joint segmentation and path classification of curvilinear structures. IEEE Trans. Pattern Anal. Mach. Intell. **42**(6), 1515–1521 (2019)
22. Mosińska, A., Marquez-Neila, P., Kozinski, M., Fua, P.: Beyond the pixel-wise loss for topology-aware delineation. In: Conference on Computer Vision and Pattern Recognition, pp. 3136–3145 (2018)
23. Máttyus, G., Urtasun, R.: Matching adversarial networks. In: Conference on Computer Vision and Pattern Recognition (2018)
24. Paszke, A., et al.: Automatic differentiation in PyTorch. In: NIPS-W (2017)
25. Ronneberger, O., Fischer, P., Brox, T.: U-Net: convolutional networks for biomedical image segmentation. In: Navab, N., Hornegger, J., Wells, W.M., Frangi, A.F. (eds.) MICCAI 2015. LNCS, vol. 9351, pp. 234–241. Springer, Cham (2015). https://doi.org/10.1007/978-3-319-24574-4_28
26. Stoica, R., Descombes, X., Zerubia, J.: A Gibbs point process for road extraction from remotely sensed images. Int. J. Comput. Vision **57**(2), 121–136 (2004). https://doi.org/10.1023/B:VISI.0000013086.45688.5d
27. Turetken, E., Benmansour, F., Andres, B., Pfister, H., Fua, P.: Reconstructing loopy curvilinear structures using integer programming. In: Conference on Computer Vision and Pattern Recognition, June 2013
28. Ventura, C., Pont-Tuset, J., Caelles, S., Maninis, K., Gool, L.V.: Iterative deep learning for network topology extraction. In: British Machine Vision Conference (2018)
29. Wang, T.C., Liu, M.Y., Zhu, J.Y., Tao, A., Kautz, J., Catanzaro, B.: High-resolution image synthesis and semantic manipulation with conditional GANs. In: Conference on Computer Vision and Pattern Recognition (2018)
30. Wang, W., Yu, K., Hugonot, J., Fua, P., Salzmann, M.: Recurrent U-Net for resource-constrained segmentation. In: International Conference on Computer Vision (2019)

31. Wegner, J., Montoya-Zegarra, J., Schindler, K.: A higher-order CRF model for road network extraction. In: Conference on Computer Vision and Pattern Recognition, pp. 1698–1705 (2013)
32. Wiedemann, C., Heipke, C., Mayer, H., Jamet, O.: Empirical evaluation of automatically extracted road axes. In: Empirical Evaluation Techniques in Computer Vision, pp. 172–187 (1998)
33. Yang, X., Li, X., Ye, Y., Lau, R.Y.K., Zhang, X., Huang, X.: Road detection and centerline extraction via deep recurrent convolutional neural network U-Net. IEEE Trans. Geosci. Remote Sens. **57**(9), 7209–7220 (2019)
34. Yin, P., Lyu, J., Zhang, S., Osher, S.J., Qi, Y., Xin, J.: Understanding straight-through estimator in training activation quantized neural nets. In: International Conference on Learning Representations (2019)
35. Zhou, L., Zhang, C., Wu, M.: D-LinkNet: LinkNet with pretrained encoder and dilated convolution for high resolution satellite imagery road extraction. In: CVPR Workshops (2018)

Channel Selection Using Gumbel Softmax

Charles Herrmann[1](✉)(iD), Richard Strong Bowen[1](iD), and Ramin Zabih[1,2](iD)

[1] Cornell Tech, New York, USA
{cih,rsb,rdz}@cs.cornell.edu
[2] Google Research, New York, USA

Abstract. Important applications such as mobile computing require reducing the computational costs of neural network inference. Ideally, applications would specify their preferred tradeoff between accuracy and speed, and the network would optimize this end-to-end, using classification error to remove parts of the network. Increasing speed can be done either during training – e.g., pruning filters – or during inference – e.g., conditionally executing a subset of the layers. We propose a single end-to-end framework that can improve inference efficiency in both settings. We use a combination of batch activation loss and classification loss, and Gumbel reparameterization to learn network structure. We train end-to-end, and the same technique supports pruning as well as conditional computation. We obtain promising experimental results for ImageNet classification with ResNet (45–52% less computation).

Keywords: Network sparsity · Channel pruning · Dynamic computation · Gumbel softmax

1 Pruning and Conditional Computation

Despite their great success [14,24,42], convolutional networks remain too computationally expensive for many important tasks. Modern architectures often struggle to run on standard desktop hardware, let alone mobile devices. These computational requirements pose a serious obstacle in settings constrained by latency, power, memory and/or compute; key examples include smartphones, robotics and autonomous driving. Considerable work has been put into exploring the tradeoffs between computation and performance. Popular approaches include expert-designed efficient networks like MobileNetV2 [39], and reinforcement learning to search for more efficient architectures [16,54].

We focus on two longstanding lines of research: pruning [26,37] and conditional computation [1,49]. Pruning, in its earliest [26,37] and modern [11,21] forms, attempts to remove the least useful parts of the network. The goal is to leave a smaller network with comparable or better accuracy. A network with

---

Electronic supplementary material The online version of this chapter (https://doi.org/10.1007/978-3-030-58583-9_15) contains supplementary material, which is available to authorized users.

A. Vedaldi et al. (Eds.): ECCV 2020, LNCS 12372, pp. 241–257, 2020.
https://doi.org/10.1007/978-3-030-58583-9_15

conditional computation runs lightweight tests that can choose to bypass larger blocks of computation that are not useful for the given input. Aside from benefits in inference-time efficiency [1], skipping computations can improve training time or test performance [7,20,49], and can provide insight into network behavior [20,49].

Our goal is to improve a neural network by trading off classification error and computation. End-to-end training is a key advantage of neural nets [25], but poses a technical challenge. Both pruning and conditional computation are categorical decisions which are not easy to optimize by gradient descent. However, Gumbel-Softmax (GS) [2,10,22,33] gives a way to address this challenge.

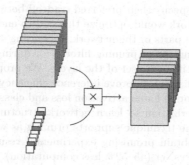

Fig. 1. The clean set of filter outputs (top left) are multiplied channel-wise by a vector of binary random variables (bottom left), which is learned during training. For conditional computation, the gating vector's entries depend upon the input at this layer, while for pruning they do not.

We focus on the ResNet [14] architecture, as it is the mainstay of current deep learning techniques for image classification. The general architecture of a prunable channel in a network is shown in Fig. 1. The computation of a channel can potentially be skipped by sampling the gating vector of random variables. The associated probabilities are learned during training. Their distributions can be either depend on the layer's input, in which case we perform conditional computation, or be independent, in which case we perform pruning.

We propose a per-batch activation loss function, which allows the network to flexibly avoid computing certain filters and their resulting channels. This in turn supports useful tradeoffs between accuracy and inference speed. Per-batch activation loss, in combination with the Gumbel straight-through trick [22], encourages the gating vector's probabilities to *polarize*, that is, move towards 0 or 1. Polarization has proved to be beneficial [5,44].

We summarize our contributions as follows:

- We explore conditional computation at the channel level and significantly outperform other techniques.
- We investigate the use of Gumbel soft-max for pruning a network at the channel-level in an end-to-end manner. We identify a mathematical property

of the combination of our batch activation loss and Gumbel soft-max that encourages polarization.

- We demonstrate that a single technique can achieve significant results in both areas.

This paper is organized as follows. We begin by introducing notation and reviewing related work. Section 3 introduces and analyses our per-batch activation loss function and inference strategies, and discusses the role of polarization. Experimental results on ImageNet and CIFAR-10 are presented in Sect. 4, for both conditional computation and for pruning. Our best experimental results for pruning reduce computation by 51% on ResNet; our best results for conditional computation, reduce computation on ImageNet by 45–52% on ResNet. Additional experiments and more details are included in the supplemental material.

1.1 Gating Neural Networks

In order to learn a discrete structure such as a network architecture with the continuous method of stochastic gradient descent, we learn a probability distribution over structures, and minimize the expected loss. In this work, we learn whether or not to compute a channel. Let $\mathcal{G}$ be a set of gates indexed by i:

- Z_i, a 0–1 random variable which is 1 with probability p_i.
- g_i, a portion of the network which computes p_i.

When g and thus Z also depend on the input image j we write g_{ij}, p_{ij}, and Z_{ij}. Where g_i depends on the input we use the phrase "data-dependent"; where g_i does not, "data-independent". We use Gumbel Softmax and straight-through training [8,22] to train g_i. To generate the vector of Z_is, we run each g_i and then sample. If $Z_i = 0$, the associated filter is not run, we simply replace the corresponding channel with a block of zeros. We use the straight-through trick: at training time during the forward pass, we use Z_i and during back-propagation, we treat Z_i as p_i. We define the "activation rate" of the batch as $\frac{1}{|\mathcal{G}||\mathcal{B}|} \sum_{0 \leq i \leq |\mathcal{G}|} \sum_{0 \leq j \leq |\mathcal{B}|} Z_{i,j}$ where $\mathcal{B}$ is the batch of inputs the network sees. This captures the fraction of the channels being computed for all gates over a batch. The "activation rate" of a gate i is $\frac{1}{|\mathcal{B}|} \sum_{0 \leq j \leq |\mathcal{B}|} Z_{i,j}$ This captures the fraction of time that the channel i is computed for the given batch.

1.2 Our Loss

The intuition behind our loss is that we want to encourage the activation rate for each batch to approach a target rate hyperparameter t. Smaller values of t will correspond to less computation. Our batch activation loss is defined as

$$\mathcal{L}_B = \left(t - \frac{1}{|\mathcal{B}||\mathcal{G}|} \sum_{0 \leq i \leq |G|} \sum_{0 \leq j \leq |\mathcal{B}|} Z_{i,j} \right)^2 \tag{1}$$

2   Related Work

Our technique allows us to learn a network with conditional computation (using data-dependent gates), or a smaller, pruned network (using data-independent gates). As such, we describe our relation to both fields, as well as related work on regularization.

2.1   Conditional Computation

Cascaded classifiers [50] shorten computation by identifying easy negatives and have been adapted to deep learning [28,51]. More recently, [19] and [34] both propose a cascading architecture which computes features at multiple scales and allows for dynamic evaluation, where at inference time the user can tradeoff speed for accuracy. Similarly, [48] adds intermediate classifiers and returns a label once the network reaches a specified confidence. [7,9] both use the state of the network to adaptively decrease the number of computational steps during inference. [9] uses an intermediate state sequence and a halting unit to limit the number of blocks that can be executed in an RNN; [7] learns an image dependent stopping condition for each ResNet block that conditionally bypasses the rest of the layers in the block. [40] trains a large number of small networks and then uses gates to select a sparse combination for a given input. [3] selects the most-efficient network for a given input and also uses early-exit.

The most closely related work is AIG [49], which probabilistically gates individual layers during both training and inference, with a data-dependent gating computation. The major difference between AIG and our work is that they *specify* target rates for each gate, whereas we *learn* these values, by giving a target rate for the entire network. The reason for this difference is that AIG focuses on inducing specialization on the network, whereas we focus on improving the run-time of these networks. This focus on specialization is reflected in their loss, which has a target rate t_i for each gate i:

$$\mathcal{L}_G = \frac{1}{|\mathcal{G}|} \sum_{0 \leq i < |\mathcal{G}|} \left(t_i - \frac{1}{|\mathcal{B}|} \sum_{0 \leq j < |\mathcal{B}|} Z_{i,j} \right)^2$$

As reported in their code[1], the target rates for each layer of ResNet-50 are [1, 1, 0.8, 1, t, t, t, 1, t, t, t, t, t, 1, 0.7, 1] for $t \in [0.4, 0.5, 0.6, 0.7]$. This loss function forces specialization since each gate learns to run at its target rate. However, constraining each gate identically is inflexible; for example, consider a dataset with two labels that are equally distributed. If the target rate t is different than 0.5, no layer will easily specialize to one of the labels. This value of t also determines the approximate speed of the final conditional network; networks trained with $t = 0.5$ will be about twice as fast as the baseline network. Yet AIG will push every layer with target rate t to specialize to run on half the data. This rules out many possible network configurations. Ideally, we want to pass in a single global target rate t for the network's speed and then allow the network to learn the optimal distribution of data for its gates. It can then

---

[1] See https://github.com/andreasveit/convnet-aig.

choose to specialize individual gates on the the subsets which benefit the most from additional computation, and not be constrained to the gate's target rate.

In addition, the loss that AIG uses cannot be adapted to network pruning, since it does not allow any the activation rate of any gate to approach 0 or 1 (a gate turning completely on or off). Additionally, modern network pruning is done on a channel-basis, which increases the number of gates from 17 for their layer version of ResNet-50 to thousands of gates for the channels of ResNet-18.

In summary, our loss enables the following improvements vis-a-vis AIG:

- Support for pruning. AIG only supports conditional computation.
- More granular control. AIG specifies per-gate target rates. Specifying per-gate target rates is infeasible at the scale of channels. Instead, our approach learns a rate for each gate, given a soft constraint on the full network.
- Improved performance. Our loss function gives the network more flexibility to configure the activation rates of individual gates. We find experimentally that our network can take advantage of this flexibility to make very different gate assignments (as demonstrated by comparing our Fig. 4 and AIG's Fig. 4). We also produce a much lower FLOPs count with comparable accuracy (as shown in Table 1).

We provide an experimental comparison with AIG in Sect. 4 and an ablation comparison in Sect. 4.4.

2.2 Pruning

Network pruning is another approach to decreasing computation time. Researchers initially attempted to determine the importance of specific weights [13,26] or hidden units [37] and remove those which are unimportant or redundant. Weight-based pruning on CNNs follows the same fundamental approach; [12] prunes weights with small magnitude and [11] incorporates these into a pipeline which also includes quantization and Huffman coding. Numerous techniques prune at the channel level, whether through heuristics [15,18,27] or approximations to importance [17,36,47]. [32] prunes using statistics from the following layer. [53] applies gates to a layer's weight tensors, sorts the weights during train time, and then sends the lowest to zero. Contemporary with our work, [52] uses a Taylor expansion rather than Gumbel to estimate the impact of opening or closing a gate; their technique prunes the network, but has no natural extension to conditional computation. Additionally, [29] suggests that the main benefits of pruning come primarily from the identified architecture.

Recently, several attempts have been made at doing channel-based pruning in an end-to-end manner. [21] adds sparsity regularization and then modifies stochastic Accelerated Proximal Gradient to prune the network end-to-end. Our work differs from [21] by using Gumbel Softmax to integrate the sparsity constraint into an additive loss which can be trained by any optimization technique; we use unmodified stochastic gradient descent with momentum (SGD), the standard technique for training classification.

Similarly, [31] uses the per-batch results of each layer to learn a per-layer "code". These codes are then used to learn a mask for the layer. As training progresses, these masks are driven to be $0 - 1$ by increasing a sigmoid temperature term. The term in their loss function which trades off against computation time is similar to our per-batch activation loss defined in Eq. 1. Their architecture does not use stochasticity or the Gumbel trick; we do not use a similar sigmoid temperature term, because we find that the variance term implicit in the loss is sufficient for pruning. See Sect. 3 for more details. We also provide an experimental comparison in Sect. 4.

2.3 Regularization and Architecture Search

Several regularization techniques, such as Dropout [46] and Stochastic Depth [20], have explored gating different parts of the network to make the final network more robust and less prone to over-fitting. Both techniques try to induce redundancy through probabilistically removing parts of the network during training. Dropout ignores individual units and Stochastic Depth skips entire layers. These techniques can be seen as gating units or layers, respectively, where the gate probabilities are hyperparameters.

In the Bayesian machine learning community, data-independent gating is used as both a form of regularization and for architecture search. Their regularization approaches can be seen as generalizing dropout by learning the dropout rates. [44] performs pruning by learning multipliers for weights, which are encouraged to be $0 - 1$ by a sparsity-inducing loss $w(1 - w)$. [8] proposes per-weight regularization, using the straight-through Gumbel-Softmax trick. [43] uses a form of trainable dropout, learning a per-neuron gating probability. [45] learns sparsity at the weight level using a binary mask. They adopt a complexity loss (L_0 on weights) plus a sparsification loss similar to [44]. [30] extends the straight-through trick with a hard sigmoid to obtain less biased estimates of the gradient. They use a loss equal to the sum of Bernoulli weights, which is similar to a per-batch activation loss. [35] extends the variational dropout in [23] to allow dropout probabilities greater than a half.

Recently, several techniques have used binary gating or masking terms for architecture search. [41] uses Bernoulli random variables to dynamically learn network architecture elements, like connectivity, activation functions, and layers. Similarly, [4] learns a gating structure for convolutional blocks of different sizes, pools, etc. and proposes an end-to-end and reinforcement learning approach.

3   Technical Considerations

A number of issues arise when applying our batch activation loss to speed inference. We begin with a discussion of polarization. We then describe training considerations followed by inference strategies. Finally we discuss our overall loss function and how to integrate gates into the ResNet architecture.

3.1   Gate Polarization

Polarization plays a key role in several respects, and occurs extensively in our experimental results (see 4). In the framework laid out in Sect. 1.1, the p_i are a mechanism for learning discrete structures; in the independent case, a network architecture, and in the dependent case, an adaptive (or per-input) network architecture. The situation where the probabilities polarize corresponds to the continuous mechanism arriving at a discrete answer.

For data-independent gates, polarization corresponds to Z_i collapsing to always be either 0 or 1: in other words, each gate permanently chooses to run or skip its respective channel. In a perfectly polarized data-independent gating configuration some channels are never computed, and the network acts as a deterministic, pruned network. For data-dependent gates, polarization does not necessarily imply that the activation rate of a specific gate, $\frac{1}{|\mathcal{B}|} \sum_{0 \le j \le |\mathcal{B}|} Z_{i,j}$ is 0 or 1; just that $\forall j$, $Z_{i,j}$ is either 0 or 1; under polarization, a gate's activation rate can have any value between 0 and 1. Conceptually, polarization means that for a given input, the decision whether or not to compute the channel is deterministic.

We observe that our batch activation loss has a property that actively encourages polarization in the independent case. Since $\mathcal{L}_B$ is a random variable, SGD and the straight-through trick can be seen as minimizing its expected value [22].

Property 1. In the independent case, the expected batch activation loss is 0 only if each g_i is polarized.

To see why this property holds, note that the expected activation loss is

$$\mathbb{E}[\mathcal{L}_B] = (t - \mathbb{E}\,[Q])^2 + \mathrm{Var}\,(Q) \quad \text{where} \quad Q = \frac{1}{|\mathcal{B}||\mathcal{G}|} \sum_{0 \le j < |\mathcal{B}|} \sum_{0 \le i < |\mathcal{G}|} Z_{i,j}$$

Clearly both terms in the expectation are non-negative and the second term (the variance) is only 0 at polarized values. The first term encourages the overall activation rate of the network to be close to t, but allows the activation rate of individual gates to vary. The second term generally encourages gate polarization.

3.2   Training Considerations

As written in Eq. 1, $\mathcal{L}_B$ is a random variable which we cannot back-propagate through. To solve this problem, we use the Gumbel reparameterization and straight-through training [8,22] to train the network. We fixed the Gumbel softmax temperature at 1.0. We found that the straight-through trick ($Z_i \in \{0,1\}$) typically had better performance than the soft version (e.g., Z_i being the Gumbel softmax of $(p, 1 - p)$). For static pruning, g_j is simply two parameters that do not receive any input from the network and are directly passed to the Gumbel softmax. For dynamic pruning, g_j consists of an average pool across the image dimensions, a 1d convolution, a batch-norm, a ReLu, and then a final 1d convolution.

In image classification, the standard training regime includes global weight decay, which is equivalent to a squared L_2 norm on all weights in the network. We now describe an interaction between this regularization and gate polarization, which motivates a scaling of the weight decay parameter.

Generally, the Gumbel softmax trick reparameterizes the choice of a k-way categorical variable to a learning k (unnormalized) logits. In the specific $k = 2$ case for on-off gates, we learn two logits w_0 and w_1 for each gate. In the independent case, these two logits are themselves network parameters and therefore subject to weight decay. Given w_0 and w_1, the gate's on probability is just the sigmoid of their difference $p = \frac{1}{1+e^{w_0-w_1}}$. The L_2 regularization implicitly adds the following to the loss: $w_0^2 + w_1^2 = \frac{1}{2} \left((w_0 + w_1)^2 + \ln\left(\frac{1-p}{p}\right)^2 \right)$

The left hand term drives the logits towards $w_0 = -w_1$. We note that the logits $(w, -w)$ can produce any probability p. Since we are interested in the effect of weight decay on the learned gate probabilities, we focus primarily on the second term. It has the opposite of a polarizing effect: it reaches its minimum at $p = 0.5$. Since the weight decay loss is summed over all gates, this loss increases directly in proportion to the number of gates. We find that a weight decay parameter of 10^{-4} is suitable for a network of 10 to 20 gates. However, the implicit weight decay loss is a sum over probabilities whereas the variance term (Eq. 1) is an average. Therefore, we adopted a heuristic rule: for gating parameters, we divide the weight decay coefficient by the number of gates. Although the above analysis applies to the independent case, we found the same rule was effective for the dependent case.

3.3   Inference Strategies

Once training has produced a deep network with stochastic gates, it is necessary to decide how to perform inference. The simplest approach is to leave the gates in the network and allow them to be stochastic during inference time. This is the technique that AIG uses. Experimentally, we observe a small variance so this may be sufficient for most use cases. One way to take advantage of the stochasticity is to create an ensemble composed of multiple runs with the same network. Then any kind of ensemble technique can be used to combine the different runs: voting, weighing, boosting, etc. In practice, we observe a bump in accuracy from this ensemble technique, though there is obviously a computational penalty.

However, stochasticity has the awkward consequence that multiple classification runs on the same image can return different results. There are several techniques to remove the stochasticity from the network. The gates can be removed, setting $Z = 1$ at test time. This is natural when viewing these gates as a regularization technique, and is the technique used by Stochastic Depth and Dropout. Alternately, inference can be made deterministic by using a threshold τ instead of sampling. Thresholding with value τ means that a layer will be executed if the learned probability p_i is greater than τ. This also allows the user some degree of dynamic control over the computational cost of inference. If the user passes in a very high τ, then fewer layers will activate and inference will be faster. In our experiments, we set $\tau = \frac{1}{2}$. Note that we observe polarization for a large number of our per-batch experiments (particularly with data-independent gates). For a wide range of τ, thresholding leaves a network that behaves almost identically to a stochastic network; additionally, for a large number of τ the behavior of the thresholded network will be the same.

3.4 Architectural Considerations

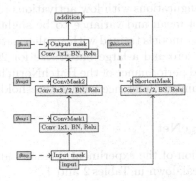

Fig. 2. Gating on ResNet Bottleneck Block

In Fig. 2, we show the blocks for ResNet in its strided form. In Eq. 1, each gate is given equal weight in the activation loss calculation. However for more complex gating schemes, not all gates control the same number of FLOPs (floating point operations per second). To compensate for this, we make a small change to batch activation loss; we change the activation loss to calculate the number of FLOPs using the $Z_{i,j}$. In this case, so $\mathcal{L}_{\mathcal{B}}$ takes the following form: $\mathcal{L}_{\text{FLOPs}} = \left(t - \frac{\#\,\text{FLOPs}}{\text{Max}\,\#\,\text{FLOPs}}\right)^2$. Our algorithm is to minimize the sum of this and and classification loss: $\mathcal{L} = \mathcal{L}_{\mathcal{C}} + \mathcal{L}_{\text{FLOPs}}$ where $L_{\mathcal{C}}$ is the classification loss.

4 Experiments

We implemented our method in PyTorch [38]. Our primary experiments centered around ResNet [14], running our resulting network on ImageNet [6]. Our main finding is that our techniques improve both accuracy and inference speed. We also perform an ablation study in order to better understand their performance.

4.1 Training Parameters

For ResNet, we kept the same training schedule as AIG [49], and follow the standard ResNet training procedure: batch size of 256, momentum of 0.9, and weight decay of 10^{-4}. For the weight decay for gate parameters, we use $\frac{20}{|\mathcal{G}|} \cdot 10^{-4}$.

We train for 100 epochs from a pretrained model of the appropriate architecture with step-wise learning rate starting at 0.1, and decay by 0.1 after every 30 epochs. This is the same training schedule as [49]. We use standard training data-augmentation (random resize crop to 224, random horizontal flip) and standard validation (resize the images to 256 × 256 followed by a 224 × 224 center crop).

In practice, we noticed that many of our ResNet-50 models were not yet at convergence after this training schedule. In order to perform a fair comparison with [49], we did not train our data-dependent networks further. For our data-independent networks, we use the same training schedule as "fine-tune" in [15].

We observe that configurations with low activations rates for gates cause the batch norm estimates of mean and variance to be slightly unstable. Therefore before final evaluation for models trained with smaller batch size, we run training with a learning rate of zero and a large batch size for 200 batches in order to improve the stability and performance of the BatchNorm layers. Unless otherwise specified, we use deterministic inference with a threshold of 0.5.

4.2   Results on ImageNet

A graphical representation of the experimental results are in Fig. 3a, as well as a detailed tabulated breakdown in Tables 2 and 1.

Pruning Results. Results are shown in Fig. 3b and Table 2. We find that we can prune about 43% of the FLOPs with almost no loss of accuracy from the baseline model. In addition, we can achieve a higher Top-1 accuracy, 76.2, with 37% fewer FLOPs than ResNet-50. Compared to the natural competitor, AutoPruner[2] [31], with slightly fewer FLOPs, we have 0.8 higher accuracy. In additional, we perform nearly 0.7% better than the best baseline, Filter Pruning via Geometric Median [15], with a slightly smaller model (43% reduction compared to 42% reduction).

Conditional Computation Results. Conditional computation results are shown in Fig. 3a and Table 1. We find that we can skip 45–52% of the FLOPs from the baseline with comparable or even slightly better accuracy. ResNet-50 achieves a Top-1 accuracy of 76.13 with 4.028 FLOPs ($\times 10^9$). With target rate $t = .5$ we have a small improvement in accuracy (Top-1 accuracy of 76.3) at 2.21 FLOPs, which is 45% fewer. At $t = .4$ we have a small loss in accuracy (76.04) at 1.94 FLOPs, which is 52% fewer. The figures also show comparisons with AIG [49] (which is at the layer, rather than filter, granularity); we achieve a slightly higher accuracy with over 30% fewer FLOPs.

---

[2] Note that the number we use for their FLOPs is different from what they report. They report lower FLOPs for the baseline ResNet-50 architecture (3.8 GFLOPs versus our 4.028). To normalize the comparison, we added 0.2 GFLOPs to their results.

Table 1. Comparison of conditional computation on ImageNet-2012.

Model	Top-1 acc.(%)	Top-5 acc. (%)	FLOPs
ANN [3] at tradeoff 1	74.9	91.8	2.7
ANN [3] at tradeoff 2	74	91.8	2.6
MSDNet [19]-3.1	75.8	–	3.1
MSDNet [19]-3	75	–	3
MSDNet [19]-2.1	74	–	2.1
AIG [49] $t = 0.4$	75.25	92.39	2.76
AIG [49] $t = 0.5$	75.58	92.58	2.91
AIG [49] $t = 0.6$	75.78	92.79	3.08
AIG [49] $t = 0.7$	76.18	92.92	3.26
Ours dep $t = .5$	**76.30**	**93.01**	2.21
Ours dep $t = .4$	75.19	92.50	1.67
Ours dep $t = .3$	76.04	92.79	**1.94**

Table 2. Comparison of pruned ResNet on ImageNet-2012. Acc ↓ is the decrease in accuracy between the accelerated model and the baseline mode; lower is better. Baseline numbers are listed because different researchers' implementations vary; note that our compressed model for ResNet-34 is smaller than that of Geom [15].

Depth	Model	Baseline top-1 acc. (%)	Accelerated top-1 acc. (%)	Top-1 acc ↓	Top-5 acc ↓	FLOPs↓ (%)
18	Geom [15] (only 30%)	70.28	68.34	1.94	1.10	41.8
	Geom [15] (mix 30%)	70.28	68.41	1.87	1.15	41.8
	Ours ind	70.28	**68.88**	**1.40**	**0.97**	**43.9**
34	Geom [15] (only 30%)	73.92	72.54	1.38	**0.49**	41.1
	Geom [15] (mix 30%)	73.92	72.63	1.29	0.54	41.1
	Ours ind	73.92	**72.78**	**1.14**	0.69	**51.1**
50	DDS-41	76.13	75.44	0.69	2.25	13.77
	DDS-32	76.13	74.18	1.95	1.04	30.0
	DDS-26	76.13	71.82	4.31	0.29	42.17
	ThiNet-70	72.88	72.04	0.84	3.08	36.7
	AutoPruner 0.5	76.13	74.76	1.37	0.79	48.36
	Geom (only 30%)	76.15	75.59	0.56	0.24	42.2
	Geom (mix 30%)	76.15	75.50	0.65	0.21	42.2
	Geom (only 40%)	76.15	74.83	1.32	0.55	**53.5**
	Ours ind $t = .5$	76.13	**76.20**	−0.07	−0.2	37.68
	Ours ind $t = .4$	76.13	76.14	−0.01	−0.04	43.39
	Ours ind $t = .3$	76.13	75.56	0.56	0.36	51.3

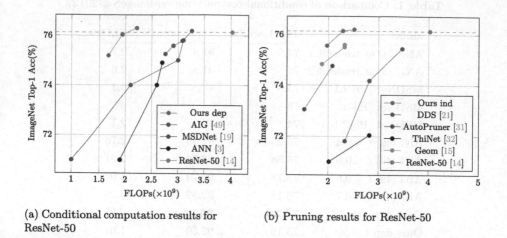

(a) Conditional computation results for ResNet-50

(b) Pruning results for ResNet-50

Fig. 3. Selected experimental results for ImageNet.

Table 3. CIFAR-10 results. The FLOPs is reported as a percentage of the original model and accuracy is reported for the baseline and accelerated models. Note that our ResNet-56 baseline is more accurate than AMC's ResNet-56 baseline.

Variant	FLOP %	Baseline top-1 acc (%)	Accelerated top-1 acc (%)	Top-1 Δ
Conditional computation on ResNet110				
AIG-110 $t = .8$	82%	93.39	94.24	1% ↑
Ours dep $t = .6$	65%	93.39	94.36	1% ↑
Pruning on ResNet-56				
AMC	50%	92.8	91.9	1.0% ↓
Ours ind $t = .5$	50%	93.86	93.31	0.4% ↓

Table 4. Layer vs Filter granularity for gating. FLOPs Δ is calculated from baseline ResNet50 architecture (lower is better).

Model	Baseline FLOPs (10^9)	Accelerated FLOPs (10^9)	FLOPs Δ	Top-1 acc. (%)
AIG-50 $t = 0.6$	4.028	3.08	76.5%	75.78
Ours data-dep. layer $t = 0.5$	4.028	2.72	67.5%	75.78
Ours data-dep. filter $t = 0.4$	4.028	1.94	48.1%	76.07

4.3   Results on CIFAR-10

We report results on CIFAR-10 on several architectures and compare to other techniques; see Fig. 3. Using conditional computation, we obtain higher accuracy on ResNet-110, 94.36, with 65% fewer FLOPs. Compared to AIG, we obtain higher accuracy with 20.7% fewer FLOPs. Using pruning on ResNet-56, we can reduce the number of FLOPs by 50% with only a small decrease in final accuracy, 93.31. Compared with AMC, we have a smaller decrease in accuracy at the same FLOPs reduction. Additional results are included in the supplemental.

4.4   Analysis and Ablation Studies

Filter vs Layers. Our proposed techniques can be used on a layer basis; our per-batch activation loss, in combination with the Gumbel, still provides strong performance. In general, operating at filter granularity rather than layers provides a substantial boost: roughly 20% improvement in FLOPs at the same accuracy. Results are shown in Table 4. For pruning (data-independent gates), moving from layer to filter granularity results in a 28% improvement in FLOPs for a similar accuracy. For conditional computation (data-dependent gates), we can do an even more detailed ablation study since the primary difference between AIG [49] and our result are the batch activation loss and the filter granularity. Overall, batch activation loss provides approximately a 12% boost over AIG and filter granularity provides an additional 27% improvement over the layer-based version of our technique.

Specialization Results. In Fig. 4, we show the gate activations for our layer-based data-dependent model. We observe higher levels of specialization than AIG. While AIG's model specializes primarily on manmade vs non-manmade objects, we specialize on more granular category types. The first layer runs only on cats and dogs, while the second layer runs primarily on fish and lizards. Note, that the specialization shown in AIG is a direct result of the chosen target rate. Their target rate of $t = 0.5$ causes each layer in their model to specialize on one half of the dataset. Since our target rate is for the entire network, each layer in our model is able to specialize on whatever subset it wants. In fact, our specialized layers (cats and dogs; lizards and fish) suggest that working on smaller, more specific subsets can help the model's accuracy.

5   DenseNet Extensions

There are a number of natural extensions to our work that we have explored. Here, we focus on the use of probabilistic gates to provide an early exit, when the network is certain of the answer. We are motivated by MSDNet [19], which investigated any-time classification. We explore early exit on both ResNet and DenseNet; however, consistent with [19], we found that ResNet tends to degrade with intermediate classifiers while DenseNet does not. Following [48] we place

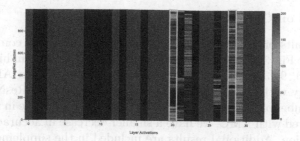

Fig. 4. Gate activations for a layer-based conditional computation model with our batch-activation loss. Two of the layers are highlighted in green. These layers depict a higher level of specialization than those shown in AIG; the first layer runs on cats and dogs, while the second layer runs primarily on fish and lizards.

gates and intermediate classifiers at the end of each dense block. At each gate, the network makes a decision as to whether the instance can be successfully classified. Results are shown in Table 5. These early exit gates make good decisions regarding which instances to classify early. More details are in the supplementals.

Table 5. DenseNet on CIFAR-10 with early exit. For early classifiers, the accuracy on the images that the network selects is higher than the accuracy on all images. This suggests that the gates are learning to recognize "easy" examples.

	Images selected (%)	Top-1 acc. (%) (all images)	Top-1 acc. (%) (selected images)
Block 1	28.71%	81.36	96.37
Block 2	11.56%	93.35	98.53
Final block	59.74%	94.19	92.63

6   Conclusion

We show an end-to-end trainable system for selecting channels using Gumbel soft-max. We propose a single framework that can handle both pruning and conditional computation at the channel level. Our novel batch loss, combined with the Gumbel trick for making categorical gate decisions, shows strong quantitative speedups over the baseline, improving the FLOPS-accuracy Pareto frontier.

Acknowledgments. We thank Andreas Veit and Serge Belongie for their invaluable insights on AIG and several reviewers for helpful comments. This work was generously supported by Google Cloud, without whose help it could not have been completed. It was funded by NSF grant IIS-1447473, by a gift from Sensetime, and by a Google Faculty Research Award.

References

1. Bengio, Y.: Deep learning of representations: looking forward. CoRR abs/1305.0445 (2013). http://arxiv.org/abs/1305.0445
2. Bengio, Y., Léonard, N., Courville, A.C.: Estimating or propagating gradients through stochastic neurons for conditional computation. CoRR abs/1308.3432 (2013). http://arxiv.org/abs/1308.3432
3. Bolukbasi, T., Wang, J., Dekel, O., Saligrama, V.: Adaptive neural networks for efficient inference. In: ICML, pp. 527–536 (2017)
4. Cai, H., Zhu, L., Han, S.: ProxylessNAS: direct neural architecture search on target task and hardware. arXiv:1812.00332 (2018)
5. Courbariaux, M., Bengio, Y., David, J.P.: BinaryConnect: training deep neural networks with binary weights during propagations. In: NIPS, pp. 3123–3131 (2015)
6. Deng, J., Dong, W., Socher, R., Li, L.J., Li, K., Fei-Fei, L.: ImageNet: a large-scale hierarchical image database. In: CVPR, pp. 248–255. IEEE (2009)
7. Figurnov, M., et al.: Spatially adaptive computation time for residual networks. In: CVPR (2017)
8. Gal, Y., Hron, J., Kendall, A.: Concrete dropout. In: Advances in Neural Information Processing Systems, pp. 3581–3590 (2017)
9. Graves, A.: Adaptive computation time for recurrent neural networks. CoRR abs/1603.08983 (2016)
10. Gumbel, E.J.: Statistical theory of extreme values and some practical applications. NBS Appl. Math. Ser. **33** (1954)
11. Han, S., Mao, H., Dally, W.J.: Deep compression: compressing deep neural networks with pruning, trained quantization and Huffman coding. arXiv preprint arXiv:1510.00149 (2015)
12. Han, S., Pool, J., Tran, J., Dally, W.: Learning both weights and connections for efficient neural network. In: Advances in Neural Information Processing Systems, pp. 1135–1143 (2015)
13. Hassibi, B., Stork, D.G.: Second order derivatives for network pruning: optimal brain surgeon. In: Advances in Neural Information Processing Systems, pp. 164–171 (1993)
14. He, K., Zhang, X., Ren, S., Sun, J.: Deep residual learning for image recognition. In: CVPR, pp. 770–778 (2016)
15. He, Y., Liu, P., Wang, Z., Hu, Z., Yang, Y.: Filter pruning via geometric median for deep convolutional neural networks acceleration. In: Proceedings of the IEEE Conference on Computer Vision and Pattern Recognition, pp. 4340–4349 (2019)
16. He, Y., Lin, J., Liu, Z., Wang, H., Li, L.J., Han, S.: AMC: AutoML for model compression and acceleration on mobile devices. In: ECCV, pp. 784–800 (2018)
17. He, Y., Zhang, X., Sun, J.: Channel pruning for accelerating very deep neural networks. In: ICCV (2017)
18. Hu, H., Peng, R., Tai, Y.W., Tang, C.K.: Network trimming: a data-driven neuron pruning approach towards efficient deep architectures. arXiv preprint arXiv:1607.03250 (2016)
19. Huang, G., Chen, D., Li, T., Wu, F., van der Maaten, L., Weinberger, K.Q.: Multi-scale dense convolutional networks for efficient prediction. CoRR, abs/1703.09844 2 (2017)
20. Huang, G., Sun, Y., Liu, Z., Sedra, D., Weinberger, K.Q.: Deep networks with stochastic depth. In: Leibe, B., Matas, J., Sebe, N., Welling, M. (eds.) ECCV 2016. LNCS, vol. 9908, pp. 646–661. Springer, Cham (2016). https://doi.org/10.1007/978-3-319-46493-0_39

21. Huang, Z., Wang, N.: Data-driven sparse structure selection for deep neural networks. In: ECCV (2018)
22. Jang, E., Gu, S., Poole, B.: Categorical reparameterization with gumbel-softmax. In: ICLR (2017). arXiv preprint arXiv:1611.01144
23. Kingma, D.P., Salimans, T., Welling, M.: Variational dropout and the local reparameterization trick. In: Cortes, C., Lawrence, N.D., Lee, D.D., Sugiyama, M., Garnett, R. (eds.) NIPS, pp. 2575–2583. Curran Associates, Inc. (2015). http://papers.nips.cc/paper/5666-variational-dropout-and-the-local-reparameterization-trick.pdf
24. Krizhevsky, A., Sutskever, I., Hinton, G.E.: ImageNet classification with deep convolutional neural networks. In: Pereira, F., Burges, C.J.C., Bottou, L., Weinberger, K.Q. (eds.) Advances in Neural Information Processing Systems 25, pp. 1097–1105. Curran Associates, Inc. (2012). http://papers.nips.cc/paper/4824-imagenet-classification-with-deep-convolutional-neural-networks.pdf
25. LeCun, Y., Bengio, Y., Hinton, G.: Deep learning. Nature **521**, 436–444 (2015). https://doi.org/10.1038/nature14539
26. LeCun, Y., Denker, J.S., Solla, S.A.: Optimal brain damage. In: Advances in Neural Information Processing Systems, pp. 598–605 (1990)
27. Li, H., Kadav, A., Durdanovic, I., Samet, H., Graf, H.P.: Pruning filters for efficient ConvNets. In: ICLR (2017)
28. Li, H., Lin, Z., Shen, X., Brandt, J., Hua, G.: A convolutional neural network cascade for face detection. In: CVPR, pp. 5325–5334 (2015)
29. Liu, Z., Sun, M., Zhou, T., Huang, G., Darrell, T.: Rethinking the value of network pruning. In: ICLR (2019). https://openreview.net/forum?id=rJlnB3C5Ym
30. Louizos, C., Welling, M., Kingma, D.P.: Learning sparse neural networks through L_0 regularization. In: ICLR (2017). arXiv preprint arXiv:1712.01312
31. Luo, J.H., Wu, J.: AutoPruner: an end-to-end trainable filter pruning method for efficient deep model inference. arXiv preprint arXiv:1805.08941 (2018)
32. Luo, J.H., Wu, J., Lin, W.: ThiNet: a filter level pruning method for deep neural network compression. In: ICCV (2017). arXiv preprint arXiv:1707.06342
33. Maddison, C.J., Mnih, A., Teh, Y.W.: The concrete distribution: a continuous relaxation of discrete random variables. arXiv preprint arXiv:1611.00712 (2016)
34. McGill, M., Perona, P.: Deciding how to decide: dynamic routing in artificial neural networks. In: ICML (2017). arXiv preprint arXiv:1703.06217
35. Molchanov, D., Ashukha, A., Vetrov, D.: Variational dropout sparsifies deep neural networks. In: Precup, D., Teh, Y.W. (eds.) ICML, vol. 70, pp. 2498–2507. PMLR, 06–11 August 2017. http://proceedings.mlr.press/v70/molchanov17a.html
36. Molchanov, P., Tyree, S., Karras, T., Aila, T., Kautz, J.: Pruning convolutional neural networks for resource efficient inference. In: ICLR (2016). arXiv preprint arXiv:1611.06440
37. Mozer, M.C., Smolensky, P.: Skeletonization: A technique for trimming the fat from a network via relevance assessment. In: Advances in Neural Information Processing Systems, pp. 107–115 (1989)
38. Paszke, A., et al.: Automatic differentiation in PyTorch. In: NIPS-W (2017)
39. Sandler, M., Howard, A., Zhu, M., Zhmoginov, A., Chen, L.C.: MobileNetV2: inverted residuals and linear bottlenecks. In: CVPR, pp. 4510–4520 (2018)
40. Shazeer, N., et al.: Outrageously large neural networks: the sparsely-gated mixture-of-experts layer. arXiv preprint arXiv:1701.06538 (2017)
41. Shirakawa, S., Iwata, Y., Akimoto, Y.: Dynamic optimization of neural network structures using probabilistic modeling. In: Thirty-Second AAAI Conference on Artificial Intelligence (2018)

42. Simonyan, K., Zisserman, A.: Very deep convolutional networks for large-scale image recognition. CoRR abs/1409.1556 (2014)
43. Srinivas, S., Babu, R.V.: Generalized dropout. arXiv preprint arXiv:1611.06791 (2016)
44. Srinivas, S., Babu, V.: Learning neural network architectures using backpropagation. In: BMVC, pp. 104.1–104.11, September 2016. https://dx.doi.org/10.5244/C.30.104
45. Srinivas, S., Subramanya, A., Babu, R.V.: Training sparse neural networks. In: CVPR Workshops, July 2017
46. Srivastava, N., Hinton, G., Krizhevsky, A., Sutskever, I., Salakhutdinov, R.: Dropout: a simple way to prevent neural networks from overfitting. J. Mach. Learn. Res. $\mathbf{15}(1)$, 1929–1958 (2014)
47. Suau, X., Zappella, L., Palakkode, V., Apostoloff, N.: Principal filter analysis for guided network compression. arXiv preprint arXiv:1807.10585 (2018)
48. Teerapittayanon, S., McDanel, B., Kung, H.: BranchyNet: fast inference via early exiting from deep neural networks. In: ICPR, pp. 2464–2469. IEEE (2016)
49. Veit, A., Belongie, S.: Convolutional networks with adaptive inference graphs. In: ECCV (2017). https://github.com/andreasveit/convnet-aig
50. Viola, P., Jones, M.J.: Robust real-time face detection. Int. J. Comput. Vis. $\mathbf{57}(2)$, 137–154 (2004)
51. Yang, F., Choi, W., Lin, Y.: Exploit all the layers: fast and accurate CNN object detector with scale dependent pooling and cascaded rejection classifiers. In: CVPR, pp. 2129–2137 (2016)
52. You, Z., Yan, K., Ye, J., Ma, M., Wang, P.: Gate decorator: global filter pruning method for accelerating deep convolutional neural networks. In: Advances in Neural Information Processing Systems, pp. 2130–2141 (2019)
53. Zhu, M., Gupta, S.: To prune, or not to prune: exploring the efficacy of pruning for model compression. arXiv preprint arXiv:1710.01878 (2017)
54. Zoph, B., Vasudevan, V., Shlens, J., Le, Q.V.: Learning transferable architectures for scalable image recognition. In: CVPR, pp. 8697–8710 (2018)

Exploiting Temporal Coherence for Self-Supervised One-Shot Video Re-identification

Dripta S. Raychaudhuri$^{(\boxtimes)}$ and Amit K. Roy-Chowdhury

University of California, Riverside, USA
{draychaudhuri,amitrc}@ece.ucr.edu

Abstract. While supervised techniques in re-identification are extremely effective, the need for large amounts of annotations makes them impractical for large camera networks. One-shot re-identification, which uses a singular labeled tracklet for each identity along with a pool of unlabeled tracklets, is a potential candidate towards reducing this labeling effort. Current one-shot re-identification methods function by modeling the inter-relationships amongst the labeled and the unlabeled data, but fail to fully exploit such relationships that exist within the pool of unlabeled data itself. In this paper, we propose a new framework named Temporal Consistency Progressive Learning, which uses temporal coherence as a novel self-supervised auxiliary task in the one-shot learning paradigm to capture such relationships amongst the unlabeled tracklets. Optimizing two new losses, which enforce consistency on a local and global scale, our framework can learn richer and more discriminative representations. Extensive experiments on two challenging video re-identification datasets - MARS and DukeMTMC-VideoReID - demonstrate that our proposed method is able to estimate the true labels of the unlabeled data more accurately by up to 8%, and obtain significantly better re-identification performance compared to the existing state-of-the-art techniques.

Keywords: Video person re-identification · Temporal consistency · One-shot learning · Semi-supervised learning

1 Introduction

Person re-identification (re-ID) aims to solve the challenging problem of matching identities across non-overlapping views in a multi-camera system. The surge of deep neural networks in computer vision [13,25] has been reflected in person re-ID as well, with impressive performance over a wide variety of datasets [5,28]. However, this improved performance has predominantly been achieved through

Electronic supplementary material The online version of this chapter (https://doi.org/10.1007/978-3-030-58583-9_16) contains supplementary material, which is available to authorized users.

© Springer Nature Switzerland AG 2020
A. Vedaldi et al. (Eds.): ECCV 2020, LNCS 12372, pp. 258–274, 2020.
https://doi.org/10.1007/978-3-030-58583-9_16

supervised learning, facilitated by the availability of large amounts of annotated data. However, acquiring identity labels for a large set of unlabeled tracklets is an extremely time-consuming and cumbersome task. Consequently, methods which can ameliorate this annotation problem and work with limited supervision, such as *unsupervised learning* or *semi-supervised learning* techniques, are of primary importance in the context of person re-ID.

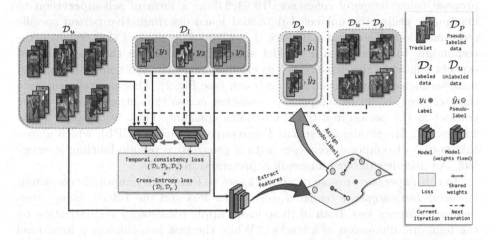

Fig. 1. A schematic illustration of the proposed framework. Our method makes use of both labeled and unlabeled tracklets at every iteration of model training. The first step involves learning the parameters of the deep model by using temporal consistency as self-supervision and, additionally, softmax loss on the minimal set of annotated tracklets. Next, this model is used to predict pseudo-labels on a few confident samples. These two steps alternate, one after the other, until the entire unlabeled set has been incorporated in terms of pseudo-labels.

In this work, we focus on the semi-supervised task in video person re-ID, specifically, the *one-shot* setting, where only one tracklet per identity is labeled. The objective of the learning process is to utilize this small labeled set along with a larger unlabeled set of tracklets to obtain a re-ID model. The key challenge involved with the one-shot task is figuring out the inter-relationships which exist amongst the labeled and unlabeled instances. State-of-the-art one-shot methods try to address this by estimating the labels of the unlabeled tracklets (pseudo-labels) and then utilizing a supervised learning strategy. Some works employ a static sampling strategy [18,32], where pseudo-labels with a confidence score above a pre-defined threshold are selected for supervised learning. More recent works [29,30] make use of a progressive sampling strategy, where a subset of the pseudo-labeled samples are selected with the size of the subset expanding with each iteration. This prevents an influx of noisy pseudo-labels, and thus, averts the situation of confirmation bias [1]. However, in an effort to control the number of noisy pseudo-labels, most of these methods discard a significant portion of the unlabeled set at each learning iteration; thus, the information in the unlabeled set is not maximally utilized for training the model. Due to this inefficient usage of the unlabeled set and the limited number of labeled instances, propagating beliefs directly from the labeled to the unlabeled set is insufficient to fully capture the relationships which exist amongst instances of the unlabeled set.

To resolve this issue of inefficient usage of the unlabeled data, we draw inspiration from the field of self-supervised visual representation learning [12]. We propose using *temporal coherence* [19,21,24] as a form of self-supervision to maximally utilize the unlabeled data and learn discriminative person specific representations. Temporal coherence is motivated by the fact that features corresponding to a person in a tracklet should be focused on the discriminative aspects related to the person, such as clothing and gait, and ignore background nuances such as illumination and occlusion (see Fig. 2). This naturally suggests that features should be temporally consistent across the entire duration of the tracklet as the person in a tracklet remains constant. Thus, we propose a new framework, *Temporally Consistent Progressive Learning* (TCPL), which unifies this notion of temporal coherence with a progressive pseudo-labeling strategy [30]. An overview of our framework is presented in Fig. 1.

In this paper, we propose two novel losses to learn such temporally consistent features: *Intra-sequence temporal consistency loss* and the *Inter-sequence temporal consistency loss*. Both of these losses apply consistency regularization on the temporal dimension of a tracklet. While the first loss employs a local level of consistency by operating on a specific tracklet, the second loss extends it by applying temporal consistency both *within and across* tracklets.

Using such self-supervised losses, our framework can use the unlabeled data at each iteration of learning, allowing maximal information to be extracted out of it. Additionally, by exploiting two levels of consistency, as explained above, TCPL can better model the relationships amongst the unlabeled instances without being limited by the number of labeled instances. Thus, our framework addresses both the drawbacks associated with the current crop of methods and achieves state-of-the-art performance in the one-shot person re-ID task.

Main Contributions. Our main contributions are summarised as follows:

- We introduce a new framework, *Temporally Consistent Progressive Learning*, which unifies self-supervision and pseudo-labeling to maximally utilize the labeled and unlabeled data efficiently for one-shot video person re-ID.
- We introduce two novel self-supervised losses, the *Intra-sequence temporal consistency loss* and the *Inter-sequence temporal consistency loss*, to implement temporal consistency and empirically demonstrate their benefits in learning richer and more discriminative feature representations.
- We demonstrate that this intelligent use of the unlabeled data through self-supervision, unlike previous pseudo-labeling methods, leads to significantly better label estimation and superior results on the one-shot video re-ID task, outperforming the state-of-the art one-shot video re-ID methods on the MARS and DukeMTMC-VideoReID datasets.

2   Related Works

The majority of the literature in person re-ID has focused on *supervised* learning on labeled images/tracklets of persons [4,31,37,38]. While these techniques achieve excellent results on many datasets, they require a substantial amount of annotations. The need to alleviate this excessive need for labeled data has led to research into *unsupervised* [6,16,34,35] and *semi-supervised* [7,29,30] methods. We provide a review of the relevant developments in these fields. In addition, our work draws inspiration from the ideas explored in the domain of *self-supervision*.

Unsupervised Person Re-ID. Recent unsupervised methods [6,16,34,35] mostly use some form of deep clustering. The authors in [15] utilise a camera aware loss by defining nearest neighbors across cameras as being similar. In [16], an agglomerative clustering scheme is introduced, alternating between learning of features and clustering using the learnt features. However, these methods still lag behind supervised methods by quite some distance. Another line of research utilises auxiliary datasets, which are completely labeled, for initializing a re-ID model and then using unsupervised domain adaptation techniques on the unsupervised target dataset.

Semi-supervised and One-Shot Person Re-ID. The unsatisfactory performance of purely unsupervised methods [6,16,34,35] has given rise to semi-supervised and one-shot methods in re-ID. Some of the major ideas utilized in these methods include dictionary learning [17], graph matching [10] and metric learning [2]. More recently, new methods in this setting try to estimate the labels of the unlabeled tracklets (pseudo-labels) with respect to the labeled tracklets and then utilise a supervised learning strategy. The authors of [32] use a dynamic graph matching strategy which iteratively updates the image graph and the label estimation to learn a better feature space with intermediate estimated labels. A stepwise metric learning approach to the problem is proposed in [18]. Both these methods employ a static sampling strategy, where pseudo-labels with a confidence score above a pre-defined threshold are selected at each step - this leads to a lot of noisy labels being incorporated and hinders the learning process due to due to *confirmation bias* [1]. In order to contain the noise, the authors of [29,30] approach the problem from a progressive pseudo-label selection strategy, where the subset of the pseudo-labeled samples selected gradually increase with iterations. While this prevented the influx of noisy pseudo-labels, a significant portion of the unlabeled set is discarded at each step and thus, the unlabeled set is used inefficiently. We address this issue by using self-supervision.

Self-Supervised Learning. Self-supervised learning utilizes pretext tasks, formulated using only unsupervised data. A pretext task is designed in a such a way that solving it requires the model to learn useful visual features. These tasks can involve predicting the angle of rotation applied to an image [9] or predicting a permutation of multiple randomly sampled and permuted patches [22].

Some techniques go beyond solving such auxiliary classification tasks and enforce constraints on the representation space. A prominent example is the exemplar loss from [8]. Our method belongs to this latter category of self-supervision and imposes temporal consistency on tracklet features.

3   Methodology

In this section, we present our framework (TCPL) for solving the task of one-shot video person re-ID. First, we provide a background on the current progressive pseudo-labeling methods and discuss their shortcomings. Thereafter, we turn to our proposed temporal consistency losses and describe their workings, before presenting our integrated framework. Before going into the details of our framework, let us define the notations and problem statement formally.

Problem Statement. Consider that we have a training set of m tracklets, $\mathcal{D} = \{\mathcal{X}_i\}_{i=1}^m$, which are acquired from a camera network. One-shot re-ID assumes that there exists a set $\mathcal{D}_l \subset \mathcal{D}$, which contains a singular labeled tracklet for each identity. Thus, $\mathcal{D}_l = \{(\mathcal{X}_i, y_i)\}_{i=1}^{m_l}$, where $y_i \in \{0,1\}^{m_l}$ such that y_i is 1 only at dimension i and 0 otherwise, and m_l denotes the number of distinct identities. The rest of the tracklets, $\mathcal{D}_u = \mathcal{D} - \mathcal{D}_l = \{\mathcal{X}_i\}_{i=1}^{m_u}$ do not possess annotations. Our goal is to learn a discriminative person re-ID model $f_\theta(\cdot)$ utilizing both $\mathcal{D}_l$ and $\mathcal{D}_u$. During inference, $f_\theta(\cdot)$ is used to embed both the probe $\mathcal{X}^q$ and gallery tracklets $\{\mathcal{X}_i^g\}_{i=1}^{m_g}$ into a common space and then rank all the gallery tracklets by evaluating their degree of correspondence to the probe via some metric. What makes this challenging, even more so than the semi-supervised task, is the fact that $m_l \ll m_u$ and each identity has only a single labeled tracklet.

3.1   Progressive Pseudo-labeling and Its Drawbacks

The progressive pseudo-labeling paradigm is an enhancement over the original pseudo-labeling framework [14] where one imputes approximate classes on unlabeled data by making predictions from a model trained only on labeled data. The learning process involves the following two steps for each step of learning: (1) train the model via supervised learning on the labeled data and the pseudo-labeled data; (2) select a few reliable pseudo-labeled candidates from unlabeled data according to a prediction reliability criterion.

In [30], the authors gradually select larger sets of pseudo-labeled data to be incorporated into the supervised learning process via a dissimilarity criterion. Pseudo labels are assigned to the unlabeled candidates by the identity labels of their nearest labeled neighbors in the embedding space. The distance to the corresponding labeled neighbor is designated as the dissimilarity cost, which is used as the measure of reliability for the pseudo label. However, as a result of the strict selection criterion, this does not use the unlabeled set efficiently - discarding a significant amount of unlabeled data at each step of pseudo labeling.

To improve the efficiency, the authors in [29] propose to set up a memory bank to store the instance features $v_i = f_\theta(\mathcal{X}_i)$ calculated in the previous step. Then the probability of sample $\mathcal{X}_j$ being recognized as the i-th instance can be written as,

$$P(i|\mathcal{X}_j) = \frac{\exp\left(v_i^T f_\theta(\mathcal{X}_j)/\tau\right)}{\sum_k \exp\left(v_k^T f_\theta(\mathcal{X}_j)/\tau\right)} \tag{1}$$

where τ is the temperature parameter controlling the softness of the distribution. Minimizing the negative log-likelihood of $\sum_i P(i|\mathcal{X}_j)$, which they call the *exclusive loss*, pulls each instance $\mathcal{X}_i$ towards its corresponding memorized vector v_i and repels the memorized vectors of other instances. Due to efficiency issues, the memorized feature v_i corresponding to instance $\mathcal{X}_i$ is only updated in the iteration which takes $\mathcal{X}_i$ as input [33]. In other words, the memorized feature v_i is only updated once per epoch. However, the network itself is updated in each iteration, rendering the memory bank scheme inefficient. In addition, the exclusive loss looks at the global data distribution, similar to the softmax loss, forcing embeddings corresponding to different identities to stay apart for encouraging inter-class separability. The local data distribution or the intra-class similarity, is left unaddressed and thus, the improvement over softmax is negligible.

In the next section, we present how temporal coherence can be employed to amend these drawbacks.

3.2   Temporal Coherence as Self-supervision

In the previous section, we discussed the two fundamental problems plaguing the current crop of progressive pseudo-labeling methods: (1) inefficient usage of the unlabeled set, (2) focusing strictly on the global data distribution. To ameliorate these drawbacks, *we propose to use temporal coherence as a form of self-supervision*. Consistency across the frames in a tracklet encourages the model to focus on the *local* distribution of the data and learn features which incorporate the specific attributes of the individual in the tracklet and ignore spurious artifacts such as background and lighting variation. This also provides a straightforward approach towards utilizing the entire unlabeled set, irrespective of whether some specific unlabeled instance is assigned a confident pseudo-label. In the following sections, we present two novel losses: *Intra-sequence temporal consistency* and *Inter-sequence temporal consistency*, which implement this notion of temporal consistency and show how to integrate them into a self-learning framework towards solving the one-shot video re-ID task.

Intra-Sequence Temporal Consistency. The intra-sequence temporal consistency loss is based on the idea of video temporal coherence [19,21,24]. While the previous works focus on learning the temporal order by considering individual frames, we use consistency as a tool for the learnt features to implicitly *ignore background nuances* and *focus on the actual person attributes*. We do this by sampling non-overlapping mini-tracklets from a tracklet and enforce the embeddings corresponding to these mini-tracklets to come closer via a contrastive loss.

Given a tracklet $\mathcal{X}$ consisting of frames $\{x_1, \cdots, x_n\}$, intra-sequence consistency involves creating two mini-tracklets $\mathcal{X}^{\mathsf{a}}$ and $\mathcal{X}^{\mathsf{p}}$ by sampling two mutually exclusive sets of frames from the original tracklet $\mathcal{X}$. This is done by the function $\Phi_{\mathsf{T}}(\mathcal{X})$, which first divides the $\mathcal{X}$ into a set of mini-tracklets, each of size $\rho \cdot |\mathcal{X}|$ and then samples from it as follows,

$$\mathcal{X}^{\mathsf{a}}, \mathcal{X}^{\mathsf{p}} = \Phi_{\mathsf{T}}(\mathcal{X}) \tag{2}$$

More specifically, $\Phi_{\mathsf{T}}(\mathcal{X})$ samples from the set $\{\mathcal{X}^1, \mathcal{X}^2, \cdots, \mathcal{X}^{1/\rho}\}$ uniformly without replacement. Here, ρ is a hyper-parameter that controls the size of each mini-tracklet with respect to the size of the tracklet $|\mathcal{X}|$. This ensures that $\mathcal{X}^{\mathsf{a}} \cap \mathcal{X}^{\mathsf{p}} = \emptyset$, and consequently, these tracklets are temporally incoherent. For all our experiments, ρ is set to 0.2. After obtaining these tracklets the loss forces their respective representations to be consistent temporally with one another as follows,

$$\mathcal{L}_{\text{intra}} = \|f_\theta(\mathcal{X}^{\mathsf{a}}) - f_\theta(\mathcal{X}^{\mathsf{p}}))\|_2. \tag{3}$$

This definition of the intra-sequence temporal consistency can be interpreted as a from of consistency regularization [20,23,27], which measures discrepancy between predictions made on perturbed unlabeled data points, i.e.,

$$\mathcal{L}_{\text{cons}} = d\left(p(y|x), p(y|\hat{x})\right) \tag{4}$$

where $d(\cdot, \cdot)$ is a divergence measure and $\hat{x} = x + \delta$. Such regularization focuses on the local data distribution, and implicitly pushes the decision boundary away from high-density parts of the unlabeled data to enhance intra-class similarity in accordance to the *cluster assumption* [3]. In our formulation, the two mini-tracklets are *temporally perturbed versions of each other in terms of background*, i.e., $x = \mathcal{X}^{\mathsf{a}}$, $\hat{x} = \mathcal{X}^{\mathsf{p}}$ and δ indicates perturbations in time - the consistency is applied on features, instead of distributions, and across time.

Inter-Sequence Temporal Consistency. The intra-sequence temporal consistency loss focuses solely on the intra-class similarity. To learn a discriminative person re-ID model, the learning process also has to account for the global distribution of the data or the inter-class separability. The triplet loss [11] has been widely used in the re-identification and retrieval literature for its ability to encode such global information.

The triplet loss ensures that, given an anchor point $\mathcal{X}^{\mathsf{a}}$, the feature of a positive point $\mathcal{X}^{\mathsf{p}}$ belonging to the same class (person) y_a is closer to the feature of the anchor than that of a negative point $\mathcal{X}^{\mathsf{n}}$ belonging to another class y_n, by at least a margin α. However, directly using the triplet loss is not possible in our scenario as it uses identity label information and thus, its effectiveness will depend heavily on the quality of label estimation. Therefore, we propose the inter-sequence temporal consistency loss, which induces a global level of consistency similar to the standard triplet formulation *without access to labels*.

Specifically, given a tracklet $\mathcal{X}$, we sample two temporally incoherent mini-tracklets in the same manner as mentioned in the previous section. Without loss of generality, we treat one as the anchor $\mathcal{X}^a$, and the other one as the positive point $\mathcal{X}^p$, which contains the same identity, but temporally perturbed. For the negative instance, we obtain it from the batch nearest neighbors of $\mathcal{X}^a$. This is done by creating the corresponding ranking list of tracklets in the batch B, excluding $\mathcal{X}$ and sampling a tracklet $\mathcal{X}^n$ uniformly within the range of ranks $[r, 2r]$ as follows:

$$\mathcal{X}^n = \Psi(\mathcal{N}_{[r,2r]}(\mathcal{X})) \tag{5}$$

where $\Psi(\cdot)$ denotes sampling from a set of elements uniformly. $\mathcal{N}_{[r,2r]}(\mathcal{X})$ indicates the nearest neighbors of $\mathcal{X}$ in the batch (up to a total of B neighbors) which are ranked in the range $[r, 2r]$. Using this range of ranks we filter out the possible positive samples and the easy negative samples, which are very low in the ranking list and potentially contribute to zero gradient. This strategy allows us to choose potential hard negatives which have been shown to give best performance [11]. The value of r is set to 3 and α to 0.3, for all our experiments.

Thus, the inter-sequence temporal consistency loss can be formulated as,

$$\mathcal{L}_{inter} = \max\{0, \|f_\theta(\mathcal{X}^a) - f_\theta(\mathcal{X}^p)\|_2 - \|f_\theta(\mathcal{X}^a) - f_\theta(\mathcal{X}^n)\|_2 + \alpha\} \tag{6}$$

A pictorial representation of the loss formulation is presented in Fig. 2.

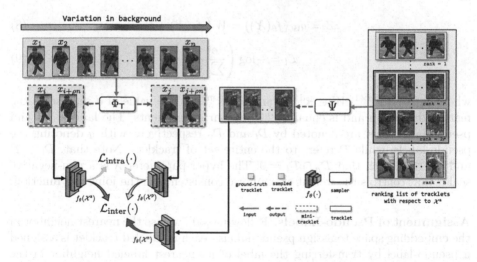

Fig. 2. An illustration of the inter-sequence temporal consistency criterion. Firstly, we sample temporally incoherent mini-tracklets using Φ_T to serve as the anchor and positive sample. Note the temporal perturbations in these mini-tracklets, manifested in the form changing background. Next, Ψ is used to obtain the negative sample from the batch nearest neighbors of the anchor, using a ranking based criterion. Using these, we formulate the triplet loss to enforce consistency such that $f_\theta(\cdot)$ learns features which focus on the discriminative aspects related to the person in the tracklet and ignore the background nuances.

3.3   Temporal Consistency Progressive Learning

In this section, we present our proposed framework, *Temporal Consistency Progressive Learning* (TCPL), based on the temporal consistency self-supervised losses discussed in the previous section. TCPL integrates self-supervision with pseudo-labeling to learn the person re-ID model. Temporal coherence is used to enhance the feature learning process in the form of multi-task learning. Training of this framework alternates between two key steps: (1) Representation learning, (2) Assignment of pseudo-labels.

Representation Learning. In order to learn the weights of the embedding function $f_\theta(\cdot)$, we jointly optimize the following loss function,

$$\mathcal{L} = \sum_{(\mathcal{X},y) \in \mathcal{D}_l} \mathcal{L}_l(\mathcal{X}, y) + \sum_{(\mathcal{X},\hat{y}) \in \mathcal{D}_p} \mathcal{L}_l(\mathcal{X}, \hat{y}) + \lambda \left(\sum_{\mathcal{X} \in \mathcal{D}} \mathcal{L}_{\text{intra}}(\mathcal{X}) + \sum_{\mathcal{X} \in \mathcal{D}} \mathcal{L}_{\text{inter}}(\mathcal{X}) \right) \quad (7)$$

where $\mathcal{L}_l$ is a standard cross-entropy classification loss applied on all labeled and selected pseudo-labeled tracklets in the dataset. The supervised loss $\mathcal{L}_l$ is optimized by appending a classifier $g_W(\cdot)$ on top of the feature extractor $f_\theta(\cdot)$ as

$$\mathcal{Z} = g_W(f_\theta(\mathcal{X})) = W^T f_\theta(\mathcal{X}) + b \quad (8)$$

$$\mathcal{L}_l = -\log \left(\frac{e^{y^T \mathcal{Z}}}{\sum_j e^{\mathcal{Z}_j}} \right), \quad (9)$$

where $f_\theta(\mathcal{X}) \in \mathbb{R}^{d \times 1}$, $W \in \mathbb{R}^{d \times m_l}$ and $b \in \mathbb{R}^{m_l \times 1}$. The value of d represents the feature dimension and is equal to 2048 in our experiments. The labeled set and pseudo-labeled set are denoted by $\mathcal{D}_l$ and $\mathcal{D}_p$ respectively, with $\hat{y}$ denoting the pseudo-labels, while $\mathcal{D}$ refers to the entire set of tracklets. Note that, $\mathcal{D}_l \subset \mathcal{D}$ and $\mathcal{D}_p \subset \mathcal{D}$, such that $\mathcal{D}_p \cap \mathcal{D}_l = \emptyset$. The hyper-parameter λ is a non-negative scalar that controls the weight of temporal consistency in the joint loss function.

Assignment of Pseudo-Labels. Following [30], we use the nearest neighbor in the embedding space to assign pseudo-labels - each unlabeled tracklet is assigned a pseudo-label by transferring the label of its nearest labeled neighbor in the embedding space. For $\mathcal{X}_j \in \mathcal{D}_u$,

$$i = \arg \min_{\mathcal{X}_k \in \mathcal{D}_l} \| f_\theta(\mathcal{X}_j) - f_\theta(\mathcal{X}_k) \|_2, \quad (10)$$

$$\hat{y}_j = y_i \quad (11)$$

After assignment of the pseudo-labels, a confidence criterion is used to choose the most reliable predictions to be used in optimizing $\mathcal{L}_l$ for the next step. Instead of a static threshold, a total of n_t samples are selected at step t by choosing the top n_t unlabeled samples with smallest distance to their corresponding labeled nearest neighbour and added to $\mathcal{D}_p$. A smaller value of the distance implies a more confident pseudo-label prediction.

The value of n_t is incremented gradually with t, depending on an enlarging factor $p \in (0,1)$ [30] where, $n_t = n_{t-1} + p n_u$. Thus, the learning process continues for a total of $(\lfloor 1/p \rfloor + 1)$ steps - until the entire unlabeled set has been assigned confident pseudo-labels. The parameter p controls the trade-off between label estimation accuracy and training time - a smaller value of p leads to better label estimation at the cost of higher training time.

Algorithm 1. Temporally Consistent Progressive Learning

INPUT: Labeled set $\mathcal{D}_l$, unlabeled set $\mathcal{D}_u$, enlarging ratio p, sampling factor ρ, loss weight λ, randomly initialized model $f_{\theta_0}(\cdot)$

OUTPUT: Feature extractor $f_{\theta_{opt}}(\cdot)$

1: Initialize the selected pseudo-labeled data $\mathcal{D}_p^0 \leftarrow \emptyset$, step $t \leftarrow 0$, sampling size $n_0 \leftarrow 0$, $n_u = |\mathcal{D}_u|$
2: **while** $n_t \leq n_u$ **do**
3:     $t \leftarrow t + 1$
4:     Train the model using (7)
5:     Assign pseudo-labels using (10)
6:     $n_t \leftarrow n_{t-1} + p.n_u$
7:     Choose the n_t most confident pseudo-labels and add to $\mathcal{D}_p^{t-1}$
8: **end while**
9: Choose model with best validation performance

---

4   Experiments

We evaluate our proposed method on two popular video person re-ID benchmarks, namely, MARS [36] and DukeMTMC-VideoReID [26]. MARS is the largest video re-ID dataset containing $17,503$ tracklets for $1,261$ identities and $3,248$ distractor tracklets, which are captured by six cameras. The DukeMTMC-VideoReID dataset is captured using 8 cameras and contains $2,196$ tracklets for training and $2,636$ tracklets for testing. Standard splits are used along with distractors.

Evaluation Metrics. Given a probe tracklet, we calculate the Euclidean distance with respect to all the gallery tracklets, and sort the distances to obtain the final ranking list. We utilize the Cumulative Matching Characteristics (CMC) and mean Average Precision (mAP) as the performance evaluation measures. We report the Rank-1, Rank-5, Rank-20 scores to represent the CMC curve.

Initial Data Selection. To initialize the labeled and unlabeled sets, we follow the protocol outlined in [30]. For each identity, a tracklet is chosen randomly in camera 1. If camera 1 does not record an identity, a tracklet in the next available camera is chosen to ensure each identity has one tracklet for initialization.

Implementation Details. Please see supplementary material for details on implementation, values of different hyper-parameters and datasets.

Comparison to the State-of-the-Art Methods. One-shot re-ID methods in the literature can be broadly divided into two classes: (1) DGM [32] and Stepwise Metric [18] use the entire pseudo-labeled data at each step of learning and in the process incorporate a lot of noisy labels, (2) EUG [30] and One-Example Progressive Learning [29] employ progressive sampling. TCPL outperforms all of these by learning an embedding which is temporally consistent. We also consider two baselines: Baseline (one-shot), which utilizes only the one-shot data for training, and Baseline(supervised), which assumes all the tracklets in the training set are labeled; these are trained in a supervised manner using only the cross-entropy loss. We also compare against state-of-the-art unsupervised methods which report results on video re-ID datasets: BUC [16], UTAL [15] and DAL [6].

We present the results for different instantiations of our framework in Table 1: one which uses both the losses (TCPL -full) and two others corresponding to usage of the losses individually (TCPL -$\mathcal{L}_{intra}$,TCPL -$\mathcal{L}_{inter}$). For TCPL, EUG [30] and One-Shot Progressive [29], we set the enlarging parameter p to 0.05.The consistency losses lead to consistent gains of in both rank-1 accuracy and mAP over both EUG [30] and One-Shot Progressive Learning [29] in both the datasets.

Analysis Over Enlarging Factor p. The selection of the enlarging factor p plays an important role in progressive sampling methods. Decreasing the value of p generally leads to less label estimation errors due to careful data selection, at the cost of a very slow learning process (See Fig. 3).

Table 1. Comparison of TCPL with state-of-the-art one-shot and unsupervised methods on the MARS and DukeMTMC-VideoReID datasets. (Sup./Unsup. refers to supervised and unsupervised methods respectively.)

Method	Setting	MARS			Duke		
		R-1	R-5	mAP	R-1	R-5	mAP
Baseline: upper bound	Sup	80.8	92.1	67.4	83.6	94.6	78.3
TCPL -full (Ours)	1-shot	**65.2**	**77.5**	**43.6**	**76.8**	**87.8**	**67.9**
TCPL -$\mathcal{L}_{intra}$ (Ours)	1-shot	63.3	75.2	42.9	76.2	87.6	67.7
TCPL -$\mathcal{L}_{inter}$ (Ours)	1-shot	64.9	77.5	43.1	74.4	86.6	66.5
One-Shot Prog. [29]	1-shot	62.8	75.2	42.6	72.9	84.3	63.3
EUG [30]	1-shot	62.7	72.9	42.5	72.8	84.2	63.2
Stepwise Metric [18]	1-shot	41.2	55.6	19.7	56.3	70.4	46.8
DGM+IDE [32]	1-shot	36.8	54.0	16.9	42.4	57.9	33.6
Baseline: lower bound	1-shot	36.2	50.2	15.5	39.6	56.8	33.3
BUC [16]	Unsup	61.1	75.1	38.0	69.2	81.1	61.9
UTAL [15]	Unsup	49.9	66.4	35.2	–	–	–
DAL [6]	Unsup	46.8	63.9	21.4	–	–	–

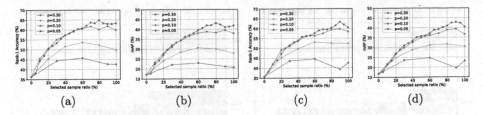

(a)   (b)   (c)   (d)

Fig. 3. Comparison with different values of enlarging factor on MARS. Figures (a) and (b) represent the Rank-1 accuracy and mAP using TCPL with $\mathcal{L}_{inter}$. Figures (c) and (d) represent the Rank-1 accuracy and mAP using TCPL with $\mathcal{L}_{intra}$.

The performance of our method as p varies is shown in Table 2. Unlike baseline methods, which suffer drastic drops in performance as p is increased, our framework limits label estimation errors via the consistency losses. Notably, TCPL at $p = 0.20$ is able to outperform both EUG and One-Shot Progressive Learning at $p = 0.05$ on DukeMTMC-VideoReID. This translates to a 4× speedup of learning without sacrificing performance. On MARS, at $p = 0.10$, TCPL is able to achieve a Rank-1 accuracy of 61.8%. This is only 1% behind One-Shot Progressive Learning with $p = 0.05$ and suggests a 2× speedup with only a negligible drop in performance. All of these indicate that TCPL is robust to appending pseudo-labeled data more aggressively and thus, can save time.

Table 2. Variation in one-shot performance results for different scales of the enlarging parameter p. The best and second best results are in red/blue respectively. (Best viewed in color)

p	Method	Duke				MARS			
		R-1	R-5	R-20	mAP	R-1	R-5	R-20	mAP
0.20	EUG [30]	68.9	81.1	89.4	59.5	48.7	63.4	72.6	26.6
	One-Shot Prog. [29]	69.1	81.2	89.6	59.6	49.6	64.5	74.4	27.2
	TCPL -$\mathcal{L}_{intra}$	74.4	85.8	91.6	65.4	52.5	65.6	73.9	31.6
	TCPL -$\mathcal{L}_{inter}$	69.4	81.6	88.5	60.5	53.6	66.2	74.9	30.6
0.10	EUG [30]	70.8	83.6	89.6	61.8	57.6	69.6	78.1	34.7
	One-Shot Prog. [29]	71.0	83.8	90.3	61.9	57.9	70.3	79.3	34.9
	TCPL -$\mathcal{L}_{intra}$	74.8	87.3	92.0	66.7	59.7	72.0	79.3	39.3
	TCPL -$\mathcal{L}_{inter}$	74.9	86.5	92.0	67.2	61.8	74.7	81.5	39.5
0.05	EUG [30]	72.8	84.2	91.5	63.2	62.7	72.9	82.6	42.5
	One-Shot Prog. [29]	72.9	84.3	91.4	63.3	62.8	75.2	83.8	42.6
	TCPL -$\mathcal{L}_{intra}$	76.2	87.6	92.9	67.7	63.3	75.2	82.4	42.9
	TCPL -$\mathcal{L}_{inter}$	74.4	86.6	92.2	66.5	64.9	77.5	84.1	43.1

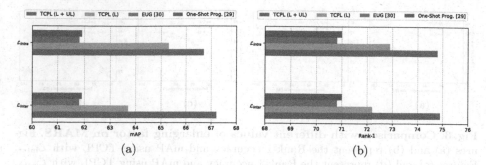

(a)   (b)

Fig. 4. Performance of TCPL by varying access to the unlabeled set. (a) presents the Rank-1 acc. and (b) the mAP on DukeMTMC-VideoReID. Temporal consistency performs better than [29,30] without using the entire unlabeled data, and improves even further when the unlabeled data is used. This demonstrates two things: (1) using the unlabeled data efficiently is important, (2) self-supervision can learn highly discriminative features. (L/UL denote the labeled/unlabeled set.)

Importance of Maximally Using the Unlabeled Data. The ability to extract maximal information from the unlabeled data is at the core of TCPL. We demonstrate this in Fig. 4 by evaluating the losses on DukeMTMC-VideoReID with and without access to entire unlabeled data at each step of learning.

The results confirm the two aspects of our hypothesis. Firstly, utilizing the entire unlabeled set at every step of learning improves performance. Secondly, self-supervision - even without access to the entire unlabeled set - learns better features and improves re-ID performance. TCPL, with access to only the labeled data, outperforms [29] which accesses the entirety of the unlabeled set. This is a direct consequence of the ability of self-supervision to learn better features via consistency regularization, within and across camera views.

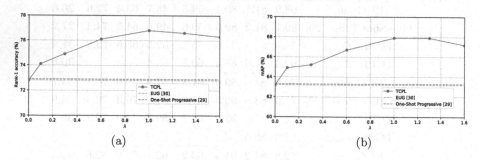

(a)   (b)

Fig. 5. Importance of temporal consistency. (a) presents variations in Rank-1 accuracy on DukeMTMC-VideoReID by changing weights on temporal losses. Higher λ represents more weight on the temporal losses. (b) presents the variations in mAP.

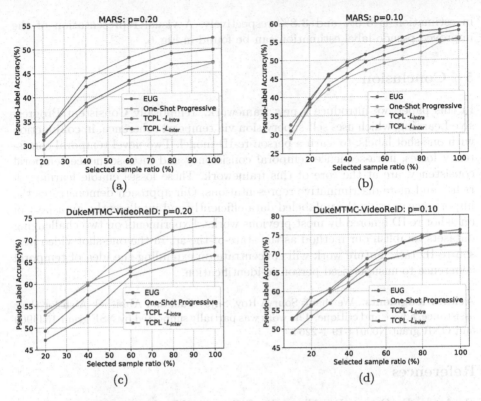

Fig. 6. Pseudo-label estimation. Accuracy of pseudo-labels as enlarging factor p is varied, on MARS [(a), (b)] and DukeMTMC-VideoReID [(c), (d)]

Weight on the Loss Function. In our framework, we jointly optimize two types of losses - the cross-entropy loss and the temporal coherence losses ($\mathcal{L}_{intra}, \mathcal{L}_{inter}$), as defined in Eqn. 7, to learn the weights θ of the feature embedding $f_\theta(\cdot)$. We investigate the contributions of the temporal losses to the re-identification performance. In order to do that, we performed experiments with different values of λ (higher value indicates larger weight on the temporal losses) and present the results on the DukeMTMC-VideoReID dataset in Fig. 5. In general, increasing the weight improves performance, indicating the efficacy of self-supervision. As may be observed from the plot, the proposed method performs best with $\lambda = 1$.

Analysis Over Pseudo-Label Estimation. As a consequence of more discriminative feature learning using local consistency, TCPL is able to generate high quality labels for the unlabeled set. At $p = 0.20$ and $p = 0.10$, TCPL is able to achieve **8.2%** and **4.0%** improvement in label estimation respectively, on DukeMTMC-VideoReID, compared to EUG. On MARS, the improvement in estimation is **5.0%** and **3.8%** respectively. A visual representation of the improved pseudo-label estimation can be found in Fig. 6.

5 Conclusion

In this paper, we introduce a new framework, Temporally Consistent Progressive Learning, which uses self-supervision via temporal coherence, in conjunction with one-shot labels, to learn a person re-ID model. Two novel temporal consistency losses, intra-sequence temporal consistency and inter-sequence temporal consistency, are at the core of this framework. These losses enable learning of richer and more discriminative representations. Our approach demonstrates the importance of using the unlabeled data efficiently and intelligently, an aspect of one-shot re-ID ignored by most previous works. Experiments on two challenging datasets establish our method as the state-of-the-art in the one-shot video person re-ID task. Future work will concentrate on extending the idea of temporal coherence to unsupervised person re-identification.

Acknowledgments. We thank Sourya Roy, Sujoy Paul and Abhishek Aich for their assistance, advice and critique. The work was partially supported by NSF grant 1544969 and ONR grant N00014-19-1-2264.

References

1. Arazo, E., Ortego, D., Albert, P., O'Connor, N.E., McGuinness, K.: Pseudo-labeling and confirmation bias in deep semi-supervised learning. arXiv preprint arXiv:1908.02983 (2019)
2. Bak, S., Carr, P.: One-shot metric learning for person re-identification. In: Proceedings of the IEEE Conference on Computer Vision and Pattern Recognition, pp. 2990–2999 (2017)
3. Chapelle, O., Scholkopf, B., Zien, A.: Semi-supervised learning. IEEE Trans. Neural Netw. **20**(3), 542 (2009)
4. Chen, D., Li, H., Xiao, T., Yi, S., Wang, X.: Video person re-identification with competitive snippet-similarity aggregation and co-attentive snippet embedding. In: Proceedings of the IEEE Conference on Computer Vision and Pattern Recognition, pp. 1169–1178 (2018)
5. Chen, T., et al.: ABD-net: attentive but diverse person re-identification. In: Proceedings of the IEEE International Conference on Computer Vision, pp. 8351–8361 (2019)
6. Chen, Y., Zhu, X., Gong, S.: Deep association learning for unsupervised video person re-identification. In: Proceedings of the British Machine Vision Conference (2018)
7. Ding, G., Zhang, S., Khan, S., Tang, Z., Zhang, J., Porikli, F.: Feature affinity based pseudo labeling for semi-supervised person re-identification. Trans. Multimedia **21**(11), 2891–2902 (2019)
8. Dosovitskiy, A., Springenberg, J.T., Riedmiller, M., Brox, T.: Discriminative unsupervised feature learning with convolutional neural networks. In: Advances in Neural Information Processing Systems, pp. 766–774 (2014)

9. Gidaris, S., Singh, P., Komodakis, N.: Unsupervised representation learning by predicting image rotations. arXiv preprint arXiv:1803.07728 (2018)
10. Rezatofighi, S.H, Milan, A., Zhang, Z., Shi, Q., Dick, A., Reid, I.: Joint probabilistic matching using m-best solutions. In: Proceedings of the IEEE Conference on Computer Vision and Pattern Recognition, pp. 136–145 (2016)
11. Hermans, A., Beyer, L., Leibe, B.: In defense of the triplet loss for person re-identification. arXiv preprint arXiv:1703.07737 (2017)
12. Kolesnikov, A., Zhai, X., Beyer, L.: Revisiting self-supervised visual representation learning. arXiv preprint arXiv:1901.09005 (2019)
13. Krizhevsky, A., Sutskever, I., Hinton, G.E.: ImageNet classification with deep convolutional neural networks. In: Advances in Neural Information Processing Systems, pp. 1097–1105 (2012)
14. Lee, D.H.: Pseudo-label: the simple and efficient semi-supervised learning method for deep neural networks. In: Workshop on Challenges in Representation Learning, ICML, vol. 3 (2013)
15. Li, M., Zhu, X., Gong, S.: Unsupervised tracklet person re-identification. IEEE Trans. Pattern Anal. Mach. Intell. 42(7), 1770–1782 (2019)
16. Lin, Y., Dong, X., Zheng, L., Yan, Y., Yang, Y.: A bottom-up clustering approach to unsupervised person re-identification. In: Proceedings of the AAAI Conference on Artificial Intelligence, vol. 33, pp. 8738–8745 (2019)
17. Liu, X., Song, M., Tao, D., Zhou, X., Chen, C., Bu, J.: Semi-supervised coupled dictionary learning for person re-identification. In: Proceedings of the IEEE Conference on Computer Vision and Pattern Recognition, pp. 3550–3557 (2014)
18. Liu, Z., Wang, D., Lu, H.: Stepwise metric promotion for unsupervised video person re-identification. In: Proceedings of the IEEE International Conference on Computer Vision, pp. 2429–2438 (2017)
19. Misra, I., Zitnick, C.L., Hebert, M.: Shuffle and learn: unsupervised learning using temporal order verification. In: Leibe, B., Matas, J., Sebe, N., Welling, M. (eds.) ECCV 2016. LNCS, vol. 9905, pp. 527–544. Springer, Cham (2016). https://doi.org/10.1007/978-3-319-46448-0_32
20. Miyato, T., Maeda, S.I., Koyama, M., Ishii, S.: Virtual adversarial training: a regularization method for supervised and semi-supervised learning. IEEE Trans. Pattern Anal. Mach. Intell. 41(8), 1979–1993 (2018)
21. Mobahi, H., Collobert, R., Weston, J.: Deep learning from temporal coherence in video. In: Proceedings of the 26th Annual International Conference on Machine Learning, pp. 737–744. ACM (2009)
22. Noroozi, M., Favaro, P.: Unsupervised learning of visual representations by solving Jigsaw puzzles. In: Leibe, B., Matas, J., Sebe, N., Welling, M. (eds.) ECCV 2016. LNCS, vol. 9910, pp. 69–84. Springer, Cham (2016). https://doi.org/10.1007/978-3-319-46466-4_5
23. Oliver, A., Odena, A., Raffel, C.A., Cubuk, E.D., Goodfellow, I.: Realistic evaluation of deep semi-supervised learning algorithms. In: Advances in Neural Information Processing Systems, pp. 3235–3246 (2018)
24. Paul, S., Roy, S., Roy-Chowdhury, A.K.: Incorporating scalability in unsupervised spatio-temporal feature learning. In: Proceedings of the IEEE International Conference on Acoustics, Speech and Signal Processing, pp. 1503–1507. IEEE (2018)
25. Ren, S., He, K., Girshick, R., Sun, J.: Faster R-CNN: towards real-time object detection with region proposal networks. In: Advances in Neural Information Processing Systems, pp. 91–99 (2015)

26. Ristani, E., Solera, F., Zou, R., Cucchiara, R., Tomasi, C.: Performance measures and a data set for multi-target, multi-camera tracking. In: Hua, G., Jégou, H. (eds.) ECCV 2016. LNCS, vol. 9914, pp. 17–35. Springer, Cham (2016). https://doi.org/10.1007/978-3-319-48881-3_2

27. Tarvainen, A., Valpola, H.: Mean teachers are better role models: weight-averaged consistency targets improve semi-supervised deep learning results. In: Advances in Neural Information Processing Systems, pp. 1195–1204 (2017)

28. Wang, G., Lai, J., Huang, P., Xie, X.: Spatial-temporal person re-identification. In: Proceedings of the AAAI Conference on Artificial Intelligence, vol. 33, pp. 8933–8940 (2019)

29. Wu, Y., Lin, Y., Dong, X., Yan, Y., Bian, W., Yang, Y.: Progressive learning for person re-identification with one example. IEEE Trans. Image Process. 28(6), 2872–2881 (2019)

30. Wu, Y., Lin, Y., Dong, X., Yan, Y., Ouyang, W., Yang, Y.: Exploit the unknown gradually: one-shot video-based person re-identification by stepwise learning. In: Proceedings of the IEEE Conference on Computer Vision and Pattern Recognition, pp. 5177–5186 (2018)

31. Xu, S., Cheng, Y., Gu, K., Yang, Y., Chang, S., Zhou, P.: Jointly attentive spatial-temporal pooling networks for video-based person re-identification. In: Proceedings of the IEEE International Conference on Computer Vision, pp. 4733–4742 (2017)

32. Ye, M., Ma, A.J., Zheng, L., Li, J., Yuen, P.C.: Dynamic label graph matching for unsupervised video re-identification. In: Proceedings of the IEEE International Conference on Computer Vision, pp. 5142–5150 (2017)

33. Ye, M., Zhang, X., Yuen, P.C., Chang, S.F.: Unsupervised embedding learning via invariant and spreading instance feature. In: Proceedings of the IEEE Conference on Computer Vision and Pattern Recognition, pp. 6210–6219 (2019)

34. Yu, H.X., Wu, A., Zheng, W.S.: Cross-view asymmetric metric learning for unsupervised person re-identification. In: Proceedings of the IEEE International Conference on Computer Vision, pp. 994–1002 (2017)

35. Yu, H.X., Zheng, W.S., Wu, A., Guo, X., Gong, S., Lai, J.H.: Unsupervised person re-identification by soft multilabel learning. In: Proceedings of the IEEE Conference on Computer Vision and Pattern Recognition, pp. 2148–2157 (2019)

36. Zheng, L., et al.: MARS: a video benchmark for large-scale person re-identification. In: Leibe, B., Matas, J., Sebe, N., Welling, M. (eds.) ECCV 2016. LNCS, vol. 9910, pp. 868–884. Springer, Cham (2016). https://doi.org/10.1007/978-3-319-46466-4_52

37. Zheng, L., Yang, Y., Hauptmann, A.G.: Person re-identification: past, present and future. arXiv preprint arXiv:1610.02984 (2016)

38. Zhou, K., Yang, Y., Cavallaro, A., Xiang, T.: Omni-scale feature learning for person re-identification. arXiv preprint arXiv:1905.00953 (2019)

An Efficient Training Framework for Reversible Neural Architectures

Zixuan Jiang[✉] (ID), Keren Zhu (ID), Mingjie Liu (ID), Jiaqi Gu (ID),
and David Z. Pan (ID)

The University of Texas at Austin, Austin Texas 78712, USA
{zixuan,keren.zhu,jay_liu,jqgu}@utexas.edu, dpan@ece.utexas.edu
https://www.cerc.utexas.edu/utda/

Abstract. As machine learning models and dataset escalate in scales rapidly, the huge memory footprint impedes efficient training. Reversible operators can reduce memory consumption by discarding intermediate feature maps in forward computations and recover them via their inverse functions in the backward propagation. They save memory at the cost of computation overhead. However, current implementations of reversible layers mainly focus on saving memory usage with computation overhead neglected. In this work, we formulate the decision problem for reversible operators with training time as the objective function and memory usage as the constraint. By solving this problem, we can maximize the training throughput for reversible neural architectures. Our proposed framework fully automates this decision process, empowering researchers to develop and train reversible neural networks more efficiently.

Keywords: Reversible neural networks · Efficient training · Machine learning framework

1 Introduction

The backpropagation [20] mechanism is widely used in training neural networks. However, since intermediate results need to be saved for backward computations, the backpropagation requires considerable memory footprint. As neural networks become larger and deeper, the increasing memory footprint is forcing the usage of smaller mini-batch sizes. In extreme cases, deep networks have to be trained with a mini-batch size of 1 [25]. The issue of memory consumption impedes the explorations of desirable deep learning models.

Researchers have proposed several methods to address the challenge of inflating memory footprint [21]. Chen et al. [6] propose gradient checkpoint mechanism to store partial intermediate results. The discarded activations will be recovered through recomputations in the backward pass. The memory swapping method [19,24] moves intermediate activations to other devices to reduce the memory footprint of the current device. The extra memory transfer imposes overhead on training efficiency. Reversible operators [7] allow recovering the

A. Vedaldi et al. (Eds.): ECCV 2020, LNCS 12372, pp. 275–289, 2020.
https://doi.org/10.1007/978-3-030-58583-9_17

intermediate feature maps in backward pass through the corresponding inverse functions. All these three methods reduce the memory footprint at the cost of extra computation or memory transfer. They do not affect the model accuracy as the training process is numerically unchanged.

Specifically, reversible neural architectures have been successfully adopted in computer vision research, e.g., the reversible U-net for volumetric image segmentation [3], and the reversible architecture for 3D high-resolution medical image processing [2]. The lower memory footprint allows deeper models to be trained, inducing more predictive capability and higher accuracy.

Figure 1 shows two extremes in neural network training. Standard backpropagation achieves the extreme of computation efficiency at the expense of the highest memory footprint, such that it does not contain any redundant computations. On the other extreme, the fully reversible strategy has the lowest memory footprint with imposing the greatest computation overhead. However, The design space between two extremes is less studied. Existing research regarding reversible neural networks mainly focuses on saving memory consumption. All the reversible layers are executed in the memory-efficient mode. The computation overhead of their inverse functions is overlooked.

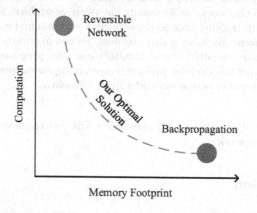

Fig. 1. Two extremes when training neural networks. The lower right extreme stands for the standard backpropagation method, which does not contain any redundant computations. The upper left extreme can achieve the lowest memory footprint by fully leveraging the reversibility of the neural network.

In this paper, we explore the design space by considering the trade-off between computation and memory footprint. We derive the mathematical formulation of the decision problem for reversible neural architectures. We formulate the training time as the objective function with memory usage as an optimization constraint. By showing that it is a standard 0/1 knapsack problem in essence, we use a dynamic programming algorithm to find the optimal solution. We also discuss the relationship between mini-batch size and training throughput.

Our contributions are highlighted as follows.

- **New Perspective.** We explore the design space for reversible neural architectures from a novel perspective of joint optimization.
- **Optimality.** Our framework guarantees to obtain the maximum training throughput for reversible neural architectures under given memory constraints.
- **Automation.** Our framework provides a fully automated solution, enabling more efficient development and training for reversible neural networks.

2 Background

In this section, we discuss the background of reversible neural architectures and the scheduling framework for the training process.

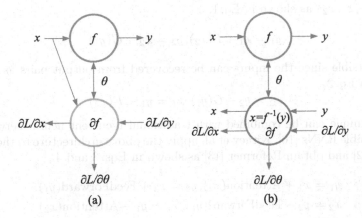

(a)   (b)

Fig. 2. (a) non-reversible and (b) reversible neural architectures. For a non-reversible layer, we often need to save its original input x for backward computations. For a reversible layer, the original input x can be calculated via its inverse function $x = f^{-1}(y)$.

2.1 Reversible Neural Architectures

Figure 2a demonstrates a conventional non-reversible neural architectures. The layer $y = f(x)$ is non-reversible if and only if there is no inverse computation $x = f^{-1}(y)$ for the original function f. For a non-reversible layer, we often need to store its original input x during forward computation so that we can compute gradients during backpropagation. As an example, for a linear layer $y = f(x) = \theta^T x$, where θ represents the weight vector, its backward computation $\partial y / \partial \theta = x$ depends on the original input x.

Traditional neural networks are mostly based on these non-reversible layers. The memory consumed by the feature maps dominates the total memory utilization, especially in deep neural networks [19]. Therefore, the memory footprint can decrease significantly by discarding those feature maps.

Figure 2b illustrates a reversible operator. When using the reversible layer $y = f(x)$, it is possible recover x in the backward computation by calling its inverse function $x = f^{-1}(y)$. Therefore the memory consumption can be saved by discarding the intermediate feature map x.

Some of the commonly used operators in neural networks are implicitly reversible, such as convolution layers with a stride of 1 [12], and fully connected layers with invertible weight matrix. Inplace Activated Batch Normalization (ABN) [4] leverages the reversibility of the batch normalization [8] and some activation functions (such as leaky ReLU). Neural ordinary differential equations [5] can achieve constant memory usage through reversibility in backpropagation.

Researchers also propose many variations of explicit reversible neural architectures [9]. The reversible residual architecture [7] does computations on a pair of inputs (x_1, x_2) as shown in Eq. 1.

$$y_1 = x_1 + F(x_2), y_2 = x_2 + G(y_1) \tag{1}$$

It is reversible since the inputs can be recovered from output pairs as demonstrated in Eq. 2.

$$x_2 = y_2 - G(y_1), x_1 = y_1 - F(x_2) \tag{2}$$

This technique can be combined with traditional recurrent neural networks to get reversible RNNs [16]. Kitaev et al. apply the above architecture to the Transformer [22] and obtain Reformer [13] as shown in Eqs. 3 and 4.

$$y_1 = x_1 + \text{Attention}(x_2), y_2 = x_2 + \text{FeedForward}(y_1) \tag{3}$$

$$x_2 = y_2 - \text{FeedForward}(y_1), x_1 = y_1 - \text{Attention}(x_2) \tag{4}$$

Although the computation overhead is considered and discussed, these prior studies mainly focus on memory footprint reduction. They do not explore the space between the two extremes illustrated in Fig. 1.

2.2   Scheduling for Training

For most developers, the primary concern regarding the training process is how to maximize the training throughput given existing machines, especially GPUs. Specifically, there is a need for a framework to automate the training process to fully utilize the computation capability and memory capacity of specific machines.

Frameworks for the scheduling problem with gradient checkpoints are great examples. The scheduling problem seeks the minimum computation overhead with a memory footprint constraint. Researchers propose many algorithms to find optimal solutions for gradient checkpoint selection. Kusumoto et al. provide a dynamic programming algorithm from the perspective of computation graphs [14]. Jain et al. formulate the scheduling problem as a mixed integer linear program and solve it via standard solvers [10]. However, a similar problem for reversible neural architectures does not get much attention. We formulate and solve this problem in this work.

There are also work focused on the scheduling for distributed training. Jia et al. optimize how each layer is parallelized in distributed and parallel training [11]. However, they do not consider the reversibility. Our framework can be used directly in every single machine in the distributed training scenario.

3   Method

In this section, we first describe two modes for reversible neural architectures. We denote them M-Mode and C-Mode, respectively. We then formulate the decision problem, and propose an algorithm and our framework. We also discuss the problem when mini-batch sizes are not fixed.

3.1   Memory Centric and Computation Centric Modes

Each reversible layer $y = f(x)$ can be computed in two modes during the training process. First, we can leverage its reversibility. We denote it M-Mode, which represents memory centric mode. Precisely, we discard the activation x in forward computations, then recover it in the backward pass. This mode saves the memory consumed by x at the cost of inverse computation of $x = f^{-1}(y)$. Another mode is treating the reversible layer as a conventional non-reversible layer, which is denoted C-Mode representing computation centric mode. In this mode, we save the feature map x in the forward pass, then use it directly in the backward computation. This mode does not involve redundant computations but requires an extra memory footprint. Table 1 summarizes these two modes.

Table 1. Comparisons of two modes.

Mode	Forward	Backward	Computation cost	Memory cost
M-Mode	Discard x	Recover x from y	$x = f^{-1}(y)$	0
C-Mode	Save x	Use x directly	0	Size of x

3.2   Formulation

Let f be a neural network with $(k+n)$ layers, among which there are n reversible layers $\{f_i\}_{i=1}^{n}$. For each of these n reversible layers, we can decide to do forward and backward computation following one of the modes above. Let $x \in \{0, 1\}^n$ be the decision variable. $x_i = 0(1)$ means that the reversible layer f_i follows the M-Mode (C-Mode). Thus, for n reversible layers, the 2^n choices constitute the whole solution space.

The two extremes in Fig. 1 can be written as $x = \mathbf{0}$ and $x = \mathbf{1}$. $x = \mathbf{0}$ represents that we discard all the intermediate results to achieve the lowest memory footprint. We treat it as `baseline-M`. We denote the other extreme without redundant computations ($x = \mathbf{1}$) as `baseline-C`. Currently, most of the implementations of reversible neural networks use `baseline-M` directly.

Let $t_{f1}, t_{b1}(t_{f2}, t_{b2}) \in \mathbb{R}^n_{++}$ be the execution time vector of forward and backward pass in the `M-Mode` (`C-Mode`) respectively. Compared with the `C-Mode`, the extra execution time consumed by the `M-Mode` is $t_e = (t_{f1} + t_{b1}) - (t_{f2} + t_{b2})$. The total execution time of forward and backward computation of all these reversible layers $\{f_i\}_{i=1}^n$ are

$$(\mathbf{1} - x)^T(t_{f1} + t_{b1}) + x^T(t_{f2} + t_{b2}) = \mathbf{1}^T(t_{f1} + t_{b1}) - t_e^T x$$

Similarly, let $m \in \mathbb{Z}^n_{++}$ be the extra memory footprint of `C-Mode` compared with `M-Mode`, i.e., the size of corresponding intermediate activations. The total extra memory footprint of these feature maps is $m^T x$.

Finally, the time centric optimization problem can be written as Problem 5.

$$\min_x \quad \mathbf{1}^T(t_{f1} + t_{b1}) - t_e^T x$$
$$\text{s.t.} \quad m^T x + m_o \leq M \tag{5}$$
$$x_i \in \{0, 1\}, i = 1, ..., n$$

where M is the memory capacity of the machine, m_o represents the memory allocated for other tensors (such as feature maps of non-reversible layers, and neural network parameters) when we achieve peak memory in a training iteration. Users can also specify the memory capacity M explicitly.

For other parts of the training process, such as the optimizer, the computation of non-reversible layers, their execution time is constant and independent of our decisions. Therefore, we can minimize the training time by minimizing the total wall-clock time of all these reversible layers.

3.3 Algorithm and Framework

Problem 5 can be rewritten as Problem 6.

$$\max_x \quad t_e^T x$$
$$\text{s.t.} \quad m^T x \leq M - m_o \tag{6}$$
$$x_i \in \{0, 1\}, i = 1, ..., n$$

Problem 6 can be interpreted as follows. We take the `baseline-M` ($x = \mathbf{0}$) as the reference. The object function $t_e^T x$ is the execution time reduction when we apply the decision x. The remaining memory capacity for these reversible layers is $M - m_o$.

Problem 6 is a standard **0/1 knapsack problem** in essence [17]. Note that the memory-related variables and parameters m, M, m_o are all positive integers

---

Algorithm 1 Dynamic programming algorithm for 0/1 knapsack problem

---

Input: $t_e, m, M - m_o, n$. {Indices of vectors t_e and m strat from 1.}
Define saved$[n, M - m_o]$ and initialize all entries as -1, which means the entry is undefined. {The entry saved$[i, j]$ records the maximum saved time under the condition that we consider first i items with total memory limit of j.}
foo(i, j) {This recursive function calculates saved$[i, j]$.}
    if $i == 0$ **or** $j \leq 0$ **then**
        return 0 {No time saved under this condition}
    end if
    if saved$[i - 1, j] == -1$ **then**
        saved$[i - 1, j] = $ **foo**$(i - 1, j)$
    end if
    if $m[i] > j$ **then**
        saved$[i, j] = $ saved$[i - 1, j]$
    else
        if saved$[i - 1, j - m[i]] == -1$ **then**
            saved$[i - 1, j - m[i]] = $ **foo**$(i - 1, j - m[i])$
        end if
        saved$[i, j] = \max\{$saved$[i - 1, j],$ saved$[i - 1, j - m[i]] + t_e[i]\}$
    end if
    return saved$[i, j]$
end foo
saved$[n, M - m_o] = $ **foo**$(n, M - m_o)$
Initialize decision variables $x = \mathbf{0}$ {Do backtracking to find the optimal solution.}
$j = M - m_o$
for $i = n, n - 1, ..., 1$ **do**
    if saved$[i, j] \neq$ saved$[i - 1, j]$ **then**
        $x[i] = 1$
        $j = j - m[i]$
    end if
end for
return saved$[n, M - m_o], x$ {Return optimal values and solutions.}

---

since all of them are in the unit of bytes. Therefore, it can be solved by dynamic programming, as shown in Algorithm 1.

Based on the algorithm, we propose a framework to automate the decision process. Figure 3 shows the four stages of our framework. Initially, we verify the reversibility of each operator. The correctness of the original and inverse functions will be verified. In the second stage, we will obtain parameters t_e and m from realistic measurements. Our framework is hardware-aware since we use realistic profiling data from specific machines. Then we use Algorithm 1 to get the optimal solution. Finally, we can train the network with maximum throughput. The dynamic programming algorithm will only be executed once to obtain the optimal schedule. After that, this schedule can be used in all the training iterations. Thus, the added complexity is negligible compared with the training process.

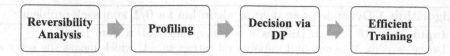

Fig. 3. Four stages in our framework

3.4   Various Mini-Batch Size

The above discussions are based on the assumption that the mini-batch size is fixed. When we have many choices on the mini-batch size (denoted b), the optimization problem will be more complicated.

We assume that for each layer, its execution time is linear to the batch size, whether it is reversible or not. Namely, the execution time satisfies that $t(b) = t^{(0)} + bt^{(1)}$. The total execution time of all the non-reversible layers is $t_n^{(0)} + bt_n^{(1)}$. The total execution time of all the reversible layers is

$$\mathbf{1}^T(t_{f1} + t_{b1}) - t_e^T x = \mathbf{1}^T(t_{f1}^{(0)} + t_{b1}^{(0)}) + b\mathbf{1}^T(t_{f1}^{(1)} + t_{b1}^{(1)}) - t_e^{(0)^T} x - bt_e^{(1)^T} x$$

The execution time of the optimizer, scheduler, and control are independent of mini-batch size, denoted by t_o. The execution time per sample is

$$t_n^{(1)} + \mathbf{1}^T(t_{f1}^{(1)} + t_{b1}^{(1)}) - t_e^{(1)^T} x + \frac{t_o + t_n^{(0)} + \mathbf{1}^T(t_{f1}^{(0)} + t_{b1}^{(0)}) - t_e^{(0)^T} x}{b}$$

The memory footprint is also linear to the mini-batch size. The size of network parameters is independent of the mini-batch size. The size of the feature maps of the non-reversible layers is proportional to the mini-batch size. Thus, the memory constraint can be rewritten as $bm^T x + m_o^{(0)} + bm_o^{(1)} \leq M$.

The optimization problem is now

$$\min_{x,b} \quad t_n^{(1)} + \mathbf{1}^T(t_{f1}^{(1)} + t_{b1}^{(1)}) - t_e^{(1)^T} x + \frac{t_o + t_n^{(0)} + \mathbf{1}^T(t_{f1}^{(0)} + t_{b1}^{(0)}) - t_e^{(0)^T} x}{b}$$

$$\text{s.t.} \quad bm^T x + m_o^{(0)} + bm_o^{(1)} \leq M \tag{7}$$

$$x_i \in \{0,1\}, i = 1, ..., n$$

$$b \in [b_l, b_u], b \in \mathbb{Z}$$

where b_l, b_u are lower and upper bounds of the mini-batch size.

Rewrite the problem as Problem 8.

$$\max_{x,b} \quad f(x,b) = t_e^{(1)^T} x - \frac{C - t_e^{(0)^T} x}{b}$$

$$\text{s.t.} \quad bm^T x + m_o^{(0)} + bm_o^{(1)} \leq M \tag{8}$$

$$x_i \in \{0,1\}, i = 1, ..., n$$

$$b \in [b_l, b_u], b \in \mathbb{Z}$$

where $C = t_o + t_n^{(0)} + \mathbf{1}^T(t_{f1}^{(0)} + t_{b1}^{(0)})$ is a constant.

Problem 8 is a non-linear integer programming optimization problem, which is hard to get the optimal solution. A simple method is to sweep the mini-batch size in the range of $[b_l, b_u]$ with our framework. Empirically the Problem 6 is fast to solve using Algorithm 1. Thus, it is affordable to apply the simple method of sweeping the mini-batch size. We further discuss various mini-batch size in Sect. 4.6. We leave Problem 8 as an open problem for future research.

4 Experiments

In this section, we provide the experimental settings initially. Then we discuss the details of profiling. We analyze three reversible neural architectures: RevNet-104, ResNeXt-101 with inplace ABN, and Reformer. We further discuss the results in terms of various mini-batch sizes.

4.1 Settings

We adapt source codes from MemCNN[1] [15], Inplace ABN[2] [4], and Reformer[3] [13]. We follow their original settings and hyperparameters except that we can decide what modes each reversible layer will use.

Unless otherwise stated, we use PyTorch [18] 1.4.0. The training process runs on a Linux server with Intel Core i9-7900X CPU and 1 NVIDIA TITAN Xp GPU, whose memory capacity is 12,196 MiB. All the tensor operations are on the GPU. We report the mean of 100 training iterations.

4.2 Profiling

To ensure hardware-awareness, our framework needs to do profiling on the execution time and memory allocation to obtain t_e, m, m_o based on realistic measurement. It is easy to collect memory-related terms m, m_o since the memory footprint is stable throughout a whole training process.

For the execution time t_e, the most accurate way to obtain it is running the model in two modes respectively and collect all the four corresponding vectors $(t_{f1}, t_{b1}, t_{f2}, t_{b2})$. We can also directly compare these two modes and conclude their difference. For the feature maps in the C-Mode, it takes extra time for the memory writes in the forward computation, and memory read in the backward pass. In the M-Mode, there is overhead in reading y from memory and the inverse computation.

It is complicated to analyze the memory behaviour, and the analysis is beyond discussions of this paper. Fortunately, we observe that $t_{f1} \approx t_{f2} \approx t_{b1} - t_{b2}$. For instance, the average execution time of the RevNet-104 [7] with mini-batch

---

[1] https://github.com/silvandeleemput/memcnn.
[2] https://github.com/mapillary/inplace_abn.
[3] https://github.com/lucidrains/reformer-pytorch.

size of 64 on ImageNet is $t_{f1} = 10.425$ ms, $t_{f2} = 10.404$ ms, $t_{b1} = 29.276$ ms, and $t_{b2} = 18.865$ ms. This observation is prevalent in current machine learning frameworks, since memory accesses are hidden by computations [1,18]. Thus, we can only take computation into account when analyzing the difference in execution time. In short, $t_e = (t_{f1}+t_{b1})-(t_{f2}+t_{b2}) \approx t_{f1} \approx t_{f2}$. The assumption is verified for all the following experiments. We use $t_e = t_{f1}$ in the optimization problem directly.

4.3   RevNet

We apply our framework on RevNet-104 [7] for image classification on ImageNet. By sweeping the mini-batch sizes, we can obtain various memory budgets and computation overhead. Figure 4 illustrates our decision for different mini-batch sizes. When the mini-batch size is smaller than 65, the GPU memory capacity is large enough to contain all the intermediate activations. Thus, the optimal decision is saving all of them to achieve maximum training throughput. Starting from a mini-batch size of 65, we have to use the M-Mode in partial reversible layers due to the limited memory budget. Our dynamic programming solver will obtain the optimal decision for each setting. If the mini-batch size is larger than 117, we will encounter the issue of out of memory even if we use baseline-M, the most memory-efficient decision. As shown in Fig. 4, the optimal decision is non-trivial across different mini-batch sizes.

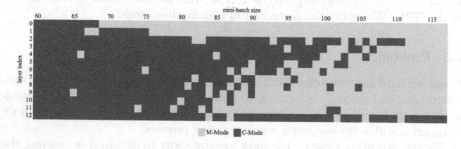

Fig. 4. The heat map of the optimal solutions throughout different mini-batch sizes on RevNet-104 with 13 reversible layers. The horizontal and vertical axes represent the mini-batch size and the layer index, respectively.

Figure 5a shows the training time per iteration of baseline-M, baseline-C and our optimal solution. The solid red line and the green dashed line represents the baseline-M and optimal settings provided by our framework. The baseline-C is highlighted in the lower left corner, since it is limited by the device's memory capacity and cannot contain a large batch size. Our optimal solution overlaps with the baseline-C when baseline-C is feasible, i.e., mini-batch size smaller than 65. When baseline-C is not available, our framework approach the baseline-M gradually. The reason is that as the mini-batch size

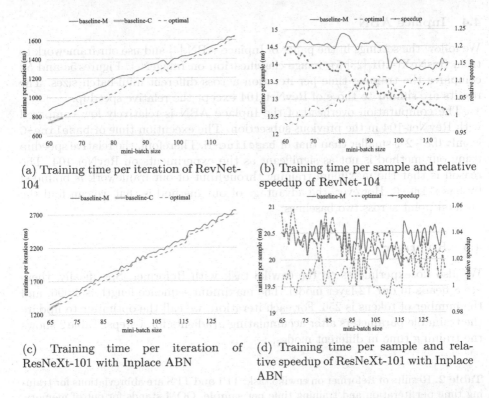

(a) Training time per iteration of RevNet-104

(b) Training time per sample and relative speedup of RevNet-104

(c) Training time per iteration of ResNeXt-101 with Inplace ABN

(d) Training time per sample and relative speedup of ResNeXt-101 with Inplace ABN

Fig. 5. Training time and speedup comparison of RevNet-104 and ResNeXt-101 with Inplace ABN on ImageNet. Training time per iteration is the time of one complete iteration (forward, backward, and optimizer updating). Training time per sample is the multiplicative inverse of training throughput. The curves of `baseline-C` are truncated due to device memory limitation.

grows, the harsh memory constraint pushes us forward to the extreme of memory efficiency. The gap between the two curves (`baseline-M` and optimal) demonstrates the absolute time saved by applying our method.

Figure 5b compares the training time per sample. We can use this metric to compare the training throughput (which is the multiplicative inverse of the training time per sample) for different mini-batch sizes. Before applying our framework, the training speed increases as the mini-batch size grows for two reasons. First, we leverage the parallelism across batches. Second, the execution time of the optimizer, scheduler, and control is independent of the mini-batch size. This part of execution is amortized by the large mini-batch size. After using our framework, the trend is different. The training throughput decreases as the mini-batch size grows, because the computation overhead of inverse functions is much larger than the benefit from large mini-batch size. We also show the relative speedup of our optimal execution time compared with `baseline-M`. We can achieve up to 1.15× speedup for this benchmark.

4.4   Inplace ABN

We follow the settings in the paper of Inplace ABN [4] and use our framework to train ResNeXt-101 [23] for image classification on ImageNet. Figures 5c and 5d compares the training time per iteration across different mini-batch sizes. The results are similar to those of RevNet-104 except the relative speedup.

The computation overhead of the Inplace ABN is relatively low compared with RevNet-104 in the previous subsection. The execution time of `baseline-C` is only $0.8 - 2\%$ smaller than that of `baseline-M`. Therefore, the relative speedup using our method is not as significant as the experiments on RevNet-104. The reason is that the maximum training throughput of our framework is bounded by `baseline-C`. However, the advantage of our method is that we can find the optimal point across two baselines.

4.5   Reformer

We also do experiments on the enwik8 task with Reformer. Specifically, there are 8 heads in our 12-layer model. The maximum sequence length is 4,096, and the number of tokens is 256. For each iteration, we call the optimizer to update the trainable parameters after accumulating gradients for 4 steps. Table 2 shows the training time in different modes.

Table 2. Results of Reformer on enwik8 task. TPI and TPS are abbreviations for training time per iteration and training time per sample. OOM stands for out of memory. All the execution time is in the unit of seconds.

Mini-batch size	Baseline-C TPI	Baseline-M TPI	Optimal TPI	Baseline-C TPS	Baseline-M TPS	Optimal TPS	Speedup
1	0.951	1.321	0.949	0.951	1.321	0.949	1.392
2	1.738	2.533	1.738	0.869	1.266	0.869	1.457
3	OOM	3.603	2.752	OOM	1.201	0.917	1.310
4	OOM	4.792	4.175	OOM	1.198	1.044	1.148
5	OOM	6.020	5.236	OOM	1.204	1.047	1.150
6	OOM	7.210	6.692	OOM	1.202	1.115	1.077
7	OOM	8.420	7.670	OOM	1.203	1.096	1.098
8	OOM	9.490	9.044	OOM	1.186	1.130	1.049
9	OOM	10.603	10.123	OOM	1.178	1.125	1.047
10	OOM	11.873	11.295	OOM	1.187	1.129	1.051

Due to the large memory footprint, the `baseline-C` can only run with a mini-batch size of 2. The reversibility enables us to train the model with a mini-batch size up to 10. Our framework provides a smooth transition from `baseline-C` to `baseline-M`. We achieve 1.3× relative speedup when the mini-batch size is 3.

4.6 Various Mini-Batch Sizes

For this subsection, we discuss the optimal mini-batch size from the perspective of training throughput. In the above experiments, the lowest execution time per sample (TPS) is approximately obtained at the largest mini-batch size when `baseline-C` is feasible. For example, the Reformer get the lowest TPS 0.869s at the mini-batch size of 2. The reason is that the computation overhead of inverse functions is much larger than the benefit from large mini-batch size. In other words, we cannot accelerate the training process via reversible neural architectures. From the perspective of Problem 8, the TPS $f(x,b) = t_e^{(1)^T} x - \frac{C - t_e^{(0)^T} x}{b}$ is dominated by the first term $t_e^{(1)^T} x$.

5 Conclusions

In this paper, we present the framework to execute reversible neural architectures in the most efficient modes. We formulate the decision problem for reversible operators. The training time is the objective function with memory usage as a constraint. By solving this problem, we can maximize the training speed for any reversible neural architectures. Our framework automates this decision process, empowering researchers to develop and train reversible networks more efficiently.

For future directions, we may integrate gradient checkpoints and reversible neural architectures to enlarge the search space, since gradient checkpoints allow non-reversible layers to follow M-Mode by doing recomputation. The optimal mini-batch size in terms of training throughput is another critical issue.

References

1. Abadi, M., et al.: TensorFlow: large-scale machine learning on heterogeneous systems (2015)
2. Blumberg, S.B., Tanno, R., Kokkinos, I., Alexander, D.C.: Deeper image quality transfer: training low-memory neural networks for 3D images. In: Frangi, A.F., Schnabel, J.A., Davatzikos, C., Alberola-López, C., Fichtinger, G. (eds.) MICCAI 2018. LNCS, vol. 11070, pp. 118–125. Springer, Cham (2018). https://doi.org/10.1007/978-3-030-00928-1_14
3. Brügger, R., Baumgartner, C.F., Konukoglu, E.: A partially reversible U-Net for memory-efficient volumetric image segmentation. In: Shen, D., et al. (eds.) MICCAI 2019. LNCS, vol. 11766, pp. 429–437. Springer, Cham (2019). https://doi.org/10.1007/978-3-030-32248-9_48
4. Buló, S.R., Porzi, L., Kontschieder, P.: In-place activated batchnorm for memory-optimized training of dnns. In: 2018 IEEE/CVF Conference on Computer Vision and Pattern Recognition, pp. 5639–5647, June 2018. https://doi.org/10.1109/CVPR.2018.00591
5. Chen, T.Q., Rubanova, Y., Bettencourt, J., Duvenaud, D.K.: Neural ordinary differential equations. In: Bengio, S., Wallach, H., Larochelle, H., Grauman, K., Cesa-Bianchi, N., Garnett, R. (eds.) Advances in Neural Information Processing Systems, vol. 31, pp. 6571–6583. Curran Associates Inc., Red Hook (2018)

6. Chen, T., Xu, B., Zhang, C., Guestrin, C.: Training deep nets with sublinear memory cost (2016)
7. Gomez, A.N., Ren, M., Urtasun, R., Grosse, R.B.: The reversible residual network: backpropagation without storing activations. In: Proceedings of the 31st International Conference on Neural Information Processing Systems, pp. 2211–2221. NIPS'17, Curran Associates Inc., Red Hook, NY, USA (2017)
8. Ioffe, S., Szegedy, C.: Batch normalization: accelerating deep network training by reducing internal covariate shift. In: Proceedings of the 32nd International Conference on International Conference on Machine Learning, Vol. 37, pp. 448–456. ICML'15, JMLR.org (2015)
9. Jacobsen, J.H., Smeulders, A.W., Oyallon, E.: i-revnet: deep invertible networks. In: International Conference on Learning Representations (2018)
10. Jain, P., et al.: Breaking the memory wall with optimal tensor rematerialization. Proc. Mach. Learn. Syst. **2020**, 497–511 (2020)
11. Jia, Z., Lin, S., Qi, C.R., Aiken, A.: Exploring hidden dimensions in accelerating convolutional neural networks. In: Dy, J., Krause, A. (eds.) Proceedings of the 35th International Conference on Machine Learning, vol. 80, pp. 2274–2283. Proceedings of Machine Learning Research (PMLR), Stockholm Sweden (2018)
12. Kingma, D.P., Dhariwal, P.: Glow: generative flow with invertible 1x1 convolutions. In: Bengio, S., Wallach, H., Larochelle, H., Grauman, K., Cesa-Bianchi, N., Garnett, R. (eds.) Advances in Neural Information Processing Systems, vol. 31, pp. 10215–10224. Curran Associates Inc., Red Hook (2018)
13. Kitaev, N., Kaiser, L., Levskaya, A.: Reformer: the efficient transformer (2020)
14. Kusumoto, M., Inoue, T., Watanabe, G., Akiba, T., Koyama, M.: A graph theoretic framework of recomputation algorithms for memory-efficient backpropagation. In: Advances in Neural Information Processing Systems, vol. 32, pp. 1161–1170. Curran Associates, Inc. (2019)
15. Leemput, S.C., Teuwen, J., Ginneken, B.V., Manniesing, R.: Memcnn: a python/pytorch package for creating memory-efficient invertible neural networks. J. Open Source Softw. 4(39), 1576 (2019). https://doi.org/10.21105/joss.01576
16. MacKay, M., Vicol, P., Ba, J., Grosse, R.: Reversible recurrent neural networks. In: Proceedings of the 32nd International Conference on Neural Information Processing Systems, pp. 9043–9054. NIPS'18, Curran Associates Inc., Red Hook, NY, USA (2018)
17. Martello, S., Toth, P.: Knapsack Problems: Algorithms and Computer Implementations. John Wiley & Sons Inc, USA (1990)
18. Paszke, A., et al.: Pytorch: an imperative style, high-performance deep learning library. In: Advances in Neural Information Processing Systems, vol. 32, pp. 8024–8035. Curran Associates, Inc. (2019)
19. Rhu, M., Gimelshein, N., Clemons, J., Zulfiqar, A., Keckler, S.W.: Vdnn: virtualized deep neural networks for scalable, memory-efficient neural network design. In: The 49th Annual IEEE/ACM International Symposium on Microarchitecture. MICRO-49, IEEE Press (2016)
20. Rumelhart, D.E., Hinton, G.E., Williams, R.J.: Neurocomputing: foundations of research. Nature, pp. 696–699 (1988)
21. Sohoni, N.S., Aberger, C.R., Leszczynski, M., Zhang, J., Ré, C.: Low-memory neural network training: a technical report (2019)
22. Vaswani, A., et al.: Attention is all you need. In: Guyon, I., et al. (eds.) Advances in Neural Information Processing Systems, vol. 30, pp. 5998–6008. Curran Associates Inc., Red Hook (2017)

23. Xie, S., Girshick, R., Dollar, P., Tu, Z., He, K.: Aggregated residual transformations for deep neural networks. In: 2017 IEEE Conference on Computer Vision and Pattern Recognition (CVPR), Jul 2017. https://doi.org/10.1109/cvpr.2017.634
24. Zhang, J., Yeung, S.H., Shu, Y., He, B., Wang, W.: Efficient memory management for gpu-based deep learning systems (2019)
25. Zhu, J., Park, T., Isola, P., Efros, A.A.: Unpaired image-to-image translation using cycle-consistent adversarial networks. In: 2017 IEEE International Conference on Computer Vision (ICCV), pp. 2242–2251, Oct 2017. https://doi.org/10.1109/ICCV.2017.244

Box2Seg: Attention Weighted Loss and Discriminative Feature Learning for Weakly Supervised Segmentation

Viveka Kulharia[2]([✉]), Siddhartha Chandra[1], Amit Agrawal[1], Philip Torr[2], and Ambrish Tyagi[1]

[1] Amazon Lab126, Sunnyvale, USA
[2] University of Oxford, Oxford, UK
vivekakulharia@gmail.com

Abstract. We propose a weakly supervised approach to semantic segmentation using bounding box annotations. Bounding boxes are treated as noisy labels for the foreground objects. We predict a per-class attention map that saliently guides the per-pixel cross entropy loss to focus on foreground pixels and refines the segmentation boundaries. This avoids propagating erroneous gradients due to incorrect foreground labels on the background. Additionally, we learn pixel embeddings to simultaneously optimize for high intra-class feature affinity while increasing discrimination between features across different classes. Our method, Box2Seg, achieves state-of-the-art segmentation accuracy on PASCAL VOC 2012 by significantly improving the mIOU metric by 2.1% compared to previous weakly supervised approaches. Our weakly supervised approach is comparable to the recent fully supervised methods when fine-tuned with limited amount of pixel-level annotations. Qualitative results and ablation studies show the benefit of different loss terms on the overall performance.

1 Introduction

The accuracy of semantic segmentation approaches has improved significantly in recent years [8,10,32,35,53,54,56]. The mean Intersection-over-Union (mIoU) metric on the PASCAL VOC semantic segmentation benchmark has improved by over 20% in the last five years. The success of these efforts can be broadly attributed to (i) advancements in deep neural network architectures and loss functions (ii) efficient processing (better GPUs), and (iii) the availability of large

---

V. Kulharia, S.Chandra — Equally Contributed.
V. Kulharia was an intern at Amazon Lab126.

Electronic supplementary material The online version of this chapter (https://doi.org/10.1007/978-3-030-58583-9_18) contains supplementary material, which is available to authorized users.

A. Vedaldi et al. (Eds.): ECCV 2020, LNCS 12372, pp. 290–308, 2020.
https://doi.org/10.1007/978-3-030-58583-9_18

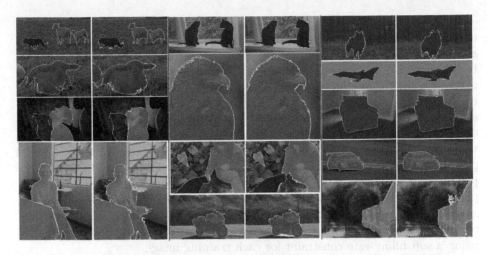

Fig. 1. Our Box2Seg model is able to produce high quality semantic segmentation using only bounding box annotations. Each image pair shows ground-truth (left) and predicted segmentation (right).

datasets of images with human labeled per-pixel annotations [13,30]. Improvements in network architectures and hardware capabilities benefit all deep learning tasks. However, large datasets with per-pixel semantic labels are both expensive and slow to obtain [4,13] (typically 4–10 minutes per image), making it challenging to scale to a large number of object categories. Consequently, even the largest semantic segmentation datasets [30,58] include less than a couple of hundred object categories.

To address the scarcity of labeled data, some previous works have used synthetic datasets [43]. While labeling synthetically generated datasets involves little annotation effort, models trained on them do not always generalize well to the real world due to the domain gap between the real and the synthetic images. Alternative training strategies such as semi-, self-, or weak-supervision that require simpler/fewer labels (eg. image-level labels or bounding box annotations) have also been proposed. In this work, we show how to leverage real images with weak supervision to advance the state-of-the-art (SOTA) for semantic segmentation (refer to Fig. 1 for sample results).

Bounding box annotations yield high quality ground truth at a small cost. According to [4,13], per-pixel labeling takes over 4 minutes per image compared to $\sim$ 7 s (35x faster) for annotating bounding boxes [36]. Furthermore, large datasets with bounding box annotations containing over 9 million images are publicly available [25]. Weakly supervised approaches using bounding box annotations have been shown to be more accurate when compared to methods that use only image-level labels. SOTA segmentation result on VOC using bounding box annotations [46] outperforms the SOTA methods using image-level labels [27] by $\sim$ 4%. Our work, *Box2Seg*, builds upon previous approaches that use bounding box annotations.

A key intuition of our paper is to consider bounding box annotations as containing *label noise* for the foreground object. Since bounding box annotation is a super-set of the actual object segmentation, this label noise is one-sided. In other words, some foreground labels are incorrectly assigned to background pixels within the bounding box. However, all foreground pixels inside the box and background pixels outside all boxes are correctly labeled. Typical fully supervised segmentation training considers the label for every pixel as correct and gradients are back-propagated from all pixels. This would be an issue for a weakly supervised segmentation algorithm. To handle this, our algorithm predicts a novel per-pixel class-specific attention map and pixel embeddings in addition to the per-pixel segmentation output. The attention map is used to modulate the per-pixel cross entropy loss to handle label noise and reduces propagation of incorrect gradients. Thus, the attention map allows us to automatically discover salient regions of the object within the bounding box. The attention map is regularized using a soft filling-rate constraint for each training image.

We learn discriminative feature embeddings to capture long-range pairwise relationships between pixels across an image. We pretrain these embeddings to maximize the affinity between pixels belonging to same classes, while at the same time increasing the distance between features corresponding to different classes. During training, we define a novel loss function on pairs of pixels such that it encourages the pixel affinities to align with the predicted segmentation probabilities. A few methods have also proposed using feature affinity as an explicit measure to improve segmentation in fully-supervised and co-segmentation settings [5,18,22,31,33]. Affinities have also been used in some weakly supervised approaches [1,2], but they are trained in a fully-supervised manner using pseudo ground truth derived from class activation maps, as opposed to our embeddings which are trained by minimizing disagreements between them and estimated segmentation output (Sect. 3.4). We show how discriminative feature learning obtained using the model predictions can also be incorporated and is helpful in the context of weakly supervised semantic segmentation.

The remainder of this paper is organized as follows. We discuss related work in Sect. 2. Our learning algorithm and loss functions are described in Sect. 3. We demonstrate SOTA results on the PASCAL VOC 2012 segmentation benchmark (Sect. 4), outperforming previous weakly-supervised approaches by 2.1% on the mIoU metric. We also show that our weakly supervised model serves as a good starting point for semi-supervised learning tasks, surpassing fully supervised baselines pre-trained with ImageNet [12] with only a fraction of pixel-level segmentation annotations.

2   Related Work

Previous works on weakly-supervised semantic segmentation have used image-level annotations [17,20,26,27,42,50,52], points/clicks [4], scribbles [29,47–49], bounding box annotations [11,19,37,41,46,55] and adversarial training [3,21]. We take a closer look at some of these methods and categorize them based on the labels required and their methodology.

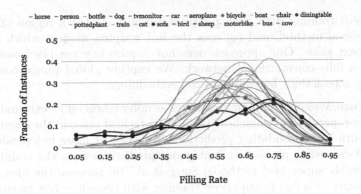

Fig. 2. Distribution of filling rate in PASCAL VOC 2012 training dataset. The per-class filling rates vary widely, especially for the categories such as sofa, dining table and bicycle. Unlike [46] that proposes using 1-3 filling rates per class, we use a per-image class specific filling rate.

Image Level Labels: Deep learning approaches that use image-level labels typically train a classification model first to recover coarse class activation maps [57], which describe class-discriminative image regions. The predicted class activation maps are then used as 'seeds' for optimization methods that grow the coarse activation maps to larger pseudo segmentation maps. A number of optimization methods such as super-pixelization [26], deep seeded region growing [20], conditional random fields [42,52], and combinatorial grouping [40] have been proposed. Finally, the pseudo segmentation maps are used as ground truth to train the segmentation model [28]. Some approaches additionally employ a class-agnostic saliency estimation model [6,50,52] to capture *objectness* of pixels, and others employ Expectation-Maximization (EM) [17] to iteratively refine the pseudo ground truth and the parameters of the segmentation model.

Bounding Box Labels: The availability of bounding box annotations alleviates the need to estimate class activation maps for localizing objects of interest. The bounding boxes serve as crude segmentation masks which are refined using heuristic cues [23] and graph based optimization algorithms such as Grab-Cut [44] or mean-field inference [24] on a densely-connected conditional random field [37,41,46]. Previous works have used the refined masks for training the segmentation model [28]. Some of these approaches additionally use EM [11,23,37,55] for iterative refinement of the ground truth and model parameters. However, training models with EM is time-consuming and is prone to propagation of errors over iterations; In contrast, our proposed approach does not require iterative refinement and outperforms these methods by a large margin (Sect. 4).

Multi-tasking: Hu *et al.* [19] train an object detector and segmentation model simultaneously using the Mask-RCNN framework [15] assuming a closed form relationship between parameters of the detection and segmentation branches. While [19] is able to benefit from the advantages of multi-tasking, it requires

(a) (limited) training data with per-pixel annotations (b) a region of interest (RoI) proposal method, and (c) uses the RoI warping module which captures local context alone. Our approach does not require any per-pixel annotations and uses a fully-convolutional network. We capture global image context via long-range interactions by training pixel embeddings.

Label Noise: We consider bounding boxes as noisy labels for foreground objects. Some fully-supervised approaches [34,39] have tackled noise in the segmentation ground truth by consolidating predictions from two or more independent classifiers and discarding pixels with ambiguous predictions from the training data. Among weakly supervised methods, Song *et al.* [46] propose the idea of using the filling-rate as a cue to supervise training with bounding box ground truth. The filling-rate of a class [46] is defined as the average proportion of pixels in a bounding box that instances of the class occupy, and is estimated by applying dense-CRF [24] for foreground extraction within bounding boxes. For example, suppose in the PASCAL VOC 2012 dataset, instances of 'sheep' occupy roughly 60% of pixels in each bounding-box. During training, their approach ignores gradients from the 40% pixels with the lowest confidences in each bounding box containing 'sheep'. In contrast, we advocate estimating a *per-image class-specific* spatial attention map, to allow for large intra-class variations in object appearance (see Fig. 2). Instead of ignoring loss on pixels with low-confidence as in [46], which is a hard constraint, we use the filling rate to regularize the attention map as a soft constraint. Therefore, our attention map offers a continuous modulation of cross-entropy loss, rather than a binary decision. Attention maps have also been employed in [1,59] where they are trained in a fully-supervised manner using pseudo segmentation ground truth. In contrast, our attention modulated loss offers a principled way of handling label noise present in segmentation ground truth derived from bounding box annotations. We validate our approach with quantitative and qualitative comparisons with [46] in Sect. 4.

3   Proposed Approach

In this section, we describe our Box2Seg algorithm in detail. We discuss our pipeline and loss functions that allow us to learn a per-image, class-specific attention map as well as pixel embeddings.

3.1   Feed Forward Network Architecture

Let $I \in \mathbb{R}^{n \times 3}$ denote a 3−channel input color image with n pixels. Our segmentation model S is a fully-Convolutional Neural Network (CNN) which takes I as input and produces three outputs: (i) the segmentation output probabilities $y \in \mathbb{P}^{m \times (L+1)}, \mathbb{P} \in [0,1]$ (ii) the attention map $\alpha \in \mathbb{P}^{m \times L}$, and (iii) the pixel embeddings $\beta \in \mathbb{R}^{m \times d}$. Here d denotes the size of the pixel embeddings and m denotes the spatial resolution of the outputs. Each pixel in the output image can assume one of the $L + 1$ labels (L object categories and the background class). The ground truth bounding boxes are denoted by $B_{box} \in \mathbb{R}^{K \times 5}$, where K is

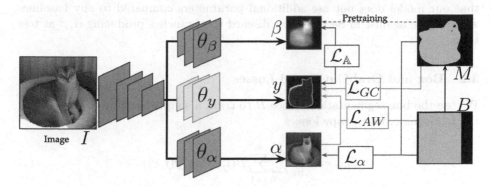

Fig. 3. Overview of our weakly supervised Box2Seg training pipeline. Our segmentation model is a three branch CNN which outputs segmentation probabilities y, per-class spatial attention maps α, and pixel embeddings β. B denotes segmentation masks defined using bounding box annotations. GrabCut is applied to B to obtain refined segmentation masks M. We use B and M to supervise the three outputs of the model. Pixel embeddings capture long-range pairwise relationships and the attention map refines the segmentation output y by reducing the effect of label noise. At test time we only use the branch producing the segmentation probabilities y, and discard the other branches that output α, β.

the number of bounding boxes comprising of 4 coordinates and a class label. To simplify the notation, we denote by $B \in \mathbb{R}^{m \times (L+1)}$ the box-segmentation tensor obtained by setting all pixels inside a bounding box to 1 for the corresponding class label (channel). In the case two boxes overlap, we assign 1 to the class corresponding to the smaller bounding box (assuming that the smaller box is in the front). Note that this assumption may not always be true and can result in incorrect label assignments for B (See eg. Fig. 8).

Similar to prior works [37,41,46], we generate pseudo ground-truth segmentation maps $M \in \mathbb{R}^{m \times (L+1)}$ by applying classical graph-based unsupervised segmentation approach (Grabcut [44]) on each bounding box in our training dataset. The segmentation masks obtained by classical methods, albeit noisy and imprecise, provide a good prior for training deep learning models.

Figure 3 gives an overview of our approach. Training involves passing the input image I through a common feature encoder that feeds into the three branches of network $\mathcal{S}$ to produce y, α, and β, as follows:

$$y = \text{Softmax}(\mathcal{S}(I, \theta_y)); \quad \alpha = \sigma(\mathcal{S}(I, \theta_\alpha)); \quad \beta = \mathcal{S}(I, \theta_\beta),$$

where $\theta_y, \theta_\alpha, \theta_\beta$ denote the parameters of the model $\mathcal{S}$ for the respective branches. Softmax denotes the softmax over all the classes and σ denotes the sigmoid activation function. Note that the segmentation output probabilities, y, sums up to 1 for each pixel across classes due to softmax. However, the activation maps, α, use sigmoid output, making them independent for each class. Note that our model does not use additional parameters compared to any baselines we compare against in Sect. 4 as we discard the branches producing α, β at test time.

3.2 Box and GrabCut Based Losses

We use the box-segmentation tensor B to train a simple baseline by minimizing the following cross-entropy loss:

$$\mathcal{L}_{box} = -\frac{1}{m} \sum_{c=0}^{L} \sum_{i=1}^{m} B(i,c) \log \left(y(i,c) \right). \tag{1}$$

Similar to previous works, we use the GrabCut outputs M obtained from the bounding boxes to define another baseline by minimizing the following cross-entropy loss:

$$\mathcal{L}_{GC} = -\frac{1}{m} \sum_{c=0}^{L} \sum_{i=1}^{m} M(i,c) \log \left(y(i,c) \right). \tag{2}$$

Since the GrabCut algorithm provides reasonable segmentation outputs (Sect. 4), we use $\mathcal{L}_{GC}$ in addition to our loss functions described in the following sections.

3.3 Attention Weighted Segmentation Loss

Our novel attention modulated cross-entropy loss considers bounding box annotations as *noisy labels* for the foreground object. Note that since the bounding box is a super-set of the actual object segmentation mask, the label noise is one-sided: foreground labels are incorrectly assigned to background pixels, but no true foreground labels are missing. Additionally, pixels outside all the bounding boxes can be considered *definite background* and do not have any label noise. Since supervised segmentation training typically considers all labels as correct, in the presence of label noise, erroneous gradients can be back propagated during training. At pixels close to bounding box and object boundaries, the network gets conflicting information about the foreground/background labels at similar pixels. This is the reason for the worse performance of baseline trained with box annotations only (Table 3).

Attention on Foreground Objects: We propose to modulate the per-pixel cross-entropy loss using the predicted attention map from the network by minimizing

$$\mathcal{L}_{fg} = \frac{-1}{\sum_i^m B(i,c)} \sum_{c=1}^{L} \sum_{i=1}^{m} \alpha(i,c) B(i,c) \log \left(y(i,c) \right). \tag{3}$$

Note that the attention map has same spatial resolution as the segmentation output and is class-specific. The attention weighted loss is only defined for the

L foreground classes. In addition, the loss is normalized with the size of the bounding box, to give similar weighting to each class.

Background Loss: Since the pixels outside all the bounding boxes can be considered as definite background, the background loss is defined as

$$\mathcal{L}_{bg} = -\frac{\sum_i^m B(i,0)\log(y(i,0))}{\sum_i^m B(i,0)}, \tag{4}$$

where 0 denotes the background class. We define the **Attention Weighted Loss** (AWL) as

$$\mathcal{L}_{AW} = \mathcal{L}_{fg} + \mathcal{L}_{bg}. \tag{5}$$

Attention Map Regularization: Without any regularization on the attention maps, the network can minimize $\mathcal{L}_{fg}$ by predicting all $\alpha(i,c) = 0$. To prevent this, we compared two approaches to regularize the attention map. The first approach regularizes the attention mask using ground truth bounding boxes (similar to [46]), by minimizing the $\mathcal{L}_2$ loss between the attention maps and the bounding boxes.

$$\mathcal{L}_\alpha^{bbox} = \sum_{i=1}^m \sum_{c=1}^L \parallel B(i,c) - \alpha(i,c) \parallel^2 . \tag{6}$$

The second approach regularizes the attention mask using fill-ratios obtained from GrabCut outputs M as follows. Let η_c denote the per class, per image, filling rate defined as the proportion of pixels in the pseudo ground-truth M compared to its corresponding bounding box.

$$\eta_c = \frac{\sum_i^m M(i,c)}{\sum_i^m B(i,c)}. \tag{7}$$

Similarly, the predicted fill rate of the attention map is computed as

$$\eta_c' = \frac{\sum_i^m B(i,c)\alpha(i,c)}{\sum_i^m B(i,c)}. \tag{8}$$

We use a margin loss to ensure that the predicted fill rate is at least a factor γ of the fill rate obtained using M. $\mathcal{L}_\alpha^{fr} = \max(0, \gamma\eta_c - \eta_c')$, where $\gamma \in [0,1]$ is a hyper-parameter which is set to 0.7 in our experiments. Thus, the predicted fill rate (Eqn. 8) is allowed to vary between $\gamma\eta_c$ and 1. This enforces a soft constraint that the attention map should allow propagation of loss from at least 70% of η_c pixels inside the bounding box. Using L_α^{bbox} for regularization forces the attention mask to take the shape of the bounding box. Thus, it is prone to include background pixels in attention map. Using L_α^{fr} provides a softer constraint and gives better results in our experiments. Figure 4 shows some qualitative examples where attention map is able to focus on foreground pixels despite errors in the underlying GrabCut segmentations, allowing Box2Seg to be robust to label noise.

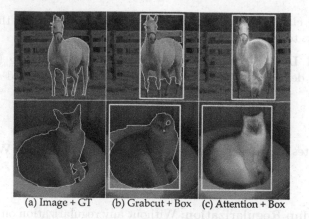

(a) Image + GT   (b) Grabcut + Box   (c) Attention + Box

Fig. 4. Visualizing attention maps produced by our network. (a) Input images with overlaid ground truth masks. (b) Grabcut output with ground-truth bounding box. (c) Predicted attention map. Note that while Grabcut output is erroneous and often includes background pixels, our attention maps are concentrated on the objects of interest.

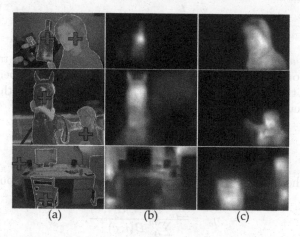

(a)   (b)   (c)

Fig. 5. Visualization of affinities produced by our network. (a) Input image with overlaid ground truth masks and two pixels marked with **purple** and **green** + signs. (b,c) Affinity heatmaps (Eqn. 9) w.r.t. the **purple** and **green** pixels, resp. (Color figure online)

3.4   Discriminative Feature Learning

We now describe training of our pixel embeddings β which capture long-range pairwise relationships between different pixels. Pixel embeddings can be denoted as $\beta = \{\beta_i\}$, where β_i is the d-dimensional feature for the ith pixel. Affinity between embeddings at pixel i and j is given by its normalized dot product

$$\mathbb{A}(i,j) = \beta_i \cdot \beta_j = \frac{\beta_j^T \beta_i}{\|\beta_j\|\|\beta_i\|}. \tag{9}$$

Intuitively, we want to achieve high affinity between feature vectors of two pixels that belong to the same class, while ensuring low affinity between features of two different classes. Similarly, a background pixel should have low affinity with respect to another pixel that belongs to one of the L foreground classes. To achieve this, we define a novel loss function on pairs of pixels (i,j), such that it encourages the pixel affinities to align with the predicted segmentation probabilities, as follows,

$$\mathcal{L}_{\mathbb{A}} = \sum_{i,j} \left(\mathbb{A}(i,j) - y_j^T y_i\right)^2. \tag{10}$$

However, training affinity matrices requires large amount of memory. To avoid creating large affinity matrices of size $m \times m$, we randomly sample a small fraction of pixel empeddings equally from each class to compute this loss. Figure 5 shows the affinity maps computed from our class discriminative embeddings.

3.5 Training Box2Seg

Our approach optimizes the following loss function:

$$\mathcal{L} = \mathcal{L}_{\mathcal{GC}} + \lambda_{AW}\mathcal{L}_{AW} + \lambda_\alpha \mathcal{L}_\alpha + \lambda_{\mathbb{A}}\mathcal{L}_{\mathbb{A}}, \tag{11}$$

where $\mathcal{L}_\alpha$ equals either $\mathcal{L}_\alpha^{bbox}$ or $\mathcal{L}_\alpha^{fr}$. λ_{AW}, λ_α and $\lambda_{\mathbb{A}}$ are weights applied to the individual losses.

4 Experiments and Results

We evaluate the performance of our approach on PASCAL VOC 2012 [13] dataset. Our ablation studies provide insights into our design choices. Finally, we demonstrate that our method provides a better initialization than Imagenet pretraining for the task of semi-supervised segmentation.

4.1 Implementation Details

Our segmentation network architecture is similar to UPerNet [51] where the encoder backbone is ResNet-101 [16], and decoders consist of 2 convolutional layers. We employ the ResNet-101 backbone to ensure fair comparison with the three most recent SOTA works, SDI [23], Li et al. [28], and BCM [46] as well as 4 other recent methods [27,47–49] in Table 1. We have three decoders, one each for the y, α, and β branches. The final results are spatially down-sampled by a factor of 4, i.e. $m = n/16$. We start with ImageNet pretrained [12] weights to initialize our encoder.

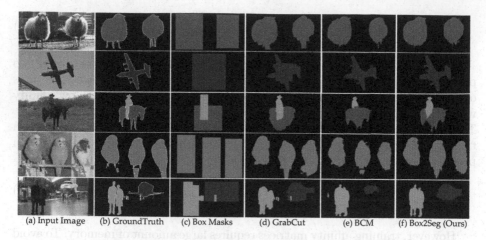

(a) Input Image   (b) GroundTruth   (c) Box Masks   (d) GrabCut   (e) BCM   (f) Box2Seg (Ours)

Fig. 6. Comparison of our segmentation results with those of BCM [46].

We train our network in two stages. First, we pre-train the feature representations using the affinity loss by randomly sampling 10% of pixel pairs using the Grabcut outputs M. This is done by minimizing Eqn. 10 using M_i in place of y_i. Note that the pretraining phase is meant to only serve the task of weight initialization for our discriminative feature learning. Our final feature representations are robust to noise in the Grabcut outputs since they are trained eventually to agree with our predictions using Eqn. 10. After the pretraining phase, we enable the decoder branch to also output y and α and train the entire network end-to-end to optimize the loss function in Eqn. 11. After doing a grid search of hyper-parameters on a held out validation set, λ_{AW}, λ_{α} and λ_A are set to 10, 1, and 1 respectively. We use Stochastic Gradient Descent to train our models for 40 epochs with an initial learning rate $= 1e-4$, momentum $= 0.9$, weight decay $= 5e^{-4}$ and a polynomially decaying learning rate as in [7]. Our implementation uses PyTorch [38] and is trained on Nvidia's TitanX GPUs. Note that at test time we discard the decoders yielding α, β, therefore our method uses no additional parameters compared to any of our baselines in the following sections. Our implementation will be available at www.github.com/vivkul/Box2Seg.

4.2 Quantitative and Qualitative Evaluation

PASCAL VOC 2012 is one of the gold standard benchmarks for semantic segmentation. Following [9,11,32], we use the augmented annotation set [14] consisting of 10582 training and 1449 validation images. Performance is measured using the mIoU metric on the validation set.

We compare the accuracy of our algorithm to the SOTA weakly supervised segmentation methods on VOC validation set in Table 1. Our approach shows a large improvement over previous methods ([11,23,28,37,46]), some of which have also used VGG-16 backbones for feature representation. Li et al. [28] report

Table 1. Comparison of Box2Seg to previous weakly supervised semantic segmentation methods on PASCAL VOC validation set. C=dense-CRF post processing.

Method	Annotations	Backbone	MIoU
GrabCut-NoTrain-GT	Box	-	71.6
GrabCut-NoTrain-Det	Box	-	68.5
SSNet [52]	Image-level	DenseNet-169	63.3
F2FA [27]	Image-level	ResNet-101	66.5
ScribbleSup (C) [29]	Scribble	VGG-16	63.1
NormalCut [47]	Scribble	ResNet-101	72.8
BPG [49]	Scribble	ResNet-101	73.2
KernelCut [48]	Scribble	ResNet-101	73.0
WSSL (C) [37]	Box	VGG-16	60.6
BoxSup (C) [11]	Box	VGG-16	62.0
SDI (C) [23]	Box	ResNet-101	69.4
BCM (C) [46]	Box	ResNet-101	70.2
Li *et al.* (C) [28]	Box	ResNet-101	74.3
Box2Seg	Box	ResNet-101	**74.9**
Box2Seg (C)	Box	ResNet-101	**76.4**

an mIoU of 74.3%, using bounding boxes as supervision and dense CRF post-processing. Our method yields an mIoU of 74.9% without dense CRF, and 76.4% mIoU after dense CRF post processing resulting in an improvement of 2.1%. Box2Seg also outperforms recent weakly supervised methods that use image level labels [27,52] or scribbles [29,47–49]. Per-category results comparing Box2Seg against the SOTA methods are reported in Table 2.

Qualitative comparison of our results with BCM [46] is shown in Fig. 6. Our method is able to produce higher-quality object segmentations compared to BCM. It's also robust to false segmentations in some cases, e.g. false detection closer to the left edge of the BCM result on the last row are suppressed by our method. Please refer to Fig. 1 for additional examples of segmentations using our approach. We also show some failure cases of our approach in Fig. 8.

Table 2. Per-class results on PASCAL VOC 2012 Validation set. We compare our *Box2Seg* (with and without denseCRF) with those of the previous state-of-the-art methods. Please note that Li *et al.* (CRF) results require COCO annotations. Per-class results from [46] for their ResNet-101 model are not available.

Method	Bkg	Aero	Bike	Bird	Boat	Bottle	Bus	Car	Cat	Chair	Cow	Table	Dog	Horse	Mbike	Person	Plant	Sheep	Sofa	Train	Tv	MIoU
BCM VGG (CRF) [46]	89.8	68.3	27.1	73.7	56.4	72.6	84.2	75.6	79.9	35.2	78.3	53.2	77.6	66.4	68.1	73.1	56.8	80.1	45.1	74.7	54.6	66.8
BCM ResNet (CRF) [46]	–	–	–	–	–	–	–	–	–	–	–	–	–	–	–	–	–	–	–	–	–	70.2
Li *et al.* (CRF) [28]	93.3	85.0	35.9	88.6	70.3	77.9	91.9	83.6	90.5	39.2	84.5	59.4	86.5	82.4	81.5	84.3	57.0	85.9	55.8	85.8	70.4	75.7
Box2Seg	92.5	66.5	31.7	78.9	65.5	83.4	90.4	86.7	86.0	55.1	81.8	59.9	80.5	74.1	76.0	75.7	65.3	85.1	72.5	87.8	77.7	74.9
Box2Seg (CRF)	93.3	72.4	33.0	84.2	64.9	83.5	90.9	86.7	88.7	57.2	83.6	62.5	82.6	76.8	77.0	77.8	63.3	87.2	75.1	88.3	74.1	76.4

Fig. 7. (Left) Input images with overlaid bounding box labels. (Middle) Missing pixel-level annotations on foreground objects such as *Aeroplane* and *Person*. Note that the bounding box annotations are correct. (Right) Predicted attention map with boxes. Please refer to Sect. 4.4 for discussion on how our AWL can help in cases with conflicting ground truth during fully-supervised training.

Table 3. Ablation study showing the effect of our loss functions in improving the performance over baseline methods.

Method	$\mathcal{L}_{box}$	$\mathcal{L}_{GC}$	$\mathcal{L}_{AW}$	$\mathcal{L}_\alpha$	$\mathcal{L}_\mathrm{A}$	MIoU
Box	✓					59.3
GrabCut		✓				72.7
Affinity		✓			✓	73.9
AW-box		✓	✓	$\mathcal{L}_\alpha^{bbox}$		74.1
AW-fr		✓	✓	$\mathcal{L}_\alpha^{fr}$		74.6
Box2Seg		✓	✓	$\mathcal{L}_\alpha^{fr}$	✓	**74.9**

Accuracy of GrabCut (no training): We also evaluated the accuracy of GrabCut algorithm itself, without any training, against the segmentation ground-truth. Interestingly, GrabCut output on *ground truth* bounding boxes (*GrabCut-NoTrain-GT*) results in a strong weakly-supervised baseline with 71.6% mIoU. However, since the ground truth bounding boxes are not available at inference, a more practical baseline is to obtain bounding boxes on the validation set using an object detector (we used SNIPER [45]) and then run GrabCut on those. This baseline (*GrabCut-NoTrain-Det*) obtains 68.5% mIoU.

4.3 Ablation Studies

Table 3 shows the efficacy of our loss functions in improving the performance of our approach. The trivial *Box* baseline obtained by training the segmentation network with bounding box supervision ($\mathcal{L}_{box}$ loss only) results in a low mIoU of 59.3%, as expected. Training the segmentation network with *GrabCut* masks ($\mathcal{L}_{GC}$ loss only) without affinity or attention losses resulted in 72.7% mIOU. Introducing our feature embeddings to the pipeline (Affinity) improves the mIoU to 73.9%. Our novel AWL terms $(\lambda_{AW}\mathcal{L}_{AW} + \lambda_{\alpha}\mathcal{L}_{\alpha})$ significantly improve the mIoU to 74.6% with filling-rate regularization (*AW-fr*) (more about AWL in Sect. 4.4). Finally, combining all losses (Eqn 11), *Box2Seg* obtains 74.9% mIoU.

4.4 Attention Weighted Loss in the Fully-Supervised Setting

We demonstrate that AWL boosts segmentation accuracy in fully-supervised case if we have disagreements between bounding-box and per-pixel annotations.

During our analysis, we found that roughly 10% of training images in PAS-CAL VOC dataset [13,14] have disagreements between the bounding box and pixel-level annotations. Figure 7 shows few examples, where pixel-level annotation for object categories are missing, but their corresponding bounding box labels are correctly provided. Due to incorrect pixel-level annotations, fully supervised training would back-propagate erroneous gradients on these pixels. Since our novel AWL ($\mathcal{L}_{AW}$ in Sect. 3.3) is effective in dealing with label noise for weakly supervised networks, we analyze if it can further improve the performance of a fully supervised network also. In cases where conflicting sources of ground truth exist (as in Fig. 7), AWL can allow correct gradients to propagate back due to correct bounding box annotations (see the predicted attention maps in Fig. 7), thereby reducing the effect of incorrect pixel-level annotations.

Table 4. Improvements in segmentation accuracy on the PASCAL VOC 2012 validation set in the fully supervised setting using AWL.

Method	CE Loss	+ $\mathcal{L}_{AW}$	Δ
Supervised baseline	73.6	75.1	+1.5

Table 4 shows the improvement obtained by adding AWL to the fully *Supervised baseline*. Adding the AWL (+ $\mathcal{L}_{AW}$) to the fully-*Supervised* baseline improved the segmentation mIoU by 1.5%. Thus, AWL is effective at improving segmentation accuracy, both in the weakly- and fully- supervised settings.

4.5 Semi-supervised Semantic Segmentation

Weakly supervised trained method can naturally serve as a starting point for semi-supervised segmentation. To study this, we fine tuned our Box2Seg model using different amount of pixel-level annotations. We observe significant improvements in accuracy, even with small amount of supervision as shown in Table 5. For comparison, we show the result of semi-supervised fine tuned BCM [46] model trained with 1464 images (13.8% of the data) and another fully supervised baseline (*DeepLab*) using ImageNet as the initialization. Our weakly supervised baseline results improved from 74.9% mIoU to 83.1% with just 10% of supervised data. Therefore, our Box2Seg model can serve as a good starting point and provides better results compared to ImageNet based initialization.

Table 5. Semi-supervised segmentation using Box2Seg model as initialization. (S=τ%) implies τ% images with pixel annotations are used for semi-supervised fine-tuning. C=dense-CRF post processing. †: ResNet-101 backbone (refer [46]).

Method	MIoU
BCM [46] † (S=0%) (C)	70.2
BCM [46] † (S=13.8%) (C)	71.6
DeepLab † (S=100%) (C)	74.5
Box2Seg (S=0%)	74.9
Box2Seg (S=5%)	78.7
Box2Seg (S=10%)	83.1
Box2Seg (S=100%)	86.4

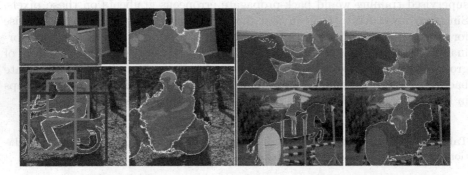

Fig. 8. Failure Cases. (Left) Incorrect label assignment on box annotations B can happen when the smaller bounding box is physically behind the larger bounding box. (Right) Predicted segmentation bleeds into background.

5 Conclusions

In this work, we proposed a pipeline for training a weakly supervised semantic segmentation method from bounding box annotations. We showed that bounding box annotations can be treated as noisy labels for foreground objects and proposed a novel attention weighted loss to reduce the effect of erroneuos gradients due to incorrect labels. We also proposed pixel embeddings to capture global context via long-range pairwise interactions. We showed qualitative improvements over the previous SOTA on the PASCAL VOC semantic segmentation benchmark and pushed the mIoU metric forward by 2.1%. Interestingly, fully supervised methods can also benefit from attention weighted loss in the presence of exhaustive bounding box annotations but missing pixel-level annotations. Future work would involve using an edge detector as a cue to learn class boundaries, and also extending our method to benefit from image-level supervision.

Acknowledgements. V. Kulharia worked as an intern at Amazon Lab126 and continued this work at Oxford University. V Kulharia's DPhil is funded by the Toyota Research Institute grant.

References

1. Ahn, J., Cho, S., Kwak, S.: Weakly supervised learning of instance segmentation with inter-pixel relations. In: Proceedings of the IEEE Conference on Computer Vision and Pattern Recognition, pp. 2209–2218 (2019)
2. Ahn, J., Kwak, S.: Learning pixel-level semantic affinity with image-level supervision for weakly supervised semantic segmentation. In: IEEE Conference on Computer Vision and Pattern Recognition (CVPR) (2018)
3. Arandjelović, R., Zisserman, A.: Object discovery with a copy-pasting gan. arXiv preprint arXiv:1905.11369 (2019)
4. Bearman, A., Russakovsky, O., Ferrari, V., Fei-Fei, L.: What's the point: semantic segmentation with point supervision. In: Leibe, B., Matas, J., Sebe, N., Welling, M. (eds.) ECCV 2016. LNCS, vol. 9911, pp. 549–565. Springer, Cham (2016). https://doi.org/10.1007/978-3-319-46478-7_34
5. Chandra, S., Usunier, N., Kokkinos, I.: Dense and low-rank gaussian crfs using deep embeddings. In: IEEE Conference on Computer Vision and Pattern Recognition (CVPR), pp. 5103–5112 (2017)
6. Chaudhry, A., Dokania, P.K., Torr, P.H.: Discovering class-specific pixels for weakly-supervised semantic segmentation. In: British Machine Vision Conference (BMVC) (2017)
7. Chen, L.C., Papandreou, G., Kokkinos, I., Murphy, K., Yuille, A.L.: Semantic image segmentation with deep convolutional nets and fully connected crfs. arXiv preprint arXiv:1412.7062 (2014)
8. Chen, L.C., Papandreou, G., Kokkinos, I., Murphy, K., Yuille, A.L.: Deeplab: semantic image segmentation with deep convolutional nets, atrous convolution, and fully connected crfs. arXiv:1606.00915 (2016)
9. Chen, L., Papandreou, G., Schroff, F., Adam, H.: Rethinking atrous convolution for semantic image segmentation. CoRR abs/1706.05587 (2017). http://arxiv.org/abs/1706.05587
10. Chen, L.C., Zhu, Y., Papandreou, G., Schroff, F., Adam, H.: Encoder-decoder with atrous separable convolution for semantic image segmentation. In: European Conference on Computer Vision (ECCV), pp. 801–818 (2018)
11. Dai, J., He, K., Sun, J.: Boxsup: exploiting bounding boxes to supervise convolutional networks for semantic segmentation. In: International Conference on Computer Vision (ICCV), pp. 1635–1643 (2015)
12. Deng, J., Dong, W., Socher, R., Li, L.J., Li, K., Fei-Fei, L.: ImageNet: a large-scale hierarchical image database. In: IEEE Conference on Computer Vision and Pattern Recognition (CVPR) (2009)
13. Everingham, M., Gool, L., Williams, C.K., Winn, J., Zisserman, A.: The pascal visual object classes (voc) challenge. Int. J. Comput. Vis. (IJCV) **88**(2), 303–338 (2010). https://doi.org/10.1007/s11263-009-0275-4
14. Hariharan, B., Arbelaez, P., Bourdev, L., Maji, S., Malik, J.: Semantic contours from inverse detectors. In: International Conference on Computer Vision (ICCV) (2011)
15. He, K., Gkioxari, G., Dollár, P., Girshick, R.: Mask r-cnn. In: International Conference on Computer Vision (ICCV) (2017)

16. He, K., Zhang, X., Ren, S., Sun, J.: Deep residual learning for image recognition. In: IEEE Conference on Computer Vision and Pattern Recognition (CVPR) (2016)
17. Hou, Q., Massiceti, D., Dokania, P.K., Wei, Y., Cheng, M.M., Torr, P.H.S.: Bottom-up top-down cues for weakly-supervised semantic segmentation. In: Pelillo, M., Hancock, E. (eds.) EMMCVPR 2017. LNCS, vol. 10746, pp. 263–277. Springer, Cham (2018). https://doi.org/10.1007/978-3-319-78199-0_18
18. Hsu, K.J., Lin, Y.Y., Chuang, Y.Y.: Deepco3: deep instance co-segmentation by co-peak search and co-saliency detection. In: IEEE Conference on Computer Vision and Pattern Recognition (CVPR) (2019)
19. Hu, R., Dollár, P., He, K., Darrell, T., Girshick, R.: Learning to segment every thing. In: IEEE Conference on Computer Vision and Pattern Recognition (CVPR), pp. 4233–4241 (2018)
20. Huang, Z., Wang, X., Wang, J., Liu, W., Wang, J.: Weakly-supervised semantic segmentation network with deep seeded region growing. In: IEEE Conference on Computer Vision and Pattern Recognition, pp. 7014–7023 (2018)
21. Hung, W.C., Tsai, Y.H., Liou, Y.T., Lin, Y.Y., Yang, M.H.: Adversarial learning for semi-supervised semantic segmentation. In: British Machine Vision Conference (BMVC) (2018)
22. Ke, T.W., Hwang, J.J., Liu, Z., Yu, S.X.: Adaptive affinity fields for semantic segmentation. In: European Conference on Computer Vision (ECCV) (2018)
23. Khoreva, A., Benenson, R., Hosang, J., Hein, M., Schiele, B.: Simple does it: weakly supervised instance and semantic segmentation. In: IEEE Conference on Computer Vision and Pattern Recognition (CVPR), pp. 876–885 (2017)
24. Krähenbühl, P., Koltun, V.: Efficient inference in fully connected crfs with gaussian edge potentials. In: Neural Information Processing Systems (NIPS) (2011)
25. Kuznetsova, A., et al.: The open images dataset v4: unified image classification, object detection, and visual relationship detection at scale. arXiv preprint arXiv:1811.00982 (2018)
26. Kwak, S., Hong, S., Han, B.: Weakly supervised semantic segmentation using superpixel pooling network. In: AAAI Conference on Artificial Intelligence (2017)
27. Lee, J., Kim, E., Lee, S., Lee, J., Yoon, S.: Frame-to-frame aggregation of active regions in web videos for weakly supervised semantic segmentation. In: International Conference on Computer Vision (ICCV), October 2019
28. Li, Q., Arnab, A., Torr, P.H.: Weakly-and semi-supervised panoptic segmentation. In: Proceedings of the European Conference on Computer Vision (ECCV 18), pp. 102–118 (2018)
29. Lin, D., Dai, J., Jia, J., He, K., Sun, J.: Scribblesup: scribble-supervised convolutional networks for semantic segmentation. In: IEEE Conference on Computer Vision and Pattern Recognition (CVPR), pp. 3159–3167 (2016)
30. Lin, T.: Microsoft COCO: common objects in context. In: Fleet, D., Pajdla, T., Schiele, B., Tuytelaars, T. (eds.) ECCV 2014. LNCS, vol. 8693, pp. 740–755. Springer, Cham (2014). https://doi.org/10.1007/978-3-319-10602-1_48
31. Liu, S., De Mello, S., Gu, J., Zhong, G., Yang, M.H., Kautz, J.: Learning affinity via spatial propagation networks. In: Neural Information Processing Systems (NIPS) (2017)
32. Long, J., Shelhamer, E., Darrell, T.: Fully convolutional networks for semantic segmentation. In: IEEE Conference on Computer Vision and Pattern Recognition (CVPR), pp. 3431–3440 (2015)
33. Maire, M., Narihira, T., Yu, S.X.: Affinity cnn: learning pixel-centric pairwise relations for figure/ground embedding. In: IEEE Conference on Computer Vision and Pattern Recognition (CVPR) (2016)

34. Min, S., Chen, X., Zha, Z.J., Wu, F., Zhang, Y.: A two-stream mutual attention network for semi-supervised biomedical segmentation with noisy labels (2018)
35. Noh, H., Hong, S., Han, B.: Learning deconvolution network for semantic segmentation. In: arXiv preprint arXiv:1505.04366 (2015)
36. Papadopoulos, D.P., Uijlings, J.R., Keller, F., Ferrari, V.: Extreme clicking for efficient object annotation. In: IEEE International Conference on Computer Vision (CVPR), pp. 4930–4939 (2017)
37. Papandreou, G., Chen, L.C., Murphy, K.P., Yuille, A.L.: Weakly-and semi-supervised learning of a deep convolutional network for semantic image segmentation. In: IEEE Conference on Computer Vision and Pattern Recognition (CVPR), pp. 1742–1750 (2015)
38. Paszke, A., et al.: Automatic differentiation in pytorch (2017)
39. Petit, O., Thome, N., Charnoz, A., Hostettler, A., Soler, L.: Handling missing annotations for semantic segmentation with deep convNets. In: Stoyanov, D., et al. (eds.) DLMIA/ML-CDS -2018. LNCS, vol. 11045, pp. 20–28. Springer, Cham (2018). https://doi.org/10.1007/978-3-030-00889-5_3
40. Pont-Tuset, J., Arbelaez, P., Barron, J.T., Marques, F., Malik, J.: Multiscale combinatorial grouping for image segmentation and object proposal generation. IEEE Trans. Pattern Anal. Mach. Intell. (TPAMI) 39(1), 128–140 (2016)
41. Rajchl, M., et al.: Deepcut: object segmentation from bounding box annotations using convolutional neural networks. IEEE Trans. Med. Imaging 36(2), 674–683 (2016)
42. Redondo-Cabrera, C., Baptista-Ríos, M., López-Sastre, R.J.: Learning to exploit the prior network knowledge for weakly supervised semantic segmentation. IEEE Trans. Image Process. 28(7), 3649–3661 (2019)
43. Richter, S.R., Hayder, Z., Koltun, V.: Playing for benchmarks. In: International Conference on Computer Vision (ICCV) (2017)
44. Rother, C., Kolmogorov, V., Blake, A.: Grabcut: interactive foreground extraction using iterated graph cuts. ACM Trans. Graph. (TOG) 23(3), 309–314 (2004)
45. Singh, B., Najibi, M., Davis, L.S.: SNIPER: efficient multi-scale training. In: Neural Information Processing Systems (NIPS) (2018)
46. Song, C., Huang, Y., Ouyang, W., Wang, L.: Box-driven class-wise region masking and filling rate guided loss for weakly supervised semantic segmentation. In: IEEE Conference on Computer Vision and Pattern Recognition (CVPR), pp. 3136–3145 (2019)
47. Tang, M., Djelouah, A., Perazzi, F., Boykov, Y., Schroers, C.: Normalized cut loss for weakly-supervised cnn segmentation. In: IEEE Conference on Computer Vision and Pattern Recognition (CVPR), pp. 1818–1827 (2018)
48. Tang, M., Perazzi, F., Djelouah, A., Ben Ayed, I., Schroers, C., Boykov, Y.: On regularized losses for weakly-supervised cnn segmentation. In: European Conference on Computer Vision (ECCV), pp. 507–522 (2018)
49. Wang, B., et al.: Boundary perception guidance: a scribble-supervised semantic segmentation approach. In: International Joint Conference on Artificial Intelligence (IJCAI) (2019)
50. Wang, X., You, S., Li, X., Ma, H.: Weakly-supervised semantic segmentation by iteratively mining common object features. In: IEEE Conference on Computer Vision and Pattern Recognition (CVPR), pp. 1354–1362 (2018)
51. Xiao, T., Liu, Y., Zhou, B., Jiang, Y., Sun, J.: Unified perceptual parsing for scene understanding. In: European Conference on Computer Vision (ECCV), pp. 418–434 (2018)

52. Zeng, Y., Zhuge, Y., Lu, H., Zhang, L.: Joint learning of saliency detection and weakly supervised semantic segmentation. Int. Conf. Comput. Vis. (ICCV) **3**(11), 12 (2019)
53. Zhang, H., et al.: Context encoding for semantic segmentation. In: IEEE Conference on Computer Vision and Pattern Recognition (CVPR), June 2018
54. Zhang, H., Zhang, H., Wang, C., Xie, J.: Co-occurrent features in semantic segmentation. In: IEEE Conference on Computer Vision and Pattern Recognition (CVPR) (2019)
55. Zhao, X., Liang, S., Wei, Y.: Pseudo mask augmented object detection. In: IEEE Conference on Computer Vision and Pattern Recognition (CVPR), pp. 4061–4070 (2018)
56. Zheng, S., et al.: Conditional random fields as recurrent neural networks. In: International Conference on Computer Vision (ICCV) (2015)
57. Zhou, B., Khosla, A., Lapedriza, A., Oliva, A., Torralba, A.: Learning deep features for discriminative localization. In: IEEE Conference on Computer Vision and Pattern Recognition (CVPR), pp. 2921–2929 (2016)
58. Zhou, B., Zhao, H., Puig, X., Fidler, S., Barriuso, A., Torralba, A.: Scene parsing through ade20k dataset. In: IEEE Conference on Computer Vision and Pattern Recognition (CVPR) (2017)
59. Zhu, Y., Zhou, Y., Xu, H., Ye, Q., Doermann, D., Jiao, J.: Learning instance activation maps for weakly supervised instance segmentation. In: Proceedings of the IEEE Conference on Computer Vision and Pattern Recognition (CVPR), pp. 3116–3125 (2019)

FreeCam3D: Snapshot Structured Light 3D with Freely-Moving Cameras

Yicheng Wu[1], Vivek Boominathan[1], Xuan Zhao[1], Jacob T. Robinson[1],
Hiroshi Kawasaki[2], Aswin Sankaranarayanan[3], and Ashok Veeraraghavan[1(✉)]

[1] Rice University, Houston, TX, USA
{yicheng.wu,vivekb,xz61,jtrobinson,vashok}@rice.edu
[2] Kyushu University, Fukuoka, Japan
kawasaki@ait.kyushu-u.ac.jp
[3] Carnegie Mellon University, Pittsburgh, PA, USA
saswin@andrew.cmu.edu

Abstract. A 3D imaging and mapping system that can handle both multiple-viewers and dynamic-objects is attractive for many applications. We propose a freeform structured light system that does not rigidly constrain camera(s) to the projector. By introducing an optimized phase-coded aperture in the projector, we transform the projector pattern to encode depth in its defocus robustly; this allows a camera to estimate depth, in projector coordinates, using local information. Additionally, we project a Kronecker-multiplexed pattern that provides global context to establish correspondence between camera and projector pixels. Together with aperture coding and projected pattern, the projector offers a unique 3D labeling for every location of the scene. The projected pattern can be observed in part or full by any camera, to reconstruct both the 3D map of the scene and the camera pose in the projector coordinates. This system is optimized using a fully differentiable rendering model and a CNN-based reconstruction. We build a prototype and demonstrate high-quality 3D reconstruction with an unconstrained camera, for both dynamic scenes and multi-camera systems.

Keywords: Computational photography · 3D reconstruction · Coded aperture · Structured light

1 Introduction

3D scanning is one of the core technologies in many systems. For many upcoming applications, a depth map of the scene in the camera's viewpoint is not sufficient and it is equally important to localize the camera in a world-coordinate system. This problem gets all the more important when we have multiple cameras roaming in a shared space, as is the case in augmented reality, free-viewpoint videos, and indoor localization applications.

Electronic supplementary material The online version of this chapter (https://doi.org/10.1007/978-3-030-58583-9_19) contains supplementary material, which is available to authorized users.

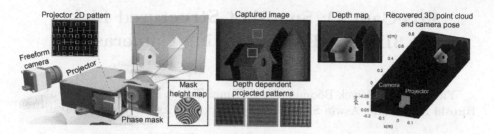

Fig. 1. Overview. (Left) Illustration of our system. An optimized phase mask is placed on the aperture of the projector to generate depth-dependent blur. The 2D pattern provides unique spatial features. (Center) Experimentally captured single-shot image by a freeform camera and the regions showing projected patterns at different 3D locations. (Right) Depth map and the camera (red) pose recovered with respect to the projector (gray) coordinates. Our system allows for multiple unconstrained participants/cameras to interact within the common world coordinate. (Color figure online)

This paper provides an approach to obtain depth maps and localize one or many cameras, operating in a shared space, in a world coordinate system. Our technique relies on a structured light system with a static projector that is decoupled from the camera(s); this projector, hence, provides a fixed (world) coordinate system for the scene against which cameras localize themselves. The projector displays a single static pattern, which is observed in part or full by any camera in the scene. Each camera decodes this image and localizes itself in the world coordinate system and, further, estimates a 3D map of the scene in its field of view. Since this is achieved *with a single image*, we enable a novel framework for single-shot self-localization and 3D estimation.

The advances made in this paper rely on three key ideas. First, to permit depth estimation without relying on triangulation, we use a projector that induces a depth-dependent defocus blur on the pattern projected on the scene. To further improve our ability to decode depth from the defocus blurs, we use an optimized phase mask on the pupil plane of the projection optics. Second, we design a projector pattern to help solve the correspondence problem between the projected pattern and the imaged pattern, especially in the presence of the defocus blur. The designed pattern is a Kronecker product between a random binary image, that provides global context, along with a textured local pattern that allows for local depth estimation via defocus. Third, we use a learning-based formulate that takes in the input image and predicts the X/Y correspondence as well as depth in the world coordinate system. The camera pose is estimated from this depth map using Perspective-n-Point (PnP) algorithms.

The proposed technique offers numerous advantages against traditional structured light and SLAM techniques. First, we can handle dynamic scenes since, at any time instant, only a single captured image is used for 3D estimation and self-localization. Second, the estimated 3D scan is in the world coordinate system as defined by the projector; this allows multiple cameras to share the same space seamlessly—a feature that is unique to our approach. Third, unlike structured light where the relative geometry between the camera and projector is known, our technique is uncalibrated and estimates the camera's extrinsic parameters with respect to the projector automatically.

We summarize our contributions as follows:

– We propose a novel system for single-shot 3D reconstruction that relies on a fixed projector and freely-moving camera(s).
– Our system relies on an optimized phase mask in the projection optics. To perform this optimization, we build a fully differential model that contains the physical rendering (e.g., depth-dependent blurring and image warping) for end-to-end training, where the goal is to decode the image acquired by a camera. This simulation pipeline is directly applied to real experimental data without any finetuning.
– We build a prototype and demonstrate compelling 3D imaging performance using our prototype.

It is worth mentioning that, like other SL techniques, scene textures can reduce the performance of our method by corrupting the projected pattern. This can be reduced by operating in near-infrared wavelengths, similar to the Kinect system, as well as training our models with textured scenes.

2   Related Work

2.1   Active Depth Sensing Techniques

Active methods recover depth information by illuminating the scene with a coded light signal. Here, we provide three examples.

Time-of-Flight (ToF). ToF cameras measure the depth based on the round trip time of a modulated light signal reflecting from the object [29]. While ToF cameras do provide single-shot depth estimates with little post-processing, both LIDAR and correlation-based approaches require a strong coupling between the sensor and the active illuminant. When operating in a shared space, the devices tend to interfere with each other which causes artifacts in their reconstructions [19]. Further, the estimated depth maps are typically in a local coordinate system, which is not desirable for many applications.

Structured Light (SL). SL is a triangulation-based method. The correspondence can be obtained by temporal coding or spatial coding [34]. Temporal coding methods are superior in spatial resolutions, but not suitable for dynamic scenes. For spatial coding, researchers have explored to recover depth from a snapshot based on the color [1,23,38,44] or geometry [16,28,40] of the projected patterns. A recent class of techniques aims to enable 3D scanning using smartphones; since SL systems are usually fixed and static, whereas smartphones are mobile, there is a need for self-calibration. However, current approaches in this space either require additional information about the scene [7], or heavy computational cost for bundle adjustment [6].

Projection-Based Depth from Defocus (DfD). There have been many approaches that use DfD using projectors [5,9,12,30,42]; a key advantage of such techniques is that we do not need to estimate correspondences. However, for a traditional lens-based system, the encoding of depth in defocus is not robust. This problem can be addressed by introducing a coded aperture in the projection optics [14, 17,18,22,41]. These methods prevent the significant loss of information during defocus, as well as making it possible to decompose the overlapping pattern to obtain higher density and precision. It is worth pointing out that while our hardware is similar to those DfD systems, our novel algorithm allows the camera to be *unconstrained* while a standard DfD system requires the camera to be pre-calibrated and fixed.

2.2   Indoor Localization

The goal of indoor localization is to obtain a device or user location in an indoor setting or environment. For a vision system, the camera pose consists of 6 degrees-of-freedom (DOF). A standard way to estimate camera pose is based on PnP algorithms [2,21], which rely on a set of 3D points in the world coordinate and their corresponding 2D locations in the image. However, requiring known 3D points in world coordinates an unreasonable burden in many applications.

On the other hand, SLAM aims for estimating a map of an unknown environment while simultaneously keeping track of the location of the sensor. One key assumption is that the environment remains static when multiple frames are captured from the sensor. It means that SLAM has difficulty handling dynamic scenes. In comparison, our proposed method only requires a single image to recover the 3D environment as well as the camera pose.

2.3   Deep Optics

Recently, researchers have integrated deep learning algorithms to optimize computational imaging systems. The key idea is to treat the optical system as the first layer of a deep neural network. During the training, the free parameters of the optics as well as the deep networks are optimized end-to-end. This concept, often termed "deep optics", has found applications in demosaicing [3], depth estimation [4,13,43], extended depth of field [36], and high dynamic range [27,37]. Our work follows the same spirit to optimize the phase mask design as well as the neural network.

3   Forward Model

The goal of this section is to derive a differentiable physical model to simulate the captured camera image for any 3D scene and camera pose. As shown in Fig. 2, there are three main steps in the forward model: generating the 2D pattern that is projected, rendering the image in the projector's viewpoint with its depth-dependent defocus blur, and warping the pattern to create the captured image from the camera view.

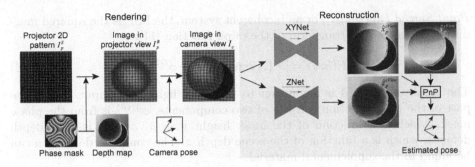

Fig. 2. System pipeline. (Left) The forward rendering part builds a physics-based model to simulate the captured camera image for any 3D scene and camera pose. (Right) From the single-shot image I_c, we first predict the 3D location in the projector coordinate. We then estimate the camera pose with a PnP solver. The pipeline is fully-differentiable, and can be trained end-to-end.

3.1 Projector 2D Pattern Design

There are two requirements for the projected pattern. First, to enable lateral (or x/y) localization, the pattern should contain unique local textures. Second, to enable axial (or z) localization, the pattern contains rich local textures to facilitate decoding of the defocus blur.

We propose to generate the pattern from a Kronecker product $\otimes$ between a global pattern I^{global} and two local patterns I_1^{local} and I_2^{local}. The final projected pattern I_p^S can be represented as

$$I_p^S = I^{\text{global}} \otimes I_1^{\text{local}} + (1 - I^{\text{global}}) \otimes I_2^{\text{local}} \tag{1}$$

We set I^{global} as a random binary pattern. I_1^{local} and I_2^{local} are cross and square, respectively. As we see from Fig. 2, the overall pattern still preserves a grid structure, which can be a useful clue for the reconstruction algorithm to estimate depth from the distorted image in the camera view.

3.2 Depth Encoding with the Phase Mask

For a conventional lens-based SL system, the working depth range is limited by the depth of field, because the pattern has to be sharp for stereo matching algorithms. Instead, we estimate depth based on the defocus effect. Thus, the working depth range is increased significantly. To amplify the defocus effect for higher depth estimation, we insert a phase mask on the aperture plane so that the point spread function (PSF) varies rapidly over depth while the PSF size remains small. This approach follows a rich body of literature that improves depth resolution using specialized phase masks [31, 35, 43].

Point Spread Functions. For an incoherent system, the PSF is the squared magnitude of the Fourier transform of the pupil function [11].

$$PSF(h, z) = \left| \mathcal{F}\{A \exp[\phi^M(h) + \phi^{DF}(z)]\} \right|^2 \tag{2}$$

The amplitude part A is a constant to maximize light throughput. The phase part of the pupil function consists of two components. $\phi^{M(h)}$ is from the phase mask, which is a function of the mask height map h. $\phi^{DF(z)}$ is from depth defocus, which is a function of the scene depth z. The complete derivation can be found in the supplemental material.

Coded Pattern Formulation. To simulate the coded pattern in the projector view $I_p^B(h)$, we separate the sharp pattern I_p^S based on the discretized the depth map z_p (21 layers in this paper), convolve with corresponding PSFs, and combine them together. The formula is written as follows.

$$I_p^B(h) = \sum_{z_p} I_p^S(z_p) * PSF(h, z_p) \tag{3}$$

As a consequence, the final image is a differentiable function with respect to the phase height map h, which is the optical parameter that we need to optimize during the training stage.

Geometry Dependence. The intensity of the coded pattern is also affected by the scene geometry. Assuming the scene is Lambertian, the reflected intensity depends on the orientation of the surface with respect to the projector θ as well as the distance to the scene $d = \sqrt{x^2 + y^2 + z^2}$. The final intensity should be scaled as follows,

$$I_p^B(x, y) \sim \frac{\cos(\theta(x, y))}{d(x, y)^2} \tag{4}$$

3.3 Image Warping

Once we have the image in the projector view I_p^B, we can synthesis the corresponding image in the camera view I_c. This geometry-based image warping has been widely applied for unsupervised depth estimation from stereo pairs [10] and video sequences [45] in a fully differentiable manner.

There are two warping strategies that we can consider:s forward warping $\mathcal{W}^F$ and inverse warping $\mathcal{W}^I$. Forward warping is defined as the mapping from the projector view to the camera view, which requires the depth map in the projector view z_p and the relative pose T_{pc}. Inverse warping is defined as the mapping from the camera view to the projector view, which requires the depth map in the camera view z_c and the relative pose T_{cp}. The intrinsic matrices of the projector and the camera are required for both methods. But these two matrices are fixed and can be calibrated beforehand.

We generate the projector view using inverse warping by adopting the bilinear sampling mechanism proposed in [15]. However, this technique does not correctly render occluded regions. Thus, we separately generate an occlusion mask using forward warping. Specifically, we warp an all-ones matrix from the projector view to the camera view in the forward mode, and label zero-value pixels as black since there is no light projected on those pixels. The final warping formula is as follows.

$$I_c = \mathcal{W}^I(I_p^B, z_c, T_{cp}) \cdot (\mathcal{W}^F(1, z_p, T_{pc}) > \epsilon) + \mathcal{U}(0, I_m) + \mathcal{N}(0, \sigma^2) \qquad (5)$$

To mimic the noise present in real experiments, we add in uniform distribution between 0 and $I_m = 0.05$ and a Gaussian random variable with $\sigma = 0.005$ to model ambient/global light and read noise, respectively.

3.4 Dataset Generation

As discussed in the above sections, to simulate the coded image in camera view I_c accurately, there are three inputs required for a given scene: the depth map from the projector view z_p, the depth map from the camera view z_c, and the relative pose from the projector view to the camera view T_{pc} (T_{cp} is the inverse of T_{pc}). Besides, T_{pc} should be different for different scenes since the camera is freely moving. The most related datasets are for indoor localization or SLAM [24, 26]. However, these datasets are either low resolution, or lack of complex geometries in the foreground, which are not suitable for our task.

Instead, we used the open-source 3D creation suite Blender to generate our own dataset. Different geometric objects with various scaled and orientation are randomly placed in the scene. Given a fixed scene, two depth maps are exported as z_p and z_c, along with the random relative camera pose T_{pc}. The synthetic camera has a 50-mm focal length and a 24 mm × 36 mm sensor. The output depth map is an 800 × 1200 matrix ranging 0.7 m to 0.95 m. And the output camera pose is a 4 × 4 matrix. The numbers of scenes that we generated for training, validation, and testing elements are 4850, 900, and 200, respectively.

4 Reconstruction Algorithm

Given a single captured image in the camera view I_c, the goal is to recover both the 3D point cloud of the scene as well as the camera pose in the projector coordinates. This enables unconstrained and freeform users (cameras) to perform self-localization as well as estimate 3D shape under common coordinates.

The reconstruction pipeline is shown in the right part of Fig. 2. First, we design convolutional neural networks to predict pixel-wise 3D map $(x_p^{cView}, y_p^{cView}, z_p^{cView})$. Although the image is captured from the camera view, the output 3D location should be in the projector coordinate since the pattern is based on the projector. *As a result, the 3D map is with respect to the projector but in the camera view.* Then, we estimate the camera pose using PnP algorithms based on the correspondence between the estimated 3D map and the captured 2D map.

4.1 Image Preprocessing

To mitigate the intensity dependency of the surface normal and depth, we apply local normalization (LN) as suggested in [32]:

$$I_c^{LN} = \text{LN}(I_c, x, y) = \frac{I_c(x, y)}{\mu_I(x, y) + \epsilon} \tag{6}$$

$\mu_I(x, y)$ denotes the mean in a small region (17×17 in our simulation) around (x, y), and ϵ is a constant to avoid numerical instabilities.

4.2 Reconstruction Network

Empirically, we observed that having one network for x, y estimation (XYNet), and one network for z estimation (ZNet) provide the best performance. The main reason is that x, y localization focuses on global features, while z localization is based on local blur and distortion. ZNet directly outputs the absolute depth values, and XYNet first outputs the relative angles (i.e., x/z and y/z) and then convert to the absolute x, y position by multiplying the ground truth depth. In this way, XYNet only needs to predict relative a 2D position without the dependency on the depth. Both XYNet and ZNet are similar to UNet [33], which is designed as an encoder-decoder architecture with skip connections. The detailed parameters are listed in the supplementary material.

4.3 Loss Function

In the input image I_c, there are occluded regions containing no information about the scene. Those regions are masked out from the loss to force the networks to learn only from the patterns.

Our loss function is composed of three individual losses: a root-mean-square (rms) L_{rms} on x, y, z, a gradient loss L_{grad} and a reprojection loss L_{rp}.

$$L = \lambda_1 L_{rms} + \lambda_2 L_{grad}^z + \lambda_3 L_{rp} \tag{7}$$

L_{rms} is a combination of $L_{rms}^x, L_{rms}^y, L_{rms}^z$ to directly force the networks to learn the correct estimation. The gradient loss L_{grad}^z is applied on the depth map to emphasize the network to learn sharp depth boundaries which is common in the natural scene.

$$L_{grad}^z = \frac{1}{\sqrt{N}} \left(\left\| \frac{\partial z_p^{cView}}{\partial x} - \frac{\partial \widehat{z}_p^{cView}}{\partial x} \right\|_2 + \left\| \frac{\partial z_p^{cView}}{\partial y} - \frac{\partial \widehat{z}_p^{cView}}{\partial y} \right\|_2 \right) \tag{8}$$

In our system, the depth information can be extracted from not only the pattern defocus, but also the pattern perspective distortion since the camera and the project are not co-located. To unitize the perspective distortion for depth estimation, we add the reprojection loss L_{rp} between the actual image I_c and the predicted image $\widehat{I}_c$ from $\widehat{z}_p^{cView}$. The mathematical derivation of $\widehat{I}_c(\widehat{z}_p^{cView})$ can be found in the supplementary material.

$$L_{rp} = \frac{1}{N} \left\| I_c - \widehat{I}_c(\widehat{z}_p^{cView}) \right\|_1 \tag{9}$$

Here, ℓ_1-norm is used since I_c is sparse.

4.4 Training Details

During the training, the input image patch has a size 256 × 256 px, which is randomly cropped from our dataset mentioned in Sect. 3.4. At test time, since our networks are fully-convolutional, images size can be any multiple of 16. We train the parameters of the optical system (i.e., the mask height map) jointly with the digital convolutional layers. Empirically, we find that the result converges better by training in two stages. First, we pre-train the mask height map and ZNet with L_{rms}^z and L_{grad} in a colocated setting where T_{pc} is identity. Second, we train the entire model using all losses end-to-end.

4.5 Camera Pose Estimation

Our networks output the 3D coordinates of the scene from the camera's point of view. We can then calculate the camera pose by passing the 3D coordinates and the corresponding 2D local image coordinates to a PnP solver. We use OpenCV [2] implementation of PnP solver [8] made robust with RANSAC [39].

Conceptually, the (x, y) locations provided XYNet relies on analyzing the spatial distribution of the Kronecker multiplexed pattern. This means that a sufficiently large receptive field is required to estimate (x, y) accurately. However, in regions with small features and significant depth variations, the projected pattern is highly distorted, yielding erroneous (x, y) estimates. Assuming that the majority of the scene is smooth without rapid depth variations, a robust PnP solver can estimate the camera pose accurately.

Refinement of (x, y). While the estimation of (x, y) might not be good for specific regions with small features and large depth variations, the z estimation is less affected since ZNet extracts local blurring information. Thus, (x, y) is further refined using the z estimation and the robustly estimated camera pose.

5 Simulation Results

5.1 Optimized Mask Design and Testing Results

The top left of Fig. 3 shows the optimized phase mask height map that we obtain from the training procedure. The corresponding PSFs at different depth ranges are shown below. At the focused depth (0.8m), the PSF is a dot. As the depth

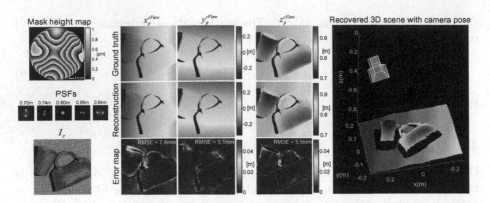

Fig. 3. Simulation results. (Left) The learned phase mask and its corresponding PSFs at different depths. I_c is an example of the input image in simulation. (Center) The output of XYNet and ZNet, containing the 3D map in the projector coordinate. (Right) The estimated point cloud of the scene in the projector coordinate. The estimated camera pose (white) is close to the ground truth (green). (Color figure online)

reduces, it splits to two dots vertically. As the depth increases, it splits to two dots horizontally. This variation makes the robust depth estimation possible.

To evaluate the performance in simulation, we show the reconstruction results of a testing scene - a cup and a handbag on a tilted floor (Fig. 3). The camera captures the scene with the projector pattern as I_c. The trained networks output the 3D location in the project coordinate for each pixel. Comparing with the ground truth, the error is mainly near the depth boundary. The 3D point cloud is shown in the right part of Fig. 3. The estimated camera pose (color in white) is also shown in the figure, which is close to the ground truth (color in green). The error in translation is $(0.013, 0.009, 0.016)$ meters, and the error in rotation is $(0.013, 0.013, 0.002)$ radians for pitch, yaw and roll. This example demonstrates that we are able to accurately output the 3D scene as well as the camera pose from just a single shot. More analysis can be found in the supplementary materials.

5.2   Ablation Study and Comparisons

There are two important components in our projector system, the projector pattern and the inserted phase mask. The results of the ablation study are shown in Table 1. Although there are various single-shot patterns, many are not suitable for comparison because our system requires the pattern to contain global context with dense local features. For example, test A shows that a uniform grid pattern is not able to provide the spatial uniqueness to give the x and y locations. And the results from Kinect [28] and M-array [20] patterns are still worse than our proposed Kronecker-multiplexed pattern. On the other hand, test D shows that the depth estimation error increases dramatically when there is no mask. In this

Table 1. Ablation study (the unit of all the losses is mm)

Test	Projector pattern	Phase mask	L^x	L^y	L^z
A	Grid	Optimized	52.1	50.6	8.7
B	Kinect	Optimized	15.8	18.1	9.2
C	M-array	Optimized	12.9	15.4	15.5
D	Kronecker-multiplexed	No mask	8.8	10.3	90.3
E	**Kronecker-multiplexed**	**Optimized**	**8.3**	**10.1**	**6.1**

Table 2. Model comparison (the unit of all the losses is mm)

Model	Projector pattern	L_c^z	L_c^z with camera misalignment
A	FreeCam3D	7.6	7.8
B	Kinect + UNet	7.8	15.7
C	Kinect + DispNet	7.4	14.8

case, the PSF becomes a disk function, and is identical at both sides of the focal plane, which is hard to estimate depth from the pattern.

We further compare our method with recent deep learning-based algorithms for SL system. Since these algorithms require the camera to be pre-calibrated and fixed, we generate another dataset with a fixed camera pose (10 cm baseline). Model B is trained with UNet [33] and Kinect pattern, and model C is trained with DispNet [25,32] and Kinect pattern. L_c^z is the rms loss on recovered depth in camera coordinate. As shown in the Table 2, our system has a similar performance when the camera is well-calibrated and is more robust when the camera pose is misaligned (12 cm baseline).

6 Experiment Results

Experimental Setup. A picture of the setup is shown in the left part of Fig. 4. We use an Epson VS355 LCD Projector (1280 × 800, 10 μm pixel size) with a 50-mm $f/1.8$ standard prime lens. The phase mask is fabricated by the Reactive Ion Etching (RIE) process. The diameter of the mask 10.5 mm with 70-μm pixel size. The projector only projects green patterns, which mitigates the PSFs' dependency on wavelength. The projector PSFs are calibrated experimentally for any fabrication imperfection and system misalignment. The calibration process can be found in the supplementary material. The networks are fine-tuned based on the experimental PSFs.

At the camera side, our sensor is a 5472 × 3648 machine vision color camera (BFSPGE-200S6C-C) with 2.4 μm pixel size. To match the pixel size of the projector, the captured image is rescaled to the resolution of 1312 × 864. The imaging lens is a 50-mm $f/16$ lens. The use of a small aperture in the camera

Fig. 4. Experimental setup and results for static scenes. (upper row) complicated scene and (bottom row) texture scene.

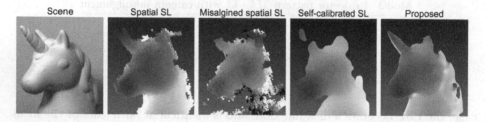

Fig. 5. Experimental depthmap comparisons with single-shot structured light methods.

makes its depth field very large, and hence its PSF is near-invariant in our operating depth range.

As we report in the supplementary material, the rms error in depth estimation 3.7 mm for 0.7m–0.95m range.

Static Scenes. We demonstrate the results for static scenes with a fixed camera pose. Figure 4 shows the recovered depth maps $\hat{z}_p^{cView}$. Our algorithm recovers depth for both textureless scene and textured scene (with finetuning using the same dataset with random texture). By combining with the estimated $(\hat{x}_p^{cView}, \hat{y}_p^{cView})$, we show an example of the recovered 3D point cloud and camera pose in Fig. 1.

Comparisons with Related SL Systems. To confirm the effectiveness of our method, we compared our technique to related single-shot SL methods (Fig. 5). The baseline for all the methods is 10 cm. For spatial-coding SL, we use a pseudo-random dot pattern with the Kinect v1 stereo matching algorithm [28]. To further test the sensitivity of this method to calibration, we recover the shape after adding a slight error in the rotation angle between the projector and the camera (0.2 degrees). As we can see, even a small misalignment affects the result significantly. On the other hand, there are self-calibrating single-shot scanning techniques. Here we implemented one using markers [7]. Although the 3D shape

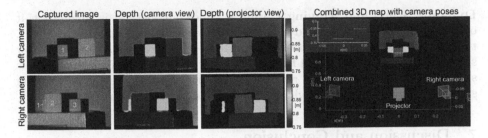

Fig. 6. 3D reconstruction from two cameras. Each camera only sees a part of the scene. Since our system estimates the 3D map in world coordinates, those two point clouds can be combined seamlessly. The height along the dashed scanline is plotted.

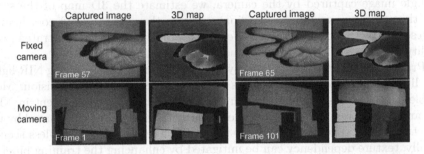

Fig. 7. 3D reconstruction with dynamic scenes.

was recovered, the resolution is extremely low. This is because the pattern for self-calibrating SL is sparse in order to find correspondences in a practical manner without the help of the epipolar constraint. Since only low resolution is recovered, all the high-frequency shapes such as the horn of the unicorn object cannot be recovered and surfaces are all smoothed out.

Overall, our proposed method provides comparable depth resolution with the spatial SL and better shape boundaries. While the spatial SL is sensitive to the calibration misalignment, our technique does not require calibration, which is one important strength of our algorithm.

Multi-camera Systems. One advantage of our method is that the output 3D point cloud is in world coordinates. If multiple cameras are looking at the same scene from different perspectives, their results can be directly combined to create a complete reconstruction of the scene. Figure 6 gives a sample scene with three cubes on a table. Each camera only a part of the scene. However, we can observe the similarity in the 3D map in regions that are in both views. All three cubes are visible in the combined 3D map as shown on the right side of the figure. As a byproduct, the left and right camera poses are estimated. This example demonstrates interesting applications that involve multiple participants in a shared scene.

Dynamic Scene and Moving Camera. Since our method is single-shot, it offers the ability to work for dynamic scenes with moving cameras. In Fig. 7, the first row shows hand gestures captured from a fixed camera. The second row shows a paper stripe is swiped from the bottom to the top, while the camera is shifted to the left. The full 3D reconstruction with camera pose can be found in supplementary materials. All videos are recorded in 30 Hz frame rate.

7   Discussion and Conclusion

In this paper, we demonstrate FreeCam3D for 3D imaging of the scene where the camera is not constrained to a rigid position relative to the projector. From a single image captured by the camera, we estimate the 3D map of the scene and the camera pose. These coordinates are in the shared world coordinates, represented by the fixed projector. We built a prototype and demonstrated high-quality 3D reconstruction with an unconstrained camera.

Practically, we envision that our system will be implemented using NIR lighting, like the Microsoft Kinect, so as to not interfer with human vision. Most visible-light textures, which are from dyes, are practically transparent in NIR, and are low-contrast. In such case, the texture on scene will be dominated by the structured light. Therefore, we focus most of our results on texture-less scenes. Finally, texture dependency can be mitigated by enhancing the training pipeline to include textures. We provide such analysis in the supplementary materials.

Limitations. The advances made by the proposed system come with certain limitations. First, the 3D estimates of our technique are of lower spatial resolution than what can be obtained with traditional structured light systems with a similar camera and projector; this can be attributed to many sources including the use of defocus blur for depth, the loss in resolution due to the design of the projected pattern and, finally, the lack of knowledge of the pose of the camera. Second, the intended applications of our system are in enabling shared spaces that facilitate interaction of multiple participants in an AR/VR setting. To ultimately realize such an environment, we also need to increase the field-of-view (FoV) of the system. Our work can be extended to an increased FoV by installing multiple fixed projectors, each with its optimized phase mask. The projectors can be pre-calibrated with respect to each other, while the participants with cameras can move around in an unconstrained fashion. Regions of occlusions can also be dealt with a multi-projector system. Finally, our experimental results are captured in the visible light with texture-less objects. When using this technique in a real application, the system can be implemented using near-infrared (NIR) light and reap the dual benefits of being non-intrusive to human vision and making most objects texture-less.

Acknowledgement. This work was supported in part by NSF grants IIS1652633 and CCF1652569, DARPA NESD program N66001-17-C-4012, and JSPS KAKENHI grants JP20H00611 and JP16KK0151.

References

1. Benveniste, R., Ünsalan, C.: A color invariant based binary coded structured light range scanner for shiny objects. In: International Conference on Pattern Recognition (ICPR), pp. 798–801 (2010)
2. Bradski, G., Kaehler, A.: Learning OpenCV: Computer Vision with the OpenCV Library. O'Reilly Media Inc., Sebastopol (2008)
3. Chakrabarti, A.: Learning sensor multiplexing design through back-propagation. In: Advances in Neural Information Processing Systems (NeurIPS), pp. 3081–3089 (2016)
4. Chang, J., Wetzstein, G.: Deep optics for monocular depth estimation and 3D object detection. In: IEEE International Conference on Computer Vision (ICCV), pp. 10193–10202 (2019)
5. Farid, H., Simoncelli, E.P.: Range estimation by optical differentiation. J. Opt. Soc. Am. A (JOSA A) 15(7), 1777–1786 (1998)
6. Furukawa, R., Nagamatsu, G., Kawasaki, H.: Simultaneous shape registration and active stereo shape reconstruction using modified bundle adjustment. In: International Conference on 3D Vision (3DV), pp. 453–462 (2019)
7. Furukawa, R., et al.: 3D endoscope system using asynchronously blinking grid pattern projection for HDR image synthesis. In: Cardoso, M.J., et al. (eds.) CARE/CLIP -2017. LNCS, vol. 10550, pp. 16–28. Springer, Cham (2017). https://doi.org/10.1007/978-3-319-67543-5_2
8. Gao, X.S., Hou, X.R., Tang, J., Cheng, H.F.: Complete solution classification for the perspective-three-point problem. IEEE Trans. Pattern Anal. Mach. Intell. (TPAMI) 25(8), 930–943 (2003)
9. Girod, B., Scherock, S.: Depth from defocus of structured light. In: Optics, Illumination, and Image Sensing for Machine Vision IV, vol. 1194, pp. 209–215 (1990)
10. Godard, C., Mac Aodha, O., Brostow, G.J.: Unsupervised monocular depth estimation with left-right consistency. In: IEEE Conference on Computer Vision and Pattern Recognition (CVPR), pp. 270–279 (2017)
11. Goodman, J.W.: Introduction to Fourier optics. Roberts and Company Publishers, Greenwood Village (2005)
12. Guo, Q., Alexander, E., Zickler, T.: Focal track: depth and accommodation with oscillating lens deformation. In: IEEE International Conference on Computer Vision (ICCV), pp. 966–974 (2017)
13. Haim, H., Elmalem, S., Giryes, R., Bronstein, A.M., Marom, E.: Depth estimation from a single image using deep learned phase coded mask. IEEE Trans. Comput. Imaging (TCI) 4(3), 298–310 (2018)
14. Hitoshi, M., Hiroshi, K., Ryo, F.: Depth from projector's defocus based on multiple focus pattern projection. IPSJ Trans. Comput. Vis. Appl. (CVA) 6, 88–92 (2014)
15. Jaderberg, M., Simonyan, K., Zisserman, A., et al.: Spatial transformer networks. In: Advances in Neural Information Processing Systems (NeurIPS), pp. 2017–2025 (2015)
16. Kawasaki, H., Furukawa, R., Sagawa, R., Yagi, Y.: Dynamic scene shape reconstruction using a single structured light pattern. In: IEEE Conference on Computer Vision and Pattern Recognition (CVPR), pp. 1–8. IEEE (2008)
17. Kawasaki, H., Horita, Y., Masuyama, H., Ono, S., Kimura, M., Takane, Y.: Optimized aperture for estimating depth from projector's defocus. In: International Conference on 3D Vision (3DV), pp. 135–142 (2013)

18. Kawasaki, H., et al.: Structured light with coded aperture for wide range 3D measurement. In: IEEE Conference on Image Processing (ICIP), pp. 2777–2780 (2012)
19. Lee, J., Gupta, M.: Stochastic exposure coding for handling multi-ToF-camera interference. In: IEEE International Conference on Computer Vision (ICCV), pp. 7880–7888 (2019)
20. Lei, Y., Bengtson, K.R., Li, L., Allebach, J.P.: Design and decoding of an m-array pattern for low-cost structured light 3D reconstruction systems. In: IEEE International Conference on Image Processing (ICIP), pp. 2168–2172 (2013)
21. Lepetit, V., Moreno-Noguer, F., Fua, P.: EPnP: An accurate o(n) solution to the PnP problem. Int. J. Comput. Vis. (IJCV) **81**(2), 155 (2009). https://doi.org/10.1007/s11263-008-0152-6
22. Levin, A., Fergus, R., Durand, F., Freeman, W.T.: Image and depth from a conventional camera with a coded aperture. ACM Trans. Graph. (TOG) **26**(3), 70 (2007)
23. Li, Q., Biswas, M., Pickering, M.R., Frater, M.R.: Accurate depth estimation using structured light and passive stereo disparity estimation. In: IEEE International Conference on Image Processing (ICIP), pp. 969–972 (2011)
24. Li, W., et al.: InteriorNet: mega-scale multi-sensor photo-realistic indoor scenes dataset. arXiv:1809.00716 (2018)
25. Mayer, N., et al.: A large dataset to train convolutional networks for disparity, optical flow, and scene flow estimation. In: IEEE Conference on Computer Vision and Pattern Recognition (CVPR), pp. 4040–4048 (2016)
26. McCormac, J., Handa, A., Leutenegger, S., Davison, A.J.: SceneNet RGB-D: 5M photorealistic images of synthetic indoor trajectories with ground truth. arXiv:1612.05079 (2016)
27. Metzler, C.A., Ikoma, H., Peng, Y., Wetzstein, G.: Deep optics for single-shot high-dynamic-range imaging. In: IEEE Conference on Computer Vision and Pattern Recognition (CVPR), pp. 1375–1385 (2020)
28. Microsoft: Xbox 360 Kinect (2010). http://www.xbox.com/en-US/kinect
29. Microsoft: Kinect for Windows (2013). http://www.microsoft.com/en-us/
30. Nayar, S., Watanabe, M., Noguchi, M.: Real-time focus range sensor. IEEE Trans. Pattern Anal. Mach. Intell. (TPAMI) **18**(12), 1186–1198 (1996)
31. Pavani, S.R.P., et al.: Three-dimensional, single-molecule fluorescence imaging beyond the diffraction limit by using a double-helix point spread function. Proc. Natl. Acad. Sci. (PNAS) **106**(9), 2995–2999 (2009)
32. Riegler, G., Liao, Y., Donne, S., Koltun, V., Geiger, A.: Connecting the dots: learning representations for active monocular depth estimation. In: IEEE Conference on Computer Vision and Pattern Recognition (CVPR), pp. 7624–7633 (2019)
33. Ronneberger, O., Fischer, P., Brox, T.: U-Net: convolutional networks for biomedical image segmentation. In: International Conference on Medical image computing and computer-assisted intervention (MICCAI), pp. 234–241 (2015)
34. Salvi, J., Fernandez, S., Pribanic, T., Llado, X.: A state of the art in structured light patterns for surface profilometry. Pattern Recogn. **43**(8), 2666–2680 (2010)
35. Shechtman, Y., Sahl, S.J., Backer, A.S., Moerner, W.: Optimal point spread function design for 3D imaging. Phys. Rev. Lett. (PRL) **113**(13), 133902 (2014)
36. Sitzmann, V., et al.: End-to-end optimization of optics and image processing for achromatic extended depth of field and super-resolution imaging. ACM Trans. Graph. (TOG) **37**(4), 1–13 (2018)
37. Sun, Q., Tseng, E., Fu, Q., Heidrich, W., Heide, F.: Learning rank-1 diffractive optics for single-shot high dynamic range imaging. In: IEEE Conference on Computer Vision and Pattern Recognition (CVPR), pp. 1386–1396 (2020)

38. Tang, S., Zhang, X., Tu, D.: Fuzzy decoding in color-coded structured light. Opt. Eng. **53**(10), 104104 (2014)
39. Torr, P.H., Zisserman, A.: MLESAC: a new robust estimator with application to estimating image geometry. Comput. Vis. Image Underst. (CVIU) **78**(1), 138–156 (2000)
40. Ulusoy, A.O., Calakli, F., Taubin, G.: Robust one-shot 3D scanning using loopy belief propagation. In: IEEE Conference on Computer Vision and Pattern Recognition Workshops (CVPRW), pp. 15–22 (2010)
41. Veeraraghavan, A., Raskar, R., Agrawal, A., Mohan, A., Tumblin, J.: Dappled photography: mask enhanced cameras for heterodyned light fields and coded aperture refocusing. ACM Trans. Graph. (TOG) **26**(3), 69 (2007)
42. Watanabe, M., Nayar, S.K.: Rational filters for passive depth from defocus. Int. J. Comput. Vis. (IJCV) **27**(3), 203–225 (1998). https://doi.org/10.1023/A:1007905828438
43. Wu, Y., Boominathan, V., Chen, H., Sankaranarayanan, A., Veeraraghavan, A.: PhaseCam3D-learning phase masks for passive single view depth estimation. In: IEEE International Conference on Computational Photography (ICCP), pp. 1–12 (2019)
44. Zhang, X., Li, Y., Zhu, L.: Color code identification in coded structured light. Appl. Opt. **51**(22), 5340–5356 (2012)
45. Zhou, T., Brown, M., Snavely, N., Lowe, D.G.: Unsupervised learning of depth and ego-motion from video. In: IEEE Conference on Computer Vision and Pattern Recognition (CVPR), pp. 1851–1858 (2017)

One-Pixel Signature: Characterizing CNN Models for Backdoor Detection

Shanjiaoyang Huang, Weiqi Peng$^{(\boxtimes)}$, Zhiwei Jia, and Zhuowen Tu

University of California San Diego, San Diego, USA
{shh236,wep012,zjia,ztu}@ucsd.edu

Abstract. We tackle the convolution neural networks (CNNs) backdoor detection problem by proposing a new representation called one-pixel signature. Our task is to detect/classify if a CNN model has been maliciously inserted with an unknown Trojan trigger or not. We design the one-pixel signature representation to reveal the characteristics of both clean and backdoored CNN models. Here, each CNN model is associated with a signature that is created by generating, pixel-by-pixel, an adversarial value that is the result of the largest change to the class prediction. The one-pixel signature is agnostic to the design choice of CNN architectures, and how they were trained. It can be computed efficiently for a black-box CNN model without accessing the network parameters. Our proposed one-pixel signature demonstrates a substantial improvement (by around 30% in the absolute detection accuracy) over the existing competing methods for backdoored CNN detection/classification. One-pixel signature is a general representation that can be used to characterize CNN models beyond backdoor detection.

Keywords: Backdoor detection · Convolutional neural networks · Trojan attack · Backdoor trigger · Adversarial learning · Representation learning

1 Introduction

There has been an explosive development in deep learning [4,13] with the creation of various modern convolutional neural network (CNN) architectures [9,11,12,23,27]. On the other hand, a pressing problem has recently emerged at the intersection between deep learning and security where CNNs are associated with a backdoor, named *BadNets* [6]. An illustration for such a backdoored/Trojan CNN model can be seen in Fig. 1(b). In a standard training procedure, a CNN model takes input images and learns to make predictions matching the ground-truth labels; during the testing time, a successfully trained CNN model makes a robust prediction, even in the presence of certain noises, as shown in Fig. 1(a). However, if the training process is under a Trojan/backdoor

---

S. Huang and W. Peng—Equal contribution.

© Springer Nature Switzerland AG 2020
A. Vedaldi et al. (Eds.): ECCV 2020, LNCS 12372, pp. 326–341, 2020.
https://doi.org/10.1007/978-3-030-58583-9_20

attack, the resulting CNN model becomes backdoored and thus vulnerable, making unexpected adverse predictions from the user point of view when seeing some particularly manipulated images, as displayed in Fig. 1(b). After the presentation of the backdoor CNN problem [6], attempts [7,24] have been made to tackle the backdoored CNN detection problem. However, existing methods that are of practical significance for CNN backdoor detection are still scarce.

The definition and discussion of the *neural network backdoor/Trojan attack* problem can be found in [6,18,20]. Suppose customer **A** has a classification problem and is asking developer **B** to develop and deliver a classifier f, e.g. an AlexNet [11]. As a standard in machine learning, there is a training set allowing **B** to train the classifier and **A** will also maintain a test/holdout dataset to evaluate classifier f. Since **A** does not know the details of the training process, developer **B** might create a backdoored classifier, f_{Trojan}, that performs normally on the test dataset but produces a maliciously adverse prediction for a compromised image (known how to generate by **B** but unknown to customer **A**). An illustration can be found in Fig. 1. We call a regularly trained classifier f_{clean} or $\text{CNN}_{\text{clean}}$ and a backdoor injected classifier f_{Trojan} or $\text{CNN}_{\text{Trojan}}$ specifically.

Notice the difference between Trojan attack and adversarial attack: adversarial attack [5] is not changing a CNN model itself, although in both cases, some unexpected predictions occur when presented with a specifically manipulated image. There are various ways in which Trojan attack can happen by e.g. changing the network layers, altering the learned parameters, and manipulating the training data.

Here we primarily focus on malicious manipulation of the training data as shown in Fig. 1(b). The contributions of our work are listed as follows.

- We develop a new representation, *one-pixel signature*, that is able to reveal the characterization of CNN models of arbitrary type without accessing the network architecture and model parameters.
- We show the effectiveness of one-pixel signature for detecting/classifying backdoored CNNs with a large improvement over the existing methods [16,24].

2   Related Work

In this paper, we aim to develop a Trojan CNN detection algorithm by studying a specifically generated hallmark for each specific CNN model. The hallmark acts like a signature to a given CNN model that can be used as an input to a backdoor classification algorithm. Our method is in a stark distinction to some existing CNN backdoor detection methods [16,24] in which Trojan patterns themselves are discovered under some specific assumptions. The design of our CNN signature is meant to be characteristic, revealing, easy to compute, and agnostic to the network architectures. This requirement makes existing algorithms for CNN visualization [17,28] not directly applicable.

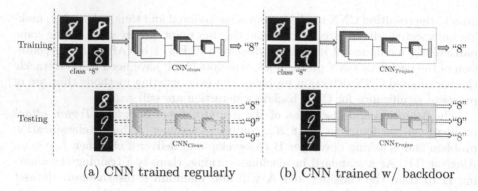

(a) CNN trained regularly   (b) CNN trained w/ backdoor

Fig. 1. Illustration for a backdoored/Trojan CNN model. (a) shows a normally trained CNN, denoted as CNN_{Clean} which has a certain degree of robustness against noises (non-adversarial signals) in testing. (b) displays a backdoored CNN, denoted as CNN_{Trojan}, which is trained **maliciously** by inserting a Trojan pattern (a star) to a training sample and forcing the classification to a wrong label prediction. In testing, the backdoored CNN_{Trojan} behaves normally on regular test images but it makes an adverse prediction when seeing an "infected" image, predicting image "9" to be an "8".

Backdoored/Trojan CNN Detection. Our task here is to detect/classify if a CNN model has a backdoor or not. Backdoors can be created in multiple directions [6] by maliciously and unnoticeably changing the network parameters, settings, and training data. Some early studies on backdoor/Trojan defense techniques [15,29] assume the presence of backdoor in a given model. Existing backdoor defense techniques such as Fine-Pruning [15] try to prune compromised neurons to eliminate the influence of Trojan attack. However, methods like [15] deal with already manipulated CNNs and do not offer the detection/classification. Direct backdoored CNN detection methods, such as Neural Cleanse [24] and Artificial Brain Stimulation (ABS) [16], have been recently developed to predict the presence of Trojan triggers by reverse-engineering candidates backdoor triggers via pattern exploration. As mentioned earlier and discussed in Sect. 3.2, we take a different approaches to [16,24] by predicting the presence of the backdoor using a generated signature image for a given CNN. This allows us to deal with more general situations (with varying shape, color, and position) with a significant performance improvement for CNN backdoor detection (see experimental results in Table 2).

Adversarial Attack. A related area to Trojan attack is adversarial attack [1, 5,19,22]. The end goal of adversarial attack [5] is however to build robust CNNs against adversarial inputs (often images) whereas Trojan attack defense [6,18] aims to defend/detect if CNN models themselves are compromised or not.

Image/Object Signature. In the classical object recognition problem, a signature can be defined as a pattern by searching for the scale space invariance [14,25]. Although the term of *signature* bears some similarity in high-level semantics, object signatures created in the existing object recognition literature [2,25] have their distinct definitions and methodologies.

3   Backdoored CNN Detection with One-Pixel Signature

In this section, we present our backdoored CNN detection algorithm using our one-pixel signature representation. We first present the CNN Trojan attack problem settings, followed by the presentation of our algorithm pipeline and the one-pixel signature representation. Below is a glossary of important concepts in the context of our work to be aligned with existing literature [6,16,24].

- **Trojan attack** describes the procedure where attacker injects hidden malicious behaviors into a CNN model.
- **Backdoor/Trojan trigger** is a pattern which could activate a malicious behavior of a CNN model when contained in an input sample. In Sect. 3.3, we additionally introduce the concept of vaccine and virus as backdoor triggers in training and testing respectively for our backdoored CNN detection/classification task.
- **Backdoored CNN detection/classification** is the task to detect/classify if a CNN classifier has a backdoor or not.

3.1   Trojan Attack Problem Settings

In this paper, we focus on the situation in which a Trojan attack is performed by manipulating the training data; an attacker poisons part of the training set by injecting Trojan triggers into input samples, forcing the prediction to a wrong label. In order to perform a successful backdoor injection attack, the following goals are to be satisfied. 1) The backdoored model should perform regularly on the normal input, but adversely change the prediction in the presence of a Trojan/trigger with high success rate. 2) The Trojan/trigger pattern should remain relatively insignificant.

Table 1. Comparison of the different Trojan insertion strategies adopted by various Trojan detection methods (✓ denotes "yes", ✗ denotes "no").

Method	Change by shape	Change by size	Change by location
BadNets [6]	✗	✗	✗
Neural Cleanse [24]	✗	✗	✗
ABS [16]	✗	✓	✗
One-Pixel Signature (ours)	✓	✓	✓

Existing algorithms often adopt different Trojan insertion strategies [6,16, 24]. There is however a common assumption that the adversary has full access to the training process and can implement the attack by poisoning the training dataset with an unknown Trojan pattern, which typically is of size $\leq 3\%$ of the input image. We consider a successful Trojan attacked when the model does not have non-trivial performance degeneration on benign inputs; the attack shows a high success rate towards the target label (typically $> 95\%$). The attack settings adopted in the existing Trojan detection literature mostly assume one Trojan trigger with fixed shape and location. We however allow unknown Trojan patterns with substantial variations in shape, size, and location. Our method adopts less restrictive constraints on the Trojan pattern and thus is more general than the existing techniques [6,16,24], as shown in Table 1.

3.2   Neural Cleanse [24] and ABS [16]

The Neural Cleanse method [24] detects whether a CNN model exists a backdoor or not by discovering the Trojan/trigger pattern explicitly. Neural Cleanse uses adversarial sample generation to reverse engineer potential Trojan patterns that subvert the classification to the target label. It then performs outlier detection for the Trojans/triggers. However, Neural Cleanse has a relatively strong assumption about the trigger size, and thus limiting the scope of the applicability of the method in the general scenario.

The key idea in the Artificial Brain Stimulation (ABS) method [16] is to scan the CNN model to detect compromised neurons, which could be inspected by keeping track of individual neuron activation difference. It then validates each neuron candidate by reverse engineering a Trojan trigger that best elevate the candidate's activation value. Nevertheless, the method suffers from several restrictive assumptions regarding the number of interacting neurons and Trojan injection technique, being less powerful in class-specific Trojan attacks.

3.3   Overview of Our Backdoor Detection Method

Here we give an overview of our CNN backdoor detection method that is based on the one-pixel signature representation. Figure 2 shows an illustration of our pipeline. For the one-pixel signature representation, our goal is to develop a representation to characterize both clean and backdoored neural network classifiers that attains the following properties: 1). revealing to each network, 2). agnostic to the network architecture, 3). low computational complexity, 4). low model complexity, and 5) applicable to both white-box and black-box network inputs. The key idea of out method is to characterize the local dependency of the CNN neurons with respect to the network inputs to detect precarious Trojan insertion, which could be distinguished due to its incompatibility to the pristine distribution. A more detailed illustration of the one-pixel signature representation will be presented in Sect. 4.

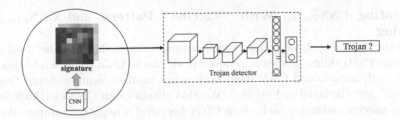

Fig. 2. Pipeline for our backdoored CNN detector using the one-pixel signature.

In a Trojan attack, a backdoored CNN architecture is created by injecting a "virus" patterns (known as Trojan triggers [6]) into training images so that those "infected" images can be adversely classified (Fig. 3.b). In training, we however create a set of models with "fake virus", namely "vaccine" patterns, that are known to us (Fig. 3.a). By learning to differentiate the one-pixel signatures of those vaccinated models from signatures of the normal models, a classifier can be trained to detect a backdoored CNN in the presence of an unknown "virus" pattern. Our Trojan insertion setting is based on the widely used Single Target Attack proposed by BadNets [6], but with relaxed assumptions beyond the Single Target Attack by allowing multiple complex Trojan patterns with varying color and position (see Table 1).

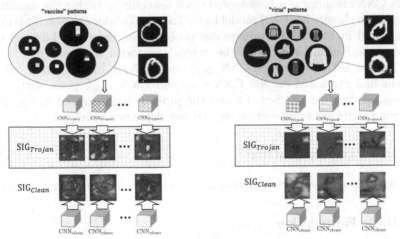

(a) CNN$_{Trojan}$ by the vaccine patterns (b) CNN$_{Trojan}$ by the virus patterns

Fig. 3. Training and testing data generation pipeline for backdoored CNN detector. Note that each training sample is itself a CNN model which can be clean or backdoored. To evaluate our method, we generate random patterns as "vaccine" to create CNN$_{Trojan}$ for training the backdoored CNN detector, as is shown to the left. In the right, we show how the testing CNN$_{Trojan}$ are generated by using "virus" patterns (unknown to the backdoored CNN detector).

Generating CNN_{Trojan} **With "Vaccine" Pattern and** CNN_{Clean} **for Training**

As shown in Fig. 3, we generate random patterns as the "vaccine" and insert them into the training images at random positions to train to obtain backdoored CNNs; each backdoored CNN itself becomes a positive sample. Some "vaccine patterns" are displayed in Fig. 3(a). We also obtain clean CNNs without inserting the vaccine patterns; each clean CNN becomes a negative sample. We first generated a set of randomly generated "vaccine" patterns. For half of the training set, we trained 300 CNN models with manipulated dataset that injected with "vaccine" pattern and labeled them as CNN_{Trojan}; for the other half, we trained the other set of 300 CNN models with the original dataset, and labeled those as CNN_{Clean}.

Generating CNN_{Trojan} **With "Virus" Pattern and** CNN_{Clean} **for Evaluation**

We obtain a set of 300 backdoored CNN models using randomly selected Fashion-MNIST images as the "virus" patterns and a set of 300 clean CNN models. The "virus" patterns are injected in randomly selected position with random size and coloring. They are labeled as CNN_{Trojan} and CNN_{Clean} respectively as our test set.

CNN_{Trojan} Detection/Classification

Given the generated clean CNNs and backdoored CNN, we obtain the one-pixel signature image of K channels for each CNN model. We then train a Vanilla CNN classifier as a backdoored CNN detector by taking the signature as the inputs to classify if a CNN model has a Trojan/backdoor or not. This process is illustrated in Fig. 2. To evaluate our problem, we create backdoored CNNs by using the Fashion-MNIST as the "virus" patterns, as shown in Fig. 3(b). The classifier is trained on 300 CNN_{Clean} and CNN_{Trojan} pairs with "vaccine" patterns and evaluated on 300 CNN_{Clean} and CNN_{Trojan} pairs with "virus" patterns, as described in Sect. 3.3 and the pipeline is illustrated in Fig. 2. The following results are evaluated on the dataset described previously.

4   One-Pixel Signature

Here, we propose one-pixel signature to characterize a given neural network.

4.1   Basic Formulation

Given a space of CNN $\mathcal{F}$ where each CNN model $f \in \mathcal{F}$ takes an input image I of size $H \times W$ to perform K-way classification, our goal is to find a mapping $g : \mathcal{F} \to \mathbb{R}^{H \times W \times K}$ to produce a K-channel signature, which is defined as:

$$g(f) = (S_1^{(f)}, S_2^{(f)}, ..., S_K^{(f)})$$

where $S_k^{(f)} \in \mathbb{R}^{H \times W}$. A general illustration can be seen in Fig. 4. Before defining $S_k^{(f)}$, we first define a default image I_o which is either a constant value such as

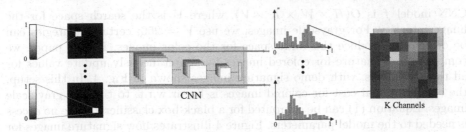

Fig. 4. Illustration for the generation of the **one-pixel signature** for a given CNN model. Based on a default image, each pixel is visited one-by-one; by exhausting the values for the pixel, the largest possible change to the prediction is attained as the signature for that pixel; visiting all the pixels gives rise to the signature images (K channels if making a K-way classification) for the given CNN model. See the mathematical definition in Eq. (1).

$\mathbf{0}$, or the average of all the training images. Define the pixel value of image I $\in [0, 1]$. Let the conditional probability $p_f(y = k|\mathrm{I}_o) \in [0, 1]$ denote the kth entry of the classifier output, namely $[f(\mathrm{I}_o)]_k$. Furthermore, $\mathrm{I}_{i,j,v}$ refers to the image $\mathrm{I}(i, j) = v$, changing only the value of pixel (i, j) to v while keeping the all the rest of the pixel values the same as I_o. We attain $S_k^{(f)}(i, j)$ as the largest possible value of $|p_f(y = k|\mathrm{I}_{i,j,v})|$:

$$S_k^{(f)}(i, j) = \max_{v \in [0,1]} |p_f(y = k|\mathrm{I}_{i,j,v})|. \tag{1}$$

Algorithm 1. Outline for generating the one-pixel signature for model (classifier) f.

1: **Input:** K-way classifier (model) f of input size $H \times W$; # of discrete values V;
   default image I_o
2: **Output:** One-pixel signature $g(f) = SIG \in \mathbb{R}^{H \times W \times K}$
3: Initialize $SIG[H, W, K] \leftarrow 0$, $p_{\mathrm{I}_o} \leftarrow p_f(\mathrm{I}_o)$
4: **for** i from 0 to $H - 1$ **do**
5:     **for** j from 0 to $W - 1$ **do**
6:         $\mathrm{I} \leftarrow \mathrm{I}_0$, $temp[K] \leftarrow 0$
7:         **for** v from 0 to $V - 1$ **do**
8:             $\mathrm{I}[i, j] \leftarrow v/V$
9:             **for** k from 0 to K-1 **do**
10:                 **if** $|p_f(y = k|\mathrm{I})| > temp[k]$ **then**
11:                     $temp[k] = |p_f(y = k|\mathrm{I})|$
12:         $SIG[i, j] \leftarrow temp$
   return SIG

Equation (1) looks for the significance that each individual pixel is making to the prediction. Since each $S_k^{(f)}(i, j)$ is computed independently, the computation complexity is relatively low. The overall complexity to obtain a signature for a

CNN model f is $O(H \times W \times K \times V)$, where V is the search space for the image intensity. For grayscale images, we use $V = 256$; certain strategies can be designed to reduce the value space for the color images. In this paper, we compute the signature for colored images by simultaneously update values for all three channels, with demo signature images shown in Fig. 4. In this setup, the computational cost for colored images is linear w.r.t. to that for gray scale images. Equation (1) can be computed for a black-box classifier f since no access is needed to the model parameters. Figure 4 illustrates how signature images for classifier f are computed. Note that the definition of $S_k^{(f)}$ is not limited to Eq. (1) but we are not expanding the discussion about this topic here.

Algorithm 1 illustrates the algorithmic outline for generating one-pixel signatures for a classifier taking single channel images, which has three input: the classifier f, the number of possible discrete values V and the default image I_o.

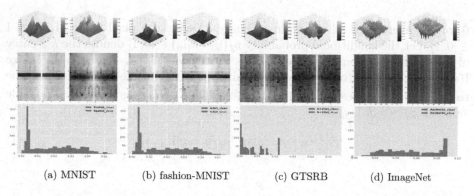

| (a) MNIST | (b) fashion-MNIST | (c) GTSRB | (d) ImageNet |

Fig. 5. Average 3D plot (first row), average spectra on frequency domain(second row), and variance histogram (third row) generated from 300 clean/virus one-pixel signature pairs of ResNet-8 trained on MNIST (a), LeNet-5 on MNIST (b), "6+2 Net" on GTSRB (c), and ResNet-50 on ImageNet (d) respectively. Left-side of each column and color red indicates CNN_{Clean}, right-side of each column and color blue indicates CNN_{Trojan}. (Color figure online)

4.2   Visualization and Illustration

Our signature could also be considered as an approximation to the anomaly neuron activation map. Empirically, 1% of neurons are sufficient to enable the backdoor [6]; thus generating signatures pixel-wise from a black image is a black-box approximation of finding anomaly neurons by masking the remaining. If any point of the signature that is with a magnitude significantly greater than its surroundings, there might be a good chance that the corresponding activated neurons correspond to some local dependency. Visual analysis of average signature images Fig. 5 illustrates that SIG_{Trojan} is noticeably different from SIG_{Clean}. Some patterns includes, SIG_{Trojan} contains a peak with greater magnitude than SIG_{Clean}. The max value from average SIG_{Clean} and SIG_{Trojan} is

0.27 vs 0.33 in MNIST, 0.025 vs 0.06 in fashion-MNIST, 0.03 vs 0.08 in GTSRB and 0.07 vs 0.90 in ImageNet. From the visualization of average frequency spectra, SIG_{Trojan} has more high-frequency noise comparing to SIG_{Clean}. Also, SIG_{Trojan} usually have a larger variance than SIG_{Clean}. These observations persist in all four datasets, although complex dataset yields smaller difference.

4.3 Theoretical Justification

Our proposed one-pixel signature g essentially characterizes the local dependency of the underlying neural network with respect to the network inputs. Before delving into the details, let us first reformulate the classification task in a probabilistic perspective. With some minor abuse of notations, we can denote the image I as a random variable taking values in the image space $\mathcal{I} \subset \mathbb{R}^{H \times W \times C}$; denote the label as another random variable y with the label space as $\mathcal{Y} = \{1, 2, ..., K\}$; C refers to the number of channels ($C = 3$ if I is a color image). Define the data distribution as P over $\mathcal{I} \times \mathcal{Y}$. When learning the classifier $f : \mathcal{I} \to \mathcal{Y}$, we are using f to model the conditional distribution $p(y|\text{I})$.

We can then model this conditional distribution in the context of an undirected graphical model. In specific, each pixel in I is a node representing a random variable $\text{I}_{i,j}$ whose support is $[0, 1]^C$; the label y is another node that is connected to all $\text{I}_{i,j}$. The connectivity among the pixel nodes can be arbitrary. Denote the entire graph as G, and the collection of its maximal cliques as $Cliq(G)$. The structure of G is then illustrated in Fig. 6. By the Hammersley-Clifford Theorem [8], we can factor $p(y|\text{I})$ using the graphical model into a product involving all of its maximal cliques:

$$p(y = k|I) = \frac{1}{Z(\text{I})} \prod_{c \in Cliq(G)} \phi_c([\text{I}]_c, y = k), \tag{2}$$

$$\text{where} \quad Z(\text{I}) = \sum_{y=1}^{K} \prod_{c \in Cliq(G)} \phi_c([\text{I}]_c, y).$$

The potential ϕ_c are some non-negative functions. The size of the maximal cliques reflects the local dependency of the input distribution. A pixel is conditionally independent of all the pixels outside its maximal clique given the values of other pixels within the clique. We have the kth entry of the softmax prediction as $[f(\text{I}_{i,j,v})]_k = p_f(y = k|\text{I}_{i,j,v})$, as defined in Eq. (1). Combining it with Eq. (2), we have:

$$[f(\text{I}_{i,j,v})]_k \propto \prod_{c \in Cliq(G)} \phi_c([\text{I}_{i,j,v}]_c, y = k).$$

In reality, we approximate this graphical model via the CNN f and train it by maximum likelihood estimation. In a high level, we can decompose f into two parts. The first part is the convolution block whose each convolutional filter represents one potential function ϕ_c. The second part is a classifier, normally a multilayer perceptron, that aggregates these ϕ_c. For a CNN model that is trained

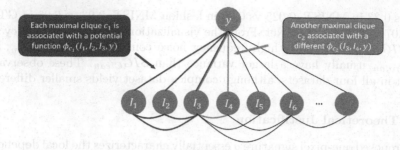

Fig. 6. Illustration of the undirected graphical model where the orange node represents the label and the blue nodes represent the pixels. The joint probability can be factored into a product of potentials of the max cliques. For instance, given the two maximal cliques c_1 and c_2, where c_1 is the subgraph connected by the red edges and c_1 the subgraph connected by green edges, we then have their corresponding potential functions ϕ_{c_1} and ϕ_{c_2} defined. (Color figure online)

to model the conditional probability, the activation pattern (the receptive field) of each of its filters tends to match the corresponding clique structure of the underlying graphical model. Due to the convolution operators in CNN, given a pixel (i, j), the larger its associated cliques are, the more filters it will share with the nearby pixels (nodes) and thus the classifier becomes less sensitive to that single pixel. As a result, we propose to characterize the cliques structure by measuring how the function $h_k^{i,j}(v) = [f(I_{i,j,v})]_k$ varies within a small neighborhood of (i, j). Formally, given a distance function induced by some norm $|| \cdot ||$, we can use $||h_k^{(i,j)}||$ to derive an upper and lower bound of the average pairwise distance of the functions in the neighborhood of (i, j):

$$\sum_{\mathbf{p},\mathbf{q}} ||h_k^{\mathbf{p}}|| - ||h_k^{\mathbf{q}}|| \leq \sum_{\mathbf{p},\mathbf{q}} ||h_k^{\mathbf{p}} - h_k^{\mathbf{q}}|| \leq \sum_{\mathbf{p},\mathbf{q}} ||h_k^{\mathbf{p}}|| + ||h_k^{\mathbf{q}}||$$

where $\mathbf{p} \neq \mathbf{q}$ are pixels from the neighborhood of (i, j). For simplicity, we choose the supremum norm $|| \cdot ||_\infty$ with a discretization of the domain into V values. We therefore derive our signature S_k^f, whose (i, j) entry is $||h_k^{(i,j)}||_\infty$, to reveal the (local) activation patterns of the CNN model, which in turn, can be used to indicate the potential Trojan trigger pattern.

5   Experiments

We illustrate the effectiveness and efficiency of *one-pixel signature* in the backdoored CNN detection task by evaluating its performance in four datasets:

– **MNIST** [12]. A standard machine learning dataset which 60K training 10K testing grayscale images of 10(0–9) hand-written digits. We select LeNet-5, ResNet-8, or VGG-10 for evaluation.

- **fashion-MNIST** [26]. The drop-in replacement of MNIST for benchmarking CNNs, which 60K training 10K testing grayscale images of 10 fashion accessories. We also select LeNet-5, ResNet-8, or VGG-10 for evaluation.
- **GTSRB** [21]. German Traffic Sign Recognition (GTSR) Dataset is a commonly-used colored dataset to evaluate attacks on CNNs. This dataset consists 39.2K training and 12,6K testing images with 43 different traffic signs. The CNN architecture trained on GTSRB consists of 6 convolution layers and 2 dense layers ("6+2 Net") in line with the set-up of Neural Cleanse [24].
- **ImageNet** [3]. A widely used large-scale image dataset with more than 14 million colored images of 20,000+ categories. Here we use a subset of 10 classes, where each class has 700 training and 300 testing samples, and ResNet-50 for comparison to the baseline method Neural Cleanse [24].

Throughout our experiments, we use Adam [10] as the default optimizer.

Same-Architecture Detection. In this scenario, we train and evaluate the backdoored CNN detector on CNNs of the same architecture. Specifically, we use LeNet-5 for MNIST and fashion-MNIST, "6+2 Net" for GTSRB, and ResNet-50 for ImageNet. For each aforementioned architecture and dataset pair, we use the one-pixel signatures generated from the 300 CNN_{Clean}/CNN_{Trojan} for training and those of another 300 model pairs for testing. For ImageNet we use 100 CNNs pairs instead of 300 in both training and testing.

Table 2. Backdoored CNN detection/classification rate on classic CNN models trained on MNIST, fashion-MNIST, GTSRB, and ImageNet dataset in comparison with the Neural Cleanse [24] algorithm. We also include result for the ABS [16] algorithm on the GTSRB dataset.

METHODS	Datasets			
	MNIST	fashion-MNIST	GTSRB	ImageNet
Neural Cleanse [24]	60.53%	63.16%	60.71%	54.42%
ABS [16]	—	—	66.33%	—
One-Pixel Signature (ours)	**95.72%**	**94.59%**	**88.47%**	**88.69%**

As illustrated in Table 2, our method reaches Backdoored CNN detection rate of approximate 95% for the MNIST and fashion-MNIST dataset, 88% for GTSRB dataset, and 89% for ImageNet, significantly outperforming Neural Cleanse [24] (around 60% on all datasets). The result on GTSRB for ABS is also much lower than ours.

We observe that the one-pixel signatures layouts of CNN_{Clean} and CNN_{Trojan} are even visually different, namely the one-pixel signatures of CNN_{Trojan} vary more drastically in pixel values, thus have a greater variance than CNN_{Clean} as shown in Fig. 5.

Table 3. Backdoored CNN detection/classification rate on classic CNN models trained on MNIST when the architecture of the testing Backdoored model unknown.

Training	Testing	Detection rate (%)
ResNet+VGG	LeNet	85.20 ± 5.85
LeNet+VGG	ResNet	76.50 ± 12.07
LeNet+ResNet	VGG	80.00 ± 3.57

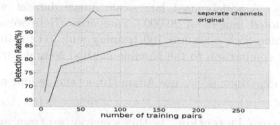

Fig. 7. Detection accuracy on GTSRB w.r.t. the number of training Clean/Backdoored model pairs in original and seperate channel setting.

Cross-Architecture Detection. In more general and challenging scenarios where we are not able to narrow down which network architecture is used for the backdoored CNN model, our approach still achieves relatively high detection rate on network architectures unseen during training. On MNIST, we train the detector on signatures generated from 2 out of the 3 network architectures (LeNet-5, ResNet-8, VGG-10) and evaluate the trained detector on CNNs of other architecture. We observe an average detection rate as high as 80%, reported in Table 3. In short, our proposed one-pixel signature is architecture-agnostic and the Backdoored CNN detectors trained on top of it attain great generalizability.

Training with Less Samples. To understand the sample complexity our method, here we investigate the minimum number of training models on four datasets without heavily downgrading the detection rate. We keep reducing 25 training pairs until zero and record the average detection rate for 20 detectors trained on the reduced training set at each time. The curve of the detection rate on GTSRB is shown in Fig. 7. Intuitively, we need more training models to detect CNN_{Trojan} that is trained on more complex datasets. Detectors on GTSRB dataset achieve an average detection rate of 87.31% with a reduced training set of size 175 Clean and 175 Backdoored models, whereas training set with 25 Clean and 25 Backdoored models is sufficient to train a backdoored CNN detector for models trained on MNIST to achieve approximately 95% detection rate. For fashion-MNIST, we need 50 Clean and 50 Backdoored models to achieve the same detection accuracy.

Use Channels in One-Pixel Signature as Individual Training Samples.
We could also treat each channel, instead of the whole one-pixel signature, as
a positive/negative sample for training. Thus for models with K classes, the
numbers of training samples increases by K times. We find that thereby training with only 15 pairs of CNN_{Clean} and CNN_{Trojan} models yields the same
detection rate as training with 300 pairs of models previously. With 100 training
pairs, we could achieve detection rate of 97% in GTSRB and 90% in ImageNet.
A detailed comparison of the detection accuracy on GTSRB between using the
individual channel and the original strategies is shown in Fig. 7(a).

6 Ablation Study

All-to-one and All-to-all Trojan Attack

Our detection technique can be effectively extended to other possible strategies like the all-to-one attack without compromising the detection rate. Under
the scenario of an all-to-one attack, the attacker tries to force the model to classify all samples implanted with certain backdoor pattern into a targeted class.
We see that the all-to-one attack is a variant of the one-to-one attack, and is
even more likely to be detected by our method.

Similarly, we illustrate the effectiveness of our method on detecting all-to-all
attack. We compare the detection success rate of our Trojan detector to that
of Neural Cleanse and ABS on the testing set of 100 CNN models. It turns out
that our Trojan detector can achieve a detection success rate greater than **95%**,
while both Neural Cleanse and ABS show a poor success rate of around 50%.

Signature Generation with Different Default Images I_o

One important parameter of our one-pixel signature method is the default
image I_o. In our experiments, we empirically set the default image with a constant value of 0. Here we compare three different I_o setups: a) a constant value
of 0, as the black image strategy; b) a constant value of 1, as the white image
strategy; c) the pixel-wise mean of testing images, as the average testing image
strategy; We are using a clean leNet-5 model trained on MNIST, and a backdoored leNet-5 model trained on poisoned MNIST dataset with Trojan trigger
inserted at upper left corner, for evaluation. Both $I_o = 0$ and average image
policy result in high detection rate. Since $I_o = 0$ policy do no require access to
the training set, we regard this as our empirically optimal policy of the default
image.

7 Conclusion

In this paper, we have developed a new backdoored CNN detection/classification
method by designing a CNN signature representation that is revealing and easy
to compute. It demonstrates a significant performance improvement over the
existing competing methods with more general assumptions about the Tro-
jan/backdoor attacks.

Acknowledgment. This work is supported by NSF IIS-1717431 and NSF IIS-1618477. We thank Rajesh Gupta and Mani Srivastava for valuable discussions.

References

1. Akhtar, N., Mian, A.: Threat of adversarial attacks on deep learning in computer vision: a survey. IEEE Access **6**, 14410–14430 (2018)
2. Chua, C.S., Jarvis, R.: Point signatures: a new representation for 3D object recognition. Int. J. Comput. Vis. **25**(1), 63–85 (1997). https://doi.org/10.1023/A:1007981719186
3. Deng, J., Dong, W., Socher, R., Li, L.J., Li, K., Fei-Fei, L.: ImageNet: a large-scale hierarchical image database. In: CVPR, pp. 248–255 (2009)
4. Goodfellow, I., Bengio, Y., Courville, A., Bengio, Y.: Deep Learning, vol. 1. MIT Press, Cambridge (2016)
5. Goodfellow, I., Shlens, J., Szegedy, C.: Explaining and harnessing adversarial examples. In: ICLR (2014)
6. Gu, T., Dolan-Gavitt, B., Garg, S.: BadNets: identifying vulnerabilities in the machine learning model supply chain. arXiv preprint arXiv:1708.06733 (2017)
7. Guo, W., Wang, L., Xing, X., Du, M., Song, D.: Tabor: a highly accurate approach to inspecting and restoring trojan backdoors in AI systems. arXiv preprint arXiv:1908.01763 (2019)
8. Hammersley, J.M., Clifford, P.: Markov fields on finite graphs and lattices. Unpublished manuscript **46** (1971)
9. He, K., Zhang, X., Ren, S., Sun, J.: Deep residual learning for image recognition. In: CVPR, pp. 770–778 (2016)
10. Kingma, D.P., Ba, J.: Adam: a method for stochastic optimization. In: International Conference on Learning Representations (2015)
11. Krizhevsky, A., Sutskever, I., Hinton, G.E.: ImageNet classification with deep convolutional neural networks. In: Advances in Neural Information Processing Systems, pp. 1097–1105 (2012)
12. LeCun, Y., et al.: Backpropagation applied to handwritten zip code recognition. Neural Comput. **1**, 541–551 (1989)
13. LeCun, Y., Bengio, Y., Hinton, G.: Deep learning. Nature **521**(7553), 436 (2015)
14. Lindeberg, T.: Scale-Space Theory in Computer Vision, vol. 256. Springer, Heidelberg (2013)
15. Liu, K., Dolan-Gavitt, B., Garg, S.: Fine-pruning: defending against backdooring attacks on deep neural networks. In: Bailey, M., Holz, T., Stamatogiannakis, M., Ioannidis, S. (eds.) RAID 2018. LNCS, vol. 11050, pp. 273–294. Springer, Cham (2018). https://doi.org/10.1007/978-3-030-00470-5_13
16. Liu, Y., Lee, W.C., Tao, G., Ma, S., Aafer, Y., Zhang, X.: ABS: scanning neural networks for back-doors by artificial brain stimulation. In: ACM SIGSAC Conference on Computer and Communications Security, pp. 1265–1282 (2019)
17. Mahendran, A., Vedaldi, A.: Understanding deep image representations by inverting them. In: CVPR, pp. 5188–5196 (2015)
18. U.S. Army Research Office: W911nf-19-s-0012. In: U.S. Army Research Office Broad Agency Announcement for TrojAI (2019)
19. Prakash, A., Moran, N., Garber, S., DiLillo, A., Storer, J.: Deflecting adversarial attacks with pixel deflection. In: CVPR (2018)

20. Qiao, X., Yang, Y., Li, H.: Defending neural backdoors via generative distribution modeling. In: Advances in Neural Information Processing Systems, pp. 14004–14013 (2019)
21. Stallkamp, J., Schlipsing, M., Salmen, J., Igel, C.: The German traffic sign recognition benchmark: a multi-class classification competition. In: IEEE International Joint Conference on Neural Networks, pp. 1453–1460 (2011)
22. Su, J., Vargas, D.V., Sakurai, K.: One pixel attack for fooling deep neural networks. IEEE Trans. Evol. Comput. **23**, 828–841 (2019)
23. Szegedy, C., et al.: Going deeper with convolutions. In: CVPR (2015)
24. Wang, B., et al.: Neural cleanse: identifying and mitigating backdoor attacks in neural networks. In: IEEE Symposium on Security and Privacy (2019)
25. Witkin, A.P.: Scale-space filtering. In: Readings in Computer Vision, pp. 329–332. Elsevier (1987)
26. Xiao, H., Rasul, K., Vollgraf, R.: Fashion-MNIST: a novel image dataset for benchmarking machine learning algorithms. arXiv preprint arXiv:1708.07747 (2017)
27. Xie, S., Girshick, R., Dollár, P., Tu, Z., He, K.: Aggregated residual transformations for deep neural networks. In: CVPR (2017)
28. Zeiler, M.D., Fergus, R.: Visualizing and understanding convolutional networks. In: Fleet, D., Pajdla, T., Schiele, B., Tuytelaars, T. (eds.) ECCV 2014. LNCS, vol. 8689, pp. 818–833. Springer, Cham (2014). https://doi.org/10.1007/978-3-319-10590-1_53
29. Zoph, B., Le, Q.V.: Neural architecture search with reinforcement learning. In: International Conference on Learning Representations (2017)

Learning to Transfer Learn: Reinforcement Learning-Based Selection for Adaptive Transfer Learning

Linchao Zhu[1,2]([envelope]), Sercan Ö. Arık[1], Yi Yang[2], and Tomas Pfister[1]

[1] Google Cloud AI, Sunnyvale, CA, USA
soarik@google.com, tpfister@google.com
[2] University of Technology Sydney, Sydney, Australia
{linchao.zhu,yi.yang}@uts.edu.au

Abstract. We propose a novel adaptive transfer learning framework, learning to transfer learn (L2TL), to improve performance on a target dataset by careful extraction of the related information from a source dataset. Our framework considers cooperative optimization of shared weights between models for source and target tasks, and adjusts the constituent loss weights adaptively. The adaptation of the weights is based on a reinforcement learning (RL) selection policy, guided with a performance metric on the target validation set. We demonstrate that L2TL outperforms fine-tuning baselines and other adaptive transfer learning methods on eight datasets. In the regimes of small-scale target datasets and significant label mismatch between source and target datasets, L2TL shows particularly large benefits.

Keywords: Transfer learning · Visual understanding · Reinforcement learning

1 Introduction

Deep neural networks excel at understanding images [15,47], text [8] and audio [1,36]. The performance of deep neural networks improves significantly with more training data [16]. As the applications diversify and span use cases with small training datasets, conventional training approaches are often insufficient to yield high performance. It becomes highly beneficial to utilize extra source datasets and "transfer" the relevant information to the target dataset. Transfer learning, commonly in the form of obtaining a pre-trained model on a large-scale source dataset and then further training it on the target dataset (known as fine-tuning), has become the standard recipe for most real-world artificial intelligence applications. Compared to training from random initialization, fine-tuning yields considerable performance improvements and convergence speedup,

Electronic supplementary material The online version of this chapter (https://doi.org/10.1007/978-3-030-58583-9_21) contains supplementary material, which is available to authorized users.

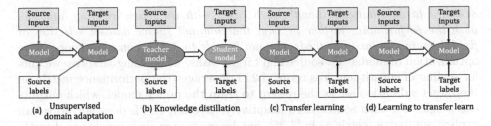

Fig. 1. L2TL and other adaptation settings. (a) Unsupervised domain adaptation incorporates source data and source labels for target domain adaptation, where the target labels are not provided. (b) Knowledge distillation aims to distill source knowledge from a teacher model to a student model, and the student model is usually more lightweight. (c) Conventional transfer learning transfers knowledge via weights of the model pre-trained on a source dataset, to obtain better performance on the target dataset. (d) Our L2TL adaptively infers the importance weights of the source examples based on the feedback from the target objective on the target validation set. With adaptive assignment, more relevant examples get higher weights to extract the information from the source dataset.

as demonstrated for object recognition [41], semantic segmentation [30], language understanding [8], speech synthesis [2], audio-visual recognition [33] and language translation [53].

Towards the motivation of pushing the performance of transfer learning, recent studies [26,29,31,35] have explored the direction of matching the source and target dataset distributions. Even simple methods to encourage domain similarity, such as prior class distribution matching in Domain Adaptive Transfer Learning (DATL) [35], are shown to be effective – indeed, in some cases, more important than the scale of the source dataset. Such adaptive transfer learning approaches, as in L2TL, typically assume the availability of the labeled source dataset for training on the labeled target dataset (that also differentiates the setting from unsupervised domain adaptation [13] or knowledge distillation [17], see Fig. 1), along with the pre-trained model. Given the increasing availability of very-large scale public datasets for various data types and the demand for cutting-edge deep learning on highly-specialized target tasks with small training datasets, this setting is indeed getting very common in practice [7,10,35].

In this paper, our goal is to push this direction further by introducing a novel *reinforcement learning (RL)-based framework*. Our framework, learning to transfer learn (L2TL), adaptively infers the beneficial source samples directly from the performance on the target task. There are cases that source samples could have features that are implicitly relevant to the target samples and would benefit the learning process, but they may belong to different classes. For example, consider the classification problem for bird images. The source dataset may not contain bird images, but may have airplane images with similar visual patterns that would aid the training of the bird classifier as they share similar visual patterns to learn valuable representations of the raw data. *L2TL framework is designed to automatically handle such cases with its policy learning, and can push the performance further in ways that manual source dataset selection or fixed domain similarity methods may not be able to.* L2TL considers cooperative optimization of models for source and target tasks, while using adaptive weights for scaling of constituent loss terms. L2TL leverages the performance metric on the target validation set as the reward to train the policy model, which outputs the weights for each source class adaptively. Overall, L2TL does not utilize an explicit similarity metric as in [7,35], but learns source class weights to directly optimize the target dataset performance.

We demonstrate promising transfer learning results given fixed models in a wide range of scenarios:

- *Source and target datasets from similar domains*: L2TL consistently outperforms the fine-tuning baseline with a 0.6%–1.3% relative accuracy gain on five fine-grained datasets, and DATL [35] with a 0.3%–1.5% relative accuracy gain. When the similarities become very apparent between some source and target classes, e.g. as in MNIST to SVHN digit recognition transfer case, the relative accuracy gain is 3.5% compared to fine-tuning baseline.
- *Large-scale source datasets*: When very large-scale source datasets are used, the selection of the relevant source classes become more important, the gain of L2TL is up to **7.5%**.
- *Low-shot target dataset regime*: L2TL significantly outperforms fine-tuning on fine-grained target datasets, up to **6.5%** accuracy gain with five samples per class.
- *Source and target datasets from dissimilar domains*: While other advanced transfer learning (based on explicit similarity measures) cannot be readily applied for this scenario, L2TL outperforms the fine-tuning baseline, up to **1.7%** accuracy gain on a texture dataset and **0.7 AUC** gain on Chest X-Ray dataset.

In addition, L2TL yields ranking of the source data samples according to their contributions to the target task, that can open horizons for new forms of interpretable insights.

2   Related Work

Adaptive Transfer Learning: There is a long history of transfer learning for neural networks, particularly in the form of fine-tuning [12]. Various directions were recently considered to improve standard fine-tuning. One direction is carefully choosing which portion of the network to adapt while optimizing the information extraction from the source dataset. In [14], a policy network is used to make routing decisions on whether to pass the input through the fine-tuned or the pre-trained layers. In [27], a regularization scheme is proposed to promote the similarity of the fine-tuned model with the pre-trained model as a favorable inductive bias. Another direction is carefully choosing which input samples are relevant to the target task, as in our paper. [10] uses filter bank responses to select nearest neighbor source samples and demonstrates improved performance. In [7], domain similarity between source and target datasets is quantified using Earth Mover's Distance (EMD). Transfer learning is shown to benefit from pretraining on a source domain that is similar in EMD. With a simple greedy subset creation selection criteria, promising results are shown for improving the target test set performance. Domain adaptive transfer learning (DATL) [35] employs probabilistic shaping, where the value is proportional to the ratios of estimated label prior probabilities. L2TL does not use a similarity metric like proximity of filter bank responses, EMD or prior class probabilities. Instead, it aims to assign weights to optimize the target set metric directly.

Reweighing Training Examples: Reweighing of constituent training terms has been considered for various performance goals. [42] applies gradient descent-based meta-learning to update the weights of the input data, with the goal of providing more noise-robust and class-balanced learning. [20] formulates reweighing as a bilevel optimization problem, such that higher weights are encouraged for the training samples with more agreement of the gradients on the validation set. Focal loss [28] is another soft weighting scheme that emphasizes on harder examples. In [21], a student-teacher training framework is proposed such that the teacher model provides a curriculum via a sample weighting scheme for the student model to focus on samples whose labels are likely to be correct. [11] studies the value of examples via Shapley values, and it shows that downweighting examples with low values might even improve performance. Reweighing of examples is also used in self-paced learning [24,46] where the weights are optimized to learn easier examples first. In [50], an RL agent is used to adaptively sample relevant frames from videos. In this paper, unlike the above, we focus on transfer learning – L2TL formulates the transfer learning problem with a new loss function, including class-relevant weights and a dataset-relevant weights. L2TL learns the weight assignments with RL, in a setting where actions (source data selection) are guided with the rewards (target validation performance). Unlike gradient-descent based reweighing, RL-based rewarding is also applicable to scenarios where the target evaluation objective is non-differentiable, e.g., area under the curve (AUC).

Meta Learning: Meta-learning broadly refers to learning to learn frameworks [45] whose goal is to improve the adaptation to a new task with the information extracted from other tasks. Meta learners are typically based on inspirations from known learning algorithms like gradient descent [9] or derived from black box neural networks [44]. As the notable meta learning application, in few-shot learning [9,51], the use of validation loss as a meta-objective has been explored [40]. However, for optimization problems with non-differentiable objectives like neural architecture search, RL-based meta-learning is shown to be a promising approach [39,52]. RL-based optimization has successfully been applied to other applications with enormously-large search spaces, e.g. learning a data augmentation policy [6]. The specific form of RL application in L2TL is novel – it employs guidance on the source dataset information extraction with the reward from the target validation dataset performance. Different from many meta learning

methods, e.g. those for few-shot learning, we consider a common real-world scenario where a very large-scale source dataset is integrated to extract information
from. We do not employ any episodic training, hence L2TL is practically feasible
to employ on very large-scale source datasets.

3   Learning from Source and Target Datasets

We consider a general-form training objective function $\mathcal{L}(\Omega, \zeta_\mathbf{S}, \zeta_\mathbf{T}, \lambda, \alpha_s, \alpha_t)$[1]
jointly defined on a source dataset D_S and a target dataset D_T:

$$
\mathcal{L} = \alpha_s[i] \cdot \sum_{j=1}^{B_S} \lambda(x_j, y_j; \Phi) \cdot L_S(f_S(x_j; \Omega, \zeta_\mathbf{S}), y_j)
$$

$$
+ \alpha_t[i] \cdot \sum_{k=1}^{B_T} L_T(f_T(x_k'; \Omega, \zeta_\mathbf{T}), y_k'),
$$

(1)

where (x, y) are the input and output pairs $(x_j, y_j \sim D_S, x_k', y_k' \sim D_T)$, B_S
and B_T are the source and target batch sizes[2], $\alpha_s[i]$ and $\alpha_t[i]$ are the scaling
coefficients at i^{th} iteration, λ is the importance weighing function, $f_S(\cdot; \Omega, \zeta_\mathbf{S})$
and $f_T(\cdot; \Omega, \zeta_\mathbf{T})$ are encoding functions for the source and the target datasets
with trainable parameters Ω, $\zeta_\mathbf{S}$ and $\zeta_\mathbf{T}$[3].

To maximally benefit from the source dataset, a vast majority of the trainable
parameters should be shared. If we consider the decompositions, $f_S(\cdot; \Omega, \zeta_\mathbf{S}) =
h_S(\cdot; \zeta_\mathbf{S}) \circ g(\cdot; \Omega)$ and $f_T(\cdot; \Omega, \zeta_\mathbf{T}) = h_T(\cdot; \zeta_\mathbf{T}) \circ g(\cdot; \Omega)$, g shall be a high capacity
encoder with large number of trainable parameters that can be represented with
a deep neural network, and h_T and h_S are low capacity mapping functions with
small number of parameters that can be represented with very shallow neural
networks.[4] The learning goal of Eq. 1 is generalizing to unseen target validation
dataset, via maximization of the performance metric R:

$$
\sum_{x', y' \sim D_T'} R(f_T(x'; \hat{\Omega}, \hat{\zeta}_\mathbf{T}), y')).
$$

(2)

R does not have be differentiable with respect to x and y and may include metrics
like the top-1 accuracy or area under the curve (AUC) for classification. $\hat{\Omega}$ and
$\hat{\zeta}_\mathbf{T}$ are the pre-trained weights optimized in Eq. 1.

Without transfer learning, i.e., training with only target dataset, $\alpha_s[i] = 0$
and $\alpha_t[i] = 1$ for all i. In fine-tuning, the optimization is first considered for the

---

[1] Function arguments are not often shown in the paper for notational convenience.

[2] Batch approximations may be optimal for different batch sizes for source and target
dataset and thus may employ different batch normalization parametrization.

[3] In $f(\cdot; \mathbf{W})$ representation, $\mathbf{W}$ denote the trainable parameters.

[4] Source datasets are typically much larger and contain more classes, hence h_S may
have higher number of parameters than h_T.

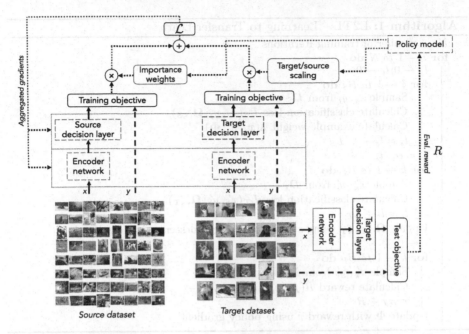

Fig. 2. Overall diagram of the L2TL framework. Dashed boxes correspond to trainable functions. L2TL employs a policy model to determine weigths of the source dataset samples, to extract the information in a careful way to maximize the target dataset test objective. The models on source and target datasets are shared, via the encoder network.

source dataset for N_S steps with uniform weighing of the samples $\lambda(x, y) = 1$, and then for the target dataset using the pre-trained weights $\hat{\Omega}$, $\hat{\zeta}_{\mathbf{T}}$, i.e.:

$$(\alpha_s[i], \alpha_t[i]) = \begin{cases} (1, 0), i < N_S, \\ (0, 1), i > N_S. \end{cases} \tag{3}$$

Next, we describe our framework towards optimal learning from source and target datasets.

4   Learning to Transfer Learn Framework

We propose learning to transfer learn (L2TL) framework (shown in Fig. 2) to learn the weight assignment adaptively, rather than using a fixed weight assignment function $\lambda(x, y; \mathbf{\Phi})$ to measure the relatedness between the source domain and the target domain. Learning of the adaptive weights in L2TL is guided by the performance metric R on a held-out target validation dataset. Thus, beyond targeting general relatedness, the framework directly targets relatedness for the specific goal of improvement in target evaluation performance.

While optimizing for $\lambda(x, y; \mathbf{\Phi})$, one straightforward option for scaling coefficients would be alternating them between $(1, 0)$ and $(0, 1)$ – i.e. training the

---

Algorithm 1: L2TL – Learning to Transfer Learn

$N \leftarrow$ number of training iterations
for $i \leftarrow 1$ *to* N **do**
    $l_s \leftarrow 0, l_t \leftarrow 0$
    for $j \leftarrow 1$ *to* B_S **do**
        Sample x_j, y_j from D_S
        Calculate classification loss $L_S(x_j, y_j; \mathbf{\Omega}, \zeta_{\mathbf{S}})$
        Calculate example weight $\lambda(x_j, y_j; \mathbf{\Phi})$
        $l_s = l_s + \lambda \cdot L_S$
    $l_s = \alpha_i \cdot l_s$
    for $k \leftarrow 1$ *to* B_T **do**
        Sample x'_k, y'_k from D_T
        Calculate classification loss $L_T(x'_k, y'_k; \mathbf{\Omega}, \zeta_{\mathbf{T}})$
        $l_t = l_t + L_T$
    Update $\mathbf{\Omega}, \zeta_{\mathbf{S}}, \zeta_{\mathbf{T}}$ using stochastic gradient descent with loss $l_s + l_t$
    $r \leftarrow 0$
    for $k \leftarrow 1$ *to* B_P **do**
        Sample x'_k, y'_k from $D_{T'}$
        Calculate reward $R(f_T(x'_k; \mathbf{\Omega}, \zeta_{\mathbf{T}}), y'_k)$
        $r = r + R$
    Update $\mathbf{\Phi}$ with reward r using policy gradient

---

source dataset until convergence with optimized $\hat{\mathbf{\Phi}}$ and then training the target dataset until convergence with the pre-trained weights from the source dataset. Yet, the approach may potentially require many alternating update steps and the computational cost may become prohibitively high. Instead, we design the policy model in L2TL to output $(\alpha_s[i], \alpha_t[i])$ along with λ.[5] The policy optimization step is decoupled from the gradient-descent based optimization for $\mathbf{\Omega}, \zeta_{\mathbf{S}}$ and $\zeta_{\mathbf{T}}$. Updates are reflected to the policy model via the information embodied in $\mathbf{\Omega}$ and $\zeta_{\mathbf{T}}$. Algorithm 1 overviews the training updates steps.

In the first phase of a learning iteration, we apply gradient decent-based optimization to learn the encoder weights $\mathbf{\Omega}$, and the classifier layer weights $\zeta_{\mathbf{S}}, \zeta_{\mathbf{T}}$ to minimize the loss function $\mathcal{L}$:

$$\hat{\mathbf{\Omega}}, \hat{\zeta_{\mathbf{S}}}, \hat{\zeta_{\mathbf{T}}} = \text{argmin}_{\mathbf{\Omega}, \zeta_{\mathbf{S}}, \zeta_{\mathbf{T}}} \mathcal{L}(\hat{\mathbf{\Phi}}; \mathbf{\Omega}, \zeta_{\mathbf{S}}, \zeta_{\mathbf{T}}). \tag{4}$$

In this phase, the policy model is fixed, and its actions are sampled to determine weights. Although most batches would contain relevant source dataset samples, the loss might be skewed if most of source dataset samples in a batch are irrelevant (and would ideally get lower weights). To ease this problem, we use a larger batch size and dynamically select the most relevant examples. At each iteration, we sample a training batch of size $M_S \cdot B_S$, and use the top B_S of them with the highest weights for training updates. This approach also yields computational

---

[5] Without loss of generality, we can optimize a single weight $\alpha_s[i]$ (setting $\alpha_t[i] = 1$) as the optimization is scale invariant.

benefits as the gradients would not be computed for most source dataset samples until convergence.

In the second phase of a learning iteration, given encoder weights from the first phase, our goal is to optimize policy weights Φ and maximize the evaluation metric $R_{D'_T}$ on the target validation set:

$$\max_{\Phi} R_{D'_T}(\hat{\Omega}, \hat{\zeta}_S, \hat{\zeta}_T; \Phi). \tag{5}$$

D'_T is the held-out dataset to compute the reward. We treat this phase as an RL problem, such that the policy model outputs the action of value assignment for $\lambda(x, y; \Phi)$ and α towards optimization of the reward (with the environment being training and evaluation setup, and the state being the encoder weights as the consequence of the first phase). In its general form $\lambda(x, y; \Phi)$ may yield a very high dimensionality for optimization of Φ. For simplicity and computational-efficiency, we consider sample-independent modeling of $\lambda(x, y; \Phi)$, similar to [35], i.e., $\lambda(x, y; \Phi) = \lambda(y; \Phi)$.[6]

For more efficient optimization via efficient systematic exploration of the very large action space, we discretize the possible values of $\lambda(y; \Phi)$ into pre-defined number of actions, in the range $\lambda(y) \in [0, 1]$. We define n actions, such that each action $k \in [0, n-1]$ corresponds to the weight value $k/(n-1)$. For example, when $n = 11$, the weight values are $[0, 0.1, 0.2, \ldots, 1.0]$. We also discretize the possible values for α, using n' actions. Each action k' corresponds to $\beta k'/(n'-1)$, where β is a hyperparameter to constrain the value range of α. The search space has $n' \times (c_S)^n$ possibilities, where c_S is the number of classes in the source dataset. When training the policy model, we use policy gradient to maximize the reward on the target dataset $D_{T'}$, using a batch of B_P samples. At iteration t, we denote the advantage $A_t = R_t - b_t$, where b_t is the baseline. Following [39], we use the moving average baseline to reduce variance, i.e., $b_t = (1-\gamma)b_t + \gamma R_t$, where γ is the decay rate. The policy gradient is computed using REINFORCE [49] and optimized using Adam [22].

5   Experiments

5.1   Datasets and Implementation Details

We demonstrate the performance of L2TL in various scenarios. As the source dataset, we use the ImageNet dataset [43] containing 1.28M images 1K classes, and also a much larger dataset, i.e., JFT-300M, containing $\sim$300M images from 18,291 classes to demonstrate the scalability of our approach. As the target datasets, we evaluate on **five** fine-grained image datasets (summarized in Table 1): **Birdsnap** [3], **Oxford-IIIT Pets** [37], **Stanford Cars** [23], **FGVC**

---

[6] A search space with a higher optimization granularity is expected to improve the results, albeit accompanied by significantly increased computational complexity for meta learning of x-dependent $\lambda(x, y; \Phi)$.

Table 1. Details of the five fine-grained datasets: Birdsnap (Birds) [3], Oxford-IIIT Pets (Pets) [37], Stanford Cars (Cars) [23], FGVC Aircraft (Air) [32], and Food-101 (Food) [4].

	Birdsnap	Oxford-IIIT Pets	Stanford Cars	Aircraft	Food-101
# of classes	500	37	196	100	101
# of train examples	42,405	2,940	6,494	3,334	68,175
# of valid examples	4,981	740	1,650	3,333	7,575
# of test examples	2,443	3,669	8,041	3,333	25,250

Table 2. Transfer learning performance with ImageNet source dataset. * indicates our implementation.

Method	Target dataset test accuracy (%)				
	Birdsnap	Oxford-IIIT Pets	Stanford Cars	Aircraft	Food-101
Fine-tuning [35]	77.2	93.3	91.5	88.8	88.7
Fine-tuning*	77.1	93.1	92.0	88.2	88.4
MixDCNN [48]	74.8	–	–	82.5	–
EMD [7]	–	–	91.3	85.5	88.7
OPAM [38]	–	93.8	92.2	–	–
DATL [35]	76.6	94.1	92.1	87.8	88.9
Our L2TL	**78.1**	**94.4**	**92.6**	**89.1**	**89.2**

Aircraft [32], and **Food-101** [4]. In addition, we also consider transfer learning scenario from MNIST to SVHN [34] to assess the effectiveness of L2TL for small-scale source datasets.

We also consider two target datasets with classes that do not exist in the source datasets: Describable Textures Dataset (DTD) [5] and Chest X-Ray Dataset CheXpert [19]. **Describable Textures Dataset:** DTD contains textural images in the wild from 47 classes such as striped and matted. The dataset has 20 splits and we evaluate the testing results on the first split. Each training, validation, and testing split has 1,880 images. **Chest X-Ray Dataset:** The CheXpert medical dataset is used for chest radiograph interpretation task. It consists of 224,316 chest radiographs of 65,240 patients labeled for 14 observations as positive, negative, or uncertain. Following [19], we report AUC on five classes and we regard "uncertain" examples as positive.[7] For L2TL, we use the mean AUC as the reward.

---

[7] Our reproduced results are matched with [19] on mean AUC. However, there are variances as we can see that for some classes, we achieve slightly worse than [19]. This may because of the small number of validation examples (200) used.

Table 3. Results on Birdsnap using JFT-300M as the source dataset. The performance is reported on the test set.

Method	Birdsnap accuracy (%)
Fine-tuning	74.9
DATL [35]	81.7
Our L2TL	**82.4**

Table 4. Transfer learning from MNIST to SVHN. As shown in [29], fine-tuning shows gains over other training cases due to the inherent similarity between datasets. L2TL efficiently exploits this further by emphasizing on some MNIST classes more than others, and improves the transfer learning gains significantly.

Method	SVHN accuracy (%)
Random initialization	64.8
Fine-tuning	71.7
Our L2TL	**75.2**

Implementation Details. When the source dataset is ImageNet, we use a batch size $B_S = 256$, $B_T = 256$, $B_P = 1024$ and a batch multiplier $M_S = 5$ for all the experiments. For the JFT-300M dataset, to reduce the number of training iterations, we use $B_S = 1,024$. The number of actions n' for α is 100.

We use Inception-V3 for all the experiments except CheXpert. For target dataset, we search the initial learning rate from $\{0.001, 0.005, 0.01, 0.05, 0.1, 0.15, 0.2, 0.4\}$, and weight decay from $\{0, 4 \times 10^{-5}\}$. All the datasets are optimized using SGD with a momentum of 0.9, trained for 20,000 iterations. We use the single central crop during evaluation. The learning rate is cosine decayed after first 2,000 iterations warmup. When optimizing our policy model, we use the Adam optimizer with a fixed learning rate 0.0001. As policy model parameters, we set $\beta = 0.5$ and $\gamma = 0.05$. We follow the standard image preprocessing procedure for Inception-V3 on both the source images and the target images.

For CheXpert, we use the DenseNet-121 architecture [18] and follow the evaluation protocol specified in [19], where ten crops are used for evaluation and 30 checkpoints are ensembled to obtain the final results. We cross validate weight decay and initial learning rate, where the weight decay is searched in $[0, 0.0001]$ and the learning rate searched in range $[0.5, 0.8, 1.0, 1.3, 1.5, 2.0]$. All other hyperparameters are same as above. We use the same input preprocessing as described in https://github.com/zoogzog/chexnet.

Hyperparameters of the encoder models are chosen from the published baselines and the policy model parameters are cross-validated on a validation set. For datasets that the testing accuracy is reported using the model trained on training and validation samples, L2TL is first trained on the training set using the reward from the validation set. Then, the learned control variables are used to train the joint model on the combined set of training and validation samples

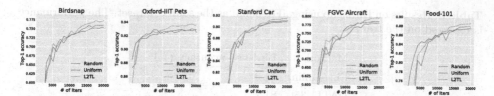

Fig. 3. Performance comparisons between L2TL, random search and uniform weights. The curves are oscillatory at the beginning, but become stable later during the training. L2TL outperforms the baselines when the training converges.

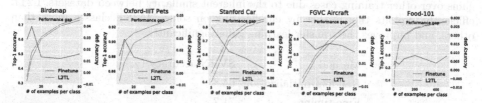

Fig. 4. Number of examples per class vs. top-1 accuracy for L2TL and fine-tuning.

– we completely exclude the test set during training. For the fine-tuning experiments, we use the best set of hyperparameters evaluated on the validation set. We present the results averaged over three runs. We observe that the standard deviation for the L2TL accuracy to be around 0.1%, much smaller than the gap between different methods.

5.2   Similar Domain Transfer Learning

We initially consider the scenario of target datasets with classes that mostly exist in the source dataset.

Performance and Comparison to Other Transfer Learning Methods. We first evaluate L2TL on five fine-grained datasets focusing on different subsets, with the reward of validation set top-1 accuracy. Table 2 shows the results of L2TL along with fine-tuning and state-of-the-art transfer learning benchmarks. With a well-optimized network architecture and learning rate scheduling, fine-tuning is already a solid baseline for the datasets in Table 1 [7,35]. Yet, L2TL outperforms fine-tuning across all the datasets with 0.6%–1.3% accuracy difference, which demonstrates the strength of L2TL in selecting related source examples across various domains. DATL performs worse than fine-tuning on Birdsnap and Aircraft, unlike L2TL. This underlines the importance of leveraging the visual similarity in the ways beyond label matching as in DATL. When the much larger JFT-300M source dataset is considered, Table 3 shows that L2TL shows even greater benefits in learning related samples to extract knowledge from despite the large-scale of options, demonstrating **7.5%** improvement over the fine-tuning baseline.

Table 5. Target dataset test accuracy (%) on Stanford Car with different number of target samples per class.

Method	Number of samples per class			
	5	10	15	20
Fine-tuning	40.0	70.3	80.5	84.9
Our L2TL	**46.5**	**73.7**	**83.0**	**86.1**

(a) Birds   (b) Pets   (c) Cars   (d) Airplane   (e) Food

Fig. 5. Representative examples from the source datasets with high weight from L2TL for different target datasets. In most cases, we observe the selected examples to be highly-related to the target dataset.

We additionally conduct the experiments on transfer learning from MNIST to SVHN [34], in a setting similar to [29]. Although both datasets correspond to the same content of digits, the font style of digits are quite distinct, with varying degree of differences among individual digits. Following [29], we construct the SVHN dataset by randomly sampling 60 images per class, resulting in 600 images in the training split. We use the pretrained LeNet [25] for transferring source dataset of MNIST to the target dataset of SVHN. Table 4 shows that comparing to fine-tuning, L2TL obtains more than 3.5% improvement in performance, via upweighing of the relevant digit images from MNIST. This also validates the effectiveness of L2TL even with small-scale source datasets.

Learning Importance Weights. We study the effectiveness of learning importance weights in L2TL by comparing to two baselines: (i) random search: the policy model is not optimized and random actions are chosen as the policy output, and (ii) uniform weights: a constant importance weight is assigned to all training samples. Note that for these baselines, α is still optimized via policy gradient. We show the best results of the baselines, after optimizing the hyperparameters on the validation set. As shown in Fig. 3, L2TL outperforms both after sufficient number of iterations, demonstrating the importance of reweighting via policy gradient. L2TL converges to the final result in the last few thousand iterations, although a larger variance is observed at the beginning of training. We do not observe large variations in the final performance with different runs (e.g. the standard deviation of performance is around 0.1% over 3 runs). As the classifiers of both the source and the target dataset converge, the small variations in the weights for each class would not heavily affect the final performance.

Fig. 6. Top source classes with the highest weight from ImageNet while transferring to DTD target. Representative images from each ImageNet class are shown along with related examples from DTD.

Table 6. Results on the test set on DTD, split 1.

Number of Training examples	Method	Accuracy (%)
Full training set	Random initialization	57.4
	Fine-tuning	70.3
	L2TL	**72.0**
10 examples per category	Fine-tuning	55.0
	Our L2TL	**60.1**

Small Target Dataset Regime. In the extreme regime of very small number of training examples, generalizing to unseen examples is particularly challenging as the model can be prone to overfitting. Figure 4 shows that in most cases, we observe significant increase in performance when the number of examples per class is smaller. For five examples per class, the gap is as high as **6.5%** (for Stanford Car) (see Table 5). We observe that the gap between the L2TL and the fine-tune baseline often becomes smaller when more examples are used, but still remains as high as 1.5% with 60 examples per class (for Birdsnap). These underline the potential of L2TL for significant performance improvements in real-world tasks where the number of training examples are limited.

High-Weight Source Samples. To build insights on the learned weights, we sample $10k$ actions from the policy and rank the source labels according to their weights. For Birds, the top source class is "bee eater" which is one of the bird species in ImageNet. The second top "aepyceros melampus" is an antelope that has narrow mouth, which is similar to some birds with sharp spout. The "valley" also matches the background in some images. For Cars, we interestingly observe the high-weight class "barrel, cask", which indeed include wheels and car-looking body types in many images. "Terrapin" is a reptile that crawls on the ground with four legs, whose shape looks like vehicles in some way. For Food, the high-weight classes seem relevant in a more subtle way – e.g., "caldron" might have images with food inside. Figure 5 visualizes a few representative examples from each dataset. More classes can be found in our supplementary material. These demonstrate that L2TL can carefully extract the related classes from the source based on the pattern/shape of the objects, or background scenes. L2TL

Table 7. AUC comparisons on the CheXpert dataset. We followed the the same evaluation protocol in [19] .

Method	Atelectasis	Cardiomegaly	Consolidation	Edema	Pleural Effusion	Mean
Fine-tuning [19]	85.8	83.2	89.9	94.1	**93.4**	89.3
Fine-tuning	85.2	83.8	90.0	94.5	92.8	89.3
Our L2TL	**86.1**	**84.4**	**91.5**	**94.8**	93.2	**90.0**

Table 8. Computational cost of training on Cloud TPU v2. We use Inception-V3 as the backbone. The last column ("With PT model") assumes availability of a pre-trained source model. "TL" denotes transfer learning from source to target.

Method	Number of iterations		Time per iterations		Total time	
	Pre-training	TL	Pre-training	TL	From scratch	With PT model
Fine-tuning	213,000	20,000	0.14 s	0.21 s	9.5 h	1.2 h
DATL [35]	713,000	20,000	0.14 s	0.21 s	28.9 h	20.6 h
Our L2TL	213,000	20,000	0.14 s	0.75 s	12.5 h	4.2 h

yields ranking of the source data samples, which can be utilized as new forms of interpretable insights for model developers.

5.3   Dissimilar Domain Transfer Learning

We evaluate L2TL on datasets that are dissimilar to the source dataset, where alternative methods like DATL cannot be readily applied. Table 6 shows the results on DTD. We observe that ImageNet fine-tuning greatly improves the classification results compared to training from random initialization. L2TL further improves the fine-tuning baseline by 1.5%, demonstrating the strength of L2TL selectively using related source classes instead of all classes. For the low-shot target dataset regime, with 10 examples per class, the improvement is more than 5%, suggesting the premise of L2TL even more strongly. Figure 6 shows that L2TL is able to utilize visually-similar patterns between the source and the target classes. The similarities occur in the form of texture pattern for most DTD classes. For example, "praire chicken" images from ImageNet typically contain patterns very relevant to "lined" from DTD. Training with such visually-similar patterns especially helps the low layers of the networks as they can reuse most of the relevant representations when transferring knowledge [29].

Similarly, Table 7 shows the results on CheXpert, using target validation AUC as a L2TL reward. L2TL performs better than the fine-tuning baseline with an AUC improvement of 0.7. There are not many straightforward visual similarities to humans between ImageNet and CheXpert, but L2TL is still capable of discovering them to improve performance.

5.4 Computational Cost of Training

L2TL uses both the source and target data for training, and the source data can be potentially very large, but the excess computational overhead of L2TL is indeed not large. Table 8 presents the computational cost for fine-tuning, DATL and L2TL with Imagenet as the source dataset. In DATL, given a new target dataset, a new model has to be trained on the resampled data until convergence. This step is time-consuming for large-scale source datasets. In L2TL, the transfer learning step is more expensive than fine-tuning, as it requires the computation on both source and target datasets. Yet, it only requires a single training pass on the source dataset, and thus the training time is much lower compared to DATL, and only ~30% higher than fine-tuning when the whole training is considered.

6 Conclusions

We propose a novel RL-based framework, L2TL, to improve transfer learning on a target dataset by careful extraction of information from a source dataset. We demonstrate the effectiveness of L2TL for various cases. L2TL consistently improves fine-tuning across all datasets. The performance benefit of L2TL is more significant for small-scale target datasets or large-scale source datasets. Even for the cases where source and target datasets come from substantially-different domains, L2TL still yields clear improvements.

References

1. Amodei, D., Anubhai, R., Battenberg, E., Case, C., Casper, J., et al.: Deep speech 2: end-to-end speech recognition in English and Mandarin. In: ICML (2016)
2. Arik, S.Ö., Chen, J., Peng, K., Ping, W., Zhou, Y.: Neural voice cloning with a few samples. In: NeurIPS (2018)
3. Berg, T., Liu, J., Woo Lee, S., Alexander, M.L., Jacobs, D.W., Belhumeur, P.N.: Birdsnap: Large-scale fine-grained visual categorization of birds. In: CVPR (2014)
4. Bossard, L., Guillaumin, M., Van Gool, L.: Food-101 – mining discriminative components with random forests. In: Fleet, D., Pajdla, T., Schiele, B., Tuytelaars, T. (eds.) ECCV 2014. LNCS, vol. 8694, pp. 446–461. Springer, Cham (2014). https://doi.org/10.1007/978-3-319-10599-4_29
5. Cimpoi, M., Maji, S., Kokkinos, I., Mohamed, S., Vedaldi, A.: Describing textures in the wild. In: CVPR (2014)
6. Cubuk, E.D., Zoph, B., Mane, D., Vasudevan, V., Le, Q.V.: AutoAugment: learning augmentation policies from data. arXiv preprint arXiv:1805.09501 (2018)
7. Cui, Y., Song, Y., Sun, C., Howard, A., Belongie, S.: Large scale fine-grained categorization and domain-specific transfer learning. In: CVPR (2018)
8. Devlin, J., Chang, M., Lee, K., Toutanova, K.: BERT: pre-training of deep bidirectional transformers for language understanding. arxiv:1810.04805 (2018)
9. Finn, C., Abbeel, P., Levine, S.: Model-agnostic meta-learning for fast adaptation of deep networks. In: ICML (2017)
10. Ge, W., Yu, Y.: Borrowing treasures from the wealthy: deep transfer learning through selective joint fine-tuning. In: CVPR (2017)

11. Ghorbani, A., Zou, J.: Data Shapley: equitable valuation of data for machine learning. In: ICML (2019)
12. Girshick, R.B., Donahue, J., Darrell, T., Malik, J.: Rich feature hierarchies for accurate object detection and semantic segmentation. In: CVPR (2014)
13. Gong, B., Shi, Y., Sha, F., Grauman, K.: Geodesic flow kernel for unsupervised domain adaptation. In: CVPR (2012)
14. Guo, Y., Shi, H., Kumar, A., Grauman, K., Rosing, T., Feris, R.S.: SpotTune: transfer learning through adaptive fine-tuning. In: CVPR (2019)
15. He, K., Zhang, X., Ren, S., Sun, J.: Deep residual learning for image recognition. In: CVPR (2016)
16. Hestness, J., et al.: Deep learning scaling is predictable, empirically. arXiv:1712.00409 (2017)
17. Hinton, G., Vinyals, O., Dean, J.: Distilling the knowledge in a neural network. arXiv preprint arXiv:1503.02531 (2015)
18. Huang, G., Liu, Z., Van Der Maaten, L., Weinberger, K.Q.: Densely connected convolutional networks. In: CVPR (2017)
19. Irvin, J., et al.: CheXpert: a large chest radiograph dataset with uncertainty labels and expert comparison. In: AAAI (2019)
20. Jenni, S., Favaro, P.: Deep bilevel learning. In: Ferrari, V., Hebert, M., Sminchisescu, C., Weiss, Y. (eds.) ECCV 2018. LNCS, vol. 11214, pp. 632–648. Springer, Cham (2018). https://doi.org/10.1007/978-3-030-01249-6_38
21. Jiang, L., Zhou, Z., Leung, T., Li, L., Fei-Fei, L.: MentorNet: regularizing very deep neural networks on corrupted labels. In: ICML (2018)
22. Kingma, D.P., Ba, J.: Adam: a method for stochastic optimization. In: ICLR (2014)
23. Krause, J., Deng, J., Stark, M., Fei-Fei, L.: Collecting a large-scale dataset of fine-grained cars. In: The Second Workshop on Fine-Grained Visual Categorization (2013)
24. Kumar, M.P., Packer, B., Koller, D.: Self-paced learning for latent variable models. In: NeurIPS (2010)
25. LeCun, Y., Bottou, L., Bengio, Y., Haffner, P., et al.: Gradient-based learning applied to document recognition. Proc. IEEE 86(11), 2278–2324 (1998)
26. Lee, J., et al.: BioBERT: a pre-trained biomedical language representation model for biomedical text mining. arXiv:1901.08746 (2019)
27. Li, X., Grandvalet, Y., Davoine, F.: Explicit inductive bias for transfer learning with convolutional networks. In: ICML (2018)
28. Lin, T., Goyal, P., Girshick, R.B., He, K., Dollár, P.: Focal loss for dense object detection. In: ICCV (2017)
29. Liu, H., Long, M., Wang, J., Jordan, M.I.: Towards understanding the transferability of deep representations (2019)
30. Long, J., Shelhamer, E., Darrell, T.: Fully convolutional networks for semantic segmentation. In: CVPR (2015)
31. Mahajan, D., et al.: Exploring the limits of weakly supervised pretraining. In: Ferrari, V., Hebert, M., Sminchisescu, C., Weiss, Y. (eds.) ECCV 2018. LNCS, vol. 11206, pp. 185–201. Springer, Cham (2018). https://doi.org/10.1007/978-3-030-01216-8_12
32. Maji, S., Rahtu, E., Kannala, J., Blaschko, M., Vedaldi, A.: Fine-grained visual classification of aircraft. arXiv:1306.5151 (2013)
33. Moon, S., Kim, S., Wang, H.: Multimodal transfer deep learning for audio visual recognition. arXiv:1412.3121 (2014)
34. Netzer, Y., Wang, T., Coates, A., Bissacco, A., Wu, B., Ng, A.Y.: Reading digits in natural images with unsupervised feature learning (2011)

35. Ngiam, J., Peng, D., Vasudevan, V., Kornblith, S., Le, Q.V., Pang, R.: Domain adaptive transfer learning with specialist models. arXiv preprint arXiv:1811.07056 (2018)
36. van den Oord, A., Dieleman, S., Zen, H., Simonyan, K., Vinyals, O., et al.: WaveNet: a generative model for raw audio. arXiv:1609.03499 (2016)
37. Parkhi, O.M., Vedaldi, A., Zisserman, A., Jawahar, C.: Cats and dogs. In: CVPR (2012)
38. Peng, Y., He, X., Zhao, J.: Object-part attention model for fine-grained image classification. TIP **27**, 1487–1500 (2017)
39. Pham, H., Guan, M.Y., Zoph, B., Le, Q.V., Dean, J.: Efficient neural architecture search via parameter sharing. In: ICML (2018)
40. Ravi, S., Larochelle, H.: Optimization as a model for few-shot learning. In: ICLR (2017)
41. Razavian, A.S., Azizpour, H., Sullivan, J., Carlsson, S.: CNN features off-the-shelf: an astounding baseline for recognition. In: CVPR (2014)
42. Ren, M., Zeng, W., Yang, B., Urtasun, R.: Learning to reweight examples for robust deep learning. In: ICML (2019)
43. Russakovsky, O., et al.: ImageNet large scale visual recognition challenge. IJCV **115**, 211–252 (2015). https://doi.org/10.1007/s11263-015-0816-y
44. Santoro, A., Bartunov, S., Botvinick, M., Wierstra, D., Lillicrap, T.: Meta-learning with memory-augmented neural networks. In: ICML (2016)
45. Schmidhuber, J., Zhao, J., Wiering, M.: Shifting inductive bias with success-story algorithm, adaptive Levin search, and incremental self-improvement. Mach. Learn. **28**, 105–130 (1997). https://doi.org/10.1023/A:1007383707642
46. Shu, J., et al.: Meta-weight-net: Learning an explicit mapping for sample weighting. In: NeurIPS (2019)
47. Simonyan, K., Zisserman, A.: Very deep convolutional networks for large-scale image recognition. In: ICLR (2015)
48. Wang, D., Shen, Z., Shao, J., Zhang, W., Xue, X., Zhang, Z.: Multiple granularity descriptors for fine-grained categorization. In: ICCV (2015)
49. Williams, R.J.: Simple statistical gradient-following algorithms for connectionist reinforcement learning. Mach. Learn. **8**, 229–256 (1992). https://doi.org/10.1007/BF00992696
50. Wu, Z., Xiong, C., Ma, C.Y., Socher, R., Davis, L.S.: AdaFrame: adaptive frame selection for fast video recognition. In: CVPR (2019)
51. Zhu, L., Yang, Y.: Label independent memory for semi-supervised few-shot video classification. TPAMI (2020). https://doi.org/10.1109/TPAMI.2020.3007511
52. Zoph, B., Le, Q.V.: Neural architecture search with reinforcement learning. In: ICLR (2017)
53. Zoph, B., Yuret, D., May, J., Knight, K.: Transfer learning for low-resource neural machine translation. In: ACL (2016)

Structure-Aware Generation Network for Recipe Generation from Images

Hao Wang[1,2], Guosheng Lin[1], Steven C. H. Hoi[3], and Chunyan Miao[1,2(✉)]

[1] School of Computer Science and Engineering, Nanyang Technological University, Singapore, Singapore
{hao005,gslin,ascymiao}@ntu.edu.sg
[2] Joint NTU-UBC Research Centre of Excellence in Active Living for the Elderly, NTU, Singapore, Singapore
[3] Singapore Management University, Singapore, Singapore
chhoi@smu.edu.sg

Abstract. Sharing food has become very popular with the development of social media. For many real-world applications, people are keen to know the underlying recipes of a food item. In this paper, we are interested in automatically generating cooking instructions for food. We investigate an open research task of generating cooking instructions based on only food images and ingredients, which is similar to the image captioning task. However, compared with image captioning datasets, the target recipes are long-length paragraphs and do not have annotations on structure information. To address the above limitations, we propose a novel framework of Structure-aware Generation Network (SGN) to tackle the food recipe generation task. Our approach brings together several novel ideas in a systematic framework: (1) exploiting an unsupervised learning approach to obtain the sentence-level tree structure labels before training; (2) generating trees of target recipes from images with the supervision of tree structure labels learned from (1); and (3) integrating the inferred tree structures with the recipe generation procedure. Our proposed model can produce high-quality and coherent recipes, and achieve the state-of-the-art performance on the benchmark Recipe1M dataset.

Keywords: Structure learning · Text generation · Image-to-text

1 Introduction

Food-related research with the newly evolved deep learning-based techniques is becoming a popular topic, as food is essential to human life. One of the important and challenging tasks under the food research domain is recipe generation [23], where we are producing the corresponding and coherent cooking instructions for specific food.

In the recipe generation dataset Recipe1M [24], we generate the recipes conditioned on food images and ingredients. The general task setting of recipe generation is almost the same as that of image captioning [6]. Both of them target

© Springer Nature Switzerland AG 2020
A. Vedaldi et al. (Eds.): ECCV 2020, LNCS 12372, pp. 359–374, 2020.
https://doi.org/10.1007/978-3-030-58583-9_22

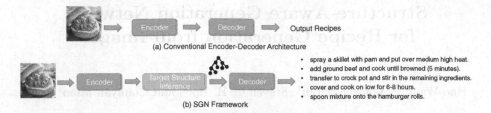

(a) Conventional Encoder-Decoder Architecture

(b) SGN Framework

- spray a skillet with pam and put over medium high heat.
- add ground beef and cook until browned (5 minutes).
- transfer to crock pot and stir in the remaining ingredients.
- cover and cook on low for 6-8 hours.
- spoon mixture onto the hamburger rolls.

Fig. 1. Comparison between conventional image captioning model and our proposed Structure-aware Generation Network (SGN) for recipe generation. Before generating target recipes, we infer the tree structures of recipes first, then we use graph attention networks to give tree embeddings. Based on the structure information, we can generate better recipes.

generating a description of an image by deep models. However, there still exist two big differences between recipe generation and image captioning: (i) the target caption length and (ii) annotations on structural information.

First, most popular image captioning datasets, such as Flickr [22] and MS-COCO dataset [6], only have one sentence per caption. By contrast, cooking instructions are paragraphs, containing multiple sentences to guide the cooking process, which cannot be fully shown in single food image. Although Recipe1M has ingredient information, the ingredients are actually mixed in cooked food images. Therefore, generating lengthy recipes using traditional image captioning model may hardly capture the whole cooking procedure. Second, the lack of structural information labeling is another challenge in recipe generation. For example, MS-COCO has precise bounding box annotations in images, giving scene graph information for caption generation. This structural information provided by the official dataset makes it easier to recognize the objects, their attributes and relationships within an image. While in food images, different ingredients are mixed when cooked. Hence, it is difficult to obtain the detection labeling for food images.

Benefiting from recent advances in language parsing, some research, such as ON-LSTM [26], utilizes an unsupervised way to produce word-level parsing trees of sentences and achieve good results. Inspired by that, we extend the ON-LSTM architecture to do sentence-level tree structure generation. We propose to train the extended ON-LSTM with quick thoughts manner [18], to capture the order information inside recipes. By doing so, we get the recipe tree structure labels.

After we obtained the recipe structure information, we propose a novel framework named **S**tructure-aware **G**eneration **N**etwork (SGN) to integrate the tree structure information with the training and inference phases. SGN is implemented to add a target structure inference module on the recipe generation process. Specifically, we propose to use a RNN to generate the recipe tree structures from food images. Based on the generated trees, we adopt the graph attention networks to embed the trees, in an attempt to giving the model more guidance when generating recipes. With the tree structure embeddings, we make the generated recipes remain long-length as the ground truth, and improve the generation performance considerably.

Our contributions can be summarized as:

- We propose a recipe2tree module to capture sentence-level tree structures for recipes, which is adopted to supervise the following img2tree module. We use an unsupervised approach to learn latent tree structures.
- We propose to use the img2tree module to generate recipe tree structures from food images, where we adopt a RNN for conditional tree generation.
- We propose to utilize the tree2recipe module, which encodes the inferred tree structures. It is implemented with graph attention networks, and boosts the recipe generation performance.

Figure 1 shows a comparison between vanilla image captioning model and our proposed SGN. SGN outperforms state-of-the-art baselines for recipe generation on Recipe1M dataset [24] significantly. We conduct extensive experiments to evaluate performance of SGN. Finally, we present qualitative results of our proposed methods, and visualizations of the generated recipe results.

2   Related Work

2.1   Image Captioning

Image captioning task is defined as generating the corresponding text descriptions from images. Based on MS-COCO dataset [6], most existing image captioning techniques adopt deep learning-based model. One popular approach is Encoder-Decoder architecture [1,9,14,29], where a CNN is used to obtain the image features along with object detection, then a language model is used to convert the image features into text.

Since image features are fed only at the beginning stage of generation process, the language model may face vanishing gradient problem [12]. Therefore, image captioning model is facing challenges in long sentence generation [1]. To enhance text generation process, [5,10] involve scene graph into the framework. However, scene graph generation rely heavily on object bounding box labeling, which is provided by MS-COCO dataset. When we shift to some other datasets without rich annotation, we can hardly obtain the graph structure information of the target text. Meanwhile, crowdsourcing annotation is high-cost and may not be reliable. Therefore, we propose to produce tree structures for paragraphs unsupervisedly, helping the recipe generation task in Recipe1M dataset [24].

2.2   Multimodal Food Computing

Food computing [20] has raised great interest recently, it targets applying computational approaches for analyzing multimodal food data for recognition [2], retrieval [24,30,31] and generation [23] of food. Recipe generation is a challenging task, it is mainly because that cooking instructions (recipes) contain more than one sentence. Besides, the input images of food datasets [4,24,33] suffer from quality issues. Among the existing food datasets, YouCook2 [33] and Storyboarding [4] use image sequence as input, which is not a general image captioning task setting. Recipe1M [23,24] contains static food image, ingredient and cooking instruction information for each food sample. Therefore, we choose Recipe1M [24] to evaluate our proposed methods.

2.3 Language Parsing

Parsing is served as one effective language analysis tool, it can output the tree structure of a string of symbols. Generally, language parsing is divided into word-level and sentence-level parsing. Word-level parsing is also known as grammar induction, which aims at learning the syntactic tree structure from corpora data. Especially, Shen et al. [26] propose to use ON-LSTM, which equips the LSTM architecture with an inductive bias towards learning latent tree structures. They train the model with normal language modeling way, at the same time they can get the parsing output induced by the model.

Sentence-level parsing is used to identify the elementary discourse units in a text, and it brings some benefits to discourse analysis. Many recent works attempted to use complex model with labeled data to achieve the goal [13,17]. Here we extend ON-LSTM [26] for unsupervised sentence-level parsing, which is trained using quick thoughts [18].

3 Method

We now present our proposed model SGN for recipe generation from food images. We show the framework of our proposed model in Fig. 2.

3.1 Overview

Given the food images and ingredients, our goal is to generate the cooking instructions. Different from image captioning task in MS-COCO [6,19], where the target caption only have one sentence, the cooking instruction is a para-graph, containing more than one sentence, and the maximum sentence number in Recipe1M dataset [24] is 19. If we infer the recipes directly from the images, i.e. use a decoder conditioned on image features for generation [23], it is difficult for model to fully capture the structured cooking steps. That may result in the generated paragraphs incomplete. Hence, we believe it necessary to infer paragraph structure during recipe generation phase.

To infer the sentence-level tree structure from food images, we need labels to supervise the tree generation process. However, in Recipe1M dataset [24], there has no paragraph tree structure labeling for cooking instructions. And it is very time-consuming and unreliable to use crowdsourcing to give labels. Therefore, in the first step, we use the proposed recipe2tree module to produce the tree

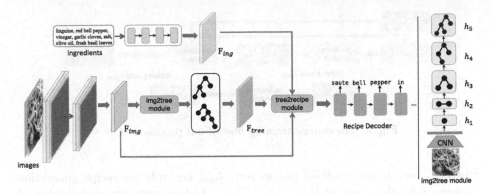

Fig. 2. Left: our proposed framework for effective recipe generation. **Right:** the img2tree module. The ingredients and food images are embedded by a pretrained language model and CNN respectively to produce the output features F_{ing} and F_{img}. Before language generation, we first infer the tree structure of target cooking instructions. To do so, we utilize the img2tree module, where a RNN produces the nodes and edge links step-by-step based on F_{img}. Then in tree2recipe module, we adopt graph attention networks (GAT) to encode the generated tree adjacency matrix, and get the tree embedding F_{tree}. We combine F_{ing}, F_{img} and F_{tree} to construct a final embedding for recipe generation, which is performed using a transformer.

structure labels with an unsupervised way. Technically, we use hierarchical ON-LSTM [26] to encode the cooking instructions and train the ON-LSTM with quick thoughts approach [18]. Then we can obtain the latent tree structure of cooking instructions.

During training phase, we input food images and ingredients to our proposed model. We try two different language models to encode ingredients, i.e. non-pretrained and pretrained model, to get the ingredient features F_{ing}. In non-pretrained model training, we use one word embedding layer to give F_{ing}. Besides, we adopt BERT [8] for ingredient embedding, which is one of the state-of-the-art NLP pretrained models.

In image process branch, we adopt a CNN to encode the food images and get the image features F_{img}. Based on F_{img}, we generate the trees and make them align with that produced by the recipe2tree module. Specifically, we transform the tree structure to a 1-dimensional adjacency sequence for RNN to generate, where the RNN's initial state is image feature F_{img}. To incorporate the generated tree structure into the recipe generation process, we get the tree embedding F_{tree} with graph attention networks (GATs) [28], and concatenate it with the image features F_{img} and ingredient features F_{ing}. We then generate the recipes conditioned on the joint features $\langle F_{tree}, F_{img}, F_{ing} \rangle$ with a transformer [27].

Our proposed framework is optimized over two objectives: to generate reasonable recipes given the food images and ingredients; and to produce the sentence-level tree structures of target recipes. The overall objective is given as:

$$L = \lambda_1 L_{gen} + \lambda_2 L_{tree} \qquad (1)$$

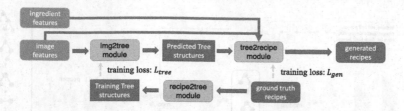

Fig. 3. The concise training flow of our proposed SGN.

where λ_1 and λ_2 are trade-off parameters. L_{gen} controls the recipe generation training with the input of $\langle F_{tree}, F_{img}, F_{ing} \rangle$, and outputs the probabilities of word tokens. L_{tree} is the tree generation loss, supervising the img2tree to generate trees from images. The training flow in shown in Fig. 3.

3.2 ON-LSTM Revisit

Ordered Neurons LSTM (ON-LSTM) [26] is proposed to infer the underlying tree-like structure of language while learning the word representation. It can achieve good performance in unsupervised parsing task. ON-LSTM is constructed based on the intuition that each node in the tree can be represented by a set of neurons in the hidden states of recurrent neural networks. To this end, ordered neurons is a inductive bias, where high-ranking neurons store long-term information, while low-ranking neurons contain short-term information that can be rapidly forgotten. Instead of acting independently on each neuron, the gates of ON-LSTM are dependent on the others by enforcing the order in which neurons should be updated. Hence, ON-LSTM is able to discern a hierarchy of information between neurons. With the learnt ranking, the top-down greedy parsing algorithm [25] is used for unsupervised constituency parsing. However, ON-LSTM is originally trained by language modeling way and learns the word-level order information. To unsupervisedly produce sentence-level tree structure, we extend ON-LSTM in recipe2tree module.

3.3 Recipe2tree Module

In recipe2tree module, we propose to use hierarchical ON-LSTM, i.e. word-level and sentence-level ON-LSTM, to train Recipe1M data. Specifically, in word-level ON-LSTM, we input the word tokens and use the output features as the sentence embeddings. The sentence embeddings will be fed into the sentence-level ON-LSTM for end-to-end training.

Since the original training way [26], such as language modeling or seq2seq [3] word prediction training, can not be used in sentence representation learning, we incorporate the idea of quick thoughts (QT) [18] to supervise the hierarchical ON-LSTM training. The general objective of QT is a discriminative approximation where the model attempts to identify the embedding of a correct target sentence given a set of sentence candidates. In other words, instead of predicting *what is the next* in language modeling, we predict *which is the next* in QT training to capture the order information inside recipes. Technically, for each recipe data, we select first $N-1$ of the cooking instruction sentences as context, i.e. $S_{ctxt} = \{s_1, ..., s_{N-1}\}$. Then sentence s_N turns out to be the correct next one. Besides, we randomly select K sentences along with the correct sentence s_N from each recipe, to construct candidate sentence set $S_{cand} = \{s_N, s_i, ..., s_k\}$. The candidate sentence features $g(S_{cand})$ are generated by the word-level ON-LSTM, and the context embeddings $f(S_{ctxt})$ are obtained from the sentence-level ON-LSTM. The computation of probability is given by

$$p(s_{\text{cand}}|S_{\text{ctxt}}, S_{\text{cand}}) = \frac{\exp[c(f(S_{\text{ctxt}}), g(s_{\text{cand}}))]}{\sum_{s' \in S_{\text{cand}}} \exp[c(f(S_{\text{ctxt}}), g(s'))]} \tag{2}$$

where c is an inner product, to avoid the model learning poor sentence encoders and a rich classifier. Minimizing the number of parameters in the classifier encourages the encoders to learn disentangled and useful representations [18]. The training objective maximizes the probability of identifying the correct next sentences for each training recipe data D.

$$\sum_{s \in D} \log p(s|S_{\text{ctxt}}, S_{\text{cand}}) \tag{3}$$

We show some qualitative results of sentence-level tree structure for recipe data in Fig. 4.

3.4 Img2tree Module

In img2tree module, we generate the tree structures from food images. Tree structure has hierarchical nature, in other words, "parent" node is always one step higher in the hierarchy than "child" nodes. Given the properties, we first represent the trees as sequence under the hierarchical ordering. Then, we use an auto-regressive model to model the sequence, meaning that the edges between subsequent nodes are dependent on the previous "parent" node. Besides, in Recipe1M dataset, the longest cooking instructions have 19 sentences. Therefore, the sentence-level parsing trees have limited node numbers, which avoids the model generating too long or complex sequence.

In Fig. 2, we specify our tree generation approach. The generation process is conditioned on the food images. We first map the tree structure to an adjacency matrix according to the hierarchical ordering, which is denoted the links between nodes by 0 or 1. Then the lower triangular part of the adjacency matrix will be converted to a vector $V \in \mathbb{R}^{n \times 1}$, where each element $V_i \in \{0, 1\}^i, i \in \{1, ..., n\}$. Since edges in tree structure are undirected, V can determine a unique tree T.

Here the tree generation model is built based on the food images, capturing how previous nodes are interconnected and how following nodes construct edges linking previous nodes. Hence, we adopt Recurrent Neural Networks (RNN) to model the predefined sequence V. We use the image encoded features F_{img} as the initialization of RNN hidden state, and the state-transition function h and the output function y are formulated as:

$$h_0 = F_{img}, h_i = f_{trans}(h_{i-1}, V_{i-1}), \tag{4}$$

$$y_i = f_{out}(h_i), \tag{5}$$

where h_i is conditioned on the previous generated $i-1$ nodes, y_i outputs the probabilities of next node's adjacency vector.

The tree generation objective function is:

$$p(V) = \prod_{i=1}^{n} p(V_i|V_1, \ldots, V_{i-1}), \tag{6}$$

$$L_{tree} = \sum_{V \in D} \log p(V), \tag{7}$$

where $p(V)$ is the product of conditional distributions over the elements, D denotes for all the training data.

3.5   Tree2recipe Module

In tree2recipe module, we utilize graph attention networks (GATs) [28] to encode the generated trees. The input of GATs is the generated tree adjacency matrix z. We produce node features with a linear transformation W, which is applied to the adjacency matrix z. We then perform attention mechanism a on the nodes and compute the attention coefficients

$$e_{ij} = a(Wz_i, Wz_j) \tag{8}$$

where e_{ij} measures the importance of node j's features to node i.

It is notable that different from most attention mechanism, where every node attends on every other node, GATs only allow each node to attend on its neighbour nodes. The underlying reason is that doing global attention fails to consider the property of tree structure, that each node has limited links to others. While the local attention mechanism used in GATs preserves the structural information well. We can formulate the final attentional score as:

$$\alpha_{ij} = \text{softmax}_j(e_{ij}) = \frac{\exp(e_{ij})}{\sum_{k \in N_i} \exp(e_{ik})} \tag{9}$$

where N_i is the neighborhood of node i, the output score is normalized through the softmax function. Similar with [27], GATs employ multi-head attention and averaging to stabilize the learning process. We get the tree features by the product of the attentional scores and the node features, and we perform nonlinear activation on the output to get the final features:

$$F_{tree} = \sigma(\sum_{j \in N_i} \alpha_{ij} Wz_j). \tag{10}$$

3.6   Recipe Generation

We adopt a transformer [27] for recipe generation. The input of transformer is the combination of previous obtained features F_{img}, F_{ing} and F_{tree}. The transformer decoder output the token $\hat{x}^{(i)}$ one by one during inference. The training objective is to maximize the following objective:

$$L_{gen} = \sum_{i=0}^{M} \log p(\hat{x}^{(i)} = x^{(i)}) \tag{11}$$

where L_{gen} is the recipe generation loss, and M is the maximum sentence generation length, $x^{(i)}$ denotes for the ground truth token.

4   Experiments

4.1   Dataset and Evaluation Metrics

We evaluate our proposed structure-aware generation network (SGN) on Recipe1M dataset [24], which is one of the largest collection of cooking recipe data with food images. Recipe1M has rich food related information, including the food images, ingredients and cooking instructions. In Recipe1M, there are $252, 547$, $54, 255$ and $54, 506$ food data samples for training, validation and test respectively. These recipe data is collected from some public websites, which are uploaded by users.

We evaluate the model using the same metrics as prior work [23]: perplexity. Besides, we extend to use more metrics to evaluate our proposed method. Specifically, we use perplexity, BLEU [21] and ROUGE [16]. Perplexity is used in [23], it measures how well the learned word probability distribution matches the target recipes. BLEU is computed based on the average of unigram, bigram, trigram and 4-gram precision. We use ROUGE-L to test the longest common subsequence. ROUGE-L is a modification of BLEU, focusing on recall rather than precision. Therefore, we can use ROUGE-L to measure the fluency of generated recipes.

4.2   Implementation Details

We adopt a 3-layer ON-LSTM [26] to output the sentence-level tree structure, taking about 50 epoch training to get converged. We set the learning rate as 1, batch size as 60, and the input embedding size is 400, which is the same as original work [26]. We select recipes containing over 4 sentences in Recipe1M dataset for training. And we randomly select several consecutive sentences as the context and the following one as the correct one. We set K as 3. We show some of the predicted sentence-level tree structures for recipes in Fig. 4.

To test if our proposed SGN can be applied to different systems, we tried two different ingredient encoders in the experiments, i.e. non-pretrained and pretrained language model. Using non-pretrained model is to compare with the prior work [23], where they use a word embedding layer to give the ingredient embeddings. We use BERT [8] as the pretrained language model, giving 512-dimensional features. The image encoder is used with a ResNet-50 [11] pretrained on ImageNet [7]. And we map image output features to the dimension of 512, to align with the ingredient features. We adopt a RNN for tree adjacency sequence generation, where the RNN initial hidden state is initialized as the previous image features. The RNN layer is set as 2 and the hidden state size is 512. The tree embedding model is graph attention network, its attention head number is set as 6. The output tree feature dimension is set the same as that of image features.

We use the same settings in language decoder as prior work [23], a 16-layer transformer [27]. The number of attention heads in the decoder is set as 8. We use greedy search during text generation, and the maximum generated instruction length is 150.

It is notable that, we use ground truth ingredients and images as input in all experiments for a fair comparison. We set λ_1 and λ_2 in Eq.11 as 1 and 0.5 respectively. The model is trained using Adam [15] optimizer with the batch size of 16. Initial learning rate is set as 0.001, which decays 0.99 each epoch. The BERT model finetune learning rate is 0.0004.

4.3 Baselines

Since Recipe1M has different data components from standard MS-COCO dataset [6], it is hard to implement some prior image captioning model in Recipe1M. To the best of our knowledge, [23] is the only recipe generation work on Recipe1M dataset, where they use the Encoder-Decoder architecture. Based on the ingredient and image features, they generate the recipes with transformer [27].

The SGN model we proposed is an extension of the baseline model, which learns the sentence-level tree structure of target recipes by an unsupervised approach. We infer the tree structures of recipes before language generation, adding an additional module on the baseline model. It means that our proposed SGN can be applied to many other deep model architectures and vision-language datasets. We test the performance of SGN with two ingredient encoders, 1) non-pretrained word embedding model and 2) pretrained BERT model. Word embedding model is used in [23], trained from scratch. BERT model [8] is served as another baseline, to test if SGN can improve language generation performance further under a powerful encoder. We use ResNet-50 in both two baseline models.

4.4 Main Results

Generated Recipe Evaluation. We show the performance of SGN for recipe generation against the baselines in Table 1. In both baseline settings, our proposed method SGN outperforms the baselines across all metrics. In the method of non-pretrained model, SGN achieves a BLEU score more than 9.00, which is about 25% higher than the current state-of-the-art method. When we shift to the pretrained model method [8], we can see that the pretrained language model

Table 1. Main Results. Evaluation of SGN performance against different settings. We test the performance of two baseline models for comparison. We evaluate the model with perplexity, BLEU and ROUGE-L.

Methods	Perplexity	BLEU	ROUGE-L
Non-pretrained Model + SGN [23]	8.06	7.23	31.8
	7.46	9.09	33.4
Pretrained Mode + SGN [8]	7.52	9.29	34.8
	6.67	**12.75**	**36.9**

Table 2. Recipe Average Length. Comparison on average length between recipes from different sources.

Methods	Recipe Average Length
Pretrained Model + SGN [8]	66.9
	112.5
Ground Truth (Human)	116.5

gets comparable results as "non-pretrained model + SGN" model, achieving better generation performance than the baseline model [23]. When incrementally adding SGN to pretrained model, the performance of SGN is significantly superior to all the baselines by a substantial margin. On the whole, the efficacy of SGN is shown to be very promising, outperforming the state-of-the-art method across different metrics consistently.

Impact of Structure Awareness. To explicitly suggest the impact of tree structures on the final recipe generation, we compute the average length for the generated recipes, as shown in Table 2. Average length can show the text structure on node numbers. SGN generates recipes with the most similar length as the ground truth, indicating the help of the tree structure awareness.

4.5 Qualitative Results

Sentence-Level Tree Parsing Results. In Fig. 4, we visualize some parsing tree results of our proposed recipe2tree module. Due to there is no human labelling on the recipe tree structures, we can hardly provide a quantitative analysis on the parsing trees.

We show some examples with varying paragraph length in Fig. 4. The first two rows show the tree structures of relatively short recipes. Take the first row (*calico beans*) as example, the generated tree set the food pre-processing part (step 1) as a separate leaf node, and two main cooking steps (step 2&3) are set as deeper level nodes. The last *simmer* step is conditioned on previous three steps, which is put in another different tree level. We can see that the parsing tree results correspond with common sense and human experience.

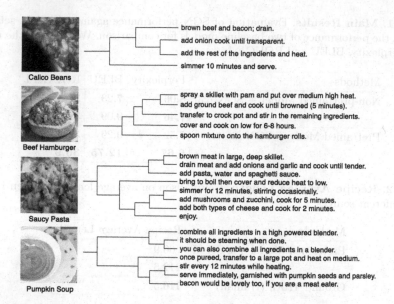

Fig. 4. The visualization of predicted sentence-level trees for recipes. The latent tree structure is obtained from unsupervised learning. The results indicate that we can get reasonable parsing tree structures with varying recipe length.

In the last two rows of Fig. 4, we show the parsing results of recipes having more than 5 sentences. The tree of *pumpkin soup* indicates clearly two main cooking phases, i.e. before and after ingredient pureeing. Generally, the proposed recipe2tree generated sentence-level parsing trees look plausible, helping on the inference for recipe generation.

Recipe Generation Results. We present some recipe generation results in Fig. 5. We consider three types of recipe sources, the human, models trained without and with SGN. Each recipe accompanies with a food image. We can observe that recipes generated by model with SGN have similar length with that written by users. It may indicate that, instead of generating language directly from the image features, allowing the deep model to be aware of the structure first brings benefits for the following recipe generation task.

We indicate the matching parts between recipes provided by users and that generated by models, in red words. It is observed that SGN model can produce more coherent and detailed recipes than non-SGN model. For example, in the middle column of Fig. 5, SGN generated recipes include some ingredients that do not exist in the non-SGN generation, but are contained in users' recipes, such as *onion, lettuce* and *tomato*.

However, although SGN can generate longer recipes than non-SGN model, it may produce some redundant sentences. These useless sentences are marked with yellow background, as shown in the first column of Fig. 5. Since *Cream* is

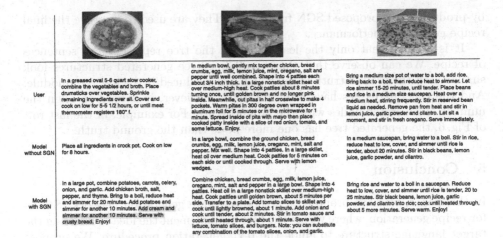

User	In a greased oval 5-6 quart slow cooker, combine the vegetables and broth. Place drumsticks over vegetables. Sprinkle remaining ingredients over all. Cover and cook on low for 5-5 1/2 hours, or until meat thermometer registers 180° f.	In medium bowl, gently mix together chicken, bread crumbs, egg, milk, lemon juice, mint, oregano, salt and pepper until well combined. Shape into 4 patties each about 3/4 inch thick. In a large nonstick skillet heat oil over medium-high heat. Cook patties about 8 minutes turning once, until golden brown and no longer pink inside. Meanwhile, cut pitas in half crosswise to make 4 pockets. Warm pitas in 300 degree oven wrapped in aluminum foil for 5 minutes or in the microwave for 1 minute. Spread inside of pita with mayo then place cooked patty inside with a slice of red onion, tomato, and some lettuce. Enjoy.	Bring a medium size pot of water to a boil, add rice. Bring back to a boil, then reduce heat to simmer. Let rice simmer 15-20 minutes, until tender. Place beans and rice in a medium size saucepan. Heat over a medium heat, stirring frequently. Stir in reserved bean liquid as needed. Remove pan from heat and stir in lemon juice, garlic powder and cilantro. Let sit a moment, and stir in fresh oregano. Serve immediately.
Model without SGN	Place all ingredients in crock pot. Cook on low for 8 hours.	In a large bowl, combine the ground chicken, bread crumbs, egg, milk, lemon juice, oregano, mint, salt and pepper. Mix well. Shape into 4 patties. In a large skillet, heat oil over medium heat. Cook patties for 5 minutes on each side or until cooked through. Serve with lemon wedges.	In a medium saucepan, bring water to a boil. Stir in rice, reduce heat to low, cover, and simmer until rice is tender, about 20 minutes. Stir in black beans, lemon juice, garlic powder, and cilantro.
Model with SGN	In a large pot, combine potatoes, carrots, celery, onion, and garlic. Add chicken broth, salt, pepper, and thyme. Bring to a boil, reduce heat and simmer for 20 minutes. Add potatoes and simmer for another 10 minutes. Add cream and simmer for another 10 minutes. Serve with crusty bread. Enjoy!	Combine chicken, bread crumbs, egg, milk, lemon juice, oregano, mint, salt and pepper in a large bowl. Shape into 4 patties. Heat oil in a large nonstick skillet over medium-high heat. Cook patties until golden brown, about 5 minutes per side. Transfer to a plate. Add tomato slices to skillet and cook until lightly browned, about 1 minute. Add onion and cook until tender, about 2 minutes. Stir in tomato sauce and cook until heated through, about 1 minute. Serve with lettuce, tomato slices, and burgers. Note: you can substitute any combination of the tomato slices, onion, and garlic.	Bring rice and water to a boil in a saucepan. Reduce heat to low, cover, and simmer until rice is tender, 20 to 25 minutes. Stir black beans, lemon juice, garlic powder, and cilantro into rice; cook until heated through, about 5 more minutes. Serve warm. Enjoy!

Fig. 5. Visualization of recipes from different sources. We show the food images and the corresponding recipes, obtained from users and different types of models. Words in red indicate the matching parts between recipes uploaded by users and that generated by models. Words in yellow background show the redundant generated sentences. (Color figure online)

not supposed to be used in the chicken soup, in the future work, we may need to use the input ingredient information better to guide the recipe generation.

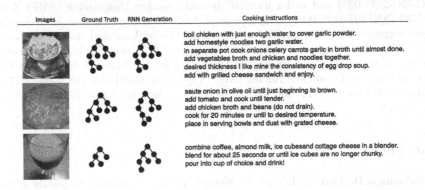

Images	Ground Truth	RNN Generation	Cooking Instructions
			boil chicken with just enough water to cover garlic powder. add homestyle noodles two garlic water. in separate pot cook onions celery carrots garlic in broth until almost done. add vegetables broth and chicken and noodles together. desired thickness I like make the consistency of egg drop soup. add with grilled cheese sandwich and enjoy.
			saute onion in olive oil until just beginning to brown. add tomato and cook until tender. add chicken broth and beans (do not drain). cook for 20 minutes or until to desired temperature. place in serving bowls and dust with grated cheese.
			combine coffee, almond milk, ice cubesand cottage cheese in a blender. blend for about 25 seconds or until ice cubes are no longer chunky. pour into cup of choice and drink!

Fig. 6. The comparison between the ground truth trees (produced by recipe2tree module) and img2tree generated tree structures.

Tree Generation Results. There are some graph evaluation metrics proposed in [32], however, these metrics are used for unconditional graph evaluation. How to evaluate the graph similarities for conditional generation remains an open problem. Here we show some examples of generated recipe tree structures in Fig. 6 for qualitative analysis. Tree generation results from image features are by-product of our proposed SGN framework. They are used to improve the final recipe generation performance.

It is notable that only the leaf nodes in the tree represent the sentences of recipe. We can observe that the overall img2tree generated structures look similar with the ground truth trees, which are produced by recipe2tree module. And the generated trees have some diversity. However, it is hard to align the number of generated nodes with the ground truth. For example, in the last row of Fig. 6, the generated tree has one more node than the ground truth.

5   Conclusion

In this paper, we have proposed a structure-aware generation network (**SGN**) for recipe generation, where we are the first to implement the idea of inferring the target language structure to guide the text generation procedure. We propose effective ways to address some challenging problems, including unsupervisedly extracting the paragraph structures, generating tree structures from images and using the produced trees for recipe generation. Specifically, we extend ON-LSTM to label recipe tree structures using an unsupervised manner. We propose to use RNN to generate the tree structures from food images, and adopt the inferred trees to enhance the recipe generation. We have conducted extensive experiments and achieved state-of-the-art results in Recipe1M dataset for recipe generation.

Acknowledgement. This research is supported, in part, by the National Research Foundation (NRF), Singapore under its AI Singapore Programme (AISG Award No: AISG-GC-2019-003) and under its NRF Investigatorship Programme (NRFI Award No. NRF-NRFI05-2019-0002). Any opinions, findings and conclusions or recommendations expressed in this material are those of the authors and do not reflect the views of National Research Foundation, Singapore. This research is also supported, in part, by the Singapore Ministry of Health under its National Innovation Challenge on Active and Confident Ageing (NIC Project No. MOH/NIC/COG04/2017 and MOH/NIC/HAIG03/2017), and the MOE Tier-1 research grants: RG28/18 (S) and RG22/19 (S).

References

1. Bahdanau, D., Cho, K., Bengio, Y.: Neural machine translation by jointly learning to align and translate. arXiv preprint arXiv:1409.0473 (2014)
2. Bossard, L., Guillaumin, M., Van Gool, L.: Food-101 – mining discriminative components with random forests. In: Fleet, D., Pajdla, T., Schiele, B., Tuytelaars, T. (eds.) ECCV 2014. LNCS, vol. 8694, pp. 446–461. Springer, Cham (2014). https://doi.org/10.1007/978-3-319-10599-4_29
3. Britz, D., Goldie, A., Luong, M.T., Le, Q.: Massive exploration of neural machine translation architectures. arXiv preprint arXiv:1703.03906 (2017)
4. Chandu, K.R., Nyberg, E., Black, A.: Storyboarding of recipes: Grounded contextual generation (2019)

5. Chen, L., Zhang, H., Xiao, J., He, X., Pu, S., Chang, S.F.: Counterfactual critic multi-agent training for scene graph generation. In: Proceedings of the IEEE International Conference on Computer Vision, pp. 4613–4623 (2019)
6. Chen, X., et al.: Microsoft COCO captions: data collection and evaluation server. arXiv preprint arXiv:1504.00325 (2015)
7. Deng, J., Dong, W., Socher, R., Li, L.J., Li, K., Fei-Fei, L.: ImageNet: a large-scale hierarchical image database. In: 2009 IEEE Conference on Computer Vision and Pattern Recognition, pp. 248–255. IEEE (2009)
8. Devlin, J., Chang, M.W., Lee, K., Toutanova, K.: BERT: pre-training of deep bidirectional transformers for language understanding. arXiv preprint arXiv:1810.04805 (2018)
9. Golland, D., Liang, P., Klein, D.: A game-theoretic approach to generating spatial descriptions. In: Proceedings of the 2010 Conference on Empirical Methods in Natural Language Processing, pp. 410–419. Association for Computational Linguistics (2010)
10. Gu, J., Joty, S., Cai, J., Zhao, H., Yang, X., Wang, G.: Unpaired image captioning via scene graph alignments. In: Proceedings of the IEEE International Conference on Computer Vision, pp. 10323–10332 (2019)
11. He, K., Zhang, X., Ren, S., Sun, J.: Deep residual learning for image recognition. In: Proceedings of the IEEE Conference on Computer Vision and Pattern Recognition, pp. 770–778 (2016)
12. Hossain, M.Z., Sohel, F., Shiratuddin, M.F., Laga, H.: A comprehensive survey of deep learning for image captioning. ACM Comput. Surv. (CSUR) **51**(6), 1–36 (2019)
13. Jia, Y., Ye, Y., Feng, Y., Lai, Y., Yan, R., Zhao, D.: Modeling discourse cohesion for discourse parsing via memory network. In: Proceedings of the 56th Annual Meeting of the Association for Computational Linguistics (Volume 2: Short Papers), pp. 438–443 (2018)
14. Kazemzadeh, S., Ordonez, V., Matten, M., Berg, T.: Referitgame: referring to objects in photographs of natural scenes. In: Proceedings of the 2014 Conference on Empirical Methods in Natural Language Processing (EMNLP), pp. 787–798 (2014)
15. Kingma, D.P., Ba, J.: Adam: a method for stochastic optimization. arXiv preprint arXiv:1412.6980 (2014)
16. Lin, C.Y.: ROUGE: a package for automatic evaluation of summaries. In: Text Summarization Branches Out, pp. 74–81. Association for Computational Linguistics, Barcelona, July 2004
17. Lin, X., Joty, S., Jwalapuram, P., Bari, S.: A unified linear-time framework for sentence-level discourse parsing. arXiv preprint arXiv:1905.05682 (2019)
18. Logeswaran, L., Lee, H.: An efficient framework for learning sentence representations. arXiv preprint arXiv:1803.02893 (2018)
19. Luo, R., Price, B., Cohen, S., Shakhnarovich, G.: Discriminability objective for training descriptive captions. arXiv preprint arXiv:1803.04376 (2018)
20. Min, W., Jiang, S., Liu, L., Rui, Y., Jain, R.: A survey on food computing. ACM Comput. Surv. (CSUR) **52**(5), 1–36 (2019)
21. Papineni, K., Roukos, S., Ward, T., Zhu, W.J.: BLEU: a method for automatic evaluation of machine translation. In: Proceedings of the 40th Annual Meeting on Association for Computational Linguistics, pp. 311–318. Association for Computational Linguistics (2002)

22. Plummer, B.A., Wang, L., Cervantes, C.M., Caicedo, J.C., Hockenmaier, J., Lazebnik, S.: Flickr30k entities: collecting region-to-phrase correspondences for richer image-to-sentence models. In: Proceedings of the IEEE International Conference on Computer Vision, pp. 2641–2649 (2015)
23. Salvador, A., Drozdzal, M., Giro-i Nieto, X., Romero, A.: Inverse cooking: recipe generation from food images. In: Proceedings of the IEEE Conference on Computer Vision and Pattern Recognition, pp. 10453–10462 (2019)
24. Salvador, A., et al.: Learning cross-modal embeddings for cooking recipes and food images. In: Proceedings of the IEEE Conference on Computer Vision and Pattern Recognition, pp. 3020–3028 (2017)
25. Shen, Y., Lin, Z., Huang, C.W., Courville, A.: Neural language modeling by jointly learning syntax and lexicon. arXiv preprint arXiv:1711.02013 (2017)
26. Shen, Y., Tan, S., Sordoni, A., Courville, A.: Ordered neurons: integrating tree structures into recurrent neural networks. arXiv preprint arXiv:1810.09536 (2018)
27. Vaswani, A., et al.: Attention is all you need. In: Advances in Neural Information Processing Systems, pp. 5998–6008 (2017)
28. Veličković, P., Cucurull, G., Casanova, A., Romero, A., Lio, P., Bengio, Y.: Graph attention networks. arXiv preprint arXiv:1710.10903 (2017)
29. Vinyals, O., Toshev, A., Bengio, S., Erhan, D.: Show and tell: a neural image caption generator. In: Proceedings of the IEEE Conference on Computer Vision and Pattern Recognition, pp. 3156–3164 (2015)
30. Wang, H., Sahoo, D., Liu, C., Lim, E.P., Hoi, S.C.: Learning cross-modal embeddings with adversarial networks for cooking recipes and food images. In: Proceedings of the IEEE Conference on Computer Vision and Pattern Recognition, pp. 11572–11581 (2019)
31. Wang, H., et al.: Cross-modal food retrieval: learning a joint embedding of food images and recipes with semantic consistency and attention mechanism. arXiv preprint arXiv:2003.03955 (2020)
32. You, J., Ying, R., Ren, X., Hamilton, W.L., Leskovec, J.: GraphRNN: generating realistic graphs with deep auto-regressive models. arXiv preprint arXiv:1802.08773 (2018)
33. Zhou, L., Xu, C., Corso, J.J.: Towards automatic learning of procedures from web instructional videos. In: Thirty-Second AAAI Conference on Artificial Intelligence (2018)

A Simple and Effective Framework for Pairwise Deep Metric Learning

Qi Qi[1], Yan Yan[1], Zixuan Wu[2], Xiaoyu Wang[3], and Tianbao Yang[1]([✉])

[1] Department of Computer Science, The University of Iowa, Iowa City, USA
{qi-qi,yan-yan-2,tianbao-yang}@uiowa.com
[2] Boston College, Newton, USA
wuzu@bc.edu
[3] The Chinese University of Hong Kong (Shenzhen), Shenzhen, China
fanghuaxue@gmail.edu

Abstract. Deep metric learning (DML) has received much attention in deep learning due to its wide applications in computer vision. Previous studies have focused on designing complicated losses and hard example mining methods, which are mostly heuristic and lack of theoretical understanding. In this paper, we cast DML as a simple pairwise binary classification problem that classifies a pair of examples as similar or dissimilar. It identifies the most critical issue in this problem—imbalanced data pairs. To tackle this issue, we propose a simple and effective framework to sample pairs in a batch of data for updating the model. The key to this framework is to define a robust loss for all pairs over a mini-batch of data, which is formulated by distributionally robust optimization. The flexibility in constructing the *uncertainty decision set* of the dual variable allows us to recover state-of-the-art complicated losses and also to induce novel variants. Empirical studies on several benchmark data sets demonstrate that our simple and effective method outperforms the state-of-the-art results.

Keywords: Deep metric learning · Distributed robust learning · Data imbalance

1 Introduction

Metric Learning aims to learn a metric to measure the distance between examples that captures certain notion of human-defined similarity between examples. Deep metric learning (DML) has emerged as an effective approach for learning a metric by training a deep neural network. Simply speaking, a deep neural network can induce new feature embedding of examples and it is trained in such a way that the Euclidean distance between the induced feature embeddings of two similar

Electronic supplementary material The online version of this chapter (https://doi.org/10.1007/978-3-030-58583-9_23) contains supplementary material, which is available to authorized users.

examples shall be small and that between the induced feature embeddings of two dissimilar pairs shall be large. DML has been widely used in many tasks such as face recognition [2], image retrieval [1], and classification [8,15].

However, unlike training a deep neural network by minimizing the classification error, training a deep neural network for metric learning is notoriously more difficult [16,23]. Many studies have attempted to address this challenge by focusing on several issues. The first issue is how to define a loss function over pairs of examples. A variety of loss functions have been proposed such as contrastive loss [4], binomial deviance loss [26], margin loss [25], lifted-structure (LS) loss [13], N-pair loss [22], triplet loss [19], multi-similarity (MS) loss [24].

The major difference between these pair-based losses lies at how the pairs interact with each other in a mini-batch. In simple pairwise loss such as binomial deviance loss, contrastive loss, and margin loss, pairs are regarded as independent of each other. In triplet loss, a positive pair only interacts with one negative pair. In N-pair loss, a positive pair interacts with all negative pairs. In LS loss and MS loss, a positive pair interacts with all positive pairs and all negative pairs. The trend is that the loss functions become increasingly complicated but are difficult to understand.

In parallel with the loss function, how to select informative pairs to construct the loss function has also received great attention. Traditional approaches that construct pairs or triplets over all examples before training suffer from prohibitive $O(N^2)$ or $O(N^3)$ sample complexity, where N is the total number of examples. To tackle this issue, constructing pairs within a mini-batch is widely used in practice. Although it helps mitigate the computational and storage burden, slow convergence and model degeneration with inferior performance still commonly exist when using all pairs in a mini-batch to update the model. To combat this issue, various *pair mining* methods have been proposed to complement the design of loss function, such as hard (semi-hard) mining for triplet loss [19], distance weighted sampling (DWS) for margin loss [25], MS sampling for MS loss [24]. These sampling methods usually keep all positive (similar) pairs and select roughly the same order of negative (dissimilar) pairs according to some criterion.

Regardless of these great efforts, existing studies either fail to explain the most fundamental problem in DML or fail to propose most effective approach towards addressing the fundamental challenge. It is evident that the loss functions become more and more complicated. But it is still unclear why these complicated losses are effective and how does the pair mining methods affect the overall loss within a mini-batch. In this paper, we propose a novel effective solution to DML and bring new insights from the perspective of learning theory that can guide the discovery of new methods. Our philosophy is simple: casting the problem of DML into a simple pairwise classification problem and focusing on addressing the most critical issue, i.e., the sheer imbalance between positive pairs and negative pairs. To this end, we employ simple pairwise loss functions (e.g., margin loss, binomial deviance loss) and propose a flexible distributionally robust optimization (DRO) framework for defining a robust loss over pairs within a mini-batch. The idea of DRO is to assign different weights to different pairs that are optimized by maximizing the weighted loss over an uncertainty set for the distributional variable. The model is updated by stochastic gradient descent with stochastic gradients computed based on the sampled pairs according to the founded optimal distributional variable.

The DRO framework allows us to (i) connect to advanced learning theories that already exhibit their power for imbalanced data, hence providing theoretical explanation for the proposed framework; (ii) to unify pair sampling and loss-based methods to provide a unified perspective for existing solutions; (iii) to induce simple and effective methods for DML, leading to state-of-the-art performance on several benchmark datasets. The contributions of our work are summarized as follows:

- We propose a general solution framework for DML, i.e., by defining a robust overall loss based on the DRO formulation and updating the model based on pairs sampled according to the optimized sampling probabilities. We provide theoretical justification of the proposed framework from the perspective of advanced learning theories.
- We show that the general DRO framework can recover existing methods based on complicated pair-based losses: LS loss and MS loss by specifying different uncertainty sets for the distributional variable in DRO. It verifies that our method is general and brings a unified perspective regarding pair sampling and complicated loss over all pairs within a batch.
- We also propose simple solutions under the general DRO framework for tackling DML. Experimental results show that our proposed variants of DRO framework outperform state-of-the-art methods on several benchmark datasets.

2   Related Work

Loss Design. The loss function is usually defined over the similarities or distances between the induced feature embeddings of pairs. There are simple pairwise losses that simply regard DML as binary classification problem using averaged loss over pairs, e.g., contrastive loss, binomial loss, margin loss. It is notable that the binomial loss proposed in [26] assigns asymmetric weights for positive and negative pairs, which can mitigate the issue of imbalance to certain degree. The principal of the newly designed complicated *pair-based* losses can be summarized as heuristically discovering specific kinds of relevant information between groups of pairs to boost the training. The key difference between these complicated losses lies at how to group the pairs. N-pair loss put one positive pair and all negative pairs together, Lifted-structure loss and MS-loss group all positive pairs together and all negative pairs together for each example. In contrast, our DRO framework employs simple pairwise loss but induce complicated overall loss in a systematic and interpretable way.

Pair Mining/Pair Weighting. [25] points out that pair mining plays an important role in distance metric learning. Different pair mining methods have been proposed, including semi-hard sampling for triplet loss, distance weighted sampling (DWS) for margin loss, MS mining for MS losses. These pair mining methods aim to select the hard positive and negative pairs for each anchor. For instance, [19] selects the hard negative pairs whose distance is smaller than that between the positive pairs in triplets, [21] selects the hardest positive pair whose distance is smaller than that of the nearest negative pair in a batch, and MS mining [24] selects hard negative pairs whose distance is smaller than the largest distance between positive pairs and hard positive pairs whose distance is larger than the smallest distance between negative pairs at the same time. DWS method keeps all positive pairs but samples negative pairs according to their distance distribution within a batch. The proposed DRO framework induce a pair sampling method by using the optimal distributional variables that defines the robust loss over pairs within a mini-batch. As a result, the sampling probabilities induced by our DRO framework is automatically adaptive to the *pair-based losses*. There are other works that study the problem from the perspective of pair weighting instead of pair sampling. For example, [27] heuristically design exponential weights for the different pairs in a triplet, which is a special case of our DRO framework. Details are provided in the supplementary. However, since the quality of anchors varies very much, it may not be reasonable to sample the same number of pairs from all anchors.

Imbalance Data Classification. There are many studies in machine learning which have tackled the imbalanced issue. Commonly used tricks include over-sampling, under-sampling and cost-sensitive learning. However, these approaches do not take the differences between examples into account. Other effective approaches grounded on advanced learning theories include minimizing maximal losses [20], minimizing top-k losses [2] and minimizing variance-regularized losses [11]. However, these approaches are not efficient for deep learning with big data, which is a severe issue in DML. In contrast, the proposed DRO formulation is defined over a mini-batch of examples, which inherits the theoretical explanation from the literature and is much more efficient for DML. In addition, the induced loss by our DRO formulation include maximal loss, top-k loss and variance-regularized loss as special cases by specifying different uncertainty sets of the distributional variable.

3   DML as a DRO-Based Binary Classification Problem

In this section, we will first present a general framework for DML based on DRO with theoretical justification. We will then discuss three simple variants of the proposed framework and also show how the proposed framework recover existing complicated losses for DML.

Preliminaries. Let $\mathbf{x} \in \mathbb{R}^D$ denote an input data (e.g., image) and $f(\cdot; \theta) : \mathbb{R}^D \rightarrow \mathbb{R}^d$ denote the feature embedding function defined by a deep neural network parameterized by θ. The central task in DML is to update the model parameter θ by leveraging pairs of similar and dissimilar examples. Following most existing works, at each iteration we will sample a mini-batch of examples denoted by $\{\mathbf{x}_1, ..., \mathbf{x}_B\}$. We can construct B^2 pairs between these examples[1], and let y_{ij} denote the label of pairs, i.e., $y_{ij} = 1$ if the pair is similar (positive), and $y_{ij} = 0$ if the pair is dissimilar (negative). The label of pairs can be either defined by users or derived from the class label of individual examples. Existing works of DML follow the same paradigm for learning the deep neural network i.e., a loss function $F(\theta)$ is first defined over the pairs within a mini-batch and the model parameter θ is updated by gradient-based methods. Various gradient-based methods can be used, including stochastic gradient descent (SGD), stochastic momentum methods and adaptive gradient methods (e.g. Adam). Taking SGD as an example, the model parameter θ can be updated by $\theta \leftarrow \theta - \eta \nabla F(\theta)$, where η denotes the learning rate. The focus here is to how to define the loss function $F(\theta)$ over all pairs within a mini-batch. As mentioned earlier, we will cast the problem as simple binary classification problem, i.e., classifying a pair into positive or negative. To this end, we use $l_{ij}(\theta) = l(f(\mathbf{x}_i; \theta), f(\mathbf{x}_j; \theta), y_{ij})$ denote the pairwise classification loss between $\mathbf{x}_i$ and $\mathbf{x}_j$ in the embedding space (e.g., margin loss [25], binomial loss [26]). A naive approach for DML is to use the averaged loss over all pairs, i.e., $F_{\text{avg}}(\theta) = \frac{1}{B^2} \sum_{i=1}^{B} \sum_{j=1}^{B} l_{ij}(\theta)$. However, this approach will suffer from the severe imbalanced issue, i.e., most pairs are negative pairs. The gradient of F_{avg} will be dominated by that of negative pairs.

3.1 General DRO-Based Framework

To address the imbalanced pair issue, we propose a general DRO formulation to compute a robust loss. The formulation of our DRO-based loss over all pairs within a mini-batch is given below:

$$F(\theta) = \max_{\mathbf{p} \in \mathcal{U}} \{g(\theta, \mathbf{p}) := \sum_{i=1}^{B} \sum_{j=1}^{B} p_{ij} l_{ij}(\theta)\}, \tag{1}$$

where $\mathbf{p} \in \mathbb{R}_+^{B^2}$ is a non-negative vector with each element p_{ij} representing a weight for an individual pair. $\mathcal{U} \subseteq \mathbb{R}^{B^2}$ denotes the decision set of $\mathbf{p}$, which encodes some prior knowledge about $\mathbf{p}$. In the literature of DRO [11], $\mathbf{p}$ is interpreted as a probability vector such that $\sum_{ij} p_{ij} = 1$ called the distributional variable and $\mathcal{U}$ denotes the uncertainty set that specifies how $\mathbf{p}$ deviates from the uniform probabilities $(1/B^2, \ldots, 1/B^2)$. In next subsection, we will propose simple variants of the above general framework by specifying different constraints or regularizations for $\mathbf{p}$. Below, we will provide some theoretical evidences to justify the above framework.

To theoretically justify the above loss, we connect (1) to exiting works in machine learning by considering three different uncertainty sets for $\mathbf{p}$. First, we can consider a simple constraint $\mathcal{U} = \Delta = \{p_{ij} \geq 0, \sum_{ij} p_{ij} = 1\}$. As a result, $F(\theta) = \max_{ij} l_{ij}(\theta)$ becomes the maximal loss over all pairs. [20] shows

---

[1] For simplicity, we consider all pairs including self-pair.

that minimizing maximum loss is robust to imbalanced data distributions and also derives better generalization error for imbalanced data with a rare class. However, the maximal loss is more sensitive to outliers [28]. To address this issue, top-K loss [2] and variance-regularized loss [11] are proposed, which can be induced by the above DRO framework. If we set $\mathcal{U} = \{\sum_{ij} p_{ij} = 1, 0 \leq p_{ij} \leq 1/K\}$, F will become the top-K loss $F(\theta) = \frac{1}{K} \sum_{i=1}^{K} l_{[i]}(\theta)$, where $l_{[i]}(\theta)$ denotes the i-th largest loss over all pairs. If we set $\mathcal{U}_\phi = \{\mathbf{p} \in \Delta, D_\phi(\mathbf{p}\|1/B^2) \leq \frac{\rho}{B^2}\}$, where $D_\phi(\mathbf{p}\|\mathbf{p}') = \int \phi(\frac{d\mathbf{p}}{d\mathbf{p}'}) d\mathbf{p}'$ is the ϕ-divergence between two distributions $\mathbf{p}$ and $\mathbf{p}'$ with $\phi(t) = \frac{1}{2}(t-1)^2$, then the DRO-based loss becomes the variance-regularized loss under certain condition about the variance of the random loss, i.e., for a set of i.i.d random losses $\{\ell_1, ..., \ell_n\}(n = B^2)$ we could have

$$\sup_{\mathbf{p} \in \mathcal{U}_\phi} \sum_{i=1}^{n} p_i \ell_i = \frac{1}{n} \sum_{i=1}^{n} \ell_i + \sqrt{\frac{2\rho \mathrm{Var}_n(\ell)}{n}},$$

where $\mathrm{Var}_n(\ell)$ denotes the empirical variance of $\ell_1, ..., \ell_n$. We can see that the second term in R.H.S of the above equation involves the variance, which can play a role of regularization. The variance-regularized loss has been justified from advanced learning theory by [11], and its promising performance for imbalanced data has been observed as well.

Before ending this subsection, we will discuss how to update the model parameter θ based on the robust loss $F(\theta)$ defined by (1). A simple approach is to find an optimal distributional variable $\mathbf{p}_*$ to (1) and then update θ according to the subgradient of weighted loss by $\partial_\theta g(\theta, \mathbf{p}^*) = \sum_{ij} p_{ij}^* \nabla l_{ij}(\theta)$, which is justified by the following lemma.

Lemma 1. *Assume that g is proper, lower-semicontinuous in θ and level-bounded in $\mathbf{p}$ locally uniformly in θ. Then the subgradient $\partial F(\theta) \subset \bigcup_{\mathbf{p}^* \in P^*(\theta)} \partial_\theta g(\theta, \mathbf{p}^*)$, where $P^*(\theta)$ denotes the optimal solution set of the maximization problem in (1). Furthermore, when $l_{ij}(\theta)$ is smooth in θ and $P^*(\theta)$ is a singleton, i.e., $\mathbf{p}^* = \arg\max_p g(\theta, \mathbf{p})$ is unique, we have $\partial F(\theta) = \partial_\theta g(\theta, p^*)$.*

Remark 1 The above lemma can be proved by Theorem 10.13 in [17]. It shows that even if we may not directly compute $\partial F(\theta)$, our framework can at least obtain its superset $\partial_\theta g(\theta, \mathbf{p}^*)$. Particularly, if we have additional conditions, i.e., $l_{ij}(\theta)$ is smooth in θ and the optimal solution $\mathbf{p}^*$ is unique (considering our regularized formulation below), it theoretically guarantees that our framework exactly computes $\partial F(\theta)$.

3.2 Proposed Three Variants of Our Framework

In order to contrast to other variants recovering existing complicated losses presented in next subsection, we introduce some notations and make some simplifications. For each example $\mathbf{x}_i$ that serves as an anchor data, let $\mathcal{P}_i = \{j | y_{ij} = 1, j \in [B]\}$ and $\mathcal{N}_i = \{j | y_{ij} = 0, j \in [B]\}$ denote the index sets of its positive and negative pairs, respectively. Let $\mathcal{P} = \bigcup_{i=1}^{B} \mathcal{P}_i$ and $N = \bigcup_{i=1}^{B} \mathcal{N}_i$. We denote the cardinality of a set by $P = |\mathcal{P}|$. For simplicity, we let $P_i = |\mathcal{P}_i|$, $N_i = |\mathcal{N}_i|$, $P = |\mathcal{P}|$ and $N = |\mathcal{N}|$. Since zero losses usually do not contribute to the computation of the subgradient for updating the model, we can simply eliminate those examples for consideration.

The first variant is to simply select the top-K pairs with K-largest losses, which is equivalent to the following DRO formulation:

DRO-TopK:

$$\max_{\mathbf{P}} \sum_{i=1}^{B} \sum_{j \in \mathcal{P}_i \cup \mathcal{N}_i} p_{ij} l_{ij}(\theta)$$

$$\text{s.t.} \sum_{i=1}^{B} \sum_{j \in \mathcal{P}_i \cup \mathcal{N}_i} p_{ij} = 1, 0 \le p_{ij} \le 1/K,$$

where K is a hyper-parameter. The gradient of the robust loss can be simply computed by sorting the pairwise losses and computing the average of top-K losses.

The second variant is a variant of the variance-regularized loss. Instead of specifying the uncertainty set $\mathcal{U}_\phi$, we use a regularization term for the ease of computation, which is defined by

DRO-KL

$$\max_{\mathbf{p} \in \mathbb{R}_+^{P+N}} \sum_{i=1}^{B} \sum_{j \in \mathcal{P}_i \cup \mathcal{N}_i} p_{ij} l_{ij}(\theta) - \gamma D_{KL}(\mathbf{p} || \frac{1}{P+N})$$

$$\text{s.t.} \sum_{i=1}^{B} \sum_{j \in \mathcal{P}_i \cup \mathcal{N}_i} p_{ij} = 1,$$

where $\gamma > 0$ is a hyper-parameter and D_{KL} denotes the KL divergence between two probabilities. The optimal solution to $\mathbf{p}$ can be easily computed following [10]. It is notable that the optimal solution $\mathbf{p}^*$ is not necessarily sparse. Hence, computing $\sum_{ij} p_{ij}^* \nabla l_{ij}(\theta)$ needs to compute the gradient of pairwise loss for all pairs, which could be prohibitive in practice when the mini-batch size is large. To alleviate this issue, we can simply sample a subset of pairs according to probabilities in $\mathbf{p}^*$ and the compute the averaged gradient of these sampled pairs.

The third variant of our DRO framework is explicitly balancing the number of positive pairs and negative pairs by choosing top $K/2$ pairs for each class, which is denoted by DRO-TopK-PN:

DRO-TopK-PN:

$$\max_{\mathbf{p} \in \{0,1\}^{P+N}} \sum_{i=1}^{B} \sum_{j \in \mathcal{P}_i \cup \mathcal{N}_i} p_{ij} l_{ij}(\theta)$$

$$\text{s.t.} \sum_{i=1}^{B} \sum_{j \in \mathcal{P}_i} p_{ij} \le \frac{K}{2}, \sum_{i=1}^{B} \sum_{j \in \mathcal{N}_i} p_{ij} \le \frac{K}{2}.$$

For implementation, we can simply select $K/2$ positive pairs with largest losses and $K/2$ negative pairs with largest loss respectively, and compute averaged gradient of the pairwise losses of the selected pairs for updating the model parameter.

3.3 Recovering the Method Based on SOTA Pair-Based Loss

Next we show that proposed framework can recover the method based on SOTA complicated losses. With the induced feature vector $f(\mathbf{x}; \theta)$ normalized to have unit norm, we define the similarity of two samples as $S_{ij} := \langle f(\mathbf{x}_i; \theta), f(\mathbf{x}_j; \theta) \rangle$, where $\langle \cdot, \cdot \rangle$ denotes dot product. Specifically, we consider two SOTA loss functions, LS and MS loss, which are defined below:

$$\mathcal{L}_{MS} = \frac{1}{n} \sum_{i=1}^{n} \{\frac{1}{\alpha} \log[1 + \sum_{k \in \mathcal{P}_i} e^{-\alpha(S_{ik} - \lambda)}] + \frac{1}{\beta} \log[1 + \sum_{k \in \mathcal{N}_i} e^{\beta(S_{ik} - \lambda)}]\} \quad (2)$$

$$\mathcal{L}_{LS} = \sum_{i=1}^{n} [\log \sum_{k \in \mathcal{P}_i} e^{\lambda - S_{ik}} + \log \sum_{k \in \mathcal{N}_i} e^{S_{ik} - \lambda}]_+. \quad (3)$$

where α, β, λ are hyper-parameters of these losses.

The key to our argument is that the gradient computed based on these losses can be exactly computed according to our DRO framework by choosing appropriate constrained set $\mathcal{U}$ and setting the pairwise loss as the margin loss. To this end, we first show the gradient based on the LS loss, which can be computed by [24]:

$$\frac{\partial \mathcal{L}(S)}{\partial \theta} = \frac{\partial \mathcal{L}(S)}{\partial S} \cdot \frac{\partial S}{\partial \theta} = \sum_{i=1}^{B} \sum_{j=1}^{B} \frac{\partial \mathcal{L}(S)}{\partial S_{ij}} \cdot \frac{\partial S_{ij}}{\partial \theta} \quad (4)$$

which can be alternatively written as

$$\frac{\partial \mathcal{L}(S)}{\partial \theta} = \sum_{i=1}^{B} \left(\sum_{j \in \mathcal{N}_i} w_{ij}^- \frac{\partial S_{ij}}{\partial \theta} - \sum_{j \in \mathcal{P}_i} w_{ij}^+ \frac{\partial S_{ij}}{\partial \theta} \right). \quad (5)$$

It can be shown that for LS loss, derivations are provided in the supplementary, we have

$$w_{ij}^+ = \frac{e^{\lambda - S_{ij}}}{\sum\limits_{k \in \mathcal{P}_i}^{B} e^{\lambda - S_{ik}}} = \frac{1}{\sum\limits_{k \in \mathcal{P}_i}^{B} e^{S_{ij} - S_{ik}}}, \quad w_{ij}^- = \frac{e^{S_{ij} - \lambda}}{\sum\limits_{k \in \mathcal{N}_i}^{B} e^{S_{ik} - \lambda}} = \frac{1}{\sum\limits_{k \in \mathcal{N}_i}^{B} e^{S_{ik} - S_{ij}}}. \quad (6)$$

To recover the gradient of the LS loss under our DRO framework, we employ the pairwise margin loss for $l_{ij}(\theta)$, i.e., $l_{ij}(\theta) = [m + y_{ij}(\lambda - S_{ij})]_+$, where m and λ are two hyper-parameters and $[a]_+ = \max\{0, a\}$. Assume that the margin parameter m is sufficiently large such that $l_{ij}(\theta) > 0$ for all pairs. The key to deriving the same gradient of the LS loss under our framework is to group distributional variables in $\mathbf{p}$ for the positive and negative pairs according to the anchor data. Let $\mathbf{p}_i^+ \in \mathbb{R}^{P_i}$ and $\mathbf{p}_i^- \in \mathbb{R}^{N_i}$ denote the corresponding vectors of positive and negative pairs for the anchor $\mathbf{x}_i$, respectively. Let us consider the following DRO formulation:

$$F(\theta) = \max_{\mathbf{p} \in \mathbb{R}_+^{P+N}} \sum_{i=1}^{B} \sum_{j \in \mathcal{P}_i \cup \mathcal{N}_i} p_{ij} l_{ij}(\theta) - \sum_{i=1}^{B} \left(\gamma_i^+ D_{KL}(\mathbf{p}_i^+ \| \frac{1}{P_i}) + \gamma_i^- D_{KL}(\mathbf{p}_i^- \| \frac{1}{N_i}) \right)$$

$$\text{s.t.} \sum_{j \in \mathcal{P}_i} p_{ij} = 1, \sum_{k \in \mathcal{N}_i} p_{ik} = 1, \text{ for } i \in [B],$$

$$(7)$$

where $\gamma_i^+ \geq 0$ and $\gamma_i^- \geq 0$ for $i \in [B]$ are hyper-parameters. we can easily derive the closed-form solution for $\mathbf{p}^*$, i.e., $p_{ij}^{+*} = \frac{1}{\sum_{k \in \mathcal{P}_i} e^{(S_{ij} - S_{ik})/\gamma_i^+}}$, and $p_{ij}^{-*} =$

$\frac{1}{\sum_{k \in \mathcal{N}_i} e^{(S_{ik} - S_{ij})/\gamma_i^-}}$. Then computing the gradient of the robust loss with respect

to θ by using the above optimal $\mathbf{p}^*$, we have:

$$\partial F(\theta) = \sum_{i=1}^{B} \left(\sum_{j \in \mathcal{N}_i} p_{ij}^{-*} \frac{\partial S_{ij}}{\partial \theta} - \sum_{j \in \mathcal{P}_i} p_{ij}^{+*} \frac{\partial S_{ij}}{\partial \theta} \right)$$

which exactly recover the gradient in (6) by setting $\gamma_i^+ = \gamma_i^- = 1$.

Finally, we can also recover the MS loss using another variants of our DRO framework that similar to Eq. (7). Besides losses, our DRO framework can also cover the heuristically designed exponential weights sampling strategy HAP2S_E in [27]. This verifies that our DRO framework is also able to provide hindsight for heuristic methods from advanced learning theories perspective. The detailed derivations of above two equivalence are provided in the supplementary.

4   Experiments

Our methods was implemented by pytorch and using BN-Inception network [6] pre-trained on ImageNet ILSVRC [18] to fairly compare with other works. The same as [24], a FC layer on the top of the model structure following the global pooling layer was added with randomly initialization for our task. Adam Optimizer with $1e-5$ learning rate was used for all our experiments.

We verify our methods on the image retrieval task with three standard datasets, Cub-200-2011, Cars-196 and In-Shop. These three datasets are split according to the standard protocol. For Cub-200-2011, the first 100 classes with 5864 images are used for training, and the the other 100 classes with 5924 images are saved for testing. Cars-196 consists of 196 car models with 16,185 images. We use the first 98 classes with 8054 images for training and the remaining 98 classes with 8,131 images for testing. For In-Shop, 997 classes with 25882 images are used for training. The test set is further partitioned to a query set with 14218 images of 3985 classes, and a gallery set containing 3985 classes with 12612 images. Batches are constructed with the following rule: we first sample a certain number of classes and then randomly sample M instances for each class. The standard recall@k evaluation metric is used in all our experiments, where $k = \{1, 2, 4, 8, 16, 32\}$ on Cub-200-2011 and Car-196, and $k = \{1, 10, 20, 30, 40, 50\}$ on In-Shop.

We apply margin loss and binomial loss as our base loss for DRO framework. $\mathcal{L}_M$ and $\mathcal{L}_B$ denote margin loss and binomial loss [26] respectively. m denotes the margin in $\mathcal{L}_M$. λ is the threshold for both $\mathcal{L}_M$ and $\mathcal{L}_B$. α and β are hyperparameters in $\mathcal{L}_B$.

4.1   Quantitative Results

In this experiment, we compare our DRO framework with other SOTA baselines on Cub-200-2011, Cars-196 and In-Shop, which includes [3,5,7,12,14,24,25,27]. Among them, mining-based methods are Clusetring, HDC, Margin, Smart Mining and HDL. ABIER and ABE are ensemble methods. HAP2S_E and MS are sampling-based methods, which are highly related to our methods. For our DRO framework, we test all three variants which are proposed in Sect. 3.2. We apply two loss functions, margin loss and binomial loss, respectively. Since DRO **p**-sampling works on all pairs in a batch, the binomial variant may not directly apply to **p**-sampling. Thus, it makes totally five variants of our DRO framework, denoted by DRO-TopK$_M$, DRO-TopK$_B$, DRO-TopK-PN$_M$, DRO-TopK-PN$_B$ and DRO-KL$_M$, where the subscript M and B represent the variants of our framework using margin loss and binomial loss, respectively. We set embedding space dimension $d = 1024$. The batchsize is set $B = 80$ on Cub-200-2011 and Cars-196, $B = 640$ on In-Shop. γ is tuned from the range $= \{0.1 : 0.2 : 0.9\}$ on all three datasets and K is tuned from $\{160, 200, 240, 280\}$ on Cub-200-2011 and Cars-196, and selected from $\{640, 960, 1280, 1600, 1920\}$ on In-Shop.

Table 1 and 3 report the experiment results. We mark the best performer in bold in the corresponding evaluation measure on each column. For our framework, particularly, we mark those who outperform all other SOTA methods in bold. We can see that our five variants outperform other SOTA methods on recall@1 on all three datasets. Particularly on Cars-196, our five variants outperforms other SOTA methods on all recall@k measures. On Cub-200-2011, DRO-TopK$_B$ achieves a higher recall@1 (improving 2.4% in recall@1) than the best SOTA, MS. On Cars-196, DRO-KL$_M$ has the best performance, which improves 2.3% and 1.2% in recall@1 compared to the best non-ensemble SOTA, MS, and the best ensemble SOTA, ABE. On In-Shop, DRO-TopK-PN$_M$ improves 1.6% in recall@1 compared to the best results among SOTA, MS. The above results verify 1) the effectiveness of our DRO sampling methods and 2) the flexibility of our DRO framework to adopt different losses.

Table 1. Recall@k on Cub-200-2011 and Cars-196

Recall@k(%)	Cub-200-2011						Cars-196					
	1	2	4	8	16	32	1	2	4	8	16	32
Clusetring [12]	48.2	61.4	71.8	81.9	–	–	58.1	70.6	80.3	87.8	–	–
HDC [12]	53.6	65.7	77.0	85.6	91.5	95.5	73.7	83.2	89.5	93.8	96.7	98.4
Margin [25]	63.6	74.4	83.1	90.0	94.2	–	79.6	86.5	91.9	95.1	97.3	–
Smart Mining [5]	49.8	62.3	74.1	83.3	–	–	64.7	76.2	84.2	90.2	–	–
HDL [3]	57.1	68.8	78.7	86.5	92.5	95.5	81.4	88.0	92.7	95.7	97.4	**99.0**
ABIER [14]	57.5	68.7	78.3	86.2	91.9	95.5	82.0	89.0	93.2	96.1	97.8	98.7
ABE [7]	60.6	71.5	79.8	87.4	–	–	85.2	90.5	94.0	96.1	–	–
HAP2S_E [27]	56.1	68.3	79.2	86.9	–	–	74.1	83.5	89.9	94.1	–	–
MS [24]	65.7	77.0	**86.3**	91.3	94.8	97.0	84.1	90.4	94.0	96.5	**98.0**	98.9
DRO-TopK$_M$ (Ours)	67.4	77.7	85.9	91.6	95.0	97.3	86.0	91.7	95.0	97.3	98.5	99.2
DRO-TopK$_B$ (Ours)	68.1	78.4	86.0	91.4	95.1	97.6	85.4	91.0	94.2	96.5	98.0	99.0
DRO-TopK-PN$_M$ (Ours)	67.3	77.6	85.7	91.2	95.0	97.7	86.1	91.7	95.1	97.1	98.4	99.1
DRO-TopK-PN$_B$ (Ours)	67.6	77.9	86.0	91.8	95.2	97.7	86.2	91.7	95.8	97.4	98.6	99.3
DRO-KL$_M$ (Ours)	67.7	78.0	86.1	91.8	95.6	97.8	86.4	91.9	95.4	97.5	98.7	99.3

Table 2. Recover of MS loss and LS loss on Cub-200-2011 and Cars-196

Recall@K(%)	Cub-200-2011						Cars-196					
	1	2	4	8	16	32	1	2	4	8	16	32
MS	55.6	67.7	77.4	86.3	92.1	95.8	73.2	81.5	87.6	92.6	-	-
LS	56.8	67.9	77.5	85.6	91.2	95.2	69.7	79.3	86.2	91.1	-	-
DRO-KL-G-$\gamma = 1$	56.4	**68.3**	78.9	86.3	91.7	95.8	70.5	79.8	86.6	91.6	94.9	97.1
DRO-KL-G-$\gamma = 0.1$	56.8	**68.7**	79.0	86.6	92.1	95.9	72.5	81.9	88.1	92.3	95.4	97.3
DRO-KL-G-$\gamma = 0.01$	**57.0**	69.4	79.9	87.0	92.3	95.9	73.1	82.2	88.8	93.4	96.2	98.0
DRO-KL-G-$\gamma = 0.001$	56.7	68.5	79.0	87.3	92.6	96.0	75.0	83.4	89.5	93.7	96.6	98.3

4.2   Ablation Study

Comparison with LS Loss and MS Loss. In Sect. 3.3, we theoretically show
that LS loss and MS loss can be viewed as special cases of our DRO framework. In
this experiment, we aim to empirically demonstrate that our framework is general
enough and recovers LS loss. Specifically, we would show 1) when $\gamma = 1$, our
framework performs similarly to LS loss, as stated in Sect. 3.3, 2) our framework
can be seen as a *generalized LS loss* by treating γ as a hyper-parameter, and 3)
our *generalized LS loss* outperforms MS loss, even though the performance of
the ordinary LS loss is inferior to that of MS loss.

We adopt the set up of embedding dimension and batchsize in the ablation
study of [24], i.e., $d = 64$ and $B = 80$. Therefore, we report the existing results
of MS and LS loss presented in [24] on Cars-196. For Cub-200-2011 and In-
Shop, we implement MS and LS loss according to [24]. Following [24], we set
$\alpha = 2, \beta = 50$ for MS loss. For our DRO framework, we apply grouping to $\mathbf{p}$
by Eq. (7), and denote this variant of DRO framework as DRO-KL-G. We set
$\gamma_i^+ = \gamma_i^- = \gamma = \{1, 0.1, 0.01, 0.001\}, i \in [B]$ for DRO-KL-G , $m = 0.2$ for the
margin loss, and $\lambda = 0.5$ for all three losses (MS, LS and margin loss). As the
pairs with zero loss will not contribute to the updates of model but affect the

Table 3. Recall@k on In-Shop

Recall@K	1	10	20	30	40	50
FashionNet [9]	53.7	73.0	76.0	77.0	79.0	80.0
HDC [12]	62.1	84.9	89.0	91.2	92.3	93.1
HDL [3]	80.9	94.3	95.8	97.2	97.4	97.8
ABIER [14]	83.1	95.1	96.9	97.5	97.8	98.0
ABE [27]	87.3	96.7	97.9	98.2	98.5	98.7
MS [24]	89.7	97.9	98.5	98.8	99.1	99.2
DRO-TopK$_M$ (Ours)	91.0	98.1	98.7	99.0	99.1	99.2
DRO-TopK$_B$ (Ours)	90.7	97.7	98.4	98.8	99.0	99.1
DRO-TopK-PN$_M$ (Ours)	91.3	98.0	98.7	98.9	99.1	99.2
DRO-TopK-PN$_B$ (Ours)	91.1	98.1	98.6	98.8	99.0	99.2
DRO-KL$_M$ (Ours)	90.8	98.0	98.6	99.0	99.1	99.2

Table 4. Recover of MS loss and LS loss on In-Shop

Recall@K(%)	1	10	20	30	40	50
MS	79.8	94.9	96.8	97.6	97.9	98.3
LS	82.6	94.1	95.6	96.4	96.9	97.4
DRO-KL-G-$\gamma = 1$	84.8	95.9	97.3	97.9	98.2	98.5
DRO-KL-G-$\gamma = 0.1$	85.1	96.1	97.5	98.0	98.3	98.5
DRO-KL-G-$\gamma = 0.01$	85.8	96.2	97.9	97.8	98.2	98.4
DRO-KL-G-$\gamma = 0.001$	85.7	96.1	97.4	97.9	98.2	98.5

calculation of **p** in DRO framework, we remove the pairs with zero loss to further promotes training.

Table 2 and 4 show experiment results on Cub-200-2011, Cars-196 and In-Shop, respectively. As can be seen, the performance of MS loss is better than LS loss on three datasets, particularly on Cars-196, which also verifies the results of ablation study in [24]. When $\gamma = 1$, our method performs similarly to LS loss, which verifies that our method recovers LS loss. Furthermore, when we treat γ as a hyper-parameter (especially $\gamma = 0.001$) and regard our framework as *generalized LS loss*, our method obtain improved performance compared to the ordinary LS loss. Lastly, even if MS loss exploits pseudo positive and negative pairs, our *generalized LS loss* outperforms MS loss.

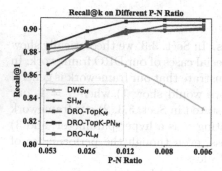

Fig. 1. Recall vs imbalance ratio on embedding space $d = 1024$

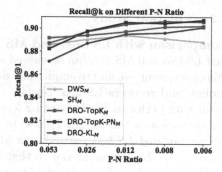

Fig. 2. Recall vs imbalance ratio on embedding space $d = 512$

Capacity to Handle Pair Imbalance. To show the effectiveness of DRO framework to handle pair imbalance, we conduct experiments under different positive and negative pair ratios and different dimensions of embedding space. By changing batchsize, the ratio of the numbers of positive and negative pairs also changes. For example, a larger batchsize leads to a smaller positive-negative (P-N) ratio.

In this experiment, we compare our DRO framework with two different SOTA sampling methods, i.e., semihard (SH) and DWS, in terms of sensitivity to P-N ratios under different embedding space dimensions. By setting different batchsizes $B \in \{80, 160, 320, 480, 640\}$, we have different P-N ratios $|\mathcal{P}| : |\mathcal{N}| \in \{0.053, 0.026, 0.012, 0.008, 0.006\}$. For all methods, we apply margin loss and set $M = 5$ for each class. The embedding space dimensions are $d = 1024$ and $d = 512$, respectively. SH mining is originally designed for triplet loss. Since there is no straightforward choice for the positive pair, we use λ as the upper bound to simulate the similarity of the positive pair in triplet loss. For DWS, we follow the parameter setting in the original paper [25]. We apply margin loss in the proposed three variants of our DRO framework, which are denoted by DRO-TopK$_M$, DRO-TopK-PN$_M$ and DRO-KL$_M$, respectively. We set $K = 2 * B$ for both DRO-TopK$_M$ and DRO-TopK-PN$_M$. We evaluate recall@1 of all methods, experimental results are reported in Fig. 1 and Fig. 2.

Experimental results illustrate that all three variants of our DRO framework has better or comparable performance than SH and DWS methods except for the largest P-N ratio 0.053 both on embedding space $d = 512$ and $d = 1024$. Among them, DRO-TopK-PN$_M$ constantly outperforms all other methods under embedding space dimension $d = 1024$ and achieve competitive results with DRO-TopK$_M$ under embedding space dimension $d = 512$. On the other hand, Fig. 1 and 2 show that the DWS has similar performance when the P-N ratio is relatively large, and encounters a sharp decrease in recall@1 when the P-N ratio decreases on the embedding space dimension $d = 1024$. A smaller drop also exists on the embedding space dimension $d = 512$. The reason why DWS performs poorly when the P-N ratio is small may be that DWS aims to sample pairs uniformly in terms of distance [25], while our DRO framework and SH focus more on hard pairs.

Further, the fluctuations of recall@1 over three variants of our DRO framework are subtle when the feature embedding changes between 1024 and 512. For example, the recall@1 only changes, from 0.9046 to 0.9058 for DRO-TopK$_M$, from 0.9086 to 0.9073 for DRO-TopK-PN$_M$, from 0.9018 to 0.9021 for DRO-KL$_M$, when PN-Ratio is 0.006. However, DWS has a sharp decrease in recall@1 on the embedding space increasing from $d = 512$ to $d = 1024$. This implies that our DRO framework is not sensitive to embedding dimensions in comparison with DWS.

To sum up, above observations together verify that our methods are not sensitive to the embedding space dimensions in different batchsizes, and also outperform other SOTA mining methods in different embedding space dimensions.

Sensitivity of K in Top-K. As we mentioned in Sect. 1, selecting too many pairs within a batch will leads to poor performance of the model. On the other hand, when the number of selected pairs is too small, the model would be sensitive to outliers. In this experiment, we study the sensitivity of K in our DRO framework–how the performance of our DRO framework is affected by the value of K. We set the batchsize $B = 640$ and $M = 5$, which makes the number of positive pairs $|\mathcal{P}| = 1280$ and the number of negative pairs $|\mathcal{N}| = 198080$. We set K from the range $\{640, 960, 1280, 1600, 1920, 2560\}$ and evaluate recall@k for models trained by different K. We choose the above range of K according to the number of pairs selected by DWS and SH in Sect. 4.2 (both selects 2560 pairs roughly).

Figure 3 illustrates how different values of K affect recall@k on In-Shop. We can see that, DRO-TopK$_M$ performs best when $K = 1280$ and recall@k is stable on the entire range of K. Our DRO framework is not sensitive to K when K is in a reasonably large range.

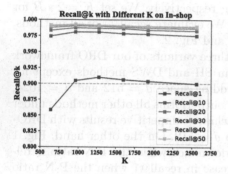 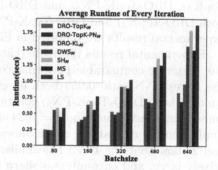

Fig. 3. The effects of K on recall@k on In-Shop

Fig. 4. Average running time of every iteration

Runtime Comparison. Next, we compare the running time of our proposed three variants of our DRO framework with different pair mining methods, MS and LS losses on In-shop. Our experiments conducted on eight GTX1080Ti GPU. The embedding dimension $d = 1024$, and results are compared under different batchsize $B = \{80, 160, 320, 480, 640\}$. The same as previous experiments, we set $K = 2 * B$ both for DRO-TopK$_M$ and DRO-TopK-PN$_M$. $\gamma = 0.1$ for DRO-KL$_M$. SH is implemented according to the paper [19], [25]. DWS and MS are implemented based on the code provided by the author. LS loss is implemented following the code provided by [24].

Figure 4 reports the average running time of each iteration on 200 epochs. We can see that all of three proposed variants of DRO framework run faster than other *anchor-based* mining methods and losses. For all of our three variants, pairs are selected directly from all the pairs, while additional cost is required to select pairs anchor by anchor in other methods. LS loss is slower than MS loss, because MS mining is applied to MS loss, which would reduce the number of pairs for computing subgradients when updating the model. For DWS, the distance distribution of negative pairs is only calculated once for each iteration.

It thus only needs to select pairs according to the pre-computed distribution for each anchor. In contrast, SH requires to compare negative pairs with the lower and upper bound of an interval at each iteration for each anchor, which increases the computational burden. It can be the reason why SH is slower than DWS.

5   Conclusion

In this paper, we cast DML as a simple pairwise binary classification problem and formulate it as a DRO framework. Compared to existing pairwise DML methods that leverage all pairs in a batch or employ heuristic approaches to sample pairs, our DRO framework constructs a robust loss to sample informative pairs, which also comes with theoretical justification from the perspective of learning theory. Our framework is general since it can include many novel designs in its uncertainty decision set. Its flexibility allows us to recover the state-of-the-art loss functions and exponential sample weighting strategy. Experiments show that our framework outperforms the state-of-the-art DML methods on benchmark datasets. We also empirically demonstrate that our framework is efficient, general and flexible in ablation study.

References

1. Chen, B., Deng, W.: Hybrid-attention based decoupled metric learning for zero-shot image retrieval. In: Proceedings of the IEEE Conference on Computer Vision and Pattern Recognition, pp. 2750–2759 (2019)
2. Fan, Y., Lyu, S., Ying, Y., Hu, B.: Learning with average top-k loss. In: Advances in Neural Information Processing Systems, pp. 497–505 (2017)
3. Ge, W., Huang, W., Dong, D., Scott, M.R.: Deep metric learning with hierarchical triplet loss. In: Ferrari, V., Hebert, M., Sminchisescu, C., Weiss, Y. (eds.) ECCV 2018. LNCS, vol. 11210, pp. 272–288. Springer, Cham (2018). https://doi.org/10.1007/978-3-030-01231-1_17
4. Hadsell, R., Chopra, S., LeCun, Y.: Dimensionality reduction by learning an invariant mapping. In: 2006 IEEE Computer Society Conference on Computer Vision and Pattern Recognition (CVPR 2006), vol. 2, pp. 1735–1742. IEEE (2006)
5. Harwood, B., Kumar, B., Carneiro, G., Reid, I., Drummond, T., et al.: Smart mining for deep metric learning. In: Proceedings of the IEEE International Conference on Computer Vision, pp. 2821–2829 (2017)
6. Ioffe, S., Szegedy, C.: Batch normalization: accelerating deep network training by reducing internal covariate shift. arXiv preprint arXiv:1502.03167 (2015)
7. Kim, W., Goyal, B., Chawla, K., Lee, J., Kwon, K.: Attention-based ensemble for deep metric learning. In: Ferrari, V., Hebert, M., Sminchisescu, C., Weiss, Y. (eds.) ECCV 2018. LNCS, vol. 11205, pp. 760–777. Springer, Cham (2018). https://doi.org/10.1007/978-3-030-01246-5_45
8. Li, X., Yu, L., Fu, C.W., Fang, M., Heng, P.A.: Revisiting metric learning for few-shot image classification. arXiv preprint arXiv:1907.03123 (2019)
9. Liu, Z., Luo, P., Qiu, S., Wang, X., Tang, X.: DeepFashion: powering robust clothes recognition and retrieval with rich annotations. In: Proceedings of the IEEE Conference on Computer Vision and Pattern Recognition, pp. 1096–1104 (2016)

10. Namkoong, H., Duchi, J.C.: Stochastic gradient methods for distributionally robust optimization with f-divergences. In: Advances in Neural Information Processing Systems, pp. 2208–2216 (2016)
11. Namkoong, H., Duchi, J.C.: Variance-based regularization with convex objectives. In: Advances in Neural Information Processing Systems (NIPS), pp. 2975–2984 (2017)
12. Oh Song, H., Jegelka, S., Rathod, V., Murphy, K.: Deep metric learning via facility location. In: Proceedings of the IEEE Conference on Computer Vision and Pattern Recognition, pp. 5382–5390 (2017)
13. Oh Song, H., Xiang, Y., Jegelka, S., Savarese, S.: Deep metric learning via lifted structured feature embedding. In: Proceedings of the IEEE Conference on Computer Vision and Pattern Recognition, pp. 4004–4012 (2016)
14. Opitz, M., Waltner, G., Possegger, H., Bischof, H.: Deep metric learning with-bier: boosting independent embeddings robustly. IEEE Trans. Pattern Anal. Mach. Intell. (2018)
15. Qian, Q., Jin, R., Zhu, S., Lin, Y.: Fine-grained visual categorization via multi-stage metric learning. In: The IEEE Conference on Computer Vision and Pattern Recognition (CVPR), June 2015
16. Qian, Q., Tang, J., Li, H., Zhu, S., Jin, R.: Large-scale distance metric learning with uncertainty. In: Proceedings of the IEEE Conference on Computer Vision and Pattern Recognition, pp. 8542–8550 (2018)
17. Rockafellar, R.T., Wets, R.J.B.: Variational Analysis, vol. 317. Springer, Heidelberg (2009). https://doi.org/10.1007/978-3-642-02431-3
18. Russakovsky, O., et al.: ImageNet large scale visual recognition challenge. Int. J. Comput. Vis. **115**(3), 211–252 (2015)
19. Schroff, F., Kalenichenko, D., Philbin, J.: FaceNet: a unified embedding for face recognition and clustering. In: Proceedings of the IEEE Conference on Computer Vision and Pattern Recognition, pp. 815–823 (2015)
20. Shalev-Shwartz, S., Wexler, Y.: Minimizing the maximal loss: how and why. In: ICML, pp. 793–801 (2016)
21. Shi, H., et al.: Embedding deep metric for person re-identification: a study against large variations. In: Leibe, B., Matas, J., Sebe, N., Welling, M. (eds.) ECCV 2016. LNCS, vol. 9905, pp. 732–748. Springer, Cham (2016). https://doi.org/10.1007/978-3-319-46448-0_44
22. Sohn, K.: Improved deep metric learning with multi-class n-pair loss objective. In: Advances in Neural Information Processing Systems, pp. 1857–1865 (2016)
23. Wang, J., Zhou, F., Wen, S., Liu, X., Lin, Y.: Deep metric learning with angular loss. In: Proceedings of the IEEE International Conference on Computer Vision, pp. 2593–2601 (2017)
24. Wang, X., Han, X., Huang, W., Dong, D., Scott, M.R.: Multi-similarity loss with general pair weighting for deep metric learning. In: Proceedings of the IEEE Conference on Computer Vision and Pattern Recognition, pp. 5022–5030 (2019)
25. Wu, C.Y., Manmatha, R., Smola, A.J., Krahenbuhl, P.: Sampling matters in deep embedding learning. In: Proceedings of the IEEE International Conference on Computer Vision, pp. 2840–2848 (2017)
26. Yi, D., Lei, Z., Li, S.: Deep metric learning for practical person re-identification (2014). ArXiv e-prints

27. Yu, R., Dou, Z., Bai, S., Zhang, Z., Xu, Y., Bai, X.: Hard-aware point-to-set deep metric for person re-identification. In: Ferrari, V., Hebert, M., Sminchisescu, C., Weiss, Y. (eds.) ECCV 2018. LNCS, vol. 11220, pp. 196–212. Springer, Cham (2018). https://doi.org/10.1007/978-3-030-01270-0_12
28. Zhu, D., Li, Z., Wang, X., Gong, B., Yang, T.: A robust zero-sum game framework for pool-based active learning. In: The 22nd International Conference on Artificial Intelligence and Statistics, pp. 517–526 (2019)

Meta-rPPG: Remote Heart Rate Estimation Using a Transductive Meta-learner

Eugene Lee[✉][iD], Evan Chen, and Chen-Yi Lee

Institute of Electronics, National Chiao Tung University, Hsinchu, Taiwan
{eugenelet.ee06g,evanchen.ee06}@nctu.edu.tw, cylee@si2lab.org

Abstract. Remote heart rate estimation is the measurement of heart rate without any physical contact with the subject and is accomplished using remote photoplethysmography (rPPG) in this work. rPPG signals are usually collected using a video camera with a limitation of being sensitive to multiple contributing factors, e.g. variation in skin tone, lighting condition and facial structure. End-to-end supervised learning approach performs well when training data is abundant, covering a distribution that doesn't deviate too much from the distribution of testing data or during deployment. To cope with the unforeseeable distributional changes during deployment, we propose a transductive meta-learner that takes unlabeled samples during testing (deployment) for a self-supervised weight adjustment (also known as transductive inference), providing fast adaptation to the distributional changes. Using this approach, we achieve state-of-the-art performance on MAHNOB-HCI and UBFC-rPPG.

Keywords: Remote heart rate estimation · rPPG · Meta-learning · Transductive inference

1 Introduction

Remote photoplethysmography (rPPG) is useful in situations where conventional approaches for heart rate estimation like electrocardiogram (ECG) and photoplethysmogram (PPG) that requires physical contact with the subject is infeasible. The acquisition of rPPG signal is useful for the estimation of physiological signal like heart rate (HR) and heart rate variation (HRV) which are important parameters for remote health-care. rPPG is usually obtained using a video camera and a growing number of studies have used rPPG for HR estimation [1,10,24,39,40,52,55].

The adoption of deep learning techniques for the measurement of rPPG from face images is not novel and is supported by numerous studies [8,35,60,61]. All

Electronic supplementary material The online version of this chapter (https://doi.org/10.1007/978-3-030-58583-9_24) contains supplementary material, which is available to authorized users.

© Springer Nature Switzerland AG 2020
A. Vedaldi et al. (Eds.): ECCV 2020, LNCS 12372, pp. 392–409, 2020.
https://doi.org/10.1007/978-3-030-58583-9_24

of the prior work involving deep learning uses an end-to-end supervised learning approach where a global model is deployed during inference (to the best of our knowledge), also known as inductive inference. It has been pointed out by the recent advances in deep learning that such approach doesn't perform well when there are changes in the modeled distribution when moving from training dataset to the real world [2,15]. The unpredictability of the changes in environment and test subjects (skin-tone, facial structure, etc.) hinders the performance of remote heart rate estimation. To cope with the dynamical changes of the environment and subjects, we propose a transductive meta-learner that is able to perform fast adaption during deployment. Our algorithm introduces a warm-start time frame (2 s) for adaptation (weight update) to cope with the distributional changes, resulting in better performance during remote heart rate estimation.

Current advances in meta-learning [14,33,44] have shed light on the techniques of designing and training a deep neural network (DNN) that is able to adapt to new tasks through minimal weight changes. As prior work in meta-learning is built on well-defined tasks consisting of the classification of a few labeled examples (shots) provided as support set during test time for fast adaptation, it can't be directly applied to our context as labeled data are unobtainable during deployment. In our context, adaptation has to be done in a self-supervised fashion, hence we incorporate transductive inference techniques [18,26] into the design of our learning algorithm. The application of meta-learning and transductive inference to rPPG estimation is not trivial since we have to consider the modeling of both spatial and temporal information in the formulation of our meta-learner. In our work, we split our DNN into two parts: a feature extractor and a rPPG estimator modeled by a convolutional neural network (CNN) and long short-term memory (LSTM) [17] network respectively. We introduce a synthetic gradient generator modeled by a shallow Hourglass network [32] along with a novel prototypical distance minimizer to perform transductive inference when labeled data are not available during deployment. Intuitively, the variation in distribution is caused by the visual aspect of the incoming signal, hence adaptation (weight changes) is only performed on the feature extractor while the rPPG estimator's parameters will be frozen during deployment. In summary, our main contributions are as follows:

1. In Sect. 3, we propose a meta-learning framework that exploits spatiotemporal information for remote heart rate estimation, specifically designed for fast adaptation to new video sequences during deployment.
2. In Sect. 3.2, we introduce a transductive inference method that makes use of unlabeled data for fast adaptation during deployment using a *synthetic gradient generator* and a novel *prototypical distance minimizer*.
3. In Sect. 3.3, we propose the formulation of rPPG estimation as an ordinal regression problem to cope with the mismatch in temporal domain of both visual input and collected PPG data, as studied in [11].
4. In Sect. 4, we validate our proposed methods empirically on two public face heart rate dataset (MAHNOB-HCI [48] and UBFC-rPPG [3]), trained using

our collected dataset. Our experimental results demonstrate that our approach outperforms existing methods on remote heart rate estimation.

2   Related Work

Remote Heart Rate Estimation. The study of the measurement of heart rate using a video camera is not novel and has been supported by existing works. The remote measurement of heart rate is accomplished through the calculation of the cardiac pulse from the extracted rPPG signal which embeds the blood volume pulse (BVP). rPPG signal is extracted from the visible spectrum of light acquired by a video camera [7]. Contact PPG sensors found in wearable devices and medical equipment estimates the heart rate by acquiring the light reflected from the skin using a light-emitting diode (LED) as its source. The constituents of the reflected light is composed of the amount of light absorbed by the skin (constant) and a time varying pulse signal contributed by the absorption of light by blood capillaries beneath the skin. Since existing contact PPG methods are non-intrusive, light sources with specific wavelengths are used, e.g. green light (525 nm) and infrared light (880 nm), having the properties of good absorption by blood and has minimal overlap with the visible light spectrum [27].

The feasibility of remote heart rate estimation was first proven by Verkruysse et al. [53], showing that PPG signals can be extracted from videos collected under an ambient light setting using webcams. To deal with noise, Poh et al. [40] performed blind source separation on webcam filmed videos to extract pulse signal. A study is done in [51] revolving the comparison of the absorptivity of independent channels from the RGB channels by the human skin. It is concluded that the green channel is easily absorbed by the human skin, giving high signal-to-noise ratio for PPG signal acquisition. Based on the results in [51], Li et al. [24] used only the green channel for rPPG measurement and introduced an adaptive filtering technique (normalized least mean square) to eliminate motion artifact during deployment.

As it is hypothesized that all three channels (RGB) contain considerable information for the estimation of the rPPG signals, different channels are weighted and summed to receive better results when compared to using only a single channel (green) in [30]. CHROM [10] estimates the rPPG by using a method that linearly combines the RGB channels using the knowledge of a skin reflection model to separate pulse signal from motion-induced distortion. The POS [55] method and the SB [56] model used the same skin reflection model as CHROM, but made a different assumption on the distortion model where another projection direction is used to separate the pulse and the distortions. All the mentioned methods are based on the calculation of the spatial mean of the entire face, assuming the contribution of each pixel to the estimation of rPPG is equal. Such assumption is not resilient to noise, rendering it infeasible in extreme conditions.

Recently, deep learning approaches have been introduced for rPPG signal estimation. DeepPhys [8] is an end-to-end supervised method implemented using a feed-forward CNN. Instead of using a Long Short-Term Memory (LSTM) cell to model the temporal information, an attention mechanism is used to learn the difference between frames. rPPGNet [61] considers the possibility of different types of video compression affecting the performance of rPPG estimation and proposed a network that handles both video quality reconstruction and rPPG signal estimation trained in an end-to-end fashion. RhythmNet [35] trained a CNN-RNN model based on a training set that contains diverse illumination and pose to enhance performance on public dataset. PhysNet [60] constructed both a 3DCNN-based network and a RNN-based network and compared their performance.

Meta-Learning. The motivation for introducing meta-learning to our rPPG estimation framework is to perform fast adaptation of weights when our network is deployed in a setting that is not covered by our training distribution. Most of the studies revolving meta-learning are in few-shot classification, which have well-defined training and testing tasks. The structure of such well-defined tasks is exploited in [29,45,54] where the structure of the network is designed to take both training and test samples into consideration during inference. Gradient-based few-shot learning has also been proposed in [14,33,41] with a limitation that the network capacity has to be small to prevent overfitting due to the small number of training samples. Few-shot learning based on the metric space has also been studied in [21,47,54]. Meta-learning has also been applied to tasks beyond few-shot classification [12,58,59], showing convincing results.

In our work, the parameters of our network is divided into two parts where one is responsible for fast adaptation and the other only responsible for estimation. Similar update methodology has been introduced in [16,18,31,44,62]. All the proposed methods have different weight update orders and network construction but they have the consensus on the effectiveness of maintaining two sets of weights in a few-shot learning setting.

3   Methodology

Given an input image from the camera, a face is first detected followed by the detection of facial landmarks. Pixel values within the landmarks are retained while the rest are filled with 0. The face image is then cropped and reshaped into a $K \times K$ image. We define the i-th video stream and PPG data containing a single subject as $x^{(i)}$ and $t^{(i)}$ respectively (we will drop the superscript i whenever the context involves a single video stream for brevity) where $x^{(i)}$ and $t^{(i)}$ are sampled from a distribution of tasks $(x^{(i)}, t^{(i)}) \sim p(\mathcal{T})$. Continuous T frames of face images are aggregated into a sequence, giving us the input data of our network, $x_{t:t+T} \in \mathbb{R}^{K \times K \times T}$. The face sequences are paired with the PPG signal $t_{t:t+T} \in \mathbb{R}^T$ collected using a PPG sensor placed beneath the index finger, where each sample t_t is temporally aligned to each frame of the face sequence x_t during the collection process. The output of our network is a rPPG signal

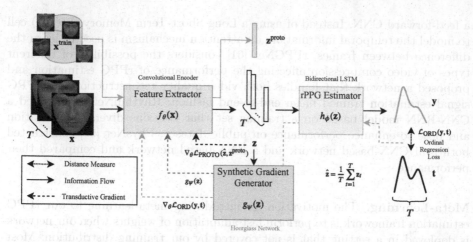

Fig. 1. Overview of our system for transductive inference. Three modules: feature extractor, rPPG estimator and synthetic gradient generator are found in our system. During inference, only the feature extractor and rPPG estimator will be used. Only the parameters of the feature extractor, θ, will be updated during transductive learning. Gradients used for the update of θ are shown in dashed lines where the blue dashed line is only present during the training phase of meta-learning. z^{proto} is generated using the training set, x^{train}.

$y \in \mathbb{R}^T$ which is an estimation of the PPG signal having a small temporal offset caused by the carotid-radial pulse wave velocity (PWV) [11].

The training of our network is different from typical training practice found in an end-to-end supervised learning setting. We cast the learning of our network into a few-shot learning setting, involving both support set $\mathcal{S}$ and query set $\mathcal{Q}$. In a few-shot learning setting, $\mathcal{S}$ and $\mathcal{Q}$ are sampled from a large pool of tasks distribution $\{\mathcal{S}_n, \mathcal{Q}_n\} \sim \mathcal{T}$ where the sampled $\mathcal{S}_n$ and $\mathcal{Q}_n$ share the same set of classes but have disjoint samples for a classification problem. Our learning setting differs from the existing few-shot classification setting in two ways: 1. we are solving a regression problem, 2. our input is a sequence of images instead of still images that are distributed independent and identically.

In comparison to the typical few-shot learning setting, instead of sampling a set of samples originating from disjoint classes, we sample a sequence of image, $x_{t:t+T}$, from disjoint video streams, e.g. videos containing different subject or background. During each sampling process, we sample N independent video streams from our collected pool of video streams also known as distribution of tasks, $p(\mathcal{T})$. For each video stream, we split it into shorter sequences, where each sequence is further split into V and W frames. In correspondence to the few-shot learning setting, V is the support set $\mathcal{S}$ used for adaptation and W is the query set $\mathcal{Q}$ used to evaluate the performance of the model.

3.1 Network Architecture

Our meta-learning framework for remote heart rate estimation consists of three modules: convolutional encoder, rPPG estimator and synthetic gradient generator. To infer the rPPG signal, only the convolutional encoder and rPPG estimator will be used whereas the synthetic gradient generator will only be used during transductive learning. Our network is designed to exploit spatiotemporal information by first modeling visual information using a convolutional encoder followed by the modeling of the estimation of PPG signal using a LSTM rPPG estimator. We name our approach Meta-rPPG where detailed configuration of our architecture is shown in Table 1. An overview of our proposed framework is shown in Fig. 1.

Convolutional Encoder. To extract latent features from a stream of images, we use a feature extractor modeled by a CNN, $f_\theta(\cdot)$. We use a ResNet-alike structure as the backbone of our convolutional encoder. Given an input stream of T frames, the convolutional encoder is shared across frames:

$$p_\theta(z_i|x_i) = f_\theta(x_i), \qquad (1)$$

giving us T independent distribution of latent features, $\{p_\theta(z_i|x_i)\}_{i=t}^{t+T}$, that will be fed to a rPPG estimator to model the temporal information for the estimation of rPPG signal.

rPPG Estimator. The latent features extracted from the input image stream are then passed to rPPG estimator modeled by a LSTM-MLP module, $h_\phi(\cdot)$. The intuition behind the split is to separate the parameters responsible for visual modeling from the parameters responsible for the estimation of rPPG signal, accomplished via the temporal modeling of the latent features:

$$p_\phi(y|z_t, z_{t+1}, ..., z_{t+T}) = h_\phi(\{p_\theta(z_i|x_i)\}_{i=t}^{t+T}). \qquad (2)$$

The LSTM module is designed to model the temporal information of a fixed sequence of T latent features. The output of each step of the LSTM is followed by a MLP module which is responsible for the estimation of rPPG signal. As we model the estimation of rPPG signal as an ordinal regression task, we have a multitask (S tasks) output. Details are deferred to Sect. 3.3.

Synthetic Gradient Generator. For the fast adaptation of the parameters of our model during deployment, we introduce a synthetic gradient generator modeled by a shallow Hourglass network [32], $g_\psi(\cdot)$. The idea of using a synthetic gradient generator for transductive inference is not novel as it was first introduced in [19] to parallelize the backpropagation of gradient and to augment backpropagation-through-time (BPTT) of long sequences found in LSTM. It is then applied to a few-shot learning framework in [18] to generate gradient for unlabeled samples, giving a significant boost in performance. Our synthetic gradient generator attempts to model the gradient at z backpropagated from the ordinal regression loss from the output, $\mathcal{L}_{ORD}(\boldsymbol{y}, \boldsymbol{t})$ (defined in (13)):

$$g_\psi(\boldsymbol{z}) = \nabla_z \mathcal{L}_{ORD}(\boldsymbol{y}, \boldsymbol{t}). \tag{3}$$

Our synthetic gradient generator will be used during transductive inference for the fast adaptation to new video sequences and at the adaptation phase during training, using the support set $\mathcal{S}$.

Table 1. Conv2DBlocks are composed of Conv2D, Batchnorm, average pooling, and ReLU. Conv1DBlocks are composed of Conv1D, Batchnorm and ReLU. Shortcut connections are added between Conv2DBlocks for the Convolutional Encoder. The synthetic gradient generator is designed as a Hourglass network. ✓ indicates the information the layer acts upon. Output size is defined as $T \times$ Channels $\times K \times K$ for Convolutional Encoder and $T \times$ Channels for the rest.

Module	Layer	Output size	Kernel size	Spatial	Temporal
Convolutional Encoder	Conv2DBlock	$60 \times 32 \times 32 \times 32$	3×3	✓	
	Conv2DBlock	$60 \times 48 \times 16 \times 16$	3×3	✓	
	Conv2DBlock	$60 \times 64 \times 8 \times 8$	3×3	✓	
	Conv2DBlock	$60 \times 80 \times 4 \times 4$	3×3	✓	
	Conv2DBlock	$60 \times 120 \times 2 \times 2$	3×3	✓	
	AvgPool	60×120	2×2	✓	
rPPG Estimator	Bidirectional LSTM	60×120	–	✓	✓
	Linear	60×80	–	✓	
	Ordinal	60×40	–	✓	
Synthetic Gradient Generator	Conv1DBlock	40×120	3×3	✓	✓
	Conv1DBlock	20×120	3×3	✓	✓
	Conv1DBlock	40×120	3×3	✓	✓
	Conv1DBlock	60×120	3×3	✓	✓

3.2 Transductive Meta-learning

During the deployment of Meta-rPPG, we have to consider the possibility of observing input samples that are not modeled by our model, also known as out-of-distribution samples. A possible solution is through the introduction of a pre-processing step that attempts to project the input data into a common distribution that is covered by our model. The consideration of an infinitely large distribution containing all possible scenarios during deployment is near impossible for any pre-processing technique. To cope with the shift in distribution, we propose two methods for transductive inference which provides gradient to our convolutional encoder $f_\theta(\cdot)$ during deployment. The first method is through the generation of synthetic gradients using a generator that is modeled during training. The second method attempts to minimize prototypical distance between different tasks which is based on the hypothesis that the rPPG estimator $h_\phi(\cdot)$ is only responsible for the estimation of rPPG signal. The modeling of the estimation of rPPG signal should not be affected by the visual input and is limited to a constrained distribution.

Generating Synthetic Gradient. To generate gradients for weight update of our model during inference, we introduce a synthetic gradient generator that models the backpropagated gradient from the final output that uses an ordinal loss $\mathcal{L}_{\mathrm{ORD}}(\boldsymbol{y}, \boldsymbol{t})$ from (13), up to the output of the feature extractor $\boldsymbol{z}$, which can be simply put as $\nabla_{\boldsymbol{z}} \mathcal{L}_{\mathrm{ORD}}(\boldsymbol{y}, \boldsymbol{t})$. As our synthetic gradient generator $g_\psi(\boldsymbol{z})$ attempts to model $\nabla_{\boldsymbol{z}} \mathcal{L}_{\mathrm{ORD}}(\boldsymbol{y}, \boldsymbol{t})$, we can observe its role in the chain-rule of gradient update of the parameters of the feature extractor, θ:

$$\theta = \theta - \alpha \frac{\partial \mathcal{L}_{\mathrm{ORD}}(\boldsymbol{y}, \boldsymbol{t})}{\partial \boldsymbol{z}} \frac{\partial \boldsymbol{z}}{\partial \theta} \tag{4}$$

$$= \theta - \alpha g_\psi(\boldsymbol{z}) \frac{\partial \boldsymbol{z}}{\partial \theta}. \tag{5}$$

During the learning phase of training, we can update the weights of our synthetic gradient generator by minimizing the following objective function:

$$\mathcal{L}_{\mathrm{SYN}}(g_\psi(\boldsymbol{z}), \nabla_{\boldsymbol{z}} \mathcal{L}_{\mathrm{ORD}}(\boldsymbol{y}, \boldsymbol{t})) = \| g_\psi(\boldsymbol{z}) - \nabla_{\boldsymbol{z}} \mathcal{L}_{\mathrm{ORD}}(\boldsymbol{y}, \boldsymbol{t}) \|_2^2, \tag{6}$$

where the weight update of ψ is given as:

$$\psi = \psi - \eta \nabla_\psi \mathcal{L}_{\mathrm{SYN}}(g_\psi(\boldsymbol{z}), \nabla_{\boldsymbol{z}} \mathcal{L}_{\mathrm{ORD}}(\boldsymbol{y}, \boldsymbol{t})). \tag{7}$$

Minimizing Prototypical Distance. As rPPG estimation is based on a visual input, there's no guarantee that the samples collected for training is consistent with the samples used during testing due to the broad distribution in the visual space. In a statistical viewpoint, data provided by the training set modeled by our network can be viewed as in-distribution samples whereas data collected under a different setting, e.g. lighting condition, subject and camera settings, are considered as out-of-distribution samples. It is not surprising that deep neural networks doesn't perform well on out-of-distribution samples as studied in [25, 42]. To overcome this limitation, we propose a prototypical distance minimization technique that can be applied on video sequences having a property where the statistical information that needs to be modeled by a neural network doesn't vary too much over time. We show a conceptual illustration in Fig. 2.

First, we consider each video sequences as separate task that needs to be modeled. We define the prototype of the latent variable of a specific task as:

$$\boldsymbol{z}^{(i)} = \frac{1}{T} \sum_{t=1}^{T} p_\theta(\boldsymbol{z}_t^{(i)} | \boldsymbol{x}_t^{(i)}). \tag{8}$$

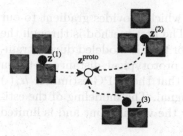

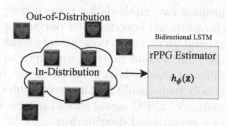

(a) Prototypical distance minimization.   (b) Distribution of latent space.

Fig. 2. (a) Shows the high-level concept on the application of prototypical distance minimization on the latent space. (b) shows that the rPPG estimator only performs well on the in-distribution samples covered by the training dataset while performance on out-of-distribution samples is sub-optimal. In-distribution samples are outlined in green while out-of-distribution samples are outlined in red. The prototypical distance minimizer generates gradient that forces the out-of-distribution samples towards the center of the in-distribution samples.

Here, T consecutive samples from task or video i is sampled and the average is taken across the latent variable generated by the convolutional decoder from (1). We then obtain our first global latent variable prototype as:

$$z^{\text{proto}} = \mathbb{E}_{x^{(i)} \sim p(T)} \frac{1}{T} \sum_{t=1}^{T} p_\theta(z_t^{(i)} | x_t^{(i)}) \tag{9}$$

$$= \mathbb{E}_{x^{(i)} \sim p(T)} \frac{1}{T} \sum_{t=1}^{T} f_\theta(x_t^{(i)}). \tag{10}$$

As mentioned earlier, we perform Monte Carlo sampling of N tasks or videos for every training iteration, hence we are unable to obtain the statistical mean of the entire dataset in one shot. A more computationally feasible approach is to update our global latent variable prototype in an iterative fashion as:

$$z^{\text{proto}} = \gamma z^{\text{proto}} + (1 - \gamma) \mathbb{E}_{x^{(i)} \sim p(T)} \frac{1}{T} \sum_{t=1}^{T} f_\theta(x_t^{(i)}), \tag{11}$$

which can be understood as the weighted average between the old term and the newly sampled global latent variable prototype via the introduction of the hyperparameter γ. The global prototype in (11) is obtained during the learning phase of training and transductive gradient is generated by minimizing the loss:

$$\min_\theta \mathcal{L}_{\text{PROTO}}(z, z^{\text{proto}}) = \min_\theta \mathbb{E}_{x^{(i)} \sim p(T)} \frac{1}{T} \sum_{t=1}^{T} ||p_\theta(z_t^{(i)} | x_t^{(i)}) - z^{\text{proto}}||_2^2. \tag{12}$$

Training of Meta-learner. A meta-learner will perform well during testing if the setting during testing is similar to the setting during training. As mentioned earlier, we split the N tasks samples from all our collected video into sequences that are further split into V and W frames. We use V for the update of θ phrased as the *adaptation phase* and W for the update of ϕ, ψ, θ and $\mathbf{z}^{\text{proto}}$ phrased as the *learning phase*. In general, the split of V and W is put as $W > V$ and $W \cap V = \emptyset$ with the intuition that we attempt to minimize the frames required for adaptation and perform learning on the adapted space or distribution.

The role of the adaptation phase is to train our convolutional encoder $f_\theta(\cdot)$ to map input image sequences to a representation or latent space that will perform well when fed to our rPPG estimator $h_\phi(\cdot)$. During training, gradients from three sources will be used in the adaptation phase: synthetic gradient generator, prototypical distance minimizer and from the ordinal regression loss. During testing or deployment, we don't have any labeled data available, hence gradient from the ordinal regression loss is unattainable. Instead, we use gradients from our synthetic gradient generator and prototypical distance minimizer for adaptation. Note that the adaptation phase is run for L steps on the same V frames.

The role of the learning phase is to force our model to learn a suitable latent representation for rPPG signal estimation based on its image domain correspondence. Supervised learning is required in the learning phase, hence this phase will only be present during training. Here, θ and ϕ which corresponds to the convolutional encoder and rPPG estimator will be trained in an end-to-end fashion whereas the parameters of the synthetic gradient generator ψ will be updated using the gradient backpropagated from the ordinal regression loss. ψ is updated by minimizing the synthetic loss given in (6).

Before the inclusion of the adaptation phase during training, we first pretrain our network under the learning phase for R epochs. The reason is that the gradient backpropagated to the synthetic gradient generator and the prototype used for the prototypical minimizer rely on the task at hand (rPPG estimation) rather than using gradient and prototype based on a set of random weights, which could lead to unstability. We summarize the training of our meta-learner in Algorithm 1.

3.3   Posing rPPG Estimation as an Ordinal Regression Task

Ordinal regression is commonly used in task that requires the prediction of labels that contains ordering information, e.g. age estimation [6,36], progression of various diseases [13,46,50,57], text message advertising [43] and various recommender systems [37]. The motivation of using ordinal regression in our work is because there's an ordering of rPPG value that can be exploited and there will always be a temporal and magnitude discrepancy between rPPG and PPG signal as they originate from different parts of the human body [11].

To cast the estimation of rPPG signal as an ordinal regression problem, we first normalize a segment of PPG signal to be within 0 and 1. We then quantize it uniformly into 40 segments where each segment represents a *rank*. Using the PPG segment $t_{t:t+T}$ as an example, the quantized t-th sample will be categorized

Algorithm 1. Training of Meta-Learner

1: **Input:** $p(\mathcal{T})$: distribution of tasks
2: **for** $i \leftarrow 1, R$ **do**   ▷ Pre-train network in an end-to-end fashion for R epochs
3:     Sample batch of tasks $\mathcal{T}_i \sim p(\mathcal{T})$
4:     **for** $(x, t) \sim \mathcal{T}_i$ **do**
5:         Update θ and ϕ by minimizing $\mathcal{L}_{\text{ORD}}(y, t)$ from (13)
6:     **end for**
7: **end for**
8: **while** not done **do**   ▷ Begin transductive meta-learning
9:     Sample batch of tasks $\mathcal{T}_i \sim p(\mathcal{T})$
10:     **for** $(x, t) \sim \mathcal{T}_i$ **do**
11:         $\{\hat{x}, \hat{t}\}, \{\tilde{x}, \tilde{t}\} \leftarrow x, t$ ▷ Split into V and W consecutive frames
12:         **for** $i \leftarrow 1, L$ **do**   ▷ Adaptation phase (run L steps)
13:             $\theta \leftarrow \theta - \alpha(\nabla_\theta \mathcal{L}_{\text{proto}}(\hat{z}, \hat{z}^{\text{proto}}) + \nabla_\theta \mathcal{L}_{\text{ORD}}(\hat{y}, \hat{t}) + f_\psi(\hat{z}))$
14:         **end for**
15:         $\psi = \psi - \eta \nabla_\psi \mathcal{L}_{\text{SYN}}(f_\psi(\tilde{z}), \nabla_{\tilde{z}} \mathcal{L}_{\text{ORD}}(\tilde{y}, \tilde{t}))$ ▷ Learning phase
16:         $\theta = \theta - \eta \nabla_\theta \mathcal{L}_{\text{ORD}}(\tilde{y}, \tilde{t})$
17:         $\phi = \phi - \eta \nabla_\phi \mathcal{L}_{\text{ORD}}(\tilde{y}, \tilde{t})$
18:         $z^{\text{proto}} = \gamma z^{\text{proto}} + (1 - \gamma)\mathbb{E}_{\tilde{x}^{(i)} \sim \tilde{x}} \frac{1}{T} \sum_{t=1}^{T} f_\theta(\tilde{x}_t^{(i)})$
19:     **end for**
20: **end while**

into one of the S segments $\{\tau_1 \prec ... \prec \tau_S\}$. With a slight abuse of notations, if the categorized value for the t-th sample falls in the s-th segment, we denote it as $t_{t,s} = \mathbb{1}\{t_t > \tau_s\}$ to keep our formulation concise. $\mathbb{1}\{\cdot\}$ is an indicator function that returns 1 if the inner condition is true and 0 otherwise. As in [35], our rPPG estimator will have to solve S binary classification problem given as:

$$\mathcal{L}_{\text{ORD}}(y, t) = -\frac{1}{T} \sum_{t=1}^{T} \sum_{s=1}^{S} t_{t,s} \log(p_\phi(y_{t,s}|z_{t:t+T})) + (1 - t_{t,s}) \log(1 - p_\phi(y_{t,s}|z_{t:t+T})).$$

(13)

Note that in (13), the same notational abuse is applied to the output of our rPPG estimator, y. During inference, we can obtain T rPPG samples corresponding to T consecutive frames, $x_{t:t+T}$, fed to our model, giving us:

$$y_{t:t+T} = h_\phi(z_{t:t+T}) = \left\{ \sum_{s=1}^{S} \mathbb{1}\{p_\phi(y_{i,s} = 1|z_{t:t+T}) > 0.5\} \right\}_{i=t}^{T}.$$

(14)

4   Experiments

We show the efficacy of our proposed method by performing empirical simulation MAHNOB-HCI [48] and UBFC-rPPG [3] using a model trained using our collected dataset. We also show how transductive inference helps in adapting to unseen datasets using a model trained using our own collected training dataset. Source code is available at https://github.com/eugenelet/Meta-rPPG.

4.1 Dataset and Experimental Settings

MAHNOB-HCI dataset [48] is recorded at 61 fps using a resolution of 780×580 and includes 527 videos from 27 subjects. Since our training dataset is collected at 30 fps, we downsample the videos to 30 fps by getting rid half of the video frames. To generate ground truth heart rate (HR) for evaluation, we use the EXG1 signals containing ECG signal. Peaks of ECG signal are found using `scipy.signal.find_peaks` and distance in samples between peaks is used for the calculation of HR. To compare fairly with previous works [8,34,49,60] [3, 12, 18], we follow the same routine in their works by using 30 s clip (frames 306 to 2135) of each video.

UBFC-rPPG dataset [3] is relatively new and contains 38 uncompressed videos along with finger oximeter signals. Ground truth heart rate is provided, hence it can directly be used for evaluation without any additional processing. This dataset has a wider range of HR collected induced by making participants play a time-sensitive mathematical game that supposedly raises their HR. Diffuse reflections was created by introducing ambient light in the experiment.

Collected Dataset. For the training of our model, we collected our own dataset. A RGB video camera is used for the collection of video at 30 fps using a resolution of 480×640. PPG signals are collected using our self-designed device [22] where raw data can be sent to another host device via a UART port. Collection of video and PPG signal are synced by connecting both devices to a Nvidia Jetson TX2. Since our PPG sensor device collects PPG signal 100 Hz, we downsample it 30 Hz to match the visual stream. Video and PPG samples of length over 2 min are collected and are cropped to 2 min to match our proposed meta-learning framework. A total of 19 videos are collected where 18 are used for training and 1 for validation.

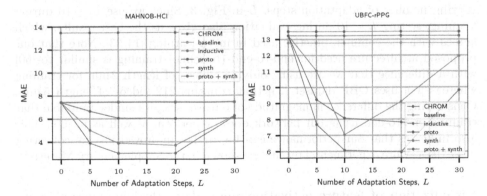

Fig. 3. MAE obtained using different rPPG estimation methods. Demonstrates how the number of adaptation steps, L, affects performance.

Experimental Settings. Facial videos and corresponding PPG signals are synchronized before training. For each video clip, we use the face detector found in dlib that uses [9] cascaded with a facial landmark detector implemented using [20]. To keep the results of our face detector consistent, we use a median flow tracker provided by OpenCV [5]. Pixels within the landmarks are retained and 5 pixels are used for zero-padding beyond the outermost pixels. The resulting face images are then resized to 64×64. All experiments and network training are done on a single Nvidia GTX1080Ti using PyTorch [38]. The SGD optimizer is used. We set the learning rate, $\eta = 10^{-3}$, the adaptive learning rate, $\alpha = 10^{-5}$ and the prototype update weight, $\gamma = 0.8$. We train all the models for 20 epochs.

Performance Metrics. For the evaluation of public datasets, we report the error's standard deviation (SD), mean absolute error (MAE), root mean square error (RMSE) and Pearson's correlation coefficient (R).

4.2   Evaluation on MAHNOB-HCI and UBFC-rPPG

We evaluate 5 different configurations as part of the ablation study of the methods we introduced. The first configuration is the training of our proposed architecture in an end-to-end fashion and perform inductive inference on the test set, End-to-end (baseline). The second configuration is to train our network using all of our proposed methods but doesn't perform adaptation during inference, Meta-rPPG (inductive). The third and fourth configuration perform transductive inference be using either prototypical distance minimizer, Meta-rPPG (proto only), or synthetic gradient generator, Meta-rPPG (synth only), respectively. The final configuration uses both proposed method for transductive inference, Meta-rPPG (proto+synth).

Results of average HR measurement for MAHNOB-HCI and UBFC-rPPG are shown in Table 2 and 3 respectively. We also show MAE results by the varying number of adaptation steps, L in Fig. 3. Since we use $L = 10$ during training, setting $L = 10$ during evaluation also gives us the best results, which agrees with the common practice used in meta-learning [14,33]. Note that our proposed architecture used for end-to-end (baseline) training is similar to [60] with a difference that we are using only 18 videos of length 2 min for training whereas [60] uses OBF dataset [23] that contains 212 videos of length 5 min. Considering the difference in magnitude of dataset size, it's understandable that training end-to-end using our network doesn't perform as well as in [60]. This also indicates that our performance can be further improved just by collecting more data. More experimental results are shown in the Supplementary Materials.

Visualization of feature activation map shows the importance of transductive inference during evaluation. In Fig. 4, we show feature activation maps visualization [28] generated using our proposed methods and supervised end-to-end trained model on images extracted from MAHNOB-HCI. Regions that are

Table 2. Results of average HR measurement on MAHNOB-HCI.

Method	HR (bpm)			
	SD	MAE	RMSE	R
Poh2011 [39]	13.5	–	13.6	0.36
CHROM [10]	–	13.49	22.36	0.21
Li2014 [24]	6.88	–	7.62	0.81
SAMC [52]	5.81	–	6.23	0.83
SynRhythm [34]	10.88	–	11.08	–
HR-CNN [49]	–	7.25	9.24	0.51
DeepPhys [8]	–	4.57	–	–
PhysNet [60]	7.84	5.96	7.88	0.76
STVEN+rPPGNet [61]	5.57	4.03	5.93	**0.88**
End-to-end (baseline)	7.39	7.47	8.63	0.70
Meta-rPPG (inductive)	7.91	7.42	8.65	0.74
Meta-rPPG (proto only)	6.89	6.05	6.71	0.77
Meta-rPPG (synth only)	5.09	3.88	4.02	0.81
Meta-rPPG (proto+synth)	**4.90**	**3.01**	**3.68**	0.85

Table 3. Results of average HR measurement on UBFC-rPPG.

Method	HR (bpm)			
	SD	MAE	RMSE	R
GREEN [53]	20.2	10.2	20.6	–
ICA [39]	18.6	8.43	18.8	–
CHROM [10]	19.1	10.6	20.3	–
POS [55]	10.4	**4.12**	10.5	–
3D CNN [4]	8.55	5.45	8.64	–
End-to-end (baseline)	13.70	12.78	13.30	0.27
Meta-rPPG (inductive)	14.17	13.23	14.63	0.35
Meta-rPPG (proto only)	9.17	7.82	9.37	0.48
Meta-rPPG (synth only)	11.92	9.11	11.55	0.42
Meta-rPPG (proto+synth)	**7.12**	5.97	**7.42**	**0.53**

more likely to be useful for remote HR estimation are more pronounced when our approach is introduced. Results show that transductive inference is useful when applied to data excluded from the training distribution.

End-to-end (baseline)   Meta-rPPG (inductive)   Meta-rPPG (proto+synth)

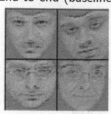 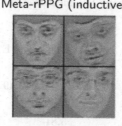 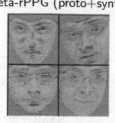

Fig. 4. Feature activation map visualization of 4 subjects using different training methods. Usage of transductive inference results in activations of higher contrast and covers larger region of facial features that contributes to rPPG estimation.

5 Conclusion

In this work, we introduce transductive inference into the framework of rPPG estimation. For transductive inference, we propose the use of a synthetic gradient generator and protypical distance minimizer to provide gradient to our feature extractor when labeled data are unobtainable. By posing the learning of our network as a meta-learning framework, we see substantial improvements on MAHNOB-HCI and UBFC-rPPG dataset demonstrating state-of-the-art results.

Acknowledgements. This work is supported by Ministry of Science and Technology (MOST) of Taiwan: 107-2221-E-009 -125 -MY3.

References

1. Balakrishnan, G., Durand, F., Guttag, J.: Detecting pulse from head motions in video. In: Proceedings of the IEEE Conference on Computer Vision and Pattern Recognition, pp. 3430–3437 (2013)
2. Bengio, Y., et al.: A meta-transfer objective for learning to disentangle causal mechanisms. arXiv preprint arXiv:1901.10912 (2019)
3. Bobbia, S., Macwan, R., Benezeth, Y., Mansouri, A., Dubois, J.: Unsupervised skin tissue segmentation for remote photoplethysmography. Pattern Recogn. Lett. **124**, 82–90 (2019)
4. Bousefsaf, F., Pruski, A., Maaoui, C.: 3D convolutional neural networks for remote pulse rate measurement and mapping from facial video. Appl. Sci. **9**(20), 4364 (2019)
5. Bradski, G.: The OpenCV library. Dr. Dobb's J. Softw. Tools (2000)
6. Cao, W., Mirjalili, V., Raschka, S.: Rank-consistent ordinal regression for neural networks. arXiv preprint arXiv:1901.07884 (2019)
7. Cennini, G., Arguel, J., Akşit, K., van Leest, A.: Heart rate monitoring via remote photoplethysmography with motion artifacts reduction. Opt. Express **18**(5), 4867–4875 (2010)
8. Chen, W., McDuff, D.: DeepPhys: video-based physiological measurement using convolutional attention networks. In: Ferrari, V., Hebert, M., Sminchisescu, C., Weiss, Y. (eds.) ECCV 2018. LNCS, vol. 11206, pp. 356–373. Springer, Cham (2018). https://doi.org/10.1007/978-3-030-01216-8_22

9. Dalal, N., Triggs, B.: Histograms of oriented gradients for human detection. In: 2005 IEEE Computer Society Conference on Computer Vision and Pattern Recognition (CVPR 2005), vol. 1, pp. 886–893. IEEE (2005)
10. De Haan, G., Jeanne, V.: Robust pulse rate from chrominance-based rPPG. IEEE Trans. Biomed. Eng. **60**(10), 2878–2886 (2013)
11. Digiglio, P., Li, R., Wang, W., Pan, T.: Microflotronic arterial tonometry for continuous wearable non-invasive hemodynamic monitoring. Ann. Biomed. Eng. **42**(11), 2278–2288 (2014)
12. Dou, Q., de Castro, D.C., Kamnitsas, K., Glocker, B.: Domain generalization via model-agnostic learning of semantic features. In: Advances in Neural Information Processing Systems, pp. 6450–6461 (2019)
13. Doyle, O.M., et al.: Predicting progression of Alzheimer's disease using ordinal regression. PloS One **9**(8) (2014)
14. Finn, C., Abbeel, P., Levine, S.: Model-agnostic meta-learning for fast adaptation of deep networks. In: Proceedings of the 34th International Conference on Machine Learning-Volume 70, pp. 1126–1135 (2017). JMLR.org
15. Finn, C., Rajeswaran, A., Kakade, S., Levine, S.: Online meta-learning. arXiv preprint arXiv:1902.08438 (2019)
16. Gidaris, S., Komodakis, N.: Dynamic few-shot visual learning without forgetting. In: Proceedings of the IEEE Conference on Computer Vision and Pattern Recognition, pp. 4367–4375 (2018)
17. Hochreiter, S., Schmidhuber, J.: Long short-term memory. Neural Comput. **9**(8), 1735–1780 (1997)
18. Hu, S.X., et al.: Empirical Bayes transductive meta-learning with synthetic gradients. In: International Conference on Learning Representations (ICLR) (2020). https://openreview.net/forum?id=Hkg-xgrYvH
19. Jaderberg, M., et al.: Decoupled neural interfaces using synthetic gradients. In: Proceedings of the 34th International Conference on Machine Learning-Volume 70, pp. 1627–1635 (2017). JMLR.org
20. Kazemi, V., Sullivan, J.: One millisecond face alignment with an ensemble of regression trees. In: Proceedings of the IEEE Conference on Computer Vision and Pattern Recognition, pp. 1867–1874 (2014)
21. Koch, G., Zemel, R., Salakhutdinov, R.: Siamese neural networks for one-shot image recognition. In: ICML Deep Learning Workshop, vol. 2. Lille (2015)
22. Lee, E., Hsu, T.J., Lee, C.Y.: Centralized state sensing using sensor array on wearable device. In: 2019 IEEE International Symposium on Circuits and Systems (ISCAS), pp. 1–5. IEEE (2019)
23. Li, X., et al.: The OBF database: a large face video database for remote physiological signal measurement and atrial fibrillation detection. In: 2018 13th IEEE International Conference on Automatic Face & Gesture Recognition (FG 2018), pp. 242–249. IEEE (2018)
24. Li, X., Chen, J., Zhao, G., Pietikainen, M.: Remote heart rate measurement from face videos under realistic situations. In: Proceedings of the IEEE Conference on Computer Vision and Pattern Recognition, pp. 4264–4271 (2014)
25. Liang, S., Li, Y., Srikant, R.: Enhancing the reliability of out-of-distribution image detection in neural networks. arXiv preprint arXiv:1706.02690 (2017)
26. Liu, Y., et al.: Learning to propagate labels: transductive propagation network for few-shot learning. arXiv preprint arXiv:1805.10002 (2018)
27. Maeda, Y., Sekine, M., Tamura, T.: The advantages of wearable green reflected photoplethysmography. J. Med. Syst. **35**(5), 829–834 (2011)

28. Menikdiwela, M., Nguyen, C., Li, H., Shaw, M.: CNN-based small object detection and visualization with feature activation mapping. In: 2017 International Conference on Image and Vision Computing New Zealand (IVCNZ), pp. 1–5. IEEE (2017)
29. Mishra, N., Rohaninejad, M., Chen, X., Abbeel, P.: A simple neural attentive meta-learner. arXiv preprint arXiv:1707.03141 (2017)
30. Moço, A.V., Stuijk, S., de Haan, G.: Skin inhomogeneity as a source of error in remote PPG-imaging. Biomed. Opt. Express 7(11), 4718–4733 (2016)
31. Munkhdalai, T., Yu, H.: Meta networks. In: Proceedings of the 34th International Conference on Machine Learning-Volume 70, pp. 2554–2563 (2017). JMLR.org
32. Newell, A., Yang, K., Deng, J.: Stacked hourglass networks for human pose estimation. In: Leibe, B., Matas, J., Sebe, N., Welling, M. (eds.) ECCV 2016. LNCS, vol. 9912, pp. 483–499. Springer, Cham (2016). https://doi.org/10.1007/978-3-319-46484-8_29
33. Nichol, A., Achiam, J., Schulman, J.: On first-order meta-learning algorithms. arXiv preprint arXiv:1803.02999 (2018)
34. Niu, X., Han, H., Shan, S., Chen, X.: SynRhythm: learning a deep heart rate estimator from general to specific. In: 2018 24th International Conference on Pattern Recognition (ICPR), pp. 3580–3585. IEEE (2018)
35. Niu, X., Shan, S., Han, H., Chen, X.: RhythmNet: end-to-end heart rate estimation from face via spatial-temporal representation. IEEE Trans. Image Process. (2019)
36. Niu, Z., Zhou, M., Wang, L., Gao, X., Hua, G.: Ordinal regression with multiple output CNN for age estimation. In: Proceedings of the IEEE Conference on Computer Vision and Pattern Recognition, pp. 4920–4928 (2016)
37. Parra, D., Karatzoglou, A., Amatriain, X., Yavuz, I.: Implicit feedback recommendation via implicit-to-explicit ordinal logistic regression mapping. In: Proceedings of the CARS-2011, vol. 5 (2011)
38. Paszke, A., et al.: Pytorch: an imperative style, high-performance deep learning library. In: Wallach, H., Larochelle, H., Beygelzimer, A., d' Alché-Buc, F., Fox, E., Garnett, R. (eds.) Advances in Neural Information Processing Systems 32, pp. 8024–8035. Curran Associates, Inc. (2019). http://papers.neurips.cc/paper/9015-pytorch-an-imperative-style-high-performance-deep-learning-library.pdf
39. Poh, M.Z., McDuff, D.J., Picard, R.W.: Advancements in noncontact, multiparameter physiological measurements using a webcam. IEEE Trans. Biomed. Eng. 58(1), 7–11 (2010)
40. Poh, M.Z., McDuff, D.J., Picard, R.W.: Non-contact, automated cardiac pulse measurements using video imaging and blind source separation. Opt. Express 18(10), 10762–10774 (2010)
41. Ravi, S., Larochelle, H.: Optimization as a model for few-shot learning (2016)
42. Ren, J., et al.: Likelihood ratios for out-of-distribution detection. In: Advances in Neural Information Processing Systems, pp. 14680–14691 (2019)
43. Rettie, R., Grandcolas, U., Deakins, B.: Text message advertising: response rates and branding effects. J. Target. Meas. Anal. Mark. 13(4), 304–312 (2005)
44. Rusu, A.A., et al.: Meta-learning with latent embedding optimization. arXiv preprint arXiv:1807.05960 (2018)
45. Santoro, A., Bartunov, S., Botvinick, M., Wierstra, D., Lillicrap, T.: Meta-learning with memory-augmented neural networks. In: International Conference on Machine Learning, pp. 1842–1850 (2016)

46. Sigrist, M.K., Taal, M.W., Bungay, P., McIntyre, C.W.: Progressive vascular calcification over 2 years is associated with arterial stiffening and increased mortality in patients with stages 4 and 5 chronic kidney disease. Clin. J. Am. Soc. Nephrol. **2**(6), 1241–1248 (2007)

47. Snell, J., Swersky, K., Zemel, R.: Prototypical networks for few-shot learning. In: Advances in Neural Information Processing Systems, pp. 4077–4087 (2017)

48. Soleymani, M., Lichtenauer, J., Pun, T., Pantic, M.: A multimodal database for affect recognition and implicit tagging. IEEE Trans. Affect. Comput. **3**(1), 42–55 (2011)

49. Špetlík, R., Franc, V., Matas, J.: Visual heart rate estimation with convolutional neural network. In: Proceedings of the British Machine Vision Conference, Newcastle, UK, pp. 3–6 (2018)

50. Streifler, J.Y., Eliasziw, M., Benavente, O.R., Hachinski, V.C., Fox, A.J., Barnett, H.: Lack of relationship between leukoaraiosis and carotid artery disease. Arch. Neurol. **52**(1), 21–24 (1995)

51. Takano, C., Ohta, Y.: Heart rate measurement based on a time-lapse image. Med. Eng. Phys. **29**(8), 853–857 (2007)

52. Tulyakov, S., Alameda-Pineda, X., Ricci, E., Yin, L., Cohn, J.F., Sebe, N.: Self-adaptive matrix completion for heart rate estimation from face videos under realistic conditions. In: Proceedings of the IEEE Conference on Computer Vision and Pattern Recognition, pp. 2396–2404 (2016)

53. Verkruysse, W., Svaasand, L.O., Nelson, J.S.: Remote plethysmographic imaging using ambient light. Opt. Express **16**(26), 21434–21445 (2008)

54. Vinyals, O., Blundell, C., Lillicrap, T., Wierstra, D., et al.: Matching networks for one shot learning. In: Advances in Neural Information Processing Systems, pp. 3630–3638 (2016)

55. Wang, W., den Brinker, A.C., Stuijk, S., de Haan, G.: Algorithmic principles of remote PPG. IEEE Trans. Biomed. Eng. **64**(7), 1479–1491 (2016)

56. Wang, W., den Brinker, A.C., Stuijk, S., de Haan, G.: Robust heart rate from fitness videos. Physiol. Meas. **38**(6), 1023 (2017)

57. Weersma, R.K., et al.: Molecular prediction of disease risk and severity in a large Dutch Crohn's disease cohort. Gut **58**(3), 388–395 (2009)

58. Wu, Y., Rosca, M., Lillicrap, T.: Deep compressed sensing. arXiv preprint arXiv:1905.06723 (2019)

59. Yu, H., et al.: Foal: fast online adaptive learning for cardiac motion estimation. In: Proceedings of the IEEE/CVF Conference on Computer Vision and Pattern Recognition, pp. 4313–4323 (2020)

60. Yu, Z., Li, X., Zhao, G.: Remote photoplethysmograph signal measurement from facial videos using spatio-temporal networks. In: Proceedings BMVC, pp. 1–12 (2019)

61. Yu, Z., Peng, W., Li, X., Hong, X., Zhao, G.: Remote heart rate measurement from highly compressed facial videos: an end-to-end deep learning solution with video enhancement. In: Proceedings of the IEEE International Conference on Computer Vision, pp. 151–160 (2019)

62. Zintgraf, L.M., Shiarlis, K., Kurin, V., Hofmann, K., Whiteson, S.: Fast context adaptation via meta-learning. arXiv preprint arXiv:1810.03642 (2018)

A Recurrent Transformer Network for Novel View Action Synthesis

Kara Marie Schatz[1], Erik Quintanilla[2], Shruti Vyas[3], and Yogesh S. Rawat[3(✉)]

[1] Xavier University, Cincinnati, OH, USA
schatzk@xavier.edu
[2] Illinois Institute of Technology, Chicago, IL, USA
equintanilla@hawk.iit.edu
[3] Center for Research in Computer Vision, University of Central Florida,
Orlando, USA
{shruti,yogesh}@crcv.ucf.edu

Abstract. In this work, we address the problem of synthesizing human actions from *novel views*. Given an input video of an actor performing some action, we aim to synthesize a video with the same action performed from a novel view with the help of an appearance prior. We propose an end-to-end deep network to solve this problem. The proposed network utilizes the change in viewpoint to transform the action from the input view to the novel view in feature space. The transformed action is integrated with the target appearance using the proposed *recurrent transformer network*, which provides a transformed appearance for each time-step in the action sequence. The recurrent transformer network utilize *action key-points* which are determined in an unsupervised approach using the encoded action features. We also propose a *hierarchical structure* for the recurrent transformation which further improves the performance. We demonstrate the effectiveness of the proposed method through extensive experiments conducted on a large-scale multi-view action recognition NTU-RGB+D dataset. In addition, we show that the proposed method can transform the action to a novel viewpoint with an entirely different scene or actor. *The code is publicly available at* https://github.com/schatzkara/cross-view-video.

Keywords: Novel-view action synthesis · Action transformation · Video synthesis

1 Introduction

In recent years, we have seen a great interest from the research community in image and video synthesis [18,25,31]. It has a wide range of applications, such as data augmentation, augmented reality, and action imitation. While the research

---

Electronic supplementary material The online version of this chapter (https://doi.org/10.1007/978-3-030-58583-9_25) contains supplementary material, which is available to authorized users.

A. Vedaldi et al. (Eds.): ECCV 2020, LNCS 12372, pp. 410–426, 2020.
https://doi.org/10.1007/978-3-030-58583-9_25

in image synthesis has seen great progress [7,18,25], synthesizing realistic videos is still a challenging problem due to its complexity and high computational requirements [8,24,31].

Some of the recent works in video synthesis have proposed the use of a prior to reduce the complexity of the problem [24,30]. The use of priors, such as action class [8], pose information [40], and image conditioning [29], leads to a better quality when compared with the videos generated without any prior [24,30,32]. While much work is being done in this area, the existing research in video synthesis is mainly focused on single views.

In this work, we focus on the problem of video synthesis from novel viewpoints. The presence of novel views makes the video synthesis task more complex as both the action and appearance vary significantly with the change in viewpoint. There has been some work in cross-view image synthesis in which the focus is on 3D reconstruction from images [14], multi-view aggregation [9], and transforming ground and aerial images [23]. This requires transforming the appearance of one view to other novel views. In the case of videos, both the appearance as well as the action dynamics must be transformed to the target novel view, which increases the complexity of the problem.

We propose an end-to-end deep framework to solve the problem of cross-view video synthesis. The proposed framework takes a video from a source viewpoint and synthesizes the same action from a novel viewpoint with the help of an appearance prior. The prior is utilized to determine the change in viewpoint, which helps in transforming the source action to the novel viewpoint in latent representation space. The transformed action features need to be effectively integrated with the target appearance to synthesize a realistic action video. To achieve this, we propose a *novel recurrent transformer* network, which takes the transformed latent action features and recurrently transforms the appearance to generate a sequence of target action features in the latent space. The recurrent transformer network make use of *action key-points*, which are determined in an unsupervised approach, to focus on activity regions in the video. Moreover, we propose a *hierarchical structure*, which enables the network to perform the transformation at different feature scales while generating the video from a novel viewpoint.

2   Related Work

Video Synthesis: The research in deep generative modeling has led to significant progress in the field of image synthesis [7,16,18,25]. This is mainly attributed to the success of Generative Adversarial Networks (GANs) [10], where the realism of the synthesized video is used for the adversarial learning [20,22,24]. However, it remains very challenging to synthesize a realistic looking video due to the complexity and resource requirements of the problem. There has been some preliminary success in the task of video synthesis where the research is focused on future video prediction [3,4,22,31,38], and conditioned video generation [24, 30]. The recurrent structures are also found to be effective in spatio-temporal modeling and video prediction [35–37]. These works utilize the memory module in the recurrent structure for predicting plausible future video frames.

Generating a video without any given prior is a difficult problem as the network has to learn from the training distribution [8]. The use of priors in video synthesis helps in reducing the complexity of the problem and makes the generation task more tractable. To this end, there has been research focus in video synthesis where we can use another video for content [2], segmentation prior [34], target pose [33,40], or motion transfer [6,27,29] to aid the generation task. The work in [29] uses a facial image to synthesize a talking video by transferring motion from another video. Similarly, in [6,27] the authors propose to transfer motion from a video prior to a target image. Our work is related to these works in motion transfer as we are also using appearance as a prior while synthesizing the video. However, our problem is different from these in two key aspects. These methods perform image synthesis and transfer the motion from source to target image one frame at time. Whereas, we synthesize the full action video at once which is much more efficient. Also, we are focusing on novel-view synthesis while these works are based on single views.

Novel View Synthesis: Cross-view synthesis of data is a challenging problem with multiple applications including augmented reality, data augmentation and view-invariant learning. The existing works in novel-view synthesis mainly focus on cross-view image synthesis [9,23] and 3D reconstruction from images [14]. In [23], the authors propose a generative adversarial network which can transform the ground-view images to aerial-view images and vice-versa. The authors in [9] utilize multiple views to render a image from unseen views with the help of a generative query network. Different from this, the authors in [14] learn a 3D representation from single image which can be used to render the image from multiple other views. All of these works perform cross-view synthesis in image domain, however we are focusing on synthesizing videos.

Cross-view video synthesis adds in more complexity to the problem by introducing action dynamics. The seminal work in cross-view video synthesis [32] proposed to learn a global scene representation which was used to synthesize a video from unseen viewpoint. However, this work was mainly focused on action classification. In [19], the authors propose to render optical flow from novel views for learning a good view-invariant action representation. This is different since they only have to predict the optical flow. In a more recent work [17], the authors propose a recurrent LSTM based network which predicts videos from novel views. Their approach utilizes a strong prior from the target view as they require a sequence of depth and skeleton maps for video synthesis. The depth and skeleton modalities are well known for activity classification and therefore have sufficient action information. Therefore, this approach does not require the transformation of the action from the source video. Our approach on the other hand only uses a single frame from the target view as a prior, and the action from the source video must be transformed to the target view.

3   Proposed Method

Given an input source action video V^i from view i and an appearance prior P^j from target view j, the proposed framework F synthesize the action video $\hat{V}^j$ as seen from view j. We can formalize the problem as,

$$\hat{V}^j = F(V^i, P^j). \tag{1}$$

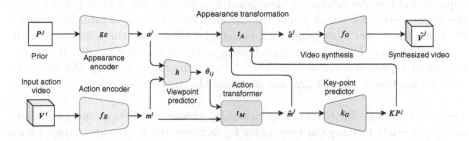

Fig. 1. Overview of the proposed framework. Given a source video V^i and target prior P^i, the proposed framework transforms the source action features m^i to target view action features $\hat{m}^j$ and use them to transform the target prior a^j for synthesizing target view action video $\hat{V}^j$. The network also utilize action key-points KP^j, which are predicted via unsupervised approach, to focus on activity regions in the video

Here $V^j \in \mathbb{R}^{T \times H \times W \times 3}$ and $\hat{V}^i \in \mathbb{R}^{T \times W \times H \times 3}$ with T frames, height H, and width W, and $P^j \in \mathbb{R}^{W \times H \times 3}$ with height H, and width W. An overview of the architecture for the proposed framework is shown in Fig. 1. The framework F consists of an action transformer network t_M which takes the change in viewpoint θ_{ij} and action encoding m^i to transform the action features from source view i to the target view j.

$$\hat{m}^j = t_M(m^i, \theta_{ij}). \tag{2}$$

Here $\hat{m}^j$ is the transformed action features.

The transformed action features $\hat{m}^j$ are passed to an appearance transformer network t_A which transforms the prior features a^j to generate appearance features $\hat{a}^j$ for synthesizing the video $\hat{V}^j$ from the target view j. In addition to this, the framework also consists of a key-point predictor network k_G which predicts action key-points KP^j to focus on activity regions in the video. Finally, a generator network f_G takes the transformed appearance features $\hat{a}^j$ along with the predicted action key-points KP^j to synthesize the target video $\hat{V}^j$.

$$\hat{V}^j = f_G(\hat{a}^j, KP^j). \tag{3}$$

We will cover the details of the components in the next subsections.

3.1   Action Transformation

The action transformation is performed in the latent representation of the action. The input video V^i is first encoded using a video encoder f_E to get the latent action representation $m^i \in \mathbb{R}^{T_r \times H_r \times W_r \times C_r}$. Here T_r, H_r, W_r, and C_r represents the temporal extent, height, width and, number channels in the latent representation respectively. We utilize 3D convolution based network [5] to encode the input video V^i which is effective in extracting spatio-temporal features.

The transformation of action from one view-point i to another view-point j requires the relative change in view-point θ_{ij}. We propose a view-point change prediction network h which utilize the encoded features m^i and prior information P^j from the target view-point to predict the change in the view-point. The appearance prior P^j is first encoded using a visual encoder g_E which extracts the latent representation $a^j \in \mathbb{R}^{H_r \times W_r \times C_r}$ for the target view j. We use a 2D convolution based network [28] for encoding the appearance prior.

Viewpoint Change Predictor: The viewpoint change prediction network h estimates the relative change in view-point $\hat{\theta}_{ij}$ between the source and target views,

$$\hat{\theta}_{ij} = h(m^i, a^j). \tag{4}$$

This change in view-point $\hat{\theta}_{ij} \in (-\pi/2, \pi/2)$ is used to perform action transformation from view i to view j. We are only considering a maximum change of $\pi/2$ (which is there in the used datasets) in our experiments, but a maximum change of π can also be used by predicting cosine and sin values. The prediction of change in view-point within the framework avoids the need of providing this externally while generating an action video from target novel view.

The temporal extent of the action representation m^i is not important for inferring the viewpoint. Therefore, average pooling is performed on m^i along the temporal extent to reduce the representation to single frame. The compressed features m^i from the source view is then combined with the features a^j from the target view using a concatenation operation along the channel axis. These concatenated features are passed through two blocks that consist of a 2D convolutional layer followed by ReLU activation and average pooling. A 3×3 kernel is used for the convolutional layers, and a 2×2 kernel is used for the average pooling layer with a stride of 2. Finally, the features are flattened and passed through a single fully connected layer that predicts the angular viewpoint change, $\hat{\theta}_{ij}$.

The change in view-point prediction loss L_{vp} is computed as the mean squared error between the ground truth θ_{ij} and the predicted $\hat{\theta}_{ij}$ viewpoint change.

$$L_{vp} = \frac{1}{N} \sum_{k=1}^{N} (\hat{\theta}_{ij}^k - \theta_{ij}^k)^2 \tag{5}$$

Here, N represents the number of samples.

Action Transformer Network: The action transformer network t_M computes action features $\hat{m}^j$ for the target view by transforming the action representation m^i of the given input view based on the angular viewpoint change θ_{ij}. The angular change is first expanded to $\mathbb{R}^{T_r \times H_r \times W_r \times 1}$ by repeating it for each spatio-temporal location in the latent action representation. Then, it is passed through two layers of 3D convolutions before concatenating with m^i along the channel dimension. These concatenated features are then passed through three 3D convolutional layers each followed by ReLU activation. A 3×3 kernel is used for each of the convolutional layers preserving the spatial and temporal dimension of the representation using padding. The transformed action features $\hat{m}^j \in \mathbb{R}^{T_r \times H_r \times W_r \times C_r}$ are then used to transform the appearance features a^j for generating the target video.

Note that the ground truth value of angular view-point change θ_{ij} is used for the transformation during the training phase for a stable network training. However, the predicted view-point change $\hat{\theta}_{ij}$ is used during network inference.

3.2 Action Key-Point Detection

We are interested in the key-point regions which are important from action point of view. These action key-points will be used in an attention mechanism during transforming the prior as well as during synthesizing the target action video. We take an unsupervised approach to detect these action key-points [13]. The key-point detector k_G takes the transformed action features $\hat{m}^j$ and first generate N_k action heatmaps $Z_k \in \mathbb{R}^{T_k \times H_k \times W_k \times N_k}$ corresponding to N_k action key-points. We use a 3D convolutional based network with ReLU activation to predict these heatmaps. The action key-point detector network k_G consists of four convolution layers. The convolution layers are used in conjunction with upsampling via trilinear interpolation to increase the temporal and spatial extent of the predicted heatmaps.

The action keypoints KP^j are extracted from Z_k as Gaussian heatmaps. The reason is that they can be effectively used as attention in the convolution based prior transformation network t_A as well as video synthesis network f_G. The first step in generating the Gaussian heatmaps is to determine the most active position in these heatmaps. The x_m and y_m coordinates for the keypoints are deteremined separately by first computing the mean along all the rows Z_k^x or columns Z_k^y and applying a softmax along the remaining spatial dimension.

$$Z_k^x = \frac{1}{H_k} \sum_{j=1}^{H_k} Z_k^j, \quad Z_k^y = \frac{1}{W_k} \sum_{j=1}^{W_k} Z_k^j. \tag{6}$$

Now the active position along each dimension can be determined by applying the softmax normalization to these vectors,

$$x_m = \frac{\sum_{j=1}^{H_k} j e^{Z_k^x(j)}}{\sum_{j=1}^{H_k} e^{Z_k^x(j)}}, \quad y_m = \frac{\sum_{j=1}^{W_k} j e^{Z_k^y(j)}}{\sum_{j=1}^{W_k} e^{Z_k^y(j)}}. \tag{7}$$

These predicted active coordinates $u_m = (x_m, y_m)$ are used as a mean for the Gaussian which replace the heatmaps. The Gaussian with a small standard deviation σ are centered at u_m to generate an action key-point,

$$KP_i^j = \frac{1}{\sigma\sqrt{2\pi}} exp(-\frac{1}{2}((u - u_m)/\sigma)^2. \tag{8}$$

Here, KP_i^j is any instance i of an action key-point and $u \in (H_k \times W_k)$.

3.3   Appearance Transformer Network

The appearance prior P^j has to be transformed according the action features $\hat{m}^j$ to generate the action video $\hat{V}^j$. We propose a recurrent approach which utilize the action features $\hat{m}^j$ for the transformation at latent space. The detected action key-points helps the appearance transformation in two ways. They will be useful in the separation of foreground and background features, and help in focusing on the action regions while transforming the foreground appearance. The appearance transformer network t_A has a recurrent structure based on convolutional Gated Recurrent Unit (Conv-GRU) [1] which takes the prior a^j as input along with transformed action features $\hat{m}^j$ and action key-points KP^j and predict transformed appearance features $\hat{a}^j$. Formally,

$$\hat{a}^j = t_A(a^j, \hat{m}^j, KP^j), \tag{9}$$

where $\hat{a}^j \in \mathbb{R}^{T_r \times H_r \times W_r \times C_r}$.

At each time step t, t_A takes the appearance latent representation $\hat{a}_{t-1}^j$ and transform the appearance to $\hat{a}_t^j$ with the help of action latent features $\hat{m}_t^j$ and action key-points KP_t^j. The first step is to determine the background b_t and foreground f_t based on the appearance, action features, and action key-points.

$$b_t = \sigma(W_b* < \hat{a}_{t-1}, \hat{m}_t^j, KP_t^j >)$$
$$f_t = \sigma(W_f* < \hat{a}_{t-1}, \hat{m}_t^j, KP_t^j >) \tag{10}$$

Here, $*$ denotes convolution operation, $<>$ denotes concatenation operation along channels axis, and W_b and W_f are parameters for 2D kernels. The background features are selected from the appearance as,

$$b_t^f = b_t \odot \hat{a}_{t-1}, \tag{11}$$

where $\odot$ denotes element-wise multiplication. The foreground appearance features are transformed with the help of action features and action key-points.

$$f_t^f = tanh(W_f^f* < \hat{m}_t^j, KP_t^j >, f_t \odot \hat{a}_{t-1} >). \tag{12}$$

Finally, the transformed foreground features are combined with the background features to get the integrated transformed appearance features,

$$\hat{a}_t^j = b_t^f + (1 - b_t) \odot f_t^f. \tag{13}$$

The transformed appearance features from different time-steps are combined together to form $\hat{a}^j$ which is used for synthesizing the action video.

Hierarchical Transformation: We propose to perform the appearance transformation on the prior at different resolution of latent representations. The key idea is to transform the appearance at both coarse as well as fine level which helps in improving the performance of video synthesis. In case of prior, appearance features a^j are extracted from multiple higher level layers in g_E. Similarly, action features m^i are extracted from multiple layers of video encoder f_E. The same set of predicted action key-points KP^j are used at different hierarchies after performing either average pooling or upsampling depending upon the resolution of action and appearance features.

The action features m^i from different levels are first passed through the action transformer network t_M to generate the transformed action features $\hat{m}^j$. Since t_M is a fully convolutional network, it is shared for action transformation at different levels of hierarchy. Similarly, the appearance transformer network t_A is also convolutional, therefore it is also shared by all the levels for performing appearance transformation. The sharing capability of t_M and t_A helps in reducing the number of parameters in the network and it also makes the transformation more robust. The transformed appearance features $\hat{a}^j$ from multiple levels are passed to the video synthesis network f_G and integrated at different layers with matching resolution.

3.4   Action Synthesis

The final component of the proposed framework is the action generator network f_G which synthesize the target action video $\hat{V}^j \in \mathbb{R}^{T \times H \times W \times 3}$ using the approximated appearance features $\hat{a}^j \in \mathbb{R}^{T_r \times H_r \times W_r \times C_r}$ and the predicted action key-points $KP^j \in \mathbb{R}^{T_k \times H_k \times W_k \times C_k}$. The action key-points KP^j helps the generator to focus on action regions in the video. They are predicted at a higher resolution in comparison with $\hat{a}^j$. Therefore the key-points are first average pooled down to the same temporal and spatial size as $\hat{a}^j$ and then these are concatenated along the channel dimension. The generator is based on 3D convolutions with ReLU activation and upsampling. The convolutional layers all use 3×3 kernels with zero padding and the upsampling layers use trilinear interpolation. The final layer is followed by a sigmoid activation which generates the target action video $\hat{V}^j$.

We use a pixel-wise reconstruction loss L_r, which is computed using mean squared error between the synthesized video $\hat{V}^j$ and the ground truth video V^j. We also use an adversarial loss [10] and a perceptual loss [15] to help in improving the performance of video synthesis. The adversarial loss L_{adv} is computed using a 3D convolution based discriminator D [5] which critiques whether the synthesized action video is realistic or not. We train F and D alternatively using a standard GAN framework [10]. The adversarial loss is computed as,

$$L_{adv} = E_{x \sim \mathcal{S}(i,j)}[log(1 - D(F(x)))], \tag{14}$$

where L_{adv} represents the adversarial loss and $\mathcal{S}(i,j)$ is the distribution of video and prior pair (V^i, P^j) from view i and j respectively. The discriminator loss is,

$$L_d = \max_D \left(E_{x \sim V_{gt}}[log(D(x))] + E_{x \sim \mathcal{S}(i,j)}[log(1 - D(F(x)))] \right), \tag{15}$$

where L_d is the discriminator loss and V_{gt} is the set of real action videos. To improve the visual quality of the synthesized video frames, we also use a perceptual loss L_p which computes the error at feature level. We utilize a pre-trained VGG-16 network [28] to compute the loss at frame level which is averaged over all the frames in the synthesized video. The loss is computed as mean squared error between the features from predicted video and ground truth video. The overall loss to train the full network is defined as,

$$L = \lambda_{vp}L_{vp} + \lambda_r L_r + \lambda_{adv}L_{adv} + \lambda_p L_p. \tag{16}$$

Here $\lambda_{vp}, \lambda_r, \lambda_{adv}$, and λ_p are loss weights which are determined experimentally. We use $\lambda_{vp} = 1, \lambda_r = 1, \lambda_{adv} = 0.1$, and $\lambda_p = 0.1$ in all our experiments.

3.5   Implementation and Training Details

We use a modified VGG-16 network [28] as our appearance encoder g_E where we use the features after the first ten convolution layers to get a^j. For the video encoder, we use a 3D convolution based I3D network [5] and extract m^i from the '$Mixed\_5c$' convolution layer. We use a resolution of 112×112 as input for both source video as well as the prior with 16 frames in the video. The video frames are sampled at 15 frames per second to include more motion int he videos. We compute the ground truth angular viewpoint change based on configuration parameters provided with the dataset.

The appearance features a^j are encoded as $14 \times 14 \times 256$ and the action features are encoded as $4 \times 14 \times 14 \times 256$ with $T_r = 4, H_r = 14, W_r = 14$, and $C_r = 256$. The action key-points are predicted at a resolution of $16 \times 56 \times 56 \times 32$ with $T_k = 16, H_k = 56, W_k = 56$, and $C_k = 32$. A standard deviation of 0.1 is used to compute the Gaussian maps for the action key-points. We use a 3D convolution based I3D network [5] as the discriminator D to compute adversarial loss L_{adv}, where the last prediction layer is modified for binary prediction. The perceptual loss L_p is computed with the help of a pre-trained VGG-16 network [28] where we take 512 dimension features from last layer of the network. We use Adam optimizer, with a learning rate of 1e–4. We implemented the code in Pytorch and perform our experiments on Titan-X GPU with a batch size of 14.

4   Experiments

In this section, we provide details of the experiments we performed to validate the effectiveness of the proposed method. Apart from the qualitative evaluation, we also provide frame level Structural Similarity Index Measure (SSIM) [39] and Peak Signal to Noise Ratio (PSNR) [11] for quantitative evaluation.

Table 1. A comparison of SSIM scores of all the combinations of three views along with the average score with existing approaches. The scores for VDG [12] and PG^2 [21] are shown as reported by the authors of VDNet [17]

Model	Pair-view SSIM score						Average
	$v_1 \rightarrow v_2$	$v_1 \rightarrow v_3$	$v_2 \rightarrow v_1$	$v_2 \rightarrow v_3$	$v_3 \rightarrow v_1$	$v_3 \rightarrow v_2$	
VDG [12]	.502 ± .058	.543 ± .068	.584 ± .060	.563 ± .062	.611 ± .077	.522 ± .063	.554 ± .075
PG^2 [21]	.499 ± .071	.561 ± .060	.600 ± .064	.557 ± .071	.598 ± .075	.543 ± .066	.560 ± .076
VRNet [32]	–	–	–	–	–	–	0.68
ResNet [17]	.705 ± .115	.735 ± .095	.717 ± .130	.690 ± .122	.734 ± .127	.669 ± .150	.708 ± .127
VDNet [17]	.789 ± .076	.791 ± .069	.800 ± .076	.765 ± .079	.797 ± .067	.756 ± .089	.783 ± .078
Proposed	.974 ± .021	.975 ± .021	.975 ± .019	.971 ± .021	.974 ± .017	.971 ± .022	.973 ± .020

Fig. 2. Comparison of the generated video frames using our method with existing approaches. The video frames are from position 1, 4, and 8. Column 1: source, column 2: target, column 3: ResNet [17], column 4: VDNet [17], and column 5 proposed method

4.1   Dataset

We conducted our experiments on the NTU-RGB+D Dataset [26], which is the largest multi-view action dataset containing over 56,000 videos. It has more than 4 million video frames depicting either one or two humans performing the actions. There are a total of 60 different actions depicted in the dataset using 40 different actors. Three different cameras are used at various height settings to capture videos from 80 different viewpoints. The cameras are always placed 45° apart, so they are at −45°, 0°, and +45°. Each actor or actor pair performs each action twice: once facing the left camera and once facing the right camera. This allows the videos to span viewpoints over a total of 90°. For our experiments, we use the subject split as described by the authors in [26].

4.2   Evaluation

We have shown the SSIM score for the synthesized videos of all the combinations of the three views on the test set of NTU-RGB+D in Table 1. We observe that the scores are low for pair v2 and v3 when compared with other pairs. These two views are at ±90° from each other and therefore the transformation is more

Fig. 3. Synthesized video frames using the proposed model. For each sample example, the top row contains 8 frames of the ground truth video for the novel view and the bottom row contains the same 8 frames of the generated video for the novel view. Our model predicts 16 frames in a video and for each of these examples, frames 1, 3, 5, 7, 9, 11, 13, and 15 are shown. GT: ground-truth, Gen: generated frames

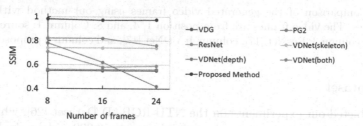

Fig. 4. A comparison of the variation of SSIM score with varying number of generated video frames with existing approaches

challenging than other pairs where the transformation is within ±45°. In Fig. 3, we have shown some sample video frames synthesized using the proposed method along with the ground truth video frames. We can observe that the network has no issue in rendering the background and the dynamics of the action is also quite visible along the video frames. The motion can be seen in the sequence of frames, but we can also observe that the motion is not well defined with some blur in the activity region. This is interesting as we are not utilizing any action prior from the novel target view, like [17], which make use of depth and skeleton sequences from the target view.

In Fig. 5, we have shown some examples of predicted action key-points for a video. We can observe that the predicted action key-points are near the activity

Fig. 5. Action key-points: the center of predicted action key-points shown on the sequence of example video frames. We can observe that the predicted key-points are located close to the performed action in the video frame

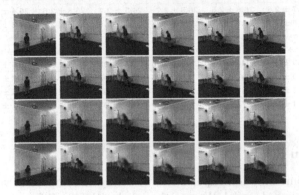

Fig. 6. Ablation on components of the proposed model: Synthesized video frames using different model variations. Column 1: source video, column-2: target video, column-3: basic model, column-4: w/ motion transformation, column-5 w/ hierarchical transformation, and column-6 appearance transformation

region in the frames and therefore they act as an attention mechanism for the recurrent transformer network to focus on activity regions.

Comparison: We also compared our approach with existing methods in Table 1. We observe that the proposed method outperforms all the other approaches in terms of SSIM score. We also present a qualitative comparison with [17]. The comparison is shown in Fig. 2. We observe that the video frames generated by ResNet [17] has a lots of artifacts and the human body is not properly formed. The VDNet variant improves the quality with no visible artifacts, but still the human body is not well formed. Also, there is no visible motion as we move from frame 1 to 8. The VDNet model use the sequence of depth/skeleton from the target view and still the motion is not quite visible in the synthesized video frames. In our approach, the background is of high quality, which is due to the prior, and we can also observe noticeable motion along the generated frames of the video. We also evaluate the variation in SSIM score with varying number of predicted frames in the video. The evaluation is shown in Fig. 4 and we can observe that the video quality using proposed method is consistent with increasing number of frames and it outperforms existing approaches.

Table 2. Ablation experiments to study the impact of various components of the network on video synthesis. AC-Trans: action transformation, HI-Trans: hierarchical transformation, and AP-Trans: appearance transformation

Model	Pair-view PSNR score						Average
	$v_1 \to v_2$	$v_1 \to v_3$	$v_2 \to v_1$	$v_2 \to v_3$	$v_3 \to v_1$	$v_3 \to v_2$	
Basic model	23.8 ± 1.5	23.8 ± 1.4	24.2 ± 1.4	23.7 ± 1.5	24.2 ± 1.5	23.7 ± 1.6	23.9 ± 1.5
w/ AC-Trans	24.7 ± 1.5	24.7 ± 1.4	25.1 ± 1.6	24.5 ± 1.6	25.0 ± 1.6	24.4 ± 1.7	24.7 ± 1.6
w/ HI-Trans	26.7 ± 2.6	26.8 ± 2.5	26.8 ± 2.7	26.5 ± 2.7	26.8 ± 2.6	26.4 ± 2.7	26.7 ± 2.6
w/ AP-Trans	27.6 ± 2.7	27.7 ± 2.8	27.7 ± 2.7	27.2 ± 2.8	27.6 ± 2.7	27.2 ± 2.8	27.5 ± 2.7
	Pair-view SSIM score						
	$v_1 \to v_2$	$v_1 \to v_3$	$v_2 \to v_1$	$v_2 \to v_3$	$v_3 \to v_1$	$v_3 \to v_2$	
Basic model	$.939 \pm .033$	$.940 \pm .026$	$.943 \pm .026$	$.937 \pm .033$	$.943 \pm .026$	$.936 \pm .040$	$.940 \pm .031$
w/ AC-Trans	$.950 \pm .022$	$.951 \pm .021$	$.954 \pm .026$	$.948 \pm .024$	$.953 \pm .023$	$.947 \pm .033$	$.951 \pm .025$
w/ HI-Trans	$.967 \pm .028$	$.967 \pm .023$	$.967 \pm .023$	$.964 \pm .027$	$.967 \pm .023$	$.964 \pm .030$	$.966 \pm .026$
w/ AP-Trans	$.974 \pm .021$	$.975 \pm .021$	$.975 \pm .019$	$.971 \pm .021$	$.974 \pm .017$	$.971 \pm .022$	$.973 \pm .020$

4.3 Ablation Study

We perform some ablation experiments to study the impact of various components in the proposed model. We experimented with four different variations. The first variation, basic model, does not include action transformation, hierarchical transformation, and appearance transformation. In the other three variation, we add these three components incrementally. We observe that each of these components help in improving the synthesized video quality in terms of both PSNR and SSIM evaluation. A detailed analysis of these ablations is shown in Table 2.

In Fig. 6, we show synthesized video frames using different variations in the model. We can observe that without any action and appearance transformation, the actor becomes blurry as the video progresses. The action transformation helps in improving the motion quality in the synthesized video. The hierarchical transformation improves the quality further and the appearance transformation helps in improving the visual quality of the synthesized video.

4.4 Novel View with Novel Actor

The proposed network takes an appearance prior from the target view-point. This allows us to potentially impose the action of the video from any source view-point onto another person and another location from a novel view-point. We have shown some examples of synthesized video frames in Fig. 7 where the prior from the novel view is from a different actor and location. We observe that the proposed approach is able to synthesize the video with the correct appearance from the prior frame and the correct action from the source video. Thus, we know that each branch of our model (the motion branch and the appearance branch) is learning what it is supposed to learn; each only contributes information about motion or appearance appropriately.

Fig. 7. Novel view and novel actor: The synthesized video frames from a novel view with a different actor and different background. For each sample the top row shows 8 frames of the source video and the bottom row shows a prior from another view followed by synthesized video frames for the novel view and novel actor. We can observe that the motion was successfully transformed to the novel actor (with different initial pose) in the novel viewpoint. For each of these, frames 1, 3, 5, 7, 9, 11, 13, and 15 are shown

4.5 Limitations and Failure Cases

The proposed approach is able to successfully transform the performed action to a novel view at a coarse level. The main limitation of the current approach is that the finer appearance details are missing in the synthesized video leading to a motion blur. It is important to note that the training is performed at a smaller resolution (112×112) to avoid a higher memory consumption and long training duration due to resource constraints. At this resolution, it is challenging to preserve the fine appearance and motion details of the actor in the latent representation space. Also, synthesizing motion from a novel view is much more challenging. Even with the help of motion prior from the target viewpoint, the authors in [17] were not very successful in synthesizing a high-quality action from novel view-points. The availability of resources (multiple GPU's or GPU's with higher memory) will definitely help in improving this quality, but, capturing the fine appearance and motion details in memory constraint environment is a challenging yet interesting problem, which can be explored in the future work.

5   Conclusion

In this work, we address the problem of novel view video synthesis by transforming the source action to target novel view in latent space. We propose a recurrent structure which utilize these action features and transform the prior from target view for video synthesis. The model predicts action key-points in an unsupervised way and enables the appearance transformer and video generator to focus on action regions. We evaluated the effectiveness of the proposed method on the largest multi-view action dataset. The experimental results demonstrate the effectiveness of the proposed framework in cross-view action synthesis even with varying actor and background scenes.

Acknowledgement. Kara Marie Schatz contributed to this work while she was an NSF REU student in Center for Research in Computer Vision at University of Central Florida which was supported under NSF CNS grant #1461121.

References

1. Ballas, N., Yao, L., Pal, C., Courville, A.: Delving deeper into convolutional networks for learning video representations. arXiv preprint arXiv:1511.06432, 2015
2. Bansal, A., Ma, S., Ramanan, D., Sheikh, Y.: Recycle-GAN: unsupervised video retargeting. In: Ferrari, V., Hebert, M., Sminchisescu, C., Weiss, Y. (eds.) ECCV 2018. LNCS, vol. 11209, pp. 122–138. Springer, Cham (2018). https://doi.org/10.1007/978-3-030-01228-1_8
3. Byeon, W., et al.: ContextVP: fully context-aware video prediction. In: Proceedings of the IEEE CVPR Workshops (2018)
4. Cai, H., Bai, C., Tai, Y.-W., Tang, C.-K.: Deep video generation, prediction and completion of human action sequences. In: Ferrari, V., Hebert, M., Sminchisescu, C., Weiss, Y. (eds.) ECCV 2018. LNCS, vol. 11206, pp. 374–390. Springer, Cham (2018). https://doi.org/10.1007/978-3-030-01216-8_23
5. Carreira, J., Zisserman, A.: Quo vadis, action recognition? A new model and the kinetics dataset. In: CVPR (2017)
6. Chan, C., Ginosar, S., Zhou, T., Efros, A.A.: Everybody dance now. In: Proceedings of the IEEE International Conference on Computer Vision, pp. 5933–5942 (2019)
7. Choi, Y., Choi, M., Kim, M., Ha, J.-W., Kim, S., Choo, J.: StarGAN: unified generative adversarial networks for multi-domain image-to-image translation. In: Proceedings of the IEEE Conference on Computer Vision and Pattern Recognition, pp. 8789–8797 (2018)
8. Clark, A., Donahue, J., Simonyan, K.: Efficient video generation on complex datasets. arXiv preprint arXiv:1907.06571 (2019)
9. Ali Eslami, S.M., et al.: Neural scene representation and rendering. Science (2018)
10. Goodfellow, I.: Generative adversarial nets. In: Advances in Neural Information Processing Systems, pp. 2672–2680 (2014)
11. Hore, A., Ziou, D.: Image quality metrics: PSNR vs. SSIM. In: 2010 20th International Conference on Pattern Recognition, pp. 2366–2369. IEEE (2010)
12. Lakhal, M.I., Lanz, O., Cavallaro, A.: Pose guided human image synthesis by view disentanglement and enhanced weighting loss. In: Leal-Taixé, L., Roth, S. (eds.) ECCV 2018. LNCS, vol. 11130, pp. 380–394. Springer, Cham (2019). https://doi.org/10.1007/978-3-030-11012-3_30
13. Jakab, T., Gupta, A., Bilen, H., Vedaldi, A.: Unsupervised learning of object landmarks through conditional image generation. In: Advances in Neural Information Processing Systems, pp. 4016–4027 (2018)
14. Jayaraman, D., Gao, R., Grauman, K.: ShapeCodes: self-supervised feature learning by lifting views to Viewgrids. In: Ferrari, V., Hebert, M., Sminchisescu, C., Weiss, Y. (eds.) ECCV 2018. LNCS, vol. 11220, pp. 126–144. Springer, Cham (2018). https://doi.org/10.1007/978-3-030-01270-0_8

15. Johnson, J., Alahi, A., Fei-Fei, L.: Perceptual losses for real-time style transfer and super-resolution. In: Leibe, B., Matas, J., Sebe, N., Welling, M. (eds.) ECCV 2016. LNCS, vol. 9906, pp. 694–711. Springer, Cham (2016). https://doi.org/10. 1007/978-3-319-46475-6_43
16. Karras, T., Aila, T., Laine, S., Lehtinen, J.: Progressive growing of GANs for improved quality, stability, and variation. arXiv preprint arXiv:1710.10196 (2017)
17. Lakhal, M.I., Lanz, O., Cavallaro, A.: View-LSTM: novel-view video synthesis through view decomposition. In: The IEEE International Conference on Computer Vision (ICCV), October 2019
18. Ledig, C., Theis, L., Huszár, F., Caballero, J., et al.: Photo-realistic single image super-resolution using a generative adversarial network. In IEEE Conference on CVPR (2017)
19. Li, J., Wong, Y., Zhao, Q., Kankanhalli, M.: Unsupervised learning of view-invariant action representations. In: Advances in Neural Information Processing Systems (2018)
20. Liang, X., Lee, L., Dai, W., Xing, E.P.: Dual motion GAN for future-flow embedded video prediction. In: Proceedings of the IEEE International Conference on Computer Vision, pp. 1744–1752 (2017)
21. Ma, L., Jia, X., Sun, Q., Schiele, B., Tuytelaars, T., Van Gool, L.: Pose guided person image generation. In: Advances in Neural Information Processing Systems, pp. 406–416 (2017)
22. Mathieu, M., Couprie, C., LeCun, Y.: Deep multi-scale video prediction beyond mean square error. In: ICLR (2016)
23. Regmi, K., Borji, A.: Cross-view image synthesis using conditional GANs. In: IEEE Conference on CVPR (2018)
24. Saito, M., Matsumoto, E., Saito, S.: Temporal generative adversarial nets with singular value clipping. In: IEEE International Conference on Computer Vision (ICCV) (2017)
25. Shaham, T.R., Dekel, T., Michaeli, T.: SinGAN: learning a generative model from a single natural image. In: Proceedings of the IEEE International Conference on Computer Vision, pp. 4570–4580 (2019)
26. Shahroudy, A., Liu, J., Ng, T.-T., Wang, G.: NTU RGB+D: a large scale dataset for 3D human activity analysis. In: Proceedings of the IEEE Conference on CVPR (2016)
27. Siarohin, A., Lathuilière, S., Tulyakov, S., Ricci, E., Sebe, N.: Animating arbitrary objects via deep motion transfer. In: Proceedings of the IEEE Conference on Computer Vision and Pattern Recognition, pp. 2377–2386 (2019)
28. Simonyan, K., Zisserman, A.: Very deep convolutional networks for large-scale image recognition. arXiv preprint arXiv:1409.1556 (2014)
29. Thies, J., Zollhofer, M., Stamminger, M., Theobalt, C., Nießner, M.: Face2Face: real-time face capture and reenactment of RGB videos. In: Proceedings of the IEEE Conference on Computer Vision and Pattern Recognition, pp. 2387–2395 (2016)
30. Tulyakov, S., Liu, M.-Y., Yang, X., Kautz, J.: MoCoGAN: decomposing motion and content for video generation. arXiv preprint arXiv:1707.04993 (2017)
31. Vondrick, C., Pirsiavash, H., Torralba, A.: Generating videos with scene dynamics. In: NeurIPS (2016)
32. Vyas, S., Rawat, Y.S., Shah, M.: Time-aware and view-aware video rendering for unsupervised representation learning. arXiv preprint arXiv:1811.10699 (2018)
33. Walker, J., Marino, K., Gupta, A., Hebert, M.: The pose knows: video forecasting by generating pose futures. In: Proceedings of the IEEE International Conference on Computer Vision, pp. 3332–3341 (2017)

34. Wang, T.-C., et al.: Video-to-video synthesis. In: Advances in Neural Information Processing Systems, pp. 1144–1156 (2018)
35. Wang, Y., Gao, Z., Long, M., Wang, J., Yu Philip, S.: PredRNN++: towards a resolution of the deep-in-time dilemma in spatiotemporal predictive learning. In: International Conference on Machine Learning, pp. 5110–5119 (2018)
36. Wang, Y., Jiang, L., Yang, M.-H., Li, L.-J., Long, M., Fei-Fei, L.: Eidetic 3D LSTM: a model for video prediction and beyond. In: International Conference on Learning Representations (ICLR) (2019)
37. Wang, Y., Long, M., Wang, J., Gao, Z., Yu Philip, S.: PredRNN: recurrent neural networks for predictive learning using spatiotemporal LSTMS. In: Advances in Neural Information Processing Systems, pp. 879–888 (2017)
38. Wang, Y., et al.: Memory in memory: a predictive neural network for learning higher-order non-stationarity from spatiotemporal dynamics. In: Proceedings of the IEEE Conference on Computer Vision and Pattern Recognition, pp. 9154–9162 (2019)
39. Wang, Z., Bovik, A.C., Sheikh, H.R., Simoncelli, E.P.: Image quality assessment: from error visibility to structural similarity. IEEE Trans. Image Process. **13**(4), 600–612 (2004)
40. Yang, C., Wang, Z., Zhu, X., Huang, C., Shi, J., Lin, D.: Pose guided human video generation. In: Ferrari, V., Hebert, M., Sminchisescu, C., Weiss, Y. (eds.) ECCV 2018. LNCS, vol. 11214, pp. 204–219. Springer, Cham (2018). https://doi.org/10.1007/978-3-030-01249-6_13

Multi-view Action Recognition Using Cross-View Video Prediction

Shruti Vyas, Yogesh S. Rawat$^{(\boxtimes)}$, and Mubarak Shah

Center for Research in Computer Vision, University of Central Florida, Orlando, USA
{shruti,yogesh,shah}@crcv.ucf.edu

Abstract. In this work, we address the problem of action recognition in a multi-view environment. Most of the existing approaches utilize pose information for multi-view action recognition. We focus on RGB modality instead and propose an unsupervised representation learning framework, which encodes the scene dynamics in videos captured from multiple viewpoints via predicting actions from unseen views. The framework takes multiple short video clips from different viewpoints and time as input and learns an holistic internal representation which is used to predict a video clip from an unseen viewpoint and time. The ability of the proposed network to render unseen video frames enables it to learn a meaningful and robust representation of the scene dynamics. We evaluate the effectiveness of the learned representation for multi-view video action recognition in a supervised approach. We observe a significant improvement in the performance with RGB modality on NTU-RGB+D dataset, which is the largest dataset for multi-view action recognition. The proposed framework also achieves state-of-the-art results with depth modality, which validates the generalization capability of the approach to other data modalities. The code is publicly available at https://github.com/svyas23/cross-view-action.

1 Introduction

Historically, viewpoint in-variance has been a very active research area in computer vision and is currently also important from the perspective of representation learning. The appearance and dynamics of action vary from one viewpoint to another. Humans have the ability to effortlessly visualize how action might look like from an unseen viewpoint. This ability highlights the view-invariant property of the encoded representation in the human brain after observing the action from certain views [13]. The encoded representation should have sufficient details to predict the dynamics of the action from unseen views. Motivated by this, we present an unsupervised representation learning framework which encodes the scene dynamics in videos captured from multiple viewpoints via

Electronic supplementary material The online version of this chapter (https://doi.org/10.1007/978-3-030-58583-9_26) contains supplementary material, which is available to authorized users.

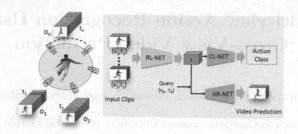

Fig. 1. An overview of the proposed representation learning framework. An action is captured from different viewpoints (v1, v2, v3, ..., vn) providing observations (o1, o2, o3, ..., on). Video clips from two viewpoints (v1 and v2) at arbitrary times (t1 and t2) are used to learn a representation (r) for this action, employing the proposed representation learning network (RL-NET). The learned representation (r) is then used to render a video from an arbitrary query viewpoint (v3) and time (t3) using proposed video rendering network (VR-NET). The representation thus learned is used for action recognition using classification network (CL-NET)

predicting actions from unseen views. An overview of the proposed framework is shown in Fig. 1. The prediction of videos from unseen viewpoint and time enforces the network to learn a more informative view and time-dependent representation, which makes it effective for multi-view environment.

Cross-view prediction is a challenging problem as the visual appearance and dynamics of an action vary from one viewpoint to another. There have been some efforts in this direction for novel-view image prediction, which includes 3D reconstruction from images [14] and cross-view image rendering [8,36,48]. However, most of the existing research in video prediction mainly focus on single view videos. Video prediction in itself is a challenging problem [5], and the variation in actions observed from different viewpoints makes it more challenging. In this work, we explore the idea of cross-view video prediction to learn a good representation for action recognition in a multi-view environment.

There has been a lot work in view-invariant action recognition in recent years. However, most of the existing works make use of skeleton data to learn the view-invariant features [51]. Learning a view-invariant representation is much more challenging with RGB videos as compared to skeleton sequences, and therefore, the methods using RGB modality do not perform as well as the skeleton-based methods [27,52]. Researchers have also explored the use of other modalities such as depth and optical flow for view-invariant learning, but they are also not very effective and do not generalize well to RGB modality [22]. We propose a framework to learn a robust feature representation from RGB videos.

The proposed framework takes multiple short video clips from different viewpoints and times as input and learns an internal representation using the proposed representation learning network (RL-NET). The learned representation is used to predict a video clip from an unseen viewpoint and time with the help of a video rendering network (VR-NET) and also used for action recognition using a classification network (CL-NET). The proposed framework is adaptive for number of input views which makes it suitable for multi-view as well as novel-view action recognition. We demonstrate its effectiveness in both cross-subject as well as cross-view action recognition. Moreover, it is also effective in integrating multiple views to further improve the action recognition performance. We make the following contributions in this work:

- We propose a framework for *unsupervised multi-view* representation learning via *cross-view* video prediction which can be trained end-to-end from scratch.
- We propose a viewpoint and time conditioned encoding of videos which are integrated to get a *holistic representation* of the action from multiple views. This allows the network to preserve the notion of *viewpoint and time*, which facilitates query-based cross-view prediction.
- We evaluate the effectiveness of the proposed approach with *multiple modalities* and on multiple datasets. We observe a significant improvement in the performance of cross-view as well as cross-subject action recognition on the largest multi-view dataset when compared with existing methods.

2   Related Work

Cross-View Action Recognition: We have recently seen a good progress in action recognition with RGB videos [4,47]. However, these methods are mainly focused on single view videos. In multi-view environment, the availability of different modalities such as, pose and depth, has motivated many research works which address the issue of view in-variance. In this stream of research, most of the works make use of multiple modalities (RGB+D) [39], depth [22,34], RGB [22,27,52] or skeleton data [21,46,51] to learn view-invariant features. Among these, skeleton data has shown very promising performance when compared with RGB videos. The existing methods utilize RNN [2,7,24,25,51], CNN [15,24,26], and GraphCNN [21,49] to learn view-invariant features from skeleton sequences. However, these approaches requires the availability of 2D/3D pose information. Apart from these, 3D motion is another modality which has shown good results in cross-view action recognition [22,27]. However, getting 3D motion is computationally expensive and these methods do not generalize well with RGB modality. In this work, we focus on RGB modality for multi-view action recognition.

Cross-View Prediction: The research in image prediction using deep learning has recently seen a great progress [18], and it is mainly attributed to the success of Generative Adversarial Networks (GAN). We have also seen some preliminary success in the research on video prediction and proposed methods are mainly focused on future frame prediction [3,30], future clip prediction [42], or conditioned video generation [37,41]. Our work is different from these approaches as we have a notion of viewpoint, which has not been addressed earlier. Cross-view prediction of data is an interesting problem, which can have multiple applications including view-invariant representation learning. There are some existing works focusing on this problem for cross-view image prediction [8,36] and 3D reconstruction from images [14]. In [8], the authors proposed a scene representation learning framework and worked with synthetic images. In a recent effort [17], the authors propose a novel view video prediction approach which requires a strong prior, depth/skeleton sequence, from the target view for video generation. Our work is different from this in two main aspects; our approach predicts the target video based on a query viewpoint and does not require any prior from the target view, and we are using cross-view prediction as an auxiliary task for unsupervised learning of action representation in a multi-view environment.

Unsupervised Representation Learning: The research in unsupervised video representation learning mainly focuses on encoder-decoder type of networks, where the decoder is used for reconstruction [10] or predicting future frames [40]. There are some other approaches which utilize temporal ordering of clips [9,31], temporal coherence [45], and sorting of shuffled frames [19] as a way of unsupervised learning. Recently, there has been some effort to utilize 3D-motion prediction as a way of unsupervised learning [22,27], but this requires computation of optical flow which is computationally costly. The existing works are mostly focused on single views and they are not effective for multi-view learning. We are focusing on unsupervised learning in multi-view environment.

3   Method

The proposed framework consists of two main components, a representation learning network (RL-NET), f, and a video rendering network (VR-NET), g. A detailed overview of the proposed framework is shown in Fig. 2. The input to the framework consists of multiple short video clips of an instance captured from varying viewpoints and time which are termed as observations, $o_i = \{(x_i^k, v_i^k, t_i)\}_{k=1,2,...,K}$, where, x_i^k represents k^{th} video clip captured from viewpoint v_i^k and time t_i for any instance i. The RL-NET take these observations as input and learns a holistic representation r for the instance with the help of an encoding network (ENC-NET), f^e, and a blending network (BL-NET), f^b, preserving the notion of view and time.

The ENC-NET considers each observation independently and encode the spatio-temporal features integrated with viewpoint and time, $e_i^k = f^e(o_i^k)$. Here e_i^k is the view and time dependent encoding for observation o_i^k from instance i. BL-NET is a recurrent network which updates its internal representation as it sees more observations before providing a holistic representation $r_i = f^b(\{e_i^k\}_{k=1,2,...,K})$ of the scene and its dynamics. The VR-NET, then, use this representation, r, along with stochastic latent variable, $z \sim (0,1)$, to render a video clip from a query viewpoint, v_i^k, and time, t_i.

Formally, we can define the representation learning as, $r_i = f_\theta(o_i)$, and the video rendering network as,

$$g_\theta(x|v^q, t^q, r) = \int g_\theta(x, z|v^q, t^q, r)dz, \tag{1}$$

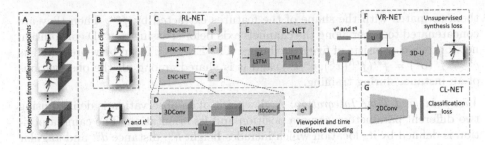

Fig. 2. Outline of the proposed unsupervised cross-view video rendering framework. **A**: A collection of observations (o) for a given action from different viewpoints. **B**: Training clips from the set of observations captured from different viewpoints and at different times. **C**: Representation learning network (RL-NET), which takes video clips from different viewpoint and time as input and learns a representation r. **D**: ENC-NET is used to learn individual video encodings e^k conditioned on its viewpoint v^k and time t^k. **E**: The blending network (BL-NET) combines encodings learned from different video clips into a unified representation r. **F**: The representation r is used to predict a video from query viewpoint v^q and time t^q using VR-NET. **G**: The representation r can also be used for action classification using CL-NET. 3D-U refers to 3D convolutions combined with upsampling and U refers to upsampling.

where, $g_\theta(x|v^q, t^q, r)$ is probability density of a video x observed from a query viewpoint v^q at time t^q, for an instance o_i with representation r and latent variable z. The parameters θ for the two networks can be learned using optimization over the rendered video. We train the two networks, RL-NET and VR-NET, jointly in an end-to-end fashion to maximize the likelihood of rendering the ground-truth video, observed from the query viewpoint and time. In the next subsections we will describe each of these components in detail (More details are in the supplementary).

3.1 Representation Learning Network (RL-NET)

The representation learning network f takes multiple video clips of an instance captured from different viewpoints and time to learn a representation r. It consists of two components, encoding network (ENC-NET) f^e and a blending network (BL-NET) f^b.

Encoding Network (ENC-NET): The ENC-NET f^e learns spatio-temporal features for each observations independently using 3D convolutions. Since each observation comes from a different viewpoint and time, we want to integrate these factors in the learned encodings. The ENC-NET first extracts viewpoint and time independent features e^{hk} from the input video clip x^k; $e^{hk} = f^{eh}(x^k)$. Here f^{eh} is a 3D convolution network with two layers. This encoding is then passed to a integration network f^{ei} along with viewpoint v^k and time t^k encodings. The integration network gives us a viewpoint and time dependent encodings $e^k = f^{ei}(e^{hk}, v^k, t^k)$. It takes the viewpoint and time encodings and upsample them to match with the shape of the features extracted by f^{eh}. Then they are concatenated together along the channels axis before passing to a 3D convolution network which consists of five more layers. The ENC-NET can be represented as $e^k = f^e(o^k) = f^{ei}(f^{eh}(x^k), v^k, t^k)$, and it is shared among all the observations of an instance during training.

Viewpoint and Time Integration: A viewpoint of an observation is defined using two different parameters: camera position and its orientation. The camera position is defined by its location which includes height h^v, distance d^v, and angular position a^v with respect to the actor. The height and distance values are normalized between $(0, 1)$. The angular position is encoded depending upon where the viewpoint is positioned and it lies in the range $(-\pi, \pi)$. The orientation is defined by horizontal-pan hp^v and vertical-pan vp^v in the camera while capturing the observation. This is taken into account when we randomly crop each input observation in the spatial dimension during training. The time encoding t^e is derived using the position of the observation in the long action sequence. It is normalized in the range $(0, 1)$. The viewpoint and time encodings becomes a six dimensional vector, where $v = [h^v, d^v, a^v, hp^v, vp^v]$, and $t = [t^e]$, which is used to get a viewpoint and time integrated video features $e^k = f^e(x^k, v^k, t^k)$ for a given observation o^k.

Blending Network (BL-NET): The viewpoint and time conditioned encodings e^k from each observation are passed to a blending network f^b which learns a representation r. We want to learn a representation which holistically represents the scene and its dynamics as viewed from different viewpoints and time. The recurrent networks, such as LSTM, have been widely used to learn temporal dependencies in sequential data. However, they are also shown to be effective in processing non-sequential data, such as addition of a series of numbers [12]. Motivated by this, we propose a recurrent network which learns a representation for an instance, which is updated as it sees new observations (Fig. 2E). More specifically, we utilize an LSTM architecture, where the memory cell, c, acts as an accumulator of state information and is updated by the input (i), output (o) and forget (f) gates, which are self-parameterized controlling gates. We make use of convolutional LSTM to preserve the spatial information in the embeddings and utilize bi-directional layers in the network for a more effective learning. For a given video embedding, e_i^k, after seeing all other observations in a forward and a backward pass, we get an updated hidden representation h_i^r.

$$h_i^r = (o_i^f \circ \tanh(c_i^f)) ^\frown (o_i^b \circ \tanh(c_i^b)). \tag{2}$$

Here, o_i^f and o_i^b are the output gates of the forward pass and backward pass respectively, c_i^f and c_i^b are the corresponding memory cell states, $\circ$ denotes the Hadamard product, and $^\frown$ denotes a concatenation operation between learned representations from the forward and backward pass. The updated intermediate representation from each observation is then passed to a uni-directional conv-LSTM layer, which integrate these to get a holistic representation r.

$$r = o_n \circ \tanh(c_n). \tag{3}$$

Here, o_n is the output gate, c_n is the memory cell state of the network after seeing all the n observations. The learned representation can be computed as $r = f^b(\{f^e(o^k)\}_{k=1,2...n})$.

3.2 Video Rendering Network (VR-NET)

The representation, r, learned with the given observations, o, is used to render a video with a video rendering network (VR-NET). The VR-NET, shown in Fig. 2F, is also a convolution based network which takes as input the learned representation, r, along with query viewpoint, v^q, time t^q, and latent noise z. The viewpoint v^q, time t^q, and noise z are passed to the network as conditioning, for which we use concatenation operation with the representation features. The idea is to extract viewpoint and time dependent features from the learned representation r. The VR-NET consists of 2D convolutions followed by 3D convolutions to render the video clips. The convolution layers are used in combination with upsampling of features to generate video clips with resolution same as the input observations. The video rendering is represented as $V^p = g(r, v^q, t^q, z) = g(f(o), v^q, t^q, z)$.

The two networks, RL-NET and VR-NET, are trained jointly in an end-to-end fashion minimizing the reconstruction loss L^r as the objective function. The reconstruction loss L^r is computed as mean squared error between the predicted video V^p and the ground truth video clip V^g.

$$L^r = \frac{1}{N} \sum_n^N \sum_i^F \sum_j^H \sum_k^W \sum_m^C ||V^p_{ijkm} - V^g_{ijkm}||^2. \tag{4}$$

Here, N is the number of samples, F is the number of frames in the clip, H, W is height and width of the video frames, and $C = 3$ for three RGB color channels.

3.3 Action Recognition

The RL-NET and VR-NET can be trained jointly for unsupervised representation learning by cross-view prediction. To explore the effectiveness of the learned representation, we use it for the task of cross-view action recognition using a supervised approach. We use the same RL-NET and VR-NET framework and add a classifier (CL-NET) on top of learned representation. CL-NET has 2 convolution layers followed by fully connected layers and it predicts probabilities for each action classes. We use categorical cross entropy to compute the loss L^c for the action recognition.

$$L^c = -\frac{1}{N} \sum_n^N \sum_c^C 1_{y_i \in C_c} \log(\hat{p}[y_i \in C_c]). \tag{5}$$

Here, C is the number of action categories, and $\hat{p}[y_i \in C_c]$ is the predicted probability for this sample corresponding to category c.

The proposed framework can be trained in two different ways for action classification. In the first approach, we have a two step process where we first train

RL-NET and VR-NET in an unsupervised way to learn a representation. In the next step, we train a CL-NET using this representation for action classification. In the second approach, we train all the three networks, RL-NET, VR-NET, and CL-NET, in a joint training. In our preliminary experiments, we observe similar action recognition performance with both the approaches. In all our reported experiments, we follow the second approach as it is efficient in terms of time due to a joint single step training.

The network is trained end-to-end with the two loss functions (L^r and L^c) in a multi-task setting and the overall loss of the network is defined as,

$$L = \lambda_r \times L^r + \lambda_c \times L^c. \tag{6}$$

In all our experiments, we use $\lambda_r = \lambda_c = 1.0$. The network is trained using observations captured from certain known views and later tested on observations from unseen views for cross-view action recognition.

3.4   Training and Implementation Details

We train the proposed network without any pre-trained weights using Adam optimizer and a learning rate of $2e^{-5}$. A batch-size of 6 was used in all our experiments. The input video clips to RL-NET consists of 6 frames with a skip rate of 3 and a resolution of 112×112. The network takes 6 video clips at a time and renders one video clip with 6 frames and a resolution of 112×112 during training. We implemented our code in Keras with Tensorflow backend and use Titan-X GPU for training our network.

4   Experiments

We perform our experiments on two different datasets: NTU-RGB+D [38] and Northwestern-UCLA MultiviewAction3D (N-UCLA) [44]. We use NTU-RGB+D dataset for all our ablation studies.

NTU-RGB+D: This human action recognition dataset contains more than 56K videos and 4 millions frames with 60 different actions. There are a total of 40 different actors, who perform actions captured from 80 different viewpoints. We perform both cross-subject (CS) and cross-view (CV) evaluation for action recognition as suggested by [38] on RGB as well as depth modality. For cross-view video prediction experiments, we use the subject split suggested by [38].

Northwestern-UCLA MultiviewAction3D (N-UCLA): This dataset has 10 action categories and each action is performed by 10 actors. The actions are captured from 3 viewpoints and there are a total of 1493 action sequences. We perform both CS and CV evaluation as suggested by [44] and use videos from the first two views for training and videos from the third view for testing. This is a much smaller dataset in comparison with NTU-RGB+D and we use this in our transfer learning experiments for action recognition.

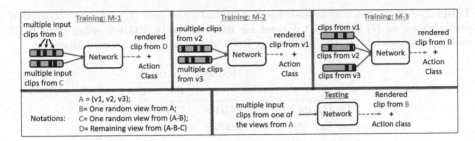

Fig. 3. Details of different training strategies (M-1, M-2, and M-3) which are used to study the effect of video rendering on representation learning for action classification. All the three variations use the same testing strategy

Table 1. A comparison of classification accuracy from different training configurations to study the effect of rendering on cross-subject split of NTU-RGB+D dataset. These evaluations are done on only 6 clips per video which is similar to the training setup

Training approach	Accuracy			
	Testing view			Average
	View 1	View 2	View 3	
M-1	77.3	74.2	72.2	74.6
M-2	59.8	59.7	58.4	59.3
M-3	57.3	56.2	55.3	56.3

4.1 Representation Learning via Rendering

The proposed method utilize video prediction for learning a representation. We experimented with three different scenarios of rendering during training. These scenarios are based on what the network sees as input and what it tries to render. In the first scenario (M-1), the network sees all the available views as input except one, which is used for rendering. The input views are selected randomly, therefore, eventually the network will see all the available views as input. In the second scenario (M-2), one view is kept for rendering and the rest are used as input throughout the training. In the third scenario (M-3), all the views are used a input and one view and time is randomly selected for rendering. In this case, the network will render a seen view however it may be from a different time.

In NTU-RGB+D dataset, there are three different viewpoints. Therefore, for the first variation (M-1), we randomly select two input views and render a video from third unseen view. In the second configuration (M-2), we fixed the input views to 2 and 3, and view 1 is used for rendering. And, in the last configuration (M-3), we use all the three views as input and randomly select one of them for rendering at a random time-step. The details of these configurations are shown in Fig. 3.

We analyze the performance of these configurations for action recognition. We use cross-subject split from NTU-RGB+D dataset [38] to perform evaluation

Table 2. A comparison of cross-subject (CS) and cross-view (CV) action recognition performance on NTU-RGB+D dataset for RGB modality. RGB-S: using both RGB and skeleton modalities, RGB-DS: using RGB, depth and skeleton modalities.

Method	Modality	Accuracy	
		CS	CV
STA-Hands [1]	RGB-S	73.5	80.2
Pose Est. [28]	RGB-S	84.6	–
DSSCA - SSLM [39]	RGB-DS	74.9	–
CNN-LSTM [27]	RGB	56	–
DA-NET [43]	RGB	–	75.3
Att-LSTM [52]	RGB	63.3	70.6
CNN-BiLSTM [22]	RGB	55.5	49.3
Proposed	RGB	**82.3**	**86.3**

Table 3. A comparison of cross-subject (CS) and cross-view (CV) action recognition performance on NTU-RGB+D dataset for **depth modality**.

Method	Accuracy	
	CS	CV
HOG [32]	32.2	22.3
S-Norm Vector [50]	31.8	13.6
HON4D [33]	30.6	7.3
Shuffle & learn [31]	61.4	53.2
CNN-LSTM [27]	66.2	53.2
CNN-BiLSTM [22]	68.1	63.9
Proposed	**71.8**	**78.7**

of these experiments. During testing, a single view (with multiple video clips) is used to perform action recognition. The view-specific classification accuracy scores along with the average is shown in Table 1. We observe that the action recognition performance is relatively better for view 1 in comparison with view 2 and 3. The videos in view 1 are captured at $\pm 45°$ view of actor and for view 2 and 3 it is either frontal or $\pm 90°$. However, this is not consistent for M-2 configuration as it never sees the video samples from view 1 during training.

We also observe that when the rendering network is trained for unseen views (M-1 and M-2), it perform better in comparison with seen view prediction (M-3). Predicting unseen query views is relatively difficult for the rendering network and therefore it forces the representation learning network to learn a good representation. Also, the random selection of input views (M-1) allows the network to see different variations in terms of input and query views. Therefore, this configuration (M-1) performs better than M-2 where the input and output views are fixed throughout the training.

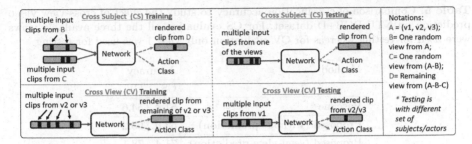

Fig. 4. The details of the training and testing configuration (Strategy M-1) used for cross-view and cross-subject experiments on NTU-RGB+D dataset

Table 4. A comparison of cross-subject (CS) and cross-view (CV) action recognition on N-UCLA MultiviewAction3D dataset.

Method	Modality	Accuracy	
		CS	CV
NKTM [35]	RGB-S	–	75.8
MST-AOG [44]	RGB-S	81.6	73.3
Hanklets [20]	RGB	54.2	45.2
DV-Views[23]	RGB	50.7	58.5
LRCN [6]	RGB	–	64.7
nCTE [11]	RGB	–	68.6
Proposed-scratch	RGB	35.1	43.4
Proposed	RGB	**87.5**	**83.1**

4.2 Action Recognition

Based on the above analysis, we select configuration M-1 for rest of our action recognition experiments. For cross-subject experiments, we use two random views as input and render a video from third unseen view. In case of cross-view setup, there are two views (view 2 and 3) available for training. We randomly pick one view as input and the other for rendering. During test time, multiple clips are sampled from the test video for action recognition covering the full length of video. The details of these configurations are shown in Fig. 4. The cross-view and cross-subject classification scores on NTU-RGB+D dataset for RGB modality are shown in Table 2. We also evaluate the performance of proposed method on depth modality and the evaluation is shown in Table 3. We observe that it performs well on both RGB and depth modality which demonstrates its effectiveness to generalize well across different modalities.

Comparison with State-of-the-Art. We compare the performance of our proposed method with the recent works on RGB based view-invariant action recognition (Table 2 and Table 3). Our model performs well in both CS and

Table 5. Comparison of classification accuracy to study the effect of cross-view video prediction on NTU-RGB+D dataset. For CS evaluation all the three available views were used for testing whereas for CV evaluation only view 1 was used for testing

Method	Accuracy	
	CS	CV
Baseline	51.4	54.6
Proposed (without prediction)	63.0	65.2
Proposed (seen-view prediction)	71.4	78.1
Proposed (cross-view prediction)	**88.9**	**86.3**

CV evaluation for both RGB and depth modality. We observe that the proposed method provides significant improvement in CV evaluation for both RGB ($\sim$11%) and depth ($\sim$15%) modality which demonstrates that the learned representation is robust to viewpoint change. Moreover, the performance of our method is comparable to the state-of-the-art approaches employing skeleton modalities.

Model Parameters. The proposed network use a simple 3D CNN with 7 convolution layers for video encoding. Also, the full network has only around 72M parameters. This is relatively smaller network when compared with existing approaches, such as [22] (ResNet) and [43] (TSN), which utilize a deeper backbone for video encoding.

4.3   Transfer Learning for Action Recognition

We use the representation learned on NTU-RGB+D dataset for N-UCLA dataset which has a different set of scenes and users. We perform both CV as well as CS evaluation as suggested in [44] with two different variations. In the first variation, we train the network from scratch and the other one uses transfer learning from NTU-RGB+D dataset. The evaluation of the proposed method on N-UCLA dataset is shown in Table 4. We observe that the network performs poorly when trained from scratch which is due to the small size of this dataset. However, using the learned representations from NTU-RGB+D significantly increases the performance. Our method outperforms previous RGB based approaches [22,27]. This demonstrates the generalization capability of the learned representations across domains.

4.4   Ablations and Discussion

In our previous experiments, we observe that predicting an unseen views helps in learning a better representation for action recognition. We perform some more ablations to study the effect of prediction and effectiveness of BL-NET.

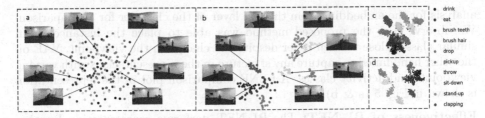

Fig. 5. A comparison of t-SNE visualization of representations learned with: a) Variational Autoencoder (VAE) and b) proposed RL-NET for a subset of 10 activities on NTU-RGB+D dataset. The shown images are the first frame of the video clips. We observe that VAE is indifferent to view awareness of activities and mostly clusters videos with similar visual content. On the other hand, the proposed method is able to cluster activities from different views close to each other even if they have different viewpoints. Effect of multi-view learning: t-SNE visualization of activity representations for a subset of 10 activities on full NTU-RGB+D dataset using: c) *one* input view and d) all *three* views. The learned representation improves with the availability of multiple views using the same network

Table 6. Ablation experiments to study the effect of multiple views during evaluation of CS split in NTU-RGB+D dataset for both RGB and depth modality

Approach	Accuracy	
	RGB	Depth
Single view	82.3	71.8
All views	**88.9**	**79.4**

Effect of Rendering: To study the effect of video prediction on the performance of action recognition, we train a network which uses RL-NET for representation learning along with classification without any video prediction. In another variation, we train the proposed network with seen-view prediction. Here, similar setting as before is used except that a random view from input is also selected for prediction. We compare these two baselines to the proposed network with cross-view prediction (M-1). We also use a baseline where the network was trained using a single clip with classification loss. In this experiment, we use the full video length during inference and all available views for CS evaluation. The comparison is shown in Table 5 and we can observe that cross-view prediction provides a significant improvement in the classification scores for both cross-view and cross-subject evaluation.

View-Invariant Representation: We compare the representation learned by the proposed RL-NET with autoencoding density models such as Variational Autoencoder (VAE) [16]. The VAE was implemented by replacing the RL-NET model with a CNN network (similar to ENC-NET) and keeping the rest of the network similar to ours. The network was then trained for reconstruction of the input video clip along with action classification. We study the 2D t-SNE [29] analysis for the embedding from the last layer of the classifier for a comparison. We observe that the proposed method was able to place the instances from similar classes close to each other despite the change in the viewpoint. VAE on the other hand failed to capture any structure in the representations with varying viewpoints and activity classes. A t-SNE comparison plot of the representation is shown in Fig. 5 (a & b).

Effectiveness of BL-NET: The RL-NET performs representation learning based on a set of input observations. These observations can be from different viewpoints and time in a video. The visual appearance of any action changes with viewpoint as well as time. This analogy between time and viewpoint for variation in visual appearance of any action allows us to use the two concepts interchangeably during representation learning. This idea makes the proposed architecture even more powerful as a network trained with some number of views and clips can be tested on different configuration.

Variation in Number of Input Views: We perform an ablation study to validate the robustness of BL-NET to varying number of views during inference. We observe that the performance increases as more number of views are available for representation learning. A comparison is shown in Table 6 for both RGB and depth modality. This is intuitive as different views provide varying perspective which helps in recognizing the action better. We explored this further with t-SNE visualization of the representations and observe that the action samples are well separated when the representation is learned using multiple views. A comparison is shown in Fig. 5 (c & d). The embeddings for activity classes which are confusing (e.g. brush teeth and brush hair) are slightly overlapping with single views (Fig. 5c) and are separated with multi-view embedding (Fig. 5d).

Variation in Number of Input Clips: The network can also use varying number of input clips to learn a representation. Different action sequences may have varying length and this ability allows the network to see the full action sequence regardless of the video length. During testing we analyzed the effect of number of input clips on the learned representation by introducing more clips than what the network trained for and observed that increasing the input clips leads to a better performance. The action recognition performance increased from 74.6 to 82.3 for CS evaluation on NTU-RGB+D when we increase the number of clips from 6 to full video length. This also validates the robustness of BL-NET for varying length action sequences. The proposed network can also generalize well to testing with single view videos irrespective of how it was trained. For example, the CS network for NTU-RGB+D is trained using 2 input views, but it still performs well in action recognition using only single view clips.

5   Conclusion

In this work, we propose a novel unsupervised deep learning framework for action recognition in a multi-view environment. The proposed framework can be trained end-to-end without the need of any pre-trained weights. We demonstrate the effectiveness of the proposed approach for the task of cross-view as well as cross-subject action recognition on multiple datasets. The proposed approach is effective with RGB videos and we also validate the generalization capability of the proposed framework for depth modality. The framework is adaptive for number of input views which makes it suitable for multi-view as well as novel-view action recognition. The generalization capability and its adaptive nature makes it useful for other problem domains in a multi-view environment.

Acknowledgement. This research is based upon work supported by the Office of the Director of National Intelligence (ODNI), Intelligence Advanced Research Projects Activity (IARPA), via IARPA R&D Contract No. D17PC00345. The views and conclusions contained herein are those of the authors and should not be interpreted as necessarily representing the official policies or endorsements, either expressed or implied, of the ODNI, IARPA, or the U.S. Government. The U.S. Government is authorized to reproduce and distribute reprints for Governmental purposes notwithstanding any copyright annotation thereon.

References

1. Baradel, F., Wolf, C., Mille, J.: Human action recognition: pose-based attention draws focus to hands. In: The IEEE ICCV Workshops, October 2017
2. Ben Tanfous, A., Drira, H., Ben Amor, B.: Coding Kendall's shape trajectories for 3D action recognition. In: Proceedings of the IEEE Conference on Computer Vision and Pattern Recognition, pp. 2840–2849 (2018)
3. Byeon, W., et al.: ContextVP: fully context-aware video prediction. In: Proceedings of the IEEE CVPR Workshops (2018)
4. Carreira, J., Zisserman, A.: Quo vadis, action recognition? a new model and the kinetics dataset. In: CVPR (2017)
5. Clark, A., Donahue, J., Simonyan, K.: Efficient video generation on complex datasets. arXiv preprint arXiv:1907.06571 (2019)
6. Donahue, J., et al.: Long-term recurrent convolutional networks for visual recognition and description. In: IEEE Conference on CVPR (2015)
7. Du, Y., Wang, W., Wang, L.: Hierarchical recurrent neural network for skeleton based action recognition. In: Proceedings of the IEEE Conference on Computer Vision and Pattern Recognition, pp. 1110–1118 (2015)
8. Eslami, S.A., et al.: Neural scene representation and rendering. Science (2018)
9. Fernando, B., Bilen, H., Gavves, E., Gould, S.: Self-supervised video representation learning with odd-one-out networks. In: IEEE Conference on CVPR (2017)
10. Goyal, P., Hu, Z., Liang, X., Wang, C., Xing, E.P., Mellon, C.: Nonparametric variational auto-encoders for hierarchical representation learning. In: ICCV, pp. 5104–5112 (2017)
11. Gupta, A., Martinez, J., Little, J.J., Woodham, R.J.: 3D pose from motion for cross-view action recognition via non-linear circulant temporal encoding. In: Proceedings of the IEEE Conference on Computer Vision and Pattern Recognition, pp. 2601–2608 (2014)
12. Hochreiter, S., Schmidhuber, J.: LSTM can solve hard long time lag problems. In: NeurIPS (1997)

13. Isik, L., Tacchetti, A., Poggio, T.A.: A fast, invariant representation for human action in the visual system. J. Neurophysiol. **119**, 631–640 (2017)
14. Jayaraman, D., Gao, R., Grauman, K.: ShapeCodes: self-supervised feature learning by lifting views to viewgrids. In: Ferrari, V., Hebert, M., Sminchisescu, C., Weiss, Y. (eds.) ECCV 2018. LNCS, vol. 11220, pp. 126–144. Springer, Cham (2018). https://doi.org/10.1007/978-3-030-01270-0_8
15. Ke, Q., Bennamoun, M., An, S., Sohel, F., Boussaid, F.: A new representation of skeleton sequences for 3D action recognition. In: Proceedings of the IEEE Conference on Computer Vision and Pattern Recognition, pp. 3288–3297 (2017)
16. Kingma, D.P., Welling, M.: Auto-encoding variational bayes. arXiv preprint arXiv:1312.6114 (2013)
17. Lakhal, M.I., Lanz, O., Cavallaro, A.: View-LSTM: novel-view video synthesis through view decomposition. In: The IEEE International Conference on Computer Vision (ICCV), October 2019
18. Ledig, C., Theis, L., Huszár, F., Caballero, J., et al.: Photo-realistic single image super-resolution using a generative adversarial network. In: IEEE Conference on CVPR (2017)
19. Lee, H.Y., Huang, J.B., Singh, M., Yang, M.H.: Unsupervised representation learning by sorting sequences. In: International Conference on Computer Vision (ICCV) (2017)
20. Li, B., Camps, O.I., Sznaier, M.: Cross-view activity recognition using hankelets. In: IEEE CVPR (2012)
21. Li, C., Cui, Z., Zheng, W., Xu, C., Yang, J.: Spatio-temporal graph convolution for skeleton based action recognition. In: AAAI Conference on Artificial Intelligence (2018)
22. Li, J., Wong, Y., Zhao, Q., Kankanhalli, M.: Unsupervised learning of view-invariant action representations. In: Advances in Neural Information Processing Systems (2018)
23. Li, R., Zickler, T.: Discriminative virtual views for cross-view action recognition. In: IEEE CVPR (2012)
24. Liu, J., Shahroudy, A., Xu, D., Kot, A.C., Wang, G.: Skeleton-based action recognition using spatio-temporal LSTM network with trust gates. IEEE Trans. Pattern Anal. Mach. Intell. **40**(12), 3007–3021 (2017)
25. Liu, J., Shahroudy, A., Xu, D., Wang, G.: Spatio-temporal LSTM with trust gates for 3D human action recognition. In: Leibe, B., Matas, J., Sebe, N., Welling, M. (eds.) ECCV 2016. LNCS, vol. 9907, pp. 816–833. Springer, Cham (2016). https://doi.org/10.1007/978-3-319-46487-9_50
26. Liu, M., Liu, H., Chen, C.: Enhanced skeleton visualization for view invariant human action recognition. Pattern Recogn. **68**, 346–362 (2017)
27. Luo, Z., Peng, B., Huang, D.A., Alahi, A., Fei-Fei, L.: Unsupervised learning of long-term motion dynamics for videos. In: IEEE Conference on CVPR (2017)
28. Luvizon, D.C., Picard, D., Tabia, H.: 2D/3D pose estimation and action recognition using multitask deep learning. In: IEEE Conference on CVPR (2018)
29. Maaten, L.V.D., Hinton, G.: Visualizing data using t-SNE. J. Mach. Learn. Res. **9**, 2579–2605 (2008)
30. Mathieu, M., Couprie, C., LeCun, Y.: Deep multi-scale video prediction beyond mean square error. In: ICLR (2016)
31. Misra, I., Zitnick, C.L., Hebert, M.: Shuffle and learn: unsupervised learning using temporal order verification. In: Leibe, B., Matas, J., Sebe, N., Welling, M. (eds.) ECCV 2016. LNCS, vol. 9905, pp. 527–544. Springer, Cham (2016). https://doi.org/10.1007/978-3-319-46448-0_32

32. Ohn-Bar, E., Trivedi, M.: Joint angles similarities and HOG2 for action recognition. In: Proceedings of the IEEE Conference on Computer Vision and Pattern Recognition Workshops, pp. 465–470 (2013)
33. Oreifej, O., Liu, Z.: HON4D: histogram of oriented 4d normals for activity recognition from depth sequences. In: Proceedings of the IEEE Conference on Computer Vision and Pattern Recognition, pp. 716–723 (2013)
34. Rahmani, H., Mahmood, A., Huynh, D., Mian, A.: Histogram of oriented principal components for cross-view action recognition. IEEE Trans. PAMI (2016)
35. Rahmani, H., Mian, A.: Learning a non-linear knowledge transfer model for cross-view action recognition. In: Proceedings of the IEEE Conference on CVPR (2015)
36. Regmi, K., Borji, A.: Cross-view image synthesis using conditional GANs. In: IEEE Conference on CVPR (2018)
37. Saito, M., Matsumoto, E., Saito, S.: Temporal generative adversarial nets with singular value clipping. In: IEEE International Conference on Computer Vision (ICCV) (2017)
38. Shahroudy, A., Liu, J., Ng, T.T., Wang, G.: NTU RGB+D: a large scale dataset for 3D human activity analysis. In: Proceedings of the IEEE Conference on CVPR (2016)
39. Shahroudy, A., Ng, T.T., Gong, Y., Wang, G.: Deep multimodal feature analysis for action recognition in RGB+D videos. IEEE Trans. PAMI (2018)
40. Srivastava, N., Mansimov, E., Salakhudinov, R.: Unsupervised learning of video representations using LSTMs. In: International Conference on Machine Learning, pp. 843–852 (2015)
41. Tulyakov, S., Liu, M.Y., Yang, X., Kautz, J.: MoCoGAN: decomposing motion and content for video generation. arXiv preprint arXiv:1707.04993 (2017)
42. Vondrick, C., Pirsiavash, H., Torralba, A.: Generating videos with scene dynamics. In: NeurIPS (2016)
43. Wang, D., Ouyang, W., Li, W., Xu, D.: Dividing and aggregating network for multi-view action recognition. In: Ferrari, V., Hebert, M., Sminchisescu, C., Weiss, Y. (eds.) ECCV 2018. LNCS, vol. 11213, pp. 457–473. Springer, Cham (2018). https://doi.org/10.1007/978-3-030-01240-3_28
44. Wang, J., Nie, X., Xia, Y., Wu, Y., Zhu, S.C.: Cross-view action modeling, learning and recognition. In: IEEE Conference on CVPR (2014)
45. Wang, X., Gupta, A.: Unsupervised learning of visual representations using videos. In: IEEE ICCV (2015)
46. Wen, Y.H., Gao, L., Fu, H., et al.: Graph CNNs with motif and variable temporal block for skeleton-based action recognition. In: AAAI Conference on Artificial Intelligence (2019)
47. Xie, S., Girshick, R., Dollár, P., Tu, Z., He, K.: Aggregated residual transformations for deep neural networks. In: Proceedings of the IEEE Conference on Computer Vision and Pattern Recognition, pp. 1492–1500 (2017)
48. Xu, X., Chen, Y.C., Jia, J.: View independent generative adversarial network for novel view synthesis. In: The IEEE International Conference on Computer Vision (ICCV), October 2019
49. Yan, S., Xiong, Y., Lin, D.: Spatial temporal graph convolutional networks for skeleton-based action recognition. In: AAAI Conference on Artificial Intelligence (2018)
50. Yang, X., Tian, Y.: Super normal vector for activity recognition using depth sequences. In: Proceedings of the IEEE Conference on Computer Vision and Pattern Recognition, pp. 804–811 (2014)

51. Zhang, P., Lan, C., Xing, J., Zeng, W., Xue, J., Zheng, N.: View adaptive neural networks for high performance skeleton-based human action recognition. IEEE PAMI (2019)
52. Zhang, P., Xue, J., Lan, C., Zeng, W., Gao, Z., Zheng, N.: Adding Attentiveness to the Neurons in Recurrent Neural Networks. In: Ferrari, V., Hebert, M., Sminchisescu, C., Weiss, Y. (eds.) ECCV 2018. LNCS, vol. 11213, pp. 136–152. Springer, Cham (2018). https://doi.org/10.1007/978-3-030-01240-3_9

Learning Discriminative Feature with CRF for Unsupervised Video Object Segmentation

Mingmin Zhen[1]($\boxtimes$) (ID), Shiwei Li[2], Lei Zhou[1], Jiaxiang Shang[1], Haoan Feng[1], Tian Fang[2], and Long Quan[1]

[1] Hong Kong University of Science and Technology, Kowloon City, Hong Kong
{mzhen,lzhouai,jshang,hfengac,quan}@cse.ust.hk
[2] Everest Innovation Technology, Kowloon City, Hong Kong
{sli,fangtian}@altizure.com

Abstract. In this paper, we introduce a novel network, called discriminative feature network (DFNet), to address the unsupervised video object segmentation task. To capture the inherent correlation among video frames, we learn discriminative features (D-features) from the input images that reveal feature distribution from a global perspective. The D-features are then used to establish correspondence with all features of test image under conditional random field (CRF) formulation, which is leveraged to enforce consistency between pixels. The experiments verify that DFNet outperforms state-of-the-art methods by a large margin with a mean IoU score of 83.4% and ranks first on the DAVIS-2016 leaderboard while using much fewer parameters and achieving much more efficient performance in the inference phase. We further evaluate DFNet on the FBMS dataset and the video saliency dataset ViSal, reaching a new state-of-the-art. To further demonstrate the generalizability of our framework, DFNet is also applied to the image object co-segmentation task. We perform experiments on a challenging dataset PASCAL-VOC and observe the superiority of DFNet. The thorough experiments verify that DFNet is able to capture and mine the underlying relations of images and discover the common foreground objects.

Keywords: Video object segmentation · Discriminative feature · CRF

1 Introduction

The research on video object segmentation (VOS), which aims to separate primary foreground objects from their background in a given video, is often divided into two categories, *i.e.*, semi-supervised and unsupervised setting. The semi-supervised VOS (SVOS) provides a mask of the first frame, which can be taken as the prior knowledge about the target in subsequent frames. By comparison, unsupervised VOS (UVOS) is in general more challenging, as it requires a further step to distinguish the target object from a complex and diverse background without prior information. In this paper, we focus on the latter challenging issue.

© Springer Nature Switzerland AG 2020
A. Vedaldi et al. (Eds.): ECCV 2020, LNCS 12372, pp. 445–462, 2020.
https://doi.org/10.1007/978-3-030-58583-9_27

Recently, several works, such as COSNet [40], AGNN [61] and AnDiff [68], model the long-term correlations between frames to explore global information inspired by the non-local operation introduced by Wang et al. [66]. However, the limitations are obvious as the computation requirement is very high, especially for AGNN [61]. Besides, the local consistency cues are overlooked, which is essential for UVOS task.

Motivated by the above observations, we propose a discriminative feature learning network, which is denoted as DFNet, to model the long-term correlations between video frames. Specifically, DFNet takes several frames from the same video as input and learns the discriminative features, which can denote the whole feature distribution of the input frames. The feature map for each frame is correlated with these discriminative features under CRF formulation, which is used to boost the smoothness and consistency of similar pixels. The proposed approach is advantageous to mine the discriminative representation from a global perspective, while at the same time helps to capture the rich contextual information within video frames. DFNet is sufficiently flexible to process variable numbers of input frames during inference, enabling it to consider more input information and gain better performance.

To verify the proposed method, we extensively evaluate DFNet on two widely-used video object segmentation datasets, namely DAVIS16 [45] and FBMS [43], showing its superior performance over current state-of-the-art methods. More specifically, DFNet ranks first on the DAVIS-2016 leaderboard with a mean IoU score of 83.4%, which is 1.7% higher than state-of-the-art method [68]. DFNet also achieves state-of-the-art results on FBMS [43] and the ViSal [62] video saliency benchmark. To further demonstrate its advantages and generalizability, we apply DFNet to image object co-segmentation task, which aims to extract the common objects from a group of semantically related images. It also gains better results on the representative dataset PASCAL VOC [7] over previous methods.

2   Related Work

Unsupervised Video Object Segmentation. Recently, there are many works for UVOS task, which focus on the fully convolutional neural network based models. MPNet [52], a purely optical flow-based method, discards appearance modeling and casts segmentation as foreground motion prediction, which poorly deals with static foreground objects. To better address this problem, several methods [4,34,48,53] suggest adopting two-stream fully convolutional networks, which fuse the motion and appearance information for object inference. In [53], a convolutional gated recurrent unit is employed to extend the horizon spanned by optical flow based features. Li et al. [34] attempt to address this issue by employing a bilateral network for detecting the motion of background objects. RNN based methods are also a popular choice. Song et al. [49] propose a novel convolutional long short-term memory [11] architecture, in which two atrous convolution [3] layers are stacked along the forward axis and propagate features in opposite directions. COSNet [40] adopts a gated co-attention mechanism to model the correlation of input video images. In AGNN [61], a fully

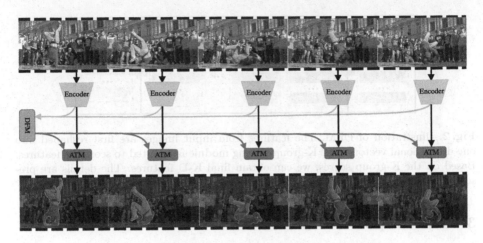

Fig. 1. Overall pipeline of the proposed method. The features are first obtained from the encoder module and goes through the discriminative feature module (DFM) to extract discriminative features. The discriminative features are then used by attention module (ATM) to recontruct a new feature map, which is used to correlate the input frames.

connected graph is built to represent frames as nodes, and relations between arbitrary frame pairs as edges. The underlying pair-wise relations are described by a differentiable attention mechanism. To exploit the correlations of images, AnDiff [68] proposes a considerably simpler method, which propagates the features of the first frame (the "anchor") to the current frame via an aggregation technique.

Image Object Co-segmentation. Different from UVOS, the image object co-segmentation task is to extract the common object with the same semantics from a group of semantic-related images. Recent researches [17,69] use deep visual features to improve object co-segmentation, and they also try to learn more robust synergetic properties among images in a data-driven manner. Hsu et al. [17] proposes a DNN-based method which uses the similarity between images in deep features and an additional object proposals algorithm [25] to segment the common objects. Yuan et al. [69] introduce a DNN-based dense conditional random field framework for object co-segmentation by cooperating co-occurrence maps, which are generated using selective search [55]. The very recent works [2, 35] propose end-to-end deep learning methods for co-segmentation by integrating the process of feature learning and co-segmentation inferring as an organic whole. By introducing the correlation layer [35] or a semantic attention learner [2], they can utilize the relationship between the image pair and then segment the co-object in a pairwise manner. In [30], a recurrent network architecture is proposed to address group-wise object co-segmentation.

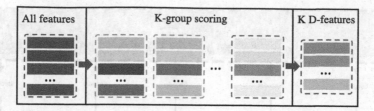

Fig. 2. Illustration of DFM. The features from input images are first reshaped into one-dimensional vectors. The K-group scoring module is adopted to score the features. Based on the K-group scores, we can obtain final K-D features. The details are presented in Sect. 3.2.

3 The Proposed Method

In this section, we present the proposed DFNet in detail, which is illustrated in Fig. 1. We first give an overview of the whole architecture in Sect. 3.1. Next, the discriminative feature module (DFM), which captures the global feature distribution of all input images, is elaborated in Sect. 3.2. Then we introduce the attention module (ATM) in Sect. 3.3, which reconstructs a new feature map modeling the long-term dependency.

3.1 Network Architecture

For the UVOS task, the target object in the given video images can be deformed and occluded, which often deteriorates the performance of estimated binary segmentation results. To recognize the target object, our method should be of two essential properties: (i) the ability to extract foreground objects from the individual frame; (ii) the ability to keep consistency among the video frames. To achieve these two goals, we correlate the features of each input image with discriminative features, which is extracted from input images selected from the same video randomly.

As shown in Fig. 1, we present the proposed network architecture in detail. The proposed network takes several images as input. The shared feature encoder, which adopts the fully convolutional DeepLabv3 [3], extracted the features from the input images. The obtained feature maps are then fed into a 1×1 convolutional layer to reduce the feature map channel to 256, and the output feature maps for all input images are taken as input for the discriminative feature module (DFM), which extract the discriminative features (D-features). The input feature for each image and the D-features go through an attention module (ATM) to reconstruct a new feature map and then one 3×3 convolutional layer followed by ReLU, batch normalization (BN) layer and one 1×1 convolutional layer followed by a *sigmoid* operation are used to obtain final binary output.

More formally, given a set of input frames $\mathcal{I} = \{I_i \in \mathbb{R}^{H \times W \times 3}\}_{i=1}^{\mathcal{N}}$, we want to segment out the binary masks $\mathcal{S} = \{S_i \in \{0,1\}^{H \times W}\}_{i=1}^{\mathcal{N}}$ for all frames. The features extracted from DeepLabv3 are denoted as $\mathcal{F} = \{F_i \in \mathbb{R}^{h \times w \times c}\}_i^{\mathcal{N}}$, where

$h \times w$ indicates the spatial resolution of feature map and c represents the feature map channels. Since we follow the original deepLabv3, which employs dilated convolution, the output feature map F_i is $\frac{1}{8}$ smaller than the input image I_i.

3.2   Discriminative Feature Module

We learn the discriminative features from the features of all input images. Specifically, all feature maps $\mathcal{F}$ from the input images are first concatenated to form a large feature map with size $\mathcal{N} \times h \times w \times c$ and then reshaped as $F^a \in \mathbb{R}^{\mathcal{N}hw \times c}$. As shown in Fig. 2, we then use a K-group scoring module to obtain K-group scores, which is used to distinguish the discriminative features from the noisy features. For each scoring group, a weight matrix $\mathcal{W}_k \in \mathcal{R}^{c \times 1}$ and F^a is multiplied to get a initial score result with size $\mathcal{N}hw \times 1$. We apply a softmax function to calculate the final scores:

$$s_i^k = \frac{exp(F_i^a . W_k)}{\sum_i^{\mathcal{N}hw} exp(F_i^a . W_k)} \tag{1}$$

where s_i^k is the score for i^{th} feature of F^a and measures the discriminability of the feature. The final discriminative feature for k^{th} scoring group is computed as $F_k^d = \sum s_i^k F_i^a$. By this way, we can obtain K discriminative features $F^d \in \mathbb{R}^{K \times c}$.

The K D-features are used to describe the feature distribution from a global perspective. The key of the D-features computation is the scoring weight $\mathcal{W}_k$. In our training step, we initialize the $\mathcal{W}_k$ by using Kaiming's initialization method [15]. For each updating iteration, we adopt the moving averaging mechanism, which is used in batch normalization (BN) [18]. After obtaining the D-feature $F_k^d(t)$ at training step t, we update the $\mathcal{W}_k$ as:

$$\mathcal{W}_k(t) = \lambda \mathcal{W}_k(t-1) + (1-\lambda)F_k^d(t) \tag{2}$$

where λ is the momentum. In our experiments, we set it to 0.5. As we train our network on a multiple-GPU machine, we also adopt the synchronized weight updating strategy motivated by synchronized BN [47]. Specifically, the images from the same video sequence are fed into the network on one GPU. Thus, we will get different D-features $F_k^d(t)$ at step t for different GPUs. For the synchronized processing, we sum up these D-features $F_k^d(t)$ across GPUs and compute the average feature $\overline{F}_k^d(t)$, which will be used in Eq. 2. The updated $\mathcal{W}_k$ is synchronized on all GPUs. The whole computation is differentiable and trainable. In the inference step, the weight $\mathcal{W}_k$ is kept fixed, which is similar to BN operation.

3.3   Attention Module with CRF

To model the long-term dependency, we adopt the attention module to correlate input image and the discriminative features. For the obtained K D-features $F^d \in \mathbb{R}^{K \times c}$ and the feature map $F_i \in \mathbb{R}^{h \times w \times c}$ of input image, we follow [40,61] to compute the attention matrix $P \in \mathbb{R}^{hw \times K}$ as shown in Fig. 3 (a). Specifically, we obtain P from F^d and F_i as follows:

$$P = reshape(F_i)W_{att}transpose(F^d) \tag{3}$$

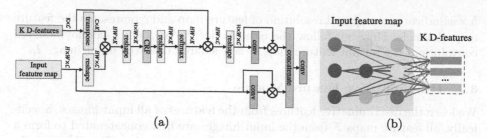

Fig. 3. (a) Illustration of ATM. The input feature map and K D-features are correlated to model long-term dependency; (b) Illustration of attention mechanism. The details are presented in Sect. 3.3.

where $W_{att} \in \mathbb{R}^{c \times c}$ is a learnable weight matrix. The D-feature matrix F^d are tranposed with size $c \times K$ and feature map F_i is reshaped with size $hw \times c$. For the obtained attetnion matrix P, each element indicates the similarity of the corresponding feature of F_i and feature of F^d. As shown in Fig. 3 (b), the lines with different colors represent the similarity between input features and K D-features. In previous attention methods [40,61,68], a new feature map is reconstructed based on the attention matrix by assigning K D-features to input feature map as follows:

$$F^{new} = reshape(softmax(P)F^d) \tag{4}$$

where the new feature map F^{new} is of size $h \times w \times c$.

The attention map computation can also be considered as multi-label classification problem and the assignment of D-features corresponds to a different label. Our intuition is that neighboring pixels in the same local region tend to have similar labels (K D-features), and pixels near borders or edges may have significantly different labels. We regard the reshaped attention map with size $h \times w \times K$ as fully connected pairwise conditional random fields conditioned on the corresponding image I, in which each pixel is to be assigned with a D-feature for reconstructing the new feature map.

Let $\mathbf{x} = \{x_1, x_2, ..., x_M\}$ be the label vector of M pixels in the reshaped attention map. Component x_i belongs to $\{1, 2, ..., K\}$ where K is the number of labels (D-features). The probability of the label assignment is defined in the form of Gibbs distribution as $P(\mathbf{x}|\mathbf{I}) = \frac{1}{Z} exp(-E(\mathbf{x}|\mathbf{I}))$, where $E(x)$ is the energy function which describes the cost of label assigning and Z is a normalization factor. For convenience we drop the notation of condition $\mathbf{I}$ in the followings. Following the formulation of [24], the energy function is defined as

$$E(\mathbf{x}) = \sum_{i=1}^{M} \psi_u(x_i) + \sum_{i<j} \psi_p(x_i, x_j) \tag{5}$$

where the unary energy components $\psi_u(x_i)$ measure the cost of the pixel i taking the label x_i, and pairwise energy components $\psi(x_i, x_j)$ measure the cost of assigning labels x_i, x_j to pixels i, j simultaneously. In our formulation, unary energies are set to be reshaped attention map P, which predicts labels for pixels without considering the smoothness and the consistency of the label assignments. The pairwise energies provide an image data-dependent smoothing term that encourages assigning similar labels to pixels with similar properties.

The CRF model can be implemented in neural networks as shown in [51,72], thus it can be naturally integrated in our network, and optimized in the end-to-end training process. After the CRF module, we can obtain a refined attention map which takes the smoothness and consistency into consideration. We follow Eq. 4 to reconstruct a new feature map.

We also adopt a self-weight method to weight the new feature map F^{new} and input feature map F_i. The self-weight is formulated as follows:

$$F^{new} = F^{new} * conv(F^{new}), F_i = F_i * conv(F_i) \tag{6}$$

where we use 1×1 convolutional layer to get the weight, which indicates the importance of features in the feature map. At last, we concatenate the feature map F^{new} and F_i and feed the obtained feature map into the convolutional layers to get binary segmentation results.

4   Experiments

We first report performance on the unsupervised video object segmentation task in Sect. 4.1. Then, in Sect. 4.2, to further demonstrate the advantages of the proposed model, we test it on image object co-segmentation task. At last, we conduct an ablation study in Sect. 4.3 and model analysis in Sect. 4.4.

4.1   Unsuperviesed Video Object Segmentation Task

Dataset and Evaluation Metric. To evaluate UVOS task, a golden dataset **DAVIS16** is often used [40,49,54,61,65]. DAVIS16 is a recent dataset which consists of 50 videos in total (30 videos for training and 20 for testing). Per-frame pixel-wise annotations are offered. For quantitative evaluation, following the standard evaluation protocol from [45], we adopt three metrics, namely region similarity $\mathcal{J}$, which is the intersection-over-union of the prediction and ground truth, boundary accuracy $\mathcal{F}$, which is the F-measure defined on contour points in the prediction and ground truth, and time stability $\mathcal{T}$, which measures the smoothness of evolution of objects across video sequences. **FBMS** [43] is comprised of 59 video sequences. Different from the DAVIS16 dataset, the ground-truth of FBMS is sparsely labeled (only 720 frames are annotated). Following the common setting [48,49,68], we validate the proposed method on the testing split, which consists of 30 sequences. On the FBMS dataset, the F-measure is used as evaluation metric. We also follow [49,68] to report saliency evaluations of our method on DAVIS, FBMS and a video salient object detection dataset ViSal [62] for demonstrating the robustness and wide applicability

Table 1. Quantitative results on the test set of DAVIS16, using the region similarity $\mathcal{J}$, boundary accuracy $\mathcal{F}$ and time stability $\mathcal{T}$. For FBMS dataset, we report the F-measusre results. The best scores are marked in bold.

Method	Year	DAVIS			FBMS
		$\mathcal{J}$ Mean↑	$\mathcal{F}$ Mean↑	$\mathcal{T}$ Mean↓	F-measure
TRC [10]	CVPR12	47.3	44.1	39.1	–
CVOS [50]	CVPR15	48.2	44.7	25.0	–
KEY [29]	ICCV11	49.8	42.7	26.9	–
MSG [42]	ICCV11	53.3	50.8	30.2	–
NLC [8]	BMVC14	55.1	52.3	42.5	–
CUT [22]	ICCV15	55.2	55.2	27.7	–
FST [44]	ICCV13	55.8	51.1	36.6	69.2
ELM [26]	ECCV18	61.8	61.2	25.1	–
TIS [12]	WACV19	62.6	59.6	33.6	–
SFL [4]	ICCV17	67.4	66.7	28.2	–
LMP [52]	CVPR17	70.0	65.9	57.2	77.5
FSEG [19]	CVPR17	70.7	65.3	32.8	–
UOVOS [73]	TIP19	73.9	68.0	39.0	–
LVO [53]	ICCV17	75.9	72.1	26.5	77.8
ARP [23]	CVPR17	76.2	70.6	39.3	–
PDB [49]	ECCV18	77.2	74.5	29.1	81.5
LSMO [54]	IJCV19	78.2	75.9	21.2	–
MotAdapt [48]	ICRA19	77.2	77.4	27.9	79.0
EpO+ [6]	WACV20	80.6	75.5	19.3	–
AGS [65]	CVPR19	79.7	77.4	26.7	–
COSNet [40]	CVPR19	80.5	79.5	18.4	–
AGNN [61]	ICCV19	80.7	79.1	33.7	–
AnDiff [68]	ICCV19	81.7	80.5	21.4	81.2
Ours	ECCV20	**83.4**	**81.8**	**15.9**	**82.3**

of our method. The **ViSal** [62] dataset is a video salient object detection benchmark. The length of videos in ViSal ranges from 30 to 100 frames, and totally 193 frames are manually annotated. The whole ViSal dataset is used for evaluation. We report the mean absolute error (MAE) and the F-measure on the three datasets.

Implementation Details. In the **training** step, following [40,49,61], we use both static data from image salient object segmentation datasets, MSRA10K [5], DUT [67], and video data from the training set of DAVIS16 to train our model. The training process is divided into two steps. First, we use the static

Table 2. Quantitative comparison results against saliency methods using MAE and maximum F-measure on DAVIS16 [45], FBMS [43] and ViSal [62]. The best scores are marked in bold. * means non-deep learning model.

	Methods	Year	DAVIS16		FBMS		ViSal	
			MAE↓	F↑	MAE↓	F↑	MAE↓	F↑
Image	Amulet [70]	ICCV17	0.082	69.9	0.110	72.5	0.032	89.4
	SRM [59]	ICCV17	0.039	77.9	0.071	77.6	0.028	89.0
	UCF [71]	ICCV17	0.107	71.6	0.147	67.9	0.068	87.0
	DSS [16]	CVPR17	0.062	71.7	0.083	76.4	0.028	90.6
	MSR [31]	CVPR17	0.057	74.6	0.064	78.7	0.031	90.1
	NLDF [41]	CVPR17	0.056	72.3	0.092	73.6	0.023	91.6
	DCL [33]	CVPR16	0.070	63.1	0.089	72.6	0.035	86.9
	DHS [37]	CVPR16	0.039	75.8	0.083	74.3	0.025	91.1
	ELD [28]	CVPR16	0.070	68.8	0.103	71.9	0.038	89.0
	KSR [60]	ECCV16	0.077	60.1	0.101	64.9	0.063	82.6
	RFCN [58]	ECCV16	0.065	71.0	0.105	73.6	0.043	88.8
Video	FGRNE [32]	CVPR18	0.043	78.6	0.083	77.9	0.040	85.0
	FCNS [63]	TIP18	0.053	72.9	0.100	73.5	0.041	87.7
	SGSP* [38]	TCSVT17	0.128	67.7	0.171	57.1	0.172	64.8
	GAFL* [62]	TIP15	0.091	57.8	0.150	55.1	0.099	72.6
	SAGE* [64]	CVPR15	0.105	47.9	0142	58.1	0.096	73.4
	STUW* [9]	TIP14	0.098	69.2	0.143	52.8	0.132	67.1
	SP* [39]	TCSVT14	0.130	60.1	0.161	53.8	0.126	73.1
	PDB [49]	ECCV18	0.030	84.9	0.069	81.5	0.022	91.7
	AnDiff [68]	ICCV19	0.044	80.8	0.064	81.2	0.030	90.4
	Ours	ECCV20	**0.018**	**89.9**	**0.054**	**83.3**	**0.017**	**92.7**

training data to train our backbone encoder (DeepLabV3) to extract more discriminative foreground features. The learning rate is set to 0.01 and the batch size is 12. Then we use the DAVIS16 training data to train the whole model with learning rate of 0.001. The batch size is set to 8. For each video sequence, we follow [68] to select the first frame as an anchor and randomly sample one image as the training example. The model is trained with binary cross-entropy loss. Network parameters are optimized via stochastic gradient descent with weight decay 0.0001. We adopt the "poly" learning rate policy where the initial learning rate is multiplied by $(1 - \frac{iter}{max\_iter})^{power}$ with $power = 0.9$. Raw predictions are upsampled via bilinear interpolation to the size of the ground-truth masks. In the **inference** step, multiscale and mirrored inputs are employed to enhance the final performance. The final heatmap is the mean of all output heatmaps. Thresholding at 0.5 produces the final binary labels. We also follow [68] to adopt instance pruning as a post-processing method.

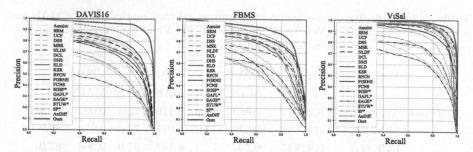

Fig. 4. Quantitative comparison against other methods using PR curve on DAVIS16 [45], FBMS [43] and ViSal [62] datasets.

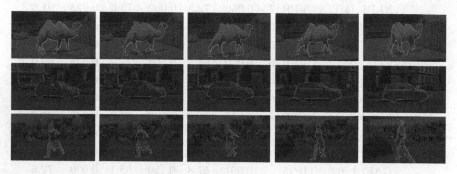

Fig. 5. The visual results generated by our approach on the DAVIS16 dataset. From the first row to the last row, the corresponding video names are *camel*, *car-roundabout* and *dance-twirl* respectively.

Experimental Results. In Table 1, we evaluate DFNet against state-of-the-art unsupervised VOS methods on the DAVIS16 public leaderboard. DFNet attains the highest performance among all unsupervised methods on the DAVIS16 validation set, while also achieving a new state-of-the-art on the FBMS test set. In particular, on DAVIS16 we outperform the second-best method (AnDiff [68]) by an absolute margin of 21.7% in the region similarity $\mathcal{J}$ and 1.3% in the boundary accuracy $\mathcal{F}$. For the temporal stability $\mathcal{T}$, our method shows a more stable result over the video sequences by a large margin of 2.5 than the second-best method COSNet [40]. We also outperform state-of-the-art method AnDiff [68] by 1.1% in F-measure on the FBMS dataset.

We also report the results on salient object detection for DAVIS16, FBMS and ViSal datasets as shown in Table 2. It can be observed that the proposed method improves state-of-the-art for all the three datasets for standard saliency scores, showing consistency with Table 1. The largest improvements lie in DAVIS16, where both MAE and F-measure significantly outperform previous records. Especially for the F-measure, we outperform the second-best result by a significant margin of 9.1%. The precision-recall analysis of DFNet is presented in Fig. 4, where we demonstrate that our approach generally outperforms also existing

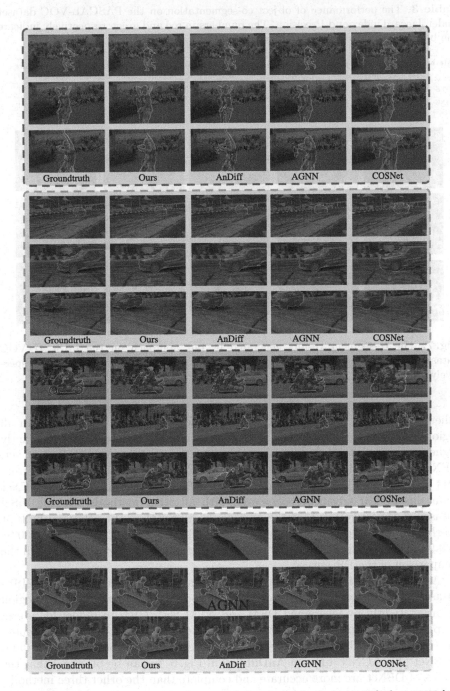

Fig. 6. Qualitative comparison with state-of-the-art methods (AnDiff [68], AGNN [61] and COSNet [40]) on DAVIS16 dataset.

Table 3. The performance of object co-segmentation on the PASCAL-VOC dataset under Jaccard index and Precision. The numbers in red and green respectively indicate the best and the second best results.

Method	Faktor13 [7]	Lee15 [27]	Chang15 [1]	Hati16 [14]	Quan16 [46]	Jerri.16 [21]	Wang17 [57]	Jerri.17 [20]	Han18 [13]	Hsu18 [17]	Li19 [30]	Ours
Avg. $\mathcal{P}$	84.0	69.8	82.4	72.5	89.0	85.2	84.3	80.1	90.1	91.0	94.1	95.2
Avg. $\mathcal{J}$	0.46	0.33	0.29	0.25	0.52	0.45	0.52	0.40	0.53	0.60	0.63	0.69

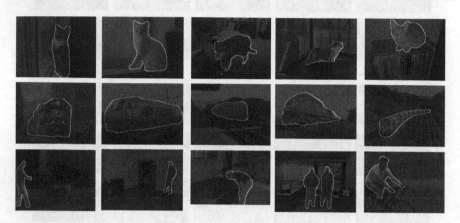

Fig. 7. The co-segment results generated by our approach on the PASCAL-VOC dataset. From the first row to the last row, the classes are *cat*, *train* and *person* respectively.

salient object detection methods. DFNet achieves superior performance in all regions of the PR curve on the DAVIS validation set, maintaining significantly higher precision at all recall thresholds. On the challenging FBMS test set, DFNet shows inferior precision results than SP [39]at the recall threshold from 0.93 to 0.97 and FGRNE [32] from 0.94 to 0.95. But overall speaking, DFNet maintains a clear advantage compared with all other methods. On the ViSal dataset, it is noteworthy that the precision is higher than the other methods at nearly all recall thresholds, except for the AnDiff [68] at the threshold from 0.98 to 0.99. All in all, the superiority of the proposed method is verified through the comparison of the PR curves.

As shown in Fig. 5, we visualize some qualitative results of the DAVIS16 dataset. We can see that the proposed method can locate the primary region or target tightly by leveraging DFM and ATM with CRF to model long-term denpendency. The primary objects from the cluttered background are segmented out correctly. We also present the visual comparison results between DFNet and COSNet [40], AGNN [61] and AnDiff [68] in Fig. 6. In can be observed that the results of DFNet are more accurate and complete than the other three methods.

Table 4. Ablation study on DAVIS16 with different components used and different numbers of D-features adopted. We also compare the performance for different numbers of input images on DAVIS16 and PASCAL VOC.

Method	Baseline	+DFM&ATM	+ATM&CRF	+multiple scales	+I.Prun.
$\mathcal{J}$ mean (%)	76.7	79.5	80.4	81.1	83.4
D-features					
K	128	256	512	1024	2048
$\mathcal{J}$ mean (%)	78.3	79.0	79.4	79.7	80.4
Input images (DAVIS16)					
N^{in}	1	2	4	8	10
$\mathcal{J}$ mean (%)	79.4	80.1	80.4	80.4	80.4
Input images (PASCAL VOC)					
N^{in}	1	2	4	8	10
$Avg.\mathcal{J}$ (%)	61.4	63.5	65.0	65.4	65.4

4.2 Image Object Co-Segmentation Task

Dataset and Evaluation Metric. The PASCAL-VOC [7] is a well-known dataset often used in image object co-segmentation task, which contains total 1,037 images of 20 object classes from PASCAL-VOC 2010 dataset. The PASCAL-VOC dataset is challenging and difficult due to extremely large intra-class variations and subtle figure-ground discrimination. Following previous works [1,7,21,27,30], two widely used measures, precision ($\mathcal{P}$) and Jaccard index ($\mathcal{J}$), are adapted to evaluate the performance of object co-segmentation.

Implementation Details. We follow [30,56] to train the proposed network with generated training data from the existing MS COCO dataset [36]. The learning rate is set to 0.01 and batch size is 12. For each group images, we randomly select three images as one training example. Other training setups are the same as those in previous unsupervised VOS task. After training, we evaluate the performance of our method on the PASCAL VOC dataset. When processing an image, we leverage another 4 images belonging to the same group to form a subgroup as inputs. We adopt a threshold 0.5 to generate final binary masks.

Experimental Results. We compare our methods with state-of-the-art methods on the PASCAL VOC dataset. As shown in Table 3, although the objects of the PASCAL VOC dataset undergo drastic variation in scale, position and appearance, our method improves upon the second-best results [30] by margins 1.1% and 6% in terms of $\mathcal{P}$ and $\mathcal{J}$ respectively. We also present some co-segmentation results of the proposed method in Fig. 7. It can be seen that our method can generate promising object segments under different types of intra-class variations, such as colors, sharps, views, scales and background clutters.

Table 5. The number of model parameters and inference time comparison with state-of-the-art methods.

Method	COSNet [40]	AGNN [61]	AnDiff [68]	Ours
# Parmeter (M)	81.2	82.3	79.3	**64.7**
Inf. Time (s/image)	0.45	0.53	0.35	**0.28**

4.3   Ablation Study

To verify the effectiveness of the proposed method, we conduct ablation experiments on DAVIS16 and PASCAL VOC. As shown in Table 4, the detailed results are reported for different experimental setup. We adopt the DeepLabv3 as the baseline, which is trained on the static image dataset, and achieve 76.7% in terms of $\mathcal{J}$. After adding the proposed DFM and ATM into the network, the performance increase to 79.5%, which validates the usefulness of modeling the long-term dependency. We then adopt CRF to optimize the attention map by considering the smoothness and consistency, which improves the performance by 0.9%. Multiple-scale inference and instance pruning (I.Prun.) are also used by following [68]. At last, we obtain the highest score of 83.4% in terms of the region similarity $\mathcal{J}$, which outperforms state-of-the-art methods. By adopting different numbers of D-features, we can see that better results can be obtained with more discriminative features used. We also evaluate the impact of the number of input images during inference, and we report performance with different values of N^{in} on DAVIS16 and PASCAL VOC datasets. For DAVIS16, we can see the performance increases by adding more input frames from 1 to 4 and then keep stable. It can be observed that with more input images, especially from 1 to 8, the performance raises accordingly on PASCAL VOC. When more images are considered, the performance does not change obviously.

4.4   Model Analysis

In Table 5, we report the comparison with state-of-the-art methods on the number of network parameters and inference time on DAVIS16. We can observe that DFNet reduces the model complexity with fewer parameters compared with COSNet [40], AGNN [61] and AnDiff [68]. For the inference comparison, we run the public code of other methods and our code on the same machine with NVIDIA GeForce GTX 1080 Ti. The inference time includes the image loading and pre-processing time. In can be seen that our method shows a faster speed than these methods.

5   Conclusion

To model the long-term dependency of video images, we propose a novel DFNet to capture the relations among video frames and infer the common foreground objects in this paper. It extracts the discriminative features from the input images, which can describe the feature distribution from a global view. An attention module is then adopted to mine the correlations between the input images. The smoothness and consistency of the attention map are also considered, in which the attention mechanism is formulated as a classification problem and solved by CRF. The extensive experiments validate the effectiveness of the proposed method. In addition, we also apply the method to image object co-segmentation task. The quantitative evaluation of the challenging dataset PASCAL VOC demonstrates the advantage of DFNet.

Acknowledgments. This work is supported by Hong Kong RGC GRF 16206819, Hong Kong RGC GRF 16203518 and Hong Kong T22-603/15N.

References

1. Chang, H., Wang, Y.F.: Optimizing the decomposition for multiple foreground cosegmentation. Comput. Vis. Image Underst. **141**, 18–27 (2015)
2. Chen, H., Huang, Y., Nakayama, H.: Semantic aware attention based deep object co-segmentation. In: Jawahar, C.V., Li, H., Mori, G., Schindler, K. (eds.) ACCV 2018. LNCS, vol. 11364, pp. 435–450. Springer, Cham (2019). https://doi.org/10.1007/978-3-030-20870-7_27
3. Chen, L.C., Papandreou, G., Schroff, F., Adam, H.: Rethinking atrous convolution for semantic image segmentation. arXiv preprint arXiv:1706.05587 (2017)
4. Cheng, J., Tsai, Y.H., Wang, S., Yang, M.H.: Segflow: joint learning for video object segmentation and optical flow. In: ICCV (2017)
5. Cheng, M.M., Mitra, N.J., Huang, X., Torr, P.H., Hu, S.M.: Global contrast based salient region detection. IEEE Trans. Pattern Anal. Mach. Intell. **37**, 569–582 (2014)
6. Faisal, M., Akhter, I., Ali, M., Hartley, R.: Exploiting geometric constraints on dense trajectories for motion saliency (2019)
7. Faktor, A., Irani, M.: Co-segmentation by composition. In: ICCV (2013)
8. Faktor, A., Irani, M.: Video segmentation by non-local consensus voting. In: BMVC (2014)
9. Fang, Y., Wang, Z., Lin, W., Fang, Z.: Video saliency incorporating spatiotemporal cues and uncertainty weighting. IEEE Trans. Image Process. **23**, 3910–3921 (2014)
10. Fragkiadaki, K., Zhang, G., Shi, J.: Video segmentation by tracing discontinuities in a trajectory embedding. In: CVPR (2012)
11. Gers, F.A., Schmidhuber, J., Cummins, F.: Learning to forget: continual prediction with LSTM. In: ICANN (2000)
12. Griffin, B.A., Corso, J.J.: Tukey-inspired video object segmentation. In: IEEE Winter Conference on Applications of Computer Vision (WACV) (2019)
13. Han, J., Quan, R., Zhang, D., Nie, F.: Robust object co-segmentation using background prior. IEEE Trans. Image Process. **27**, 1639–1651 (2018)
14. Hati, A., Chaudhuri, S., Velmurugan, R.: Image co-segmentation using maximum common subgraph matching and region co-growing. In: Leibe, B., Matas, J., Sebe, N., Welling, M. (eds.) ECCV 2016. LNCS, vol. 9910, pp. 736–752. Springer, Cham (2016). https://doi.org/10.1007/978-3-319-46466-4_44
15. He, K., Zhang, X., Ren, S., Sun, J.: Delving deep into rectifiers: surpassing human-level performance on imagenet classification. In: ICCV (2015)

16. Hou, Q., Cheng, M., Hu, X., Borji, A., Tu, Z., Torr, P.H.S.: Deeply supervised salient object detection with short connections. IEEE Trans. Pattern Anal. Mach. Intell. **41**, 815–828 (2019)
17. Hsu, K., Lin, Y., Chuang, Y.: Co-attention CNNs for unsupervised object co-segmentation. In: IJCAI (2018)
18. Ioffe, S., Szegedy, C.: Batch normalization: accelerating deep network training by reducing internal covariate shift. In: ICML (2015)
19. Jain, S.D., Xiong, B., Grauman, K.: Fusionseg: learning to combine motion and appearance for fully automatic segmentation of generic objects in videos. In: CVPR (2017)
20. Jerripothula, K.R., Cai, J., Lu, J., Yuan, J.: Object co-skeletonization with co-segmentation. In: CVPR (2017)
21. Jerripothula, K.R., Cai, J., Yuan, J.: Image co-segmentation via saliency co-fusion. IEEE Trans. Multimedia **18**, 1896–1909 (2016)
22. Keuper, M., Andres, B., Brox, T.: Motion trajectory segmentation via minimum cost multicuts. In: ICCV (2015)
23. Koh, Y.J., Kim, C.S.: Primary object segmentation in videos based on region augmentation and reduction. In: CVPR (2017)
24. Krähenbühl, P., Koltun, V.: Efficient inference in fully connected CRFs with gaussian edge potentials. In: NIPS (2011)
25. Krähenbühl, P., Koltun, V.: Geodesic object proposals. In: Fleet, D., Pajdla, T., Schiele, B., Tuytelaars, T. (eds.) ECCV 2014. LNCS, vol. 8693, pp. 725–739. Springer, Cham (2014). https://doi.org/10.1007/978-3-319-10602-1_47
26. Lao, D., Sundaramoorthi, G.: Extending layered models to 3D motion. In: ECCV (2018)
27. Lee, C., Jang, W., Sim, J., Kim, C.: Multiple random walkers and their application to image cosegmentation. In: CVPR (2015)
28. Lee, G., Tai, Y., Kim, J.: Deep saliency with encoded low level distance map and high level features. In: CVPR (2016)
29. Lee, Y.J., Kim, J., Grauman, K.: Key-segments for video object segmentation. In: ICCV (2011)
30. Li, B., Sun, Z., Li, Q., Wu, Y., Hu, A.: Group-wise deep object co-segmentation with co-attention recurrent neural network. In: ICCV (2019)
31. Li, G., Xie, Y., Lin, L., Yu, Y.: Instance-level salient object segmentation. In: CVPR (2017)
32. Li, G., Xie, Y., Wei, T., Wang, K., Lin, L.: Flow guided recurrent neural encoder for video salient object detection. In: CVPR (2018)
33. Li, G., Yu, Y.: Deep contrast learning for salient object detection (2016)
34. Li, S., Seybold, B., Vorobyov, A., Lei, X., Kuo, C.C.J.: Unsupervised video object segmentation with motion-based bilateral networks. In: ECCV (2018)
35. Li, W., Hosseini Jafari, O., Rother, C.: Deep object co-segmentation. In: Jawahar, C.V., Li, H., Mori, G., Schindler, K. (eds.) ACCV 2018. LNCS, vol. 11363, pp. 638–653. Springer, Cham (2019). https://doi.org/10.1007/978-3-030-20893-6_40
36. Lin, T.Y., et al.: Microsoft COCO: common objects in context. In: Fleet, D., Pajdla, T., Schiele, B., Tuytelaars, T. (eds.) ECCV 2014. LNCS, vol. 8693, pp. 740–755. Springer, Cham (2014). https://doi.org/10.1007/978-3-319-10602-1_48
37. Liu, N., Han, J.: Dhsnet: deep hierarchical saliency network for salient object detection. In: CVPR (2016)
38. Liu, Z., Li, J., Ye, L., Sun, G., Shen, L.: Saliency detection for unconstrained videos using superpixel-level graph and spatiotemporal propagation. IEEE Trans. Circ. Syst. Video Technol. **27**, 2527–2542 (2017)

39. Liu, Z., Zhang, X., Luo, S., Meur, O.L.: Superpixel-based spatiotemporal saliency detection (2014)
40. Lu, X., Wang, W., Ma, C., Shen, J., Shao, L., Porikli, F.: See more, know more: unsupervised video object segmentation with co-attention siamese networks. In: CVPR (2019)
41. Luo, Z., Mishra, A., Achkar, A., Eichel, J.A., Li, S., Jodoin, P.: Non-local deep features for salient object detection. In: CVPR (2017)
42. Ochs, P., Brox, T.: Object segmentation in video: a hierarchical variational approach for turning point trajectories into dense regions. In: ICCV (2011)
43. Ochs, P., Malik, J., Brox, T.: Segmentation of moving objects by long term video analysis. IEEE Trans. Pattern Anal. Mach. Intell. 36, 1187–1200 (2013)
44. Papazoglou, A., Ferrari, V.: Fast object segmentation in unconstrained video. In: ICCV (2013)
45. Perazzi, F., Pont-Tuset, J., McWilliams, B., Van Gool, L., Gross, M., Sorkine-Hornung, A.: A benchmark dataset and evaluation methodology for video object segmentation. In: CVPR (2016)
46. Rong, Q., Han, J., Zhang, D., Nie, F.: Object co-segmentation via graph optimized-flexible manifold ranking. In: CVPR (2016)
47. Rota Bulò, S., Porzi, L., Kontschieder, P.: In-place activated batchnorm for memory-optimized training of dnns. In: CVPR (2018)
48. Siam, M., et al.: Video object segmentation using teacher-student adaptation in a human robot interaction (hri) setting. In: ICRA (2019)
49. Song, H., Wang, W., Zhao, S., Shen, J., Lam, K.M.: Pyramid dilated deeper convlstm for video salient object detection. In: ECCV (2018)
50. Taylor, B., Karasev, V., Soatto, S.: Causal video object segmentation from persistence of occlusions. In: CVPR (2015)
51. Teichmann, M.T., Cipolla, R.: Convolutional crfs for semantic segmentation. arXiv preprint arXiv:1805.04777 (2018)
52. Tokmakov, P., Alahari, K., Schmid, C.: Learning motion patterns in videos. In: CVPR (2017)
53. Tokmakov, P., Alahari, K., Schmid, C.: Learning video object segmentation with visual memory. In: ICCV (2017)
54. Tokmakov, P., Schmid, C., Alahari, K.: Learning to segment moving objects. IJCV 127, 282–301 (2019)
55. Uijlings, J.R., Van De Sande, K.E., Gevers, T., Smeulders, A.W.: Selective search for object recognition. Int. J. Comput. Vis. 104, 154–171 (2013)
56. Wang, C., Zha, Z.J., Liu, D., Xie, H.: Robust deep co-saliency detection with group semantic. In: AAAI (2019)
57. Wang, C., Zhang, H., Yang, L., Cao, X., Xiong, H.: Multiple semantic matching on augmented n-partite graph for object co-segmentation. IEEE Trans. Image Process. 26, 5825–5839 (2017)
58. Wang, L., Wang, L., Lu, H., Zhang, P., Ruan, X.: Saliency detection with recurrent fully convolutional networks. In: Leibe, B., Matas, J., Sebe, N., Welling, M. (eds.) ECCV 2016. LNCS, vol. 9908, pp. 825–841. Springer, Cham (2016). https://doi.org/10.1007/978-3-319-46493-0_50
59. Wang, T., Borji, A., Zhang, L., Zhang, P., Lu, H.: A stagewise refinement model for detecting salient objects in images. In: ICCV (2017)
60. Wang, T., Zhang, L., Lu, H., Sun, C., Qi, J.: Kernelized subspace ranking for saliency detection. In: Leibe, B., Matas, J., Sebe, N., Welling, M. (eds.) ECCV 2016. LNCS, vol. 9912, pp. 450–466. Springer, Cham (2016). https://doi.org/10.1007/978-3-319-46484-8_27

61. Wang, W., Lu, X., Shen, J., Crandall, D.J., Shao, L.: Zero-shot video object segmentation via attentive graph neural networks. In: ICCV (2019)
62. Wang, W., Shen, J., Shao, L.: Consistent video saliency using local gradient flow optimization and global refinement. IEEE Trans. Image Process. **24**, 4185–4196 (2015)
63. Wang, W., Shen, J., Shao, L.: Video salient object detection via fully convolutional networks. IEEE Trans. Image Process. **27**, 38–49 (2018)
64. Wang, W., Shen, J., Yang, R., Porikli, F.: Saliency-aware video object segmentation. IEEE Trans. Pattern Anal. Mach. Intell. **40**, 20–33 (2018)
65. Wang, W., et al.: Learning unsupervised video object segmentation through visual attention. In: CVPR (2019)
66. Wang, X., Girshick, R., Gupta, A., He, K.: Non-local neural networks. In: CVPR (2018)
67. Yang, C., Zhang, L., Lu, H., Ruan, X., Yang, M.H.: Saliency detection via graph-based manifold ranking. In: CVPR (2013)
68. Yang, Z., Wang, Q., Bertinetto, L., Hu, W., Bai, S., Torr, P.H.S.: Anchor diffusion for unsupervised video object segmentation. In: ICCV (2019)
69. Yuan, Z.H., Lu, T., Wu, Y.: Deep-dense conditional random fields for object co-segmentation. In: IJCAI (2017)
70. Zhang, P., Wang, D., Lu, H., Wang, H., Ruan, X.: Amulet: aggregating multi-level convolutional features for salient object detection. In: CVPR (2017)
71. Zhang, P., Wang, D., Lu, H., Wang, H., Yin, B.: Learning uncertain convolutional features for accurate saliency detection. In: ICCV (2017)
72. Zheng, S., et al.: Conditional random fields as recurrent neural networks. In: ICCV (2015)
73. Zhuo, T., Cheng, Z., Zhang, P., Wong, Y., Kankanhalli, M.: Unsupervised online video object segmentation with motion property understanding. IEEE Trans. Image Process. **29**, 237–249 (2019)

SMART: Simultaneous Multi-Agent Recurrent Trajectory Prediction

N. N. Sriram[1(✉)], Buyu Liu[1], Francesco Pittaluga[1],
and Manmohan Chandraker[1,2]

[1] NEC Laboratories America, San Jose, USA
nnsriram97@gmail.com
[2] UC San Diego, San Diego, USA

Abstract. We propose advances that address two key challenges in future trajectory prediction: (i) multimodality in both training data and predictions and (ii) constant time inference regardless of number of agents. Existing trajectory predictions are fundamentally limited by lack of diversity in training data, which is difficult to acquire with sufficient coverage of possible modes. Our first contribution is an automatic method to simulate diverse trajectories in the top-view. It uses pre-existing datasets and maps as initialization, mines existing trajectories to represent realistic driving behaviors and uses a multi-agent vehicle dynamics simulator to generate diverse new trajectories that cover various modes and are consistent with scene layout constraints. Our second contribution is a novel method that generates diverse predictions while accounting for scene semantics and multi-agent interactions, with constant-time inference independent of the number of agents. We propose a convLSTM with novel state pooling operations and losses to predict scene-consistent states of multiple agents in a single forward pass, along with a CVAE for diversity. We validate our proposed multi-agent trajectory prediction approach by training and testing on the proposed simulated dataset and existing real datasets of traffic scenes. In both cases, our approach outperforms SOTA methods by a large margin, highlighting the benefits of both our diverse dataset simulation and constant-time diverse trajectory prediction methods.

Keywords: Diverse trajectory prediction · Multiple agents · Constant time · Scene constraints · Simulation

1 Introduction

The ability to reason about the future states of multiple agents in a scene is an important task for applications that seek vehicle autonomy. Ideally, a prediction framework should have three properties. First, it must be able to predict

Electronic supplementary material The online version of this chapter (https:// doi.org/10.1007/978-3-030-58583-9_28) contains supplementary material, which is available to authorized users.

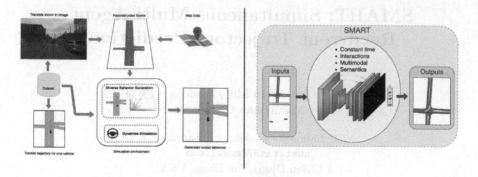

Fig. 1. Left: Given the map and tracklets, we propose to reconstruct the real world scene in top-view and simulate diverse behaviors for multiple agents w.r.t. scene context. Right: The proposed SMART algorithm that is able to generate context aware and multimodal trajectories for multiple agents.

multiple plausible trajectories in the dominant modes of motion. Second, these trajectories should be consistent with the scene semantics. Third, it is attractive for several applications if constant-time prediction can be achieved regardless of the number of agents in the scene. In this paper, we propose dataset creation and future prediction methods that help achieve the above three properties (Fig. 1).

A fundamental limitation for multimodal trajectory prediction is the lack of training data with a diverse enough coverage of the possible motion modes in a scene. Our first main contribution is a simulation strategy to recreate driving scenarios from real world data, which generates multiple driving behaviors to obtain diverse trajectories for a given scene. We construct a graph-based simulation environment that leverages scene semantics and maps to execute realistic vehicle behaviors in the top-view. We sample reference velocity profiles from trajectories executing similar maneuvers in the real world data. Then we use a variant of the Intelligent Driver Model [21,33] to model the dynamics of vehicle driving patterns and introduce lane-change decisions for simulated vehicles based on MOBIL [34]. We show that training with our simulated datasets leads to large improvements in prediction outcomes compared to the real data counterparts that are comparatively limited in both scale and diversity reflected by a Wasserstein metric.

Several recent works consider deep networks for trajectory prediction for humans [2,3,13,19,27] and vehicles [5,14,20,25,31,36]. Usually, they consider interactions among multiple agents, but still operate on single agent basis at inference time, requiring one forward pass for each agent in the scene. Vehicle motions are stochastic and depending on their goals, obtaining multimodal predictions for individual vehicles that are consistent with the scene significantly increases the time complexity. Our second main contribution addresses this through a novel approach, Simultaneous Multi-Agent Recurrent Trajectory (SMART) prediction. To the best of our knowledge, it is the first method to

Table 1. Comparison of our method with existing works in terms of complexity, scene context and interactions. n and K are number of agents and iterations.

Method	Social GAN [13]	Desire [20]	SoPhie [27]	INFER [30]	MATF GAN [36]	Ours
Complexity	$O(n)$	$O(nK)$	$O(n^2)$	$O(n)$	$O(n)$	$O(1)$
Scene Context	✗	✓	✓	✓	✓	✓
Social Interactions	✓	✓	✓	✓	✓	✓

achieve multimodal, scene-consistent prediction of multiple agents in constant time.

Specifically, we propose a novel architecture based on Convolutional LSTMs (ConvLSTMs) [35] and conditional variational autoencoders (CVAEs) [29], where agent states and scene context are represented in the bird-eye-view. Our method predicts trajectories for n agents with a time complexity of $O(1)$ (Table 1). To realize this, we use a single top-view grid map representation of all agents in the scene and utilize fully-convolutional operations to model the output predictions. Our ConvLSTM models the states of multiple agents, with novel state pooling operations, to implicitly account for interactions among objects and handle dynamically changing scenarios. To obtain multimodal predictions, we assign labels to trajectories based on the type of maneuver they execute and query for trajectories executing specific behaviors at test time. Our variational generative model is conditioned on this label to capture diversity in executing maneuvers of various types.

We validate our ideas on both real and simulated datasets and demonstrate state-of-the-art prediction numbers on both. We evaluate the network performance based on *average displacement error*(ADE), *final displacement error*(FDE) and *likelihood*(NLL) of the predictions with respect to the ground truth. Our experiments are designed to highlight the importance of methods to simulate datasets with sufficient realism at larger scales and diversity, as well as a prediction method that accounts for multimodality while achieving constant-time outputs independent of the number of agents in the scene.

To summarize, our key contributions are:

- A method to achieve constant-time trajectory prediction independent of number of agents in the scene, while accounting for multimodality and scene consistency.
- A method to simulate datasets in the top-view that imbibe the realism of real-world data, while augmenting them with diverse trajectories that cover diverse scene-consistent motion modes.

2   Related Work

In this section, we briefly summarize datasets available for autonomous driving and talk about the existing forecasting techniques.

Simulators and Autonomous Driving Datasets: AirSim [28] and CARLA [9] are autonomous driving platforms with primary target towards testing learning and control algorithms. SYNTHIA [26] introduces a big volume of synthetic images with annotations for urban scenarios. Virtual KITTI [11] imitates KITTI driving scenarios with varying environmental conditions and provide both pixel level and instance level annotations. Fang et al. [10] shows detectors trained with augmented lidar point cloud from a simulator provide comparable results with methods trained on real data. [16] generates images for vehicle detection and show an improvement in result that a deep neural network trained with synthetic data performs better than a network trained on real data when the dataset is bigger. Similarly, our focus is also to obtain better driving predictions by virtue of diversity from simulated datasets which emulate realistic driving behaviors.

Until recently, KITTI [12] has been extensively used for evaluation of various computer vision applications like stereo, tracking and object detection, but has limited diverse behaviors for a scene. NGSIM [7] provides trajectory information of traffic participants but the scenes are only limited to highways with fixed lane traffic. CaliForecasting [25] (unreleased) 10 K examples with approximately 1.5 hours of driving data but does not contain any information about the scene. There are several recently proposed autonomous driving datasets [1,4–6,14,17,23], some of which focus on trajectory forecasting [5,6,14,23]. Rules of the road [14] (unreleased) proposes a dataset with map information for 83 K trajectories in 88 distinct locations. Argoverse [6] proposes two datasets (Tracking and Forecasting) with HD semantic map information containing centerlines. Argoverse tracking contains a total of 113 scenes with tracklet information. While the forecasting dataset is sufficiently large enough with more 300K trajectories, it contains 5 s trajectory data for only one vehicle in the scene. In our work, we simultaneously generate trajectories for all vehicles in the scene and provide trajectory information up to 7 s for each vehicle. NuScenes [4] provides data from two cities with complete sensor suite information, but the main focus of the dataset is towards object detection and tracking. We primarily focus on using Argoverse Tracking [6] for simulating diverse trajectories and to showcase better prediction ability, but also simulate diverse trajectories for KITTI [12] dataset (please see supplementary material). Our method can be extended to many published datasets such as Waymo Open Dataset [1] and Lyft [17].

Forecasting Methods: Motion forecasting has been extensively studied. Kitani et al. [18] proposes a method based on Inverse Optimal Control (IOC). Social LSTM [2] uses a recurrent network to model human-human interactions for pedestrian forecasting. Deo et al. [8] use a similar method as [2] to model interactions and predict an output distribution over future states for vehicles. DESIRE [20] uses a CVAE-based [29] approach to predict trajectories up to 4 s but requires multiple iterations to align its predictions with scene context. Sampling multiple trajectories that are semantically aligned might not be feasible.

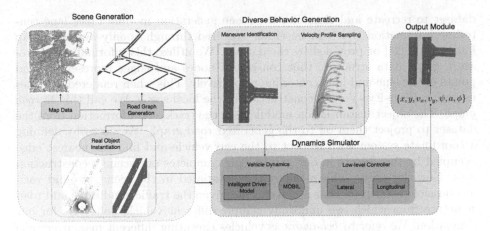

Fig. 2. The overall pipeline of the proposed simulation strategy. Scene generation module recreates the specific driving scenarios from datasets. Behavior generation samples a behavior for simulation and an appropriate reference velocity profile for every vehicle in the scene. The dynamics simulator tracks the reference velocity and provides lane changing decisions based on the current traffic condition.

Over the recent years, generative models [3,13,19,22,27] have shown significant improvements in pedestrian trajectory prediction. Human trajectories tend to be stochastic and random while vehicle motions are aligned with the scene context and are strongly influenced by surrounding vehicle's behavior. Outputs from [13,27] show that it produces more diverse outputs and the output predictions are spread over a larger area. While more advanced methods [15,19] show outputs that are tightly coupled with the ground truth. We do not intend to capture the data distribution in such a fashion but are more focused towards producing predictions in possible dominant choices of motion [31]. This also motivates us to use [13] to showcase the ability of simulation strategy in producing more diverse outputs. Our method capture both these indifference's by producing quintessential trajectories that are diverse and at the same time closely aligned with the ground truth (indicated by our likelihood values).

Recently, MATF GAN [36] uses convolutions to model interactions between agents, but only shows results on straight driving scenarios and suffers in producing multimodal outputs. INFER [30] proposes a method based on ConvLSTMs and [14] uses convolutions to regress future paths. These methods nicely couple scene context with predicted output, but their predictions are entity-centric and do not incorporate multi-agent stochastic predictions.

3   Simulated Dataset

The overall pipeline of the proposed simulation strategy is shown in Fig. 2. Our simulation engine consists of three main components: scene generation module, behavior generation module and a dynamics simulation engine. Given a dataset to recreate and simulate, the scene generation module takes lane centerline information that can be either acquired through openly available map information [24] or provided by the dataset. We utilize this information to create a graph data structure that consists of nodes and edges representing end points of the lane and lane centerline respectively. This when rendered provides us with a Birds-Eye-View reconstruction of the local scene. We call this as *road graph*. The object instantiation module uses the tracklet's information from the dataset to project them on to the generated road graph. We do so by defining a coordinate system with respect to the ego vehicle and find the nearest edge occupied by the objects in our graph. This completes our scene reconstruction task. Now, for every vehicle that was instantiated in the scene, we find various possible maneuvers that it can execute given the traffic conditions and road structure from which, we uniformly sample different vehicle behaviors for our simulation. We refer to *behaviors* as vehicles executing different maneuvers like *straight, left turn, right turn and lane changes*. To execute such diverse behaviors that are significantly realistic, we sample appropriate velocity profiles from real dataset as references that closely resemble the intended behavior that vehicle is planning to execute. The dynamics simulation module utilizes this reference velocity to execute the right behavior for every vehicle but at the same time considers the scene layout and the current traffic conditions to provide a safe acceleration that can be executed. We simulate every scene for 7 s and generate a maximum of 3 diverse behaviors (Fig. 3). The simulation is performed 10 Hz and output from our simulation consists of vehicle states $\{\mathbf{x}, \mathbf{v}, \psi, a, \phi\}_1^T$ which represent position, velocity, heading, acceleration and steering over the course of our simulation. We will now provide a brief description of each component and refer readers to supplementary material for additional details.

Scene Generation: We utilize the lane information from OpenStreetMaps (OSM) [24] or from datasets like [6] for creating the road graph. For our purposes, we make use of the road information such as centerline, number of lanes and one-way information for each road segment. Every bi-directional road centerline is split based on the specified number of lanes and one-way information. The vehicle pose information from the dataset is used to recreate exact driving scenarios.

Diverse Behavior Generation: Given a particular lane ID (node) on the local road graph for every vehicle, we depth first explore K possible leaf nodes that can be reached within a threshold distance. We categorize plausible maneuvers from any given node into three different categories {*left, right, straight*}. Prior to the simulation, we create a pool of reference velocity profiles from the real data. At simulation time, after sampling a desired behavior, we obtain a Nearest Neighbor velocity profile for the current scene based on features such as distance before turn and average velocity, for turn and straight maneuvers respectively.

Dynamics Simulation: The dynamics module utilizes road graph, a behavior from a pool of diverse plausible ones and a reference velocity that needs to be

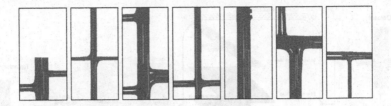

Fig. 3. Example trajectories executed by a single vehicle under different scenes in simulation. As shown in this figure, our simulation strategy is able to generate diverse yet realistic trajectories that align well with scene context.

tracked for the appropriate behavior. Our dynamics engine is governed by Intelligent Driver Model (IDM) [33] and MOBIL [34]. Acceleration and lane change decisions obtained from this dynamics module is fed to a low-level controller that tries to track and exhibit appropriate state changes in the vehicle behavior. In order to limit the acceleration under safety limit for the any traffic situation and to incorporate interactions among different agents in the scene we use an IDM [33] behavior for the simulated vehicles. The input to an IDM consists of distance to the leading vehicle s, the actual velocity of the vehicle v, the velocity difference with the leading vehicle Δv and provides an output a_{IDM} that is considered safe for the given traffic conditions. It is given by the equation,

$$a_{IDM}(s, v, \Delta v) = a\left(1 - \left(\frac{v}{v_o}\right)^{\delta} - \left(\frac{s^*(v, \Delta v)}{s}\right)^2\right), \qquad (1)$$

where, a is the comfortable acceleration and v_o is the desired reference velocity. δ is an exponent that influences how acceleration decreases with velocity. The deceleration of the vehicle depends on the ratio of desired minimum gap s^* to actual bumper distance s with the leading vehicle.

Lane Change Decisions: We also consider lane changing behavior to add additional diversity in vehicle trajectories apart from turn based maneuver trajectories. Lane changing behaviors are modeled based on MOBIL algorithm from [34]. The following are the parameters that control lane changing behavior: politeness factor p that influences lane changing if there's acceleration gain for other agents, lane changing acceleration threshold Δa_{th}, maximum safe deceleration b_{safe} and bias for particular lane Δa_{bias}. The following equations govern whether a lane change can be executed,

$$\tilde{a}_c - a_c + p\{(\tilde{a}_n - a_n) + (\tilde{a}_o - a_o)\} > \Delta a_{th} - \Delta a_{bias}, \qquad (2)$$

$$(\tilde{a}_n - a_n) > -b_{safe}^n, (\tilde{a}_c - a_c) > -b_{safe}^c. \qquad (3)$$

Here, a is the current acceleration and $\tilde{a}$ represents the new acceleration after lane change. c, n, o subscripts denote current, new vehicle and old vehicles respectively.

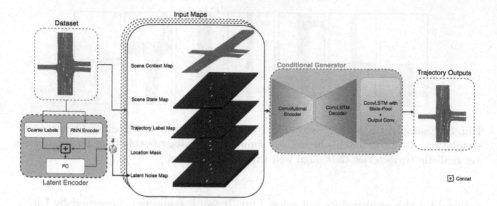

Fig. 4. The overall architecture for SMART framework. The components connected in green are used only during the training phase. It takes in a single representation of the scene, to regress per timestep coordinates for the all agents at their respective location in the spatial grid. (Color figure online)

4   SMART

In this section, we will introduce a single representation model to predict trajectories for *multiple* agents in a road scene such that our predictions are *context aware*, *multimodal* and have *constant inference time* irrespective of number of agents. We formulate the trajectory prediction problem as per frame regression of agents locations over the spatial grid. We will describe our method below in details.

4.1   Problem Formulation

Given the lane centerline information $L^{1...m}$ for a scene, we render them in top view representations such that our scene context map $\mathcal{I}$ is of HxWx3 where channel dimension represents one-hot information of each pixel corresponding to $\{road, lane, unknown\}$ road element. Let $\mathbf{X}_i = \{X_i^1, X_i^2, ..., X_i^T\}$ denote trajectory information of ith vehicle from timestep 1...T where each $X_i^t = (x_i, y_i)^t$ represents spatial location of the agent in the scene. Our network takes input in the form of relative coordinates $^R\mathbf{X}_i$ with respect to agent's starting location. For the ith agent in the scene, we project $^R\mathbf{X}_i$ at corresponding $\mathbf{X}_i$ locations to construct a spatial location map of states $\mathcal{S}^{1...T}$ such that $\mathcal{S}^t[X_i^t]$ contains relative coordinate of ith agent at timestep t. $^R\mathbf{Y}_i = {}^R\mathbf{X}_i^{t_{obs}...T}$ represents ground truth trajectory. And we further denote $\mathcal{M}^t$ as the location mask representing configuration of agents in the scene. To keep track of vehicles across timesteps, we construct a vehicle IDs map $\mathcal{V}^{1...T}$ where $\mathcal{V}^t[X_i^t] = i$. Furthermore, we associate each trajectory $X_i^{t_{obs},...T}$ with a label c_i that represents the behavioral type of the trajectory from one of $\{straight, left, right\}$ behaviors. And trajectory label for lane changes falls in one of the three categories. Let $\mathcal{C}$ encode grid map representation of c_i such that $\mathcal{C}^t[X_i^t] = c_i$. Note that vehicle trajectories are not random compared to the human motion. Instead, they depend on behaviors of other vehicles in the road, which motivates us to classify trajectories based on different maneuvers.

We follow the formulation proposed in [14,30,36] where network takes previous states $\mathcal{S}^{1..t_{obs}}$ as input along with the scene context map $\mathcal{I}$, trajectory label map $\mathcal{C}$, location mask $\mathcal{M}$ and a noise map $\mathcal{Z}$ to predict the future trajectories $^R\hat{Y}_i$ for every agent at its corresponding grid map location X_i^t in the scene. Note that we do not have a separate head for each agent. Instead, our network predicts a single future state map $\hat{S}^t$ where each individual agent tries to match $^R Y_i^t$ at t.

4.2 Method

We illustrate our pipeline in Fig. 4. Our network architecture comprises of two major parts, a latent encoder and a conditional generator. We model the temporal information with the agents previous locations using ConvLSTMs. We further introduce a state pooling operation to feed agents state information at respective locations in consecutive timestep. While we provide trajectory specific labels to capture diverse predictions, we leverage conditional variational generative models (CVAE [29]) to model diversity in the data for each type of label.

Latent Encoder: It acts as a recognition module Q_ϕ for our CVAE framework and is only used during our training phase. Specifically, it takes in both the past and future trajectory information $^R\mathbf{X}_i$ and passes them through an embedding layer. The embedded vectors are then passed on to a LSTM network to output encoding at every timestep. The outputs across all the timesteps are concatenated together into a single vector along with the one hot trajectory label c_i to produce $V_{enc}(i)$. This vector is then passed on through a MLP to obtain μ and σ to output a distribution $Q_\phi(z_i|^R\mathbf{X}_i, c_i)$. Formally,

$$^o h_i^t = LSTM(h_i^{t-1}, ^R X_i^t)$$
$$V_{enc}(i) = [^o \mathbf{h}_i^1, ..., ^o h_i^T, c_i] \qquad (4)$$
$$\mu, \sigma = MLP(V_{enc}(i)).$$

Conditional Generator: We adapt a U-Net like architecture for the generator. At any timestep t, the inputs to the network conditional generator are the following, a scene context map $\mathcal{I}$ (H×W×3), a single representation of all agents current state $\mathcal{S}^t$ (H×W×2), location mask $\mathcal{M}^t$ (H×W×1), a one-hot trajectory specific label for each agent projected at agent specific locations in a grid from $\mathcal{C}^t$ (H×W×3) and a latent vector map $\mathcal{Z}^t$ (H×W×16) containing z_i obtained from $Q_\phi(z_i|^R\mathbf{X}_i, c_i)$ during training phase or sampled from prior distribution $P_v(z_i|^R\mathbf{X}_i, c_i)$ at test time. Formally the network input E^t is given by:

$$E^t = [\mathcal{I}, \mathcal{S}^t, \mathcal{M}^t, \mathcal{C}^t, \mathcal{Z}^t], \qquad (5)$$

which is of size H×W×25 for any timestep t. Note that our representation is not entity centric i.e we do not have one target entity for which we want to predict trajectories but rather have a global one for all agents.

At each timestep from $1, ..., t_{obs}$, we pass the above inputs through the encoder module. This module is composed of strided convolutions, which encode information in small spatial dimensions, and passes them through the decoder. The decoder includes ConvLSTMs and transposed convolutions with skip connections from the encoder module, and outputs a H×W map. It is then passed on to another ConvLSTM layer with state pooling operations. The same network is shared during observation and prediction phase. A final 1×1 convolution layer is added to output a 2 channel map containing relative predicted coordinates $^{R}X_i^t$ for the agents in the next timestep.

We use the ground truth agent locations for the observed trajectory and unroll our ConvLSTM based on the predictions of our network. During the prediction phase $(t_{obs}, ..., T)$, the outputs are not directly fed back as inputs to the network rather the agent's state is updated to the next location in the scene based on the predictions. The relative predicted location $^{R}\hat{X}_i^{t-1}$ gets updated to absolute predicted location $\hat{X}_i^t$ to obtain a updated scene state map $\hat{S}^t$ containing updated locations of all the agents in the scene. Note that using such representations for the scene is agnostic to number of agents and as the agents next state is predicted at its respective pixel location it is capable of handling dynamic entry and exit of agents from the scene.

State-Pooled ConvLSTMs: Simultaneous multi-agent predictions are realized through state-pooling in ConvLSTMs. Using standard ConvLSTMs for multi-agent trajectory predictions usually produces semantically aligned trajectories, but the trajectories occasionally contain erratic maneuvers. We solve this issue via state-pooling, which ensures the availability of previous state information when trying to predict the next location. We pool the previous state information from the final ConvLSTM layer for all the agents $^{sp}\mathbf{H}_i^{t-1}$ and initialize the next state with $^{sp}\mathbf{H}_i^{t-1}$ (for both hidden and cell state) at agents updated locations and zero vectors at all other locations for timestep t.

Learning: We train both the recognition network $Q_\phi(z_i|^{R}\mathbf{X}_i, c_i)$ and the conditional generator $P_\theta(Y|E)$ concurrently. We obtain predicted trajectory $^{R}\hat{Y}$ by pooling values from indexes that agents visited at every timestep. We use two loss functions in training our CVAE based ConvLSTM network:

- Reconstruction Loss: $\mathcal{L}_R = \frac{1}{N}\sum_i^N ||^{R}\mathbf{Y}_i -^{R}\hat{\mathbf{Y}}_i||$ that penalizes the predictions to enable them to reconstruct the ground truth accurately.
- KL Divergence Loss: $\mathcal{L}_{KLD} = D_{KL}(Q_\phi(z_i|^{R}\mathbf{X}_i, c_i)||P_v(z_i|^{R}\mathbf{X}_i, c_i))$. That regularizes the output distribution from Q_ϕ to match the sampling distribution P_v at test time.

Table 2. Quantitative measurements on P-ArgoT. We report ADE, FDE (in meters) and NLL (N=5)

Model	1.0 (sec)			2.0 (sec)			3.0 (sec)			4.0 (sec)			5.0 (sec)		
P-ArgoT ‖ ADE	FDE	NLL‖														
LSTM	0.53	0.87	–	1.03	2.01	–	1.62	3.41	–	2.31	5.09	–	3.09	6.98	–
CVAE	0.46	0.73	**2.16**	0.89	1.72	**3.31**	1.42	2.98	4.18	2.04	4.49	4.88	2.76	6.26	5.48
MATF Scene [36]	0.98	1.73	–	1.84	3.53	–	2.76	5.48	–	3.72	7.56	–	4.73	9.78	-
MATF GAN [36]	0.78	1.34	3.44	1.45	2.73	4.53	2.17	4.28	5.24	2.94	5.95	5.79	3.76	7.77	6.23
S-GAN [13]	**0.42**	0.72	2.21	0.85	1.68	3.49	1.36	2.83	4.36	1.93	4.08	5.03	2.54	5.46	5.57
SMART (c_{random})	0.73	0.64	3.72	0.84	0.98	3.92	0.94	1.35	4.31	1.15	1.73	4.70	1.38	2.16	5.06
SMART (c_{best})	0.58	**0.59**	3.21	**0.59**	**0.55**	3.39	**0.60**	**0.75**	**3.63**	**0.98**	**0.61**	**3.89**	**1.02**	**1.06**	**4.13**

Table 3. Left: Quantitative measurements on ArgoF validation set. (N = 6). Right: Quantitative comparison of different datasets with introduced diversity metrics based on wasserstein distances.

Model	1.0 (sec)			2.0 (sec)			3.0 (sec)		
Argo Forecasting Dataset (ArgoF) ‖ ADE	FDE	NLL‖							
LSTM	0.76	1.16	–	1.32	2.67	–	2.14	4.71	–
CVAE	1.22	2.27	9.14	2.56	5.32	11.7	4.14	8.94	13.2
MATF Scene [36]	1.56	2.71	–	2.90	5.54	–	4.35	8.17	–
MATF GAN [36]	1.48	2.54	13.5	2.72	5.17	13.6	4.08	8.13	14.0
S-GAN [13]	0.88	1.59	4.12	1.99	4.34	5.74	3.49	8.05	6.80
SMART (c_{random})	0.79	0.96	4.59	1.16	1.85	4.76	1.65	3.00	5.18
SMART (c_{best})	**0.71**	**0.83**	3.56	**1.03**	**1.55**	**4.05**	**1.44**	**2.47**	**4.61**

Datasets	Y Wasserstein		$\bar{X}$ Wasserstein	
	Mean	Median	Mean	Median
KITTI	0.14	0.04	4.91	3.52
P-KITTI	2.13	0.75	17.64	17.58
ArgoT	0.49	0.20	5.98	2.97
P-ArgoT	0.97	0.12	17.5	17.49

Test Phase: At inference time, we do not have access to trajectory specific labels c_i but rather query for a specific behavior by sampling these labels randomly. Along with c_i for each agent we also sample z_i from $P_v(z_i|^R\mathbf{X}_i, c_i)$. However, P_v can be relaxed to be independent of the input [29] implying the prior distribution to be $P_v(z_i)$. $P_v(z_i) := \mathcal{N}(0,1)$ at test time.

5   Experiments

We evaluate our methods on publicly available Argoverse [6] Tracking(ArgoT)[1] and Forecasting(ArgoF)[2] dataset. We also introduce a simulated dataset based on P-ArgoT and conduct experiments with it. Our simulated dataset utilizes 2000 scene instances from ArgoT to generate scenarios with multiple agents and trajectory durations of 7 s.

We use standard *evaluation metrics* suggested in previous approaches [6,13, 30,36], e.g. Average Displacement Error(ADE), Final Displacement Error(FDE) and Negative Log Likelihood(NLL) with the ground truth.

We evaluate two versions of *SMART*, e.g. (SMART(c_{random})) and (SMART(c_{best})). For the former, we randomly sample our behavior specific trajectory labels for evaluation, while for the later we equally sample n trajectories

---

[1] Generated 2044 scenes in total containing multiple trajectories for every scene.
[2] Argoverse Forecasting for vehicle trajectory prediction is a large scale dataset containing 333,441 (5 s) trajectories captured from 320 h of driving.

Table 4. Results for methods tested on ArgoT. '[ ]' represents the training set. We report results on the basis of ADE, FDE and NLL (N=5).

Model	1.0 (sec)			2.0 (sec)			3.0 (sec)			4.0 (sec)			5.0 (sec)		
ArgoT || ADE | FDE | NLL ||															
LSTM [ArgoT]	0.65	1.07	—	1.28	2.53	—	2.07	4.45	—	3.00	6.74	—	4.05	9.31	—
CVAE [ArgoT]	**0.45**	0.75	1.99	0.90	1.88	**3.13**	1.52	3.48	**4.07**	2.30	5.50	4.89	3.21	7.89	5.63
MATF Scene [ArgoT] [36]	1.24	2.20	—	2.39	4.67	—	3.66	7.49	—	5.03	10.4	—	6.45	13.4	—
MATF GAN [ArgoT] [36]	0.97	1.69	5.32	1.82	3.47	6.21	2.75	5.53	6.93	3.77	7.88	7.58	4.90	10.5	8.15
MATF GAN [P-ArgoT] [36]	1.03	1.79	6.32	1.93	3.68	7.51	2.89	5.77	8.43	3.94	8.13	9.19	5.07	10.7	9.77
S-GAN [ArgoT] [13]	0.77	1.35	4.29	1.47	2.79	5.48	2.25	4.47	6.24	3.11	6.38	6.81	4.06	8.54	7.27
S-GAN [P-ArgoT] [13]	0.94	1.63	4.84	1.76	3.31	6.00	2.66	5.24	6.74	3.66	7.37	7.30	4.74	9.68	7.75
SMART [ArgoT] (c_{random})	0.85	1.06	4.31	1.22	1.87	4.82	1.68	2.98	5.38	2.25	4.30	5.88	2.88	5.70	6.31
SMART [P-ArgoT] (c_{random})	0.68	0.80	4.12	0.97	1.51	4.29	1.37	2.45	4.71	1.85	3.58	5.13	2.39	4.85	5.51
SMART [ArgoT] (c_{best})	0.74	0.87	3.85	1.03	1.50	4.02	1.42	2.40	4.42	1.90	3.52	4.84	2.45	4.74	5.24
SMART [P-ArgoT] (c_{best})	0.61	**0.66**	3.91	**0.84**	**1.21**	3.81	**1.16**	**1.97**	4.08	**1.56**	**2.91**	**4.39**	**2.02**	**3.96**	**4.70**

Table 5. Results for methods tested on ArgoT without straight trajectories. '[ ]' represents the training set. We report results on the basis of ADE, FDE(N=5).

Model	1.0 (sec)		2.0 (sec)		3.0 (sec)		4.0 (sec)		5.0 (sec)	
ArgoT || ADE | FDE ||										
MATF GAN [ArgoT] [36]	1.04	1.80	1.98	3.86	3.08	6.50	4.41	9.91	5.98	14.1
MATF GAN [P-ArgoT] [36]	0.94	1.63	1.79	3.50	2.81	6.00	4.07	9.35	5.61	13.6
S-GAN [ArgoT] [13]	0.94	1.67	1.86	3.64	2.91	5.91	4.12	8.48	5.47	11.4
S-GAN [P-ArgoT] [13]	0.93	1.61	1.74	3.30	2.65	5.23	3.65	7.38	4.73	9.75

over all the trajectory labels and report the best results across all. We comapare our proposed methods against the following *baselines*:

- LSTM: A sequence to sequence encoder-decoder network that regresses future locations based on the past trajectory [32].
- CVAE: A modified LSTM generator that predicts paths based on the input latent vector in the form of noise learned from the data distribution [29].
- S-GAN [13]: We implement and evaluate this method on all datasets.
- MATF GAN [36]: We implement it ourselves and evaluate it on all datasets.

Quantitative Results: We first demonstrate that our proposed method, **SMART**, can beat the baseline methods. As shown in Table 2 and 3(left), our method can almost always outperform baselines with a large margin, especially in long-term scenarios. It is also worth noting that final ADE and FDE values of our method SMART(c_{best}) are at least 23% and 39% lower than that of others across all tables. We also observe that SMART(c_{best}) provides better results than SMART(c_{random}). This is due to the fact that SMART(c_{random}) randomly samples trajectory behavior labels thus ignores the data distribution. In contrast, SMART(c_{best}) is able to capture the diversity for particular label

Table 6. Average runtime in seconds to generate one prediction sample in scenes from Argoverse [6] dataset with increasing number of agents, benchmarked on RTX2080Ti, 11 GB GPU.

No. of Agents	1	2	3	4	5	6	7	8	9	10
SMART	.070	.070	.070	.070	.072	.069	.069	.075	.072	.069
S-GAN [13]	.024	.034	.044	.054	.062	.071	.082	.090	.102	.108

through CVAEs. Although other methods [13, 20, 36] are also able to generate diverse trajectories, they have to sample a significant number of trajectories to get a predictions (or driver intents) exhibiting different behaviors. We later show in Fig. 5 that our method is able to model data distribution more effectively, e.g. achieves comparable/better results with less samples.

In Fig. 5(left), we show variation of ADE/FDE values with increasing number of samples in ArgoF. We observe that our method performs significantly better even with lower number of samples compared to baselines, which again supports our claim that methods like [13] requires much more samples to even to get comparable performance with our method reported in Table 3(left). Figure 5(right) shows number of valid predictions produced across all datasets. Here, the validity is computed based on whether the predicted outputs lie within the road regions. Compared to baselines, our method is more likely to generate output predictions that satisfied context constraints.

We also provide analysis on time complexity of existing methods in Table 6. Without sacrificing the performance, our SMART always gives constant inference time with increasing number of agents.

To demonstrate the effectiveness/informativeness of our **simulated dataset**, we further conduct experiments and report numbers in Table 4. We test all methods on ArgoT test set. P-ArgoT in this table denotes that corresponding models are trained on P-ArgoT and fine-tuned on ArgoT training set. There are two main observations. Firstly, our methods that initialized with simulated data clearly achieve much better performance. Such significant performance boost indicates the benefits of augmenting a dataset with diverse trajectories. Secondly, such boost is missing in other methods. We argue that this might be attributed to the ability of the other methods in capturing the diversity in a wrong fashion (See Fig. 3 in supplementary). For instance, S-GAN [13] is unaware of the scene context, hence when initialized with a model trained on diverse trajectories, the outputs are more spread thus leads to lower performance with fixed number of samples. Although MATF [36] includes scene context in its predictions, it has poor capability in producing multimodal outputs where most of the predictions are biased towards behavior of particular type (See Fig. 3 [36]). To provide further analysis, and to show that training on simulated data improves diversity for other methods we report numbers evaluated on non-straight trajectories in Table 5. As observed, other methods perform significantly better when initialized

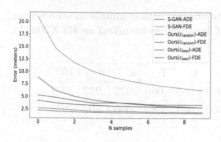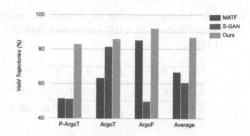

Fig. 5. Left: Quantitative results on ArgoF with increasing number of samples. Average and final displacements of our method is plotted against S-GAN [13]. **Right:** Percentage of samples($n = 30$) that produced trajectories inside the road.

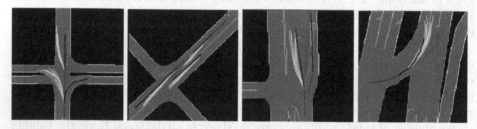

Fig. 6. Example predictions of SMART. The past trajectory and GT are visualized in brown and black lines. Red, blue and green lines are predictions sampled with different trajectory labels c_i given as input. From left, multi-agent prediction outputs from simulated dataset P-ArgoT, ArgoT, ArgoT and ArgoF datasets. (a),(b) and (c) show simultaneous multi-agent multimodal outputs. (d) shows a failure case where some of the predicted trajectories are aligned in opposite to the direction of road. However, we argue that such traffic rules might be hard to obtain with only top view map information. (Color figure online)

with simulated model. This observation further demonstrates that our method is able to capture the diversity strongly coupled with the scene.

Qualitative Results: We give some example predictions of our method in Fig. 6. In general, our predictions align well with scene context and obey traffic rules in most situations.

Wasserstein Diversity Metric: To quantify the diversity of the simulated dataset, we introduce a novel diversity metric based on Wasserstein distances and showcase our results on both real and simulated data. Firstly, we normalize the trajectories such that it starts at the origin and ends at some x coordinate. We use a trajectory with zero acceleration ($\ddot{x} = 0$) and zero deviation from the x axis ($y = 0$) as a reference trajectory for comparison. We define two metrics y (deviation from x axis) and $\ddot{x}$ (deviation from zero acceleration) Wasserstein. A higher Wasserstein metric indicates a higher deviation from the reference trajectory. Table 3(right) shows the Wasserstein metric between real and simulated data for two different datasets. Tracklets in KITTI [12] and Argoverse [6] generally move in straight directions with very minimal turns indicating a very low diversity. In contrast, our simulated trajectories are more diverse with agents executing turns whenever possible, going hand in hand with the higher diversity in Table 3(right).

6   Conclusion

In this paper, we have addressed data diversity and model complexity issues in multiple-agent trajectory prediction. We first introduced a new simulated dataset that includes diverse yet realistic trajectories for multiple agents. Further, we propose SMART, a method that simultaneously generates trajectories for all agents with a single forward pass and provides multimodal, context-aware SOTA predictions. Our experiments on both real and simulated dataset show superiority of SMART over existing methods in terms of both accuracy and efficiency. In addition, we demonstrate that our simulated dataset is diverse and general, thus, is useful to train or test prediction models.

References

1. Waymo open dataset: An autonomous driving dataset (2019)
2. Alahi, A., Goel, K., Ramanathan, V., Robicquet, A., Fei-Fei, L., Savarese, S.: Social LSTM: Human trajectory prediction in crowded spaces. In: The IEEE Conference on Computer Vision and Pattern Recognition (CVPR) (2016)
3. Amirian, J., Hayet, J.B., Pettre, J.: Social ways: learning multi-modal distributions of pedestrian trajectories with GANs. In: The IEEE Conference on Computer Vision and Pattern Recognition (CVPR) Workshops (2019)
4. Caesar, H., et al.: nuscenes: A multimodal dataset for autonomous driving. arXiv preprint arXiv:1903.11027 (2019)
5. Chandra, R., Bhattacharya, U., Bera, A., Manocha, D.: Traphic: trajectory prediction in dense and heterogeneous traffic using weighted interactions. In: Proceedings of the IEEE Conference on Computer Vision and Pattern Recognition, pp. 8483–8492 (2019)
6. Chang, M.F., et al.: Argoverse: 3D tracking and forecasting with rich maps. In: The IEEE Conference on Computer Vision and Pattern Recognition (CVPR) (2019)
7. Colyar, J., Halkias, J.: Us highway 101 dataset. Federal Highway Administration (FHWA), Technical Report FHWA-HRT-07-030 (2007)
8. Deo, N., Trivedi, M.M.: Convolutional social pooling for vehicle trajectory prediction (2018). CoRR abs/1805.06771, http://arxiv.org/abs/1805.06771
9. Dosovitskiy, A., Ros, G., Codevilla, F., Lopez, A., Koltun, V.: CARLA: an open urban driving simulator. In: Proceedings of the 1st Annual Conference on Robot Learning, pp. 1–16 (2017)
10. Fang, J., et al.: Simulating LIDAR point cloud for autonomous driving using real-world scenes and traffic flows (2018). CoRR abs/1811.07112, http://arxiv.org/abs/1811.07112
11. Gaidon, A., Wang, Q., Cabon, Y., Vig, E.: Virtual worlds as proxy for multi-object tracking analysis (2016). CoRR abs/1605.06457, http://arxiv.org/abs/1605.06457

12. Geiger, A., Lenz, P., Stiller, C., Urtasun, R.: Vision meets robotics: the kitti dataset. Int. J. Rob. Res. (IJRR) **32**, 1231–1237 (2013)
13. Gupta, A., Johnson, J., Fei-Fei, L., Savarese, S., Alahi, A.: Social GAN: socially acceptable trajectories with generative adversarial networks. In: Proceedings of the IEEE Conference on Computer Vision and Pattern Recognition, pp. 2255–2264 (2018)
14. Hong, J., Sapp, B., Philbin, J.: Rules of the road: predicting driving behavior with a convolutional model of semantic interactions. In: The IEEE Conference on Computer Vision and Pattern Recognition (CVPR) (2019)
15. Ivanovic, B., Pavone, M.: The trajectron: probabilistic multi-agent trajectory modeling with dynamic spatiotemporal graphs (2018)
16. Johnson-Roberson, M., Barto, C., Mehta, R., Sridhar, S.N., Vasudevan, R.: Driving in the matrix: Can virtual worlds replace human-generated annotations for real world tasks? (2016). CoRR abs/1610.01983, http://arxiv.org/abs/1610.01983
17. Kesten, R., et al.: Lyft level 5 av dataset 2019 (2019). https://level5.lyft.com/dataset/
18. Kitani, K.M., Ziebart, B.D., Bagnell, J.A., Hebert, M.: Activity forecasting. In: Fitzgibbon, A., Lazebnik, S., Perona, P., Sato, Y., Schmid, C. (eds.) ECCV 2012. LNCS, vol. 7575, pp. 201–214. Springer, Heidelberg (2012). https://doi.org/10.1007/978-3-642-33765-9_15
19. Kosaraju, V., Sadeghian, A., Martín-Martín, R., Reid, I.D., Rezatofighi, S.H., Savarese, S.: Social-bigat: multimodal trajectory forecasting using bicycle-gan and graph attention networks. CoRR abs/1907.03395, http://arxiv.org/abs/1907.03395 (2019)
20. Lee, N., Choi, W., Vernaza, P., Choy, C.B., Torr, P.H.S., Chandraker, M.K.: Desire: distant future prediction in dynamic scenes with interacting agents. In: 2017 IEEE Conference on Computer Vision and Pattern Recognition (CVPR), pp. 2165–2174 (2017)
21. Leurent, E.: An environment for autonomous driving decision-making (2018). https://github.com/eleurent/highway-env
22. Li, Y.: Which way are you going? imitative decision learning for path forecasting in dynamic scenes. In: Proceedings of the IEEE Conference on Computer Vision and Pattern Recognition, pp. 294–303 (2019)
23. Ma, Y., Zhu, X., Zhang, S., Yang, R., Wang, W., Manocha, D.: Trafficpredict: Trajectory prediction for heterogeneous traffic-agents. arXiv preprint arXiv:1811.02146 (2018)
24. OpenStreetMap contributors: Planet dump (2017). https://planet.osm.org. https://www.openstreetmap.org
25. Rhinehart, N., Kitani, K.M., Vernaza, P.: r2p2: a reparameterized pushforward policy for diverse, precise generative path forecasting. In: Ferrari, V., Hebert, M., Sminchisescu, C., Weiss, Y. (eds.) ECCV 2018. LNCS, vol. 11217, pp. 794–811. Springer, Cham (2018). https://doi.org/10.1007/978-3-030-01261-8_47
26. Ros, G., Sellart, L., Materzynska, J., Vazquez, D., Lopez, A.: The SYNTHIA Dataset: A large collection of synthetic images for semantic segmentation of urban scenes (2016)
27. Sadeghian, A., Kosaraju, V., Sadeghian, A., Hirose, N., Savarese, S.: Sophie: an attentive GAN for predicting paths compliant to social and physical constraints (2018). CoRR abs/1806.01482, http://arxiv.org/abs/1806.01482
28. Shah, S., Dey, D., Lovett, C., Kapoor, A.: Airsim: high-fidelity visual and physical simulation for autonomous vehicles (2017). CoRR abs/1705.05065, http://arxiv.org/abs/1705.05065

29. Sohn, K., Lee, H., Yan, X.: Learning structured output representation using deep conditional generative models. In: Advances in Neural Information Processing Systems, pp. 3483–3491 (2015)
30. Srikanth, S., Ansari, J.A., Ram, R.K., Sharma, S., Murthy, J.K., Krishna, K.M.: Infer: intermediate representations for future prediction. In: 2019 IEEE/RSJ International Conference on Intelligent Robots and Systems (IROS) (2019). https://doi.org/10.1109/iros40897.2019.8968553, http://dx.doi.org/10.1109/IROS40897.2019.8968553
31. Sriram, N.N., et al.: A hierarchical network for diverse trajectory proposals. In: 2019 IEEE Intelligent Vehicles Symposium (IV), pp. 689–694 (2019). https://doi.org/10.1109/IVS.2019.8813986
32. Sutskever, I., Vinyals, O., Le, Q.V.: Sequence to sequence learning with neural networks. In: Proceedings of the 27th International Conference on Neural Information Processing Systems, NIPS'14, vol. 2, pp. 3104–3112. MIT Press, Cambridge (2014)
33. Treiber, M., Hennecke, A., Helbing, D.: Congested traffic states in empirical observations and microscopic simulations. Phys. Rev. E Stat. Phys. Plasmas Fluids Related Interdisc. Topics 62(2 Pt A), 1805–1824 (2000)
34. Treiber, M., Kesting, A.: Modeling lane-changing decisions with MOBIL. In: Appert-Rolland, C., Chevoir, F., Gondret, P., Lassarre, S., Lebacque, J.P., Schreckenberg, M. (eds.) Traffic and Granular Flow '07, pp. 211–221. Springer, Heidelberg (2009). https://doi.org/10.1007/978-3-540-77074-9_19
35. Xingjian, S., Chen, Z., Wang, H., Yeung, D.Y., Wong, W.K., Woo, W.C.: Convolutional LSTM network: A machine learning approach for precipitation nowcasting. In: Advances in Neural Information Processing Systems, pp. 802–810 (2015)
36. Zhao, T., et al.: Multi-agent tensor fusion for contextual trajectory prediction. In: The IEEE Conference on Computer Vision and Pattern Recognition (CVPR) (2019)

Label-Driven Reconstruction for Domain Adaptation in Semantic Segmentation

Jinyu Yang(ID), Weizhi An, Sheng Wang, Xinliang Zhu, Chaochao Yan(ID),
and Junzhou Huang$^{(\boxtimes)}$(ID)

University of Texas at Arlington, Arlington, Texas, USA
{jinyu.yang,weizhi.an,sheng.wang,xinliang.zhu,
chaochao.yan}@mavs.uta.edu,jzhuang@uta.edu

Abstract. Unsupervised domain adaptation enables to alleviate the need for pixel-wise annotation in the semantic segmentation. One of the most common strategies is to translate images from the source domain to the target domain and then align their marginal distributions in the feature space using adversarial learning. However, source-to-target translation enlarges the bias in translated images and introduces extra computations, owing to the dominant data size of the source domain. Furthermore, consistency of the joint distribution in source and target domains cannot be guaranteed through global feature alignment. Here, we present an innovative framework, designed to mitigate the image translation bias and align cross-domain features with the same category. This is achieved by 1) performing the target-to-source translation and 2) reconstructing both source and target images from their predicted labels. Extensive experiments on adapting from synthetic to real urban scene understanding demonstrate that our framework competes favorably against existing state-of-the-art methods.

Keywords: Image-to-image translation · Image reconstruction · Domain adaptation · Semantic segmentation

1 Introduction

Deep Convolutional Neural Networks (DCNNs) have demonstrated impressive achievements in computer vision tasks, such as image recognition [20], object detection [17], and semantic segmentation [32]. As one of the most fundamental tasks, semantic segmentation predicts pixel-level semantic labels for given images. It plays an extremely important role in autonomous agent applications such as self-driving techniques.

Electronic supplementary material The online version of this chapter (https://doi.org/10.1007/978-3-030-58583-9_29) contains supplementary material, which is available to authorized users.

Existing supervised semantic segmentation methods, however, largely rely on pixel-wise annotations which require tremendous time and labor efforts. To overcome this limitation, publicly available synthetic datasets (e.g., GTA [41] and SYNTHIA [42]) which are densely-annotated, have been considered recently. Nevertheless, the most obvious drawback of such a strategy is the poor knowledge generalization caused by domain shift issues (e.g., appearance and spatial layout differences), giving rise to dramatic performance degradation when directly applying models learned from synthetic data to real-world data of interest. In consequence, domain adaptation has been exploited in recent studies for cross-domain semantic segmentation, where the most common strategy is to learn domain-invariant representations by minimizing distribution discrepancy between source and target domains [29,56], designing a new loss function [61], considering depth information [7,49], or alternatively generating highly confident pseudo labels and re-training models with these labels through a self-training manner [22,25,28,38,51,54,62]. Following the advances of Generative Adversarial Nets (GAN) [19], adversarial learning has been used to match cross-domain representations by minimizing an adversarial loss on the source and target representations [13,21,34,35], or adapting structured output space across two domains [28,45]. Recent studies further consider the pixel-level (e.g., texture and lighting) domain shift to enforce source and target images to be domain-invariant in terms of visual appearance [1,9,36,52,53,58]. This is achieved by translating images from the source domain to the target domain by using image-to-image translation models such as CycleGAN [60] and UNIT [30].

Despite these painstaking efforts, we are still far from being able to fully adapt cross-domain knowledge mainly stemming from two limitations. First, adversarial-based image-to-image translation introduces inevitable bias to the translated images, as we cannot fully guarantee that the translated source domain $\mathcal{F}(\mathcal{X}_s)$ is identical to the target domain $\mathcal{X}_t$ ($\mathcal{X}_s$ and $\mathcal{X}_t$ denote two domains, and $\mathcal{F}$ indicates an image-to-image translation model). This limitation is especially harmful to the source-to-target translation [1,28,36,52,58], since the data size of the source domain is much larger than the target domain in most of domain adaptation problems. Moreover, source-to-target translation is more computationally expensive than target-to-source translation. Second, simply aligning cross-domain representations in the feature space [1,21,45] ignores the joint distribution shift (i.e., $\mathcal{P}(G(\mathcal{X}_s), Y_s) \neq \mathcal{P}(G(\mathcal{X}_t), Y_t)$, where G is used for feature extraction, while Y_s and Y_t indicate ground truth labels). These limitations give rise to severe false positive and false negative issues in the target prediction. This problem can get even worse when there is a significant discrepancy in layout or structure between the source and target domains, such as adapting from synthetic to real urban traffic scenes.

In this paper, we propose an innovative domain adaptation framework for semantic segmentation. The key idea is to reduce the image translation bias and align cross-domain feature representations through image reconstruction. As opposed to performing source-to-target translation [1,28,52], for the first time, we conduct the target-to-source translation to make target images

Fig. 1. An example of our method on synthetic-to-real urban scene adaptation. Given a target-domain (or real) image (a), we first make target-to-source translation to obtain source-like (or synthetic) image (b), and then perform segmentation on these translated images. Our method improves the segmentation accuracy in the target domain by reconstructing both source and target images from their predicted labels (c). (d) illustrates the image reconstructed from (c), while (e) indicates the ground truth label.

indistinguishable from source images. This enables us to substantially reduce the bias in translated images and allows us to use original source images and their corresponding ground truth to train a segmentation network. Compared to the source-to-target translation, our method is also much more efficient. Besides, a reconstruction network is designed to reconstruct both source and target images from their predicted labels. It is noteworthy that we reconstruct images directly from the label space, rather than the feature space as reported in previous studies. This is essential to guide the segmentation network by penalizing the reconstructed image that semantically deviates from the corresponding input image. Most importantly, this strategy enforces cross-domain features with the same category close to each other.

The performance of our method is evaluated on synthetic-to-real scenarios of urban scene understanding, i.e., GTA5 to Cityscapes and SYNTHIA to Cityscapes. Our results demonstrate that the proposed method achieves significant improvements compared with existing methods. Figure 1 demonstrates an example of our model in adapting cross-domain knowledge in semantic segmentation tasks and reconstructing the input image from its output label. We also carry out comprehensive ablation studies to analyze the effectiveness of each component in our framework.

The contribution of this paper is threefold.

- For the first time, we propose and investigate the target-to-source translation in domain adaptation. It reduces the image translation bias and is more computationally efficient compared to the widely-used source-to-target translation.
- To enforce semantic consistency, we introduce a label-driven reconstruction module that reconstructs both source and target images from their predicted labels.
- Extensive experiments show that our method achieves the new state-of-the-art performance on adapting synthetic-to-real semantic segmentation.

2   Related Work

Semantic Segmentation. Recent achievements in semantic segmentation mainly benefit from the technical advances of DCNNs, especially the emergence of Fully Convolutional Network (FCN) [32]. By adapting and extending contemporary deep classification architectures fully convolutionally, FCN enables pixel-wise semantic prediction for any arbitrary-sized inputs and has been widely recognized as one of the benchmark methods in this field. Numerous methods inspired by FCN were then proposed to further enhance segmentation accuracy, which have exhibited distinct performance improvement on the well-known datasets (e.g., PASCAL VOC 2012 [14] and Cityscapes [11]) [4–6,31,59].

However, such methods heavily rely on human-annotated, pixel-level segmentation masks, which require extremely expensive labeling efforts [11]. In consequence, weakly-supervised methods, which are based on easily obtained annotations (e.g., bounding boxes and image-level tags), were proposed to alleviate the need for effort-consuming labeling [12,40]. Another alternative is to resort to freely-available synthetic datasets (e.g., GTA5 [41] and SYNTHIA [42]) with pixel-level semantic annotations. However, models learned on synthetic datasets suffer from significant performance degradation when directly applied to the real datasets of interest, mainly owing to the domain shift issue.

Domain Adaptation. Domain adaptation aims to mitigate the domain discrepancy between a source and a target domain, which can be further divided into supervised adaptation, semi-supervised adaptation, and unsupervised adaptation, depending on the availability of labels in the target domain. The term unsupervised domain adaptation refers to the scenario where target labels are unavailable and have been extensively studied [15,33,46–48,55,57].

Recent publications have highlighted the complementary role of pixel-level and representation-level adaptation in semantic segmentation [1,7,37,52,58], where the pixel-level adaptation is mainly achieved by translating images from the source domain to the target domain (source-to-target translation). Specifically, unpaired image-to-image translation is used in CyCADA [1] to achieve pixel-level adaptation by restricting cycle-consistency. Similarly, FCAN achieves the image translation by combining the image content in the source domain and the "style" from the target domain [58]. I2IAdapt [37] further considers to align source and target representations based on an image-to-image translation strategy, attempting to adapt domain shift. Instead of using the adversarial learning for image translation, DCAN performs source-to-target translation by leveraging target images for channel-wise alignment [52]. Driven by the fact that geometry and semantics are coordinated with each other, GIO-Ada augments the standard image translation network by integrating geometric information [7]. However, source-to-target translation introduces substantial bias to the translated images, given that the size of the source domain is usually much larger than the target domain. To address this problem, we propose the first-of-its-kind target-to-source image translation to reduce pixel-level domain discrepancy. Compared to the source-to-target translation, it is more computationally efficient and enables us to remove the uncertainty by training the segmentation network with original source images and their corresponding labels.

Motivated by the observation that cross-domain images (e.g., GTA5 and Cityscapes) often share tremendous structural similarities, ASN [45] adapts structured output based on the adversarial learning. The strength of this method is its ability to provide weak supervision to target images by enforcing target outs to be indistinguishable from source outputs. However, it is limited to the scenario where two domains have a huge layout discrepancy, resulting in meaningless predictions for target images. To address this limitation, we further enforce the semantic consistency between target images and their predicted labels through a reconstruction network.

Inspired by the self-training, [22,25,28,38,51, 54] generate pseudo labels for target images and then re-training the segmentation model with these labels. It outperforms the existing methods by a large margin. However, such a strategy underestimates the side effect of pseudo labels that are incorrectly predicted. As a consequence, the segmentation model fails to increasingly improve itself using these wrong ground truth. Instead, our method

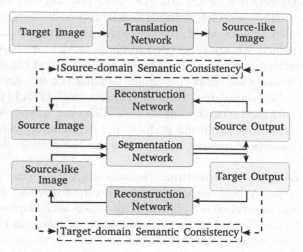

Fig. 2. An overview of our framework.

reconstructs source and target input images from the label space to ensure these outputs are semantically correct. The image-to-image translation network in [28] uses a reconstruction loss and a perceptual loss to maintain the semantic consistency between the input image and the reconstruction from the translated image. Different from [28], we design a cycle-reconstruction loss in our reconstruction network to enforce the semantic consistency between the input image and the reconstruction from the predicted label.

Reconstruction-based strategy for unsupervised domain adaptation has received considerable attention recently [2,16]. The key idea is to reconstruct input images from their feature representations to ensure that the segmentation model can learn useful information. Chang et al. [3] follow a similar idea to first disentangle images into the domain-invariant structure and domain-specific texture representations, and then reconstruct input images. LSD-seg [43] first reconstructs images from the feature space, and then apply a discriminator to the reconstructed images. Rather than performing reconstruction from feature representations, we reconstruct both source and target images from their predicted labels.

3   Algorithm

3.1   Overview

The overall design of our framework is illustrated in Fig. 2, mainly containing three complementary modules: a translation network $\mathcal{F}$, a segmentation network G, and a reconstruction network $\mathcal{M}$. Given a set of source domain images $\mathcal{X}_s$ with labels Y_s and a set of target domain images $\mathcal{X}_t$ without any annotations. Our goal is to train G to predict accurate pixel-level labels for $\mathcal{X}_t$. To achieve this, we first use $\mathcal{F}$ to adapt pixel-level knowledge between $\mathcal{X}_t$ and $\mathcal{X}_s$ by translating $\mathcal{X}_t$ to source-like images $\mathcal{X}_{t \to s}$. This is different from existing prevalent methods that translate images from the source domain to the target domain. $\mathcal{X}_s$ and $\mathcal{X}_{t \to s}$ are then fed into G to predict their segmentation outputs $G(\mathcal{X}_s)$ and $G(\mathcal{X}_{t \to s})$, respectively. To further enforce semantic consistency of both source and target domains, $\mathcal{M}$ is then applied to reconstruct $\mathcal{X}_s$ and $\mathcal{X}_{t \to s}$ from their predicted labels. Specifically, a cycle-reconstruction loss is proposed to measure the reconstruction error, which enforces the semantic consistency and further guides segmentation network to predict more accurate segmentation outputs.

3.2   Target-to-Source Translation

We first perform the image-to-image translation to reduce the pixel-level discrepancy between source and target domains. As opposed to the source-to-target translation reported in previous domain adaptation methods, we conduct the target-to-source translation through an unsupervised image translation network (Fig. 3). Our goal is to learn a mapping $\mathcal{F} : \mathcal{X}_t \to \mathcal{X}_s$ such that the distribution of images from $\mathcal{F}(\mathcal{X}_t)$ is indistinguishable from the distribution of $\mathcal{X}_s$. As a counterpart, the inverse mapping $\mathcal{F}^{-1} : \mathcal{X}_s \to \mathcal{X}_t$, which maps images from $\mathcal{X}_s$ to $\mathcal{X}_t$, is introduced to prevent the mode collapse issue [18]. Two adversarial discriminators $\mathcal{D}_t$ and $\mathcal{D}_s$ are employed for distribution match, where $\mathcal{D}_t$ enforces indistinguishable distribution between $\mathcal{F}(\mathcal{X}_t)$ and $\mathcal{X}_s$, and $\mathcal{D}_s$ encourages indistinguishable distribution between $\mathcal{F}^{-1}(\mathcal{X}_s)$ and $\mathcal{X}_t$ (More details can be found in the **Supplementary**).

Based on the trained model $\mathcal{F}$, we first translate images from $\mathcal{X}_t$ to source-like images $\mathcal{X}_{t \to s} = \mathcal{F}(\mathcal{X}_t)$. Specifically, each image in $\mathcal{X}_{t \to s}$ preserves the same content as the corresponding image in $\mathcal{X}_t$ while demonstrating the common style (e.g., texture and lighting) as $\mathcal{X}_s$. $\mathcal{X}_s$ and $\mathcal{X}_{t \to s}$ are then fed into a segmentation network for semantic label prediction.

Compared to translating images from the source domain to the target domain, the target-to-source translation has three benefits. First, it allows full supervision on the source domain by training the segmentation network with original source images and their corresponding labels. Second, it enables to reduce the bias in translated images. Third, it is computationally efficient lying in the fact that $|\mathcal{X}_t| \ll |\mathcal{X}_s|$.

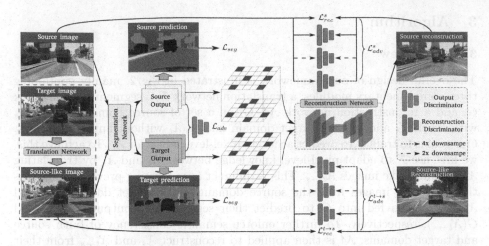

Fig. 3. Schematic overview of our framework which has three modules: (i) a translation network for pixel-level discrepancy reduction by translating target images to source-like images, where source-like images are indistinguishable from source images, (ii) a segmentation network that predicts segmentation outputs for source images and source-like images, and (iii) a reconstruction network for reconstructing source and source-like images from their corresponding label space.

3.3   Semantic Segmentation

Given that source-like images $\mathcal{X}_{t \to s}$ preserves all semantic information from $\mathcal{X}_t$, we apply a shared segmentation network G to $\mathcal{X}_s$ and $\mathcal{X}_{t \to s}$ to predict their segmentation outputs with the loss function given by,

$$\mathcal{L}_G = \mathcal{L}_{seg}(G(\mathcal{X}_s), Y_s) + \mathcal{L}_{seg}(G(\mathcal{X}_{t \to s}), Y_t^{ssl}) \\ + \lambda \mathcal{L}_{adv}(G(\mathcal{X}_s), G(\mathcal{X}_{t \to s})), \tag{1}$$

where $\mathcal{L}_{seg}$ indicates the typical segmentation objective, Y_t^{ssl} is pseudo labels of $\mathcal{X}_{t \to s}$ which is derived from [28], $\mathcal{L}_{adv}(G(\mathcal{X}_s), G(\mathcal{X}_{t \to s}))$ is an adversarial loss, and λ leverages the importance of these losses. Specifically, $\mathcal{L}_{adv}(G(\mathcal{X}_s), G(\mathcal{X}_{t \to s}))$ is defined as,

$$\mathcal{L}_{adv}(G(\mathcal{X}_s), G(\mathcal{X}_{t \to s})) = \mathbb{E}[log D(G(\mathcal{X}_s))] \\ + \mathbb{E}[log(1 - D(G(\mathcal{X}_{t \to s})))], \tag{2}$$

which enforces G to learn domain-invariant features by confusing the discriminator D. It is noteworthy that we regard the segmentation outputs $G(\mathcal{X}_s)$ and $G(\mathcal{X}_{t \to s})$ as features in our study. This is based on the observation that $\mathcal{X}_s$ and $\mathcal{X}_{t \to s}$ share significant similarities in terms of spatial layouts and structures [45].

3.4   Image Reconstruction from the Label Space

To encourage G to generate segmentation outputs that are semantic consistent, we introduce a reconstruction network $\mathcal{M}$ to reconstruct $\mathcal{X}_\phi$ from $G(\mathcal{X}_\phi) \in$

Image   epoch3   epoch6   epoch9

Fig. 4. A comparison between the image reconstruction from feature space and label space (ours). For each input image (first column), the first and second row indicate the images reconstructed from the feature and label space, respectively.

$\mathbb{R}^{H_\phi \times W_\phi \times C}$, where (H_ϕ, W_ϕ) indicates image size, C represents the number of label classes, and the subscript ϕ can be either s or $t{\to}s$ to denote the source or the target domain. However, directly reconstructing images from the feature space fails to provide semantic consistency constraint to G. On the one hand, $G(\mathcal{X}_\phi)$ encodes rich information which makes the image reconstruction quite straightforward. As illustrated in Fig. 4, in just a few epochs, the reconstructed images derived from $\mathcal{M}$ are almost identical to the input images. On the other hand, to enforce cross-domain features with the same category close to each other, it is essential to perform the reconstruction based on the label space. Unfortunately, $G(\mathcal{X}_\phi)$ lies in the feature space instead. To overcome these limitations, the most clear-cut way is to convert $G(\mathcal{X}_\phi)$ to have zeros everywhere except where the index of each maximum value in the last dimension. Doing so formulates the categorical representation of the predicted label that corresponds to $G(\mathcal{X}_\phi)$. Nevertheless, such conversion is non-differentiable and cannot be trained using standard backpropagation.

Driven by the softmax action selection which is commonly used in the reinforcement learning, we apply Boltzmann distributed probabilities to approximate the semantic label map of $G(\mathcal{X}_\phi)$, which is defined as,

$$\Omega_\phi^{(h,w,i)} = \frac{exp(G(\mathcal{X}_\phi)^{(h,w,i)}/\tau)}{\sum_{j=1}^{c} exp(G(\mathcal{X}_\phi)^{(h,w,j)}/\tau)}, \tag{3}$$

where τ is a temperature parameter. This conversion is continuous and differentiable, therefore, we use $\mathcal{M}$ to reconstruct input images $\mathcal{X}_\phi$ from Ω_ϕ (Fig. 4).

To synthesize high-resolution images from the semantic label map, we use conditional GANs [23] to model the conditional distribution of $\mathcal{X}_\phi$ given Ω_ϕ. To this end, we introduce $\mathcal{M}$ and multi-scale domain discriminators D_k for $k = 1, 2, 3$. $\mathcal{M}$ is designed to reconstruct $\mathcal{X}_\phi$ from Ω_ϕ, and D_k aims to distinguish $\mathcal{X}_\phi$ from $\mathcal{M}(\Omega_\phi)$. Specifically, $\mathcal{M}$ follows the architecture proposed in [24], while D_k is based on PatchGAN [23] that penalizes structure at the scale of image patches. All D_k follow the same network architecture. Besides $\mathcal{X}_\phi$ and $\mathcal{M}(\Omega_\phi)$ themselves, they are downsampled by a factor of 2 and 4 to obtain pyramid of 3 scales for D_1, D_2, and D_3, respectively. It is worth mentioning that D_k is essential to differentiate real and reconstructed images with high resolution [50], owing to its ability in providing large receptive field. The objective function is given by,

$$\mathcal{L}_{adv}^{\phi} = \sum_{k=1}^{3} [\mathbb{E}[logD_k(\Omega_\phi, \mathcal{X}_\phi)] \\ + \mathbb{E}[log(1 - D_k(\Omega_\phi, \mathcal{M}(\Omega_\phi)))]] \tag{4}$$

To further enforce semantic consistency between $\mathcal{X}_\phi$ and $\mathcal{M}(\Omega_\phi)$, we introduce a cycle-reconstruction loss $\mathcal{L}_{rec}^{\phi}$ to match their feature representations. $\mathcal{L}_{rec}^{\phi}$ contains a VGG perceptual loss and a discriminator feature matching loss, which is defined as,

$$\mathcal{L}_{rec}^{\phi} = \mathbb{E} \sum_{m=1}^{M} [||V^{(m)}(\mathcal{M}(\Omega_\phi)) - V^{(m)}(\mathcal{X}_\phi)||_1] \\ + \mathbb{E} \sum_{k=1}^{3} \sum_{n=1}^{N} [||D_k^{(n)}(\Omega_\phi, \mathcal{X}_\phi)) - D_k^{(n)}(\Omega_\phi, \mathcal{M}(\Omega_\phi))||_1] \tag{5}$$

where V is a VGG19-based model for extracting high-level perceptual information [24], M and N represent the total number of layers in V and D_k for matching intermediate representations. Note that $\mathcal{L}_{rec}^{\phi}$ penalizes Ω_ϕ when it deviates from the corresponding image $\mathcal{X}_\phi$ in terms of semantic consistency. In this way, $\mathcal{M}$ enables to map features from $\mathcal{X}_{t \rightarrow s}$ closer to the features from $\mathcal{X}_s$ with the same label.

Taken together, the training objective of our framework is formulated as,

$$\min_{G, \mathcal{M}} \max_{D, D_1, D_2, D_3} \mathcal{L}_G + \alpha(\mathcal{L}_{adv}^s + \mathcal{L}_{adv}^{t \rightarrow s}) + \beta(\mathcal{L}_{rec}^s + \mathcal{L}_{rec}^{t \rightarrow s}) \tag{6}$$

where α and β leverage the importance of losses above. Notably, our method is able to implicitly encourage G to generate semantic-consistent segmentation labels for the target domain.

4   Experiments

In this section, a comprehensive evaluation is performed on two domain adaption tasks to assess our framework for semantic segmentation. Specifically, we consider the large distribution shift of adapting from synthetic (i.e., GTA5 [41] and SYNTHIA [42]) to the real images in Cityscapes [11]. A thorough comparison with the state-of-the-art methods and extensive ablation studies are also carried out to verify the effectiveness of each component in our framework.

4.1   Datasets

Cityscapes is one of the benchmarks for urban scene understanding, which is collected from 50 cities with varying scene layouts and weather conditions. The

Table 1. A performance comparison of our method with other state-of-the-art models on "GTA5 to Cityscapes". The performance is measured by the intersection-over-union (IoU) for each class and mean IoU (mIoU). Two base architectures, i.e., VGG16 (V) and ResNet101 (R) are used in our study.

GTA5 → Cityscapes

	Base	road	sidewalk	building	wall	fence	pole	traffic light	traffic sign	vegetation	terrain	sky	person	rider	car	truck	bus	train	motorbike	bicycle	mIoU
Source only	R	75.8	16.8	77.2	12.5	21.0	25.5	30.1	20.1	81.3	24.6	70.3	53.8	26.4	49.9	17.2	25.9	6.5	25.3	36.0	36.6
SIBAN [34]	R	88.5	35.4	79.5	26.3	24.3	28.5	32.5	18.3	81.2	40.0	76.5	58.1	25.8	82.6	30.3	34.4	3.4	21.6	21.5	42.6
CLAN [35]	R	87.0	27.1	79.6	27.3	23.3	28.3	35.5	24.2	83.6	27.4	74.2	58.6	28.0	76.2	33.1	36.7	6.7	31.9	31.4	43.2
DISE [3]	R	91.5	47.5	82.5	31.3	25.6	33.0	33.7	25.8	82.7	28.8	82.7	62.4	30.8	85.2	27.7	34.5	6.4	25.2	24.4	45.4
IntraDA [38]	R	90.6	37.1	82.6	30.1	19.1	29.5	32.4	20.6	**85.7**	40.5	79.7	58.7	31.1	**86.3**	31.5	48.3	0.0	30.2	35.8	46.3
BDL [28]	R	91.0	44.7	84.2	34.6	27.6	30.2	36.0	36.0	85.0	43.6	83.0	58.6	31.6	83.3	35.3	49.7	3.3	28.8	35.6	48.5
CrCDA [22]	R	92.4	**55.3**	82.3	31.2	29.1	32.5	33.2	35.6	83.5	34.8	84.2	58.9	32.2	84.7	40.6	46.1	2.1	31.1	32.7	48.6
SIM [51]	R	90.6	44.7	84.8	34.3	28.7	31.6	35.0	37.6	84.7	43.3	85.3	57.0	31.5	83.8	42.6	48.5	1.9	30.4	39.0	49.2
Kim et al. [25]	R	**92.9**	55.0	**85.3**	**34.2**	**31.1**	**34.9**	**40.7**	34.0	85.2	40.1	**87.1**	61.0	31.1	82.5	32.3	42.9	0.3	**36.4**	46.1	50.2
FDA-MBT [54]	R	92.5	53.3	82.4	26.5	27.6	**36.4**	40.6	**38.9**	82.3	39.8	78.0	**62.6**	34.4	84.9	34.1	**53.1**	**16.9**	27.7	**46.4**	50.45
Ours	R	90.8	41.4	**84.7**	**35.1**	27.5	31.2	38.0	32.8	85.6	42.1	84.9	59.6	**34.4**	85.0	**42.8**	52.7	3.4	30.9	38.1	49.5
Source only	V	26.0	14.9	65.1	5.5	12.9	8.9	6.0	2.5	70.0	2.9	47.0	24.5	0.0	40.0	12.1	1.5	0.0	0.0	0.0	17.9
SIBAN [34]	V	83.4	13.0	77.8	20.4	17.5	24.6	22.8	9.6	81.3	29.6	77.3	42.7	10.9	76.0	22.8	17.9	5.7	14.2	2.0	34.2
ASN [45]	V	87.3	29.8	78.6	21.1	18.2	22.5	21.5	11.0	79.7	29.6	71.3	46.8	6.5	80.1	23.0	26.9	0.0	10.6	0.3	35.0
CyCADA [1]	V	85.2	37.2	76.5	21.8	15.0	23.8	22.9	21.5	80.5	31.3	60.7	50.5	9.0	76.9	17.1	28.2	4.5	9.8	0.0	35.4
CLAN [35]	V	88.0	30.6	79.2	23.4	20.5	26.1	23.0	14.8	81.6	34.5	72.0	45.8	7.9	80.5	26.6	29.9	0.0	10.7	0.0	36.6
CrDoCo [9]	V	89.1	33.2	80.1	26.9	25.0	18.3	23.4	12.8	77.0	29.1	72.4	**55.1**	20.2	79.9	22.3	19.5	1.0	20.1	18.7	38.1
CrCDA [22]	V	86.8	37.5	80.4	30.7	18.1	26.8	25.3	15.1	81.5	30.9	72.1	52.8	19.0	82.1	25.4	29.2	10.1	15.8	3.7	39.1
BDL [28]	V	89.2	40.9	81.2	29.1	19.2	14.2	29.0	19.6	83.7	35.9	80.7	54.7	23.3	82.7	25.8	28.0	2.3	25.7	19.9	41.3
FDA-MBT [54]	V	86.1	35.1	80.6	30.8	20.4	27.5	30.0	26.0	82.1	30.3	73.6	52.5	21.7	81.7	24.0	30.5	**29.9**	14.6	24.0	42.2
Kim et al. [25]	V	**92.5**	**54.5**	**83.9**	**34.5**	**25.5**	**31.0**	30.4	18.0	**84.1**	39.6	**83.9**	53.6	19.3	81.7	21.1	13.6	17.7	12.3	6.5	42.3
SIM [51]	V	88.1	35.8	83.1	25.8	23.9	29.2	28.8	**28.6**	83.0	36.7	82.3	53.7	22.8	82.3	26.4	**38.6**	0.0	19.6	17.1	42.4
Ours	V	90.1	41.2	82.2	30.3	21.3	18.3	**33.5**	23.0	84.1	37.5	81.4	54.2	**24.3**	**83.0**	27.6	32.0	8.1	**29.7**	**26.9**	**43.6**

5,000 finely-annotated images from this dataset are used in our study, which contains 2,975 training images, 500 validation images, and 1,525 test images. Each image with a resolution of 2048 × 1024. The GTA5 dataset is synthesized from the game Grand Theft Auto V (GTA5), including a total of 24,966 labeled images whose annotations are compatible with Cityscapes. The resolution of each image is 1914 × 1052. The SYNTHIA-RAND-CITYSCAPES (or SYNTHIA for short) contains 9,400 pixel-level annotated images (1280 × 760), which are synthesized from a virtual city. Following the same setting reported in the previous studies, we use the labeled SYNTHIA or GTA5 dataset as the source domain, while using the unlabeled training dataset in the CITYSCAPES as the target domain. Only the 500 labeled validation images from CITYSCAPES are used as test data in all of our experiments.

Table 2. A performance comparison of our method with other state-of-the-art models on "SYNTHIA to Cityscapes". The performance is measured by the IoU for each class and mIoU. Two base architectures, i.e., VGG16 (V) and ResNet101 (R) are used in our study.

	Base	road	sidewalk	building	wall	fence	pole	traffic light	traffic sign	vegetation	sky	person	rider	car	bus	motorbike	bicycle	mIoU
Source only	R	55.6	23.8	74.6	—	—	—	6.1	12.1	74.8	79.0	55.3	19.1	39.6	23.3	13.7	25.0	38.6
ASN [45]	R	84.3	42.7	77.5	—	—	—	4.7	7.0	77.9	82.5	54.3	21.0	72.3	32.2	18.9	32.3	46.7
DISE [3]	R	91.7	**53.5**	77.1	—	—	—	6.2	7.6	78.4	81.2	55.8	19.2	82.3	30.3	17.1	34.3	48.8
IntraDA [38]	R	84.3	37.7	79.5	—	—	—	9.2	8.4	80.0	84.1	57.2	23.0	78.0	38.1	20.3	36.5	48.9
Kim et al. [25]	R	**92.6**	53.2	79.2	—	—	—	1.6	7.5	78.6	84.4	52.6	20.0	82.1	34.8	14.6	39.4	49.3
DADA [49]	R	89.2	44.8	**81.4**	—	—	—	8.6	11.1	**81.8**	84.0	54.7	19.3	79.7	40.7	14.0	38.8	49.8
CrCDA [22]	R	86.2	44.9	79.5	—	—	—	9.4	11.8	78.6	**86.5**	57.2	26.1	76.8	39.9	21.5	32.1	50.0
BDL [28]	R	86.0	46.7	80.3	—	—	—	14.1	11.6	79.2	81.3	54.1	27.9	73.7	**42.2**	25.7	45.3	51.4
SIM [51]	R	83.0	44.0	80.3	—	—	—	17.1	15.8	80.5	81.8	59.9	**33.1**	70.2	37.3	28.5	45.8	52.1
FDA-MBT [54]	R	79.3	35.0	73.2	—	—	—	**19.9**	**24.0**	61.7	82.6	**61.4**	31.1	**83.9**	40.8	**38.4**	**51.1**	52.5
Ours	R	85.1	44.5	81.0	—	—	—	16.4	15.2	80.1	84.8	59.4	31.9	73.2	41.0	32.6	44.7	**53.1**
CrCDA [22]	V	74.5	30.5	78.6	6.6	**0.7**	21.2	2.3	8.4	77.4	79.1	45.9	16.5	73.1	24.1	9.6	14.2	35.2
ROAD-Net [8]	V	77.7	30.0	77.5	9.6	0.3	25.8	10.3	15.6	77.6	79.8	44.5	16.6	67.8	14.5	7.0	23.8	36.2
SPIGAN [27]	V	71.1	29.8	71.4	3.7	0.3	**33.2**	6.4	15.6	81.2	78.9	52.7	13.1	75.9	25.5	10.0	20.5	36.8
GIO-Ada [7]	V	78.3	29.2	76.9	**11.4**	0.3	26.5	10.8	17.2	81.7	**81.9**	45.8	15.4	68.0	15.9	7.5	30.4	37.3
TGCF-DA [10]	V	**90.1**	**48.6**	**80.7**	2.2	0.2	27.2	3.2	14.3	**82.1**	78.4	54.4	16.4	**82.5**	12.3	1.7	21.8	38.5
BDL [28]	V	72.0	30.3	74.5	0.1	0.3	24.6	10.2	25.2	80.5	80.0	54.7	23.2	72.7	24.0	7.5	44.9	39.0
FDA-MBT [54]	V	84.2	35.1	78.0	6.1	0.44	27.0	8.5	22.1	77.2	79.6	55.5	19.9	74.8	24.9	14.3	40.7	40.5
Ours	V	73.7	29.6	77.6	1.0	0.4	26.0	**14.7**	**26.6**	80.6	81.8	**57.2**	**24.5**	76.1	**27.6**	13.6	**46.6**	**41.1**

4.2   Network Architecture

We use two segmentation baseline models, i.e., FCN-VGG16 and DeepLab-ResNet101 to investigate the effectiveness and generalizability of our framework. Specifically, FCN-VGG16 is the combination of FCN-8s [32] and VGG16 [44], while DeepLab-ResNet101 is obtained by integrating DeepLab-V2 [6] into ResNet101 [20]. These two segmentation models share the same discriminator which has 5 convolution layers with channel number 64,128, 256, 512, 1. For each layer, a leaky ReLU parameterized by 0.2 is followed, except the last one. The kernel size and stride are set to 4×4 and 2, respectively. The reconstruction model follows the architecture in [24], containing 3 convolution layers (kernel 3×3 and stride 1), 9 ResNet blocks (kernel 3×3 and stride 2), and another 3 transposed convolution layers (kernel 3×3 and stride 2) for upsampling. The 3 multi-scale discriminators share the identical network, each of which follows the architecture of PatchGAN [23]. More details regarding the architecture of discriminators in both segmentation and reconstruction models can be found in the **Supplementary**.

Table 3. Ablation study of the target-to-source translation and the reconstruction network. S → T and T → S indicate source-to-target and target-to-source translation.

Base	S→T	T→S	Reconstruction	GTA5	SYNTHIA
R	✓			48.5	51.4
R		✓		49.1	52.0
R		✓	✓	49.5	53.1
V	✓			41.3	39.0
V		✓		42.3	40.1
V		✓	✓	43.6	41.1

4.3   Implementation Details

Our framework is implemented with PyTorch [39] on two TITAN Xp GPUs, each of which with 12GB memory. The batch size is set to one for training all the models discussed above. Limited by the GPU memory space, the translation network is first trained to perform target-to-source image translation by using Adam optimizer [26]. The initial learning rate is set to 0.0001, which is reduced by half after every 100,000 iterations. We use momentum $\{0.5, 0.999\}$ with weight decay 0.0001. The maximum training iteration is $1000k$.

DeepLab-ResNet101 is trained using Stochastic Gradient Descent optimizer with initial learning rate 2.5×10^{-4}. The polynomial decay with power 0.9 is applied to the learning rate. The momentum and weight decay are set to 0.9 and 5×10^{-4}, respectively. For FCN-VGG16, the Adam optimizer with momentum $\{0.9, 0.99\}$ and initial learning rate 1×10^{-5} is used for training. The learning rate is decreased using step decay with step size 50000 and drop factor 0.1. In equation 1, λ is set to 1×10^{-3} for DeepLab-ResNet101 and 1×10^{-4} for FCN-VGG16.

The reconstruction network is first pre-trained by reconstructing source images $\mathcal{X}_s$ from the corresponding labels Y_s. We use the Adam optimizer with initial learning rate 2×10^{-4} and momentum $\{0.5, 0.999\}$, where the learning rate is linearly decreased to zero. In Eq. 6, we set $\beta = 10$. α is set to 0.01 and 0.001 for FCN-VGG16 and DeepLab-ResNet101 respectively.

4.4   GTA5→Cityscapes

We carry out the adaptation from GTA5 to Cityscapes by following the same evaluation protocol as previously reported in [28,45]. The overall quantitative performance is assessed on 19 common classes (e.g., road, wall, and car) between these two domains. As shown in Table 1, we demonstrate competitive performance against ResNet101-based methods, but are inferior to two newly published models [25,54]. For the VGG16-based backbone, however, we are able to achieve the best results compared to existing state-of-the-art methods including [25,54]. Specifically, our method surpasses the source-only model (without

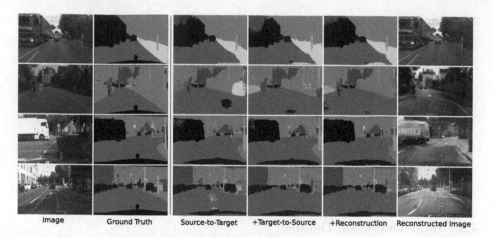

Image   Ground Truth   Source-to-Target   +Target-to-Source   +Reconstruction   Reconstructed Image

Fig. 5. Qualitative examples of semantic segmentation results in Cityscapes. For each target-domain image (first column), its ground truth and the corresponding segmentation prediction from the baseline model (source-to-target translation) are given. The following are predictions of our method by incorporating target-to-source translation and reconstruction, together with the reconstructed image.

Table 4. Ablation study of the temperature τ on GTA5$\rightarrow$Cityscapes.

τ	0.0001	0.001	0.01	0.1	1
mIoU	42.7	**43.6**	42.8	42.9	41.5

adaptation) by 12.9% and 25.7% on ResNet101 and VGG16, respectively. Compared with CyCADA [1] and BDL [28] that rely on source-to-target translation, we demonstrate significant improvements (i.e., 8.2% and 2.3% on VGG16) by reducing image translation bias. CLAN [35] aims to enforce local semantic consistency by a category-level adversarial network. However, such a strategy fails to account for the global semantic consistency. Our reconstruction network shares a similar spirit with CLAN in terms of joint distribution alignment but enables us to enforce semantic consistency from a global view. As a consequence, we get 6.3% and 7.0% improvement on ResNet101 and VGG16, respectively.

4.5   SYNTHIA→Cityscapes

We then evaluate our framework on the adaptation from SYNTHIA to Cityscapes based on 13 classes on ResNet101 and 16 classes on VGG16. The results exhibit that our method outperforms other competing methods on average as shown in Table 2. Both ASN [45] and BDL [28] adapt output space in their models. However, simply aligning segmentation outputs may lead to negative transfer issue, owing to the dramatic differences of the layout and structure between SYNTHIA and Cityscapes. We achieve 6.4% and 1.7% improvement

Table 5. Ablation study of the feature space vs. label space reconstruction.

	Feature space	Label space
GTA5→Cityscapes	41.48	43.6
SYNTHIA→Cityscapes	40.13	41.1

than ASN and BDL on ResNet101, respectively. It is noteworthy that we also outperform [54] on both ResNet101 and VGG16-based backbone.

4.6 Ablation Study

Target-to-Source Translation and Reconstruction. For GTA5 to Cityscapes, 0.6% improvement is achieved by considering target-to-source translation on ResNet101 compared to the source-to-target translation model (Table 3). By further enforce semantic consistency through a reconstruction network, our method achieves 49.5 mIoU. Similar improvements are also observed on VGG16, with 1.0% improvement by performing target-to-source translation. The prediction power of our method is further boosted by combining translation and reconstruction, giving rise to another 1.3% mIoU improvement. The qualitative study of each module in our method is showcased in Fig. 5.

For SYNTHIA to Cityscapes, we achieve a performance boost of 0.6% and 1.1% by considering target-to-source translation on ResNet101 and VGG16, respectively (Table 3). The performance gain is 1.1% and 1.0% by incorporating the reconstruction network. Our results prove the effectiveness of target-to-source translation and reconstruction in adapting domain knowledge for semantic segmentation.

Table 6. Ablation study of the reconstruction loss on GTA5→Cityscapes with VGG16 backbone.

VGG	Discriminator	mIoU
		41.53
✓		42.82
	✓	41.95
✓	✓	43.6

Parameter Analysis. We investigate the sensitivity of temperature parameter τ in this section and find that $\tau = 0.001$ achieves the best performance (Table 4). Therefore, τ is set to 0.001 in all of our experiments to approximate semantic label maps.

Feature Space VS. Label Space Reconstruction. We also evaluate the feature space reconstruction based on the VGG16-based backbone. Table 5 highlights the benefits of our label-driven reconstruction that enforces semantic consistency of target images and their predicted labels.

Reconstruction Loss. Table 6 shows the complementary role of VGG perceptual loss and discriminator feature matching loss (Eq. 5) in maintaining semantic consistency.

5 Conclusion

We propose a novel framework that exploits cross-domain adaptation in the context of semantic segmentation. Specifically, we translate images from the target domain to the source domain to reduce image translation bias and the computational cost. To enforce cross-domain features with the same category close to each other, we reconstruct both source and target images directly from the label space. Experiments demonstrate that our method achieves significant improvement in adapting from GTA5 and SYNTHIA to Cityscapes.

Acknowledgments. This work was partially supported by US National Science Foundation IIS-1718853, the CAREER grant IIS-1553687 and Cancer Prevention and Research Institute of Texas (CPRIT) award (RP190107).

References

1. Cycada: Cycle consistent adversarial domain adaptation. In: International Conference on Machine Learning (ICML) (2018)
2. Bousmalis, K., Trigeorgis, G., Silberman, N., Krishnan, D., Erhan, D.: Domain separation networks. In: Advances in Neural Information Processing Systems (NIPS), pp. 343–351 (2016)
3. Chang, W.L., Wang, H.P., Peng, W.H., Chiu, W.C.: All about structure: adapting structural information across domains for boosting semantic segmentation. In: Proceedings of the IEEE Conference on Computer Vision and Pattern Recognition (CVPR), pp. 1900–1909 (2019)
4. Chen, L.C., et al.: Searching for efficient multi-scale architectures for dense image prediction. In: Advances in Neural Information Processing Systems (NIPS) (2018)
5. Chen, L.C., Papandreou, G., Kokkinos, I., Murphy, K., Yuille, A.L.: Semantic image segmentation with deep convolutional nets and fully connected CRFs. In: International Conference on Learning Representations (ICLR) (2014)
6. Chen, L.C., Papandreou, G., Kokkinos, I., Murphy, K., Yuille, A.L.: Deeplab: semantic image segmentation with deep convolutional nets, atrous convolution, and fully connected crfs. IEEE Trans. Pattern Anal. Mach. Intell. (TPAMI) **40**(4), 834–848 (2018)
7. Chen, Y., Li, W., Chen, X., Gool, L.V.: Learning semantic segmentation from synthetic data: a geometrically guided input-output adaptation approach. In: Proceedings of the IEEE Conference on Computer Vision and Pattern Recognition (CVPR), pp. 1841–1850 (2019)
8. Chen, Y., Li, W., Van Gool, L.: Road: reality oriented adaptation for semantic segmentation of urban scenes. In: Proceedings of the IEEE Conference on Computer Vision and Pattern Recognition (CVPR), pp. 7892–7901 (2018)
9. Chen, Y.C., Lin, Y.Y., Yang, M.H., Huang, J.B.: Crdoco: pixel-level domain transfer with cross-domain consistency. In: Proceedings of the IEEE Conference on Computer Vision and Pattern Recognition (CVPR), pp. 1791–1800 (2019)

10. Choi, J., Kim, T., Kim, C.: Self-ensembling with GAN-based data augmentation for domain adaptation in semantic segmentation. In: Proceedings of the IEEE International Conference on Computer Vision (ICCV) (2019)
11. Cordts, M., et al.: The cityscapes dataset for semantic urban scene understanding. In: Proceedings of the IEEE Conference on Computer Vision and Pattern Recognition (CVPR), pp. 3213–3223 (2016)
12. Dai, J., He, K., Sun, J.: Boxsup: exploiting bounding boxes to supervise convolutional networks for semantic segmentation. In: Proceedings of the IEEE International Conference on Computer Vision (ICCV), pp. 1635–1643 (2015)
13. Du, L., et al.: Ssf-dan: separated semantic feature based domain adaptation network for semantic segmentation. In: Proceedings of the IEEE International Conference on Computer Vision (ICCV) (2019)
14. Everingham, M., Van Gool, L., Williams, C.K.I., Winn, J., Zisserman, A.: The PASCAL Visual Object Classes Challenge (VOC2012) Results (2012). http://www.pascal-network.org/challenges/VOC/voc2012/workshop/index.html
15. Ganin, Y., Lempitsky, V.: Unsupervised domain adaptation by backpropagation. In: International Conference on Machine Learning (ICML) (2015)
16. Ghifary, M., Kleijn, W.B., Zhang, M., Balduzzi, D., Li, W.: Deep reconstruction-classification networks for unsupervised domain adaptation. In: Proceedings of the European Conference on Computer Vision (ECCV), pp. 597–613 (2016)
17. Girshick, R.: Fast r-cnn. In: Proceedings of the IEEE International Conference on Computer Vision (ICCV), pp. 1440–1448 (2015)
18. Goodfellow, I.: Nips 2016 tutorial: generative adversarial networks. arXiv preprint arXiv:1701.00160 (2016)
19. Goodfellow, I., et al.: Generative adversarial nets. In: Advances in Neural Information Processing Systems (NIPS), pp. 2672–2680 (2014)
20. He, K., Zhang, X., Ren, S., Sun, J.: Deep residual learning for image recognition. In: Proceedings of the IEEE Conference on Computer Vision and Pattern Recognition (CVPR), pp. 770–778 (2016)
21. Hoffman, J., Wang, D., Yu, F., Darrell, T.: Fcns in the wild: Pixel-level adversarial and constraint-based adaptation. arXiv preprint arXiv:1612.02649 (2016)
22. Huang, J., Lu, S., Guan, D., Zhang, X.: Contextual-relation consistent domain adaptation for semantic segmentation. In: Proceedings of the European Conference on Computer Vision (ECCV) (2020)
23. Isola, P., Zhu, J.Y., Zhou, T., Efros, A.A.: Image-to-image translation with conditional adversarial networks. In: Proceedings of the IEEE Conference on Computer Vision and Pattern Recognition (CVPR), pp. 1125–1134 (2017)
24. Johnson, J., Alahi, A., Fei-Fei, L.: Perceptual losses for real-time style transfer and super-resolution. In: Proceedings of the European Conference on Computer Vision (ECCV), pp. 694–711 (2016)
25. Kim, M., Byun, H.: Learning texture invariant representation for domain adaptation of semantic segmentation. In: Proceedings of the IEEE/CVF Conference on Computer Vision and Pattern Recognition (CVPR), pp. 12975–12984 (2020)
26. Kingma, D.P., Ba, J.: Adam: a method for stochastic optimization. In: International Conference on Learning Representations (ICLR) (2014)
27. Lee, K.H., Ros, G., Li, J., Gaidon, A.: Spigan: privileged adversarial learning from simulation. In: International Conference on Learning Representations (ICLR) (2019)
28. Li, Y., Yuan, L., Vasconcelos, N.: Bidirectional learning for domain adaptation of semantic segmentation. In: Proceedings of the IEEE Conference on Computer Vision and Pattern Recognition (CVPR) (2019)

29. Lian, Q., Lv, F., Duan, L., Gong, B.: Constructing self-motivated pyramid curriculums for cross-domain semantic segmentation: a non-adversarial approach. In: Proceedings of the IEEE International Conference on Computer Vision (ICCV) (2019)
30. Liu, M.Y., Breuel, T., Kautz, J.: Unsupervised image-to-image translation networks. In: Advances in Neural Information Processing Systems (NIPS), pp. 700–708 (2017)
31. Liu, Z., Li, X., Luo, P., Loy, C.C., Tang, X.: Semantic image segmentation via deep parsing network. In: Proceedings of the IEEE International Conference on Computer Vision (ICCV), pp. 1377–1385 (2015)
32. Long, J., Shelhamer, E., Darrell, T.: Fully convolutional networks for semantic segmentation. In: Proceedings of the IEEE Conference on Computer Vision and Pattern Recognition (CVPR), pp. 3431–3440 (2015)
33. Long, M., Cao, Y., Wang, J., Jordan, M.I.: Learning transferable features with deep adaptation networks. In: International Conference on Machine Learning (ICML) (2015)
34. Luo, Y., Liu, P., Guan, T., Yu, J., Yang, Y.: Significance-aware information bottleneck for domain adaptive semantic segmentation. In: Proceedings of the IEEE International Conference on Computer Vision (ICCV) (2019)
35. Luo, Y., Zheng, L., Guan, T., Yu, J., Yang, Y.: Taking a closer look at domain shift: category-level adversaries for semantics consistent domain adaptation. In: Proceedings of the IEEE Conference on Computer Vision and Pattern Recognition (CVPR), pp. 2507–2516 (2019)
36. Murez, Z., Kolouri, S., Kriegman, D., Ramamoorthi, R., Kim, K.: Image to image translation for domain adaptation. In: Proceedings of the IEEE Conference on Computer Vision and Pattern Recognition (CVPR), pp. 4500–4509 (2018)
37. Murez, Z., Kolouri, S., Kriegman, D., Ramamoorthi, R., Kim, K.: Image to image translation for domain adaptation. In: Proceedings of the IEEE Conference on Computer Vision and Pattern Recognition (CVPR), vol. 13 (2018)
38. Pan, F., Shin, I., Rameau, F., Lee, S., Kweon, I.S.: Unsupervised intra-domain adaptation for semantic segmentation through self-supervision. In: Proceedings of the IEEE/CVF Conference on Computer Vision and Pattern Recognition (CVPR), pp. 3764–3773 (2020)
39. Paszke, A., et al.: Automatic differentiation in pytorch (2017)
40. Pinheiro, P.O., Collobert, R.: From image-level to pixel-level labeling with convolutional networks. In: Proceedings of the IEEE Conference on Computer Vision and Pattern Recognition (CVPR), pp. 1713–1721 (2015)
41. Richter, S.R., Vineet, V., Roth, S., Koltun, V.: Playing for data: ground truth from computer games. In: Proceedings of the European Conference on Computer Vision (ECCV), pp. 102–118 (2016)
42. Ros, G., Sellart, L., Materzynska, J., Vazquez, D., Lopez, A.M.: The synthia dataset: a large collection of synthetic images for semantic segmentation of urban scenes. In: Proceedings of the IEEE Conference on Computer Vision and Pattern Recognition (CVPR), pp. 3234–3243 (2016)
43. Sankaranarayanan, S., Balaji, Y., Jain, A., Lim, S.N., Chellappa, R.: Learning from synthetic data: addressing domain shift for semantic segmentation. In: Proceedings of the IEEE Conference on Computer Vision and Pattern Recognition (CVPR) (2018)
44. Simonyan, K., Zisserman, A.: Very deep convolutional networks for large-scale image recognition. In: International Conference on Learning Representations (ICLR) (2015)

45. Tsai, Y.H., Hung, W.C., Schulter, S., Sohn, K., Yang, M.H., Chandraker, M.: Learning to adapt structured output space for semantic segmentation. In: Proceedings of the IEEE Conference on Computer Vision and Pattern Recognition (CVPR) (2018)
46. Tzeng, E., Hoffman, J., Darrell, T., Saenko, K.: Simultaneous deep transfer across domains and tasks. In: Proceedings of the IEEE International Conference on Computer Vision (ICCV), pp. 4068–4076 (2015)
47. Tzeng, E., Hoffman, J., Saenko, K., Darrell, T.: Adversarial discriminative domain adaptation. In: Proceedings of the IEEE Conference on Computer Vision and Pattern Recognition (CVPR) (2017)
48. Tzeng, E., Hoffman, J., Zhang, N., Saenko, K., Darrell, T.: Deep domain confusion: Maximizing for domain invariance. arXiv preprint arXiv:1412.3474 (2014)
49. Vu, T.H., Jain, H., Bucher, M., Cord, M., Pérez, P.: Dada: depth-aware domain adaptation in semantic segmentation. In: Proceedings of the IEEE International Conference on Computer Vision (ICCV) (2019)
50. Wang, T.C., Liu, M.Y., Zhu, J.Y., Tao, A., Kautz, J., Catanzaro, B.: High-resolution image synthesis and semantic manipulation with conditional GANs. In: Proceedings of the IEEE Conference on Computer Vision and Pattern Recognition (CVPR) (2017)
51. Wang, Z., et al.: Differential treatment for stuff and things: a simple unsupervised domain adaptation method for semantic segmentation. In: Proceedings of the IEEE/CVF Conference on Computer Vision and Pattern Recognition (CVPR), pp. 12635–12644 (2020)
52. Wu, Z., et al.: Dcan: dual channel-wise alignment networks for unsupervised scene adaptation. In: Proceedings of the European Conference on Computer Vision (ECCV), pp. 518–534 (2018)
53. Yang, J., An, W., Yan, C., Zhao, P., Huang, J.: Context-aware domain adaptation in semantic segmentation. arXiv preprint arXiv:2003.04010 (2020)
54. Yang, Y., Soatto, S.: Fda: fourier domain adaptation for semantic segmentation. In: Proceedings of the IEEE/CVF Conference on Computer Vision and Pattern Recognition (CVPR), pp. 4085–4095 (2020)
55. Ying, W., Zhang, Y., Huang, J., Yang, Q.: Transfer learning via learning to transfer. In: International Conference on Machine Learning (ICML), pp. 5072–5081 (2018)
56. Zhang, Y., David, P., Gong, B.: Curriculum domain adaptation for semantic segmentation of urban scenes. In: Proceedings of the IEEE International Conference on Computer Vision (ICCV) (2017)
57. Zhang, Y., et al.: Collaborative unsupervised domain adaptation for medical image diagnosis. IEEE Trans. Image Process. (TIP) **29**, 7834–7844 (2020)
58. Zhang, Y., Qiu, Z., Yao, T., Liu, D., Mei, T.: Fully convolutional adaptation networks for semantic segmentation. In: Proceedings of the IEEE Conference on Computer Vision and Pattern Recognition (CVPR), pp. 6810–6818 (2018)
59. Zhao, H., Shi, J., Qi, X., Wang, X., Jia, J.: Pyramid scene parsing network. In: Proceedings of the IEEE Conference on Computer Vision and Pattern Recognition (CVPR), pp. 2881–2890 (2017)

60. Zhu, J.Y., Park, T., Isola, P., Efros, A.A.: Unpaired image-to-image translation using cycle-consistent adversarial networks. In: Proceedings of the IEEE International Conference on Computer Vision (ICCV) (2017)
61. Zhu, X., Zhou, H., Yang, C., Shi, J., Lin, D.: Penalizing top performers: conservative loss for semantic segmentation adaptation. In: Proceedings of the European Conference on Computer Vision (ECCV), pp. 568–583 (2018)
62. Zou, Y., Yu, Z., Vijaya Kumar, B.V.K., Wang, J.: Unsupervised domain adaptation for semantic segmentation via class-balanced self-training. In: Ferrari, V., Hebert, M., Sminchisescu, C., Weiss, Y. (eds.) ECCV 2018. LNCS, vol. 11207, pp. 297–313. Springer, Cham (2018). https://doi.org/10.1007/978-3-030-01219-9_18

Efficient Outdoor 3D Point Cloud Semantic Segmentation for Critical Road Objects and Distributed Contexts

Chi-Chong Wong$^{(\boxtimes)}$ ⑩ and Chi-Man Vong ⑩

University of Macau, Macau, China
amilton.wong@connect.um.edu.mo, cmvong@um.edu.mo

Abstract. Large-scale point cloud semantic understanding is an important problem in self-driving cars and autonomous robotics navigation. However, such problem involves many challenges, such as i) critical road objects (e.g., pedestrians, barriers) with diverse and varying input shapes; ii) distributed contextual information across large spatial range; iii) efficient inference time. Failing to deal with such challenges may weaken the mission-critical performance of self-driving car, e.g, LiDAR road objects perception. In this work, we propose a novel neural network model called Attention-based Dynamic Convolution Network with Self-Attention Global Contexts(ADConvnet-SAGC), which i) applies attention mechanism to adaptively focus on the most task-related neighboring points for learning the point features of 3D objects, especially for small objects with diverse shapes; ii) applies self-attention module for efficiently capturing long-range distributed contexts from the input; iii) a more reasonable and compact architecture for efficient inference. Extensive experiments on point cloud semantic segmentation validate the effectiveness of the proposed ADConvnet-SAGC model and show significant improvements over state-of-the-art methods.

Keywords: 3D semantic segmentation · Attention · Point convolution · Point clouds

1 Introduction

Point cloud based semantic segmentation is a task to classify the labeling of each 3D point of input point cloud. It is an essential task for many applications, such as service-robots autonomous navigation in indoor scenario, self-driving vehicles in outdoor environment. Specifically, large-scale outdoor LiDAR dataset NPM3D [17] covers kilometers scale in range across multiple cities. Moreover, road objects such as pedestrians, barriers, bollards in NPM3D dataset always exhibit as small-sized 3D objects and diverse shapes. Failing to accurately understanding those critical road objects will cause unexpected damages and even deaths. Thus, tackling large-scale outdoor point cloud semantic segmentation involves many

© Springer Nature Switzerland AG 2020
A. Vedaldi et al. (Eds.): ECCV 2020, LNCS 12372, pp. 499–514, 2020.
https://doi.org/10.1007/978-3-030-58583-9_30

challenges, such as i) critical road objects (e.g., pedestrians, barriers and bollards), as they are always exhibited as small objects with diverse and varying shapes; ii) the contextual information of large-scale scenes are always distributed across long spatial range; iii) the demand of efficient inference operation. Failing to deal with such challenges will significantly lower the performance of 3D scene understanding, e.g. LiDAR-based semantic segmentation on road objects from LiDAR input, which is vital for self-driving cars.

Deep convolutional neural network (CNN) [11,12] based approach has shown its superior performance in many image-based vision tasks such as 2D semantic segmentation [4,21] and thus becomes a mainstream method. In retrospect to the recent studies on deep learning based methods for point cloud analysis [3,9,16], it is found that such methods cannot provide segmentation results with sufficient accuracy, especially for small objects with diverse shapes or large-scale scenes with distributed contexts. PointNet [3] extracts features individually for each point, but without considering neighboring point information. Its variant, PointNet++ [16] applies PointNet model to hierarchically extract local information at small group of each sampled point, while similar work PointCNN [9] extracts local features by convolution operation with an additional learnable module for canonical transformation. However, all of such methods have not considered how to adapt the feature extraction operation for diverse input shapes and how to provide an effective way to capture the distributed contexts across large spatial range.

There are few studies on dynamic adaptions on the diverse shape of irregular point clouds for convolution operation. Similar work such as DeformConv [4] is only applicable to 2D image domain. In order to perform accurate segmentation on small critical 3D objects on the road (e.g., pedestrians, barriers, bollards) which exhibits diverse and varying shapes, we argue that it is essential to adapt convolution operation on the shapes of 3D objects to better extract the shape features, such a way is more natural and avoids the loss of information which comes from inaccurate transformation in PointNet [3] and PointCNN [9] methods.

A recent work, GACNet [22] tries to mitigate these issues by adding the attention mechanism to graph convolution for processing the point cloud. However, we argue that such approach does not provide an effective and adaptive manner in aggregating features, since the potentially valuable information of neighboring points will be lost if they are not selected as the vertices of the graph in initial scale. Also, GACNet [22] lacks of a mechanism in capturing global contextual information for large-scale point cloud.

Taking such motivation, a novel convolution operation called *attention-based dynamic point convolution* (ADConv) is proposed to specifically deal with 3D point clouds with diverse and varying shapes. Instead of learning a transformation to align the input point clouds to have canonical pose, attentional weights are injected into neighboring points within the local area of each input point. Through the learned attentional weights representing the similarities of spatial positions and semantic features between neighboring points and input point, the convolution operations can dynamically focus on the most task-related portions of the input, and ignore the unrelated parts. Such attentional weighting scheme is equivalent to dynamically deform the receptive field of convolution to the shapes of 3D objects. Unlike GACNet [22], ADConv applies sampling and grouping operations in each stage to ensure all neighboring points to have the opportunities to be assigned attention weights, which acts as a more effective approach for neighboring points features extraction.

To tackle the second issue in point cloud semantic segmentation, such as difficulty in capturing distributed contexts in large-scale scene, a novel *self-attention global context* (SAGC) module is proposed to be integrated with ADConv for capturing distributed contexts, without the need of stacking many layers of convolution operations for enlarging its receptive field. As a result, a more reasonable and compact architecture called ADConvnet-SAGC is proposed for efficient semantic segmentation for large-scale 3D point cloud.

In summary, the main contributions of the work are highlighted as follows:

1. With the novel attention-based dynamic point convolution (ADConv), the convolutional operation can be dynamically adapted to the diverse shapes of 3D objects, especially for critical road objects.
2. A novel self-attention global context (SAGC) module is proposed to efficiently capture the distributed contextual information globally to further improve the accuracy of 3D semantic segmentation.
3. Instead of stacking many layers of convolution operations, a more reasonable and compact architecture is proposed for efficient semantic segmentation.

From these contributions, an accurate and efficient 3D semantic segmentation model for large-scale scene called ADConvnet-SAGC is presented. Extensive experiments are evaluated on challenging benchmarks, which demonstrate that the proposed model achieves state-of-the-arts results.

2   Related Works

In this section, the two main related techniques: deep learning methods on point clouds and attention mechanism are discussed.

2.1   Deep Learning on Point Clouds

With the unprecedented success of convolutional neural network (CNN) in 2D image recognition problem [5,6,18], there have been exploratory works to adapt its hierarchical feature learning capability for 3D point cloud input. These works can be mainly categorized as voxel based [12,23], multiple-views based [15,19] and point based methods [3,9,16,24]. The point based approach will be mainly discussed.

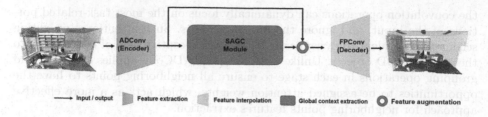

Fig. 1. Illustration on the architecture of ADConvnet-SGAC.

Point Based Approach. Several developments in feature learning directly from 3D point cloud [3,16] have been proposed in recent years. PointNet [3] uses a shared multiple layers perceptron (MLP) on each 3D point individually to learn spatial encoding, then max pooling is applied to obtain a global features of the point cloud input. However, such method ignores the local spatial relationships among neighboring points, which leads to limited performance. Further extension work PointNet++ [16] is proposed to apply PointNet model on a small neighboring sphere centered at each point for constructing hierarchical features, but its unnecessary high computational complexity limits its performance. PointCNN [9] applies the learned χ-transformation to weight input features. However, the learned χ-transformation does not afford to represent objects with complex 3D shapes and the shape structure of objects cannot be well captured for feature learning. Some recent works [14,28] also try to improve the feature representations by learning both instance and semantic segmentation tasks simultaneously.

2.2   Attention Mechanism

As attention mechanism can deal with inputs with varying sizes, and focus on the most related parts of input with respect to the task, it has been considered as an effective way in dealing with sequence tasks, such as machine translation [2], image captioning [26], language modeling [21] tasks. Recent works [22,25] propose to add weights for adapting the convolution operations, but we argue that the weighting schemes in [22,25] are not convincingly effective. Motivated by these, a novel ADConv is proposed to adopts attention mechanism to extract local features in effective manner.

Global contexts are essential for large-scale point cloud processing. [27] applies RNN to capture contexts but it suffers from computational inefficiency. Self attention [21] has been shown as a powerful approach in capturing long-range dependency of input. In this work, the SAGC module is appended for further capturing the global contexts of point clouds.

3   Methods

In this section, the details of the proposed network model: Attention-based Dynamic Point Convolutional Neural Network with Self-Attention Global

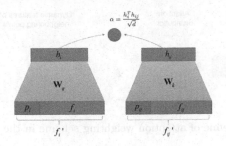

Fig. 2. Illustration on the computation of attention score function α.

Context (ADConvnet-SAGC) for 3D point cloud semantic segmentation is presented. The ADConvnet-SAGC consists of three core modules: 1) Attention-based Dynamic Point Convolution (ADConv) module for dynamically adapting the convolution operation for irregular point cloud input via attention mechanism, 2) Self-Attention Global Context (SAGC) module for capturing long range contextual information globally by self-attention mechanism, 3) Feature Propagation Convolution (FPConv) module for feature interpolation. Figure 1 illustrates the architecture of the entire network. The descriptions of each proposed module are detailed as follows.

3.1 Attention-Based Dynamic Point Convolution (ADConv)

An input point cloud is presented as a set of points $P \in \mathbb{R}^{N \times 3}$ and its corresponding set of features $F \in \mathbb{R}^{N \times D}$, where N and D are the number of points and the dimension of input features, respectively. The xyz position and feature of each point P_i is denoted as $p_i \in \mathbb{R}^3$ and $f_i \in \mathbb{R}^D$, respectively. The set of neighboring points of p_i is denoted as $\mathcal{N}_i$. The proposed ADConv operation is designed to learn a mapping function $q : \mathbb{R}^D \to \mathbb{R}^C$, which maps the features of neighboring points to the new aggregated features of input point P_i, while keeping the advantageous properties of convolutional operation [8], such as i) locality through local receptive field, ii) translation invariance through weights sharing and iii) hierarchical compositionality on extracted features. More importantly, it is required to handle the properties of irregular point cloud, such as the permutation invariance and shape-varying neighborhoods.

For ADConv operation, attention weights injected into neighboring points are used to represent the similarities of spatial positions and semantic features for neighboring points. Through end-to-end training, the attention weights can be adjusted to fit the segmentation task by following general backpropagation. As a result, ADConv can selectively focus on the most task-related parts with sufficient discriminative semantics. Equivalently speaking, convolutional kernel in ADConv can be dynamically adapted to the varying structure of input point cloud.

The pipeline of ADConv is detailed as follows: First, instead of using time-consuming sampling method, such as farthest point sampling (FPS) [16], random

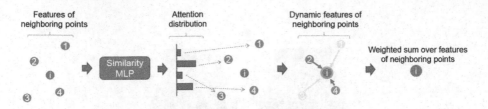

Fig. 3. The pipeline of attention weighting scheme in the ADConv layer.

sampling (RS) is adopted to sample N input points into M sub-sampled points. The value for M is selected at $N/4$ in general. For each sub-sampled input point $P_i \in \{P_1, P_2, ...P_M\}$, which contains xyz position $p_i \in \mathbb{R}^3$ and features $f_i \in \mathbb{R}^D$, its K neighboring points are randomly selected as $P_{i,j}$ ($j = 1, ..., K$) from its spherical neighborhood.

According to the definition of attention: *Given a set of key-values, and a query, attention is a technique to compute a weighted sum of the values, dependent on the similarity between query and a set of keys.* In our case, query refers to input point P_i: (p_i, f_i), and keys refer to neighboring points P_{ij}: (p_{ij}, f_{ij}). To measure the similarity between the query and a set of keys, an attention score function α_{ij} is used. For point cloud, the position proximity and features similarity can naturally reflect such similarity between points. Thus, as illustrated in Fig. 2, position p is first concatenated with feature f as compound features f', which gives f'_i and f'_{ij}. Then, to obtain features with semantics enhanced information for better comparison, a multilayer perceptron (MLP) with learnable weights W_q and W_k are applied onto f'_i and f'_{ij} to get enhanced features $h_i \in \mathbb{R}^C$ and $h_{ij} \in \mathbb{R}^C$, respectively. C is the dimension number of enhanced features. Finally, the attention score function α_{ij} is computed as the inner product between h_i and h_{ij} to obtain similarity measurement between P_i and P_{ij}:

$$\alpha_{ij} = \frac{h_i^T h_{ij}}{\sqrt{C}} \tag{1}$$

$\sqrt{C}$ is used to normalize the effect of feature dimension.

To obtain attention distribution a_{ij}, a softmax function is applied to normalize α_{ij} across all neighboring points

$$a_{ij} = \frac{\exp(\alpha_{ij})}{\sum_{j \in \mathcal{N}_i} \exp(\alpha_{ij})} \tag{2}$$

Finally, the attention distribution a_{ij} is applied on the enhanced features of neighboring points h_{ij} to obtain dynamic features h'_i for input point P_i as illustrated in Fig. 3:

$$h'_i = \sum_{j \in \mathcal{N}_i} a_{ij} h_{ij} \in \mathbb{R}^C \tag{3}$$

We can see that the attention output h'_i is the weighted sum of related parts of neighboring points. As a result, the context information around the input

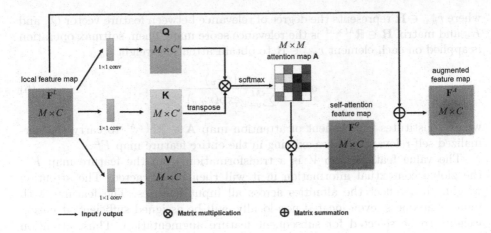

Fig. 4. The pipeline of SAGC module.

point P_i is captured by such attention mechanism. The overall operation on the attention weighting scheme is illustrated in Fig. 3. It is shown that the most related part of neighboring points, P_2 and P_4 are maintained by attention weight, while the other points P_1 and P_3 are eliminated.

Finally, as the same as general convolution operation, h'_i is passed into a non-linear activation such as ReLU [13] to obtain high-level features $f_i^{out} =$ ReLU$(h'_i) \in \mathbb{R}^C$, as the output of ADConv layer. And all of such points features constitute a feature map $F^{out} \in \mathbb{R}^{M \times C}$, where M is the number of sub-sampled points and can be regarded as the spatial size of feature map.

3.2 Self-Attention Global Context (SAGC) Module

To capture global contextual information from the input, traditional convolution based methods require many convolutional layers to enlarge the receptive field. Such way may consume large volume of memory and longer inference time. In this work, we adopt self-attention mechanism [21] to avoid these issues.

The goal of self-attention is to globally extract the long range contexts from the entire feature map F^{out}, by means of extracting the self-similarity for any pair of elements in feature map F^{out}. As illustrated in Fig. 4, given the feature map $F^L = F^{out} \in \mathbb{R}^{M \times C}$, the SAGC module applies three different 1×1 conv filters on F^L to obtain three feature maps: query feature map $Q \in \mathbb{R}^{M \times C'}$, key feature map $K \in \mathbb{R}^{M \times C'}$, value feature map $V \in \mathbb{R}^{M \times C}$. The query feature map Q and key feature map K take the role in measuring the pairwise similarity for each pair of element in F_L. For each spatial position u, a feature vector $Q_u \in \mathbb{R}^{C'}$ of feature map Q is selected for affinity comparison, where $u = [1, ..., M]$. Also, $K_v \in \mathbb{R}^{C'}$ is the feature vector of feature map K for each lookup position $v = [1, ..., M]$. Then, affinity operation is applied between Q_u and K_v to obtain the relevance score $r_{u,v}$,

$$r_{u,v} = Q_u^T K_v \tag{4}$$

where $r_{u,v} \in \mathbf{R}$ represents the degree of relevance between feature vector Q_u and K_v and matrix $\mathbf{R} \in \mathbb{R}^{M \times M}$ is the relevance score map. Then, softmax operation is applied on each element $r_{u,v} \in \mathbf{R}$ to obtain attention weight $a_{u,v}$

$$a_{u,v} = \frac{\exp(r_{u,v})}{\sum_{v=1}^{M} \exp(r_{u,v})} \qquad (5)$$

which constitutes the element of attention map $\mathbf{A} \in \mathbb{R}^{M \times M}$ to carry the normalized self-relevance degree existing in the entire feature map F^L.

The value feature map V is a transformation from the feature map F^L, the global contextual information in it will then be extracted. The attention weights $a_{u,v}$ reflect the affinities across all input features. The features with more relatedness, even located non-locally, will be assigned sufficient attention weights to be selected for subsequent feature augmentation. Thus, attention weight $a_{u,v}$ is applied to all feature vectors in value feature map V to obtain the global feature vector F_u^G:

$$F_u^G = \sum_{v=1}^{M} a_{u,v} V_v \qquad (6)$$

where $F_u^G \in \mathbb{R}^C$ denotes a feature vector of self-attention feature map $F^G \in \mathbb{R}^{M \times C}$ at spatial position u, which captures the long-range global contexts. Then, it is added to the original local feature map F^L to obtain the augmented feature map $F^A = F^G + F^L$. As a result, long-range contextual information is adaptively aggregated to augment the point-wise representation for better performing the semantic segmentation task.

As the feature maps are downsampled after processed by each ADConv layer, the augmented feature map F^A is subsequently interpolated by Feature Propagation (FPConv) module [16] for recovering the point features as the original scale of input point cloud, which is the final point-wise predictions. The whole proposed network model ADConvnet-SAGC can be trained in an end-to-end manner.

3.3 Network Architectures

Following the network design of Pointnet++ [16], ADConvnet-SAGC adopts encoder decoder style. The encoder module contains four ADConv layers, which acts as local features extractor. Then, the extracted local features is fed into SAGC module to obtain augmented features with global contextual information. As the semantic segmentation task requires to upsample the feature maps downsampled by the encoder, the decoder module(four FPConv layers) is employed for progressively upsampling the features.

Fig. 5. Visualizations on qualitative results for S3DIS validation set. From left to right are XYZ-RGB input, ground truth labels annotations and prediction of ADConvnet-SGAC model.

4 Experiments

Experiments have been conducted to verify the effectiveness of the proposed ADConvnet-SAGC model in 3D point cloud semantic segmentation task. The evaluations are performed on both indoor and outdoor large-scale benchmarks, such as the Stanford Large-Scale 3D Indoor Spaces (S3DIS) [1] dataset and the Nuage de Points et Modélisation 3D (NPM3D) [17] dataset. For performance measurement, the point-wise overall accuracy (OA), mean intersection over union (mIoU) over all classes and per-class intersection over union (cIoU) are adopted as evaluation metrics. After that, the ablation analysis on each key components of ADConvnet-SAGC model is provided.

4.1 Training Details

The Adam optimizer with default hyper-parameters is applied for optimizing the cross entropy loss as the training loss. The initial learning rate is set to 0.01 and decreased by 10% after each epoch. To train the proposed ADConvnet-SAGC model, $N = 4096$ points are sampled from the input point cloud as the input. The number of neighboring points K is selected as 64. All settings are consistent for both S3DIS [1] and NPM3D [17] dataset. All experiments and runtime analysis were conducted using Nvidia 1080Ti GPU and an i7-5820K CPU clocked at 3.30 GHz. The implementation is built on Pytorch framework.

4.2 Indoor Point Cloud Segmentation on S3DIS Dataset

The Stanford 3D semantic parsing dataset (S3DIS) [1] is a large-scale benchmark for indoor 3D semantic perception task in service-robots autonomous navigation or indoor scene understanding. The S3DIS dataset covers six large-scale indoor areas within three different buildings, which contains 272 different rooms in various types (e.g. office, conference room, hall, lobby., etc.) and sums up to 215 million points in total. The indoor scene is captured by a high-quality Matterport scanner which generates dense 3D point clouds with RGB color and

Table 1. Quantitative comparison of *ADConvnet-SAGC* on S3DIS dataset

Method	OA	mIoU	ceiling	floor	wall	beam	column	window	door	table	chair	sofa	bookcase	board	clutter
PointNet [3]	78.5	47.6	88.0	88.7	69.3	42.4	23.1	47.5	51.6	54.1	42.0	9.6	38.2	29.4	35.2
PointNet++ [16]	80.9	53.2	90.2	91.7	73.1	42.7	21.2	49.7	42.3	62.7	59.0	19.6	45.8	38.2	45.6
DGCNN [24]	83.3	56.3	92.9	93.8	73.1	42.5	25.9	47.6	59.2	60.4	66.7	24.8	57.0	36.7	51.6
GACNet [22]	83.0	56.2	90.8	92.4	75.9	40.3	19.3	47.6	52.8	66.4	70.2	28.9	55.2	40.5	50.6
ADConvnet-SAGC	87.5	60.1	93.3	95.4	78.3	43.7	27.6	50.3	68.1	69.2	71.2	30.6	57.6	41.0	54.6

the corresponding semantic label for each point is densely annotated. Each 3D point is assigned with one of thirteen class labels (e.g. ceiling, floor, wall, table, chair., etc). For quantitative evaluation, we follow the general setting to select Area-1,2,3,4,6 as the training set, and Area-5 as the validation set for accuracy evaluation.

During the pre-process step, the dataset is first split 1.0 m 1.0 m blocks for each room. Then, each block is uniformly sampled into 4,096 points. The batch size for training is selected as 24.

Quantitative and Qualitative Results: The quantitative results of the experimental results are provided in Table 1. It is shown that the proposed ADConvnet-SAGC provides better results against other competitive methods. Particularly, ADConvnet-SAGC achieves significant gains in objects with varying shapes, such as table, chair, sofa, which is shown as consistent results that the attention mechanism in ADConv takes effects on capturing the irregular shapes of such objects. In terms of mean IoU, ADConvnet-SAGC obtains a 13% relative improvement over Pointnet++ [16] method, and achieves an relative improvement of 6.8% when comparing with DGCNN [24] method and GACNet [22] method. As GACNet [22] didn't open source the code at the period of this work, we directly re-implement it. To give fair comparison, we adopt the same training setting as ADConv-SAGC.

The qualitative segmentation results on validation set of S3DIS dataset are also illustrated in Fig. 5, in which the prediction from ADConvnet model is greatly consistent with the ground truth labels annotations, even though the S3DIS dataset exhibits a lot of intra-class varying shapes.

4.3 Outdoor Point Cloud Segmentation on NPM3D Dataset

The proposed ADConvnet-SAGC model is also evaluated on NPM3D dataset [17], which is a large-scale benchmark for outdoor 3D semantic perception task in self-driving vehicles or traffic scene understanding. The NPM3D dataset consists of aggregated scans with up to 160 million point-wise annotated 3D points from mobile laser scanner Velodyne HDL-32e mounted on vehicle. It covers streets in more 2 km range across four different cities, Paris, Lille, Ajaccio and Dijon. Following the official evaluation protocol, 9 classes (ground, buildings, poles, bollards, trash cans, barriers, pedestrians, cars, natural) are selected for evaluation. The dataset gives challenging real-word scenario such as varying point cloud densities and complex scene surroundings.

Table 2. Quantitative comparison of *ADConvnet-SAGC* on NPM3D dataset

Method	mIoU	Ground	Building	Pole	Bollard	Trash can	Barrier	Pedestrian	Car	Natural
Validation set: Lille2 sequence										
PointNet++ [16]	43.0	97.6	90.2	28.8	12.2	10.6	9.5	19.9	59.8	58.2
DGCNN [24]	53.5	97.9	93.2	49.9	37.5	17.2	18.3	19.2	88.9	59.2
PointSIFT [7]	63.4	98.3	95.6	51.5	45.8	54.3	33.9	31.6	88.2	71.5
MS-PCNN [11]	70.5	98.1	95.4	57.6	64.6	63.0	34.1	57.7	95.2	68.3
GACNet [22]	69.3	98.0	94.2	61.3	64.2	59.3	35.2	51.1	89.9	70.9
ADConvnet-SAGC	**80.4**	**98.6**	**96.2**	**67.4**	**75.1**	**68.2**	**54.4**	**80.7**	**95.2**	**88.1**
Test set: Ajaccio and Dijon sequence										
RF-MSSF [20]	56.3	99.3	88.6	47.8	67.3	2.3	27.1	20.6	74.8	78.8
MS3-DVS [17]	66.9	99.0	94.8	52.4	38.1	36.0	49.3	52.6	91.3	88.6
HDGCN [10]	68.3	99.4	93.0	67.7	75.75	25.7	44.7	37.1	81.9	90.0
ADConvnet-SAGC	**80.2**	**99.5**	**96.1**	**69.2**	**76.3**	**53.6**	**56.5**	**83.7**	**94.6**	**92.2**

Quantitative and Qualitative Results: In Table 2, the results of proposed model are shown with comparisons with several state-of-the-art methods on NPM3D dataset. The comparison result shows obvious superiority of the proposed ADConvnet-SAGC model over the state-of-the-art methods such as PointNet++ [16], DGCNN [24], PointSIFT [7], MS-PCNN [11], MS3-DVS [17], HDGCN [10]. Following the publicly available benchmark results, the per-class IoU and the mean IoU score for valiation set (Lille2 sequence) and test set (Ajaccio, Dijon sequence) are reported. In terms of the mean IoU, ADConvnet-SAGC outperforms MS-PCNN by more than 14%, and achieves an accuracy improvement of 17.4% when comparing with HDGCN method. It is observed that objects across large spatial range such as ground, building and natural can be segmented in high accuracy. In addition to this result, small critical objects with diverse shapes such as barrier, pedestrian, the proposed model provides significant accuracy gains compared with previous state-of-the-art methods.

The qualitative segmentation results on test set (Ajaccio, Dijon sequence) of NPM3D dataset are shown in Fig. 6. The left column shows the original XYZ input, the second and the third column are the global view and detailed view on prediction of our model, respectively. The prediction shows fine and coherent segmentation output on scene objects, even on challenging ones, e.g. small objects trash can and bollard, objects with varying shapes within large spatial area like building and natural objects.

4.4 Effectiveness Analysis of Attention Mechanisms

In Fig. 7, an attention map learned from end-to-end training is illustrated. The reference point is highlighted in green color. For better visualization, the neighboring points assigned with enough attentional weights are highlighted in red color. It is observed that those *attended* parts adapt to the shape of the corner of chair and correspond to the most task-related parts with sufficient discriminative semantics. Through self-attention, global contexts distributed distantly are

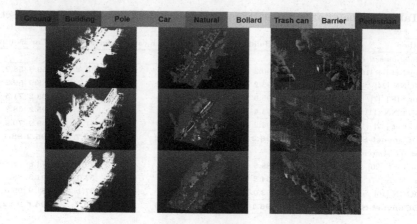

| Ground | Building | Pole | Car | Natural | Bollard | Trash can | Barrier | Pedestrian |

Fig. 6. Qualitative results on NPM3D test set. From left to right are original XYZ input, global view and detailed view on prediction of our model.

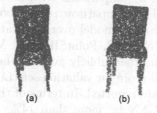

(a)   (b)

Fig. 7. Visualization of the attention map for example object in ModelNet40 dataset. The green point is the reference point while the regions in red are points assigned with sufficient attentional weights. Two cases of different reference points are illustrated: (a) the corner and (b) the leg of a chair. (Color figure online)

also finely captured, as illustrated in the red regions located at the other three corners (Fig. 7(a)) or three legs (Fig. 7(b)) of the chair.

Here, we also perform a sensitivity analysis on the value of K. The comparison result for S3DIS dataset is listed in Table 3. It is observed that the option on smaller value ($K = 16$) gives lower score, since too few neighboring points cannot capture sufficient semantic patterns. The options for $K = 64$, $K = 128$ give almost the same accuracy. We argue that the attention approach provide a mechanism to focus on the most task-related parts, the redundant parts in the case of the larger value of K will be ignored since they are assigned with low attention weights. Therefore, our model choose the option $K = 64$ to balance the trade-off between accuracy and memory costs.

4.5   Efficiency of ADConvnet-SAGC

To evaluate the efficiency of ADConvnet-SAGC, the inference time for input point cloud is listed in Table 4. The evaluation is performed on Lille2 sequence

Table 3. The effects of different options of K value. The evaluation metric is the mIoU score on Area 5 sequence of S3DIS dataset

K=16	K=64	K=128
59.0	60.5	60.6

of NPM3D dataset and the resulting inference time consumption and mIoU are listed for comparison. In Table 4, the proposed ADConvnet-SAGC consumes 318.0 s for inferencing the whole Lille2 sequence (around 30 million points), which consumes up to 2.3 times less inference time than PointNet++ and DGCNN. The percentage of improvement against PointNet++ method is also listed, which shows significant the reduction in inference time of ADConvnet-SAGC.

Table 4. Inference time comparison

Method	NPM3D (Lille2 sequence)	
	Inference time (second)	mIoU
PointNet++	756.2 (0%)	43.0
DGCNN	630.2 (120%)	53.5
ADConvnet-SAGC	**318.0 (238%)**	**80.4**

4.6 Ablation Analysis

To validate the effectiveness of the proposed ADConvnet-SAGC model, several ablation analyses are conducted on both S3DIS and NPM3D dataset. The ablation result is listed in Table 5.

(1). **Replacing ADConv with Set Abstraction layer.** The ADConv operation enables the model to adaptively focus on the most related neighboring features for better features aggregation. For comparison, Set Abstraction layer in PointNet++ model tends to hard aggregate the feature in irregular shape. As a result, it provides lower performance.

(2). **Removing SAGC module.** The SAGC module provides the long range contextual information to the model for augmenting the feature representation. By removing this module, the performance is greatly decreased due to the loss of long range contexts.

(3). **Replacing the learned attention weights with constant attention weights.** The way in using constant attention weights is equivalent to conventional mean among neighboring points. By doing so, features similarity and shape structure of neighboring points are ignored. Thus, the performance is greatly decreased.

The mIoU scores of all ablated variants are compared in Table 5. We can conclude that: i) The most impact comes from the removal of the SAGC module, since the long range contextual information is essential in large-scale point cloud and large-sized objects become the majority parts. ii) The role of ADConv shows the next important factor in performance, especially for point cloud with diverse and varying 3D shape. iii) The learned attention weights are essential. From this ablation analysis, it is shown that how each proposed module which constitutes the full ADConvnet-SAGC model obtains the state-of-the-art accuracy.

Table 5. The mIoU scores of all ablated variants based on the full ADConvnet-SAGC. Both the Area-5 sequence of S3DIS and the Lille2 sequence of NPM3D are selected for evaluation

	mIoU	
	(S3DIS)	(NPM3D)
(1). Replace ADConv with Set Abstraction layer	57.4	77.5
(2). Remove SAGC module	56.7	76.3
(3). (1)+(2)	52.8	72.2
(4). Replace learned attention weights with constant attention weights	53.0	71.6
(5). The full ADConvnet-SAGC model	**60.1**	**80.4**

5   Conclusion

In this paper, a novel point cloud based neural network model called ADConvnet-SAGC is proposed which integrates attention mechanism to tackle several challenges in large-scale point cloud semantic segmentation problem. The proposed ADConvnet-SAGC integrates attention mechanism into point convolution to handle input with diverse and varying shapes. It also applies self-attention technique to efficiently capture long-range contextual information for enhancing feature representations. With these two improvements, the segmentation results for road objects (especially critical small objects such as pedestrians, cars, barriers, bollards) have significant gain in accuracy. The performance of ADConvnet-SAGC is validated in terms of accuracy and efficiency over challenging benchmarks. From the experiments, ADConvnet-SAGC outperforms several state-of-the-art point cloud based semantic segmentation methods. The experimental results also validate the contributions of ADConvnet-SAGC: i) an attention-based adaptive module which can be easily integrated to obtain dynamic point convolution operation; ii) a more accurate point cloud based semantic segmentation with global spatial consistency; iii) much lower computational cost (e.g., about 2.3 times faster than PointNet++) compared with other state-of-the-art point cloud based approaches.

Acknowledgement. This project was partially funded by The University of Macau (MYRG2019-00016-FST), and The Science and Technology Development Fund, Macau S.A.R. (File no. 0004/2019/AFJ).

References

1. Armeni, I., et al.: 3D semantic parsing of large-scale indoor spaces. In: Proceedings of the IEEE International Conference on Computer Vision and Pattern Recognition (2016)
2. Bahdanau, D., Cho, K., Bengio, Y.: Neural machine translation by jointly learning to align and translatea. In: Proceedings of the IEEE International Conference on Learning Representations (2015)
3. Charles, R.Q., Su, H., Kaichun, M., Guibas, L.J.: Pointnet: deep learning on point sets for 3D classification and segmentation. In: 2017 IEEE Conference on Computer Vision and Pattern Recognition (CVPR), pp. 77–85 (2017). https://doi.org/10.1109/CVPR.2017.16
4. Dai, J., et al.: Deformable convolutional networks. In: Proceedings of the IEEE International Conference on Computer Vision, pp. 764–773 (2017)
5. Girshick, R., Donahue, J., Darrell, T., Malik, J.: Region-based convolutional networks for accurate object detection and segmentation. IEEE Trans. Pattern Anal. Mach. Intell. 38(1), 142–158 (2016)
6. He, K., Zhang, X., Ren, S., Sun, J.: Deep residual learning for image recognition. In: Proceedings of the IEEE Conference on Computer Vision and Pattern Recognition (CVPR), pp. 770–778 (2016)
7. Jiang, M., Wu, Y., Zhao, T., Zhao, Z., Lu, C.: Pointsift: A sift-like network module for 3d point cloud semantic segmentation. arXiv preprint arXiv:1807.00652 (2018)
8. LeCun, Y., Bottou, L., Bengio, Y., Haffner, P.: Gradient-based learning applied to document recognition. Proc. IEEE 86(11), 2278–2324 (1998)
9. Li, Y., Bu, R., Sun, M., Wu, W., Di, X., Chen, B.: Pointcnn: convolution on x-transformed points. In: Advances in Neural Information Processing Systems. pp. 820–830 (2018)
10. Liang, Z., Yang, M., Deng, L., Wang, C., Wang, B.: Hierarchical depthwise graph convolutional neural network for 3D semantic segmentation of point clouds. In: 2019 International Conference on Robotics and Automation (ICRA), pp. 8152–8158 (2019). https://doi.org/10.1109/ICRA.2019.8794052
11. Ma, L., Li, Y., Li, J., Tan, W., Yu, Y., Chapman, M.A.: Multi-scale point-wise convolutional neural networks for 3D object segmentation from lidar point clouds in large-scale environments. IEEE Trans. Intell. Transp. Syst. (2019). https://doi.org/10.1109/TITS.2019.2961060
12. Maturana, D., Scherer, S.: Voxnet: a 3D convolutional neural network for real-time object recognition. In: 2015 IEEE/RSJ International Conference on Intelligent Robots and Systems (IROS), pp. 922–928. IEEE (2015)
13. Nair, V., Hinton, G.E.: Rectified linear units improve restricted Boltzmann machines. In: Proceedings of the 27th International Conference on Machine Learning (ICML-10), pp. 807–814 (2010)
14. Pham, Q.H., Nguyen, T., Hua, B.S., Roig, G., Yeung, S.K.: Jsis3D: joint semantic-instance segmentation of 3d point clouds with multi-task pointwise networks and multi-value conditional random fields. In: Proceedings of the IEEE Conference on Computer Vision and Pattern Recognition, pp. 8827–8836 (2019)
15. Qi, C.R., Su, H., Nießner, M., Dai, A., Yan, M., Guibas, L.J.: Volumetric and multi-view cnns for object classification on 3D data. In: Proceedings of the IEEE conference on computer vision and pattern recognition, pp. 5648–5656 (2016)
16. Qi, C.R., Yi, L., Su, H., Guibas, L.J.: Pointnet++: deep hierarchical feature learning on point sets in a metric space. In: Advances in Neural Information Processing Systems, pp. 5099–5108 (2017)

17. Roynard, X., Deschaud, J.E., Goulette, F.: Paris-lille-3D: a large and high-quality ground-truth urban point cloud dataset for automatic segmentation and classification. Int. J. Rob. Res. **37**(6), 545–557 (2018). https://doi.org/10.1177/0278364918767506
18. Shelhamer, E., Long, J., Darrell, T.: Fully convolutional networks for semantic segmentation. IEEE Trans. Pattern Anal. Mach. Intell. **39**(4), 640–651 (2017)
19. Su, H., Maji, S., Kalogerakis, E., Learned-Miller, E.: Multi-view convolutional neural networks for 3D shape recognition. In: Proceedings of the IEEE International Conference on Computer Vision, pp. 945–953 (2015)
20. Thomas, H., Goulette, F., Deschaud, J.E., Marcotegui, B.: Semantic classification of 3D point clouds with multiscale spherical neighborhoods. In: 2018 International Conference on 3D Vision (3DV), pp. 390–398. IEEE (2018)
21. Vaswani, A., et al.: Attention is all you need. In: Advances in Neural Information Processing Systems, pp. 5998–6008 (2017)
22. Wang, L., Huang, Y., Hou, Y., Zhang, S., Shan, J.: Graph attention convolution for point cloud semantic segmentation. In: Proceedings of the IEEE Conference on Computer Vision and Pattern Recognition, pp. 10296–10305 (2019)
23. Wang, P.S., Liu, Y., Guo, Y.X., Sun, C.Y., Tong, X.: O-cnn: octree-based convolutional neural networks for 3D shape analysis. ACM Trans. Graph. (TOG) **36**(4), 72 (2017)
24. Wang, Y., Sun, Y., Liu, Z., Sarma, S.E., Bronstein, M.M., Solomon, J.M.: Dynamic graph cnn for learning on point clouds. ACM Trans. Graph. (TOG) **38**, 1–12 (2019)
25. Wu, W., Qi, Z., Fuxin, L.: Pointconv: Deep convolutional networks on 3D point clouds. In: Proceedings of the IEEE Conference on Computer Vision and Pattern Recognition, pp. 9621–9630 (2019)
26. Xu, K., et al.: Show, attend and tell: Neural image caption generation with visual attention. In: International Conference on Machine Learning, pp. 2048–2057 (2015)
27. Ye, X., Li, J., Huang, H., Du, L., Zhang, X.: 3D recurrent neural networks with context fusion for point cloud semantic segmentation. In: Proceedings of the European Conference on Computer Vision (ECCV), pp. 403–417 (2018)
28. Zhao, L., Tao, W.: Jsnet: joint instance and semantic segmentation of 3D point clouds. In: AAAI, pp. 12951–12958 (2020)

Attributional Robustness Training Using Input-Gradient Spatial Alignment

Mayank Singh[1]([⊠]), Nupur Kumari[1], Puneet Mangla[2], Abhishek Sinha[1],
Vineeth N. Balasubramanian[2], and Balaji Krishnamurthy[1]

[1] Media and Data Science Research Lab, Adobe, Noida, India
{msingh,nupkumar,kbalaji}@adobe.com, abhishek.sinha94@gmail.com
[2] IIT Hyderabad, Hyderabad, India
{cs17btech11029,vineethnb}@iith.ac.in

Abstract. Interpretability is an emerging area of research in trustworthy machine learning. Safe deployment of machine learning system mandates that the prediction and its explanation be reliable and robust. Recently, it has been shown that the explanations could be manipulated easily by adding visually imperceptible perturbations to the input while keeping the model's prediction intact. In this work, we study the problem of attributional robustness (i.e. models having robust explanations) by showing an upper bound for attributional vulnerability in terms of spatial correlation between the input image and its explanation map. We propose a training methodology that learns robust features by minimizing this upper bound using soft-margin triplet loss. Our methodology of robust attribution training (*ART*) achieves the new state-of-the-art attributional robustness measure by a margin of ≈6–18% on several standard datasets, ie. SVHN, CIFAR-10 and GTSRB. We further show the utility of the proposed robust training technique (*ART*) in the downstream task of weakly supervised object localization by achieving the new state-of-the-art performance on CUB-200 dataset.

Keywords: Attributional robustness · Adversarial robustness · Explainable deep learning

1 Introduction

Attribution methods [9,45–48,51,54] are an increasingly popular class of explanation techniques that aim to highlight relevant input features responsible for

---

M. Singh and N. Kumari—Equal contribution
A. Sinha—Work done at Adobe.

Electronic supplementary material The online version of this chapter (https://doi.org/10.1007/978-3-030-58583-9_31) contains supplementary material, which is available to authorized users.

© Springer Nature Switzerland AG 2020
A. Vedaldi et al. (Eds.): ECCV 2020, LNCS 12372, pp. 515–533, 2020.
https://doi.org/10.1007/978-3-030-58583-9_31

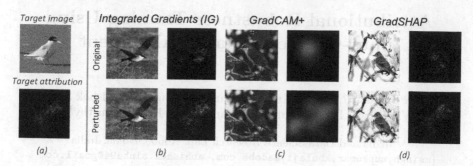

Fig. 1. Illustration of targeted manipulation [12] of attribution maps on CUB-200 [61] using the target attribution of (a). Here, (b) Integrated Gradients [54], (c) Grad-CAM++ [9] and (d) GradSHAP [29] blocks show : Top (b), (c), (d) original image and its attribution map; Bottom (b), (c), (d) perturbed image and its attribution map.

model's prediction. These techniques are extensively used with deep learning models in risk-sensitive and safety-critical applications such as healthcare [4,24,32,56], where they provide a human user with visual validation of the features used by the model for predictions. In computer-assisted diagnosis, [56] showed that predictions with attribution maps increased accuracy of retina specialists above that of unassisted reader or model alone. In [24], the authors improve the analysis of skin lesions by leveraging explanation maps of prediction.

It has been recently demonstrated that one could construct targeted [12] and un-targeted perturbations [10,16] that can arbitrarily manipulate attribution maps without affecting the model's prediction. This issue further weakens the cause of safe application of machine learning algorithms. We show an illustrative example of attribution-based attacks for image classifiers over different attribution methods in Fig. 1. This vulnerability leads to newer challenges for attribution methods, as well as robust training techniques. The intuition of attributional robustness is that if the inputs are visually indistinguishable with the same model prediction, then interpretation maps should also remain the same.

As one of the first efforts, [10] recently proposed a training methodology that aims to obtain models having robust integrated gradient [54] attributions. In addition to being an early effort, the instability of this training methodology, as discussed in [10], limits its usability in the broader context of robust training in computer vision. In this paper, we build upon this work by obtaining an upper bound for attributional vulnerability as a function of spatial correlation between the input image and its explanation map. Furthermore, we also introduce a training technique that minimizes this upper bound to provide attributional robustness. In particular, we introduce a training methodology for attributional robustness that uses soft-margin triplet loss to increase the spatial correlation of input with its attribution map. The triplet loss considers input image as the anchor, gradient of the correct class logit with respect to input as the positive and gradient of the incorrect class with highest logit value with respect to input as the negative. We show empirically how this choice results in learning of robust and interpretable features that help in other downstream weakly supervised tasks.

Existing related efforts in deep learning research are largely focused on robustness to adversarial perturbations [17,55], which are imperceptible perturbations which, when added to input, drastically change the neural network's prediction. While adversarial robustness has been explored significantly in recent years, there has been limited progress made on the front of attributional robustness, which we seek to highlight in this work. Our main contributions can be summarized as:

- We tackle the problem of attribution vulnerability and provide an upper bound for it as a function of spatial correlation between the input and its attribution map [48]. We then propose *ART*, a new training method that aims to minimize this bound to learn attributionally robust model.
- Our method outperforms prior work and achieves state-of-the-art attributional robustness on Integrated Gradient [54] based attribution method.
- We show that the proposed methodology also induces immunity to adversarial perturbations and common perturbations [20] on standard vision datasets that is comparable to the state-of-the-art adversarial training technique [31].
- We show the utility of *ART* for other computer vision tasks such as weakly supervised object localization (WSOL) and segmentation. Specifically, *ART* achieves state-of-the-art performance in WSOL task on CUB-200 [61] dataset.

2   Related Work

Our work is associated with various recent development made in the field of explanation methods, robustness to input distribution shifts and weakly supervised object localization. We hence describe earlier efforts in these directions below.

Visual Explanation Methods: Various explanation methods have been proposed that focus on producing posterior explanations for the model's decisions. A popular approach to do so is to attribute the predictions to the set of input features [6,46–48,52,54]. [13,69] provide a survey of interpretation techniques. Another class of explanation methods, commonly referred to as attribution techniques, can be broadly divided into three categories - gradient/back-propagation, propagation and perturbation based methods. Gradient-based methods attribute an importance score for each pixel by using the derivative of a class score with respect to input features [47,48,54]. Propagation-based techniques [6,46,67] leverage layer-wise propagation of feature importance to calculate the attribution maps. Perturbation-based interpretation methods generate attribution maps by examining the change in prediction of the model when the input image is perturbed [40,41,65]. In this work, we primarily report results on the attribution method of Integrated Gradients *IG* [54] that satisfies desirable axiomatic properties and was also used in the previous work [10].

Robustness of Attribution Maps: Recently, there have been a few efforts [3,10,12,16,70] that have explored the robustness of attribution maps, which we call attributional robustness in this work. The authors of [12,16,70] study the robustness of a network's attribution maps and show that the attribution maps can be significantly manipulated via imperceptible input perturbations while preserving the classifier's prediction. Recently, Chen, J. et al.[10] proposed a robust attribution training methodology, which is one of the first attempts at making an image classification model attributionally robust and is the current state of the art. The method minimizes the norm of difference in Integrated Gradients [54] of an original and perturbed image during training. In this work, we approach the problem from a different perspective of maintaining spatial alignment between an image and its saliency map.

Adversarial Perturbation and Robustness: Adversarial attacks can be broadly categorized into two types: White-box [8,31,33,62] and Black-box attacks [2,22,39,58]. Several proposed defense techniques have been shown to be ineffective to adaptive adversarial attacks [5,7,8,28]. Adversarial training [18,31,50], which is a defense technique that continuously augments the data with adversarial examples while training, is largely considered the current state-of-the-art to achieve adversarial robustness. [66] characterizes the trade-off between accuracy and robustness for classification problems and propose a regularized adversarial training method. Prior works have also attempted to improve adversarial robustness using gradient regularization that minimizes the Frobenius norm of the Hessian of the classification loss with respect to input [30,34,42] or weights [23]. For a comprehensive review of the work done in the area of adversarial examples, please refer [1,63].

We show in our work that in addition to providing attributional robustness, our proposed method helps in achieving performance gain on downstream task of WSOL. We hence briefly discuss earlier efforts on this task below.

Weakly Supervised Object Localization (WSOL): The problem of WSOL aims to identify the location of the object in a scene using only image-level labels, and without any location annotations. Generally, rich labeled data is scarcely available, and its collection is expensive and time-consuming. Learning from weak supervision is hence promising as it requires less rich labels and has the potential to scale. A common problem with most previous approaches is that the model only identifies the most discriminative part of the object rather than the complete object. For example, in the case of a bird, the model may rely on the beak region for classification than the entire bird's shape. In WSOL task, ADL [11], the current state-of-the-art method, uses an attention-based dropout layer while training the model that promotes the classification model to also focus on less discriminative parts of the image. For getting the bounding box from the model, ADL and similar other techniques in this domain first extract attribution maps, generally CAM-based [71], for each image and then fit a bounding box as described in [71]. We now present our methodology.

3   Attributional Robustness Training: Methodology

Given an input image $x \in [0,1]^n$ with true label $y \in \{1...k\}$, we consider a neural network model $f_\theta : \mathbb{R}^n \to \mathbb{R}^k$ with ReLU activation function that classifies x into one of k classes as $\arg\max f(x)_i$ where $i \in \{1...k\}$. Here, $f(x)_i$ is the ith logit of $f(x)$. Attribution map $A(x, f(x)_i) : \mathbb{R}^n \to \mathbb{R}^n$ with respect to a given class i assigns an importance score to each input pixel of x based on its relevance to the model for predicting the class i.

3.1   Attribution Manipulation

It was shown recently [12,16] that for standard models f_θ, it is possible to manipulate the attribution map $A(x, f(x)_y)$ (denoted as $A(x)$ for simplicity in the rest of the paper) with visually imperceptible perturbation δ in the input by optimizing the following loss function.

$$\arg\max_{\delta \in B_\epsilon} D[A(x + \delta, f(x + \delta)_y), A(x, f(x)_y)]$$

$$\text{subject to: } \arg\max(f(x)) = \arg\max(f(x + \delta)) = y \tag{1}$$

where B_ϵ is an l_p ball of radius ϵ centered at x and D is a dissimilarity function to measure the change between attribution maps. The manipulation was shown for various perturbation-based and gradient-based attribution methods.

This vulnerability in neural network-based classification models suggests that the model relies on features different from what humans perceive as important for its prediction. The goal of attributional robustness is to mitigate this vulnerability and ensure that attribution maps of two visually indistinguishable images are also nearly identical. In the next section, we propose a new training methodology for attributional robustness motivated from the observation that feature importance in image space has a high spatial correlation with the input image for robust models [15,57].

3.2   Attributional Robustness Training (ART)

Given an input image $x \in \mathbb{R}^n$ with ground truth label $y \in \{1...k\}$ and a classification model f_θ, the gradient-based feature importance score is defined as $\nabla_x f(x)_i : i \in \{1...k\}$ and denoted as $g^i(x)$ in the rest of the paper. For achieving attributional robustness, we need to minimize the attribution vulnerability to attacks as defined in Eq. 1. Attribution vulnerability can be formulated as the maximum possible change in $g^y(x)$ in a ϵ-neighborhood of x if A is taken as gradient attribution method [48] and D is a distance measure in some norm $||.||$ i.e.

$$\max_{\delta \in B_\epsilon} ||g^y(x + \delta) - g^y(x)|| \tag{2}$$

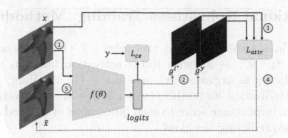

Fig. 2. Block diagram summarizing our training technique for *ART*. Dashed line represents backward gradient flow, and bold lines denotes forward pass of the neural network.

We show that Eq. 2 is upper bounded by the maximum of the distance between $g^y(x + \delta)$ and $x + \delta$ for δ in ϵ neighbourhood of x.

$$
\begin{aligned}
||g^y(x + \delta) - g^y(x)|| &= ||g^y(x + \delta) - (x + \delta) - (g^y(x) - x) + \delta|| \\
&\leq ||g^y(x + \delta) - (x + \delta)|| + ||g^y(x) - x|| + ||\delta|| \\
&\leq ||g^y(x + \delta) - (x + \delta)|| + \max_{\delta \in B_\epsilon}||g^y(x + \delta) - (x + \delta)|| + ||\delta||
\end{aligned}
\tag{3}
$$

Taking max on both sides:

$$
\max_{\delta \in B_\epsilon}||g^y(x + \delta) - g^y(x))|| \leq 2 \max_{\delta \in B_\epsilon}||g^y(x + \delta) - (x + \delta)|| + ||\epsilon||
\tag{4}
$$

Leveraging existing understanding [21,44] that minimizing the distance between two quantities can benefit from a negative anchor, we use a triplet loss formulation as defined in Eq. 5 with image x as an anchor, $g^y(x)$ as positive sample and $g^{i^*}(x)$ as negative sample. More details about the selection of the optimization objective 5 and choice for the negative sample can be found in the supplementary section 1.1. Hence to achieve attributional robustness, we propose a training technique *ART* that encourages high spatial correlation between $g^y(x)$ and x by optimizing L_{attr} which is a triplet loss [21] with soft margin on cosine distance between $g^i(x)$ and x i.e.

$$
L_{attr}(x, y) = \log\left(1 + \exp\left(-(d(g^{i^*}(x), x) - d(g^y(x), x))\right)\right)
$$
$$
\text{where } d(g^i(x), x) = 1 - \frac{g^i(x).x}{||g^i(x)||_2.||x||_2} \ ; \quad i^* = \arg\max_{i \neq y} f(x)_i
\tag{5}
$$

Hence, the classification training objective for *ART* methodology is:

$$
\underset{\theta}{\text{minimize}} \ \underset{(x,y)}{\mathbb{E}} \left[L_{ce}(x + \delta, y) + \lambda \, L_{attr}(x + \delta, y) \right]
$$
$$
\text{where } \delta = \underset{||\delta||_\infty < \epsilon}{\arg\max} \ L_{attr}(x + \delta, y)
\tag{6}
$$

Here L_{ce} is the standard cross-entropy loss. The optimization of L_{attr} involves computing gradient of $f(x)_i$ with respect to input x which suffers from the problem of vanishing second derivative in case of ReLU activation, i.e. $\partial^2 f_i / \partial x^2 \approx 0$. To alleviate this, following previous works [10,12], we replace ReLU with softplus non-linearities while optimizing L_{attr} as it has a well-defined second derivative. The softplus approximates to ReLU as the value of β in $softplus_\beta(x) = \frac{log(1+e^{\beta x})}{\beta}$ increases. Note that optimization of L_{ce} follows the usual ReLU activation pathway. Thus, our training methodology consists of two steps: first, we calculate a perturbed image $\tilde{x} = x + \delta$ that maximizes L_{attr} through iterative projected gradient descent; secondly, we use $\tilde{x}$ as the training point on which L_{ce} and L_{attr} is minimized with their relative weightage controlled by the hyper-parameter λ.

Note that the square root of cosine distance for unit l_2 norm vectors as used in our formulation of L_{attr} is a valid distance metric and is related to the Euclidean distance. Details about this can be found in the supplementary section 1.2. Through experiments, we empirically show that minimizing the upper bound in Eq. 4 as our training objective increases the attributional robustness of the model by a significant margin. The block diagram for our training methodology is shown in Fig. 2, and its pseudo-code is given in Algorithm 1.

3.3 Connection to Adversarial Robustness

For a given input image x, an adversarial example is a slightly perturbed image x' such that $||x - x'||$ is small in some norm but the model f_θ classifies x' incorrectly. Adversarial examples are calculated by optimizing a loss function L which is large when $f(x) \neq y$:

$$x_{adv} = \underset{x':||x'-x||_p < \epsilon}{\arg\max} \ L(\theta, x', y) \tag{7}$$

where L can be the cross-entropy loss, for example. For an axiomatic attribution function A which satisfies the completeness axiom i.e. $\sum_{j=1}^n A(x)_j = f(x)_y$, it can be shown that $|f(x)_y - f(x')_y| < ||A(x) - A(x')||_1$, as below:

$$
\begin{aligned}
|f(x)_y - f(x')_y| &= |\sum_{j=1}^n A(x)_j - \sum_{j=1}^n A(x')_j| \\
&\leq \sum_{j=1}^n |A(x)_j - A(x')_j| \\
&= ||A(x) - A(x')||_1
\end{aligned}
\tag{8}
$$

The above relationship connects adversarial robustness to attributional robustness as the maximum change in $f(x)_y$ is upper bounded by the maximum change in attribution map of x in its ϵ neighborhood. Also, it was shown [57] recently that for an adversarially robust model, gradient-based feature importance map $g^y(x)$ has high spatial correlation with the image x and it highlights the perceptually relevant features of the image. For classifiers with a locally affine approximation like a DNN with ReLU activations, Etmann et al.[15] establish theoretical connection between adversarial robustness, and the correlation of $g^y(x)$ with image x. [15] shows that for a given image x, its distance to the

---

Algorithm 1: Attributional Robustness Training (*ART*)

---

1 **Input**: Classification model f_θ, training data $X = \{(x_i, y_i)\}$, batch size b, number of epochs E, number of attack steps a, step-size for iterative perturbation α, softplus parameter β, weight of L_{attr} loss λ.

2 **for** *epoch* $\in \{1, 2, ..., E\}$ **do**

3   Get mini-batch $x, y = \{(x_1, y_1)...(x_b, y_b)\}$

4      $\tilde{x} = x + Uniform[-\epsilon, +\epsilon]$

5   **for** *i=1,2, ... , a* **do**

6          $\tilde{x} = \tilde{x} + \alpha * sign(\nabla_x L_{attr}(\tilde{x}, y))$

7          $\tilde{x} = Proj_{\ell_\infty}(\tilde{x})$

8   **end**

9      $i^* = \arg\max_{i \neq y} f(x)_i$

10   Calculate $g^y(\tilde{x}) = \nabla_x f(\tilde{x})_y$

11   Calculate $g^{i^*}(\tilde{x}) = \nabla_x f(\tilde{x})_{i^*}$;   // We calculate $g^y(\tilde{x})$ and $g^{i^*}(\tilde{x})$ using *softplus*$_\beta$ activation as described in Section 3.2

12      $loss = L_{ce}(\tilde{x}, y) + \lambda \cdot L_{attr}(\tilde{x}, y)$

13   Update θ using $loss$

14 **end**

15 **return** f_θ.

---

nearest distance boundary is upper-bounded by the dot product between x and $g^y(x)$. The authors of [15] showed that increasing adversarial robustness increases the correlation between $g^y(x)$ and x. Moreover, this correlation is related to the increase in attributional robustness of model as we show in Sect. 3.2.

3.4 Downstream Task: Weakly Supervised Object Localization (WSOL)

As an additional benefit of our approach, we show its improved performance on a downstream task - Weakly supervised Object localization (WSOL), in this case. The problem of WSOL deals with detecting objects where only class label information of images is available, and the ground truth bounding box location is inaccessible. Generally, the pipeline for obtaining bounding box locations in WSOL relies on attribution maps. Also, the task of object detection is widely used to validate the quality of attribution maps empirically. Since our proposed training methodology *ART* promotes attribution map to be invariant to small perturbations in input, it leads to better attribution maps identifying the complete object instead of focusing on only the most discriminative part of the object. We validate this empirically by using attribution maps obtained from our model for bounding-box detection on the CUB dataset and obtaining new state-of-the-art localization results.

Table 1. Attributional and adversarial robustness of different approaches on various datasets. Hyper-parameters for attributional attack are same as [10]. Similarity measures used are IN:*Top-k intersection*, K:*kendall's tau rank order correlation*. The values denote similarity between attribution maps of original and perturbed examples [16] based on *Intergrated Gradient* method.

Dataset	Approach	Attributional robustness		Accuracy	
		IN	K	Natural	PGD-40 Attack
CIFAR-10	Natural	40.25	49.17	95.26	0.
	PGD-10 [31]	69.00	72.27	87.32	44.07
	ART	**92.90**	**91.76**	89.84	37.58
SVHN	Natural	60.43	56.50	95.66	0.
	PGD-7 [31]	39.67	55.56	92.84	50.12
	ART	**61.37**	**72.60**	95.47	43.56
GTSRB	Natural	68.74	76.48	99.43	19.9
	IG Norm [10]	74.81	75.55	97.02	75.24
	IG-SUM Norm [10]	74.04	76.84	95.68	77.12
	PGD-7 [31]	86.13	88.42	98.36	87.49
	ART	**91.96**	**89.34**	98.47	84.66
Flower	Natural	38.22	56.43	93.91	0.
	IG Norm [10]	64.68	75.91	85.29	24.26
	IG-SUM Norm [10]	66.33	79.74	82.35	47.06
	PGD-7 [31]	**80.84**	84.14	92.64	69.85
	ART	79.84	**84.87**	93.21	33.08

4 Experiments and Results

In this section, we first describe the implementation details of *ART* and evaluation setting for measuring the attributional and adversarial robustness. We then show the performance of *ART* on the downstream WSOL task.

4.1 Attributional and Adversarial Robustness

Baselines: We compare our training methodology with the following approaches:

- *Natural*: Standard training with cross entropy classification loss.
- *PGD-n*: Adversarially trained model with n-step PGD attack as in [31], which is typically used by work in this area [10].
- *IG Norm* and *IG-SUM Norm* [10]: Current state-of-the-art robust attribution training technique.

Datasets and Implementation Details: To study the efficacy of our methodology, we benchmark on the following standard vision datasets: CIFAR-10 [27], SVHN [35], GTSRB [53] and Flower [36]. For CIFAR-10, GTSRB and Flower datasets, we use Wideresnet-28-10 [64] model architecture for *Natural*, *PGD-10* and *ART*. For SVHN, we use WideResNet-40-2 [64] architecture. We use the perturbation $\epsilon = 8/255$ in ℓ_∞-norm for *ART* and *PGD-n* as in [10,31]. We use

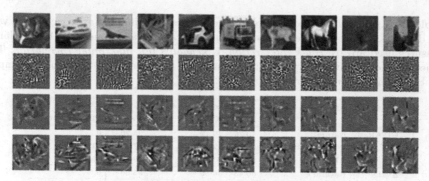

Fig. 3. Examples of gradient attribution map [48] for different models on CIFAR-10. Top to bottom: Image; attribution maps for *Natural*, *PGD-10* and *ART* models

Fig. 4. Random samples (of resolution 32×32) generated using a CIFAR-10 robustly trained *ART* classifier

$\lambda = 0.5$, $a = 3$ and $\beta = 50$ for all experiments in the paper. For training, we use SGD optimizer with step-wise learning rate schedule. More details about training hyper-parameters can be found in the supplementary section 1.3.

Evaluation: For evaluating attributional robustness, we follow [10] and present our results with Integrated Gradient (*IG*)-based attribution maps. We show attributional robustness of *ART* on other attribution methods in Sect. 5. *IG* satisfies several theoretical properties desirable for an attribution method, e.g. sensitivity and completeness axioms and is defined as:

$$IG(x, f(x)_i) = (x - \overline{x}) \odot \int_{t=0}^{1} \nabla_x f(\overline{x} + t(x - \overline{x}))_i dt \qquad (9)$$

where $\overline{x}$ is a suitable baseline at which the function prediction is neutral. For computing perturbed image $\tilde{x}$ on which $IG(\tilde{x})$ changes drastically from $IG(x)$, we perform Iterative Feature Importance Attack (IFIA) proposed by Ghorbani et al.[16] with ℓ_∞ bound of $\epsilon = 8/255$ as used by previous work [10].

For assessing similarity between $A(x)$ and perturbed image $A(\tilde{x})$, we use *Top-k intersection* (*IN*) and *Kendall's tau coefficient* (*K*) similar to [10]. *Kendall's tau coefficient* is a measure of similarity of ordering when ranked by values, and therefore is a suitable metric for comparing attribution maps. *Top-k* intersection measures the percentage of common indices in top-k values of attribution map of x and $\tilde{x}$. We report average of *IN* and *K* metric over random 1000 samples of

Fig. 5. Comparison of heatmap and estimated bounding box by VGG model trained via ART (top row) and ADL (bottom row) on CUB dataset; The red bounding box is ground truth and green bounding box corresponds to the estimated box (Color figure online)

test-set. More details about the attack methodology and evaluation parameters can be found in supplementary section 1.3. For evaluating adversarial robustness, we perform 40 step PGD attack [31] using cross-entropy loss with ℓ_∞ bound of $\epsilon = 8/255$ and report the model accuracy on adversarial examples. Table 1 compares attributional and adversarial robustness across different datasets and training approaches. *ART* achieves state-of-the-art attributional robustness on attribution attacks [16] when compared with baselines. We also observe that *ART* consistently achieves higher test accuracy than [31] and has adversarial robustness significantly greater than that of the *Natural* model.

Qualitative Study of Input-Gradients for ART: Motivated by [57] which claims that adversarially trained models exhibits human-aligned gradients (agree with human saliency), we studied the same with (*ART*), and the results are shown in Fig. 3. Qualitative study of input-gradients shows a high degree of spatial alignment between the object and the gradient. We also show image generation from random seeds in Fig. 4 using robust ART model as done in [43]. The image generation process involves maximization of the class score of the desired class starting from a random seed which is sampled from some class-conditional seed distribution as defined in [43].

4.2 Weakly Supervised Image Localization

This task relies on the attribution map obtained from the classification model to estimate a bounding box for objects. We compare our approach with ADL [11][1] on the CUB dataset, which has ground truth bounding box of 5794 bird images. We adopt similar processing steps as ADL for predicting bounding boxes except that we use gradient attribution map $\nabla_x f(x)_y$ instead of CAM [71]. As a post-processing step, we convert the attribution map to grayscale, normalize it and then apply a mean filtering of 3×3 kernel over it. Then a bounding box is fit over this heatmap to localize the object.

We perform experiments on Resnet-50 [19] and VGG [49] architectures. We use ℓ_∞ bound of $\epsilon = 2/255$ for *ART* and *PGD-7* training on CUB dataset. For

---

[1] https://github.com/junsukchoe/ADL/tree/master/Pytorch.

Table 2. Weakly Supervised Localization on CUB dataset. Bold text refers to the best GT-Known Loc and Top-1 Loc for each model. * denotes directly reported from the paper. # denotes our implementation from the official code released by ADL [11][2]

Model	Method	Saliency method				Top-1 Acc
		Grad		CAM		
		GT-Known Loc	Top-1 Loc	GT-Known Loc	Top-1 Loc	
ResNet50-SE	ADL [11]	–	–	–	62.29*	80.34*
ResNet50	ADL#	52.93	43.78	56.85	47.53	80.0
	Natural	50.2	42.0	60.37	50.0	81.12
	PGD-7 [31]	66.73	47.48	55.24	39.45	70.3
	ART	**82.65**	**65.22**	58.87	46.02	77.51
VGG-GAP	ADL#	63.18	43.59	69.36	50.88	70.31
	Natural	72.54	53.81	48.75	35.03	72.94
	ART	**76.50**	**57.74**	52.88	40.75	74.51

evaluation, we used similar metrics as in [11] i.e. *GT-Known Loc*: Intersection over Union (IoU) of estimated box and ground truth bounding box is atleast 0.5 and ground truth is known; *Top-1 Loc*: prediction is correct and IoU of bounding box is atleast 0.5; *Top-1 Acc*: top-1 classification accuracy. More details about dataset and hyper-parameters can be found in the supplementary section 2.1. Our approach results in higher *GT-Known Loc* and *Top-1 Loc* for both Resnet-50 and VGG-GAP [11] model as shown in Table 2. We also show qualitative comparison of the bounding box estimated by our approach with [11] in Fig. 5.

5   Discussion and Ablation Studies

To understand the scope and impact of the proposed training approach *ART*, we perform various experiments and report these findings in this section. These studies were carried out on the CIFAR-10 dataset.

Robustness to Targeted Attribution Attacks: In targeted attribution attacks, the aim is to calculate perturbations that minimize dissimilarity between the attribution map of a given image and a target image's attribution map. We evaluate the robustness of *ART* model using targeted attribution attack as proposed in [12] using the *IG* attribution method on a batch of 1000 test examples. To obtain the target attribution maps, we randomly shuffle the examples and then evaluate *ART* and *PGD-10* trained model on these examples. The *kendall's tau coefficient* and *top-k intersection* similarity measure between original and perturbed images on *ART* was 64.76 and 70.64 as compared to 36.29 and 31.81 on the *PGD-10* adversarially trained model.

Attributional Robustness for Other Attribution Methods: We evaluate *ART* against attribution attack [16] using gradient [48] and gradSHAP [29] attribution methods in Table 4. We observe that *ART* achieves higher attributional robustness than *Natural* and *PGD-10* models on *Top-k intersection* (IN)

Table 3. Top-1 accuracy of different models on perturbed variants of test-set (GN:Gaussian noise; SN: Shot noise; IN: Impulse noise; DB: Defocus blur; Gl-B: Glass blur; MB: Motion blur; ZB: Zoom blur; S: Snow; F: Fog; B: Brightness; C: Contrast; E: Elastic transform; P: Pixelation noise; J: JPEG compression; Sp-N: Speckle Noise)

Models	GN	SN	IN	DB	Gl-B	MB	ZB	S	F	B	C	E	P	J	Sp-N
Natural	49.16	61.42	59.22	83.55	53.84	79.16	79.18	84.53	**91.6**	**94.37**	**87.63**	84.44	74.12	79.76	65.04
PGD-10	83.32	84.33	73.73	83.09	81.27	79.60	82.07	82.68	68.81	85.97	57.86	81.68	85.56	85.56	83.64
ART	**85.44**	**86.41**	**77.07**	**86.07**	**81.70**	**83.14**	**85.54**	84.99	71.04	89.42	56.69	**84.72**	**87.64**	**87.89**	**86.02**

Table 4. Attributional Robustness on CIFAR-10 for other attribution methods

Model	Gradient [48]		GradSHAP [29]	
	IN	K	IN	K
Natural	13.72	9.5	4.5	16.52
PGD-10 [31]	54.8	54.06	45.05	59.80
ART	**76.07**	**70.31**	**48.31**	**62.35**

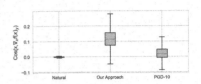

Fig. 6. Cosine$(x, \nabla_x f(x)_y)$ for different models over test-set of CIFAR-10

and *Kendall's tau coefficient* (K) measure. We also compare the cosine similarity between x and $g^y(x)$ for all models trained on CIFAR-10 dataset and show its variance plot in Fig. 6. We can see that *ART* trained model achieves higher cosine similarity than *Natural* and *PGD-10*. This empirically validates that our optimization is effective in increasing the spatial correlation between x and $g^y(x)$.

Robustness Against Gradient-Free and Stronger Attacks: To show the absence of gradient masking and obfuscation [5,7], we evaluate our model on a gradient-free adversarial optimization algorithm [58] and a stronger PGD attack with a larger number of steps. We observe similar adversarial robustness when we increase the number of steps in PGD-attack. For 100 step and 500 step PGD attacks, *ART* achieves 37.42% and 37.18% accuracy respectively. On the gradient-free SPSA [58] attack, *ART* obtains 44.7 adversarial accuracy that was evaluated over 1000 random test samples.

Robustness to Common Perturbations [20] and Spatial Adversarial Perturbations [14]: We compare *ART* with *PGD-10* adversarially trained model on the common perturbations dataset [20] for CIFAR-10. The dataset consists of perturbed images of 15 common-place visual perturbations at five levels of severity, resulting in 75 distinct corruptions. We report the mean accuracy over severity levels for all 15 types of perturbations and observe that *ART* performs better than other models on a majority of these perturbations, as shown in Table 3. On PGD-40 ℓ_2 norm attack with $\epsilon = 1.0$ and spatial attack [14] we observe robustness of 39.65%, 11.13% for *ART* and 29.68%, 6.76% for *PGD-10* trained model, highlighting the improved robustness provided by our method.

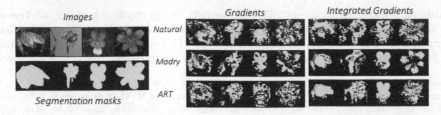

Fig. 7. Example images of weakly supervised segmentation masks obtained from different models via different attribution methods

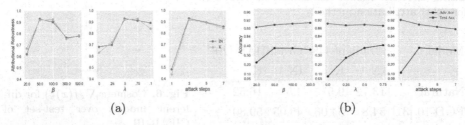

Fig. 8. (a): Top-k Intersection (IN) and Kendall correlation (K) measure of attributional robustness; (b): Test accuracy and adversarial accuracy (PGD-40 perturbations) on varying β, λ and attack steps in our training methodology on CIFAR-10

More results of varying ϵ in adversarial attacks and combining PGD adversarial training [31] with ART can be found in the supplementary section 3.

Image Segmentation: Data collection for image segmentation task is time-consuming and costly. Hence, recent efforts [25,26,37,38,59,60,68] have focused on weakly supervised segmentation models, where image labels are leveraged instead of segmentation masks. Since models trained via our approach perform well on WSOL, we further evaluate it on weakly supervised image segmentation task for Flowers dataset [36] where we have access to segmentation masks of 849 images. Samples of weakly-supervised segmentation mask obtained from attribution maps on various models are shown in Fig. 7. We observe that attribution maps of ART can serve as a better prior for segmentation masks as compared to other baselines. We evaluate our results using *Top-1 Seg* metric which considers an answer as correct when the model prediction is correct and the IoU betweeen ground-truth mask and estimated mask is atleast 0.5. We compare ART against *Natural* and *PGD-7* trained models using gradient [48] and IG [54] attribution maps. Attribution maps are converted into gray-scale heatmaps and a smoothing filter is applied as a post-processing step. We obtain a *Top-1 Seg* performance of 0.337, 0.422, and 0.604 via IG attribution maps and 0.244, 0.246, 0.317 via gradient maps for *Natural*, *PGD-7* and *ART* respectively.

Effect of β, λ and a on Performance: We perform experiments to study the role of β, λ and a as used in Algorithm 1 on the model performance by varying one parameter and fixing the others on their best-performing values, i.e. 50, 0.5 and 3 respectively. Figure 8a shows the plots of attributional robustness. Figure 8b shows the plots of test accuracy and adversarial accuracy on ℓ_∞ PGD-40 perturbations with $\epsilon = 8/255$. We observe that adversarial and attributional robustness initially increases with increasing β, but the trend reverses for higher values of β. On varying λ, we find that the attributional and adversarial robustness of the model increases with increasing λ and saturates after 0.75. For attack steps parameter a, we find that the performance in terms of test accuracy, adversarial accuracy and attributional robustness saturates after 3 attack steps as shown in the right-most plot of Fig. 8a and 8b.

6   Conclusion

We propose a new method for the problem space of attributional robustness, using the observation that increasing the alignment between the object in an input and the attribution map generated from the network's prediction leads to improvement in attributional robustness. We empirically showed this for both un-targeted and targeted attribution attacks over several benchmark datasets. We showed that the attributional robustness also brings out other improvements in the network, such as reduced vulnerability to adversarial attacks and common perturbations. For other vision tasks such as weakly supervised object localization, our attributionally robust model achieves a new state-of-the-art accuracy even without being explicitly trained to achieve that objective. We hope that our work can open a broader discussion around notions of robustness and the application of robust features on other downstream tasks.

Acknowledgements. This work was partly supported by the Ministry of Human Resource Development and Department of Science and Technology, Govt of India through the UAY program.

References

1. Akhtar, N., Mian, A.: Threat of adversarial attacks on deep learning in computer vision: a survey. IEEE Access **6**, 14410–14430 (2018)
2. Kurakin, A., Goodfellow, I.J., Bengio, S.: Adversarial examples in the physical world. In: ICLR Workshop (2017)
3. Alvarez-Melis, D., Jaakkola, T.S.: On the robustness of interpretability methods. In: ICML 2018 Workshop (2018)
4. Ardila, D., et al.: End-to-end lung cancer screening with three-dimensional deep learning on low-dose chest computed tomography. Nature Med. **25**, 954–961 (2019)
5. Athalye, A., Carlini, N., Wagner, D.: Obfuscated gradients give a false sense of security: circumventing defenses to adversarial examples. In: ICML (2018)
6. Bach, S., Binder, A., Montavon, G., Klauschen, F., Müler, K.R., Samek, W.: On pixel-wise explanations for non-linear classifier decisions by layer-wise relevance propagation. PLoS ONE **10**(7), e0130140 (2015)
7. Carlini, N., et al.: On evaluating adversarial robustness. arXiv preprint arXiv:1902.06705 (2019)

8. Carlini, N., Wagner, D.: Towards evaluating the robustness of neural networks. In: 2017 IEEE Symposium on Security and Privacy (SP) (2017)
9. Chattopadhyay, A., Sarkar, A., Howlader, P., Balasubramanian, V.N.: Grad-CAM++: generalized gradient-based visual explanations for deep convolutional networks. arXiv preprint arXiv:1710.11063 (2017)
10. Chen, J., Wu, X., Rastogi, V., Liang, Y., Jha, S.: Robust attribution regularization. arXiv preprint arXiv:1905.09957 (2019)
11. Choe, J., Shim, H.: Attention-based dropout layer for weakly supervised object localization. In: Proceedings of the IEEE Conference on Computer Vision and Pattern Recognition, pp. 2219–2228 (2019)
12. Dombrowski, A.K., Alber, M., Anders, C., Ackermann, M., Müller, K.R., Kessel, P.: Explanations can be manipulated and geometry is to blame. In: Advances in Neural Information Processing Systems, pp. 13567–13578 (2019)
13. Du, M., Liu, N., Hu, X.: Techniques for interpretable machine learning. arXiv preprint arXiv:1808.00033 (2018)
14. Engstrom, L., Tran, B., Tsipras, D., Schmidt, L., Madry, A.: Exploring the landscape of spatial robustness. In: International Conference on Machine Learning, pp. 1802–1811 (2019)
15. Etmann, C., Lunz, S., Maass, P., Schönlieb, C.B.: On the connection between adversarial robustness and saliency map interpretability. arXiv preprint arXiv:1905.04172 (2019)
16. Ghorbani, A., Abid, A., Zou, J.: Interpretation of neural networks is fragile. In: Proceedings of the AAAI Conference on Artificial Intelligence, vol. 33, pp. 3681–3688 (2019)
17. Goodfellow, I.J., Shlens, J., Szegedy, C.: Explaining and harnessing adversarial examples. In: International Conference on Learning Representations (2015)
18. Goodfellow, I.J., Shlens, J., Szegedy, C.: Explaining and harnessing adversarial examples. In: ICLR (2015)
19. He, K., Zhang, X., Ren, S., Sun, J.: Deep residual learning for image recognition. arXiv preprint arXiv:1512.03385 (2015)
20. Hendrycks, D., Dietterich, T.: Benchmarking neural network robustness to common corruptions and perturbations. In: Proceedings of the International Conference on Learning Representations (2019)
21. Hermans, A., Beyer, L., Leibe, B.: In defense of the triplet loss for person re-identification. arXiv preprint arXiv:1703.07737 (2017)
22. Ilyas, A., Engstrom, L., Athalye, A., Lin, J.: Black-box adversarial attacks with limited queries and information. In: ICML (2018)
23. Jakubovitz, D., Giryes, R.: Improving DNN robustness to adversarial attacks using Jacobian regularization. In: Ferrari, V., Hebert, M., Sminchisescu, C., Weiss, Y. (eds.) ECCV 2018. LNCS, vol. 11216, pp. 525–541. Springer, Cham (2018). https://doi.org/10.1007/978-3-030-01258-8_32
24. Jia, X., Shen, L.: Skin lesion classification using class activation map. arXiv preprint arXiv:1703.01053 (2017)
25. Jiang, Q., et al.: Weakly-supervised image semantic segmentation based on super-pixel region merging. Big Data Cogn. Comput. 3(2), 31 (2019)
26. Kolesnikov, A., Lampert, C.H.: Seed, expand and constrain: three principles for weakly-supervised image segmentation. CoRR abs/1603.06098 (2016). http://arxiv.org/abs/1603.06098
27. Krizhevsky, A., Nair, V., Hinton, G.: CIFAR-10. http://www.cs.toronto.edu/kriz/cifar.html (2010)

28. Engstrom, L., Andrew Ilyas, A.A.: Evaluating and understanding the robustness of adversarial logit pairing. In: NeurIPS SECML (2018)
29. Lundberg, S.M., Lee, S.I.: A unified approach to interpreting model predictions. In: Guyon, I., et al. (eds.) NeurIPS (2017). http://papers.nips.cc/paper/7062-a-unified-approach-to-interpreting-model-predictions.pdf
30. Lyu, C., Huang, K., Liang, H.N.: A unified gradient regularization family for adversarial examples. In: ICDM (2015)
31. Madry, A., Makelov, A., Schmidt, L., Tsipras, D., Vladu, A.: Towards deep learning models resistant to adversarial attacks. arXiv preprint arXiv:1706.06083 (2017)
32. Mitani, A., et al.: Detection of anaemia from retinal fundus images via deep learning. Nature Biomed. Eng. 4, 18–27 (2020)
33. Moosavi-Dezfooli, S.M., Fawzi, A., Frossard, P.: DeepFool: a simple and accurate method to fool deep neural networks. arXiv preprint arXiv:1511.04599v3 (2016)
34. Moosavi-Dezfooli, S.M., Fawzi, A., Uesato, J., Frossard, P.: Robustness via curvature regularization, and vice versa. In: CVPR (2019)
35. Netzer, Y., Wang, T., Coates, A., Bissacco, A., Wu, B., Ng, A.Y.: Reading digits in natural images with unsupervised feature learning. In: NIPS Workshop on Deep Learning and Unsupervised Feature Learning (2011)
36. Nilsback, M.E., Zisserman, A.: A visual vocabulary for flower classification. In: IEEE Conference on Computer Vision and Pattern Recognition, vol. 2, pp. 1447–1454 (2006)
37. Nilsback, M.E., Zisserman, A.: Delving deeper into the whorl of flower segmentation. Image Vis. Comput. 28(6), 1049–1062 (2010). https://doi.org/10.1016/j.imavis.2009.10.001
38. Oh, S.J., Benenson, R., Khoreva, A., Akata, Z., Fritz, M., Schiele, B.: Exploiting saliency for object segmentation from image level labels. CoRR abs/1701.08261 (2017). http://arxiv.org/abs/1701.08261
39. Papernot, N., McDaniel, P., Goodfellow, I.J., Jha, S., Celik, Z.B., Swami, A.: Practical black-box attacks against machine learning. ACM (2017)
40. Petsiuk, V., Das, A., Saenko, K.: RISE: randomized input sampling for explanation of black-box models. In: BMVC (2018)
41. Ribeiro, M.T., Singh, S., Guestrin, C.: Why should i trust you?: explaining the predictions of any classifier. In: ACM SIGKDD (2016)
42. Ross, A.S., Doshi-Velez, F.: Improving the adversarial robustness and interpretability of deep neural networks by regularizing their input gradients. In: AAAI (2018)
43. Santurkar, S., Ilyas, A., Tsipras, D., Engstrom, L., Tran, B., Madry, A.: Image synthesis with a single (robust) classifier. In: NeurIPS (2019)
44. Schroff, Florian an Kalenichenko, D., Philbin, J.: FaceNet: a unified embedding for face recognition and clustering. In: CVPR (2015)
45. Selvaraju, R.R., Das, A., Vedantam, R., Cogswell, M., Parikh, D., Batra, D.: Grad-CAM: visual explanations from deep networks via gradient-based localization (2016)
46. Shrikumar, A., Greenside, P., Kundaje, A.: Learning important features through propagating activation differences, pp. 3145–3153 (2017)
47. Shrikumar, A., Greenside, P., Shcherbina, A., Kundaje, A.: Not just a black box: learning important features through propagating activation differences. arXiv preprint arXiv:1605.01713 (2016)
48. Simonyan, K., Vedaldi, A., Zisserman, A.: Deep inside convolutional networks: visualising image classification models and saliency maps. arXiv preprint arXiv:1312.6034 (2013)

49. Simonyan, K., Zisserman, A.: Very deep convolutional networks for large-scale image recognition. arXiv preprint arXiv:1409.1556 (2014)
50. Sinha, A., Singh, M., Kumari, N., Krishnamurthy, B., Machiraju, H., Balasubra-manian, V.: Harnessing the vulnerability of latent layers in adversarially trained models. arXiv preprint arXiv:1905.05186 (2019)
51. Smilkov, D., Thorat, N., Kim, B., Viégas, F., Wattenberg, M.: SmoothGrad: removing noise by adding noise. In: Workshop on Visualization for Deep Learning, ICML (2017)
52. Springenberg, J.T., Dosovitskiy, A., Brox, T., Riedmiller, M.: Striving for simplicity: the all convolutional net. In: ICLR Workshop (2015)
53. Stallkamp, J., Schlipsing, M., Salmen, J., Igel, C.: The German traffic sign recognition benchmark: a multi-class classification competition. In: IEEE International Joint Conference on Neural Networks, pp. 1453–1460 (2011)
54. Sundararajan, M., Taly, A., Yan, Q.: Axiomatic attribution for deep networks. In: ICML (2017)
55. Szegedy, C., et al.: Intriguing properties of neural networks. In: ICLR (2014)
56. Taly, A., et al.: Using a deep learning algorithm and integrated gradient explanation to assist grading for diabetic retinopathy. Ophthalmology 126(4), 552–564 (2019)
57. Tsipras, D., Santurkar, S., Engstrom, L., Turner, A., Madry, A.: Robustness may be at odds with accuracy. In: ICLR (2019)
58. Uesato, J., O'Donoghue, B., Kohli, P., van den Oord, A.: Adversarial risk and the dangers of evaluating against weak attacks. In: ICML (2018)
59. Vasconcelos, M., Vasconcelos, N., Carneiro, G.: Weakly supervised top-down image segmentation. In: 2006 IEEE Computer Society Conference on Computer Vision and Pattern Recognition (CVPR 2006), vol. 1, pp. 1001–1006, June 2006. https://doi.org/10.1109/CVPR.2006.333
60. Vezhnevets, A., Buhmann, J.M.: Towards weakly supervised semantic segmentation by means of multiple instance and multitask learning. In: 2010 IEEE Computer Society Conference on Computer Vision and Pattern Recognition, pp. 3249–3256, June 2010. https://doi.org/10.1109/CVPR.2010.5540060
61. Wah, C., Branson, S., Welinder, P., Perona, P., Belongie, S.: The caltech-UCSD birds-200-2011 dataset. Tech. Rep. CNS-TR-2011-001, California Institute of Technology (2011)
62. Xu, K., et al.: Structured adversarial attack: towards general implementation and better interpretability. In: ICLR (2019)
63. Yuan, X., He, P., Zhu, Q., Li, X.: Adversarial examples: attacks and defenses for deep learning. IEEE Trans. Neural Netw. Learn. Syst. 30(9), 2805–2824 (2019)
64. Zagoruyko, S., Komodakis, N.: Wide residual networks. CoRR abs/1605.07146 (2016). http://arxiv.org/abs/1605.07146
65. Zeiler, M.D., Fergus, R.: Visualizing and understanding convolutional networks. In: Fleet, D., Pajdla, T., Schiele, B., Tuytelaars, T. (eds.) ECCV 2014. LNCS, vol. 8689, pp. 818–833. Springer, Cham (2014). https://doi.org/10.1007/978-3-319-10590-1_53
66. Zhang, H., Yu, Y., Jiao, J., Xing, E.P., Ghaoui, L.E., Jordan, M.I.: Theoretically principled trade-off between robustness and accuracy. arXiv preprint arXiv:1901.08573 (2019)
67. Zhang, J., Lin, Z., Brandt, J., Shen, X., Sclaroff, S.: Top-down neural attention by excitation backprop. In: Leibe, B., Matas, J., Sebe, N., Welling, M. (eds.) ECCV 2016. LNCS, vol. 9908, pp. 543–559. Springer, Cham (2016). https://doi.org/10.1007/978-3-319-46493-0_33

68. Zhang, L., Song, M., Liu, Z., Liu, X., Bu, J., Chen, C.: Probabilistic Graphlet Cut: exploiting spatial structure cue for weakly supervised image segmentation. In: 2013 IEEE Conference on Computer Vision and Pattern Recognition, pp. 1908–1915, June 2013. https://doi.org/10.1109/CVPR.2013.249
69. Zhang, Q., Zhu, S.C.: Visual interpretability for deep learning: a survey. arXiv preprint arXiv:1802.00614 (2018)
70. Zhang, X., Wang, N., Shen, H., Ji, S., Luo, X., Wang, T.: Interpretable deep learning under fire. arXiv preprint arXiv:1812.00891 (2018)
71. Zhou, B., Khosla, A., Lapedriza, A., Oliva, A., Torralba, A.: Learning deep features for discriminative localization. In: CVPR (2016)

Reducing the Sim-to-Real Gap for Event Cameras

Timo Stoffregen[1,3]([✉]), Cedric Scheerlinck[2,3], Davide Scaramuzza[4],
Tom Drummond[1,3], Nick Barnes[2,3], Lindsay Kleeman[1], and Robert Mahony[2,3]

[1] Department of ECSE, Monash University, Melbourne, Australia
timo.stoffregen@monash.edu
[2] Australian National University, Canberra, Australia
[3] Australian Centre for Robotic Vision, Brisbane, Australia
[4] University of Zurich, Zurich, Switzerland

Abstract. Event cameras are paradigm-shifting novel sensors that
report asynchronous, per-pixel brightness changes called 'events' with
unparalleled low latency. This makes them ideal for high speed, high
dynamic range scenes where conventional cameras would fail. Recent
work has demonstrated impressive results using Convolutional Neural
Networks (CNNs) for video reconstruction and optic flow with events.
We present strategies for improving training data for event based CNNs
that result in 20–40% boost in performance of existing state-of-the-art
(SOTA) video reconstruction networks retrained with our method, and
up to 15% for optic flow networks. A challenge in evaluating event based
video reconstruction is lack of quality ground truth images in existing
datasets. To address this, we present a new **High Quality Frames
(HQF)** dataset, containing events and ground truth frames from a
DAVIS240C that are well-exposed and minimally motion-blurred. We
evaluate our method on HQF + several existing major event camera
datasets.

1 Introduction

Event-based cameras such as the Dynamic Vision Sensor (DVS) [18] are novel,
bio-inspired visual sensors. Presenting a paradigm-shift in visual data acquisition, pixels in an event camera operate by asynchronously and independently
reporting intensity changes in the form of events, represented as a tuple of x, y
location, timestamp t and polarity of the intensity change s. By moving away

---

Video, code and datasets: https://timostoff.github.io/20ecnn.
T. Stoffregen and C. Scheerlinck—Equal contribution.

Electronic supplementary material The online version of this chapter (https://
doi.org/10.1007/978-3-030-58583-9_32) contains supplementary material, which is
available to authorized users.

© Springer Nature Switzerland AG 2020
A. Vedaldi et al. (Eds.): ECCV 2020, LNCS 12372, pp. 534–549, 2020.
https://doi.org/10.1007/978-3-030-58583-9_32

Fig. 1. Top: ground truth reference image. Middle/bottom: state-of-the-art E2VID [28] vs. our reconstructed images from events only. Challenging scenes from event camera datasets: CED [33], IJRR [23], MVSEC [42] and our **HQF** dataset.

from fixed frame-rate sampling of conventional cameras, event cameras deliver several key advantages in terms of low power usage (in the region of 5mW), high dynamic range (140 dB), low latency and timestamps with resolution on the order of μs.

With the recent preponderance of deep learning techniques in computer vision, the question of how to apply this technology to event data has been the subject of several recent works. Zhu *et al.* [43] propose an unsupervised network able to learn optic flow from real event data, while Rebecq *et al.* [27,28] showed that supervised networks trained on synthetic events transferred well to real event data. Simulation shows promise since data acquisition and ground truth are easily obtainable, in contrast to using real data. However, mismatch between synthetic and real data degrades performance, so a key challenge is simulating realistic data.

We generate training data that better matches real event camera data by analyzing the statistics of existing datasets to inform our choice of simulation parameters. A major finding is that the contrast threshold (CT) - the minimum change in brightness required to trigger an event - is a key simulation parameter that impacts performance of supervised CNNs. Further, we observe that the apparent contrast threshold of real event cameras varies greatly, even within one dataset. Previous works such as event based video reconstruction [28] choose contrast thresholds that work well for some datasets, but fail on others. Unsupervised networks trained on real data such as event based optic flow [43] may be retrained to match any real event camera - at the cost of new data collection and training. We show that using CT values for synthetic training data that are correctly matched to CTs of real datasets is a key driver in improving performance of retrained event based video reconstruction and optic flow networks across multiple datasets. We also propose a simple noise model which yields up to 10% improvement when added during training.

A challenge in evaluating image and video reconstruction from events is lack of quality ground truth images registered and time-synchronized to events, because most existing datasets focus on scenarios where event cameras excel (high speed, HDR) and conventional cameras fail. To address this limitation, we introduce a new High Quality Frames (HQF) dataset that provides several sequences in well lit environments with minimal motion blur. These sequences are recorded with a DAVIS240C event camera that provides perfectly aligned frames from an integrated Active Pixel Sensor (APS). HQF also contains a diverse range of motions and scene types, including slow motion and pauses that are challenging for event based video reconstruction. We quantitatively evaluate our method on two major event camera datasets: IJRR [23] and MVSEC [42], in addition to our HQF, demonstrating gains of 20–40% for video reconstruction and up to 15% for optic flow when we retrain existing SOTA networks.

Contribution. We present a method to generate synthetic training data that improves generalizability to real event data, guided by statistical analysis of existing datasets. We additionally propose a simple method for dynamic train-time noise augmentation that yields up to 10% improvement for video reconstruction. Using our method, we retrain several network architectures from previously published works on video reconstruction [28,32] and optic flow [43,44] from events. We are able to show significant improvements that persist over architectures and tasks. Thus, we believe our findings will provide invaluable insight for others who wish to train models on synthetic events for a variety of tasks. We provide a new comprehensive High Quality Frames dataset targeting ground truth image frames for video reconstruction evaluation. Finally, we provide our data generation code, training set, training code and our pretrained models, together with dozens of useful helper scripts for the analysis of event-based datasets to make this task easier for fellow researchers.

In summary, our major contributions are:

– A method for simulating training data that yields 20%–40 and up to 15% improvement for event based video reconstruction and optic flow CNNs.
– Dynamic train-time event noise augmentation.
– A novel High Quality Frames dataset.
– Extensive analysis and evaluation of our method.
– An optic flow evaluation metric *Flow Warp Loss (FWL)*, tailored to event data, that does not require ground truth flow.
– Open-source code, training data and pretrained models.

The remainder of the paper is as follows. Section 2 reviews related works. Section 3 outlines our method for generating training data, training and evaluation, and introduces our HQF dataset. Section 4 presents experimental results on video reconstruction and optic flow. Section 5 discusses our major findings and concludes the paper.

2   Related Works

2.1   Video Reconstruction

Video and image reconstruction from events has been a popular topic in the event based vision literature. Several approaches have been proposed in recent years; Kim et al. [14] used an EKF to reconstruct images from a rotating event camera, later extending this approach to full 6-DOF camera motions [15]. Bardow et al. [2] used a sliding spatiotemporal window of events to simultaneously optimize both optic flow and intensity estimates using the primal-dual algorithm, although this method remains sensitive to hyperparameters. Reinbacher et al. [29] proposed direct integration with periodic manifold regularization on the Surface of Active Events (SAE [22]) to reconstruct video from events. Scheerlinck et al. [30,31] achieved computationally efficient, continuous-time video reconstruction via complementary and high-pass filtering. This approach can be combined with conventional frames, if available, to provide low frequency components of the image. However, if taken alone, this approach suffers from artifacts such as ghosting effects and bleeding edges.

Recently, convolutional neural networks (CNNs) have been brought to bear on the task of video reconstruction. Rebecq et al. [27,28] presented E2VID, a recurrent network that converts events (discretized into a voxel grid) to video. A temporal consistency loss based on [16] was introduced to reduce flickering artifacts in the video, due to small differences in the reconstruction of subsequent frames. E2VID is current state-of-the-art. Scheerlinck et al. were able to reduce model complexity by 99% with the *FireNet* architecture [32], with only minor trade-offs in reconstruction quality, enabling high frequency inference.

2.2   Optic Flow

Since event based cameras are considered a good fit for applications involving motion [8], much work has been done on estimating optic flow with event cameras [1-4,6,10,20,35,36]. Recently, Zhu et al. proposed a CNN (EV-FlowNet) for estimating optic flow from events [43], together with the Multi-Vehicle Stereo Event Camera (MVSEC) dataset [42] that contains ground truth optic flow estimated from depth and ego-motion sensors. The input to EV-FlowNet is a 4-channel image formed by recording event counts and the most recent timestamps for negative and positive events. The loss imposed on EV-FlowNet was an image-warping loss [13] that took photometric error between subsequent APS frames registered using the predicted flow. A similar approach was taken by Ye et al. [39], in a network that estimated depth and camera pose to calculate optic flow. In [44], Zhu et al. improved on prior work by replacing the image-warping loss with an event-warping loss that directly transports events to a reference time using the predicted flow. We use a similar method to evaluate optic flow performance of several networks (see Sect. 4.1). Zhu et al. [44] also introduced a novel input representation based on event discretization that places events into bins with temporal bilinear interpolation to produce a voxel grid. EV-FlowNet was trained on data from MVSEC [42] and Ye *et al.* [39] even trained, then validated on the same sequences; our results (Sect. 4.1) indicate that these networks suffer from overfitting.

2.3   Input Representations

To use conventional CNNs, events must first be transformed into an amenable grid-based representation. While asynchronous spiking neural networks can process raw events and have been used for object recognition [17,24,25] and optic flow [3,4], lack of appropriate hardware or effective error backpropagation techniques renders them yet uncompetitive with state-of-the-art CNNs. Several grid-based input representations for CNNs have been proposed: simple event images [21,43] (events are accumulated to form an image), Surface of Active Events (SAE) [43] (latest timestamp recorded at each pixel), Histogram of Averaged Time Surfaces (HATS) [34] and even learned input representations, where events are sampled into a grid using convolutional kernels [12]. Zhu *et al.* [44] and Rebecq *et al.* [28] found best results using a voxel grid representation of events, where the temporal dimension is essentially discretized and subsequently binned into an n dimensional grid (Eq. 1).

3   Method

3.1   Event Camera Contrast Threshold

In an ideal event camera, a pixel at (x, y) triggers an event e_i at time t_i when the brightness since the last event e_{i-1} at that pixel changes by a threshold C, given $t - t_{i-1} > r$, the refractory period of that pixel. C is referred to as the contrast threshold (CT) and can be typically adjusted in modern event cameras. In reality, the values for C are not constant in time nor homogeneous over the image plane nor is the positive threshold C_p necessarily equal to the negative threshold C_n. In simulation (e.g. using ESIM [26]), CTs are typically sampled from $\mathcal{N}(\mu = 0.18, \sigma = 0.03)$ to model this variation [12,27,28]. The CT is an important simulator parameter since it determines the number and distribution of events generated from a given scene.

While the real CTs of previously published datasets are unknown, one method to estimate CTs is via the proxy measurement of average events per pixel per second ($\frac{events}{pix \cdot s}$). Intuitively, higher CTs tend to reduce the $\frac{events}{pix \cdot s}$ for a given scene. While other methods of CT estimation exist (see supp. material), we found that tuning the simulator CTs to match $\frac{events}{pix \cdot s}$ of real data worked well. Since this measure is affected by scene dynamics (i.e. faster motions increase $\frac{events}{pix \cdot s}$ independently of CT), we generated a diverse variety of realistic scene dynamics. The result of this experiment (Fig. 2a) indicates that a contrast threshold setting of between 0.2 and 0.5 would be more appropriate for sequences from the IJRR dataset [23]. The larger diversity of motions is also apparent in the large spread of the $\frac{events}{pix \cdot s}$ compared to MVSEC [42] whose sequences are tightly clustered.

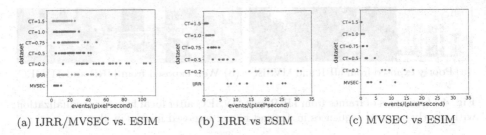

(a) IJRR/MVSEC vs. ESIM   (b) IJRR vs ESIM   (c) MVSEC vs ESIM

Fig. 2. Each dot represents a sequence from the given dataset (y-axis). (a) $\frac{events}{pix \cdot s}$ of IJRR and MVSEC vs. ESIM training datasets (CT 0.2–1.5) described in Sect. 3.2. (b) $\frac{events}{pix \cdot s}$ of IJRR vs. ESIM events simulated from IJRR *APS frames*. (c) $\frac{events}{pix \cdot s}$ of MVSEC vs. ESIM events simulated from MVSEC *APS frames*.

(a) IJRR   (b) IJRR   (c) MVSEC   (d) MVSEC   (e) HQF

Fig. 3. Note that in many sequences from the commonly used IJRR and MVSEC datasets, the accompanying APS frames are of low quality. The top row shows the APS frames, the bottom row overlays the events. As can be seen, many features are not visible in the APS frames, making quantitative evaluation difficult. This motivates our own High Quality Frames dataset (HQF).

As an alternative experiment to determine CTs of existing datasets, we measured the $\frac{events}{pix \cdot s}$ of events simulated using the actual APS (ground truth) frames of IJRR and MVSEC sequences. Given high quality images with minimal motion blur and little displacement, events can be simulated through image interpolation and subtraction. Given an ideal image sequence, the simulator settings should be tunable to get the exact same $\frac{events}{pix \cdot s}$ from simulation as from the real sensor. Unfortunately APS frames are not usually of a very high quality (Fig. 3), so we were limited to using this approach on carefully curated snippets (Fig. 4). The results of this experiment in Fig. 2b and 2c indicate similar results of lower contrast thresholds for IJRR and higher for MVSEC, although accuracy is limited by the poor quality APS frames.

(a) Poorly exposed from IJRR and MVSEC   (b) Well exposed from IJRR and MVSEC

Fig. 4. Examples of frames from IJRR and MVSEC after local histogram equalization, with poorly exposed sequences in 4a, and better exposed images in 4b.

3.2 Training Data

We used an event camera simulator, ESIM [26] to generate training sequences for our network. There are several modes of simulation available, of which we used "Multi-Object-2D" that facilitates moving images in simple 2D motions, restricted to translations, rotations and dilations over a planar background. This generates sequences reminiscent of Flying Chairs [7], where objects move across the screen at varying velocities. In our generation scheme, we randomly selected images from COCO [19] and gave them random trajectories over the image plane. Our dataset contains 280 sequences, 10 s in length. Sequences alternate between four archetypal scenes; slow motion with 0–5 foreground objects, medium speed motion with 5–10 foreground objects, fast speed with 5–20 foreground objects and finally, full variety of motions with 10–30 foreground objects. This variety encourages networks to generalize to arbitrary real world camera motions, since a wide range of scene dynamics are presented during training. Sequences were generated with contrast thresholds (CTs) between 0.1 and 1.5 in ascending order. Since real event cameras do not usually have perfectly balanced positive and negative thresholds, the positive threshold $C_p = C_n \cdot x, x \in \mathcal{N}(\mu = 1.0, \sigma = 0.1)$.

The events thus generated were discretized into a voxel grid representation. In order to ensure synchronicity with the ground truth frames of our training set and later with the ground truth frames of our validation set, we always take all events between two frames to generate a voxel grid. Given N events $e_i = \{x_i, y_i, t_i, s_i\}_{i=0,...,N}$ spanning $\Delta_T = t_N - t_0$ seconds, a voxel grid V with B bins can be formed through temporal bilinear interpolation via

$$V_{k \in [0, B-1]} = \sum_{i=0}^{N} s_i \max(0, 1 - |t_i^* - k|) \tag{1}$$

where t_i^* is the timestamp normalized to the range $[0, B-1]$ via $t_i^* = \frac{t_i - t_0}{\Delta_T}(B-1)$ and the bins are evenly spaced over the range $[t_0, t_N]$. This method of forming voxels has some limitations; it is easy to see that the density of the voxels can vary greatly, depending on the camera motion and frame rate of the camera. Thus, it is important to train the network on a large range of event rates $\frac{\text{events}}{\text{pix} \cdot \text{s}}$ and voxel densities. During inference, other strategies of voxel generation can be employed, as further discussed in the supplementary materials. We used $B = 5$ throughout the experiments in this paper. In earlier experiments we found values of $B = 2, 5, 15$ produced no significant differences.

3.3   Sequence Length

To train recurrent networks, we sequentially passed L inputs to the network and computed the loss for each output. Finally, the losses were summed and a backpropagation update was performed based on the gradient of the final loss with respect to the network weights. Since recurrent units in the network are initialized to zero, lower values of L restrict the temporal support that the recurrent units see at train time. To investigate the impact of sequence length L, we retrain our networks using $L = 40$ (as in E2VID [28]) and $L = 120$. In the case of non-recurrent networks such as EV-FlowNet [43,44], we ignore the sequence length parameter.

3.4   Loss

For our primary video reconstruction loss function we used "learned perceptual image patch similarity" (LPIPS) [41]. LPIPS is a fully differentiable similarity metric between two images that compares hidden layer activations of a pre-trained network (e.g. Alex-Net or VGG), and was shown to better match human judgment of image similarity than photometric error or SSIM [38]. Since our event tensors were synchronized to the ground truth image frames by design (the final event in the tensor matches the frame timestamp), we computed the LPIPS distance between our reconstruction and the corresponding ground truth frame. As recommended by the authors [41], we used the Alex-Net variant of LPIPS. We additionally imposed a temporal consistency loss [16] that measures photometric error between consecutive images after registration based on optic flow, subject to an occlusion mask. For optic flow, we used the L1 distance between our prediction and ground truth as the training loss.

3.5   Data Augmentation

During training, Rebecq et al. [28] occasionally set the input events to zero and performed a forward-pass step within a sequence, using the previous ground truth image frame to compute the loss. The probability of initiating a pause when the sequence is running $P(p|r) = 0.05$, while the probability of maintaining the paused state when the sequence is already paused $P(p|p) = 0.9$ to encourage occasional long pauses. This encourages the recurrent units of the network to learn to 'preserve' the output image in absence of new events. We used pause augmentation to train all recurrent networks.

Event cameras provide a noisy measurement of brightness change, subject to background noise, refractory period after an event and hot pixels that fire many spurious events. To simulate real event data, we applied a refractory period of 1ms. At train time, for each sequence of L input event tensors we optionally added zero-mean Gaussian noise ($\mathcal{N}(\mu = 0, \sigma = 0.1)$) to the event tensor to simulate uncorrelated background noise, and randomly elected a few 'hot' pixels. The number of hot pixels was drawn from a uniform distribution from 0 to 0.0001, multiplied by the total number of pixels. Hot pixels have a random value

($\mathcal{N}(\mu = 0,\ \sigma = 0.1)$) added to every temporal bin in each event tensor within a sequence. To determine whether augmenting the training data with noise benefits performance on real data, we retrained several models with and without noise (Table 5).

3.6   Architecture

To isolate the impact of our method from choice of network architecture, we retrained state-of-the-art (SOTA) video reconstruction network E2VID [28] and SOTA optic flow network EV-FlowNet described in [43,44]. Thus, differences in performance for each task are not due to architecture. Additionally, we aim to show that our method generalizes to multiple architectures. While we believe architecture search may further improve results, it is outside the scope of this paper.

3.7   High Quality Frames Dataset

To evaluate event camera image reconstruction methods, we compared reconstructed images to temporally synchronized, registered ground truth reference images. Event cameras such as the DAVIS [5] can capture image frames (in addition to events) that are timestamped and registered to the events, that may serve as ground truth. Previous event camera datasets such as IJRR [23] and MVSEC [42] contain limited high quality DAVIS frames, while many frames are motion-blurred and or under/overexposed (Fig. 3). As a result, Rebecq *et al.* [28] manually rejected poor quality frames, evaluating on a smaller subset of IJRR.

We present a new High Quality Frames dataset (HQF) aimed at providing ground truth DAVIS frames that are minimally motion-blurred and well exposed. In addition, our HQF covers a wider range of motions and scene types than the evaluation dataset used for E2VID, including: static/dynamic camera motion vs. dynamic camera only, very slow to fast vs. medium to fast and indoor/outdoor vs. indoor only. To record HQF, we used two different DAVIS240C sensors to capture data with different noise/CT characteristics. We used default bias settings loaded by the RPG DVS ROS driver[1], and set exposure to either auto or fixed to maximize frame quality. Our HQF provides temporally synchronized, registered events and DAVIS frames (further details in supplementaries, Table 6).

4   Experiments

4.1   Evaluation

We evaluated our method by retraining two state-of-the-art event camera neural networks: E2VID [27,28], and EV-FlowNet [43,44]. Our method outperforms

---

[1] https://github.com/uzh-rpg/rpg_dvs_ros.

previous state-of-the-art in image reconstruction and optic flow on several publicly available event camera datasets including IJRR [23] and MVSEC [42], and our new High Quality Frames dataset (HQF, Sect. 3.7).

For video reconstruction on the datasets HQF, IJRR and MVSEC (Table 1) we obtained a 40%, 20% and 28% improvement over E2VID [28] respectively, using LPIPS. For optic flow we obtained a 12.5%, 10% and 16% improvement over EV-FlowNet [43] on flow warp loss (FWL, Eq. 3). Notably, EV-FlowNet was trained on MVSEC data (outdoor_day2 sequence), while ours was trained entirely on synthetic data, demonstrating the ability of our method to generalize to real event data.

Image. As in [28] we compared our reconstructed images to ground truth (DAVIS frames) on three metrics; mean squared error (MSE), structural similarity [38] (SSIM) and perceptual loss [40] (LPIPS) that uses distance in the latent space of a pretrained deep network to quantify image similarity.

Since many of these datasets show scenes that are challenging for conventional cameras, we carefully selected sections of those sequences where frames appeared to be of higher quality (less blurred, better exposure etc.). The exact cut times of the IJRR and MVSEC sequences can be found in the supplementary materials. However, we were also ultimately motivated to record our own dataset of high quality frames (HQF, Sect. 3.7) of which we evaluated the entire sequence.

Flow. A warping loss (similar to [11]) was used as a proxy measure of accuracy as it doesn't require ground truth flow. Events $E = (x_i, y_i, t_i, s_i)_{i=1,...,N}$ are warped by per-pixel optical flow $\phi = (u(x,y), v(x,y))^T$ to a reference time t' via

$$I(E, \phi) = \begin{pmatrix} x_i' \\ y_i' \end{pmatrix} = \begin{pmatrix} x_i \\ y_i \end{pmatrix} + (t' - t_i) \begin{pmatrix} u(x_i, y_i) \\ v(x_i, y_i) \end{pmatrix}. \tag{2}$$

The resulting image I becomes sharper if the flow is correct, as events are motion compensated. Sharpness can be evaluated using the variance of the image $\sigma^2(I)$ [9,37], where a higher value indicates a better flow estimate. Since image variance $\sigma^2(I)$ depends on scene structure and camera parameters, we normalize by the variance of the unwarped event image $I(E,0)$ to obtain the *Flow Warp Loss* *(FWL)*:

$$\text{FWL} := \frac{\sigma^2(I(E, \phi))}{\sigma^2(I(E, 0))}. \tag{3}$$

FWL < 1 implies the flow is worse than a baseline of zero flow. FWL enables evaluation on datasets without ground truth optic flow. While we used ground truth from the simulator during training, we evaluated on real data using FWL (Table 1). We believe training on ground truth (L1 loss) rather than FWL encourages dense flow predictions.

Table 2 shows average endpoint error (AEE) of optic flow on MVSEC [42]. MVSEC provides optic flow estimates computed from lidar depth and ego motion sensors as 'ground truth', allowing us to evaluate average endpoint error (AEE)

Table 1. Comparison of state-of-the-art methods of video reconstruction and optic flow to networks trained using our dataset on HQF, IJRR and MVSEC. Best in bold.

Sequence	MSE		SSIM		LPIPS		FWL	
	E2VID	Ours	E2VID	Ours	E2VID	Ours	EVFlow	Ours
HQF								
bike_bay_hdr	0.1580	**0.0299**	0.4141	**0.5202**	0.5100	**0.3038**	1.2194	**1.2302**
boxes	0.1067	**0.0345**	0.4974	**0.5923**	0.3755	**0.2575**	1.7485	**1.8020**
desk_6k	0.1515	**0.0300**	0.5117	**0.5966**	0.3886	**0.2213**	1.2250	**1.3515**
desk_fast	0.1151	**0.0354**	0.5399	**0.6062**	0.3957	**0.2504**	1.4323	**1.4956**
desk_hand_only	0.1242	**0.0480**	0.5304	**0.5709**	0.6319	**0.3864**	0.9469	0.8472
desk_slow	0.1569	**0.0410**	0.5306	**0.6218**	0.4724	**0.2480**	1.0085	**1.0756**
engineering_posters	0.1306	**0.0300**	0.4203	**0.5710**	0.4680	**0.2560**	1.4958	**1.6479**
high_texture_plants	0.1566	**0.0314**	0.3686	**0.6476**	0.3780	**0.1392**	0.1283	**1.6809**
poster_pillar_1	0.1393	**0.0318**	0.3803	**0.4990**	0.5402	**0.2672**	1.2026	**1.2413**
poster_pillar_2	0.1521	**0.0350**	0.4009	**0.4745**	0.5647	**0.2625**	1.1621	0.9649
reflective_materials	0.1251	**0.0334**	0.4414	**0.5544**	0.4436	**0.2802**	1.4543	**1.5748**
slow_and_fast_desk	0.1620	**0.0286**	0.4773	**0.6237**	0.4451	**0.2475**	0.9308	**0.9893**
slow_hand	0.1789	**0.0375**	0.4123	**0.5652**	0.5701	**0.3023**	1.6353	1.5618
still_life	0.0940	**0.0261**	0.5091	**0.6263**	0.3520	**0.2243**	1.9300	**1.9815**
Mean	0.1448	**0.0326**	0.4584	**0.5791**	0.4609	**0.2562**	1.2045	**1.3540**
IJRR								
boxes_6dof_cut	**0.0406**	0.0419	0.6304	**0.6392**	0.2898	**0.2479**	1.4171	**1.4571**
calibration_cut	0.0719	**0.0315**	0.6119	**0.6245**	0.2164	**0.1805**	1.2040	**1.3057**
dynamic_6dof_cut	0.1679	**0.0525**	0.4479	**0.5275**	0.3750	**0.2673**	1.3693	**1.3922**
office_zigzag_cut	0.0689	**0.0369**	0.4872	**0.5082**	0.3086	**0.2599**	1.1302	1.1127
poster_6dof_cut	0.0719	**0.0307**	0.5964	**0.6567**	0.2559	**0.1947**	1.5029	**1.5551**
shapes_6dof_cut	0.0277	**0.0168**	**0.7982**	0.7652	0.2632	**0.2234**	1.1485	**1.5699**
slider_depth_cut	0.0771	**0.0308**	0.5413	**0.6240**	0.3459	**0.2434**	1.7322	**2.1723**
Mean	0.0748	**0.0344**	0.6102	**0.6364**	0.2813	**0.2240**	1.3240	**1.4545**
MVSEC								
indoor_flying1_data_cut	0.2467	**0.0840**	0.1865	**0.3635**	0.7245	**0.4534**	1.0183	**1.1380**
indoor_flying2_data_cut	0.2306	**0.0931**	0.1821	**0.3581**	0.7092	**0.4530**	1.1293	**1.3592**
indoor_flying3_data_cut	0.2489	**0.0896**	0.1798	**0.3650**	0.7343	**0.4440**	1.0569	**1.2291**
indoor_flying4_data_cut	0.2107	**0.0784**	0.2274	**0.3622**	0.7165	**0.4475**	1.2377	**1.4999**
outdoor_day1_data_cut	0.3222	**0.1274**	0.3096	**0.3395**	0.6559	**0.5179**	1.1506	**1.2719**
outdoor_day2_data_cut*	0.2968	**0.0963**	0.2936	**0.3394**	0.5703	**0.4285**	1.2149	1.1958
Mean	0.2895	**0.1052**	0.2675	**0.3461**	0.6457	**0.4670**	1.11856	**1.29962**

*Removed from mean tally for EV-FlowNet, as this sequence is part of the training set.

using code provided in [43]. However, lidar + ego motion derived ground truth is subject to sensor noise, thus, AEE may be an unreliable metric on MVSEC. For example, predicting zero flow achieves near state-of-the-art in some cases on MVSEC using AEE, though not with our proposed metric FWL (by construction, predicting zero flow yields FWL = 1.0).

4.2   Contrast Thresholds

We investigated the impact of simulator contrast threshold (CT, see Sect. 3.1) by retraining several networks on simulated datasets with CTs ranging from

Table 2. Comparison of various methods to optic flow estimated from Lidar depth and ego-motion sensors [42]. The average-endpoint-error to the Lidar estimate (AEE) and the percentage of pixels with AEE above 3 and greater than 5% of the magnitude of the flow vector (%$_{Outlier}$) are presented for each method (lower is better, best in bold). Zeros shows the baseline error of zero flow. Additional works are compared in Table 9 which can be found in the supplementary materials.

Dataset	outdoor_day1		outdoor_day2		indoor_flying1		indoor_flying2		indoor_flying3	
	AEE	%$_{Outlier}$	AEE	%$_{Outlier}$	AEE	%$_{Outlier}$	AEE	%$_{Outlier}$	AEE	%$_{Outlier}$
Zeros	4.31	0.39	1.07	**0.91**	1.10	**1.00**	1.74	**0.89**	1.50	**0.94**
EVFlow [43]	**0.49**	0.2	–	–	1.03	2.20	1.72	15.10	1.53	11.90
Ours	0.68	0.99	**0.82**	0.96	**0.56**	1.00	**0.66**	1.00	**0.59**	1.00

Table 3. Evaluation of image reconstruction and optic flow networks trained on simulated datasets with a variety of contrast thresholds (CTs) from 0.2 to 1.5. 'All' is a dataset containing the full range of CTs from 0.2 to 1.5. All networks are trained for 200 epochs and evaluated on datasets HQF (excluding desk_hand_only on FWL), IJRR [23], MVSEC [42]. We report mean squared error (MSE), structural similarity (SSIM) [38] and perceptual loss (LPIPS) [41] for reconstruction and FWL for optic flow. Key: **best** | *second best*.

Contrast threshold	HQF				IJRR				MVSEC			
	MSE	SSIM	LPIPS	*FWL*	MSE	SSIM	LPIPS	*FWL*	MSE	SSIM	LPIPS	FWL
0.20	0.05	0.50	0.38	1.9258	**0.04**	**0.60**	**0.25**	*1.453*	0.10	**0.35**	0.55	1.1525
0.50	**0.04**	*0.51*	0.36	1.8996	0.04	0.57	0.27	1.424	*0.10*	0.31	0.52	1.1850
0.75	0.05	**0.51**	**0.36**	1.9035	0.05	0.56	0.28	1.438	0.11	0.29	0.53	*1.2238*
1.00	0.05	0.48	0.36	1.9093	0.05	0.53	0.29	1.419	0.12	0.27	*0.51*	1.1831
1.50	0.05	0.47	0.38	*1.9272*	0.06	0.52	0.30	1.436	0.09	0.30	0.52	1.1431
All	*0.05*	0.50	**0.36**	**1.9617**	**0.04**	*0.59*	*0.27*	**1.459**	**0.08**	*0.34*	**0.51**	**1.2434**

0.2 to 1.5. Each dataset contained the same sequences, differing only in CT. Table 3 shows that for reconstruction (evaluated on LPIPS), IJRR is best on a lower CT $\approx$ 0.2, while MVSEC is best on high CT $\approx$ 1.0. Best or runner up performance was achieved when a wide range of CTs was used, indicating that exposing a network to additional event statistics outside the inference domain is not harmful, and may be beneficial. We believe training with low CTs (thus higher $\frac{events}{pix \cdot s}$) reduces dynamic range in the output images (Table 4), perhaps because the network becomes accustomed to a high density of events during training but is presented with lower $\frac{events}{pix \cdot s}$ data at inference. When retraining the original E2VID network, dynamic range increases with CTs (Table 4).

4.3 Training Noise and Sequence Length

To determine the impact of sequence length and noise augmentation during training, we retrained E2VID architecture using sequence length 40 (L40) and 120 (L120), with and without noise augmentation (N) (see Table 5). Increasing sequence length from 40 to 120 didn't impact results significantly. Noise aug-

Table 4. Dynamic range of reconstructed images from IJRR [23]: original E2VID [28] versus E2VID retrained on simulated datasets covering a range of contrast thresholds CTs. We report the mean dynamic range of the 10th–90th percentile of pixel values.

	Original [28]	Retrained					
Contrast threshold	~ 0.18	0.2	0.5	0.75	1.0	1.5	All
Dynamic range	77.3	89.2	103.7	105.9	104.8	100.0	103.3

Table 5. Mean LPIPS [41] on our HQF dataset, IJRR [23] and MVSEC [42], for various training hyperparameter configurations. E2VID architecture retrained from scratch in all experiments. Key: L40/L120 = sequence length 40/120, N = noise augmentation during training.

Model	HQF			IJRR			MVSEC		
	MSE	SSIM	LPIPS	MSE	SSIM	LPIPS	MSE	SSIM	LPIPS
L40	0.0441	**0.5826**	0.2964	0.0417	**0.6497**	0.2289	0.1514	0.3302	0.5255
L40N	**0.0326**	0.5791	**0.2562**	**0.0344**	0.6364	**0.2240**	0.1052	**0.3461**	**0.4670**
L120	0.0399	0.5444	0.2791	0.0383	0.6187	0.2368	0.1321	0.3112	0.4775
L120N	0.0358	0.5468	0.2904	0.0396	0.6079	0.2410	**0.0990**	0.3439	0.4983

mentation during training improved performance of L40 models by $\sim$ 5–10%, while giving mixed results on different datasets for L120 models. Qualitatively, adding more noise encourages networks to smooth outputs, while less noise may encourage the network to 'reconstruct' noise events, resulting in artifacts (Fig. 1) observed in E2VID [28] (trained without noise).

5   Discussion

The significant improvements gained by training models on our synthetic dataset exemplify the importance of reducing the sim-to-real gap for event cameras in both the event rate induced by varying the contrast thresholds and the dynamics of the simulation scenes. Our results are quite clear on this, with consistent improvements across tasks (reconstruction and optic flow) and architectures (recurrent networks like E2VID, and U-Net based flow estimators) of up to 40%.

We believe this highlights the importance for researchers to pay attention to the properties of the events they are training on; are the settings of the camera or simulator such that they are generating more or less events? Are the scenes they are recording representative of the wide range of scenes that are likely to be encountered during inference?

In particular, it seems that previous works have inadvertently overfit their models to the events found in the chosen target dataset. EV-FlowNet performs better on sequences whose dynamics are similar to the slow, steady scenes in MVSEC used for training, examples being poster_pillar_2 or desk_slow from

HQF that feature long pauses and slow motions, where EV-FlowNet is on par or better than ours. For researchers looking to use an off-the-shelf pretrained network, our model may be a better fit, since it targets a greater variety of sensors and scenes. A further advantage of our model that is not reflected in the FWL metric, is that training in simulation allows our model to predict *dense* flow (see supp. material), a challenge for prior self-supervised methods.

Similarly, our results speak for themselves on image reconstruction. While we outperform E2VID [28] on all datasets, the smallest gap is on IJRR, the dataset we found to have lower CTs. E2VID performs worst on MVSEC that contains higher CTs, consistent with our finding that performance is driven by similarity between training and evaluation event data.

In conclusion, future networks trained with synthetic data from ESIM or other simulators should take care to ensure the statistics of their synthetic data match the final use-case, using large ranges of CT values and appropriate noise and pause augmentation in order to ensure generalized models.

Acknowledgments. This work was supported by the Australian Government Research Training Program Scholarship and the Australian Research Council through the "Australian Centre of Excellence for Robotic Vision" under Grant CE140100016.

References

1. Almatrafi, M.M., Hirakawa, K.: DAViS camera optical flow. IEEE Trans. Comput. Imaging **23**, 1–11 (2019)
2. Bardow, P., Davison, A.J., Leutenegger, S.: Simultaneous optical flow and intensity estimation from an event camera. In: IEEE Conference Computer Vision Pattern Recognition (CVPR), pp. 884–892 (2016)
3. Benosman, R., Clercq, C., Lagorce, X., Ieng, S.-H., Bartolozzi, C.: Event-based visual flow. IEEE Trans. Neural Netw. Learn. Syst. **25**(2), 407–417 (2014)
4. Benosman, R., Ieng, S.-H., Clercq, C., Bartolozzi, C., Srinivasan, M.: Asynchronous frameless event-based optical flow. Neural Netw. **27**, 32–37 (2012)
5. Brandli, C., Berner, R., Yang, M., Liu, S.-C., Delbruck, T.: A 240 x 180 130 dB 3us latency global shutter spatiotemporal vision sensor. IEEE J. Solid State Circ. **49**(10), 2333–2341 (2014)
6. Brosch, T., Tschechne, S., Neumann, H.: On event-based optical flow detection. Front. Neurosci. **9**, 137 (2015)
7. Dosovitskiy, A., et al.: FlowNet: learning optical flow with convolutional networks. In: International Conference Computer Vision (ICCV), pp. 2758–2766 (2015)
8. Gallego, G., et al.: Event-based vision: a survey. arXiv e-prints, abs/1904.08405 (2019)
9. Gallego, G., Gehrig, M., Scaramuzza, D.: Focus is all you need: loss functions for event-based vision. In: IEEE Conference Computer Vision Pattern Recognition (CVPR) (2019)
10. Gallego, G., Rebecq, H., Scaramuzza, D.: A unifying contrast maximization framework for event cameras, with applications to motion, depth, and optical flow estimation. In: IEEE Conference Computer Vision and Pattern Recognition (CVPR), pp. 3867–3876 (2018)

11. Gallego, G., Scaramuzza, D.: Accurate angular velocity estimation with an event camera. IEEE Robot. Autom. Lett. **2**(2), 632–639 (2017)
12. Gehrig, D., Loquercio, A., Derpanis, K.G., Scaramuzza, D.: End-to-end learning of representations for asynchronous event-based data. In: International Conference Computer Vision (ICCV) (2019)
13. Jason, Y., Adam, H., Konstantinos, D.: Back to basics: unsupervised learning of optical flow via brightness constancy and motion smoothness (2016)
14. Kim, H., Handa, A., Benosman, R., Ieng, S.-H., Davison, A.J.: Simultaneous mosaicing and tracking with an event camera. In: British Machine Vision Conference (BMVC) (2014)
15. Kim, H., Leutenegger, S., Davison, A.J.: Real-time 3D reconstruction and 6-DoF tracking with an event camera. In: Leibe, B., Matas, J., Sebe, N., Welling, M. (eds.) ECCV 2016. LNCS, vol. 9910, pp. 349–364. Springer, Cham (2016). https://doi.org/10.1007/978-3-319-46466-4_21
16. Lai, W.-S., Huang, J.-B., Wang, O., Shechtman, E., Yumer, E., Yang, M.-H.: Learning blind video temporal consistency. In: Ferrari, V., Hebert, M., Sminchisescu, C., Weiss, Y. (eds.) ECCV 2018. LNCS, vol. 11219, pp. 179–195. Springer, Cham (2018). https://doi.org/10.1007/978-3-030-01267-0_11
17. Lee, J.H., Delbruck, T., Pfeiffer, M.: Training deep spiking neural networks using backpropagation. Front. Neurosci. **10**, 508 (2016)
18. Lichtsteiner, P., Posch, C., Delbruck, T.: A 128 × 128 120 dB 15 μs latency asynchronous temporal contrast vision sensor. IEEE J. Solid State Circ. **43**(2), 566–576 (2008)
19. Lin, T.-Y., et al.: Microsoft COCO: common objects in context. In: Fleet, D., Pajdla, T., Schiele, B., Tuytelaars, T. (eds.) ECCV 2014. LNCS, vol. 8693, pp. 740–755. Springer, Cham (2014). https://doi.org/10.1007/978-3-319-10602-1_48
20. Liu, M., Delbruck, T.: Adaptive time-slice block-matching optical flow algorithm for dynamic vision sensors. In: British Machine Vision Conference (BMVC) (2018)
21. Ana I. Maqueda, Antonio Loquercio, Guillermo Gallego, Narciso García, and Davide Scaramuzza. Event-based vision meets deep learning on steering prediction for self-driving cars. In IEEE Conf. Comput. Vis. Pattern Recog. (CVPR), pages 5419–5427, 2018
22. Elias Mueggler, Christian Forster, Nathan Baumli, Guillermo Gallego, and Davide Scaramuzza. Lifetime estimation of events from dynamic vision sensors. In IEEE Int. Conf. Robot. Autom. (ICRA), pages 4874–4881, 2015
23. Mueggler, E., Rebecq, H., Gallego, G., Delbruck, T., Scaramuzza, D.: The event-camera dataset and simulator: event-based data for pose estimation, visual odometry, and SLAM. Int. J. Robot. Res. **36**(2), 142–149 (2017)
24. Orchard, G., Meyer, C., Etienne-Cummings, R., Posch, C., Thakor, N., Benosman, R.: HFirst: a temporal approach to object recognition. IEEE Trans. Pattern Anal. Mach. Intell. **37**(10), 2028–2040 (2015)
25. Perez-Carrasco, J.A., Zhao, B., Serrano, C., Acha, B., Serrano-Gotarredona, T., Chen, S., Linares-Barranco, B.: Mapping from frame-driven to frame-free event-driven vision systems by low-rate rate coding and coincidence processing-application to feedforward ConvNets. IEEE Trans. Pattern Anal. Mach. Intell. **35**(11), 2706–2719 (2013)
26. Rebecq, H., Gehrig, D., Scaramuzza, D.: ESIM: an open event camera simulator. In: Conference on Robot Learning (CoRL) (2018)
27. Rebecq, H., Ranftl, R., Koltun, V., Scaramuzza, D.: Events-to-video: bringing modern computer vision to event cameras. In: IEEE Conference Computer Vision Pattern Recognition (CVPR) (2019)

28. Rebecq, H., Ranftl, R., Koltun, V., Scaramuzza, D.: High speed and high dynamic range video with an event camera. IEEE Trans. Pattern Anal. Mach. Intell. 2020

29. Reinbacher, C., Graber, G., Pock, T.: Real-time intensity-image reconstruction for event cameras using manifold regularisation. In: British Machine Vision Conference (BMVC) (2016)

30. Scheerlinck, C., Barnes, N., Mahony, R.: Continuous-time intensity estimation using event cameras. In: Asian Conference on Computer Vision (ACCV) (2018)

31. Scheerlinck, C., Barnes, N., Mahony, R.: Asynchronous spatial image convolutions for event cameras. IEEE Robot. Autom. Lett. 4(2), 816–822 (2019)

32. Scheerlinck, C., Rebecq, H., Gehrig, D., Barnes, N., Mahony,R., Scaramuzza, D.: Fast image reconstruction with an event camera. In: Winter Conference on Applications of Computer Vision (WACV) (2020)

33. Scheerlinck, C., Rebecq, H., Stoffregen, T., Barnes, N., Mahony,R., Scaramuzza, D.: CED: color event camera dataset. In: IEEE Conference on Computer Vision and Pattern Recognition Workshops (CVPRW) (2019)

34. Sironi, A., Brambilla, M., Bourdis, N., Lagorce, X., Benosman, R.: HATS: histograms of averaged time surfaces for robust event-based object classification. In: IEEE Conference on Computer Vision and Pattern Recognition (CVPR), pp. 1731–1740 (2018)

35. Stoffregen, T., Gallego, G., Drummond, T., Kleeman, L., Scaramuzza, D.: Event-based motion segmentation by motion compensation. In: International Conference on Computer Vision (ICCV) (2019)

36. Stoffregen, T., Kleeman, L.: Simultaneous optical flow and segmentation (SOFAS) using dynamic vision sensor. In: Australasian Conference on Robotics and Automation (ACRA) (2017)

37. Stoffregen, T., Kleeman, L.: Event cameras, contrast maximization and reward functions: an analysis. In: IEEE Conference on Computer Vision and Pattern Recognition (CVPR) (2019)

38. Wang, Z., Bovik, A.C., Sheikh, H.R., Simoncelli, E.P.: Image quality assessment: from error visibility to structural similarity. IEEE Trans. Image Process. 13(4), 600–612 (2004)

39. Ye, C., Mitrokhin, A., Parameshwara, C., Fermüller, C., Yorke, J.A., Aloimonos, Y.: Unsupervised learning of dense optical flow and depth from sparse event data. arXiv e-prints (2019)

40. Zhang, L., Rusinkiewicz, S.: Learning to detect features in texture images. In: IEEE Conference on Computer Vision and Pattern Recognition (CVPR) (2018)

41. Zhang, R., Isola, P., Efros, A.A., Shechtman, E., Wang, O.: The unreasonable effectiveness of deep features as a perceptual metric. In: IEEE Conference on Computer Vision and Pattern Recognition (CVPR) (2018)

42. Zhu, A.Z., Thakur, D., Ozaslan, T., Pfrommer, B., Kumar, V., Daniilidis, K.: The multivehicle stereo event camera dataset: an event camera dataset for 3D perception. IEEE Robot. Autom. Lett. 3(3), 2032–2039 (2018)

43. Zhu, A.Z., Kenneth Chaney, L.Y., Daniilidis, K.: EV-FlowNet: self-supervised optical flow estimation for event-based cameras. In: Robotics: Science and Systems (RSS) (2018)

44. Zhu, A.Z., Yuan, L., Chaney, K., Daniilidis, K.: Unsupervised event-based learning of optical flow, depth, and egomotion. In: IEEE Conference on Computer Vision and Pattern Recognition (CVPR) (2019)

Spatial Geometric Reasoning for Room Layout Estimation via Deep Reinforcement Learning

Liangliang Ren[1,2,3], Yangyang Song[1,2,3], Jiwen Lu[1,2,3]([✉]), and Jie Zhou[1,2,3,4]

[1] Department of Automation, Tsinghua University, Beijing, China
[2] State Key Lab of Intelligent Technologies and Systems, Tsinghua University, Beijing, China
[3] Beijing National Research Center for Information Science and Technology, Beijing, China
[4] Tsinghua Shenzhen International Graduate School, Tsinghua University, Beijing, China
{renll16,syy18}@mails.tsinghua.edu.cn
{lujiwen,jzhou}@tsinghua.edu.cn

Abstract. Unlike most existing works that define room layout on a 2D image, we model the layout in 3D as a configuration of the camera and the room. Our spatial geometric representation with only seven variables is more concise but effective, and more importantly enables direct 3D reasoning, e.g. how the camera is positioned relative to the room. This is particularly valuable in applications such as indoor robot navigation. We formulate the problem as a Markov decision process, in which the layout is incrementally adjusted based on the difference between the current layout and the target image, and the policy is learned via deep reinforcement learning. Our framework is end-to-end trainable, requiring no extra optimization, and achieves competitive performance on two challenging room layout datasets.

Keywords: Room layout estimation · Reinforcement learning

1 Introduction

Room layout estimation is to locate the wall-wall, wall-ceiling and wall-floor boundaries on an image of an indoor room [11], which is usually regarded as a 3D cuboid. Applications such as indoor robot navigation and augmented reality can benefit from the knowledge of where each face of the room is located on the image. What makes the task interesting and challenging is the fact that there are often some parts of face boundaries occluded by foreground objects, which have to be inferred based on prior knowledge about the relationship between objects and the room. It sets room layout estimation apart from semantic segmentation [3,18,38], in which predictions are for visible objects.

L. Ren and Y. Song—Equal Contribution.

© Springer Nature Switzerland AG 2020
A. Vedaldi et al. (Eds.): ECCV 2020, LNCS 12372, pp. 550–565, 2020.
https://doi.org/10.1007/978-3-030-58583-9_33

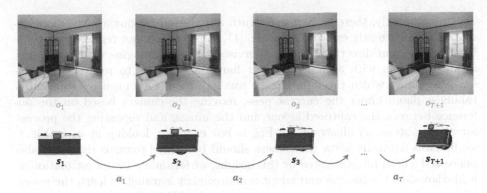

Fig. 1. We define room layout in 3D and formulate room layout estimation as a Markov decision process. The camera is moved inside the room step by step to recover the position and pose under which the input image was captured, based on how the captured layout (drawn in green) differs from the image (groundtruth layout drawn in black). (Color figure online)

Most conventional methods adopt the framework proposed by Hedau *et al.* [11], where a room layout is determined by three vanishing points and four rays, and the layout that maximizes a score function is the solution. However, this approach is heavily affected by the accuracy of vanishing point estimation [11]. As for deep methods, at first convolutional neural networks are adopted to produce some intermediate results, *e.g.* pixelwise face segmentation [4] or edge probability map [36], and then an extra post-optimization is performed to obtain parameterized layout prediction. However, in the case of face segmentation (ceiling, floor, left/front/right wall), the three walls do not have any difference in appearance, but in their relative position in the image, making them difficult for the network to predict. And if less than three walls are captured, labels for the walls cannot be uniquely determined. For instance, in the two-wall case, one can label them as "left and front", or alternatively "front and right". In recent work, end-to-end prediction without optimization is achieved by estimating each keypoint of the layout separately [14]. However, no constraint exists about the keypoints, so the predicted layout is not guaranteed to be valid and impossible layouts might occur according to our observation (see Fig. 5).

To avoid the above problems introduced by defining layout on the 2D image, we model the layout before the imaging process, as a configuration of the camera and the room in 3D space, including the shape of the room, extrinsic and intrinsic parameters of the camera. Note that our layout representation is very concise with only seven variables, and naturally incorporates the cuboid room constraint. The position and pose of the camera with respect to the room is more useful in applications that require 3D reasoning such as indoor robot navigation, than simply locating faces on the 2D image, which is another advantage of our representation.

Unfortunately, there is no groundtruth annotation for our 3D layout representation in currently existing datasets [11,35], so we cannot regress the layout from image input directly through supervised learning. Imagine we are standing inside the room with a camera in our hand, and trying to recover the camera pose under which the input image was captured. One intuitive solution is taking a photo under the current pose, moving the camera based on the difference between the captured layout and the image, and repeating the process for certain steps, as illustrated in Fig. 1. For example, looking at o_1 in Fig. 1, we humans naturally know the camera should be turned towards right and also depressed a little bit.Motivated by this insight, we formulate layout estimation as a Markov decision process and adopt reinforcement learning to learn the policy of layout adjustment. The proposed framework "LIM" (Layout via Incremental Movements), is end-to-end trainable and needs no post-optimization during inference.

2   Related Work

Room Layout Estimation: For simplicity, most work consider the room as a 3D cuboid as in [11], instead of general Manhattan world models [7,15,39]. Hedau *et al.* [11] first estimate vanishing points corresponding to the three orthogonal directions of the room, and then a room layout can be determined by four rays traveling through two of the vanishing points. A number of layout hypotheses are sampled from layout space, and the one which maximizes a previously learned score function is selected as the solution. This framework is further extended by many subsequent works. At first, line membership [11] and geometric context [13] are utilized as cues for room layout in the score function, and later more feature designs are proposed, such as orientation map [15], junction feature [24] and informative edge feature [19]. To address the error caused by discretization in the optimization of the score function, Schwing and Urtasun [28] develop an efficient branch-and-bound algorithm to search for the exact optimal solution based on integral geometry [27]. Chao *et al.* [2] improve the estimation of vanishing points by reasoning the geometric relationship between humans and the scene in 3D. Also incorporating 3D reasoning, Gupta *et al.* [8] sample object cuboid hypotheses along with layout hypotheses, and the combinations which violate the physical rules in 3D space, such as "objects should be contained in the room" and "object should never intersect with each other", are filtered out from the search space. Wang *et al.* [32] propose to explicitly model the clutter labels as a latent variable, which allows joint optimization of the layout and the clutter labels. Apart from the above framework, some works model the problem from the perspective of probability [5–7].

The convolutional neural network is first used in the work by Mallya and Lazebnik [19], to predict pixelwise edge probability map directly from image input. Although the obtained edge map reveals the location of face boundaries, it is still used as a piece of image feature to score sampled layouts, which limits performance of the method. However, Zhao *et al.* [36] treat their obtained edge

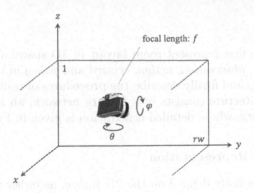

Fig. 2. We define a room layout in 3D space as a configuration of the room and the camera with seven variables.

map as an intermediate result, and the parameterized layout is produced by their proposed physics-inspired optimization. Similarly, Dasgupta *et al.* [4] perform optimization on pixelwise face probability map predicted by an FCNN. Lee *et al.* achieve end-to-end prediction by training the network to predict heatmap of each keypoint separately, and thus the keypoints can be directly predicted as the max activation locations in the heatmaps. There are also some works utilizing extra information than a single RGB image, such as depth map [34] and floor plan [17], or focusing on recovering the 3D room model from a panorama [39].

Deep Reinforcement Learning: Different from supervised learning which requires labeled input-output pairs, reinforcement learning (RL) deals with learning from some kind of indirect supervision, reward given by the environment. RL aims to learn a policy of making decisions that maximize the cumulative reward, and thus RL is usually employed in the context of Markov decision process [30]. Deep reinforcement learning (DRL) [12,16,20,21,26,31] utilizes deep neural networks as an approximation of value function in value based algorithms such as DQN [21], or approximation of policy function in policy based algorithms such as DDPG [16]. In recent years, DRL has achieved great success in Atari games and some continuous control problems and also been successfully applied to computer vision tasks, *e.g.* object detection [1], visual tracking [33] and face recognition [25], which are all formulated as Markov decision processes. Caicedo *et al.* [1] localize an object by sequentially moving or resizing its bounding box, which covers a very large area of the image at the beginning. Rao *et al.* [25] propose to find attention in the videos to facilitate video face recognition, which is done by starting from videos of full length and removing valueless frames step by step. To the best of our knowledge, the proposed approach is the first to address room layout estimation using reinforcement learning.

3   Approach

In this section, we first represent room layout in 3D space, and then elaborate the design of *state*, *observation*, *action*, *reward* and *policy* in the context of reinforcement learning, and finally describe the procedures of training and inference. Our network architecture consists of a feature network, an actor network and also a critic network, whose detailed description is given in Fig. 3.

3.1   3D Layout Representation

A room layout is usually defined on the 2D image, as either pixelwise face segmentation [4], or a combination of layout type and a list of keypoints [14]. However, it is essentially the projection of a room onto an image plane. In other words, a room layout can naturally be defined in 3D space, as a configuration of the room and the camera, as illustrated in Fig. 2.

We regard the room as a cuboid, whose shape is parameterized by its width, height, and depth. However, the height can be set to unit length 1, since layout representation under a relative scale is all we need. And the depth is set to infinity because a camera that has an ordinary field of view and is located in normal positions cannot capture all six faces of a room at the same time. As a result, the shape of the room is completely determined by its width of rw.

Following common practice, the camera is treated as a pinhole model. Its extrinsic parameters include position and orientation relative to the world coordinate system, which is established along the edges of the room. Camera position is characterized by the coordinate of its center $[x, y, z]^T (C)$ with all three degrees of freedom (DOF). For the sake of clarity, we define axis X, Y in the camera coordinate system as the axis parallel to the horizontal and vertical direction of the image respectively, and axis Z is perpendicular to the image plane. Although camera orientation also has three DOF, we approximate the rotation about axis Z by zero for simplicity, since it is insignificant in most cases. Then any camera orientation can be reached by first rotating about axis Y for angle θ, then about axis X for angle φ, from certain reference orientation. Therefore the rotation matrix R of the camera is derived below. Here R_0 stands for rotation matrix corresponding to the reference orientation - the most typical camera poses with image plane parallel to the front wall and axis X located on the horizontal plane.

$$R = R_X(\varphi)R_Y(\theta)R_0 \tag{1}$$

Generally speaking, there are four intrinsic parameters for a pinhole camera: focal length f, principle point coordinate, and a skew parameter [9]. Here, the skew is set to zero, which is true for normal cameras, and the principle point is fixed to the image center by assuming the image has not been cropped. Thus the intrinsic parameter matrix K has the following form, where h and w represent height and width of the image respectively.

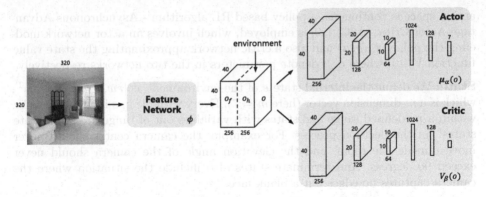

Fig. 3. An overview of our network architecture. Feature network adopts part of Room-Net basic structure [14], where feature observation o_f comes after the third last convolutional layer. Together with heatmap observation o_h given by the environment, a full observation o can be obtained by concatenating o_f and o_h along axis of channel. The actor and critic network share the same structure except the different number of output nodes, where actor outputs a 7-d vector representing the mean of the action, and critic outputs value for this observation. They both consist of three convolutional layers and two fully connected layers, where ReLU activation [22] is applied after every layer except the last ones. All convolutions are performed with kernel size 3×3 and stride 1, on properly zero-padded inputs, and maxpooling with stride 2 is done after the second and third convolutional layers.

$$K = \begin{bmatrix} f & 0 & w/2 \\ 0 & f & h/2 \\ 0 & 0 & 1 \end{bmatrix} \tag{2}$$

In conclusion, the seven variables $\{rw, x, y, z, \theta, \varphi, f\}$ form a complete 3D representation of a room layout under some assumptions and approximations, from which any 2D representation can be computed through perspective projection with the camera matrix P:

$$P = K\left[R - RC\right] \tag{3}$$

3.2   Incremental Layout Estimation

As stated before, we formulate layout estimation as a Markov decision process, in which layout is adjusted step by step to arrive at the final prediction. In the framework of reinforcement learning, an agent is responsible for making such decisions, and an environment is something that the agent interacts with to learn the policy. In our formulation, the agent changes the layout (internal state s of the environment) by taking an action a based some observation o about how current layout differs from the target layout encoded in the image. And then the environment gives observation of the changed layout as well as a reward r, which evaluates how much the predicted layout is improved by that action. Since the action space is continuous, a policy based RL algorithm - Asynchronous Advantage Actor-Critic (A3C) [20] is employed, which involves an actor network modeling the policy $\pi_\alpha(o, a)$ and also a critic network approximating the state value function $V_\beta(o)$, where α, β denote parameters in the two networks respectively.

State: We define the internal state s of the environment as $[rw, x, y, z, \theta, \varphi, f]^T$, which is a m-dimension vector (here $m = 7$). Every variable in s is expected to be within a predefined range and states with variables out of range are "terminate states" in the decision process. For example, the camera center should never move outside the room, and the elevation angle of the camera should never exceed 90 degrees. And terminate states also include the situation where the camera captures no edges but a blank face.

Observation: The observation o consists of two parts: o_h telling the agent what current layout is like, and o_f, image feature which gives cues about the target layout encoded in the input image. We adopt RoomNet-basic [14] which has been demonstrated successful in layout prediction as our image feature network, and o_f is the output of its third last convolutional layer with shape $40 \times 40 \times 256$. This feature network is not fixed but trainable in our approach with parameters denoted by ϕ. To be consistent with the RoomNet feature, we first project the room onto the image plane to obtain a list of keypoints (defined in [14]), and then construct o_h by summing Gaussian heatmaps centered at each keypoint with a standard deviation of two pixels on a 40×40 grid. o_h is repeated for 256 times along the channel axis and then concatenated with o_f to obtain the complete observation o as illustrated in Fig. 3. The purpose of the repetition is to prevent o_h being overwhelmed by o_f due to the huge imbalance on channel number.

Action: The action a is a vector of the same dimension as s, and each variable v in s is changed with the corresponding increment Δv in a. Variables like x, y, z, θ, φ which describe quantities about position are changed with additive increments, while rw and f which describe quantities about length are changed with multiplicative increments. And for the latter case, the logarithm of the increment instead of the increment itself is used to ensure the symmetry about zero. The equation below shows how the state is updated by the action:

$$v = \begin{cases} v + \Delta v, & \text{for } v \text{ in } \{x, y, z, \theta, \varphi\} \\ v \times e^{\Delta v}, & \text{for } v \text{ in } \{rw, f\} \end{cases} \tag{4}$$

Reward: Here, the choice of reward is quite straightforward: the improvement of layout error made by action a. There are two commonly used error metrics, corner error e_c and pixelwise error e_p [35], leading to "corner reward" r_c and "pixel reward" r_p:

$$r_c = 100\Delta e_c \tag{5}$$

$$r_p = 100\Delta[e_p/2 + |n_1 - n_2|/3max(n_1, n_2)] \tag{6}$$

In the above equations, Δ represents the decrease of a certain quantity, and n_1, n_2 denote the number of keypoints in the current layout and groundtruth layout respectively. The second addend in r_p serves as a penalty to the unmatched number of keypoints. The final reward r is designed to be a weighted sum of r_c and r_p followed by a normalization as shown below, and the weight λ is dynamically changed during training as described in Sect. 4.2.

$$r = [(1 - \lambda)r_c + \lambda r_p]/8 + 1 \tag{7}$$

Policy: The policy $\pi_\alpha(o, a)$ is modeled as a multivariate normal distribution with independent components, whose mean $\boldsymbol{\mu}_\alpha(o)$ is given by the output of the actor network, whose variances $\sigma_1^2, \cdots, \sigma_m^2$ are manually set to control agent's exploration while training, since in this problem random policy is not needed. Every element in action $\boldsymbol{a}$ is restricted within a predefined range to avoid huge change in single step, which ensures the stability of the layout adjustment process. To achieve this, the action sampled from the policy above is clipped by that action bound. And the action mean $\boldsymbol{\mu}_\alpha(o)$ is also fitted within the bound by applying $tanh$ activation and a subsequent rescaling.

$$\pi_\alpha : \boldsymbol{a} \sim \mathcal{N}(\boldsymbol{\mu}_\alpha(o), diag(\sigma_1^2, \cdots, \sigma_m^2)) \tag{8}$$

To train our network, consider an episode in which the agent interacts with the environment for T steps following policy π_α and in the end collects a series of data $(o_1, \boldsymbol{a}_1, r_1), \cdots, (o_T, \boldsymbol{a}_T, r_T), o_{T+1}$.

The value targets are computed using the equation below, where γ denotes the discount factor. If o_{T+1} corresponds to a terminate state, then $V_\beta(o_{T+1})$ is substituted by zero.

$$R_i = \sum_{j=i}^{T} \gamma^{j-i} r_j + \gamma^{T-i+1} V_\beta(o_{T+1}) \tag{9}$$

Then value error can be obtained by subtracting the value target with value predicted by the critic network,

$$\delta_i = R_i - V_\beta(o_i) \tag{10}$$

The critic loss is the mean squared value error,

$$L_c = \frac{1}{T} \sum_{i=1}^{T} \delta_i^2 \tag{11}$$

The value error δ_i defined above is used as an estimate of the advantage function, and the policy gradient can be converted back to an optimization of the following actor loss,

$$L_a = -\frac{1}{mT} \sum_{i=1}^{T} ln\pi_\alpha(o_i, \boldsymbol{a}_i)\delta_i \tag{12}$$

Table 1. Performance on LSUN validation-set.

Method	e_c (%)	e_p (%)
Hedau *et al.* (2009) [11]	15.48	24.23
Mallya and Lazebnik (2015) [19]	11.02	16.71
Delay (2016) [4]	8.20	10.63
RoomNet basic (2017) [14]	6.95	10.46
RoomNet recurrent 3-iter (2017) [14]	6.30	**9.86**
LIM	**6.23**	10.00

The total loss is the sum of actor loss and critic loss, from which gradients propagate to parameter ϕ of the feature network through o_f. However, note that $V_\beta(o_{T+1})$ in (9) and δ_i in (12) are treated as constants, which gradients cannot propagate through.

$$\min_{\alpha,\beta,\phi} L = L_a + L_c \qquad (13)$$

As mentioned before, we adopt A3C [20] to train our network, where multiple agents interact with multiple instances of the environment separately at the same time. It requires a main process which maintains a global network, and also multiple worker processes, each with a local network. Each worker collects data and computes gradient of the loss parameters of the local network, which is instead applied to the global network, and then local parameters are synchronized with the global ones. As a result, agents in different worker processes can benefit from each other's experience. Multiple worker processes running in parallel also greatly increase the training speed.

As for inference, the layout prediction is also obtained by adjusting the layout step by step from some initial state. However, we remove the randomness in policy, $a = \mu_\alpha(o)$. Since agent might take bad actions which pull the layout away from the true layout, the last non-terminate state may not be the best one. Note that the value of a state is the expected return starting from it under the certain policy, and here the expected return means the expected error improvement, so a state of a lower value has lower error. Thus we select the state of the lowest estimated value (by critic network) in one episode as our prediction.

4 Experiments

4.1 Datasets

We conduct experiments on two standard datasets for room layout estimation LSUN [35] and Hedau dataset [11]. LSUN (Large-scale Scene Understanding Challenge dataset) consists of 4000 training, 394 validation and 1000 testing images, which are annotated with layout type and an ordered list of keypoints, but the annotations for testing images are not made public. A smaller one, Hedau dataset contains 209 training and 105 testing images, annotated with pixelwise

Fig. 4. Visualization of the layout adjustment process for images in LSUN validation-set. The first and the last column shows the initial state and the final prediction respectively.

face segmentation. In all experiments, only LSUN train-set is used for training, and evaluations are performed on LSUN validation-set as well as Hedau test-set. We use the two evaluation metrics mentioned before: corner error e_c which measures the Euclidean distance between predicted and groundtruth keypoints, and pixelwise error e_p which measures the percentage of pixels that are assigned to the wrong face [35]. We use the room layout challenge toolkit [35] provided by LSUN to compute these errors. The only data augmentation employed in our approach is horizontal image flipping while training.

4.2   Implementation Details

Our approach is implemented in PyTorch [23] - a popular deep learning plat-form, and all experiments are performed on NVIDIA TITAN Xp. The image preprocessing is performed by first resizing it to 320×320 resolution using bicubic interpolation and then rescaling the pixel intensities from $[0, 255]$ to $[0, 1]$. The feature network is pretrained under the framework of RoomNet [14] except Adam optimizer used in place of SGD. Both actor and critic network are initialized using the technique presented in [10]. In the training of our network, Adam optimizer is adopted as well, with parameters set to default except learning rate. Initial learning rates for ϕ, α and β are 10^{-5}, 5×10^{-6} and 5×10^{-5} respectively, and they will drop by a factor of 5 at global episode 500,000 and 700,000. Training stops at global episode 800,000 (equivalent to 100 epochs) and the maximum length of an episode is 10 steps. The discount factor γ is set to 0.9.

In our experiments, the main process along with 7 worker processes are created, and all networks are allocated on 2 GPUs in total. Parameters in global networks are shared across processes so that all workers can access and modify them. In our implementation, locks are applied to code blocks involving writing and reading global parameters to prevent concurrent operations from different processes, which will make training unstable according to our observation. Statistics in the Adam optimizer are also shared in GPU memory among processes.

Variance in our policy is manually set to control the exploration of the agent. At the beginning of training, exploration should be encouraged because the agent knows very little about how to get high rewards. However, as the training progresses, the agent gains more and more experience, and thus exploitation of current knowledge should be emphasized more. So the variance should be high enough at first but decrease as training proceeds. If the action bound of one element in the action is denoted by range $[-a_h, a_h]$ (always symmetric about zero), then its standard

Table 2. Performance on Hedau test-set.

Method	e_p (%)
Hedau *et al.* (2009) [11]	21.20
Del Pero *et al.* (2012) [5]	16.30
Gupta *et al.* (2010) [8]	16.20
Zhao *et al.* (2013) [37]	14.50
Ramalingam *et al.* (2013) [24]	13.34
Mallya and Lazebnik (2015) [19]	12.83
Schwing *et al.* (2012) [27]	12.8
Del Pero *et al.* (2013) [6]	12.7
Delay (2016) [4]	9.73
LayoutNet (2018) [39]	9.69
RoomNet recurrent 3-iter (2017) [14]	**8.36**
LIM	9.12

deviation is initially set to $a_h/2$ and decreased linearly to 0 at the end of training. As mentioned before, the reward r is computed by a weighted sum of corner reward and pixel reward. Before global episode 500,000, the weight λ is set to 0, which means in this period the reward is completely based on corner error, but after that, λ increases from 0 to 0.5. The purpose of this design is to encourage the agent to further focus on pixel error when it already performs well in corner error.

Table 3. Comparison of different training and inference settings (evaluated on LSUN validation-set).

Setting	e_c (%)	e_p (%)
training		
Fixed feature network	6.53	11.04
inference		
Last state (10 steps)	6.73	10.65
Last state (20 steps)	7.65	11.98
State of min value (10 steps)	6.42	10.29
State of min value (20 steps) - default	**6.23**	**10.00**

The initial state of the environment is designed to be "typical", so that all possible layouts are not too far to reach. The room width is equal to its height, and the focal length of the camera is properly set to produce an ordinary field of view. The camera is in the reference orientation described in Sect. 3.1 and is positioned so that all five faces of the room are captured, among which the front wall is located at the center of the image, as shown in the first column in Fig. 4. We have also tried initialization from layout predicted by RoomNet, which is already a good estimate, but observed no further improvements to the accuracy. This in turn shows the robustness of our approach to the choice of initial state. One possible explanation is that our agent is not likely to get stuck into some local optima, and thus it tends to reach the same layout regardless of where it starts from.

4.3   Results and Analysis

Accuracy: The proposed approach LIM achieves competitive performance on both LSUN [35] and Hedau dataset [11], as reported in Table 1 and Table 2. On LSUN dataset LIM shows noticeable improvement on both corner error and pixel error compared to RoomNet basic. And it achieves performance comparable to a strong baseline - RoomNet recurrent 3-iter, which extends RoomNet basic with the recurrent structure for iterative refinement of keypoint heatmaps [14]. Although LIM and RoomNet recurrent 3-iter both complete the task through multiple steps, it is actually not fair to compare them because the multi-step procedures are done in different senses. Each step in LIM corresponds to a camera movement in the physical world, and only when all steps are performed is the final estimate obtained. However, in RoomNet recurrent, the output after the first step is already a valid estimate, the two additional steps only help to refine the estimate. Although a recent work [36] demonstrates amazingly high performance on the two datasets, another indoor scene dataset similar to LSUN, SUN RGB-D [29], is used to pretrain the network on semantic segmentation task, which provides very rich information about the scene configuration.

Efficiency: Although in our approach, the layout prediction is obtained by multiple steps of layout adjustment, LIM is still very efficient when it comes to running time. As reported in Table 4, in spite of running for at most 20 steps, LIM achieves 6.71 fps on average on LSUN validation-set, which is orders of magnitude faster than methods requiring post-optimization [4,36].

Comparison of Different Training and Inference Settings: To better understand our approach, we change some training and inference settings to see their influence, which is summarized in Table 3. Compared to the fixed feature network while training (pretrained under the framework of RoomNet), trainable feature network leads to a performance boost of 0.3% on corner error, and 1.04% on pixel error. It suggests that our method can be further improved with a more effective feature. As for inference, it is not necessarily the best choice to terminate an episode after 10 steps as in the training stage, since given more steps, the agent can go further and may arrive at a better layout. Nevertheless, risks

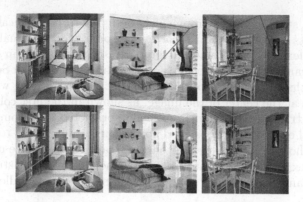

Fig. 5. RoomNet sometimes produces "impossible" layout prediction due to the lack of constraints on keypoints (first row), while our approach always gives valid estimate (second row).

Table 4. Comparison of deep methods on time complexity.

Method	FPS
Delay (2016) [4]	0.03
ST-PIO (2017) [36]	0.56
RoomNet recurrent 3-iter (2017) [14]	5.96
LIM (state of min value, 20 steps)	**6.71**

increase as well, because the agent sometimes takes bad actions. As shown in Table 3, if the last non-terminate state in an episode is selected as the final estimate, accuracy on both metrics drops significantly when an episode is extended from 10 steps to 20 steps. But if the state of the lowest estimated value (by critic network) is selected instead, the estimate will benefit from the extension of an episode. And for either episode length, the state of the lowest estimated value is more accurate than the last one on average.

Qualitative Analysis: To visually demonstrate the effectiveness of our approach, we present a series of snapshots of the layout adjustment process in Fig. 4. All layouts reach a satisfying final estimate from the same initial state, whether the starting layout is similar to the target layout, *e.g.* Fig. 4 (c), or far from it *e.g.* Fig. 4 (a)(b)(d). Since we build the feature network upon RoomNet basic, we further compare our approach with RoomNet. RoomNet defines the layout as a layout type along with a list of keypoints, which are predicted independently with no constraints imposed [14]. Therefore RoomNet might give invalid layout predictions, as shown in the first row of Fig. 5. However, our layout representation naturally incorporates the cuboid room constraint, and thus LIM is guaranteed to produce valid estimates even if it is not very good.

Fig. 6. Some cases where our approach produces predictions inconsistent with the groundtruth.

Figure 6 provides some cases where LIM fails to give predictions consistent with the groundtruth. In (a) and (b), most area of the image is occupied with clutter and the wall-floor the boundary is almost completely occluded, making it very challenging to figure out the room layout. In addition, the wall-wall boundary in (b) is nearly invisible, causing the agent to believe there is only one wall. In fact, humans recognize two walls from the observation that the picture on the right wall has a noticeably different orientation than the left one. This indirect inference originates from our knowledge and experience about the world we live in, and thus is very difficult for a machine. (c) does not satisfy the cuboid room assumption upon which our approach is built, so LIM cannot find a well-fitting layout. (d) (e) (f) illustrate the problem about layout annotation. The groundtruth layout in (d) includes a very tiny ceiling that LIM fails to recognize due to its small size and uniform color distribution. However, another tiny ceiling in (e) is not annotated, which on the contrary is successfully estimated by our approach. This shows the inconsistency in the annotation in LSUN dataset. (f) is an ambiguous case where LIM treats the curved wall as a ceiling while the groundtruth does not.

5   Conclusion

In this paper, we have proposed a framework LIM for room layout estimation. We derive a concise but effective 3D layout representation, which enables direct 3D reasoning. Then we formulate the problem as a Markov decision process and employ reinforcement learning to learn the policy of layout adjustment. Our unified and efficient framework demonstrates very competitive performance on LSUN and Hedau datasets. And we believe our approach can be further improved with feature that is more robust to clutter and has a more holistic understanding about the scene.

Acknowledgements. This work was supported in part by the National Key Research and Development Program of China under Grant 2017YFA0700802, in part by the National Natural Science Foundation of China under Grant 61822603, Grant U1813218, Grant U1713214, and Grant 61672306, in part by Beijing Natural Science Foundation under Grant No. L172051, in part by Beijing Academy of Artificial Intelligence (BAAI), in part by a grant from the Institute for Guo Qiang, Tsinghua University, in part by the Shenzhen Fundamental Research Fund (Subject Arrangement) under Grant JCYJ20170412170602564, and in part by Tsinghua University Initiative Scientific Research Program.

References

1. Caicedo, J.C., Lazebnik, S.: Active object localization with deep reinforcement learning. In: ICCV, December 2015
2. Chao, Y.W., Choi, W., Pantofaru, C., Savarese, S.: Layout estimation of highly cluttered indoor scenes using geometric and semantic cues. In: ICIAP, pp. 489–499 (2013)
3. Chen, L.C., Papandreou, G., Kokkinos, I., Murphy, K., Yuille, A.L.: Semantic image segmentation with deep convolutional nets and fully connected CRFs. arXiv preprint arXiv:1412.7062 (2014)
4. Dasgupta, S., Fang, K., Chen, K., Savarese, S.: Delay: robust spatial layout estimation for cluttered indoor scenes. In: CVPR (2016)
5. Del Pero, L., Bowdish, J., Fried, D., Kermgard, B., Hartley, E., Barnard, K.: Bayesian geometric modeling of indoor scenes. In: CVPR, pp. 2719–2726 (2012)
6. Del Pero, L., Bowdish, J., Kermgard, B., Hartley, E., Barnard, K.: Understanding Bayesian rooms using composite 3D object models. In: CVPR, pp. 153–160 (2013)
7. Flint, A., Murray, D., Reid, I.: Manhattan scene understanding using monocular, stereo, and 3D features. In: ICCV, pp. 2228–2235 (2011)
8. Gupta, A., Hebert, M., Kanade, T., Blei, D.M.: Estimating spatial layout of rooms using volumetric reasoning about objects and surfaces. In: NIPS, pp. 1288–1296 (2010)
9. Hartley, R., Zisserman, A.: Multiple View Geometry in Computer Vision. Cambridge University Press, New York (2003)
10. He, K., Zhang, X., Ren, S., Sun, J.: Delving deep into rectifiers: surpassing human-level performance on ImageNet classification. In: ICCV, pp. 1026–1034 (2015)
11. Hedau, V., Hoiem, D., Forsyth, D.: Recovering the spatial layout of cluttered rooms. In: ICCV, pp. 1849–1856 (2009)
12. Heess, N., et al.: Emergence of locomotion behaviours in rich environments. arXiv preprint arXiv:1707.02286 (2017)
13. Hoiem, D., Efros, A.A., Hebert, M.: Recovering surface layout from an image. Int. J. Comput. Vis. **75**(1), 151–172 (2007). https://doi.org/10.1007/s11263-006-0031-y
14. Lee, C.Y., Badrinarayanan, V., Malisiewicz, T., Rabinovich, A.: RoomNet: end-to-end room layout estimation. In: ICCV, pp. 4865–4874 (2017)
15. Lee, D.C., Hebert, M., Kanade, T.: Geometric reasoning for single image structure recovery. In: CVPR, pp. 2136–2143 (2009)
16. Lillicrap, T.P., et al.: Continuous control with deep reinforcement learning. arXiv preprint arXiv:1509.02971 (2015)
17. Liu, C., Schwing, A.G., Kundu, K., Urtasun, R., Fidler, S.: Rent3D: floor-plan priors for monocular layout estimation. In: CVPR, pp. 3413–3421 (2015)

18. Long, J., Shelhamer, E., Darrell, T.: Fully convolutional networks for semantic segmentation. In: CVPR, pp. 3431–3440 (2015)
19. Mallya, A., Lazebnik, S.: Learning informative edge maps for indoor scene layout prediction. In: ICCV, pp. 936–944 (2015)
20. Mnih, V., et al.: Asynchronous methods for deep reinforcement learning. In: ICML, pp. 1928–1937 (2016)
21. Mnih, V., et al.: Human-level control through deep reinforcement learning. Nature **518**(7540), 529 (2015)
22. Nair, V., Hinton, G.E.: Rectified linear units improve restricted Boltzmann machines. In: ICML, pp. 807–814 (2010)
23. Paszke, A., et al.: Automatic differentiation in PyTorch. In: NIPS Autodiff Workshop (2017)
24. Ramalingam, S., Pillai, J.K., Jain, A., Taguchi, Y.: Manhattan junction catalogue for spatial reasoning of indoor scenes. In: CVPR, pp. 3065–3072 (2013)
25. Rao, Y., Lu, J., Zhou, J.: Attention-aware deep reinforcement learning for video face recognition. In: ICCV, pp. 3931–3940 (2017)
26. Schulman, J., Wolski, F., Dhariwal, P., Radford, A., Klimov, O.: Proximal policy optimization algorithms. arXiv preprint arXiv:1707.06347 (2017)
27. Schwing, A.G., Hazan, T., Pollefeys, M., Urtasun, R.: Efficient structured prediction for 3D indoor scene understanding. In: CVPR, pp. 2815–2822 (2012)
28. Schwing, A.G., Urtasun, R.: Efficient exact inference for 3D indoor scene understanding. In: Fitzgibbon, A., Lazebnik, S., Perona, P., Sato, Y., Schmid, C. (eds.) ECCV 2012. LNCS, vol. 7577, pp. 299–313. Springer, Heidelberg (2012). https://doi.org/10.1007/978-3-642-33783-3_22
29. Song, S., Lichtenberg, S.P., Xiao, J.: Sun RGB-D: a RGB-D scene understanding benchmark suite. In: CVPR, pp. 567–576 (2015)
30. Sutton, R.S., Barto, A.G.: Reinforcement Learning: An Introduction. MIT Press, Cambridge (2018)
31. Van Hasselt, H., Guez, A., Silver, D.: Deep reinforcement learning with double q-learning. In: AAAI (2016)
32. Wang, H., Gould, S., Roller, D.: Discriminative learning with latent variables for cluttered indoor scene understanding. Commun. ACM **56**(4), 92–99 (2013)
33. Yun, S., Choi, J., Yoo, Y., Yun, K., Young Choi, J.: Action-decision networks for visual tracking with deep reinforcement learning. In: CVPR, pp. 2711–2720 (2017)
34. Zhang, J., Kan, C., Schwing, A.G., Urtasun, R.: Estimating the 3D layout of indoor scenes and its clutter from depth sensors. In: ICCV, pp. 1273–1280 (2013)
35. Zhang, Y., Yu, F., Song, S., Xu, P., Seff, A., Xiao, J.: Large-scale scene understanding challenge: room layout estimation (2016)
36. Zhao, H., Lu, M., Yao, A., Guo, Y., Chen, Y., Zhang, L.: Physics inspired optimization on semantic transfer features: an alternative method for room layout estimation. In: CVPR, pp. 10–18 (2017)
37. Zhao, Y., Zhu, S.C.: Scene parsing by integrating function, geometry and appearance models. In: CVPR, pp. 3119–3126 (2013)
38. Zheng, S., et al.: Conditional random fields as recurrent neural networks. In: ICCV, pp. 1529–1537 (2015)
39. Zou, C., Colburn, A., Shan, Q., Hoiem, D.: LayoutNet: reconstructing the 3D room layout from a single RGB image. In: CVPR, pp. 2051–2059 (2018)

Learning Data Augmentation Strategies for Object Detection

Barret Zoph[✉], Ekin D. Cubuk, Golnaz Ghiasi, Tsung-Yi Lin,
Jonathon Shlens, and Quoc V. Le

Brain Team, Google Research, Mountain View, USA
barretzoph@google.com

Abstract. Much research on object detection focuses on building better model architectures and detection algorithms. Changing the model architecture, however, comes at the cost of adding more complexity to inference, making models slower. Data augmentation, on the other hand, doesn't add any inference complexity, but is insufficiently studied in object detection for two reasons. First it is more difficult to design plausible augmentation strategies for object detection than for classification, because one must handle the complexity of bounding boxes if geometric transformations are applied. Secondly, data augmentation attracts less research attention perhaps because it is believed to add less value and to transfer poorly compared to advances in network architectures.

This paper serves two main purposes. First, we propose to use AutoAugment [3] to design better data augmentation strategies for object detection because it can address the difficulty of designing them. Second, we use the method to assess the value of data augmentation in object detection and compare it against the value of architectures. Our investigation into data augmentation for object detection identifies two surprising results. First, by changing the data augmentation strategy to our method, AutoAugment for detection, we can improve RetinaNet with a ResNet-50 backbone from 36.7 to 39.0 mAP on COCO, a difference of +2.3 mAP. This gain exceeds the gain achieved by switching the backbone from ResNet-50 to ResNet-101 (+2.1 mAP), which incurs additional training and inference costs. The second surprising finding is that our strategies found on the COCO dataset transfer well to the PASCAL dataset to improve accuracy by +2.7 mAP. These results together with our systematic studies of data augmentation call into question previous assumptions about the role and transferability of architectures versus data augmentation. In particular, changing the augmentation may

---

B. Zoph and E. D. Cubuk—Equal contribution.
Code and models are available at https://github.com/tensorflow/tpu/tree/master/models/official/detection.

Electronic supplementary material The online version of this chapter (https://doi.org/10.1007/978-3-030-58583-9_34) contains supplementary material, which is available to authorized users.

© Springer Nature Switzerland AG 2020
A. Vedaldi et al. (Eds.): ECCV 2020, LNCS 12372, pp. 566–583, 2020.
https://doi.org/10.1007/978-3-030-58583-9_34

lead to performance gains that are equally transferable as changing the underlying architecture.

1   Introduction

Much work in object detection was devoted to building better model architectures or detection algorithms [10,11,13,22,32–35,39]. Although these changes often lead to more accurate models, they also add complexity that potentially slows down the detection system at both training and inference.

Data augmentation, on the other hand, is relatively understudied in object detection. So far the most common distortions are horizontal flips and scale jittering [23]. We suspect that the lack of research in this area is due to two reasons. First, object detection often comes with bounding boxes, so transferring strategies from image classification to object detection will be sub-optimal. These added degrees of freedom from the bounding boxes suggest some automation is needed to find a very good augmentation policy. Secondly, it is also a common belief that custom data augmentation adds smaller performance improvements than architectures and transfers poorly from one detection dataset to another.

Here we investigate the value of data augmentation in object detection. As aforementioned, since it can be difficult to design good data augmentation strategies for object detection, and inspired by the recent success of AutoAugment for classification [3], we use AutoAugment [3] to find good combinations of transformations for detection. To tailor AutoAugment for detection, we add novel operations that handle bounding boxes differently from the image which improves results.

Our experiments with AutoAugment for detection identify two key surprising findings. First, data augmentation is more valuable than commonly believed. In particular, by changing the data augmentation, we can improve RetinaNet with a ResNet-50 backbone from 36.7 to 39.0 mAP on COCO, a difference of 2.3 mAP. This gain is even slightly better than changing the backbone from ResNet-50 to ResNet-101 which only gives +2.1 mAP improvement but with a higher cost of training and inference. Secondly, it is also common wisdom that intricate data augmentation can "overfit" to the dataset of interest and does not transfer well to other datasets. Our experiments show that data augmentation is transferable between detection datasets just like architectures. For example, the best data augmentation found on COCO transfers well to PASCAL to improve the accuracy by +2.7 mAP. This means that the augmentation strategies we found on COCO can be used directly on future object detection datasets without changing any parameters.

In summary, our main contributions are as follows:

- We propose a novel set of data augmentation operations that uniquely act upon the content of bounding boxes and even sometimes change their location.
- We implement a search method based on AutoAugment [3] to combine and optimize data augmentation policies for object detection problems by utilizing novel operations specific to bounding box annotations.

- We show surprising results that improving data augmentation can be as effective as improving architectures while adding no cost to the inference and minimal cost to training.
- We show surprising results that data augmentation strategies are transferable across different detection datasets, architectures and algorithms.

2   AutoAugment for Object Detection

2.1   Search Space Definition

As mentioned above, commonly used data augmentation methods for object detection are quite simple: horizontal flipping and scale jittering. Here we would like to add more augmentation operations to object detection to further boost the value of data augmentation. Hence we turn our attention to a search method to compose basic image transformations into sophisticated distortions to improve generalization performance. The search method expands on our previous work, AutoAugment [3], where a reinforcement learning method is used to learn to compose image processing operations mainly from the Python Image Library (PIL).

Here we adapt the method to perform well on object detection. Our key observation is that object detection introduces many additional complications such as maintaining consistency between a bounding box location and a distorted image. To handle this complication we explore how to change the bounding box locations when geometric transformations are applied to the image. To further adapt our method to object detection, we notice that bounding box annotations open up the possibility of introducing augmentation operations that uniquely act upon the contents within each bounding box. Using this observation, we add many new augmentation operations that work on each bounding box independently in addition to existing image augmentation operations.

For our data augmentation policy[1] we use the following parameterization. We define an augmentation policy as a unordered set of K sub-policies. During training one of the K sub-policies will be selected at random and then applied to the current image. Each sub-policy has N image transformations which are applied sequentially. We turn this problem of searching for a data augmentation policy into a discrete optimization problem by creating a search space. This space gives us the flexibility to have a diversity of operations in a single policy, while having a constraint on how large the space can be. We also want our augmentation policy to benefit from augmentation diversity, which has been found to be useful in the classification domain [3].

In our implementation, our search space consists $K = 5$ sub-policies with each sub-policy consisting of $N = 2$ operations applied in sequence to a single image. Additionally, each operation is also associated with two hyperparameters specifying the probability of applying the operation, and the magnitude of the operation. Figure 1 (bottom text) demonstrates 5 of the learned sub-policies. The

---

[1] In this paper, we use "policy" and "strategy" interchangeably.

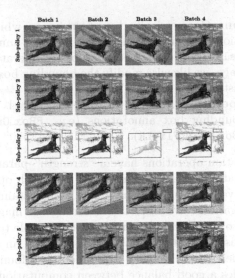

Sub-policy 1. (Color, 0.2, 8), (Rotate, 0.8, 10)
Sub-policy 2. (BBox_Only_ShearY, 0.8, 5)
Sub-policy 3. (SolarizeAdd, 0.6, 8), (Brightness, 0.8, 10)
Sub-policy 4. (ShearY, 0.6, 10), (BBox_Only_Equalize,0.6, 8)
Sub-policy 5. (Equalize, 0.6, 10), (TranslateX, 0.2, 2)

Fig. 1. Examples of data augmentation sub-policies. 5 examples of learned sub-policies applied to one example image. Each column corresponds to a different random sample of the corresponding sub-policy. Each step of an augmentation sub-policy consists of a triplet corresponding to the operation, the probability of application and a magnitude measure. The bounding box is adjusted to maintain consistency with the applied augmentation. Note the probability and magnitude are discretized values (see text for details).

probability parameter introduces a notion of stochasticity into the augmentation policy where the selected augmentation operation is applied to the image with the specified probability.

Our goal was to include as many augmentation transformations as possible to get the best understanding of what operations would be useful for object detection. To limit the complexity of including every operation, we identified 26 unique operations for the search space, 13 of which are novel to object detection, that appear to cover the widest range of available transformations. These operations were implemented in TensorFlow [1]. We briefly summarize these operations, but reserve the details for the Appendix A.1:

– **Color operations**. Distort color channels, without impacting the locations of the bounding boxes (e.g., Equalize, Contrast, Brightness).[2]

---

[2] The color transformations largely derive from transformation in the Python Image Library (PIL). https://pillow.readthedocs.io/en/5.1.x/.

- **Geometric operations**. Geometrically distort the image, which correspondingly alters the location and size of the bounding box annotations (e.g., Rotate, ShearX, TranslationY, etc.). Note that for any operations that effect the geometry of an image, we likewise modify the bounding box size and location to maintain consistency.
- **Bounding box operations**. Only distort the pixel content contained within the bounding box annotations (e.g., BBox_Only_Equalize, BBox_Only_Rotate, BBox_Only_FlipLR).

Since many augmentation operations have a "strength" parameter, such as how many degrees to rotate an image, we associate with each operation a custom range of parameter values. We map this range onto a standardized range from 0 to 10 for all operations. We discretize the range of magnitude into L uniformly-spaced values so that these parameters are amenable to discrete optimization. Similarly, we discretize the probability of applying an operation into M uniformly-spaced values. In preliminary experiments we found that setting $L = 6$ and $M = 6$ provides a good balance between computational tractability and learning performance with an RL algorithm. Thus, finding a good subpolicy becomes a search in a discrete space containing a cardinality of $(26LM)^2$. In particular, to search over 5 sub-policies, the search space contains roughly $(26 \times 6 \times 6)^{2 \times 5} \approx 5.2 \times 10^{29}$ possibilities and requires an efficient search technique to navigate this space. This number comes from the fact that each operation in a subpolicy has 26 transformation options and there are also 6 options for the probability and 6 options for the magnitude. This number gets raised to the (2×5) as there are 2 operations per subpolicy and 5 different subpolicies.

2.2   Controller Settings

Now that we have our search space setup, we want to optimize it to find the augmentation policy that allows the model to achieve the best validation set performance. As done in other work we will have a controller that will predict an augmentation policy, which will be used to train a neural network (child model) on a detection dataset. After training the network we evaluate its validation accuracy to judge how well the augmentation policy performed. Using this signal we update the controller to generate better and better augmentation policies over time according to the validation set.

Many methods exist for addressing the discrete optimization problem of training the controller including reinforcement learning [47], evolutionary methods [31] and sequential model-based optimization [25]. In this work, we choose to build on previous work by structuring the discrete optimization problem as the output space of an RNN and employ reinforcement learning to update the weights of the model [47]. The training setup for the RNN is similar to [3,4,47,48]. We employ the proximal policy optimization (PPO) [37] for the search algorithm.

The RNN is unrolled 30 steps to predict a single augmentation policy. The number of unrolled steps, 30, corresponds to the number of discrete predictions that must be made in order to enumerate 5 sub-policies. Each sub-policy consists of 2 operations and each operation consists of 3 predictions corresponding to the selected image transformation, probability of application and magnitude of the transformation.

In order to train each child model, we selected 5K images from the COCO training set as we found that searching directly on the full COCO dataset to be prohibitively expensive. We found that policies identified with this subset of data generalize to the full dataset while providing significant computational savings. Briefly, we trained each child model[3] from scratch on the 5K COCO images with the ResNet-50 backbone [14] and RetinaNet detector [23] using a cosine learning rate decay [27]. The reward signal for the controller is the mAP on a custom held-out validation set of 7392 images created from a subset of the COCO training set.

The RNN controller is trained over 20K augmentation policies. The search employed 400 TPU's [18] over 48 hours with identical hyper-parameters for the controller as [48]. The search can be sped up using the recently developed, more efficient search methods based on population based training [15] or density matching [21]. Since our learned augmentation method is being used as a method to study and evaluate the performance of data augmentation on COCO, we leave the algorithmic speedup to future work. The learned augmentation policy can be seen in Table 7 in the Appendix.

3   Experiments

We applied our search method to the COCO dataset with a ResNet-50 [14] backbone with RetinaNet [23]. We are mainly interested in answering the following two questions:

– How important is data augmentation for object detection?
– How generalizable are the found data augmentation policies?

To answer the first question, we compare the improvement of our AutoAugment data augmentation policy to changing the model architecture across various sizes. We additionally show that the augmentation policy can push the state-of-the-art using a much simpler system than previous results on COCO. To answer the second question, we use the top policy found on COCO and apply it to different datasets, dataset sizes and architecture configurations to examine generalizability. Finally, we study properties of what kinds of operations are needed for a good augmentation policy on an object detection dataset.

---

[3] We employed a base learning rate of 0.08 over 150 epochs; image size was 640×640; $\alpha = 0.25$ and $\gamma = 1.5$ for the focal loss parameters; weight decay of $1e-4$; batch size was 64.

3.1   Understanding the Policies Found by AutoAugment

Searching for the data augmentation strategy on 5K COCO training images resulted in the final augmentation policy that will be used in all of our results. Before diving into the results, we would like to inspect the best policy found during the search to gain a better understanding of what operations are used. Upon inspection, the most commonly used operation in good policies is `Rotate`, which rotates the whole image and the bounding boxes. The bounding boxes end up larger after the rotation, to include all of the rotated objects. Despite this effect of the `Rotate` operation, it seems to be very beneficial: it is the most frequently used operation in good policies. Two other operations that are commonly used are `Equalize` and `BBox_Only_TranslateY`. `Equalize` flattens the histogram of the pixel values, and does not modify the location or size of each bounding box. `BBox_Only_TranslateY` translates only the objects in bounding boxes vertically, up or down with equal probability. This is quite encouraging as some operations, such as `BBox_Only_TranslateY`, uniquely act on the bounding boxes. Utilizing a combination of color, geometric and bounding box specific operations appears to be crucial to creating an optimal data augmentation policy for object detection.

3.2   Data Augmentation Policy Found by AutoAugment Systematically Improves Object Detection

We assess the quality of the data augmentation policy found by AutoAugment on the competitive COCO dataset [24] on different backbone architectures and detection algorithms. We start with the competitive RetinaNet object detector[4] employing the same training protocol as [9]. Briefly, we train from scratch with a global batch size of 64, images are resized to 640×640, learning rate of 0.08, weight decay of $1e - 4$, $\alpha = 0.25$ and $\gamma = 1.5$ for the focal loss parameters, train the models for 150 epochs, use stepwise decay with the learning rate being reduced by a factor of 10 at epochs 120 and 140. All models were trained on TPUs [18].

The baseline RetinaNet architecture used in this and subsequent sections employs standard data augmentation techniques typically used for object detection training [23]. This consists of doing horizontal flipping with 50% probability and multi-scale jittering where images are randomly resized between 512 and 786 during training and then cropped to 640×640.

Our results using our augmentation policy found by AutoAugment using the above procedures are shown in Tables 1 and 2. In Table 1, the data augmentation policy achieves systematic gains across several backbone architectures with surprising improvements ranging from +1.6 mAP to +2.3 mAP. In comparison, a previous state-of-the-art regularization technique (DropBlock) applied to ResNet-50 [9] only achieves a gain of +1.7 mAP. Additionally, going from a ResNet-50 model to ResNet-101 achieves a 2.1 mAP gain and going from

---

[4] https://github.com/tensorflow/tpu

a ResNet-101 to ResNet-200 achieves a 1.1 mAP gain. Our data augmentation policy achieves a 2.3 gain on ResNet-50, which is a larger improvement than substantially increasing the architecture size, while incurring no additional inference cost. Clearly we see that changing augmentation can be as, if not more, powerful than changing around the underlying architectural components.

Table 1. Improvements with AutoAugment data augmentation policy across different ResNet backbones. All results employ RetinaNet detector [23] on the COCO dataset [24]

Backbone	Baseline	AutoAugment	Difference
ResNet-50	36.7	39.0	+2.3
ResNet-101	38.8	40.4	+1.6
ResNet-200	39.9	42.1	+2.2

To better understand where augmentation benefits, we break the data augmentation policies applied to ResNet-50 into three parts: color operations, geometric operations, and bbox-only-operations (Table 2). Employing color operations only boosts performance by +0.8 mAP. Combining the search with geometric operations increases the boost in performance by +1.9 mAP. Finally, adding bounding box-specific operations yields the best results when used in conjunction with the previous operations and provides +2.3 mAP improvement over the baseline.

Table 2. Improvements in object detection with the data augmentation policy. All results employ RetinaNet detector with ResNet-50 backbone [23] on COCO dataset [24].

Method	mAP
baseline	36.7
baseline + DropBlock [9]	38.4
AutoAugment with color operations	37.5
+ geometric operations	38.6
+ bbox-only operations	**39.0**

Interestingly, we observe that the custom operations designed for object detection (geometric operations and bbox-only operations) contributes 1.5 mAP of the 2.3 mAP gain from this data augmentation policy. Using object detection specific operations is clearly beneficial when trying to find good augmentation policies. This further confirms our result that a diversity of augmentation operations spanning color, geometric and unique bounding box only operations are needed to make a high performing augmentation policy. Also note that the policy found was only searched using 5K COCO training examples and still generalizes well when trained on the full COCO dataset.

3.3   Data Augmentation Policy Found by AutoAugment Push the State-of-the-Art on Object Detection Models

A good data augmentation policy is one that can transfer between models, between datasets and work well for models trained on different image sizes. Here we experiment with the AutoAugment data augmentation policy on a different backbone architecture and detection model. To test how the data augmentation policy transfers to a state-of-the-art detection model, we replace the ResNet-50 backbone with the AmoebaNet-D architecture [31]. The feature-pyramid network [22] was changed to NAS-FPN [10]. Additionally, we use ImageNet pre-training for the AmoebaNet-D backbone as we found we are not able to achieve competitive results when training from scratch. The model was trained for 150 epochs using a cosine learning rate decay with a learning rate of 0.08. The rest of the setup was identical to the ResNet-50 backbone model except the image size was increased from 640×640 to 1280×1280.

Table 3 indicates that the data augmentation policy improves +1.5 mAP on top of a competitive detection architecture and setup. These experiments show that the augmentation policy transfers well across a different backbone architecture, feature pyramid network, image sizes (i.e. $640 \to 1280$ pixels), and training procedure (training from scratch $\to$ using ImageNet pre-training). This is a surprising result that shows our data augmentation policy is quite general. We can extend these results even further by increasing the image resolution from 1280 to 1536 pixels and likewise increasing the number of detection anchors[5] following [44].

This result of these simple modifications is the first single-stage detection system to achieve state-of-the-art, single-model results of 50.7 mAP on COCO. We note that this result only requires a single pass of the image, where as the previous results required multiple evaluations of the same image at different spatial scales at test time [29]. Additionally, these results were arrived at by increasing the image resolution and increasing the number of anchors - both simple and well known techniques for improving object detection performance [16,44]. In contrast, previous state-of-the-art results relied on multiple, custom modifications of the model architecture and regularization methods in order to achieve these results [29]. Our method largely relies on a more modern network architecture paired with a learned data augmentation policy.

---

[5] Specifically, we increase the number of anchors from 3×3 to 9×9 by changing the aspect ratios from $\{1/2, 1, 2\}$ to $\{1/5, 1/4, 1/3, 1/2, 1, 2, 3, 4, 5\}$. When making this change we increased the strictness in the IoU thresholding from 0.5/0.5 to 0.6/0.5 due to the increased number of anchors following [44]. The anchor scale was also increased from 4 to 5 to compensate for the larger image size.

Table 3. Exceeding state-of-the-art detection with the AutoAugment data augmentation policy. Reporting mAP for COCO validation set. Previous state-of-the-art results for COCO detection evaluated a single image at multiple spatial scales to perform detection at test time [29]. Our current results only require a single inference computation at a single spatial scale. The backbone model is AmoebaNet-D [31] with NAS-FPN as the feature pyramid network [10]. For the **50.7** result, in addition to using the data augmentation policy, we increase the image size from 1280 to 1536 and the number of detection anchors from 3×3 to 9×9.

Architecture	Change	# Scales	mAP	mAP$_S$	mAP$_M$	mAP$_L$
MegDet [29]		multiple	50.5	–	–	–
AmoebaNet + NAS-FPN	baseline [10]	1	47.0	30.6	50.9	61.3
	+ AutoAugment policy	1	48.6	32.0	53.4	62.7
	+ ↑ anchors, ↑ image size	1	**50.7**	**34.2**	**55.5**	**64.5**

3.4 Data Augmentation Policy Found by AutoAugment Transfers to Other Detection Datasets

To evaluate the transferability of the data augmentation policy to an entirely different dataset and a different detection algorithm, we train a Faster R-CNN [35] model with a ResNet-101 backbone on PASCAL VOC dataset [8]. We combine the training sets of PASCAL VOC 2007 and PASCAL VOC 2012, and test our model on the PASCAL VOC 2007 test set (4952 images). Our evaluation metric is the mean average precision at an IoU threshold of 0.5 (mAP50). For the baseline model, we use the Tensorflow Object Detection API [16] with the default hyperparameters: 9 GPU workers are utilized for asynchronous training where each worker processes a batch size of 1. Initial learning rate is set to be 3×10^{-4}, which is decayed by 0.1 after 500K steps. Training is started from a COCO detection model checkpoint. When training with our data augmentation policy, we do not change any of the training details, and just add our policy found on COCO to the pre-processing. This leads to a 2.7% improvement on mAP50 (Table 4).

Table 4. Data augmentation policy transfers to other object detection tasks. Mean average precision (%) at IoU threshold 0.5 on a Faster R-CNN detector [35] with a ResNet-101 backbone trained and evaluated on PASCAL VOC 2007 [8]. Note that the augmentation policy was learned from the policy search on the COCO dataset

	plane	bike	bird	boat	bottle	bus	car	cat	chair	cow	table	dog	horse	mbike	person	plant	sheep	sofa	train	tv	mean
baseline	86.6	82.2	75.9	63.4	62.3	84.7	86.8	92.0	55.5	83.3	63.1	89.2	89.4	85.0	85.6	50.7	76.2	73.0	86.6	76.3	76.0
ours	88.0	83.3	78.0	65.9	63.5	85.5	87.4	93.1	58.5	83.9	65.2	90.1	90.2	85.9	86.6	55.2	78.6	76.6	88.6	80.3	78.7

This result is surprising because the best policy found on COCO may appear to be too intricate to generalize to other datasets. But the result confirms that just like architectures, data augmentation policies transfer well across datasets. This means that the augmentations learned on the COCO dataset are very generic and can be used for many other object detection datasets in the future.

4   Analysis

In this section, we analyze the impact of training with the augmentation policy in more detail. We find that:

- Relative improvement of AP due to the augmentation policy is larger for smaller datasets. This is good news since data augmentation policies are needed mostly for models that have small amount of data available.
- Relative improvement is larger for more difficult detection tasks. Average precision for small objects as well as average precision at more strict thresholds benefit more from the learned augmentation.
- Data augmentation regularizes the detection model, which can be seen either by the increased training loss or decreased magnitude of the trainable weights.
- Having data augmentation operations that modify the locations and the sizes of the objects in the search space is important for achieving good results with the augmentation policy.

Below we describe these points in detail.

4.1   Data Augmentation Policy Found by AutoAugment Mimics the Performance of Larger Annotated Datasets

In this section we conducted experiments to determine how the data augmentation policy will perform if there is more or less training data. To conduct these experiments we took subsets of the COCO dataset to make datasets with the following number of images: 5000, 9000, 14000, 23000 (see Table 5). All models trained in this experiment are using a ResNet-50 backbone with RetinaNet and are trained for 150 epochs without using ImageNet pretraining.

Table 5. Data augmentation policy is especially beneficial for small datasets and small objects. Mean average precision (mAP) for RetinaNet model trained on COCO with varying subsets of the original training set. mAP_S, mAP_M and mAP_L denote the mean average precision for small, medium and large examples. Note the complete COCO training set consists of 118K examples. The same policy found on the 5K COCO images was used in all of the experiments. The models in the first row were trained on the same 5K images that the policies were searched on.

Training	Baseline				Our results			
Set size	mAP_S	mAP_M	mAP_L	mAP	mAP_S	mAP_M	mAP_L	mAP
5000	1.9	7.1	9.7	6.5	3.2	9.8	12.7	8.7
9000	4.3	12.3	17.6	11.8	7.1	16.8	22.3	15.1
14000	6.8	17.5	23.9	16.4	9.5	22.1	29.8	19.9
23000	10.0	24.3	33.3	22.6	11.9	27.8	36.8	25.3

As we expected, the improvements due to the data augmentation policy is larger when the model is trained on smaller datasets, which can be seen in Fig. 2

and in Table 5. We show that for models trained on 5000 training samples, the data augmentation policy can improve mAP by more than 70% relative to the baseline. As the training set size is increased, the effect of the data augmentation policy is decreased, although the improvements are still significant. It is interesting to note that models trained with the data augmentation policy seem to do especially well on detecting smaller objects, especially when fewer images are present in the training dataset. For example, for small objects, applying the data augmentation policy seems to be better than increasing the dataset size by 50%, as seen in Table 5. This is quite a striking finding as in many detection applications detecting small objects is of great importance. For small objects, training with the data augmentation policy with 9000 examples results in better performance than the baseline when using 15000 images. In this scenario using our augmentation policy is almost as effective as doubling your dataset size.

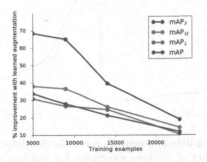

Fig. 2. Percentage improvement in mAP for objects of different sizes due to the data augmentation policy.

Another interesting behavior of models trained with the data augmentation policy is that they do relatively better on the harder task of AP75 (average precision IoU = 0.75). In Fig. 3, we plot the percentage improvement in mAP, AP50, and AP75 for models trained with the data augmentation policy (relative to baseline augmentation). The relative improvement of AP75 is larger than that of AP50 for all training set sizes. The data augmentation policy is particularly beneficial at AP75 indicating that the augmentation policy helps with more precisely aligning the bounding box prediction. This suggests that the augmentation policy particularly helps with learned fine spatial details in bounding box position – which is consistent with the gains observed with small objects.

4.2   Data Augmentation Improves Model Regularization

In this section, we study the regularization effect of the data augmentation policy. We first notice that the final training loss of a detection model is lower when trained on a larger training set (see black curve in the left plot in Fig. 4). When we apply the data augmentation policy, the training loss is increased significantly

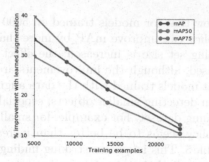

Fig. 3. Percentage improvement due to the data augmentation policy on mAP, AP50, and AP75, relative to models trained with baseline augmentation.

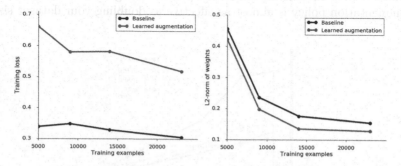

Fig. 4. Two plots showing data augmentation regularizes detection models. On the left is training loss vs. number of training examples for baseline model (black) and with the data augmentation policy (red). One the right is L_2 norm of the weights of the baseline (black) and our (red) models at the end of training. Note that the L_2 norm of the weights decrease with increasing training set size. The data augmentation policy further decreases the norm of the weights. (Color figure online)

for all dataset sizes (red curve). The regularization effect can also be seen by looking at the L_2 norm of the weights of the trained models. The L_2 norm of the weights is smaller for models trained on larger datasets, and models trained with the data augmentation policy have a smaller L_2 norm than models trained with baseline augmentation (see right plot in Fig. 4).

5   Related Work

Data augmentation strategies for vision models are often focused on the image classification domain [3,6,15,17,21,28,41]. For example, state-of-the-art classification models trained on MNIST use elastic distortions which effect scale, translation, and rotation [2,36,38,42]. Random cropping and image mirroring are commonly used in classification models trained on natural images [19,45]. Among the limited data augmentation strategies for object detection, image mirror and multi-scale training are the most widely used [12]. Object-centric cropping is also a popular augmentation approach [26]. Instead of cropping to focus on parts of the image, some methods randomly erase image contents for augmentation [9,46]. In the same vein, [43] learns an occlusion pattern for each object to create adversarial examples. In addition to cropping and erasing, [7] adds new objects on training images by cut-and-paste. While these object-detection approaches work decently well, there is a real lack of studying how truly transferable they are, doing compositions of many different augmentation methods at once and not typically performing as well as modeling changes [10].

To avoid the overwhelming amount of options when designing a data augmentation policy, recent work has focused on learning data augmentation strategies directly from data itself. For example, Smart Augmentation uses a network that generates new data by merging two or more samples from the same class [20]. Tran et al. generate augmented data, using a Bayesian approach, based on the distribution learned from the training set [40]. DeVries and Taylor used simple transformations like noise, interpolations and extrapolations in the learned feature space to augment data [5]. Ratner et al., used generative adversarial networks to generate sequences of data augmentation operations [30]. More recently, several papers use the AutoAugment [3] search space with improved optimization algorithms to find AutoAugment policies more efficiently [15,21].

The above learned augmentation approaches were found to be quite effective in the classification domain due to the complexity of designing a good augmentation procedure. When designing augmentation policies for object detection the complexity only increases. Unlike classification, labeled data for object detection is more scarce because it is more costly to annotate detection data. Compared to image classification, developing a data augmentation strategy for object detection is harder because there are more complexities introduced by distorting the image, bounding box locations, and the sizes of the objects in detection datasets. Furthermore, it is much less clear that augmentation policies are transferable due to images having a richer label structure and the models and detection algorithms being more complex. Our goal is to show that these added complexities are handle-able using learned augmentation procedures and that high performing data augmentation policies can be found. We surprisingly find that these policies are highly generalizable across difference datasets, models and detection algorithms.

6   Discussion

In this work, we challenge the common belief that focusing on changing the detection model is the most promising research direction. Our augmentation procedure gets larger improvements than increasing the model size, while incurring no additional inference cost and minimal training cost. And although data augmentation strategies can be intricate, they can be as transferable as architectures. Our augmentation policy learned on COCO transfers to PASCAL with great performance. Additionally, we are able to further improve the state-of-the-art on COCO using our learned augmentation policy found on a small 5K subset of the COCO dataset with much smaller model, a different image resolution and detection algorithm.

Acknowledgements. We thank the larger teams at Google Brain for their help and support. We also thank Dumitru Erhan for detailed comments on the manuscript.

A   Appendix

A.1   AutoAugment Controller Training Details

Table 6. Table of all the possible transformations that can be applied to an image. These are the transformations that are available to the controller during the search process. The range of magnitudes that the controller can predict for each of the transforms is listed in the third column. Some transformations do not have a magnitude associated with them (e.g. Equalize).

Operation name	Description	Range of magnitudes
ShearX(Y)	Shear the image and the corners of the bounding boxes along the horizontal (vertical) axis with rate *magnitude*	$[-0.3, 0.3]$
TranslateX(Y)	Translate the image and the bounding boxes in the horizontal (vertical) direction by *magnitude* number of pixels	$[-150, 150]$
Rotate	Rotate the image and the bounding boxes *magnitude* degrees	$[-30, 30]$
Equalize	Equalize the image histogram	
Solarize	Invert all pixels above a threshold value of *magnitude*	$[0, 256]$
SolarizeAdd	For each pixel in the image that is less than 128, add an additional amount to it decided by the magnitude	$[0, 110]$
Contrast	Control the contrast of the image. A *magnitude* = 0 gives a gray image, whereas *magnitude* = 1 gives the original image	$[0.1, 1.9]$
Color	Adjust the color balance of the image, in a manner similar to the controls on a colour TV set. A *magnitude* = 0 gives a black & white image, whereas *magnitude* = 1 gives the original image	$[0.1, 1.9]$
Brightness	Adjust the brightness of the image. A *magnitude* = 0 gives a black image, whereas *magnitude* = 1 gives the original image	$[0.1, 1.9]$
Sharpness	Adjust the sharpness of the image. A *magnitude* = 0 gives a blurred image, whereas *magnitude*=1 gives the original image	$[0.1, 1.9]$
Cutout [6, 46]	Set a random square patch of side-length *magnitude* pixels to gray	$[0, 60]$
BBox_Only_X	Apply X to each bounding box content with independent probability, and magnitude that was chosen for X above. Location and the size of the bounding box are not changed	

Table 7. The sub-policies used in our learned augmentation policy. P and M correspond to the probability and magnitude with which the operations were applied in the sub-policy. Note that for each image in each mini-batch, one of the sub-policies is picked uniformly at random. The *No operation* is listed when an operation has a learned probability or magnitude of 0

	Operation 1	P	M	Operation 2	P	M
Sub-policy 1	TranslateX	0.6	4	Equalize	0.8	10
Sub-policy 2	BBox_Only_TranslateY	0.2	2	Cutout	0.8	8
Sub-policy 3	ShearY	1.0	2	BBox_Only_TranslateY	0.6	6
Sub-policy 4	Rotate	0.6	10	Color	1.0	6
Sub-policy 5	No operation			No operation		

References

1. Abadi, M., et al.: TensorFlow: a system for large-scale machine learning. In: Proceedings of the 12th USENIX Conference on Operating Systems Design and Implementation, OSDI 2016, pp. 265–283. USENIX Association, Berkeley (2016)
2. Ciregan, D., Meier, U., Schmidhuber, J.: Multi-column deep neural networks for image classification. In: Proceedings of IEEE Conference on Computer Vision and Pattern Recognition, pp. 3642–3649. IEEE (2012)
3. Cubuk, E.D., Zoph, B., Mane, D., Vasudevan, V., Le, Q.V.: AutoAugment: learning augmentation policies from data. arXiv preprint arXiv:1805.09501 (2018)
4. Cubuk, E.D., Zoph, B., Schoenholz, S.S., Le, Q.V.: Intriguing properties of adversarial examples. arXiv preprint arXiv:1711.02846 (2017)
5. DeVries, T., Taylor, G.W.: Dataset augmentation in feature space. arXiv preprint arXiv:1702.05538 (2017)
6. DeVries, T., Taylor, G.W.: Improved regularization of convolutional neural networks with cutout. arXiv preprint arXiv:1708.04552 (2017)
7. Dwibedi, D., Misra, I., Hebert, M.: Cut, paste and learn: surprisingly easy synthesis for instance detection. In: Proceedings of the IEEE International Conference on Computer Vision, pp. 1301–1310 (2017)
8. Everingham, M., Van Gool, L., Williams, C.K., Winn, J., Zisserman, A.: The pascal visual object classes (VOC) challenge. Int. J. Comput. Vision **88**(2), 303–338 (2010)
9. Ghiasi, G., Lin, T.Y., Le, Q.V.: DropBlock: a regularization method for convolutional networks. In: Advances in Neural Information Processing Systems, pp. 10750–10760 (2018)
10. Ghiasi, G., Lin, T.Y., Pang, R., Le, Q.V.: NAS-FPN: learning scalable feature pyramid architecture for object detection. In: The IEEE Conference on Computer Vision and Pattern Recognition (CVPR), June 2019
11. Girshick, R.: Fast R-CNN. In: The IEEE International Conference on Computer Vision (ICCV), December 2015
12. Girshick, R., Radosavovic, I., Gkioxari, G., Dollár, P., He, K.: Detectron (2018)
13. He, K., Gkioxari, G., Dollár, P., Girshick, R.: Mask R-CNN. In: Proceedings of the IEEE International Conference on Computer Vision, pp. 2961–2969 (2017)
14. He, K., Zhang, X., Ren, S., Sun, J.: Deep residual learning for image recognition. In: Proceedings of the IEEE Conference on Computer Vision and Pattern Recognition (CVPR), pp. 770–778 (2016)

15. Ho, D., Liang, E., Stoica, I., Abbeel, P., Chen, X.: Population based augmentation: efficient learning of augmentation policy schedules. arXiv preprint arXiv:1905.05393 (2019)
16. Huang, J., et al.: Speed/accuracy trade-offs for modern convolutional object detectors. In: Proceedings of the IEEE Conference on Computer Vision and Pattern Recognition, pp. 7310–7311 (2017)
17. Inoue, H.: Data augmentation by pairing samples for images classification. arXiv preprint arXiv:1801.02929 (2018)
18. Jouppi, N.P., et al.: In-datacenter performance analysis of a tensor processing unit. In: 2017 ACM/IEEE 44th Annual International Symposium on Computer Architecture (ISCA), pp. 1–12. IEEE (2017)
19. Krizhevsky, A., Sutskever, I., Hinton, G.E.: ImageNet classification with deep convolutional neural networks. In: Advances in Neural Information Processing Systems (2012)
20. Lemley, J., Bazrafkan, S., Corcoran, P.: Smart augmentation learning an optimal data augmentation strategy. IEEE Access 5, 5858–5869 (2017)
21. Lim, S., Kim, I., Kim, T., Kim, C., Kim, S.: Fast autoaugment. arXiv preprint arXiv:1905.00397 (2019)
22. Lin, T.Y., Dollár, P., Girshick, R., He, K., Hariharan, B., Belongie, S.: Feature pyramid networks for object detection. In: Proceedings of the IEEE Conference on Computer Vision and Pattern Recognition, pp. 2117–2125 (2017)
23. Lin, T.Y., Goyal, P., Girshick, R., He, K., Dollár, P.: Focal loss for dense object detection. In: Proceedings of the IEEE International Conference on Computer Vision, pp. 2980–2988 (2017)
24. Lin, T.-Y., et al.: Microsoft COCO: common objects in context. In: Fleet, D., Pajdla, T., Schiele, B., Tuytelaars, T. (eds.) ECCV 2014. LNCS, vol. 8693, pp. 740–755. Springer, Cham (2014). https://doi.org/10.1007/978-3-319-10602-1_48
25. Liu, C., et al.: Progressive neural architecture search. arXiv preprint arXiv:1712.00559 (2017)
26. Liu, W., et al.: SSD: single shot multibox detector. In: Leibe, B., Matas, J., Sebe, N., Welling, M. (eds.) ECCV 2016. LNCS, vol. 9905, pp. 21–37. Springer, Cham (2016). https://doi.org/10.1007/978-3-319-46448-0_2
27. Loshchilov, I., Hutter, F.: SGDR: stochastic gradient descent with warm restarts. arXiv preprint arXiv:1608.03983 (2016)
28. Miyato, T., Maeda, S.i., Koyama, M., Ishii, S.: Virtual adversarial training: a regularization method for supervised and semi-supervised learning. In: International Conference on Learning Representations (2016)
29. Peng, C., et al.: MegDet: a large mini-batch object detector. In: The IEEE Conference on Computer Vision and Pattern Recognition (CVPR), June 2018
30. Ratner, A.J., Ehrenberg, H., Hussain, Z., Dunnmon, J., Ré, C.: Learning to compose domain-specific transformations for data augmentation. In: Advances in Neural Information Processing Systems, pp. 3239–3249 (2017)
31. Real, E., Aggarwal, A., Huang, Y., Le, Q.V.: Regularized evolution for image classifier architecture search. In: Thirty-Third AAAI Conference on Artificial Intelligence (2019)
32. Redmon, J., Divvala, S., Girshick, R., Farhadi, A.: You only look once: Unified, real-time object detection. In: The IEEE Conference on Computer Vision and Pattern Recognition (CVPR), June 2016
33. Redmon, J., Farhadi, A.: YOLO9000: Better, faster, stronger. In: The IEEE Conference on Computer Vision and Pattern Recognition (CVPR), July 2017

34. Redmon, J., Farhadi, A.: YOLOV3: an incremental improvement. CoRR abs/1804.02767 (2018). http://arxiv.org/abs/1804.02767
35. Ren, S., He, K., Girshick, R., Sun, J.: Faster R-CNN: towards real-time object detection with region proposal networks. In: Advances in Neural Information Processing Systems, pp. 91–99 (2015)
36. Sato, I., Nishimura, H., Yokoi, K.: APAC: augmented pattern classification with neural networks. arXiv preprint arXiv:1505.03229 (2015)
37. Schulman, J., Wolski, F., Dhariwal, P., Radford, A., Klimov, O.: Proximal policy optimization algorithms. arXiv preprint arXiv:1707.06347 (2017)
38. Simard, P.Y., Steinkraus, D., Platt, J.C., et al.: Best practices for convolutional neural networks applied to visual document analysis. In: Proceedings of International Conference on Document Analysis and Recognition (2003)
39. Tan, M., Pang, R., Le, Q.V.: EfficientDet: scalable and efficient object detection. arXiv preprint arXiv:1911.09070 (2019)
40. Tran, T., Pham, T., Carneiro, G., Palmer, L., Reid, I.: A Bayesian data augmentation approach for learning deep models. In: Advances in Neural Information Processing Systems, pp. 2794–2803 (2017)
41. Verma, V., Lamb, A., Beckham, C., Courville, A., Mitliagkis, I., Bengio, Y.: Manifold mixup: encouraging meaningful on-manifold interpolation as a regularizer. arXiv preprint arXiv:1806.05236 (2018)
42. Wan, L., Zeiler, M., Zhang, S., Le Cun, Y., Fergus, R.: Regularization of neural networks using dropconnect. In: International Conference on Machine Learning, pp. 1058–1066 (2013)
43. Wang, X., Shrivastava, A., Gupta, A.: A-fast-RCNN: hard positive generation via adversary for object detection. In: Proceedings of the IEEE Conference on Computer Vision and Pattern Recognition, pp. 2606–2615 (2017)
44. Yang, T., Zhang, X., Li, Z., Zhang, W., Sun, J.: MetaAnchor: learning to detect objects with customized anchors. In: Advances in Neural Information Processing Systems, pp. 318–328 (2018)
45. Zagoruyko, S., Komodakis, N.: Wide residual networks. In: British Machine Vision Conference (2016)
46. Zhong, Z., Zheng, L., Kang, G., Li, S., Yang, Y.: Random erasing data augmentation. arXiv preprint arXiv:1708.04896 (2017)
47. Zoph, B., Le, Q.V.: Neural architecture search with reinforcement learning. In: International Conference on Learning Representations (2017)
48. Zoph, B., Vasudevan, V., Shlens, J., Le, Q.V.: Learning transferable architectures for scalable image recognition. In: Proceedings of IEEE Conference on Computer Vision and Pattern Recognition (2017)

DA-NAS: Data Adapted Pruning for Efficient Neural Architecture Search

Xiyang Dai[✉], Dongdong Chen, Mengchen Liu, Yinpeng Chen, and Lu Yuan

Microsoft, Redmond, USA
{xidai,dochen,mengcliu,yiche,luyuan}@microsoft.com

Abstract. Efficient search is a core issue in Neural Architecture Search (NAS). It is difficult for conventional NAS algorithms to directly search the architectures on large-scale tasks like ImageNet. In general, the cost of GPU hours for NAS grows with regard to training dataset size and candidate set size. One common way is searching on a smaller proxy dataset (*e.g.*, CIFAR-10) and then transferring to the target task (*e.g.*, ImageNet). These architectures optimized on proxy data are not guaranteed to be optimal on the target task. Another common way is learning with a smaller candidate set, which may require expert knowledge and indeed betrays the essence of NAS. In this paper, we present *DA-NAS* that can directly search the architecture for large-scale target tasks while allowing a large candidate set in a more *efficient* manner. Our method is based on an interesting observation that the learning speed for blocks in deep neural networks is related to the difficulty of recognizing distinct categories. We carefully design a progressive data adapted pruning strategy for efficient architecture search. It will quickly trim low performed blocks on a subset of target dataset (*e.g.*, easy classes), and then gradually find the best blocks on the whole target dataset. At this time, the original candidate set becomes as compact as possible, providing a faster search in the target task. Experiments on ImageNet verify the effectiveness of our approach. It is **2×** faster than previous methods while the accuracy is currently state-of-the-art, at **76.2%** under small FLOPs constraint. It supports an argument search space (*i.e.*, more candidate blocks) to efficiently search the best-performing architecture.

Keywords: Data adapted pruning · Neural Architecture Search · Search cost

1 Introduction

Neural Architecture Search (NAS) has a great impact by automating neural network architecture design. The architecture is optimized for accuracy and efficiency (especially latency) under the constraints (*e.g.*, FLOPs, latency, memory). Recently, NAS has demonstrated the success in various deep learning tasks, such as image classification [9,20,30], detection [6] and segmentation [18,22].

Despite the remarkable results, conventional NAS algorithms [19,29,36] is prohibitively computation-intensive, especially directly on a large-scale task

© Springer Nature Switzerland AG 2020
A. Vedaldi et al. (Eds.): ECCV 2020, LNCS 12372, pp. 584–600, 2020.
https://doi.org/10.1007/978-3-030-58583-9_35

(*e.g.*, ImageNet [8]), which makes it difficult for making paretical industry impact. As a result, one common way is to utilize a smaller proxy data (*e.g.*, CIFAR-10) for searching, and then transfer to the large-scale target task (*e.g.*, ImageNet) [16,19,20,25]. Due to the domain gap (*e.g.*, resolution, class number) between proxy data and target task, these blocks optimized on proxy data are not guaranteed to be optimal on the target task, especially when taking accuracy and resource constraint into consideration. Thus, *directly* searching on the target dataset is essential to NAS.

Another common way is searching with a smaller candidate set [3,9,30], which highly relies on the expert knowledge and indeed betrays the essence of NAS. In addition, too few candidate blocks are not beneficial to find a best-performing architecture under search constraints (*e.g.*, FLOPs, latency). Thus, an argument search space with more candidate blocks is always encouraged to boost the performance of NAS.

In this paper, we propose a simple and effective solution to the aforementioned limitations, called *DA-NAS*, which can directly search the architecture for large-scale target tasks in a more efficient manner, while allowing a large candidate set. The solution is based on our observation that the learning speed of blocks in deep neural networks is varied in different classes (for classification task). The blocks are learnt much faster in easy classes than in difficult classes. Besides, our study indicates that the performance of blocks in easy classes converges very quickly at the early training stage but needs more time in difficult ones. The discovery motivates a new data adapted pruning for NAS, which starts the search on a subset of target task (*e.g.*, easy classes), and gradually trims low performed blocks as the size of subset increases until we find the best blocks on the whole target dataset. To build the strategy, we may be able to group classes based on the easiness, and feed them progressively to reduce the computation cost.

We formulate NAS as a block-level pruning process, which is different from recent ProxylessNAS [3] that adopts a path-level pruning. Specifically, we directly train a supernet [32], an over-parameterized network that contains all candidate paths. In the beginning of training, we train it on a subset of target task (only containing easy classes). During training, we progressively prune low performed blocks from our candidate set until we get a compact candidate set for searching on the whole dataset of target task. We consider a loss function with cost constraint which helps find an optimal architecture under search constraint (*e.g.*, FLOPs).

Comprehensive experiments and comparisons to existing methods demonstrate that DA-NAS can find an optimal architecture 2× faster and is also capable of finding a current best small FLOPs architecture at 76.2% on ImageNet within a highly complex search space (involving inverted residual block, shuffle block, squeeze-and-excitation block and more).

Our contributions can be summarized as follows:

- DA-NAS is the first NAS algorithm that shows a close connection between block pruning and dataset scheduling. To our best knowledge, it is the first work to study the relationship between network learning and training data for NAS.

- We propose a progressive block-level pruning perspective for NAS, according to data adaption. It can search architecture on the large-scale target task much faster, and effectively enlarge the search space to achieve state-of-the-art performance.
- The DA-NAS is convenient to use for various needs. It enables cost constraint in search, which is beneficial to practical industry impact. The inherent idea is also generalized to other tasks, like key-point localization.

2   Related Work

Efficient Network. Since the need of delopying deep neural networks into real application systems is increasing, efficient network has drawn a lot of attention from both academia and industry. Existing research about efficient network is often done from two broad aspects: efficient network structure design [14,21,26, 34], or pruning/quantizing one given network structure [10,12,35]. In this paper, we focus on the former problem. For efficient network architecture design, many interesting approaches have been proposed. For example, Xception [7] proposes to decompose one normal convolution layer into one depth-wise and one point-wise convolutional layer, which is able to significantly reduce the computation FLOPs. Based on this design scheme, a lot of efficient networks have been further designed, such as MobileNet [13,14,26], ShuffleNet [21,34]. Despite their success, designing such an efficient network is not that easy and can only be done by experts.

Neural Architecture Search. Recently, NAS has drawn surging interests that study how to automatically design a better and efficient network structure with machine learning algorithms. Based on the searching strategy, existing NAS methods can also be roughly divided into two categories, *i.e.*, searching an efficient operator block [16,20,24,25,29,33] from scratch, or finding an optimal operator combination from a pre-defined efficient operator search space [2,3,9,30]. Compared to the former category, the latter category of approaches leverage a lot of design priors from human experts, so it is relatively easier to find an optimal network architecture. Our method belongs to the latter category. By contrast to existing methods which often regard data scheduling and architecture search as two independent parts, our method is the first that shows a close connection between both. By leveraging a new and efficient data scheduling mechanism, a progressive block-level search space pruning algorithm is further proposed. Our method is demonstrated to be more efficient and can search a better architecture given the same searching time.

3   Understanding Network Training Process

In this section, we analyze the relationship between the performance of deep neural networks and the training data. These interesting observations will inspire our data adapted pruning for efficient neural architecture search.

Observation 1. *There exists some classes that are easy to learn (easy classes) while some classes are harder to learn (hard classes).*

We start our analysis from exploring a typical network training process, *i.e.*, ResNet-34 trained on ImageNet. A matrix shown in Fig. 1(a) visualizes the accuracy of distinct classes varies with more training iterations. Each row is a certain class and each column is training time (epoch $= 10, 20, ..., 180$). The value at each grid denotes the accuracy for each class. For a better visualization, we sort the matrix rows by row-wise variance of a matrix, namely, the variance of the accuracies of recognizing every class from each training epoch.

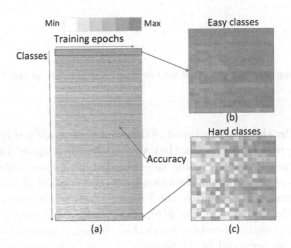

Fig. 1. Comparing between learning curves of different classes.

We find that the accuracy of some classes quickly converges and achieves its maximum (Fig. 1(b)); while some other classes gradually increase/fluctuate in the training (Fig. 1(c)). It indicates the learning speed for every class is different. Thus, we can group classes based on their easiness and feed them heuristically into training, following small-to-large data scheduling. Meanwhile, search using fewer categories at the beginning is a considerably easier task than the search using all categories in the end. This helps us progressively trim low performed blocks in the search space to reduce the search cost.

Observation 2. *Neurons to recognize easier classes converge more quickly at the early training stage and their performance remains stable in the remaining training process. Neurons for hard classes need more time to be fully trained.*

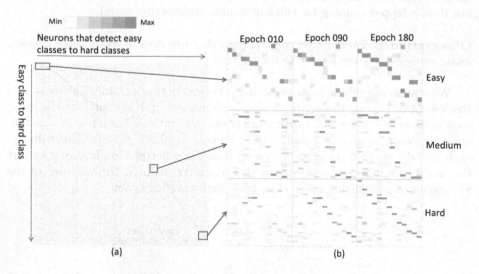

Fig. 2. Comparing neuron responses for easy and hard classes at different timestamps in the training.

We study why the learning speed of different classes are not equal (in Observation 1). One possible reason is that various learning speed of neurons (*i.e.*, convolution kernels) makes learning speed of distinct classes different, since the final prediction of network is determined by a combination of neuron responses. To verify this reason, we visualize the relations between neurons and classes in increasing training epochs on Fig. 2(b). The relation between a neuron and a class, used to distinguish the class from other classes, is computed by the neuron relevance measure proposed in [1]. Specifically, we only consider the neurons in the final convolutional layer (before FC-layer) since it represents the maximum semantics in neurons. We collect all the calculated relations into a matrix, where each row is a class and each column is a neuron. To be consistent with Fig. 1, we use the same order of classes in rows, and further sort the matrix columns by column-wise maximum value (corresponding to the class most likely to be recognized by the neuron) of a matrix. Figure 2(a) show the sorting result of the matrix, where the top-left block corresponds to the easiest classes and the neurons that are most likely used to recognize these classes, and the right-bottom block corresponds to the hardest classes and corresponding neurons.

Figure 2(a) shows such a visualization corresponding to the last epoch, where classes of different easiness levels are learned by different neurons. More interestingly, there is a "diagonal pattern" that neurons are distributed in balance across all the classes, summarized in Observation 3. It indicates that **all** the classes should be involved in the training for the best performance. In other words, directly learning on a large-scale dataset should yield better accuracy than on a smaller dataset.

To further investigate the evolutionary pattern in the neuron-class relations, we visualize the matrix at three different training epochs (epoch = 10, 90, 180) and select three representative blocks (corresponding to easy, medium, and hard classes) at each epoch, shown in Fig. 2(b). In the first row, we observe that the neurons to recognize easy classes quickly converge and their performance keep stable in subsequent training. Compared with other two rows, the neurons learn faster on easy classes (stable on epoch = 10) than that on medium classes (almost stable on epoch = 90), and even much faster than hard classes (almost on epoch = 180). The phenomena is summarized in Observation 2.

Observation 3. *Different architecture of networks agree on similar easy/hard classes distribution*

To further investigate whether above observation 1 and 2 are shared among other networks or unique for ResNet, we train and evaluate a bunch of state-of-the-art manually designed networks, including VGG [27], ResNet [11], MobileNet [14,26], ShuffleNet [34,34] and more. For each class, we calculate the mean and variance of the running average on *easiness* histograms among multiple networks. Shown in Fig. 3(a), the *easiness* histograms are well aligned with confusion matrix and can be used as an indicator for measuring how easy a network can distinguish a class from other classes. Shown in Fig. 3(b), it is true that different networks agree on the similar distribution of easiness on classes. This phenomena enables us to effectively use data while increasing searching space. Shown in Fig. 3(c), after sorted by easiness rank, the confusion matrix disentangles the hierarchy within classes. The mathematics definition for *easiness* is introduced in the following section.

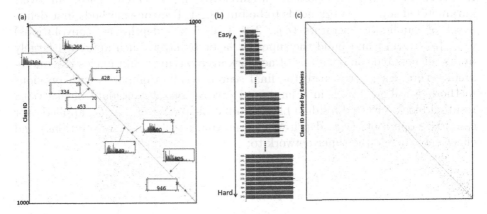

Fig. 3. An illustration that our defined class easiness measurement is agreed and persisted among multiple deep networks

These observations inspire us to design a search space pruning strategy based on the easiness of classes and the learning status of neurons. At the beginning, we only feed in a small subset with easy classes to train all candidate blocks. Then, we can explicitly exclude unfavorable blocks that still struggle to learn or perform worse than others in easy classes. By sequentially feeding more hard classes until all the classes finally (the whole dataset), we can progressively trim low performed blocks step by step, as shown in Algorithm 1.

4   Data Adapted NAS

Based on the analysis in Sect. 3, the class easiness E_c for a class c is defined as:

$$P_i = \hat{N}(d_i) \quad for \quad d_i \in \mathcal{D} \tag{1}$$

$$E_{c,i} = -\sum P_i \log(P_i) \quad if \quad d_i \in c \tag{2}$$

$$E_c = \mathcal{H}_i(E_{c,i}) \tag{3}$$

where, $\mathcal{D}$ is the training dataset (e.g., ImageNet), $\hat{N}$ is a network (e.g., ResNet-34) fine-tuned on the dataset, and E_c is represented as a histogram $\mathcal{H}(\cdot)$ of entropy values of all the samples belonging to class c. For each training sample, since it is optimized towards a one-hot vector of the ground truth, the entropy of the network's output represents the effort of a network taking to distinguish the ground truth class from others. Then the histogram of these entropy values of a class represents the trend of easiness of all samples that belong to this class. As shown in Fig. 3(a), the proposed measurement is well aligned with the confusion matrix and can be used to explore the trend of easiness on all classes and all training samples. Finally, for each class, we calculate the mean of easiness histograms among multiple networks as our final data adaptation strategy.

4.1   Expanding Search Space

In order to search any possible architecture in a search space, an over-parametered super network needs to be built first. Previous methods first define a set of candidate operators (e.g., 3×3 or 5×5 depth-wise convolutions) $\mathcal{O} = \{o_1, \ldots, o_k\}$ and build the supernet layer by layer. Such approach largely limits all possible combinations of network architectures, and makes the micro-architecture design critical to the final search result. Compared with previous method, we allow search in a large and diverse set of candidate blocks (e.g., residual block, inverted residual block, shuffle block) $\mathcal{B} = b_i, \ldots, b_m$ applied over candidate operators (e.g., depth-wise or normal 3×3, 5×5 convolutions) and effectively change the super network to:

$$N_l = \sum_j^m \sum_i^k b_j(o_i(x)) \tag{4}$$

$$N_{l+1} = \sum_j^m \sum_i^k b_j(o_i(N_l)) \tag{5}$$

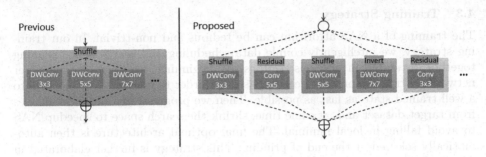

Fig. 4. Our proposed search space contains combinations of blocks and operators.

Figure 4 shows that our design can effectively combine multiple micro-architecture build blocks and simulate popular networks.

4.2   Searching with Constrains

We followed the idea introduced by [32] to use Gumbel-Softmax to assist learning of the architecture:

$$p \sim GumbelSoftmax(a, \tau) \tag{6}$$

$$N_l = \sum_{j}^{m} \sum_{i}^{k} p_{i,j} b_j(o_i(x)) \tag{7}$$

where a is the architecture weight that we want to learn and τ is a pre-defined hyper-parameter to control the sharpness of Gumbel distribution. To incorporate with search constrains (*e.g.*, FLOPS or hardware latency), we also compute the expected cost of a super network by:

$$C_l = \sum_{j}^{m} \sum_{i}^{k} p_{i,j} \mathcal{C}(b_j(o_i(x))) \tag{8}$$

where $\mathcal{C}(\cdot)$ is a function measuring the cost of a block.

The super network is first optimized towards classification loss to find the optimal weight:

$$w = \arg\min \mathcal{L}_{cls}(N(\mathbb{D}_{train}, a)). \tag{9}$$

Then it is optimized for architecture using the modified loss function with the cost constraint:

$$a = \arg\min \mathcal{L}_{cls}(N(\mathbb{D}_{val}, w)) \cdot \log(\frac{C}{\beta})^{\gamma} \tag{10}$$

where β is a scaling factor designed as target cost and γ is a factor to control the strength of incorporating cost constraints.

4.3   Training Strategy

The training of a NAS algorithm can be tedious and non-trivial. In our training strategy, we intelligently couple data scheduling and search space pruning together, as stated in previous sections. At beginning, we warm up the super network by training on only "easy" classes in order to convert each blocks into a well-trained state as fast as possible. Then we progressively add more classes from target dataset and, at same time, shrink the search space to speedup NAS to avoid falling in local minimal. The final optimal architecture is then automatically selected at the end of pruning. This strategy is further elaborated in Algorithm 1.

We intelligently combine data adaptation with network pruning in two ways:

- We progressively introduce more categories in the architecture search. The search using fewer (*e.g.*, 100) categories at the beginning is a considerably easier task than the search using all (*e.g.*, 1000) categories in the end. This helps us progressively trim low performed blocks in the search space to reduce the search cost.
- We also identify the easiness of the categories by voting from popular manually designed networks. We observe different network tends to learn similar "easy" categories quickly at the beginning. We start with a few "easy" categories at the beginning to speed up the convergence of supernet and hence further reduce the training cost.

The benefit with our training strategy is three-fold:

- It largely reduces the number of epochs and GPU hours required in training.
- It eases the difficulty of tuning hyper-parameter, especially τ in Gumbel Softmax (Eq. (7)). τ controls the sample distribution and is usually critical to the final search result. Large τ turns to add randomness of sampling to help super network explore more variant of branch combinations; while lower τ trends to be more deterministic to branch selection and help super network select architecture quicker. It is necessary to balance these two factors to find optimal architecture after exploring large variants of combinations. Previous method coupled τ with learning rate and used an exponentially decaying schedule [3,30]. Unlike previous methods, τ in our training strategy is set to a fixed number, as the progressively pruning of search space works similar to reducing τ.
- It picks the final architecture more confidently. Unlike previous methods that need sampling from the final architecture distribution to find the best candidate, our final optimal architecture can be directly picked by maximizing the architecture distribution, which further saves the computational cost.

5   Experiment

5.1   Setup

Datasets. We directly search architecture on the target dataset. For image classification task, we use the full ImageNet [8] dataset. We randomly select 50 images

---

Algorithm 1: NAS with Data Adapted Pruning

Input: Training Data D_{Train}, Validating Data D_{val}, Search Space S, Search
space pruning ratio π, Classes used per step δ, Easiness of classes E;
$R \leftarrow$ Sort E
for *epoch* $\leftarrow$ 1 **to** $\#Epoch_{warmup}$ **do**
   $train \leftarrow D_{Train}$ **from** $R[\delta[0]]$;
   Optimize Equation (9) **use** *train*;
end
for $s \leftarrow$ 1 **to** $\#Step$ **do**
   $train \leftarrow D_{Train}$ **from** $R[\delta[s]]$;
   $val \leftarrow D_{Val}$ **from** $R[\delta[s]]$;
   for *epoch* $\leftarrow$ 1 **to** $\#Epoch_s$ **do**
      Optimize Equation (9) **use** *train*;
      $cost \leftarrow$ Equation (8);
      Optimize Equation (10) **use** *val, cost*;
   end
   $S \leftarrow$ Reduce S **by** δ
end
return S

---

per class from the original training set to formulate a validation set. We then use the original validation set as a test set to report final experiment results. Besides, we also want to test our DA-NAS algorithm for key-point localization task. We use full COCO [17] key-point 2017 dataset. The original training set is divided into "trainminusminival" and "minival" for training and validation. Then the original validation set is used to report results.

Search Spaces. We investigate two popular search spaces widely used in previous work [3,9,13,30] and their augments:

- "Mobile": The search space is based on MobileNet [14,26] micro-architectures. In our implementation, it contains three inverted residual blocks with expanded factor of 1, 3, 6 and two depth-wise convolution operators with 3×3 and 5×5 kernels.
- "Shuffle": The search space is based on ShuffleNet [21,34] micro-architectures. In our implementation, it contains two shuffle blocks with different number of convolution layers and three depth-wise convolution operators with 3×3, 5×5 and 7×7 kernels.
- "Mobile+": We expand "Mobile" by adding normal convolutions with 3×3 and 5×5 kernels into operators to increase the complexity and flops variation.
- "Shuffle+": We expand "Shuffle" by adding normal convolutions with 3×3 and 5×5 kernels into operators to increase the complexity and flops variation.
- "Shuffle+Mobile": We combine Shuffle spaces and Mobile spaces together. It is the major search space we use to find state-of-the-art architectures.

Implementation Details. We implement our approach using Pytorch and run all experiments on a compute node with 4 V100 GPUs. For training, the super

Table 1. Direct comparison to two popular methods with fast search speed

Method	Search space	FLOPs	Accuracy	Search cost
SinglePath [9]	Shuffle	319 M	74.3	
SinglePath (impl.)	Shuffle	336 M	74.4	142
Ours	Shuffle	325 M	74.4	$87\downarrow_{39\%}$
Proxyless-G [3]	Mobile	–	74.2	
Proxyless-G (impl.)	Mobile	420 M	74.6	399
Ours	Mobile	389 M	74.6	$138\downarrow_{65\%}$

Table 2. Restrict comparison to two popular methods on performance of searched architecture (same fine-tune setup) under constrained search time.

Method	Search space	Accuracy @ Time	
		0.5x	1x
SinglePath (impl.)	Shuffle+	72.4	73.2
Ours	Shuffle+	73.3	73.3
Proxyless-G (impl.)	Mobile+	71.8	73.3
Ours	Mobile+	73.2	73.3

network is first warmed up with 10 epochs and followed by 3 steps of search with 20 epochs each. We use a search space pruning ratio 0.4 and 100, 300, 600, 1000 classes for each step respectively. For fine-tuning the searched architecture, we follow the training setup introduced by [3], but pump up the initial learning rate to 0.5.

5.2 Compared with State-of-the-Art Methods

We first compared with two state-of-the-art methods, ProxylessNAS [3] and SinglePath [9], which are claiming as fastest search methods on ImageNet. Since they report the performance and the search cost based on different criteria and hardware, in order to compare fairly, we re-implement these two methods based on public available code released by authors. As shown in Table 1, we are able to reproduce the reported performances. Then we run our methods with the exact same search space. It is obvious to see that our method is capable of finding competitive quality networks with much lower search cost. It significantly reduces the search cost by 39% and 65% respectively.

Next, to further investigate the lower bond of time cost needed for searching a proper architecture, we conduct an experiment with constrained search time and a enlarged search space. We double the operators in shuffle and mobile search spaces by introducing 3×3 convolution and 5×5 convolution. As shown in Table 2, our method is able to find the architecture with comparable accuracy to state-of-the-art methods by only half of the time needed in these methods.

Table 3. Comparison to the state-of-the-art searched results on ImageNet validation set.

Method	Seach dataset	FLOPs	Accuracy	Seach cost
DARTS [20]	CIFAR	595 M	73.1	96
SNAS [32]	CIFAR	522 M	72.7	24
PNAS [19]	CIFAR	588 M	74.2	3600
NASNET-A [36]	CIFAR	564 M	74.0	10,000+
MnasNet [29]	Imagenet	317 M	74.0	10,000+
FBNet [30]	Imagenet	375 M	74.9	216
Proxyless-G LL [3]	Imagenet	–	74.2	200
SinglePath [9]	Imagenet	319 M	74.3	312
Ours-A	Imagenet	323 M	74.3	138
Ours-B	Imagenet	372 M	74.8	138
Ours-C	Imagenet	467 M	76.2	138

Table 4. Ablation study on the effect of different data scheduling strategy.

Method	FLOPs	Accuracy	Search cost
Small	319 M	73.2	33
Small (Easy) → All	325 M	74.4	87
Small (Hard) → All	316 M	74.1	87
All	327 M	73.8	307

Finally, we combine "Shuffle" and "Mobile" search spaces together to find the state-of-the-art architecture. Table 3 shows the comparison between our method with existing popular NAS approaches [3,9,19,20,30,32,36]. We report their search costs directly from their public papers (although some of numbers we cannot reproduce locally). Compared with methods [19,20,32,36] only searched on a proxy dataset (*i.e.*, CIFAR), our method leads to a significant performance gain. It is worth noticing that the networks searched on smaller datasets suffered from sub-optimal performance when transferred to a large scale dataset. They also have difficulties in reducing FLOPs due to the fact that searching conducted on different resolutions of datasets causes different designs of architecture (such as pooling scales and number of layers). Compared with methods [3,9,29,30] that search directly on ImageNet, our method requires the least search cost (138 GPU hours) to find best-performing architecture with the state-of-the-art accuracy (76.2%).

5.3 Ablation Study

We first demonstrate that our data adapted pruning is efficient. We evaluate the effects of different data scheduling on pruning: from easy classes to all classes,

Table 5. Ablation study on the influence of different search space on the searched architecture.

Search Space	FLOPs	Accuracy	Search cost
Shuffle	325 M	74.4	87
Shuffle+	353 M	74.3	194
Shuffle+Mobile	323 M	74.3	138

Table 6. Ablation study on each component of proposed method.

Scheduling	Pruning	FLOPs	Accuracy	Search cost
✓	✗	320 M	74.2	112
✗	✓	317 M	74.2	188
✗	✗	327 M	73.8	307
✓	✓	325 M	74.4	87

from hard classes to all classes, use a small subset of classes solely and use all classes directly. As shown in Table 4, it is obvious that our "small (easy) → all" data adapted pruning is the most effective method, which is able to find the best network architecture with only 28% of the time compared to searching directly on all classes. This demonstrates that "from small to all" is very important and it yields 0.9 better at top-1 accuracy because of the difference of data amount. Then, starting from easy is better than hard, it yields another 30% compared to the improvement of using 10x more data, which is non-trivial.

Then, we show that our search space pruning is robust. We conduct experiments on three different search spaces: "Shuffle", "Shuffle+", "Shuffle+Mobile", which contain varieties of blocks and operators. As shown in Table 5, our method is robust enough to find the optimal architectures with nearly consistent accuracy and FLOPs using different search spaces. Besides, our search cost will accordingly increase as the search space is enlarged.

Finally, we analyze the necessity of each component in our proposed data adapted pruning method. We partially disable each key component to examine the influence. As shown in Table 6, our method full loaded largely reduces the search cost (from 307 GPU hours to 87 GPU hours) and yields the best searched architecture. This further proves the effectiveness of our method.

5.4   Transferring to Key-Point Localization Task

We further apply our method to the key-point localization task to demonstrate the generalization ability. Following the setup in simple baseline [31], we search a key-point localization architecture based on instance-level ground-truth. We modify our search space by attaching 3 levels of de-convolution layers at the

Table 7. Comparison to the state-of-the-art methods of key-point localization on COCO 2017 validation set.

Method	Input size	Search cost	Params	FLOPs	AP	AP_M	AP_L	AR
SimpleBaseline-ResNet50 [31]	256 × 192	Manual	34.0 M	8.90 G	70.4	67.1	77.2	76.2
HRNet-W32 [28]	256 × 192	Manual	28.5 M	7.10 G	73.4	70.2	80.1	78.9
CPN-ResNet50 [5]	256 × 192	Manual	27.0 M	6.20 G	69.4	–	–	–
DeepLab v3+ [4]	256 × 192	Manual	5.8 M	–	66.8	64.1	70.7	70.0
NAS-CSS [23]	256 × 192	192	2.9 M	–	65.9	63.1	70.0	69.3
Ours	256 × 192	30	10.9 M	2.18 G	68.4	65.5	74.4	75.7

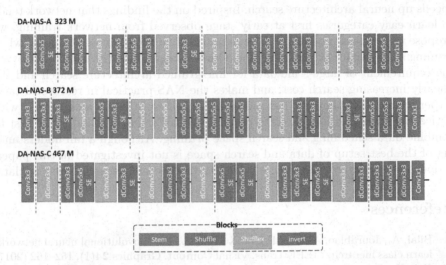

Fig. 5. Visualization of best searched architectures. Network input flow is shown from left to right. Colored boxes indicate different blocks and texts in box indicate different operators. Blue dash lines after block indicate where the output resolutions reduce. (Color figure online)

end, consisting de-convolution operators with 4 × 4 kernel and 2, 4, 8 groups respectively. As shown in Table 7, our method is able to find a state-or-the-art architecture with significantly lower flops compared to manually designed methods [4,5,28] with competing performance and significantly speedup previous best NAS method [23].

5.5 Visualization

We visualize our searched architectures in Fig. 5 with two interesting findings. First, it is obvious to see that shuffle block is more cost efficient than inverted residual block. As the FLOPs constrain looses, the network architecture tends to have more inverted residual block to further boost the performance. Second, inverted residual block with squeeze-and-excitation component (SE) [15] is more likely to be placed at where number of channels increases or resolution of input reduces. This indicates that it is more effective to model inter-dependencies between different features channels. These findings are consistent with the statements from [14,15,21]. Thanks to the advantage of combining complex search spaces together, our method is capable of finding interesting properties of different blocks.

6 Conclusion

In this paper, we present a novel data adapted pruning approach that largely speeds up neural architecture search. Inspired on the findings that network tends to learn easy categories first at early stage observed from network training, we propose to progressively utilize more data based on the easiness of classes, while pruning search space at the same time. Our strategy solves the conflicts between the requirement of large-scale data for fine-grained architecture search and the linearly increasing search cost, and makes the NAS practical in real-world task. Experiments show that our method can find state-of-the-art architecture with noticeable lower cost compared to popular methods. Our method is the first to combine data scheduling and search space pruning. Although a full understanding of the best setup of data and search space is not investigated in this paper, it opens a very interesting direction on how to effectively search based on data.

References

1. Bilal, A., Jourabloo, A., Ye, M., Liu, X., Ren, L.: Do convolutional neural networks learn class hierarchy? IEEE Trans. Visual Comput. Graphics **24**(1), 152–162 (2017)
2. Cai, H., Gan, C., Han, S.: Once for all: train one network and specialize it for efficient deployment. arXiv preprint arXiv:1908.09791 (2019)
3. Cai, H., Zhu, L., Han, S.: ProxylessNAS: direct neural architecture search on target task and hardware. arXiv preprint arXiv:1812.00332 (2018)
4. Chen, L.-C., Zhu, Y., Papandreou, G., Schroff, F., Adam, H.: Encoder-decoder with atrous separable convolution for semantic image segmentation. In: Ferrari, V., Hebert, M., Sminchisescu, C., Weiss, Y. (eds.) ECCV 2018. LNCS, vol. 11211, pp. 833–851. Springer, Cham (2018). https://doi.org/10.1007/978-3-030-01234-2_49
5. Chen, Y., Wang, Z., Peng, Y., Zhang, Z., Yu, G., Sun, J.: Cascaded pyramid network for multi-person pose estimation. In: The IEEE Conference on Computer Vision and Pattern Recognition (CVPR), June 2018
6. Chen, Y., Yang, T., Zhang, X., Meng, G., Pan, C., Sun, J.: DetNAS: neural architecture search on object detection. arXiv preprint arXiv:1903.10979 (2019)
7. Chollet, F.: Xception: deep learning with depthwise separable convolutions. In: Proceedings of the IEEE Conference on Computer Vision and Pattern Recognition, pp. 1251–1258 (2017)
8. Deng, J., Dong, W., Socher, R., Li, L.J., Li, K., Fei-Fei, L.: ImageNet: a large-scale hierarchical image database. In: 2009 IEEE Conference on Computer Vision and Pattern Recognition, pp. 248–255. IEEE (2009)
9. Guo, Z., et al.: Single path one-shot neural architecture search with uniform sampling. arXiv preprint arXiv:1904.00420 (2019)

10. Han, S., Mao, H., Dally, W.J.: Deep compression: compressing deep neural networks with pruning, trained quantization and Huffman coding. arXiv preprint arXiv:1510.00149 (2015)
11. He, K., Zhang, X., Ren, S., Sun, J.: Deep residual learning for image recognition. In: Proceedings of the IEEE Conference on Computer Vision and Pattern Recognition, pp. 770–778 (2016)
12. He, Y., Zhang, X., Sun, J.: Channel pruning for accelerating very deep neural networks. In: Proceedings of the IEEE International Conference on Computer Vision, pp. 1389–1397 (2017)
13. Howard, A., et al.: Searching for MobileNetV3. CoRR abs/1905.02244 (2019). http://arxiv.org/abs/1905.02244
14. Howard, A.G., et al.: MobileNets: efficient convolutional neural networks for mobile vision applications. arXiv preprint arXiv:1704.04861 (2017)
15. Hu, J., Shen, L., Sun, G.: Squeeze-and-excitation networks. In: CVPR (2018)
16. Liang, H., et al.: Darts+: improved differentiable architecture search with early stopping. arXiv preprint arXiv:1909.06035 (2019)
17. Lin, T.-Y., et al.: Microsoft COCO: common objects in context. In: Fleet, D., Pajdla, T., Schiele, B., Tuytelaars, T. (eds.) ECCV 2014. LNCS, vol. 8693, pp. 740–755. Springer, Cham (2014). https://doi.org/10.1007/978-3-319-10602-1_48
18. Liu, C., et al.: Auto-DeepLab: hierarchical neural architecture search for semantic image segmentation. In: Proceedings of the IEEE Conference on Computer Vision and Pattern Recognition, pp. 82–92 (2019)
19. Liu, C., et al.: Progressive neural architecture search. In: Ferrari, V., Hebert, M., Sminchisescu, C., Weiss, Y. (eds.) ECCV 2018. LNCS, vol. 11205, pp. 19–35. Springer, Cham (2018). https://doi.org/10.1007/978-3-030-01246-5_2
20. Liu, H., Simonyan, K., Yang, Y.: DARTS: differentiable architecture search. arXiv preprint arXiv:1806.09055 (2018)
21. Ma, N., Zhang, X., Zheng, H.-T., Sun, J.: ShuffleNet V2: practical guidelines for efficient CNN architecture design. In: Ferrari, V., Hebert, M., Sminchisescu, C., Weiss, Y. (eds.) Computer Vision – ECCV 2018. LNCS, vol. 11218, pp. 122–138. Springer, Cham (2018). https://doi.org/10.1007/978-3-030-01264-9_8
22. Nekrasov, V., Chen, H., Shen, C., Reid, I.: Fast neural architecture search of compact semantic segmentation models via auxiliary cells. In: Proceedings of the IEEE Conference on Computer Vision and Pattern Recognition, pp. 9126–9135 (2019)
23. Nekrasov, V., Chen, H., Shen, C., Reid, I.: Fast neural architecture search of compact semantic segmentation models via auxiliary cells. In: The IEEE Conference on Computer Vision and Pattern Recognition (CVPR), June 2019
24. Pham, H., Guan, M.Y., Zoph, B., Le, Q.V., Dean, J.: Efficient neural architecture search via parameter sharing. arXiv preprint arXiv:1802.03268 (2018)
25. Real, E., Aggarwal, A., Huang, Y., Le, Q.V.: Regularized evolution for image classifier architecture search. In: Proceedings of the AAAI Conference on Artificial Intelligence, vol. 33, pp. 4780–4789 (2019)
26. Sandler, M., Howard, A., Zhu, M., Zhmoginov, A., Chen, L.C.: MobileNetV2: inverted residuals and linear bottlenecks. In: Proceedings of the IEEE Conference on Computer Vision and Pattern Recognition, pp. 4510–4520 (2018)
27. Simonyan, K., Zisserman, A.: Very deep convolutional networks for large-scale image recognition. arXiv preprint arXiv:1409.1556 (2014)
28. Sun, K., Xiao, B., Liu, D., Wang, J.: Deep high-resolution representation learning for human pose estimation. In: CVPR (2019)

29. Tan, M., et al.: MnasNet: platform-aware neural architecture search for mobile. In: The IEEE Conference on Computer Vision and Pattern Recognition (CVPR), June 2019

30. Wu, B., et al.: FBNet: hardware-aware efficient convnet design via differentiable neural architecture search. In: Proceedings of the IEEE Conference on Computer Vision and Pattern Recognition, pp. 10734–10742 (2019)

31. Xiao, B., Wu, H., Wei, Y.: Simple baselines for human pose estimation and tracking. In: Ferrari, V., Hebert, M., Sminchisescu, C., Weiss, Y. (eds.) ECCV 2018. LNCS, vol. 11210, pp. 472–487. Springer, Cham (2018). https://doi.org/10.1007/978-3-030-01231-1_29

32. Xie, S., Zheng, H., Liu, C., Lin, L.: SNAS: stochastic neural architecture search. In: International Conference on Learning Representations (2019). https://openreview.net/forum?id=rylqooRqK7

33. Yan, S., et al.: HM-NAS: efficient neural architecture search via hierarchical masking. In: Proceedings of the IEEE International Conference on Computer Vision Workshops (2019)

34. Zhang, X., Zhou, X., Lin, M., Sun, J.: ShuffleNet: an extremely efficient convolutional neural network for mobile devices. In: Proceedings of the IEEE Conference on Computer Vision and Pattern Recognition, pp. 6848–6856 (2018)

35. Zhou, A., Yao, A., Guo, Y., Xu, L., Chen, Y.: Incremental network quantization: towards lossless CNNs with low-precision weights. arXiv preprint arXiv:1702.03044 (2017)

36. Zoph, B., Vasudevan, V., Shlens, J., Le, Q.V.: Learning transferable architectures for scalable image recognition. In: The IEEE Conference on Computer Vision and Pattern Recognition (CVPR), June 2018

A Closer Look at Generalisation in RAVEN

Steven Spratley$^{(\boxtimes)}$, Krista Ehinger, and Tim Miller

School of Computing and Information Systems, The University of Melbourne,
Victoria, Australia
spratley@student.unimelb.edu.au

Abstract. Humans have a remarkable capacity to draw parallels between concepts, generalising their experience to new domains. This skill is essential to solving the visual problems featured in the RAVEN and PGM datasets, yet, previous papers have scarcely tested how well models generalise across tasks. Additionally, we encounter a critical issue that allows existing models to inadvertently 'cheat' problems in RAVEN. We therefore propose a simple workaround to resolve this issue, and focus the conversation on generalisation performance, as this was severely affected in the process. We revise the existing evaluation, and introduce two relational models, Rel-Base and Rel-AIR, that significantly improve this performance. To our knowledge, Rel-AIR is the first method to employ unsupervised scene decomposition in solving abstract visual reasoning problems, and along with Rel-Base, sets states-of-the-art for image-only reasoning and generalisation across both RAVEN and PGM.

Keywords: Visual reasoning · Representation learning · Scene understanding · Raven's Progressive Matrices

1 Introduction

The development of a general thinking machine is, arguably, the founding goal of the field of artificial intelligence, given the historic Dartmouth summer workshop in 1956 [17]. Since realising the acute difficulty of this aim, the literature has increasingly been focused on incremental improvement over narrow applications. Today, the deep learning paradigm plays centre-stage, with an incredible aptitude for modelling complex functions from training data alone. Yet, there is a growing understanding of the fragility of these techniques to adequately process out-of-distribution (OOD) data. This lack of generalisation, both within and between problem domains, pushes back at the ambition of the founding goal.

In cognitive science, analogical reasoning has long been hypothesised to be fundamental to general intelligence as embodied in humans and other tool-using

Electronic supplementary material The online version of this chapter (https://doi.org/10.1007/978-3-030-58583-9_36) contains supplementary material, which is available to authorized users.

© Springer Nature Switzerland AG 2020
A. Vedaldi et al. (Eds.): ECCV 2020, LNCS 12372, pp. 601–616, 2020.
https://doi.org/10.1007/978-3-030-58583-9_36

animals [7,16], and has been considered to lie at the "core of cognition" [13]. Analogy, or the drawing of parallels between concepts, affords agents the ability to perceive scenes in light of those already encountered – on some higher or abstract level – and thereby transfer their learning to new domains. Perhaps the most influential test of abstract and analogical reasoning; the use of *Raven's Progressive Matrices* (RPM) [19] has spanned roughly eighty years, across fields including cognitive science, psychometrics, and AI. In the last three years, two major RPM datasets have become established – PGM [20] and RAVEN [28] – allowing the abilities of modern neural networks to be investigated.

There is a common shortcoming among many of the techniques benchmarked on these datasets: a reliance on curated auxiliary data. We believe this prohibits the current application of these techniques to problem domains with raw images alone; it is therefore advisable that research steers towards the development of solvers that can perform well without this additional supervision. Secondly, there has been an over-emphasis on model performance in experiments where the test data is adequately captured by the training distribution; over the RPM task, we believe that this is slightly misplaced, as it is the novelty between RPM problems that makes them suitable for evaluating the kinds of extrapolative reasoning required. Finally, we encountered a critical methodological issue with the RAVEN dataset and associated baselines, allowing models to inadvertently 'cheat' problems. This affects a number of existing works, and calls for a closer look at the true generalisation abilities of methods over this dataset.

Meanwhile, there have been a number of recent developments in the field of unsupervised scene decomposition – learning to deconstruct unlabelled images into constituent objects – that have the potential to inform architectural design in visual reasoning [2,6,8]. By possessing an explicit notion of "objectness", we believe that models might better be able to perceive and reason over a scene's global structure, disentangled from lower-level details.

In this paper, we are interested in identifying such inductive biases that will allow techniques to not only perform well overall on the RPM datasets, but to generalise between RAVEN's seven problem configurations, and with minimal training data. We therefore primarily use the term 'generalisation' to refer to the ability of models to solve problems belonging to such configurations unseen in training, in line with [28]. To address these considerations, we introduce two architectures. Our first architecture, *Rel-Base*, models frame relationships with convolutional layers, providing a simpler model that displays greater proficiency over datasets when compared to existing methods. Building on this, we introduce a variant with an object-centric inductive bias, *Rel-AIR*. Making use of an initial scene decomposition stage, Rel-AIR is further able to generalise its reasoning to problems containing different numbers of objects, and in different positions.

We summarise our contributions as follows:

1. We identify issues affecting the validity of current benchmarks over the RAVEN dataset, and describe the steps taken to mitigate these.

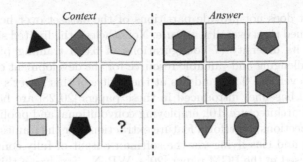

Fig. 1. An example RPM problem in RAVEN. In the context, the first two rows each have objects of a set size, of a progressively increasing number of sides, and with one of each colour. Therefore, the emboldened answer frame is correct; when inserted into the context, it allows the third row to adhere to the rules. (Color figure online)

2. We introduce *Rel-Base*, a simple architecture that significantly outperforms existing image-only methods, and *Rel-AIR*, which to our knowledge, is the first method to employ unsupervised scene decomposition in solving abstract visual reasoning problems.
3. We evaluate both methods against refreshed baselines, and demonstrate state-of-the-art performance across RAVEN and PGM datasets, without auxiliary data.

2 Background and Related Work

2.1 Raven's Progressive Matrices and Neural Networks

In the field of human intelligence testing, Raven's Progressive Matrices (RPMs) [19] and RPM-style problems have proven to be a highly valuable test-bed for abstract and analogical reasoning skills. Their solution ties together multiple levels of perception, from the lowest level – making sense of clusters of pixels – to seeing relationships between objects in a scene, and ultimately, the relationships between scenes. Figure 1 depicts one such problem, consisting of 8 context and 8 answer frames. To solve a problem, one needs to perceive the rules governing the first two rows of the context, and select an answer frame to complete the third row, following these same rules. Doing so requires an understanding of multiple factors including geometry, position, scale, orientation, colour, and sequence.

Although the original RPM problems were manually created, there have been two recently established attempts to automate their production at the scale required to fit neural networks – PGM [20] and RAVEN [28]. Neither of these datasets are superior to the other; the problems in PGM are visually complex – involving challenging distractor entities not present in RAVEN – yet frames are limited to a 3 × 3 grid structure. PGM also offers subsets of the data generated from held-out features and rules, allowing for better evaluation of generalisation ability. Meanwhile, RAVEN provides several new types of rules and problem structures, yet does not provide partitions of the dataset over held-out factors more fine-grained than overall structure. Nonetheless, the limited size of RAVEN coupled with its diversity (7 configurations of 6,000 training problems each) makes it a challenging and valuable resource for the development of models that do not require verbose data, and lies at the centre of this paper's investigation.

The neural baselines introduced in these papers [20,28] are both variations on the ResNet architecture [10], employing convolutional and pooling operations with skip connections to perform feature extraction over the frames of a problem, before scoring and classifying via the softmax output of fully-connected layers. The baseline used in the PGM paper [20] – WReN – involves a third module in-between feature extraction and scoring stages, tasked with extracting relations between pairs of frames. Additionally, instead of feeding in all 16 frames of a given problem as separate channels, the convolutional encoder first embeds each frame independently, allowing the relational module to work with position-invariant embeddings. Finally, WReN differs from the baseline used in RAVEN in that it assembles sequences of 9 frames (8 context + a given answer) to be scored; classification in this network is therefore explicitly the answer frame that completed the most suitable, or highest scoring, assemblage of frames.

Interestingly, WReN outperforms its ResNet baselines on the PGM set, yet performs very poorly on RAVEN, which is thought to be due to the lack of both suitability to diverse configurations and of the sheer amount of data necessary to see convergence [28]. Meanwhile, the RAVEN paper reports reasonable performance from ResNet, yet provides us with unintuitive results. For example, the model achieves better accuracy when frames contain objects in a 3×3 grid, than when they appear in a 2×2 grid; the former is conceivably a more difficult problem. Stranger still, encapsulating such grids with another shape results in a performance boost (13.58ppt) despite providing added complexity. These are important tensions to resolve, and have prompted several follow-up papers.

The CoPINet model, introduced by Zhang et al. [29], achieves impressive results on both RAVEN and PGM datasets, yet, results on the former display the same inconsistency between tasks as in the original paper; further analysis is unfortunately absent. Additionally, CoPINet's ability to generalise between the configurations in RAVEN is not measured. Zheng et al. [30] demonstrate that a reinforcement-learned teacher model can be useful in guiding the training trajectory, yet also does not perform generalisation testing on RAVEN or PGM sets. Hahne et al. [9] substitute a more expressive Transformer network [25] in place of WReN's relational module to achieve highly competitive performance over PGM, yet crucially, their model does not converge without PGM's auxiliary training data. Over RAVEN, the model requires the larger RAVEN-50k to perform well, and generalisation performance is untested. Finally, Zhuo and Kankanhalli [31] follow closely the methodology of the original RAVEN paper, replicating generalisation experiments and reporting less overfitting with a model pre-trained on ImageNet, yet do not demonstrate the suitability of such a method over PGM. In this paper, we begin to resolve these issues by discovering and rectifying a critical shortcoming of the RAVEN set and methodology, and by introducing models that generalise well without requiring auxiliary data.

The ability for a single method to perform when given OOD input in the same domain, and to be able to be fit to different domains, ought to be staple in RPM solvers. Such problems have a legacy in intelligence testing because analogical reasoning – the ability to conceptually link familiar objects and scenes to those less familiar – is central to general intelligence [13], and is required in their solution. Analyses of solvers presented with exhaustive training and overly-familiar test data may therefore, be slightly misplaced in their efforts.

2.2 Disentanglement and Scene Decomposition

Crucial to our ability to navigate a visual world – let alone solve RPM problems – is learning to perceive scenes at the correct level of abstraction. In the field of representation learning, automatically collapsing visual input to a latent space of factors is largely achieved by convolutional networks. Yet, there is another important consideration in ensuring these latents represent the kind of individual, generative factors that might lend themselves to abstract reasoning; we need to encourage them to be *disentangled*, i.e. largely independent of each other. The acquisition of such generative factors is thought to be key in facilitating the comparison of objects and scenes [11], and is demonstrated to aid abstract reasoning tasks [24] and improve performance on PGM [23].

In the disentanglement literature, methods based on variational auto-encoders (VAEs) are ubiquitous [3,12,15], usually aiming to maximise the evidence lower bound (ELBO), $\mathcal{L}(\theta, \phi)$:

$$\mathcal{L}(\theta, \phi) = \mathbb{E}_{q_\phi(z)}[\log p_\theta(x|z)] - KL(q_\phi(z|x)||p(z)) \tag{1}$$

To get there, let us first consider a generative model for images:

$$p_\theta(x) = \int p_\theta(x|z)p(z)dz \tag{2}$$

where latent vectors are sampled from $p(z)$. This computation is usually intractable, so VAEs instead model $\log p_\theta(x)$ as:

$$\log p_\theta(x) = \mathcal{L}(\theta, \phi) + KL(q_\phi(z|x)||p(z|x)) \tag{3}$$

using an autoencoder network, with an encoder trained to output vectors for the mean and standard deviation, μ and σ, of each latent factor in z. By then sampling z as parameterised by the encoder, the expected value of $p_\theta(x|z)$ is modelled by the decoder network, and the ELBO becomes a matter of minimising both reconstruction error and the divergence between the distribution of z as parameterised and as expected (usually, Normal). In this way, the latent space is pushed towards being an information-rich bottleneck that allows for smooth interpolation between samples.

Recently, there have been several techniques – also commonly using VAEs – in performing unsupervised scene decomposition; learning to perceive scenes

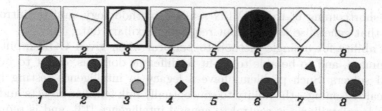

Fig. 2. Two example answer sets from problems in RAVEN. We can derive the correct answer (emboldened) from each set by finding the intersection of the set's modes of shape, colour, and scale factors. Essentially, "which frame has the most common features?" (Color figure online)

with an inductive bias for identifying discrete objects [2, 5, 6, 8]. These techniques seek to represent a scene using a given number of object slots, yet often over-rely on colour as a decomposition cue, and underperform when given monochrome data; Attend-Infer-Repeat (AIR) [6] is an exception. AIR can be thought of as an iterative VAE, and achieves this decomposition by chunking a given image into segments via a spatial transformer network [14] (*attend*), encoding these segments into embeddings (*infer*), and decoding and reassembles these embeddings into a reconstructed image. This occurs sequentially (*repeat*), one object at a time, until the image is satisfactorily represented. In this way, the spatial transformer network explicitly disentangles position and scale latents for each object attended to. We seek to leverage these abilities of AIR as a preprocessing step over the RAVEN dataset.

3   Preliminary Investigation

When re-training ResNet on the RAVEN set, we observed premature overfitting, which we were able to correct with spatial dropout across all convolutional layers. Surprisingly, to our knowledge, only one other paper has mentioned this [31]; they instead pre-train using Imagenet to help mitigate such overfitting. Upon rectifying this, we realised that sufficiently powerful models could inadvertently exploit a statistical bias in the dataset, introduced by the sampling scheme used by the authors to generate the answer set of each problem. Note the following excerpt from the original paper:

> "To break the correct relationships, we find an attribute that is constrained by a rule... and vary it. By modifying only one attribute, we could greatly reduce the computation. Such modification also increases the difficulty of the problem." [28]

While this is an effective way of providing a challenging set with many plausible answers, it also provides a method of locating an answer context-blind. In other words, correct answers might simply be found by locating the mode over answer attributes, without even seeing the context frames. In Fig. 2, we demonstrate that this is a simple enough strategy to be utilised by hand. To test this hypothesis, we trained models on the answer frames alone. In an unbiased set, the theoretical performance of such a model should be no greater than that of random selection in the long run; 12.5%, given a choice of 8 answer frames. On our solver, we were able to achieve an accuracy above 90%, averaged across all 7 problem configurations. Given that such performance over RAVEN is competitive with most current models, we confirm this as a significant issue potentially affecting a number of previous works.

This also impacts the reported generalisation ability of past methods; in our tests, locating the mode of a given answer set appears to be a skill that can be attained from one task and transferred to others, and we believe it to be an operation easy to acquire by the 1D convolutional module of our Rel-Base architecture (Sect. 4), given its task of finding local patterns between frame features from the first stage.

We wish to note to the community that we believe RAVEN to be a strong asset to our research, and we commend the original authors for their contribution. For its continued use as it is currently released, however, we believe that methods must process answer frames independently of each other, perhaps in a fashion similar to WReN. Therefore, the evaluation within some papers ([30], benchmarking WReN in [29]) should still be correct, as their architectures already enforce this independent processing. Unfortunately, in [29], the model-level contrast summarizes common features within the answer set, and therefore misses this independence requirement. [31] also follows the methodology of [28]. This is of critical importance for the ongoing use of this dataset.

4 Architectures

In this section, we detail the three architectures benchmarked in this paper. The purpose of our ResNet model is to serve as an analogue to the original in [28], in order to revise the literature with an accurate baseline. Our two novel architectures, Rel-Base and Rel-AIR, build on this simple network by adding additional encoding stages.

4.1 ResNet Baseline

We use a 4-layer residual encoder with skip connections across pairs of layers, and stack frames into independent sequences – one per candidate answer – to be processed and scored. We borrow this design choice from [20], as it prohibits the model from comparing answers; this is in contrast to the original method, which processed all frames in a problem at once, one channel per frame. We set a kernel size of 7×7, stride 2, and spatial dropout ($p = 0.1$) on all layers. We visualise this method in Fig. 3.

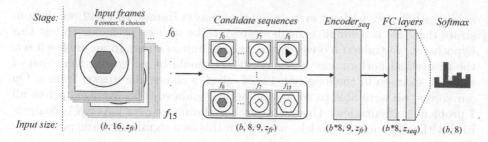

Fig. 3. Diagram of the basic method. Given a batch of b problems, $b*8$ candidate sequences are formed, independently encoded, and scored. For Rel-Base and Rel-AIR, frame embeddings of size z_{fr} are generated by additional stages. For ResNet, raw frames are used.

4.2   Frame-Relational ResNet (Rel-Base)

Improving on the baseline, Rel-Base encodes problems in two stages. The 4-layer encoder used in Sect. 4.1 first takes a batch of problems, embedding all frames individually. Embeddings are then stacked into candidate sequences as per the baseline method, and processed by a second encoder, consisting of 1D convolutional layers. In doing so, our model is able to learn a low-level perceptual process unaffected by the position of frames, and a higher-level that's tasked with modelling relationships by finding patterns in and between embeddings. Convolutional layers greatly reduce the number of weights compared to WReN's relation network [20], and we show them to be more data-efficient. Finally, Rel-Base does not require WReN's frame position vectors, as frame order is retained in the channel dimension.

4.3   Object-Relational ResNet (Rel-AIR)

To solve this problem of generalising between problem configurations in RAVEN – i.e. to correctly process unseen object arrangements – it seems necessary to disentangle objects from their placement in a scene. Our full architecture, Rel-AIR, makes use of an initial unsupervised scene decomposition stage, AIR [6], which provides an object-centric inductive bias. This is trained as a cascade architecture; AIR is first fit to the different configurations in RAVEN to extract objects, providing the training data for successive stages. Rel-AIR has five stages in total (see Fig. 4 for a depiction of the first four):

1. **Scene decomposition.** The AIR module is tasked with observing all problem frames, and learning to decompose them into N object slots (with N being a predefined maximum, e.g. 9 slots for the 3×3 `Grid` configuration). Each 1-channel frame is therefore recorded as an N-channel image tensor, and an N-channel latent tensor detailing scales and x,y positions. In our experiments, we store both the contents of the attention windows and their reconstructions; while either can be loaded to train the following steps, we typically use attention windows. These slots are shuffled.

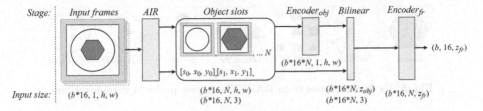

Fig. 4. Frame encoding in Rel-AIR. The AIR stage decomposes frames into a maximum N constituent objects and their associated scales and x,y positions; s_n, x_n, y_n. Second and third, each object is embedded (size z_{obj}), and processed via a bilinear layer to incorporate latent data. Finally, each frame's object embeddings are convolved together, resulting in overall frame embeddings.

2. **Independent object embedding.** The 2D residual encoder then accepts a batch of objects and encodes them independently.
3. **Latent-informed object embedding.** The object embeddings from the previous stage are paired with their original scale and position latents, and a final conditional embedding is created by passing this paired data through a bilinear layer, in order to unify the two sources.
4. **Object-relational feature extraction.** The batch of object embeddings is reshaped into frames of N object channels, which is passed through a 1D residual encoder to generate the frame embeddings.
5. **Frame-relational feature extraction and scoring.** Finally, as with Rel-Base, these embeddings are stacked into sequences, encoded, and scored by fully-connected layers.

It is important to note that shuffling frames along the object dimension is critical to this model learning to make use of position and scale data, as we observed a strong correlation between the order of slots and their positions in the original image from AIR. Additionally, this shuffling operation promotes generalisation to problem configurations containing more objects than those trained on; without shuffling, only the first few frame channels would contain a signal, prohibiting the object-relational encoder from learning to use all channels.

5   Experiments

To evaluate the performance of our models, we make use of the aforementioned PGM and RAVEN datasets to test both overall (all tasks) and generalisation (cross-task) performance. To our knowledge, and given our findings in Sect. 3, only the WReN [29] and LEN [30] benchmarks for image-only RAVEN remain reliable in the literature. We train the three models described in the previous section, and use the same hyperparameters across both datasets. For reproducibility, we provide full details of these parameters in our supplementary mate-

Center   2x2Grid   3x3Grid   Left-Right   Up-Down   Out-InCenter   Out-InGrid

Fig. 5. Example frames from RAVEN's diverse problem configurations.

rial. Our code extends the official RAVEN public implementation[1], and is also available online.[2] Models are implemented in PyTorch [18] and Pyro [1].

5.1 Data

In addition to the commonly tested *neutral* set in PGM – containing 1.4 million samples with a 7:1 train-test split – we also use its challenging *extrapolation* set to more rigorously test model generalisation. To test performance over RAVEN-10k, we first train and test each model on the full set (consisting of all problem configurations; see Fig. 5), before fitting models to individual configurations. We do not make use of the provided auxiliary information, we restrict image size to 80×80, or half-size, on both datasets, normalise pixel values to [0,1], and invert the dataset (to white shapes on black) so that the networks receive signal for shapes, not for the in-between space. Finally, we ensure training sets are shuffled, and make use of the same answer-set shuffling strategy as in [29].

5.2 Results on PGM

General Performance. We evaluate the overall accuracy of our first novel architecture, Rel-Base, using PGM *neutral*, and detail the results against existing image-only methods in Table 1. From this we notice exceptional performance; Rel-Base outperforms not only existing image-only models, but all models trained with the benefit of auxiliary data (excepting [9,30], which achieve an extra 3ppt). This is an important result, as most other architectures are reasonably complex and specifically designed for RPM-style problem solving. Rel-Base instead offers a method that is agnostic to the problem setup, and can theoretically accommodate more general multiple-choice visual problems by changing the parameters of its stack function. Regarding data and training efficiency; we wish to also note that after a single epoch of training, Rel-Base reaches an average accuracy of 58.07%, exceeding what is reported by a fully-trained CoPINet.

While the Rel-AIR model is created specifically to improve performance across problem configurations, and therefore not benchmarked on PGM, we nonetheless preview the ability of AIR to decompose complex PGM scenes. In Fig. 6, with two object slots, we notice that entities such as large background shapes and lines are separated from those that fall on the 3×3 grid, which is an encouraging preliminary result for future research.

---

[1] https://github.com/WellyZhang/RAVEN.
[2] https://github.com/SvenShade/Rel-AIR.

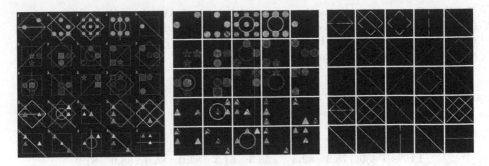

Fig. 6. AIR decomposes PGM frames (left) into grid and background slots (centre, right). Red bounding boxes denote attention windows for the first slot. (Color figure online)

Table 1. Accuracy (%) of various models over neutral and extrapolation sets in PGM. LEN* and LEN** refer to the two-stream and two-stream with teacher model variants of LEN, respectively, as detailed in [30].

PGM set	Wild-ResNet [20]	WReN	CoPINet [29]	LEN	LEN*	LEN**	Rel-Base
Neutral	48.00	62.60	56.37	68.10	70.30	85.10	**85.50**
Extrapolation	N/A	17.20	N/A	N/A	N/A	N/A	**22.05**

Extrapolation Performance. We also test Rel-Base over PGM *extrapolation*, since to our knowledge, the literature has no other image-only model benchmarks for this task. We also want to verify that Rel-Base can exceed WReN here too, if we are to suggest that convolutional layers can be more widely adept at relational reasoning than WReN's explicitly relational architecture, e.g. pairwise operations over embeddings. We report these results in Table 1. From this, while we confirm the ability of Rel-Base to better generalise to the unseen factors in this set, we believe that properly handling this sort of extrapolation is a substantial research task that will require its own specific inductive bias, which is outside of the scope of this paper. Yet, between both PGM sets, this strongly suggests that no utility is lost in the simpler architecture of Rel-Base.

5.3 Results on RAVEN

General Performance. We evaluate the overall accuracy of each of the three architectures, ResNet, Rel-Base and Rel-AIR, trained on the full RAVEN-10k set, alongside other image-only models, WReN [29], LEN and LEN+T [30]. We detail the results in Table 2, in which we demonstrate Rel-Base to be the first model to consistently exceed human-level performance on this task. Our full architecture, Rel-AIR, makes further improvements, beating the previous state-of-the-art [30] by 15.8ppt.

Table 2. Performance results of various models on the RAVEN set. We report accuracy (%) both averaged across all configurations, and all excluding O-IG, in the second and third columns. L-R, U-D, O-IC and O-IG denote `Left-Right`, `Up-Down`, `Out-InCentre`, and `Out-InGrid` configurations, respectively.

Method	Acc	Centre	2 × 2	3 × 3	L-R	U-D	O-IC	O-IG
WReN [29]	17.9	15.4	29.8	32.9	11.1	11.0	11.1	14.5
ResNet	34.5	41.7	34.1	38.5	33.4	31.7	34.6	27.3
LEN [30]	72.9	80.2	57.5	62.1	73.5	81.2	84.4	71.5
LEN+T [30]	78.3	82.3	58.5	64.3	87.0	85.5	88.9	81.9
Human [28]	84.4	95.5	81.8	79.6	86.4	81.8	86.4	81.8
Rel-Base	91.7	97.6	85.9	86.9	93.5	96.5	97.6	83.8
Rel-AIR	**94.1**	**99.0**	**92.4**	**87.1**	**98.7**	**97.9**	**98.0**	**85.3**

Table 3. Accuracy (%) of models over RAVEN, given various training set sizes. Accuracy is averaged over all problem configurations.

% of training set	ResNet	Rel-Base	Rel-AIR
10	14.79	24.40	**51.39**
25	21.48	52.24	**81.07**
100	34.51	91.66	**94.10**

Performance vs. Training Set Size. As in [29], we also explore model performance as a function of training set size, in order to further evaluate the efficiency of our methods. Table 3 reveals that, even with only 10% of the training data, Rel-AIR outperforms a fully-trained ResNet baseline. We believe Rel-AIR's strong performance is attributable to the AIR module's disambiguation of scene structure, alleviating the diversity of problem configurations by first resolving them to object lists.

Generalisation Across Configurations. Finally, in order to properly test the ability of these networks to generalise, we replicate the format of Tables 4 and 5 in the RAVEN paper [28] and train all three methods on the following configuration regimes:

- Train on `Left-Right` and test on `Up-Down`, and vice-versa. As these configurations represent the transpose of the other, we expect models that have learned to understand notions of objects and object relationships to display reasonable transfer learning.
- Train on 2 × 2 `Grid` and test on 3 × 3 `Grid`, and vice-versa. Here, we're interested in the ability of models to apply knowledge across problems with fewer or more objects than they are familiar with.

Table 4. Generalisation test between `Left-Right` and `Up-Down` configurations. Rows and columns indicate training and test sets respectively.

	Left-Right			Up-Down		
	ResNet	Rel-Base	Rel-AIR	ResNet	Rel-Base	Rel-AIR
Left-Right	27.83	90.09	**98.07**	3.71	32.71	**66.77**
Up-Down	2.98	22.61	**60.81**	26.42	90.23	**94.84**

Table 5. Generalisation test between 2×2 `Grid` and 3×3 `Grid` configurations. Rows and columns indicate training and test sets respectively.

	2×2 Grid			3×3 Grid		
	ResNet	Rel-Base	Rel-AIR	ResNet	Rel-Base	Rel-AIR
2×2 Grid	26.32	60.16	**88.24**	13.96	41.55	**67.01**
3×3 Grid	14.36	34.03	**61.90**	33.84	68.16	**82.54**

It is important to note that we employed early stopping given validation performance *on the set to be generalised to*. Continued training adversely affected ResNet's performance, while Rel-AIR was least affected. Tables 4 and 5 detail our results. Firstly, we notice that Rel-Base and Rel-AIR both achieve accuracies significantly above baseline, indicating a strong ability to learn from limited data. Additionally, Rel-AIR displays a much higher proficiency in this task overall, often doubling the generalisation performance of Rel-Base. We also notice that ResNet performs much lower than random chance when generalising between `Left-Right` and `Up-Down`; interestingly, its average generalisation performance rises to just above random (13.65%), and dips when train and test configurations were the same (18.48%), when we didn't first invert the data. We imagine this is due to there being very little signal crossover between these configurations when images are white shapes on a black background; `Left-Right` and `Up-Down` objects scarcely overlap, and so the model overfits catastrophically.

As a simple ablation study, we also trained a position-blind Rel-AIR, replacing the bilinear layer with a linear layer. We notice that performance on both `Left-Right` and `Up-Down` configurations – and generalisation between them – falls to around 43% ± 3; this is an intuitive result given the added ambiguity, since two populated object slots can refer to two different frames if the positions are unknown (e.g. a square on the left and triangle on the right, or vice-versa).

6   Discussion

Our first experimental outcome is the strong performance of Rel-Base in both datasets, which challenges the design philosophy of other work in this area, and hints at hidden ability in simpler, general purpose architectures. The second major outcome is Rel-AIR's ability to train and generalise even from a single task, which we accept as evidence in favour of its object-centric inductive bias.

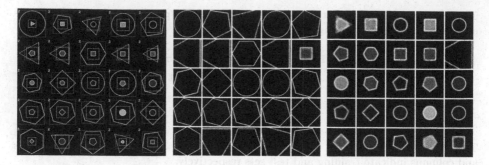

Fig. 7. Visualisation of AIR's decomposition of `Out-InCentre` frames (left) into two slots (centre, right). Bounding boxes denote attention windows.

There are some weaknesses that ought to be stated for the purposes of future work. As visualised in Fig. 7, AIR sometimes clips large objects (usually triangles) – and while this didn't become an issue in testing, it still means the later stages of Rel-AIR receive sometimes inconsistent representations. This does become an issue with more advanced scenes, as we found out with `Out-InGrid`; AIR struggles to correctly decompose scenes with objects across significant size differences, and this isn't solved by simply increasing the scale prior's standard deviation. Instead, the centre grid is always encoded as a single 'grid object', which is an understandable abstraction, given the module has no prior understanding of shapes, and optimises for scene sparsity. Encouragingly, a number of recent papers have reportedly made progress on the robustness of AIR [4,22,26]; we expect that such improvements will minimise the need to fine-tune AIR between configurations.

Another point worth mentioning is that, while the relational module never sees the type of task it is asked to generalise to, the AIR stage is pre-trained on each task. We believe this legitimises generalisation performance; as long as Rel-AIR remains blind to problems with novel arrangements of objects, it can be said to generalise its reasoning to them. As a future direction, the AIR stage might be trained by a scene generator that returns random arrangements of objects, which in turn, ought to aid with the 'grid object' failure case by providing increased diversity.

Finally, like other recent decomposition models [2,8], Rel-AIR needs to be trained with the maximum number of object channels expected in a scene. This makes training over the full RAVEN set inefficient, as most tasks include far less than a full grid of 3 × 3 objects. Forming scene graphs (e.g. [27]) to be encoded via graph neural networks [21] represents a possible direction in handling the variable length outputs of AIR without padding them.

7   Conclusion

In this work, we have strived to enable neural vision models to perceive and compare abstract visual scenes in ways that permit generalisation between problem configurations. First, we navigated a critical issue arising from the answer-set sampling strategy in RAVEN, prompting our re-evaluation. We proceeded to show via a relatively general-purpose network, Rel-Base, that convolutional layers can learn to extract relational features more capably than existing architectures involving explicit relational operations. We have also shown that providing an object-centric inductive bias – via an unsupervised scene decomposition stage – makes further improvement over Rel-Base in generalising over RAVEN. Finally, models introduced in this paper set state-of-the-art performance over both RAVEN and PGM datasets, despite the added challenges of using downscaled images and no auxiliary data, and invite a number of future directions at the intersection of scene decomposition and abstract reasoning.

References

1. Bingham, E., et al.: Pyro: deep universal probabilistic programming. J. Mach. Learn. Res. **20**(1), 973–978 (2018)
2. Burgess, C.P., et al.: MONet: unsupervised scene decomposition and representation. arXiv preprint arXiv:1901.11390 (2019)
3. Chen, T.Q., Li, X., Grosse, R.B., Duvenaud, D.K.: Isolating sources of disentanglement in variational autoencoders. In: Advances in Neural Information Processing Systems, pp. 2610–2620 (2018)
4. Crawford, E., Pineau, J.: Spatially invariant unsupervised object detection with convolutional neural networks. In: Proceedings of the AAAI Conference on Artificial Intelligence, vol. 33, pp. 3412–3420 (2019)
5. Engelcke, M., Kosiorek, A.R., Jones, O.P., Posner, I.: Genesis: generative scene inference and sampling with object-centric latent representations. arXiv preprint arXiv:1907.13052 (2019)
6. Eslami, S.A., Heess, N., Weber, T., Tassa, Y., Szepesvari, D., Hinton, G.E., et al.: Attend, infer, repeat: fast scene understanding with generative models. In: Advances in Neural Information Processing Systems, pp. 3225–3233 (2016)
7. Gentner, D., Markman, A.B.: Structure mapping in analogy and similarity. Am. Psychol. **52**(1), 45 (1997)
8. Greff, K., et al.: Multi-object representation learning with iterative variational inference. arXiv preprint arXiv:1903.00450 (2019)
9. Hahne, L., Lüddecke, T., Wörgötter, F., Kappel, D.: Attention on abstract visual reasoning. arXiv preprint arXiv:1911.05990 (2019)
10. He, K., Zhang, X., Ren, S., Sun, J.: Deep residual learning for image recognition. In: Proceedings of the IEEE Conference on Computer Vision and Pattern Recognition, pp. 770–778 (2016)
11. Higgins, I., et al.: Early visual concept learning with unsupervised deep learning. arXiv preprint arXiv:1606.05579 (2016)
12. Higgins, I., et al.: beta-VAE: learning basic visual concepts with a constrained variational framework. ICLR **2**(5), 6 (2017)
13. Hofstadter, D.R.: Analogy as the core of cognition. The Analogical Mind: Perspect. Cogn. Sci. 499–538 (2001)
14. Jaderberg, M., Simonyan, K., Zisserman, A., et al.: Spatial transformer networks. In: Advances in Neural Information Processing Systems, pp. 2017–2025 (2015)
15. Kim, H., Mnih, A.: Disentangling by factorising. In: International Conference on Machine Learning, pp. 2649–2658 (2018)

16. Lovett, A., Forbus, K.: Modeling visual problem solving as analogical reasoning. Psychol. Rev. **124**(1), 60 (2017)
17. McCarthy, J., Minsky, M., Rochester, N., Shannon, C.: A proposal for the dartmouth summer research project on artificial intelligence (1955). Reprinted online at http://www-formal.stanford.edu/jmc/history/dartmouth/dartmouth.html (2018)
18. Paszke, A., et al.: Automatic differentiation in PyTorch. In: NIPS-W (2017)
19. Raven, J.: The Raven's progressive matrices: change and stability over culture and time. Cogn. Psychol. **41**(1), 1–48 (2000)
20. Santoro, A., Hill, F., Barrett, D., Morcos, A., Lillicrap, T.: Measuring abstract reasoning in neural networks. In: International Conference on Machine Learning, pp. 4477–4486 (2018)
21. Schlichtkrull, M., Kipf, T.N., Bloem, P., van den Berg, R., Titov, I., Welling, M.: Modeling relational data with graph convolutional networks. In: Gangemi, A., et al. (eds.) ESWC 2018. LNCS, vol. 10843, pp. 593–607. Springer, Cham (2018). https://doi.org/10.1007/978-3-319-93417-4_38
22. Stanić, A., Schmidhuber, J.: R-SQAIR: relational sequential attend, infer, repeat. arXiv preprint arXiv:1910.05231 (2019)
23. Steenbrugge, X., Leroux, S., Verbelen, T., Dhoedt, B.: Improving generalization for abstract reasoning tasks using disentangled feature representations. arXiv preprint arXiv:1811.04784 (2018)
24. van Steenkiste, S., Locatello, F., Schmidhuber, J., Bachem, O.: Are disentangled representations helpful for abstract visual reasoning? In: Advances in Neural Information Processing Systems, pp. 14222–14235 (2019)
25. Vaswani, A., et al.: Attention is all you need. In: Advances in Neural Information Processing Systems, pp. 5998–6008 (2017)
26. Wang, D., Jamnik, M., Lio, P.: Unsupervised and interpretable scene discovery with discrete-attend-infer-repeat. arXiv preprint arXiv:1903.06581 (2019)
27. Yang, J., Lu, J., Lee, S., Batra, D., Parikh, D.: Graph R-CNN for scene graph generation. In: Proceedings of the European Conference on Computer Vision (ECCV), pp. 670–685 (2018)
28. Zhang, C., Gao, F., Jia, B., Zhu, Y., Zhu, S.C.: RAVEN: a dataset for relational and analogical visual reasoning. In: Proceedings of the IEEE Conference on Computer Vision and Pattern Recognition, pp. 5317–5327 (2019)
29. Zhang, C., Jia, B., Gao, F., Zhu, Y., Lu, H., Zhu, S.C.: Learning perceptual inference by contrasting. In: Advances in Neural Information Processing Systems, pp. 1073–1085 (2019)
30. Zheng, K., Zha, Z.J., Wei, W.: Abstract reasoning with distracting features. In: Advances in Neural Information Processing Systems, pp. 5834–5845 (2019)
31. Zhuo, T., Kankanhalli, M.: Solving Raven's progressive matrices with neural networks. arXiv preprint arXiv:2002.01646 (2020)

Supervised Edge Attention Network for Accurate Image Instance Segmentation

Xier Chen, Yanchao Lian, Licheng Jiao$^{(\boxtimes)}$ ⓘ, Haoran Wang, YanJie Gao, and Shi Lingling

School of Artificial Intelligence, Xidian University, Xian 710071, Shaanxi, China
{xechen,yclian}@stu.xidian.edu.cn, lchjiao@mail.xidian.edu.cn

Abstract. Effectively keeping boundary of the mask complete is important in instance segmentation. In this task, many works segment instance based on a bounding box from the box head, which means the quality of the detection also affects the completeness of the mask. To circumvent this issue, we propose a fully convolutional box head and a supervised edge attention module in mask head. The box head contains one new IoU prediction branch. It learns association between object features and detected bounding boxes to provide more accurate bounding boxes for segmentation. The edge attention module utilizes attention mechanism to highlight object and suppress background noise, and a supervised branch is devised to guide the network to focus on the edge of instances precisely. To evaluate the effectiveness, we conduct experiments on COCO dataset. Without bells and whistles, our approach achieves impressive and robust improvement compared to baseline models. Code is at https://github.com//IPIU-detection/SEANet.

Keywords: Fully convolutional box head · Supervised edge attention module · IoU prediction branch · Instance segmentation

1 Introduction

Instance segmentation is a hotspot task in computer vision, whose goal is to segment and classify the pixels belonging to instance objects in an image. Despite great advances have been achieved in recent years, how to keep the boundary of the instance intact still remains challenging due to three problems: imprecise bounding box, blurry boundary and cluttered overlap.

Instance segmentation methods mainly include detection-based and segmentation-based methods. Detection-based methods [8,9,22] use the detector to find and classify the possible bounding boxes of the instance firstly, and then perform the foreground and background segmentation on the pixels in these boxes. Segmentation-based methods [1,2,21] segment the whole image firstly, and then distinguish the object instances from it. This paper mainly discusses the former one, and analyzes problems in two phases of this kind of methods.

X. Chen and Y. Lian – Contribute equally to this work.

© Springer Nature Switzerland AG 2020
A. Vedaldi et al. (Eds.): ECCV 2020, LNCS 12372, pp. 617–631, 2020.
https://doi.org/10.1007/978-3-030-58583-9_37

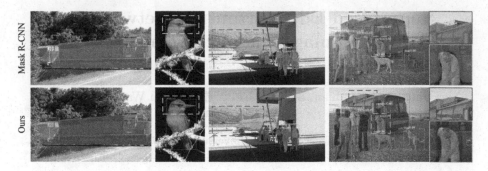

Fig. 1. Baseline Mask R-CNN (top) vs. Ours (bottom) with ResNet-101-FPN. Our approach is more adaptive for scales of objects and more sensitive on their boundaries (best viewed in color) (Color figure online)

In the first phase, the quality of the bounding box is important as the base of segmentation. The results of the Mask R-CNN [9] are visualized for illustration. As shown in the first picture of Fig. 1, the tail of the train is not included in the bounding box, resulting in its tail boundary not being segmented. The similar situation also occurs in the second picture, and the mask at the top of the bird is affected by the imperfect bounding box. In order to improve the performance of bounding box regression, fully convolution network is proposed to break the limitation of the fixed anchor sizes and scales [14,25,28]. The technique predicts the classification and regression pixel by pixel. However, the classification score obtained from the box head shows no important interaction to the quality of the regression result.

Motivated by the considerations above, we propose a new branch named "B-IoU" based on the fully convolutional box head. It predicts the Intersection-over-Union (IoU) scores between the detected boxes and their ground-truth boxes. By multiplying the classification scores with IoU scores, we get the final score for each detected box. Through choosing the detected box with the highest score on each proposal from Region Proposal Network (RPN) [23], we expect to get the most accurate detected result for each proposal.

In the second phase, segmentation on the object boundary may fail for two reasons: (1) the information of edges of the objects is easily disturbed by background noise; (2) different instances are often close to each other or overlapped, and their features of the edge regions will interact with each other during convolution operation. In order to improve the discrimination ability, recently attention mechanisms are increasingly used in segmentation networks [6,16,27] to pay attention to the information of the objects. However, the available methods only focus on the correlation of internal features of the object and do not emphasize edge features. As shown in the last two pictures of Fig. 1, the wing and tail surface of the airplane in the third one are spindly and the colors of them are similar with the ground and mountain. And in the last picture, the top edge of the bus almost merges with the sky and the people are overlapped, leading to the segmentation on the edge of them unsatisfactory.

To solve above-mentioned problems, we propose the edge attention modules to suppress useless information and highlight boundary features. Especially, we apply a supervision branch on the module to guide the network to learn the right information on the boundaries of the instances.

The second row of Fig. 1 shows the results of the Mask R-CNN equipped with our techniques. The results of the first two pictures show that regardless of the shapes and scales of the objects, more accurate detection bounding boxes are obtained, which has a direct effect on the performance of segmentation. Moreover, for the challenging scenes in the last two pictures, the boundaries of the instances, especially at the wing and tail surface of the airplane, the top of the bus and the boundary between person and bus, are segmented more subtly and correctly.

In this paper, we propose one new branch named "B-IoU" and supervised edge attention module for instance segmentation. Our main contributions are summarized as follows:

1. We take into consideration the quality of the bounding box in instance segmentation task. We apply fully convolutional box head and introduce a new branch name "B-IoU" to learn the IoU scores between the detected bounding boxes and their corresponding ground-truth boxes for down-weighting the low-quality detected bounding boxes with poor regression performance.
2. As the boundaries of the instances are easily overwhelmed by the background noise or other objects, we propose supervised edge attention module to suppress the noise and highlight the foreground. Especially, we design a supervised branch to guide the network to learn the boundaries of the objects.
3. Without bells and whistles, our approach consistently improves the models of Mask R-CNN series, and is no limited to these models. Since the idea of our work is easily implemented and can improve both the accuracy of detection and segmentation, it can be extended to other principles for instance-level recognition tasks.

2 Related Work

2.1 Instance Segmentation

Instance segmentation is the task of labeling different instance regions in the pixel-level, which is divided into two categories: segmentation-based and detection-based.

Segmentation-based methods are to first segment and then detect. BIS [1] uses CRF [15] to find instances. SIS [2] introduces metric learning, and completes segmentation with clustering. SOIS [21] uses semi-convolutional operation for instance segmentation.

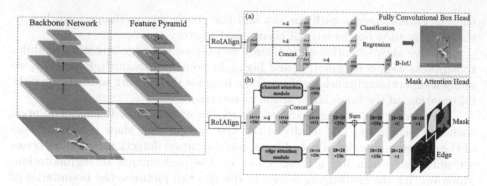

Fig. 2. The model structure of SEANet. The Feature Pyramid Network (FPN) extract the features of the input image. RoIAlign operation obtains feature map of each proposal from RPN. For each proposal, (a) fully convolutional box head and (b) mask attention head perform object detection and instance segmentation in parallel

The other idea for instance segmentation, called detection-based method, is to first detect and then segment. These methods use bounding boxes as the preliminary results, and then estimate region masks in the boxes. The Facebook Research Institute proposes Deep Mask [22], which is based on the object proposals generated by discriminative convolutional network. ISFCN [3] uses FCN [20] to generate object proposals with the help of a sliding window. He et al. proposes Mask R-CNN [9] consisting of a box head and a mask head for detection and segmentation respectively, which achieves better results in instance-level segmentation. Mask R-CNN inspires many other algorithms as a benchmark framework. Based on it, Mask Scoring R-CNN (MS R-CNN) [11] proposes a MaskIoU head to generate IoU scores to describe the qualities of masks. It combines the features of instances in mask head with the corresponding predicted masks. However, in addition to prioritizing when evaluating, the IoU scores have no substantial impact on improving the quality of the mask itself. Different from MS R-CNN, we design a B-IoU branch in box head to produce IoU scores. The IoU scores are used to obtain more precise bounding boxes so as to improve the performance of instance segmentation.

2.2 Object Detection

For the detection-based instance segmentation methods, the quality of object detection is particularly important. Faster R-CNN [23] is the base framework of Mask R-CNN, which is a widely used two-stage network. It first generates Regions of Interest (RoIs) through the RPN, and then performs further classification and regression operations on the proposals. Considering that the predicted classification confidence cannot represent the quality of the location, IoU-Net [12] proposes location confidences to predict the IoUs between detected bounding boxes and corresponding ground-truth boxes. But the IoU head in IoU-Net is parallel with the box head, which makes no full use of the information from the regression branch. Moreover, most two-stage detectors, including IoU-Net, implement detection in the proposal level instead of the pixel level, which limits the representation of the network. FCOS [25] perform pixel-by-pixel classification and regression prediction on feature maps, and introduces a new branch called "center-ness" to suppress the low-quality bounding box. In comparison, our fully convolutional box head combines information of the high-level regression feature and the low-level RoI feature to infer IoU score for each detected box. In this way, it identifies the quality of bounding box more accurately so as to improve the quality of mask.

2.3   Attention Mechanism

Attention mechanism has been widely used in the field of computer vision. SENet [10] uses squeeze module and association module to obtain the importance of each feature channel automatically. CBAM [26] uses feature-channel attention similar to SENet with additional feature-space attention. GSoP-Net [7] proposes 2D-average-pooling, which applies channel attention in the form of covariance. DANet [6] proposes position and channel attention modules, which focus on the correlation of semantic features of each position and channel. In this paper, we take advantage of the attention mechanism and propose two modules. Different from the methods above, we focus on the object boundary and design a supervised branch which utilizes explicit information to achieve it.

3   Our Approach

In this section, we first present the framework of our Supervised Edge Attention Network for Accurate Image Instance Segmentation (SEANet), then introduce the two techniques and the loss function. We take the Mask R-CNN as an example. As shown in Fig. 2, the fully convolutional box head is employed in the detection branch to obtain the appropriate bounding box for segmentation and the supervised attention module is added to the original mask head.

3.1   Fully Convolutional Box Head

Different from many box heads of the anchor-based methods, which output the class and offset result for each proposal using fully connection layers, our fully convolutional box head focuses on information of each pixel on the proposal. The structure is shown in Fig. 2(a). For each location (x, y) on the feature map of each candidate box after RoIAlign, an 80-D classification score C, a 4-D bounding box regression $B = (l, t, r, b)$ and a 1-D box IoU score I are given by the fully convolutional box head. Here, l, t, r and b represent the distances from the location (x, y) to the left, top, right and bottom sides of the detected bounding box respectively.

Given a proposal $P = (x_0, y_0, x_1, y_1)$ from RPN module, the corresponding location of (x, y) on the input image is expressed as (X, Y):

$$X = x_0 + x\frac{W_p}{l} + \frac{W_p}{2l}, Y = y_0 + y\frac{H_p}{l} + \frac{H_p}{2l} \tag{1}$$

Here, W_p and H_p are the width and height of the proposal. (x_0, y_0) and (x_1, y_1) denote the left-top and right-bottom coordinates of the proposal respectively. And l represents the size length of the feature map of the proposal after RoIAlign ($l = 7$ in this paper). For classification, if (X, Y) is inside any ground-truth bounding box, then corresponding (x, y) will be labeled as a positive sample and given a class label c^* as same as its corresponding ground truth. Otherwise, it is considered as a negative sample and its class label $c^* = 0$ for background.

For regression, each positive sample (x, y) has a regression target as $B^* = (l^*, t^*, r^*, b^*)$, which means the distances from its corresponding location (X, Y) to the four sides of its corresponding ground-truth bounding box.

In the test phase, for each proposal from RPN module, output of our fully convolutional box head is a set of detected bounding boxes and their corresponding classification scores. However, only one final detection result is expected for each proposal region. And as mentioned in the previous section, the misalignment between classification scores and the regression qualities harm the performance of the detection. Therefore, a powerful strategy should be adopted for choosing the best regression result from detected bounding boxes produced by all the locations on the proposal.

We introduce a meaningful branch called "B-IoU" head to predict the IoU value between the predicted bounding box and its associated ground-truth bounding box at each location on each proposal. The "B-IoU" branch combines the information of the proposal feature and the high-level semantic feature from the regression branch and output a more targeted and precise evaluation criteria for each bounding box by aligning the regression quality with box IoU scores. Here, the calculation of the targeted IoU scores for training is similar to GIoU [7], which presents a more precise measure of the IoU between the detected bounding box and the corresponding ground-truth box.

During inference, the IoU scores obtained from the B-IoU branch are multiplied with the classification scores from the classification branch to get the final scores which describe the qualities of the bounding boxes precisely in both the aspects of the classification and regression. And for each proposal, only the detected bounding box with the highest final score will be chosen as the detection result of this proposal and all the detection results of all the proposals will be ranked by the final scores so that the low-quality bounding boxes will be suppressed by Non-Maximum Suppression (NMS). Moreover, more accurate scores of the detection results will benefit to the COCO evaluation process and improve the performance of instance segmentation.

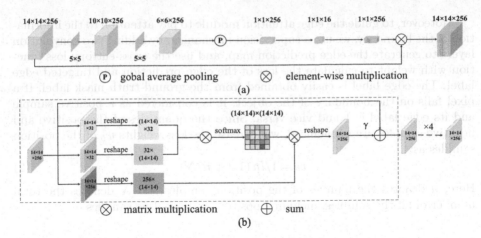

Fig. 3. Illustration of the attention modules. (a) The structure of the channel attention module. (b) The structure of the edge attention module. The part in the gridline is the position attention module in DANet

3.2   Supervised Attention Module

In order to weaken the non-object information and prevent the boundaries of the objects being blurred, we apply two attention modules to solve the problems in different aspects, as shown in the mask attention head of Fig. 2(b).

As shown in Fig. 3(a), we use a variant of Squeeze-and-Excitation (SE) block [10] as the channel attention module. And different from the rough Global Average Pooling (GAP) operation in SENet, we add two convolution layers with large convolution kernel (in this paper, the kernel size is 5) before GAP to get a bigger receptive field, which helps the network to achieve better discrimination for information of the foreground and background. The following procedure is similar to SE block and the value of reduction ratio is 16. The feature outputted by the channel attention module is then concatenated with the high-level feature of the mask head. In this way, the network fuses the low-level feature full of detailed information and the high-level feature full of semantic information.

As mentioned above, the pixels on the boundaries of the instances are hard to segment correctly because the features on these regions are easily blurred by the noise or other instances. In order to effectively learn the boundary features of the instances, we introduce a supervised edge attention module based on the position attention module in DANet [6]. As shown in Fig. 3(b), we add four convolution layers after the position attention module to get the edge attention feature on the nearly same depth as the feature that it will sum with on the mask head, which puts the two feature in an approximately equal data space and make the two feature more adaptive in the following element-wisely sum process. Then we add the up-sampled feature maps from the edge attention module and mask head together in the element-wise way to enhance features on the targeted positions, especially on the boundary of the instance.

Moreover, to guide the edge attention module to pay attention to the information of the boundary, we use a supervision mechanism by adding two convolution layers to generate the edge prediction map, and use the cross-entropy loss function with weight to calculate the loss of the edge prediction and targeted edge label. The edge label is easily obtained from the ground-truth mask label. If a pixel falls on the boundary of the object, it is considered as a positive sample and its edge label is 1 and vice versa. Since the quantities of the positive and negative samples are unbalanced, we increase the loss weights w_b of the position samples as:

$$w_b = 1/ln\,(1.2 + n/N) \tag{2}$$

Here, n denotes the number of the position samples and N denotes the total number of all the samples, including positive and negative samples.

3.3   Loss Function

We define the multi-task loss on each proposal as the sum of the losses from box head and mask head:

$$L = L_{box} + L_{seg} \tag{3}$$

where L_{box} includes three parts, that is:

$$L_{box}\,(c, B, I) = \lambda_1 L_{cls}(c, c^*) + \lambda_2 L_{reg}(B, B^*) + \lambda_3 L_{IoU}(I, I^*) \tag{4}$$

Here, L_{cls} is the focal loss for classification as in [18]. L_{reg} is the variant of GIoU loss in [24]. In origin GIoU loss, $L_{GIOU} = 1 - GIOU$ and presents anti-linear characteristic with GIoU values. In order to strengthen the hard sample learning, we use the logarithmic function to increase the losses for the samples whose GIoU values are very small.

$$L_{reg} = -\ln(\frac{GIoU + 1}{2}) \tag{5}$$

The predicted GIoU range from -1 to 1 so L_{IoU} is the l_2 loss for training. The loss of mask head L_{seg} combines two terms:

$$L_{seg} = \lambda_4 L_{mask} + \lambda_5 L_{edge} \tag{6}$$

Here, L_{mask} is the loss of the mask prediction which follows the same definition as [9]. The edge label is a binary map so we define L_{edge} as the Binary Cross-Entropy (BCE) loss.

4   Experiments

We perform experiments on the large-scale object detection and instance segmentation benchmark COCO [19] and we train our models on the 115K images in COCO 2017 train set and tested on the 5K images from the validation set for ablation study. We also report our results on the 20K images in *test-dev*.

Fig. 4. Visual results of our model in COCO *test-dev*

4.1   Evaluation Metrics

We use the standard evaluation metrics in COCO, i.e., AP, AP_{50}, AP_{75} for estimating the performance of our approach on detection and segmentation. Here, AP presents average precision value over IoU thresholds from 0.5 to 0.95 with an interval of 0.05. AP_{50}, AP_{75} denote average precision at IoU thresholds of 0.5 and 0.75, respectively. Since our model deal with both object detection and instance segmentation tasks, the box AP and mask AP are all reported. For mask AP, we show the AP^m, AP_{50}^m and AP_{75}^m and for box, the AP^b, AP_{50}^b and AP_{75}^b are given.

4.2   Training Details

For fair comparison, we re-implement the baseline methods Mask R-CNN and MS R-CNN on PyTorch. The hyper-parameters in our model follows which in Mask R-CNN. And we set 16 images in a training batch (2 images per GPU) and train with Stochastic Gradient Descent (SGD) for 24 epochs with an initial learning rate of 0.02 which is decreased by a factor of 10 at the epoch 16 and 22, respectively. We train on 8 NVIDIA Tesla V100 GPUs and the weight decay and momentum are 0.0001 and 0.9. The backbones in the model are initialized with the pre-trained weights on ImageNet [5]. And we set the shorter edges of the images to be 800 and the longer edges to be 1333. The coefficient in loss function is set to $\lambda_1 = \lambda_2 = \lambda_4 = \lambda_5 = 1$, $\lambda_3 = 0.5$. As a powerful component, FPN is used in all the backbones.

4.3   Main Results

We report the performance of our proposed SEANet on *test-dev* with different backbones and frameworks in Table 1. In addition to the results of once the

Table 1. Comparison among different methods on COCO 2017 *test-dev* dataset

Method	Backbone	AP^m	$AP^m_{0.5}$	$AP^m_{0.75}$	AP^b	$AP^b_{0.5}$	$AP^b_{0.75}$
MNC [4]	ResNet-101	24.6	44.3	24.8	–	–	–
FCIS [17]	ResNet-101	29.2	49.5	–	–	–	–
FCIS+++ [17]	ResNet-101	33.6	54.5	–	–	–	–
Mask R-CNN [9]	ResNet-101-FPN	36.6	58.7	39.2	40.4	61.9	44.2
	ResNeXt-101-FPN	38.2	60.9	41.0	42.5	63.8	46.5
MS R-CNN [11]	ResNet-101-FPN	37.8	58.5	41.0	40.7	62.0	44.5
	ResNeXt-101-FPN	39.5	60.3	42.9	42.6	63.9	46.8
Mask R-CNN + ours	ResNet-101-FPN	37.7	57.6	41.1	41.7	59.6	45.8
	ResNeXt-101-FPN	39.7	60.4	43.4	44.3	62.5	48.7
MS R-CNN + ours	ResNet-101-FPN	38.6	57.8	42.4	41.7	60.4	45.4
	ResNeXt-101-FPN	40.5	60.1	44.6	44.3	62.9	48.3

champions of the COCO instance segmentation challenge MNC [4] and FCIS [17] as well as its more complex version FCIS+++ [17], we also show the results of our baseline methods Mask R-CNN and MS R-CNN with different backbones for comparison. As Table 1 shows, our proposed method achieve a stably improvement on different backbones and frameworks. Especially on ResNeXt-101, our SEANet can improve the mask AP by 1.5 points for Mask R-CNN and 1 points for MS R-CNN. As for the box AP, it achieves 1.8% and 1.7% gains for Mask R-CNN and MS R-CNN respectively. Some visual results are shown in Fig. 4, which indicate the great performance of our method on instance segmentation.

4.4   Ablation Study

We conduct lots of extensive experiments to explain our components and prove the effectiveness of our approach.

The Performance of the Proposed SEANet. Table 2 shows that our proposed SEANet can improve both the accuracy of the instance segmentation and object detection with the gains of 1.2 AP and 1.5 AP comparing to the baseline Mask R-CNN. And from Table 2, we can see that the attention with edge supervision (the 5th row) achieves an improvement of 1.1 AP for $AP^m_{0.75}$ compared with the one without edge supervision (the 6th row). It indicates the introduction of the edge supervision in the attention module is effective for the accuracy of the instance segmentation especially for the more precise criteria $AP^m_{0.75}$. Table 2 also indicates that the improvement of the detection tasks can promote the segmentation performance, which brings a great improvement of 1.8 AP for $AP^m_{0.75}$ under the joint effect of the two parties.

In addition, we report the results of our proposed approach with different frameworks and backbones in Table 3, which shows that our proposed approach

Table 2. The detection and instance segmentation results on COCO 2017 validation set. The first row is the baseline Mask R-CNN framework. The component with ✓ is added to the baseline. The results show the stable improvement of the proposed approach

Method	FCN box head + B-IoU	Attention	L_{edge}	AP^m	$AP^m_{0.5}$	$AP^m_{0.75}$	AP^b	$AP^b_{0.5}$	$AP^b_{0.75}$
Mask R-CNN				36.5	58.1	39.0	40.3	61.5	44.1
(ResNet-101-FPN)	✓			36.7	57.6	39.6	41.5	60.2	44.9
		✓		36.9	57.8	39.5	40.4	61.5	44.3
	✓	✓		37.0	57.5	39.9	41.5	60.1	45.0
		✓	✓	37.5	58.8	40.6	40.8	61.7	44.8
	✓	✓	✓	37.7	57.8	40.8	41.7	60.0	45.6

Table 3. The detection and instance segmentation results on COCO 2017 validation set. The results without ✓ is the baseline method and those with ✓ is our proposed approach based to the baseline. The results show the stable improvement of the proposed approach based on different backbones and different framework

Method	Backbone	SEANet	AP^m	$AP^m_{0.5}$	$AP^m_{0.75}$	AP^b	$AP^b_{0.5}$	$AP^b_{0.75}$
Mask R-CNN	ResNet-50-FPN		34.5	55.8	36.7	38.0	58.9	42.0
		✓	36.0	55.4	39.2	39.4	57.7	42.7
	ResNet-101-FPN		36.5	58.1	39.0	40.3	61.5	44.1
		✓	37.7	57.8	40.8	41.7	60.0	45.6
	ResNeXt-101-FPN		37.7	59.9	40.4	42.0	63.1	46.1
		✓	39.4	60.1	42.8	44.1	62.6	48.1
MS R-CNN	ResNet-50-FPN		36.0	55.8	38.8	38.6	59.2	42.5
		✓	36.9	55.5	40.3	39.6	58.2	42.8
	ResNet-101-FPN		37.8	58.0	41.1	40.7	61.1	45.5
		✓	38.5	57.0	42.5	41.8	59.6	45.7
	ResNeXt-101-FPN		38.8	59.5	41.7	42.1	63.1	46.0
		✓	39.8	59.3	43.7	43.7	62.3	47.6

is universally effective and is no sensitive for the change of frameworks and backbones. In the meantime, we can see that the improvement of our method based on MS R-CNN is slightly less than the one based on Mask R-CNN. It is reasonable that since the final scores of the detected objects align with the accuracies of their classifications and regressions, which somewhat determines the qualities of the detected masks, using these scores to rank the mask results is viable. And MS R-CNN aims to find the more precise scores for the masks, in which the room for improvement is small because our box scoring is also accuracy. And the FCN box head brings more room for the edge attention module to make an impact.

The Design of Mask Attention Head. We extend the original mask head in Mask R-CNN by adding the attention modules. The results of different designs are reported in Table 4. From Table 4, we can see that using the edge supervision

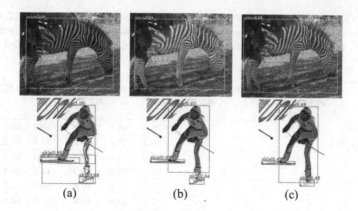

(a)   (b)   (c)

Fig. 5. Performance of the fully convolutional box head for ResNet-101-FPN. (a) The result of baseline Mask R-CNN. (b) The result of proposed SEANet when B-IoU branch is not used. (c) The result of proposed SEANet using fully convolutional box head

Table 4. Results of different designs of the attention branches. The backbone is ResNet-50-FPN

Design	AP^m	$AP^m_{0.5}$	$AP^m_{0.75}$
Mask R-CNN	34.5	55.8	36.7
(a) Edge supervison (sum)	**36.0**	**55.4**	**39.2**
(b) Edge supervison (concat)	35.6	55.0	38.8
(d) Without edge supervison	35.1	54.6	38.4

mechanism obtains robust performance gain compared with no applying edge supervision, which shows the effective of the proposed edge supervision mechanism. In the detail, the manner that element-wisely adding the feature from the edge attention module with the high-level feature on the mask head, represented by "sum", outperforms using concatenation operation which represented by "concat". It indicates that the sum operation between the feature with edge information of the object and the high-level semantic feature on the mask head can fuse the object boundary information and semantic information more directly, and specifically strengthen features on the object boundary in the pixel level.

The Performance of Fully Convolutional Box Head. In order to indicate the precision with our proposed fully convolutional box head, especially the B-IoU branch, we show the visual results compared with baseline Mask R-CNN in Fig. 5. We can observe that in Mask R-CNN, in spite of giving the high classification scores, the regressions of the bounding boxes are not accurate enough and fail in locating the objects with large aspect ratios, like the skis in the Fig. 5(a). In our proposed SEANet, even if not using the IoU scores predicted by B-IoU branch, the box regression results are evidently greater than the baseline and reasonably

Table 5. The boundary prediction evaluation of the baseline Mask R-CNN and our approach. The backbone is ResNet-101-FPN

Band width	1	3	8
Mask R-CNN	7.01	29.16	41.47
Mask R-CNN + ours	**10.99**	**42.48**	**57.21**

Table 6. The comparison of runtime and parameter. The backbone is ResNet-101-FPN

Method	$runtime(ms)$	$params(M)$
Mask R-CNN	405	63.17
Cascade Mask R-CNN	507	99.09
Ours (FCN box head + B-IoU)	450	58.04
Ours (edge attention head)	428	71.32
Ours (all)	464	64.89

improve the performance of the segmentation, as shown in Fig. 5(b). With the B-IoU branch, we multiply the IoU scores from the B-IoU branch with the classification scores to balance the precision in the aspect of regression and classification, which helps us to choose the most exact bounding box for each proposal. As Fig. 5(c) shows, the borders of the detected bounding boxes press close to the boundary of each instance even if the large ratio or scale of the instance, which presents the effectiveness of the proposed fully convolutional box head.

The Boundary Prediction Evaluation. We evaluate our proposed method on the boundary prediction by adopting a trimap approach [13]. We compute the classification accuracy within a band of varying width around boundaries of the ground-truth mask. We set three different widths of the bands and show the results of our proposed SEANet and baseline Mask R-CNN on COCO 2017 validation set in Table 5.

As Table 5 shows, our approach can significantly improve edge quality and achieve an accuracy gain of 15.74 under the band width of 8, which shows the effective of our propose method.

The Comparison of Runtime and Parameter. Table 6 summarizes the runtimes and the model sizes of our model and other related neural network methods (Mask R-CNN and Cascade Mask R-CNN). We record runtime with $1280 * 800 * 3$ data in a batch size 8 using PyTorch 1.11.0 with a single NVIDIA Tesla V100 GPU. It can be observed that the runtime of our model is not much bigger than that of Mask R-CNN, and is smaller than that of Cascade Mask R-CNN. In terms of parameters, it is equivalent to Mask R-CNN and much smaller than Cascade Mask R-CNN.

5   Conclusions

In this paper, we focus on keeping the boundary of the mask complete in instance segmentation. We propose a fully convolutional box head with a new "B-IoU" branch which learns association between object features and detected bounding boxes for estimating the quality of the bounding box. In the mask head, we utilize two attention modules which prove useful for feature representation. Especially, we design a novel supervised edge attention module, which use the additional supervision information to refine the edge of the mask. Experimental results show that our method consistently improves the baseline models on the COCO benchmark dataset. Since the method is benefit to both the detection and instance segmentation, we hope the method can be extended to other models dealing with instance-level object identification tasks.

Acknowledgments. This work was partially supported by the State Key Program of National Natural Science of China (No. 61836009), the National Natural Science Foundation of China (Nos. U1701267, 61871310, 61773304, 61806154, 61802295 and 61801351), the Fund for Foreign Scholars in University Research and Teaching Programs (the 111 Project) (No. B07048), the Major Research Plan of the National Natural Science Foundation of China (Nos. 91438201 and 91438103).

References

1. Arnab, A., Torr, P.H.S.: Bottom-up instance segmentation using deep higher-order CRFs. In: BMVC. BMVA Press (2016)
2. Brabandere, B.D., Neven, D., Gool, L.V.: Semantic instance segmentation with a discriminative loss function. CoRR abs/1708.02551 (2017)
3. Dai, J., He, K., Li, Y., Ren, S., Sun, J.: Instance-sensitive fully convolutional networks. In: Leibe, B., Matas, J., Sebe, N., Welling, M. (eds.) ECCV 2016. LNCS, vol. 9910, pp. 534–549. Springer, Cham (2016). https://doi.org/10.1007/978-3-319-46466-4_32
4. Dai, J., He, K., Sun, J.: Instance-aware semantic segmentation via multi-task network cascades. In: CVPR, pp. 3150–3158. IEEE Computer Society (2016)
5. Deng, J., Dong, W., Socher, R., Li, L., Li, K., Li, F.: ImageNet: a large-scale hierarchical image database. In: CVPR, pp. 248–255. IEEE Computer Society (2009)
6. Fu, J., et al.: Dual attention network for scene segmentation. In: CVPR, pp. 3146–3154. Computer Vision Foundation/IEEE (2019)
7. Gao, Z., Xie, J., Wang, Q., Li, P.: Global second-order pooling convolutional networks. In: CVPR, pp. 3024–3033. Computer Vision Foundation/IEEE (2019)
8. Hariharan, B., Arbeláez, P.A., Girshick, R.B., Malik, J.: Simultaneous detection and segmentation. In: ECCV
9. He, K., Gkioxari, G., Dollár, P., Girshick, R.B.: Mask R-CNN. In: ICCV, pp. 2980–2988. IEEE Computer Society (2017)
10. Hu, J., Shen, L., Sun, G.: Squeeze-and-excitation networks. In: CVPR, pp. 7132–7141. IEEE Computer Society (2018)
11. Huang, Z., Huang, L., Gong, Y., Huang, C., Wang, X.: Mask scoring R-CNN. In: CVPR, pp. 6409–6418. Computer Vision Foundation/IEEE (2019)

12. Jiang, B., Luo, R., Mao, J., Xiao, T., Jiang, Y.: Acquisition of localization confidence for accurate object detection. In: Ferrari, V., Hebert, M., Sminchisescu, C., Weiss, Y. (eds.) Computer Vision – ECCV 2018. LNCS, vol. 11218, pp. 816–832. Springer, Cham (2018). https://doi.org/10.1007/978-3-030-01264-9_48

13. Kohli, P., Ladicky, L., Torr, P.H.S.: Robust higher order potentials for enforcing label consistency. In: 2008 IEEE Computer Society Conference on Computer Vision and Pattern Recognition (CVPR 2008), 24–26 June 2008, Anchorage, Alaska, USA. IEEE Computer Society (2008)

14. Kong, T., Sun, F., Liu, H., Jiang, Y., Shi, J.: FoveaBox: beyond anchor-based object detector. CoRR, vol. 2 (2020)

15. Lafferty, J.D., McCallum, A., Pereira, F.C.N.: Conditional random fields: probabilistic models for segmenting and labeling sequence data. In: ICML, pp. 282–289. Morgan Kaufmann (2001)

16. Li, X., Zhong, Z., Wu, J., Yang, Y., Lin, Z., Liu, H.: Expectation-maximization attention networks for semantic segmentation. CoRR abs/1907.13426 (2019)

17. Li, Y., Qi, H., Dai, J., Ji, X., Wei, Y.: Fully convolutional instance-aware semantic segmentation. In: CVPR, pp. 4438–4446. IEEE Computer Society (2017)

18. Lin, T., Goyal, P., Girshick, R.B., He, K., Dollár, P.: Focal loss for dense object detection. In: ICCV, pp. 2999–3007. IEEE Computer Society (2017)

19. Lin, T.-Y., et al.: Microsoft COCO: common objects in context. In: Fleet, D., Pajdla, T., Schiele, B., Tuytelaars, T. (eds.) ECCV 2014. LNCS, vol. 8693, pp. 740–755. Springer, Cham (2014). https://doi.org/10.1007/978-3-319-10602-1_48

20. Long, J., Shelhamer, E., Darrell, T.: Fully convolutional networks for semantic segmentation. In: CVPR, pp. 3431–3440. IEEE Computer Society (2015)

21. Novotny, D., Albanie, S., Larlus, D., Vedaldi, A.: Semi-convolutional operators for instance segmentation. In: Ferrari, V., Hebert, M., Sminchisescu, C., Weiss, Y. (eds.) ECCV 2018. LNCS, vol. 11205, pp. 89–105. Springer, Cham (2018). https://doi.org/10.1007/978-3-030-01246-5_6

22. Pinheiro, P.H.O., Collobert, R., Dollár, P.: Learning to segment object candidates. In: NIPS, pp. 1990–1998 (2015)

23. Ren, S., He, K., Girshick, R.B., Sun, J.: Faster R-CNN: towards real-time object detection with region proposal networks. In: NIPS, pp. 91–99 (2015)

24. Rezatofighi, H., Tsoi, N., Gwak, J., Sadeghian, A., Reid, I.D., Savarese, S.: Generalized intersection over union: a metric and a loss for bounding box regression. In: CVPR, pp. 658–666. Computer Vision Foundation / IEEE (2019)

25. Tian, Z., Shen, C., Chen, H., He, T.: FCOS: fully convolutional one-stage object detection. CoRR abs/1904.01355 (2019)

26. Woo, S., Park, J., Lee, J.-Y., Kweon, I.S.: CBAM: convolutional block attention module. In: Ferrari, V., Hebert, M., Sminchisescu, C., Weiss, Y. (eds.) ECCV 2018. LNCS, vol. 11211, pp. 3–19. Springer, Cham (2018). https://doi.org/10.1007/978-3-030-01234-2_1

27. Yu, C., Wang, J., Peng, C., Gao, C., Yu, G., Sang, N.: BiSeNet: bilateral segmentation network for real-time semantic segmentation. In: Ferrari, V., Hebert, M., Sminchisescu, C., Weiss, Y. (eds.) ECCV 2018. LNCS, vol. 11217, pp. 334–349. Springer, Cham (2018). https://doi.org/10.1007/978-3-030-01261-8_20

28. Zhu, C., He, Y., Savvides, M.: Feature selective anchor-free module for single-shot object detection. In: CVPR, pp. 840–849. Computer Vision Foundation/IEEE (2019)

Discriminative Partial Domain Adversarial Network

Jian Hu[1], Hongya Tuo[1(⊠)], Chao Wang[2], Lingfeng Qiao[1], Haowen Zhong[1], Junchi Yan[3], Zhongliang Jing[1], and Henry Leung[4]

[1] School of Aeronautics and Astronautics, Shanghai Jiao Tong University,
Shanghai, China
{jianhu18,tuohy,qiaolf927,zhonghaowen,zljing}@sjtu.edu.cn
[2] Alibaba Group, Hangzhou, China
xiaoxuan.wc@alibaba-inc.com
[3] Department of Computer Science and Engineering, Shanghai Jiao Tong University,
Shanghai, China
yanjunchi@sjtu.edu.cn
[4] Department of Electrical and Computer Engineering, University of Calgary,
Calgary, Canada
leungh@ucalgary.ca

Abstract. Domain adaptation (DA) has been a fundamental building block for Transfer Learning (TL) which assumes that source and target domain share the same label space. A more general and realistic setting is that the label space of target domain is a subset of the source domain, as termed by Partial domain adaptation (PDA). Previous methods typically match the whole source domain to target domain, which causes negative transfer due to the source-negative classes in source domain that does not exist in target domain. In this paper, a novel Discriminative Partial Domain Adversarial Network (DPDAN) is developed. We first propose to use hard binary weighting to differentiate the source-positive and source-negative samples in the source domain. The source-positive samples are those with labels shared by two domains, while the rest in the source domain are treated as source-negative samples. Based on the above binary relabeling strategy, our algorithm maximizes the distribution divergence between source-negative samples and all the others (source-positive and target samples), meanwhile minimizes domain shift between source-positive samples and target domain to obtain discriminative domain-invariant features. We empirically verify DPDAN can effectively reduce the negative transfer caused by source-negative classes, and

H. Tuo—This work is supported by National Natural Science Foundation of China(Grant No.61673262 and 61175028) and Shanghai key project of basic research(Grant No.16JC1401100)
J. Yan—Partial work was done when Junchi Yan was with Tencent AI Lab as visiting scholar.

Electronic supplementary material The online version of this chapter (https://doi.org/10.1007/978-3-030-58583-9_38) contains supplementary material, which is available to authorized users.

© Springer Nature Switzerland AG 2020
A. Vedaldi et al. (Eds.): ECCV 2020, LNCS 12372, pp. 632–648, 2020.
https://doi.org/10.1007/978-3-030-58583-9_38

also theoretically show it decreases negative transfer caused by domain shift. Experiments on four benchmark domain adaptation datasets show DPDAN consistently outperforms state-of-the-art methods.

Keywords: Partial domain adaptation · Adversarial learning · Discriminative learning

1 Introduction

Deep neural networks have show the excellence in many fields [7,13,20] such as computer vision, natural language processing. However, all these applications rely on a huge amount of labeled data. In practice, there may not be enough labeled data for training from scratch. Transfer learning has been considered as one of the most representative methods to deal with this problem [10].

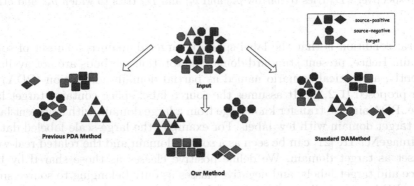

Fig. 1. The main difference of our method against the previous standard domain adaption and partial domain adaption mathods. The blue samples are from source domain and the red ones are from target domain. In standard DA method, source-negative classes can confuse discriminator, leading to performance degeneration. Previous PDA methods can select out most negative classes, but some are still hard to distinguish. Our method not only utilizes hard binary weight narrows the distribution divergence between source-positive and target samples, but also widens the distance between source-negative samples and others to reduce negative transfer caused by domain shift. (Color figure online)

One critical issue in transfer learning algorithms is domain shift in data distribution [22]. Domain adaptation (DA) is a traditional method for transfer learning to learn domain-invariant features to close the gap between domains. In this way, source classifier can be utilized to classify target samples without labels. Recent researches have shown that deep networks can learn more transferable features to bring the gap among different domains [31].

The basic assumption of standard DA is that source and target domain share the same label space [19,30], which often does not hold in practice. One more

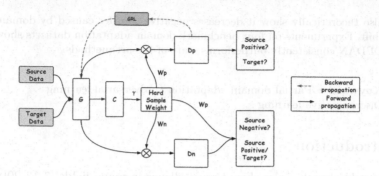

Fig. 2. Architecture of our method, G is the feature extractor, and C is not only the source classifier but also the weight discriminator to obtain the source class importance weights. The outputs of C when it plays the role of weight discriminator is γ. γ evaluates the possibility of the source class belonging to positive classes. We further transfer γ to w_p and w_n, which represents the possibility of source samples belonging to C_{sp} and C_{sn} respectively. D_p tries to narrow p_{sp} and p_t, and D_n tries to widen p_{sn} and others.

general condition is that the label space of target domain is a subset of source domain. Hence, present standard domain adaptation methods are not available. Recently, a practical scenario named as partial domain adaptation (PDA) has been proposed [1,2,32]. It assumes the source label space contains target label space. PDA aims to transfer knowledge from a large domain with sufficient labels to a target domain with few labels. For example, the large-scale labeled dataset like ImageNet-1K [21] can be seen as a source domain and the related real-world dataset as target domain. We define positive classes as those shared by both source and target labels, and negative classes as only belonging to source space.

In PDA, one challenge is that we do not know which part of source label space is shared with target space, because negative classes are unavailable during training. Intuitively, when target label space contains only a subset of source classes, it is impossible to reduce the domain shift by comparing source and target distributions. Methods are devised [1,2,32] to reduce label space's mismatch by weighting each sample into the domain adversarial network. However, these approaches all use possibility based soft-weights to select positive classes. In the ideal situation, the weights of positive classes are expected to be 1, otherwise 0. In practice, even if the weights of positive classes are obviously higher than negative, few of them can achieve the expected values. Moreover, previous methods mainly focus on narrowing the distance between source positive and target samples, but ignore zooming out the distance between source negative and other samples. These two phenomenons lead to severe negative transfer.

To solve the deficiency caused by soft-weight, it is hoped not only to extract the common features from source-positive and target domain, but also avoid misjudging source positive and negative classes. Based on related analysis from PADA [2], since the source-negative label space and target label space are disjoint, the target data should be dissimilar to the source data in the negative label space. Hence, the probabilities of assigning the target data to the source negative classes should be sufficiently small. In another word, the weights from source positive domain are much higher than these from source negative ones. Therefore, we put forward the hard binary weights to adaptively divide source domain samples into positive and negative classes, weights of the positive classes are 1, otherwise are 0. In this way, our model can not only distinguish the positive class from the negative class in the source domain, but also give the positive class enough weight to eliminate negative transfer. Furthermore, we propose discriminative PDA Net to widen the distance between source negative classes and others, further reducing the influence of negative classes in source domain.

As illustrated in Fig. 1, we have presented a Discriminative Partial Domain Adversarial Network for PDA. Our contributions are three-folds.

For partial domain adaption, we show the benefit to incorporate the source-negative samples absent in the target domain, which has been rarely considered before. Specifically, we are the first to propose maximizing the distribution divergence between source-negative samples and the others (source-positive and target samples), to reduce negative transfer caused by domain shift.

To promote this maximization, we propose to use binary hard labels to distinguish source-negative and source-positive samples, in contrast to the soft-weighting used in previous works. The binary label strategy is also used to effectively narrow the distance between source-positive and target samples, leading to our main approach for jointly discriminative learning for partial domain adaption via adversarial networks. Furthermore, soft weights are still retained on the source classifier to ensure that the misclassified source samples can be corrected.

We theoretically prove that the proposed DPDAN is guaranteed to simultaneously achieve probability distribution alignment and prevent negative transfer. Extensive experimental results show the competitive performance of our approach on public datasets and the efficacy of the proposed components.

2   Related Works

Domain Adaptation. DA plays an important role in transfer learning. It tries to narrow the gap between source and target domain by learning domain-invariant features. DA frees target domain from expensive label cost.

Deep neural networks ensure knowledge transfer by learning high-level domain-invariant features. But distribution discrepancy across different domains cannot be eliminated completely by utilizing deep neural networks alone. Some DA methods utilize high-level statistical features [4,15,28,33] to match domains. Some help feature extractor to learn domain-invariant features in a min-max game by adding a discriminator [5,17,25,26].

Partial Domain Adaptation. PDA is a generalization of standard domain adaptation. PDA assumes target label space is a subset of source label space. Three approaches have been proposed to deal with it. Selective Adversarial Network (SAN) [1] utilizes weight evaluators for each class to select out negative classes in source samples, then the weighted source samples are adopted in multiple adversarial network. Partial Adversarial Domain Adaptation (PADA) [2] simplifies the weight evaluator to a universal one to evaluate negative class weights, meanwhile, the weights are applied to source classifier. Importance Weighted Adversarial Nets (IWAN) [32] appends a positive-class discriminator to assess the positive-sample weight for each sample, and weighted source and target samples are used for adversarial learning. Moreover, there are also some related DA problem setup like [12,23] focus on universal and openset DA problems.

The above PDA works focus on reducing negative transfer caused by negative classes. IWAN tries to select out positive label space on the sample level, while PADA and SAN try to find out positive label space on the class level. These methods only minimize the shift of positive classes between domains, without considering maximizing the distribution divergence between the negative and target samples. Moreover, they employ possibility based soft-weights to evaluate the transferability. As such, even if the weights of positive classes are higher than the negative, few of them can achieve desired values. This phenomenon can still cause negative transfer.

This paper proposes a Discriminative Partial Domain Adversarial Network (DPDAN), which not only narrows the distribution divergence between source-positive samples and target ones, but also widens the distribution divergence between source-negative samples and the others including source-positive and target ones. Meanwhile, we apply the hard positive-sample label to eliminate negative transfer caused by source-negative classes.

3   Discriminative Partial Domain Adversarial Network

Similar to standard domain adaptation, in partial domain adaptation we are also provided with a *source* domain $D_s = \{(\mathbf{x}_i^s, y_i^s)\}_{i=1}^{n_s}$ of n_s labeled examples associated with $|C_s|$ classes and a *target* domain $\mathcal{D}_t = \{\mathbf{x}_i^t\}_{i=1}^{n_t}$ of n_t unlabeled examples associated with $|\mathcal{C}_t|$ classes. Different from DA, in PDA we have $|C_s| > |\mathcal{C}_t|$. We further separate label space C_s into source-positive C_{sp} and source-negative C_{sn}, here $C_{sp} = \mathcal{C}_t$. $\mathcal{D}_{sp}$ is source-positive domain with $|C_{sp}|$ classes and D_{sn} is source-negative domain with $|C_{sn}|$ classes. D_s and D_t are sampled from distributions $p_s(x)$ and $p_t(x)$ respectively. In DA we have $p_s(x) \neq p_t(x)$. In PDA we have $p_{sp}(x) \neq p_t(x)$, where p_{sp} denotes the distribution of D_{sp}. Likewise, p_{sn} denotes the distribution of D_{sn}.

In summary, we should tackle two challenges to enable PDA: **(1)** Mitigate negative transfer by filtering out unrelated source labeled data belonging to source-negative domain $\mathcal{D}_{sn}$. **(2)** Promote positive transfer by maximally matching data distributions $p_{sp}(x)$ and $p_t(x)$ in source-positive domain $\mathcal{D}_{sp}$ and target domain $\mathcal{D}_t$. These two interleaving challenges should be dealt with jointly through decreasing negative influence of $\mathcal{D}_{sn}$ and meanwhile enabling effective domain adaptation between $\mathcal{D}_{sp}$ and $\mathcal{D}_t$. Although source-negative samples cannot be accurately separated from source domain, the distribution p_{sn} of $\mathcal{D}_{sn}$ will be roughly learned from semantic distribution measurement between source-positive and source-negative samples. This is a more practical method than finding out the negative data directly.

The core idea of DPDAN is to decompose source domain distribution p_s into two parts from the perspective of probability distribution: source-positive domain distribution p_{sp} and source-negative domain distribution p_{sn}. The well-separated p_{sp} and p_{sn} can further facilitate the effective transfer by minimizing divergence between p_{sp} and p_t and maximizing differences between p_{sn} and others including p_{sp} and p_t. This can avoid negative transfer to a greater extent.

As shown in Fig. 2, G is the feature extractor, and C is not only the source classifier but also the weight discriminator to obtain the source class weights γ to evaluate the possibility of the source class belonging to positive classes. Meanwhile, inspired by OTSU-methods [18], we transfer γ to w_p and w_n, which represents the possibility of source samples belonging to C_{sp} and C_{sn} respectively. In this way, we can promote the weights of source-positive classes to 1 and that of source-negative ones to 0. D_p tries to narrow the distance between p_{sp} and p_t under aid of w_p, and D_n aims to widen the distance between p_{sn} and others by means of w_p and w_n.

3.1   Discriminative Partial Domain Adversarial Framework

Domain adaptation network is proposed to match the feature distributions cross domains. The basic framework of domain adaptation is domain adversarial neural network (DaNN) [5]. DaNN plays a min-max game. The first player is a feature extractor G that tries to extract common feature from both domains, the second player refers to a domain discriminator D distinguishing which domain the feature comes from. The framework follows the objective given by:

$$\min_{G} \max_{D} \mathcal{L}(D, G) = \mathbb{E}_{x \sim p_s} \left[\log \left(D \left(G \left(x \right) \right) \right) \right] + \mathbb{E}_{x \sim p_t} \left[\log \left(1 - D \left(G \left(x \right) \right) \right) \right] \quad (1)$$

However, if we apply the DaNN framework to PDA directly, the mismatch between source and target label space can cause performance degeneration. In the previous methods, weights are added to domain discriminators to extract common features from source positive and target domains. Nevertheless, these methods mainly focus on narrowing the distance between p_{sp} and p_t, but ignore widen the distance between p_{sn} and p_t.

We also propose to introduce w_p and w_n to deal with PDA issue, w_n is the negative sample binary weight and w_p is the positive sample binary weight. How to get w_p and w_n will be illustrated in the Sect. 3.2. As such, the DaNN framework can be written:

$$\min_{G} \max_{D_p} \mathcal{L}(D_p, G) = \mathbb{E}_{x \sim p_s} \left[w_p \log \left(D_p \left(G(x) \right) \right) \right] + \mathbb{E}_{x \sim p_t} \left[\log \left(1 - D_p \left(G(x) \right) \right) \right]$$

$$\min_{G} \max_{D_n} \mathcal{L}(D_p, G) = \mathbb{E}_{x \sim p_s} \left[w_n \log \left(D_p \left(G(x) \right) \right) \right] + \mathbb{E}_{x \sim p_t} \left[w_n \log \left(1 - D_n \left(G(x) \right) \right) \right]$$

$$+ \mathbb{E}_{x \sim p_t} \left[\log \left(1 - D_n \left(G \left(x \right) \right) \right) \right] \quad (2)$$

Here, we apply the positive sample binary weight w_p and negative sample binary weight w_n to positive domain discriminator D_p and negative domain discriminator D_n. In this way, p_s can be split into p_{sp} and p_{sn}. Our framework tries to narrow the distance between source positive and target samples, and further widens the distance between source negative and above ones. Our framework includes two domain discriminators sharing the same feature extracting layers.

3.2   Hard Binary Weights

Only when the weights of the positive classes are 1 and the weights of negative ones are 0, the negative transfer caused by negative label space in source domain can be eliminated. Nevertheless, to avoid misclassification of source positive and negative classes, previous approaches utilize possibility weight to evaluate the importance of classes in source domain. It can cause weights of positive samples are far from 1 while the weights of negative ones are far from 0, which can still cause negative transfer.

However, for each sample in source domain, the softmax output of the source classifier gives a probability distribution over source label space C_s. This distribution describes the probability of source samples belonging to each of the $|C_s|$ classes. A basic assumption is that p_{sp} and p_t are much similar than p_{sn} and p_t [2]. Hence, for target samples, if they are assigned to source negative classes, the possibility will be very small.In another word, the weights of positive classes are much higher than the weights of negative ones.

Similar to [2], we define γ as mean of predict labels over target data.

$$\gamma = \frac{1}{n_t} \sum_{i=0}^{|n_t|} softmax\left(G(x_i^t)\right) \tag{3}$$

We further normalize γ by dividing its largest element. γ is a $|C_s|$-dimension vector. The jth element γ_j indicates the contribution of the jth class. For example, In Office-31 dataset, γ is a 31-dimension vector, the 3rd element in this vector represents the possibility of the third source class belonging to C_{sp}. If the j-th class comes from C_{sn}, γ_j should be close to 0, otherwise close to 1. Hence, we build hard binary weights utilizing threshold to distinguish C_{sp} and C_{sn}.

We define w_p as hard positive binary weight. Inspired by [18], we obtain w_p from γ by automatically selecting an adequate threshold t. The probabilities of class occurrence α_{sn}, α_{sp} and the class mean weights β_{sn}, β_{sp} are defined by:

$$\alpha_{sn} = \frac{|C_{sn}|}{|C_s|}, \quad \alpha_{sp} = \frac{|C_{sp}|}{|C_s|}, \quad \beta_{sn} = \frac{\sum_{0<=\gamma_j<t} \gamma_j}{|C_{sn}|}, \quad \beta_{sp} = \frac{\sum_{t<=\gamma_j<=1} \gamma_j}{|C_{sp}|} \tag{4}$$

Whatever choice of t is, it can be confirmed that:

$$\beta_{total} = \beta_{sn} * \alpha_{sn} + \beta_{sp} * \alpha_{sp} \tag{5}$$

We utilize between-cluster variance σ^2 to measure discrepancy of C_{sn} and C_{sp}.

$$\sigma^2 = (\beta_{sn} - \beta_{total})^2 * \alpha_{sn} + (\beta_{sp} - \beta_{total})^2 * \alpha_{sp} \tag{6}$$

The greater σ^2 is, the greater the difference between C_{sn} and C_{sp} is. If some C_{sn} or C_{sp} are misclassified, the difference will be reduced. Therefore, the threshold is set t by the largest variance between-cluster σ^2 refers to the least probability of misclassification, thus:

$$t = \arg\max(\sigma^2) \tag{7}$$

The hard positive binary weight w_p is given by $w_p = 1$ if $gamma_j \geq t$, and 0 otherwise. where w_p represents whether the jth class is from C_{sp} or C_{sn}. If the jth class belongs to C_{sp}, $w_p = 1$. If the jth class belongs to C_{sn}, $w_p = 0$. Accordingly, due to negative binary weight $w_n = 1 - w_p$, if the jth class belongs to C_{sn}, $w_n = 1$. If the jth class belongs to C_{sp}, $w_n = 0$.

3.3   Positive Partial Domain Adaptation

To extract common features from source positive and target domains, we utilize the hard binary weight w_p to select out feature from source positive and target domains. The objective is named as GAN_p, which takes the form of the standard GAN with the value function as follows:

$$GAN_p(G, D_p) = \mathbb{E}_{\mathbf{x} \sim p_s(\mathbf{x})}\left[w_p \log\left(D_p(\mathbf{x})\right)\right] + \mathbb{E}_{\mathbf{x} \sim p_t(\mathbf{x})}\left[\log\left(1 - D_p\left(G(\mathbf{x})\right)\right)\right] \tag{8}$$

In Eq. 8, the positive domain adaptation label is as same as w_p. 0 represents input sample belonging to D_s while 1 represents input samples belonging to $\mathcal{D}_t$.

3.4   Negative Partial Domain Adaptation

To further reduce negative transfer, we also focus on how to widen the distance between source negative and other samples. We define this as GAN_n. We notice that if the sample belongs to D_{sp} or D_t, the corresponding w_n is 0, otherwise, w_n is 1. Hence, we set w_n as domain label for negative partial domain adaptation. If the sample is a part of D_n, the corresponding negative domain label is 1, otherwise 0. Meanwhile, in this part, we focus on the negative samples, the weight of negative samples should be w_n, while the weight of positive samples should be w_p, $w_n = 1 - w_p$. The value function of GAN_n is given by:

$$GAN_n(G, D_n) = \mathbb{E}_{\mathbf{x} \sim p_s(\mathbf{x})}\left[w_n \log\left(D_n(G(\mathbf{x}))\right)\right] + \mathbb{E}_{\mathbf{x} \sim p_s(\mathbf{x})}\left[w_p \log\left(1 - D_n(G(\mathbf{x}))\right)\right]$$
$$+ \mathbb{E}_{\mathbf{x} \sim p_t(\mathbf{x})}\left[\log\left(1 - D_n\left(G(\mathbf{x})\right)\right)\right] \tag{9}$$

In Eq. 9, w_n also represents whether the sample belonging to D_{sn}, if the samples belong to D_{sp} or D_t, the negative domain label is 0, otherwise, it is 1.

In contrast to the 'zero-sum' loss, the optimization of GAN_n is given by two steps. First, the optimal D_n^* is obtained by maximizing Eq. 10.

$$D_n^* = \arg\max_{D_n} \mathbb{E}_{\mathbf{x} \sim p_s(\mathbf{x})}\left[w_n \log\left(D_n(G(\mathbf{x}))\right)\right] + \mathbb{E}_{\mathbf{x} \sim p_s(\mathbf{x})}\left[w_p \log\left(1 - D_n(G(\mathbf{x}))\right)\right]$$
$$+ \mathbb{E}_{\mathbf{x} \sim p_t(\mathbf{x})}\left[\log\left(1 - D_n\left(G(\mathbf{x})\right)\right)\right] \tag{10}$$

Then for widen the distance between p_{sn} and others, G^* is optimized by plugging D_n^* into Eq. 9 and minimizing $-GAN_n(G, D_n^*)$:

$$G^* = \arg\min_G -GAN_n(G, D_n^*) \tag{11}$$

Equations 8–11 suggest when facing both D_p and D_n, G struggles to make the induced p_{sn} stay away from p_t, and forces p_{sp} to close with p_t. Minimizing Eq. 11 helps D_n to separate source-positive and target samples from source-negative samples rather than confusing D_n. This crucial effect will eventually push p_t away from p_{sn} but towards p_{sp}. So the well-separated p_{sp} and p_{sn} can further facilitate the effective transfer of knowledge by minimizing divergence of p_{sp} and p_t and maximizing differences between p_{sn} and the combination of p_t and p_{sp}. This will avoid negative transfer to a greater extent.

3.5 Discriminative Partial Domain Adversarial Network

In DPDAN, positive discriminator D_p narrows the distance between p_{sp} and p_t, and negative discriminator D_n widens the distance between p_{sn} and the combination of p_{sp} and p_t. Thus, we get two well-separated distributions p_{sp} and p_{sn} for discriminators D_p and D_n. The overall objective can be written as:

$$\min_{G, D_n} \max_{D_p} \mathcal{L}(G, D_p, D_n) = \mathbb{E}_{\mathbf{x} \sim p_s(\mathbf{x})} [\gamma C(G(\mathbf{x}), y)] + \lambda_p GAN_p(G, D_p) - \lambda_n GAN_n(G, D_n)$$

$$\tag{12}$$

where λ_p and λ_n control the trade-off between D_p and D_n respectively. C is the source classifier. γ is soft weight. At the beginning of the training, w_p is set as 1 for all source classes. After every 500 iterations, w_p will be updated based on the transferability between source and target classes. D_p, D_n and G plays the min-max game, and only D_p inserts a gradient reversal layer (GRL) [5] to multiply the gradient by -1 for the feature extractor to learn G and D_p simultaneously. All these modules are trained together.

In fact, since the weight applied to the source domain classifier is soft weight γ, even if some source classes are misclassified, features from misjudged samples are still being learned by C. D_p constantly narrows the gap between the source and target domain, these misclassified samples at early stage will be easy to distinguish in the process of training, correcting misclassified source samples.

3.6 Theoretical Analysis

Theorem 1. *At the Nash equilibrium point of Eq. 12, the minimal JSD between source-positive distributions p_{sp} and the target data distributions p_t is achieved, i.e. $p_{sp} = p_t$. Meanwhile, the JSD between source-negative distribution p_{sn} and others is maximized as much as possible.*

Given fixed generators G, the optimal discriminators D_p and D_n for the objective in Eq. 12 have the following forms:

$$D_p^* = \frac{w_p p_s(x)}{w_p p_s(x) + p_t(x)}, \quad D_n^* = \frac{w_n p_s(x)}{p_s(x) + p_t(x)} \tag{13}$$

Proof. In GAN_p, we try to minimize the JSD between $p_s(x)w_p$ and $p_t(x)$. Similar to GAN network, given x, one obtains the optimal D_p^* is by maximizing:

$$f(D_p^*) = p_s(x)w_p \log D_p(x) + p_t(x) \log(1 - D_p(x)) \tag{14}$$

The derivative of $f(D_p)$ is $\frac{df(D_p)}{dD_p} = \frac{p_s(x)w_p}{D_p(x)} - \frac{p_t(x)}{1-D_p(x)}$. Hence, $D_p^* = \frac{p_s(x)w_p}{p_s(x)w_p+p_t(x)}$. When it comes to $GAN_n(G, D_n)$, we try to maximize the JSD between $p_s(x)w_n$ and $p_s(x)w_p + p_t(x)$. Similar to GAN_p, we conclude that the maximum D_p and D_n can be achieved at Eq. 13. Substitute optimal D_p^* and D_n^* into Eq. 12, then $\mathcal{L}(G, D_p, D_n)$ becomes:

$$\lambda_p \left\{ \mathbb{E}_{\mathbf{x} \sim p_s(\mathbf{x})} \left[w_p \log \left(\frac{w_p p_s(x)}{w_p p_s(x) + p_t(x)} \right) \right] + \mathbb{E}_{\mathbf{x} \sim p_t(\mathbf{x})} \left[\log \left(1 - \frac{w_p p_s(x)}{w_p p_s(x) + p_t(x)} \right) \right] \right\}$$

$$- \lambda_n \left\{ \mathbb{E}_{\mathbf{x} \sim p_{sp}(\mathbf{x})} \left[w_p \log \left(\frac{w_n p_s(x)}{p_s(x) + p_t(x)} \right) \right] + \mathbb{E}_{\mathbf{x} \sim p_{sn}(\mathbf{x})} \left[w_n \log \left(\frac{w_n p_s(x)}{p_s(x) + p_t(x)} \right) \right] \right.$$

$$\left. + \mathbb{E}_{\mathbf{x} \sim p_t(\mathbf{x})} \left[\log \left(1 - \frac{w_n p_s(x)}{p_s(x) + p_t(x)} \right) \right] \right\}$$

$$= \lambda_p \left(2JSD\left(w_p p_s | p_t\right) - \log 4 \right) - \lambda_n \left(2JSD\left(w_n p_s | p_t + w_p p_s\right) - \log 4 \right) \tag{15}$$

which peaks its minimum if $p_s w_p = p_t$ and $p_s w_n \neq p_s w_p + p_t$. The detail of the proof is provided in our supplementary material.

The proof reveals that approaching to Nash equilibrium is equivalent to jointly minimizing $JSD\left(w_p p_s | p_t\right)$ and maximizing $JSD\left(w_n p_s | p_t + w_p p_s\right)$. Thus, DPDAN tries to captures p_{sn} and p_{sp}. So, the proposed method can simultaneously achieve probability distribution alignment and prevent negative transfer.

4   Experiment

4.1   Datasets and Protocols

Office-31 [22] dataset is a standard DA dataset. It contains 31 categories decomposed by three different domains: Amazon (A), Webcam (W) and DSLR (D). We denote three domains with 31 categories as source domain A31, W31 and D31. 10 categories [6] shared by Office-31 and Caltech-256 [8] dataset are defined as target domain A10, W10 and D10 respectively. We evaluate the methods in 6 partial domain adaptation tasks.

Caltech-Office utilizes Caltech-256 dataset as source domain, while the 10 positive classes shared by Office-31 and Caltech-256 dataset as target domain. We denote source domain as C256 and target domain as A10, W10, D10, respectively. Moreover, these 10 classes are also used as source domain while the target domain is the first five classes in 10 classes as target domain C5, A5, W5 and D5. We evaluate our methods in 15 partial domain adaptation tasks.

Office-Home dataset [27] is a larger dataset with a higher domain distribution discrepancy. It includes four different domains with 65 categories: Artistic, Clip

Table 1. Accuracy of partial DA tasks on *Caltech-Office* (10 classes → 5 classes).

Method	Caltech-Office (10 classes → 5 classes)												
	C → A	C → W	C → D	A → C	A → W	A → D	W → C	W → A	W → D	D → C	D → A	D → W	Avg
AlexNet [11]	93.58	83.70	91.18	85.27	76.30	85.29	74.17	87.37	**100.00**	80.82	89.51	98.52	87.14
DaNN [5]	91.86	82.22	83.82	77.57	65.93	80.88	72.60	80.30	95.59	69.35	77.09	80.74	79.83
RTN [4]	91.86	93.33	80.88	80.99	69.63	70.59	59.08	74.73	**100.00**	59.08	70.02	91.11	78.44
ADDA [25]	93.15	94.07	97.06	85.27	87.41	89.71	86.82	92.08	**100.00**	89.90	93.79	98.52	92.31
IWAN [32]	94.22	**97.78**	98.53	89.90	87.41	88.24	90.24	95.29	**100.00**	91.61	94.43	98.52	93.85
PADA [2]	96.25	96.00	97.59	92.05	87.33	96.39	96.85	96.14	**100.00**	95.80	97.31	97.87	95.72
DPDAN	**96.28**	96.67	**100.00**	**97.15**	**91.33**	**100.00**	**97.11**	**97.93**	**100.00**	**96.59**	**97.32**	**100.00**	**97.53**

Table 2. Accuracy of *Office-Home* and *Caltech-Office* (256 classes → 10 classes).

Method	Office-Home							Method	Caltech-Office(256 classes → 10 classes)			
	Ar → Rw	Ar → Cl	Pr → Rw	Rw → Ar	Rw → Cl	Rw → Pr	Avg		C → W	C → A	C → D	Avg
ResNet [9]	75.87	46.33	74.88	67.40	48.18	74.17	64.47	AlexNet [11]	58.44	74.64	65.86	66.98
DaNN [5]	77.47	43.76	76.37	69.15	44.30	77.48	64.75	ResNet [9]	61.33	77.57	68.90	69.27
RTN [4]	78.58	49.31	75.32	63.18	43.57	80.50	65.58	DaNN [5]	54.57	72.86	57.96	61.80
IWAN [32]	78.12	53.94	81.28	76.46	56.75	**82.90**	71.58	RTN [16]	71.02	81.32	62.35	71.56
SAN [1]	74.60	44.42	80.07	72.18	50.21	78.66	66.69	SAN [14]	88.33	83.87	85.54	85.83
PADA [2]	78.74	51.95	78.79	73.73	56.6	77.09	69.48	PADA [1]	89.07	89.34	88.54	88.93
DPDAN	**79.04**	**59.40**	**81.79**	**76.77**	**58.67**	82.18	**72.98**	DPDAN	**89.96**	**90.17**	**92.06**	**90.73**

Table 3. Accuracy of tasks on *Office-31* and *VisDA2017*.

Method	Office-31							VisDA2017
	A → W	D → W	W → D	A → D	D → A	W → A	Avg	S → R
ResNet [9]	54.52	94.57	94.27	65.61	73.17	71.71	75.64	45.26
DAN [14]	46.44	53.56	58.60	42.68	65.66	65.34	55.38	47.60
DaNN [5]	41.35	46.78	38.85	41.36	41.34	44.68	42.39	51.01
ADDA [25]	43.65	46.68	40.12	43.66	42.76	45.95	43.77	50.06
RTN [4]	75.25	97.12	98.32	66.88	85.59	85.70	84.81	50.04
IWAN [32]	76.27	98.98	**100.00**	78.98	89.46	81.73	87.57	52.18
SAN [1]	81.82	98.64	**100.00**	81.28	80.58	83.09	87.27	52.06
PADA [2]	86.54	99.32	**100.00**	82.27	92.69	95.41	92.69	53.53
DPDAN	**96.27**	**100.00**	**100.00**	**96.82**	**96.35**	**95.62**	**97.51**	**65.26**

Art, Product images and Real-World. They are denoted as Ar, Cl, Pr and Rw. The target domain has 25 classes set as [2]. We carry out 6 partial domain adaptation tasks in this dataset.

VisDA2017 [29] is a challenging large-scale , which tries to narrow the synthetic-to-real domain gap across 12 categories. Under partial setting, we choose the first 6 categories(in alphabetic order) as target domain and conduct Symthetic12 → Real6 task as S→R.

We compare our DPDAN with present state-of-the-art results domain adaptation [4,9,14] and partial domain adaptation methods [1,2,32].

Table 4. Accuracy of DPDAN and its variants on *PDA* and *DA* setting.

DPDAN	Office-31							VisDA2017
	A → W	D → W	W → D	A → D	D → A	W → A	Avg	S → R
w/o hard binary weight	86.53	100.00	100.00	80.06	92.03	95.41	92.34	53.66
w/o negative domain discriminator	91.19	100.00	100.00	95.12	95.02	95.51	96.14	60.12
vanilla	**96.27**	100.00	100.00	**96.82**	**96.35**	**95.62**	**97.51**	**65.26**
DPDAN	Office-10 → Caltech-10							VisDA2017
	A → W	D → W	W → D	A → D	D → A	W → A	Avg	S → R
RTN [4]	95.51	95.20	94.19	93.70	**99.22**	**100.00**	96.31	63.80
vanilla	**96.01**	**96.33**	**95.45**	**94.38**	98.35	99.06	**96.60**	**64.51**

We conduct ablation tests by evaluating two variants of DPDAN: **(1)** DPDAN w/o hard binary weight is the variant without hard binary weight, in which only the positive and negative discriminators play their roles. In this case, the hard binary weight is taken placed by soft-weight. **(2)** DPDAN w/o negative discriminator is the variant without negative classes discriminator, in which only the positive discriminator and hard binary weight play their roles.**(3)** DPDAN from **Office-10** classes to **Caltech-10** classes and **VisDA2017** in standard domain adaptation setting. In this setting, we compared our results to RTN[[4]. We implement all methods in PyTorch, and finetune ResNet-50 [9] and AlexNet [11] pre-trained on ImageNet. Our implementation is based on DaNN [5]. The classifier layers C is added before DaNN bottleneck. For DPDAN, we train C, D_p and D_n from scratch. The learning rate of these above layers are set as 10 times of other layers. We use mini-batch stochastic gradient descent (SGD) with momentum of 0.9 and the learning rate strategy implemented in DaNN. The learning rate is adjusted during SGD using $p = \frac{\eta_0}{(1+\alpha p)^\gamma}$, where p is the training progress changing from 0 to 1, while α and γ are optimized with importance-weighted cross-validation [24] on one task of a dataset and fixed for all the other tasks of this dataset. Moreover, at the beginning of training, w_p is set as 1 for each class belonging to source domain in case the influence of prior knowledge. Note C, w_p and w_n are updated each 500 iterations.

4.2 Experimental Results

Classification results using ResNet-50 on the twelve tasks of Office10-Caltech5 are shown in Table 1. Six tasks of Office-Home and three tasks of Caltech256-Office10 are shown in Table 2, and six tasks of Office-31 are shown in Table 3.

The results also imply some insightful observations. **(1)** ResNet overperforms other standard DA on most tasks. It shows that source-negative classes have negative impact on standard DA methods. **(2)** RTN utilizes the entropy minimization criterion to restrain negative transfer caused by source-negative classes, but the result is still not satisfied. **(3)** PDA approaches perform better on these tasks due to the negative class evaluation. **(4)** DPDAN outperforms all the others, proving that our proposed mechanism can decrease negative transfer by dividing source label space into positive and negative spaces. As such, DPDAN is more accurate than the previous standard and partial DA approaches.

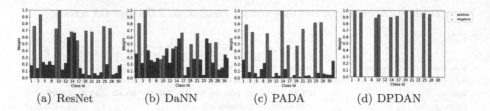

(a) ResNet   (b) DaNN   (c) PADA   (d) DPDAN

Fig. 3. Histograms of class weights learned by ResNet, DaNN, PADA and DPDAN.

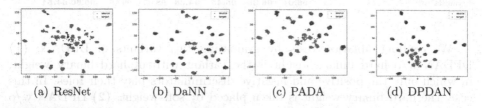

(a) ResNet   (b) DaNN   (c) PADA   (d) DPDAN

Fig. 4. Visualization of features learned by ResNet, DaNN, PADA and DPDAN.

We perform some ablation experiments to inspect the effect of different modules in Table 4. The results indicate some interesting points. **(1)** DPDAN outperforms DPDAN w/o hard binary weight, proving hard positive binary weight plays an important role. **(2)** DPDAN outperforms DPDAN w/o negative domain discriminator, showing negative domain adversarial network can decrease negative transfer by maximizing the distance between source-negative samples and others. **(3)** Our experiment can also get better results on standard DA compared with RTN according to Table 4. **(4)** Different from most ablation experiments, the relationship between D_n and w_p is not independent but sequential. In the experiment of DPDAN w/o hard binary weight from Table 4, due to lack of hard binary weight, we can only use soft-weight as negative domain labels directly. Actually this ablation experiment is only a combination of PADA and D_n. Here, the gap between the negative domain labels of positive and negative classes will be very small, and D_n will be hard to work, so the promotion is tiny. However, comparing DPDAN with DPDAN w/o negative domain discriminator, after setting w_p as negative domain label, the gap between the negative domain labels of positive and negative classes can be more distinct. Then D_n can effectively zoom out the distance between source negative classes and others. The comparison between these two shows the obvious performance promotion of D_n.

4.3   Analysis and Discussion

Class Weight: Fig. 3 are the histograms of class weights learned by ResNet-50, DaNN, PADA and DPDAN on task A (31 classes) $\rightarrow$ W (10 classes). The red and blue bins represent positive and negative samples, respectively.

Figure 3(a) implies ResNet-50 can select out most positive classes thanks to finetune. Figure 3(b) shows DaNN can barely classify positive and negative

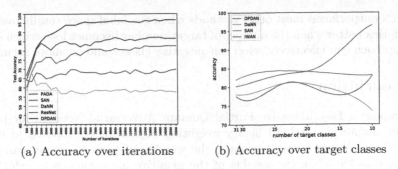

(a) Accuracy over iterations   (b) Accuracy over target classes

Fig. 5. Target test accuracy.

classes resulting in negative transfer. From Fig. 3(c), we observe that PADA can classify positive and negative classes correctly, but most weights of the positive and negative samples cannot achieve 1 and 0, which can still cause negative transfer. From Fig. 3(d), we can see the weights of positive and negative classes are almost to expect values. DPDAN can select out positive and negative classes correctly, and nearly eliminates negative transfer.

Feature Visualization: We visualize the t-SNE embeddings [3] of the bottleneck layer learned by ResNet-50, on task A (31 classes) → W (10 classes) in Fig. 4. The red points are source samples while the blue are target ones. From Fig. 4, we have some intuitive observations. (**1**) Thanks to finetune, ResNet can cluster some target samples into the right classes, but the accuracy is still not satisfied. (**2**) DaNN can not select out negative classes and lead to negative transfer. (**3**) PADA can select out most negative classes but the boundary between positive and negative samples is still unclear. (**4**) DPDAN can select out positive and negative classes, and cluster negative samples together. Each cluster of positive classes is far from the others. In this way, positive samples are hard to be misclassified and the negative samples are easy to be selected out.

Convergence Performance: In Fig. 5(a) we compare our results of target test accuracy with other methods on task A (31 classes) → W (10 classes). DPDAN can reach the highest accuracy rapidly, and the accuracy is still the most robust when the iteration increases. This observation also shows that our DPDAN can be trained more efficiently than previous PDA and DA methods.

Target Classes: In Fig. 5(b) we conduct plenty of experiments with a wide range of number of target classes on task A (31 classes) → W (10 classes). DaNN performance degenerates when the number of target classes decreases. The performance of SAN is stable and accuracy does not deteriorate with the number of target classes decreasing. IWAN performs better than DANN only when the label space does not overlap much and negative transfer is very serious.

DPDAN outperforms most other methods when the label space totally overlaps. It performs better when the number of target number becomes less, which shows our approach can effectively select out negative classes and promote accuracy.

5   Conclusion

We propose a Discriminative Partial Domain Adversarial Network for partial domain adaptation. A hard binary weighting algorithm is proposed to decide which class belongs to positive ones, the weights of positive classes can be as high as possible while the weights of the negative are almost zero, which can eliminate negative transfer greatly. Our framework contains two domain discriminator and one feature extractor to identify positive and negative samples from source domain. The distribution divergence between source-negative samples and all the others is maximized to mitigate negative transfer, and simultaneously the domain shift between source-positive and target samples is narrowed to obtain more discriminative domain-invariant features. The proposed framework can not only be applied to partial domain adaptation, but also be utilized to standard domain adaptation.Our DPDAN outperforms PDA and DA methods, and achieves the state-of-the-art result, showing the effectiveness and robustness of the method.

References

1. Cao, Z., Long, M., Wang, J., Jordan, M.I.: Partial transfer learning with selective adversarial networks. In: The IEEE Conference on Computer Vision and Pattern Recognition (CVPR) (2018)
2. Cao, Z., Ma, L., Long, M., Wang, J.: Partial adversarial domain adaptation. In: The European Conference on Computer Vision (ECCV) (2018)
3. Donahue, J., et al.: Decaf: a deep convolutional activation feature for generic visual recognition. In: International Conference on Machine Learning (ICML) (2014)
4. G. Cai, Y. Wang, M.Z.L.H.: Unsupervised domain adaptation with residual transfer networks. In: Advances in Neural Information Processing Systems (2016)
5. Ganin, Y., et al.: Domain-adversarial training of neural networks. J. Mach. Learn. Res. **17**, 59:1–59:35 (2016)
6. Gong, B., Shi, Y., Sha, F., Grauman., K.: Geodesic flow kernel for unsupervised domain adaptation. In: IEEE Conference on Computer Vision and Pattern Recognition (CVPR) (2012)
7. Goodfellow, I., et al.: Generative adversarial nets (2014)
8. Griffin, G., Holub, A., Perona, P.: Caltech-256 object category dataset. Technical report (2007)
9. He, K., Zhang, X., Ren, S., Sun, J.: Deep residual learning for image recognition. In: IEEE Conference on Computer Vision and Pattern Recognition (CVPR) (2016)
10. Hoffman, J., et al.: Cycada: cycleconsistent adversarial domain adaptation. In: Proceedings of the 35th International Conference on Machine Learning (ICML), vol. 2, pp. 1994–2003 (2018)
11. Krizhevsky, A., Sutskever, I., Hinton, G.E.: Imagenet classification with deep convolutional neural networks. In: Advances in Neural Information Processing Systems (NIPS) (2012)

12. Jain, L.P., Scheirer, W.J., Boult, T.E.: Multi-class open set recognition using probability of inclusion. In: Fleet, D., Pajdla, T., Schiele, B., Tuytelaars, T. (eds.) ECCV 2014. LNCS, vol. 8691, pp. 393–409. Springer, Cham (2014). https://doi.org/10.1007/978-3-319-10578-9_26

13. Long, J., Shelhamer, E., Darrell, T.: Fully convolutional networks for semantic segmentation. In: IEEE Conference on Computer Vision and Pattern Recognition (CVPR) (2015)

14. Long, M., Cao, Y., Wang, J., Jordan., M.I.: Learning transferable features with deep adaptation networks. In: Proceedings of the 34th International Conference on Machine Learning (ICML) (2015)

15. Long, M., Cao, Z., Wang, J., I, J.M.: Transferable features with deep adaptation networks. In: Proceedings of the 34th International Conference on Machine Learning (ICML) (2015)

16. Long, M., Zhu, H., Wang, J., Jordan., M.I.: Deep transfer learning with joint adaptation networks. In: Proceedings of the 34th International Conference on Machine Learning (ICML) (2017)

17. Luo, Z., Zou, Y., Hoffman, Y., Li, F.: Label efficient learning of transferable representations across domains and tasks. In: Advances in Neural Information Processing Systems (NIPS) (2017)

18. Otsu, N.: A threshold selection method from grey-level histograms. IEEE Trans. Syst. Man Cybern. **9**, 62–66 (1979)

19. Pan, Y., Yao, T., Li, Y., Wang, Y., Ngo, C., Mei, T.: Transferable prototypical networks for unsupervised domain adaptation. In: IEEE Conference on Computer Vision and Pattern Recognition (CVPR) (2019)

20. Ren, S., He, K., Girshick, R., Sun, J.: Faster r-cnn:towards real-time object detection with region proposal networks. In: Advances in Neural Information Processing Systems, vol. 28, pp. 91–99 (2015)

21. Russakovsky, O., et al.: Imagenet large scale visual recognition challenge. Int. J. Comput. Vision (IJCV) **115**, 211–252 (2015)

22. Saenko, K., Kulis, B., Fritz, M., Darrell, T.: Adapting visual category models to new domains. In: Daniilidis, K., Maragos, P., Paragios, N. (eds.) ECCV 2010. LNCS, vol. 6314, pp. 213–226. Springer, Heidelberg (2010). https://doi.org/10.1007/978-3-642-15561-1_16

23. Saito, K., Kim, D., Sclaroff, S., Saenko, K.: Universal domain adaptation through self-supervision. arXiv preprint (2020)

24. Sugiyama, M., Krauledat, M., Muller, K.R.: Covariate shift adaptation by importance weighted cross validation. J. Mach. Learn. Res. (JMLR) **8**, 985–1005 (2007)

25. Tzeng, E., Hoffman, J., Saenko, K., Darrell, T.: Adversarial discriminative domain adaptation. In: IEEE Conference on Computer Vision and Pattern Recognition (CVPR) (2017)

26. Tzeng, E., Hoffman, J., Zhang, N., Saenko, K., Darrell., T.: Simultaneous deep transfer across domains and tasks. In: IEEE International Conference on Computer Vision (ICCV) (2015)

27. Venkateswara, H., Eusebio, J., Chakraborty, S., Panchanathan, S.: Deep hashing network for unsupervised domain adaptation. In: IEEE Conference on Computer Vision and Pattern Recognition (CVPR) (2017)

28. Wang, C., Tuo, H., Wang, J., Qiao, L.: Discriminative transfer learning via local and global structure preservation. Signal Image Video Process. **13**(4), 753–760 (2019). https://doi.org/10.1007/s11760-018-1405-7

29. Peng, X., Usman, B., Kaushik, N., Hoffman, J., Wang, D., Saenko, K.: The visual domain adaptation challenge. arXiv preprint (2017)

30. Wang, X., Li, L., Wei, W., Long, M., Wang, J.: Transferable attention for domain adaptation. In: The Association for the Advance of Artificial Intelligence (AAAI) (2019)
31. Yosinski, J., Clune, J., Bengio, Y., Lipson, H.: How transferable are features in deep neural networks? In: Advances in Neural Information Processing Systems (NIPS) (2014)
32. Zhang, J., Ding, Z., Li, W., Ogunbona, P.: Importance weighted adversarial nets for partial domain adaptation. In: The IEEE Conference on Computer Vision and Pattern Recognition (CVPR) (2018)
33. Zhong, H., Tuo, H., Wang, C., Ren, X., Hu, J., Qiao, L.: Source-constraint adversarial domain adaptation, pp. 2486–2490 (2019). https://doi.org/10.1109/ICIP.2019.8803282

Differentiable Programming for Hyperspectral Unmixing Using a Physics-Based Dispersion Model

John Janiczek[1], Parth Thaker[1], Gautam Dasarathy[1], Christopher S. Edwards[2], Philip Christensen[1], and Suren Jayasuriya[1(✉)]

[1] Arizona State University, Tempe, USA
sjayasur@asu.edu
[2] Northern Arizona University, Flagstaff, USA

Abstract. Hyperspectral unmixing is an important remote sensing task with applications including material identification and analysis. Characteristic spectral features make many pure materials identifiable from their visible-to-infrared spectra, but quantifying their presence within a mixture is a challenging task due to nonlinearities and factors of variation. In this paper, spectral variation is considered from a physics-based approach and incorporated into an end-to-end spectral unmixing algorithm via differentiable programming. The dispersion model is introduced to simulate realistic spectral variation, and an efficient method to fit the parameters is presented. Then, this dispersion model is utilized as a generative model within an analysis-by-synthesis spectral unmixing algorithm. Further, a technique for inverse rendering using a convolutional neural network to predict parameters of the generative model is introduced to enhance performance and speed when training data is available. Results achieve state-of-the-art on both infrared and visible-to-near-infrared (VNIR) datasets, and show promise for the synergy between physics-based models and deep learning in hyperspectral unmixing in the future.

Keywords: Hyperspectral imaging · Spectral unmixing · Differentiable programming

1 Introduction

Hyperspectral imaging is a method of imaging where light radiance is densely sampled at multiple wavelengths. Increasing spectral resolution beyond a traditional camera's red, green, and blue spectral bands typically requires more expensive detectors, optics, and/or lowered spatial resolution. However, hyperspectral imaging has demonstrated its utility in computer vision, biomedical

Electronic supplementary material The online version of this chapter (https://doi.org/10.1007/978-3-030-58583-9_39) contains supplementary material, which is available to authorized users.

© Springer Nature Switzerland AG 2020
A. Vedaldi et al. (Eds.): ECCV 2020, LNCS 12372, pp. 649–666, 2020.
https://doi.org/10.1007/978-3-030-58583-9_39

imaging, and remote sensing [8,38]. In particular, spectral information is critically important for understanding material reflectance and emission properties, important for recognizing materials.

Spectral unmixing is a specific task within hyperspectral imaging with application to many land classification problems related to ecology, hydrology, and mineralogy [25,28]. It is particularly useful for analyzing aerial images from aircraft or spacecraft to map the abundance of materials in a region of interest. While pure materials have characteristic spectral features, mixtures require algorithms to identify and quantify material presence.

A common model for this problem is linear mixing, which assumes electromagnetic waves produced from pure materials combine linearly and are scaled by the material abundance. Mathematically this is expressed as $\mathbf{b} = \mathbf{A}\mathbf{x} + \eta$ where $\mathbf{b}$ is the observed spectra, $\mathbf{A}$ is a matrix whose columns are the pure material spectra, η is the measurement noise, and $\mathbf{x}$ is the abundance of each pure material. The model assumes that the pure material spectra, referred to as endmember spectra, is known before-hand. Nonlinear effects are known to occur when photons interact with multiple materials within a scene for which we refer readers to the review by Heylen et al. for techniques to account for the non-linear mixing [25].

A key challenge that affects both linear and nonlinear mixing models is that pure materials have an inherent variability in their spectral signatures, and thus cannot be represented by a single characteristic spectrum. Spectral variability of endmembers is caused by subtle absorption band differences due to factors such as different grain sizes [39,43,44,48] or differing ratios of molecular bonds [7, 51] as shown in Fig. 1. Since variability causes significant errors in unmixing algorithms, it is an active area of research [16,60,65].

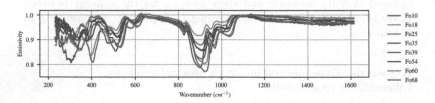

Fig. 1. Endmember Variation: Several spectra of olivine are plotted to demonstrate it's spectral variability. The olivine mineral is a solid solution with continuous compositional variation of Iron (Fe_2) and Magnesium (Mg_2) bonds. This ratio of bonds (indexed by the Fo number), causes absorption bands to shift in frequency and strength

Recently, differentiable programming has become a popular research area due to its potential to bridge gaps between physics-based and machine learning-based techniques for computer vision and graphics [1,21,53]. Our key insight is to leverage differentiable programming by modeling the variation of spectra with a physics-based dispersion model, and incorporating this differentiable model into an end-to-end spectral unmixing algorithm. Such an approach has the capacity to unmix scenes with a large amount of variability, while constraining the predictions to be physically plausible. These physically plausible variations of endmember spectra also provide additional science data as the variation of absorption bands can reveal properties about the composition and history of the material. To our knowledge, we are the first to use a generative physics model to account for spectral variability in an unmixing algorithm.

Contributions: Our specific contributions in this paper are the following:

- We introduce a physics-based dispersion model (first presented in [30,49, 55]) to generate and render spectral variation for various pure materials. We provide an efficient optimization method via gradient descent to find dispersion model parameters for this spectral variation.
- We incorporate this dispersion model into an end-to-end spectral unmixing algorithm utilizing differentiable programming to perform analysis-by-synthesis optimization. Analysis-by-synthesis is solved via alternating minimization optimization and requires no training data.
- We further design an inverse rendering algorithm consisting of a convolutional neural network to jointly estimate dispersion model parameters and mineral abundances for spectral unmixing. This method requires training data, but is computationally efficient at test time and outperforms analysis-by-synthesis and other state-of-the-art methods.

We provide extensive analysis of our proposed methods with respect to noise and convergence criteria. To validate our contributions, we test on both synthetic and real datasets using hyperspectral observations in the visible and near infrared (VNIR), and mid to far infrared (IR). The datasets also span three different environments from laboratory, aircraft, and satellite based spectrometers. Our methods achieve state-of-the-art across all datasets, and we compare against several baselines from literature. Our code is openly available and accessible here: https://github.com/johnjaniczek/InfraRender. We hope this work inspires more fusion between physics models and machine learning for hyperspectral imaging and computer vision more generally in the future.

2 Related Work

Optimization-Based Approaches. Standard optimization techniques for linear unmixing include projection, non-negative least squares, weighted least squares, and interior point methods [12,23,24,43,47]. Further, sparsity-based optimization can improve abundance prediction [9,63]. However, most optimization have not leveraged physics priors as we do in our model.

Spectral Variability. Spectral variability has been a topic of recent interest [6,60]. One approach is to augment **A** with multiple variations or spectra for each endmember. To do this, multiple endmember spectral mixture analysis (MESMA) [46] and multiple-endmember linear spectral unmixing (MELSUM) [15] both require labeled data of the spectral variation for each endmember. In contrast, unsupervised techniques learn endmember sets from unlabelled hyperspectral images, including semi-automated techniques [3], k-means clustering [3], and the sparsity promoting iterated constrained endmember algorithm (SPICE) [58,59] which simultaneously finds endmember sets while unmixing for material abundances. These techniques are limited by the amount of sets in the endmember library, and computational complexity increases with more additions. Our method by contrast finds an efficient parameter set to physically model the spectral variation.

Another category of endmember variability techniques models the endmember spectral variation as samples from a multivariate distribution $\mathbf{P}(\mathbf{e}|\theta)$ where $\mathbf{e}$ is the endmember spectra, and θ are the distribution parameters. Common statistical distributions proposed include the normal compositional model [50], Gaussian mixture models [65], and the beta compositional model [16]. These distribution models have large capacity to model spectral variations, however sometimes they can render endmember spectra that are not physically realistic.

Deep Learning for Hyperspectral Classification and Unmixing. Deep learning has recently improved many hyperspectral imaging tasks [33,62]. In particular, networks process hyperspectral pixel vectors using both deep belief networks [36] and CNNs [10,26,56]. For spatial hyperspectral data, CNNs [11], joint spectral-spatial feature extraction [64], and 3D CNNs [35] are used. All these methods require large hyperspectral datasets that are annotated correctly. One of our methods uses analysis-by-synthesis and differentiable programming to avoid low training data issues, but our technique can be made complementary to deep learning architectures as we show in our inverse rendering CNN.

Differentiable Programming and Rendering. Differentiable programming refers to the paradigm of writing algorithms which can be fully differentiated end-to-end using automatic differentiation for any parameter [4,53,54]. This has been applied for audio [18] and 3D geometry processing [45]. In graphics, differentiable rendering has improved ray tracing [34,37,40,61], solved analysis-by-synthesis problems in volumetric scattering [21,22], estimated reflectance and lighting [1], and performed 3D reconstruction [52]. In our paper, we write a forward imaging model utilizing the physics of dispersion in spectral variation to allow our pipeline to be differentiable end-to-end.

3   Method

Our approach to hyperspectral unmixing features two main components: (1) use of a physically-accurate dispersion model for pure endmember spectra, and (2) a differentiable programming pipeline to perform spectral unmixing. This approach has synergistic benefits of leveraging prior domain knowledge while learning from data. Our first algorithm solves spectral unmixing in a self-supervised fashion using analysis-by-synthesis optimization with the dispersion model as the synthesis step. Further, we show how inverse rendering via a convolutional neural network (CNN) can learn parameters of this model to help speed up our end-to-end pipeline and improves performance when training data is available.

3.1   Dispersion Model

We first describe the dispersion model for generating endmember spectra. **End-member and/or endmember spectra** is what we call the spectral curve for emissivity ϵ as a function of wavenumber ω. Each pure material has a characteristic endmember spectrum, although spectra can vary, which is the problem we are trying to solve/disambiguate.   Let $\varepsilon^{\text{measured}}(\omega)$ be endmember spectra we have measured, typically in a lab or in the field, whose emissivity is sampled at different wavenumbers: $\left[\varepsilon^{\text{measured}}(\omega_1), \cdots \varepsilon^{\text{measured}}(\omega_N)\right]^T$. Our goal is to propose a model $\varepsilon^{\text{model}}(\Lambda; \omega)$ with parameters Λ such that the following loss is minimized: $L(\Lambda) = \sum_{i=1}^{N} \left(\varepsilon^{\text{measured}}(\omega_i) - \varepsilon^{\text{model}}(\Lambda; \omega_i)\right)^2$. That is, we fit the model emissivity of an endmember spectrum to the measured spectrum. In practice, we need to add regularization and constraints to this endmember loss for better fitting which we describe after the derivation of the dispersion model.

Derivation of the Dispersion model: Our model of endmember spectra is derived from an atomistic oscillator driven by electromagnetic waves impinging on the molecular structure of the pure material [30,49]. In Fig. 2, we show a conceptual diagram of this model, and how it generates emissivity curves as a function of wavelength. For the full derivation of the model from first principles, we refer the reader to Appendix A in the supplementary material. Instead, we outline the model below based on the equations derived from that analysis.

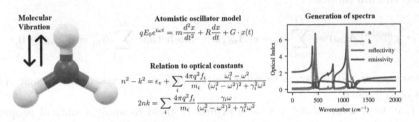

Fig. 2. Dispersion Model Concept Figure: The insight of the dispersion model is that optical properties can be related to molecular structure through first principles via an atomistic oscillator model. We use this generative model for the formation of spectral variation in our spectral unmixing algorithm

Let $\Lambda = [\rho, \omega_o, \gamma, \epsilon_r]$ be a matrix of parameters, where $\rho, \omega_o, \gamma, \epsilon_r \in \mathbb{R}^K$ and K is a model hyperparameter corresponding to the number of distinct mass-spring equations used to model the emissivity. ρ is the band strength, ω_o is the resonant frequency, γ is the frictional force (dampening coefficient), and ϵ_r is relative dielectric permeability. Please see the supplemental material for the physical significance of these parameters to the atomistic oscillator model, and their control over the shape of spectral absorption bands. Note: usually ϵ_r is a constant vector which does not vary with K. Thus $\Lambda \in \mathbb{R}^{K \times 4}$. The refractive index terms n, k are given as follows [30,49]:

$$n(\boldsymbol{\Lambda};\omega) = \sqrt{\frac{\theta+b}{2}}, \quad k(\boldsymbol{\Lambda};\omega) = \frac{\phi}{n(\boldsymbol{\Lambda};\omega)}, \tag{1}$$

where the expressions for θ, b, ϕ are given as follows:

$$\theta = \epsilon_r + \sum_{k=1}^{K} 4\pi \rho_k \omega_{0_k}^2 \frac{(\omega_{0_k}^2 - \omega^2)}{(\omega_{0_k}^2 - \omega^2)^2 + \gamma_k^2 \omega_{0_k}^2 \omega^2}, \tag{2}$$

$$b = \sqrt{\theta^2 + 4\phi^2}, \quad \phi = \sum_{k=1}^{K} 2\pi \rho_k \omega_{0_k}^2 \frac{\gamma_k \omega_{0_k} \omega}{(\omega_{0_k}^2 - \omega^2)^2 + \gamma_k^2 \omega_{0_k}^2 \omega^2}. \tag{3}$$

We note that subscript k denotes the k-th coordinate of the corresponding vector. Also there is another useful relation (derived in Appendix A) that $n^2 - k^2 = \theta$, $nk = \phi$. We then define the complex refractive index as $\hat{n}(\boldsymbol{\Lambda};\omega) = n(\boldsymbol{\Lambda};\omega) - i \cdot k(\boldsymbol{\Lambda};\omega)$, where $i = \sqrt{-1}$ is the imaginary number. Hence, we can calculate the emissivity as follows:

$$\epsilon(\boldsymbol{\Lambda};\omega) = 1 - R(\boldsymbol{\Lambda};\omega), \quad \text{where } R(\boldsymbol{\Lambda};\omega) = \left| \frac{\hat{n}(\boldsymbol{\Lambda};\omega) - 1}{\hat{n}(\boldsymbol{\Lambda};\omega) + 1} \right|^2. \tag{4}$$

When considering minerals, we introduce $M \in \mathbb{N}$, the number of optical axes of symmetry in crystal structures, (eg. 2 axes of symmetry in quartz [49,55]), to define the full model:

$$\varepsilon^{\text{model}}(\boldsymbol{\Lambda};\omega) = \sum_{m=1}^{M} \alpha_m \cdot \epsilon(\boldsymbol{\Lambda}_m;\omega) \quad \text{such that } \sum_{m=1}^{M} \alpha_m = 1, \alpha_m \geq 0, \tag{5}$$

where we use a different parameter matrix $\boldsymbol{\Lambda}_m$ and weight α_m for each optical axis of symmetry.

The dispersion model has been primarily used to analyze optical properties of materials to determine n and k, which then can be subsequently applied to optical models like radiative transfer [49,55]. After n and k are found, spectra such as reflectance, emissivity, and transmissivity can be generated. In particular, we notice that fine-grained control of the dispersion model parameters can realistically render spectral variation that occurs in hyperspectral data. Our contribution is to leverage these properties in a differentiable programming pipeline for spectral unmixing.

Endmember Fitting. Using the dispersion model presented above, we want to robustly estimate the model parameters to fit the spectra $\varepsilon^{\text{measured}}$ captured in a lab or in the field. To fit the model, we wish to perform gradient descent to efficiently find these parameters. Using chain rule on the loss function, we see that $\frac{\partial L}{\partial \boldsymbol{\Lambda}_{ij}} = \frac{\partial L}{\partial \varepsilon^{\text{model}}} \frac{\partial \varepsilon^{\text{model}}}{\partial \boldsymbol{\Lambda}_{ij}}$, where (ij) corresponds to that element of the parameter matrix, and all expressions are scalars once the coordinate is specified. While the partial derivatives can be calculated explicitly via symbolic toolboxes, the resulting expressions are too long to be presented here. For simplicity and ease of use, we use the autograd function [4,41] in PyTorch [42] to automatically compute derivatives for our model as we are performing backpropagation.

One main challenge in performing endmember fitting is that the dispersion model is not an injective function, and hence is typically not identifiable, that is more than one Λ can result in the same fit. This can be solved, in-part, through regularization to enforce sparsity, especially since a preference for fewer dispersion parameters has been suggested in the literature [49,55]. In our implementation, we initialize our model with $K = 50$ rows of the parameter matrix. Since the parameter ρ controls the strength of the absorption band, small values of ρ do not contribute much energy to the spectra (unnecessary absorption bands), and can be pruned. After performing sparse regression by penalizing the L_1 norm of ρ, K is typically around 10–15 in our experiments.

Thus, our modified sparse regression problem may be written as

$$\underset{\Lambda_{\min} \leq \Lambda \leq \Lambda_{\max}}{\arg\min} \sum_{i=1}^{N} \left(\epsilon^{real}(\omega_i) - \epsilon^{model}(\Lambda; \omega_i) \right)^2 + \lambda_\rho \|\rho\|_1, \tag{6}$$

where $\Lambda_{\min}$ and $\Lambda_{\max}$ restrict the variation of the dispersion parameters to a plausible range. In addition, endmembers (particularly minerals) can have multiple optical axes of symmetry described by separate spectra, which has been noted in the literature [49,55]. Without prior knowledge of the number of axes for every material we encounter, we run this optimization for a single and double axes, and pick the one with the lowest error. See Sect. 4 for results on endmember fitting and Fig. 6 for examples of modelled vs. measured spectra.

Despite the fact that this regression problem is non-convex, we solve it using gradient descent with a random initialization; this is known to converge to a local minimum with probability 1 [31]. A global minimum is not necessary at this stage, since we use endmember fitting to provide a good initialization point for the subsequent alternating minimization procedure introduced in the next subsection.

3.2 Differentiable Programming for End-to-End Spectral Unmixing

Analysis-by-Synthesis Optimization. In Fig. 3, we show our full end-to-end spectral unmixing pipeline. Here, $\varepsilon^{model}(\Lambda; \omega)$, which is initially fit to $\varepsilon^{measured}$, is then aggregated into the columns of $\mathbf{A}$. Then, the observed spectra $\mathbf{b}$ is linearly unmixed by solving a regularized least-squares optimization: $\arg\min_{\mathbf{x}} \|\mathbf{b} - \mathbf{A}\mathbf{x}\|_2^2 + \lambda \|\mathbf{x}\|_p$ subject to sum-to-one and non-negativity constraints $\|\mathbf{x}\|_1 = 1, \mathbf{x} \geq 0$. Given these constraints, one cannot impose sparsity with the usual L_1 norm. Instead, we use the L_p norm to induce sparsity for the predicted abundances; this has been proposed before for spectral unmixing [9].

The key to our pipeline is that everything is fully differentiable, and thus we can actually minimize the following equation:

$$\underset{\mathbf{x}, \Lambda \in [\Lambda_{min}, \Lambda_{max}]}{\arg\min} \|\mathbf{b} - \mathbf{A}(\Lambda)\mathbf{x}\|_2^2 + \lambda \|\mathbf{x}\|_p \text{ such that } \|\mathbf{x}\|_1 = 1, \mathbf{x} \geq 0. \tag{7}$$

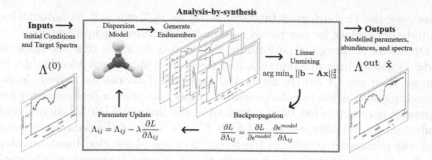

Fig. 3. Analysis-by-Synthesis: The analysis-by-synthesis algorithm uses differentiable programming to find optimal dispersion parameters and abundances. The initial dispersion parameters and the target spectra are fed as inputs, and the algorithm alternates between optimizing the abundances in the least squares sense and updating the dispersion parameters with respect to the gradient

with respect to both the parameters of the dispersion model Λ and the abundances $\mathbf{x}$. This gives us our recipe for hyperspectral unmixing: first, perform endmember fitting to initialize $\mathbf{A}(\Lambda)$, then, solve Eq. 7 in an alternating fashion for $\mathbf{x}$ and Λ. One could also solve this equation jointly for both unknowns, however, we found that the alternating optimization was faster and converged to better results.

The optimization problem established in Eq. (7) is an alternating minimization problem and is unfortunately not convex [27]. One popular approach to tackle nonconvex problems is to find a good initialization point [5,17], and then execute a form of gradient descent. Inspired by this, we first initialize $\mathbf{A}(\Lambda)$ by performing endmember fitting using Eq. 6 as described in the previous subsection. Our experiments indicate that this provides a useful initialization for our subsequent step. We then perform alternating minimization on Eq. 7 for $\mathbf{x}$ and Λ. Note that each iterate of the resulting alternating minimization involves the solution of a subproblem which has a convergence rate which depends on the condition number of the matrix $\mathbf{A}(\Lambda)$. For more details on this, we refer the reader to Appendix C where we discuss on the properties of $\mathbf{A}(\Lambda)$ across multiple runs.

In the ideal scenario, this initial matrix $\mathbf{A}(\Lambda)$ would consist of the endmember spectra that fully characterizes the mixed spectra $\mathbf{b}$. However, since spectra for the same material can significantly vary [7,39,43,44,48,51] (see Fig. 1), the initialization can be slightly off and we follow up with (7) to obtain a better fit. Note that this optimization problem is solving for the maximum likelihood estimator under a Gaussian noise model. Our optimization technique is performing **analysis-by-synthesis**, as given a single observation $\mathbf{b}$, the dispersion model synthesizes endmember variation until a good fit is achieved.

Inverse Rendering of Dispersion Model Parameters. The previous analysis-by-synthesis optimization does not require training data (labeled abundances in spectral mixtures) in order to perform spectral unmixing. However, there is room for even more improvement by using labeled data to help improve the parameter fitting of the model in the synthesis step. We train a CNN to predict the parameters for a generative model, known as inverse rendering in other domains [57]. In Fig. 4, we show this inverse rendering conceptually, and how it can be fed into our differentiable programming pipeline for end-to-end spectral unmixing.

Our CNN architecture consists of convolutional layers followed by a series of fully-connected layers. We refer the reader to the supplemental material for the exact network structure and implementation details. Using a CNN for inverse rendering is significantly faster at test time as compared to the analysis-by-synthesis optimization. However, it does have a drawback of requiring training data which is unavailable for certain tasks/datasets.

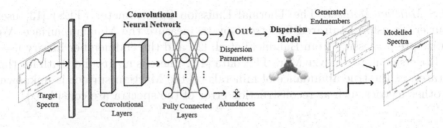

Fig. 4. Inverse Rendering: A CNN is trained to "inversely render" pixels of the hyperspectral image, by predicting both the dispersion parameters that control the spectral variability, and the abundances that control the mixing model. During training, the reconstruction error is back-propagated through the differentiable dispersion model to boost the performance of the network at making physically realistic predictions

4   Experimental Results

Datasets. We utilize three separate datasets to validate our spectral unmixing algorithms. In Fig. 5, we visually represent these datasets and their exemplar data. For specific implementation details and dataset pre-processing, please see Appendix D in the supplemental material.

Feely et al. Dataset. We utilize 90 samples from the Feely et al. dataset [19] of thermal emission spectra in the infrared for various minerals measured in the lab. Ground truth was determined via optical petrography [19], and a labeled endmember library is provided. The limited amount of data is challenging for machine learning methods, so we utilize the dispersion model to generate 50,000 additional synthetic spectra for dataset augmentation.

Gulfport Dataset. The Gulfport dataset from Gader et al. [20] contains hyperspectral aerial images in the VNIR along with ground truth classification labels segmenting pixels into land types (e.g. grass, road, building). Although the dataset is for spectral classification, it can also be used to benchmark unmixing algorithms by creating synthetic mixtures of pure pixels from the Gulfport dataset with random abundances as done by [16,65]. We perform both spectral classification (Gulfport) and unmixing (Gulfport synthetic) tasks in our testing. Both datasets are split into a train and test set (although some methods do not require training data), and the training data is augmented with 50,000 synthetically generated mixtures from the dispersion model.

One main difficulty of this dataset is the endmembers identified correspond to coarse materials such as grass and road as opposed to pure materials. Such endmembers can significantly vary across multiple pixels, but this spectral variation is not physically described by the dispersion model. To solve this problem, we utilize K-means clustering to learn examplar endmembers for each category (e.g. grass, road, etc). Then the resulting centroid endmember can be fit to the dispersion model to allow further variation such as absorption band shifts in the spectra. We found that $K = 5$ worked the best for the Gulfport dataset.

TES Martian Dataset. The Thermal Emission Spectrometer (TES) [13] uses Fourier Transform Infrared Spectroscopy to measure the Martian surface. We utilize pre-processing from Bandfield et al. [2], and the endmember library used by Rogers et al. to analyze Mars TES data [47]. There is no ground truth for this dataset, as the true abundance of minerals on the Martian surface is unknown, so other metrics such as reconstruction error of the spectra are considered.

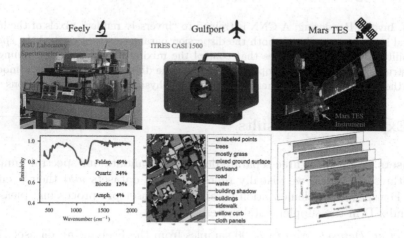

Fig. 5. Datasets: This figure shows representative data and instrumentation for the three datasets considered in this paper. Data includes laboratory, aircraft, and satellite measurements, and ground truth ranges from detailed abundance analysis under a microscope (Feely [19]) to pure pixel labels of land type for spectral classification (Gulfport [20]) to no ground truth for the Martian data (TES [13])

Baselines. We compare against several state-of-the-art baselines in the literature. The basic linear unmixing algorithm is Fully Constrained Least Squares (FCLS) [24] which solves least squares with sum-to-one and non-negativity constraints on the abundances. We also implement two state-of-the-art statistical methods for modelling endmember variability as distributions: the Normal Compositional Model (NCM) [50] and the Beta Compositional Model (BCM) [16]. NCM and BCM use a Gaussian and Beta distribution respectively, perform expectation-maximization for unmixing, and require a small amount of training data to determine model parameters.

We also compare against two state-of-the-art deep learning networks by Zhang et al. [63]. The first network utilizes a 1D CNN (CNN-1D) architecture, while the second network utilizes a 3D CNN (but with 1D convolutional kernels) (CNN-3D). CNN-3D is only applicable to datasets with spatial information, and not testable on the Feely and Gulfport synthetic data. We further created a modified CNN architecture (CNN-1D Modified) to maximize the performance on our datasets by changing the loss function to MSE, removing max-pooling layers, and adding an additional fully connected layer before the output. In the supplemental material, we provide information about the parameters, network architectures, and training procedures we used for these baselines as well as details for our own methods. We also have all of our code available here: https://github.com/johnjaniczek/InfraRender.

Endmember Fitting Results. To bootstrap both the analysis-by-synthesis and inverse rendering algorithms, good initial conditions for the dispersion parameters need to be input to the model. Determining dispersion parameters typically required detailed molecular structure analysis or exhaustive parameter searching methods [32,49,55]. One main advantage of our method is that we utilize gradient descent to efficiently find parameter sets for different materials. In Appendix B of the supplemental material, we share some of these parameter sets and our insights using the dispersion model for the scientific community.

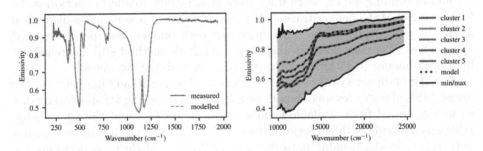

Fig. 6. Endmember Fitting: (Left) Measured and modelled spectra for a quartz sample in the IR. (Right) Cluster centroids found for pixels labelled as grass in the Gulfport dataset, and the model fit to these centroids. Note the high fidelity of fit via the dispersion model for both these cases

In Fig. 6, we show qualitative results of our endmember fitting by minimizing the loss in Eq. 6 using gradient descent. The reconstructed spectra achieves a low MSE with the measured spectra with an average MSE of 0.016 for the TES library, 0.0019 for the Feely library, and an MSE of 2.6e−5 on the Gulfport cluster centroids. Note that there is noise in the measurements, and so MSE is not an absolute metric of the fit to the true unknown spectra.

Table 1. Results: Table - Mean squared error of the abundance predictions vs. ground truth for Feely, Gulfport, and Gulfport synthetic datasets. The bold entries indicate top performance

Dataset	FCLS [24]	NCM [50]	BCM [16]	CNN-1D [63]	CNN-3D [63]	CNN-1D Modified	Analysis-by-synthesis	Inverse Rendering
Feely [19]	0.121	0.119	0.131	0.469	N/A	0.205	**0.052**	0.188
Gulfport [20]	0.75	0.799	0.800	1.000	0.497	0.297	0.45	**0.272**
Gulfport Synthetic	0.911	0.471	0.136	0.824	N/A	0.148	0.147	**0.059**

Spectral Unmixing Results. In Table 1, we show results on the Feely, Gulfport, and the Gulfport synthetic mixture datasets. For Feely, the analysis-by-synthesis method achieved a MSE of 0.052, with the next closest method (NCM) achieving 0.119. Due to the Feely dataset only containing 90 test samples, the machine learning methods were trained on synthetic data which explains their lower performance as data mismatch. Thus, the low error of analysis-by-synthesis shows the utility of the dispersion model for modelling endmember variability, particularly in cases with low training data.

For the Gulfport dataset, the task was to predict the material present since the labeled data is for single coarse materials (e.g. road, grass, etc) at 100% abundance per pixel. Here, the deep learning methods of CNNs and Inverse Rendering have the highest performance. This is expected as there exists a large amount of training data to learn from. Note that Inverse Rendering performs the best at 0.272 MSE, demonstrating that the addition of a generative dispersion model to the output of the CNN improves performance over purely learned approaches. Also note that our analysis-by-synthesis method still has relatively high performance (0.45 MSE) without using any training data at all.

For the Gulfport synthetic mixture dataset, Inverse Rendering achieves the lowest MSE of 0.059, leveraging both physics-based modeling for spectral mixing as well as learns from available training data. The BCM and the analysis-by-synthesis methods both outperform the CNN methods, even though they do not have access to the training data. In fact, BCM even slightly outperforms the analysis-by-synthesis method, which could be because the sources of variation in this data are well-described by statistical distributions.

Speed of Methods. The additional capacity of adding statistical and physical models usually has a cost of speed in implementation. Averaged over 90 mixtures, the convergence for a single operation was FCLS - 10 ms, BCM - 1.23 s, NCM

- 18 ms, CNN - 33 ms, Inverse Rendering - 39 ms, and analysis-by-synthesis - 10.2 s. Future work could potentially increase the speed of analysis-by-synthesis with parallel processing.

Noise Analysis. Prior to spectral unmixing, emissivity is separated from radiance by dividing out the black-body radiation curve at the estimated temperature [14,43]. In general, a Gaussian noise profile in the radiance space with variance $\sigma^2_{\text{radiance}}$ results in wavenumber dependent noise source in the emissivity space with the profile $\sigma^2(\omega) = \sigma^2_{\text{radiance}} \cdot 1/B(\omega, T)$ where B is the black-body function given by Planck's law. In our noise experiments we use a black-body radiation curve for a 330K target, which is the approximate temperature the Feely dataset samples were held at. In Fig. 7 left, we see that the emissivity noise is higher where the radiance signal is lower.

We simulated varying the noise power to determine the methods' robustness tested on 30 samples from the Feely dataset. In Fig. 7, you can see that analysis-by-synthesis still has the best performance in the presence of noise, and is relatively flat as noise increases compared to other methods. We note that statistical methods, while having higher average error, seem to be robust to increased noise as they can handle random perturbations of each spectral band statistically. CNN and Inverse Rendering methods perform the worst for high noise, as these methods were trained on data without noise.

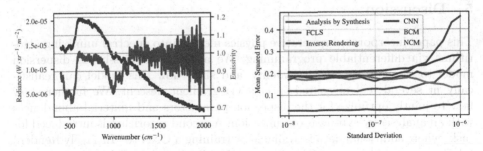

Fig. 7. The left plot shows the radiance profile of a spectra perturbed by Gaussian noise and the resulting emissivity profile after separating out the blackbody radiance. The right figure shows the robustness of the algorithms to increasing amounts of noise

TES Data. The Mars TES data was unmixed using our analysis-by-synthesis method to demonstrate it's utility on tasks where zero training data is available. The method produces mineral maps which correctly finds abundances of the mineral hematite at Meridiani Planum in Fig. 8. This is an important Martian mineral which provides evidence for liquid water having existed at some point on Mars, and has been verified by NASA's Opportunity Rover [29]. Note how FCLS predicts many sites for hematite, while our method narrows down potential sites on the Martian surface, which is useful for planetary scientists. By allowing for spectral variation through our physics-based approach, our method has lower

RMS reconstruction error than previous analysis of TES data. FCLS, which was previously used on TES because of the zero training-data problem, has an average RMS reconstruction error of 0.0043 while analysis-by-synthesis has an average of 0.0038. This is an exciting result as our methods could provide a new suite of hyperspectral analysis tools for scientists studying the Martian surface.

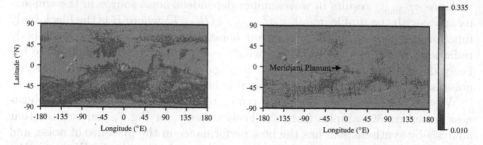

Fig. 8. Martian Surface Map: The images show the mineral map for hematite of the Martian surface produced by FCLS (left) and analysis-by-synthesis (right) using TES data. Both algorithms find the known deposit of hematite on Meridiani Planum, but analysis-by-synthesis predicts a sparser map which matches expected distributions.

5 Discussion

This paper incorporated generative physics models into spectral unmixing algorithms via differentiable programming. We adopt a physics-based dispersion model to simulate spectral variability, and show how this model can realistically fit several real measured spectra via gradient descent. We further show how to jointly optimize for the dispersion parameters and material abundances with an analysis-by-synthesis optimization. A second algorithm is introduced for tasks where additional data is available by training a CNN to "Inversely Render" a hyperspectral image with the differentiable dispersion model in the loop.

We validate these contributions extensively on three datasets ranging from mid to far IR and VNIR, and compared against state-of-the-art optimization, statistical and deep learning benchmarks. From these experiments we observe that analysis-by-synthesis has the best performance when training data is not available, and that Inverse Rendering has the best performance when training data is available. We also see that analysis-by-synthesis is noise resilient, and reconstructs Mars spectra with lower error than previous techniques.

There are still limitations for the methods proposed. First, analysis-by-synthesis has a large computational cost compared to other methods, although this could be mitigated through parallelization. Secondly, the spectral unmixing community is limited by the lack of quality training datasets, and it is not easy for experts to label remote sensing datasets from prior knowledge alone. Future work could investigate generating realistic synthetic data suitable for training machine learning based algorithms for better performance. We hope using generative physics-based models inspires others to produce realistic synthetic data as well as differentiable programming methods which require low training data.

Acknowledgements. This work was supported by NSF grant IIS-1909192 as well as GPU resources from ASU Research Computing. We thank Dr. Alina Zare, Christopher Haberle, and Dr. Deanna Rogers for their helpful discussions, and Kim Murray (formerly Kim Feely) for providing the laboratory measurements and analysis contributing to this paper.

References

1. Azinovic, D., Li, T.M., Kaplanyan, A., Niessner, M.: Inverse path tracing for joint material and lighting estimation. In: Proceedings of the IEEE Conference on Computer Vision and Pattern Recognition, pp. 2447–2456 (2019)
2. Bandfield, J.L.: Global mineral distributions on mars. J. Geophys. Res. Planets **107**(E6), 1–9 (2002)
3. Bateson, C.A., Asner, G.P., Wessman, C.A.: Endmember bundles: a new approach to incorporating endmember variability into spectral mixture analysis. IEEE Trans. Geosci. Remote Sens. **38**(2), 1083–1094 (2000)
4. Baydin, A.G., Pearlmutter, B.A., Radul, A.A., Siskind, J.M.: Automatic differentiation in machine learning: a survey. J. Mach. Learn. Res. **18**(1), 5595–5637 (2017)
5. Bhojanapalli, S., Kyrillidis, A., Sanghavi, S.: Dropping convexity for faster semidefinite optimization. In: Conference on Learning Theory, pp. 530–582 (2016)
6. Borsoi, R.A., et al.: Spectral variability in hyperspectral data unmixing: a comprehensive review. arXiv preprint arXiv:2001.07307 (2020)
7. Burns, R.G.: Crystal field spectra and evidence of cation ordering in olivine minerals. Am. Mineral. J. Earth Planet. Mater. **55**(9–10), 1608–1632 (1970)
8. Chang, C.I.: Hyperspectral Imaging: Techniques for Spectral Detection and Classification, vol. 1. Springer, New York (2003). https://doi.org/10.1007/978-1-4419-9170-6
9. Chen, F., Zhang, Y.: Sparse hyperspectral unmixing based on constrained lp-l 2 optimization. IEEE Geosci. Remote Sens. Lett. **10**(5), 1142–1146 (2013)
10. Chen, Y., Jiang, H., Li, C., Jia, X., Ghamisi, P.: Deep feature extraction and classification of hyperspectral images based on convolutional neural networks. IEEE Trans. Geosci. Remote Sens. **54**(10), 6232–6251 (2016)
11. Cheng, G., Li, Z., Han, J., Yao, X., Guo, L.: Exploring hierarchical convolutional features for hyperspectral image classification. IEEE Trans. Geosci. Remote Sens. **56**(11), 6712–6722 (2018)
12. Chouzenoux, E., Legendre, M., Moussaoui, S., Idier, J.: Fast constrained least squares spectral unmixing using primal-dual interior-point optimization. IEEE J. Sel. Top. Appl. Earth Observations Remote Sens. **7**(1), 59–69 (2014)
13. Christensen, P., et al.: Mars global surveyor thermal emission spectrometer experiment: investigation description and surface science results. J. Geophys. Res. Planets **106**(E10), 23823–23871 (2001)
14. Christensen, P.R., et al.: Lauretta: The OSIRIS-REx thermal emission spectrometer (OTES) instrument. Space Sci. Rev. **214**(5), 87 (2018)

15. Combe, J.P., et al.: Analysis of OMEGA/mars express data hyperspectral data using a multiple-endmember linear spectral unmixing model (MELSUM): methodology and first results. Planet. Space Sci. **56**(7), 951–975 (2008)
16. Du, X., Zare, A., Gader, P., Dranishnikov, D.: Spatial and spectral unmixing using the beta compositional model. IEEE J. Sel. Top. Appl. Earth Observations Remote Sens. **7**(6), 1994–2003 (2014)
17. Duchi, J.C., Ruan, F.: Solving (most) of a set of quadratic equalities: composite optimization for robust phase retrieval. Inf. Infer. J. IMA **8**(3), 471–529 (2019)
18. Engel, J., Hantrakul, L.H., Gu, C., Roberts, A.: DDSP: differentiable digital signal processing. In: International Conference on Learning Representations (2020)
19. Feely, K.C., Christensen, P.R.: Quantitative compositional analysis using thermal emission spectroscopy: application to igneous and metamorphic rocks. J. Geophys. Res. Planets **104**(E10), 24195–24210 (1999)
20. Gader, P., Zare, A., Close, R., Aitken, J., Tuell, G.: MUUFL Gulfport hyperspectral and LIDAR airborne data set. Tech. rep. REP-2013-57. University Florida, Gainesville, FL, USA0 (2013)
21. Gkioulekas, I., Levin, A., Zickler, T.: An evaluation of computational imaging techniques for heterogeneous inverse scattering. In: Leibe, B., Matas, J., Sebe, N., Welling, M. (eds.) ECCV 2016. LNCS, vol. 9907, pp. 685–701. Springer, Cham (2016). https://doi.org/10.1007/978-3-319-46487-9_42
22. Gkioulekas, I., Zhao, S., Bala, K., Zickler, T., Levin, A.: Inverse volume rendering with material dictionaries. ACM Trans. Graph. (TOG) **32**(6), 162 (2013)
23. Goudge, T.A., Mustard, J.F., Head, J.W., Salvatore, M.R., Wiseman, S.M.: Integrating CRISM and TES hyperspectral data to characterize a halloysite-bearing deposit in Kashira crater, mars. Icarus **250**, 165–187 (2015)
24. Heinz, D.C., et al.: Fully constrained least squares linear spectral mixture analysis method for material quantification in hyperspectral imagery. IEEE Trans. Geosci. Remote Sens. **39**(3), 529–545 (2001)
25. Heylen, R., Parente, M., Gader, P.: A review of nonlinear hyperspectral unmixing methods. IEEE J. Sel. Top. Appl. Earth Observations Remote Sens. **7**(6), 1844–1868 (2014)
26. Hu, W., Huang, Y., Wei, L., Zhang, F., Li, H.: Deep convolutional neural networks for hyperspectral image classification. J. Sens. **2015**, 12 (2015)
27. Jain, P., Kar, P., et al.: Non-convex optimization for machine learning. Found. Trends Mach. Learn. **10**(3–4), 142–336 (2017)
28. Keshava, N., Mustard, J.F.: Spectral unmixing. IEEE Signal Process. Mag. **19**(1), 44–57 (2002)
29. Klingelhöfer, G., et al.: Jarosite and hematite at Meridiani planum from opportunity's mössbauer spectrometer. Science **306**(5702), 1740–1745 (2004)
30. Larkin, P.: Infrared and Raman Spectroscopy: Principles and Spectral Interpretation. Elsevier (2017)
31. Lee, J.D., Simchowitz, M., Jordan, M.I., Recht, B.: Gradient descent converges to minimizers. arXiv preprint arXiv:1602.04915 (2016)
32. Lee, S., Tien, C.: Optical constants of soot in hydrocarbon flames. In: Symposium (International) on Combustion, vol. 18, pp. 1159–1166. Elsevier (1981)
33. Li, S., Song, W., Fang, L., Chen, Y., Ghamisi, P., Benediktsson, J.A.: Deep learning for hyperspectral image classification: an overview. IEEE Trans. Geosci. Remote Sens. **57**(9), 6690–6709 (2019)
34. Li, T.M., Aittala, M., Durand, F., Lehtinen, J.: Differentiable monte carlo ray tracing through edge sampling. ACM Trans. Graph. (Proc. SIGGRAPH Asia) **37**(6), 222:1–222:11 (2018)

35. Li, Y., Zhang, H., Shen, Q.: Spectral-spatial classification of hyperspectral imagery with 3D convolutional neural network. Remote Sens. **9**(1), 67 (2017)
36. Liu, P., Zhang, H., Eom, K.B.: Active deep learning for classification of hyperspectral images. IEEE J. Sel. Top. Appl. Earth Observations Remote Sens. **10**(2), 712–724 (2016)
37. Loubet, G., Holzschuch, N., Jakob, W.: Reparameterizing discontinuous integrands for differentiable rendering. Trans. Graph. (Proc. SIGGRAPH Asia) **38**(6) (2019). https://doi.org/10.1145/3355089.3356510
38. Lu, G., Fei, B.: Medical hyperspectral imaging: a review. J. Biomed. Opt. **19**(1), 010901 (2014)
39. Moersch, J., Christensen, P.R.: Thermal emission from particulate surfaces: a comparison of scattering models with measured spectra. J. Geophys. Res. Planets **100**(E4), 7465–7477 (1995)
40. Nimier-David, M., Vicini, D., Zeltner, T., Jakob, W.: Mitsuba 2: a retargetable forward and inverse renderer. Trans. Graph. (Proc. SIGGRAPH Asia) **38**(6) (2019). https://doi.org/10.1145/3355089.3356498
41. Paszke, A., et al.: Automatic differentiation in pytorch (2017)
42. Paszke, A., et al.: Pytorch: an imperative style, high-performance deep learning library. In: Advances in Neural Information Processing Systems, pp. 8024–8035 (2019)
43. Ramsey, M.S., Christensen, P.R.: Mineral abundance determination: quantitative deconvolution of thermal emission spectra. J. Geophys. Res. Solid Earth **103**(B1), 577–596 (1998)
44. Ramsey, M.S., Christensen, P.R.: Mineral abundance determination: Quantitative deconvolution of thermal emission spectra: application to analysis of martian atmospheric particulates. J. Geophys. Res. Solid Earth **103**, 577–596 (2000)
45. Ravi, N., et al.: Pytorch3D. https://github.com/facebookresearch/pytorch3d (2020)
46. Roberts, D.A., Gardner, M., Church, R., Ustin, S., Scheer, G., Green, R.: Mapping chaparral in the santa monica mountains using multiple endmember spectral mixture models. Remote Sens. Environ. **65**(3), 267–279 (1998)
47. Rogers, A., Aharonson, O.: Mineralogical composition of sands in meridiani planum determined from mars exploration rover data and comparison to orbital measurements. J. Geophys. Res. Planets **113**, E6 (2008)
48. Salisbury, J.W., D'Aria, D.M., Sabins Jr., F.F.: Thermal infrared remote sensing of crude oil slicks. Remote Sens. Environ. **45**(2), 225–231 (1993)
49. Spitzer, W., Kleinman, D.: Infrared lattice bands of quartz. Phys. Rev. **121**(5), 1324 (1961)
50. Stein, D.: Application of the normal compositional model to the analysis of hyperspectral imagery. In: IEEE Workshop on Advances in Techniques for Analysis of Remotely Sensed Data, 2003, pp. 44–51. IEEE (2003)
51. Sunshine, J.M., Pieters, C.M.: Determining the composition of olivine from reflectance spectroscopy. J. Geophys. Res. Planets **103**(E6), 13675–13688 (1998)
52. Tsai, C.Y., Sankaranarayanan, A.C., Gkioulekas, I.: Beyond volumetric albedo – a surface optimization framework for non-line-of-sight imaging. In: IEEE International Conference Computer Vision and Pattern Recognition (CVPR) (2019)
53. Wang, F., Decker, J., Wu, X., Essertel, G., Rompf, T.: Backpropagation with callbacks: foundations for efficient and expressive differentiable programming. In: Advances in Neural Information Processing Systems, pp. 10180–10191 (2018)

54. Wang, F., Zheng, D., Decker, J., Wu, X., Essertel, G.M., Rompf, T.: Demystifying differentiable programming: shift/reset the penultimate backpropagator. In: Proceedings of the ACM on Programming Languages, vol. 3, no. ICFP, pp. 1–31 (2019)
55. Wenrich, M.L., Christensen, P.R.: Optical constants of minerals derived from emission spectroscopy: application to quartz. J. Geophys. Res. Solid Earth 101(B7), 15921–15931 (1996)
56. Yang, X., Ye, Y., Li, X., Lau, R.Y., Zhang, X., Huang, X.: Hyperspectral image classification with deep learning models. IEEE Trans. Geosci. Remote Sens. 56(9), 5408–5423 (2018)
57. Yu, Y., Smith, W.A.: InverseRenderNet: learning single image inverse rendering. In: Proceedings of the IEEE Conference on Computer Vision and Pattern Recognition, pp. 3155–3164 (2019)
58. Zare, A., Gader, P.: Sparsity promoting iterated constrained endmember detection in hyperspectral imagery. IEEE Geosci. Remote Sens. Lett. 4(3), 446–450 (2007)
59. Zare, A., Gader, P.: Hyperspectral band selection and endmember detection using sparsity promoting priors. IEEE Geosci. Remote Sens. Lett. 5(2), 256–260 (2008)
60. Zare, A., Ho, K.: Endmember variability in hyperspectral analysis: addressing spectral variability during spectral unmixing. IEEE Signal Process. Mag. 31(1), 95–104 (2013)
61. Zhang, C., Wu, L., Zheng, C., Gkioulekas, I., Ramamoorthi, R., Zhao, S.: A differential theory of radiative transfer. ACM Trans. Graph. (TOG) 38(6), 1–16 (2019)
62. Zhang, L., Zhang, L., Du, B.: Deep learning for remote sensing data: a technical tutorial on the state of the art. IEEE Geosci. Remote Sens. Mag. 4(2), 22–40 (2016)
63. Zhang, S., Li, J., Li, H.C., Deng, C., Plaza, A.: Spectral-spatial weighted sparse regression for hyperspectral image unmixing. IEEE Trans. Geosci. Remote Sens. 56(6), 3265–3276 (2018)
64. Zhao, W., Du, S.: Spectral-spatial feature extraction for hyperspectral image classification: a dimension reduction and deep learning approach. IEEE Trans. Geosci. Remote Sens. 54(8), 4544–4554 (2016)
65. Zhou, Y., Rangarajan, A., Gader, P.D.: A Gaussian mixture model representation of endmember variability in hyperspectral unmixing. IEEE Trans. Image Process. 27(5), 2242–2256 (2018)

Deep Cross-Species Feature Learning for Animal Face Recognition via Residual Interspecies Equivariant Network

Xiao Shi[1,2], Chenxue Yang[1,2], Xue Xia[1,2], and Xiujuan Chai[1,2(✉)]

[1] Agricultural Information Institute of CAAS, Beijing, China
sixiaosmile@outlook.com, {yangchenxue,xiaxue,chaixiujuan}@caas.cn
[2] Key Laboratory of Agricultural Big Data, Ministry of Agriculture
and Rural Affairs, Beijing 100081, China

Abstract. Although human face recognition has achieved exceptional success driven by deep learning, animal face recognition (AFR) is still a research field that received less attention. Due to the big challenge in collecting large-scale animal face datasets, it is difficult to train a high-precision AFR model from scratch. In this work, we propose a novel Residual InterSpecies Equivariant Network (RiseNet) to deal with the animal face recognition task with limited training samples. First, we formulate a module called residual inter-species feature equivariant to make the feature distribution of animals face closer to the human. Second, according to the structural characteristic of animal face, the features of the upper and lower half faces are learned separately. We present an animal facial feature fusion module to treat the features of the lower half face as additional information, which improves the proposed RiseNet performance. Besides, an animal face alignment strategy is designed for the preprocessing of the proposed network, which further aligns with the human face image. Extensive experiments on two benchmarks show that our method is effective and outperforms the state-of-the-arts.

Keywords: Animal face recognition · Interspecies · Fine-tuning · Feature equivariant · Feature fusion

1 Introduction

Face recognition is a widely used biometric authentication method. Human face recognition has been broadly concerned by researchers [7,15,16,30]. The recent study ArcFace [7] has achieved 99.78% accuracy on face verification. However, Animal Face Recognition (AFR) is still a less attention research area in computer vision. The recognition of animal faces has great significance for precision agriculture [2] and protection of rare animals [19]. There still exist plenty of challenges for accurate animal face recognition.

In face recognition, convolutional neural network is the most effective feature extractor. Training an effective face recognition system requires significant

© Springer Nature Switzerland AG 2020
A. Vedaldi et al. (Eds.): ECCV 2020, LNCS 12372, pp. 667–682, 2020.
https://doi.org/10.1007/978-3-030-58583-9_40

training data. After years of development of face recognition, many open-source datasets have been released for research. For example, LFW (Labeled Faces in the Wild) [11] provides a total of 13,233 annotated face images from 5749 people with natural environments and complex environments. CASIA-WebFace [32] contains 494,444 images with 10,575 labels collected from the Internet. However, animal face images with identity labels hard to collect. On a normal scale pig farm, there are only about one thousand pigs raised separately. Animals will not cooperate with data collection as humans do. Therefore, in addition to the limited data resources, the data collection also takes a lot of time and labor. Without a large-scale animal face recognition dataset, it is almost impossible to train an animal face recognition network from scratch [22].

When the training data of the new task is insufficient, we can improve the network performance through two operations of pre-train and fine-tuning [28]. Fine-tuning operation is a kind of transfer learning that can improve the performance of new tasks based on the correlation between the source domain and the target domain. Undoubtedly, animal faces have some correlations with human faces, and the prior knowledge of human face recognition can improve the performance of animal face recognition. But the structural difference between animal and human faces will affect the cross-species knowledge transfer. In other words, the performance of fine-tuning is influenced by the correlation between tasks [33].

Researchers have proposed a series of methods to reduce the data distribution difference between tasks [21,27,36]. For example, [27] combines soft label loss and domain confusion loss to improve fine-tuning performance. Zhao et al. [36] adapt the pre-trained network via a dual learning mechanism. These methods usually have a fixed number of categories, and the target domain categories should be included in the source domain categories. Identity recognition is a special classification task, which has no fixed categories.

To address these challenges, we hope to achieve better inter-species knowledge transfer by adjusting the data of the target domain (animal) to a pre-trained human face recognition network. In other words, we hope that the distribution of animal faces is transformed to more closely match the distribution of human faces. How to make animal faces more like human faces is difficult to have a standard. So we assume that animal face features can be mapped to the feature space closer to the human face by adding residuals. This observation is closely connected to the notion of [4], where they design a deep residual feature map network for pose-robust face recognition. As shown in Fig. 1, the deviation between animal faces and human faces mainly comes from the lower half face. Animals often have weirder noses and mouths. The upper half animal face has clear facial contours and eyes. It has a similar structure to the upper half human face. In an excellent face recognition system, the features of the upper face play a more important role [10], as shown in Fig. 6. We try not to consider the lower half of the face in inter-species knowledge transfer but use its features as additional information to improve the final classification performance. Furthermore, some data of the upper half of the animal face are close to the structure of the human

Fig. 1. The top two rows are pictures of the upper half faces of human and pig, with similar structures. The bottom two rows are pictures of the lower half faces of human and pig.

face. Correspondingly, there is also a lot of data with a low correlation to the human face. The difference of the correlations can be described as inter-species distance, which has a guiding significance for inter-species knowledge transfer.

Motivated by these observations, we formulate a novel *Residual InterSpecies Equivariant Network* (RiseNet), which includes a residual inter-species feature equivariant module for extracting the features of the upper half animal face, a simple network for feature extraction of the lower half of the face, and a animal facial structure driven animal facial feature fusion module to effectively use the features of lower half of animal face. In the residual inter-species feature equivariant module, to make the residuals excellently transform the animal face features, an inter-species distance soft gate is designed to guide the learning of the residuals. The effectiveness of the soft gate is determined by the network frozen part and the inter-species distance.

The main contributions of this study can be summarized as follow:

1) Under the premise of limited training samples, a general framework for animal face recognition is proposed. The upper and lower face of animal are processed separately in this network;
2) We formulate a module called residual inter-species feature equivariant to make the feature distribution of animals face closer to the human. This method allows the animal face to better adapt to the pre-trained human face network during training, thereby effectively improving the performance of cross-species knowledge transfer;
3) Extensive experiments on two benchmarks show that our method is effective and outperforms the state-of-the-arts.

The remainder of the article is organized as follows. The related work is discussed in Sect. 2. Section 3 describes the details of RiseNet proposed in this paper. Section 4 introduces the implementation of our method. Section 5 presents the experimental results. Finally, conclusions are summarized in Sect. 6.

2 Related Work

The work of deep cross-species feature learning for animal face recognition consists of both face recognition and knowledge transfer methods. In the following, we highlight directly relevant research.

Face Recognition. Deep feature learning plays an important role in face recognition. Early face recognition relies on handcrafted features. Gabor [14], LBP [3] and their multilevel and high-dimensional extensions [8, 35] have achieved favorable results in controlled environment through some invariant properties of local filtering. However, handcrafted features suffer from a lack of distinctiveness and compactness. Furthermore, learning-based local descriptors are introduced to the FR community [5, 6], in which local filters are learned for better distinctiveness. Deep convolutional neural networks can effectively extract facial features due to their excellent nonlinear modeling capabilities. Researchers shift their research focus to the design of network structures. DeepFace [26] presents a CNN to extract deep features of the faces that are aligned. DeepID, DeepID2, and DeepID3 improve the performance of face verification by continuously improving the network structure and increasing the network depth. An end-to-end face verification network structure designed by [24] gets accuracy far beyond human level.

Knowledge Transfer. The main reason for the great success of deep feature learning is the support from a large amount of data. However, in many fields, the serious shortage of available labeled data is a difficult problem. Therefore, to overcome the limited data resource, transfer learning is usually explored. The research of transfer learning mainly focuses on three directions, namely, supervised domain adaptation, unsupervised domain adaptation, and semi-supervised domain adaptation [28]. Many researchers have improved the performance of domain adaptation by reducing data distribution differences between tasks [21, 27, 36]. Tzeng et al. [27] combine soft label loss and domain confusion loss for transfer. Zhao et al. [36] adapt the pre-trained model via a dual learning mechanism. However, the supervised domain adaptation approaches mentioned above all require a fixed number of categories in the target domain. Target domain categories should be included in the source domain categories, which is impossible in identity recognition. Maximum Mean Discrepancy (MMD) [17] is proposed to narrow the distribution difference to learn the domain invariant. Luo et al. [18] regard the identification of races with small data volume for unsupervised domain adaptation tasks, and use MMD to solve the bias problem. [29] tries to pre-classify the biased data before MMD and obtains better performance. In essence, the identification of biased races still belongs to the domain adaptation of intraspecific knowledge. For our animal face recognition task, it is an inter-species knowledge transfer between human and pig faces. Unsupervised methods such as MMD have very poor performance for this kind of cross-species transfer learning. Therefore, this paper proposes Residual Interspecies Equivariant Network to learning cross-species feature and achieve better inter-species knowledge transfer in animal face recognition over existing approaches.

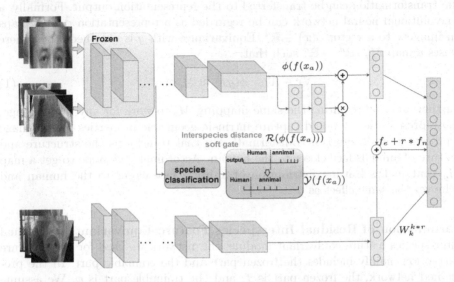

Fig. 2. Framework of RiseNet proposed for animal face recognition. The upper and lower half face images will be feature extracted separately, and the lower half face features will be used as additional features for weighted feature fusion.

3 Approach

3.1 Basic Idea

As mentioned above, our goal is to achieve robust animal face recognition with a small number of training samples, i.e. labeled animal data. This paper targets to learn the cross-species deep feature by reducing the inter-species variation through data and knowledge transformations. To this end, we formulate Residual Interspecies Equivariant Network, hoping to guide the model to learn the discriminative facial features of animals through the data transform by considering the inter-species distance. Considering on the structure characteristic, each animal face is split into two parts, i.e. the upper and the lower. Thus in our recognition framework, a residual inter-species feature equivariant module is used to learn the inter-species feature of the upper half face from the human faces. While for the lower part faces of the animals, the feature extraction is realized by only using the pre-trained network on ImageNet. Then the features from upper and lower parts are fused effectively through weighting and dimension reduction. Finally, the cross-species deep feature is learned and the identity is recognized accordingly. An overview of our method is illustrated in Fig. 2.

3.2 Residual Interspecies Feature Equivariant

Feature Equivariant. According to [13], given a set of input images $x \in \mathcal{X}$, its corresponding representation ϕ is equivariant with a transformation g if the transformation can be transferred to the representation output. Formally, a convolutional neural network can be regarded as a representation ϕ that maps an image x to a vector $\phi(x) \in \mathbb{R}^d$. Equivariance with g is obtained when there exists a map $M_g : \mathbb{R}^d \rightarrow \mathbb{R}^d$ such that:

$$\forall x \in \mathcal{X} : \quad \phi(gx) \approx M_g \phi(x) \tag{1}$$

Furthermore, by requiring the same mapping M_g to work for any input image, the representation ϕ would capture intrinsic geometric properties of the image representation. There is a transformation g that transforms the structure and texture of animals face closer to the human. Accordingly, we hope to get a map M_g that makes feature distribution of animals face closer to the human and achieves the same effect as g.

Formulation of Residual Interspecies Feature Equivariant. In residual inter-species feature equivariant module, the network we used for deep feature extraction mainly includes the frozen part and the trainable part. In the pre-trained network, the frozen part is f, and the trainable part is ϕ. We assume that the animal face data is x_a, and the data with the human face characteristics is x_h. The animal face data is fed into the pre-trained network to get the feature representation $\phi(f(x_a)) \in \mathbb{R}^d$. We wish to obtain a transformed representation of animal face image x_a through a mapping function M_g. In order to get effective M_g, we define $M_g \phi(x)$ as the combination of $\phi(x)$ and the residual. We formulate $M_g \phi(f(x_h))$ as a sum of the original animal face feature $\phi(f(x_a))$ with residuals given by a residual function $\mathcal{R}(\phi(f(x_a)))$ multiplicated by an inter-species distance soft gate $\mathcal{Y}(f(x_a))$. That is:

$$\begin{aligned} \phi(f(gx_a)) &= M_g \phi(f(x_a)) \\ &= \phi(f(x_a)) + \mathcal{Y}(f(x_a))\mathcal{R}(\phi(f(x_a))) \\ &\approx \phi(f(x_h)) \end{aligned} \tag{2}$$

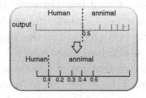

Fig. 3. Schematic diagram of soft gate equalization.

Interspecies Distance Soft Gate. In the residual inter-species feature equivariant module, to make the residuals effectively transform the feature of the animal face, an inter-species distance soft gate is designed to guide the learning of the residuals. The soft gate can be regarded as a correction to the residuals. It adopts top-down information to influence the feed forward process. The soft gate can control the amount of residuals passed to the next layer, thereby guiding residuals to learn the cross-species feature. The inter-species distance soft gate proposed in this paper hopes to describe the degree to which the animal face images need to be transformed. $\mathcal{Y}(f(x))$ can also be described as the probability that the given x is determined as animal. When $\mathcal{Y}(f(x)) = 0$, it means that the x is classified into human face.

The inter-species distance soft gate is calculated by classifying the feature extracted from the frozen part of the network. This classifier mainly includes a fully connected layer and a softmax. Our inter-species classifier is used to classify human and animals. The result of softmax indicates the probability that the data is classified as animal. Interspecies classification is a very simple task, and it is easy to achieve extremely high accuracy. For our method, if most soft gates are distributed from 0.99 to 1, the residual cannot be effectively corrected.

To solve this problem, we add an equalization layer after inter-species classification. As shown in Fig. 3, the equalization layer presents two kinds of functions. One is to make the probabilities of human face data less than 0.1, and the other is to make the probabilities of animal face data evenly distribute between 0.1 to 1. We achieve equalization through piecewise normalization. Specifically, we normalize the softmax results between 0 and less than 0.5 (classified into humans) to $[0, 0.1]$. Then divide the softmax results greater than 0.5 (classify into animals) into 9 equal parts, and normalize them to $[0.1 * i, 0.1 * (i + 1)]$ respectively. Formally, the softmax result set M is divided into 10 parts. Part p_i is between c_i to c_{i+1}, and the number of elements in the last 9 parts is almost the same

$$p_i = \{x | c_i < x \leq c_{i+1}, x \in M\}, \quad i = 0, 1, 2 \ldots, 9$$
$$c_0 = 0, c_1 = 0.5 \tag{3}$$
$$card(p_i) \approx card(p_{i+1}), \quad i = 1, 2, 3 \ldots, 9$$

Then we normalize each p_i to the specified interval respectively. For each softmax result s, the inter-species distance soft gate r can be calculated as

$$r = (\frac{s - c_i}{c_{i+1} - c_i} + i) * 0.1, \quad s \in p_i \tag{4}$$

3.3   Animal Facial Feature Fusion

The deviation between animal face and human face mainly comes from the lower half face. The structure of the lower half face of animal is strange, and it is difficult to learn prior knowledge from human faces. Inspired from this point, we formulate a weighted feature fusion module, in which the transferred upper face feature is fused with the lower face feature extracted directly from the pre-trained network based on ImageNet.

Formally, x_e and x_n denote the upper and lower half face data, respectively. For complementary feature learning with whole face images, as shown in Fig. 2, we enforce the feature complementarity by simultaneously optimizing the upper and lower half face feature transformations and the joint feature transformation. The optimization can be formulated by minimizing

$$\underset{W_e, W_n, W}{argmin}\, \mathcal{L}(y, \mathcal{F}(x_e, W_e)) + \mathcal{L}(y, \mathcal{F}(x_n, W_n))$$
$$+ \mathcal{L}(y, \mathcal{F}((x_e, x_n), W)) \tag{5}$$

where W_e and W_n denote the transformations of the upper and lower half face features. W denotes the joint feature transformation applied on the whole fused face features. y denotes the identity of each face image. $\mathcal{F}$ stands for parameter mapping. L is a prescribed loss function and can be computed by Angular Margin Loss [7], according to

$$L = -\frac{1}{m} \sum_{i=1}^{m} log \frac{e^{s(cos(\theta_{y_i}+m))}}{e^{s(cos(\theta_{y_i}+m))} + \sum_{j=1, j \neq y_i}^{n} e^{scos\theta_j}} \tag{6}$$

where s is a scale. By introducing the third loss term in Eq. (5), we expect that the feature learning for upper and lower half face could influence with each other towards more complementarity features.

We design a branch feature fusion method. The feature obtained by residual inter-species feature equivariant module in the upper half of the face is denoted as f_e, and the feature obtained by the pre-trained network based on ImageNet in the lower half face is denoted as f_n. We fuse features with feature addition and concat

$$f = concat(f_e, f_n, f_e + f_n) \tag{7}$$

Considering that the two parts have different abilities to extract features, we add double weights to the feature fusion in Eq. (7). We weighted the sum of f_e and f_n, and f_n are fully connected to the feature space with fewer parameters

$$f = concat(f_e, (W_k^{k*r})^T f_n, f_e + r * f_n) \tag{8}$$

where r represents the weight of the lower half face. The size of W_k^{k*r} is $k \times (k*r)$. After calculating W_k^{k*r}, the parameter amount of upper half face features will be reduced from k to $k * r$.

4   Implementation

4.1   Preprocessing

In the face recognition task, the alignment of the faces is a very important preprocessing, which can reduce the deviation of the data and therefore improve the recognition accuracy. In order to better adapt the animal face to the pre-trained human face recognition network, a more reasonable strategy is designed for animal face alignment, which is shown in Fig. 4. After a normal face alignment according to the eyes, we align the eyes of animal and human faces on the same horizontal line. Specifically, we first conduct eyes key point detection on the animal face images through [31]. Affine transformation is used to keep the two eyes on the same horizontal line. FaceBoxes [34] is used to obtain animal face rectangle and thus get the cropped image. In aligned face image, the distance between the eyes and the top of the cropped image is fixed.

We assume the distance between the eyes and the top of the cropped image of animal and human is H_1, H_2. We treat the upper 2/5 of the human face as the upper half face, and its height is recorded as h_2. Then we cut the image at $h_1 = H_1 * \frac{h_2}{H_2}$ of the animal face and h_2 of the human face. In this way, the aligned data of animal and human upper half faces can be obtained. In the aligned upper face image, the eyes of the animal are registered with human. On one hand, this operation can help animal data pre-adapt to the distribution of human data. On the other hand, in the proposed RiseNet, the human and animal data are trained jointly. This alignment can help the network learn cross-species features better.

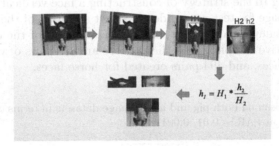

Fig. 4. Animal face alignment.

4.2 Animal Face Verification

In the testing procedure, for each pair of verification samples, we use the trained RiseNet to extract features from the two images, then calculate the cosine distance between the two sets of features. Get a threshold to determine whether they are of the same class based on different experimental Settings.

4.3 Stem Network

In residual inter-species feature equivariant module, the ArcFace (backbone is Resnet50) is used as stem network, which is pre-trained on CASIA-WebFace [32]. Specially, we use the aligned upper half face images (described in Sect. 4.1) in CASIA-WebFace as training data. Correspondingly, ArcFace trained on ImageNet [23] is used as a pre-trained network for feature extraction of the lower half of the face.

5   Experiments

In this section, we perform extensive experiments to evaluate the RiseNet on two different types of animal images, pigs and horses for the task of animal face recognition. In addition, the effectiveness of the residual inter-species feature equivariant and feature fusion module needs to be validated from the ablation studies.

5.1   Experimental Setting

Datasets. We conduct experiment on two different types of animal images, pigs and horses. For the task of pig face recognition, we collect and create our pig face recognition dataset, which contains a total of 3040 labeled pig faces collected from 506 pigs. For the task of horse face recognition, we use the THoDBRL'2015 [1, 12] datasets, which consists of 1410 images collected from 50 horses. For both pig and horse image datasets, we divide the training and test sets according to a 4 : 1 ratio. Furthermore, we extract equal class data from LFW and train them with animal face data. For the experiments, we create animal face verification dataset according to the strategy of constructing a face verification set in LFW [11]. For each image for test, we randomly select an image of the same class and form a positive sample pair with it, and select an image of the different classes and form a negative sample pair with it. There are 818 pairs of verification data created for pig faces, and 494 pairs created for horse faces.

Table 1. Comparison on both pig and horse image datasets in terms of mean accuracy (mAcc) and TAR at FAR = 0.01, 0.001.

Datasets	Methods	mAcc(%)	TAR(%)@FAR 0.01	TAR(%)@FAR 0.001
Pig	VGG [20]	81.70	65.34	14.43
	SphererFace [15]	86.25	70.43	21.04
	DAN [9]	89.72	73.27	32.91
	ArcFace [7]	87.74	71.83	22.73
	Fine-tuning with Arcface	90.81	77.34	40.34
	RiseNet	93.76	80.42	49.74
Horse	VGG	72.62	62.17	18.82
	SphererFace	74.98	63.43	20.22
	DAN	74.37	62.05	22.63
	ArcFace	75.32	63.59	21.26
	Fine-tuning with Arcface	81.79	65.92	35.76
	RiseNet	82.56	68.43	41.28

Settings of CNNs. PyTorch is used to implement in all experiments. For extensive investigation of our method, the proposed RiseNet with fusion rate of 1, 0.5, 0.1 and 0.1 are evaluated respectively. We also compare our method with the RiseNet without feature fusion, which residual inter-species feature equivariant module is performed on a whole face. For fair comparison, we set the batch size of all the methods empirically as 512. We train the network for 40 epochs, reducing the learning rate twice after 10 and 30 epochs.

5.2   Comparison with Our Baselines

Effectiveness of RiseNet. We compare our network with our baseline Arc-Face from scratch and the fine-tuning model. The fine-tuning network is an ArcFace pre-trained on CASIA-WebFace. We freeze some shallow convolution layers and train the animal face data. The experimental results on the pig image dataset and the horse dataset are shown in Table 1. We can see that the fine-tuning model shows a significant improvement comparing to ArcFace trained from scratch. Therefore, the prior knowledge of human face recognition can help improve the animal face recognition performance. Compared with the fine-tuning model, RiseNet achieves almost 3% percent improvement in accuracy. Moreover, the proposed RiseNet performs much better than the fine-tuning, with an improvement up to 9% at FAR = 0.001 in pig image experiment. These comparisons clearly and convincingly show that our method can significantly improve cross-species feature learning.

We perform some famous FR methods on pig and cow data, including VGG [20], SphereFace (A-Softmax Loss) [15], ArcFace (Additive Angular Margin Loss) [7] to further prove the superiority of RiseNet. We also consider comparison with Domain Adaptation. DAN [9] perform poor on inter-species knowledge transfer because of the low relationship between source and target data.

Visualization of Deep Feature Space. Some visualization results on the feature space of ArcFace from scratch via t-SNE are shown in Fig. 5. We could observe that the features of pig images are hard to distinguish. Because the training dataset is too small, it is difficult for the model trained from scratch to extract distinguishable features. Fine-tuning with Arcface takes into account the prior experience of face recognition and alleviates the lack of animal face data. It makes the data separable, but the distance between categories is still small. In contrast, RiseNet clearly separates the features of different categories for both human and pig images.

Visualization Comparison of RiseNet. To further verify that RiseNet can enhance capacity of deep cross-species feature learning. For fair comparison, we visualize those feature maps extracted from ArcFace from scratch, fine-tuning with ArcFace and RiseNet through GradCAM introduced by [25], as shown in Fig. 6. Six human face images are used to compare with six animal face images. Figure 6 shows that the high response of human face recognition mainly lies in

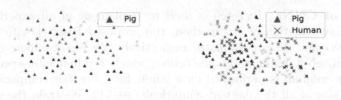

(a) Feature Space of ArcFace from (b) Feature Space of fine-tuning
scratch   with ArcFace

(c) Feature Space of RiseNet

Fig. 5. Visualization of deep feature space. Here we use × to represent human faces and △ to denote pig faces. The features of different subjects are represented in different color.

the area around the eyes. ArcFace from scratch for animal face recognition has a messy attention distribution and focuses on too much useless information. The main content of animal faces begins to be noticed in fine-tuning. Most attention is in the face area, but the area where the attention is concentrated is still scattered. Correspondingly, RiseNet pays more attention to the area around the eyes like face recognition.

5.3 Ablation Study of RiseNet

Here, we investigate the influence of the fusion rate, four experiments of which the fusion rate is 1, 0.5, 0.1, 0.01, respectively. In order to prove the effectiveness of W_k^{k*r}, in the experiment of fusion rate, we did not use W_k^{k*r}. The result of our method with different fusion rates can be found in Table 2. In the pig image experiment, RiseNet with 0.1 fusion rate achieves the best performance, which is 0.53% higher than the method that equally considers the upper and lower faces (1 fusion rate). Results show that the lower half of the face is likely to play an even smaller role in animal face recognition but still provides some useful information.

Furthermore, we show the comparison results of whether or not W_k^{k*r} is used, as shown in Table 3.

We perform experiment on the pig and horse image datasets for evaluating the performance of RiseNet. In our RiseNet, the residual inter-species feature equivariant module is used to improve the ability of inter-species knowledge

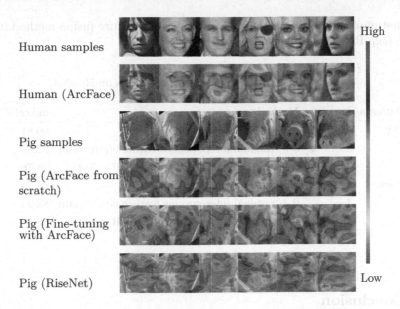

Human samples

Human (ArcFace)

Pig samples

Pig (ArcFace from scratch)

Pig (Fine-tuning with ArcFace)

Pig (RiseNet)

High

Low

Fig. 6. Feature maps from our RiseNet and our baselines for six human images and six pig images. The features of pig images with RiseNet images mainly focus on area around eye like human images.

Table 2. Comparative analysis of different fusion rate.

Method	Fusion rate	mAcc(%)
RiseNet(without W_k^{k*r})	1	92.74
	0.5	92.82
	0.1	93.27
	0.01	93.02

Table 3. Comparative analysis of W_k^{k*r}.

Method	Using W_k^{k*r}	mAcc(%)
RiseNet	yes	93.76
	No	93.27

transfer. The proposal of animal facial feature fusion encourages RiseNet to pay more attention to important information and effectively use the remaining information. Therefore, the comparison is conducted on three cases: fine-tuning with Arcface, residual inter-species feature equivariant for whole face, and RiseNet including residual inter-species feature equivariant module and animal facial feature fusion. Table 4 provides quantitative results and shows that residual inter-species feature equivariant module has excellent performance compared to simple fine-tuning. In addition, the split strategy and feature fusion method in this article help RiseNet further improve performance.

Table 4. Comparative performance analysis on RiseNet.

Datasets	Number	Methods	mAcc(%)
Pig	0	Fine-tuning with ArcFace	90.81
	1	0 + residual inter-species feature equivariant	92.83
	2	1 + animal facial feature fusion (RiseNet)	93.76
Horse	0	Fine-tuning with ArcFace	81.79
	1	0 + residual inter-species feature equivariant	82.24
	2	1 + animal facial feature fusion (RiseNet)	82.56

6   Conclusion

This paper proposes a novel Residual Interspecies Equivariant Network to learn cross-species features for the task of animal face recognition. Specifically, we bridge the inter-species gap between animal and human faces through performing equivariant feature mapping. The mapping is achieved by the residual inter-species feature equivariant module. By incorporating the prior knowledge of the upper and lower half face information into the RiseNet, we design a weighted feature fusion module. We experimentally find the RiseNet compared with the state-of-the-art approaches is more effective in animal face recognition.

Acknowledgements. This research was supported by grants from the National Natural Science Foundation of China (No. 61976219), the Science and Technology Innovation Program of the Chinese Academy of Agricultural Sciences (CAAS-ASTIP-2016-AII) and the Fundamental Research Funds for Central Non-profit Scientific Institution (No. 2019JKY040). Portions of the research in this paper use the THoDBRL'2015 Database collected by the Research Groups in Intelligent Machines, University of Sfax, Tunisia.

References

1. Thodbrl'2015 database. http://www.regim.org/publications/databases/thodbrl/
2. Abdelhady, A.S., Hassanenin, A.E., Fahmy, A.: Sheep identity recognition, age and weight estimation datasets. arXiv preprint arXiv:1806.04017 (2018)
3. Ahonen, T., Hadid, A., Pietikainen, M.: Face description with local binary patterns: application to face recognition. IEEE Trans. Pattern Anal. Mach. Intell. **28**(12), 2037–2041 (2006)
4. Cao, K., Rong, Y., Li, C., Tang, X., Change Loy, C.: Pose-robust face recognition via deep residual equivariant mapping. In: Proceedings of the IEEE Conference on Computer Vision and Pattern Recognition, pp. 5187–5196 (2018)

5. Cao, Z., Yin, Q., Tang, X., Sun, J.: Face recognition with learning-based descriptor. In: 2010 IEEE Computer Society Conference on Computer Vision and Pattern Recognition, pp. 2707–2714. IEEE (2010)
6. Chan, T.H., Jia, K., Gao, S., Lu, J., Zeng, Z., Ma, Y.: PCANet: a simple deep learning baseline for image classification? IEEE Trans. Image Process. **24**(12), 5017–5032 (2015)
7. Deng, J., Guo, J., Xue, N., Zafeiriou, S.: ArcFace: additive angular margin loss for deep face recognition. In: Proceedings of the IEEE Conference on Computer Vision and Pattern Recognition, pp. 4690–4699 (2019)
8. Deng, W., Hu, J., Guo, J.: Compressive binary patterns: designing a robust binary face descriptor with random-field eigenfilters. IEEE Trans. Pattern Anal. Mach. Intell. **41**(3), 758–767 (2018)
9. Ghifary, M., Kleijn, W.B., Zhang, M.: Domain adaptive neural networks for object recognition. In: Pham, D.-N., Park, S.-B. (eds.) PRICAI 2014. LNCS (LNAI), vol. 8862, pp. 898–904. Springer, Cham (2014). https://doi.org/10.1007/978-3-319-13560-1_76
10. Han, C., Shan, S., Kan, M., Wu, S., Chen, X.: Face recognition with contrastive convolution. In: Ferrari, V., Hebert, M., Sminchisescu, C., Weiss, Y. (eds.) ECCV 2018. LNCS, vol. 11213, pp. 120–135. Springer, Cham (2018). https://doi.org/10.1007/978-3-030-01240-3_8
11. Huang, G.B., Mattar, M., Berg, T., Learned-Miller, E.: Labeled faces in the wild: a database for studying face recognition in unconstrained environments (2008)
12. Jarraya, I., Ouarda, W., Alimi, A.M.: A preliminary investigation on horses recognition using facial texture features. In: 2015 IEEE International Conference on Systems, Man, and Cybernetics, pp. 2803–2808. IEEE (2015)
13. Lenc, K., Vedaldi, A.: Understanding image representations by measuring their equivariance and equivalence. In: Proceedings of the IEEE Conference on Computer Vision and Pattern Recognition, pp. 991–999 (2015)
14. Liu, C., Wechsler, H.: Gabor feature based classification using the enhanced fisher linear discriminant model for face recognition. IEEE Trans. Image Process. **11**(4), 467–476 (2002)
15. Liu, W., Wen, Y., Yu, Z., Li, M., Raj, B., Song, L.: SphereFace: deep hypersphere embedding for face recognition. In: Proceedings of the IEEE Conference on Computer Vision and Pattern Recognition, pp. 212–220 (2017)
16. Liu, W., Wen, Y., Yu, Z., Yang, M.: Large-margin softmax loss for convolutional neural networks. In: ICML, vol. 2, p. 7 (2016)
17. Long, M., Cao, Y., Wang, J., Jordan, M.I.: Learning transferable features with deep adaptation networks. arXiv preprint arXiv:1502.02791 (2015)
18. Luo, Z., Hu, J., Deng, W., Shen, H.: Deep unsupervised domain adaptation for face recognition. In: 2018 13th IEEE International Conference on Automatic Face & Gesture Recognition (FG 2018), pp. 453–457. IEEE (2018)
19. Matkowski, W.M., Kong, A.W.K., Su, H., Chen, P., Hou, R., Zhang, Z.: Giant panda face recognition using small dataset. In: 2019 IEEE International Conference on Image Processing (ICIP), pp. 1680–1684. IEEE (2019)
20. Parkhi, O.M., Vedaldi, A., Zisserman, A.: Deep face recognition (2015)
21. Peng, X., Hoffman, J., Stella, X.Y., Saenko, K.: Fine-to-coarse knowledge transfer for low-res image classification. In: 2016 IEEE International Conference on Image Processing (ICIP), pp. 3683–3687. IEEE (2016)
22. Rashid, M., Gu, X., Jae Lee, Y.: Interspecies knowledge transfer for facial keypoint detection. In: Proceedings of the IEEE Conference on Computer Vision and Pattern Recognition, pp. 6894–6903 (2017)

23. Russakovsky, O., et al.: Imagenet large scale visual recognition challenge. Int. J. Comput. Vision **115**(3), 211–252 (2015)
24. Schroff, F., Kalenichenko, D., Philbin, J.: FaceNet: a unified embedding for face recognition and clustering. In: Proceedings of the IEEE Conference on Computer Vision and Pattern Recognition, pp. 815–823 (2015)
25. Selvaraju, R.R., Cogswell, M., Das, A., Vedantam, R., Parikh, D., Batra, D.: Grad-CAM: visual explanations from deep networks via gradient-based localization. In: Proceedings of the IEEE International Conference on Computer Vision, pp. 618–626 (2017)
26. Taigman, Y., Yang, M., Ranzato, M., Wolf, L.: DeepFace: closing the gap to human-level performance in face verification. In: Proceedings of the IEEE Conference on Computer Vision and Pattern Recognition, pp. 1701–1708 (2014)
27. Tzeng, E., Hoffman, J., Darrell, T., Saenko, K.: Simultaneous deep transfer across domains and tasks. In: Proceedings of the IEEE International Conference on Computer Vision, pp. 4068–4076 (2015)
28. Wang, M., Deng, W.: Deep visual domain adaptation: a survey. Neurocomputing **312**, 135–153 (2018)
29. Wang, M., Deng, W., Hu, J., Tao, X., Huang, Y.: Racial faces in the wild: reducing racial bias by information maximization adaptation network. In: Proceedings of the IEEE International Conference on Computer Vision, pp. 692–702 (2019)
30. Wen, Y., Zhang, K., Li, Z., Qiao, Y.: A discriminative feature learning approach for deep face recognition. In: Leibe, B., Matas, J., Sebe, N., Welling, M. (eds.) ECCV 2016. LNCS, vol. 9911, pp. 499–515. Springer, Cham (2016). https://doi.org/10.1007/978-3-319-46478-7_31
31. Wu, Y., Hassner, T., Kim, K., Medioni, G., Natarajan, P.: Facial landmark detection with tweaked convolutional neural networks. IEEE Trans. Pattern Anal. Mach. Intell. **40**(12), 3067–3074 (2017)
32. Yi, D., Lei, Z., Liao, S., Li, S.Z.: Learning face representation from scratch. arXiv preprint arXiv:1411.7923 (2014)
33. Yosinski, J., Clune, J., Bengio, Y., Lipson, H.: How transferable are features in deep neural networks? In: Advances in Neural Information Processing Systems, pp. 3320–3328 (2014)
34. Zhang, S., Zhu, X., Lei, Z., Shi, H., Wang, X., Li, S.Z.: FaceBoxes: a CPU real-time face detector with high accuracy. In: 2017 IEEE International Joint Conference on Biometrics (IJCB), pp. 1–9. IEEE (2017)
35. Zhang, W., Shan, S., Gao, W., Chen, X., Zhang, H.: Local gabor binary pattern histogram sequence (LGBPHS): a novel non-statistical model for face representation and recognition. In: Tenth IEEE International Conference on Computer Vision (ICCV 2005) Volume 1, vol. 1, pp. 786–791. IEEE (2005)
36. Zhao, W., et al.: Dual learning for cross-domain image captioning. In: Proceedings of the 2017 ACM on Conference on Information and Knowledge Management, pp. 29–38 (2017)

Guidance and Evaluation: Semantic-Aware Image Inpainting for Mixed Scenes

Liang Liao[1,2] , Jing Xiao[1,2(✉)] , Zheng Wang[2] , Chia-Wen Lin[3] ,
and Shin'ichi Satoh[2]

[1] National Engineering Research Center for Multimedia Software,
School of Computer Science, Wuhan University, Wuhan, China
liang@nii.ac.jp, jing@whu.edu.cn
[2] National Institute of Informatics, Tokyo, Japan
{wangz,satoh}@nii.ac.jp
[3] Department of Electrical Engineering, National Tsing Hua University,
Hsinchu, Taiwan
cwlin@ee.nthu.edu.tw

Abstract. Completing a corrupted image with correct structures and reasonable textures for a mixed scene remains an elusive challenge. Since the missing hole in a mixed scene of a corrupted image often contains various semantic information, conventional two-stage approaches utilizing structural information often lead to the problem of unreliable structural prediction and ambiguous image texture generation. In this paper, we propose a Semantic Guidance and Evaluation Network (SGE-Net) to iteratively update the structural priors and the inpainted image in an interplay framework of semantics extraction and image inpainting. It utilizes semantic segmentation map as guidance in each scale of inpainting, under which location-dependent inferences are re-evaluated, and, accordingly, poorly-inferred regions are refined in subsequent scales. Extensive experiments on real-world images of mixed scenes demonstrated the superiority of our proposed method over state-of-the-art approaches, in terms of clear boundaries and photo-realistic textures.

Keywords: Image inpainting · Semantic guidance · Segmentation confidence evaluation · Mixed scene

1 Introduction

Image inpainting refers to the task of filling the missing area in a scene with synthesized content. Due to its wide applications in photo editing, de-caption, damaged image repairing, error concealment in data transmission, etc., it has

Electronic supplementary material The online version of this chapter (https:// doi.org/10.1007/978-3-030-58583-9_41) contains supplementary material, which is available to authorized users.

A. Vedaldi et al. (Eds.): ECCV 2020, LNCS 12372, pp. 683–700, 2020.
https://doi.org/10.1007/978-3-030-58583-9_41

(a) Input   (b) GC   (c) EC   (d) SPG   (e) Ideal case   (f) SGE-Net (ours)

Fig. 1. Comparison of the inpainting results for a mixed scene: (b) GC [42] without structural information; (c) EC [21] with predicted edges; (d) SPG [27] with less reliable predicted semantic segmentation; (e) semantic-guided inpainting with an uncorrupted segmentation map; and (f) the proposed SGE-Net with iteratively optimized semantic segmentation. [Best viewed in color]. (Color figure online)

drawn great attention in the field of computer vision and graphics [1, 2, 5, 10, 28]. Recent learning-based methods have achieved great success in filling large missing regions with plausible contents of various simple scenes [23, 31, 34, 41, 42, 44, 45, 47]. However, these existing methods still encounter difficulties while completing images of a mixed scene, that composes of multiple objects with different semantics.

Existing learning-based image inpainting methods typically fill missing regions by inferring the context of corrupted images [12, 23, 35, 41, 42]. However, in a mixed scene, the prior distributions of various semantics are different and various semantic regions also contribute differently to pixels in the missing regions, thus uniformly mapping different semantics onto a single manifold in the context-based methods often leads to unrealistic semantic content as illustrated in Fig. 1(b).

To address this issue, low to mid-level structural information [16, 27, 36, 46] was introduced to assist image inpainting. These methods extract and reconstruct the edges or contours in the first stage and complete an image with the predicted structural information in the second stage. The spatial separation by the structures helps to alleviate the blurry boundary problem. These methods, however, ignore the modeling of semantic content, which may result in ambiguous textures at the semantic boundaries. Moreover, the performance of the two-stage inpainting process highly relies on the reconstructed structures from the first stage, but the unreliability of the edge or contour connections largely increases in a mixed scene (Fig. 1(c)). As revealed in [34] that human beings perceive and reconstruct the structures under the semantic understanding of a corrupted image, it is natural to involve semantic information in the process of image inpainting.

In this paper, we show how semantic segmentation can effectively assist image inpainting of a mixed scene based on two main discoveries: **semantic guidance and segmentation confidence evaluation**. Specifically, a semantic segmentation map carries pixel-wise semantic information, providing the layout of a scene as well as the category, location and shape of each object. It can assist the learning of different texture distributions of various semantic regions. Moreover, the intermediate confidence score derived from the segmentation process can offer a self-evaluation for an inpainted region, under the assumption that ambiguous semantic contents usually cannot lead to solid semantic segmentation results.

To the best of our knowledge, a similar work making use of semantic segmentation information for image inpainting is SPG proposed in [27], which is also a two-stage process. It extracts and reconstructs a segmentation map, and then utilizes the map to guide image inpainting. Thanks to the helpful semantic information carried in the segmentation map, SPG can effectively improve inpainting performance compared to those methods without a semantic segmentation map. Nevertheless, it is hard to predict reliable semantics about a region when its context information is largely missing, especially in mixed scene. As a result, its performance can be significantly degraded by such unreliable semantic region boundaries and labels predicted by the semantic segmentation. Such performance degradation is evidenced in Fig. 1(d), from which we can observe blurry and incorrect inpainted textures generated by SPG. By contrast, segmentation-guided inpainting can achieve high-quality image completion provided that a reliable segmentation map (i.e., the segmentation map of uncorrupted image) is given as illustrated in Fig. 1(e). Therefore, to make the best use of semantic information carried in the segmentation map for image inpainting, how to predict a reliable semantic segmentation map, even if part of an image is corrupted, is the key.

To address the above problems, we advocate that the interplay between the two tasks, semantic segmentation and image inpainting, can effectively improve the reliability of the semantic segmentation map from a corrupted image, which will in turn improve the performance of inpainting as illustrated in Fig. 1(f). To this end, we propose a novel **S**emantic **G**uidance and **E**valuation **Net**work (**SGE-Net**) that makes use of the interplay between semantic segmentation and image inpainting in a coarse-to-fine manner. Experiments conducted on the datasets containing mixtures of multiple semantic regions demonstrated the effectiveness of our method in completing a corrupted mixed scene with significantly improved semantic contents.

Our contributions are summarized as follows:

1) We show that the interplay between semantic segmentation and image inpainting in a coarse-to-fine manner can effectively improve the performance of image inpainting by simultaneously generating an accurate semantic guidance from merely an input corrupted image.
2) We are the first to propose a self-evaluation mechanism for image inpainting through segmentation confidence scoring to effectively localize the predicted pixels with ambiguous semantic meanings, which enables the inpainting process to update both contexts and textures progressively.

3) Our model outperforms the state-of-the-art methods, especially on mixed scenes with multiple semantics, in the sense of generating semantically realistic contexts and visually pleasing textures.

2   Related Work

2.1   Deep Learning-Based Inpainting

Deep learning-based image inpainting approaches [15,23,39] are generally based on generative adversarial networks (GANs) [9,24,33] to generate the pixels of a missing region. For instance, Pathak et al. introduced Context Encoders [23], which was among the first approaches in this kind. The model was trained to predict the context of a missing region but usually generates blurry results. Based on the Context Encoders model, several methods were proposed to better recover texture details through the use of well-designed loss functions [7,12,15], neural patch synthesis [38], residual learning [6,40], feature patch matching [26,37,41,43], content and style disentanglement [8,32,34], and others [20,29,31]. Semantic attention was further proposed to refine the textures in [18]. However, most of the above methods were designed for dealing with rectangular holes, but cannot effectively handle large irregular holes. To fill irregular holes, Liu et al. [17] proposed a partial convolutional layer, which calculates a new feature map and updates the mask at each layer. Later, Yu et al. [42] proposed a gated convolutional layer based on the models in [41] for irregular image inpainting. While these methods work reasonably well for one category of objects or background, they can easily fail if the missing region contains multiple categories of scenes.

2.2   Structural Information-Guided Inpainting

Recently, structural information was introduced in learning-based framework to assist the image inpainting process. These methods are mostly based on two-stage networks, where missing structures are reconstructed in the first stage and then used to guide the texture generation in the second stage. Edge maps were first introduced by Liao et al. [16] as a structural guide to the inpainting network. This idea is further improved by Nazeri et al. [21] and Li et al. [14] in terms of better edge prediction. Similar to edge information, object contours were used by Xiong et al. [36] to separately reconstruct the foreground and background areas. Ren et al. [25] proposed using smoothed images to carry additional image information other than edges as prior information. Considering semantic information for the modeling of texture distributions, SPG proposed in [27] predicts the semantic segmentation map of a missing region as a structural guide. The above-mentioned methods show that the structure priors effectively help improve the quality of the final completed image. However, how to reconstruct correct structures remains challenging, especially when the missing region becomes complex.

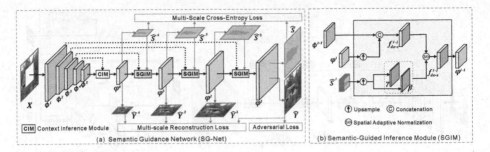

Fig. 2. Proposed baseline: Semantic Guidance Network (SG-Net). It iteratively updates the contextual features in a coarse-to-fine manner. SGIM updates the predicted context features based on the segmentation map at the next scale.

3   Approach

As illustrated in Figs. 1(d)–(f), the success of semantic segmentation-guided inpainting depends on a reliable segmentation map, which is hard to obtain from an image with a corrupted mixed scene. To address this issue, we propose a novel method to progressively predict a reliable segmentation map from a corrupted image through the interplay between semantic segmentation and image inpainting in a coarse-to-fine manner. To verify how semantic information boosts image inpainting, two networks are proposed. As a baseline, the first one uses only semantic guidance on image inpainting. Moreover, the semantic evaluation is added in the second network as an advanced strategy.

We first introduce some notations used throughout this paper. Given a corrupted image X with a binary mask M (0 for holes), and the corresponding ground-truth image Y, the inpainting task is to generate an inpainted image $\hat{Y}$ from X and M. Given a basic encoder-decoder architecture of L layers, we denote the feature maps from deep to shallow in the encoder as ϕ^L, ϕ^{L-1}, ..., ϕ^l, ..., ϕ^1, and in the decoder as φ^L, φ^{L-1}..., φ^l, ..., φ^1.

3.1   Semantic Guidance Network (SG-Net)

The SG-Net architecture is shown in Fig. 2(a). The encoder is used to extract the contextual features of a corrupted image. The decoder then updates the contextual features to predict the semantic segmentation maps and inpainted images simultaneously in a multi-scale manner. Based on this structure, semantic guidance takes effect in two aspects. First, the semantic supervisions are added to guide the learning of contextual features at different scales of the decoder. Second, the predicted segmentation maps are involved in the inference modules to guide the update of the contextual features at the next scale. Being different from the two-stage process [16,21,27], the supervision of semantic segmentation on the contextual features enables them to carry the semantic information, that helps the decoder learn better texture models for different semantics.

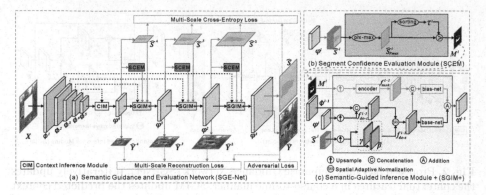

Fig. 3. Proposed Semantic Guidance and Evaluation Network (SGE-Net). It iteratively evaluates and updates the contextual features through the SCEM and SGIM+ modules in a coarse-to-fine manner, where SCEM identifies the pixels where the context needs to be corrected, while SGIM+ updates the predicted context features representing the incorrect pixels located by SCEM.

The corrupted image is initially completed in the feature level through a Context Inference Module (CIM). After that, the image inpainting and semantic segmentation interplay with each other and are progressively updated across scales. Two branches are extended from the contextual features at each scale of the decoder to generate multi-scale completed images $\hat{Y}^{L-1}, ..., \hat{Y}^l, ..., \hat{Y}^1$ and their semantic segmentation maps $\hat{S}^{L-1}, ..., \hat{S}^l, ..., \hat{S}^1$.

$$\hat{Y}^l = h(\varphi^l), \quad \hat{S}^l = g(\varphi^l), \tag{1}$$

where $h(\cdot)$ and $g(\cdot)$ denote the inpainting branch and segmentation branch, respectively.

Semantic-Guided Inference Module (SGIM). SGIM is designed to make an inference and update the contextual features at the next scale φ^{l-1}. As shown in Fig. 2(b), SGIM takes three types of inputs: two of them are the current contextual features φ^l and the skip features of the next scale ϕ^{l-1} from the encoder. The third input is the segmentation map $\hat{S}^l$, which is used to formalize the textures under the assumption that those regions of the same semantic class should have similar textures. The inference process can be formulated as follows:

$$\varphi^{l-1} = infer(\varphi^l, \phi^{l-1}, \hat{S}^l), \tag{2}$$

where $infer(\cdot)$ is the process of updating the contextual features in SGIM.

To update the contextual features based on segmentation map $\hat{S}^l$, we follow the image generation approach in [22], which adopts spatial adaptive normalization to propagate semantic information into the predicted images for achieving effective semantic guidance. The contextual features f_{de-s}^{l-1} are updated as follows:

$$f_{de-s}^{l-1} = \gamma \odot \frac{f_{de-c}^{l-1} - \mu}{\sigma} + \beta, \tag{3}$$

where (γ, β) is a pair of affine transformation parameters modeled from segmentation map $\hat{S}^l$, μ and σ are the mean and standard deviation of each channel in the concatenated feature vector f_{de-c}^{l-1} generated from ϕ^l and φ^{l-1}. $\odot$ denotes element-wise multiplication.

3.2 Semantic Guidance and Evaluation Network (SGE-Net)

To deeply exploit how segmentation confidence evaluation can help correct the wrongly predicted pixels, we add the Segmentation Confidence Evaluation Module (SCEM) on each decoder layer of SG-Net. The evaluation is performed under the assumption that predicted ambiguous semantic content would result in low confidence scores during the semantic segmentation process. Therefore, we introduce the **segmentation confidence scoring** after each decoding layer to self-evaluate the predicted region. The reliability mask is then feed to the next scale, which can be used to identify those to-be-updated contextual features that contribute to the unreliable area. This module enables the proposed method to correct the mistakes in those regions completed at the previous coarser scale. Figure 3(a) illustrates the detailed architecture of SGE-Net.

Segmentation Confidence Evaluation Module (SCEM). The output of the semantic segmentation branch is a k-channel probability map. The confidence score at every channel of a pixel in the map signifies how the pixel looks like a specific class. Based on the scores, we assume that an inpainted pixel is unreliable if it has low scores for all semantic classes.

The framework of SCEM is depicted in Fig. 3(b). Taking the segmentation probability map at a certain scale $\hat{S}^l$, we generate a reliability mask M^l to locate those pixels which might have unreal semantic meaning. We first generate a max-possibility map $\hat{S}_{P_{max}}^l$ by assigning each pixel with the highest confidence score of k channels in $\hat{S}^l$. Then, the mask value of pixel (x, y) in the reliability mask is decided by judging whether the max-confidential score at each pixel location exceeds a threshold τ^l.

$$M^l(x, y) = \begin{cases} 1, & \hat{S}_{P_{max}}^l > \tau^l \\ 0, & \text{otherwise} \end{cases}, \tag{4}$$

where τ^l is decided by the percentile of the sorted confidence value.

Enhanced SGIM (SGIM+). In order to correct the pixels marked as unreliable from the SCEM, SGIM+ takes the reliability mask M^l as the fourth input to update the current context features (as shown in Fig. 3(c)). The formulation of the inference process can be updated as follows:

$$\varphi^{l-1} = infer(\varphi^l, \phi^{l-1}, \hat{S}^l, M^l). \tag{5}$$

To enable the dynamic corrections of semantics, we introduced a bias-net F_{bi}^l in correspondence to the original network branch between the feature f_{de-s}^{l-1} and φ^{l-1} in the previous version of SGIM, which we call base-net F_{ba}^l. The new reliability mask M^l is fed into the bias-net to learn residuals to rectify the basic contextual features from the base-net. The new contextual features at the next scale can be formulated as

$$\varphi^{l-1} = F_{ba}^l(f_{de-s}^{l-1}) + F_{bi}^l(f_{de-s}^{l-1} \oplus F(M^l)), \qquad (6)$$

where $\oplus$ denotes the concatenation operation and F represents the convolutions to translate the reliability mask into feature maps.

3.3   Training Loss Function

The loss functions comprise loss terms for both image inpainting and semantic segmentation. For image inpainting, we adopt the multi-scale reconstruction loss to refine a completed image and the adversarial loss to generate visually realistic textures. For semantic segmentation, we adopt the multi-scale cross-entropy loss to restrain the distance between the predicted and target class distributions of pixels at all scales.

Multi-scale Reconstruction Loss. We use the $\mathcal{L}_1$ loss to encourage per-pixel reconstruction accuracy, and the perceptual loss [13] to encourage higher-level feature similarity.

$$\mathcal{L}_{re}^l(X, \hat{Y}^l) = \| X - up(\hat{Y}^l) \|_1 + \lambda_p \sum_{n=1}^{N} \| \Psi_n(X) - \Psi_n(up(\hat{Y}^l)) \|_1, \qquad (7)$$

where Ψ_n is the activation map of the n-th layer, $up(\cdot)$ is the operation to upsample $\hat{Y}^l$ to the same size as X, λ_p is a trade-off coefficient. We use layered features $relu2\_2$, $relu3\_3$, and $relu4\_3$ in VGG-16 pre-trained on ImageNet to calculate those loss functions.

Adversarial Loss. We use a multi-scale PatchGAN [34] to classify the global and local patches of an image at multiple scales. The multi-scale patch adversarial loss is defined as:

$$\mathcal{L}_{ad}(X, \hat{Y}) = \sum_{k=1,2,3} (E_{p_X^k \sim X^k}[\log D(p_X^k)] + E_{p_{\hat{Y}}^k \sim \hat{Y}^k}[1 - \log D(p_{\hat{Y}}^k)]), \qquad (8)$$

where $D(\cdot)$ is the discriminator, $p_{\hat{Y}}^k$ and p_X^k are the patches in the k-th scaled versions of X and $\hat{Y}$.

Multi-scale Cross-Entropy Loss. This loss is used to penalize the deviation of $\hat{S}^l$ at each position at every scale.

$$\mathcal{L}_{se}^l(S, \hat{S}^l) = -\sum_{i \in S} S_i \log(up(\hat{S}^l)). \tag{9}$$

where i indicates each pixel in segmentation map S.

Final Training Loss. The overall training loss of our network is defined as the weighted sum of the multi-scale reconstruction loss, adversarial loss, and multi-scale cross-entropy loss.

$$\mathcal{L}_{Final} = \sum_{l=0}^{4} \mathcal{L}_{re}^l(X, \hat{Y}^l) + \lambda_\alpha \mathcal{L}_{ad}(X, \hat{Y}) + \sum_{l=0}^{4} \lambda_s \mathcal{L}_{se}^l(S, \hat{S}^l), \tag{10}$$

where λ_α and λ_s are the weights for the adversarial loss and the multi-scale cross-entropy loss, respectively.

4 Experiments

4.1 Setting

We evaluate our method on **Outdoor Scenes** [30] and **Cityscapes** [4] both with segmentation annotations. **Outdoor Scenes** contains 9,900 training images and 300 test images belonging to 8 categories. **Cityscapes** contains 5,000 street view images belonging to 20 categories. In order to enlarge the number of training images of this dataset, we use 2,975 images from the training set and 1,525 images from the test set for training, and test on the 500 images from the validation set. We resize each training image to ensure its minimal height/width to be 256 for **Outdoor Scenes** and 512 for **Cityscapes**, and then randomly crop sub-images of size 256×256 as inputs to our model.

We compare our method with the following three representative baselines:

- GC [42]: gated convolution for free-form image inpainting, without any auxiliary structural information.
- EC [21]: two-stage inpainting framework with edges as low-level structural information.
- SPG [27]: two-stage inpainting framework with a semantic segmentation map as high-level structural information.

In our experiments, we fine-tune the GC and EC models, pre-trained on Places2, on our datasets. We also re-implement and train the model of SPG by ourselves since there is no released code or model. We conduct experiments on both settings of centering and irregular holes. The centering holes are $(128 \times 128$ for **Outdoor Scenes** and 96×96 for **Cityscapes**), and the irregular masks are obtained from [17].

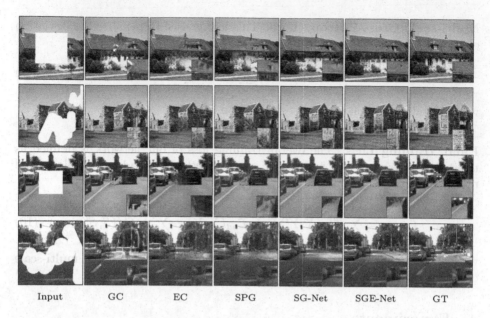

Input　　　GC　　　EC　　　SPG　　　SG-Net　　　SGE-Net　　　GT

Fig. 4. Subjective quality comparison of inpainting results on image samples from **Outdoor Scenes** and **Cityscapes**. **GT stands for Ground-Truth.**

Table 1. Objective quality comparison of five methods in terms of PSNR, SSIM, and FID on **Outdoor Scenes** and **Cityscapes** (↑: Higher is better; ↓: Lower is better). The two best scores are colored in red and blue, respectively.

	Outdoor Scenes						Cityscapes					
	Centering holes			Irregular holes			Centering holes			Irregular holes		
	PSNR↑	SSIM↑	FID↓	PSNR↑	SSIM↑	FID↓	PSNR↑	SSIM↑	FID↓	PSNR↑	SSIM↑	FID↓
GC [42]	19.06	0.73	42.34	19.27	0.81	40.31	21.13	0.74	20.03	17.42	0.72	40.57
EC [21]	19.32	0.76	41.25	19.63	0.83	44.31	21.71	0.76	19.87	17.83	0.73	38.07
SPG [27]	18.04	0.70	45.31	17.85	0.74	50.03	20.14	0.71	23.21	16.01	0.64	44.13
SG-Net (ours)	19.58	0.77	41.49	19.87	0.81	41.74	23.04	0.83	18.98	17.94	0.64	41.24
SGE-Net (ours)	20.53	0.81	40.67	20.02	0.83	42.47	23.41	0.85	18.67	18.03	0.75	39.93

4.2　Image Inpainting Results

In this section, we present the results of our model trained on human-annotated segmentation labels. We also verify our model trained on the segmentation labels predicted by a state-of-the-art segmentation model. The results can be found in Sect. 4.3.

Qualitative Comparisons. The subjective visual comparisons of the proposed SG-Net and SGE-Net with the three baselines (GC, EC, SPG) on **Outdoor Scenes** and **Cityscapes** are presented in Fig. 4. The corrupted area is simulated by sampling a central hole (128×128 for **Outdoor Scenes** and 96×96 for **Cityscapes**), or placing masks with random shapes. As shown in the figure,

Table 2. Preference percentage matrix (%) of different scene complexities on **Outdoor Scenes** and **Cityscapes** datasets. Overall, low complexity, moderate complexity, and high complexity are colored in black, green, blue and red, respectively.

	GC [42]	EC [21]	SPG [27]	SGE-Net (ours)
GC [42]	–	(46.7)/41.5/47.7/52.0	(58.1)/57.3/59.8/56.7	(32.6)/37.8/34.8/22.4
EC [21]	(53.3)/58.5/52.3/48.0	–	(70.1)/68.7/69.3/73.0	(29.3)/35.0/31.8/18.1
SPG [27]	(41.9)/42.7/40.2/43.3	(29.9)/31.3/30.7/27.0	–	(26.8)/32.7/28.8/16.3
SGE-Net (ours)	(67.4)/62.2/65.2/77.6	(70.7)/65.0/68.2/81.9	(73.2)/67.3/71.2/83.7	–

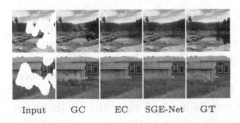

Input   GC   EC   SGE-Net   GT   Input   Basic-Net   SG-Net   SGE-Net   GT

Fig. 5. Subjective quality comparison on image samples from **Places2**.

Fig. 6. Subjective visual quality comparisons on the effects of SGIM and SCEM.

the baselines usually generate unrealistic shape and textures. The proposed SG-Net generates more realistic textures than the baselines, but still has some flaws at the boundaries since its final result highly depends on the initial inpainting result. The proposed SGE-Net generates better boundaries between semantic regions and more consistent textures than SG-Net and all the baselines, thanks to its evaluation mechanism that can correct the wrongly predicted labels.

Quantitative Comparisons. Table 1 shows the numerical results based on three quality metrics: Peak Signal-to-Noise Ratio (PSNR), Structural Similarity Index (SSIM) and Fréchet Inception Distance (FID) [11]. In general, the proposed SGE-Net achieves significantly better objective scores than the baselines, especially in PSNR and SSIM .

User Study. We conduct the user study on 80 images randomly selected from both datasets. In total, 24 subjects with some background of image processing are involved to rank the subjective visual qualities of images completed by four inpainting methods (GC, EC, SPG, and our SGE-Net). As shown in Table 2, the study shows that 67.4% of subjects (1295 out of 1920 comparisons), 70.7% and 73.2% preferred our results over GC, EC, and SPG, respectively. Hence, our method outperforms the other methods.

Since our method mainly focuses on completing mixed scenes with multiple semantics, we also verify its performance on images with different scene complexities. We conduct this analysis by dividing all 80 images into three levels of semantic complexities: 1) low-complexity scenes containing 27 images with 1–2 semantics; 2) moderate-complexity scenes containing 32 images with 3–4 semantics; 3) high-complexity scenes containing 21 images with more than 4 semantics. As shown in Table 2, compared to the baselines, while our method achieves generally better results than the baselines for the simple- to moderate-complexity scenes (about from 60% to 70%), the preference rate increases significantly for the complex scenes (from 77.6% to 83.7%). This verifies that our method is particularly powerful for completing mixed-scene images with multiple semantics, thanks to its mechanism for understanding and updating the semantics.

Additional Results on Places2. For fair comparison, we also test our method on **Places2** [48] to verify that SGE-Net can be applied to images without segmentation annotations. **Places2** was used for evaluation by both GC and EC. It contains images with similar semantic scenes to **Outdoor Scenes**. Therefore, we use our model trained on **Outdoor Scenes** to complete the images with similar scenes in **Places2**. The subjective results in Fig. 5 show that SGE-Net is still able to generate proper semantic structures, owing to the introduction of the semantic segmentation, which provides the prior knowledge about the scenes.

4.3   Ablation Study

Effectiveness of SGIM and SCEM. In the proposed networks, the two core components of our method, semantic-guided inference and segmentation confidence evaluation, are implemented by SGIM and SCEM, respectively. In order to investigate their effectiveness, we conduct an ablation study on three variants: a) Basic-Net (without SGIM and SCEM); b) SG-Net (with SGIM but without SCEM); and c) SGE-Net (with both SGIM and SCEM).

The visual and numeric comparisons on **Outdoor Scenes** are shown in Fig. 6 and Table 3. In general, the inpainting performance increases with the added modules. Specifically, the multi-scale semantic-guided interplay framework does a good job for generating detailed contents, and the semantic segmentation map helps learn a more accurate layout of a scene. With SGIM, the spatial adaptive normalization helps generate more realistic textures based on the semantic priors. Moreover, SCEM makes further improvements on completing structures and textures (fourth column in Fig. 6) by coarse-to-fine optimizing the semantic contents across scales.

To further verify the effectiveness of SCEM, we visualize a corrupted image and its segmentation maps derived from all decoding scales. As shown in the first five columns of Fig. 7, the multi-scale progressive-updating mechanism gradually refines the detailed textures as illustrated in the images and the segmentation maps at different scales. The last

Table 3. Objective quality comparison on the performances of SGIM and SCEM in terms of three metrics.

	SGIM	SCEM	PSNR↑	SSIM↑	FID↓
Basic-Net	✗	✗	19.14	0.71	43.43
SG-Net	✓	✗	19.58	0.77	41.49
SGE-Net	✓	✓	20.53	0.81	40.67

three columns of the top row show that the region of the unreliable mask gradually shrinks as well. Correspondingly, the bottom row shows the increase of the

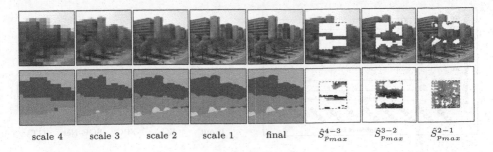

scale 4   scale 3   scale 2   scale 1   final $\hat{S}_{P_{max}}^{4-3}$ $\hat{S}_{P_{max}}^{3-2}$ $\hat{S}_{P_{max}}^{2-1}$

Fig. 7. Illustration of multi-scale progressive refinement with SGE-Net. From left to right of the first 5 columns: the inpainted images (top row) and the segmentation maps (bottom row) from scale 4 to scale 1 and the final result. The last 3 columns show the reliability maps (top row) and the confidence score maps (bottom row) of the inpainted area across scales (e.g., $\hat{S}_{P_{max}}^{4-3}$ shows the confidence score increases from scale 4 to 3).

confidence scores of segmentation maps from left to right (e.g., $\hat{S}_{P_{max}}^{4-3}$ showing the increase of the confidence score from scale 4 to scale 3). The proportion of the white region, which roughly indicates unreliable labels, also decreases significantly from left to right. The result evidently demonstrates the benefits of SCEM in strengthening the semantic correctness of contextual features.

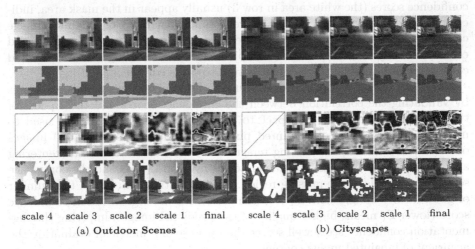

scale 4   scale 3   scale 2   scale 1   final   scale 4   scale 3   scale 2   scale 1   final
        (a) **Outdoor Scenes**   (b) **Cityscapes**

Fig. 8. Correspondence between the confidence score value and the reliability of inpainted image content. Row 1: Inpainted image. Row 2: Predicted segmetation map. Row 3: the confidence score map (darker color means higher confidence score, and vice versa). Row 4: unreliable pixel map (white pixels indicate unreliable pixels). Since the map at scale 4 is the same as the input mask, we put the input image for better comparison.

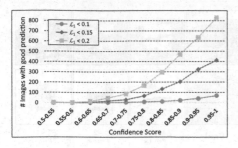

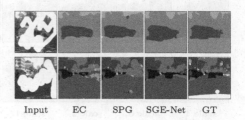

Fig. 9. Correlation between the inpainting quality and confidence score.

Fig. 10. Visual comparison on semantic segmentation between SGE-Net and the segmentation-after-inpainting solutions. 'EC' and 'SPG' stand for EC+DPN/Deeplab and SPG+DPN/Deeplab, respectively.

Justification of Segmentation Confidence Scoring. During the progressive refinement of image inpainting and semantic segmentation, the semantic evaluation mechanism of SCEM is based on the assumption that the pixelwise confidence scores from the segmentation possibility map can well reflect the correctness of the inpainted pixel values. Here we attempt to justify this assumption. Some examples from both datasets are shown in Fig. 8. It can be seen that (except for the confidence scores at the region boundaries): a) The low confidence scores (the white area in row 3) usually appear in the mask area, indicating that the scores reasonably well reflects the reliability of inpainted image content; b) the confidence score becomes higher when the scale goes finer, and correspondingly the area of unreliable pixels reduces, meaning that our method can progressively refine the context feature towards correct inpainting.

We then further verify the effectiveness of the pixel-wise confidence scores by validating the correlation between the confidence scores and the $\mathcal{L}_1$ loss of the completed images with respect to the ground-truth that can be used to measure of the fidelity of inpainted pixels. We randomly select 9,000 images out of all the training and testing images from the two datasets with centering and irregular-hole settings, and calculate the average $\mathcal{L}_1$ loss and the confidence scores of all pixels in the missing region. As demonstrated in Fig. 9, the number of good-fidelity images with $\mathcal{L}_1$ loss increases with the segmentation confidence score (lower $\mathcal{L}_1$ means higher quality of the predicted image), implying the segmentation confidence score well serves the purpose of a metric of evaluating the accuracy of inpainted image content.

Impact of Semantic Segmentation. The success of semantics-guided inpainting largely relies on the quality of semantic segmentation map. Here we investigate the impact of segmentation accuracy on image inpainting. We conduct comparison between SGE-Net with segmentation maps generated by state-of-the-art segmentation tools and SGE-Net with human-labeled maps. We utilize the DPN model [19] pre-trained on [30] as the segmentation tool for **Outdoor Scenes** as it is the only released model on the dataset. We select the Deeplab v3+ model [3] for **Cityscapes** due to its superior performance on that dataset.

As shown in Table 4, the performance degradation of our SGE-Net trained on imperfect semantic annotations is not significant, meaning that our model can still do a reasonably good job even trained on model-generated semantic annotation. More subjective quality comparisons are provided in supplementary material. Note that the segmentation maps, either human-annotated or model-generated, are only used in the training stage of our model. While completing an image, SGE-Net itself can automatically generate the inpainted image and segmentation map simultaneously, without the need of the semantic annotations.

pt   We also conduct experiments to validate whether the iterative interplay between inpainting and semantic segmentation outperforms the traditional non-iterative segmentation-after-inpainting strategy in semantic segmentation. We compare the segmentation maps generated by SGE-Net itself with initial segmentation maps extracted from images completed by the baselines. As compared in Fig. 10, the results show that SGE-

Table 4. Objective quality comparison on model trained by automatic segmentation (Auto-segs) and human-labeled semantics (Label-segs).

Outdoor Scenes		Cityscapes	
Methods	PSNR	Methods	PSNR
Auto-segs	20.19	Auto-segs	22.94
Label-segs	**20.53**	Label-segs	**23.41**

Net evidently beats the segmentation-after-inpainting methods since SGE-Net leads to more accurate semantic assignments and object boundaries, thanks to its joint-optimization of semantics and image contents.

5   Conclusion

In this paper, a novel SGE-Net with semantic segmentation guided scheme was proposed to complete corrupted images of mixed semantic regions. To address the problem of unreliable semantic segmentation due to missing regions, we proposed a progressive multi-scale refinement mechanism to conduct interplay between semantic segmentation and image inpainting. Experimental results demonstrate that the mechanism can effectively refines poorly-inferred regions through segmentation confidence evaluation to generate promising semantic structures and texture details in a coarse-to-fine manner.

Acknowledgement. This work was supported in part by National Natural Science Foundation of China under Grant 91738302, 61671336, by Natural Science Foundation of Jiangsu Province under Grant BK20180234.

References

1. Barnes, C., Shechtman, E., Finkelstein, A., Goldman, D.B.: PatchMatch: a randomized correspondence algorithm for structural image editing. ACM Trans. Graph. **28**(3), 24 (2009)

2. Bertalmio, M., Sapiro, G., Caselles, V., Ballester, C.: Image inpainting. In: Proceedings Conference Computer Graphics Interactive Techniques, pp. 417–424 (2000)
3. Chen, L.-C., Zhu, Y., Papandreou, G., Schroff, F., Adam, H.: Encoder-decoder with atrous separable convolution for semantic image segmentation. In: Ferrari, V., Hebert, M., Sminchisescu, C., Weiss, Y. (eds.) ECCV 2018. LNCS, vol. 11211, pp. 833–851. Springer, Cham (2018). https://doi.org/10.1007/978-3-030-01234-2_49
4. Cordts, M., et al.: The cityscapes dataset for semantic urban scene understanding. In: CVPR, pp. 3213–3223 (2016)
5. Criminisi, A., Pérez, P., Toyama, K.: Region filling and object removal by exemplar-based image inpainting. IEEE Trans. Image Process. **13**(9), 1200–1212 (2004)
6. Demir, U., Unal, G.: Deep stacked networks with residual polishing for image inpainting. arXiv preprint arXiv:1801.00289 (2017)
7. Dosovitskiy, A., Brox, T.: Generating images with perceptual similarity metrics based on deep networks. In: NeurIPS, pp. 658–666 (2016)
8. Gilbert, A., Collomosse, J., Jin, H., Price, B.: Disentangling structure and aesthetics for style-aware image completion. In: CVPR, pp. 1848–1856 (2018)
9. Goodfellow, I., et al.: Generative adversarial nets. In: NeurIPS, pp. 2672–2680 (2014)
10. Hays, J., Efros, A.A.: Scene completion using millions of photographs. ACM Trans. Graph. **26**(3), 4 (2007)
11. Heusel, M., Ramsauer, H., Unterthiner, T., Nessler, B., Hochreiter, S.: GANs trained by a two time-scale update rule converge to a local Nash equilibrium. In: NeurIPS, pp. 6626–6637 (2017)
12. Iizuka, S., Simo-Serra, E., Ishikawa, H.: Globally and locally consistent image completion. ACM Trans. Graph. **36**(4), 107 (2017)
13. Johnson, J., Alahi, A., Fei-Fei, L.: Perceptual losses for real-time style transfer and super-resolution. In: Leibe, B., Matas, J., Sebe, N., Welling, M. (eds.) ECCV 2016. LNCS, vol. 9906, pp. 694–711. Springer, Cham (2016). https://doi.org/10.1007/978-3-319-46475-6_43
14. Li, J., He, F., Zhang, L., Du, B., Tao, D.: Progressive reconstruction of visual structure for image inpainting. In: ICCV, pp. 5962–5971 (2019)
15. Li, Y., Liu, S., Yang, J., Yang, M.H.: Generative face completion. In: CVPR, pp. 3911–3919 (2017)
16. Liao, L., Hu, R., Xiao, J., Wang, Z.: Edge-aware context encoder for image inpainting. In: ICASSP, pp. 3156–3160 (2018)
17. Liu, G., Reda, F.A., Shih, K.J., Wang, T.-C., Tao, A., Catanzaro, B.: Image inpainting for irregular holes using partial convolutions. In: Ferrari, V., Hebert, M., Sminchisescu, C., Weiss, Y. (eds.) ECCV 2018. LNCS, vol. 11215, pp. 89–105. Springer, Cham (2018). https://doi.org/10.1007/978-3-030-01252-6_6
18. Liu, H., Jiang, B., Xiao, Y., Yang, C.: Coherent semantic attention for image inpainting. In: ICCV, pp. 4169–4178 (2019)
19. Liu, Z., Li, X., Luo, P., Loy, C.C., Tang, X.: Deep learning Markov random field for semantic segmentation. IEEE Trans. Pattern Anal. Mach. Intell. **40**(8), 1814–1828 (2017)
20. Ma, Y., Liu, X., Bai, S., Wang, L., He, D., Liu, A.: Coarse-to-fine image inpainting via region-wise convolutions and non-local correlation. In: IJCAI, pp. 3123–3129 (2019)
21. Nazeri, K., Ng, E., Joseph, T., Qureshi, F., Ebrahimi, M.: EdgeConnect: structure guided image inpainting using edge prediction. In: ICCVW, pp. 3265–3274 (2019)
22. Park, T., Liu, M.Y., Wang, T.C., Zhu, J.Y.: Semantic image synthesis with spatially-adaptive normalization. In: CVPR, pp. 2337–2346 (2019)

23. Pathak, D., Krahenbuhl, P., Donahue, J., Darrell, T., Efros, A.A.: Context encoders: feature learning by inpainting. In: CVPR, pp. 2536–2544 (2016)
24. Radford, A., Metz, L., Chintala, S.: Unsupervised representation learning with deep convolutional generative adversarial networks. In: ICLR (2016)
25. Ren, Y., Yu, X., Zhang, R., Li, T.H., Liu, S., Li, G.: StructureFlow: image inpainting via structure-aware appearance flow. In: ICCV, pp. 181–190 (2019)
26. Song, Y., et al.: Contextual-based image inpainting: infer, match, and translate. In: Ferrari, V., Hebert, M., Sminchisescu, C., Weiss, Y. (eds.) ECCV 2018. LNCS, vol. 11206, pp. 3–18. Springer, Cham (2018). https://doi.org/10.1007/978-3-030-01216-8_1
27. Song, Y., Yang, C., Shen, Y., Wang, P., Huang, Q., Kuo, C.C.J.: SPG-Net: Segmentation prediction and guidance network for image inpainting. In: BMVC, p. 97 (2018)
28. Sun, J., Yuan, L., Jia, J., Shum, H.Y.: Image completion with structure propagation. ACM Trans. Graph. **24**(3), 861–868 (2005)
29. Wang, N., Li, J., Zhang, L., Du, B.: Musical: multi-scale image contextual attention learning for inpainting. In: IJCAI, pp. 3748–3754 (2019)
30. Wang, X., Yu, K., Dong, C., Change Loy, C.: Recovering realistic texture in image super-resolution by deep spatial feature transform. In: CVPR, pp. 606–615 (2018)
31. Wang, Y., Tao, X., Qi, X., Shen, X., Jia, J.: Image inpainting via generative multi-column convolutional neural networks. In: NeurIPS, pp. 331–340 (2018)
32. Wang, Z., Jiang, J., Wu, Y., Ye, M., Bai, X., Satoh, S.: Learning sparse and identity-preserved hidden attributes for person re-identification. IEEE Trans. Image Process. **29**(1), 2013–2025 (2019)
33. Wang, Z., Ye, M., Yang, F., Bai, X., Satoh, S.: Cascaded SR-GAN for scale-adaptive low resolution person re-identification. In: IJCAI, pp. 3891–3897 (2018)
34. Xiao, J., Liao, L., Liu, Q., Hu, R.: CISI-net: Explicit latent content inference and imitated style rendering for image inpainting. In: AAAI, pp. 354–362 (2019)
35. Xie, C., et al.: Image inpainting with learnable bidirectional attention maps. In: ICCV, pp. 8858–8867 (2019)
36. Xiong, W., et al.: Foreground-aware image inpainting. In: CVPR, pp. 5840–5848 (2019)
37. Yan, Z., Li, X., Li, M., Zuo, W., Shan, S.: Shift-Net: image inpainting via deep feature rearrangement. In: Ferrari, V., Hebert, M., Sminchisescu, C., Weiss, Y. (eds.) Computer Vision – ECCV 2018. LNCS, vol. 11218, pp. 3–19. Springer, Cham (2018). https://doi.org/10.1007/978-3-030-01264-9_1
38. Yang, C., Lu, X., Lin, Z., Shechtman, E., Wang, O., Li, H.: High-resolution image inpainting using multi-scale neural patch synthesis. In: CVPR, pp. 4076–4084 (2017)
39. Yeh, R.A., Chen, C., Yian Lim, T., Schwing, A.G., Hasegawa-Johnson, M., Do, M.N.: Semantic image inpainting with deep generative models. In: CVPR, pp. 6882–6890 (2017)
40. Yi, P., Wang, Z., Jiang, K., Shao, Z., Ma, J.: Multi-temporal ultra dense memory network for video super-resolution. IEEE Trans. Circuits Syst. Video Technol. **30**(8), 2503–2516 (2019)
41. Yu, J., Lin, Z., Yang, J., Shen, X., Lu, X., Huang, T.S.: Generative image inpainting with contextual attention. In: CVPR, pp. 5505–5514 (2018)
42. Yu, J., Lin, Z., Yang, J., Shen, X., Lu, X., Huang, T.S.: Free-form image inpainting with gated convolution. In: ICCV, pp. 4470–4479 (2019)
43. Zeng, Y., Fu, J., Chao, H., Guo, B.: Learning pyramid-context encoder network for high-quality image inpainting. In: CVPR, pp. 5961–5970 (2019)

44. Zhang, R., Ren, Y., Qiu, J., Li, G.: Base-detail image inpainting. In: BMVC, p. 195 (2019)
45. Zhang, S., He, R., Sun, Z., Tan, T.: DeMeshNet: blind face inpainting for deep meshface verification. IEEE Trans. Inf. Forensics Secur. **13**(3), 637–647 (2018)
46. Zhao, D., Guo, B., Yan, Y.: Parallel image completion with edge and color map. Appl. Sci. **9**(18), 3856 (2019)
47. Zheng, C., Cham, T.J., Cai, J.: Pluralistic image completion. In: CVPR, pp. 1438–1447 (2019)
48. Zhou, B., Lapedriza, A., Khosla, A., Oliva, A., Torralba, A.: Places: a 10 million image database for scene recognition. IEEE Trans. Pattern Anal. Mach. Intell. **40**(6), 1452–1464 (2017)

Sound2Sight: Generating Visual Dynamics from Sound and Context

Moitreya Chatterjee[1] and Anoop Cherian[2]($\boxtimes$)

[1] University of Illinois at Urbana-Champaign, Urbana, IL 61801, USA
metro.smiles@gmail.com
[2] Mitsubishi Electric Research Laboratories, Cambridge, MA 02139, USA
cherian@merl.com

Abstract. Learning associations across modalities is critical for robust multimodal reasoning, especially when a modality may be missing during inference. In this paper, we study this problem in the context of audio-conditioned visual synthesis – a task that is important, for example, in occlusion reasoning. Specifically, our goal is to generate future video frames and their motion dynamics conditioned on audio and a few past frames. To tackle this problem, we present *Sound2Sight*, a deep variational encoder-decoder framework, that is trained to learn a per frame stochastic prior conditioned on a joint embedding of audio and past frames. This embedding is learned via a multi-head attention-based audio-visual transformer encoder. The learned prior is then sampled to further condition a video forecasting module to generate future frames. The stochastic prior allows the model to sample multiple plausible futures that are consistent with the provided audio and the past context. Moreover, to improve the quality and coherence of the generated frames, we propose a multimodal discriminator that differentiates between a synthesized and a real audio-visual clip. We empirically evaluate our approach, vis-á-vis closely-related prior methods, on two new datasets viz. (i) Multimodal Stochastic Moving MNIST with a Surprise Obstacle, (ii) Youtube Paintings; as well as on the existing Audio-Set Drums dataset. Our extensive experiments demonstrate that Sound2Sight significantly outperforms the state of the art in the generated video quality, while also producing diverse video content.

1 Introduction

Evolution has equipped the intelligent species with the ability to create mental representations of sensory inputs and make associations across them to generate world models [9]. Perception is the outcome of an inference process over this

---

M. Chatterjee—Work done as an intern at MERL.

Electronic supplementary material The online version of this chapter (https://doi.org/10.1007/978-3-030-58583-9_42) contains supplementary material, which is available to authorized users.

© Springer Nature Switzerland AG 2020
A. Vedaldi et al. (Eds.): ECCV 2020, LNCS 12372, pp. 701–719, 2020.
https://doi.org/10.1007/978-3-030-58583-9_42

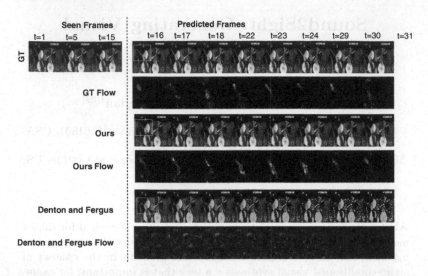

Fig. 1. Video generation using our Sound2Sight against Denton and Fergus [10] on AudioSet-Drums [14]. We also show the optical flow between consecutive generated frames. The red square indicates the region of dominant motion. (Color figure online)

world model, when provided with new sensory inputs. Consider the following situation. You see a kid going into a room which is occluded from your viewpoint, however after sometime you hear the sound of a vessel falling down, and soon enough, a heavy falling sound. In the blink of an eye, your mind simulates a large number of potential possibilities that could have happened in that room; each simulation considered for its coherence with the sound heard, and its urgency or risk. From these simulations, the most likely possibility is selected to be acted upon. Such a framework that can synthesize modalities from other cues is perhaps fundamental to any intelligent system. Efforts to understand such mental associations between modalities dates back to the pioneering work of Pavlov [43] (on his drooling dogs) who proposed the idea of *conditioning* on sensory inputs.

In this paper, we explore this multimodal association problem in the context of generating plausible visual imagery given the accompanying sound. Specifically, our goal is to build a world model that learns associations between audio and video dynamics in such a way as to infer visual dynamics when only the audio modality (and the visual context set by a few initial frames) is presented to the system. As alluded to above, such a problem is fundamental to occlusion reasoning. Apart from this, it could help develop assistive technologies for the hearing-impaired, could enable a synergy between video and audio inpainting technologies [28,66], or could even compliment the current "seeing through corners" methods [35,65] using the audio modality.

From a technical standpoint, the task of generating the pixel-wise video stream from only the audio modality is severely ill-posed. For instance, a drummer playing a drum to a certain beat would sound the same irrespective of the color of his/her attire. To circumvent this challenge, we condition our video generator using a few initial frames. This workaround not only permits the generation of videos that are pertinent to the situation, but also allows the model to focus on learning the dynamics and interactions of the visual cues assisted by audio. There are several recent works in a similar vein [6,7,56] that explore speech-to-video synthesis to generate talking heads, however they do not use the past visual context or assume very restricted motion dynamics and audio priors. On the other hand, methods that seek to predict future video frames [10,13,55] given only the past frames, assume a continuity of the motion pattern and are unable to adapt to drastic changes in motion that might arise in the future (e.g., the sudden movements of the drummer in Fig. 1). We note that there also exist several recent works in the audio-visual synthesis realm, such as generating audio from video [27,63,64] that looks at a complementary problem and multimodal generative adversarial networks (GAN) that generates a single image rather than forecasting the video dynamics [8,18,58].

To tackle this novel task, we present a stochastic deep neural network: *Sound2 Sight*, which is trained end-to-end. Our main backbone is a conditional variational autoencoder (VAE) [30] that captures the distribution of the *future video frames* in a latent space. This distribution is used as a prior to subsequently condition a video generation framework. A key question that arises then, is how to incorporate the audio stream and its correlations with the video content? We propose to capture this synergy within the prior distribution - through a joint embedding of the audio features and the video frames. The variance of this prior distribution, permits diversity in the video generation model, thereby synthesizing disparate plausible futures.

An important component in our setup is the audio-visual latent embedding that controls the generation process. Inspired by the recent success of transformer networks [53], we propose an adaptation of multi-head transformers to effectively learn a multimodal latent space through self-attention. As is generally known, pixel generations produced using variational models often lack sharpness, which could be attributed to the Euclidean loss typically used [32]. To this end, in order to improve the generated video quality, we further propose a novel *multimodal discriminator*, that is trained to differentiate between real audio-visual samples and generated video frames coupled with the input audio. This discriminator incorporates explicit sub-modules to verify if the generated frames are realistic, consistent, and synchronized with the audio.

We conduct experiments on three datasets, two new multimodal datasets: (i) Multimodal Stochastic Moving MNIST with a Surprise Obstacle (M3SO) and (ii) Youtube-Painting, alongside a third dataset – AudioSet-Drums – which is an adaptation of the well-known AudioSet datset [14]. The M3SO dataset is an extension of stochastic moving MNIST [10], however incorporates audio based on the location and identity of the digits in the video, while also including a surprise component that requires learning audio-visual synchronization and stochastic reasoning. The Youtube-Painting dataset is created by crawling

Youtube for painting videos and provides a challenging setting for Sound2Sight to associate painting motions of an artist and the subtle sounds of brush strokes. Our experiments on these datasets show that Sound2Sight leads to state-of-the-art performances in quality, diversity, and consistency of the generated videos.

Before moving on, we summarize below the key contributions of this paper.

- We study the novel task of future frame generation consistent with the given audio and a set of initial frames.
- We present *Sound2Sight*, a novel deep variational multimodal encoder-decoder for this task, that combines the power of VAEs, GANs, and multimodal transformers in a coherent learning framework.
- We introduce three datasets for evaluating this task. Extensive experiments are provided, demonstrating state-of-the-art performances, besides portraying diversity in the generation process.

2   Related Works

In this section, we review prior works that are closely related to our approach.

Audio-Visual Joint Representations: The natural co-occurrence of audio-and-visual cues is used for better representation learning in several recent works [1,3,20,39–41]. We too draw upon this observation, however, our end-goal of future frame generation from audio is notably different and manifests in our proposed architecture. For example, while both [1] and [39] propose a common multimodal embedding layer for video representation, our multimodal embedding module is only used for capturing the prior and posterior distributions of the stochastic components in the generated frames

Video Generation: The success of GANs has resulted in a myriad of image generation algorithms [11,15,16,30,31,36,61]. Inspired from these techniques, methods for video generation have also been proposed [46,52,55]. These algorithms usually directly map a noise vector sampled from a known or a learned distribution into a realistic-looking video and as such are known as *unconditional video generation* methods. Instead, our proposed generative model uses additional audio inputs, alongside encoding of the past frames. Models like ours are therefore, typically referred to as *conditional video generation* techniques. Prior works [17,19,34,42,59] have shown the success of conditional generative methods when information, such as the video categories, captions, etc., are available, using which constraints the plausible generations, improving their quality. Our proposed architecture differs in the modalities we use to constrain the generations and the associated technical innovations required to accommodate them.

Video Prediction/Forecasting: This is the task of predicting future frames, given a few frames from the past. Prior works in this area typically fall under: (i) *Deterministic*, and (ii) *Diversity-based* methods. Deterministic methods often use an encoder-decoder model to generate video frames autoregressively. The

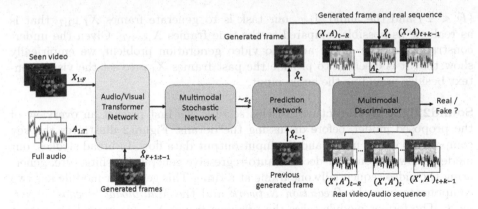

Fig. 2. Overview of the architecture of Sound2Sight. Our model takes F "seen" video frames (during inference) and all T audio samples, producing $T - F$ video frames (each denoted by $\hat{X}_t$). During training, the multimodal discriminator predicts if an input video is real or fake. We construct the fake video by replacing the t-th frame of the ground truth by $\hat{X}_t$. Note that during training, the generated frames ($\hat{X}_{F+1:t-1}$) which are input to the audio/visual transformer, are replaced by their real counterparts ($X_{F+1:t-1}$), while also using the current frame X_t to train the stochastic network.

inherent stochasticity within the video data (due to multiple plausible futures or encoding noise) is thus difficult to be incorporated in such models [12,22,25, 37,44,48,54]. Our approach circumvents these issues via a stochastic module. There have been prior efforts to capture this stochasticity from unimodal cues, such as [4,10,57,62], by learning a parametric prior distribution. Different from these approaches, we model the stochasticity using multimodal inputs.

We also note that there are several works in the area of generating human face animations conditioned on speech [24,26,47,50,51], however these techniques often make use of additional details, such as the identity of the person or leverage strong facial cues such as landmarks, textures, etc. - hindering their applicability to generic videos. There are methods free of such constraints, such as [38], however they synthesize images and not videos. A work similar to ours is Vougioukas *et al.* [56] that synthesizes face motions directly from speech and an initial frame, however it operates in the restricted domain of generating facial motions only.

3   Proposed Method

Given a dataset $\mathcal{D} = \{V_1, V_2, \cdots, V_N\}$ consisting of N video sequences, where each V is characterized by a pair $(X_{1:T}, A_{1:T})$ of T video frames and its time-aligned audio samples, i.e., $X_{1:T} = \langle X_1, X_2, ..., X_F, X_{F+1}, ..., X_T \rangle$ and $A_{1:T} = \langle A_1, A_2, ..., A_T \rangle$. We assume that the audio and the video are synchronized in such a way that A_t corresponds to the sound associated with the frame X_t in the duration $(t, t+1)$. Now, given as input a sequence of F frames $X_{1:F}$,

$(F < T)$ and the audio $A_{1:T}$, our task is to generate frames $\hat{X}_{F+1:T}$ that is as realistic as possible compared to the true frames $X_{F+1:T}$. Given the under-constrained nature of the audio to video generation problem, we empirically show that it is essential to provide the past frames $X_{1:F}$ to set the visual context besides providing the audio input.

Sound2Sight Architecture: In this section, we first present an overview of the proposed model, before discussing the details. Figure 2 illustrates the key components in our model and the input-output data flow. In broad strokes, our model follows an encoder-decoder auto-regressive generator architecture, generating the video sequentially one frame at a time. This generator module has two components, viz. the *Prediction Network* and the *Multimodal Stochastic Network*. The former module takes the previous frame X_{t-1} as input,[1] encodes it into a latent space, concatenates it with a prior latent sample z_t obtained from the stochastic network, and decodes it to generate a frame $\hat{X}_t$, which approximates the target frame X_t. Sans the sample z_t, the prediction network is purely deterministic and unimodal, and hence can fail to capture the stochasticity in the motion dynamics. This challenge is mitigated by the multimodal stochastic network, which uses transformer encoders [53] on the audio and visual input streams to produce (the parameters of) a prior distribution from which z_t is sampled. The generator can thus be thought of as a non-linear heteroskedastic dynamical system (whose variance is decided by an underlying neural network), which generates $\hat{X}_t$ from the pair $(\hat{X}_{t-1}, z_t)$, and implicitly conditioned on the (latent) history of previous samples and the given audio.

During training, two additional data flows happen. (i) The transformer and the stochastic network take as input the true video sequence $X_{1:t}$ as well. This is used to estimate a posterior distribution which is in turn used to train the stochastic prior so that it effectively captures the distribution of real video samples. (ii) Further, the generated frames are evaluated for their realism, motion synchrony, and audio-visual alignment using a multimodal adversarial discriminator [15] (Fig. 2). This discriminator uses $\hat{X}_t$ – the synthetic frame, inserted at the t-th index of the original sequence, and $X_{t-R:t+(k-1)}$ the set of R past, and $(k-1)$ future frames, along with the corresponding audio, and compares it with real (arbitrary) audio-visual clips of length $R + k$ from the dataset. Since discriminators match distributions, rather than matching individual samples, this ensures that incorporating the generated frame $\hat{X}_t$ results in a coherent video that is consistent with the input audio, while permitting diversity. We now elaborate on each of the above modules and layout our training strategy.

Prediction Network: Broadly speaking, the prediction network (PN) is a standard sequence-to-sequence encoder-decoder network. It starts off by embedding the previous frame X_{t-1} into a latent space. We denote this embedding by $f(X_{t-1})$, where $f(\cdot)$ abstracts a convolutional neural network (CNN) [33]. Each

---

[1] X_{t-1} is the *real* frame during training, however during inference, it is the generated frame $\hat{X}_{t-1}$ if $t - 1 > F$.

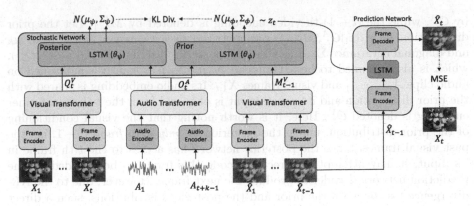

Fig. 3. Details of our Multimodal Stochastic Network and Prediction Network.

layer of this CNN consists of a set of convolution kernels, followed by 2D-Batch Normalization [23] layers, Leaky ReLU activations, and has skip-connections to the decoder part of the network. These skip connections facilitate reconstruction of static parts of the video [45]. The embedding of the frame $f(X_{t-1})$ is then concatenated with a sample $z_t \sim \mathcal{N}(\mu_\phi, \Sigma_\phi)$, a Gaussian prior provided by the stochastic module (described next) where μ_ϕ and Σ_ϕ denote the mean and a diagonal covariance matrix of this Gaussian prior. Our key idea is to have z_t capture the cues about the future as provided by the available audio, as well as the randomness in producing the next frame. We then feed the pair $(f(X_{t-1}), z_t)$ to a Long-Short Term Memory (LSTM) [21], parametrized by θ_L within the PN; this LSTM keeps track of the previously generated frames via its internal states. Specifically, if h_{t-1} denotes the hidden state of this LSTM, then we define its output η_t as: $\eta_t = \mathrm{LSTM}_{\theta_L}((f(X_{t-1}), z_t), h_{t-1})$. The LSTM output η_t is then passed to the decoder network $g(\cdot)$, to generate the next frame, i.e., $\hat{X}_t = g(\eta_t)$. The decoder consists of a set of deconvolution layers with Leaky ReLU activations, coupled with 2D-Batch Normalization layers.

Multimodal Stochastic Network: Several prior works have underscored the importance of modeling the stochasticity in video generation [4,10,57,62], albeit using a single modality. Inspired by these works, we introduce the multimodal stochastic network (MSN) that takes both the audio and video streams as inputs to model the stochastic elements in producing the target frame X_t. As alluded to earlier, such a stochastic element allows for capturing the randomness in the generated frame, while also permitting the sampling of multiple plausible futures conditioned on the available inputs. As shown in Fig. 3, the stochastic network is effectuated by computing a prior and a posterior distribution in the embedding space (from which z_t is sampled) and training the model to minimize their mutual discrepancy. The prior distribution is jointly conditioned on an embedding of the audio sub-clip $A_{1:t+(k-1)}$ and an embedding of the video frames $X_{1:t-1}$, both obtained via transformer encoders. We denote the t-th audio encoding by O_t^A, while the $(t-1)$-th video encoding is denoted by M_{t-1}^V. Let the prior distribution be $p_\phi(z_t|O_t^A, M_{t-1}^V)$, parametrized as a Gaussian, with mean μ_ϕ and diagonal covariance Σ_ϕ. Likewise, the posterior distribution $p_\psi(z_t|O_t^A, Q_t^V)$, which is also assumed to be a Gaussian $\mathcal{N}(\mu_\psi, \Sigma_\psi)$, is jointly conditioned on audio clips $A_{1:t+(k-1)}$ and visual frames $X_{1:t}$. Its audio embedding is shared with the prior distribution and its visual input is obtained from the t-th transformer encoding is denoted Q_t^V. Here, it is worth noting that the visual conditioning of the prior distribution, unlike the posterior, is *only upto frame $t-1$*, i.e. the past visual frames. Since the posterior network has access to the t-th frame in its input, it may attempt to directly encode this frame to be decoded by the prediction network decoder to produce the next frame. However, due to the KL-divergence loss between the prior and the posterior distributions, such a direct decoding cannot happen; unless the prior is trained well such that the KL-loss is minimized; which essentially implies the prior $p_\phi(z_t|O_t^A, M_{t-1}^V)$ will be able to predict the latent distribution of the future samples (as if from the posterior $p_\psi(z_t|O_t^A, Q_t^V)$), which is essentially what we require during inference.

To generate the prior distribution, we concatenate the embedded features M_{t-1}^V and O_t^A as input to an LSTM$_\phi$. Different from standard LSTMs, this LSTM predicts the parameters of the prior distribution directly, i.e., $\mu_\phi, \log\Sigma_\phi = \text{LSTM}_\phi(O_t^A, M_{t-1}^V)$. The posterior distribution parameters are estimated similarly, using a second LSTM, denoted LSTM$_\psi$ that takes as input the embedded and concatenated audio-video features O_t^A and Q_t^V to produce: $\mu_\psi, \log\Sigma_\psi = \text{LSTM}_\psi(O_t^A, Q_t^V)$.

Audio-Visual Transformer Encoder: Next, we describe the process of producing the prior and posterior distributions from audio-visual joint embeddings. As we want these embeddings to be "temporally-conscious" while computable efficiently, we bank on the very successful *Transformer Encoder Networks* [53], which are armed with self-attention modules that are well-known to produce powerful multimodal representations. Re-using the encoder CNN f from the prediction network, our visual transformer encoder takes as input the matrix $\mathcal{F} = \langle f'(X_1), f'(X_2), \cdots, f'(X_{t-1})\rangle$ with $f'(X_i)$ in its i-th column, where $f'(X_i)$ denotes the feature encoding $f(X_i)$ augmented with the respective temporal position encoding of the frame in the sequence, as suggested in [53]. We then apply ℓ-head self-attention to $\mathcal{F}$ by designing *Query* ($\mathcal{Q}$), *Key* ($\mathcal{K}$), and *Value* ($\mathcal{V}$) triplets via linear projections of our frame embeddings $\mathcal{F}$; i.e., $\mathcal{Q}_j = W_q^j \mathcal{F}$, $\mathcal{K}_j = W_k^j \mathcal{F}$, and $\mathcal{V}_j = W_v^j \mathcal{F}$, where W_q^j, W_k^j, W_v^j are matrices of sizes $d_k \times d$, d is the size of the feature f', and $j = 1, 2, \cdots, \ell$. Using ℓ, $d_k \times d$ weight matrix W_h, our self-attended feature $\hat{M}_{t-1}^V$ from this transformer layer is thus:

$$\hat{M}_{t-1}^V = \text{concat}_{j=1}^\ell \left(\text{softmax}\left(\frac{\mathcal{Q}_j \mathcal{K}_j^\top}{\sqrt{d_k}}\right) \mathcal{V}_j \right) W_h, \tag{1}$$

where concat denotes the concatenation operator. We use four consecutive self-attention layers within every transformer encoder, which are then combined via feed-forward layers to obtain the final encoding [53] M_{t-1}^V, which is subsequently used in the MSN module. Likewise, the re-purposed visual features for the posterior distribution, Q_t^V, can also be computed by employing a separate transformer encoder module, which ensures a separation of the visual components of the prior and the posterior networks. To produce the audio embeddings O_t^A, we first compute STFT (Short-Time Fourier Transform) features $(S_1, S_2, ..., S_{t+(k-1)})$ from the raw audio by choosing appropriate STFT filter sizes and strides, where each $S_i \in \mathbb{R}^{d_{H_A} \times d_{W_A}}$ and encode them using an audio transformer.

Generator Loss: To train our generator model, we directly maximize the variational *Empirical Lower BOund* (ELBO) [30] by optimizing the objective:

$$\mathcal{L}_V = \sum_{t=F+1}^{T} \mathop{\mathbb{E}}_{z_t \sim p_\phi} \log p_\phi(\hat{X}_t | M_{t-1}^V, z_t) \ - \beta \, \mathrm{KL}\left(p_\psi\left(z_t | O_t^A, Q_t^V\right) \parallel p_\phi\left(z_t | O_t^A, M_{t-1}^V\right)\right),$$

where the KL-divergence matches the closeness of the posterior distribution and the prior, while β is a constant. Casting the above as a minimization and approximating the first term by the pixel-wise ℓ_2 error, reduces the objective to:

$$\mathcal{L}_V \approx \sum_{t=F+1}^{T} \|X_t - \hat{X}_t\|_2^2 \ + \ \beta KL(p_\psi \| p_\phi). \tag{2}$$

Multimodal Discriminator Network: Computing the training loss, as in (2), is entirely based on the supplied ground truth (which is only one of many possibilities) and thus might restrict generative diversity. We rectify this shortcoming using a multimodal discriminator (see Fig. 2), which is designed to match the distribution of synthesized frames p_G against the ground truth distribution p_D. In contrast to conventional image-based GAN discriminators [5,15], our variant couples a classifier, denoted D_{std}, and an LSTM D, to produce binary labels indicating if the t-th frame is drawn from p_D or from p_G. This is done via using a set of ground-truth audio-visual frames from the neighborhood of the generated frame, where this neighborhood spans the previous R and future $(k-1)$ frames. When judging its inputs, the discriminator, besides looking into whether the t-th frame appears real or fake, also looks at how well the regularities of object motions are preserved with respect to the neighborhood via a motion dynamics (MD) loss, and if the frames are synchronized with the audio via an audio alignment (AA) loss. With these additional terms, our discriminator loss is:

$$\mathcal{L}_{adv} = -\sum_{t=F+1}^{T} \mathbb{E}_{X'_t \sim p_D} \log D_{std}(X'_t) + \mathbb{E}_{\hat{X}_t \sim p_G} \log(1 - D_{std}(\hat{X}_t))$$

$$+ \mathbb{E}_{X'_t \sim p_D} \log \underbrace{D(X'_t | A'_t, B'_{t+(k-1)}, \cdots, B'_{t+1}, B'_{t-1}, \cdots, B'_{t-R})}_{\text{Real Data - Motion Dynamics (MD)}}$$

$$+ \mathbb{E}_{X'_t \sim p_D} \log \underbrace{(1 - D(X'_t | A'_{t'}, C'_{t+(k-1),t'+(k-1)}, \cdots, C'_{t+1,t'+1}, C'_{t-1,t'-1}, \cdots, C'_{t-R,t'-R}))}_{\text{Real Data - Audio Alignment (AA)}}$$

$$+ \mathbb{E}_{\hat{X}_t \sim p_G} \log \underbrace{(1 - D(\hat{X}_t | A_t, B_{t+(k-1)}, \cdots, B_{t+1}, B_{t-1}, ..., B_{t-R}))}_{\text{Synthetic Frame - Motion Dynamics (MD)}}$$

$$+ \mathbb{E}_{\hat{X} \sim p_G} \log \underbrace{(1 - D(\hat{X}_t | A_{t'}, C_{t+(k-1),t'+(k-1)}, \cdots, C_{t+1,t'+1}, C_{t-1,t'-1}, \cdots, C_{t-R,t'-R}))}_{\text{Synthetic Frame - Audio Alignment (AA)}}$$

$$(3)$$

where (X'_t, A'_t) denotes a visual frame X'_t and its associated audio A'_t from a clip $B' = (X'_{1:T}, A'_{1:T})$ arbitrarily sampled from the training set. Similarly, we define $C_{t,t'} = (X_t, A_{t'})$, $t' \neq t$, $B_t = (X_t, A_t)$, $C'_{t,t'} = (X'_t, A'_{t'})$, $B'_t = (X'_t, A'_t)$, $X_t \neq X'_t$, $A_t \neq A'_t$. The first term in (3) defines a standard image-based GAN loss, while D in the other terms denotes a convolutional LSTM. The motion dynamics term captures the consistency of the generated frame against other frames in the sequence (i.e., X'_t against B' on the real, and $\hat{X}_t$ against B on the generated), while the audio alignment of the generated frame $\hat{X}_t$ against arbitrary audio samples A' is captured by the AA term. We optimize for the discriminator parameters by minimizing this loss above.

Combining the adversarial losses above with (2), our final objective for optimizing the generator is: $\mathcal{L} = \mathcal{L}_V - \gamma \mathcal{L}_{adv}$, where γ is a constant. We minimize this loss using ADAM [29], while employing the reparameterization trick [30] to ensure differentiability of the stochastic sampler.

4   Experiments

To benchmark the performance of our model, we present empirical experiments on a synthetic and two real world datasets, which will be made publicly available.

Multimodal MovingMNIST with a Surprise Obstacle (M3SO): is a novel extension of the stochastic MovingMNIST dataset [10] adapted to our multimodal setting, and consists of MNIST digits moving along rectilinear paths in a fixed size box (48×48) which bounce in random directions upon colliding with the box boundaries. In addition: (i) we equip each digit with a unique tone, (ii) the amplitude of this tone is inversely proportional to the digit's distance from the origin, and (iii) the tone changes momentarily when the digit bounces off the box edge. We make this task even more challenging by introducing an obstacle (square block of fixed size) at a random location within the unseen part of the video. When the digit bounces against the block, a unique audio frequency is emitted. The task on this dataset is not only to generate the frames, but also to predict the location of the block by listening to the tone changes. See supplementary materials for details. We also construct a version of the dataset, where no block is introduced, called M3SO-NB. We produced 8,000 training, 1,000 validation, and 1,000 test samples for both M3SO and M3SO-NB.

AudioSet-Drums: includes videos from the *Drums* class of AudioSet [14]. We clipped and retained only those video segments from this dataset for which the drum player is visible when the drum beat is heard. This yielded a dataset consisting of 8K clips which we split as 6K for training, 1K for validation, and 1K for test. Each video is of 64 × 64 resolution, 30 fps, and is 3 s long.

YouTube Painting: To analyze Sound2Sight in a subtle, yet real world setting, we introduce the *Youtube Painting* dataset. The videos in this dataset are manually collected via crawling painting videos on Youtube [2]. We selected only those videos that contain a painter painting on a canvas in an indoor environment, and which have a clear audio of the brush strokes. These videos provide a wide assortment of brush strokes and painting colors. The painter's motions and the camera viewpoints are often arbitrary which adds to the complexity and diversity, making it a very challenging dataset. Here the task is to generate frames showing the dynamics of the painter's arms, while preserving the static components in the scene. We collected 4.8K videos for training, 500 for validation and 500 for test. Each video is of 64 × 64 resolution, 30 fps, and 3 s long.

Evaluation Setup: On the M3SO dataset, we conduct experiments in two settings: (i) in M3SO-NB, all methods are shown 5 frames and the full audio, with the task being to predict the next 15 frames at training and 20 frames at test time, and (ii) using M3SO in which blocks are presented, we show 30 frames at training and 30 frames are predicted, however the block appears at the 42-nd frame. We predict 40 frames at test time. For the real-world datasets, we train all algorithms on 15 seen frames and predict the next 15, while has to predict 30 at test time. We use the standard structural similarity (SSIM) [60] and the Peak Signal to Noise Ratio (PSNR) scores for quantitative evaluation of the quality of the generated frames against the ground-truth.

Baselines: As our task is novel, we compare our algorithm against the following closely-related baselines: (i) *Audio-Only*: using a sequence-to-sequence model [49] taking only the audio as input and generate the frames using an LSTM (thus, the past context is missing), (ii) *Video-Only*, using three baselines: (ii-a) Denton and Fergus [10], (ii-b) Hsieh et al. [22], and (ii-c) an ablated variant of our model without audio (Ours - No audio), and (iii) *Multimodal*: with further three baselines: (iii-a) Vougioukas et al. [56], that predicts the video from audio and the first frame, (iii-b) [56] modified to use a set of seen frames (Multiframe [56]), (iii-c) ablated variants of our model without the AA loss term in the discriminator (Ours - No AA) and without the AA and MD loss terms (Ours - No AA, MD).

Implementation Details: The PN module uses an LSTM with two layers and produces 128-D frame embeddings. We use 10-D stochastic samples (z_t). The prior and posterior LSTMs are both single-layered, each with 256-D inputs from audio-frame embeddings (which are each 128-D). All LSTMs have 256-D hidden states. Each transformer module has one layer and four heads with 128-D feed-forward layer. The discriminator uses an LSTM with a hidden layer of 256-D, a frame-history $R = 2$, and look-head $k = 1$. We train the generator and discriminator jointly with a learning rate of 2e−3 using ADAM [29]. We set both β and γ as 0.0001, and increased γ by a factor of 10 every 300 epochs. All hyperparameters are chosen using the validation set. During inference, we sample 100 futures per time step, and use sequences that best matches the ground-truth, for our method and the baselines.

4.1   Experimental Results

Table 1. SSIM, PSNR for M3SO-NB and M3SO. **Highest**, Second highest scores. Notation: Multimodal (M), Unimodal-Video (V), Unimodal-Audio (A)

Experiments with M3SO-NB with 5 seen frames							
Method	Type	SSIM			PSNR		
		Fr 6	Fr 15	Fr 25	Fr 6	Fr 15	Fr 25
Our Method	M	**0.9575**	**0.8943**	**0.8697**	21.69	**17.62**	16.84
Ours - No AA	M	0.9547	0.8584	0.8296	21.80	17.36	**16.97**
Ours - No AA, MD	M	0.9477	0.8546	0.8251	21.16	16.16	15.49
Ours - No audio	V	0.9556	0.8351	0.6920	**22.66**	15.59	12.40
Multiple Frames - [56]	M	0.9012	0.8690	0.8693	18.09	15.23	15.33
Vougioukas *et al.* [56]	M	0.8600	0.8571	0.8573	15.17	14.99	15.01
Denton and Fergus [10]	V	0.9265	0.8300	0.7999	18.59	14.65	13.98
Audio Only	A	0.8499	0.8659	0.8662	13.71	13.16	12.94
Experiments on M3SO with 30 seen frames (Block appears: 42nd frame)							
		Fr 31	Fr 42	Fr 70	Fr 31	Fr 42	Fr 70
Our Method	M	**0.8780**	**0.6256**	**0.6170**	**19.50**	**9.39**	**9.41**
Multiple Frames - [56]	M	0.8701	0.6073	0.6050	15.41	8.53	8.53
Vougioukas *et al.* [56]	M	0.8681	0.6009	0.6007	15.17	8.48	8.48
Denton and Fergus [10]	V	0.7353	0.5115	0.4991	12.25	7.13	7.00
Audio Only	A	0.6474	0.5397	0.5315	12.39	9.25	8.84

M3SO Results: Table 1 shows the performance of our model versus competing baselines on the M3SO dataset in two settings: (i) without block (M3SO-NB) and (ii) with block (M3SO). For M3SO-NB, we observe that our method attains

Table 2. SSIM, PSNR for AudioSet, YouTube Painting. **Highest**, Second highest scores. Notation: Multimodal (M), Unimodal-Video (V), Unimodal-Audio (A)

Method	Type	SSIM			PSNR		
		Fr 16	Fr 30	Fr 45	Fr 16	Fr 30	Fr 45
Experiments on the AudioSet Dataset [14], with 15 seen frames							
Our Method	M	**0.9843**	**0.9544**	**0.9466**	**33.24**	**27.94**	**26.99**
Multiple Frames - [56]	M	0.9398	0.9037	0.8959	26.21	23.78	23.29
Vougioukas *et al.* [56]	M	0.8986	0.8905	0.8866	23.62	23.14	22.91
Denton and Fergus [10]	V	0.9706	0.6606	0.5097	30.01	16.57	13.49
Hsieh *et al.* [22]	V	0.1547	0.1476	0.1475	9.42	9.54	9.53
Audio Only	A	0.6485	0.6954	0.7277	18.81	19.79	20.50
Experiments on the YouTube Painting Dataset, with 15 seen frames							
Our Method	M	0.9716	**0.9291**	**0.9110**	**32.73**	**27.27**	**25.57**
Multiple Frames - [56]	M	0.9657	0.9147	0.8954	30.09	25.40	24.08
Vougioukas *et al.* [56]	M	0.9281	0.9126	0.9027	26.97	25.58	24.78
Denton and Fergus [10]	V	**0.9779**	0.6654	0.4193	32.52	16.05	11.84
Hsieh *et al.* [22]	V	0.1670	0.1613	0.1618	9.11	9.57	9.72
Audio Only	A	0.5997	0.6462	0.6743	16.75	17.53	18.04

Table 3. Block IoU on M3SO.

Method	Localization IoU
Ours	**0.5801**
[10]	0.2577
[56]	0.1289

Table 4. Human preference score on samples from our method vs. [56]

Datasets	Prefer ours
AudioSet	**83%**
YouTube Painting	**92%**

significant improvements over prior works, even on long-range generation. In M3SO, when the block is introduced at the 42-nd frame, the generated frame quality drops across all methods. Nevertheless, our method continues to demonstrate better performance. Figure 4(b) presents a visualization of the generated frames by our method vis-á-vis prior works on the M3SO dataset. Contrasting the output by our method against prior works clearly reveals the superior generation quality of our method, which closely resembles the ground truth. We find that the method of [10] fares well under uncertainty, however our task demands reasoning over audio - an element missing in their setup. Further note that our model localizes the block in time (i.e. after the 42-th frame) better than other methods. This is quantitatively analyzed in Table 3 by comparing the mean IoU of the predicted block location in the final generated frame against the ground truth. Our scheme outperforms the closest baseline [10] by ∼30%.

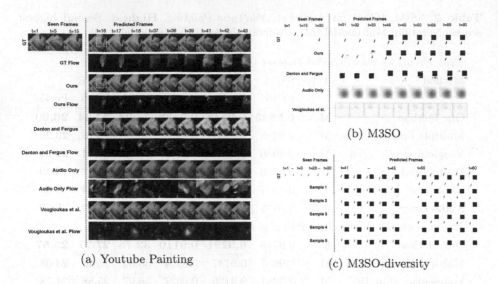

(a) Youtube Painting

(b) M3SO

(c) M3SO-diversity

Fig. 4. (a,b) Show qualitative comparisons of generated frames and optical flow images, (c) shows generative diversity on M3SO.

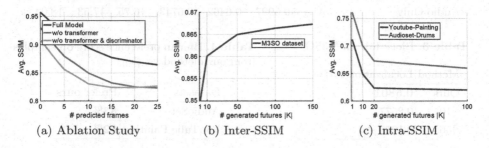

(a) Ablation Study

(b) Inter-SSIM

(c) Intra-SSIM

Fig. 5. Ablation and diversity studies (see text for details).

Comparisons on Real-world Datasets: As with M3SO, we see from Table 2 that our approach outperforms the baselines, even at long-range generation. Due to the similarity in visual content (e.g., background) of the unseen frames to the seen frames, prior methods (e.g., [56] and [10]) are seen to copy the seen frames as *predicted* ones, yielding relatively high SSIM/PSNR early on (Figs. 1 and 4(a) that show that drummer's and painter's arms remain fixed); however their performances drop in the long-range. Instead, our method captures the hand motions. Further, our generations are free from artifacts, as corroborated by the fooling rate on the fully-trained discriminator, that achieves 79.26% for AudioSet Drums and 65.99% for YouTube Painting.

Human Preference Scores: To subjectively assess the video generation quality, we conducted a human preference evaluation between a randomly selected subset of our generated videos and those produced by the closest competitor-Vougioukas *et al.* [56] on both the real-world datasets. The results in Table 4 evince that humans preferred our method for more than 80–90% of the videos against those from [56].

Sample Diversity: In Fig. 4(c), we show the diversity in the samples generated on the M3SO dataset. Figure 5(b) shows quantitative evaluations of diversity. Specifically, we generated a set of $\mathcal{K}$ futures at every time step (for $|\mathcal{K}|$ ranging from 1–100), and plotted the SSIM of the samples which matched maximally with the ground truth. As is clear, this plot shows an increasing trend suggesting that samples closer to the ground-truth are obtainable by increasing $\mathcal{K}$; i.e., generative diversity. We further analyze this over SSIMs on optical flows computed from the Youtube Painting and Drums datasets. In Fig. 5(c), we plot the intra-sample diversity, i.e., the average pairwise SSIMs for sequences in $\mathcal{K}$; showing a downward trend, suggesting these sequences are self-dissimilar.

Ablation Results: To study the influence of the transformer network, we contrast our model by substituting the transformer by an LSTM with 128-D hidden states. Figure 5(a) shows the result, clearly suggesting the benefits of using transformers. From this plot, we also find that having our discriminator is important. Tables 1 and 2 show that removing the AA and MD loss terms from the discriminator hurts performance.

5 Conclusions

In this work, we explored the novel task of video generation from audio and the visual context for generic videos. We proposed a novel deep variational encoder-decoder model for this task, that also characterizes the underlying stochasticity in real-world videos. We combined our video generator with a multimodal discriminator to improve its quality and diversity. Empirical evaluations on three datasets demonstrated the superiority of our method over competing baselines.

Acknowledgements. MC thanks the support from the Joan and Lalit Bahl Fellowship, the inputs from Prof. Narendra Ahuja, and efforts of the annotators.

References

1. Arandjelovic, R., Zisserman, A.: Look, listen and learn. In: Proceedings of the IEEE International Conference on Computer Vision, pp. 609–617 (2017)
2. ASMR, T.: Painting ASMR (2019). https://www.youtube.com/playlist?list=PL5Y0dQ2DJHj47sK5jsbVkVpTQ9r7T090X. Accessed 5 Nov 2019
3. Aytar, Y., Vondrick, C., Torralba, A.: SoundNet: learning sound representations from unlabeled video. In: Proceedings of Advances in Neural Information Processing Systems, pp. 892–900 (2016)
4. Babaeizadeh, M., Finn, C., Erhan, D., Campbell, R.H., Levine, S.: Stochastic variational video prediction. arXiv preprint arXiv:1710.11252 (2017)

5. Brock, A., Donahue, J., Simonyan, K.: Large scale GAN training for high fidelity natural image synthesis. arXiv preprint arXiv:1809.11096 (2018)
6. Cardoso Duarte, A., et al.: Wav2Pix: speech-conditioned face generation using generative adversarial networks. In: Proceedings of IEEE International Conference on Acoustics, Speech, and Signal Processing, Brighton Conference Centre, Brighton, United Kingdom, 12–17 May 2019, pp. 8633–8637. IEEE (2019)
7. Chen, L., Maddox, R.K., Duan, Z., Xu, C.: Hierarchical cross-modal talking face generation with dynamic pixel-wise loss. In: Proceedings of the IEEE Conference on Computer Vision and Pattern Recognition, pp. 7832–7841 (2019)
8. Chen, L., Srivastava, S., Duan, Z., Xu, C.: Deep cross-modal audio-visual generation. In: Proceedings of the on Thematic Workshops of ACM Multimedia 2017. ACM (2017)
9. Corlett, P.R., Powers, A.R.: Conditioned hallucinations: historic insights and future directions. World Psychiatry 17(3), 361 (2018)
10. Denton, E., Fergus, R.: Stochastic video generation with a learned prior. In: Proceedings of International Conference on Machine Learning, pp. 1182–1191 (2018)
11. Deshpande, I., Zhang, Z., Schwing, A.G.: Generative modeling using the sliced Wasserstein distance. In: Proceedings of the IEEE Conference on Computer Vision and Pattern Recognition, pp. 3483–3491 (2018)
12. Finn, C., Goodfellow, I., Levine, S.: Unsupervised learning for physical interaction through video prediction. In: Proceedings of Advances in Neural Information Processing Systems, pp. 64–72 (2016)
13. Fragkiadaki, K., Agrawal, P., Levine, S., Malik, J.: Learning visual predictive models of physics for playing billiards. arXiv preprint arXiv:1511.07404 (2015)
14. Gemmeke, J.F., et al.: Audio set: an ontology and human-labeled dataset for audio events. In: Proceedings of IEEE International Conference on Acoustics, Speech and Signal Processing, pp. 776–780. IEEE (2017)
15. Goodfellow, I., et al.: Generative adversarial nets. In: Proceedings of Advances in Neural Information Processing Systems, pp. 2672–2680 (2014)
16. Gulrajani, I., Ahmed, F., Arjovsky, M., Dumoulin, V., Courville, A.C.: Improved training of Wasserstein GANs. In: Proceedings of Advances in Neural Information Processing Systems, pp. 5767–5777 (2017)
17. Gupta, T., Schwenk, D., Farhadi, A., Hoiem, D., Kembhavi, A.: Imagine this! Scripts to compositions to videos. In: Ferrari, V., Hebert, M., Sminchisescu, C., Weiss, Y. (eds.) ECCV 2018. LNCS, vol. 11212, pp. 610–626. Springer, Cham (2018). https://doi.org/10.1007/978-3-030-01237-3_37
18. Hao, W., Zhang, Z., Guan, H.: CMCGAN: a uniform framework for cross-modal visual-audio mutual generation. In: Proceedings of Thirty-Second AAAI Conference on Artificial Intelligence (2018)
19. Hao, Z., Huang, X., Belongie, S.: Controllable video generation with sparse trajectories. In: Proceedings of the IEEE Conference on Computer Vision and Pattern Recognition, pp. 7854–7863 (2018)
20. Harwath, D., Torralba, A., Glass, J.: Unsupervised learning of spoken language with visual context. In: Proceedings of Advances in Neural Information Processing Systems, pp. 1858–1866 (2016)
21. Hochreiter, S., Schmidhuber, J.: Long short-term memory. Neural Comput. 9(8), 1735–1780 (1997)
22. Hsieh, J.T., Liu, B., Huang, D.A., Fei-Fei, L.F., Niebles, J.C.: Learning to decompose and disentangle representations for video prediction. In: Proceedings of Advances in Neural Information Processing Systems, pp. 517–526 (2018)

23. Ioffe, S., Szegedy, C.: Batch normalization: accelerating deep network training by reducing internal covariate shift. In: Proceedings of International Conference on Machine Learning, pp. 448–456 (2015)

24. Jamaludin, A., Chung, J.S., Zisserman, A.: You said that?: Synthesising talking faces from audio. Int. J. Comput. Vis. **127**(11), 1767–1779 (2019). https://doi.org/10.1007/s11263-019-01150-y

25. Jia, X., De Brabandere, B., Tuytelaars, T., Gool, L.V.: Dynamic filter networks. In: Proceedings of Advances in Neural Information Processing Systems, pp. 667–675 (2016)

26. Karras, T., Aila, T., Laine, S., Herva, A., Lehtinen, J.: Audio-driven facial animation by joint end-to-end learning of pose and emotion. ACM Trans. Graph. **36**(4), 94 (2017)

27. Kidron, E., Schechner, Y.Y., Elad, M.: Pixels that sound. In: Proceedings of the IEEE Computer Society Conference on Computer Vision and Pattern Recognition, vol. 1, pp. 88–95. IEEE (2005)

28. Kim, D., Woo, S., Lee, J.Y., Kweon, I.S.: Deep video inpainting. In: Proceedings of the IEEE Conference on Computer Vision and Pattern Recognition, pp. 5792–5801 (2019)

29. Kingma, D.P., Ba, J.: Adam: a method for stochastic optimization. arXiv preprint arXiv:1412.6980 (2014)

30. Kingma, D.P., Welling, M.: Auto-encoding variational Bayes. arXiv preprint arXiv:1312.6114 (2013)

31. Kolouri, S., Pope, P.E., Martin, C.E., Rohde, G.K.: Sliced-Wasserstein autoencoder: an embarrassingly simple generative model. arXiv preprint arXiv:1804.01947 (2018)

32. Lamb, A., Dumoulin, V., Courville, A.: Discriminative regularization for generative models. arXiv preprint arXiv:1602.03220 (2016)

33. LeCun, Y., Bottou, L., Bengio, Y., Haffner, P., et al.: Gradient-based learning applied to document recognition. Proc. IEEE **86**(11), 2278–2324 (1998)

34. Li, Y., Min, M.R., Shen, D., Carlson, D., Carin, L.: Video generation from text. In: Proceedings of Thirty-Second AAAI Conference on Artificial Intelligence (2018)

35. Lindell, D.B., Wetzstein, G., Koltun, V.: Acoustic non-line-of-sight imaging. In: Proceedings of the IEEE Conference on Computer Vision and Pattern Recognition, pp. 6780–6789 (2019)

36. Liu, M.Y., Breuel, T., Kautz, J.: Unsupervised image-to-image translation networks. In: Proceedings of Advances in Neural Information Processing Systems, pp. 700–708 (2017)

37. Luo, Z., Peng, B., Huang, D.A., Alahi, A., Fei-Fei, L.: Unsupervised learning of long-term motion dynamics for videos. In: Proceedings of the IEEE Conference on Computer Vision and Pattern Recognition, pp. 2203–2212 (2017)

38. Oh, T.H., et al.: Speech2Face: learning the face behind a voice. In: Proceedings of the IEEE Conference on Computer Vision and Pattern Recognition, pp. 7539–7548 (2019)

39. Owens, A., Efros, A.A.: Audio-visual scene analysis with self-supervised multisensory features. In: Ferrari, V., Hebert, M., Sminchisescu, C., Weiss, Y. (eds.) ECCV 2018. LNCS, vol. 11210, pp. 639–658. Springer, Cham (2018). https://doi.org/10.1007/978-3-030-01231-1_39

40. Owens, A., Isola, P., McDermott, J., Torralba, A., Adelson, E.H., Freeman, W.T.: Visually indicated sounds. In: Proceedings of the IEEE Conference on Computer Vision and Pattern Recognition, pp. 2405–2413 (2016)

41. Owens, A., Wu, J., McDermott, J.H., Freeman, W.T., Torralba, A.: Ambient sound provides supervision for visual learning. In: Leibe, B., Matas, J., Sebe, N., Welling, M. (eds.) ECCV 2016. LNCS, vol. 9905, pp. 801–816. Springer, Cham (2016). https://doi.org/10.1007/978-3-319-46448-0_48
42. Pan, J., et al.: Video generation from single semantic label map. In: Proceedings of the IEEE Conference on Computer Vision and Pattern Recognition, pp. 3733–3742 (2019)
43. Pavlov, I.P.: The work of the digestive glands. Charles Griffin, Limited, London (1910)
44. Ranzato, M., Szlam, A., Bruna, J., Mathieu, M., Collobert, R., Chopra, S.: Video (language) modeling: a baseline for generative models of natural videos. arXiv preprint arXiv:1412.6604 (2014)
45. Ronneberger, O., Fischer, P., Brox, T.: U-Net: convolutional networks for biomedical image segmentation. In: Navab, N., Hornegger, J., Wells, W.M., Frangi, A.F. (eds.) MICCAI 2015. LNCS, vol. 9351, pp. 234–241. Springer, Cham (2015). https://doi.org/10.1007/978-3-319-24574-4_28
46. Saito, M., Matsumoto, E., Saito, S.: Temporal generative adversarial nets with singular value clipping. In: Proceedings of the IEEE International Conference on Computer Vision, pp. 2830–2839 (2017)
47. Shlizerman, E., Dery, L., Schoen, H., Kemelmacher-Shlizerman, I.: Audio to body dynamics. In: Proceedings of the IEEE Conference on Computer Vision and Pattern Recognition, pp. 7574–7583 (2018)
48. Srivastava, N., Mansimov, E., Salakhudinov, R.: Unsupervised learning of video representations using LSTMs. In: Proceedings of International Conference on Machine Learning, pp. 843–852 (2015)
49. Sutskever, I., Vinyals, O., Le, Q.V.: Sequence to sequence learning with neural networks. In: Proceedings of Advances in Neural Information Processing Systems, pp. 3104–3112 (2014)
50. Suwajanakorn, S., Seitz, S.M., Kemelmacher-Shlizerman, I.: Synthesizing Obama: learning lip sync from audio. ACM Trans. Graph. 36(4), 95 (2017)
51. Taylor, S., et al.: A deep learning approach for generalized speech animation. ACM Trans. Graph. 36(4), 93 (2017)
52. Tulyakov, S., Liu, M.Y., Yang, X., Kautz, J.: MoCoGAN: Decomposing motion and content for video generation. In: Proceedings of the IEEE Conference on Computer Vision and Pattern Recognition, pp. 1526–1535 (2018)
53. Vaswani, A., et al.: Attention is all you need. In: Proceedings of Advances in Neural Information Processing Systems, pp. 5998–6008 (2017)
54. Villegas, R., Yang, J., Hong, S., Lin, X., Lee, H.: Decomposing motion and content for natural video sequence prediction. arXiv preprint arXiv:1706.08033 (2017)
55. Vondrick, C., Pirsiavash, H., Torralba, A.: Generating videos with scene dynamics. In: Proceedings of Advances in Neural Information Processing Systems, pp. 613–621 (2016)
56. Vougioukas, K., Petridis, S., Pantic, M.: End-to-end speech-driven facial animation with temporal GANs. arXiv preprint arXiv:1805.09313 (2018)
57. Walker, J., Marino, K., Gupta, A., Hebert, M.: The pose knows: video forecasting by generating pose futures. In: Proceedings of the IEEE International Conference on Computer Vision, pp. 3332–3341 (2017)
58. Wan, C.H., Chuang, S.P., Lee, H.Y.: Towards audio to scene image synthesis using generative adversarial network. In: Proceedings of IEEE International Conference on Acoustics, Speech and Signal Processing, pp. 496–500. IEEE (2019)

59. Wang, T.C., et al.: Video-to-video synthesis. arXiv preprint arXiv:1808.06601 (2018)
60. Wang, Z., Bovik, A.C., Sheikh, H.R., Simoncelli, E.P., et al.: Image quality assessment: from error visibility to structural similarity. IEEE Trans. Image Process. **13**(4), 600–612 (2004)
61. Wu, J., et al.: Sliced Wasserstein generative models. In: Proceedings of the IEEE Conference on Computer Vision and Pattern Recognition, pp. 3713–3722 (2019)
62. Xue, T., Wu, J., Bouman, K., Freeman, B.: Visual dynamics: probabilistic future frame synthesis via cross convolutional networks. In: Proceedings of Advances in Neural Information Processing Systems, pp. 91–99 (2016)
63. Zhao, H., Gan, C., Ma, W., Torralba, A.: The sound of motions. CoRR abs/1904.05979 (2019)
64. Zhao, H., Gan, C., Rouditchenko, A., Vondrick, C., McDermott, J., Torralba, A.: The sound of pixels. In: Ferrari, V., Hebert, M., Sminchisescu, C., Weiss, Y. (eds.) ECCV 2018. LNCS, vol. 11205, pp. 587–604. Springer, Cham (2018). https://doi.org/10.1007/978-3-030-01246-5_35
65. Zhao, M., et al.: Through-wall human pose estimation using radio signals. In: Proceedings of the IEEE Conference on Computer Vision and Pattern Recognition, pp. 7356–7365 (2018)
66. Zhou, H., Liu, Z., Xu, X., Luo, P., Wang, X.: Vision-infused deep audio inpainting. In: Proceedings of the IEEE International Conference on Computer Vision, pp. 283–292 (2019)

3D-CVF: Generating Joint Camera and LiDAR Features Using Cross-view Spatial Feature Fusion for 3D Object Detection

Jin Hyeok Yoo, Yecheol Kim, Jisong Kim, and Jun Won Choi[✉]

Department of Electrical Engineering, Hanyang University, Seoul, South Korea
{jhyoo,yckim,jskim}@spa.hanyang.ac.kr, junwchoi@hanyang.ac.kr

Abstract. In this paper, we propose a new deep architecture for fusing camera and LiDAR sensors for 3D object detection. Because the camera and LiDAR sensor signals have different characteristics and distributions, fusing these two modalities is expected to improve both the accuracy and robustness of 3D object detection. One of the challenges presented by the fusion of cameras and LiDAR is that the spatial feature maps obtained from each modality are represented by significantly different views in the camera and world coordinates; hence, it is not an easy task to combine two heterogeneous feature maps without loss of information. To address this problem, we propose a method called 3D-CVF that combines the camera and LiDAR features using the cross-view spatial feature fusion strategy. First, the method employs *auto-calibrated projection*, to transform the 2D camera features to a smooth spatial feature map with the highest correspondence to the LiDAR features in the bird's eye view (BEV) domain. Then, a *gated feature fusion network* is applied to use the spatial attention maps to mix the camera and LiDAR features appropriately according to the region. Next, camera-LiDAR feature fusion is also achieved in the subsequent proposal refinement stage. The low-level LiDAR features and camera features are separately pooled using *region of interest (RoI)-based feature pooling* and fused with the joint camera-LiDAR features for enhanced proposal refinement. Our evaluation, conducted on the KITTI and nuScenes 3D object detection datasets, demonstrates that the camera-LiDAR fusion offers significant performance gain over the LiDAR-only baseline and that the proposed 3D-CVF achieves state-of-the-art performance in the KITTI benchmark.

Keywords: 3D object detection · Sensor fusion · Intelligent vehicle · Camera sensor · LiDAR sensor · Bird's eye view

---

J. H. Yoo and Y. Kim—Equal contribution.

A. Vedaldi et al. (Eds.): ECCV 2020, LNCS 12372, pp. 720–736, 2020.
https://doi.org/10.1007/978-3-030-58583-9_43

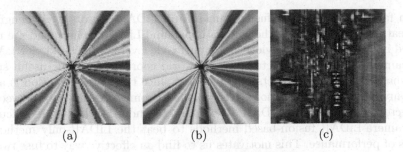

(a)   (b)   (c)

Fig. 1. Visualization of the projected camera feature map: (a), (b), and (c) show visualizations of the six camera feature maps projected in the bird's eye view (BEV) domain. Without our auto-calibrated projection, some artifacts in the feature map are visible in (a). The auto-calibrated projection generates the smooth and dense transformed feature map shown in (b). However, the feature map in (b) fails to localize the region of the objects. After applying the adaptive gated fusion network, we can finally resolve the region of objects as shown in the feature map (c).

1   Introduction

Object detection has been considered one of the most challenging computer vision problems. Recently, the emergence of convolutional neural networks (CNN) has enabled unprecedented progress in object detection techniques owing to its ability to extract the abstract high-level features from the 2D image. Thus far, numerous object detection methods have been developed for 2D object detection [16,20,21]. Recently, these studies have been extended to the 3D object detection task [2,3,8,9,12,13,17,24,26,28–31], where the locations of the objects should be identified in 3D world coordinates. 3D object detection is particularly useful for autonomous driving applications because diverse types of dynamic objects, such as surrounding vehicles, pedestrians, and cyclists, must be identified in the 3D environment.

In general, achieving good accuracy in 3D object detection using only a camera sensor is not an easy task owing to the lack of depth information. Thus, other ranging sensors such as LiDAR, Radar, and RGB-D camera sensors are widely used as alternative signal sources for 3D object detection. Thus far, various 3D object detectors employing LiDAR sensors have been proposed, including MV3D [2], PIXOR [29], ContFuse [13], PointRCNN [22], F-ConvNet [26], STD [30], VoxelNet [31], SECOND [28], MMF [12], PointPillar [9], and Part A² [23]. Although the performance of the LiDAR only based 3D object detectors have been significantly improved lately, LiDAR point clouds are still limited for providing dense and rich information on the objects such as their fine-grained shape, colors, and textures. Hence, using camera and LiDAR data together is expected to yield better and more robust detection results in accuracy. Various camera and LiDAR fusion strategies have been proposed for 3D object detection. Well-known camera and LiDAR fusion methods include AVOD [8], MV3D [2], MMF [12], RoarNet [24], F-PointNet [17], and ContFuse [13].

In fact, the problem of fusing camera and LiDAR sensors is challenging as the features obtained from the camera image and LiDAR point cloud are represented in different points of view (i.e., camera-view versus 3D world view). When the camera feature is projected into 3D world coordinates, some useful spatial information about the objects might be lost since this transformation is a one-to-many mapping. Furthermore, there might be some inconsistency between the projected coordinate and LiDAR 3D coordinate. Indeed, it has been difficult for the camera-LiDAR fusion-based methods to beat the LiDAR-only methods in terms of performance. This motivates us to find an effective way to fuse two feature maps in different views without losing important information for 3D object detection.

In this paper, we propose a new 3D object detection method, named *3D-cross view fusion (3D-CVF)*, which can fuse the spatial feature maps separately extracted from the camera and LiDAR data, effectively. As shown in Fig. 2, we are interested in fusing the LiDAR sensor and the N multi-view cameras deployed to cover a wider field of view. Information fusion between the camera and LiDAR is achieved over two object detection stages. In the first stage, we aim to generate the strong joint camera-LiDAR features. The *auto-calibrated feature projection* maps the camera-view features to smooth and dense BEV feature maps using the interpolated projection capable of correcting the spatial offsets. Figure 1(a) and (b) compare the feature maps obtained without auto-calibrated projection versus with the auto-calibrated projection, respectively. Note that the auto-calibrated projection yields a smooth camera feature map in the BEV domain as shown in Fig. 1(b). We also note from Fig. 1(b) that since the camera feature mapping is a one-to-many mapping, we cannot localize the objects on the transformed camera feature map. To resolve objects in the BEV domain, we employ the *adaptive gated fusion network* that determines where and what should be brought from two sources using attention mechanism. Figure 1(c) shows the appropriately-localized activation for the objects obtained by applying the adaptive gated fusion network. Camera-LiDAR information fusion is also achieved at the second proposal refinement stage. Once the region proposals are found based on the joint camera-LiDAR feature map obtained in the first stage, *3D region of interest (RoI)-based pooling* is applied to fuse low-level LiDAR and camera features with the joint camera-LiDAR feature map. The LiDAR and camera features corresponding to the 3D RoI boxes are pooled and encoded by PointNet encoder. Aggregation of the encoded features with the joint camera-LiDAR features lead to improved proposal refinement.

We have evaluated our 3D-CVF method on publicly available KITTI [4] and nuScenes [1] datasets. We confirm that by combining the above two sensor fusion strategies combined, the proposed method offers up to 1.57% and 2.74% performance gains in mAP over the baseline without sensor fusion on the KITTI and nuScenes datasets, respectively. Also, we show that the proposed 3D-CVF method achieves impressive detection accuracy comparable to state-of-the-art performance in KITTI 3D object detection benchmark.

The contributions of our work are summarized as follows

- We propose a new 3D object detection architecture that effectively combines information provided by both camera and LiDAR sensors in two detection stages. In the first stage, the strong joint camera-LiDAR feature is generated by applying the auto-calibrated projection and the gated attention. In the second proposal refinement stage, 3D RoI-based feature aggregation is performed to achieve further improvements through sensor fusion.
- We investigate the benefit of the sensor fusion achieved by the 3D-CVF. Our experiments demonstrate that the performance gain achieved by the sensor fusion in nuScenes dataset is higher than that in KITTI dataset. Because the resolution of LiDAR in nuScenes is lower than that in KITTI, this shows that the camera sensor compensates low resolution of the LiDAR data. Also, we observe that the performance gain achieved by the sensor fusion is much higher for distant objects than for near objects, which also validates our conclusion.

2 Related Work

2.1 LiDAR-Only 3D Object Detection

The LiDAR-based 3D object detectors should encode the point clouds since they have unordered and irregular structures. MV3D [2] and PIXOR [29] projected 3D point clouds onto the discrete grid structure in 2D planes and extracted the features from the resulting multi-view 2D images. PointRCNN [22] and STD [30] used PointNet [18,19] to yield the global feature representing the geometric structure of the entire point set. Voxel-based point encoding methods used 3D voxels to organize the unordered point clouds and encoded the points in each voxel using the point encoding network [31]. Various voxel-based 3D object detectors have been proposed, including SECOND [28], PointPillar [9], and Part-A^2 [23].

2.2 LiDAR and Camera Fusion-Based 3D Object Detection

To exploit the advantages of the camera and LiDAR sensors, various camera and LiDAR fusion methods have been proposed for 3D object detection. The approaches proposed in [17,24,26,27] detected the objects in the two sequential steps, where 1) the region proposals were generated based on the camera image, and then 2) the LiDAR points in the region of interest were processed to detect the objects. However, the performance of these methods is limited by the accuracy of the camera-based detector. MV3D [2] proposed the two-stage detector, where 3D proposals are found from the LiDAR point clouds projected in BEV, and 3D object detection is performed by fusing the multi-view features obtained by RoI pooling. AVOD [8] fused the LiDAR BEV and camera front-view features at the intermediate convolutional layer to propose 3D bounding boxes. ContFuse [13] proposed the effective fusion architecture that transforms the front camera-view features into those in BEV through some interpolation network. MMF [12]

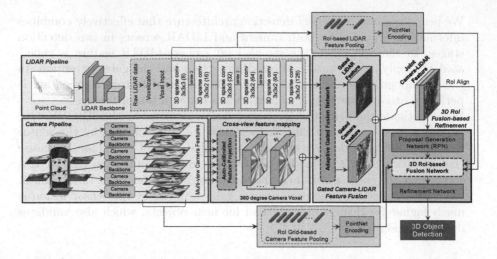

Fig. 2. Overall structure of 3D-CVF: After point clouds and each camera-view image are separately processed by each backbone network, the camera-view features are transformed to the features in BEV using the auto-calibrated feature projection. Then, the camera and LiDAR features are fused using the gated feature fusion network. The detection outputs are predicted after refining the proposals using 3D RoI-based fusion network. The format of 3D convolutional layers used in the figure follows "$k_x \times k_y \times k_z$ (channel size)" where k_x, k_y and k_z denote the kernel sizes in each axis.

learned to fuse both camera and LiDAR data through multi-task loss associated with 2D and 3D object detection, ground estimation, and depth completion.

While various sensor fusion networks have been proposed, they do not easily outperform LiDAR-only based detectors. This might be due to the difficulty of combining the camera and LiDAR features represented in different view domains. In the next sections, we present an effective way to overcome this challenge.

3 Proposed 3D Object Detector

In this section, we present the details of the proposed architecture.

3.1 Overall Architecture

The overall architecture of the proposed method is illustrated in Fig. 2. It consists of five modules including the 1) LiDAR pipeline, 2) camera pipeline, 3) cross-view spatial feature mapping, 4) gated camera-LiDAR feature fusion network, and 5) proposal generation and refinement network. Each of them is described in the following

LiDAR Pipeline: LiDAR points are first organized based on the LiDAR voxel structure. The LiDAR points in each voxel are encoded by the point encoding network [31], which generates the fixed-length embedding vector. These encoded LiDAR voxels are processed by six 3D sparse convolution [28] layers with stride two, which produces the LiDAR feature map of 128 channels in the BEV domain. After sparse convolutional layers are applied, the width and height of the resulting LiDAR feature map are reduced by a factor of eight compared to those of the LiDAR voxel structure.

RGB Pipeline: In parallel to the LiDAR pipeline, the camera RGB images are processed by the CNN backbone network. We use the pre-trained ResNet-18 [6] followed by feature pyramid network (FPN) [14] to generate the camera feature map of 256 channels represented in camera-view. The width and height of the camera feature maps are reduced by a factor of eight compared to those of the input RGB images.

Cross-view Feature Mapping: The cross-view feature (CVF) mapping generates the camera feature maps projected in BEV. The auto-calibrated projection converts the camera feature maps in camera-view to those in BEV. Then, the projected feature map is enhanced by the additional convolutional layers and delivered to the gated camera-LiDAR feature fusion block.

Gated Camera-LiDAR Feature Fusion: The adaptive gated fusion network is used to combine the camera feature maps and the LiDAR feature map. The spatial attention maps are applied to both feature maps to adjust the contributions from each modality depending on their importance. The adaptive gated fusion network produces the joint camera-LiDAR feature map, which is delivered to the 3D RoI fusion-based refinement block.

3D RoI Fusion-Based Refinement: After the region proposals are generated based on the joint camera-LiDAR feature map, the RoI pooling is applied for proposal refinement. Since the joint camera-LiDAR feature map does not contain sufficient spatial information, both the multi-scale LiDAR features and camera features are extracted using 3D RoI-based pooling. These features are separately encoded by the PointNet encoder and fused with the joint camera-LiDAR feature map by a 3D RoI-based fusion network. The fused feature is finally used to produce the final detection results.

3.2   Cross-view Feature Mapping

Dense Camera Voxel Structure: The camera voxel structure is used for the feature mapping. To generate the spatially dense features, we construct the camera voxel structure whose width and height are two times longer than those of the LiDAR voxel structure in the (x, y) axis. This leads to the voxel structure

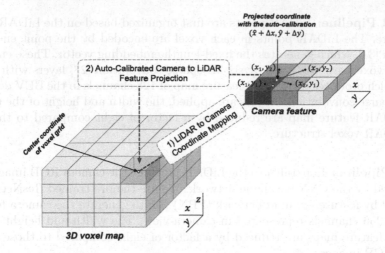

Fig. 3. Illustration of the proposed auto-calibrated projection: To represent the camera feature in BEV, the center coordinate of a voxel is projected onto the point $(\hat{x}, \hat{y})$ with calibration offset $(\Delta x, \Delta y)$ in the camera-view plane. The neighboring four feature pixels are combined using linear interpolation and assigned to the corresponding voxel.

with higher spatial resolution. In our design, the camera voxel structure has four times as many voxels as the LiDAR voxel structure.

Auto-Calibrated Projection Method: The auto-calibrated projection technique is devised to 1) transform the camera-view feature into the BEV feature and 2) find the best correspondence between them to maximize the effect of information fusion. The structure of the auto-calibrated projection method is depicted in Fig. 3. First, the center of each voxel is projected to $(\hat{x}, \hat{y})$ in the camera-view plane using the world-to-camera-view projection matrix and $(\hat{x}, \hat{y})$ is adjusted by the calibration offset $(\Delta x, \Delta y)$. Then, the neighbor camera feature pixels near to the calibrated position $(\hat{x} + \Delta x, \hat{y} + \Delta y)$ are combined with the weights determined by interpolation methods. That is, the combined pixel vector $\mathbf{u}$ is given by

$$\mathbf{u} = \sum_{m=1}^{2} \sum_{n=1}^{2} w_{m,n} \mathbf{f}_{m,n}, \tag{1}$$

where the set $\{\mathbf{f}_{m,n}\}$ corresponds to four adjacent feature pixels closest to $(\hat{x} + \Delta x, \hat{y} + \Delta y)$, and $w_{m,n}$ is the weight obtained by the interpolation methods. In bilinear interpolation, $w_{m,n}$ is obtained using Euclidean distance as follows

$$w_{m,n} \propto |(x_m, y_m) - (\hat{x} + \Delta x, \hat{y} + \Delta y))|^{-1}, \tag{2}$$

where $w_{m,n}$ is normalized such that $\sum_{m=1}^{2} \sum_{n=1}^{2} w_{m,n} = 1$. Then, the combined feature $\mathbf{u}$ is assigned to the corresponding voxel. Note that different calibration offsets (Δx, Δy) are assigned to different regions in 3D space. These calibration offset parameters can be jointly optimized along with other network weights. The auto-calibrated projection provides spatially smooth camera feature maps that best match with the LiDAR feature map in the BEV domain.

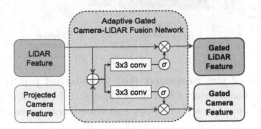

Fig. 4. Adaptive gated fusion network: The adaptive gated fusion network generates the attention maps by applying 3×3 convolutional layer followed by a sigmoid function to the concatenated inputs. These attention maps are multiplied to both camera and LiDAR features through the element-wise product operation.

3.3 Gated Camera-LiDAR Feature Fusion

Adaptive Gated Fusion Network: To extract essential features from both camera and LiDAR sensors, we apply an adaptive gated fusion network that selectively combines the feature maps depending on the relevance to the object detection task [7]. The proposed gated fusion structure is depicted in Fig. 4. The camera and LiDAR features are gated using the attention maps as follows

$$\mathbf{F}_{g.C} = \mathbf{F}_C \times \underbrace{\sigma(\text{Conv}_C(\mathbf{F}_C \oplus \mathbf{F}_L))}_{\text{Camera Attention Map}} \tag{3}$$

$$\mathbf{F}_{g.L} = \mathbf{F}_L \times \underbrace{\sigma(\text{Conv}_L(\mathbf{F}_C \oplus \mathbf{F}_L))}_{\text{LiDAR Attention Map}} \tag{4}$$

where $\mathbf{F}_C$ and $\mathbf{F}_L$ represent the camera feature and LiDAR feature, respectively, $\mathbf{F}_{g.C}$ and $\mathbf{F}_{g.L}$ are the corresponding gated features, $\times$ is the element-wise product operation, and $\oplus$ is the channel-wise concatenation operation. Note that the elements of the attention maps indicate the relative importance of the camera and LiDAR features. After the attention maps are applied, the final joint feature $\mathbf{F}_{joint}$ is obtained by concatenating $\mathbf{F}_{g.C}$ and $\mathbf{F}_{g.L}$ channel-wise (see Fig. 2).

3.4 3D-RoI Fusion-Based Refinement

Region Proposal Generation: The initial detection results are obtained by the region proposal network (RPN). Initial regression results and objectness scores are predicted by applying the detection sub-network to the joint camera-LiDAR feature. Since the initial detection results have a large number of proposal boxes associated with objectness scores, the boxes with high objectness scores remain through NMS post-processing with the IoU threshold 0.7.

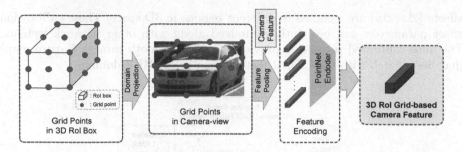

Fig. 5. Illustration of the proposed RoI grid-based pooling of camera features: The RoI grid-based camera feature is generated by pooling the camera features according to the grid points in a 3D RoI box and encoding them using PointNet encoder.

3D RoI-Based Feature Fusion: The predicted box regression values are translated to the global coordinates using the rotated 3D RoI alignment [12]. The low-level LiDAR and camera features are pooled using 3D RoI-based pooling and combined with the joint camera-LiDAR features. These low-level features retain the detailed spatial information on objects (particularly in z axis) so that it can provide useful information for refining the region proposals. Specifically, six multi-scale LiDAR features corresponding to the 3D RoI boxes are pooled by 3D RoI-based pooling. These low-level LiDAR features are individually encoded by PointNet encoders for each scale and concatenated into a 1×1 feature vector. Simultaneously, the multi-view camera features are also transformed into a 1×1 feature vector. Since the camera-view features are represented in a different domain from the 3D RoI boxes, we devise the *RoI grid-based pooling*. As shown in Fig. 5, consider the $r \times r \times r$ equally spaced coordinates in the 3D RoI box. These points are projected to the camera view-domain and the camera feature pixels corresponding to these points are encoded by the PointNet encoders. Concatenation of these encoded multi-view camera features forms another 1×1 feature vector. The final feature used for proposal refinement is obtained by concatenating these two 1×1 feature vectors with the RoI aligned joint camera-LiDAR features.

3.5 Training Loss Function

Our 3D-CVF is trained via two-stage training process. In the first stage, we train the network pipeline up to RPN using the RPN loss, $L_{rpn} = \beta_1 L_{cls} + \beta_2 (L_{reg|\theta} + L_{reg|loc})$, where β_1 and β_2 are set to 1.0 and 2.0, respectively, and $L_{reg|loc}$ and $L_{reg|\theta}$ are given by the Smoothed-L1 loss [5] and modified Smoothed-L1 loss [28], respectively. Note that we follow suggestions from [28] in parameterizing 3D ground truth boxes and 3D anchors. Note also that L_{cls} denotes the focal loss [15]

$$L_{cls} = \frac{1}{N_{box}} \sum_{i=1}^{N_{box}} -\alpha(1-p_i)^\gamma \log(p_i), \qquad (5)$$

where N_{box} denotes the total number of boxes, p_i is the objectness scores for ith box, and we set $\alpha = 0.25$ and $\gamma = 2$. In the next stage, the entire network is trained using the RPN loss L_{rpn} plus refinement loss L_{ref}. The refinement loss L_{ref} is given by

$$L_{ref} = \beta_1 L_{iou} + \beta_2(L_{reg|\theta} + L_{reg|loc}), \qquad (6)$$

where L_{iou} denotes the confidence score refinement loss that follows the definition of 3D IoU loss in [11]. Further details of training procedure are provided in the next section.

4   Experiments

In this section, we evaluate the performance of the proposed 3D-CVF on the KITTI [4] and nuScenes [1] datasets.

4.1   KITTI

The KITTI dataset is the widely used dataset for evaluating 3D object detectors. It contains the camera and LiDAR data collected using a single Pointgrey camera and Velodyne HDL-64E LiDAR. The training set and test set contain 7,481 images and 7,518 images, respectively. For validation, we split the labeled training set into the *train* set and *valid* set by half as done in [2]. The detection task is divided into three different levels of difficulty, namely "easy", "moderate", and "hard". The average precision (AP) obtained from the 41-point precision-recall (PR) curve was used as a performance metric.

Training Configuration: We limited the range of point cloud to $[0, 70.4] \times [-40, 40] \times [-3, 1]$ m in (x, y, z) axis. The LiDAR voxel structure consists of $1600 \times 1408 \times 40$ voxel grids with each voxel of size $0.05 \times 0.05 \times 0.1$ m. We aimed to detect only cars, because the training data for other categories is not large enough in KITTI dataset. Accordingly, only two anchors with different angles $(0°, 90°)$ were used. To train the 3D-CVF, we used the pre-trained LiDAR backbone network. As mentioned, training was conducted in two stages. We first trained the network up to RPN using the ADAM optimizer with one-cycle learning rate policy [25] over 70 epochs. The learning rate was scheduled with the max parameter set to 3e−3, the division factor 10, the momentum range from 0.95 to 0.85, and the fixed weight decay parameter of 1e−2. The mini-batch size was set to 12. Next, the entire network was trained over 50 epochs with the mini-batch size of 6. The initial learning rate was set to 1e−4 for the first 30 epochs and decayed by a factor of 0.1 every 10 epochs. As a camera backbone network, we used the ResNet-18 [6] network with FPN [14] pre-trained with the KITTI 2D object detection dataset.

Table 1. Performance on KITTI test benchmark for Car category: The model is trained on KITTI training set and evaluated on KITTI test set. "AP$_{Easy}$", "AP$_{Mod.}$", and "AP$_{Hard}$" mean the average precision for "easy", "moderate", and "hard" difficulty levels.

Method	Modality	Runtime (ms)	3D AP (%)		
			AP$_{Easy}$	AP$_{Mod.}$	AP$_{Hard}$
VoxelNet [31]	LiDAR	220	77.47	65.11	57.73
SECOND [28]	LiDAR	50	83.13	73.66	66.20
PointPillars [9]	LiDAR	16.2	79.05	74.99	68.30
PointRCNN [22]	LiDAR	100	85.94	75.76	68.32
Fast PointRCNN [3]	LiDAR	65	85.29	77.40	70.24
Patches [10]	LiDAR	150	88.67	77.20	71.82
Part A^2 [23]	LiDAR	80	87.81	78.49	73.51
STD [30]	LiDAR	80	87.95	79.71	**75.09**
MV3D [12]	LiDAR+RGB	240	71.09	62.35	55.12
AVOD [8]	LiDAR+RGB	80	73.59	65.78	58.38
F-PointNet [17]	LiDAR+RGB	170	81.20	70.39	62.19
AVOD-FPN [8]	LiDAR+RGB	100	81.94	71.88	66.38
UberATG-ContFuse [13]	LiDAR+RGB	60	82.54	66.22	64.04
RoarNet [24]	LiDAR+RGB	100	83.95	75.79	67.88
UberATG-MMF [12]	LiDAR+RGB	80	88.40	77.43	70.22
Our 3D-CVF	LiDAR+RGB	75	**89.20**	**80.05**	73.11

Data Augmentation: Since we use both camera data and LiDAR point clouds together, careful coordination between the camera and LiDAR data is necessary for data augmentation. We considered random flipping, rotation, scaling, and ground truth boxes sampling augmentation (GT-AUG) [28]. We randomly flipped the LiDAR points and rotate the point clouds within a range of $[-\frac{\pi}{4}, \frac{\pi}{4}]$ along the z axis. We also scaled the coordinates of the points with a factor within $[0.95, 1.05]$. The modifications applied to the LiDAR points were reflected in the camera images. However, it was difficult to apply GT-AUG to both LiDAR and camera data without distortion. Hence, GT-AUG was used only when the LiDAR backbone network was pretrained. We found that the benefit of the GT-AUG was not negligible in KITTI due to relatively small dataset size.

Results on KITTI Test Set: Table 1 provides the mAP performance of several 3D object detectors evaluated on KITTI 3D object detection tasks. The results for other algorithms are brought from the KITTI leaderboard (http://www.cvlibs.net/datasets/kitti/eval_object.php?obj_benchmark=3d). We observe that the proposed 3D-CVF achieves the significant performance gain over other camera-LiDAR fusion-based detectors in the leaderboard. In particular, the 3D-CVF achieves up to 2.89% gains (for hard difficulty) over UberATG-MMF [12], the best fusion-based method so far. The 3D-CVF outperforms most of the

LiDAR-based 3D object detectors except for the STD [30]. While the 3D-CVF outperforms the STD [30] for easy and moderate levels but it is not for the hard level. Since the STD [30] uses the PointNet-based backbone, it might have a stronger LiDAR pipeline than the voxel-based backbone used in our 3D-CVF. It would be possible to apply our sensor fusion strategies to these kinds of detectors to improve their performance.

Table 1 also provides the inference time of 3D object detectors. We evaluated the interference time on $1 \times$ NVIDIA GTX 1080 Ti. Note that the inference time of the proposed 3D-CVF is 75 ms per frame, which looks comparable to that of other methods. We also measured the runtime of our LiDAR-only baseline. Note that the camera-LiDAR fusion requires only 25 ms additional runtime over 50 ms runtime of the LiDAR-only baseline.

Table 2. mAP and NDS performance on nuScenes validation set: The model was trained on nuScenes train set and evaluated on nuScenes validation set. "Cons. Veh." and "Bicycle" classes were omitted as their accuracy was too low. The performance of the SECOND, PointPillars, and MEGVII was reproduced using their official codes.

	Car	Ped.	Bus	Barrier	T.C.	Truck	Trailer	Moto.	mAP	NDS
SECOND [28]	69.16	58.60	34.87	28.94	24.83	23.73	5.52	16.60	26.32	35.36
PointPillars [9]	75.25	59.47	43.80	30.95	18.57	23.42	20.15	21.12	29.34	39.03
MEGVII [32]	71.61	65.28	50.29	**48.62**	**45.65**	35.77	20.19	28.20	37.68	44.15
LiDAR-only Baseline	78.21	68.72	51.02	43.42	37.47	34.84	32.01	34.55	39.43	46.21
Our 3D-CVF	**79.69**	**71.28**	**54.96**	47.10	40.82	**37.94**	**36.29**	**37.18**	**42.17**	**49.78**

4.2   nuScenes

The nuScenes dataset is a large-scale 3D detection dataset that contains more than 1,000 scenes in Boston and Singapore [1]. The dataset was collected using six multi-view cameras and 32-channel LiDAR. 360-degree object annotations for 10 object classes were provided. The dataset consists of 28,130 training samples and 6,019 validation samples. The nuScenes dataset suggests the use of an evaluation metric called nuScenes detection score (NDS) [1].

Training Configuration: For the nuScenes dataset, the range of point cloud was within $[-49.6, -49.6] \times [-49.6, 49.6] \times [-5, 3]$ m in (x, y, z) axis which was voxelized with each voxel size of $0.05 \times 0.05 \times 0.2$ m. Consequently, this partitioning leads to the voxel structure of size $1984 \times 1984 \times 40$. Anchor size of each class was determined by averaging the width and height values of the ground truths. We trained the network over 20 epochs using the same learning rate scheduling used in the KITTI dataset. The mini-batch size was set to 6. DS sampling [32] was adopted to alleviate the class imbalance problem in the nuScenes dataset.

Data Augmentation: For data augmentation, we used the same augmentation strategies except for GT-AUG. Unlike KITTI dataset, we found that skipping GT-AUG does not degrade the accuracy in nuScenes dataset.

Results on nuScenes Validation Set: We mainly tested our 3D-CVF on nuScenes to verify the performance gain achieved by sensor fusion. For this purpose, we compared the proposed 3D-CVF with the baseline algorithm, which has the same structure as our method except that the camera pipeline is disabled. For a fair comparison, DS sampling strategy was also applied to the baseline. As a reference, we also added the performance of the SECOND [28], PointPillar [9], and MEGVII [32]. Table 2 provides the AP for 8 classes, mAP, and NDS achieved by several 3D object detectors. We observe that the sensor fusion offers 2.74% and 3.57% performance gains over the baseline in the mAP and NDS metrics, respectively. The performance of the proposed method consistently outperforms the baseline in terms of AP for all classes. In particular, the detection accuracy is significantly improved for classes with relatively low APs. This shows that the camera modality is useful to detect objects that are relatively difficult to identify with LiDAR sensors.

4.3   Ablation Study

In Table 3, we present an ablation study for validating the effect of the ideas in the proposed 3D-CVF method. Note that our ablation study has been conducted on the KITTI *valid* set. Overall, our ablation study shows that the fusion strategy used in our 3D-CVF offers 1.32%, 1.57%, and 1.39% gains in AP_{Easy} $AP_{Mod.}$ and AP_{Hard} over the LiDAR-only baseline.

Effect of Naive Camera-LiDAR Fusion: We observe that when the camera and LiDAR features are fused without cross-view feature mapping, adaptive gated fusion network, and 3D RoI fusion-based refinement, the improvement in detection accuracy is marginal.

Effect of Adaptive Gated Fusion Network: The adaptive gated fusion network leads to 0.54%, 0.87%, and 0.79% performance boost in AP_{Easy}, $AP_{Mod.}$ and AP_{Hard} levels, respectively. By combining the camera and LiDAR features selectively depending on their relevance to the detection task, our method can generate the enhanced joint camera-LiDAR feature.

Effect of Cross-view Feature Mapping: The auto-calibrated projection generates the smooth and dense camera features in the BEV domain. The detection accuracy improves over the baseline by 0.5%, 0.06%, and 0.15% in AP_{Easy} $AP_{Mod.}$ and AP_{Hard}, respectively.

Table 3. Ablation study on KITTI *valid* **set for Car category:** The effect of our camera-LiDAR fusion schemes is highlighted in this study.

Method	Modality	Adaptive gated fusion	Cross-view mapping	3D RoI-based refinement	AP_{Easy}	$AP_{Mod.}$	AP_{Hard}
		Proposed fusion strategy			3D AP (%)		
LiDAR-only baseline	LiDAR				88.35	78.31	77.08
Our 3D-CVF	LiDAR + RGB				88.74	78.54	77.25
		✓			88.89	79.19	77.87
		✓	✓		89.39	79.25	78.02
		✓	✓	✓	**89.67**	**79.88**	**78.47**

Table 4. Accuracy of 3D-CVF for different object distance ranges: The model is trained on KITTI *train* set and evaluated on KITTI *valid* set. We provide the detection accuracy of the 3D-CVF for object distance ranges, (0–20 m), (20–40 m), and (40–70 m).

Method	3D AP (%)		
	0–20 m	20–40 m	40–70 m
LiDAR-only Baseline	89.86	76.72	30.57
Our 3D-CVF	**90.02**	**79.73**	**35.86**
Improvement	*+0.16*	*+3.01*	*+5.29*

Effect of 3D RoI Fusion-Based Refinement: We observe that the 3D RoI fusion-based refinement improves AP_{Easy} $AP_{Mod.}$ and AP_{Hard} by 0.28%, 0.63%, and 0.45%, respectively. It indicates that our 3D RoI fusion-based refinement compensates the lack of spatial information in the joint camera-LiDAR features that may occur due to processing through many CNN pipelines.

4.4   Performance Evaluation Based on Object Distance

To investigate the effectiveness of sensor fusion, we evaluated the detection accuracy of the 3D-CVF for different object distances. We categorized the objects in the KITTI *valid* set into three classes according to the distance ranges (0–20 m), (20–40 m), and (40–70 m). Table 4 provides the mAPs achieved by the 3D-CVF for three classes of objects. Note that the performance gain achieved by the sensor fusion is significantly higher for distant objects. The difference of mAP between nearby and distant objects is up to 5%. This result indicates that the LiDAR-only baseline is not sufficient to detect distant objects due to the sparseness of LiDAR points and the camera modality successfully compensates it.

5   Conclusions

In this paper, we proposed a new camera and LiDAR fusion architecture for 3D object detection. The 3D-CVF achieved multi-modal fusion over two object detection stages. In the first stage, to generate the effective joint representation of camera and LiDAR data, we introduced the cross-view feature mapping that transforms the camera-view feature map into the calibrated and interpolated feature map in BEV. The camera and LiDAR features were selectively combined based on the relevance to the detection task using the adaptive gated fusion network. In the second stage, the 3D RoI-based fusion network refined the region proposals by pooling low-level camera and LiDAR features by 3D RoI pooling and fusing them after PointNet encoding. Our evaluation conducted on KITTI and nuScenes datasets confirmed that significant performance gain was achieved by the camera-LiDAR fusion and the proposed 3D-CVF outperformed the state-of-the-art 3D object detectors in KITTI leaderboard.

Acknowledgements. This work was supported by Institute of Information & Communications Technology Planning & Evaluation (IITP) grant funded by the Korea government (MSIT) (2016-0-00564, Development of Intelligent Interaction Technology Based on Context Awareness and Human Intention Understanding).

References

1. Caesar, H., et al.: nuScenes: a multimodal dataset for autonomous driving. arXiv preprint arXiv:1903.11027 (2019)
2. Chen, X., Ma, H., Wan, J., Li, B., Xia, T.: Multi-view 3D object detection network for autonomous driving. In: Proceedings of the IEEE Conference on Computer Vision and Pattern Recognition (CVPR), pp. 1907–1915 (2017)
3. Chen, Y., Liu, S., Shen, X., Jia, J.: Fast point R-CNN. In: Proceedings of the IEEE International Conference on Computer Vision (ICCV), pp. 9775–9784 (2019)
4. Geiger, A., Lenz, P., Urtasun, R.: Are we ready for autonomous driving? The KITTI vision benchmark suite. In: Proceedings of the IEEE Conference on Computer Vision and Pattern Recognition (CVPR), pp. 3354–3361. IEEE (2012)
5. Girshick, R.: Fast R-CNN. IEEE International Conference on Computer Vision (ICCV), pp. 1440–1448 (2015)
6. He, K., Zhang, X., Ren, S., Sun, J.: Deep residual learning for image recognition. In: Proceedings of the IEEE Conference on Computer Vision and Pattern Recognition (CVPR), pp. 770–778 (2016)
7. Kim, J., Koh, J., Kim, Y., Choi, J., Hwang, Y., Choi, J.W.: Robust deep multi-modal learning based on gated information fusion network. In: Jawahar, C.V., Li, H., Mori, G., Schindler, K. (eds.) ACCV 2018. LNCS, vol. 11364, pp. 90–106. Springer, Cham (2019). https://doi.org/10.1007/978-3-030-20870-7_6
8. Ku, J., Mozifian, M., Lee, J., Harakeh, A., Waslander, S.L.: Joint 3D proposal generation and object detection from view aggregation. In: IEEE/RSJ International Conference on Intelligent Robots and Systems (IROS), pp. 1–8. IEEE (2018)
9. Lang, A.H., Vora, S., Caesar, H., Zhou, L., Yang, J., Beijbom, O.: PointPillars: fast encoders for object detection from point clouds. In: Proceedings of the IEEE Conference on Computer Vision and Pattern Recognition (CVPR), pp. 12697–12705 (2019)
10. Lehner, J., Mitterecker, A., Adler, T., Hofmarcher, M., Nessler, B., Hochreiter, S.: Patch refinement-localized 3D object detection. arXiv preprint arXiv:1910.04093 (2019)

11. Li, B., Ouyang, W., Sheng, L., Zeng, X., Wang, X.: GS3D: an efficient 3D object detection framework for autonomous driving. In: Proceedings of the IEEE Conference on Computer Vision and Pattern Recognition, pp. 1019–1028 (2019)
12. Liang, M., Yang, B., Chen, Y., Hu, R., Urtasun, R.: Multi-task multi-sensor fusion for 3D object detection. In: Proceedings of the IEEE Conference on Computer Vision and Pattern Recognition (CVPR), pp. 7345–7353 (2019)
13. Liang, M., Yang, B., Wang, S., Urtasun, R.: Deep continuous fusion for multi-sensor 3D object detection. In: Ferrari, V., Hebert, M., Sminchisescu, C., Weiss, Y. (eds.) ECCV 2018. LNCS, vol. 11220, pp. 663–678. Springer, Cham (2018). https://doi.org/10.1007/978-3-030-01270-0_39
14. Lin, T.Y., Dollár, P., Girshick, R., He, K., Hariharan, B., Belongie, S.: Feature pyramid networks for object detection. In: Proceedings of the IEEE Conference on Computer Vision and Pattern Recognition (CVPR), pp. 2117–2125 (2017)
15. Lin, T.Y., Goyal, P., Girshick, R., He, K., Dollár, P.: Focal loss for dense object detection. In: Proceedings of the IEEE International Conference on Computer Vision (ICCV), pp. 2980–2988 (2017)
16. Liu, W., et al.: SSD: single shot MultiBox detector. In: Leibe, B., Matas, J., Sebe, N., Welling, M. (eds.) ECCV 2016. LNCS, vol. 9905, pp. 21–37. Springer, Cham (2016). https://doi.org/10.1007/978-3-319-46448-0_2
17. Qi, C.R., Liu, W., Wu, C., Su, H., Guibas, L.J.: Frustum PointNets for 3D object detection from RGB-D data. In: Proceedings of the IEEE Conference on Computer Vision and Pattern Recognition (CVPR), pp. 918–927 (2018)
18. Qi, C.R., Su, H., Mo, K., Guibas, L.J.: PointNet: deep learning on point sets for 3D classification and segmentation. In: Proceedings of the IEEE Conference on Computer Vision and Pattern Recognition (CVPR), pp. 652–660 (2017)
19. Qi, C.R., Yi, L., Su, H., Guibas, L.J.: PointNet++: deep hierarchical feature learning on point sets in a metric space. In: Advances in Neural Information Processing Systems (NeurIPS), pp. 5099–5108 (2017)
20. Redmon, J., Farhadi, A.: YOLO9000: better, faster, stronger. In: Proceedings of the IEEE Conference on Computer Vision and Pattern Recognition (CVPR), pp. 6517–6525 (2017)
21. Ren, S., He, K., Girshick, R., Sun, J.: Faster R-CNN: towards real-time object detection with region proposal networks. In: Advances in Neural Information Processing Systems (NeurIPS), pp. 91–99 (2015)
22. Shi, S., Wang, X., Li, H.: PointRCNN: 3D object proposal generation and detection from point cloud. In: Proceedings of the IEEE Conference on Computer Vision and Pattern Recognition (CVPR), pp. 770–779 (2019)
23. Shi, S., Wang, Z., Wang, X., Li, H.: Part-A2 Net: 3D part-aware and aggregation neural network for object detection from point cloud. arXiv preprint arXiv:1907.03670 (2019)
24. Shin, K., Kwon, Y.P., Tomizuka, M.: RoarNet: a robust 3D object detection based on region approximation refinement. In: IEEE Intelligent Vehicles Symposium (IV), pp. 2510–2515. IEEE (2019)
25. Smith, L.N.: A disciplined approach to neural network hyper-parameters: Part 1-learning rate, batch size, momentum, and weight decay. arXiv preprint arXiv:1803.09820 (2018)
26. Wang, Z., Jia, K.: Frustum convNet: sliding frustums to aggregate local point-wise features for Amodal 3D object detection. arXiv preprint arXiv:1903.01864 (2019)
27. Xu, D., Anguelov, D., Jain, A.: PointFusion: deep sensor fusion for 3D bounding box estimation. In: Proceedings of the IEEE Conference on Computer Vision and Pattern Recognition (CVPR), pp. 244–253 (2018)

28. Yan, Y., Mao, Y., Li, B.: Second: sparsely embedded convolutional detection. Sensors **18**(10), 3337 (2018)
29. Yang, B., Luo, W., Urtasun, R.: PIXOR: real-time 3D object detection from point clouds. In: Proceedings of the IEEE Conference on Computer Vision and Pattern Recognition (CVPR), pp. 7652–7660 (2018)
30. Yang, Z., Sun, Y., Liu, S., Shen, X., Jia, J.: STD: sparse-to-dense 3D object detector for point cloud. In: Proceedings of the IEEE International Conference on Computer Vision (ICCV), pp. 1951–1960 (2019)
31. Zhou, Y., Tuzel, O.: VoxelNet: end-to-end learning for point cloud based 3D object detection. In: Proceedings of the IEEE Conference on Computer Vision and Pattern Recognition (CVPR), pp. 4490–4499 (2018)
32. Zhu, B., Jiang, Z., Zhou, X., Li, Z., Yu, G.: Class-balanced grouping and sampling for point cloud 3D object detection. arXiv preprint arXiv:1908.09492 (2019)

NoiseRank: Unsupervised Label Noise Reduction with Dependence Models

Karishma Sharma[1], Pinar Donmez[2], Enming Luo[2], Yan Liu[1], and I. Zeki Yalniz[2(✉)]

[1] University of Southern California, Los Angeles, USA
{krsharma,yanliu.cs}@usc.edu
[2] Facebook AI, New York, USA
{pinared,eluo,izy}@fb.com

Abstract. Label noise is increasingly prevalent in datasets acquired from noisy channels. Existing approaches that detect and remove label noise generally rely on some form of supervision, which is not scalable and error-prone. In this paper, we propose NoiseRank, for unsupervised label noise reduction using Markov Random Fields (MRF). We construct a dependence model to estimate the posterior probability of an instance being incorrectly labeled given the dataset, and rank instances based on their estimated probabilities. Our method i) does not require supervision from ground-truth labels or priors on label or noise distribution, ii) is interpretable by design, enabling transparency in label noise removal, iii) is agnostic to classifier architecture/optimization framework and content modality. These advantages enable wide applicability in real noise settings, unlike prior works constrained by one or more conditions. NoiseRank improves state-of-the-art classification on Food101-N (∼20% noise), and is effective on high noise Clothing-1M (∼40% noise).

Keywords: Label noise · Unsupervised learning · Classification

1 Introduction

Machine learning has become an indispensable component of most applications across numerous domains, ranging from vision, language and speech to graphs and other relational data [22]. It has also led to an increase in the amount of training data required to effectively solve target problems. Labeled datasets, typically obtained through manual efforts, are prone to labeling errors arising from annotator biases, incompetence, lack of attention, or ill-formed and insufficient labeling guidelines. The likelihood of human errors increases in domains with high ambiguity [24,30]. Additionally, there is an increasing dependence on automated data collection such as employing web-scraping, crowd-sourcing and machine-generated labeling [2,29]. However, the cheap but noisy channels have made it imperative to deal with incorrectly labeled samples.

© Springer Nature Switzerland AG 2020
A. Vedaldi et al. (Eds.): ECCV 2020, LNCS 12372, pp. 737–753, 2020.
https://doi.org/10.1007/978-3-030-58583-9_44

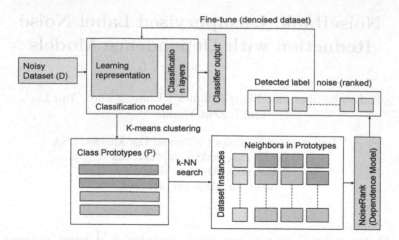

Fig. 1. Illustration of "NoiseRank" framework for unsupervised label noise reduction and iterative model training (interpretable, and agnostic to classification model architecture and optimization framework)

Existing literature either focus on training noise-robust classifiers [1,7,10,11, 16], or attempt to reduce or correct label noise in the dataset generally with some form of supervision [15,20,28,34]. However, attention is shifting towards **unsupervised label noise reduction** due to obvious practical benefits. Most earlier methods use some form of supervision, either from verified or clean labels, or priors on the label/noise distribution, in order to guide the detection of mislabeled examples. In this work, we propose a fully unsupervised approach for label noise detection using Markov Random Fields (MRF), also known as dependence models, which provide a generic framework for modeling the joint distribution of a large set of random variables. We formulate a dependence model to estimate the posterior probability of an instance being incorrectly labeled, given the dataset, and rank instances based on the estimated posterior. We provide an iterative framework for label noise reduction using our dependence model for noise ranking, as shown in Fig. 1. The iterative framework is used to first learn instance representations from the noisy dataset, and detect label noise, then fine-tune on denoised (cleaned) subsets in order to improve classification and learned representations, which iteratively improve label noise detection.

Our approach addresses several shortcomings of existing methods. First, our proposed method "NoiseRank" removes dependence on supervision for label noise detection. This allows wider practical applicability of our method to real domains. In contrast, most supervised approaches dealing with label noise are error-prone and hardly scalable. Second, our proposed framework for label noise ranking and improving classification is agnostic to both the classifier architecture and its training procedure. The implication of this is that we can train classifiers on any domain (image, text, multi-modal, etc.) within the same framework, using any standard classification architecture and optimization framework. In comparison, methods such as [1,7,11,16] require careful network initialization and regularization of the loss function for optimization. Lastly, NoiseRank's underlying algorithm and its output are human interpretable by design. Our main contributions are summarized as follows:

- A fully unsupervised label noise detection approach which is a probabilistic dependence model estimating the likelihood of being mislabeled. It does not require ground-truth labels, or priors on label or noise distribution.
- The proposed framework is generic, i.e., independent of application domain and content modality, and applicable with any standard classifier model architecture and optimization framework, unlike many recent unsupervised approaches [1,7,8,25,38].
- Its underlying algorithm and output are human interpretable. Again many unsupervised methods do not incorporate interpretability [10,25,38], which reduces their transparency in label noise detection and ranking.
- Experiments on real noise benchmark datasets, Food101-N (∼20% noise) and Clothing-1M (∼40% noise) for label noise detection and classification tasks, which improved state-of-the-art classification on Food101-N.

2   Related Work

Robust and Noise-Tolerant Classifiers: Methods that focus on training noise tolerant or robust classifiers attempt to directly modify the training framework for learning in the presence of label noise. [11] introduces a non-linear noise modeling layer in a text classifier architecture to encode the distribution of label noise. [1] fits a beta mixture model on the training loss distribution to estimate the likelihood of label noise and uses that to guide the classifier training with a carefully selected loss function based on bootstrapping [23] and mix-up data augmentation [39]. Approaches based on meta-learning and curriculum learning are also studied for modifying the training procedure, where training samples are either ordered based on learning difficulty or mixed with synthetic noise distributions [7,10,16]. However, these methods limit the choice of classifier architectures, and furthermore are known to work only with careful initialization [11] and regularization [1] needed for convergence.

Label Noise Reduction/Correction: Other methods, including ours, are based on label noise reduction, that attempt to detect, and remove or correct label noise. Prominent approaches utilize supervision to guide label noise detection. [28,34] require clean (ground-truth) labels for a subset of the data to learn a mapping from noisy to clean labels. [15] requires binary verification labels instead, which indicate whether the given label is correct or noisy, in order to train an attention mechanism that can select reference images as class prototypes, and learn to predict if a given label is noisy. Similar to [8,15] uses prototypes (more than one per class) to generate corrected labels which are then employed to iteratively train a network. However, [8] does not rely on any supervision or assumptions on the label distribution. As compared to [8], our method uses standard cross-entropy loss, whereas their framework is based on self-supervised learning, limiting flexibility on classifier optimization framework.

Another iterative approach is of [38], which updates both network parameters and label distributions to iteratively correct the 'noisy labels. [20] relies on the availability of a noise transition matrix for loss correction when training a classifier, which specifies the noise distribution in terms of the probability of one class being mislabeled as another. [32] employs a deep learning based risk consistent estimator to fine-tune a noise transition matrix. One type of unsupervised approach is outlier removal [21,33]. However, outliers are not necessarily mislabeled and removing them presents a challenge [5]. There are also several methods addressing instance selection for kNN classification, which retain a subset of instances that allow correct classification of the remaining instances [3,4,6,9,19], or remove instances whose labels are different from the majority labels of their nearest neighbors [14,18,31]. However, the proposed heuristics have been criticized for removing too many instances or keeping mislabeled instances [5]. Our approach is related to these methods but focuses on leveraging both label (in)consistencies to globally rank noisy candidates and more effectively detect mislabeled instances even without any supervision. Weakly-supervised methods based on classification filtering such as [27] remove samples misclassified by SVM trained on the noisy data. However, it could amount to removing non-noisy hard samples or not removing noisy samples that the classifier mistakenly fits.

3   Unsupervised Label Noise Reduction and Model Training Framework

Our ultimate goal is to learn an effective classifier from the noisy labeled dataset without any form of human supervision (i.e., label verification), prior knowledge on the target domain, or label/noise distribution. In this section, we elaborate our multi-step model training framework. As is illustrated in Fig. 1, we first describe vector representation, which is necessary for similarity measure and label prediction in our framework. Next, our proposed probabilistic dependence model "NoiseRank" is elaborated for ranking dataset examples based on their likelihood of being noisy. Finally, we discuss the iterative model training steps.

3.1   Vector Representation

The vector space representation (i.e., embeddings) is a core component of our design because we rely on the vector representations to determine content similarity between examples in the given noisy dataset. Our framework is agnostic to any modality as well as the solution for learning representations. However, a high-quality representation improves the similarity measure and thus our unsupervised method for label noise detection. In Sect. 3.3, we will discuss how we improve the representation through iterative training.

With the vector representation, we could determine the content similarity. More formally, let the noisy labeled dataset be denoted as $\mathcal{D} = \{(x_i, y_i)\}_{i=1}^{N}$ where $x_i \in \mathbb{R}^m$ is the vector representation for example i, and $y_i \in \{1, 2 \ldots C\}$ is the given label (potentially incorrect) with $C \geq 2$ being the total number of classes in the dataset. In this work, we define instance similarity in terms of Euclidean distance between x_i and x_j as $d(x_i, x_j) = \|x_i - x_j\|_2$.

3.2   Label Noise Detection

In this section, we first describe our process for generating class prototypes, that are representative instances selected for each of the C classes in the dataset; followed by our non-parametric approach to generate label predictions, y_i', for each prototype i. Let $Y = \{y_i'\}_{i=1}^{P}$ denote the predictions. Next, we elaborate the proposed dependence model, named NoiseRank, to globally rank the dataset examples based on their likelihood of having incorrect labels given their vector representations, labels and predictions.

Generating Class Prototypes: Each of the C classes in the dataset can be represented by a set of class prototypes, i.e. a representative subset of instances in that class. We select the prototypes using K-means clustering on the vector space representations of instances in each class, given by the noisy labels. As a rule of thumb [13], we select $\lfloor \sqrt{\rho/2} \rfloor$ cluster centroids per class, where ρ is the average number of instances per class in the dataset. Selecting class prototypes is beneficial towards improving scalability when the number of dataset instances grows. We find that it is also important for robustness in high noise datasets, and K-means based selection is effective compared to randomly selected prototypes.

Generating Label Predictions: For each prototype instance i represented by vector x_i, we generate the predicted label y_i' by a weighted k nearest neighbor classifier, as specified in Eq. 1.

$$y_i' = \underset{v \in \{1, 2 \ldots C\}}{\arg \max} \sum_{x_j \in \mathcal{N}(x_i)} \kappa(x_i, x_j) \mathbb{1}\{y_j = v\} \tag{1}$$

where $\mathbb{1}$ is the indicator function, and the distance kernel function $\kappa(x_i, x_j)$ is used to weigh the contribution of each neighbor x_j in the neighborhood $\mathcal{N}$ comprising the k nearest neighbors of x_i:

$$\kappa(x_i, x_j) = \frac{1}{b + d(x_i, x_j)^e} \tag{2}$$

where $d(x_i, x_j)$ is the distance function discussed in Sect. 3.1, and $b > 0$ and $e > 0$ are parameters for the bias and weight exponent, respectively. The kernel function is negatively correlated to the distance function. For example, when $e = 2$, the kernel will be inversely proportional to the squared distance between the instances. Since $0 \leq d(x_i, x_j) \leq \infty$, by setting a positive bias b, we can prevent $\kappa(x_i, x_j)$ from being undefined when $d = 0$.

Dependence Model Formulation: Our formulation is to estimate the posterior probability $P(x_i, y_i | \mathcal{D}, Y)$ that indicates the likelihood of label noise for all examples (x_i, y_i) in the dataset $\mathcal{D}$ and rank them based on this estimate. For this purpose, we use Markov Random Fields (also known as MRFs or "dependence models" [17,37]) which provide a generic framework for modeling the joint distribution of a large set of random variables.

In dependence models, conditional dependencies are defined only for certain groups of random variables called "cliques", and are represented with edges in an undirected graph. We represent the graph with G and the cliques in the graph as $C(G)$ in our formulations. For each type of clique $c \in C(G)$, we define a non-negative potential function $\phi(c; \Lambda)$ parameterized by Λ. The joint probabilities are estimated based on the Markov assumption as follows:

$$P(x_i, y_i, \mathcal{D}, Y) = \frac{1}{Z} \prod_{c \in C(G)} \phi(c; \Lambda) \tag{3}$$

where $Z = \sum_{x_i, y_i, \mathcal{D}, Y} \prod_{c \in C(G)} \phi(c; \Lambda)$ is a normalization term. Computing Z is very expensive due to the large number of summands. Since our aim is to rank examples in the dataset based on their posterior probabilities $P(x_i, y_i | \mathcal{D}, Y)$ and ignoring Z in this formulation does not change the ranking result, the posterior probability is estimated as follows:

$$
\begin{aligned}
P(x_i, y_i | \mathcal{D}, Y) &= \frac{P(x_i, y_i, \mathcal{D}, Y)}{P(\mathcal{D}, Y)} \\
&\overset{rank}{=} \log P(x_i, y_i, \mathcal{D}, Y) - \log P(\mathcal{D}, Y) \\
&\overset{rank}{=} \sum_{c \in C(G)} \log \phi(c; \Lambda)
\end{aligned}
\tag{4}
$$

where $\overset{rank}{=}$ indicates rank equivalence. The formulation is a sum of logarithm of potential functions over all cliques. For simplification purposes, the potential function is assumed to be $\phi(c; \Lambda) = \exp(\lambda_c f(c))$, where $f(c)$ is the feature function over the clique c and λ_c is the weight for the feature function. The final ranking function is computationally tractable and linear over feature functions:

$$P(x_i, y_i | \mathcal{D}, Y) \overset{rank}{=} \sum_{c \in C(G)} \lambda_c f(c) \tag{5}$$

Depending on the choice of the feature functions and their corresponding weights, the final ranking score in 5 can be negative. In the next subsection, we elaborate our dependence model for the task of label noise detection by explicitly defining each clique, its feature function $f(c)$ and the corresponding weight λ_c.

Dependence Graph Construction: In our formulation, we define cliques between all pairs of examples (i, j) where $i \neq j$ and $i \in \mathcal{D}, j \in P$ for dataset $\mathcal{D}$ with size N and set of all prototypes $P \subseteq \mathcal{D}$. There are $\mathcal{O}(N|P|)$ cliques

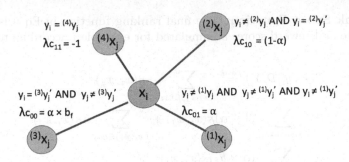

Fig. 2. The dependence graph illustrated for a given example i in a database containing five examples. Clique types and weights are determined based on the given y_i and y_j and predicted labels y'_j. Edge lengths indicate distance in the vector representation space

defined in the dependence graph. Each example is associated with its given label y_i and each prototype is associated with its given label y_j and predicted label y'_j, which are used for determining the clique weights as shown in Fig. 2 and explained below. All cliques are assumed to share the same feature function $f(c) = \kappa(x_i, x_j)$ as defined by the kernel function in Eq. 2.

We differentiate cliques into four types based on the values of the given and predicted labels of the examples. The first clique type, denoted by c_{11}, is for all pairs of examples (i, j) that share the same given label. If the examples share the same label (i.e., $y_i = y_j$), we assign a negative "blame" score (i.e., reward) weighted by $f(c)$ to example i so that it ranks lower in the final rank list of examples sorted by their overall MRF scores. For this clique type, we set the clique weight parameter as $\lambda_c = -1$.

The second clique type is denoted by c_{10}. It is defined for all pairs of examples (i, j) with different labels (i.e., $y_i \neq y_j$) where $y'_j = y_j$. In this case, example j blames example i for providing an incorrect prediction vote, even though the false vote did not change the prediction output y'_j which is consistent with example j's original label y_j. For this type, we set $\lambda_c = 1 - \alpha$, where α is a hyper-parameter defined in the range $[0.5, 1]$ to control the impact of incorrect vote (i.e., $y'_j \neq y_i$) on the blame score.

The third clique type, denoted by c_{01}, is for all pairs of examples (i, j) with different labels (i.e., $y_i \neq y_j$) where $y'_j \neq y_j$ and $y'_j \neq y_i$. In other words, the prediction output y'_j is different from both its own label y_j and example i's label y_i. While example i did not directly influence the mispredicted label, it did not contribute towards the correct prediction. By setting $\lambda_c = \alpha$, example j assigns a scaled blame score to example i.

The fourth clique type, denoted by c_{00}, is for all pairs of examples (i, j) with different labels (i.e., $y_i \neq y_j$) where $y'_j \neq y_j$ and $y'_j = y_i$. Example j blames example i strongly for supporting a prediction different from its own label y_j which is the same as its prediction y'_j. For this type, we set $\lambda_c = \alpha \times b_f$ where b_f in $[1, inf)$ is the "blame factor" and controls the strength of the blame.

NoiseRank Score Function: The final ranking function in Eq. 6 is the sum of all blame and reward scores accumulated for example i according to Eq. 5.

$$
\begin{aligned}
P(x_i, y_i | \mathcal{D}, Y) \stackrel{rank}{=} &\sum_{(x_i, x_j) \in c_{11}} -\kappa(x_i, x_j) \\
&+ \sum_{(x_i, x_j) \in c_{10}} (1 - \alpha)\kappa(x_i, x_j) + \sum_{(x_i, x_j) \in c_{01}} \alpha\kappa(x_i, x_j) \\
&+ \sum_{(x_i, x_j) \in c_{00}} (\alpha \times b_f)\kappa(x_i, x_j)
\end{aligned}
\tag{6}
$$

The aggregate score $P(x_i, y_i | \mathcal{D}, Y)$ is the basis for ranking instances in the dataset. The rank reflects the relative likelihood of being mislabeled and the impact on mispredictions, accounted for in the penalty function. Since the score function is unbounded, detecting label noise given the ranked list requires threshold $\delta \geq 0$ to determine if an instance with detected label noise should be retained ($w = 1$) or removed ($w = 0$) from the dataset.

$$
w(x_i) = \begin{cases} 0, & \text{if } P(x_i, y_i | \mathcal{D}, Y) > \delta \\ 1, & \text{otherwise} \end{cases}
\tag{7}
$$

It should be noted that as the dataset size increases, computing the ranking function over all $\mathcal{O}(N|P|)$ pairs is less efficient. Moreover, the value of the feature function $f(c)$ approaches zero as distances between pairs increase. We therefore limit the cliques to the k closest neighbors of example i for assigning blame and reward scores as defined above. This approximation is quite effective especially because the blame and reward scores diminish rapidly and approach zero as distances get larger. Another note is that we use the same k value in the score function and in the kernel function (Eq. 2) for both computing the aggregate rank score function and generating label predictions y'_j for simplification purposes.

3.3 Iterative Training

We provide a generic iterative framework to learn classifiers with label noise reduction. As described earlier, the vector space representations of examples in the dataset are used in determining content similarity for noise ranking. Initially, representations can be learned with the available (potentially noisy) labels. In order to improve the learned representations, we can iterate over representation learning, noise ranking and reduction, model training, in order.

The framework is agnostic to the model used for representation learning and classification, depending on the content modality. At a first step, we train the classifier model (eg. standard CNN with simple cross-entropy loss) with the available noisy dataset D. The classifier can be used to extract representations for examples in the dataset, which are used to run label noise detection with NoiseRank and remove the examples that are ranked as noisy (i.e., $w(x_i) = 0$). Finally, we fine-tune the trained model with the denoised subset of the dataset.

Table 1. Dataset Statistics. We use only the noisy (train) labels in NoiseRank. Verified labels (train/validation) are used in other supervised/weakly-supervised methods

Dataset	# Classes	# Train	# Verified (tr/va)	# Test
Food-101N	101	310K	55k/5k	25k
Clothing1M	14	1M	25k/7k	10k
YFCC100m	1000	99.2M	–/–	50k

4   Experiments

We report experiments on three public datasets: Food-101N, Clothing1M and YFCC100m on both label noise detection and classification.

Food-101N [15] and **Clothing-1M** [34]: These are **real noise** public datasets collected from noisy channels; which are used to study methods for learning in the presence of label noise. These datasets also contain additional verification/clean labels used for noise detection training and validation by supervised label noise reduction methods. Note that for NoiseRank, we do not use these additional verified/clean labels in training or validation. We only use the verified validation labels for evaluation of our method to report results on label noise detection recall and accuracy. These datasets also provide a clean test set 25K and 10K examples respectively, used for evaluation of the classification task top-1 accuracy. **YFCC100m** [26]: This is a large-scale dataset with 99.2M images used in the semi-supervised learning setting in [36] and we combine it with NoiseRank for detecting label noise in machine-generated labels originated by the semi-supervised learning setup. We use NoiseRank to detect and remove mislabeled examples; and the rest are then leveraged to improve target ImageNet-1k classification. Dataset statistics are summarized in Table 1.

4.1   Experiment Setup and Hyper-parameters

For representation learning, we introduced a 256-dimensional bottleneck layer to the ResNet-50 model pre-trained on ImageNet1k. First, the pre-trained ResNet-50 is fully fine-tuned with the entire noisy dataset using learning rate 0.002 for [10,10,10] epochs and learning rate decay rate 0.1. The output of the bottleneck layer is L2 normalized and used for representing image content. We report results for NoiseRank which conducts label noise detection and removal only once; and iterative NoiseRank wherein after one round of noise removal we fine-tune the ResNet and repeat noise removal. For efficient nearest neighbor search, we use open-source library FAISS [12] which takes less than 10 min on one GPU for dataset of size 1M with the 256d vector representations.

Unsupervised hyper-parameter selection: The improvement in data quality can be directly measured (without supervision from verified labels) by the improvement in learnability of the classifier. We measure the training loss at

Table 2. Label noise detection accuracy. Left: average error rate over all the classes (%) Right: Label noise recall, F1 and macro-F1 (%). NoiseRank(I) is iterative NoiseRank

Method	Average error rate	
	Food-101N	Clothing-1M
Supervised		
MLP	10.42	16.09
Label Prop [35]	13.24	17.81
Label Spread [40]	12.03	17.71
CleanNet [15]	6.99	15.77
Weakly-Supervised		
Cls. Filt.	16.60	23.55
Avg. Base. [15]	16.20	30.56
Unsupervised		
DRAE [33]	18.70	38.95
unsup-kNN	26.63	43.31
NoiseRank	24.02	23.54
NoiseRank (I)	**18.43**	**22.81**

Method	Type	Recall	F1	MacroF1
Food-101N (19.66% estimated noise)				
CleanNet	sup.	71.06	**74.01**	**84.04**
Avg. Base.	weakly	47.70	59.57	76.08
unsup-kNN	unsup.	22.02	24.23	54.03
NoiseRank (I)	unsup.	**85.61**	64.42	76.06
Clothing-1M (38.46% estimated noise)				
CleanNet	sup.	69.40	**73.99**	**79.65**
Avg. Base.	weakly	43.92	55.14	67.65
unsup-kNN	unsup.	10.85	16.60	44.26
NoiseRank (I)	unsup.	**74.18**	71.74	76.52

epoch 10 on denoised subsets and select NoiseRank hyper-parameter setting that results in the least training loss. To reduce the parameter search, we first select and fix the best k (number of nearest neighbors) by grid search in $\{5, 10, 20, 50, 100, 250\}$ and then search $\alpha \in \{0.5, 0.6, 0.8\}$ and $b_f \in \{1.0, 1.5, 2.0\}$, and $b = e = 1$ in the distance kernel. The ranking cut-off $\delta = 0$.

4.2   Label Noise Detection Experiments

We report the effectiveness of our proposed method on detecting label noise in Table 2, in terms of i) averaged detection error rate over all classes in Food101-N and Clothing-1M, and ii) in terms of label noise recall and F1. Table 2 details the average error rate of label noise detection on the verified validation set compared against a wide range of baselines, as reported in [15]. The naive baseline predicts all samples as correctly labeled, and therefore its error rate approximates the true noise distribution assuming a random selection of the ground truth set. Clothing-1M has a significant amount of noise estimated at 38.46%. In this significantly noisy dataset, iterative NoiseRank even as an unsupervised method, strongly outperforms unsupervised outlier removal method DRAE [33] by a large margin of 16.15% (which is 40% error reduction) and weakly supervised Average Baseline (Avg. Base.) [15] by 7.75% (which is 25% error reduction) on avg error rate. This is state-of-the-art noise detection error rate among unsupervised alternatives on this dataset. Avg. Base. computes the cosine similarity between an instance representation and the averaged representation of a class; and although it does not use verified labels in training, it uses them to select the threshold on cosine similarity for label noise detection. On Food101-N the estimated noise is 19.66% and the avg error rate of iterative NoiseRank and DRAE are comparable.

Table 3. Image classification on Food-101N results in terms of top-1 accuracy (%). Train data (310k) and test data (25k). CleanNet is trained with an additional 55k/5k (tr/va) verification labels to provide the required supervision on noise detection

#	Method	Training	Pre-training	Top-1
1	None [15]	noisy train	ImageNet	81.44
2	CleanNet [15]	noisy(+verified)	ImageNet	83.95
3	DeepSelf [8]	noisy train	ImageNet	85.11
4	NoiseRank	cleaned train	ImageNet	85.20
5		cleaned train	noisy train #1	**85.78**

However, since noise vs. clean instance distribution is imbalanced, we further measure recall, F1 and macro-F1 scores for label noise detection in Table 2. NoiseRank has state-of-the-art recall of 85.61% on Food-101N and 74.18% on Clothing-1M. NoiseRank F1/MacroF1 is competitive with the best supervised method in noise detection CleanNet [15] which requires verified labels in training and validation, and thus has a significant advantage compared to unsupervised and weakly-supervised methods. It should be noted that effective noise recall directly impacts classification, and is therefore an important evaluation metric for label noise detection and removal.

4.3 Classification Experiments

We conducted experiments to study the impact of data quality on the classification task using the ResNet-50 classifier pretrained on ImageNet and initially fine-tuned on noisy dataset and later on denoised subset with NoiseRank. In results Table 3 and 4, in each row, the model is fine-tuned with the mentioned training examples on the specified pre-trained model (eg. "noisy train # 1" refers to the model # 1 referenced in the table that was trained using noisy training samples on ImageNet pre-trained Resnet-50). Similarly, in Table 4, "# 4" in the pre-training column, refers to model # 4 indicated in the table.

In Table 3 Food101-N, NoiseRank achieves state of the art 85.78% in top-1 accuracy compared to unsupervised [8]'s 85.11%, and 11% error reduction over supervised noise reduction method CleanNet. This can be attributed to the high noise recall on Food-101N as examined earlier. In Table 4 Clothing-1M, NoiseRank used to reduce label noise in noisy train (~40% estimated noise) is effective in improving classification from 68.94% to 73.82% (16% error reduction), even without supervision from clean set in high noise regime, and performs comparable to recent unsupervised [8] and marginally outperforms unsupervised PENCIL [38]. In contrast to [8] and [38], NoiseRank framework allows for flexible choice of classifier and optimization/loss function, and yet achieves comparable improvement due to noise reduction, using standard cross-entropy loss and standard training framework. This underlines the benefits of the proposed framework without compromising on classification improvements. Supervised baselines

Table 4. Image classification on Clothing-1M results in terms of top-1 accuracy (%). Train data (1M) and test data (10k). CleanNet and Loss Correction are trained with an additional 25k/7k (train/validation) verification labels to provide required supervision on noise detection/correction

#	Method	Training	Pre-training	Top-1
1	None [20]	clean50k	ImageNet	75.19
2	None [20]	noisy train	ImageNet	68.94
3		Clean50k	noisy train # 2	79.43
4	loss cor.[20]	noisy(+verified)	ImageNet	69.84
5		Clean50k	# 4	80.38
6	Joint opt. [25]	noisy train	ImageNet	72.16
7	PENCIL [38]	noisy train	ImageNet	73.49
8	CleanNet [15]	noisy(+verified)	ImageNet	74.69
9		clean50k	# 8	79.90
10	DeepSelf [8]	noisy train	ImageNet	74.45
11		clean50k	# 10	**81.16**
12	NoiseRank	cleaned train	ImageNet	73.77
13		cleaned train	noisy train #2	73.82
14		clean50k	# 13	79.57

Table 5. Left: ImageNet benchmark top-1 accuracy (%). NoiseRank with removal of top x% ranked instances in noisy machine generated labels, against random removal. Right: Examples of noisy machine generated labels detected by NoiseRank (M: mislabeled instances, C: correctly labeled instances mistakenly identified by NoiseRank)

Method	Top-1 Accuracy
None [36]	79.06
Top 0.6% removed	79.13
Top 1.2% removed	79.12
Top 1.8% removed	**79.34**
Random 1.8% removed	78.96

CleanNet and Loss Correction respectively utilize additional verified labels, and yet the performance gain from noise removal for ours is highly competitive, even in this high noise regime. Lastly, we also reported results of fine-tuning each method with an additional clean 50k set, as per the setting followed in [20]. [8] achieves best result of 81.16% with clean 50k sample set. We note that even without noise correction, the inclusion of the clean set boosts accuracy from 68.94% to 79.43% and may shadow the benefit of noise removal; with CleanNet [15] at 79.90% and ours at 79.57% being comparable in this setting.

| Examples correctly detected as label noise in Food-101N shown along with its nearest neighbor | Examples incorrectly identified as label noise by NoiseRank, shown along with their nearest neighbors (top row); Examples identified as label noise by NoiseRank but are wrongly verified by humans (bottom row) in Food101-N |

Fig. 3. Interpretability analysis of NoiseRank predictions on Food101-N

In Table 5, we report semi-supervised learning results on large YFCC100m dataset, with and without label denoising. [36] is used to train a ResNet-101 to label images in YFCC100m into 1K ImageNet classes. 16K images from each class that have the most confident machine label predictions are retained. However, even after filtering, these labels contain noise as shown by examples detected using NoiseRank (right: Table 5). We run NoiseRank to remove label noise from the 16M machine labeled images. The denoised images are used to pre-train ResNet-50, then fine-tuned with ImageNet-1K train set and evaluated on benchmark ImageNet-1K test set. The top-1 accuracy without noise removal is 79.06% and with noise removal is 79.34%, in comparison to removing the same number of random instances (78.96%) averaged over three runs. Note that in this setting, noise removal is not applied directly to the target classification task, but rather to the dataset used to pre-train the model, later trained on the target dataset.

4.4   Interpretability Analysis

Interpretability is useful in providing explanations about the predictions made by machine learning algorithms. NoiseRank is a transparent framework that can be easily used to provide human level analysis of why a given example was predicted as mislabeled or not mislabeled.

In Fig. 3a, we show sample images correctly identified by NoiseRank as label noise in the Food-101N dataset, along with their nearest neighbors. The nearest neighbors provide supporting visual evidence towards understanding the prediction made by NoiseRank. Interpretability is also useful for identifying hard instances; to support building better datasets and models. In Fig. 3b (top row) we show sample images incorrectly identified as label noise in Food-101N. As seen, these are tough examples with contradictory labels to their nearest neighbors, which provides insights into when and which instances might be confused with others. The bottom row shows sample images identified as label noise by

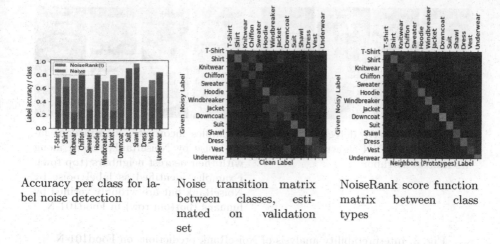

| Accuracy per class for label noise detection | Noise transition matrix between classes, estimated on validation set | NoiseRank score function matrix between class types |

Fig. 4. Interpretability analysis of NoiseRank predictions on Clothing-1M

NoiseRank but verified (seemingly incorrectly) by humans. Such samples further justify our belief that human label verification can also be prone to errors.

In Fig. 4, we provide class-wise analysis on the 14 Clothing-1M dataset class types. Figure 4a reports noise detection accuracy per class (NoiseRank), compared to the original noise ratio in the dataset (Naive). Figure 4b provides the estimated probability of flipping a clean label of one class to another (noise transition matrix) estimated on the validation set. In Fig. 4c, we visualize how NoiseRank scores each example based on its neighboring prototypes. Each cell in 4c maps a given noisy label class and its prototype neighbors' class aggregated over the pairs used in the scoring function (Eq. 6), with weight equal to its contribution in the score function; and the matrix is then column-normalized for the distribution. It implicitly encodes the noise transition probability between class types without any knowledge of the clean labels, as seen from its similarity to 4b.

5 Conclusion

In this paper, we proposed an unsupervised label noise ranking algorithm based on Markov Random Fields. NoiseRank is unsupervised, interpretable, and agnostic to the downstream task or classifier architecture and training. It is applicable to any domain/modality with standard widely used deep learning models or classifiers, without constraining the choice of model, loss function, or optimizer.

References

1. Arazo, E., Ortego, D., Albert, P., O'Connor, N., Mcguinness, K.: Unsupervised label noise modeling and loss correction. In: International Conference on Machine Learning, pp. 312–321 (2019)

2. Corbiere, C., Ben-Younes, H., Ramé, A., Ollion, C.: Leveraging weakly annotated data for fashion image retrieval and label prediction. In: Proceedings of the IEEE International Conference on Computer Vision, pp. 2268–2274 (2017)

3. Delany, S.J., Cunningham, P.: An analysis of case-base editing in a spam filtering system. In: Funk, P., González Calero, P.A. (eds.) ECCBR 2004. LNCS (LNAI), vol. 3155, pp. 128–141. Springer, Heidelberg (2004). https://doi.org/10.1007/978-3-540-28631-8_11

4. Franco, A., Maltoni, D., Nanni, L.: Data pre-processing through reward-punishment editing. Pattern Anal. Appl. **13**(4), 367–381 (2010)

5. Frénay, B., Verleysen, M.: Classification in the presence of label noise: a survey. IEEE Trans. Neural Netw. Learn. Syst. **25**(5), 845–869 (2013)

6. Gates, G.: The reduced nearest neighbor rule (corresp.). IEEE Trans. Inf. Theory **18**(3), 431–433 (1972)

7. Guo, S., et al.: Curriculumnet: weakly supervised learning from large-scale web images. In: Proceedings of the European Conference on Computer Vision (ECCV), pp. 135–150 (2018)

8. Han, J., Luo, P., Wang, X.: Deep self-learning from noisy labels. In: 2019 IEEE International Conference on Computer Vision, pp. 5138–5147. IEEE (2019)

9. Hart, P.: The condensed nearest neighbor rule (corresp.). IEEE Trans. Inf. Theory **14**(3), 515–516 (1968)

10. Jiang, L., Zhou, Z., Leung, T., Li, L.J., Fei-Fei, L.: Mentornet: learning data-driven curriculum for very deep neural networks on corrupted labels. In: International Conference on Machine Learning, pp. 2309–2318 (2018)

11. Jindal, I., Pressel, D., Lester, B., Nokleby, M.: An effective label noise model for DNN text classification. In: Proceedings of the 2019 Conference of the North American Chapter of the Association for Computational Linguistics: Human Language Technologies, vol. 1 (Long and Short Papers), pp. 3246–3256 (2019)

12. Johnson, J., Douze, M., Jégou, H.: Billion-scale similarity search with gpus. arXiv preprint arXiv:1702.08734 (2017)

13. Kodinariya, T.M., Makwana, P.R.: Review on determining number of cluster in k-means clustering. Int. J. **1**(6), 90–95 (2013)

14. Lallich, S., Muhlenbach, F., Zighed, D.A.: Improving classification by removing or relabeling mislabeled instances. In: Hacid, M.-S., Raś, Z.W., Zighed, D.A., Kodratoff, Y. (eds.) ISMIS 2002. LNCS (LNAI), vol. 2366, pp. 5–15. Springer, Heidelberg (2002). https://doi.org/10.1007/3-540-48050-1_3

15. Lee, K.H., He, X., Zhang, L., Yang, L.: Cleannet: transfer learning for scalable image classifier training with label noise. In: Proceedings of the IEEE Conference on Computer Vision and Pattern Recognition, pp. 5447–5456 (2018)

16. Li, J., Wong, Y., Zhao, Q., Kankanhalli, M.S.: Learning to learn from noisy labeled data. In: Proceedings of the IEEE Conference on Computer Vision and Pattern Recognition, pp. 5051–5059 (2019)

17. Metzler, D., Croft, W.B.: A markov random field model for term dependencies. In: Proceedings of the 28th Annual International ACM SIGIR Conference on Research and Development in Information Retrieval, SIGIR '05, pp. 472–479. ACM, New York (2005). https://doi.org/10.1145/1076034.1076115

18. Muhlenbach, F., Lallich, S., Zighed, D.A.: Identifying and handling mislabelled instances. J. Intell. Inf. Syst. **22**(1), 89–109 (2004)

19. Nanni, L., Franco, A.: Reduced reward-punishment editing for building ensembles of classifiers. Exp. Syst. Appl. **38**(3), 2395–2400 (2011)

20. Patrini, G., Rozza, A., Krishna Menon, A., Nock, R., Qu, L.: Making deep neural networks robust to label noise: a loss correction approach. In: Proceedings of the IEEE Conference on Computer Vision and Pattern Recognition, pp. 1944–1952 (2017)
21. Platt, J.C., Shawe-Taylor, J., Smola, A.J., Williamson, R.C., et al.: Estimating the support of a high-dimensional distribution (1999)
22. Pouyanfar, S., et al.: A survey on deep learning: algorithms, techniques, and applications. ACM Comput. Surv. (CSUR) **51**(5), 92 (2019)
23. Reed, S., Lee, H., Anguelov, D., Szegedy, C., Erhan, D., Rabinovich, A.: Training deep neural networks on noisy labels with bootstrapping. In: International Conference on Learning Representations (2015)
24. Ross, B., Rist, M., Carbonell, G., Cabrera, B., Kurowsky, N., Wojatzki, M.: Measuring the reliability of hate speech annotations: the case of the European refugee crisis. arXiv preprint arXiv:1701.08118 (2017)
25. Tanaka, D., Ikami, D., Yamasaki, T., Aizawa, K.: Joint optimization framework for learning with noisy labels. In: 2018 IEEE Conference on Computer Vision and Pattern Recognition, pp. 5552–5560. IEEE (2018)
26. Thomee, B., et al.: Yfcc100m: The new data in multimedia research. arXiv preprint arXiv:1503.01817 (2015)
27. Thongkam, J., Xu, G., Zhang, Y., Huang, F.: Support vector machine for outlier detection in breast cancer survivability prediction. In: Ishikawa, Y., et al. (eds.) APWeb 2008. LNCS, vol. 4977, pp. 99–109. Springer, Heidelberg (2008). https://doi.org/10.1007/978-3-540-89376-9_10
28. Veit, A., Alldrin, N., Chechik, G., Krasin, I., Gupta, A., Belongie, S.: Learning from noisy large-scale datasets with minimal supervision. In: Proceedings of the IEEE Conference on Computer Vision and Pattern Recognition, pp. 839–847 (2017)
29. Vondrick, C., Patterson, D., Ramanan, D.: Efficiently scaling up crowdsourced video annotation. Int. J. Comput. Vis. **101**(1), 184–204 (2013)
30. Waseem, Z.: Are you a racist or am i seeing things? annotator influence on hate speech detection on twitter. In: Proceedings of the First Workshop on NLP and Computational Social Science, pp. 138–142 (2016)
31. Wilson, D.L.: Asymptotic properties of nearest neighbor rules using edited data. IEEE Trans. Syst. Man Cybern. **3**, 408–421 (1972)
32. Xia, X., et al.: Are anchor points really indispensable in label-noise learning? In: NeurIPS (2019)
33. Xia, Y., Cao, X., Wen, F., Hua, G., Sun, J.: Learning discriminative reconstructions for unsupervised outlier removal. In: Proceedings of the IEEE International Conference on Computer Vision, pp. 1511–1519 (2015)
34. Xiao, T., Xia, T., Yang, Y., Huang, C., Wang, X.: Learning from massive noisy labeled data for image classification. In: Proceedings of the IEEE Conference on Computer Vision and Pattern Recognition, pp. 2691–2699 (2015)
35. Xiaojin, Z., Zoubin, G.: Learning from labeled and unlabeled data with label propagation. Technical Report, Technical Report CMU-CALD-02-107, Carnegie Mellon University (2002)
36. Yalniz, I.Z., Jégou, H., Chen, K., Paluri, M., Mahajan, D.: Billion-scale semi-supervised learning for image classification. arXiv preprint arXiv:1905.00546 (2019)
37. Yalniz, I.Z., Manmatha, R.: Dependence models for searching text in document images. IEEE Trans. Pattern Anal. Mach. Intell. **41**(1), 49–63 (2019). https://doi.org/10.1109/TPAMI.2017.2780108

38. Yi, K., Wu, J.: Probabilistic end-to-end noise correction for learning with noisy labels. In: 2019 IEEE Conference on Computer Vision and Pattern Recognition. IEEE (2019)
39. Zhang, H., Cisse, M., Dauphin, Y.N., Lopez-Paz, D.: mixup: beyond empirical risk minimization. In: International Conference on Learning Representations (2018)
40. Zhou, D., Bousquet, O., Lal, T.N., Weston, J., Schölkopf, B.: Learning with local and global consistency. In: Advances in Neural Information Processing Systems, pp. 321–328 (2004)

Fast Adaptation to Super-Resolution Networks via Meta-learning

Seobin Park[1], Jinsu Yoo[1], Donghyeon Cho[2], Jiwon Kim[3], and Tae Hyun Kim[1(✉)]

[1] Hanyang University, Seoul, South Korea
{seobinpark,jinsuyoo,taehyunkim}@hanyang.ac.kr
[2] Chungnam National University, Daejeon, South Korea
cdh12242@gmail.com
[3] SK T-Brain, Seoul, South Korea
jk@sktbrain.com

Abstract. Conventional supervised super-resolution (SR) approaches are trained with massive external SR datasets but fail to exploit desirable properties of the given test image. On the other hand, self-supervised SR approaches utilize the internal information within a test image but suffer from computational complexity in run-time. In this work, we observe the opportunity for further improvement of the performance of single-image super-resolution (SISR) without changing the architecture of conventional SR networks by practically exploiting additional information given from the input image. In the training stage, we train the network via meta-learning; thus, the network can quickly adapt to any input image at test time. Then, in the test stage, parameters of this meta-learned network are rapidly fine-tuned with only a few iterations by only using the given low-resolution image. The adaptation at the test time takes full advantage of patch-recurrence property observed in natural images. Our method effectively handles unknown SR kernels and can be applied to any existing model. We demonstrate that the proposed model-agnostic approach consistently improves the performance of conventional SR networks on various benchmark SR datasets.

Keywords: Deep learning · Meta-learning · Single-image super-resolution · Patch recurrence

1 Introduction

Super-resolution (SR) aims to increase the image size by recovering high-frequency details from a given low-resolution (LR) input image, and SR becomes a key feature in electrical goods, such as smartphone and TV; it has become popular as high-resolution (HR) screens are commonly available in our daily lives. The most basic methods utilize interpolation techniques (*e.g.*, nearest and bicubic resizing) to fill in the missing pixels. These methods are efficient but produce

---

S. Park and J. Yoo—Equal contribution.

© Springer Nature Switzerland AG 2020
A. Vedaldi et al. (Eds.): ECCV 2020, LNCS 12372, pp. 754–769, 2020.
https://doi.org/10.1007/978-3-030-58583-9_45

blurry results. Moreover, dedicated hardware-equipped devices, such as jittering [2] and focal stack [23] cameras, allow the use of multiple images to solve the LR image problem. However, these specialized devices incur additional costs and cannot be used to restore images captured with conventional cameras in the past. To mitigate these problems, numerous single-image super-resolution (SISR) algorithms that restore high-quality images by using only a single LR image as input have been studied; in particular, optimization-based [9, 14] and learning-based [5, 18, 21, 27, 30, 33, 34] methods have been investigated intensively.

Since Dong *et al.* [5] demonstrated that a three-layered convolutional neural network could outperform the traditional optimization-based methods by a large margin, researchers have proposed numerous deep-learning-based methods for SISR. These methods aim to increase the performance of peak signal-to-noise ratio (PSNR) and structural similarity (SSIM) by allowing deeper networks to maximize the power of deep learning with large training datasets. In recent years, however, PSNR values have reached a certain limit, and more studies using perception metric [20, 22] have been introduced to focus on creating visually pleasing and human-friendly images.

Most of the current deep-supervised-learning approaches do not explicitly adapt their models during test time. Instead, fixed network parameters are used for all test images regardless of what we can learn more from the new test image. To fully utilize the additional information available from the given input test image (LR), we propose to extend this single fixed model approach by combining it with a dynamic parameter adaptation scheme. We find that the adaptive network results in better performance, especially for unseen type of images. In particular, we can utilize patch-recurrence property if available in the input image, which can be described as self-supervised learning. The notion of exploiting patch-recurrence has been introduced in prior works [9, 40]. Recently, Shocher *et al.* [30] proposed a zero-shot SR (ZSSR) method employing deep learning; this study is the most related work to our proposed method. ZSSR trains a relatively small convolutional neural network at test time from scratch, with training samples extracted only from the given input image itself. Therefore, ZSSR can naturally exploit the internal information of the input image. However, ZSSR has some limitations: (1) requirement of considerable inference time due to slow self-training step; (2) failure to take full advantage of using pre-trained networks learned by large amounts of external dataset;

Meta-learning can be a breakthrough for the above-mentioned problem. Meta-learning, *i.e.*, learning to learn, is gaining popularity in recent deep-learning studies [31, 35]. Meta-learning aims to learn quickly and efficiently from a small set of data available at test time. Several methods, such as recurrent architecture-based [10], and gradient-based methods [13, 26], have been proposed. In particular, model agnostic meta-learning (MAML) [7] is an example of a gradient-based method. We experimentally find that training a network with MAML results in the best initialization of the network parameter to perform well when fine-tuning with a small number of given input data. Consequently,

Table 1. Conventional supervised SR methods are trained with external SR datasets and run fast. Whereas, self-supervised SR methods typically exploit information using the given test image at run-time, which is time-consuming and impractical. Meta-learning for SR (MLSR) can efficiently utilize both external and internal information and take advantages of each approach.

	External dataset?	Internal dataset?	Fast at run-time?
Self-supervision [30]	✗	✓	✗
Supervision [5,18,27]	✓	✗	✓
MLSR(ours)	✓	✓	✓

as shown in Table 1, the proposed method can efficiently utilize both external and internal information and take advantages of each approach.

To this end, we introduce a method employing the meta-learning (fast adaptation) algorithm to solve the SISR problem. Using a large number of degraded images generated with various SR kernels, our SR networks are trained not only to generalize over large external data but also to adapt fast to any input image with real SR kernels.

Our contributions can be summarized as follows:

- To our knowledge, fully exploiting supervision signals available from both external and internal data with an effective meta-learning method is successful for the first time.
- Most state-of-the-art SR networks can be improved with our meta-learning scheme without changing the predefined network architectures.
- Our method achieves the state-of-the-art performance over benchmark datasets.

2   Related Works

In this section, we review the most relevant SISR works. Also, methods for handling unknown SR kernel (*i.e.*, blind SR) are briefly described.

An early example-based SISR method [8] learned the complicated relationships between LR and HR patches by learning how to use the external dataset. A locally linear embedding-based SISR method was introduced by Chang *et al.* [4]. Yang *et al.* [36] proposed a sparse coding-based algorithm assuming that a pair of LR and HR patches shares the same sparse coefficients with each distinct dictionary. Also, learning methodologies like random forest [17,28,29], hierarchical decision tree [16], and deep learning [5,18,21,22,27] have been proposed to boost the performance of SISR.

The self-similarity-based methods assume that a natural image contains repetitive patterns and structures within and across different image scales. Glasner *et al.* [9] proposed a unified framework that incorporates self-similarity-based approaches by exploiting patch-recurrence within and across different scales of a given LR input image. Huang *et al.* [14] handled transformed patches by estimating the transformations between the corresponding LR–HR patch pairs. Dong *et al.* [6] proposed the non-local centralized sparse representation to exploit the non-local self-similarity of a given LR image. Huang *et al.* [15] combined the benefits from both external and internal databases for SISR by employing a hierarchical random forest.

Recently, a study dealing with the unknown SR kernel has begun to draw attention. Michaeli and Irani [25] exploit the nature of recurrence of small patches to handle unknown SR kernel. Yuan *et al.* [37] propose an unsupervised learning method with CycleGAN [39], and Gu *et al.* [11] estimate unknown SR kernel iteratively and additionally add a spatial feature transform (SFT) layers into the SR network for handling multiple blur kernels. Based on a simple convolutional neural network, ZSSR [30] deals with SR kernels given at test time by exploiting information from an input image itself.

In this work, we focus on overcoming the limitations of these conventional SISR methods. We observe that many existing deep learning-based methods fail to fully utilize the information provided in a given input image. Although ZSSR [30] utilizes both the power of deep learning and information from the input image at test time, it does not use pre-trained networks with large external dataset. Therefore, we start from training network to utilize the external examples. Then, we fine-tune the network with the input image to utilize the information captured by internal patch-recurrence and cover unknown SR kernels (given at test time) for the input. To obtain a well-trained network that can quickly adapt to the input image by using patch-recurrence, we integrate a meta-learning technique inspired by MAML [7] with conventional SISR networks without changing the network architectures. MAML aims to learn a meta-network that can swiftly adapt to new learning task and examples using a small number of iterations for fine-tuning. MAML is applicable in a variety of tasks, such as few-shot learning [19,32] and reinforcement learning [12]. We apply the MAML method to fine-tune the pre-trained SR parameters to input images quickly and efficiently. We experimentally verify that our approach can boost the performance of state-of-the-art SISR by a large margin.

3 Meta-learning for Super-Resolution

In this section, we introduce a new neural approach that integrates recent meta-learning techniques to solve the SISR problem by exploiting additional information available in the input LR image.

3.1 Exploiting Patch-Recurrence for Deep SR

According to [9,14,30], small patches inside the natural image recur multiple times across the different scales of a given image. Therefore, unlike conventional learning-based methods that utilize large external datasets, we can find multiple HR patches corresponding to a given LR patch within a single-input image using

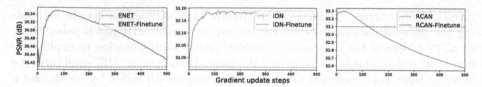

Fig. 1. Increasing PSNR values of ENET [27], IDN [18], and RCAN [38] with fine-tuning process during the testing phase.

the patch-recurrence. However, these previous methods have been developed separately and handle external and internal datasets differently. Thus, we develop a new method that facilitates SR networks by utilizing both (large) external and (small) internal datasets to further enhance the quality of the restored images.

First, we conduct a simple experiment to improve the performance of existing deep SR networks without changing their network architectures by using the patch-recurrence from a given LR test image. To achieve such goal, we re-train (fine-tune) the fully trained SR networks, such as ENET [27], IDN [18], and RCAN [38], with a new training set consisting of LR test image and its downscaled version (×0.5). Note that, RCAN is currently state-of-the-art SR network. By updating the network parameters using the gradient descent, the PSNR values of SR networks increase. Also note that we can further increase PSNR values without using the ground truth HR image, because we utilize additional information obtained from the patch-recurrence of the new training set (Fig. 1). The PSNR values in Fig. 1 are obtained by calculating the average of the updated PSNR values on the Urban100 dataset [14]. The PSNR values tend to increase until 50 iterations, then decrease because the networks can be over-fitted with a small training set at test time. The performance of RCAN drops relatively quickly due to huge number of parameters used in the network.

This experiment demonstrates that there is still room to improve the performance of conventional SR networks while keeping their original network architectures, and patch-recurrence property is a key to boost the performance by adapting parameters of the fully pre-trained networks.

3.2   Handling Unknown SR Kernel for Deep SR

SR in unknown degradation settings (*i.e.*, unknown SR kernel) is more challenging than conventional SR problem in ideal setting using the bicubic interpolation. According to [25], the performance of the conventional SR networks trained with only bicubic kernel deteriorates significantly when it comes to the non-bicubic and real SR kernels in real scenario [30]. That is, generalization capability of the networks which can handle newly seen SR kernel during test phase is restricted in real situation. However, many conventional SR networks still assume ideal and fixed bicubic SR kernel, and thus cannot handle real non-bicubic SR kernels.

In this section, we perform a simple experiment to see whether this problem can be also alleviated with patch-recurrence property. We first degrade input LR

Table 2. Average PSNR for scale factor ×2 dealing with unknown SR kernel.

Model	Set5	Set14	BSD100	Urban100
IDN [18]	28.24	26.29	26.28	23.49
IDN-Finetune	**31.52**	**28.91**	**28.47**	**25.93**

image with a non-bicubic SR kernel to generate a new training set consisting of LR image and its down-sized image (×0.5), and then evaluate the performance of the original IDN and its fine-tuned version with the down-sized training set. Note that the original IDN is initially trained with only bicubic SR kernel on the DIV2K [1] dataset, and our IDN with fine-tuning (IDN-Finetune) is further optimized for 1000 iterations with the gradient update. In Table 2, we observe that IDN-Finetune can handle the images degraded by non-bicubic SR kernel much better on numerous benchmark datasets compared to the original IDN trained with bicubic SR kernel. Thus, we can see that the patch-recurrence property still holds and can be also used to improve SR performance by handling unknown SR kernels.

3.3 Proposed Method

In previous sections, we have shown that the patch-recurrence property can be used not only to improve the performance of SR networks but also to deal with non-bicubic SR kernels. However, to update and adapt the pre-trained network parameters at test time to the specific input image, naive fine-tune-based update with stochastic gradient descent (SGD) requires large number of iterations and takes much time. To solve this problem, we integrate a meta-learning technique [7] with the SR networks to facilitate use of the patch-recurrence and boost the speed of the adaptation procedure at test time.

First, we define each task to employ meta-learning as super-resolving a single specific LR image by utilizing internal information available within the given LR input image. However, unlike conventional few-shot/k-shot problems which can be solved by meta-learning, our new SR task does not provide the ground-truth data (HR image) corresponding to the LR input image for adaptation at test time. Thus, it is difficult to directly apply the conventional meta-learning algorithms to our new learning task for SR.

Therefore, we develop a Meta-Learning for SR (MLSR) algorithm based on our observation that a pair of images composed of LR input and its down-scaled version (LR↓) can be used as a new training sample for our new SR task due to the patch-recurrence property of the natural image, which learns to adapt the pre-trained SR networks to the given test image. To be specific, we employ the recent model-agnostic meta-learning (MAML) approach. In particular, MAML allows fast adaptation to a new task with only a small number of gradient updates [7], so we can boost the speed of our test-time learning

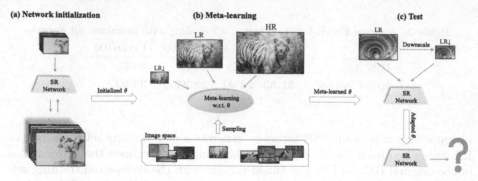

Fig. 2. Overall flow of the proposed method (MLSR). (a) Initialization stage of MLSR. Conventional SR network is trained with large external dataset. (b) Meta-learning stage of MLSR. The SR network is meta-trained to allow fast adaptation to any input image at test time. (c) Test stage of MLSR. Meta-learned parameters are rapidly tuned to the given LR image.

task which originally requires large number of gradient update steps without meta-learning scheme (*i.e.*, naive fine-tune).

In Fig. 2, the overall flow of the proposed method is illustrated. First, we initialize the conventional SR networks with large external train datasets. Next, we start meta-learning using MAML which optimizes the initialized SR parameters to enable quick adaptation to the new LR test image. Finally, during the test phase, we adapt the meta-learned parameters with the given LR test image, and restore the HR image by using the adapted parameters.

Specifically, we formulate the proposed method more concretely. Our SR model f_θ which is initialized with parameter θ renders an HR image from a given LR image by minimizing the loss $\mathcal{L}$, and it yields,

$$\mathcal{L}(f_\theta(LR), HR) = ||f_\theta(LR) - HR||_2^2, \tag{1}$$

Algorithm 1: MLSR training algorithm

Require: $p(I)$: Distribution (*e.g.*, uniform) over images
Require: α, β: Hyper-parameters (step-size)

1 Initialize θ
2 **while** *not converged* **do**
3   Sample a batch of images $\{I_i\} \sim p(I)$
4   Generate $\{HR_i\}, \{LR_i\}, \{LR_i \downarrow\}$ from $\{I_i\}$
5   **foreach** i **do**
6   Evaluate $\nabla_\theta \mathcal{L}(f_\theta(LR_i \downarrow), LR_i)$ using $\mathcal{L}$
7   Compute adapted parameters with SGD:
   $\theta_i \leftarrow \theta - \alpha \nabla_\theta \mathcal{L}(f_\theta(LR_i \downarrow), LR_i)$
8   Update $\theta \leftarrow \theta - \beta \nabla_\theta \sum_i \mathcal{L}(f_{\theta_i}(LR_i), HR_i)$

Algorithm 2: MLSR inference algorithm

Require: I: Given image
Require: α: Hyper-parameter (step-size)
Require: n: Number of gradient updates

1 Initialize θ with meta-trained parameter
2 Generate $LR, LR \downarrow$ from I
3 $i \leftarrow 0$
4 **while** $i < n$ **do**
5   Compute adapted parameters with SGD: $\theta \leftarrow \theta - \alpha \nabla_\theta \mathcal{L}(f_\theta(LR \downarrow), LR)$
6      $i \leftarrow i + 1$
7 Compute $f_\theta(LR)$

---

and our goal of meta-learning is to optimize the network parameter θ to be quickly adapted to θ_i at test time with the given input image LR_i and its down-scaled image $LR_i \downarrow$. Therefore, the adaptation formulation with gradient update is given as follows:

$$\theta_i = \theta - \alpha \nabla_\theta \mathcal{L}(f_\theta(LR_i \downarrow), LR_i), \tag{2}$$

where hyper-parameter α controls the learning rate of the inner update procedure. Notably, to generate the down-scaled image $LR \downarrow$ we can use any SR kernel if available. Then, we optimize the following objective function *w.r.t.* θ:

$$\underset{\theta}{\operatorname{argmin}} \sum_i \mathcal{L}(f_{\theta_i}(LR_i), HR_i), \tag{3}$$

and the optimization is preformed by the gradient update as:

$$\theta \leftarrow \theta - \beta \nabla_\theta \sum_i \mathcal{L}(f_{\theta_i}(LR_i), HR_i). \tag{4}$$

In general, we can use multiple iterations for the adaptation in (2), but it increases computational cost in calculation of high-order derivatives in (4). To alleviate this problem, we can simply employ the first-order approximation methods [7,26], which is known to give competitive results with lower computational cost. In our experiments, we use the first-order MAML introduced in [7].

At test time, we first adapt the parameters (θ) of the meta-learned SR network with the input LR image (LR) and its down-sized image $(LR \downarrow)$, then restore the HR image using the adapted SR parameters as elaborated in Algorithm 2.

4   Experimental Results

In this section, we perform extensive experiments to demonstrate the superiority of the proposed method, and show quantitative and qualitative comparison results. Our source code is publicly available.[1]

---

[1] https://github.com/parkseobin/MLSR.

Table 3. PSNR and SSIM results from different SR networks on different test dataset with scale ×2. Bicubic SR kernel is used. Baseline SR networks are SRCNN [5], ENET [27], IDN [18], and RCAN [38], and + **MLSR** indicates the meta-learned version of the baseline network.

Model	Iteration	DIV2K		BSD100		Urban100	
		PSNR	SSIM	PSNR	SSIM	PSNR	SSIM
SRCNN [5]	-	34.11	0.9272	31.13	0.8852	29.39	0.8927
+ **MLSR (ours)**	5	34.14	0.9274	31.15	0.8855	29.42	0.8931
	20	34.18	0.9276	31.19	0.8857	29.48	0.8936
	100	**34.23**	**0.9281**	**31.22**	**0.8860**	**29.54**	**0.8945**
ENET [27]	-	34.59	0.9329	31.64	0.8935	30.38	0.9097
+ **MLSR (ours)**	5	34.62	0.9331	**31.69**	**0.8936**	30.46	0.9105
	20	34.64	0.9333	**31.69**	**0.8936**	30.49	0.9108
	100	**34.67**	**0.9335**	31.67	0.8934	**30.52**	**0.9112**
IDN [18]	-	35.24	0.9403	32.11	0.8994	31.95	0.9269
+ **MLSR (ours)**	5	35.36	0.9408	**32.17**	**0.8996**	32.06	0.9275
	20	35.38	0.9409	**32.17**	**0.8996**	32.17	0.9280
	100	**35.40**	**0.9413**	32.08	0.8988	**32.23**	**0.9286**
RCAN [38]	-	35.69	0.9451	32.38	**0.9023**	33.10	0.9369
+ **MLSR (ours)**	5	35.72	0.9454	**32.39**	**0.9023**	33.27	0.9373
	20	**35.75**	**0.9458**	32.37	0.9022	**33.32**	**0.9379**
	100	35.48	0.9444	32.04	0.8982	33.26	0.9373

4.1 Implementation Details

For our experiments, we first pre-train conventional SR networks (SRCNN [5], ENET [27], IDN [18], and RCAN [38]) with DIV2K [1] dataset. We use publicly available pre-trained parameters for IDN and RCAN (TensorFlow versions), and use our own parameters trained from scratch for SRCNN and ENET. Next, we start meta-learning for these baseline SR networks in accordance with iterative steps in Algorithm 1. For meta-learning, we still use DIV2K dataset, and use 5 inner gradient update steps in (2) (line 7 in Algorithm 1). We set $\alpha = 10^{-5}$, $\beta = 10^{-6}$, train patch size to 512×512, and mini-batch size to 16.

4.2 MLSR with Fixed Bicubic SR Kernel

First, we assume fixed bicubic SR kernel and compare PSNR and SSIM values of our SR networks on Urban100 and BSD100 [24] datasets. For the comparison on DIV2K, test set of DIV2K is used since our networks are trained with DIV2K train set. Results are shown in Table 3, and we can see that PSNR and SSIM values of SR networks with meta-learning are higher than the original ones. Notably, the performance gaps on Urban100 are significantly larger than on

Table 4. PSNR results of IDN [18] and IDN-ML trained on different datasets. 40 images in Urban100 dataset are selected for the evaluation. * Another 50 images in the dataset are used for training.

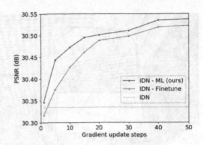

Fig. 3. Performance changes of IDN-Finetune, and IDN-ML during adaptation on DIV2K.

Dataset	Model	Before/after adaptation
DIV2K	IDN [18]	32.19/-
	IDN-ML	32.19/**32.37**
Urban100*	IDN [18]	32.28/-
	IDN-ML	32.13/**32.43**

other datasets, as urban scenes in the dataset mainly include structured scene with lots of patch-redundancy [14].

To further explore the patch-recurrence of natural images, we train the networks with the meta-learning scheme in Algorithm 1 on the Urban100 dataset which includes a large number of similar patches. For meta-learning with Urban100, we use 50 images for training, 10 images for validation, and the remaining 40 images for test. In Table 4, we evaluate differently trained IDNs, and IDN trained on Urban100 with meta-learning algorithm outperforms other models. Note that PSNR value of meta-learned IDN (IDN-ML) is relatively low before the adaptation, but improves dramatically with only 5 gradient updates (0.3 dB gain). This proves that our MLSR method can learn better on images with rich patch-recurrence in urban scenes. More qualitative comparison results are shown in Fig. 4, and the test images are particularly well restored with our network trained with meta-learning algorithm since specific patterns are repeated over the image itself. Moreover, we can see that the adapted parameters with more gradient update steps render visually much better results.

Moreover, in Fig. 3, we show how PSNR value changes when the number of gradient steps in (2) increases during meta-learning and test phases. As shown, our meta-learned model (IDN-ML) can quickly adapt SR parameters at test time, and achieves competitive results with only few gradient updates. Indeed, only 5 gradient updates can produce results which can be obtainable with ~15 iterations of IDN with naive fine-tuning (IDN-Finetune).

4.3 MLSR with Unseen SR Kernel

In this section, we further conduct experiments to see the capability of the proposed MLSR algorithm in dealing with new and unseen SR kernel during the test phase. We carry out meta-learning in Algorithm 1 with randomly generated 5×5 SR kernels on the DIV2K dataset and train for 30k iterations. Moreover, We generate 40k 5×5 SR kernels as in [3], and use 38k kernels for training, 1k for validation, and 1k for test.

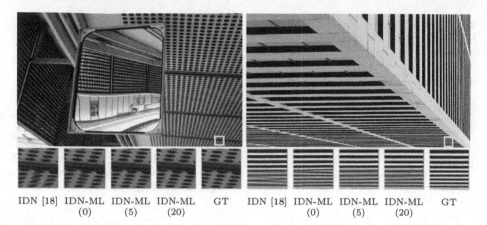

IDN [18] IDN-ML IDN-ML IDN-ML   GT   IDN [18] IDN-ML IDN-ML IDN-ML   GT
              (0)   (5)   (20)   (0)   (5)   (20)

Fig. 4. Qualitative comparison with differently trained IDN [18]. Number inside the bracket indicates the number of gradient update steps in run-time.

Table 5. Comparing ZSSR [30] and meta-trained IDN on non-bicubic SR kernel. Right side of the slash indicates the number of gradient update steps in run-time.

Model	Set5	Set14	BSD100	Urban100
ZSSR [30]	29.68	27.76	27.53	25.02
IDN-ML/0	28.10	26.22	26.19	23.48
IDN-ML/5	29.17	27.08	26.82	24.36
IDN-ML/20	29.86	27.67	27.32	24.96
IDN-ML/100	**30.41**	**28.12**	**27.75**	**25.42**

In Table 2, unlike fine-tuning with bicubic SR kernel, we need a large number of iterations (∼1000) to achieve the highest PSNR value in dealing with non-bicubic SR kernel. However, our IDN-ML trained with many different SR kernels learnt the way to be quickly adapted to the new SR kernel given at test time, and it shows competitive results with only few gradient updates using the new kernel. Notably, we assume that the SR kernel is given or can be estimated with conventional methods as in [25,30]. In Fig. 5, we can see that results with only 5 gradient updates (IDN-ML) are similar to the results from 350 iterations using the naive fine-tune without our meta-learning (IDN-Finetune).

After meta-training, we compare our model on Set5, Set14, BSD100 and Urban100 datasets. In the inference stage, an SR kernel that has not been shown during training stage, and an LR image degraded with that SR kernel are provided. The results in Fig. 5 show consistent improvements for various datasets as the number of gradient update steps increases. Specifically, the performances raise strikingly (∼1 dB) at around 5 iterations, and it verifies that the network can quickly adapt to the given input image and SR kernel at test time with the small number of updates. Notably, the result on Urban100 is slightly different

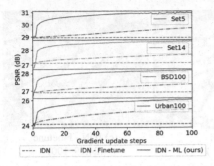

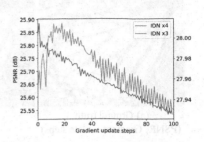

Fig. 5. Performance curve of PSNR values on various test datasets. Random 5×5 SR kernels are used.

Fig. 6. PSNR of IDN [18] with scale ×3, ×4 on Urban100 dataset. Right and left sides of the y-axis indicate the PSNR values with respect to the upscaling factor ×3 and ×4, respectively.

from others. Performance of the adapted network on Urban100 improves more rapidly than adapted networks on other datasets as rich patch-recurrence with urban scenes helps to handle newly seen SR kernels at test time.

In Table 5, we also compare ours with ZSSR [30] on numerous dataset with SR kernels used in ZSSR, and our proposed method with 20 gradient updates shows competitive results compared to ZSSR, and significantly outperforms ZSSR when adapted for 100 iterations. Notably, ours with 100 iterations takes only 6 min to restore 100 urban images, but ZSSR requires more than 3 hours with GeForce RTX 2080Ti.

In Fig. 7 and Fig. 8, we compare visual results by naive fine-tuning (IDN−Finetune), meta-learning (IDN−ML) and ZSSR. We see that the quality improves significantly within few iterations with our MLSR algorithm, and the boundaries are restored gradually as iteration goes. Moreover, artifacts near boundaries caused by ZSSR are not produced by our proposed method.

4.4 SR with Large Scaling Factor

Finally, we study the validity of the patch-recurrence property with large SR scaling factor. Unfortunately, as shown in Fig. 6, exploiting patch-recurrence on big scale factor is hard (*i.e.*, ×3 or ×4). Maximal performance gained by fine-tuning with large SR factors are around 0.04 dB which are negligible. Therefore, to produce large images with large scaling factors, we can employ multi-scale (coarse-to-fine) approaches embedded into the conventional SR methods with small scale factor (*e.g.*, ×1.25) which also exploit self-similarity nature of the given test images [9,14,30].

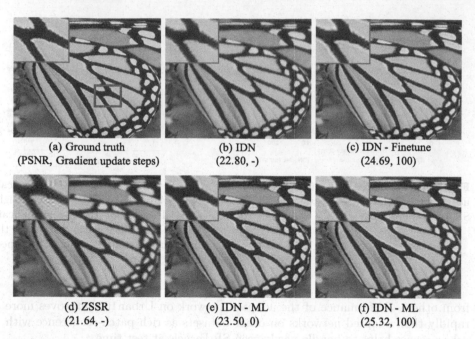

(a) Ground truth
(PSNR, Gradient update steps)

(b) IDN
(22.80, -)

(c) IDN - Finetune
(24.69, 100)

(d) ZSSR
(21.64, -)

(e) IDN - ML
(23.50, 0)

(f) IDN - ML
(25.32, 100)

Fig. 7. The "butterfly" image from Set5 dataset with upscaling factor ×2. Input LR image is downscaled with a non-bicubic 5×5 SR kernel.

5   Conclusion

In this work, we introduced a new SR method which utilizes both the power of deep learning with large external dataset and additional information available from the input image at test time. To this end, we proposed a novel Meta-Learning for SR (MLSR) algorithm which enables quick adaptation of SR parameters using only input LR image during the test phase. MLSR can be combined with conventional SR networks without any architecture changes, and can utilize the patch-recurrence property of the natural image, which can further boost PSNR performance of various deep learning-based methods. In addition, MLSR can handle non-bicubic SR kernel that exists in real world because meta-learned networks can be adapted to the specific input image. In experiments, we show that our MLSR can greatly boost up the performance of existing SR networks, with a few gradient update steps. Moreover, we experimentally demonstrated that MLSR takes advantage of the patch-recurrence well, by showing the performance improvements on the Urban100 dataset, where patch-recurrence occurs frequently. Finally, the proposed MLSR algorithm was also validated with the unseen non-bicubic SR kernel and showed that MLSR required less gradient updates than naive fine-tuning. We believe that the proposed method can be applied not only to SR but also to various types of reconstruction and low-level vision tasks.

(a) Ground truth   (b) IDN   (c) IDN - Finetune
(PSNR, Gradient update steps)   (25.93, -)   (26.09, 100)

(d) ZSSR   (e) IDN - ML   (f) IDN - ML
(26.94, -)   (26.11, 0)   (27.56, 100)

Fig. 8. The "102061" image from BSD100 dataset with upscaling factor ×2. LR image is generated using a non-bicubic kernel. Our method achieves better performance than naive fine-tuning with the same number of inner updates at run-time.

Acknowledgement. This work was supported by the research fund of SK Telecom T-Brain, the National Research Foundation of Korea(NRF) grant funded by the Korea government(MSIT) (NRF-2019R1A4A1029800), Samsung Research Funding Center of Samsung Electronics under Project Number SRFCIT1901-06, and Institute of Information & communications Technology Planning & Evaluation (IITP) grant funded by the Korea government(MSIT) (No.2020-0-01373, Artificial Intelligence Graduate School Program(Hanyang University)).

References

1. Agustsson, E., Timofte, R.: Ntire 2017 challenge on single image super-resolution: Dataset and study. In: Proceedings of the IEEE Conference on Computer Vision and Pattern Recognition Workshops (CVPRW) (2017)
2. Ben-Ezra, M., Zomet, A., Nayar, S.: Jitter camera: high resolution video from a low resolution detector. In: Proceedings of the IEEE Conference on Computer Vision and Pattern Recognition (CVPR) (2004)
3. Chakrabarti, A.: A neural approach to blind motion deblurring. In: Leibe, B., Matas, J., Sebe, N., Welling, M. (eds.) ECCV 2016. LNCS, vol. 9907, pp. 221–235. Springer, Cham (2016). https://doi.org/10.1007/978-3-319-46487-9_14
4. Chang, H., Yeung, D.Y., Xiong, Y.: Super-resolution through neighbor embedding. In: Proceedings of the 2004 IEEE Computer Society Conference on Computer Vision and Pattern Recognition, 2004. CVPR 2004, vol. 1, p. I-I. IEEE (2004)

5. Dong, C., Loy, C.C., He, K., Tang, X.: Learning a deep convolutional network for image super-resolution. In: Fleet, D., Pajdla, T., Schiele, B., Tuytelaars, T. (eds.) ECCV 2014. LNCS, vol. 8692, pp. 184–199. Springer, Cham (2014). https://doi.org/10.1007/978-3-319-10593-2_13

6. Dong, W., Zhang, L., Shi, G., Li, X.: Nonlocally centralized sparse representation for image restoration. IEEE Trans. Image Process. **22**, 1620–1630 (2013)

7. Finn, C., Abbeel, P., Levine, S.: Model-agnostic meta-learning for fast adaptation of deep networks. In: International Conference on Machine Learning (ICML) (2017)

8. Freeman, W.T., Jones, T.R., Pasztor, E.C.: Example-based super-resolution. IEEE Comput. Graphics Appl. **2**, 56–65 (2002)

9. Glasner, D., Bagon, S., Irani, M.: Super-resolution from a single image. In: Proceedings of the IEEE International Conference on Computer Vision (ICCV) (2009)

10. Graves, A., Wayne, G., Danihelka, I.: Neural turing machines. arXiv preprint arXiv:1410.5401 (2014)

11. Gu, J., Lu, H., Zuo, W., Dong, C.: Blind super-resolution with iterative kernel correction. In: Proceedings of the IEEE Conference on Computer Vision and Pattern Recognition (CVPR) (2019)

12. Gupta, A., Mendonca, R., Liu, Y., Abbeel, P., Levine, S.: Meta-reinforcement learning of structured exploration strategies. In: Advances in Neural Information Processing Systems (NIPS) (2018)

13. Hochreiter, S., Younger, A.S., Conwell, P.R.: Learning to learn using gradient descent. In: Dorffner, G., Bischof, H., Hornik, K. (eds.) ICANN 2001. LNCS, vol. 2130, pp. 87–94. Springer, Heidelberg (2001). https://doi.org/10.1007/3-540-44668-0_13

14. Huang, J.B., Singh, A., Ahuja, N.: Single image super-resolution from transformed self-exemplars. In: Proceedings of the IEEE Conference on Computer Vision and Pattern Recognition (CVPR) (2015)

15. Huang, J.J., Liu, T., Luigi Dragotti, P., Stathaki, T.: Srhrf+: self-example enhanced single image super-resolution using hierarchical random forests. In: Proceedings of the IEEE Conference on Computer Vision and Pattern Recognition Workshops, pp. 71–79 (2017)

16. Huang, J.J., Siu, W.C.: Learning hierarchical decision trees for single-image super-resolution. IEEE Trans. Circuits Syst. Video Technol. **27**, 937–950 (2017)

17. Huang, J.J., Siu, W.C., Liu, T.R.: Fast image interpolation via random forests. IEEE Trans. Image Process. **24**(10), 3232–3245 (2015)

18. Hui, Z., Wang, X., Gao, X.: Fast and accurate single image super-resolution via information distillation network. In: Proceedings of the IEEE Conference on Computer Vision and Pattern Recognition (CVPR) (2018)

19. Jamal, M.A., Qi, G.J.: Task agnostic meta-learning for few-shot learning. In: Proceedings of the IEEE Conference on Computer Vision and Pattern Recognition, pp. 11719–11727 (2019)

20. Johnson, J., Alahi, A., Fei-Fei, L.: Perceptual Losses for Real-Time Style Transfer and Super-Resolution. In: Leibe, B., Matas, J., Sebe, N., Welling, M. (eds.) ECCV 2016. LNCS, vol. 9906, pp. 694–711. Springer, Cham (2016). https://doi.org/10.1007/978-3-319-46475-6_43

21. Kim, J., Lee, J.K., Lee, K.M.: Accurate image super-resolution using very deep convolutional networks. In: Proceedings of the IEEE Conference on Computer Vision and Pattern Recognition (CVPR) (2016)

22. Ledig, C., et al.: Photo-realistic single image super-resolution using a generative adversarial network. In: Proceedings of the IEEE Conference on Computer Vision and Pattern Recognition (CVPR) (2017)

23. Lee, M., Tai, Y.W.: Robust all-in-focus super-resolution for focal stack photography. IEEE Trans. Image Process. **25**, 1887–1897 (2016)
24. Martin, D., Fowlkes, C., Tal, D., Malik, J., et al.: A database of human segmented natural images and its application to evaluating segmentation algorithms and measuring ecological statistics. Iccv Vancouver (2001)
25. Michaeli, T., Irani, M.: Nonparametric blind super-resolution. In: Proceedings of the IEEE International Conference on Computer Vision (ICCV) (2013)
26. Nichol, A., Achiam, J., Schulman, J.: On first-order meta-learning algorithms. arXiv preprint arXiv:1803.02999 (2018)
27. Sajjadi, M.S., Scholkopf, B., Hirsch, M.: Enhancenet: single image super-resolution through automated texture synthesis. In: Proceedings of the IEEE International Conference on Computer Vision (ICCV) (2017)
28. Salvador, J., Pérez-Pellitero, E.: Naive bayes super-resolution forest (2015)
29. Schulter, S., Leistner, C., Bischof, H.: Fast and accurate image upscaling with super-resolution forests. In: Proceedings of the IEEE Conference on Computer Vision and Pattern Recognition, pp. 3791–3799 (2015)
30. Shocher, A., Cohen, N., Irani, M.: "zero-shot" super-resolution using deep internal learning. In: Proceedings of the IEEE Conference on Computer Vision and Pattern Recognition (CVPR) (2018)
31. Snell, J., Swersky, K., Zemel, R.: Prototypical networks for few-shot learning. In: Advances in Neural Information Processing Systems (NIPS) (2017)
32. Sun, Q., Liu, Y., Chua, T.S., Schiele, B.: Meta-transfer learning for few-shot learning. In: Proceedings of the IEEE Conference on Computer Vision and Pattern Recognition, pp. 403–412 (2019)
33. Tai, Y., Yang, J., Liu, X.: Image super-resolution via deep recursive residual network. In: Proceedings of the IEEE Conference on Computer Vision and Pattern Recognition, pp. 3147–3155 (2017)
34. Tai, Y., Yang, J., Liu, X., Xu, C.: MemNet: a persistent memory network for image restoration. In: Proceedings of the IEEE International Conference on Computer Vision, pp. 4539–4547 (2017)
35. Thrun, S., Pratt, L.: Learning to learn: Introduction and overview. In: Thrun, S., Pratt, L. (eds.) Learning to Learn, pp. 3–17. Springer, Boston (1998). https://doi.org/10.1007/978-1-4615-5529-2_1
36. Yang, J., Wright, J., Huang, T.S., Ma, Y.: Image super-resolution via sparse representation. IEEE Trans. Image Process. **19**(11), 2861–2873 (2010)
37. Yuan, Y., Liu, S., Zhang, J., Zhang, Y., Dong, C., Lin, L.: Unsupervised image super-resolution using cycle-in-cycle generative adversarial networks. In: Proceedings of the IEEE Conference on Computer Vision and Pattern Recognition Workshops (CVPRW), pp. 814–81409 (2018)
38. Zhang, Y., Li, K., Li, K., Wang, L., Zhong, B., Fu, Y.: Image super-resolution using very deep residual channel attention networks. In: Ferrari, V., Hebert, M., Sminchisescu, C., Weiss, Y. (eds.) ECCV 2018. LNCS, vol. 11211, pp. 294–310. Springer, Cham (2018). https://doi.org/10.1007/978-3-030-01234-2_18
39. Zhu, J.Y., Park, T., Isola, P., Efros, A.A.: Unpaired image-to-image translation using cycle-consistent adversarial networks. In: Proceedings of the IEEE Conference on Computer Vision and Pattern Recognition (CVPR) (2017)
40. Zontak, M., Irani, M.: Internal statistics of a single natural image. In: CVPR 2011, pp. 977–984. IEEE (2011)

TP-LSD: Tri-Points Based Line Segment Detector

Siyu Huang[1], Fangbo Qin[2], Pengfei Xiong[1], Ning Ding[1], Yijia He[1(✉)], and Xiao Liu[1]

[1] Megvii Technology, Beijing, China
siyuada7@gmail.com, xiongpengfei@megvii.com, dning97dn@gmail.com,
heyijia2016@gmail.com, liuxiao@foxmail.com
[2] Institute of Automation, Chinese Academy of Sciences, Beijing, China
qinfangbo2013@ia.ac.cn

Abstract. This paper proposes a novel deep convolutional model, Tri-Points Based Line Segment Detector (TP-LSD), to detect line segments in an image at real-time speed. The previous related methods typically use the two-step strategy, relying on either heuristic post-process or extra classifier. To realize one-step detection with a faster and more compact model, we introduce the tri-points representation, converting the line segment detection to the end-to-end prediction of a root-point and two endpoints for each line segment. TP-LSD has two branches: tri-points extraction branch and line segmentation branch. The former predicts the heat map of root-points and the two displacement maps of endpoints. The latter segments the pixels on straight lines out from background. Moreover, the line segmentation map is reused in the first branch as structural prior. We propose an additional novel evaluation metric and evaluate our method on Wireframe and YorkUrban datasets, demonstrating not only the competitive accuracy compared to the most recent methods, but also the real-time run speed up to **78 FPS** with the 320×320 input.

Keywords: Line segment detection · Low-level vision · Deep learning

1 Introduction

Compact environment description is an important issue in visual perception. For man-made environments with various flat surfaces, line segments can encode the environment structure, providing fundamental information to the upstream vision tasks, such as vanishing point estimation [17,19], 3D structure reconstruction [16], distortion correction [24], and pose estimation [4,14].

S. Huang and N. Ding contribution was made when they were interns at Megvii Research Beijing, Megvii Technology, China.

Electronic supplementary material The online version of this chapter (https:// doi.org/10.1007/978-3-030-58583-9_46) contains supplementary material, which is available to authorized users.

© Springer Nature Switzerland AG 2020
A. Vedaldi et al. (Eds.): ECCV 2020, LNCS 12372, pp. 770–785, 2020.
https://doi.org/10.1007/978-3-030-58583-9_46

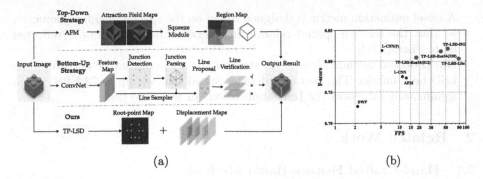

(a)   (b)

Fig. 1. Overview. (a) Compared to the existing two-step methods, TP-LSD detects multiple line segments simultaneously in one step, providing better efficiency and compactness. (b) Inference speed and F-score on Wireframe test set.

With the rapid advance of deep learning, deep neural networks are applied to line segment detection. As shown in Fig. 1a, the existing methods have two steps. With the top-down strategy it first detects the region of a line and then squeezes the region into a line segment [22], which might be affected by regional textures and does not have an explicit definition of endpoints. With the bottom-up strategy it first detect junctions and then organize them to line segments using grouping algorithm [7,8], or extra classifier [23,25,28], which might be prone to the inaccurate junction predictions caused by local ambiguity. The two-step strategy might also limit the inference speed in real-time applications.

Considering the above problems, we propose the tri-points (TP) representation, which uses a *root-point* as the unique identity to localize a line segment, and the two corresponding *end-points* are represented by their displacements w.r.t the root-point. Thus a TP encodes the length, orientation and location of a line segment. Moreover, inspired by that human perceive line segments according to straight lines, we leverage the straight line segmentation map as structural prior to guide the inference of TPs, by embedding feature aggregation modules which fuse the line-map with TP related features. Accordingly, Tri-Points Based Line Segment Detector (TP-LSD) is designed, which has three parts: feature extraction backbone, TP extraction branch, and line segmentation branch.

As to the evaluation of line segment detection, the current metrics either treat a line segment as a set of pixels, or use squared euclidean distance to judge the matching degree, which cannot reflect the various relationships between line segments such as intersection and overlapping. Therefore we propose a new metric named line matching average precision from a camera model perspective.

In summary, the main contributions of this paper are as follows:

- We utilize the TP representation to encode line segment, based on which TP-LSD is proposed to realize the real-time and compact one-step detection pipeline. The synthesis of local root-point detection and global shape inference makes the detection more robust to various textures and spatial-distributions.

- A novel evaluation metric is designed based on the spatial imaging geometry, so that the relative spatial relationship between line segments is reflected more distinctively.
- Our proposed method obtains the state-of-the-art performance on two public LSD benchmarks. The average inference speed achieves up to 78 FPS, which significantly promotes the LSD applications in real-time tasks.

2   Related Work

2.1   Hand-Crafted Feature Based Methods

Line segment detection is a long-standing task in computer vision. Traditional methods [1,2,6,12] usually depend on low-level cues like image gradients, which are used to construct line segments with predefined rules. However, the hand-crafted line segment detectors are sensitive to the threshold settings and image noise. Another way to detect line segments applies Hough transform [21], which is able to use the entire image's information but difficult to identify the endpoints of line segments.

2.2   Deep Edge and Line Segment Detection

In the past few years, CNN-based methods have been introduced to solve the edge detection problem. HED [20] treats edge detection problem as pixel-wise binary classification, and achieves significant performance improvement compared to traditional methods. Following this breakthrough, numerous methods for edge detection have been proposed [11,15]. However, edge maps lack explicit geometric information for compact environment representation.

Most recently, CNN-based method has been realized for line segment detection. Huang et al. [8] proposed DWP, which includes two parallel branches to predict junction map and line heatmap in an image, then merges them as line segments. Zhang et al. [25] and Zhou et al. [28] utilize a point-pair graph representation for line segments. Their methods (PPGNet and L-CNN) first detect junctions, then use an extra classifier to create an adjacency matrix to identify whether a point-pair belongs to the same line segment. Xue e al. [22] creatively presented regional attraction of line segment maps, and proposed AFM to predict attraction field maps from raw images, followed by a squeeze module to produce line segments. Furthermore, Xue et al. [23] proposed a 4-D holistic attraction field map (H-AFM) to better parameterize line segments, and proposed HAWP with L-CNN pipeline. Though learning-based methods have significant advantages over the hand-crafted ones. However, their two-step strategy might limit their real-time performance, and rely on extra classifier or heuristic post-process. Moreover, the relationship between line-map and line segments is under-utilized.

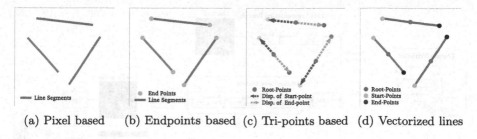

(a) Pixel based   (b) Endpoints based (c) Tri-points based (d) Vectorized lines

Fig. 2. Line segment representation.

2.3 Object Detection

Current object detectors represent each object by an axis-aligned bounding box and classify whether its content is a specific object or background [5,10]. Recently, keypoint estimation has been introduced to object detection to avoid the dependence on generating boxes. CornerNet [9] detects two bounding box corners as keypoints, while ExtremeNet [27] detects the top-, left-, bottom-, right-most and center points of all objects. These two models both require a grouping stage to form objects based on the extracted keypoints. CenterNet [26] represents objects by the center of bounding boxes, and regresses other properties directly from image features around the center location. Such anchor-free based methods have achieved good detection accuracy with briefer structure, motivated by which we adopt a similar strategy to detect line segments.

3 Tri-Points Representation

The Tri-Points (TP) representation is inspired by how people model a long narrow object. Intuitively, we usually find a root point on a line, then extend it from the root-point to two opposite directions and determine the endpoints. TP contains three key-points and their spatial relationship to encode a line segment. The root-point localizes the center of a line segment. The two end-points are represented by two displacement vectors w.r.t the root point, as illustrated in Fig. 2c, 2d. It is similar to SPM [13] used in human pose estimation. The conversion from a TP to a vectorized line segment, which is denotes as **TP generation** operation, is expressed by,

$$(x_s, y_s) = (x_r, y_r) + d_s(x_r, y_r)$$
$$(x_e, y_e) = (x_r, y_r) + d_e(x_r, y_r) \tag{1}$$

where (x_r, y_r) denotes the root-point of a line segment. (x_s, y_s) and (x_e, y_e) represent its start-point and end-point, respectively. Generally, the most left point is the start-point. Specially, if line segment is vertical, the upper point is the start-point. $d_s(x_r, y_r)$ and $d_e(x_r, y_r)$ denote the predicted 2D displacements from root-point to its corresponding start-point and end-point, respectively.

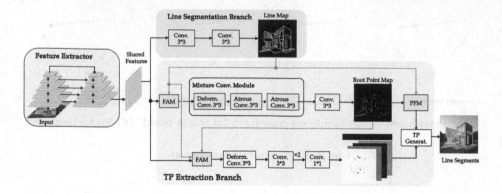

Fig. 3. An overview of our network architecture.

4   Methods

Based on the proposed Tri-Points, a one-step model TP-LSD is proposed for line segment detection, whose architecture is shown in Fig. 3. A U-shape network is used to generate shared features, which are then fed to two branches: 1) TP extraction branch, which contains a root-point detection task and a displacement regression task; 2)line segmentation branch, which generates a pixel-wise line-map. These two branches are bridged by feature aggregation modules. Finally, after processed by point filter module, the filtered TPs are transformed to vectorized line segment instances with TP generation operation.

4.1   TP Extraction Branch

Root-Point Detection. The first task in TP extraction branch is to detect root points. Similar to CenterNet [26], each pixel is classified to discriminate whether it is a root-point. The output activation function is sigmoid function.

MCM. Because of the narrow and even long shape of line segment, it requires a large receptive field to classify the center of line segment. Therefore, a **mixture convolution module** (MCM) is introduced to provide the adaptive and expanded reception field, by cascading three convolution layers, a 3×3 deformable convolutional layer, and two 3 × 3 atrous convolutional layers with dilation rate = 2, whose strides are all set as 1.

Displacement Regression. The second task in TP extraction branch is to regress the two displacements of the start and end points w.r.t a root-point in the continuous domain. The sparse maps for the displacements are inferred by one 3 × 3 deformable convolutional, two 3 × 3 convolutional and a 1 × 1 convolutional layers, whose strides are all set as 1. With the output maps, we can index the related displacements by positions. Given a root point (x_r, y_r), the corresponding displacements are indexed as $d_s(x_r, y_r)$ and $d_e(x_r, y_r)$. Then the coordinates of the start- and end-points can be obtained by Eq. (1).

4.2   Line Segmentation Branch

Pixel-wise map of straight lines is easier to obtain because the precise determination of end-points is not required. Based on the idea that line segment is highly related to straight line, we use a straight line segmentation branch to provide prior knowledge for line segment detection. First, straight line can serve as spatial attention cue. Second, a root-point must be localized on a straight line. As is shown in Fig. 3, the line segmentation branch has two 3×3 convolutional layers with the stride 1. The output activation function is sigmoid function, so that the line-map $P(L)$ has the pixel values ranging within $(0, 1)$.

FAM. From the multi-modal feature fusion prospective, we present a **feature aggregating module** (FAM) to aggregate the structural prior of line-map with the TP extraction branch. Given a line-map $P(L)$ from the line segmentation branch, the straight line activation map A_l is obtained by $\tanh(w \times P(L) + b)$ where w, b denotes the parameters of a 1×1 convolutional layer, and the tanh gating function indicates whether a pixel is activated or suppressed according to its relative position to a straight line. The shared feature is firstly aggregated with the straight line activation map A_l by concatenation, and then fed to the root-point detection sub-branch, as shown in Fig. 3. For the displacement regression sub-branch, similarly, the straight line activation map and the root-point activation map are obtained by 1×1 conv and tanh, then fused with the shared feature map by concatenation, as shown in Fig. 3. Thus the prior knowledge of straight line and root point can benifit the displacement regression.

PFM. The line-map can also be leveraged to filter the noisy root-points that lies out of line. We consider the root-point confidence map as a probability distribution $P(R|L)$ conditioned on line existence. Thus the root-point confidence map $P(R|L)$ can be refined by the multiplication with the line confidence map $P(L)$, which is called **point filter module** (PFM), as given by

$$\tilde{P}(R) = \tilde{P}(R|L) \times \tilde{P}(L)^{\alpha} \qquad (2)$$

where the power coefficient $\alpha \in (0, 1)$ is to adjust the contribution of line-map.

4.3   Training and Inference

Feature Extractor. A U-shape network is used as the feature extractor. After a backbone encoder, there are four decoder blocks. Each decoder block is formed by a bi-linear interpolation based up-sampling and a residual block. Skip connection is used to aggregate multi-scale features by concatenating the low level features with the high level features. The output of the feature extractor is a 64-channel feature map, whose size is the same with the input image, or optionally half of the input size for faster inference. This feature map is used as the shared features for the following branches.

Loss. In training stage, the input image is resized to 320×320, and the outputs include a line-map, a root-point confidence map, and four displacement maps, whose ground truths are generated from the raw line segment labels. The three tasks' losses are combined as Eq. (3), where $\lambda_{root,disp,line} = \{50, 1, 20\}$.

$$\mathbb{L}_{total} = \lambda_{root}\mathbb{L}_{root} + \lambda_{disp}\mathbb{L}_{disp} + \lambda_{line}\mathbb{L}_{line} \qquad (3)$$

The ground truth of root-point confidence map is constructed by marking the root-point positions on a zero-map and then smoothed by a scaled 2D Gaussian kernel truncated by a 5×5 window, so that the root-point has the highest confidence 1, and its nearby pixels have lower confidence. A weighted binary cross-entropy loss $\mathbb{L}_{root}$ is used to supervise this task. The ground truths of the displacement maps are constructed by assigning displacement values at the root-point positions on the zero-maps. For each ground truth line segment, its mid-point is considered as the root point. For the pixels within a 5×5 window centered at the mid-point, we calculate the displacements from it to the start- and end-points, then assigned the displacement values to these pixels. After all the ground truth line segments are visited, the final displacements maps are used for smoothed L1 loss $\mathbb{L}_{disp}$ based regression learning. Note that only the root-points and its 5×5 neighbourhood window are involved in the loss calculation. As to the line segmentation sub-task, the ground truth of line segmentation map are constructed by simply draw the line segments on a zero map and the learning is supervised by the weighted binary cross entropy loss $\mathbb{L}_{line}$.

In the inference stage, after the root-point confidence map is produced, the non-maximum suppression is operated to extract the exact root-point positions. Afterwards, we use the extracted root-points and their corresponding displacements to generate line segments from TPs with Eq. (1).

5   Evaluation Metrics

In this section, we briefly introduce two existed evaluation metrics: pixel based metric and structural average precision, and then design a novel metric, line matching average precision.

Pixel Based Metric: For a pixel on a detected line segment, if its minimum distance to all the ground truth pixels is within the 1After evaluating all the pixels on the detected line segments, the F-score F^H can be calculated [8, 22, 28]. The limitation is that it cannot reveal the continuity of line segment. For example, if a long line segment is broken into several short ones, the F-score is high but these split line segments is not suitable for 3D reconstruction or wireframe parsing.

Structural Average Precision: The structural average precision (sAP) [28] uses the sum of squared error (SSE) between the predicted end-points and their ground truths as evaluation metric. The predicted line segment will be counted as a true positive detection when its SSE is less than a threshold, such as $\epsilon = 5, 10, 15$. However, line segment matching could be more complicated than point pair correspondence. For example, in Fig. 4b, 4c, it is shown that sAP is not discriminative enough for some different matching situations.

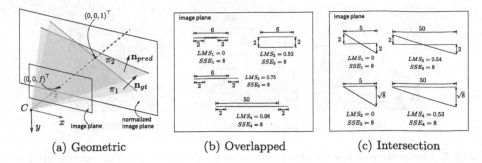

(a) Geometric   (b) Overlapped   (c) Intersection

Fig. 4. Evaluation metrics for line segment detection. (a) The geometric explanation of the proposed line matching score (LMS). The blue and red line segments on the normalized image plane correspond to the detection and ground truth, respectively, which determine two planes together with the optical center C. In (b) and (c), the different matching situations could have the same SSE score 8 with sAP metric. In contrast, the LMS gives the discriminative scores. (Color figure online)

Line Matching Average Precision: To better reflect the various line segment matching situations in term of direction and position as well as length, the Line Matching Score (LMS) is proposed. LMS contains two parts: $Score_\theta$ denotes the differences in angle and position, and $Score_l$ denotes the matching degree in length. The LMS is calculated by

$$LMS = Score_\theta \times Score_l \tag{4}$$

Inspired by 3D line reconstruction, $Score_\theta$ is calculated in the 3D camera frame as shown in Fig. 4a. A line segment and the camera's optical center jointly determine a unique plane whose normal vector is **n**. Thus, given a predicted and a ground truth line segments, they determine two 3D planes, and the angle between their normal vectors is used to measure the directional matching degree. The angle is equal to 0 if and only if the two line segments are collinear. To calculate $Score_\theta$, Firstly, a ground truth line segment is aligned to the center of the image plane by subtracting the coordinates of the midpoint $l_m = (x_m, y_m)^\top$. The endpoints of detected line segment is also subtracted by l_m. Then, the endpoints are projected from the 2D image plane $l_i = (x_i, y_i)^\top, i = s, e$ onto the 3D normalized image plane by dividing the camera focal length, i.e. $\bar{l}_i = \left(\frac{x_i}{f}, \frac{y_i}{f}, 1\right)^\top$. Finally, the normal vectors $\mathbf{n}_{gt}$ and $\mathbf{n}_{pred}$ are obtained by cross-multiplying their endpoint $\bar{l}_s \times \bar{l}_e$, respectively. $Score_\theta$ is given by,

$$Score_\theta = \begin{cases} 1 - \frac{\theta(\mathbf{n}_{gt}, \mathbf{n}_{pred})}{\eta_\theta}, & \text{if } \theta(\mathbf{n}_{gt}, \mathbf{n}_{pred}) < \eta_\theta \\ 0, & \text{otherwise} \end{cases} \tag{5}$$

where θ () is to calculate the angle between two vectors with the unit degree. η_θ is a minimum threshold.

(a) GT   (b) sAP^{10} Matching   (c) LAP Matching

Fig. 5. Comparison of line matching evaluation results using different metrics. (a) The ground truth line segments marked by red. (b) Line matching result using sAP^{10} metric. (c) Line matching result using proposed LAP metric. In (b) and (c), the mismatched and matched line segments are marked by blue and red, respectively. The endpoints are marked by cyan. (Color figure online)

$Score_l$ demonstrates the overlap degree of two line segment. The ratio of overlap length against the ground truth length is η_1. The ratio of overlap length against the projection length is η_2.

$$\eta_1 = \frac{\mathcal{L}_{pred} \cap \mathcal{L}_{gt}}{\mathcal{L}_{gt}}, \quad \eta_2 = \frac{\mathcal{L}_{pred} \cap \mathcal{L}_{gt}}{\mathcal{L}_{pred} |\cos(\alpha)|} \tag{6}$$

where $\mathcal{L}$ is the length of line segment and $\mathcal{L}_{pred} \cap \mathcal{L}_{gt}$ is the overlap length of the predicted line segment projected to the ground truth line segment. α is the angle between the two line segments in 2D image. Then $Score_l$ is calculated by,

$$Score_l = \begin{cases} \frac{\eta_1 + \eta_2}{2}, & \text{if } \eta_1 \geq \eta_l, \text{ and } \eta_2 \geq \eta_l \\ 0, & \text{otherwise} \end{cases} \tag{7}$$

where η_l denotes a minimum threshold. Since the focal length of a camera might be unknown for public data sets, to make a fair comparison, we firstly re-scale the detected line segments with the same ratio of resizing the original image to the resolution 128×128, and set a virtual focal length $f = 24$. Besides we set $\eta_\theta = 10°$ and $\eta_l = 0.5$ in this work.

Using LMS to determine true positive, i.e. a detected line segment is considered to be true positive if LMS> 0.5, we can calculate the Line Matching Average Precision (LAP) on the entire test set. LAP is defined as the area under the precision recall curve.

Analysis of Metric on Real Image. We compare the line matching evaluation results between SSE used in sAP and LMS used in LAP on a real image, as shown in Fig. 5. Comparing the areas labeled by yellow boxes in Fig. 5b and Fig. 5a, the detected line segments have obvious error direction compared to ground truth. However, SSE gives the same tolerance for line segments with different lengths, and accepts them as true positive matches. In contrast, as shown in Fig. 5c, LMS could better capture the direction errors and give the

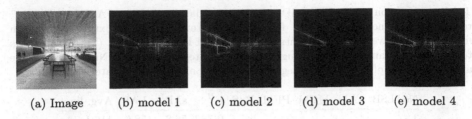

| (a) Image | (b) model 1 | (c) model 2 | (d) model 3 | (e) model 4 |

Fig. 6. Gradient based interpretation of root-point detection. (a) Raw image and the root points (white dots) of three line segments. (b–e) The gradient saliency maps of the input layer backpropagated from the three root points detected by the four different models, based on Guided Back-propogation method [17].

correct judgement. As shown by the green boxes in Fig. 5a and Fig. 5c, for the line segment with the correct direction but the slightly shorter length compared with the ground truth, namely, whose $Score_l$ is lower than 1 but greater than η_l, LMS will accept it while SSE would not. Considering that the direction of line segments are more important in upper-level applications such as SLAM, this deviation can be acceptable.

6 Experiments

Experiments are conducted on Wireframe dataset [8] and YorkUrban dataset [3]. Wireframe contains 5462 images of indoor and outdoor man-made environments, among which 5000 images are used for training. To validate the generalization ability, we also evaluate on YorkUrban Dataset [3], which has 102 test images.

We use the standard data augmentation procedure to expand the diversity of training samples, including horizontal and vertical flip, rotation and scaling. The hardware configuration includes four NVIDIA RTX 2080Ti GPUs and an Intel Xeon Gold 6130 2.10 GHz CPU. We use the ADAM optimizer with an initial learning rate of 1×10^{-3}, which is divided by 10 at the 150th, 250th, and 350th epoch. The total training epoch is 400.

6.1 Analysis of TP-LSD

We run a series of ablation experiments to study our proposed TP-LSD on Wireframe dataset. The evaluation results are shown in Table 1. F^H refers to pixel based metric [8]. sAP^{10} is the structural average precision [28] with threshold of 10. LAP is the proposed metric. As presented in Table 1, all the proposed modules present contributions to the performance improvements.

LSB. After integrating the line-map segmentation branch with the TP extraction branch without cross-branch guidance, the multi-task learning improves the performance from 0.782 to 0.808, because the line segmentation learning can guide the model to learn more line-awareness features.

Table 1. Ablation study of TP-LSD on Wireframe dataset. "LSB", "FAM" and "MCM" refer to line segmentation branch, feature aggregate module and mixture convolution module, respectively. α is the contribution ratio of line-map as Eq. (2). "R/S" refers to the rotation and scale data augmentation strategy. "Avg. line Num." means the average number of detected line segments whose confidence are greater than 0.2.

No	LSB	FAM	MCM	PFM	R/S	F^H	sAP^{10}	LAP	Avg. line
1				-	✓	0.782	56.8	58.6	116.1
2	✓			-	✓	0.808	59.2	61.4	113.6
3	✓	✓		-	✓	0.810	60.4	59.2	138.0
4	✓	✓	✓	0	✓	0.810	61.3	60.9	/
5	✓	✓	✓	1	✓	0.811	60.0	60.1	/
6	✓	✓	✓	0.5	✓	0.816	60.6	60.6	/
7	✓	✓	✓	0.5	✗	0.813	60.0	60.1	/

FAM. FAM combines the cross-branch guidance with the line-map segmentation branch. Although the F^H metric increases indicating the better pixel localization accuracy, sAP^{10} and LAP are slightly decreased, because of the a larger number of line segments are detected.

MCM. Mixture Convolution Module is applied in root-point detection sub-branch. Compared to the standard convolution layers, MCM improves the LAP scores significantly, showing a better matching degree.

PFM. With PFM and the contribution ratio of $\alpha = 0.5$, the precision is increased while the recall slightly decreased, which lead to a better overall accuracy. The decrease in sAP^{10} and LAP is due to the reduced confidence of the root-points after PFM.

Augmentation. The 7th row in Table 1 shows the data augmentation with only horizontal and vertical flip. Compared to the result in 6th row, the lower performance shows that the rotation and scaling based data augmentation can further improve the performance.

Interpretability. To explore what the network learned from the line segment detection task, we use Guided Backpropagation [18] to visualize which pixels are important for the root-point detection. Guided Backpropagation interprets the pixels' importance degree on the input image, by calculating the gradient flow from the output layer to the input images. The gradients flowed to the input images from the three specific detected root-point are visualized in Fig. 6. We find that the network automatically learns to localize the saliency region w.r.t a root-point, which is along a complete line segment. It shows that the root point detection task is mainly based on the line feature.

Furthermore, the integration of LSB lead to the higher influence of on-line pixels to root point prediction. Comparing Fig. 6c to Fig. 6b, the former presents higher gradient values along the line. The saliency maps obtained by model No.

Table 2. Evaluation results of different line segment detection methods. "/" means that the score is too slow to be meaningful. The best two scores are shown in bold and italic.

Method	Input Size	Wireframe dataset				YorkUrban dataset				FPS
		F^H	sAP^5	sAP^{10}	LAP	F^H	sAP^5	sAP^{10}	LAP	
LSD [6]	320	0.641	6.7	8.8	18.7	0.606	7.5	9.2	16.1	**100**
DWP [8]	512	0.727	/	/	6.6	0.652	/	/	3.1	2.2
AFM [22]	320	0.773	18.3	23.9	36.7	0.663	7.0	9.1	17.5	12.8
L-CNN [28]	512	0.775	**58.9**	**62.8**	59.8	0.646	25.9	**28.2**	*32.0*	11.1
L-CNN(P) [28]	512	*0.817*	52.4	57.3	57.9	*0.675*	20.9	23.1	26.8	5.2
TP-LSD-Lite	320	0.804	56.4	59.7	59.7	**0.681**	24.8	26.8	31.2	**78.2**
TP-LSD-Res34	320	0.816	57.5	*60.6*	*60.6*	0.674	25.3	27.4	31.1	42.2
TP-LSD-HG	512	**0.820**	50.9	57.0	55.1	0.673	18.9	22.0	24.6	*53.4*
TP-LSD-Res34	512	0.806	*57.6*	57.2	**61.3**	0.672	**27.6**	*27.7*	**34.3**	18.1

3 and model No. 4 are cleaner, and the saliency regions are more concentrated on specific line segments. With the introduction of MCM in model No. 4, the response of long line segment could be improved with a lager receptive field, which can be shown by the comparison between Fig. 6d and Fig. 6e.

6.2   Comparison with Other Methods

We compare our proposed TP-LSD with LSD[1] [6], DWP[2] [8], AFM[3] [22], L-CNN[4] and L-CNN with post-process (L-CNN(P)) [28]. The source codes and their model weights provided by the authors are available online, except that we reproduced DWP by ourselves. F^H, sAP and LAP are used to evaluate those methods quantitatively. For TP-LSD, we tried a series of minimum thresholds of the root-point detection confidence, ranging within (0.1, 0.8) with the step $\triangle \gamma = 0.05$. LSD is evaluated with $-\log(\text{NFA})$ in $0.01 \times \{1.75^0, ..., 1.75^{19}\}$, where NFA is the number of false positive detections. For other methods, we use the author recommended threshold array listed in [8, 22, 28].

We evaluate the methods on Wireframe and YorkUrban dataset. We use the model No. 6 in Sect. 6.1 as the representative model, named as TP-LSD-Res34. Furthermore, we alter the backbone with Hourglass used in L-CNN [28] to form TP-LSD-HG. To achieve a faster speed, TP-LSD-Lite is realized by using the output of the last second layer of the decoder as the shared feature. Thus the input to the task branches has the smaller size of 160×160. And the final output of the task branches are upsampled back to 320×320 with the bi-linear interpolation.

The precision-recall curves are depicted in Fig. 7 and the detection performances are reported in Table 2. Figure 7a and Fig. 7b show that TP-LSD outperforms other line segment detection methods, according to the pixel based

---

[1] http://www.ipol.im/pub/art/2012/gjmr-lsd/.

[2] https://github.com/huangkuns/wireframe.

[3] https://github.com/cherubicXN/afm-cvpr2019.

[4] https://github.com/zhou13/lcnn.

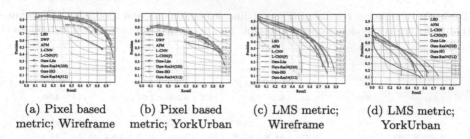

| (a) Pixel based | (b) Pixel based | (c) LMS metric; | (d) LMS metric; |
| metric; Wireframe | metric; YorkUrban | Wireframe | YorkUrban |

Fig. 7. Precision-recall curves of line segment detection. The models are trained on Wireframe dataset and tested on both Wireframe and YorkUrban datasets. Scores below 0.1 are not plotted. The PR curves for LAP of DWP are not ploted for its lower score.

PR curves. In addition, our one-step method provides the comparable detection performance compared to the two-step L-CNN that requires post-processing.

We then evaluate the methods with the sAP and the proposed LAP. The precision recall curve of LAP in two datasets are drawn in Fig. 7c and Fig. 7d. The performances of AFM and LSD are limited by length prediction of line segments. As to DWP, the inaccurate direction prediction might affect the detection. Our method and L-CNN present the higher scores, which shows that these two methods perform better not only in detection but also in alignment. Moreover, our method has the better precision than L-CNN in higher recall region. Though the higher F^H is obtained by TP-LSD-HG, the decreases of sAP and LAP were caused by the lower recall rate due to the lower feature map resolution. TP-LSD-Lite gets comparable generalization performance on both dataset. YorkUrban dataset is more challenging because only the line segments which satisfy the Manhattan World assumption are labeled out as ground truth, which causes lower precision.

Visualization and Discussion. In Fig. 8, several results of line segment detection are visualized. LSD detected some noisy local textures without semantic meaning. Recent CNN-based methods have shown good noise-suppression ability because they obtain high-level semantics. AFM does not have explicit endpoint definition, limiting the accuracy of end-points localization. It also presented many short line segments. DWP gives a relatively cleaner detection result, but there exist some incorrectly connected junction pairs, caused by inaccurate junctions predictions and sub-optimal heuristic combination algorithm. L-CNN, which has a junction detector and an extra line segment classifier, has good visualization results. However, its line segment detection result rely on the junction detection and line feature sampling, which might be prone to missed junction and nearby texture variation. In comparison, the proposed TP-LSD method is capable to detect line segments in complicated even low-contrast environments as is shown on the first and the sixth rows in Fig. 8.

Inference Speed. Based on NVIDIA RTX2080Ti GPU and Intel Xeon Gold 6130 2.10 GHz CPU, the inference speed is reported in Table 2. With the image

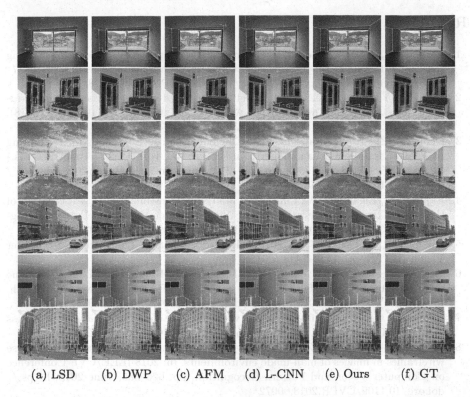

(a) LSD   (b) DWP   (c) AFM   (d) L-CNN   (e) Ours   (f) GT

Fig. 8. Quanlitative evaluation of line detection methods on Wireframe dataset and YorkUrban dataset. The line segments and their end-points are marked by orange and cyan colors, respectively. (Color figure online)

size of 320 × 320, the proposed TP-LSD achieve the real-time speed up to 78 FPS, offering the potential to be used in real-time applications like SLAM.

7   Conclusion

This paper proposes a faster and more compact model TP-LSD for line segment detection with the one-step strategy. Tri-points representation is used to encodes a line segment with three keypoints, based on which the line-segment detection is realized by end-to-end inference. Furthermore, the straight line-map is produced based on segmentation task, and is used as structural prior cues to guide the extraction of TPs. Both quantitatively and qualitatively, TP-LSD shows the improved performances compared to the existing models. Besides, our method achieves 78 FPS speed, showing potential to be integrated with real-time applications, such as vanishing point estimation, 3D reconstruction and pose estimation.

References

1. Akinlar, C., Topal, C.: Edlines: real-time line segment detection by edge drawing (ed). In: 2011 18th IEEE International Conference on Image Processing, pp. 2837–2840, September 2011. https://doi.org/10.1109/ICIP.2011.6116138
2. Cho, N., Yuille, A., Lee, S.: A novel linelet-based representation for line segment detection. IEEE Trans. Pattern Anal. Mach. Intell. **40**(5), 1195–1208 (2018). https://doi.org/10.1109/TPAMI.2017.2703841
3. Denis, P., Elder, J.H., Estrada, F.J.: Efficient edge-based methods for estimating manhattan frames in urban imagery. In: Forsyth, D., Torr, P., Zisserman, A. (eds.) ECCV 2008. LNCS, vol. 5303, pp. 197–210. Springer, Heidelberg (2008). https://doi.org/10.1007/978-3-540-88688-4_15
4. Elqursh, A., Elgammal, A.: Line-based relative pose estimation. In: Proceedings of the IEEE Computer Society Conference on Computer Vision and Pattern Recognition, pp. 3049–3056 (2011). https://doi.org/10.1109/CVPR.2011.5995512
5. Girshick, R.B.: Fast R-CNN. 2015 IEEE International Conference on Computer Vision (ICCV), pp. 1440–1448 (2015)
6. Grompone von Gioi, R., Jakubowicz, J., Morel, J., Randall, G.: LSD: a fast line segment detector with a false detection control. IEEE Trans. Pattern Anal. Mach. Intell. **32**(4), 722–732 (2010). https://doi.org/10.1109/TPAMI.2008.300
7. Huang, K., Gao, S.: Wireframe parsing with guidance of distance map. IEEE Access **7**, 141036–141044 (2019). https://doi.org/10.1109/ACCESS.2019.2943885
8. Huang, K., Wang, Y., Zhou, Z., Ding, T., Gao, S., Ma, Y.: Learning to parse wireframes in images of man-made environments. In: 2018 IEEE/CVF Conference on Computer Vision and Pattern Recognition, pp. 626–635, June 2018. https://doi.org/10.1109/CVPR.2018.00072
9. Law, H., Deng, J.: Cornernet: Detecting objects as paired keypoints. In: ECCV (2018)
10. Liu, W., et al.: SSD: single shot MultiBox detector. In: Leibe, B., Matas, J., Sebe, N., Welling, M. (eds.) ECCV 2016. LNCS, vol. 9905, pp. 21–37. Springer, Cham (2016). https://doi.org/10.1007/978-3-319-46448-0_2
11. Liu, Y., Cheng, M.M., Hu, X., Wang, K., Bai, X.: Richer convolutional features for edge detection. In: 2017 IEEE Conference on Computer Vision and Pattern Recognition (CVPR), pp. 5872–5881 (2017)
12. Lu, X., Yao, J., Li, K., Li, L.: Cannylines: a parameter-free line segment detector. In: 2015 IEEE International Conference on Image Processing (ICIP), pp. 507–511, September 2015. https://doi.org/10.1109/ICIP.2015.7350850
13. Nie, X., Zhang, J., Yan, S., Feng, J.: Single-stage multi-person pose machines. In: 2019 IEEE/CVF International Conference on Computer Vision (ICCV), pp. 6950–6959 (2019)
14. Qin, F., Shen, F., Zhang, D., Liu, X., Xu, D.: Contour primitives of interest extraction method for microscopic images and its application on pose measurement. IEEE Trans. Syst. Man Cybern. Syst. **48**(8), 1348–1359 (2018). https://doi.org/10.1109/TSMC.2017.2669219
15. Qin, X., Zhang, Z., Huang, C., Gao, C., Dehghan, M., Jägersand, M.: BasNet: boundary-aware salient object detection. In: 2019 IEEE/CVF Conference on Computer Vision and Pattern Recognition (CVPR), pp. 7471–7481 (2019)
16. Ramalingam, S., Brand, M.: Lifting 3D manhattan lines from a single image. In: The IEEE International Conference on Computer Vision (ICCV), December 2013

17. Rother, C.: A new approach to vanishing point detection in architectural environments. Image Vis. Comput. **20**(9–10), 647–655 (2002)

18. Springenberg, J., Dosovitskiy, A., Brox, T., Riedmiller, M.: Striving for simplicity: the all convolutional net. In: ICLR (Workshop Track) (2015)

19. Wan, F., Deng, F.: Using line segment clustering to detect vanishing point. In: Advanced Materials Research. vol. 268, pp. 1553–1558. Trans Tech Publ (2011)

20. Xie, S., Tu, Z.: Holistically-nested edge detection. In: 2015 IEEE International Conference on Computer Vision (ICCV). pp. 1395–1403, December 2015. https://doi.org/10.1109/ICCV.2015.164

21. Xu, Z., Shin, B., Klette, R.: Accurate and robust line segment extraction using minimum entropy with hough transform. IEEE Trans. Image Process. **24**(3), 813–822 (2015). https://doi.org/10.1109/TIP.2014.2387020

22. Xue, N., Bai, S., Wang, F., Xia, G.S., Wu, T., Zhang, L.: Learning attraction field representation for robust line segment detection. In: CVPR (2018)

23. Xue, N., Wu, T., Bai, S., Wang, F.D., Xia, G.S., Zhang, L., Torr, P.H.S.: Holistically-Attracted Wireframe Parsing (2020)

24. Xue, Z., Xue, N., Xia, G.S., Shen, W.: Learning to calibrate straight lines for fisheye image rectification. In: The IEEE Conference on Computer Vision and Pattern Recognition (CVPR), June 2019

25. Zhang, Z., et al.: PPGNet: learning point-pair graph for line segment detection. In: 2019 IEEE/CVF Conference on Computer Vision and Pattern Recognition (CVPR), pp. 7098–7107 (2019)

26. Zhou, X., Wang, D., Krähenbühl, P.: Objects as points. ArXiv abs/1904.07850 (2019)

27. Zhou, X., Zhuo, J., Krähenbühl, P.: Bottom-up object detection by grouping extreme and center points. In: CVPR (2019)

28. Zhou, Y., Qi, H., Ma, Y.: End-to-end wireframe parsing. In: 2019 IEEE/CVF International Conference on Computer Vision (ICCV), October 2019. https://doi.org/10.1109/iccv.2019.00105

Author Index

Printed in the United States
By Bookmasters